Introducing
Visual C# 2010

■ ■ ■

Adam Freeman

Apress®

Introducing Visual C# 2010

ISBN-13 (pbk): 978-1-4302-3171-4

ISBN-13 (electronic): 978-1-4302-3172-1

Printed and bound in the United States of America 9 8 7 6 5 4 3 2 1

President and Publisher: Paul Manning
Lead Editor: Ewan Buckingham
Technical Reviewer: Damien Foggon
Editorial Board: Steve Anglin, Mark Beckner, Ewan Buckingham, Gary Cornell, Jonathan Gennick, Jonathan Hassell, Michelle Lowman, Matthew Moodie, Duncan Parkes, Jeffrey Pepper, Frank Pohlmann, Douglas Pundick, Ben Renow-Clarke, Dominic Shakeshaft, Matt Wade, Tom Welsh
Coordinating Editor: Anne Collett and Kelly Moritz
Copy Editor: Kim Wimpsett and Mary Behr
Compositor: Bytheway Publishing Services
Indexer: BIM Indexing & Proofreading Services
Artist: April Milne
Cover Designer: Anna Ishchenko

Distributed to the book trade worldwide by Springer Science+Business Media, LLC., 233 Spring Street, 6th Floor, New York, NY 10013. Phone 1-800-SPRINGER, fax (201) 348-4505, e-mail orders-ny@springer-sbm.com, or visit www.springeronline.com.

For information on translations, please e-mail rights@apress.com, or visit www.apress.com.

Apress and friends of ED books may be purchased in bulk for academic, corporate, or promotional use. eBook versions and licenses are also available for most titles. For more information, reference our Special Bulk Sales–eBook Licensing web page at www.apress.com/info/bulksales.

The source code for this book is available to readers at www.apress.com.

Dedicated to my wife, Jacqui Griffyth.

Contents at a Glance

Contents

About the Author

 **Adam Freeman** is an experienced IT professional who has held senior positions in a range of companies, most recently as chief technology officer and chief operating officer of a global bank. Now retired, he spends his time writing and training for his first competitive triathlon. This is his tenth book on programming and his eighth on .NET.

About the Technical Reviewer

■ **Damien Foggon** is a developer, writer, and technical reviewer in cutting-edge technologies and has contributed to more than 50 books on .NET, C#, Visual Basic and ASP.NET. He is the co-founder of the Newcastle based user-group NEBytes (online at `http://www.nebytes.net`), is a multiple MCPD in .NET 2.0 and .NET 3.5 and can be found online at `http://blog.littlepond.co.uk`.

Acknowledgments

I would like to thank everyone at Apress for working so hard to bring this book to print. In particular, I would like to thank Anne Collett and Kelly Moritz for keeping things on track and Ewan Buckingham for commissioning and editing the book. I would also like to thank Kim Wimpsett and Damien Foggon, whose respective efforts as copy editor and technical reviewer made this book far better than it would have been without them.

PART 1

■ ■ ■

Getting Started

Welcome to the first part of this book. This is an introduction to C#, which means I have been careful to explain everything you need to know to be an effective and productive C# programmer. We are going to start slowly. In Chapter 1, I'll tell you what is in this book, what prior experience you should have, and what you can expect to find in a typical chapter. I'll also give you some useful references to other sources of information. It can often be helpful to get different treatments of the same concept when learning a new programming language.

In Chapter 2, we'll get set up and install all the software and services that we'll need as we work our way through the C# language. There are free-of-charge versions available of every package we'll need, so don't worry if you don't already own any C# or .NET software. I'll tell you where to get it and how to install it.

In Chapter 3, we will take a tour of C# and the .NET Framework. I'll explain where C# is like other languages and where it has followed a different path. I'll explain the relationship between C#, the .NET Framework, and the other .NET languages, such as Visual Basic .NET and F#. I'll also take the time to explain some of the buzzwords that surround C# and .NET so that you have a good foundation of knowledge when we come to look at C# in depth in Part II of this book.

CHAPTER 1

■■■

Introduction

I started programming in C# when version 1.0 was the current release and .NET was being billed as a Java-killer. In fact, the first C# book that I wrote was a guide to the language for Java programmers.

It's seven years later, and C# hasn't killed Java, but it has established itself as one of the most useful and expressive programming languages in use today—and one of the most widely used. C# has developed its own identity, and each new version of the language has further reinforced that identity. The current version of C#/.NET, version 4, is mature, complete, flexible, and feature rich. The development tools are good, the integration with Windows is excellent, and there is a thriving community of developers providing enhancements and add-on libraries.

I like programming in C#, and I hope you will come to like it too. I am not a language evangelist; I believe that the best language to solve a problem is usually the one that you already know. But I find myself turning to C# more and more. I find the development tools to be solid and flexible, I like the integration with Windows, and there are, for me, two killer features. The first is the excellent parallel programming features that let a program do more than one thing at a time (these features are discussed in Chapter 24 of this book). The second is the indescribably brilliant data-processing LINQ feature (covered in Chapters 27–31).

In this book, I will take you on a tour through C#, starting with the language itself, and then onto the rich APIs that are included with the .NET Framework. My main tool of instruction will be code—lots and lots of code. I don't discuss the abstractions of object-oriented programming, for example. I explain it through code samples and illustrations so that you know how it affects your programming and how to get the best results. As we go from chapter to chapter, you'll learn everything you need to know in order to write effective C# programs to solve the problems that you will face most often.

Who Should Read This Book?

This book was written for programmers who have no experience with C# and/or little to no experience with object-oriented programming. I have tried to explain every term and concept as it arises, but this is a book that teaches C# programming, rather than programming in general.

What Is Covered in This Book?

This book covers the C# language and the major .NET APIs and features. In each chapter you will find an explanation of what a feature is for and what it does, as well as all the information you need to get started using that feature effectively. There are lots of code examples, and each technique is carefully explained.

There is only so much content that you can fit into a book, and so, since this is an introduction to C#, I have focused on the features that are most commonly used and are the easiest to use. As C# has evolved, duplicate features have emerged. There are several different APIs available for processing XML data, for example. In these cases, I have included the most recent or most widely used and have omitted the others. As a new C# programmer, you don't need to know the historic value of this API or that language feature; at this stage, you just need to know how to get something done quickly, cleanly, and effectively. Once you have the basics of C# and an understanding of the current features, you can use this knowledge to work on legacy code if the need arises.

What Do You Need to Read This Book?

You could just sit and read this book, but to get the most benefit, you should be able to follow along with the examples on your own computer, which means that you will need a Windows computer. Aside from Windows, basic versions of all the software you will need are available from Microsoft free of charge. Chapter 2 tells you what you need, explains where to get it from, and shows you how to install it and get it ready for use.

What Is the Structure of This Book?

There are five parts to this book. The first part helps you get ready to use C# and to understand the building blocks of the .NET Framework. At the end of these chapters, you will have all the software you need installed and configured and be able to tell an assembly from a code file.

Part II introduces the C# language and object-oriented programming. You will learn how C# represents different kinds of data and how to create and use your own representations. C# includes some built-in data types that you will use in every program that you write, and these are covered in depth. At the end of these chapters, you will be able to write C# programs that can do useful, but basic, things.

Part III introduces some of the major APIs. This is where the complexity and utility of the programs you will be able to write really starts to take off. You will learn how to write network programs, deal with sets of data in useful ways, work with files, make your data persistent, and even how to use the C# parallel programming features. At the end of these chapters, you'll start to have some serious C# chops and be able to take on most programming problems using C#.

Part IV focuses on data and databases, which have some excellent support in C#. Most of the chapters in this part of the book relate to a feature called Language Integrated Query (LINQ). By the end of these chapters, you will be able to query and modify object data, XML data, and SQL data.

Part V covers the different feature sets that support user interfaces, which range from traditional Windows client applications to web UIs. C# has some great features for UI design and implementation, and you may be surprised how simple it can be to get some great results with very little effort.

Part VI describes some more advanced topics. You can skip these chapters and still end up with a great grasp of C# and be able to write useful and elegant programs. But at some point, you'll face a problem that can be solved only by using one of these advanced features, so I have included this information for when that happens.

What Is in Each Chapter?

The format differs slightly from chapter to chapter to best suit the topic at hand, but there are some things that are common to most of them. There are a lot of code listings in every chapter, so I have included a summary table at the start of each one to make it easier when you are looking for something specific. Table 1-1 shows part of the table from Chapter 6.

Table 1-1. Example of the Quick Problem/Solution Reference for Chapter 6

Problem	Solution	Listings
Define a new type.	Define a type using the class keyword, and add members to define functionality.	6-1 through 6-4
Create and use an object from a class.	Use the new operator.	6-5 through 6-12
Derive a class from a base type.	Specify a base type for your class.	6-13 through 6-17
Convert from one type to another.	Perform an implicit or explicit cast operation.	6-18 through 6-22

These tables help you find the code example that demonstrates a solution to a common problem. Often, there will be several code examples that show different techniques for solving the same problem, so the table will point to a range of code listings. These tables will be an invaluable time-saver once you have read this book and just need to remind yourself of a particular feature of technique.

When I introduce a new feature, I explain its use visually by showing you the anatomy of its application. Figure 1-1 is an example from Chapter 4; these figures show you the different components that you need in order to use a feature, as well as how they relate to one another.

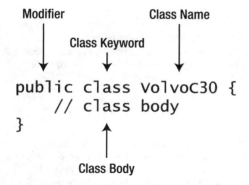

Figure 1-1. An example anatomy figure

Each chapter starts with the basics for the topic at hand and builds up your knowledge through concrete examples. Almost every C# feature throughout this book is demonstrated by a self-contained example, all of which you can download from Apress.com so that you can follow the text or experiment on your own without having to type everything in.

Getting the Example Code

All the code samples are available for download from `http://apress.com/book/sourcecode`. Each code example is self-contained. I am not a fan of building a program up over several chapters, preferring to demonstrate just the feature being described. This means that some of the examples I present are arbitrary in nature, but each one can be compiled and used on its own, and you can see exactly how to use the feature being discussed.

Finding More Information

By the time you have finished reading this book, you'll know everything you need to be an effective C# programmer—how to use the language and how to use the major API features, such as networking, data access, and user interfaces, and so on. But there is always more to learn, especially in a language with the rich library support that C# enjoys. When you are looking for more advanced information, I recommend the following sources.

The MSDN C# Programming Guide

The MSDN Library includes a useful tour of different C# features; the authors assume you are already familiar with C#, so it is not comprehensive in coverage, but it can be helpful if you want just a little more depth than I provide in this book. You can find the guide at `http://msdn.microsoft.com/en-us/library`.

Online Forums

Numerous web sites discuss C# and .NET. The one that seems to have the most knowledgeable participants and the lowest amount of useless noise is `http://stackoverflow.com`. This site is not specific to C#, but there is a very active C# community, and when you get stuck, chances are that someone has had the same problem and has asked for help.

Other Books

Introductory books—like this one—aim for breadth of coverage, introducing you to as many features as possible to get you up and running quickly. At key points in this book, I suggest other books that are entirely dedicated to a topic that I have covered in a single chapter. The information I give you will get you going for 90 percent of the problems you will face, but you'll need to dig further into the detail for the other 10 percent. Some of the books I suggest are my own, and many of them are published by Apress, but all of them provide good in-depth detail to help you build your expertise in a specific language feature.

Summary

It should be clear that I am enthusiastic about C#. I think it is a super language that can be used to great effect. It is my hope that as you read through this book you will not only learn how to program in C# but also gain your own enthusiasm. There is a lot to like about C#, and our journey through the language and its features begins here.

CHAPTER 2

■ ■ ■

Getting Ready

You need to prepare yourselves before you can start to learn C#. In this chapter, you'll install the development tools you need: Visual Studio 2010 and SQL Server, both of which are available as paid-for and free editions. You will use Visual Studio 2010 throughout this book and SQL Server in Parts IV and V of this book when you look at data and databases and user interfaces. You'll also install the latest version of the Silverlight tools, which you'll need for Chapter 35.

Once the tools are installed, I'll show you how to create the traditional Hello World application to demonstrate how to create, compile, and execute a simple project with Visual Studio.

Installing the Software

Before you can start exploring C# and the .NET Framework, you need to get set up. You'll need a PC running Windows—and it needs to be Windows 7 if you want to follow some of the Windows integration examples in Chapter 36. However, for the other chapters, older versions of Windows will be fine.

Installing Visual Studio 2010

The most important tool you will need is Visual Studio 2010, Microsoft's development environment for the .NET Framework. There are different editions of Visual Studio: Professional, Premium, and Ultimate. The Ultimate edition is the most comprehensive with all sorts of bells and whistles. It also has a significant price tag; at the time of writing, the Ultimate edition costs over $10,000. In all fairness to Microsoft, very few people will end up paying that price because of discount schemes, but nonetheless Visual Studio can be an expensive tool.

Don't worry if your budget doesn't stretch to a high sticker price; you can get everything you need for this book for free. Microsoft's entry level development tool is Visual Studio 2010 Express and is available without charge from microsoft.com/express. The Express editions lack some of the convenience features, but are still very capable. There are several editions available; for most of this book, you'll need the Visual C# 2010 Express edition, and for the ASP.NET section, you will need the Visual Web Developer 2010 edition.

VISUAL STUDIO 2008 AND EARLIER

Each version of Visual Studio is targeted at a single release of the .NET Framework. This book covers .NET version 4, which is supported by Visual Studio 2010. You won't be able to use the features added in .NET 4 with an earlier version of Visual Studio. Microsoft offers discounted upgrade prices from earlier versions or you can switch to the Express edition, which is available free of charge from `microsoft.com/express`.

If you are installing Visual Studio 2010 Professional, Premium, or Ultimate, you will need to check the options for Visual C# and Visual Web Developer when you run the installer. It doesn't matter if you have checked other options, but these two are essential for the content of this book. Figure 2-1 shows the installer for Visual Studio 2010 Ultimate with the core features checked.

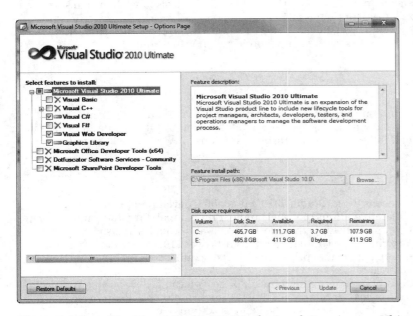

Figure 2-1. *Installing Visual Studio 2010 Professional, Premium, or Ultimate*

For the Express editions, you can either use the online installer or download an ISO file that you can burn to a DVD that contains all of the Express editions, including those for C++ and Visual Basic. You can see the installer screen from the combined installer in Figure 2-2.

The installation of the Express edition is more streamlined because there are no options, aside from installing SQL Server 2008 Express (see the next section for details). You can install the Visual C# and Visual Web Developer Express editions side-by-side on the same machine.

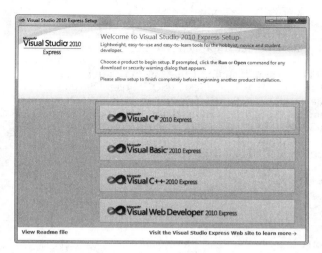

Figure 2-2. *The combined Visual Studio 2010 Express Installer*

The first thing you should do when you have finished installing the Express edition is go to the Tools menu, select Settings – Expert Settings, as shown in Figure 2-3. This makes using the Express edition more like using one of the commercial editions; the most obvious change is that the application menus will change.

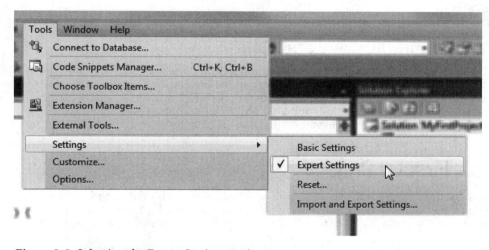

Figure 2-3. *Selecting the Expert Settings option*

Installing SQL Server 2008

All editions of Visual Studio 2010 offer to install SQL Server 2008 Express as part of the installation process, unless you already have a SQL Server installation on your machine. Much like Visual Studio,

SQL Server comes in a range of editions. SQL Server Express is the least functional, but is available for free. The main limitations are that databases are capped to 4GB of data, 1GB of memory, and will use only one CPU, but you won't be doing anything in this book that approaches these limits, which makes the Express edition perfect for your needs.

There are a couple of reasons why you might not want to install SQL Server 2008 Express as part of the Visual Studio 2010 installation process. The first is if you have a different SQL Server 2008 edition already installed. The second is the way that Visual Studio installs SQL Server leaves out the SQL Server Management Studio tool, which allows you to manage the SQL Server installation. You don't be doing anything in this book that requires Management Studio, but it is handy to have it around during normal product development. You can either download a complete SQL Server Express 2008 installer (which will include the Management Studio) or you can just download the management tools on their own; everything you need is available from `microsoft.com/sqlserver`. If you have any edition older than SQL Server 2008 SP1, you should upgrade to the current release.

Installing the Silverlight Tools

Silverlight is one of the .NET technologies that you can use to build user interfaces and is the topic of Chapter 35. You need to upgrade the Silverlight support that comes with Visual Studio 2010 to the latest version, which you do by installing the *Silverlight 4 Tools for Visual Studio 2010* package, available from this URL:

`http://go.microsoft.com/fwlink/?LinkID=177428`

Go to this web page and download and run the installer to enable to latest Silverlight development features. This package is available free of charge and can be used with all varieties of Visual Studio 2010, including the Express editions.

Downloading the Sample Code and Data

The database examples in this book all use the extended `Northwind` database that Microsoft publishes. The extended version has some additional features that were added specifically to demonstrate the features of LINQ. I have included the database as part of the source code download for this book, which you can get without charge from `Apress.com`. You don't need to have the source code, but you will need the `Northwind` files if you want to recreate the examples that use the database.

Creating Your First C# Project

Now that you have the software you need, you can create your first project. This is a book about C#, so I am not going to go into any great depth about how to use Visual Studio 2010. If you are new to Visual Studio, then this section will give you a very basic introduction to creating, compiling, and running a simple project.

Don't worry about the details at this stage. You'll explore the different types of project template available and the meaning of the different code statements as you go through the book. This section is just about getting used to the tools.

Creating the Project

If you are using one of the commercial editions of Visual Studio, select New from the File menu and select Project to open the New Project dialog, shown in Figure 2-4. What you see here will depend on the options you checked during installation and, if you checked everything, there can be a lot of different project types to choose from. Expand Visual C# in the Installed Templates section and select Console Application from the list.

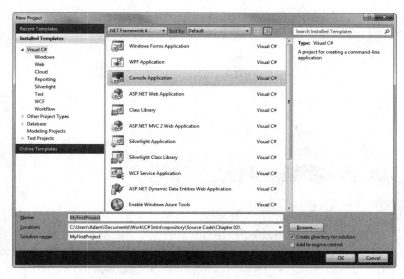

Figure 2-4. *Creating a Project with Visual Studio 2010 Ultimate*

At the bottom of the dialog you can enter the name of the project and pick the directory where the files will be stored. You can also set the name of the solution; Visual Studio lets you group projects together to form a solution. When you open a solution, Visual Studio opens all of the individual projects. If you have downloaded the source code for this book, you will find that I have created a solution for each chapter containing a project for each example. Press OK to create the project.

If you are using Visual C# 2010 Express, things are slightly different. Select New Project from the File Menu to open the New Project dialog. You will see fewer project templates, as illustrated by Figure 2-5.

Figure 2-5. Creating a Project with Visual Studio 2010 Express

There are no options to specify the name of a solution or to select where the project files are stored yet. These are handled differently in the Express editions. Select Console Application from the list, enter a name for the project, and press OK. Once the project has been created, select Save All from the File menu. This will display the Save Project dialog, shown by Figure 2-6. You can select where the project is saved and create a solution.

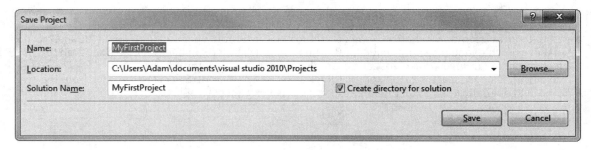

Figure 2-6. Saving a project with Visual Studio Express

Now you have created your first project. You should see something very similar to Figure 2-7. If you don't have the Properties window on the right-hand side of the window, you can open it by selecting Properties Window from the View – Other Windows menu in the Express edition and Properties Window directly from the View menu in all other editions.

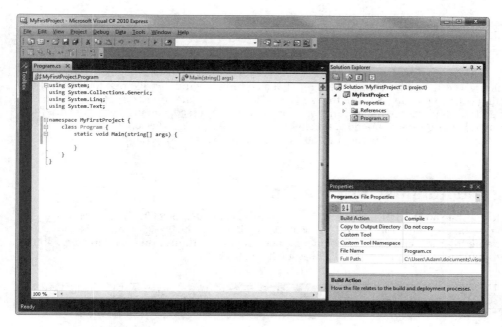

Figure 2-7. *The new project*

Visual Studio has created the project and populated it with a code file called Program.cs. The .cs suffix tells us that it is a C# file. The code file has been opened and is ready to be edited.

Editing the Code

You are going to create the classic Hello World application. Edit the code in the Program.cs file so that it matches Listing 2-1. I have emphasized the changes you need to make.

Listing 2-1. The Hello World Code

```
using System;
using System.Collections.Generic;
using System.Linq;
using System.Text;

namespace MyFirstProject {
    class Program {
        static void Main(string[] args) {

            // write our message
            Console.WriteLine("Hello, World!");

            // wait for input before exiting
            Console.WriteLine("Press enter to finish");
```

```
        Console.ReadLine();
    }
  }
}
```

You are building a console application, meaning that a command window will open to display the results of executing your code. You write out the Hello World! message and then prompt the user to hit the enter key to end the application. If you don't wait for a key to be pressed, you just see a very brief flash of the command window being opened and closed before you can read the screen. Save the changes by selecting Save from the File menu. Don't worry about the code statements; you'll learn more about them in the coming chapters.

Compiling and Running the Program

The last step is to compile and run the program. To compile the code file, select Build Solution from the Build menu. To run the program, select Start Without Debugging from the Debug menu. This does what the menu item name suggests, and executes your compiled program without using the debugger. You should see a command window appear, just like the one in Figure 2-8.

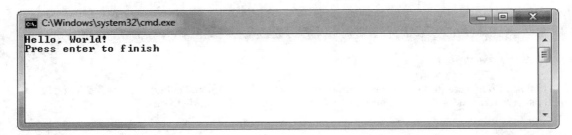

Figure 2-8. *Running the program*

You can see the Hello World message and the prompt for the user to press the enter key. If you press enter, the application will finish and the command window will disappear. When I refer to compiling and running samples throughout this book, it is this process to which I am referring. You won't be using the Visual Studio debugger, so you should always select the Start Without Debugging menu item.

Features That I Use Before Explaining Them

Listing 2-1 contains several C# features that I will use in almost every example, but which I don't explain until the relevant chapter. To help you make sense of the code listings before you get to the appropriate chapters, I'll give a quick break down of Listing 2-1 to create some context—and tell you where in the book you can find more details.

The using statements

The first lines in Listing 2-1 are *using statements*. Here they are again:

```
using System;
using System.Collections.Generic;
using System.Linq;
using System.Text;
```

To group related features together, C# has the concept of *namespaces*. A using statement makes all of the features in a given namespace available for convenient use in a code file. You can learn more about using statements in Chapter 11.

The namespace statement

The next line in Listing 2-1 is a *namespace* declaration:

```
namespace MyFirstProject {

    // other statements

}
```

The namespace keyword places anything that appears between the brace characters ({ and }) into the specified namespace. In this case, the namespace is called MyFirstProject. I tend not to use the namespace keyword in the examples in this book because they are so short, but you can find out all about namespaces in Chapter 11, which contains plenty of examples.

The class statement

The next statement defines a *class:*

```
class Program {

    // other statements

}
```

The class keyword defines a custom data type. Classes are one of the main building blocks in C#. The one in Listing 2-1 is called Program, but the names given to classes are usually more descriptive. You can learn about classes in Chapter 6.

The Main method

Methods are how you express actions that your code can perform and they are closely associated with classes. The Main method is a special kind of method; it is where the .NET Framework starts executing code statements when your program is executed. Here is the Main method from Listing 2-1:

```
static void Main(string[] args) {
    // other statements
}
```

You can find out more about methods in general and the Main method in particular in Chapter 9.

The Code Comments

There are two kinds of comment available in C# and Listing 2-1 contains the kind that I tend to use most frequently:

```
// write our message
```

Comments are ignored by the compiler and are used by the programmer to describe the intended operation of the program. You can learn about comments in Chapter 4.

The Console.WriteLine and Console.ReadLine methods

You use the `Console.WriteLine` method to write text to the console, i.e. the command line window that was used to start your program (this doesn't apply to all C# applications, only those that are text-based). Whatever you place between the parenthesis ((and)) will be written to the console, so the statement has the effect of writing `Hello, World!` to the console:

```
Console.WriteLine("Hello, World!");
```

The `Console.ReadLine` method reads a line of text entered by the user, terminated by the `Enter` key. You will see the following two statements in almost all of the examples in this book:

```
Console.WriteLine("Press enter to finish");
Console.ReadLine();
```

The first statement asks the user to press the `Enter` key and the second reads that line. If I did not add these statements, running the program from the `Debug` menu in Visual Studio would cause a new command-prompt to open, the example run, and the command-prompt to close again. Most of the examples in this book are very brief, and the effect is to have a very quick flash of black on the screen as the window opens and, a brief period later, closes again. Waiting for the user (i.e. you, the reader) to press `Enter` gives enough time to see the results that the example produces. You can learn more about the Console feature in Chapter 26.

Summary

In this chapter, you installed Visual Studio 2010 and SQL Server 2008 and upgraded the Silverlight development tools for Visual Studio. These are the key tools that you'll use throughout the book. You also created a simple application using Visual Studio and then compiled and ran it, just to get used to the basic functions of the development environment.

CHAPTER 3

■ ■ ■

Understanding C# and the .NET Framework

In this chapter, I'll introduce you to the key components of C# and the .NET Framework and explain the relationship between them. I'll also introduce the major technology building blocks that form the functionality that you'll look at throughout this book.

I'm not going to get bogged down in detail; instead, I will going to focus on the knowledge you need to put everything in context before you start learning the C# language and becoming an effective C# programmer. This chapter is about giving you a good overview that will help you form a picture of C# and .NET as you move through the book.

.NET can seem impenetrable—a wall of terms and technologies and a pit of languages and syntaxes. By the time you reach the final chapter of this book, you'll have forgotten this moment and you'll be up and running with C# and .NET. The process in between will be surprisingly easy. I use lots of examples, I don't bombard you with the tedious detail, and I tell you what you need to know to understand how to use the feature at hand.

Your interest will be piqued as you move from chapter to chapter. There are a couple of .NET features that I am particularly fond of, and I can remember wanting to dive into the details as soon as I saw them. If you are like me, you'll have the same reaction, although the features that interest you may be different. To that end, this chapter includes sources for further reading that can give you the detail on individual topics.

C# and the .NET Framework at a Glance

Let's introduce the main characters in this story – C# and the .NET Framework. Having a clear view of how the various terms and technologies associated with .NET fit together will help you when you design your C# programs and will make the process of learning about .NET easier.

Introducing C#

C# is a programming language. Like any language, C# has a syntax and a vocabulary. Programming languages, like C# or Java, differ from natural languages, such as English or French. Learning a new programming language is easier than learning a natural language. There are only a handful of words in a programming language vocabulary; C# has around 100 keywords. That may seem daunting, but you'll use some keywords more than others and you probably won't use some of them at all.

Programming languages have very rigid syntaxes—the keywords have to be used in a certain way. English is fluid and flexible because it is used for so many different reasons. Programming languages are terse and precise because they are used for one reason: to express your instructions to the computer as clearly and unambiguously as possible. Helpfully, there is a universal, authoritative specification for C#. Grammarians can vigorously debate the history and meaning of words in English, but in C# the history of all keywords is that they were defined by Microsoft and the meaning is contained in the C# language specification, which you can find at http://msdn.microsoft.com/en-us/library/ms228593.aspx. I am not suggesting that you run off and read the language specification right now; it is a dry, precise, overly-technical document in the way that formal specifications tend to be. But if you are ever in doubt about the exact meaning and use of a C# term, the specification provides the authoritative reference.

Introducing the .NET Framework

The .NET Framework runs .NET programs. For client applications, this means that the user must install the framework before running your program for the first time (although many developers include the .NET Framework in their program installers to make life easier for the user). For servers, the .NET Framework must be installed before running .NET-based services, such as web applications. There are two parts to the .NET Framework, described in the following sections.

Introducing the Common Language Runtime

The *Common Language Runtime* (CLR) is the part that actually executes .NET programs – i.e. performs the instructions that you gave using C#. The CLR (commonly referred to as the *runtime*) is a virtual machine, an idea you will be familiar with if you have used Java. In essence, the CLR provides the services that provide and enforce the .NET feature set, freeing the programmer from working directly with the operating system. The CLR lets the Microsoft .NET designers add features to make life easier for programmers (such as automatic memory management, described in the "Understanding Automatic Memory Management" section) and remove or restrict problematic features (such as unsafe code, covered in the "Understanding Unmanaged/Native Code Support" section).

The C# compiler translates your C# code into *Common Intermediate Language* (CIL) instructions, which is the language of the CLR. When you run your compiled program, the CLR loads the CIL and gets to work.

Introducing the Class Library

The second part of the .NET Framework is the .NET Framework Class Library. A class is a mix of data and program logic (I explain classes in Chapter 6). The class library is an extensive collection of functionality and features that you can use to speed up your development process and access system features. For example, you don't have to write your own classes for working with a relational database. There are classes in the class library that you can use to handle the connections, read the data, represent the SQL data types, and so on. You could use C# to implement all this functionality yourself, but you'll find that the classes in the class library are comprehensive and well-thought out.

The tasks that you can perform with the library classes range from the basic (performing basic numeric calculations—see Chapter 5), to the advanced (creating graphical user interfaces—see Chapters 32-35) and from the run-of-the-mill (handling program errors—see Chapter 14) to the cutting-edge (parallel programming—see Chapter 24).

The Relationship between C# and the .NET Framework

Understanding the relationship between C# and the .NET Framework makes learning C# easier. This relationship is shown at a high-level in Figure 3-1.

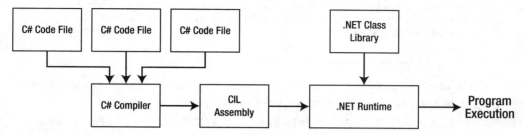

Figure 3-1. C# and the .NET Framework

You begin by writing your program using a series of C# statements (I explain the types of statement you can write and how they relate to one another in Chapters 4-15). This is not as daunting as it may sound; although there are 11 chapters dedicated to the C# language, each is focused on a particular aspect, so you will be able to write simple C# programs quite soon.

Using C# Code Files

Your program is made up of C# statements that contain instructions for the .NET runtime to follow: create some new data, change the value of some existing data, print out a message to the user, and so on. The C# statements are contained within C# code files; these are text files that have the .cs file extension. In the previous chapter, you used Visual Studio to create your first C# program. I have reproduced the code in Listing 3-1.

Listing 3-1. The Hello World Code

```
using System;
using System.Collections.Generic;
using System.Linq;
using System.Text;

namespace MyFirstProject {
    class Program {
        static void Main(string[] args) {

            // write our message
            Console.WriteLine("Hello, World!");

            // wait for input before exiting
            Console.WriteLine("Press enter to finish");
            Console.ReadLine();
        }
    }
```

}

These are the C# statements that define your program and were saved in the `Program.cs` code file. You only need one code file for such a simple program, but more complex projects can consist of many code files. C# is a *compiled* programming language. This means that the .NET runtime doesn't understand how to process C# instructions, so you have to use a compiler to convert from C# into the format that the runtime does understand—CIL. The output from compiling C# code files is an *assembly*, the .NET term for a file that contains MSIL.

■ **Tip** One of the benefits of using a compiler to transform C# to CIL is that the compiler checks your use of the C# language and reports any errors back to you. The compiler is your friend if you are, like me, more of an enthusiastic than accurate typist. Mistyped keywords, illegal syntax, and omitted characters are all detected and rejected by the C# compiler.

Assemblies are the bridge between C# and the .NET Framework. To C#, .NET is everything. You write your program instructions in the knowledge that the .NET runtime will execute them on your behalf as set out in the C# language specification. In fact, .NET doesn't really know or care about C#. It just consumes the CIL in the assemblies that compiling C# produces.

Understanding Assemblies

Assemblies have a `.exe` or `.dll` file extension. When you compiled your Hello World program in Chapter 2, the output was a file called `MyFirstProject.exe`. This is an assembly that contains the CIL produced by compiling the C# statements in Listing 3-1.

You can create assemblies that are libraries of C# functionality to be used in other projects—this is like creating your own extensions to the .NET Framework Class Library—and such files have the `.dll` file extension. Assemblies that contain programs (such as your Hello World example) produce `.exe` files.

A benefit of compiling C# to create CIL assemblies is that this process unlocks a very important feature of .NET: *cross-language interoperability*. C# is not the only language that .NET supports; Microsoft produces others including Visual Basic .NET and F#. Third-parties have produced an amazing array of languages adapted to run on the .NET Framework, everything from Ada to COBOL to Tcl/Tk. In fact, if you can name a language, the chances are that there is a .NET version of it available.

Typically, functionality written in a programming language can only be used by other programmers writing in the same language. But when you compile your C# code, you create assemblies that can then be used by other .NET languages. This relies on a .NET feature called the *Common Language Specification* (CLS)—the CIL that is created when code written using a .NET language is compiled can then be consumed by other .NET languages and vice versa.

The CLS feature means that you can mix and match code libraries without worrying about which language they were written in. Need to use a library from a third-party company that uses Visual Basic .NET? No problem. Need to build using a Managed C++ library from the guys at HQ? Don't worry. Do those guys need to use code from your C# project? Just send them your compiled assembly and they can use it in their projects. (You can create .NET code that doesn't conform to the CLS standard and therefore cannot be used by other .NET languages, but this is actually quite hard to do and not worth worrying about in this book).

When you use functionality from another assembly in your project, you create a *dependency* on that assembly. When you run your program, the .NET Runtime loads those assemblies for you, as shown in Figure 3-2.

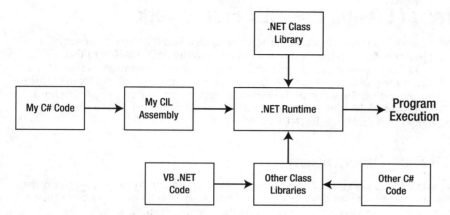

Figure 3-2. *Assemblies from different sources*

When you deploy your program to users, you must also deploy the assemblies that you rely on. You don't have to include any assemblies from the .NET Class Library because they are installed with the .NET Framework. Each assembly contains a *manifest*, which contains the following information:

- The name of the assembly

- The version number of the assembly

- The strong name of the assembly

- A list of all the files and data types in the assembly

- A list of other assemblies that this assembly depends upon

There are some other pieces of information in the manifest, but these are the ones you will care most about. If you are of a certain age, you will remember a time when Microsoft Windows was plagued with a problem called *DLL Hell*. When you installed a program on Windows, it would replace common code libraries with the versions that it required, overwriting the versions that other, already installed, programs depended on, thus making them unusable.

Things are different in .NET—dependencies between assemblies are based on the contents of the manifest. Most usefully, the version of the assembly is included in the dependency, which addresses the version upgrade issue. My project doesn't just depend on the assembly the guys from accounting produced, it depends on version 4.1.2.0 (.NET assembly versions have four parts). Your project can depend on their 3.0.0.0 release, and my program and your program can co-exist happily on the users' systems because .NET makes sure that we each get the versions we need.

This feature relies on the assembly having a *strong name*. This means that the assembly contains a digital signature and a cryptographic public key that can be used to verify that the contents of the assembly have not been altered. You don't have to create a strong name for an assembly, but it can be a good idea to do so if you intend to distribute assemblies to others. I don't cover creating strong names in this book, but that can be created as part of the Visual Studio build process. You can find more information about strong assembly names at http://msdn.microsoft.com/en-us/library/wd40t7ad.aspx.

The Key Features of C# and the .NET Framework

For the purposes of this book, it makes sense to consider the C# language and the .NET Framework as a single entity So, when I use the terms C# or .NET, I am really referring to the combination of the language and the runtime as one unit. After all, C# is your tool to make use of the features of the framework, and the framework is the platform for executing your instructions. And what a lot of features there are! In this section, I'll quickly describe some of the key features that you will rely on in this book and, where appropriate, I'll tell you which chapters cover those features. I'll also introduce you to the major technology building blocks that make up the .NET Framework.

Understanding Object-Orientation

C# is an *object-oriented* language. This is a style of programming where data and the logic that performs actions on that data are grouped together into *classes*. A class is like a blueprint. If you were creating a class to represent an employee of a company, you would define data fields to represent all of the information that you had about an employee and the actions that could be performed on that data – give a raise, issue a bonus, change department, and so on. The actions that you create in a class can change some or all of the data in that class and can rely on actions in other classes as well.

A class is like a blueprint for *all* employees. When you come to deal with a *specific* employee, you create an *object*. One class can be used to create many objects, just like one blueprint can be used to build many houses or cars. There are some significant benefits to object-oriented programming, but it can be confusing at first if you are new to this style of programming. Chapter 6 discusses how to use classes and objects—and highlights the most common causes of confusion and difficulty.

Understanding Type Safety

C# enforces a policy called *type-safety*. As mentioned previously, when you design a new type of data, you also specify what actions and operations that type of data can support. For the company employee example from the previous section, you might decide that your employee data type will support the following actions: move to a new department, leave the company, receive a promotion, and receive a bonus. If you were designing a data type to represent a number, you might support adding one number to another number, subtracting one number from another, and so on.

When it comes time to use these data types in your program, the rules of C# insist that you declare which type you are using advance: this one is a number, those other ones are employees, and so on. Once the C# compiler knows what types of data are in use, it will only let you perform the actions that you specified when you designed the data type. This means that you can't give a bonus to a car or subtract one employee from another. You *can* convert from one data type to another, but only if you have previously defined what this means.

Not all programming languages are type safe. In such languages you can define data as one type but treat it as another. Most programmers' view of type safety is driven by their prior experience. If you are used to type safe languages, it seems like a really good idea. If you are used to type unsafe languages, then type safety seems like a constraint. I have used both kinds of language over the years. I used to love the freedom that type unsafe programming gave me, but I have gradually come to appreciate the forethought that type safety requires when I design my data types and the number of errors that the C# compiler detects when it tries to compile my code.

Data types and type safety are recurring themes in C#. Details of how to create types and use them can be found in Part II of this book. I start with numeric data types in Chapter 5 and move on to more sophisticated examples in Chapters 6-15. Again, don't worry that there are a lot of chapters involved. Data types and how to use them are at the heart of any programming language, and I will take you through the C# approach by building on some simple and clear examples.

Understanding Automatic Memory Management

In some programming languages (one example being C), the programmer takes responsibility for managing the memory in which program data is stored. You allocate sufficient memory to store your data, make sure that you don't step outside of that memory, and release the memory when you are done. Memory leaks (when a program just keeps on taking up more and more of your system memory) are often caused by a programmer having forgotten to release some memory when finished with it.

C# provides automatic memory management. You say that you want a new piece of data, and C# allocates the memory for it. When you are done with the data, the memory is released automatically for you. Releasing memory automatically is handled by a feature called the *garbage collector* (GC). The garbage collector looks at all of the data you have created in your program and figures out which bits you have finished with. You can still have memory leaks in a C# program, however. These are caused when you think you have finished with some data, but the garbage collector doesn't realize it. The garbage collector and how it operates is covered in Chapter 18.

Understanding the Just-In-Time Compiler

The .NET runtime is a virtual machine—this is like a computer inside of your computer. Whereas your system's CPU executes x86 or x64 instructions, the .NET runtime executes CIL instructions. This machine-inside-a-machine approach has some serious performance problems, so to get around this, the .NET runtime includes a *just-in-time compiler* (JIT), a concept you will be familiar with if you have written in Java, for example. When you run your program, the .NET runtime compiles the CIL in your program's assemblies into native code that can be executed directly by your system CPU— i.e. the CIL is converted to x86 or x64 instructions. It doesn't give the same performance that you might get from a C program written directly to the Windows APIs, but it has a dramatic effect nonetheless; .NET can deliver performance that is suitable for all but the most computationally demanding applications. You don't have to take any explicit action to use the JIT; it is applied automatically by the runtime. For this reason, I don't go into any further details about the operation of the JIT in this book.

Understanding Parallel Processing

Modern computers can perform more than one activity at a time. In fact, most systems are sold with multi-core or multi-processor configurations. The computer that I use to write books has four cores— not an unusual configuration, or even a particularly expensive one.

You can take advantage of these cores and processors in your C# programming using the .NET feature called the Task Parallel Library. With very little effort you can create a parallel program, although some care is required to create something that works properly—you must take the time to coordinate the different tasks that your program is performing. The Task Parallel Library is the subject of Chapter 24 and a related topic is covered in Chapter 28. The .NET support for parallel programming is the best that I have seen. It replaces an older model called *threads*, which was much more complex and fiddly to work with.

Understanding Unmanaged/Native Code Support

When you take advantage of the .NET features described in this chapter—the memory management, the use of assemblies, type-safety, and so on—the runtime is said to manage your code execution. This is often referred to as *managed execution*. Your code is said to be *managed code*. Everything you do in this book is managed code. However, .NET supports *unmanaged* execution as well. You can choose to go off the managed reservation and do your own thing with memory pointers, native Windows API calls, and explicit memory management.

Using unmanaged code is a risky business. The nice and shiny .NET managed features are there to make your life simpler and your code better. But if you need the absolute highest performance, or if you need to access a custom hardware device or some legacy C or C++ code in an old DLL, then unmanaged code can be useful. I mention unmanaged code for completeness; it is a term you will often see in descriptions of .NET. I don't explain how to use unmanaged code in this book since it is a very advanced topic which is prone to creating errors and bugs.

For your purposes, what's interesting about the unmanaged support is that it is used extensively in the .NET Framework Class Library to create some very rich features that you can use in managed code. For example, the classes responsible for networking in the library have to work extensively with the native networking features of Windows. These are C APIs that don't offer the convenience and protection of the managed features. The .NET classes act as wrappers around this functionality and, in effect, act as mediators between the happy world of managed code and the minefield of unmanaged code. (As an aside, I cover the .NET support for networking in Chapter 21.)

Understanding the .NET Technology Spectrum

If you take the key features of the .NET and the mediation between managed and unmanaged code, you have the foundation for building a lot of different technologies. All you need is a legion of programmers to build some cool stuff. Microsoft has that legion of programmers and they have been busy. There are so many different technologies included in, associated with, or available for the .NET Framework that it can be hard to know where to start. Figure 3-3 shows the six high-level building blocks that you will be looking at in this book.

These are the key .NET technologies, but there are others for more specific or advanced problems. And although Figure 3-3 shows a nice division of responsibility between each of these building blocks, the reality is that there is a lot of interdependency between these technologies. For example, the Language Integrated Query (LINQ) feature allows you to query data using data models created using the ADO.NET feature called the Entity Framework and can also be used with the Task Parallel support to parallel process queries. I'll give a brief description of each of these building blocks and tell you which chapters relate to them.

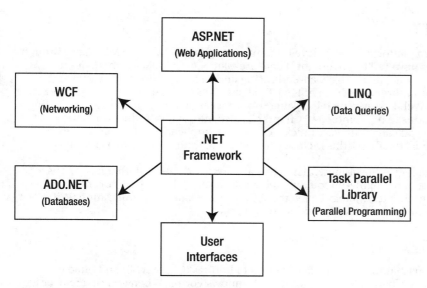

Figure 3-3. *The key .NET building blocks*

■ **Note** The breadth of the .NET Framework means that there are some technological dead-ends that have been superseded by more modern approaches. Where this has happened, I have focused on the most recent features and ignored the historical/legacy mechanisms.

Figure 3-3 doesn't give you give a sense of scale. Each of those technologies is huge and worthy of entire books. My goal in this book is to get you started on the path to being productive with each technology, but I am introducing you to each and every one, which means there are limits to how deep into each area I can go. I assume that you like to learn from books or e-books given you are reading *this* book, so I'll also recommend books that are dedicated to each topic. Some of these will be shameless plugs for my own books, and most of the others are published by Apress, but I have also recommended some that are from other publishers.

■ **Tip** Don't be dismayed by the interwoven nature of these technologies. I have structured the chapters of this book to introduce them to you gradually, so that you have a good understanding of one technology before you use it in support of another.

Understanding ASP.NET

ASP.NET is Microsoft's unified platform for web development, ranging from static HTML pages through to richly interactive interfaces powered by Silverlight. There are a lot of individual technologies in ASP.NET that are rolled together to create a truly all-embracing and wide-reaching web platform.

In this book, you will look at three aspects of ASP.NET, all of which are related to creating interactive web applications. The first is Web Forms, which is a general-purpose user-interface toolkit for creating web applications (this is introduced in Chapter 34). Chapter 34 also offers an introduction to the Dynamic Data system, which you can use to very quickly create web applications that allow users to view and edit data in a relational database (this is closely linked to the Entity Framework, which is covered in Chapter 30).

The third ASP.NET technology is Silverlight, Microsoft's answer to Adobe Flash that lets you use your C# skills to create polished and highly-interactive web applications. Silverlight is covered in Chapter 35 and is based on another technology called the Windows Presentation Foundation (WPF)—see the "Understanding User Interfaces" section later in this chapter.

Related .NET Technologies

When you come to ASP.NET in Chapter 34, you will use LINQ to Entities (Chapter 30) and build on some of the techniques you learned in Chapter 32 when you used Windows Forms. When you cover Silverlight, you will use the Windows Presentation Foundation (WPF) covered in Chapter 33 and the Windows Communication Foundation (WCF) covered in Chapter 21.

Further Reading

My own books on ASP.NET are *Pro ASP.NET 4 in C# 2010* (with Matt MacDonald) and *ASP.NET In Context*. The first one is a very comprehensive and detailed coverage of ASP.NET, while the *In Context* book is more focused on the functionality that programmers use regularly. I have also written *Pro ASP.NET MVC 3 Framework* (with Steven Sanderson) that covers an advanced ASP.NET feature (that I don't cover in this book) called MVC. I also like Christian Wenz's *ASP.NET AJAX* book, published by O'Reilly.

Understanding LINQ

LINQ stands for *Language Integrated Query* and is a very cool feature that lets you execute SQL-like queries on a wide range of data types, including XML, SQL databases, and C# data types. I'll say it several times throughout this book—LINQ is one of my favorite .NET features and I can get quite enthusiastic about it. LINQ is discussed in Chapters 27-31.

Related .NET Technologies

LINQ depends on a range of different technologies: two parts of ADO.NET called the Entity Framework and the DataSet for querying databases (Chapters 30 and 31), and the Task Parallel Library for the Parallel LINQ feature (Chapter 29). More broadly, LINQ relies on Collections (Chapter 19) and generic types (Chapter 15).

Further Reading

My own LINQ book is *Pro LINQ in C# 2010*, written with Joe Rattz and published by Apress. It is a very detailed dive into all aspects of LINQ. For more of a quick reminder once you have mastered LINQ, I like the *LINQ Pocket Reference* by Joseph Albahari, published by O'Reilly.

Understanding the Task Parallel Library

The Task Parallel Library (TPL) is a new feature that makes parallel programming simpler and quicker, although care must be taken to carefully coordinate the parallel tasks that your program performs. I explore the TPL in Chapter 25. Parallel LINQ combines LINQ and the TPL and is covered in Chapter 28. A further TPL feature, Parallel Loops, can be found in Chapter 25. The Task Parallel Library is my other favorite C#/.NET feature, along with LINQ. I have been writing parallel programs for many, many years, and the TPL is like a breath of fresh air—simple, powerful, and expressive.

Related .NET Technologies

The Task Parallel Library doesn't depend on other .NET technologies covered in this book.

Further Reading

My own book on the TPL is *Pro .NET 4 Parallel Programming in C#* and is, once again, published by Apress. The TPL is relatively new and somewhat specialized, so there aren't any other books in this area that I can recommend.

Understanding User Interfaces

.NET provides a number of different ways to create user interfaces, each of which is suited for a particular kind of program. I cover five different user-interface technologies in this book, although there are commonalities and overlaps between them.

The first is *Windows Forms*, which is the most mature of the technologies available for creating Windows programs—by which I mean programs that are installed on a Windows computer and are run locally on that machine. Windows Forms is robust, simple to use, and has been widely adopted by developers around the world. I explore Windows Forms in Chapter 32.

The second such technology is the Windows Presentation Foundation (WPF). This is the new kid on the block and can also be used to create Windows programs, just like Windows Forms. WPF doesn't have the programmer adoption of Windows Forms, but it is catching up fast. What WPF does have is rich support for handling media such as audio and video and features to create interfaces that are glossier and slicker than Windows Forms. For example, there is an extensive animation system in WPF that you can use to make elements of the interface appear, disappear, or change in some way when the user presses a button. I look at WPF in Chapter 33.

The third and fourth user-interface technologies are part of ASP.NET. Web Forms is the web equivalent of Windows Forms, and the Dynamic Data system lets you build data-centric web applications very quickly. See the "Understanding ASP.NET" section earlier in this chapter for more details of ASP.NET and Chapter 34 for details of Web Forms and Dynamic Data.

The final technology I look at is Silverlight, which is a cut-down version of the .NET Framework that is installed and runs in the user's browser (much like Adobe Flash). Silverlight uses WPF for its user interfaces, but is also closely associated with ASP.NET because Silverlight controls are usually integrated with other ASP.NET technologies and delivered to the browse using Internet Information Services (IIS), which is the application server on which ASP.NET relies.

The good news that arises from these incestuous interdependencies is that you can use your knowledge in one of these technologies to get a head start when you use another. For example, once you are familiar with how WPF works you will find that Silverlight is pretty straight-forward to learn. And even when technologies are not directly related, such as Windows Forms and WPF, you will find that a common design approach has been used. The basic mechanism for creating Windows Forms programs is very similar to the basic mechanism for creating WPF or Web Forms programs.

Related .NET Technologies

I demonstrate how to create the same set of examples in the chapters on user-interface technology. This lets me emphasize the similarities and differences of each. One of the examples is to read and display data from a SQL Server database, which means that you rely on the LINQ to Entities technology, which is the topic of Chapter 30. Silverlight is often used with the WCF, which is covered in Chapter 21. I demonstrate the combination of Silverlight and WCF in Chapter 35.

Further Reading

I have not written a book about Windows Forms. The book I'd recommend for Windows Forms is *Windows Forms Programming in C#* by Chris Sells, published by Addison Wesley. It's an old book, from 2003, but Windows Forms has received little in the way of new books for some reason.

WPF has enjoyed much more attention. I recommend Matt MacDonald's *Pro WPF in C#*, and *WPF Recipes in C#* by my old friend Allen Jones. Allen's book hasn't been revised for WPF version 4 but contains a lot of good information nonetheless.

See the "Understanding ASP.NET" section earlier in the chapter for relevant book recommendations. Silverlight tends to be covered by both ASP.NET and WPF books. There are a number of books which are just focused on Silverlight, but I have yet to find one that I would recommend.

Understanding ADO.NET

ADO.NET is another technology mammoth—a platform for data access and management that provides numerous different approaches to dealing with a wide range of data storage mechanisms, although there is a strong focus on relational databases.

You will use two ADO.NET technologies in this book. The Entity Framework lets you work with relational data using C# objects; you use this when you look at LINQ to Entities in Chapter 30. You use a lower-level approach called the *DataSet* in Chapter 31. This requires more knowledge of the database being used and more effort to get data to and from the database, but it requires less resources and can be a lot more efficient in terms of transferring data around a network.

Related .NET Technologies

When you come to look at the two parts of ADO.NET you are interested in for this book, you do so using LINQ. LINQ and ADO.NET are a natural pairing. You obtain the data using ADO.NET and then use LINQ to process it. As previously mentioned, you will use the Entity Framework to create data models for each of the user interface technologies you examine in Chapters 32-35.

Further Reading

ADO.NET-related books tend to focus on one of the individual ADO.NET technologies. I'd recommend *Pro Entity Framework 4* by Scott Klein (Apress) and *Programming Entity Framework* by Julia Lerman (O'Reilly). The Entity Framework is a key component of ADO.NET and should be the main focus for most programmers wanting to get into the detail. Coverage of other ADO.NET technologies is spotty and there isn't anything that I'd recommend as being particularly useful.

Understanding the Windows Communication Foundation

The WCF is a framework for building service applications. Another broad technology suite in its own right, you will take an introductory tour of WCF in Chapter 21 and see it used in conjunction with Silverlight in Chapter 35. If you want to build any kind of web service or complex network service, then WCF is the way to go. It is rich, flexible, and encompasses a wide range of different network and service models.

Related .NET Technologies

WCF tends to underpin programs and services that are built using other technologies; therefore, it tends to be widely used, but isn't directly tied to any one implementation approach. The use of WCF to provide services for Silverlight clients is gaining adoption.

Further Reading

The books available for WCF are a mixed bunch. The one I'd recommend is a slightly older title: *Learning WCF* by Michele Leroux Bustamante and published by O and published by O'Reilly.

Understanding .NET Cross-Platform Support

If you are familiar with Java, you might have been excited when you read that .NET uses a virtual machine and assumed that .NET can run on multiple platforms. After all, virtual machines are a common approach to platform independence.

But .NET is a Microsoft technology, which means that there is a serious gravitational pull between the features of .NET and the features of Windows and other Microsoft products. If you are using C# and .NET, you are probably expecting to deploy your program to Windows—and that's not a bad thing. Windows and Windows Server are extremely competent operating systems and having one producer control the entire technology chain has some benefits. Of course, it has some drawbacks as well, but that's a topic for another day.

That said, there are two ways in which .NET runs on other platforms. The first is Silverlight, which runs on Windows and Mac OS X computers. You don't get access to all of the .NET Framework Class Library with Silverlight, but you do get the basics, and if you want to reach non-Windows users (and there can be quite a few depending on the market segment you are after), then Silverlight might be the answer you are looking for. I introduce Silverlight in Chapter 35 and you should probably read Chapter 33, which describes the WPF used by Silverlight for user interfaces.

A more comprehensive approach is *Mono*, details of which can be found at `http://mono-project.com`. Mono is an open source implementation of the .NET Framework that runs on a range of operating systems, including the common Linux distributions, Solaris, and Mac OS X. Mono tends to lag behind the latest .NET features, but you may be surprised by just how complete the implementation is. You can build ASP.NET web applications, use LINQ, write GUI programs, and much more. There is an open source implementation of Silverlight called Moonlight and even a development environment to replace Visual Studio for programmers who want to work on platforms other than Windows (or who just don't like Visual Studio). My advice is that you should only use C# and .NET if a significant majority of your target users are on Windows, but Silverlight and Mono are worth considering if you have a minority of users on other types of system. Mono, in particular, is worth investigating.

Summary

In this chapter, I have put C# and the .NET Framework in context. You have seen the two major components of the .NET Framework and how these are related to C#. You have explored the topic of assemblies and looked at the key features of the .NET platform and how they have been used to create a wide suite of technology building blocks that give .NET its wide-ranging features and functionality. Your next step is to start learning the basics of C#. Chapter 4 starts with the fundamentals common to every language and sets the foundation for the chapters that follow.

PART 2

■ ■ ■

The C# Language

There are two parts to learning a new programming language: the language itself and the libraries that it comes with. This part of the book is concerned with the C# language—the keywords, the operators, and how you can perform basic programming tasks such as creating a variable, performing a calculation, and defining and using a new data type.

There is a lot of detail in the chapters in this part of the book, and some of the chapters are relatively long. It is easy to be overwhelmed by C#, especially if you are new to object-oriented programming and have not used a similar language such as C++ or Java. I have included lots of code samples to put things in context and diagrams that show you how C# language features are used. My advice is to spend time getting to know the content in the early chapters well. Chapter 4 sets out the fundamentals of C#, which are then covered in detail in the chapters that follow. If you start to lose track of the detail, then I recommend going back to Chapters 4-9 to ensure that you have a solid foundation in the language basics.

You should pay particular attention to Chapter 6 if you are new to object-oriented programming. There are a set of very common programming errors that you can avoid by gaining a good grasp on the difference between reference types and value types—this is a difference that bedevils new programmers.

If you *have* used a similar language (such as C++ or Java), then you'll find C# has a lot of similar features, but even so, I recommend taking the time to learn about the C#

features that other common languages do not have or which differ significantly, such as properties and delegates. A programmer new to a language tends to stick to just the features that are similar to the old language, and that would be a shame when programming in C# because there are some nice aspects that make common programming problems easier to solve.

C# Fundamentals and Keyword Reference

In this chapter, we will look at some of the most fundamental aspects of C#—the syntax, the type system, and the set of keywords and operators. We'll also look at some of the most common tasks a programmer must perform and how they can be written in C#.

This chapter is full of references to other chapters. This chapter will set out the overall structure, but you should read the other chapters to get into the detail.

This is a long chapter, and it may take you some time to work your way through all of the examples, but it is time well invested, because the topics covered in this chapter are some of the most important C# building blocks. There can be a lot to take in when learning a new language, but don't feel overwhelmed. If you do find that you struggle to take in all of the new information, then I recommend downloading the code samples for this chapter (available for free from Apress.com) and experimenting to see how the examples compile and run.

Language Fundamentals

In the following sections, we'll use a simple C# program to introduce the various elements of the C# language syntax, such as identifiers, keywords, literals, and so on. We will then look at the C# type system, in particular the differences between reference and value types. Understanding this difference is critical to effective C# programming, and it causes programmers new to C# a lot of confusion and problems.

A Simple C# Program

The best place to start with a programming language is to look at a program. Listing 4-1 contains a simple C# program.

Listing 4-1. A Simple C# Program

```
using System;

namespace ProjectNamespace {

    class Program {
```

```
static void Main(string[] args) {

    // perform a calculation
    int x = 10 * 10;

    // print out the result of the calculation
    Console.WriteLine("Result: {0}", x);
    }
  }
}
```

This is a short and simple program, but we can use it to understand how some of the fundamentals of the C# language work together. Compiling and running the code in Listing 4-1 produces the following output:

```
Result: 100
```

In the sections that follow, I'll use the program shown in Listing 4-1 to explore and demonstrate the C# fundamentals. Many of these topics are the subject of other chapters in this book, in which case I'll provide a short introduction in this chapter and point you elsewhere for further information and examples.

■ **Caution** If you select Start Debugging from Visual Studio to compile and run this program, you may see a window flash open and then immediately close again. Sometimes this happens so quickly that you won't even see the flash. This happens because Visual Studio opens a new command prompt, runs the program, and then closes the command prompt window. Select Start Without Debugging in Visual Studio to be able to see the program output. In later examples, I add some statements that keep the window open.

C# Syntax

The syntax of C# is based on the syntax of C/C++ and has a lot in common with languages such as Java. If you have used one of these languages, then you will find that C# has a familiar appearance. If you have not used an object-oriented programming language before, the syntax may seem very odd—you might want to skip ahead to Chapter 6 where I introduce some of the core object-oriented concepts.

Identifiers

Identifiers are the names assigned by the programmer to C# elements such as classes, namespaces, methods, fields, properties, and so on. These elements are described in the following chapters; for example, classes are described in Chapter 6, and fields are described in Chapter 7.

Identifiers tend to make up a lot of a C# program—not only do you use identifiers when you write your own code, but you also use other programmers' identifiers when you use the .NET Framework Library. Figure 4-1 shows the identifiers in Listing 4-1.

```
using System;

namespace ProjectNamespace {

    class Program {

        static void Main(string[] args) {

            // perform a calculation
            int x = 10 * 10;

            // print out the result of the calculation
            Console.WriteLine("Result: {0}", x);
        }
    }
}
```

Figure 4-1. The identifiers in Listing 4-1

Identifiers consist of Unicode characters and can begin with a letter or an underscore; Unicode is a public standard for encoding text that supports international characters. Identifiers are case-sensitive, and there is a strong convention in C# to use one of three capitalization styles to help illustrate the nature of the C# element being identified. Table 4-1 describes the capitalization styles.

■ **Tip** You don't have to use any of these capitalization styles, but I recommend that you do, because it will keep your code consistent when you use the code libraries from Microsoft and others.

Table 4-1. Capitalization Styles Used in C#

Style	Description	Example
Pascal case	The first letter of the identifier and the first letter of each subsequent concatenated word are capitalized.	MyValue
Camel case	The first letter of the identifier is lowercase. The first letter of each subsequent concatenated word is capitalized.	myValue
Uppercase	All letters of the identifier are capitalized. This is used only for identifiers that have two or fewer letters.	UI

These first two capitalization styles are the most widely used, and there is a preference to make C# identifiers as meaningful as possible; this often involves concatenating multiple words together. Table 4-2 describes how these styles are conventionally applied in C#, with references to the chapter that describes the C# element being identified.

Table 4-2. Capitalization Styles Used in C#

Identifier Type	Capitalization Style	Example	Chapter
Class	Pascal	`MyClass`	6
Enumeration types, Enumeration values	Pascal	`MyEnum` `MyEnumValue`	12
Event	Pascal	`MyEvent`	10
Exception classes	Pascal (and always ends with *Exception*)	`MyAppException`	14
Interface	Pascal (and always begins with letter *I*)	`IMyInterface`	12
Method	Pascal	`MyMethod`	9
Method parameter	Camel	`myParameter`	9
Namespace	Pascal	`System.Collections`	11
Property	Pascal	`MyProperty`	8
Public field	Pascal	`MyField`	7
Other fields	Camel	`myField`	7

You cannot use keywords as identifiers; keywords are reserved words that have special meaning in C# and are discussed later in this section. For example, the word `class` is a keyword, meaning that you cannot use the word `class` as an identifier. You can combine keywords with other words, however—for example, `MyClass` is allowed.

■ **Tip** You can prefix a keyword with the @ symbol to make an identifier—for example, `@class`. I recommend that you do not use this feature, because it tends to cause confusion, and there are an almost infinite number of less troublesome identifiers available for use.

Keywords

Keywords are words that have special meaning in C#; you use them to tell the C# compiler about your program or to perform a specific task or function. A reference list of C# keywords is at the end of this chapter, along with examples of their use. Figure 4-2 illustrates the keywords in Listing 4-1.

```
using System;

namespace ProjectNamespace {

    class Program {

        static void Main(string[] args) {

            // perform a calculation
            int x = 10 * 10;

            // print out the result of the calculation
            Console.WriteLine("Result: {0}", x);
        }
    }
}
```

Figure 4-2. The keywords in Listing 4-1

Literals

Literals are data items that you enter into your code by value. These are interpreted by the compiler and converted into a C# data type. Types are explained later in this chapter. Literals are a convenient way to express simple values, such as numbers, strings of characters, and Boolean values (true and false). Figure 4-3 shows the two numeric literals in Listing 4-1, both of which express the same value—the number 10. The third literal is a string literal. You can read about numeric and Boolean literals in Chapter 5 and about string and character literals in Chapter 16.

```
using System;

namespace ProjectNamespace {

    class Program {

        static void Main(string[] args) {

            // perform a calculation
            int x = 10 * 10;

            // print out the result of the calculation
            Console.WriteLine("Result: {0}", x);
        }
    }
}
```

Figure 4-3. *The literals in Listing 4-1*

Operators

Operators describe calculations or actions that are performed on one or more *operands*. If you have programmed in almost any other language, the C# operators will be familiar to you. There are three operators in Listing 4-1, as illustrated in Figure 4-4.

```
using System;

namespace ProjectNamespace {

    class Program {

        static void Main(string[] args) {

            // perform a calculation
            int x = 10 * 10;

            // print out the result of the calculation
            Console.WriteLine("Result: {0}", x);
        }
    }
}
```

Figure 4-4. *The operators in Listing 4-4*

The multiplication operator (*) is used in Listing 4-1 to calculate the product of two numeric values—multiplying 10 by 10. The assignment operator (=) sets the value of the local variable called x to the result of the multiplication operation. The C# operators are described at the end of this chapter, and examples for each are provided.

One of the most important C# operators is the one that your eye may have passed over in Figure 4-4—the dot operator (.). This operator is used for member access specify a type, member, or namespace (these terms are described later in this chapter and in Chapter 11). The dot operator joins different elements of your program together to create a chain that the C# runtime can follow to carry out an action defined in your code statement. In Listing 4-1, the dot operator combines the name of a class (Console) with the name of a method (WriteLine); this is an instruction to perform the action defined in that method, which is part of the specified class.

■ **Tip** C# lets you organize your code into related groups. You then navigate through these groups using the dot operator. For this reason, the dot operator is probably the most important operator in C#. You will see the dot operator used in every single example in this book, and you will use it in every C# program you write. A good understanding of what the dot operator does is essential for a good grasp of C#.

Punctuators

Punctuators are used to either group things together or keep things separate. There are quite a few punctuators in Listing 4-1, as shown in Figure 4-5.

```
using System;

namespace ProjectNamespace {

    class Program {

        static void Main(string[] args) {

            // perform a calculation
            int x = 10 * 10;

            // print out the result of the calculation
            Console.WriteLine("Result: {0}", x);
        }
    }
}
```

Figure 4-5. The punctuators in Listing 4-1

The semicolon (;) is used to separate some kinds of C# code statements. Because a semicolon denotes the end of a statement, you can split a statement across multiple lines. The curly braces ({}) are used to group multiple statements together into a *code block*. Code blocks are used with C# keywords and identifiers to define groups or chunks of related functionality, such as a method or class. Parentheses (()) are used to group together items such as method parameters and are also used in code statements to override the default precedence of operators.

Statements

There are different kinds of statements in C#.

- A code block groups together multiple statements where a single statement is allowed, grouping multiple statements between curly braces ({}).

- Declaration statements define variables and constants. (See Chapters 7, 8, and 10.)

- Expression statements are evaluated to produce the result of an operator—this includes calling a method, creating a new object, performing a calculation, and so on (see the "Operators" section later in this chapter).

- Selection statements select one of a number of sets of statements based on a condition (see the "Performing Selections and Selection Keywords: sections later in this chapter).

- Iteration statements repeatedly execute a code block for each item in a set of items (see the "Iterating Data Items" and "Iterator Keywords" sections later in this chapter).

- Control statements are used to transfer execution from one set of statements to another (see the "Jump Keywords" section later in this chapter).

I haven't illustrated the statements in Listing 4-1 because everything in C# is a statement of one kind of another. Examples of most of the statement types can be found later in this chapter and are dealt with in more detail in the chapters that follow.

Comments

Comments are text that helps you and other programmers understand your code, and as a general rule, the more comments you include in your code to explain your thinking and technique, the easier code becomes to understand and maintain. C# supports two kinds of comments, one of which is used in Listing 4-1 and illustrated by Figure 4-6.

```
using System;

namespace ProjectNamespace {

    class Program {

        static void Main(string[] args) {

            // perform a calculation
            int x = 10 * 10;

            // print out the result of the calculation
            Console.WriteLine("Result: {0}", x);
        }
    }
}
```

Figure 4-6. The comments in Listing 4-1

The kind of comment used in Listing 4-1 is a single-line comment. Single-line comments being with //, and anything that follows to the end of that line is ignored by the compiler. The other kind of comment is a delimited comment and can span multiple lines. Delimited comment begin with /* and do not end until the sequence */ is encountered, even if this spans multiple lines. Here is an example of a multiline-delimited comment:

```
/* This is a multiline comment. The compiler
 * ignores everything that I write in such
 * a comment until until the terminator sequence
 * is encountered */
Console.WriteLine("Result: {0}", x);
```

The asterisks at the start of the second and subsequent lines are not required, but Visual Studio will add them for you when you create a multiline comment.

The compiler ignores comments, meaning that you can use comments to temporarily disable code statements or to provide information about the actions that your code is performing.

There is a strong convention to provide comments for class methods (described in Chapter 9). These comments should provide details about what the method does, what is expected in terms of parameters, and what the result of the method will be. These comments contain XML fragments. To create such a comment, type ///, and Visual Studio will generate a template for your method that you can fill in.

Types

Every piece of data in C# must have a type. This is a key part of C# being a strongly typed programming language, as described in Chapter 3. The C# compiler and runtime both use the type of each data item to reduce some kinds of programming problems. As an example, this stops you from defining the name Joe Smith and then trying to add the name to the number 2 unless you have assigned the name to a type that has defined rules for how to add numbers to names. If you have, that's fine; if you haven't, then the compiler won't compile your program for you.

There are two kinds of types in C#: value types and reference types. The distinction between the two causes programmers new to object-oriented programming a lot of confusion.

In the following sections, I'll show you the important differences between value types and reference types. We'll revisit one particular aspect of reference types when we discuss automatic memory management in Chapter 18.

Value Types

Value-type variables directly contain their data—that is to say that the content of a value-type variable *is* its value. The following statement assigns a value of 25 to a variable called myInt. The type of the variable myInt is int, which is a value type.

```
int myInt = 25;
```

Figure 4-7 illustrates how myInt is stored in memory.

Type:	int
Name:	myInt
Value:	25

Figure 4-7. A value-type variable in memory

When storing a value-type variable, C# keeps a note of the type, the identifier, and the value. When you copy a value-type variable, you create a second, separate variable with the same type and with the same value. Here is a code statement that creates a copy of myInt:

```
int myInt2 = myInt;
```

Figure 4-8 shows the two variables as they are stored in memory.

Type:	int		Type:	int
Name:	myInt		Name:	myInt2
Value:	25		Value:	25

Figure 4-8. The effect of copying a value-type variable

These variables are unrelated. If we change the value of one, the value of the other remains the same. Here is a code statement that changes the value of the first variable:

```
myInt = 50;
```

Figure 4-9 shows the effect of this change—one of the value-type variables has been changed to a value of 50, but the other remains as it was with a value of 25.

Type:	int		Type:	int
Name:	myInt		Name:	myInt2
Value:	50		Value:	25

Figure 4-9. The effect of modifying a value-type variable

C# includes a set of predefined value types, which are described in Table 4-3. When using the numeric types, good practice is to choose the data type that uses the smallest amount of memory but that can represent all the possible values that might be assigned when your program runs; the convention in reality is to use the int type for almost everything.

Table 4-3. Predefined Value Types in C#

Value Type	Description	See Chapter
sbyte, byte	Signed and unsigned 8-bit integer values	
short, ushort	Signed and unsigned 16-bit integer values	
int, uint	Signed and unsigned 32-bit integer values	5
long, ulong	Signed and unsigned 64-bit integer values	
float, double, decimal	32-, 64- and 128-bit real values	
bool	Logical values (true and false)	
char	Character values	16

■ **Tip** You can create your own value types using the C# enum and struct features; see Chapter 12 for details, examples, and an explanation of the difference between the two features.

Reference Types

Reference types come in two parts—an object and the reference to that object. Here is a statement that creates a reference-type object:

```
StringBuilder myObject = new StringBuilder("Adam");
```

The StringBuilder type holds a string of characters and is described in Chapter 16. Figure 4-10 shows the reference type in memory. You don't deal with the object directly—instead, you work with it via the reference.

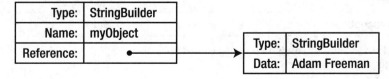

Figure 4-10. A reference type in memory

Figure 4-10 shows the reference variable and the object. The reference contains details of the variable type, the name of the variable, and a link to the object it refers to. The object contains its data but doesn't keep track of the reference—it is a one-way relationship.

When you copy a reference-type variable, you create a new copy of the reference, but not the object. The previous sentence is the most important in this chapter. It is the key to understanding object-oriented programming, and not understanding this point is the cause of most of the problems that new C# programmers encounter.

The following statements copy the reference-type variable:

```
StringBuilder myObject2 = myObject;
```

Figure 4-11 shows the effect of copying the variable.

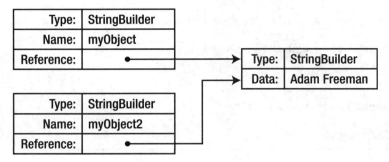

Figure 4-11. The effect of copying a reference-type variable

We have only one StringBuilder object, but now we have two references to it—one called myObject and the other called myObject2. Unlike value types, when you copy reference-type variables, the results are related because they refer to the same object. A change made to the object via one reference can be read via the second reference. This last point causes endless confusion to programmers who are new to C#.

■ **Tip** Two references to the same object can have different types. See the section on polymorphism in Chapter 6.

The C# language includes two commonly used built-in reference types, which are shown in Table 4-4. The .NET Framework library contains thousands of reference types (and many value types for that matter), and we'll explore some of these types in later parts of the book. There is a third reference type, called dynamic, but it is an advanced topic, so we won't explain its use in this book.

Table 4-4. Predefined Reference Types in C#

Reference Type	Description	See Chapter
object	The base class from which all types (including value types) are derived	6
string	A sequence of characters	16

You can create your own reference types, of course. Some of the most important C# features for doing this are classes (see Chapter 6), delegates (Chapter 10), and interfaces (Chapter 12).

Definite Assignment and Null References

C# requires that you assign a value to a variable before you read the value of the variable. The compiler checks your code to ensure that every path through your code assigns a value to every variable that you read. This is called *definite assignment*.

The assignment of a value doesn't need to occur when you declare the variable; you just have to make sure that you have made an assignment before you read the variable value. Here are some statements that demonstrate this:

```
int myInt;              // declare a variable, but don't assign to it
myInt = 20;             // assign a value to the variable
int sum = 100 + myInt;  // we can read the value because we have made an assignment
```

You don't need to make an assignment at all if you never read the value, but in this case, you have declared a variable that you neither read from nor write to, so the compiler will generate a warning for you.

When using a reference type, you can make an assignment but not have the variable refer to an object. You do this by using the special value null. Here is a statement that defines a StringBuilder object in this way:

```
StringBuilder myObject = null;
```

Figure 4-12 shows what this variable looks like in memory.

Type:	StringBuilder
Name:	myObject
Reference:	null

Figure 4-12. The effect of assigning null to a reference-type variable

We have created the reference but not the object. If we treat the variable as though it did refer to an object, then we get an exception (exceptions are the C# feature that handle errors in programs, described in Chapter 14). Here are two statements that create a reference to null and then treat the result as though there were an object available:

```
StringBuilder myObject = null;
myObject.Append("Adam");
```

Here is the exception that these statements cause:

```
Unhandled Exception: System.NullReferenceException: Object reference not set to
an instance of an object.
    at Listing_51.Main(String[] args) in C:\Listing_02\Listing_02.cs:line 41
```

Programmers often assign null to variables to avoid the compiler complaining about definite assignment, only to cause a problem when the program is running by treating a null reference as though it were an object.

Common Programming Tasks

The chapters that follow focus on the major features of C#: classes, methods, fields, parameters, delegates, and so on. These are such important topics that it can be easy to overlook the tasks that are most commonly required of programmers. In the following sections, I describe how to assign values to variables, make comparisons between values, selectively execute blocks of code, and iterate over data items.

Assigning Values

The C# assignment operator is the equals sign (=). Figure 4-13 shows how the assignment operator is used to assign a value to a variable.

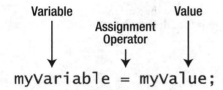

Figure 4-13. *The anatomy of a value assignment*

Listing 4-2 demonstrates defining an int variable and using the assignment operator to assign a value.

Listing 4-2. Using the Assignment Operator

```
int x = 20;
int y;
y = x;
```

The first line in Listing 4-2 defines an int variable and assigns it a value of 20 using a numeric literal in a single statement. The int type holds integer values and is discussed, along with numeric literals, in Chapter 5.

The second statement in Listing 4-2 defines a second int value, but it is not until the third statement a value is assigned to it. Note that I have used the name of the first variable. This copies the value of the first variable since int is a value type (see the previous section in this chapter for a discussion of types).

You can also use the assignment operator to assign the results of other operations to variables, like this:

```
int y = x + 20;
```

In this example, the int variable y is assigned the value of the result of x + 20. The assignment operator produces a result itself, which is the value you have assigned. This is shown by the following statement:

```
y = x = 40;
```

There are two assignments in this statement. The first assigns a value of 40 to the variable x. The second assigns the result of assigning the value of 40 to x to y. You might need to read that last sentence a couple of times for it to make sense. The result of assigning a value is the value you assigned, which you can use for further assignments. This feature of C# is not widely used—not least because it is easy to miss when scanning through pages of code.

Making Comparisons

The C# comparison operator (==) is used to determine whether two variables are the same. Listing 4-3 provides a demonstration.

Listing 4-3. Using the Comparison Operator

```
using System;
using System.Text;

class Listing_03 {

    static void Main(string[] args) {

        StringBuilder builder = new StringBuilder("Introduction to C#");
        StringBuilder builder2 = builder;

        bool sameRefs = builder == builder2;

        Console.WriteLine("References the same: {0}", sameRefs);

        // wait for input before exiting
        Console.WriteLine("Press enter to finish");
        Console.ReadLine();
    }
}
```

The code in Listing 4-3 creates two StringBuilder variables that are assigned the same value. Since StringBuilder is a reference type, this means that we have two variables that are referencing the same object (as we saw in Figure 4-11). The statement that uses the comparison operator is shown in bold in Listing 4-1 and illustrated by Figure 4-14.

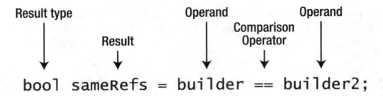

Figure 4-14. The anatomy of the comparison operator

The comparison operator is placed between the two things that you want to compare. The result of using the comparison operator is a bool value of true or false. (The bool type is described in Chapter 5.) In the listing, I have used the assignment operator to assign the result of the comparison to a bool variable called sameRefs.

For value types, the comparison operator returns true if the values contained by the two variables are the same. For reference-type variables, the comparison operator returns true if the two variables refer to the same object—compiling and running the code in Listing 4-2 produces the following output:

```
References the same: True
Press enter to finish
```

You can compare string values directly in C#; there is no need for an equivalent of the Equals method from Java, for example. Here is a simple demonstration:

```
string str1 = "Hello World";
string str2 = "Hello World";
string str3 = "Intro to C#";

bool str1EqualsStr2 = str1 == str2;
bool str1EqualsStr3 = str1 == str3;

Console.WriteLine("str1 equals str2: {0}", str1EqualsStr2);
Console.WriteLine("str1 equals str3: {0}", str1EqualsStr3);
```

Compiling and running these statements produces the following results:

```
str1 equals str2: True
str1 equals str3: False
```

In each of these comparisons, I have assigned the result to a bool variable. Often however, the comparison operator is used as a condition to a selection statement, such as an if statement. In such cases, you don't need to assign the result of the comparison operator to a variable—you can have the selection statement evaluate the comparison directly. Here's an example:

```
int i = 40;
if (i == 40) {
    Console.WriteLine("Int value is 40");
} else {
```

```
        Console.WriteLine("Int value is not 40");
}
```

Selection statements, including the if statement shown earlier, are described in the following section.

Performing Selections

Selection statements let you select blocks of code statements to be executed if a condition is met. C# supports two selection statements—the if statement and the switch statement.

Using an if Statement

With an if statement, you define a block of code statements that are performed only if a condition is met. Listing 4-4 contains an example.

Listing 4-4. Using an if Statement

```
using System;

class Listing_04 {

    static void Main(string[] args) {

        int x = 100;

        if (x == 100) {
            Console.WriteLine("Code Block Selected");
        }

        // wait for input before exiting
        Console.WriteLine("Press enter to finish");
        Console.ReadLine();
    }
}
```

The if statement in Listing 4-4 performs the statement in the code block if the value of the int local variable called x is 100. Since the variable is defined just prior to the if statement, we can sure that this code block will be selected in this example. Figure 4-15 illustrates an if statement.

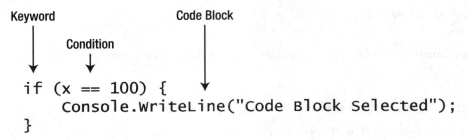

Figure 4-15. *The anatomy of an* if *statement*

The condition in an if statement is any C# expression that can be evaluated to a bool value—that is, true or false. In the listing I have used the comparison operator to check the value of a variable. You can use bool variables or fields as conditions, like this:

```
int y = 100;
bool result = y == 100;

if (result) {
    Console.WriteLine("Code Block Selected");
}
```

You can also use the literal values true and false as conditions. These values won't change when the program is running, so the if statement will always perform the same way, either always performing the statements in the code block or always stepping over them. Although I have included only one statement in the code block in Listing 4-4, you can add as many statements as you need, and those statements can include other if statements, like this:

```
int z = 100;
if (z > 50) {
    if (z == 100) {
        Console.WriteLine("Code Block Selected");
    }
}
```

You can use the C# conditional operators to combine conditions together so that one or all of a set of individual conditions are evaluated together, like this:

```
if (x > 0 && y < 200) {
    Console.WriteLine("Code Block Selected");
}
```

This if statement uses the relational operators, described later in the chapter and in Chapter 5, and the conditional AND (&&) operator to create a condition that will evaluate to true only if one variable is greater than 0 and another variable is less than 200. You can also use the conditional OR operator (||), like this:

```
if (x > 0 || y < 200) {
    Console.WriteLine("Code Block Selected");
```

```
}
```

This condition will evaluate to true if one variable is greater than 0 or the other variable is less than 200.

Adding else if Clauses

You can choose between code blocks by adding else if clauses to an if statement, like this:

```
if (x == 50) {
    Console.WriteLine("First Code Block Selected");
} else if (x == 60) {
    Console.WriteLine("Second Code Block Selected");
} else if (x == 100) {
    Console.WriteLine("Third Code Block Selected");
}
```

The conditions in an if statement with else if clauses are evaluated in turn, and the statements in the code block associated with the first condition to evaluate to true will be performed. Once a true condition has been found, no further conditions are evaluated, and at most one code block will be performed. An if statement can have many else if clauses. If none of the conditions evaluates to true, then none of the code blocks will be performed.

Adding an else Clause

An if statement can contain a single else clause that will be performed if the condition in the statement and all of the conditions in any else if clauses evaluate to false. The else clause must come at the end of the if statement, like this:

```
if (x == 100) {
    Console.WriteLine("First Code Block Selected");
} else {
    Console.WriteLine("Second Code Block Selected");
}
```

The else clause code block will not be performed if any of the conditions in the if statement have evaluated to true.

Using a switch Statement

A switch statement selects one of a set of code statements to execute by comparing a value to a set of constants. Listing 4-5 contains an example of a switch statement.

Listing 4-5. Using a switch Statement

```
string myName = "Adam Freeman";

switch (myName) {
    case "Joe Smith":
```

```
            Console.WriteLine("Name is Joe Smith");
            break;
    case "Adam Freeman":
            Console.WriteLine("Name is Adam Freeman");
            break;
    default:
            Console.WriteLine("Default reached");
            break;
}
```

In this example, the string variable myName is used as the input value for comparison in the switch statement. Figure 4-16 illustrates the switch statement in Listing 4-5.

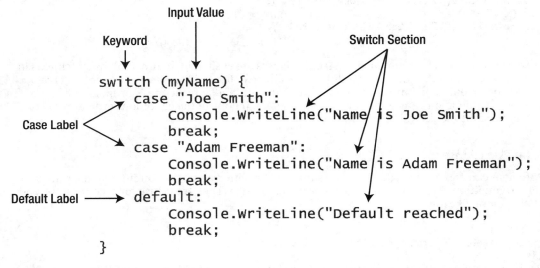

Figure 4-16. *The anatomy of a* switch *statement*

The switch statement contains one or more case labels, which contain the constant values that myName will be compared against. If the value of myName matches the constant value, then the statements in the switch sections—between the case label and the break statement—will be performed.

If none of the constant values in the case labels matches the input value, then the code statements following the default label are performed. The default section is optional in case statements.

Every switch section in a switch statement must end with a break or goto case statement—C# does not support *falling through* from one section to another. You can put multiple case statements next to each other so that the statements in a switch section will be performed if the input value matches one of a set of constant values, like this:

```
switch (myName) {
    case "Joe Smith":
        Console.WriteLine("Name is Joe Smith");
        break;
    case "Adam Freeman":
```

```
        case "Jane Jones":
        case "Peter Kent":
            Console.WriteLine("Name is Adam Freeman, Jane Jones or Peter Kent");
            break;
        default:
            Console.WriteLine("Default reached");
            break;
}
```

In this switch statement, a single switch section will be selected if the input value matches any one of three different names. The values specified in the case labels must be constant. Unlike an if statement, you can't use expressions. You can use string and character literal values (see Chapter 16), as in Listing 4-5; numeric and bool literal values (see Chapter 5); or enum values (see Chapter 12).

Jumping to Another switch Section

You can combine the statements in switch sections by using a goto case statement, which jumps to the specified section, as follows:

```
switch (myName) {
    case "Joe Smith":
        Console.WriteLine("Name is Joe Smith");
        break;
    case "Adam Freeman":
        Console.WriteLine("Name is Adam Freeman, Jane Jones or Peter Kent");
        goto case "Joe Smith";
    default:
        Console.WriteLine("Default reached");
        break;
}
```

In this switch statement, if the input value is Adam Freeman, the statement in the Adam Freeman switch section is performed, followed by the statement in the Joe Smith section.

Iterating Data Items

One of the most common programming tasks is to perform the same series of actions for each element in a sequence of data items—for example, items in an array (see Chapter 13) or a collection (see Chapter 19). C# supports four ways of performing iterations.

Using a for Loop

A for loop repeatedly performs a block of statements while a condition remains true. Before the first iteration, an *initializer* executes one or more expressions. At the end of each iteration, an *iterator* executes one or more statements. Another iteration will be performed if the condition evaluates to true. Listing 4-6 contains an example of using a for loop.

Listing 4-6. Using a for Loop

```
using System;

class Listing_06 {

    static void Main(string[] args) {


        for (int i = 0; i < 5; i++) {
            Console.WriteLine("Iteration for value: {0}", i);
        }

        // wait for input before exiting
        Console.WriteLine("Press enter to finish");
        Console.ReadLine();
    }
}
```

Figure 4-17 illustrates the for loop in Listing 4-6.

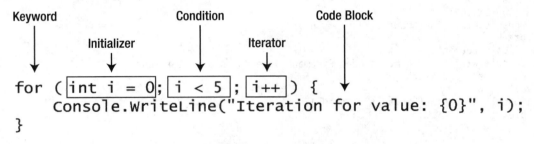

Figure 4-17. The anatomy of a for loop

The initializer, the condition, and the iterator are separated by semicolons (;). The for loop shown in Listing 4-6 is the most common kind—the initializer is used to create a local variable for use in the loop—conventionally called i. The iterator increments the local loop variable after each repetition, and the condition evaluates to true as long as the value of i is less than a predefined limit, in this case 5. This loop will iterate five times, as we can see if we compile and run the code in Listing 4-6, which produces the following results:

```
Iteration for value: 0
Iteration for value: 1
Iteration for value: 2
Iteration for value: 3
Iteration for value: 4
Press enter to finish
```

Within the loop, I can refer to the local variable i and get the current value. The initializer can define either a local variable or a series of statements separated by commas that should be performed before the first iteration. The iterator can similarly contain multiple statements, also separated by commas, like this:

```
int i, j;

for (i = 0, j = 0; i < 5; i++, j += 2) {
    Console.WriteLine("Iteration for values: i={0} and j={1}", i, j);
}
```

In this for loop, the initializer assigns values to the previously defined variables i and j. The iterator has two statements that increment the value of i by 1 and increment the value of j by 2. The increment operators are described in Chapter 5. The output of this loop is as follows:

```
Iteration for values: i=0 and j=0
Iteration for values: i=1 and j=2
Iteration for values: i=2 and j=4
Iteration for values: i=3 and j=6
Iteration for values: i=4 and j=8
```

The variables i and j were defined outside of the loop, which means that they can be used after the loop has finished iterating. In the example, i would have a value of 4, and j would have a value of 8 when the loop has finished. The initializer and iterator statements are optional, but you must still use the semicolons if you omit them, like this:

```
int i = 0;

for (; i < 5;) {
    Console.WriteLine("Iteration for value: {0}", i);
    i++;
}
```

This loop includes only the condition. The local variable that the condition relies on is defined before the loop, and its value is incremented inside the code block.

Breaking Out of a for Loop

You can terminate a for loop before the condition evaluates to false by using the break keyword, like this:

```
for (int i = 0; i < 100; i++) {
    Console.WriteLine("Iteration for value: {0}", i);
    if (i == 5) {
        break;
    }
}
```

The condition in this loop will evaluate to true until the value of the local variable i reaches 100. However, the if statement in the loop body will execute the break statement when the value of the variable is equal to 5. Here is the output from the loop:

```
Iteration for value: 0
Iteration for value: 1
Iteration for value: 2
Iteration for value: 3
Iteration for value: 4
Iteration for value: 5
```

Continuing to the Next Iteration

Normally a for loop will perform all the statements in the code block before moving on to the next iteration. By using the continue keyword, you can move to the next iteration without performing any statements that follow. Here is an example:

```
for (int i = 0; i < 5; i++) {
    Console.WriteLine("Iteration for value: {0}", i);
    if (i == 2 || i == 3) {
        continue;
    }
    Console.WriteLine("Reached end of iteration for value: {0}", i);
}
```

In this example, the continue keyword is used to advance to the next iteration without writing the last message if the value of the loop variable is 2 or 3. Here is the output from the loop:

```
Iteration for value: 0
Reached end of iteration for value: 0
Iteration for value: 1
Reached end of iteration for value: 1
Iteration for value: 2
Iteration for value: 3
Iteration for value: 4
Reached end of iteration for value: 4
```

Using a foreach Loop

A foreach loop is a convenient way of iterating over the contents of an array or collection or any class that implements the System.Collections.Generic.IEnumerable<T> interface. Listing 4-7 contains an example of using a foreach loop to iterate the contents of an array. Arrays are explained in Chapter 13, collections and the IEnumerable<T> interface are covered in Chapter 12, and details of how to make your custom types work with foreach loops can be found in Chapter 9.

Listing 4-7. Using a foreach Loop

```
using System;

class Listing_07 {
```

```
static void Main(string[] args) {

    // define an int array
    int[] array = { 2, 4, 6, 8, 10 };

    foreach (int i in array) {
        Console.WriteLine("Iteration for value: {0}", i);
    }

    // wait for input before exiting
    Console.WriteLine("Press enter to finish");
    Console.ReadLine();
  }
}
```

Figure 4-18 illustrates the foreach loop from Listing 4-7.

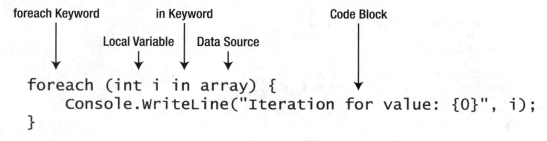

Figure 4-18. The anatomy of a foreach loop

There is no condition in a foreach loop. The statements in the code block will be executed once for each data item in the data source. In Listing 4-7, the data source is an int array with five items, so the single code statement in the code block will be executed five times.

Before each loop iteration, the value of the local variable defined in the foreach loop will be assigned to an item in the data source, and the variable can be referred to from within the code block. In the case of Listing 4-7, the local variable i will be assigned the values 2, 4, 6, and so on; the values are assigned in the order in which they appear in the data source. The type of the local variable has to match the type of the items in the data source. Compiling and running Listing 4-7 produces the following results:

```
Iteration for value: 2
Iteration for value: 4
Iteration for value: 6
Iteration for value: 8
Iteration for value: 10
Press enter to finish
```

You can use the break and continue keywords in a foreach loop as you would a for loop—see earlier in this chapter for details.

Using a do...while Loop

The third loop available in C# is a do...while loop. Listing 4-8 contains an example.

Listing 4-8. Using a do...while Loop

```csharp
using System;

class Listing_08 {

    static void Main(string[] args) {

        int x = 0;
        do {
            // write out a message
            Console.WriteLine("Iteration for value: {0}", x);

            // increment the local variable
            x++;
        } while (x < 5);

        // wait for input before exiting
        Console.WriteLine("Press enter to finish");
        Console.ReadLine();
    }
}
```

Figure 4-19 shows the do...while loop in Listing 4-8.

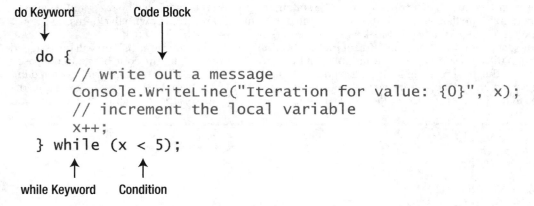

Figure 4-19. The anatomy of a do...while Loop

A do...while loop will perform the statements in the code block at least once and then continue to do so as long as the condition evaluates to true. In Listing 4-8, the code block includes a statement that increments the local variable that the condition relies on. Unlike a for loop, a do...while loop doesn't include initializer or iterator statements. Compiling and running Listing 4-8 produces the following loutput:

```
Iteration for value: 0
Iteration for value: 1
Iteration for value: 2
Iteration for value: 3
Iteration for value: 4
Press enter to finish
```

Using a while Loop

The final C# loop type is a while loop. Listing 4-9 contains an example.

Listing 4-9. Using a while Loop

```
using System;

class Listing_08 {

    static void Main(string[] args) {

        int x = 0;

        while (x < 5) {
            // write out a message
            Console.WriteLine("Iteration for value: {0}", x);
            // increment the local variable
            x++;
        }

        // wait for input before exiting
        Console.WriteLine("Press enter to finish");
        Console.ReadLine();
    }
}
```

Figure 4-20 shows the while loop in Listing 4-9 .

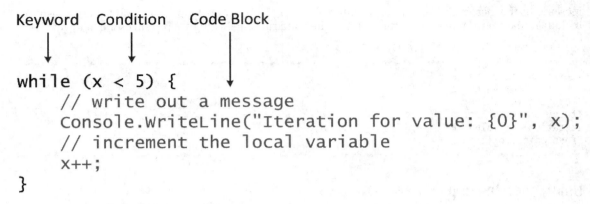

Figure 4-20. *The anatomy of a while loop*

A while loop will perform the statements in the code block while the condition evaluates to true. If the condition doesn't evaluate to true when first evaluated, the statements in the code block will never be performed; this is the key difference from the do...while loop, which will perform the statements at least once.

In Listing 4-9, the code block includes a statement that increments the local variable that the condition relies on. Unlike a for loop, a while loop doesn't include initializer or iterator statements. Compiling and running Listing 4-9 produces the following output:

```
Iteration for value: 0
Iteration for value: 1
Iteration for value: 2
Iteration for value: 3
Iteration for value: 4
Press enter to finish
```

Keyword and Operator Reference

The following sections provide a brief description of all the keywords and operators that we will encounter as we explore C# in the coming chapters. Each item is described briefly, and details of where in the book you can find further information are provided. I have not listed all the keyword and operators—just the ones that are commonly used and that are covered in this book.

These sections are not intended to be read start to finish. I suggest you use these for reference when you know what it is you want to achieve but can't remember which keyword or operator you should use. Many of the keywords are accompanied by brief examples to jog your memory in just these circumstances. The keywords are grouped by category. Table 4-3 summarizes the keywords so you can turn find what you are looking for.

Table 4-3. Keywords Grouped by Category

Category/Section	Keywords
Type Keywords	bool, byte, sbyte, char, class, decimal, double, float, delegate, dynamic, enum, interface, object, string, struct, short, ushort, int, uint, long, ulong, void, var
Modifiers	public, protected, private, internal, abstract, const, event, in, out, override, readonly, sealed, static, virtual
Selection Keywords	if, else, switch, case, default
Iterator Keywords	for, foreach, do, while
Jump Keywords	break, continue, goto, return
Exception Handling Keywords	try, catch, finally
Arithmetic Overflow Keywords	checked, unchecked
Synchronization Keywords	lock
Parameter Keywords	params, ref, out, in
Namespace Keywords	namespace, using
Literal Keywords	null, true, false, default
Object Keywords	is, as, new, typeof
LINQ Keywords	from, where, select, group, into, orderby, join, let, ascending, descending, on, equals, by, in
Other Keywords	base, get, set, value, global, implicit, explicit, operator, partial, this, yield

Type Keywords

The following C# keywords relate to types, either to support defining new types or to make use of the built-in types.

bool

The bool keyword refers to the System.Boolean value type, which is used to store true and false values. The bool type is implicitly used in the condition of selection statements.

Example

The following statement uses the bool keyword to define a bool variable and assign the value true to it:

```
bool myVariable = true;
```

References

The bool type is covered in Chapter 5. Also see the true and false keywords.

byte, sbyte

The byte and sbyte keywords refer to 8-bit signed and unsigned integer values.

Example

The following statements define a byte and sbyte local variables and assign values to them using numeric literals:

```
byte myByte = 50;
sbyte mySByte = 100;
```

References

These types are described in Chapter 5, as are numeric literals.

char

The char keyword is used to declare a single Unicode character.

Example

The following statement defines a char variable with the value a using a character literal:

```
char myChar = 'a';
```

References

The char type and character literals are discussed in Chapter 16.

class

The class keyword is used to define new reference types.

Example

The following statements define a new class:

```
class Person {
    public string Name;
    public int Age;
    public string City;

    public Person(string name, int age, string city) {
        Name = name;
        Age = age;
        City = city;
    }
}
```

The following statement creates a new local variable using the class defined earlier:

```
Person myPerson = new Person("Adam Freeman", 38, "London");
```

References

Classes and creating objects from them are covered in Chapter 6.

decimal, double, float

These keywords are used to declare variable that can contain real numbers (those with a decimal place). The types differ in the degree of precision that can be represented.

Example

The following statements define variables of each type using numeric literals and numeric suffixes:

```
decimal myDecimal = 100.23m;
double myDouble = 100.23d;
float myFloat = 100.23f;
```

References

The built-in numeric types, numeric literals, and numeric suffixes are covered in Chapter 5.

delegate

The delegate keyword is used to define a type similar to a method signature. Instances of this type can then be assigned methods.

Example

The following statement defines a new delegate type that has an int parameter and no return type:

```
delegate void MyDelegate(int pValue);
```

The following class contains a method that matches the delegate signature and demonstrates the use of the previous delegate type to assign and invoke this method to a local variable:

```
class DelegateTest {

    static void Main(string[] args) {

        // define a new instance of the delegate type
        MyDelegate del = PerformAction;

        // invoke the delegate
        del(100);

        // wait for input before exiting
        Console.WriteLine("Press enter to finish");
        Console.ReadLine();
    }

    static void PerformAction(int count) {
        Console.WriteLine("Perform action with parameter value: {0}", count);
    }
}
```

References

Delegates and some related types such as events, Actions, and Funcs are explained in Chapter 10.

dynamic

The dynamic keyword is used to declare a variable for which static type safety will not be enforced. This is an advanced feature that should not be used unless fully understood.

Example

The following statements create a dynamic type variable and invoke a method upon it:

```
dynamic myDynamicObject = new StringBuilder("Adam");
```

```
// call a method that exists
myDynamicObject.Append(" Freeman");

// call a method that does not exist
myDynamicObject.IllegalCall(200);
```

With a dynamic object reference, the compiler does not check to see whether the methods that are being called exist. In the previous code statements, the call to the Append method will work (because the method exists in the underlying StringBuilder type), but the method to IllegalCall will result in an exception when the program is run.

References

Dynamic types are explained in Chapter 15. Exceptions are described in Chapter 14.

enum

The enum keyword is used to define an enumeration, which is a type category in its own right in C#.

Example

The following statement defines a new enumeration:

```
enum DaysOfWeek {Mon, Tues, Wed, Thurs, Fri, Sat, Sun};
```

The following statement declares a local variable of the enumeration type defined earlier and assigns an initial value:

```
DaysOfWeek today = DaysOfWeek.Wed;
```

References

Enumerations are described in Chapter 12.

interface

The interface keyword is used to define new C# interfaces. Interfaces contain only the signatures of methods, properties, events, and indexes and must be implemented by a class or struct.

Example

The following statements define an interface that contains a single method:

```
public interface ICalc {

    int CalculateProduct(int x, int y);
}
```

The following class demonstrates implementing the interface:

```
public class Calculator : ICalc {

    public int CalculateProduct(int x, int y) {
        return x * y;
    }
}
```

Classes that implement interfaces are usually upcast to the interface type, like this:

```
class InterfaceTest {

    static void Main(string[] args) {

        // create a new Calculator object and upcast it to the
        // interface that it implements
        ICalc calc = new Calculator();

        // call a method through the interface
        int result = calc.CalculateProduct(10, 10);

        // print out the result
        Console.WriteLine("Result: {0}", result);

        // wait for input before exiting
        Console.WriteLine("Press enter to finish");
        Console.ReadLine();
    }
}
```

References

Interfaces and the interface keyword are described fully in Chapter 12. Upcasting is described in Chapter 6.

object

The object keyword is a convenient way of referring to the System.Object type from which all C# types, reference and value, are derived. This keyword is used when the specific type of an object is known and more generalized handling is required—for example, collection classes. The use of this keyword has declined since the introduction of generic types.

Example

The following statement creates an object and upcasts it to the System.Object type using the object keyword:

```
object myObject = new StringBuilder("Adam Freeman");
```

References

Objects in general and casting between types are discussed in Chapter 6.

string

The string keyword is a convenient way of referring to the System.String type, which represents a sequence of characters.

Example

The following statement defines a local variable and uses a string literal to assign a value to it:

```
string myString = "Introduction to C#";
```

References

Strings, characters, and string literals are all described in Chapter 16.

struct

The struct keyword is used to define struct value types, which are usually used to group small numbers of related variable together.

Example

The following statement uses the struct keyword to declare a new struct type:

```
public struct Person {
    public string Name;
    public int Age;
    public string City;

    public Person(string name, int age, string city) {
        Name = name;
        Age = age;
        City = city;
    }
}
```

The following statement demonstrates a new instance of the struct being created and assigned to a variable:

```
Person myPerson = new Person("Adam Freeman", 38, "London");
```

References

The struct keyword is described fully in Chapter 12.

short, ushort, int, uint, long, ulong

The short, ushort, int, uint, long, and ulong keywords are used to declare variables that contain 16-, 32-, and 64-bit integer values using the built-in numeric types. The unsigned types (those whose names begin with the letter *u*) can hold only positive values but can hold larger values than their signed counterparts.

Example

The following statements create variables of each of these types:

```
ushort myUshort= 100;
short myShort = -100;
uint myUint = 100;
int myInt = -100;
ulong myUlong = 100;
long myLong = -100;
```

References

The built-in numeric types are discussed in Chapter 5.

void

The void keyword is used in a method definition to indicate that no result will be returned.

Example

The following class defined a method that uses the void keyword:

```
class MyClass {

    public void PrintMessage(String str) {
        Console.WriteLine("Message: {0}", str);
    }
}
```

References

Methods, including the void keyword, are described in Chapter 9.

var

The type of variables defined with the var keyword is inferred by the compiler. This is not the same as the dynamic keyword; type constraints are still enforced only, but the compiler infers the type from your code.

The var keyword is also used with anonymous types that have no formal type name and therefore cannot be explicitly typed. Anonymous types are often used with LINQ—see Chapter 27 for examples.

Example

The following statements assign an object to a var variable and call a method on it:

```
var myInferredType = new StringBuilder("Introduction to C#");
myInferredType.Append(" 2010");
```

The following statements create a simple anonymous type:

```
var myAnonType = new {
    Name = "Adam Freeman",
    Age = 32,
    City = "London"
};

Console.WriteLine("Name: {0}", myAnonType.Name);
```

References

Anonymous types are described in Chapter 15.

Modifiers

The following keywords are applied to declarations of different kinds to create a specific kind of behavior.

public, protected, private, internal

These four keywords, known as the *access modifiers*, are used to restrict access to types (classes, structs, and so on) and their members (methods, fields, properties, and so on). There are slight variations in the meaning of these keywords because they are applied to different C# features, but Table 4-4 sums up the general meaning of them.

Table 4-4. *General Meaning of the Access Modifier Keywords*

Access Modifier	Description
public	The type or member is accessible to any code in any assembly in the program.
protected	The type or member is accessible only within the containing type or within a derived type.
internal	The type or member can be accessed only from other types inside of the same assembly.
protected internal	A combination of the protected and internal keywords—the type or member is accessible within the current assembly or to derived types in any assembly.
private	The type or member is accessible only within the body of the type that defines it (this includes nested types).

Example

The following class contains a private field and a public property that mediates access to the field:

```
class MyClass {
    private int myPrivateField = 100;

    public int MyPublicProperty {
        get {
            return myPrivateField;
        }
        set {
            myPrivateField = value;
        }
    }
}
```

References

The access modifiers are described for each C# feature they relate to, including classes (Chapter 6), fields (Chapter 7), properties (Chapter 8), and methods (Chapter 9).

abstract

The abstract keyword indicates that the thing it is applied to is missing or incomplete. For example, abstract classes contain abstract methods that must be implemented by a derived class.

Example

The following class is declared abstract and contains an abstract method:

```
abstract class MyAbstractClass {

    public abstract int CalculateProduct(int x, int y);
}
```

The following class is derived from the abstract class and implements the abstract method:

```
class MyClass : MyAbstractClass {
    public override int CalculateProduct(int x, int y) {
        return (x * y);
    }
}
```

References

The abstract keyword is discussed in Chapters 6 and 9.

const

The const modifier is used on fields or local variables to indicate that their values are constant and cannot be modified.

Example

The following statement declares a const local variable:

```
const int myConst = 100;
```

References

The const keyword is covered in Chapter 7. Also see the readonly keyword.

event

The event keyword declares an event type in a class that will publish notifications.

Example

The following class defines an event called CalculationPerformedEvent, which is invoked from within the CalculateProduct method:

```
class Calculator {
    public event EventHandler<EventArgs> CalculationPerformedEvent;

    public int CalculateProduct(int x, int y) {
        // calculate the result
        int result = x * y;

        // send an event
        CalculationPerformedEvent(this, EventArgs.Empty);

        // return the result
        return result;
    }
}
```

Objects that want to receive events use the increment operator (+=) to add a delegate to the event; this delegate is invoked when the event is invoked. The following statements demonstrate using a lambda expression to register a listener with the event defined previously:

```
// create a Calculator object
Calculator calc = new Calculator();

// subscribe to the event using a lamba expression
calc.CalculationPerformedEvent += ((object source, EventArgs args) => {
    Console.WriteLine("Event received");
});
```

References

Events are discussed in Chapter 10. Lambda expressions are discussed in Chapter 10.

in, out

The in and out modifiers support covariance and contravariance.

Example

See Chapter 15 for examples of these keywords

References

Chapter 15 describes generic types and their support for covariance and contravariance.

override

The override keyword is required to implement an abstract or virtual method or property in a base class.

Example

The following class defines a virtual and an abstract method:

```
abstract class MyAbstractClass {

    public abstract int CalculateProduct(int x, int y);

    public virtual int CalculateSum(int x, int y) {
        return 0;
    }
}
```

The following class shows how the override method is used to provide implementations of both methods in the previous class:

```
class MyDerivedClass : MyAbstractClass {

    public override int CalculateProduct(int x, int y) {
        return x * y;
    }

    public override int CalculateSum(int x, int y) {
        return x + y;
    }
}
```

References

The override keyword is described in Chapters 8 and 9. Also see the virtual and abstract keywords.

readonly

The readonly modifier is applied to fields. Fields that are readonly can be assigned values only in their declaration statement or in a constructor of the class that contains them.

Example

The following class defines a readonly field, which is assigned an initial value in its declaration statement and another value in the class constructor:

```
class MyClass {
    private readonly int myReadonlyField = 100;
```

```
    public MyClass() {
        myReadonlyField = 200;
    }
}
```

References

The readonly modifier is covered in Chapter 7. Also see the const keyword.

sealed

When applied to a class, the sealed modifier prevents any other classes being derived from the sealed class. When applied to a method along with the override keyword, no derived class can further override the method.

Example

The DerivedClass in the following statements has overridden an abstract base class method and used the sealed modifier to prevent any further derivations:

```
abstract class BaseClass {

    public abstract int CalculateProduct(int x, int y);
}

class DerivedClass : BaseClass {

    public sealed override int CalculateProduct(int x, int y) {
        return x * y;
    }
}
```

References

The sealed keyword is discussed in Chapters 6 and 9.

static

The static modifier declares a member (a method, field, property, and so on) to be static, meaning that it belongs to the type rather than an instance of a type. When applied to classes, the objects cannot be created from the class, and all class members must be static.

References

See Chapter 6 for information about static classes and Chapter 7, 8, and 9 for information about other static members.

virtual

The virtual modifier is applied to methods and properties to indicate that derived types can use the override modifier to provide more specialized implementations.

Example

See the override modifier for an example of virtual being used.

References

Chapter 6 explains class inheritance and the effect of overriding methods, and Chapter 9 provides additional information and examples.

Selection Keywords

Selection keywords allow you to selectively execute code statements. C# supports two selection statements that use five keywords, described in the following sections.

if, else

The if and else keywords are used to define an if statement, which will perform a block of statements when a condition evaluates to the bool value true.

References

The if statement is described in the "Performing Selections" section earlier in the chapter.

switch, case, default

The switch keyword is used to define a switch statement that will perform a series of statements if an input value matches a constant value. The case keyword is used to declare the constant value in a switch statement, and the default keyword defines statements that will be executed if none of the case statements matches.

References

The switch statement is described in the "Performing Selections" section earlier in the chapter.

Iterator Keywords

Iterator keywords allow you to repeatedly perform a block of code statements until some condition has been met.

for

The for keyword is used to create for loops.

References

See the "Iterating Data Items" section earlier in this chapter for details and examples.

foreach

The foreach keyword is used to create foreach loops, which perform a block of code statements for each item in a data source—typically an array or collection.

References

See the "Iterating Data Items" section earlier in this chapter for details and examples. Arrays are explained in Chapter 13, and collections are explained in Chapter 19.

do, while

The do and while keywords are used to create do...while loops.

References

See the "Iterating Data Items" section earlier in this chapter for details and examples.

Jump Keywords

In C#, code statements are usually executed in sequence. Jump keywords allow you to jump to another point, where sequential execution will resume.

break

The break keyword is used in loops to terminate the loop prematurely and in switch statements to signal the end of a switch section.

References

See the "Performing Selections" section earlier in this chapter for examples of using break as part of switch statements and the "Iterating Data Items" section for examples of using break in loops.

continue

The continue keyword is used in loops to advance prematurely to the next iteration.

References

See the "Iterating Data Items" section earlier in this chapter for examples of using the continue statement in a loop.

goto

The goto keyword is used in switch statements to jump to a different switch region.

References

See the "Performing Selections" section earlier in this chapter for details of switch statements and an example of using the goto keyword.

return

The return keyword returns a result from a method. When the result keyword is encountered, no further statements in the method are executed.

Example

The following class contains a method that uses the return keyword:

```
class Calculator {

    public int CalculateSum(int x, int y) {
        return x + y;
    }
}
```

References

See Chapter 9 for details of returning results from methods.

Exception Handling Keywords

Exceptions are the C# mechanism for flagging and dealing with error conditions.

throw

The throw keyword is used to raise an exception, indicating that an error has occurred. This keyword is used in conjunction with the System.Exception class, and classes derived from System.Exception can be used to represent specific types of error.

Example

The following statement uses the throw keyword to throw a NullReferenceException:

```
throw new NullReferenceException();
```

References

See Chapter 14 for details of throwing exceptions and creating custom exceptions that can be used to represent error conditions that are unique to your program.

try, catch, finally

The try, catch, and finally keywords are all used in try statements to handle exceptions raised with the throw keyword.

Example

The following try statement includes catch and finally clauses:

```
try {
    // code statements go here
} catch (Exception ex) {
    // print out details of the exception
    Console.WriteLine(ex.ToString());
} finally {
    // release any resources here
}
```

References

See Chapter 14 for details of using try statements to handle exceptions, including the use of catch and finally clauses.

Arithmetic Overflow Keywords

These keywords specify whether checks are made for arithmetic overflow, which occurs when an attempt is made to assign too large a value to a numeric type variable.

checked, unchecked

The checked and unchecked keywords enable and disable arithmetic overflow checking in C#.

References

Arithmetic overflow and the use of the checked and unchecked keywords are explained in Chapter 5.

Synchronization Keywords

C# has one keyword that relates to synchronization, which is a technique for parallel programming.

lock

The lock keyword marks a code block as a critical section, which can be entered by only one Thread or Task at a time.

Example

The following lock statement demonstrates how to create a critical region:

```
object myObject = new object();

lock (myObject) {

    // ... critical region code statements

}
```

References

Synchronization is explained in Chapter 24.

Parameter Keywords

C# has three keywords that are used as modifiers to method parameters.

params

The params keyword allows you to create a method with a variable number of arguments. This keyword is applied as a modifier to an array type parameter and must be the last parameter in a method definition.

Example

The following class contains a method that uses the params keyword:

```
class Calculator {

    public int CalculateSum(params int[] numbers) {
        int result = 0;
        foreach (int i in numbers) {
            result += i;
        }
        return result;
```

```
    }
}
```

The following statements show this method being used:

```
// create a Calculator object
Calculator calc = new Calculator();

// call the CalculateSum method
int result1 = calc.CalculateSum(2, 4, 6, 8, 10);
```

References

Method parameters are explained in Chapter 9.

ref

The ref keyword causes arguments to be passed by reference in a method so that any changes are reflected in the original variable.

Example

The following class contains a method with a ref parameter:

```
class Calculator {

    public void CalculateSum(ref int result, int x, int y) {
        result = x + y;
    }
}
```

The ref keyword must also be applied when calling a method that has a ref parameter. The following statements demonstrate the use of the CalculateSum method:

```
// create a Calculator object
Calculator calc = new Calculator();

// define a value-type variable that will be used as the ref parameter
int result = 0;

// call the CalculateSum method
calc.CalculateSum(ref result, 10, 10);
```

References

The ref keyword is explained in Chapter 9.

out

The out keyword works in the same way as the ref keyword, except that the variable that will be passed by reference does not have to be initialized.

Example

The following class contains a method that uses the out keyword as a modifier for a parameter:

```
class Calculator {

    public void CalculateSum(out int result, int x, int y) {
        result = x + y;
    }
}
```

The out keyword must also be used when calling a method with an out parameter, as demonstrated by these statements:

```
// create a Calculator object
Calculator calc = new Calculator();

// define a value-type variable that will be used as the ref parameter
int result;

// call the CalculateSum method
calc.CalculateSum(out result, 10, 10);
```

References

The out keyword as a parameter modifier is described in Chapter 9.

Namespace Keywords

Namespaces allow related types to be grouped together; this feature is discussed in Chapter 11. There are two keywords that support the use of namespaces.

namespace

The namespace keyword defines a new namespace.

Example

The following statements define a new namespace:

```
namespace MyNamespace {
```

```
}
```

References

Chapter 11 contains details of the C# namespaces feature.

using

The using keyword imports the contents of a namespace into your code file so that you can refer to the classes it contains without having to qualify their names.

Example

The following example uses the using keyword to import the contents of the System namespace, allowing the System.Console class to be referred to simply as Console:

```
using System;

class UsingTest {

    static void Main(string[] args) {

        Console.WriteLine("Introduction to C#");

        // wait for input before exiting
        Console.WriteLine("Press enter to finish");
        Console.ReadLine();
    }
}
```

References

Namespaces are discussed in Chapter 11. The using keyword can also be used to control the memory scope of an object; see Chapter 18 for details.

Literal Keywords

Literals allow you to define values directly in your code. Aside from the four keywords in this section, C# also supports numeric literals (covered in Chapter 5) and string and character literals (covered in Chapter 16).

null

The null keyword sets a reference-type variable so that it doesn't refer to any object.

Example

The following statement assigns `null` to an `object` variable:

```
object myObject = null;
```

References

See the "Definite Assignment and Null References" section earlier in this chapter.

true, false

The `true` and `false` keywords are the literal values for the `bool` type.

Example

The following statements assign `true` and `false` to a pair of `bool` variables:

```
bool myTrueBool = true;
bool myFalseBool = false;
```

References

See Chapter 5 for details of the `bool` type and the `true` and `false` literal keywords.

Object Keywords

These three C# type keywords allow you to create new objects from types, to check types, and to safely cast from one type to another.

is, as

The `is` keyword is used as an operator and returns `true` if an `object` is of the specified type. The `as` keyword will return the object cast to the target type only if it is legal to do so; otherwise, `null` will be returned.

References

See Chapter 6 for details of types and casting, including the use of the `is` and `as` keywords.

new

The `new` keyword creates an object from a type.

References

Chapter 6 describes how the new keyword is used.

typeof

The typeof keyword returns the type of a C# type by its name.

References

The typeof keyword is explained in Chapter XXX.

LINQ Keywords

C# defines a set of keywords for performing LINQ keywords; see Chapter 27 for details of LINQ and how the keywords are used. The LINQ keywords are as follows: from, where, select, group, into, orderby, join, let, ascending, descending, on, equals, by, in.

Other Keywords

The following keywords don't readily fall into a single category.

base

The base keyword is used to refer to the base class from a derived class. It can be used in a derived constructor to call a base class constructor and in a method or property to call the base class implementation.

Example

The following class uses the base keyword to refer to its base class constructor and the base class implementation of the overridden method:

```
class DerivedClass : BaseClass {

    public DerivedClass() : base() {
        // constructor statements go here
    }

    public override int CalculateSum(int x, int y) {
        return base.CalculateSum(x, y);
    }
}
```

References

Deriving classes, base classes, and inheritance are described in Chapter 6. Constructors and virtual/overridden methods are discussed in Chapter 9.

get, set, value

These keywords are used in properties. The get keyword defines the get accessor, the set keyword defines the set accessor, and value is used in the set accessor to access the value that has been assigned to the property.

Example

The following class has a property that uses all three keywords to mediate access to a private field:

```
class PropertyDemo {
    private string myField = "Hello";

    public string MyProperty {
        get {
            return myField;
        }
        set {
            myField = value;
        }
    }
}
```

References

Properties are explained in Chapter 8.

global

The global keyword is used with the :: operator to specify the default namespace.

References

See Chapter 11 for details of namespaces.

implicit, explicit

The limplicit and explicit keywords are used with the operator keyword to define custom conversions between types.

References

Custom conversions operators are covered in Chapter 8.

operator

The operator keyword is used to declare a custom operator in a class.

References

See Chapter 8 for details and example of custom operators.

partial

The partial keyword is used to define a class or method that is implemented across multiple code files.

References

Partial classes are discussed in Chapter 6, and partial methods are discussed in Chapter 9.

using

The using controls the memory scope of an object.

References

See Chapter 18 for details of how the using keyword is applied. The using keyword can also be used to import the contents of a namespace into a code file.

this

The this keyword refers to the current instance of the class and can also be used as a parameter modifier for extension methods.

References

See Chapter 9 for details and examples of both uses of the this keyword.

yield

The yield keyword is used in iterator blocks.

References

Iterator blocks are explained and demonstrated in Chapter 9.

Operators

The following are operators that C# supports. They look a little odd when laid out this way, but you'll quickly come to know them well, since they are used in some form in almost every C# program.

[ ] Operator

The square brackets are used to access array elements, indexers, and attributes.

References

Arrays are covered in Chapter 13, collections in Chapter 19, indexers in Chapter 8, and attributes in Chapter 17.

( ) Operator

Parentheses are used to perform explicit type casts and to group related items together, such as method parameters.

References

Type casting is covered in Chapter 6, and method parameters are covered in Chapter 9.

Dot (.) Operator

The dot operator is used for member access, either to specify the qualified name of a type or to specify the qualified name of an object member.

References

See Chapter 6 for details of using the dot operator to access methods and Chapter 11 for details of namespaces.

:: Operator

The :: operator is used with the global keyword to denote the default namespace.

References

See Chapter 11 for details of namespaces.

+, -, *, /, % Operators

These operators are known as the arithmetic operators and are responsible for addition, subtraction, multiplication, division, and modulus.

References

These operators as they apply to the built-in numeric types are discussed in Chapter 5. Chapter 8 describes how to implement these operators for custom types.

==, !=, >, >=, <, <= Operators

These are known as the comparison operators, and they return true if one value is equal to, not equal to, greater, greater or equal to, smaller, smaller, or equal to another value.

References

These operators as they apply to the built-in numeric types are discussed in Chapter 5. Chapter 8 describes how to implement these operators for custom types.

++, +=, --, -= Operators

These operators increment or decrement values.

References

These operators as they apply to the built-in numeric types are discussed in Chapter 5. Chapter 8 describes how to implement these operators for custom types.

&&, || Operators

These operators combine expressions so that they collectively return true if each individual expression returns true (for the && operator) or so that they return true if any one of the individual expressions returns true (for the || operator).

&, |, ^, ~, <<, >> Operators

These are the C# logical operators that work on the bits of a numeric type.

References

These operators as they apply to the built-in numeric types are discussed in Chapter 5.

=> Operator

The => operator is used to denote a lambda expression, which is an anonymous method delegate.

References

Delegates and lambda expressions are discussed in Chapter 10.

=, +=, -=, *=, /=, %=, &=, >>=, <<=, ^= Operators

These are the assignment operators. The equals sign (=) is used as the assignment operator in C#. The other operators combine the assignment operators with another function.

References

See the "Assigning Values" section earlier in this chapter. These operators as they apply to the built-in numeric types are discussed in Chapter 5. Chapter 8 describes how to implement these operators for custom types.

Summary

In this chapter, we looked at the fundamentals of the C# language, starting by taking a simple C# program and breaking it down to look at the different syntax elements. We looked at the type system and explored the differences between reference and value types—a distinction that causes many problems for programmers new to C#.

We looked at how you use C# to perform some of the most require programming tasks—assigning values to variables, selectively executing code statements, and iterating over data items. This chapter finished with a reference for the C# keywords and operators. These sections are very dry reading, but they can be useful when you know what you want to do but are not sure which keyword or operator will do it for you.

CHAPTER 5

■ ■ ■

Numeric and Boolean Types

Numeric types, as the name suggests, represent numbers. These types, and the operations that can be used on them, are the basis for C# mathematics support. The Boolean type allows you to express true and false values—a feature that you can use directly with the bool type or indirectly when conditions are evaluated in conditional statements.

In this chapter, you'll see the different types that are available to represent different kinds of numbers and how to define numeric values using numeric literals and the range of numeric operators that C# supports. I'll also show you how to use Boolean literals and how Booleans are used when operations are performed and conditions evaluated. Table 5-1 provides the summary for this chapter.

Table 5-1. *Quick Problem/Solution Reference for Chapter 5*

Problem	Solution	Listings
Represent a number in C#.	Use one of the predefined numeric types described in Table 5-2 or use a numeric literal.	5-1
Override the inferred type for a numeric literal value.	Use a literal suffix.	5-2
Use a hexadecimal number or specify negative literal values.	Use a literal prefix.	5-3
Convert from one numeric type to another.	Use an implicit or explicit conversion.	5-4 through 5-6
Detect overflow problems.	Use the checked keyword.	5-7 through 5-8
Determine the largest and smallest values a numeric type can represent.	Use the MaxValue and MinValue properties.	5-9
Convert a string into a numeric type.	Use the Parse or TryParse methods.	5-10
Determine the smallest detectable different between two float or double types.	Use the Epsilon property.	5-11, 5-12

Problem	Solution	Listings
Perform arithmetic calculations.	Use the arithmetic operators.	5-13 through 5-15, 5-23
Increment or decrement a value or change the sign of a value.	Use the unary operators.	5-16, 5-17
Compare two numeric values.	Use the relational operators.	5-18
Manipulate the bits that are used to represent a number.	Use the logical operators or the logical assignment operators.	5-19 through 5-22
Express a true or false value.	Use a Boolean literal value.	5-24
Convert bool values to and from strings.	Use the members of the System.Boolean struct.	5-25

Numeric Types

C# has a number of predefined numeric types that can be referred to using keywords. Table 5-2 provides an overview of these types. I tend use the keywords, rather than the type names, but different programmers have varying styles, and it is useful to know how the keywords and the types relate to each other. There is no advantage in using one style over the other; the C# compiler converts the keywords into the correct type automatically, which means that you can mix keywords and types freely, even in the same code.

Table 5-2. C# Predefined Numeric Types

C# Keyword	Type	Size	Range
sbyte	System.SByte	8 bits	−128 to 127.
byte	System.Byte	8 bits	0 to 255.
short	System.Int16	16 bits	−32,768 and 32,767.
ushort	System.UInt16	16 bits	0 and 65,535.
int	System.Int32	32 bits	−2,147,483,648 and 2,147,483,647.
uint	System.UInt32	32 bits	0 and 4,294,967,295.
long	System.Int64	64 bits	−9,223,372,036,854,775,808 and 9,223,372,036,854,775,807.

C# Keyword	Type	Size	Range
ulong	System.UInt64	64 bits	0 and 18,446,744,073,709,551,615.
float	System.Single	32 bits	See the text following this table.
double	System.Double	64 bits	See the text following this table.
decimal	System.Decimal	128 bits	See the text following this table.

An *integer* is a whole number, such as 3, 90, and 500—a number with no fractions. C# has two categories of integer type: signed and unsigned.

The sbyte, short, int, and long types hold *signed* integer values. Signed integers represent whole numbers (that is, no fractions), and one bit of the memory allocated to represent the number value is used to note whether the number is positive or negative. For routine programming, you will most likely use int the most frequently, not least because it is the numeric type that is usually used with for loops.

The byte, ushort, uint, and ulong types hold *unsigned* integer values; this means that all the memory allocated to the type is used to represent the number value so they can represent only positive numbers. If you are dealing only with positive numeric values, unsigned integers are more memory efficient (although unless you are dealing with a very large volume of numbers, the need to worry about saving 8 bits per value rarely arises).

A *real* number, often called a *floating-point* number, has a fraction; in C# this fraction is expressed using a decimal point, such as 3.5, 90.2, or 500.007. The float, double, and decimal types hold real numbers. The float and double types are usually used for scientific calculations, while the decimal type is usually used for financial calculations where extra precision is required, but that extra precision comes at the cost of lower performance when performing operations on decimal values. Listing 5-9 shows the maximum and minimum values that the float, double, and decimal can represent, but the purpose of these types is to handle accuracy following the decimal place. The double type can hold 15 significant figures, and the float type can hold seven significant figures. The decimal type can hold 28 significant figures; calculations involving the decimal type are about 10 times slower to perform that those involving the double type.

■ **Tip** The size of different numeric values is always constant in .NET—so, for example, an int is always 32 bits, even when your code is executing on a 64-bit system.

Using Numeric Literals

C# allows you to define numeric values literally so that you can just use the value of the number in a statement, like this:

```
int x = 23;
```

In this statement, I used the int keyword to define a variable called x with a value of 23. I didn't have to use the new keyword or declare the value in a special way. I just used the value I wanted, and C# took care of the rest. You can use literal definitions without making an assignment to a variable. Listing 5-1 contains some examples.

Listing 5-1. Determining Type from Numeric Literals

```csharp
using System;

class Listing_01 {

    static void Main(string[] args) {

        Type t1 = 23.GetType();
        Console.WriteLine("Value: 23 - Type: {0}", t1);

        Type t2 = 2500000000.GetType();
        Console.WriteLine("Value: 2500000000 - Type: {0}", t2);

        Type t3 = 2017.2.GetType();
        Console.WriteLine("Value: 2017.2 - Type: {0}", t3);

        // wait for input before exiting
        Console.WriteLine("Press enter to finish");
        Console.ReadLine();
    }
}
```

In this example, I have used numeric literal values as though they were instances of an object. I have expressed three numeric values and called the `GetType()` method on each of them and then printed out the value and the type that C# infers they should assigned to. Compiling and running the code in Listing 5-1 produces the following results:

```
Value: 23 - Type: System.Int32
Value: 2500000000 - Type: System.UInt32
Value: 2017.2 - Type: System.Double
Press enter to finish
```

Integers are automatically assigned to the smallest type that will accommodate the literal from the following list: int, uint, long, and ulong—the byte, sbyte, short, and ushort types are not used, even though they could all hold the value 23. However, you can force an assignment to a given type using a variable or field, for example:

```csharp
byte b = 20;
```

In this statement, the literal is assigned to a local byte variable. All literals that contain a decimal point are inferred to be double types. You can express exponential numbers using the E symbol, as follows:

```
1E05
```

Literals that include the exponential symbol are treated in the same way as literals that contain a decimal point; they are inferred to the double type. Literal type inference allows you to use numeric values more naturally in your code; you can work directly with numeric values, rather than having to declare what type should be assigned to each value. Without literal inference, simple calculation looks like this:

```
int i = 10;
double d = 20.5;
double result = i * d;
```

I had to declare that 10 is an int and 20.5 is a double. With type inference, I can rely on C# to infer the types for me and simplify my code:

```
double result = 10 * 20.5;
```

Using Literal Suffixes

If you want to use literals but don't want the types to be automatically inferred, you can use a literal suffix, which allows you to specify the numeric type you want explicitly. Listing 5-2 contains some examples.

Listing 5-2. Controlling Numeric Literal Type Inference

```
using System;

class Listing_02 {

    static void Main(string[] args) {

        Type t1 = 23L.GetType();
        Console.WriteLine("Value: 23 - Type: {0}", t1);

        Type t2 = 2500000000UL.GetType();
        Console.WriteLine("Value: 2500000000 - Type: {0}", t2);

        Type t3 = 2017.2M.GetType();
        Console.WriteLine("Value: 2017.2 - Type: {0}", t3);

        // wait for input before exiting
        Console.WriteLine("Press enter to finish");
        Console.ReadLine();
    }
}
```

I have marked the suffixes in Listing 5-2 in bold; I have applied the L, UL, and M suffixes to the literals I used in the previous example. You can see the complete set of suffixes in Table 5-3. Where there are multiple types for a suffix, the smallest possible one will be used to represent the literal. You can see the ranges that each numeric type can represent in Table 5-2.

Table 5-3. Numeric Literal Suffixes

Suffix	C# Types
No suffix (integer)	`int, uint, long, ulong`
U	`uint, ulong`
L	`long, ulong`
UL	`ulong`
No suffix (decimal)	`double`
F	`float`
D	`double`
M	`decimal`

Suffixes are not case sensitive, but the convention is to use uppercase characters so that the letter L is not mistaken for the numeral 1. Compiling and running the code in Listing 5-2 produces the following results:

```
Value: 23 - Type: System.Int64
Value: 2500000000 - Type: System.UInt64
Value: 2017.2 - Type: System.Decimal
Press enter to finish
```

By far the most common use of literal suffixes is when using real numbers. By default, literals that contain a decimal point are inferred to the `double` type, for which there is no implicit conversion to the `float` type. The following statement will generate a compiler error:

```
float f = 23.2;
```

This statement has used a literal that has been inferred to the `double` type and then assigned it to a `float` variable. To resolve this problem, the F suffix must be used:

```
float f = 23.2F;
```

You can learn more about implicit conversion later in this chapter.

Using Literal Prefixes

There are only three prefixes for numeric literals. They are described in Table 5-4.

Table 5-4. *Numeric Literal Prefixes*

Prefix	Description
0x	Specifies that the value is expressed in hexadecimal
+	Specifies that the value is positive
-	Specifies that the value is negative

Literals that have neither the + nor – prefix are assumed to be positive. Listing 5-3 demonstrates the use of the literal prefixes.

Listing 5-3. Using the Numeric Literal Prefixes

```
using System;

class Listing_03 {

    static void Main(string[] args) {

        // use the hex prefix
        int hex = 0xFF;

        // explicitly specify a positive number
        short pos = +23;

        // explicitly specify a negative number
        short neg = -23;

        // print out the values
        Console.WriteLine("Hex: {0}", hex);
        Console.WriteLine("Pos: {0}", pos);
        Console.WriteLine("Neg: {0}", neg);

        // wait for input before exiting
        Console.WriteLine("Press enter to finish");
        Console.ReadLine();
    }
}
```

Compiling and running the code in Listing 5-3 produces the following results:

```
Hex: 255
Pos: 23
Neg: -23
Press enter to finish
```

Implicit and Explicit Numeric Type Conversions

When you assign one numeric type to another, C# will try to handle the conversion for you. Some numeric type conversions can be done for you automatically; these are called *implicit* conversions. Other type conversions require you to state which type conversion is required; these are called *explicit* conversions. Implicit conversions don't require you to take any special steps. Listing 5-4 demonstrates some implicit conversions.

Listing 5-4. Implicit Numeric Type Conversions

```
long l1 = 45;
long l2 = 20 + 25;

int i = 50;
long l3 = i;
long l4 = i + 25;
```

The statements in Listing 5-4 show various implicit conversions from int to long. Remember that C# will implicitly type numeric literals to int by default if it can, so assigning a literal to a long like this is an implicit conversion from an int to a long. Implicit conversions are supported where converting from one type to another is harmless; in other words, the largest possible value represented by the original type can be represented equally well by the new type. The actual value assigned to a numeric type isn't taken into account—only the maximum possible value that the data type can represent. Table 5-5 summarizes the supported implicit numeric type conversions.

Table 5-5. Implicit Numeric Type Conversions

Original Type	Supported Types for Implicit Conversion
sbyte	short, int, long, float, double, decimal
byte	short, ushort, int, uint, long, ulong, float, double, decimal
short	int, long, float, double, decimal
ushort	int, uint, long, ulong, float, double, decimal
int	long, float, double, decimal
uint	long, ulong, float, double, decimal
long	float, double, decimal
ulong	float, double, decimal
float	double

An explicit conversion is required when converting from one numeric type to another may affect the value that is stored. To make an explicit conversion, you use the cast expression, for example:

```
int i = 20;
byte b = (byte)i;
```

In these statements, I define an int and then cast it to a byte, thereby performing an explicit conversion. Table 5-6 summarizes the supported explicit numeric conversions.

Table 5-6. Explicit Numeric Type Converions

Original Type	Supported Types for Explicit Conversion
sbyte	byte, ushort, uint, ulong
byte	sbyte
short	sbyte, byte, ushort, uint, ulong
ushort	sbyte, byte, short
int	sbyte, byte, short, ushort, uint, ulong
uint	sbyte, byte, short, ushort, int
long	sbyte, byte, short, ushort, int, uint, ulong
ulong	sbyte, byte, short, ushort, int, uint, long
float	sbyte, byte, short, ushort, int, uint, long, ulong, decimal
double	sbyte, byte, short, ushort, int, uint, long, ulong, float, decimal
decimal	sbyte, byte, short, ushort, int, uint, long, ulong, float, double

If you compare Table 5-5 and Table 5-6, you will see that every numeric type can be converted to every other numeric type, either implicitly or explicitly. Explicit conversions can be troublesome; Listing 5-5 contains an example.

Listing 5-5. Problems Performing Implicit Conversions

```
using System;

class Listing_05 {

    static void Main(string[] args) {
```

```
// define a signed value
int i = -200;
// explicitly convert to an unsigned value
uint ui = (uint)i;

Console.WriteLine("Original Value: {0}", i);
Console.WriteLine("Explicitly Converted Value: {0}", ui);

// wait for input before exiting
Console.WriteLine("Press enter to finish");
Console.ReadLine();
    }
}
```

The code in Listing 5-5 creates an int with a negative value and explicitly converts it to a uint. The uint type doesn't have any means to contain a negative value properly; it is, after all, unsigned. Compiling and running the code in Listing 5-5 produces the following results:

```
Original Value: -200

Explicitly Converted Value: 4294967096

Press enter to finish
```

We get a nonsense value—and, had we used this as the basis of a calculation, we'd get some pretty odd results. Similar problems can also arise if we explicitly convert to a type that uses less memory to store values, as demonstrated by Listing 5-6.

Listing 5-6. Explicitly Converting to a Smaller Numeric Type

```
using System;

class Listing_06 {

    static void Main(string[] args) {

        // define a short with a value greater than the
        // byte type can hold
        short s = 500;

        // explicitly convert the short to a byte
        byte b = (byte)s;

        // print out the values
        Console.WriteLine("Original value: {0}", s);
        Console.WriteLine("Explicitly converted value: {0}", b);
```

```
        // wait for input before exiting
        Console.WriteLine("Press enter to finish");
        Console.ReadLine();
    }
}
```

In this example, I define a short that is assigned a number outside the range that a byte is capable of representing and then perform an explicit conversion to a byte. This causes another unexpected value. Compiling and running the code in Listing 5-6 produces the following results:

```
Original value: 500
Explicitly converted value: 244
Press enter to finish
```

I recommend that you use explicit conversions sparingly; they tend to cause problems long after your program has been completed and sent to the user. When you wrote the code, you knew for certain that the value of this int could be safely expressed using a byte, but then something changes; the user starts dealing with larger numbers, and your program stops working. My advice is to over-allocate capacity when using numeric types; for most programs, the microscopic cost of the additional memory required is massively outweighed by the cost of identifying, fixing, and releasing a new version to resolve a problem caused by an injudicious explicit conversion. If you must use explicit conversions, then you should consider using overflow checking, described in the following section.

Using Overflow Checking

The problem in Listing 5-6 looks simple to avoid when you can see both statements in sequence. This problem usually arises when working with values passed as parameters to a method; the danger is that you make this kind of explicit conversion without realizing that the value in one type can't be represented in the other.

You can use the checked keyword when performing explicit numeric type conversions. A System.OverflowException is thrown if the value cannot be represented properly by the new numeric type. Listing 5-7 contains an example.

Listing 5-7. Using a Checked Block

```
using System;

class Listing_07 {

    static void Main(string[] args) {

        checked {
            short s = 500;
            byte b = (byte)s;
            // print out the values
            Console.WriteLine("Original value: {0}", s);
            Console.WriteLine("Explicitly converted value: {0}", b);
        }
```

```
        // wait for input before exiting
        Console.WriteLine("Press enter to finish");
        Console.ReadLine();
    }
}
```

In this example, I have used the checked keyword to surround a block of code statements. Every explicit numeric conversion inside the checked block will be examined at runtime. Compiling and running the code in Listing 5-7 produces the following results:

```
Unhandled Exception: System.OverflowException: Arithmetic operation resulted in an overflow.
    at Listing_07.Main(String[] args) in C:\Listing_07\Listing_07.cs:line 9
Press any key to continue . . .
```

You can also use the checked keyword to apply overflow checking to a single statement, as demonstrated by Listing 5-8. I use this C# feature most when I am dealing with numeric data that the user has entered; it allows me to validate my assumptions about the kind of numbers they are using.

Listing 5-8. Using the checked Keyword with a Single Statement

```
using System;

class Listing_08 {

    static void Main(string[] args) {

        short s = 500;

        byte b = checked((byte)s);

        // print out the values
        Console.WriteLine("Original value: {0}", s);
        Console.WriteLine("Explicitly converted value: {0}", b);


    // wait for input before exiting
    Console.WriteLine("Press enter to finish");
    Console.ReadLine();
    }
}
```

When using the checked keyword in this way, we use the parentheses to denote the start and end of the checked region, rather than the braces ({}) used to apply overflow checking for a block of statements. The checked statement in Listing 5-8 is shown in bold.

You can use the unchecked keyword to disable overflow checking, and you can nest checked and unchecked blocks of code, as follows:

```
checked {
    short s = 500;
    byte b = (byte)s;
    unchecked {
```

```
        // print out the values
        Console.WriteLine("Original value: {0}", s);
        Console.WriteLine("Explicitly converted value: {0}", b);
    }
}
```

In the preceding statements, the calls to the Console class are contained in an unchecked block, which is nested inside a checked block. In practice, the unchecked keyword is rarely used, since this is the default mode for explicit numeric conversions.

Using Struct Members

Each of the C# keywords for numeric types relates to a struct in the System namespace; for example, the int keyword is translated automatically to the System.Int32 struct. You can see the complete set of keyword to struct mappings in Table 5-2; you usually just use the C# keywords to work with numeric types, but the struct types behind the keywords allow the numeric types to have members and operators. All the numeric struct types are derived from System.ValueType, and since it is not possible to derive from structs, numeric types are implicitly sealed.

Common Members

There are some common members implemented by all of the numeric types. They are described in Table 5-7.

Table 5-7. Common Numeric Type Members

Member	Description
MaxValue	Returns the largest value that the type can represent.
MinValue	Returns the smallest value that the type can represent.
Parse(string)	Parses a numeric value from a string—throws an exception if a numeric value cannot be parsed. See the TryParse method for an alternative approach that doesn't throw an exception.
TryParse(string, out T)	Parses a numeric value from a string and places it in the out parameter. Returns true if parsing was successful; returns false and sets the out parameter to false otherwise. The out parameter is of the numeric type.
ToString(string)	Converts the numeric type to a string using the supplied formatting instructions; see Chapter 16 for more information.

Getting the Range of Supported Values

The static MaxValue and MinValue properties return an instance of the numeric type being used, set to the largest of smallest value that the type can represent. For example, calling MaxValue on the int type returns an int set to the largest value an int can hold. Listing 5-9 demonstrates the use of these properties.

Listing 5-9. Using the MaxValue and MinValue Properties

```
using System;

class Listing_09 {

    static void Main(string[] args) {

        Console.WriteLine("Int Max Value: {0}", int.MaxValue);
        Console.WriteLine("Int Min Value: {0}", int.MinValue);

        Console.WriteLine("ULong Max Value: {0}", ulong.MaxValue);
        Console.WriteLine("ULong Min Value: {0}", ulong.MinValue);

        Console.WriteLine("Float Max Value: {0}", float.MaxValue);
        Console.WriteLine("Float Min Value: {0}", float.MinValue);

        Console.WriteLine("Double Max Value: {0}", double.MaxValue);
        Console.WriteLine("Double Min Value: {0}", double.MinValue);

        Console.WriteLine("Decimal Max Value: {0}", decimal.MaxValue);
        Console.WriteLine("Decimal Min Value: {0}", decimal.MinValue);

        // wait for input before exiting
        Console.WriteLine("Press enter to finish");
        Console.ReadLine();
    }
}
```

Compiling and running the code in Listing 5-9 produces the following output:

```
Int Max Value: 2147483647
Int Min Value: -2147483648
ULong Max Value: 18446744073709551615
ULong Min Value: 0
Float Max Value: 3.402823E+38
Float Min Value: -3.402823E+38
Double Max Value: 1.79769313486232E+308
Double Min Value: -1.79769313486232E+308
Decimal Max Value: 79228162514264337593543950335
Decimal Min Value: -79228162514264337593543950335
Press enter to finish
```

Parsing Numeric Values

The static Parse method takes a string argument and tries to convert it into the type on which the method has been called; for example, a call to int.Parse will try to parse a string and return an int containing the parsed value. If the string argument cannot be parsed, an exception is thrown; see Chapter 14 for details of exceptions. Listing 5-10 demonstrates how to use the Parse method.

Listing 5-10. Using the Parse Method

```
using System;

class Listing_10 {

    static void Main(string[] args) {

        // parse some different numeric types
        int i = int.Parse("-346");
        long l = long.Parse("957347");
        float f = float.Parse("400.145");

        try {
            // try to parse a null string
            int x = int.Parse(null);

        } catch (ArgumentNullException ex) {
            Console.WriteLine("--- First Exception ---");
            Console.WriteLine(ex.ToString());
        }

        try {
            // try to parse something which can't
            // be converted into a number
            int x = int.Parse("Hello World");
        } catch (FormatException ex) {
            Console.WriteLine("--- Second Exception ---");
            Console.WriteLine(ex.ToString());
        }

        try {
            // try to parse a number which is too big
            // to be represented by the numeric type
            sbyte s = sbyte.Parse("500");
        } catch (OverflowException ex) {
            Console.WriteLine("---Third Exception ---");
            Console.WriteLine(ex.ToString());
        }
```

```
        // wait for input before exiting
        Console.WriteLine("Press enter to finish");
        Console.ReadLine();
    }
}
```

The code in Listing 5-10 parses strings into three different numeric types and then generates the three different kinds of exceptions that can be thrown when trying to parse a string into a numeric type. These are summarized in Table 5-8.

Table 5-8. Exceptions Thrown When Parsing Numeric Types

Exception	Error Condition
System.ArgumentNullException	Thrown when the string to be parsed is null
System.FormatException	Thrown when the string doesn't contain a number that can be parsed
System.OverflowException	Thrown when the number represented by the string is too large to be represented by the numeric type

Compiling and running the code in Listing 5-10 displays the exceptions, as follows:

```
--- First Exception ---
System.ArgumentNullException: Value cannot be null.
Parameter name: String
   at System.Number.StringToNumber(String str, NumberStyles options, NumberBuffer& number,
NumberFormatInfo info, Boolean parseDecimal)
   at System.Number.ParseInt32(String s, NumberStyles style, NumberFormatInfo info)
   at System.Int32.Parse(String s)
   at Listing_10.Main(String[] args) in C:\Listing_10\Listing_10.cs:line 14
--- Second Exception ---
System.FormatException: Input string was not in a correct format.
   at System.Number.StringToNumber(String str, NumberStyles options, NumberBuffer& number,
NumberFormatInfo info, Boolean parseDecimal)
   at System.Number.ParseInt32(String s, NumberStyles style, NumberFormatInfo info)
   at System.Int32.Parse(String s)
   at Listing_10.Main(String[] args) in C:\Listing_10\Listing_10.cs:line 24
---Third Exception ---
System.OverflowException: Value was either too large or too small for a signed byte.
   at System.SByte.Parse(String s, NumberStyles style, NumberFormatInfo info)
   at System.SByte.Parse(String s)
   at Listing_10.Main(String[] args) in C:\Listing_10\Listing_10.cs:line 33
```

Using Type-Specific Members

In addition to the common members described earlier, there are additional members available in the float, double, and decimal types. The additional members for float and double are similar, as described by Table 5-9.

Table 5-9. Additional Members of the float and double Types

Member	Description
Epsilon	Returns the smallest positive value for the type that is greater than zero. A value must be greater or less than zero by at least this amount to be considered nonzero.
NaN	Returns a special value called Not a Number, equivalent to dividing zero by zero.
PositiveInfinity NegativeInfinity	These properties return the values equivalent to dividing a positive number and a negative number by zero.
IsPositiveInfinity(V) IsNegativeInfinity(V) IsInfinity(V)	These static methods return true if the parameter value is equal to the PositiveInfinity property, the NegativeInfinity property, or either. The parameter V is a float or double value.

These additional members are rarely used in mainstream programming, but the Epsilon property demands a moment of attention. Listing 5-11 contains a demonstration.

Listing 5-11. Using the Epsilon Value

```
using System;

class Listing_11 {

    static void Main(string[] args) {

        float f1 = 0f;
        float f2 = float.Epsilon / 2;
        float f3 = float.Epsilon;

        Console.WriteLine("f2 == f1? {0}", f2 == f1);
        Console.WriteLine("f3 == f1? {0}", f3 == f1);

        // wait for input before exiting
        Console.WriteLine("Press enter to finish");
        Console.ReadLine();
    }
}
```

In the listing, I create three float values. The first has a value of 0. The second has a value of one half of Epsilon, and the third is exactly Epsilon. I then compare the float values. Compiling and running the code gives the following results:

```
f2 == f1? True
f3 == f1? False
Press enter to finish
```

You can see that the float value, which is only half of Epsilon, is reported as being equal to zero. This works only for values that are very close to zero; other float and double values don't have to differ by Epsilon to be considered different.

The decimal type has a different set of additional members, which are described in Table 5-10.

Table 5-10. *Additional Members of the decimal Type*

Member	Description
One Zero MinusOne	These static properties return values for 1, 0, and -1.
Ceiling(decimal)	Rounds up a decimal value to the nearest integer value, returned as a decimal.
Floor (decimal)	Rounds down a decimal value to the nearest integer value, returned as a decimal.
Negate(decimal)	Returns the result of multiplying a decimal value by -1.
Round(decimal)	Rounds a decimal value to the nearest integer.
Truncate(decimal)	Discards the fractional digits of a decimal value.

Listing 5-12 demonstrates some of these members. The Truncate method discards all the fractional digits of a decimal value. If you want to retain a specific number of digits—to display to a user, for example—then you can use the composite formatting feature, which is described in Chapter 16.

Listing 5-12. Using the Additional Members of the decimal Type

```
using System;

class Listing_12 {

    static void Main(string[] args) {

        // define a decimal value
        decimal d = 12345.12345M;
```

```
    // call the various members and print out the results
    Console.WriteLine("Ceiling: {0}", decimal.Ceiling(d));
    Console.WriteLine("Floor: {0}", decimal.Floor(d));
    Console.WriteLine("Negate: {0}", decimal.Negate(d));
    Console.WriteLine("Round: {0}", decimal.Round(d));
    Console.WriteLine("Truncate: {0}", decimal.Truncate(d));

    // wait for input before exiting
    Console.WriteLine("Press enter to finish");
    Console.ReadLine();
  }
}
```

In this listing, I define a decimal value and then call some of the additional members. Compiling and running the code produces the following results:

```
Ceiling: 12346
Floor: 12345
Negate: -12345.12345
Round: 12345
Truncate: 12345
Press enter to finish
```

Using Numeric Operators

Numeric types have limited value on their own; they need to be combined with operators that allow you to perform calculations and otherwise manipulate the values they represent. In the following sections, I describe the five kinds of numeric operator that C# supports.

Arithmetic Operators

C# includes basic arithmetic operators that allow you to perform basic calculations. These operators are described in Table 5-11.

Table 5-11. C# Arithmetic Operators

Operator	Name	Description
*	Multiplication operator	Multiplies two numeric values together
/	Division operator	Divides one numeric value by another
%	Modulus operator	Divides one numeric value by another and returns the remainder

Operator	Name	Description
+	Addition operator	Adds two numeric values together
-	Subtraction operator	Subtracts one numeric value from another

The arithmetic operators work as they do in most programming languages. Listing 5-13 demonstrates the use of these operators.

Listing 5-13. Using the C# Arithmetic Operators

```csharp
using System;

class Listing_13 {

    static void Main(string[] args) {

        // use the multiplication operator
        float mresult = 2.4f * 32.4f;
        Console.WriteLine("Multiplication result: {0}", mresult);

        // use the division operator
        int dresult = 3 / 2;
        Console.WriteLine("Division result: {0}", dresult);

        // use the remainder operator
        float rresult = 6.5f % 3;
        Console.WriteLine("Remainder result: {0}", rresult);

        // use the addition operator
        long x = 34;
        long aresult = 245 + x;
        Console.WriteLine("Addition result: {0}", aresult);

        // use the subtraction result
        float f1 = 2.5f;
        float f2 = 65.7f;
        float sresult = f1 - f2;
        Console.WriteLine("Subtraction result: {0}", sresult);

        // wait for input before exiting
        Console.WriteLine("Press enter to finish");
        Console.ReadLine();
    }
}
```

In the listing, I use a mix of local variables and numeric literals to demonstrate each of the operators. Compiling and running the code in Listing 5-13 produces the following results:

```
Multiplication result: 77.76001
Division result: 1
Remainder result: 0.5
Addition result: 279
Subtraction result: -63.2
Press enter to finish
```

There are two potential pitfalls when using these operators. The first potential pitfall is that when you use division operator on two integer types, the result is also an integer. If you want a result that has decimal places, you must cast the numeric types to a real-number type; this is demonstrated by Listing 5-14.

Listing 5-14. Using Integer Division

```
using System;

class Listing_14 {

    static void Main(string[] args) {

        // define two integer values
        int x = 5;
        int y = 2;

        // use the division operator
        int result1 = x / y;
        Console.WriteLine("Integer result: {0}", result1);

        // cast to a real numeric type and then use the operator
        float result2 = (float)x / (float)y;
        Console.WriteLine("Real result: {0}", result2);

        // wait for input before exiting
        Console.WriteLine("Press enter to finish");
        Console.ReadLine();
    }
}
```

In the listing, I define two int values and then use the division operator. The first division uses the ints as they are, and the second casts them to float values before performing the division. Compiling and running the code in Listing 5-14 produces the following results. You can see that I lose decimal precision in the first calculation but preserve it in the second.

```
Integer result: 2
Real result: 2.5
Press enter to finish
```

The second potential pitfall is that C# doesn't automatically resize numeric types to accommodate the results of arithmetic operations, meaning that you can easily create results that cannot be stored in the numeric type. For example, if you add two int values together, the default type of the result is also an int. Listing 5-15 demonstrates this problem.

Listing 5-15. Causing Overflow with Arithmetic Operations

```
using System;

class Listing_15 {

    static void Main(string[] args) {

        // define two large 32-bit ints
        int x = int.MaxValue;
        int y = int.MaxValue;

        // add them together and report on the result type
        Type t = (x + y).GetType();
        Console.WriteLine("Default result type: {0}", t);

        // add them together and assign the result to another int
        int result = x + y;
        Console.WriteLine("Int result: {0}", result);

        // cast them to long values
        long lresult = (long)x + (long)y;
        Console.WriteLine("Long result: {0}", lresult);

        try {
            // add the int values together, but do so
            // in a checked block
            checked {
                int ofres = x + y;
                Console.WriteLine("Overflow result: {0}", ofres);
            }
        } catch (OverflowException ex) {
            Console.WriteLine("Caught exception of type: {0}", ex.GetType());
        }

        // wait for input before exiting
        Console.WriteLine("Press enter to finish");
        Console.ReadLine();
    }
}
```

Compiling and running the code in Listing 5-15 produces the following results:

```
Default result type: System.Int32
Int result: -2
```

```
Long result: 4294967294
Caught exception of type: System.OverflowException

Press enter to finish
```

You can see that adding two int values together produces another int, even when an int is unable to represent the result. The two solutions to this problem are to cast the numeric types to ones that can accommodate the result (I used long in the example) or to use the checked keyword so that you receive an exception if there is an overflow problem; you can see further examples of using the checked keyword in the "Using Overflow Checking" section earlier in the chapter.

Unary Operators

The C# unary operators are so-called because they work on a single numeric value. The set of unary operators is described in Table 5-12.

Table 5-12. *C# Unary Operators*

Operator	Name	Description
+	Unary plus operator	Returns the value unchanged
-	Unary minus operator	Returns the value with the sign inverted
++(value) --(value)	Prefix increment and decrement operators	Increments or decrements and returns the current value of the numeric type
(value)++ (value)--	Postfix increment and decrement operators	Returns and then increments or decrements the current value of the numeric type

The unary plus operator is equivalent to returning the value of the numeric type unchanged. The unary minus operator is equivalent to subtracting the value of the numeric type from zero. Listing 5-16 demonstrates the use of these operators.

Listing 5-16. Using the Unary Plus and Minus Operators

```
using System;

class Listing_16 {

    static void Main(string[] args) {

        // define a number
        float f = 26.765f;

        // use the unary plus operator
```

```
        float up = +f;

        // use the unary minus operator
        float um = -f;

        // print out the results
        Console.WriteLine("Unary plus result: {0}", up);
        Console.WriteLine("Unary minus result: {0}", um);

        // wait for input before exiting
        Console.WriteLine("Press enter to finish");
        Console.ReadLine();
    }
}
```

Compiling and running the code in Listing 5-16 produces the following results:

```
Unary plus result: 26.765
Unary minus result: -26.765
Press enter to finish
```

The prefix and postfix increment and decrement operators are used widely, especially in for loops; see Chapter 4 for more information about for loops. These operators are a convenience that allow you to simplify your code. We start with a numeric type; let's use an int:

```
int  x = 0;
```

If we want a second int set to the current value of x and to increment x by one, we can use the following statements:

```
int y = x;
x = x + 1;
```

The value of y is zero, and the value of x is 1. We can use the postfix increment operator to get the same effect in a single statement:

```
int y = x++;
```

This statement says "assign the current value of x to y and then increment x." If the value of x is 0 before this statement is executed, y has a value of 0 and x has a value of 1 afterward. If you don't assign the result of the postfix increment operator to a variable, then the result is to increment the value of the numeric type, for example:

```
x++;
```

This statement means "increment the value of x by one." The prefix increment operator works in a similar way. Consider these statements:

```
int x = 0;

x = x + 1;
```

```
int y = x;
```

We start with an int again; this time we want to add one from the value of x and subsequently assign the value of x to y. We can achieve the same effect with the following statement:

```
int y = ++x;
```

Putting the two addition signs (++) before the variable we want to increment causes the value of x to be increased before it is assigned to y. If x has a value of 0 before this statement executes, both x and y have a value of 1 afterward. The prefix and postfix decrement operators function in the same way, but, as the name suggests, they decrement rather than increment values. Listing 5-17 demonstrates each of these operators.

Listing 5-17. Using the Prefix and Postfix Increment and Decrement Operators

```csharp
using System;

class Listing_17 {

    static void Main(string[] args) {

        // define the numeric types used in the example
        int x = 0;
        int y;

        // demonstrate postfix increment operator
        Console.WriteLine("Post-fix increment - initial value of x: {0}", x);
        y = x++;
        Console.WriteLine("Post-fix increment - new value of x: {0}", x);
        Console.WriteLine("Post-fix increment - value of y: {0}", y);

        // demonstrate prefix increment operator
        Console.WriteLine("Pre-fix increment - initial value of x: {0}", x);
        y = ++x;
        Console.WriteLine("Pre-fix increment - new value of x: {0}", x);
        Console.WriteLine("Pre-fix increment - value of y: {0}", y);

        // demonstrate postfix decrementoperator
        Console.WriteLine("Post-fix decrement value of x: {0}", x);
        y = x--;
        Console.WriteLine("Post-fix decrement - new value of x: {0}", x);
        Console.WriteLine("Post-fix decrement - value of y: {0}", y);

        // demonstrate prefix decrement operator
        Console.WriteLine("Pre-fix decrement - initial value of x: {0}", x);
        y = --x;
        Console.WriteLine("Pre-fix decrement - new value of x: {0}", x);
        Console.WriteLine("Pre-fix decrement - value of y: {0}", y);

        // wait for input before exiting
        Console.WriteLine("Press enter to finish");
        Console.ReadLine();
```

```
        }
}
```

Compiling and running the code in Listing 5-17 produces the following results:

```
Post-fix increment - initial value of x: 0
Post-fix increment - new value of x: 1
Post-fix increment - value of y: 0
Pre-fix increment - initial value of x: 1
Pre-fix increment - new value of x: 2
Pre-fix increment - value of y: 2
Post-fix decrement value of x: 2
Post-fix decrement - new value of x: 1
Post-fix decrement - value of y: 2
Pre-fix decrement - initial value of x: 1
Pre-fix decrement - new value of x: 0
Pre-fix decrement - value of y: 0
Press enter to finish
```

As with all the numeric operators, incrementing or decrementing a value can cause unexpected results if you go outside the range that a numeric type can support; see the section "Using Overflow Checking" earlier in the chapter for more details.

Relational Operators

The C# relational operators allow you to compare one numeric type to another. Table 5-13 describes these operators.

Table 5-13. C# Relational Operators

Operator	Description
==	Returns true if two numeric values are the same
!=	Returns true if two numeric values are not the same
<	Returns true if one numeric value is smaller than another
>	Returns true if one numeric value is larger than another
<=	Returns true if one numeric value is smaller or the same as another
>=	Returns true if one numeric value is larger of the same as another

The relational operators are applied to two numeric values, on either side of the operator. Each of these operators returns a bool, indicating the relationship between the numeric types; the bool type is explained in "The Boolean Type" section later in the chapter. You will typically see these operators used as conditions in selection statements, such as if statements, as follows:

```
if (x > 50) {
    ...
    // code statements
    ...
}
```

In this block, the code statements are executed if the value of x is greater than 50. See Chapter 4 for more information about selection statements. You can use these operators to compare different numeric types—for example, checking to see whether an int has the same value as a long—but the implicit and explicit conversion rules apply. See the "Implicit and Explicit Numeric Type Conversions" section earlier in this chapter for details. Listing 5-18 demonstrates the use of the relational operators.

Listing 5-18. Using the Numeric Relational Operators

```
using System;

class Listing_18 {

    static void Main(string[] args) {

        // define the values that will be used with the operators
        int x = 25;
        int y = 50;

        // use the == operator
        bool r1 = x == y;
        Console.WriteLine("== result: {0}", r1);

        // use the != operator
        bool r2 = x != y;
        Console.WriteLine("!= result: {0}", r2);

        // use the < operator
        bool r3 = x < y;
        Console.WriteLine("< result: {0}", r2);

        // use the > operator
        bool r4 = x > y;
        Console.WriteLine("> result: {0}", r4);

        // use the <= operator
        bool r5 = x <= y;
        Console.WriteLine("<= result: {0}", r5);

        // use the >= operator
        bool r6 = x >= y;
        Console.WriteLine(">= result: {0}", r6);
```

```
        // wait for input before exiting
        Console.WriteLine("Press enter to finish");
        Console.ReadLine();
    }
}
```

In this listing, I assign the result from each operator to a bool value and print it out. Compiling and running the code in Listing 5-18 produces the following results:

```
== result: False
!= result: True
< result: True
> result: False
<= result: True
>= result: False
Press enter to finish
```

Logical Operators

Logical, or bitwise, operators work on the binary digits that a numeric type uses to represent its value. In Table 5-2, earlier in the chapter, I listed each of the C# numeric types along with their sizes. These sizes are expressed in bits, and they relate to how values are stored. Figure 5-1 illustrates how this works for a byte, which uses 8 bits to represent a number.

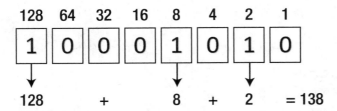

Figure 5-1. A byte with a value of 10

A bit can be set to a one or a zero. You can see the eight bits in Figure 5-1—they are the boxes with the zeros and ones in them. Starting with the rightmost bit, each is assigned a value, known as its *worth*. You can see the worth above each bit in Figure 5-1, starting at 1, then 2, 4, 8, and so on. To store a value, we set some of the bits to 1 and then add up the worth of those bits to get the value, ignoring those that are set to 0.

In the figure, you can see that the second and fourth and eighth bits from the right are set to 1 and that these have a worth of 2, 8, and 128, respectively. The byte that is demonstrated by Figure 5-1 represents a value of 138 (2, 8, and 128 added together).

We can view the binary representation of a numeric type by using the Convert.ToString method, which takes a numeric type and a base; we use a base of 2 since we want to display binary. Listing 5-19 provides a demonstration.

Listing 5-19. Displaying a Binary Representation of a Numeric Type

```
using System;

class Listing_19 {

    static void Main(string[] args) {

        // define a byte with a value of 138
        byte b = 138;

        // get the binary representation
        string br = Convert.ToString(b, 2);

        // print out the value and the binary representation
        Console.WriteLine("byte value: {0}, binary {1}", b, br);

        // wait for input before exiting
        Console.WriteLine("Press enter to finish");
        Console.ReadLine();
    }
}
```

If we compile and run the code in Listing 5-19, we get the following results:

```
byte value: 138, binary 10001010
Press enter to finish
```

You can see that the binary string that is printed matches the content of Figure 5-1. Now that we have discussed how values are stored using bits, we can look at the operators that work on them; the set of C# logical operators is described in Table 5-14. Each of these operators produces an int as the result.

Table 5-14. C# Bitwise and Logical Operators

Operator	Description
&	Logical AND of two values
|	Logical OR of two values
^	Logical XOR of two values
~	Logical NOT
<<	Left-shift operator (promotion)
>>	Right-shift operator (demotion)

The & operator takes two numeric values and compares the values of each bit; if both bits in a given position are both set to 1, then the bit with the same worth is set to 1 in the result. The | operator takes two numeric values and if either or both bits in each position are 1, then the bit in matching position in the result is set to 1. The ^ operator is similar, but the result bits are set only to 1 if one or the other, not both, of the source bits are 1.

The ~ operator is slightly different; it works on a single numeric value, and it reverses the value of the bits in the result so that a 1 in the value is a 0 in the result and a 0 in the value is a 1 in the result. Listing 5-20 demonstrates these four operators being used.

Listing 5-20. Some of the C# Logical Operators

```csharp
using System;

class Listing_20 {

    static void Main(string[] args) {

        // define the byte values that will be used
        byte b1 = 138;
        byte b2 = 129;

        // demonstrate the & operator
        Console.WriteLine("--- & Operator ---");
        Console.WriteLine("binary: {0} decimal: {1}", ConvertToBinary(b1), b1);
        Console.WriteLine("binary: {0} decimal: {1}", ConvertToBinary(b2), b2);
        int result1 = b1 & b2;
        Console.WriteLine("result: {0} decimal: {1}", ConvertToBinary(result1), result1);

        // demonstrate the | operator
        Console.WriteLine("\n--- | Operator ---");
        Console.WriteLine("binary: {0} decimal: {1}", ConvertToBinary(b1), b1);
        Console.WriteLine("binary: {0} decimal: {1}", ConvertToBinary(b2), b2);
        int result2 = b1 | b2;
        Console.WriteLine("result: {0} decimal: {1}", ConvertToBinary(result2), result2);

        // demonstrate the ^ operator
        Console.WriteLine("\n--- ^ Operator ---");
        Console.WriteLine("binary: {0} decimal: {1}", ConvertToBinary(b1), b1);
        Console.WriteLine("binary: {0} decimal: {1}", ConvertToBinary(b2), b2);
        int result3 = b1 ^ b2;
        Console.WriteLine("result: {0} decimal: {1}", ConvertToBinary(result3), result3);

        // demonstrate the ~ operator
        Console.WriteLine("\n--- ~ Operator ---");
        Console.WriteLine("binary: {0} decimal: {1}", ConvertToBinary(b1), b1);
        int result4 = (byte)~b1;
        Console.WriteLine("result: {0} decimal: {1}", ConvertToBinary(result4), result4);

        // wait for input before exiting
        Console.WriteLine("Press enter to finish");
        Console.ReadLine();
```

```
    }

    private static string ConvertToBinary(int value) {
        return String.Format("{0:00000000}", int.Parse(Convert.ToString(value, 2)));
    }
}
```

The statement in the ConvertToBinary method formats the binary string nicely; you can learn more about formatting in Chapter 16. Compiling and running the code in Listing 5-20 produces the following results; for each example, you can see the binary and decimal values and the result of the operator being applied:

```
--- & Operator ---
binary: 10001010 decimal: 138
binary: 10000001 decimal: 129
result: 10000000 decimal: 128

--- | Operator ---
binary: 10001010 decimal: 138
binary: 10000001 decimal: 129
result: 10001011 decimal: 139

--- ^ Operator ---
binary: 10001010 decimal: 138
binary: 10000001 decimal: 129
result: 00001011 decimal: 11

--- ~ Operator ---
binary: 10001010 decimal: 138
result: 01110101 decimal: 117
Press enter to finish
```

The left and right shift operators move all the bits in a value to the left or right by a specified number of places and inserting the same number of zeros to fill in the gaps. Listing 5-21 demonstrates the left- and right-shift operators.

Listing 5-21. Left- and Right-Shifting a Byte Value

```
using System;

class Listing_21 {

    static void Main(string[] args) {

        byte b = 15;

        // left shift the byte two places
        int result = b << 2;

        // show the before and after values
```

```
        Console.WriteLine("--- Left-shift Operator ---");
        Console.WriteLine("Before: {0} ({1})", ConvertToBinary(b), b);
        Console.WriteLine("After:  {0} ({1})", ConvertToBinary(result), result);

        b = 60;

        // right shift three places
        result = b >> 3;

        // show the before and after values
        Console.WriteLine("\n--- Right-shift Operator ---");
        Console.WriteLine("Before: {0} ({1})", ConvertToBinary(b), b);
        Console.WriteLine("After:  {0} ({1})", ConvertToBinary(result), result);

        // wait for input before exiting
        Console.WriteLine("Press enter to finish");
        Console.ReadLine();
    }

    private static string ConvertToBinary(int value) {
        return String.Format("{0:00000000}", int.Parse(Convert.ToString(value, 2)));
    }
}
```

The code in Listing 5-21 shifts a value two places to the left and shifts another value three places to the right. Compiling and running the code in Listing 5-21 produces the following results:

```
--- Left-shift Operator ---
Before: 00001111 (15)
After:  00111100 (60)

--- Right-shift Operator ---
Before: 00111100 (60)
After:  00000111 (7)
Press enter to finish
```

You can see that when I shift to the left, all of the 1s in the binary string are moved two places to the left. This has the effect of changing the value that is represented from 15 to 60 (see Figure 5-1 for details of why). Notice that two new zeros have been put in to the rightmost positions.

When I shift three places to the right, the bits are moved in the opposite direction—notice that one of the 1s is shifted out of the byte entirely. When this happens, the 1 value is gone for good; shifting back to the left doesn't restore it. Notice also that when a value is shifted out, it doesn't reappear on the other side (as though the values were in a loop); the positions are always filled with 0 values.

Assignment Operators

With one exception, the assignment operators allow you to conveniently apply one of the other operators and assign the result in a single step. Table 5-15 describes the assignment operators.

Table 5-15. *C# Assignment Operators*

Operator	Description
=	Assigns a value to a variable
+=	Adds to and assigns a value
-=	Subtracts from and assigns a value
*=	Multiplies and assigns a value
/=	Divides and assigns a value
%=	Remainder and assigns a variable
&=	Logical AND and assigns a variable
|=	Logical OR and assigns a variable
^=	Logical XOR and assigns a variable
<<=	Left-shift and assigns a variable
>>=	Right-shift and assigns a variable

The first item in Table 5-15 is the assignment operator, which you might be surprised to see listed in this category. But the assignment operator returns a result, which can be useful. Consider the following statements:

```
int x;
int y = x = 10;
```

Assigning a value to a variable produces a result, which in this case I have assigned to another variable. Assigning the value of 10 to the variable x produces a result of 10, which you can assign to another variable or just treat like any other numeric value; both x and y end up with a value of 10 in the previous statements. Consider these statements:

```
int x;
int y = (2 + (x = 10));
```

The result of assigning a value of 10 to x is 10, meaning that those statements are equivalent to these:

```
int x;
x = 10;
int y = 2 + x;
```

The other assignment operators allow shorthand when you want to perform an operation on a variable and assign the result to the same variable. So, these statements:

```
int x = 10;
x = x + 2;
```

can be written as follows:

```
int x = 10;
x += 2;
```

I have used the addition assignment operator to add 2 to the value of the variable x and assign the result to x. At the end of these statements, the value of x is 12. Listing 5-22 demonstrates the use of these operators.

Listing 5-22. Using the C# Assignment Operators

```
using System;

class Listing_22 {

    static void Main(string[] args) {

        // define the value we will use in this example
        int i = 100;

        // print out the initial value
        Console.WriteLine("--- Arithmetic Assignment Operators ---");
        Console.WriteLine("Initial value: {0}", i);

        // use the += operator
        i += 10;
        Console.WriteLine("Value after +=: {0}", i);

        // use the -= operator
        i -= 10;
        Console.WriteLine("Value after -=: {0}", i);

        // use the *= operator
        i *= 10;
        Console.WriteLine("Value after *=: {0}", i);

        // use the /= operator
        i /= 10;
        Console.WriteLine("Value after /=: {0}", i);

        // use the %= operator
        i %= 30;
        Console.WriteLine("Value after %=: {0}", i);

        // print out the initial binary value
```

```
        Console.WriteLine("\n--- Logical Assignment Operators ---");
        Console.WriteLine("Initial value: {0}", ConvertToBinary(i));

        // use the &= operator
        i &= 10;
        Console.WriteLine("Value after &=: {0}", ConvertToBinary(i));

        // use the |= operator
        i |= 128;
        Console.WriteLine("Value after |=: {0}", ConvertToBinary(i));

        // use the ^= operator
        i ^= 128;
        Console.WriteLine("Value after ^=: {0}", ConvertToBinary(i));

        // use the <<= operator
        i <<= 2;
        Console.WriteLine("Value after <<=: {0}", ConvertToBinary(i));

        // use the >>= operator
        i >>= 2;
        Console.WriteLine("Value after >>=: {0}", ConvertToBinary(i));

        // wait for input before exiting
        Console.WriteLine("Press enter to finish");
        Console.ReadLine();
    }

    private static string ConvertToBinary(int value) {
        return String.Format("{0:00000000}", int.Parse(Convert.ToString(value, 2)));
    }
}
```

Compiling and running the code in Listing 5-22 produces the following results:

```
--- Arithmetic Assignment Operators ---
Initial value: 100
Value after +=: 110
Value after -=: 100
Value after *=: 1000
Value after /=: 100
Value after %=: 10

--- Logical Assignment Operators ---
Initial value: 00001010
Value after &=: 00001010
Value after |=: 10001010
Value after ^=: 00001010
Value after <<=: 00101000
Value after >>=: 00001010
```

```
Press enter to finish
```

Working with Very Large Integer Values

The System.Numerics.BigInteger struct lets you work with integer values that are too large to be represented using the numeric types listed in Table 5-2. The BigInteger struct has no upper or lower bounds and so can be used to represent incredibly large numbers.

■ **Note** The System.Numerics.BigInteger struct is contained within the System.Numerics assembly. To import this assembly into your project, right-click the project in the Visual Studio Solution Explorer window, select Add Reference, click the .NET tab, and scroll down until you see System.Numerics. Click the OK button.

There are two ways to create and initialize new instances of BigInteger. If the value you want to assign can be represented using a standard numeric type, then assign the value as you would normally, as follows:

```
BigInteger bigInt = long.MaxValue;
```

This creates a new BigInteger variable called bigInt with a value equal to the maximum value that a long can represent. The problem here is that you generally want to use the BigInteger type for values that can't be expressed using numeric literals because they are too big. In such cases, you can use the static Parse method and provide the value you want as a string, like this:

```
BigInteger bigInt2 = BigInteger.Parse("92233720368547758070");
```

This statement creates a BigInteger variable called bigInt2 with a value that is ten times the largest value that a long can represent. Once you have defined and initialized a BigInteger value, you can work with it as you would other numeric types. Listing 5-23 demonstrates some basic operations.

Listing 5-23. Using the BigInteger Class

```
using System;
using System.Numerics;

class Listing_23 {

    static void Main(string[] args) {

        // create a new BigInteger using a numeric literal
        BigInteger bigInt = long.MaxValue;

        // create a new BigInteger with a value that cannot be
        // expressed using a numeric literal
        BigInteger bigInt2 = BigInteger.Parse("92233720368547758070");
```

```
        // add the two big integers together using the += operator
        bigInt += bigInt2;
        Console.WriteLine("Result after adding two BigInteger values: {0}", bigInt);

        // subtract using a numeric literal
        bigInt = bigInt2 - 500;
        Console.WriteLine("Result after subtacting a literal: {0}", bigInt);

        // multiply using a numeric type
        int i = 300;
        bigInt *= i;
        Console.WriteLine("Result after multiplung with an int: {0}", bigInt);

        // wait for input before exiting
        Console.WriteLine("Press enter to finish");
        Console.ReadLine();
    }
}
```

You can see from the code that you can perform operations on pairs of BingIntegers and on BigIntegers and the normal numeric types. Compiling and running the code in Listing 5-23 produces the following results:

```
Result after adding two BigInteger values: 101457092405402533877
Result after subtacting a literal: 92233720368547757570
Result after multiplung with an int: 27670116110564327271000
Press enter to finish
```

The Boolean Type

C# has a single Boolean type, which is used through the bool keyword. As with the numeric type keyword, this is an alias, in this case, to the System.Boolean struct. The Boolean type is used throughout C#, directly using Boolean literals and indirectly as the result of other operations and in conditional statements.

Using Boolean Literals

A bool can have only two values: true and false. You can express these values using the true and false literals—to set the value of a bool field or variable or in a conditional statement, for example. Listing 5-24 provides an illustration.

Listing 5-24. Using Boolean Literals

```
using System;

class Listing_24 {
```

```
static void Main(string[] args) {

    // assign values to a bool variable
    bool var1 = true;
    bool var2 = false;

    Console.WriteLine("Value 1: {0}", var1);
    Console.WriteLine("Value 2: {0}", var2);

    // use a bool literal in a conditional statement

    if (true) {
        Console.WriteLine("Hello");
    }

    // wait for input before exiting
    Console.WriteLine("Press enter to finish");
    Console.ReadLine();
    }
}
```

The assignment statements in Listing 5-24 use the true and false literals to assign values to a pair of bool variables. The true literal is also used as the condition in an if statement; the literal value true used on its own like this always satisfies a conditional statement, while the false literal always fails to do so.

Although you can evaluate literals values in conditional statements, it is more useful and common to evaluate bool variables or fields, like this:

```
bool x = true;
if (x) {
    // ... do something...
}
```

Notice that the if statement can evaluate the variable on its own—we don't have to use the form:

```
if (x == true) {
    // ... do something...
}
```

Using Boolean Results

You will often use the bool type implicitly as the result of other operations. The C# relational operators all return bool results; we saw how these operators relate to numeric types in Table 5-13 and how they are applied in Listing 5-19.

The most common implicit use of bool values is in conditional statements. The condition in such a statement is satisfied when the conditional expression evaluates to the bool value true. When we see statements such as these:

```
int x = 100;
if (x > 50) {
    Console.WriteLine("Hello");
```

```
}
```

we are using a convenient shorthand. We can express the same statements like this:

```
int x = 100;
bool condition = x > 50;
if (condition) {
    Console.WriteLine("Hello");
}
```

See Chapter 4 for details of the selection statements that C# supports.

Using Struct Members

The bool type has some methods and fields that make working with Booleans easier, although since Booleans are so simple, there are only a few of them. Table 5-16 describes these members.

Table 5-16. Boolean Type Members

Member	Description
TrueString FalseString	Fields that return strings representing the bool true and false values.
Parse(string)	Parses a bool value from a string; this method will throw an exception if the value cannot be parsed. See the TryParse method for an approach that won't throw an exception.
TryParse(string, out bool)	Parses a bool value from a string and places it in the out parameter. Returns true if parsing was successful; returns false and sets the out parameter to false otherwise.
ToString()	Converts the value of a bool to one of the TrueString or FalseString field values.

You can access these members through the bool keyword, through the System.Boolean type, or by using the Boolean literal keywords. Listing 5-25 demonstrates the use of these members.

Listing 5-25. Using the Members of the System.Boolean Struct

```
using System;

class Listing_25 {

    static void Main(string[] args) {

        // print out the string field values
        Console.WriteLine("TrueString: {0}", bool.TrueString);
        Console.WriteLine("FalseString: {0}", bool.FalseString);
```

```
// parse a string into a bool
bool b1 = bool.Parse("true");
Console.WriteLine("Parsed value: {0}", b1);

// use the TryParse method
bool result;
bool parseOK = bool.TryParse("true", out result);
Console.WriteLine("Parse result: {0}, bool value: {1}", parseOK, result);

// convert a bool to a string
string str = true.ToString();
Console.WriteLine("String value: {0}", str);

// wait for input before exiting
Console.WriteLine("Press enter to finish");
Console.ReadLine();
    }
}
```

Compiling and running the code in Listing 5-25 produces the following results:

```
TrueString: True
FalseString: False
Parsed value: True
Parse result: True, bool value: True
String value: True
Press enter to finish
```

Summary

In this chapter, we looked at the numeric and Boolean types that C# supports and the operations you can perform on them. These operations include basic arithmetic, working directly with the binary representation of numbers and, of course, expressing true and false values. You have seen how C# supports literals to make working with these types simpler. We used the numeric literal prefix and suffix features to control type inference and how we can convert between some types implicitly, while other conversions require the cast operator.

CHAPTER 6

■ ■ ■

Classes and Objects

You create new functionality in C# programs by defining *classes*. Classes are the blueprints used to create the *objects* that you use to represent items in your program. This chapter shows you how to define classes and then use them to create objects.

Along the way, we'll encounter three of the key concepts in object-oriented programming: inheritance, encapsulation, and polymorphism. The way that C# implements these concepts allows you to write classes with the minimum of code and maintain them with the minimum of effort.

Introducing classes and objects means referring to topics that are covered in later chapters. I have tried to provide enough information so that this chapter makes sense on its own, but a certain amount of referring to other parts of the book is inevitable. Table 6-1 provides the summary for this chapter.

■ **Tip** In this chapter and the chapters that follow, I focus on classes and the different types of class member. Classes allow you to create custom reference types. C# also allows you to create custom value types using the struct feature. See Chapter 12 for details.

Table 6-1. Quick Problem/Solution Reference for Chapter 6

Problem	Solution	Listings
Define a new type.	Define a type using the class keyword and add members to define functionality.	6-1 through 6-4
Create and use an object from a class.	Use the new operator.	6-5 through 6-12
Derive a class from a base type.	Specify a base type for your class.	6-13 through 6-17
Convert from one type to another.	Perform an implicit or explicit cast operation.	6-18 through 6-22
Cast without causing an exception.	Use the is and as operators.	6-23, 6-24

Problem	Solution	Listings
Upcast a value type to a reference type.	Box and unbox the type.	6-25, 6-26
Define a class within a class.	Create a nested class.	6-27
Create a static class.	Use the `static` modifier to create a static class.	6-28
Create a class that forces derived classes to override methods.	Use the `abstract` modifier to create an abstract class.	6-29, 6-30
Create a class that cannot be used as a base class.	Use the `sealed` modifier to create a sealed class.	6-31
Define a single class across multiple code files.	Use the `partial` modifier to create a partial class.	6-32

Creating a Basic Class

Remember that classes are the blueprints from which objects are created. Imagine we had a blueprint for a car; for the sake of an example, let's say the blueprint is for a 2010 Volvo C30. The blueprint specifies every detail of the car, but it isn't a car itself. It just describes how the car should be constructed. We have to go through the process of constructing a car from the blueprint to end up with something that we can get into and drive away, and that something will be a Volvo C30, because that's what we used as the blueprint. Listing 6-1 contains a simple class that we'll use to start our blueprint.

Listing 6-1. A Simple Class

```
public class VolvoC30 {
    // class body
}
```

This class is so simple that it doesn't do anything yet, but we'll add some features as we work through this chapter. There are four parts to the class defined in Listing 6-1, and these are illustrated in Figure 6-1.

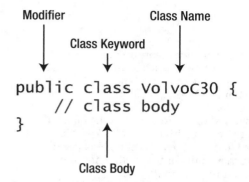

Figure 6-1. The anatomy of a simple class

All classes require the class keyword, and immediately after the keyword is the name, or identifier, of the class. You can call your class anything you like, but the convention is to name it after the category of objects that the class represents. For example, if our class represents the products we have in a warehouse, we might use the name Product or WarehouseProduct. In C#, class names are usually given Pascal case, where words are concatenated and the first letter of each word is capitalized. The class in the example is called VolvoC30. Immediately before the class keyword is the modifier; in this example, the modifier is the public keyword, which is an example of an *access modifier*. Modifiers are optional and a class can have zero, one, or multiple modifiers. Modifiers are explained in the "Using Class Modifiers" section later in this chapter.

Adding Features to a Class

The class in Listing 6-1 doesn't have any features at all. It is as though we wrote "Volvo C30" on a blueprint and then just walked away. If we gave the blueprint to someone else, they'd have only the name to go on. We have not provided any information about what features we require. We add features to a class by adding *class members*. There are a range of different categories of class members, some of which are described in the following sections. All of the different member types are described in depth in the chapters that follow.

Adding Fields

A field is a piece of information that each object created from the class will have; this can be one of the built-in value types that C# supports (such as a number or a Boolean value), or it can be another object (a reference type). If a field refers to another object, then that object can be one of those included with the .NET Framework (such as a string), or it can be a type we have created, like the VolvoC30 class. Listing 6-2 demonstrates adding some fields to our class.

Listing 6-2. Adding Fields to a Class

```
public class VolvoC30 {
    public string CarOwner;
    public string PaintColor;
    public int MilesPerGallon= 30;
```

```
}
```

There are three fields in the class in Listing 6-2, meaning that when we create an object from this class, three pieces of data will be created. Each field has a name (CarOwner, PaintColor, MilesPerGallon) and a type. The type of the CarOwner and PaintColor fields is string, meaning that these fields will be able to hold a string of characters. The type of the MilesPerGallon field is int, meaning that this field will be able to hold a numeric integer value.

You can see that I have assigned a value of 30 to the MilesPerGallon field. This has the effect of setting 30 to be the value of this field for every object that we create from this class. It is like a blueprint specifying that the driver's door window in each new Volvo be left open. It can be changed later (much as the window can be closed later), but every object starts with that value for that field. I have not specified values for the other fields; we'll use a different class feature to do that later.

You can see that all three fields have the word public in their definition. You can get full details of how this keyword affects fields as well as information about all the other things you can do with fields in Chapter 7. You can also learn about properties in that chapter; properties are closely related to fields and are worth exploring fully.

■ **Note** If you read Chapter 7, you will see that I tell you not to use public fields. I don't like going against my own advice, but I wanted the simplest possible examples for this chapter because there are some important topics that I want to focus on. This is one of those "do as I say, not as I do" moments.

Adding Methods

Methods let your object perform actions. That's a pretty wide definition, and the nature of your methods will depend on the nature of your class. If we remain with the car metaphor, then we could have methods to start the engine, open the window, plot a navigation route, and so on. If our class represented a person, we might have methods that change marital status, employment status, and relationships, with objects representing other people.

Many methods change the state of an object, typically by changing the value assigned to one of the fields. Other methods will use the value assigned to one of the fields to calculate some kind of value. Listing 6-3 shows our example class with some methods.

Listing 6-3. Adding Methods to a Class

```
public class VolvoC30 {
    public string CarOwner;
    public string PaintColor;
    public int MilesPerGallon = 30;


    public int CalculateFuelForTrip(int tripDistance) {
        return tripDistance / MilesPerGallon;
    }

    public void PrintCarDetails() {
```

```
        System.Console.WriteLine("--- Car Details ---");
        System.Console.WriteLine("Car Owner: {0}", CarOwner);
        System.Console.WriteLine("Car Color: {0}", PaintColor);
        System.Console.WriteLine("Gas Mileage: {0} mpg", MilesPerGallon);
    }
}
```

You can create different kinds of method to suit different kinds of actions. Chapter 9 covers methods in detail and explains the different types.

There are two methods in the class in Listing 6-3. The first method is called `CalculateFuelForTrip` and uses the value of the `MilesPerGallon` field and the value of a parameter to calculate the number of gallons of fuel required for a trip of a specified distance. The result of this calculation is returned as an `int`. The second method, called `PrintCarDetails`, prints out the values of the three fields to the console using the `System.Console` class.

Methods on their own don't do anything; they have to be *called* or *invoked*. Typically, when your program starts, the .NET runtime looks for a special method called the *main method* and starts performing the statements it contains. This method can then call other methods to perform actions by performing the code statements that they contain. Chapter 9 contains a lot of examples of methods and their use, including a full explanation of the main method.

Adding a Constructor

A constructor is a special method that you use when creating a new object, allowing you to provide data via parameters that will set the initial state of the object. Listing 6-4 adds a constructor to our car class.

Listing 6-4. Adding a Constructor

```
public class VolvoC30 {
    public string CarOwner;
    public string PaintColor;
    public int MilesPerGallon = 30;

    public VolvoC30(string carOwner, string paintColor) {
        CarOwner = carOwner;
        PaintColor = paintColor;
    }

    public int CalculateFuelForTrip(int tripDistance) {
        return tripDistance / MilesPerGallon;
    }

    public void PrintCarDetails() {
        System.Console.WriteLine("--- Car Details ---");
        System.Console.WriteLine("Car Owner: {0}", CarOwner);
        System.Console.WriteLine("Car Color: {0}", PaintColor);
        System.Console.WriteLine("Gas Mileage: {0} mpg", MilesPerGallon);
    }
}
```

The constructor is shown in bold. Constructors have the same name as the class that contains them, in our case, VolvoC30. This constructor has two parameters; these parameters are inputs to the construction process and are used to assign initial values to the CarOwner and PaintColor fields. We'll see how to use a constructor in the next section of this chapter.

All classes require a constructor, although if you don't provide one explicitly, the C# compiler will add a default one for you when your code is compiled. Constructors, including the default that the compiler adds, are discussed in full in the "Special Methods" section of Chapter 9.

Creating Objects from Classes

Objects are often referred to as *instances*, for example, "This object is an instance of the VolvoC30 class." This is often shortened so that it is commonly said that "This is an instance of VolvoC30." To create an object from a class, we use the new operator, sometimes referred to as the *construction* or *instantiation* operator. We tell the new operator which class to work with, and it creates a new object of the type representing by the class. Listing 6-5 demonstrates how to create a new object using our VolvoC30 class.

Listing 6-5. Creating a New Object with the new Operator

```
// create a new object of the MyClass type
VolvoC30 myCar = new VolvoC30("Adam Freeman", "Black");
```

This is a typical object creation statement. Creating objects from classes is such a common activity in C# that is it worth covering this in detail. There are six parts to the statement in Listing 6-5, and they are illustrated in Figure 6-2.

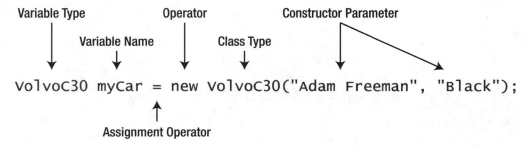

Figure 6-2. The anatomy of object construction

■ **Tip** The use of the new operator to create objects from classes is an essential C# concept; take the time to study Figure 6-2 so that you understand the various components that are involved. Classes are defined when you write the code for your program. When your program is running, you can't modify the classes themselves. Instead, you create objects from the specifications that the class represents and work with them instead. To stick with the idea of cars, the class is the plan that the designers and artists produce, and the objects are the cars that the factory produces by following the instructions in the plan.

We are going to start with the part of the statement to the right of the assignment operator:

```
new VolvoC30("Adam Freeman", "Black");
```

This is the part of the Listing 6-5 statement that creates a new object. We use the new operator, followed by name of the class we want to use as a blueprint, along with the inputs we have specified in the class constructor. We defined two parameters in our constructor, and we have to provide values for them now.

If we had defined a constructor that had no parameters or we had chosen to let the C# compiler create the default constructor for us, we would have been able to create a new object like this, without parameters:

```
new VolvoC30();
```

But we added two parameters to the constructor, which means that we have to provide values for them if we want to create objects from that class. When we create a new object, the .NET runtime creates the objects and values for the fields and assigns initial values to them. In our example class, the MilesPerGallon field has an initial value of 30. The statements in the constructor are then executed. In our example, these statements assign initial values to the CarOwner and PaintColor fields. These fields are strings and are reference types, so the runtime creates the new string objects and sets the fields to reference these objects. You can see what we end up with in Figure 6-3—a new VolvoC30 object, with references to two string objects and an int value. The VolvoC30 object also has two methods that use the fields in the object, CalculateFuelForTrip and PrintCarDetails.

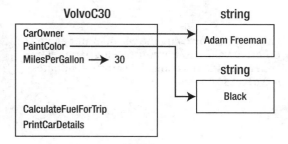

Figure 6-3. *Creating an object*

So, the part of the statement in Listing 6-5 to the right of the assignment operator has created a new VolvoC30 object, using the VolvoC30 class as a blueprint. The part of the statement to the left of the assignment operator defines a variable that will contain a reference to a VolvoC30 object. We want to do this so that we can refer to the object later and perform operations upon it. The assignment operator itself is the bridge between creating the object and assigning the reference. Here is the class that contains the statement in Listing 6-5:

```
public class Volvo_Test {

    public static void Main() {

        // create a new object of the VolvoC30 type
        VolvoC30 myCar = new VolvoC30("Adam Freeman", "Black");

        // wait for input before exiting
```

```
        Console.WriteLine("Press enter to finish");
        Console.ReadLine();
    }
}
```

The Main method is a special method that is used to start execution of a C# program. You can get full details of this method in Chapter 9. For this chapter, it is enough to know that when we compile and run the code, the .NET runtime finds the Main method in the Volvo_Test class and starts to execute the code statements it contains, including the statement that uses the new operator to create a VolvoC30 object.

When this statement has been executed, we have a VolvoC30 local variable in the Main method called myCar that contains a reference to a newly created VolvoC30 object, as illustrated in Figure 6-4.

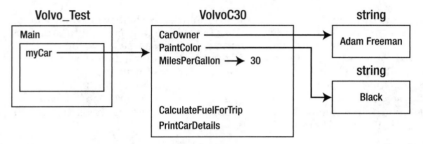

Figure 6-4. *The references between created objects*

We can use a class to create more than one object of a given type by using the new operator again. We differentiate between different objects by providing different values to the constructor parameters and giving a different name to the local variable that will reference the new object. Listing 6-6 updates the Main method in the Volvo_Test class to create multiple VolvoC30 objects.

Listing 6-6. Creating Multiple Objects from the Same Class

```
public class Volvo_Test {

    public static void Main() {

        // create a new object of the VolvoC30 type
        VolvoC30 myCar = new VolvoC30("Adam Freeman", "Black");

        // create a second VolvoC30 object
        VolvoC30 joesCar = new VolvoC30("Joe Smith", "Silver");

        // wait for input before exiting
        Console.WriteLine("Press enter to finish");
        Console.ReadLine();
    }
}
```

The statements in Listing 6-6 create two VolvoC30 objects. One has been created with the arguments Adam Freeman and Black. The other object has been created with the arguments Joe Smith and Silver.

The myCar variable has a reference to the first object, and the joesCar variable has a reference to the second object. Figure 6-5 shows the set of objects that we have created.

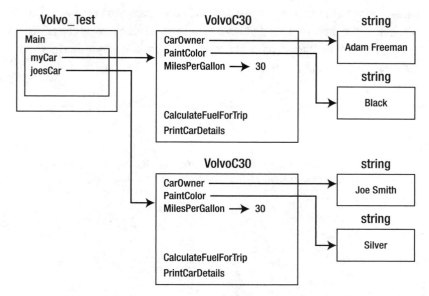

Figure 6-5. *Multiple objects and their references*

In this section, we have seen how the new operator creates an object using the class as a blueprint. By providing different values for the constructor parameters, we have been able to create two VolvoC30 objects that represent two different cars. The objects are differentiated by their fields. Fields that are defined using value types (which include int) contain a value directly, in our case a numeric value. Fields that are defined using reference types (which include string) contain references to other objects.

Using Objects

Once we have created an object, we can work with it using the members we defined in the class. Working with an object typically means doing one of two things: changing the value of a field to change the state of an object or using one of the objects methods to perform an action. Methods can modify the value of fields as well, so sometimes you'll be performing a calculation and modifying the state of an object in one go.

■ **Tip** The state of an object is the collected values of all of its internal data: the values assigned to its fields and properties (fields are discussed in Chapter 7, and properties are discussed in Chapter 8). Because you can assign different values to fields and properties, objects of the same type can be in different states. Modifying one or more fields or properties is said to *change the state* of an object, and reading the values of the fields and properties is said to be *getting the state* of an object.

Reading and Modifying Fields

To read the value of a field, we use the dot operator (.) to combine the name we have given to the object instance and the name of the field we want to access. Listing 6-7 provides a demonstration.

Listing 6-7. Reading an Object Field

```
public class Volvo_Test {

    public static void Main() {

        // create a new object of the VolvoC30 type
        VolvoC30 myCar = new VolvoC30("Adam Freeman", "Black");

        // create a second VolvoC30 object
        VolvoC30 joesCar = new VolvoC30("Joe Smith", "Silver");

        // read the value of the myCar.CarOwner field
        string owner = myCar.CarOwner;

        Console.WriteLine("Field value: {0}", owner);

        // wait for input before exiting
        Console.WriteLine("Press enter to finish");
        Console.ReadLine();
    }
}
```

The bold statement in Listing 6-7 reads the value of one of the VolvoC30 objects—the one that is referenced by the myCar variable. Here is the statement:

```
string owner = myCar.CarOwner;
```

To the right of the assignment operator, you can see that the dot operator (.) is used to combine the object reference (myCar) with the field name (CarOwner). This reads the current value of the field. To the left of the assignment operator, the statement defines a new string local variable called owner and references the result of the dot operator, in this case the field value. The value of owner is then printed out using the Console class. Compiling and running the code in Listing 6-7 produces the following results:

```
Field value: Adam Freeman
Press enter to finish
```

To modify the value of a field, we use the same operators but in a different order. Listing 6-8 contains an example.

Listing 6-8. Modifying a Field

```
public class Volvo_Test {

    public static void Main() {

        // create a new object of the VolvoC30 type
        VolvoC30 myCar = new VolvoC30("Adam Freeman", "Black");

        // create a second VolvoC30 object
        VolvoC30 joesCar = new VolvoC30("Joe Smith", "Silver");

        // modify the value of the myCar.CarOwner field
        myCar.CarOwner = "Jane Doe";

        // read the value of the myCar.CarOwner field
        string owner = myCar.CarOwner;

        Console.WriteLine("Field value: {0}", owner);

        // wait for input before exiting
        Console.WriteLine("Press enter to finish");
        Console.ReadLine();
    }
}
```

The statement in bold changes the CarOwner field of the VolvoC30 object referenced by the myCar variable to Jane Doe, like this:

```
myCar.CarOwner = "Jane Doe";
```

Once again we have combined the variable name with the field naming using the dot operator, but this time we have used the assignment value to set a new value, rather than read the current one.

Only one of the two VolvoC30 objects that we created in Listing 6-8 has been affected by modifying the field value, as shown by Figure 6-6.

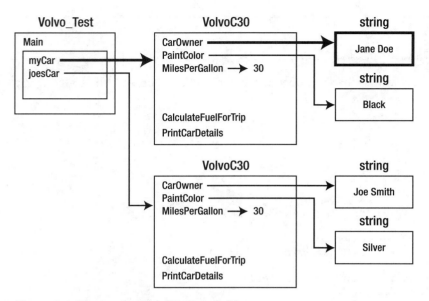

Figure 6-6. *The result of modifying a field*

The CarOwner field of the other object remains unchanged. The owner is still Joe Smith. The other fields in the modified object also remain unchanged; we modified only one field in one object, as shown by Figure 6-6.

References to Common Objects

In the previous example, we made a change that affected just one object, leaving the other object we had created unmodified. There is an important variation on this example that warrants careful attention. If you have been wondering why I keep laboring the difference between reference and value types, well, this is one of the reasons.

Let's start with a value type and add a new member to our VolvoC30 class. Here is the modified class:

```
public class VolvoC30 {
    public string CarOwner;
    public string PaintColor;
    public int MilesPerGallon = 30;
    public int ServiceInterval;

    public VolvoC30(string newOwner, string paintColor, int serviceInt) {
        CarOwner = newOwner;
        PaintColor = paintColor;
        ServiceInterval = serviceInt;
    }

    public int CalculateFuelForTrip(int tripDistance) {
        return tripDistance / MilesPerGallon;
```

```
    }

    public void PrintCarDetails() {
        System.Console.WriteLine("--- Car Details ---");
        System.Console.WriteLine("Car Owner: {0}", CarOwner);
        System.Console.WriteLine("Car Color: {0}", PaintColor);
        System.Console.WriteLine("Gas Mileage: {0} mpg", MilesPerGallon);
        System.Console.WriteLine("Service Interval: {0} miles", ServiceInterval);
    }
}
```

I have added a new field called ServiceInterval. This field contains an int, which is a value type. The initial value of this field is set from the value of a new constructor parameter. Listing 6-9 demonstrates the modified VolvoC30 class being used.

Listing 6-9. Using a Shared Value Type

```
public class Volvo_Test {

    public static void Main() {

        // define a common service interval variable
        int serviceInterval = 40000;

        // create a new object of the VolvoC30 type
        VolvoC30 myCar = new VolvoC30("Adam Freeman", "Black", serviceInterval);

        // create a second VolvoC30 object
        VolvoC30 joesCar = new VolvoC30("Joe Smith", "Silver", serviceInterval);

        // modify the value of service interval in myCar
        myCar.ServiceInterval = 50000;

        // read and print out the ServiceInterval field for both objects
        Console.WriteLine("myCar field value: {0}", myCar.ServiceInterval);
        Console.WriteLine("joesCar field value: {0}", joesCar.ServiceInterval);

        // wait for input before exiting
        Console.WriteLine("Press enter to finish");
        Console.ReadLine();
    }
}
```

In this listing, I start by defining a local int variable called serviceInterval, to which I assign a value of 40,000. I then create two VolvoC30 objects, using the local serviceInterval variable as a parameter for both objects. Because an int is a value type, this statement in the VolvoC30 constructor:

```
        ServiceInterval = serviceInt;
```

causes the parameter value to be copied into the ServiceInterval field. This is illustrated in Figure 6-7.

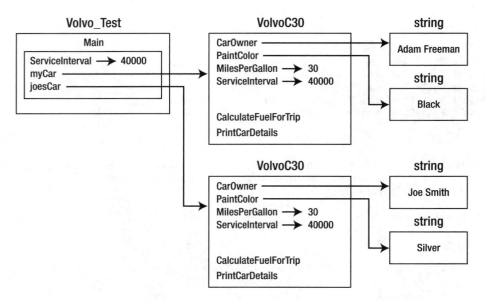

Figure 6-7. Using a common value type as a constructor argument

The serviceInterval variable in the Main method and the ServiceInterval fields in the two VolvoC30 objects are all separate. Making a change to one of them has no effect on the others, as we can see when I change one of the fields to 50000 and then print out the values for both objects. Compiling and running the code in Listing 6-9 produces the following results:

```
myCar field value: 50000
joesCar field value: 40000
Press enter to finish
```

Now let's turn our attention to a reference type. To do this, we'll create a second class and create a field on our VolvoC30 class that is of the new type. Listing 6-10 contains the code.

Listing 6-10. A Reference Type Field

```
public class EngineSpec {
    public int EngineCapacity;
    public string FuelType;

    public EngineSpec(int capacity, string type) {
        EngineCapacity = capacity;
        FuelType = type;
    }
}

public class VolvoC30 {
```

```
    public string CarOwner;
    public string PaintColor;
    public int MilesPerGallon = 30;
    public EngineSpec Engine;

    public VolvoC30(string newOwner, string paintColor, EngineSpec engineSpec) {
        CarOwner = newOwner;
        PaintColor = paintColor;
        Engine = engineSpec;
    }

    public int CalculateFuelForTrip(int tripDistance) {
        return tripDistance / MilesPerGallon;
    }

    public void PrintCarDetails() {
        System.Console.WriteLine("--- Car Details ---");
        System.Console.WriteLine("Car Owner: {0}", CarOwner);
        System.Console.WriteLine("Car Color: {0}", PaintColor);
        System.Console.WriteLine("Gas Mileage: {0} mpg", MilesPerGallon);
        System.Console.WriteLine("Engine Capacity: {0} cc", Engine.EngineCapacity);
        System.Console.WriteLine("Fuel Type: {0}", Engine.FuelType);
    }
}
```

Our new class is called EngineSpec, and it contains two fields describing a car's engine. The EngineCapacity field is an int, and the FuelType field is a string. The VolvoC30 class has a field of the type EngineSpec, the initial value of which is set using a parameter argument. The following code creates a single EngineSpec object and uses it as a parameter value in the creation of two VolvoC30 instances:

```
public class Volvo_Test {

    public static void Main() {

        // create an EngineSpec object
        EngineSpec spec = new EngineSpec(2000, "Diesel");

        // create a new object of the VolvoC30 type
        VolvoC30 myCar = new VolvoC30("Adam Freeman", "Black", spec);

        // create a second VolvoC30 object
        VolvoC30 joesCar = new VolvoC30("Joe Smith", "Silver", spec);

        // read and print out the Engine.EngineCapacity field of both objects
        // and the local variable
        Console.WriteLine("--- Values Before Change ---");
        Console.WriteLine("Local EngineSpec Variable: {0}", spec.EngineCapacity);
        Console.WriteLine("myCar field value: {0}", myCar.Engine.EngineCapacity);
        Console.WriteLine("joesCar field value: {0}", joesCar.Engine.EngineCapacity);

        // modify the capacity of the local variable
        spec.EngineCapacity = 2500;
```

```
        // read and print out the Engine.EngineCapacity field of both objects
        // and the local variable
        Console.WriteLine("--- Values After Change ---");
        Console.WriteLine("Local EngineSpec Variable: {0}", spec.EngineCapacity);
        Console.WriteLine("myCar field value: {0}", myCar.Engine.EngineCapacity);
        Console.WriteLine("joesCar field value: {0}", joesCar.Engine.EngineCapacity);

        // wait for input before exiting
        Console.WriteLine("Press enter to finish");
        Console.ReadLine();
    }
}
```

After creating the two VolvoC30 objects, I print out the value of EngineCapacity field from the local variable and both of the objects. I then change the value of the EngineCapcity field in the local variable and print out the three EngineCapacity values again. Compiling and running this code produces the following results:

```
--- Values Before Change ---
Local EngineSpec Variable: 2000
myCar field value: 2000
joesCar field value: 2000
--- Values After Change ---
Local EngineSpec Variable: 2500
myCar field value: 2500
joesCar field value: 2500
Press enter to finish
```

You can see that even though I made only one change, all three values report the new number. To understand what has happened here, we need to look at the references between the objects I created; these are illustrated by Figure 6-8.

When you copy a reference type, you get a copy of the reference, not the object that is referred to. When I created a EngineSpec object, I assigned a reference to the local variable spec. That was one reference. When I used the value of the spec variable as a constructor parameter to the two VolvoC30 objects, each object received its own copy of the reference, but all three references pointed to the same object—the one I created in this statement:

```
EngineSpec spec = new EngineSpec(2000, "Diesel");
```

When I changed the value of the EngineCapacity field using one of the references, I was making a change in the object that all three references point to. When reading the value of the EngineCapacity field, I was reading the field of the same object again and again. I was just using different references to it.

This is one of the foundations of object-oriented programming and is the cause of countless problems as programmers come to terms with the differences between value types and reference types. Remember, copy a value type, and you get a duplicate, separate value type. Copy a reference type, and you get a separate reference to the same object; a new object isn't created automatically.

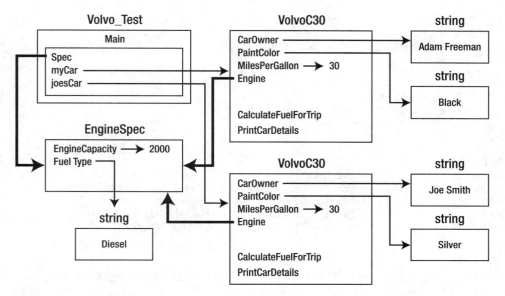

Figure 6-8. Multiple references to a single object

Using Static Fields

The fields in all the examples in the previous sections have been *instance fields,* meaning that each object has its own field. This is why we have to use the object reference with the dot operator to access the field. We have to tell the .NET runtime which object's field we want to work with.

We can also create *static fields,* where all objects share the same field and value. Listing 6-11 contains an example.

■ **Tip** Static fields are useful when you want to define a value that applies to all objects of a given type, typically because the real-world objects they represent share a common characteristic. For example, all Volvo C30 cars have four wheels. By using a static field, you can define this characteristic once, and all VolvoC30 objects will share the same value. When you change a static field, the new value is available to all the VolvoC30 objects. You don't need to go to each one you have created and change the values one by one.

Listing 6-11. Defining a Static Field

```
public class VolvoC30 {
    public string CarOwner;
    public string PaintColor;
    public int MilesPerGallon = 30;
```

```
    public static int EngineCapacity = 2000;

    public VolvoC30(string newOwner, string paintColor) {
        CarOwner = newOwner;
        PaintColor = paintColor;
    }

    public int CalculateFuelForTrip(int tripDistance) {
        return tripDistance / MilesPerGallon;
    }

    public void PrintCarDetails() {
        System.Console.WriteLine("--- Car Details ---");
        System.Console.WriteLine("Car Owner: {0}", CarOwner);
        System.Console.WriteLine("Car Color: {0}", PaintColor);
        System.Console.WriteLine("Gas Mileage: {0} mpg", MilesPerGallon);
        System.Console.WriteLine("Engine Capacity: {0} cc", EngineCapacity);
    }
}
```

You create a static field by using the static keyword, as shown in bold in the listing. To access a static field, you use the class name with the dot operator, as follows:

```
int value = VolvoC30.EngineCapacity;
```

You don't need to create an instance from the class before accessing a static field. You can just access it directly via the class name. You can get more information about static classes (classes that contain only static members) later in this chapter, static fields in Chapter 7, and static methods in Chapter 9.

Calling Methods

A new object doesn't just get a set of fields and properties; it also gets its own set of methods. In our VolvoC30 class, we defined two methods, called PrintCarDetails and CalculateFuelForTrip. Listing 6-12 shows these methods.

Listing 6-12. Revisiting the VolvoC30 Class

```
public class VolvoC30 {
    public string CarOwner;
    public string PaintColor;
    public int MilesPerGallon = 30;

    public VolvoC30(string newOwner, string paintColor) {
        CarOwner = newOwner;
        PaintColor = paintColor;
    }

    public int CalculateFuelForTrip(int tripDistance) {
        return tripDistance / MilesPerGallon;
    }
```

```
    public void PrintCarDetails() {
        System.Console.WriteLine("--- Car Details ---");
        System.Console.WriteLine("Car Owner: {0}", CarOwner);
        System.Console.WriteLine("Car Color: {0}", PaintColor);
        System.Console.WriteLine("Gas Mileage: {0} mpg", MilesPerGallon);
    }
}
```

The methods in Listing 6-12 are shown in bold. The terminology for using a method is to either *call* or *invoke* it. Both terms have the same meaning, namely, to ask the object to perform the code statements contained in the method body. Until a method is called from another method (and ultimately from the Main method), the code statements are dormant. It is not until the method is called that the code statement is executed and the action defined by the method is performed. The following code demonstrates how to invoke the methods in a VolvoC30 object:

```
public class Volvo_Test {

    public static void Main() {

        // create a new VolvoC30 object
        VolvoC30 myCar = new VolvoC30("Adam Freeman", "Black");

        // call the CalculateFuelForTrip for a 1000 mile trip
        int fuelRequired = myCar.CalculateFuelForTrip(1000);
        Console.WriteLine("Fuel Required: {0} gallons", fuelRequired);

        // call the PrintCarDetails method
        myCar.PrintCarDetails();

        // wait for input before exiting
        Console.WriteLine("Press enter to finish");
        Console.ReadLine();
    }
}
```

The statements that call the methods are marked in bold. These are instance methods, and to access them, we use the reference to the object with the dot operator (.) and the method name, like this:

```
int fuelRequired = myCar.CalculateFuelForTrip(1000);
```

This statement calls the CalculateFuelForTrip method, passing a parameter value of 1000. The result of calling this method is an int. In this statement, I assign the result to a local variable called fuelRequired. Methods parameters and results are covered in detail in Chapter 9.

If we look at the statement inside the CalculateFuelTrip method, we can see that one of the object's fields is referred to:

```
public int CalculateFuelForTrip(int tripDistance) {
    return tripDistance / MilesPerGallon;
}
```

When the statement refers to the MilesPerGallon field, it gets the value from the object that contains the method, in other words, the object we have selected using the dot operator. The PrintCarDetails method performs an action that that doesn't provide a result; this is denoted by the void keyword used in place of a return type when defining the method:

```
public void PrintCarDetails() {
    System.Console.WriteLine("--- Car Details ---");
    System.Console.WriteLine("Car Owner: {0}", CarOwner);
    System.Console.WriteLine("Car Color: {0}", PaintColor);
    System.Console.WriteLine("Gas Mileage: {0} mpg", MilesPerGallon);
}
```

You can see that the PrintCarDetails method doesn't require any parameters. We call such a method using the dot operator to combine the object reference and the method name, but we use empty parentheses (()) because there are no parameters, like this:

```
myCar.PrintCarDetails();
```

Compiling and running the previous code produces the following results:

```
Fuel Required: 33 gallons
--- Car Details ---
Car Owner: Adam Freeman
Car Color: Black
Gas Mileage: 30 mpg
Press enter to finish
```

Both of the methods in the VolvoC30 class are *instance methods*, meaning that they belong to a specific instance of VolvoC30. You can also create *static methods*, which like static fields are shared by all objects created from the same class. Static methods are explained more fully in Chapter 9.

Class Inheritance

One of the big features of object-oriented programming is that one object can inherit features from another. You can write C# programs without using the inheritance features, but you'll quickly find that your code becomes hard to maintain.

The VolvoC30 class we used in the previous sections is fine as far as it goes, but what if our program calls for us to work with different kinds of car? We could just create a new class for each type of car that we are interested in. This is demonstrated in Listing 6-13.

Listing 6-13. Creating Multiple Unrelated Classes

```
public class VolvoC30 {
    public string CarOwner;
    public string PaintColor;
    public int MilesPerGallon = 30;

    public VolvoC30(string newOwner, string paintColor) {
        CarOwner = newOwner;
        PaintColor = paintColor;
```

```
    }

    public int CalculateFuelForTrip(int tripDistance) {
        return tripDistance / MilesPerGallon;
    }

    public void PrintCarDetails() {
        System.Console.WriteLine("--- Car Details ---");
        System.Console.WriteLine("Car Owner: {0}", CarOwner);
        System.Console.WriteLine("Car Color: {0}", PaintColor);
        System.Console.WriteLine("Gas Mileage: {0} mpg", MilesPerGallon);
    }
}

public class FordFiesta {
    public string CarOwner;
    public string PaintColor;
    public int MilesPerGallon = 30;

    public FordFiesta(string newOwner, string paintColor) {
        CarOwner = newOwner;
        PaintColor = paintColor;
    }

    public int CalculateFuelForTrip(int tripDistance) {
        return tripDistance / MilesPerGallon;
    }

    public void PrintCarDetails() {
        System.Console.WriteLine("--- Car Details ---");
        System.Console.WriteLine("Car Owner: {0}", CarOwner);
        System.Console.WriteLine("Car Color: {0}", PaintColor);
        System.Console.WriteLine("Gas Mileage: {0} mpg", MilesPerGallon);
    }
}
```

These two classes represent two kinds of car; the VolvoC30 class represents a Volvo C30 car, and the FordFiesta class represents a Ford Fiesta. We can do this for every car model we need for our project, or for every kind of object we need if our project doesn't involve cars. And we can use these objects just as we did when we had only one to work with:

```
using System;

class CarTest {

    static void Main(string[] args) {

        // create a VolvoC30 object
        VolvoC30 myVolvo = new VolvoC30("Adam Freeman", "Black");

        // create a FordFiesta object
        FordFiesta myFord = new FordFiesta("Joe Smith", "Green");
```

```
        // call the PrintCarDetails method on both car objects
        myVolvo.PrintCarDetails();
        myFord.PrintCarDetails();

        // wait for input before exiting
        Console.WriteLine("Press enter to finish");
        Console.ReadLine();
    }
}
```

In the Main method of the previous CarTest class, I create a VolvoC30 object and a FordFiesta object and call the PrintCarDetails method on each of them. The results of compiling and running this code are as follows:

```
--- Car Details ---
Car Owner: Adam Freeman
Car Color: Black
Gas Milage: 30 mpg
--- Car Details ---
Car Owner: Joe Smith
Car Color: Green
Gas Milage: 30 mpg
Press enter to finish
```

This approach is OK when there are two classes to work with, but we would hit one of two problems if we needed classes for 20, 50, or even 100 different models of car.

The first problem is the amount of time needed to make a change. Let's imagine that we needed to add a field to all the car classes to represent the maximum speed. We'd have to add this field and update the PrintCarDetails method (to print out the value of the field) in all 100 classes. It takes a long time to change 100 different classes, and it takes a lot longer to make those changes correctly.

The second problem is that we need to change any code that uses our classes. If we add a new car class or change an existing class, then any code that needs to create an object or work with an object from that class also needs to change.

Both of these problems are addressed through the three pillars of object-oriented programming: inheritance, encapsulation, and polymorphism. In fact, these three pillars do more than solve these problems, but since these are the problems that most programmers face most often, they will be the ones I focus on as we look at each of these pillars in turn.

Don't be put off by the grandiose titles given to each pillar. These concepts are central to C# programming, but they are reasonably straightforward once you have wrapped your head around them. The best thing to do as you read the following sections is to remain focused on *why* these features are useful. I have included lots of code samples and some (I hope helpful) diagrams to help put things in a practical context.

Understanding Inheritance

The first pillar is *specialization* or *inheritance*, which means that you can use an existing class to derive a new class and the new class can be more specialized than the existing class. To understand what this means and how it works, we need to introduce a new class, shown in Listing 6-14.

Listing 6-14. A Common Base Class

```
class Car {
    public string CarOwner;
    public string PaintColor;
    public int MilesPerGallon;

    public Car(string newOwner, string paintColor, int mpg) {
        CarOwner = newOwner;
        PaintColor = paintColor;
        MilesPerGallon = mpg;
    }

    public virtual int CalculateFuelForTrip(int tripDistance) {
        return tripDistance / MilesPerGallon;
    }

    public virtual void PrintCarDetails() {
        System.Console.WriteLine("--- Car Details ---");
        System.Console.WriteLine("Car Owner: {0}", CarOwner);
        System.Console.WriteLine("Car Color: {0}", PaintColor);
        System.Console.WriteLine("Gas Mileage: {0} mpg", MilesPerGallon);
    }
}
```

Listing 6-14 contains a Car class. In this class I have placed the fields and methods from the FordFiesta and VolvoC30 classes we used in the previous section. This class contains the features that are common to all cars: every single car of every single model made by every single manufacturer has an owner, a paint color, and a fuel economy (we'll ignore electric cars for these examples).

Now we can create a new class using the Car class in Listing 6-14. Here is a class that represents any car made by Volvo and that is called VolvoCar:

```
class VolvoCar : Car {
    public string VolvoSoundSystem;

    public VolvoCar(string owner, string paint, int mpg, string sound)
        : base(owner, paint, mpg) {

        // set the value of the VolvoSoundSystem
        VolvoSoundSystem = sound;
    }

    public override void PrintCarDetails() {
        base.PrintCarDetails();
        System.Console.WriteLine("VolvoSoundSystem: {0}", VolvoSoundSystem);
```

```
    }
}
```

The VolvoCar class is *derived* from the Car class; this is commonly described as the VolvoCar class being a *subclass* of the Car class. The Car class is the *base class* to VolvoCar; this is often described as Car being the *superclass* to VolvoCar. A base class is specified by appending a colon and the name of the base class after the name of the derived class, as illustrated by Figure 6-9.

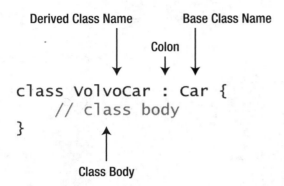

Figure 6-9. The anatomy of a class derivation

When you create a derived class, it inherits the features from the base class; this is often referred to as *inheritance*. Here is a demonstration:

```
VolvoCar myVolvo = new VolvoCar("Adam Freeman", "Black", 30, "High Performance");
int fuelRequired = myVolvo.CalculateFuelForTrip(1000);
Console.WriteLine("Fuel Required: {0} gallons", fuelRequired);
```

The key part of these statements is marked in bold. I created a VolvoCar object and then called the CalculateFuelForTrip method, even though this method is defined in the base class, Car.

■ **Note** In C# you can derive from only one base class; this is called *single inheritance*. C++-style support for multiple inheritance is not available.

In fact, even when you don't name a base class explicitly, C# still adds one. This is because all C# objects are derived, at least indirectly, from the System.Object type, which you can refer to using the object keyword. This means two things in terms of inheritance. The first is that this class definition:

```
class MyClass {
    // class body
}
```

is the same as this one:

```
class MyClass: object {
    // class body
}
```

The second thing is that all object features inherit from the System.Object class and any other base classes. When you derive a class, you create an additional specialization. The System.Object class is the ultimate base class; it has the features that are common to all C# objects. The Car class derives from System.Object, and it adds features that are special to cars. The VolvoCars class derives from the Car class and adds features that are special to cars made by Volvo. For these three classes, System.Object is the more general, and VolvoCars is the most specialized. As each class is derived, it becomes more specialized and inherits features from the base class, as illustrated by Figure 6-10.

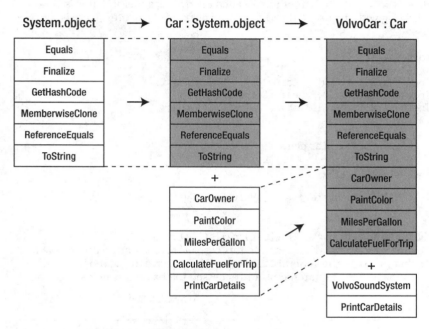

Figure 6-10. Inheritance through class derivation

The VolvoCar class is the most specialized, and it has inherited members from Car and System.Object. (The methods that are inherited from System.Object are explained later in this chapter and elsewhere in the book.)

As we continue to add classes to represent different cars, we can place new features where they most make sense. For example, the VolvoCar class contains a feature that is unique to Volvo cars—a field representing which fixed set of Volvo in-car entertainment options has been installed.

If I had added this feature to the Car class, any class derived from Car would inherit the VolvoSoundSystem field. We don't want to do that because this field has no relevance to cars made by, say, Ford. If I had added the VolvoSoundSystem to a class derived from VolvoCar, I would have to duplicate the field in every other class that derives from VolvoCar. When considering where to place a field, method, or other class member, try to find the sweet spot that doesn't add irrelevant features to classes and doesn't require duplication in peer-level classes.

Overriding Methods

The VolvoCar class has its own implementation of the PrintCarDetails method. The method of the same name in the base class (referred to as the *base method*) doesn't know how to take advantage of the specialized addition to the VolvoCar class; inheritance works in only one direction.

To solve this, VolvoCar provides its own implementation of this method that builds on the base method and adds extra information that is specific to Volvo. For this to work, the virtual keyword has to be applied as a modifier to the base method (indicating that derived classes are free to provide their own versions of the method) and the method in the derived class (known as the derived method) has to use the override keyword as a modifier to indicate that it is providing a specialized implementation of the base method.

Providing a more specialized version of a base method is called *overriding* a method; this is discussed further in Chapter 9, along with the use of the virtual and override keywords. Here is the base method from the Car class:

```
public virtual void PrintCarDetails() {
    System.Console.WriteLine("--- Car Details ---");
    System.Console.WriteLine("Car Owner: {0}", CarOwner);
    System.Console.WriteLine("Car Color: {0}", PaintColor);
    System.Console.WriteLine("Gas Mileage: {0} mpg", MilesPerGallon);
}
```

Here is the derived method from the VolvoCar class:

```
public override void PrintCarDetails() {
    base.PrintCarDetails();
    System.Console.WriteLine("VolvoSoundSystem: {0}", VolvoSoundSystem);
}
```

You can see that the derived method calls base.PrintCarDetails(). This calls the base method. Derived classes can access the members of their base class. In this case, it means that we don't have to duplicate the code statements that print out the general Car details. I didn't have to use the base implementation; I could have duplicated those statements and accessed the base class fields from the derived class.

■ **Tip** Base classes don't have to grant derived classes access to every member. See Chapters 7 and 9 for details of access modifiers, and see this chapter and Chapter 9 for details of the sealed keyword.

The following statements create a VolvoCar object and call the PrintCarDetails method:

```
VolvoCar myVolvo = new VolvoCar("Adam Freeman", "Black", 30, "High Performance");
myVolvo.PrintCarDetails();
```

The output from these methods is as follows:

```
--- Car Details ---
Car Owner: Adam Freeman
Car Color: Black
Gas Mileage: 30 mpg
VolvoSoundSystem: High Performance
Press enter to finish
```

You can see that we have the output from the base method and the output from the derived method. With just a few lines of code, we have been able to create a derived class that adds features that are specialized to a specific subclass of objects and that inherits the characteristics and features of the base class.

Inheriting Derivations

When you override a method, any further derived classes inherit the overridden method. Listing 6-15 adds three new classes to our set: VolvoC30, FordCar, and FordFiesta.

Listing 6-15. Additional Derived Classes

```
class FordCar : Car {
    public string FordWheelsOption;

    public FordCar(string owner, string paint, int mpg, string wheels)
        : base(owner, paint, mpg) {

        // set the value for the wheels
        FordWheelsOption = wheels;
    }
}

class VolvoC30 : VolvoCar {

    public VolvoC30(string owner, string paint, int mpg, string sound)
        : base(owner, paint, mpg, sound) {

    }
}

class FordFiesta : FordCar {

    public FordFiesta(string owner, string paint, int mpg, string wheels)
        : base(owner, paint, mpg, wheels) {

    }
}
```

157

The FordCar class is derived from the Car class, the VolvoC30 class is derived from VolvoCar, and the FordFiesta class is derived from FordCar. Neither the VolvoC30 nor the FordFiesta class adds new features. The relationship between our classes is shown in Figure 6-11.

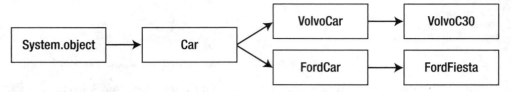

Figure 6-11. *The derivations for the car-related classes*

The VolvoCar overrode the PrintCarDetails method from the Car class, and it is this version of the method that is inherited by the VolvoC30 class. The FordCar class didn't override this method, so the FordFiesta class inherits the original version from the Car class. The following statements create objects from the VolvoC30 and FordFiesta classes and call the PrintCarDetails methods on each of them:

```
VolvoC30 myC30 = new VolvoC30("Adam Freeman", "Black", 30, "High Performance");
myC30.PrintCarDetails();
FordFiesta myFiesta = new FordFiesta("Joe Smith", "Yellow", 35, "18 inch sports");
myFiesta.PrintCarDetails();
```

The output from these statements is as follows:

```
--- Car Details ---
Car Owner: Adam Freeman
Car Color: Black
Gas Mileage: 30 mpg
VolvoSoundSystem: High Performance
--- Car Details ---
Car Owner: Joe Smith
Car Color: Yellow
Gas Mileage: 35 mpg
Press enter to finish
```

The output from the VolvoC30 class includes the additional feature that was introduced to the VolvoCar class. The output from the FordFiesta class doesn't include the additional feature that was added to the FordCar class. From this output, we can see that objects inherit overridden versions of methods from their base classes.

The value of this comes when we make changes. We have to define a method implementation in only a single place for it to be inherited, and so we have to make changes in only a single place as well. Rather than having to update the implementation of a method in 100 related classes, we can just modify the base class, and the change will be automatically inherited by any class that is derived from the modified base class.

Understanding Encapsulation

The second pillar of object-oriented programming we will look at is *encapsulation*. The idea behind encapsulation is that the interface of a class is separated from its implementation. Listing 6-16 contains two classes that provide a simple demonstration of encapsulation.

Listing 6-16. A Demonstration of Encapsulation

```
using System;

class Car {
    public string CarOwner;
    public string PaintColor;
    public int MilesPerGallon;

    public Car(string newOwner, string paintColor, int mpg) {
        CarOwner = newOwner;
        PaintColor = paintColor;
        MilesPerGallon = mpg;
    }

    public int CalculateFuelForTrip(int tripDistance) {
        return tripDistance / MilesPerGallon;
    }
}

class EncapsulationTest {

    static void Main(string[] args) {

        // create a new instance of Car
        Car myCar = new Car("Adam Freeman", "Black", 30);

        // invoke the CalculateFuelForTrip method
        int fuelRequired = myCar.CalculateFuelForTrip(1000);

        // print out the result
        Console.WriteLine("Fuel required: {0} gallons", fuelRequired);

        // wait for input before exiting
        Console.WriteLine("Press enter to finish");
        Console.ReadLine();
    }
}
```

The first class in the listing is a simplified version of the Car class we used earlier in the chapter. The Car class contains a method called CalculateFuelForTrip. A class that provides a method for other classes to use is called a *server*. The Car class is a server for the CalculateFuelForTrip method.

The second class, called EncapulationTest, creates a Car object and calls the CalculateFuelForTrip method. When a class uses a method in another class, it is called a *client* of the method. The EncapsulationTest class is a client of the CalculateFuelForTrip method in the Car class.

Encapsulation means that I can change the implementation of a method in the server without affecting the client, as long as I don't change the definition of the method. The `CalculateFuelForTrip` takes an `int` parameter and returns an `int` result. This, plus the method name, is like a contract to the client; it says, if you give me the number of miles that you want to travel as an `int`, I'll give you back the amount of fuel you'll need.

The client isn't entitled to know how a method in a server class will perform an action or calculation—only that it will. I can change the implementation of the `CalculateFuelForTrip` method in the `Car` class, and as long as I don't change the name, the parameter, or the result, the `EncapsulationTest` class won't have to be modified or even recompiled. This is especially important when you share your classes with others as precompiled assemblies.

■ **Note** Interfaces in the sense of encapsulation is slightly different from the C# language feature also called *interfaces*. See Chapter 12 for details of the language feature.

If you do change the name, the parameters, or the result of a method (or make any alteration that affects a member that other classes access), then you have broken the encapsulation contract with your clients. The client classes will have to be modified and/or recompiled to take account of the changes you have made. Sometimes, you will have no choice but to make breaking changes, but you should do everything you can to avoid this.

Understanding Polymorphism

There are two parts to polymorphism, the third pillar of object orientation. We have already touched on the first part, which is that classes can override methods in the base class and provide their own implementations.

The second part is that objects created from a derived class can be treated as objects of the base class. This is a powerful feature because it allows us to add new classes that increase specialization but that can still be used by code that was written before the new classes were created. Listing 6-17 contains two classes that set the stage for a demonstration of polymorphism.

Listing 6-17. Classes to Demonstrate Polymorphism

```
using System;

class Car {
    public string CarOwner;
    public string PaintColor;
    public int MilesPerGallon;

    public Car(string newOwner, string paintColor, int mpg) {
        CarOwner = newOwner;
        PaintColor = paintColor;
        MilesPerGallon = mpg;
    }
```

```
        public int CalculateFuelForTrip(int tripDistance) {
            return tripDistance / MilesPerGallon;
        }
}

class TripPrinter {

    public void PrintTripDetails(Car myCar) {
        int[] distances = { 50, 100, 250, 500 };

        Console.WriteLine("--- Trip details ---");
        foreach (int dist in distances) {

            Console.WriteLine("{0} miles requires: {1} gallons",
                dist,
                myCar.CalculateFuelForTrip(dist));
        }
    }
}
```

The Car class is a simplified version of the class we used previously in the chapter. The TripPrinter class contains a single method called PrintTripDetails, which takes a Car object as a parameter and calls the CalculateFuelForTrip method to determine how much fuel is required for trips of different lengths. (This method uses an array, which is explained in Chapter 13, and a foreach loop, explained in Chapter 4.)

The important point to note here is that the TripPrinter class has been written to work with Car objects and specifically calls a method defined in the Car class. The following statements demonstrate these two classes being used together:

```
using System;

class PolymorphismTest {

    static void Main(string[] args) {

        // create an instance of Car
        Car myCar = new Car("Adam Freeman", "Black", 30);

        // call the TripPrinter.PrintTripDetails method
        TripPrinter printer = new TripPrinter();
        printer.PrintTripDetails(myCar);

        // wait for input before exiting
        Console.WriteLine("Press enter to finish");
        Console.ReadLine();
    }
}
```

This class creates an instance of Car and uses it to call the PrintTripDetails method on a TripPrinter object. The results of compiling and running this code are as follows:

```
--- Trip details ---
50 miles requires: 1 gallons
100 miles requires: 3 gallons
250 miles requires: 8 gallons
500 miles requires: 16 gallons
Press enter to finish
```

Now let's derive a new class from Car. Here it is:

```
class VolvoCar : Car {
    public string VolvoSoundSystem;

    public VolvoCar(string owner, string paint, int mpg, string sound)
        : base(owner, paint, mpg) {

        // set the value of the VolvoSoundSystem
        VolvoSoundSystem = sound;
    }
}
```

The derived class is called VolvoCar, and it adds a Volvo-specific field. Polymorphism means that because the VolvoCar class is derived from the Car class, we can use VolvoCar objects where Car objects are expected, as demonstrated by these statements:

```
class PolymorphismTest {

    static void Main(string[] args) {

        // create an instance of VolvoCar
        VolvoCar myVolvo = new VolvoCar("Adam Freeman", "Black", 30, "High Performance");

        // call the TripPrinter.PrintTripDetails method
        TripPrinter printer = new TripPrinter();
        printer.PrintTripDetails(myVolvo);

        // wait for input before exiting
        Console.WriteLine("Press enter to finish");
        Console.ReadLine();
    }
}
```

These statements create a VolvoCar object and assign it to a local variable called myVolvo. This variable is then used as a parameter to call the PrintTripDetails method in a TripPrinter object. The PrintTripDetails method expects a Car object as a parameter, but I am able to use the VolvoCar object, and I am able to do this without making any changes to the TripPrinter class.

We can go a step further and assign a derived object to a local variable that has been typed for a base class, like this:

```
Car myCar = new VolvoCar("Adam Freeman", "Black", 30, "High Performance");
```

In this statement, I assign create a VolvoCar object and assign it to a Car variable. Treating a derived object as though it were an instance of a base object is called *upcasting*, and it means that we can add classes to our program, and objects created from these classes can still be handled using their base types.

When you *upcast* an object, you lose access to any specializations that have been introduced over the base class. In the case of the previous code statement, I can use the object assigned to the myCar variable as a Car, but not VolvoCar. I cannot access the additional field that VolvoCar introduces, and this makes sense; otherwise, you'd end up with some Car instances that had special features that other instances didn't.

If a derived class has overridden a method from the base class using the override keyword, it is the derived implementation that is used when the method is called, as demonstrated by Listing 6-18.

Listing 6-18. Polymorphism and Derived Method Implementations

```
using System;

class Car {
    public string CarOwner;
    public string PaintColor;
    public int MilesPerGallon;

    public Car(string newOwner, string paintColor, int mpg) {
        CarOwner = newOwner;
        PaintColor = paintColor;
        MilesPerGallon = mpg;
    }

    public virtual int CalculateFuelForTrip(int tripDistance) {
        return tripDistance / MilesPerGallon;
    }
}

class VolvoCar : Car {
    public string VolvoSoundSystem;

    public VolvoCar(string owner, string paint, int mpg, string sound)
        : base(owner, paint, mpg) {

        // set the value of the VolvoSoundSystem
        VolvoSoundSystem = sound;
    }

    public override int CalculateFuelForTrip(int tripDistance) {
        System.Console.WriteLine("Derived Method Called");
        return base.CalculateFuelForTrip(tripDistance);
    }
}

class Listing_18 {

    static void Main(string[] args) {
```

```
        // create a new instance fof VolvoCar and upcast it to Car
        Car myCar = new VolvoCar("Adam Freeman", "Black", 30, "Premium");

        // call the CalculateFuelForTrip method and print out the result
        int result = myCar.CalculateFuelForTrip(1000);
        Console.WriteLine("Result: {0} gallons", result);

        // wait for input before exiting
        Console.WriteLine("Press enter to finish");
        Console.ReadLine();
    }
}
```

In this example, the derived class, VolvoCar, has overridden the CalculateFuelForTrip method defined in the base class, Car. The derived version of the method prints out a message to the console and then calls the base implementation to calculate the result.

The Main method of the Listing_17 class creates an instance of VolvoCar and upcasts it by assigning it to a Car variable. The CalculateFuelForTrip method is called, and the result from the method is printed out. Here are the results of compiling and running Listing 6-18:

```
Derived Method Called
Result: 33 gallons
Press enter to finish
```

The results show the behavior I described. When you upcast an object, the overridden implementations of methods are used, but you are no longer able to access any members that are not defined in the type you have upcast to.

■ **Note** Derived classes can hide a base member rather than override it. When this happens, the derived implementation is used when the object is referred to by its declared type, and the base implementation is referenced when the object is upcast. In effect, the behavior you get from your object can be made to vary if it is upcast. You can see examples of hiding a method in Chapter 9, hiding a field in Chapter 7, and hiding a property in Chapter 8.

You can upcast to any of the base types of an object, not just the immediate base type. The demonstration of this is simple. Remember that all classes are derived from System.Object. We can upcast any C# object to this type. Listing 6-19 contains a simple demonstration using the Car and VolvoCar classes from the previous example.

Listing 6-19. Casting to Any Base Type

```
class Listing_19 {

    static void Main(string[] args) {

        // create an instance of VolvoCar
        VolvoCar myVolvo = new VolvoCar("Adam Freeman", "Black", 30, "Premium");

        // upcast from VolvoCar to Car
        Car myCar = myVolvo;

        // upcast from Car to object
        object myObject = myCar;

        // wait for input before exiting
        Console.WriteLine("Press enter to finish");
        Console.ReadLine();
    }
}
```

In this example, I created a VolvoCar object and upcast it to Car and then upcast again to System.Object (for which C# allows you to use the object keyword). Although I upcast from VolvoCar to object in steps in the example, you can directly upcast to any base class of an object, like this:

```
object myObject = new VolvoCar("Adam Freeman", "Black", 30, "Premium");
```

Casting Objects and Type Checking

Casting is the process of converting an object of one type into another. We saw examples of this when we looked at upcasting in the section on polymorphism. We say that an object of one type is cast to another type, for example, that a VolvoCar object was cast to Car. In this section, we'll look at the different C# features that support casting and those that can help ensure that casting doesn't cause problems in your program.

■ **Note** The examples in the following sections are focused on reference objects, but you can also cast between value types; see Chapter 5 for examples of casting and converting between numeric types.

Implicit vs. Explicit Casting

There are two kinds of casting available in C#: *implicit* and *explicit* casting. We have already seen examples of implicit casting when we were upcasting in the section covering polymorphism. Implicit casting, also known as *coercion*, is performed automatically by the compiler when it is safe to do so. Listing 6-20 contains two examples.

Listing 6-20. Implicit Casting

```
using System;

class Car {
    public string CarOwner;
    public string PaintColor;
    public int MilesPerGallon;

    public Car(string newOwner, string paintColor, int mpg) {
        CarOwner = newOwner;
        PaintColor = paintColor;
        MilesPerGallon = mpg;
    }
}

class VolvoCar : Car {
    public string VolvoSoundSystem;

    public VolvoCar(string owner, string paint, int mpg, string sound)
        : base(owner, paint, mpg) {

        // set the value of the VolvoSoundSystem
        VolvoSoundSystem = sound;
    }
}

class Listing_20 {

    static void Main(string[] args) {

        // create a VolvoCar object
        VolvoCar myVolvo = new VolvoCar("Adam Freeman", "Black", 30, "Premium");

        // perform an implicit cast by upcasting
        Car myCar = myVolvo;

        // perform an implicit cast by calling a method
        // that takes a base type as a parameter
        PrintCarDetails(myVolvo);

        // wait for input before exiting
        Console.WriteLine("Press enter to finish");
        Console.ReadLine();
    }

    static void PrintCarDetails(Car car) {
        Console.WriteLine("--- Car Details ---");
        Console.WriteLine("Owner: {0}", car.CarOwner);
        Console.WriteLine("Color: {0}", car.PaintColor);
        Console.WriteLine("Mileage: {0}", car.MilesPerGallon);
```

```
    }
}
```

The first example is a simple upcast from VolvoCar to Car, much as we saw in the previous section of this chapter. The second example occurs when the VolvoCar object is passed to the PrintCarDetails method of the Listing_20 class; this method expects a Car object and calls the members defined in the Car class. Compiling and running the code in Listing 6-20 produces the following results:

```
--- Car Details ---
Owner: Adam Freeman
Color: Black
Mileage: 30
Press enter to finish
```

The casts can be performed automatically because a derived class can always be treated as an instance of one of its base classes. These are examples of implicit casts, so-called because we didn't have to instruct the compiler to perform the conversion.

Explicit casts are so-named because we have to make an explicit instruction to the compiler to perform the conversion. Listing 6-21 contains an example.

Listing 6-21. Performing an Explicit Cast

```
class Listing_21 {

    static void Main(string[] args) {

        // create a VolvoCar object and upcast it to object
        object myObject = new VolvoCar("Adam Freeman", "Black", 30, "Premium");

        // perform an explicit cast of myObject to Car
        Car myCar = (Car)myObject;

        // read a field from the Car object
        Console.WriteLine("Owner: {0}", myCar.CarOwner);

        // wait for input before exiting
        Console.WriteLine("Press enter to finish");
        Console.ReadLine();
    }
}
```

The explicit cast instruction, shown in bold in Listing 6-21, is to convert an instance of object into an instance of Car. The .NET runtime doesn't keep track of previous conversions, so it doesn't know that the reference myObject is pointing to a VolvoCar, which can be safely cast to its base class, Car. If I compile and run the code in Listing 6-21, I get the following results:

```
Owner: Adam Freeman
Press enter to finish
```

The cast operation in Listing 6-21 is an example of *downcasting*, meaning that an object is converted to a more derived type. For this to work, the type that I am converting to has to be the type of the object or one of its base types. There are three parts to an explicit cast, and they are illustrated in Figure 6-12.

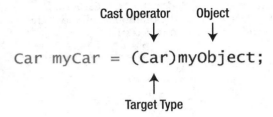

Figure 6-12. The anatomy of an explicit cast

The explicit cast operator consists of the type you want to convert the object to, surrounded by parentheses. The cast operation in Figure 6-12 is converting the object referred to by the variable myObject to the Car type.

I have shown the left side of the statement in Figure 6-12 grayed out because assigning the result of a cast operation to a variable is optional. The result of a cast operation is an object of the target type, but you can pass this directly as a parameter to a method call, as shown in Listing 6-22.

Listing 6-22. Performing an Explicit Cast on a Method Parameter

```
class Listing_22 {

    static void Main(string[] args) {

        // create a VolvoCar object and upcast it to object
        object myObject = new VolvoCar("Adam Freeman", "Black", 30, "Premium");

        // call the PrintCarDetails method and explicitly cast the
        // object in a single statement
        PrintCarDetails((Car)myObject);

        // wait for input before exiting
        Console.WriteLine("Press enter to finish");
        Console.ReadLine();
    }

    static void PrintCarDetails(Car car) {
        Console.WriteLine("--- Car Details ---");
        Console.WriteLine("Owner: {0}", car.CarOwner);
        Console.WriteLine("Color: {0}", car.PaintColor);
        Console.WriteLine("Mileage: {0}", car.MilesPerGallon);
    }
}
```

In this example, the cast to the Car type is performed within the call to the PrintCarDetails method. You can even mix implicit and explicit casting in a single statement, like this:

```
object myObject = new VolvoCar("Adam Freeman", "Black", 30, "Premium");
Car myCar = (VolvoCar)myObject;
```

In the second of these statements, an instance of System.Object is explicitly cast to the VolvoCar type and then assigned to a local variable of the Car type, which causes an implicit upcasting to be performed.

Type Conversion Exceptions

The reason that C# requires explicit instruction for downcasting is that the operation may not work. As I mentioned, the runtime doesn't keep track of the original type of a reference type, so it is possible that the target type you are casting to isn't one that the object can perform. Listing 6-23 provides a demonstration.

Listing 6-23. Performing an Illegal Explicit Cast

```
using System;

class Car {
    public string CarOwner;
    public string PaintColor;
    public int MilesPerGallon;

    public Car(string newOwner, string paintColor, int mpg) {
        CarOwner = newOwner;
        PaintColor = paintColor;
        MilesPerGallon = mpg;
    }
}

class Bicycle {
    public string BikeOwner;
    public int NumberOfGears;
    public string SaddleType;

    public Bicycle(string owner, int gears, string saddle) {
        BikeOwner = owner;
        NumberOfGears = gears;
        SaddleType = saddle;
    }
}

class Listing_23 {

    static void Main(string[] args) {

        // create an instance of Bicycle and upcast it to object
        object myObject = new Bicycle("Adam Freeman", 24, "Comfort");

        // perform an explicit cast to Car
```

```
        Car myCar = (Car)myObject;

        // wait for input before exiting
        Console.WriteLine("Press enter to finish");
        Console.ReadLine();
    }
}
```

The code in Listing 6-23 creates a Bicycle object and implicitly upcasts it to System.Object. The result of the implicit cast is then used in an explicit cast to the Car type. Car is not the declared type or one of the base types of the object, so the runtime doesn't know how to perform the cast operation. If we compile and run the code in Listing 6-23, we get the following results:

```
Unhandled Exception: System.InvalidCastException: Unable to cast object of type 'Bicycle' to
type 'Car'.
    at Listing_23.Main(String[] args) in C:\ Listing_22\Listing_22.cs:line 35
```

This is an exception telling us that you can't cast from Bicycle to Car. Exceptions are the C# mechanism for creating and handling errors and are covered in Chapter 14. The C# compiler tries to minimize problems with explicit casting by refusing to compile statements between types that are not related. In Listing 6-23, we were trying to downcast from object to Car. This might of worked because Car is derived from object. If you were to try to cast from and to types that the compiler can tell are unrelated, then you'll get an error when you try to compile your code. Here's an example:

```
// create an instance of Bicycle
Bicycle myBike = new Bicycle("Adam Freeman", 24, "Comfort");

// perform an explicit cast to Car
Car myCar = (Car)myBike;
```

The cast in this statement will never work, and the compiler can tell because the type of the object and the target type in the cast operation are unrelated.

■ **Tip** We could provide C# with the ability to convert between the Bicycle and Car types by implementing a *custom conversion operator*. You can learn more about this feature and see some examples in Chapter 8.

Avoiding Explicit Cast Exceptions

Explicit casting must be used with care because of the risk of encountering problems. C# provides some features that can help you reduce the likelihood of problems when performing explicit casts.

Testing an Object's Type

You can check the type of an object by using the is operator. Listing 6-24 provides an example.

Listing 6-24. Using the **is** *Operator to Test an Object's Type*

```
using System;

class Car {
    public string CarOwner;
    public string PaintColor;
    public int MilesPerGallon;

    public Car(string newOwner, string paintColor, int mpg) {
        CarOwner = newOwner;
        PaintColor = paintColor;
        MilesPerGallon = mpg;
    }
}

class Bicycle {
    public string BikeOwner;
    public int NumberOfGears;
    public string SaddleType;

    public Bicycle(string owner, int gears, string saddle) {
        BikeOwner = owner;
        NumberOfGears = gears;
        SaddleType = saddle;
    }
}

class Listing_24 {

    static void Main(string[] args) {

        // create an instance of Bicycle and upcast it to object
        object myObject = new Bicycle("Adam Freeman", 24, "Comfort");

        // use the is keyword to check the type
        bool isCar = myObject is Car;
        bool isBike = myObject is Bicycle;
        bool isObject = myObject is object;

        Console.WriteLine("Is Car? {0}", isCar);
        Console.WriteLine("Is Bike? {0}", isBike);
        Console.WriteLine("Is Object? {0}", isObject);

        // wait for input before exiting
        Console.WriteLine("Press enter to finish");
        Console.ReadLine();
    }
}
```

In this example, an instance of Bicycle is upcast to the object and then tested using the is operator. The results of the tests are written to the console. The is operator is used following an object reference and is itself followed by the type you want to test for. If the object is of the specified type or the specified type is a base class for the object, the is operator returns true; otherwise, it returns false. Compiling and running the code in Listing 6-24 produces the following results:

```
Is Car? False
Is Bike? True
Is Object? True
Press enter to finish
```

You can use the is operator to check an object's type before performing an explicit cast, like this:

```
if (myObject is Bicycle) {
    Bicycle myBike = (Bicycle) myObject;
} else if (myObject is Car) {
    Car myCar = (Car) myObject;
}
```

Casting Without Exceptions

You can perform a cast without causing an exception by using the as operator. Listing 6-25 provides a demonstration.

*Listing 6-25. Using the **as** Operator*

```
class Listing_25 {

    static void Main(string[] args) {

        // create an instance of Bicycle and upcast it to object
        object myObject = new Bicycle("Adam Freeman", 24, "Comfort");

        // use the as operator to convert the type
        Bicycle myBike = myObject as Bicycle;

        // try to convert the object to a Car
        Car myCar = myObject as Car;

        // print out the result of the as operations
        Console.WriteLine("myBike is null? {0}", myBike == null);
        Console.WriteLine("myCar is null? {0}", myCar == null);

        // wait for input before exiting
        Console.WriteLine("Press enter to finish");
        Console.ReadLine();
    }
}
```

The as operator returns the object cast to the target type if the conversion can be performed. No exception is thrown if the conversion cannot be performed. Instead, the as operator will return null. In Listing 6-25, a Bicycle object is upcast to object, and the as operator is applied to try to convert the object to an instance of Bicycle and Car. The result of compiling and running the code in Listing 6-25 is as follows:

```
myBike is null? False
myCar is null? True
Press enter to finish
```

You can see from these results that the as operator was able to cast the object to an instance of Bicycle but returned null when asked to convert the object to be an instance of Car.

Boxing and Unboxing

When you upcast a reference type, the object remains unaffected; only the reference to it changes. When you upcast a value type, the value is copied and contained within an object, which is known as *boxing*.

When the value type is unpacked from the object, known as *unboxing*, the value is copied once again. This can cause confusion if you are expecting changes to the value type to be reflecting in the boxed value. Listing 6-26 contains a demonstration.

Listing 6-26. Boxing and Unboxing a Value Type

```csharp
using System;

class Listing_26 {

    static void Main(string[] args) {

        // create a value-type
        int x = 100;

        // box the int as an object
        object myObject = x;

        // update the original value type
        x = 200;

        // unbox the int
        int unboxed = (int)myObject;

        // print out the values
        Console.WriteLine("Variable value: {0}", x);
        Console.WriteLine("Unboxed value: {0}", unboxed);

        // wait for input before exiting
        Console.WriteLine("Press enter to finish");
        Console.ReadLine();
```

```
        }
}
```

You can see from Listing 6-26 that boxing can be done implicitly but that unboxing requires an explicit cast. This is consistent with upcasting and downcasting reference types. Compiling and running the code in Listing 6-26 produces the following results:

```
Variable value: 200
Unboxed value: 100
Press enter to finish
```

The change that I made to the int variable didn't affect the boxed value. This is different behavior than what you will see when working with reference types. Listing 6-27 contains an example of performing the same sequence of steps on a reference type.

Listing 6-27. Making a Change to a Reference Type That Has Been Upcast

```
using System;

class Car {
    public string CarOwner;
    public string PaintColor;
    public int MilesPerGallon;

    public Car(string newOwner, string paintColor, int mpg) {
        CarOwner = newOwner;
        PaintColor = paintColor;
        MilesPerGallon = mpg;
    }
}

class Listing_27 {

    static void Main(string[] args) {

        // create a Car object
        Car myCar = new Car("Adam Freeman", "Black", 30);

        // upcast the Car to an object
        object myObject = myCar;

        // make a change to the Car via the original reference
        myCar.MilesPerGallon = 40;

        // downcast the object back to a Car
        Car downcast = (Car)myObject;

        // print out the values of the fields
        Console.WriteLine("Mileage: {0}", downcast.MilesPerGallon);
```

```
        // wait for input before exiting
        Console.WriteLine("Press enter to finish");
        Console.ReadLine();
    }
}
```

In this case, the changes I make to the myCar object affect the upcast reference as well. This is because the two references point to the same object; only the types of the references are different. Compiling and running the code in Listing 6-27 produces the following results:

```
Mileage: 40
Press enter to finish
```

Using Nested Classes

Class can contain different kinds of members. You have seen some of the most commonly used in this chapter and other kinds are described other chapters in this section of the book. One kind of member whose description belongs in this chapter is a nested class. That is to say, classes can contain other classes. Nested classes are also referred to as *inner classes*. Listing 6-28 contains an example.

Listing 6-28. Defining an Nested Class

```
using System;

class Car {
    public string CarOwner;
    public string PaintColor;
    public int MilesPerGallon;
    public Engine EngineSpec;

    public Car(string newOwner, string paintColor, int mpg, Engine enginespec) {
        CarOwner = newOwner;
        PaintColor = paintColor;
        MilesPerGallon = mpg;
        EngineSpec = enginespec;
    }

    public class Engine {
        public int Capacity;
        public string FuelType;
        public string Transmission;

        public Engine(int capacity, string type, string transmission) {
            Capacity = capacity;
            FuelType = type;
            Transmission = transmission;
        }
    }
}
```

}

In Listing 6-28, the Engine class is nested within the Car class. By default, nested classes are inaccessible to other classes, but I have used the public keyword to make Engine accessible outside of the Car class. See the "Using Class Modifiers" section for details of the public keyword.

Nested classes are referred to by using the dot operator (.) to combine the name of the enclosing class and the nested class name. In the case of Listing 6-28, the nested class is called Car.Engine. The following statements demonstrate creating and using the nested class:

```
class NestedClass_Test {

    static void Main(string[] args) {

        // create a Car.Engine object
        Car.Engine engine = new Car.Engine(2000, "Diesel", "6-speed Automatic");

        // create a new instance of Car, including a new
        // instance of the nested class
        Car myCar = new Car("Adam Freeman", "Black", 30, engine);

        // wait for input before exiting
        Console.WriteLine("Press enter to finish");
        Console.ReadLine();
    }
}
```

Nested classes can access private members defined by the containing type, often referred to as the *outer class*. The private keyword is described in the "Using Class Modifiers" section of this chapter.

There is no strong convention on using nested classes in C#, but I tend to use them when I need to define a class that is used solely by the outer class or to provide implementations of interfaces. Interfaces are described in Chapter 12.

Using Class Modifiers

C# supports several keywords that can be used to modify the behavior of a class. These keywords are explained and demonstrated in the following sections. Many of these modifiers work in conjunction with modifiers applied to class members to change the overall behavior of a class.

Creating Static Classes

A static class cannot be instantiated. In other words, the new keyword cannot be used to create objects from a static class. All of the members in a static class must also be static. For more details of static methods, see Chapter 9, and for static fields, see Chapter 7. Static classes are usually used to contain a set of related utility methods. Listing 6-29 contains an example of a static class.

Listing 6-29. A Static Class

```csharp
public static class Calculator {

    public static int CalculateSum(int x, int y) {
        return x + y;
    }

    public static int CalculateProduct(int x, int y) {
        return x * y;
    }
}
```

Static members are accessed by using the dot operator (.) to combine the name of the class and the name of the member. The following statements demonstrate the use of the methods defined in Listing 6-29:

```csharp
using System;

class Listing_29 {

    static void Main(string[] args) {

        // call the methods of the static class
        int result1 = Calculator.CalculateSum(10, 120);
        int result2 = Calculator.CalculateProduct(10, 120);

        // print out the results
        Console.WriteLine("Sum Result: {0}", result1);
        Console.WriteLine("Product Result: {0}", result2);

        // wait for input before exiting
        Console.WriteLine("Press enter to finish");
        Console.ReadLine();
    }
}
```

The calls to the static methods are shown in bold. Compiling and running this code produces the following results:

```
Sum Result: 130
Product Result: 1200
Press enter to finish
```

Creating Abstract Classes

Abstract classes cannot be instantiated directly. Instead, they force a derived class to provide an implementation for any methods or properties that are modified with the abstract keyword. Listing 6-30 contains an example of an abstract class.

Listing 6-30. An Abstract Class

```
abstract class AbstractCalculator {

    public abstract int CalculateSum(int x, int y);

    public abstract int CalculateProduct(int x, int y);
}
```

The class in Listing 6-30 defines two methods but doesn't provide method bodies for them. A derived class must override these methods and implement them before it can be instantiated, as demonstrated by Listing 6-31.

Listing 6-31. Deriving from an Abstract Class

```
class CalculatorImplementation : AbstractCalculator {

    public override int CalculateSum(int x, int y) {
        return x + y;
    }

    public override int CalculateProduct(int x, int y) {
        return x * y;
    }
}
```

Derived classes that implement all the abstract members in the base class can be instantiated and used as regular classes, but usually objects are created and then upcast to the abstract class type, as follows:

```
using System;

class Listing_31 {

        static void Main(string[] args) {

                // create an instance of the derived class
                // and upcast it to the abstract type
                AbstractCalculator calc = new CalculatorImplementation();

                // call the methods defined in the abstract class
                int result1 = calc.CalculateSum(100, 120);
                int result2 = calc.CalculateProduct(100, 120);

                // print out the results
```

```
            Console.WriteLine("Sum Result: {0}", result1);
            Console.WriteLine("Product Result: {0}", result2);

            // wait for input before exiting
            Console.WriteLine("Press enter to finish");
            Console.ReadLine();
        }
    }
}
```

The statement that creates the derived object is shown in bold. Chapter 9 contains more detail about abstract methods, and Chapter 8 does the same for abstract properties.

Creating Sealed Classes

You can prevent a class being used as a base class by using the sealed modifier. Listing 6-32 provides a demonstration.

Listing 6-32. Sealing a Class

```
public sealed class Calculator {

    public int CalculateSum(int x, int y) {
        return x + y;
    }

    public int CalculateProduct(int x, int y) {
        return x * y;
    }
}
```

This class can be instantiated and used as normal, but it cannot be derived from, and its members cannot be overridden. Extension methods can be used on sealed classes. See Chapter 9 for details of extension methods.

Creating Partial Classes

Partial classes are comprised of more than one class definition. The compiler combines all the partial definitions to create a regular class. The definitions are usually split across multiple code files, although this is not a requirement. Listing 6-33 demonstrates a partial class. Related to partial classes are *partial methods*, which are described in Chapter 9.

Listing 6-33. A Partial Class

```
public partial class Calculator {

    public int CalculateProduct(int x, int y) {
        return x * y;
    }
```

```
}

public partial class Calculator {

    public int CalculateSum(int x, int y) {
        return x + y;
    }
}
```

In this example, there are two partial definitions of the Calculator class. (These would usually be in two different code files, but it is hard to show this in a book.) Each class definition describes part of the class, and they are combined by the compiler. The following statements demonstrate the use of the partial class:

```
class Listing_33_Test {

    static void Main(string[] args) {

        // create an instance of the sealed class
        Calculator calc = new Calculator();

        // call the methods of the partial class
        int result1 = calc.CalculateSum(10, 120);
        int result2 = calc.CalculateProduct(10, 120);

        // print out the results
        Console.WriteLine("Sum Result: {0}", result1);
        Console.WriteLine("Product Result: {0}", result2);

        // wait for input before exiting
        Console.WriteLine("Press enter to finish");
        Console.ReadLine();
    }
}
```

As you can see, using a partial class is no different from using a regular class. Partial classes allow you to define a method in one part and implement it in another; see Chapter 9 for details and examples.

Using Access Modifiers

You can restrict the use of a class by applying an access modifier to the class definition. The access modifiers are described in Table 6-2. You can apply these same modifiers to members within your class; see Chapter 9 for details of restricting access to methods, Chapter 8 for properties, and Chapter 7 for fields.

Table 6-2. *Access Modifiers for Classes*

Access Modifier	Description
public	The class can be accessed anywhere.
protected	The class can be accessed only by the containing class (for nested classes) or derived classes.
internal	The class can accessed by any class in the same assembly, but not other assemblies.
protected internal	The class can be accessed by any class in the same assembly or any class in any assembly that derives from the containing class.
private	The class can be accessed only by the containing class (for nested classes).

Summary

In this chapter, we have examined two of the fundamental building blocks of C# programming: classes and objects. We have seen how classes act as blueprints for the creation of objects and how those objects can be modified to reflect changes in state and used to perform actions and calculations.

We also covered the three pillars of object orientation as they apply to classes and objects and learned how inheritance, encapsulation, and polymorphism can be used to create classes with less code that are easy to modify, extend, and maintain.

We saw how object reference can be converted from one type to another using implicit and explicit casting and how this differs from the boxing and unboxing approach used for value types. In looking at how C# supports casting, we saw how the is and as operators can be used to avoid problems when downcasting to a more specialized type.

Finally, we looked at the modifiers you can apply to classes to change their behavior, ranging from classes that cannot be derived to those that force derived classes to provide implementations of methods and other members before they can be used to instantiate objects. In the coming chapters, we'll look at the different types of members that a class (and therefore an object) can contain.

CHAPTER 7

■ ■ ■

Fields

A field is a variable that is associated with a class or with an instance of a class, and the set of fields contained with a class collectively represent an object's state. In this chapter, we'll explore the definition and use of fields, how to expose your fields to other classes directly and through properties, and the different modifiers you can use to change the way that your field works.

Fields are really important; they are at the heart of classes and are closely related to properties and methods (which I cover in Chapters 8 and 9, respectively). Without fields, we'd have no way to differentiate objects from one another and no basis on which to reflect the progression of our programs. Table 7-1 provides the summary for this chapter.

Table 7-1. *Quick Problem/Solution Reference for Chapter 7*

Problem	Solution	Listings
Set an initial value for a field.	Supply an initial value when defining the field or in the constructor of the containing class.	7-2 through 7-4
Update the value of a field.	Assign a new value directly or via a property that mediates access to the field, or call a method that updates the field indirectly.	7-5 through 7-9
Create a single copy of a field that is shared by all instances of the containing class.	Use the `static` modifier when defining the field.	7-10, 7-11
Create a read-only/constant value.	Use the `const` modifier when defining the field.	7-12, 7-13
Create read-only field that can be updated during class construction.	Use the `readonly` modifier when defining the field.	7-14, 7-15
Hide a field of the same name in the base class.	Use the `new` keyword when defining the field.	7-16, 7-17

Defining and Using Fields

There are three key stages in the life cycle of a field, and understanding each of these states helps us understand the overarching life cycle of types. In each of the following sections, I'll describe each one of these stages.

Defining Fields

To define a field, you add a statement to a class that contains the type of the field and the name you want it to have. The field type can be any value or reference type, including custom types that you have created in your project. Listing 7-1 contains a class that has two properties defined.

Listing 7-1. Simple Field Definitions

```
class Product {
    int itemsInStock;
    string productName;
}
```

The two fields are marked in bold. The first field is an `int` called `itemsInStock`, and the second field is a `string` called `productName`. These fields are part of the class, meaning that any object that is created using this class will have these fields.

FIELD NAMING CONVENTIONS

The convention for naming C# fields is to use camel case, where the first letter of the name is lowercase and the first letter of any concatenated works is uppercase, for example, `itemsInStock`.

For `public` and `static` fields, the convention is to use Pascal case, where the first letter of the name and the first letter of any concatenated words is uppercase, for example, `ItemsInStock`. However, there is an even stronger convention against using `public` or `static` fields, preferring properties instead.

You can find more details about `public` and `static` fields in the "Applying Field Modifiers" section of this chapter. For information about properties and how to use them, see Chapter 8.

The fields defined in Listing 7-1 are the simplest kind of fields. There are keywords you can use in conjunction with fields to control the behavior of a field; see the "Applying Field Modifiers" section later in this chapter for details.

Initializing Fields

Fields can be assigned values when we create a new object. These initial values can be specified as part of the field definition, which means that every instance of a class starts with the same value for a given field. Listing 7-2 contains an example.

Listing 7-2. Initializing Fields with Class Values

```
class Product {
    int itemsInStock = 210;
    string productName = "Banana";
}
```

The fields in Listing 7-2 are illustrated in Figure 7-1.

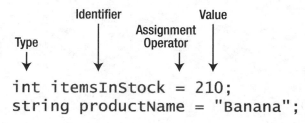

Figure 7-1. The anatomy of a field

The `itemsInStock` field is initialized with a value of `210` and the `productName` field with a value of `Banana`. Every instance of the `Product` class that is created will have the same initial values for these two fields. The values can be changed later (as we'll see in a moment), but they will all start the same.

If your field is a reference type, you can construct an object of the field type using the `new` keyword and the class constructor, as shown in Listing 7-3. The differences between reference types and value types are discussed in Chapter 4.

Listing 7-3. Initializing a Field Using the Field Type Constructor

```
class Supplier {
    // class body
}

class Product {
    int itemsInStock = 210;
    string productName = "Banana";
    Supplier productSupplier = new Supplier();
}
```

The `productSuppler` field is of the `Supplier` type, which is also defined in Listing 7-3. The `productSupplier` field is initialized with a new instance of `Supplier`. The `Supplier` class doesn't have any fields yet, but we'll add some in a moment. In Listing 7-3, every instance of the `Product` class will have the same field values.

The initial values for fields can also be supplied when an object is created; this means that different objects of the same type can have different initial field values. This is achieved using the class constructor. We cover constructors fully when we come to discuss methods in Chapter 9. Listing 7-4 contains an example of using the constructor in this way.

Listing 7-4. Setting Field Values Using a Constructor

```
class Supplier {
    string supplierName;

    public Supplier(string name) {
        supplierName = name;
    }
}

class Product {
    int itemsInStock = 210;
    string productName;
    Supplier productSupplier;

    public Product(string pname, string sname) {
        productName = pname;
        productSupplier = new Supplier(sname);
    }
}
```

The constructor for the Product class takes has two parameters, which are used to set the initial values for the productName and productSupplier fields. The code statements in the constructor are executed when a new instance of the Product class is created. We can supply different values for the constructor arguments, and these will result in instances of Product with different values for the fields.

In Listing 7-4, the Supplier class has a field and a constructor, too. In the constructor of the Product class, I set the value of the productSuppler field to be a new instance of the Supplier class and use one of the constructor parameters to initialize the supplierName field in the Supplier class via the Supplier constructor. The following statements create new instances of the Product class with different field values:

```
Product prod1 = new Product("Bananas", "Bob's Banana Shop");
Product prod2 = new Product("Apples", "Apples R Us");
```

If you define but don't initialize a field, the field value will be the default value for the field type, such as 0 for numeric types, null for reference types, and so on. A similar effect can also be achieved by supplying initial values to accessible fields when a new instance of a class is created; see the "Constructors" section in Chapter 9 for details.

Reading and Updating Fields

The values assigned to fields are the *state* of an object, and as a program runs, we need to be able to read the fields to determine the state of the object and update the values of the field as the state evolves.

For example, consider the Product class in Listing 7-4, which has a field called itemsInStock. If we sell some of the product, we need to reduce the field value to reflect the sale. If we receive a delivery, we need to increase the field value to reflect the new stock that has arrived.

Working Directly with Field Values

You can read and modify field values directly within your class. Listing 7-5 contains an example of the Product class and a method that reads and modifies the itemsInStock field. Methods are described fully in Chapter 9.

Listing 7-5. Working Directly with Fields Inside a Class

```
class Supplier {
    string supplierName;

    public Supplier(string name) {
        supplierName = name;
    }
}

class Product {
    int itemsInStock = 210;
    string productName;
    Supplier productSupplier;

    public Product(string pname, string sname) {
        productName = pname;
        productSupplier = new Supplier(sname);
    }

    public void ReadAndModifyFields() {
        // read the itemsInStock field value
        int readValue = itemsInStock;
        System.Console.WriteLine("Stock level: {0}", readValue);

        // modify the stock level
        itemsInStock = 10;

        // write out the (modified) itemsInStock field value
        System.Console.WriteLine("Stock level: {0}", itemsInStock);
    }
}

class Listing_05 {

    static void Main(string[] args) {

        // create a new instance of the Product type
        Product prod = new Product("Bananas", "Bob's Banana Shop");

        prod.ReadAndModifyFields();

        // wait for input before exiting
        System.Console.WriteLine("Press enter to finish");
        System.Console.ReadLine();
```

```
    }
}
```

The method is marked in bold. We read the value of the field with this statement:

```
int readValue = itemsInStock;
```

We have created a new local variable called **readValue** and assigned it the current value of the **itemsInStock** field. Local variables are described in Chapter 9, but the key point to note here is that we have read the value of the field. We modify the field using this statement:

```
itemsInStock = 10;
```

We have set the value of the field to be **10**, replacing the previous value. If we compile and run the code in Listing 7-5, we get the following result:

```
Stock level: 210
Stock level: 10
Press enter to finish
```

You can see that when we read the **itemsInStock** field, we get the initial value specified in the **Product** class definition, 210. Then we set the value to 10, which we can see takes effect when we write out the value again using the **System.Console.WriteLine** method.

Allowing Other Classes to Read and Modify Properties

The previous example showed an object reading and modifying its own properties in one of its methods, but often you want to allow other types to change the state of your object. You have some choices about how to do this.

Exposing Fields Directly

The simplest way of allowing others to modify the state of your object is to use an access modifier to expose the fields, allowing other objects to read and write the field values directly. The full set of access modifiers for fields is described in the "Applying Field Modifiers" section later in the chapter, but Listing 7-6 demonstrates a **Product** class that uses the **public** modifier, meaning that any object can read and write the **ItemsInStock** field. If you do not apply an access modifier to a field, the access level defaults to **private**, meaning that the field is not accessible outside of the object in which it has been defined.

Listing 7-6. Exposing a Field Using the Public Access Modifier

```
class Supplier {
    string supplierName;

    public Supplier(string name) {
        supplierName = name;
    }
}
```

```
class Product {
    public int ItemsInStock = 210;
    string productName;
    Supplier productSupplier;

    public Product(string pname, string sname) {
        productName = pname;
        productSupplier = new Supplier(sname);
    }
}

class Listing_06 {

    static void Main(string[] args) {

        // create a new instance of the Product type
        Product prod = new Product("Bananas", "Bob's Banana Shop");

        // read the itemsInStock field value
        int readValue = prod.ItemsInStock;
        System.Console.WriteLine("Stock level: {0}", readValue);

        // modify the stock level
        prod.ItemsInStock = 10;

        // write out the (modified) itemsInStock field value
        System.Console.WriteLine("Stock level: {0}", prod.ItemsInStock);

        // wait for input before exiting
        System.Console.WriteLine("Press enter to finish");
        System.Console.ReadLine();
    }
}
```

The Listing_06 class creates a new Product object and assigns it to the variable called prod. Because the ItemsInStock field is public, the Listing_06 class is able to read and modify the field value directly, using the period notation (that is, prod.ItemsInStock).

■ **Note** You will notice that I have changed the case of the name of the field in Listing 7-6 to ItemsInStock. This is the naming convention for public fields; see the "Field Naming Conventions" sidebar earlier in the chapter for details.

Exposing Properties with Field Values

Using public fields is poor programming practice because it makes it difficult to maintain the Product class. Imagine that we decide to record stock based on the number of boxes we receive, rather than individual items. We have to find and update all of the classes that access the `ItemsInStock` field so that they follow the new policy. This becomes especially troublesome when your class is used by other programmers and impossible if your class is publically available as a library and some of those programmers work in a different company. Consider using properties to mediate access to your fields. Properties are detailed fully in Chapter 8, but Listing 7-7 contains an example of using a property to read and modify a private field.

Listing 7-7. Using a Field to Allow Access to a Private Field

```
class Supplier {
    string supplierName;

    public Supplier(string name) {
        supplierName = name;
    }
}

class Product {
    int itemsInStock = 210;
    string productName;
    Supplier productSupplier;

    public Product(string pname, string sname) {
        productName = pname;
        productSupplier = new Supplier(sname);
    }

    public int ItemsInStock {
        get { return itemsInStock; }
        set { itemsInStock = value; }
    }
}

class Listing_07 {

    static void Main(string[] args) {

        // create a new instance of the Product type
        Product prod = new Product("Bananas", "Bob's Banana Shop");

        // read the itemsInStock field value
        int readValue = prod.ItemsInStock;
        System.Console.WriteLine("Stock level: {0}", readValue);

        // modify the stock level
        prod.ItemsInStock = 10;

        // write out the (modified) itemsInStock field value
        System.Console.WriteLine("Stock level: {0}", prod.ItemsInStock);

        // wait for input before exiting
```

```
        System.Console.WriteLine("Press enter to finish");
        System.Console.ReadLine();
    }
}
```

The property in the **Product** class is shown in bold. I am not going to get into the detail of properties here; you can get that in Chapter 8. But it is worth showing how properties can help make your code easier to maintain, because programmers who come to C# from languages where public fields are common can be resistant to using properties. First, notice that the code in **Listing_07** is identical to that in **Listing_06** where we used a public field instead of a property. Using a property isn't any more difficult or verbose than using a field.

But now let's imagine we have to make a change. Let's imagine that we want to track stock by the crate, and each crate contains ten items. Listing 7-8 demonstrates a modified **Product** class that handles this change.

Listing 7-8. Using Properties to Abstract Changes in Fields

```
class Product {
    int cratesInStock = 21;
    string productName;
    Supplier productSupplier;

    public Product(string pname, string sname) {
        productName = pname;
        productSupplier = new Supplier(sname);
    }

    public int ItemsInStock {
        get { return cratesInStock * 10; }
        set { cratesInStock = value / 10; }
    }

    public int CratesInStock {
        get { return cratesInStock; }
        set { cratesInStock = value; }
    }
}
```

You can see that I have removed the **itemsInStock** field and replaced it with **cratesinStock**, which is initialized to **21** (one-tenth of the initialization value used for the original field). I have added a new property that mediates access to the **cratesInStock** field, called **CratesInStock**. These may look like the same names, but they used different capitalization styles, as is the C# convention. But, critically, because I can add code to a property, I have been able to preserve compatibility with those classes that work in units and not crates, such as the **Listing_07** class from the previous example, by leaving the **ItemsInStock** property in place and converting to and from the old units as needed. You can see Chapter 8 for full details of properties and how you can use them, but I hope this example will convince you that there are good reasons not to use public properties and that a good alternative exists in C#.

Understanding Reference Type Fields

If you find that you get unexpected results when you read your object fields, you might have fallen into a trap that catches a lot of programmers new to C#. When you assign a new value to a field that is of a reference type, you are creating a new reference to an object. If you modify that object, your modifications will be reflected when you read back the property. This can be confusing, so Listing 7-9 contains an example.

Listing 7-9. Using Reference Type Fields

```
class Supplier {
    string supplierName;

    public Supplier(string name) {
        supplierName = name;
    }

    public string SupplierName {
        get { return supplierName; }
        set { supplierName = value; }
    }
}

class Product {
    string productName;
    Supplier productSupplier;

    public Product(string pname, Supplier supplier) {
        productName = pname;
        productSupplier = supplier;
    }

    public Supplier Supplier {
        get { return productSupplier; }
    }
}

class Listing_09 {

    static void Main(string[] args) {

        // create a new supplier
        Supplier supp = new Supplier("Bob's Banana Shop");

        // create a new instance of the Product type
        Product bananaProduct = new Product("Bananas",  supp);

        // update the supplier name
        supp.SupplierName = "Apples R Us";

        // create a new instance of the Product type
```

```
        Product appleProduct = new Product("Apples", supp);

        // get the supplier names from the products
        System.Console.WriteLine("Banana Name: {0}", bananaProduct.Supplier.SupplierName);
        System.Console.WriteLine("Apple Name: {0}", appleProduct.Supplier.SupplierName);

        // wait for input before exiting
        System.Console.WriteLine("Press enter to finish");
        System.Console.ReadLine();
    }
}
```

The listing contains a modified version of the **Product** class from the other example, but this one takes a **Supplier** object as a constructor argument and assigns it to the **productSupplier** field. The **Listing_09** class creates a new instance of **Supplier** and then uses it to create a new instance of **Product**. At this point, our **Product** object is all about bananas. The supplier name is **Bob's Banana Shop**, and the product name is **Bananas**.

Then I modify the name of the **Supplier** and use it to create a second product. This one is for apples. And here's the problem: when you assign a value to a reference type field, you are just assigning a reference to the object. Since I used the same instance of **Supplier** to create two **Product** instances, they both now have a reference to the same object. When I updated the name of the **Supplier**, the change becomes reflected in both **Product** instances. When I compile and run the code in Listing 7-9, I get the following results:

```
Banana Name: Apples R Us
Apple Name: Apples R Us
Press enter to finish
```

Both of my products have the same supplier name, which is not what I wanted. The simplest way to avoid this problem is not to reuse objects in this way—to create a new instance of **Supplier** for each instance of **Product**, like this:

```
// create a new supplier
Supplier supp = new Supplier("Bob's Banana Shop");

// create a new instance of the Product type
Product bananaProduct = new Product("Bananas",  supp);

// create a new supplier
supp = new Supplier("Apples R Us");

// create a new instance of the Product type
Product appleProduct = new Product("Apples", supp);
```

The Fourth Stage of the Life Cycle

Although I said that there are three stages to the field life cycle, there is a fourth one, known as *destruction*. This is where the object that contains the fields is no longer required, and the resources it occupies are required elsewhere. At this point, most fields values are simply removed from memory, but you can handle things differently; see the "Destructors" section in Chapter 17 for details.

Applying Field Modifiers

As with most class members, you can apply modifiers to tailor the behavior of your field to meet your programming needs. The following sections detail each of the available modifier keywords.

Creating Static Fields

If you don't use the `static` keyword as a modifier for your field, you create what is known as an *instance field*, meaning that each instance of a class has its own copy of the field, and changing the field value for in one instance doesn't affect any of the other instances. All the examples you have seen so far in this chapter have been instance fields.

You can create a *static field* by using the `static` keyword; this is where all instances of the class share the same copy of the field and where any changes affect all instances. Listing 7-10 demonstrates a static field.

Listing 7-10. Using the `static` Keyword

```
class Product {
    string productName;
    static string productCategory;

    public Product(string prodName, string prodCat) {
        productName = prodName;
        productCategory = prodCat;
    }

    public string ProductCategory {
        get { return productCategory; }
        set { productCategory = value; }
    }
}

class Listing_10 {

    static void Main(string[] args) {

        // create a new instance of the Product type
        Product bananaProduct = new Product("Bananas", "Fruit");

        // create another new instance of the Product type
        Product appleProduct = new Product("Apples", "Fruit");

        // change the banana category
        bananaProduct.ProductCategory = "Fresh Fruit";

        // print out the category values
```

```
        System.Console.WriteLine("Banana Category: {0}", bananaProduct.ProductCategory);
        System.Console.WriteLine("Apple Category: {0}", appleProduct.ProductCategory);

        // wait for input before exiting
        System.Console.WriteLine("Press enter to finish");
        System.Console.ReadLine();
    }
}
```

In the example, the ProductCategory property modifies the static productCategory field. Since this is a static field, any modifications affect all instances of the Product class, so modifying the field for the instance called bananaProduct also has the effect of modifying it for the instance called appleProduct. Compiling and running the code in Listing 7-10 produces the following output:

```
Banana Category: Fresh Fruit
Apple Category: Fresh Fruit
Press enter to finish
```

You can also create static properties, and this is the usual way that you provide access to a static field. You can see an example of a static property in Chapter 8. If you have created a static field that is available outside your class (through the public or internal access modifiers, for example), then the field is available through the class name instead of through instances of the class. Listing 7-11 contains an example.

Listing 7-11. Accessing a Public static Field

```
class Product {
    string productName;
    public static string ProductCategory;

    public Product(string prodName) {
        productName = prodName;
    }
}

class Listing_11 {

    static void Main(string[] args) {

        // create a new instance of the Product type
        Product bananaProduct = new Product("Bananas");

        // create another new instance of the Product type
        Product appleProduct = new Product("Apples");

        // change the banana category
        Product.ProductCategory = "Fresh Fruit";

        // print out the category values
        System.Console.WriteLine("Product Category: {0}", Product.ProductCategory);
```

```
        // wait for input before exiting
        System.Console.WriteLine("Press enter to finish");
        System.Console.ReadLine();
    }
}
```

In the example, the Listing_11 class accesses the public static field by calling
Product.ProductCategory, that is, the name of the class, followed by a period, followed by the name of
the field. Once again, though, let me say that you should use a public static property in preference to a
public static field.

Creating Read-Only Fields

C# supports two slightly different read-only fields, which are available through the const and readonly
keywords.

Using the const keyword

The const keyword creates a field that can be assigned a value only when it is defined, known as a
constant. Listing 7-12 contains an example. The key statement in this example is shown in bold.

Listing 7-12. Using the const Keyword

```
class Product {
    const int unitsPerCrate = 10;
    int cratesInStock = 21;
    string productName;

    public Product(string pname, int crates) {
        productName = pname;
        cratesInStock = crates;
    }

    public int ItemsInStock {
        get { return cratesInStock * unitsPerCrate; }
        set { cratesInStock = value / unitsPerCrate; }
    }
}

class Listing_12 {

    static void Main(string[] args) {

        // create a new instance of the Product type
        Product bananaProduct = new Product("Bananas", 21);

        // write out the number of items in stock
```

```
        System.Console.WriteLine("Units in Stock: {0}", bananaProduct.ItemsInStock);

        // wait for input before exiting
        System.Console.WriteLine("Press enter to finish");
        System.Console.ReadLine();
    }
}
```

The unitsPerCrate field is initialized with a value of 10. Any attempt to change the value of a const field will result in a compiler error; you can't initialize the field in your class constructor, and you can change the value in a method, property, or other class member. If you apply the const keyword with an access modifier that allows other types to access the field, such as public, then other types refer to the field using the class name, as demonstrated in Listing 7-13.

Listing 7-13. Using the const Keyword on a Public Field

```
class Product {
    public const int UnitsPerCrate = 10;
}

class Listing_13 {

    static void Main(string[] args) {

        // access the public const field
        System.Console.WriteLine("Units in Stock: {0}", Product.UnitsPerCrate);

        // wait for input before exiting
        System.Console.WriteLine("Press enter to finish");
        System.Console.ReadLine();
    }
}
```

A public const field is not the same as a public static field. The value assigned to a static field can be changed after it has been defined, whereas a const field's value cannot be modified.

Using the readonly Keyword

The readonly keyword offers a variation on the read-only fields created by the const keyword. A readonly field can be assigned a value when it is defined or in a class constructor but is otherwise immutable. Listing 7-14 contains an example.

Listing 7-14. Using the readonly Keyword

```
class Product {
    readonly int unitsPerCrate = 5;

    public Product(int units) {
        if (units > 10) {
            unitsPerCrate = units;
```

```
        }
    }

    public int UnitsPerCrate {
        get { return unitsPerCrate; }
    }
}
```

The Product class in Listing 7-14 defines a readonly field called unitsPerCrate, which is assigned a value of 5. So far, this is just like a const field—until we look at the constructor. Constructors are explained fully in Chapter 9, but for now it is enough to know that these special methods are called when a new instance of the Product class is created using the new keyword.

The constructor for the Product class in the example has one parameter, representing the units in each crate. If the parameter value is greater than 10, then I assign the parameter value to the readonly field. The code in Listing 7-15 demonstrates the effect of the readonly field in Listing 7-14.

Listing 7-15. The Effect of a readonly Field

```
class Listing_15 {

    static void Main(string[] args) {

        // create an instance of product using the default constructor
        Product p1 = new Product(8);

        // get the number of units per crate
        System.Console.WriteLine("Units in Stock: {0}", p1.UnitsPerCrate);

        // create an instance of product
        Product p2 = new Product(20);

        // get the number of units per crate
        System.Console.WriteLine("Units in Stock: {0}", p2.UnitsPerCrate);

        // wait for input before exiting
        System.Console.WriteLine("Press enter to finish");
        System.Console.ReadLine();
    }
}
```

I create an instance of Product by providing a parameter value of 8. Looking at the code statements in the constructor for the Product class in Listing 7-14, we can see that no new value will be assigned to the unitsPerCrate field, which means that the value of the field will remain as 5. I then create a second Product instance using a parameter value of 20; this causes the constructor to update the value of the readonly field. Compiling and running the code in Listing 7-15 produces the following results:

```
Units in Stock: 5
Units in Stock: 20
Press enter to finish
```

Allowing a `readonly` field to be modified during object construction is a useful feature. It means that you can create a per-instance constant value, which depends on the way in which your object was constructed. In Listing 7-15, the instances of `Product` each had a constant field with a different constant value. Once constructed, the object cannot change the value assigned this field, which can be useful for avoiding inadvertent modifications.

Applying Access Modifiers

You can control access to individual fields by using access modifiers, described in Table 7-2. For any modifier other than `private`, consider using a property instead of granting access directly to the field; see the "Reading and Updating Fields" section of this chapter for a brief example of using properties, or see Chapter 8 for full details.

■ **Tip** If you do not provide an access modifier when you define a field, the access level defaults to private.

Table 7-2. Access Modifiers and Their Effect on Properties

Access Modifier	Description
public	The field can be accessed anywhere; use a public property instead of a public field.
protected	The field can be accessed only by the containing class or derived classes; use a protected property instead of a protected field.
internal	The field can be accessed by any code in the current assembly but not other assemblies; use an internal property instead of an internal field.
protected internal	The field can be accessed by any code in the current assembly or any class in any assembly that derives from the containing class; use a protected internal property instead of a protected internal field.
private	The field can be accessed only by the containing class.

Hiding Base Class Fields

If you want to define a field with the same name as a field in your base class, you can do so by using the `new` keyword. Class inheritance and base classes are covered in Chapter 6. Listing 7-16 illustrates field hiding.

Listing 7-16. Using the new Keyword to Explicitly Hide a Base Field

```
class Product {
    protected int myField;
}

class DerivedProduct : Product {
    private new string myField;

    public int MyIntProperty {
        get { return base.myField; }
        set { base.myField = value; }
    }

    public string MyStringProperty {
        get { return this.myField; }
        set { this.myField = value; }
    }
}
```

In the listing, the `DerivedProduct` class is derived from the `Product` class. The `DerivedProduct` class implements a field called `myField`, which conflicts with the protected field of the same name in the base class. To address this, we use the `new` keyword when we define the field in the derived class.

If the derived class needs to access the hidden field, it can do so by prefixing the field name with `base`, followed by a period, that is, `base.myField`. The local field can be accessed by name (that is, `myField`), but I find it useful to be explicit about which field I am accessing and prefix the field name with the `this` keyword, followed by a period, that is, `this.myField`. You can see how the different fields are accessed in the properties of the `DerivedProduct` class.

Hiding fields is related to polymorphism, which is described more fully in Chapter 6. In short, if an object created from a class that hides a base field is upcast to a base type, then the hidden field will be the one that is accessed by other classes. If the same object is referred to by its declared type, then the new field is access. This is demonstrated by Listing 7-17.

Listing 7-17. The Effect of Upcasting on Hidden Fields

```
using System;
class BaseProduct {
    public string myField = "Base Value";
}

class DerivedProduct : BaseProduct {
    public new string myField = "Derived Value";
}

class Listing_17 {

    static void Main(string[] args) {

        // create an object from the derived class
        DerivedProduct derivedObject = new DerivedProduct();
```

```
        // upcast the objet to the base type
        BaseProduct upcastObject = derivedObject;

        // print out the field values
        Console.WriteLine("Derived Field: {0}", derivedObject.myField);
        Console.WriteLine("Base Field: {0}", upcastObject.myField);

        // wait for input before exiting
        System.Console.WriteLine("Press enter to finish");
        System.Console.ReadLine();
    }
}
```

The derived class in this example hides a field from the base class. Both fields are initialized with default values. The Main method in the Listing_17 class creates a DerivedProduct object and upcasts it to the base type by assigning it to a BaseProduct local variable. The results of reading the myField value are printed to the console. The results of compiling and running the code in Listing 7-17 are as follows:

```
Derived Field: Derived Value
Base Field: Base Value
Press enter to finish
```

You can see that upcasting an object has the effect of "unhiding" the field in the base class. When hiding fields, you must be confident of how objects created from your class are going to be treated, since upcasting changes the way that they behave.

Using the volatile Keyword

The volatile modifier is applied to fields that may be accessed by multiple threads without the use of the lock keyword or other synchronization mechanisms. This keyword prevents some compiler optimizations that assume access by a single thread. You can learn more about synchronization when we explore parallel and multithreaded programming techniques later in the book.

Summary

In this chapter, we have seen how to define, initialize, modify, and use fields, and we have seen how to expose those fields to other types using properties and directly. Fields, be they the regular kind or static or whether or not have constant values, are the backbone of classes, and we use them in C# to maintain the state of our program as it runs. In later chapters, we will see some specialized kinds of field, such as events and delegates, which we can use to build on the basic model to achieve very specific effects.

CHAPTER 8

■ ■ ■

Properties, Indexers, and Operators

Properties are class members that allow you to expose a characteristic of an object. Indexers are members that allow you to treat a class as though it were an array, using the same index syntax ([ ]) that is described in Chapter 13.

Properties and indexers both allow you to control access to the fields in your class and give you more control than exposing a field directly. As you'll see when we get into the detail, properties and indexers are very flexible; in fact, they are so rich that they can sometimes blur the distinction between fields and methods.

Custom operators allow you to implement custom operations using standard notation such as + and ++ and allow you to control the implicit and explicit conversion from one type to another.

If you are coming to C# from a language that doesn't have anything like these features, you might wonder why you should use them. I certainly felt that way when I started writing in C# after years of Java coding. The truth is that these features are largely syntactic sugar; they are nice-to-have features that reduce the code clutter that methods can cause. But they *are* nice-to-have. I am a firm convert, especially to properties and indexers. Give them a try in your programs, and you might become a convert too. Table 8-1 provides the summary for this chapter.

Table 8-1. Quick Problem/Solution Reference for Chapter 8

Problem	Solution	Listings
Use a property to mediate access to a field.	Use a field-backed property.	8-2
Use a property to validate values for a field.	Add validation code to the set accessor of a field-backed property.	8-2
Implement a property without defining a field.	Use an automatically implemented property.	8-3, 8-4
Create a read-only or write-only property.	Implement only the get or set accessor in a property.	8-5
Compute the value of a property on demand.	Add code to compute the result in the accessors.	8-6
Map the type of a property to a differently typed field.	Add translation code to the accessors.	8-7

Problem	Solution	Listings
Restrict the access to a property.	Apply an access modifier to the entire property or apply a more restrictive modifier to one of the accessors.	8-8
Create a virtual, abstract, sealed or static property.	Apply the appropriate keyword to the property.	8-9 through 8-12
Add array-like support for a class.	Add an indexer.	8-13, 8-14, 8-16
Use an indexer that validates access to a field.	Add validating code statements in the get and set accessors.	8-15
Implement custom unary and binary operators for custom types.	Use the operator keyword.	8-17 through 8-20
Provide support for converting between different types.	Use the conversion keyword.	8-21, 8-22

Creating a Property

Properties are very flexible. You can use this language feature to achieve several different results. In fact, properties are so flexible that you can end up creating something that might be mistaken for a method. In the following sections, I show you how to use the different models available for properties and how you can apply the same keywords available for other member types to get fine-grained control over how your properties function.

Creating a Field-Backed Property

The standard way of using a property is to use it as a mediator to a field, typically to ensure that other classes cannot set the field to a value that would create an exceptional state for your class. Listing 8-1 demonstrates the problem that this kind of property can help avoid.

Listing 8-1. The Illegal Field Value Problem

```
using System;

class Product {
    public int ItemsInStock;
    public double PricePerItem;

    public double GetTotalValueOfStock() {
        return ItemsInStock * PricePerItem;
    }
}
```

```
}

class Listing_01 {

    static void Main(string[] args) {

        // create a new instance of the Product class
        Product prod = new Product();

        // set the value of the fields
        prod.ItemsInStock = -20;
        prod.PricePerItem = 5.23;

        // get the total value of the products in stock
        Console.WriteLine("Total stock value: {0}", prod.GetTotalValueOfStock());

        // wait for input before exiting
        Console.WriteLine("Press enter to finish");
        Console.ReadLine();
    }
}
```

In Listing 8-1, the Product class has two public fields, representing the number of items in stock and the price per item. There is also a method, GetTotalValueOfStock, which uses the two fields to perform a calculation.

In the Main method of the Listing_01 class, I create a new instance of Product and set the values for the fields. I set the value for ItemsInStock to -20. Now, from the point of view of the calling class, this might make sense—perhaps a negative value is intended to indicate that there are 20 orders for the product to be shipped when a new delivery arrives. The problem is that the Product class doesn't share the same view of a negative value and so doesn't take this into account in the GetTotalValueOfStock method. If we compile and run the code in Listing 8-1, we get the following output:

```
Total stock value: -104.6
Press enter to finish
```

The output values the stock for the Product instance as a negative number. If you had lots of Product instances and tried to calculate the combined value of all your stock, having a negative value in the mix will give you the wrong result.

Properties can help you avoid this problem by allowing you to validate the value set for a field. Listing 8-2 contains an example.

Listing 8-2. Using a Property to Validate Field Values

```
using System;

class Product {
    private int itemsInStock;
    public double PricePerItem;
```

```
    public int ItemsInStock {

        get { return itemsInStock; }

        set {
            if (value >= 0) {
                itemsInStock = value;
            } else {
                throw new ArgumentOutOfRangeException();
            }
        }
    }

    public double GetTotalValueOfStock() {
        return itemsInStock * PricePerItem;
    }
}
```

The Product class in Listing 8-2 contains a property, called ItemsInStock, which mediates access to the itemsInStock field, which is now private and cannot be accessed directly. There are six parts to the property defined in Listing 8-2, illustrated in Figure 8-1, with the code statements omitted from one of the accessors for brevity.

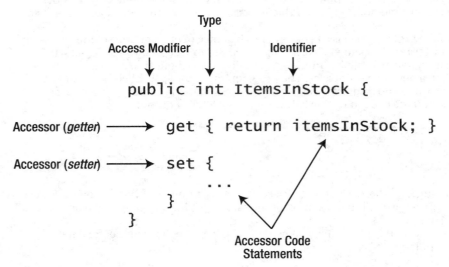

Figure 8-1. The anatomy of a property

The property identifier is the name that you will use to access the property. The convention for naming properties is the same as for fields—Pascal case for publicly accessible identifiers (capitalized first letter and first letter of each concatenated word, such as ItemsInStock) and camel case for private properties (lowercase first letter and uppercase first letter of each concatenated word, such as itemsInStock).

The accessors get and set the value of the property; they are often known as the getter and setter. The getter returns a value of the same type as the property type, int in the example. For the example property, the getter accessor is very simple:

```
get { return itemsInStock; }
```

We start with the get keyword and follow with a code block that returns a value of the type of the property, which we defined as int in the definition. In this case, we want to return the value of a field in the same class called itemsInStock, so we just say return itemsInStock.

The setter is slightly more complicated. Here it is:

```
set {
    if (value >= 0) {
        itemsInStock = value;
    } else {
        throw new ArgumentOutOfRangeException();
    }
}
```

We start with the set keyword, indicating that this is the setter. Setters are passed an instance of the property type using the special parameter called value. In this example, it is an int. The code statements in the example setter validate value to make sure that it is greater or equal to zero, and, if it is, the value is assigned to the class field. If the value is negative, then I throw an ArgumentOutOfRange exception instead. You can learn more about exceptions in Chapter 14. The remaining part of the property is the access modifier; these are discussed in the "Using Access Modifiers" section later in this chapter.

Using a Property

Using a property is just like using a field. To get the value, you use the property name, and to assign a new value, you use the property name and the assignment operator (=). The following code demonstrates using the property and public field defined in Listing 8-2:

```
class Listing_02_Test {

    static void Main(string[] args) {

        // create a new instance of the Product class
        Product prod = new Product();

        // set the value of the fields
        prod.ItemsInStock = -20;
        prod.PricePerItem = 5.23;

        // get the total value of the products in stock
        Console.WriteLine("Total stock value: {0}", prod.GetTotalValueOfStock());

        // wait for input before exiting
        Console.WriteLine("Press enter to finish");
        Console.ReadLine();
    }
}
```

If we compile and run the previous statements and the class in Listing 8-2, we get the following results:

```
Unhandled Exception: System.ArgumentOutOfRangeException: Specified argument was
out of the range of valid values.
   at Product.set_ItemsInStock(Int32 value)
...
Press any key to continue . . .
```

Creating an Automatically Implemented Property

The previous example included code statements that validated the value in the set accessor. Often, though you will just want your property to mediate access to a field because it is good practice. It means you can add features such as validation or transformation later without having to update the classes that call your properties. The property in Listing 8-3 demonstrates simply exposing a private field.

Listing 8-3. A Field Mediation Property

```
class Product {
    private int itemsInStock;

    public int ItemsInStock {
        get { return itemsInStock; }
        set { itemsInStock = value; }
    }
}
```

You can see what's happening here; the private field itemsInStock is mediated by the public property ItemsInStock. The get accessor returns the field value, and the set access assigns the provided value to the field. C# has a nice simplification of this pattern, which is called an *automatically implemented property*; Listing 8-4 contains an example.

Listing 8-4. Using an Automatically Implemented Property

```
class Product {

    public int ItemsInStock {
        get;
        set;
    }
}
```

There are no bodies for the accessors in an automatically implemented property. You just use the get and set keywords, followed by a semicolon. Most importantly, there is no field either. Automatically implemented properties allow you to reduce the clutter in your code if you are just using a property to get and set the value of a field. When you compile your class, the C# system creates a variable that is of the same type as the property and generates accessors just like the ones in Listing 8-3. We don't have any access to the variable or even know its name. We can only use the property to get and set its value.

Creating an Asymmetric Property

You don't have to implement both accessors in a property. If you omit the set accessor, you create a read-only property, and if you omit the get accessor, you create a write-only property. Listing 8-5 contains examples of both kinds.

Listing 8-5. Read-Only and Write-Only Properties

```
class Product {
    private int unitsInStock;
    private double pricePerItem;

    public int ItemsInStock {
        get { return unitsInStock; }
    }

    public double PricePerItem {
        set { pricePerItem = value; }
    }
}
```

The ItemsInStock property is read-only, meaning that the value of the private field cannot be set outside of the class. The PricePerItem property is write-only, meaning that the value of the pricePerItem field can be set, but not read, from outside the class; write-only properties are not that frequently used.

Creating a Computed Property

Properties are very flexible and need not be used just to mediate access to fields. They can also be used to access values that are computed on the fly. Listing 8-6 contains an example.

Listing 8-6. Using a Computed Property

```
class Product {

    public int ItemsInStock { get; set; }
    public double PricePerItem { get; set; }

    public double TotalValueOfStock {
        get {
            return ItemsInStock * PricePerItem;
        }
    }
}
```

In this listing, there are two automatically implemented properties, ItemsInStock and PricePerItem, and a read-only computed property called TotalValueOfStock, which uses the other two properties to return a result. When the get accessor for this property is used, the values of the other two properties are multiplied together. There is no field backing this property. The result is generated dynamically each time the get accessor is used. Using a computed property blurs the distinction between a method and property; where you draw the line is a matter of personal style. I tend to use computed properties only if

209

the computation is very simple, like the one in the example. If the computation is more complex, I tend to go with a method instead.

Mapping a Property Type to a Field Type

The field-backed properties I've given in the examples so far have all had the same type as the field they mediate access to, but this is not a requirement. You can use a property of one type to mediate access to a field of a different type by implementing the conversion between types in the accessors. Listing 8-7 contains an example that maps a string property to a double field.

Listing 8-7. Mapping One Type to Another with a Property

```
class Product {
    private double pricePerItem;

    public string PricePerItem {

        get {
            return string.Format("{0:0.00}", pricePerItem);
        }

        set {
            pricePerItem = double.Parse(value);
        }
    }
}
```

Don't worry about the string.Format or double.Parse methods for this example. You can learn more about string formatting in Chapter 16 and numeric values in Chapter 5. The important thing is that my property gets and sets string values that are converted to and from double values to match the field type. I end up using this kind of property when I have had to change the type of the field but don't want to (or can't) refactor all the types that rely on the property. This is, to me, the real value of the abstraction that properties can provide.

Using Access Modifiers

You apply access modifiers to properties as you would for any other class member. Table 8-2 shows the set of modifiers and how they work with properties.

Table 8-2. Access Modifiers and Their Effect on Properties

Access Modifier	Description
public	The property can be accessed anywhere.
protected	The property can be accessed only by the containing class or derived classes.

Access Modifier	Description
internal	The property can be accessed by any code in the current assembly but not other assemblies.
protected internal	The property can be accessed by any code in the current assembly or any class in any assembly that derives from the containing class.
private	The property can be accessed only by the containing class.

You can see the public access modifier applied to properties in some of the example listings in earlier sections of this chapter. But you can also apply the access modifiers to the get and set accessors to get fine-grained control over your property. Listing 8-8 contains a demonstration.

Listing 8-8. Applying an Access Modifier to an Accessor

```
class Product {

    public int ItemsInStock {
        private get;
        set;
    }

    public double PricePerItem { get; set; }

    public double TotalValueOfStock {
        get {
            return ItemsInStock * PricePerItem;
        }
    }
}
```

In Listing 8-8, the ItemsInStock property is public. This is the access modifier that will apply to the accessors by default. But I have used the private modifier on the get accessor. This means that anyone can set the value of the property, but it can only be read within the class that contains the property, the Product class in this example. The access modifier you apply to the accessor must be more restrictive than the modifier applied to the property overall, so, for example, you can't use the public modifier on an accessor for a private property.

Using Other Modifiers

You can use the same keywords available for other kinds of member on properties. In the following sections, I demonstrate how to use the virtual, overrides, abstract, sealed, and static keywords. There are some subtleties introduced when using these modifiers with properties because implementing the get and set accessors allow you to use these keywords more selectively than is possible for, say, a method.

Using the virtual and override Modifiers

You can use the `virtual` modifier to make a property virtual and allow derived classes to specialize the implementation of the accessors with the `override` keyword. This works just as for methods, which are covered in detail in Chapter 9. If you don't want to override a virtual property in a base class but want to create a property with the same name in the derived class, you can use the new keyword, just as with methods; however, this can cause unexpected results when your object is upcast to a base type. See Chapter 6 for details of polymorphism and the effects of upcasting.

When overriding properties, derived classes can choose to implement one or both of the accessors. If only one is overridden, then the other accessor from the inherited property is used. Listing 8-9 contains an example of an overridden property that only implements the get accessor.

Listing 8-9. Using the Virtual Modifier

```
class Product {
    protected int itemsInStock;

    public virtual int ItemsInStock {
        get {
            Console.WriteLine("Original Get Accessor");
            return itemsInStock;
        }
        set {
            Console.WriteLine("Original Set Accessor");
            itemsInStock = value;
        }
    }
}

class DerivedProduct : Product {

    public override int ItemsInStock {
        get {
            Console.WriteLine("Derived Get Accessor");
            return itemsInStock * 2;
        }
    }
}

class Listing_09 {

    static void Main(string[] args) {

        // create a new instance of the Product class
        DerivedProduct dp = new DerivedProduct();
        Product prod = dp;

        // set the value of the fields
        prod.ItemsInStock = 20;

        Console.WriteLine("Stock DP {0}", dp.ItemsInStock);
```

```
        Console.WriteLine("Stock P  {0}", prod.ItemsInStock);

        // wait for input before exiting
        Console.WriteLine("Press enter to finish");
        Console.ReadLine();
    }
}
```

Compiling and running the code in Listing 8-9 produces the following results:

```
Original Set Accessor
Derived Get Accessor
Stock DP 40
Derived Get Accessor
Stock P  40
Press enter to finish
```

Using the abstract Modifier

You can mark a property as abstract if it is part of an abstract class. You must specify which accessors derived classes are required to implement by including the get or set keywords in the abstract property definition. Listing 8-10 demonstrates an abstract property that requires both accessors to be implemented and a derived class that uses an automatically implemented property to comply with the requirements of the inherited class.

Listing 8-10. Defining an abstract Property

```
abstract class Product {

    public abstract int ItemsInStock {
        get;
        set;
    }
}

class DerivedProduct : Product {

    public override int ItemsInStock {
        get; set;
    }
}
```

Using the sealed Keyword

You use the sealed keyword to stop derived classes from overriding the implementation of a property, just as for methods. You can get full details of methods in Chapter 9. Listing 8-11 demonstrates a sealed property.

*Listing 8-11. Using the sealed **Keyword***

```
abstract class Product {

    public abstract int ItemsInStock {
        get;
        set;
    }
}

class DerivedProduct : Product {

    public sealed override int ItemsInStock {
        get;
        set;
    }
}
```

Using the static Keyword

You can create static properties that belong to a class type instead of an instance. Once again, using this keyword is just like using it on a method, which you can read more about in Chapter 9. Listing 8-12 contains an example of a static property being defined and then used.

Listing 8-12. Using the static Keyword

```
using System;

class Product {

    public static string DefaultProductName {
        get;
        set;
    }
}

class Listing_12 {

    static void Main(string[] args) {

        // set the static property in the class
        Product.DefaultProductName = "Oranges";

        // get the static property value
        Console.WriteLine("Default name: {0}", Product.DefaultProductName);

        // wait for input before exiting
        Console.WriteLine("Press enter to finish");
        Console.ReadLine();
    }
```

```
}
```

Creating an Indexer

Indexers allow you to expose the data contained by an object using array notation ([ ]). Arrays are described fully in Chapter 13. Indexers look a lot like properties, as you can see in Listing 8-13.

Listing 8-13. An Indexer

```
using System;

class Product {
    private string[] productNames
        = new string[] { "orange", "apple", "pear",
            "banana", "cherry" };

    public string this[int index] {
        get { return productNames[index]; }
        set { productNames[index] = value; }
    }
}
```

There are seven parts to the indexer in Listing 8-13, which is shown in bold. The parts are illustrated in Figure 8-2.

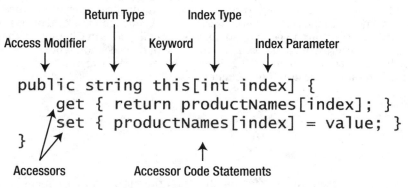

Figure 8-2. The anatomy of an indexer

Access modifiers for indexers work in the same way as for properties and are described in the "Using Access Modifiers" section earlier in the chapter.

Indexers are defined using the name this and have get and set accessors. In addition to the value parameter that we saw in properties, indexers also have the index parameter, which is of the type declared by the index type. In the example, the index type is int, and the name assigned to the parameter is index. The get accessor must return a value of the return type, and the set accessor will be passed a value of the same type in the special value parameter.

The indexer in Listing 8-13 mediates access to a field, which is a string array. Requests for values are provided as integers and are mapped to and from values in the field array. The following code demonstrates using the indexer from Listing 8-13:

```
class Listing_13_Test {

    static void Main(string[] args) {

        // create a new product
        Product p = new Product();

        // get some values via the indexer
        Console.WriteLine("Indexer value 0: {0}", p[0]);
        Console.WriteLine("Indexer value 1: {0}", p[1]);

        // set a value via the indexer
        p[2] = "guava";

        // wait for input before exiting
        Console.WriteLine("Press enter to finish");
        Console.ReadLine();
    }
}
```

You can see from the Main method in the previous class that using an indexer is just like using an array. I get and set values in the Product class using the array notation. The listing demonstrates the most common use of indexers, known as the *collection-backed* indexer. A collection is a kind of class that you can use to organize related objects. You can get more details about collections in Chapter 19. In this example, the indexer is mediating access to an array, which is the most basic collection type.

When an indexer is mediating access to a field that has its own indexers, like arrays, the get and set accessors are responsible for mapping requests to the mediated field:

```
get { return productNames[index]; }
set { productNames[index] = value; }
```

Using Multiple Indexers

A class can contain more than one indexer. One nice feature that this brings is that you can mediate access to a collection field, but doing so allows different characteristics to be mapped in different ways. Listing 8-14 contains a simple example.

Listing 8-14. Using Several Indexers in a Class

```
class Product {
    private string[] productNames
        = new string[] { "orange", "apple", "pear",
            "banana", "cherry" };

    public string this[int index] {
```

```
        get { return productNames[index]; }
        set { productNames[index] = value; }
    }

    public int this[string name] {
        get {
            return Array.IndexOf(productNames, name);
        }
    }
}
```

In the listing, there are two indexers. The first takes an integer index parameter and returns a string result. This indexer handles requests by mapping them to the array field in the class. The second indexer takes a string argument and returns an int. This indexer returns the index of the first item in the array field with the same value as the argument. You can have as many different indexers as you like in a class, as long as the signature (the combination of the return type and the arguments) is unique.

Creating a Validating Indexer

Just like properties, you can put code into the indexer accessors that validates get and set requests. Listing 8-15 contains an example that checks to see whether a numeric argument is within the bounds of an array field and returns a default value rather than throw an exception if it is not.

Listing 8-15. Validating Field Access with an Indexer

```
using System;

class Product {
    private string[] productNames
        = new string[] { "orange", "apple", "pear",
            "banana", "cherry" };

    public string this[int index] {
        get {
            if (index >= 0 && index < productNames.Length) {
                return productNames[index];
            } else {
                return "no name";
            }
        }
    }
}

class Listing_15 {

    static void Main(string[] args) {

        // create a new product
        Product p = new Product();
```

```
        // get some values via the indexer
        Console.WriteLine("Indexer value -1: {0}", p[-1]);
        Console.WriteLine("Indexer value 0: {0}", p[0]);

        // wait for input before exiting
        Console.WriteLine("Press enter to finish");
        Console.ReadLine();
    }
}
```

The indexer in Listing 8-15 is read-only because it implements only the get accessor. The code statements in the accessor check to see that the requested index is with the bounds of the array field. If the index is in bounds, then the array value at the index is returned. If the index is out of bounds, the no name string is returned. Compiling and running the code in Listing 8-15 produces the following results:

```
Indexer value -1: no name
Indexer value 0: orange
Press enter to finish
```

Creating an Indexer with Multiple Arguments

One difference between indexers and properties is that indexers can have arguments. In fact, they can have more than one argument. Listing 8-16 contains an example, which also demonstrates the use of a computed indexer, where the return values are not obtained from an underlying collection field.

Listing 8-16. An Indexer with Multiple Arguments

```
using System;

class Product {

    public int this[int arg1, int arg2] {
        get {
            return arg1 * arg2;
        }
    }
}

class Listing_16 {

    static void Main(string[] args) {

        // create a new product
        Product p = new Product();

        // get some values via the indexer
        Console.WriteLine("Indexer value [10, 20]: {0}", p[10, 20]);

        // wait for input before exiting
```

```
        Console.WriteLine("Press enter to finish");
        Console.ReadLine();
    }
}
```

In the listing, the indexer has two int arguments, although there is no requirement that arguments be of the same type. This is a computed index, and the result is calculated by multiplying the two arguments together. This example demonstrates that you can use indexers where methods would usually be used (although just because you can do something doesn't mean that you should, especially if other people are going to work with your classes). Compiling and running the code in Listing 8-16 produces the following result:

```
Indexer value [10, 20]: 200
Press enter to finish
```

Creating Custom Operators

In Chapter 5, we looked at the operators that you can apply to numeric types. C# allows you to define custom implementations of these operators so that you can apply them to any class that you define. In this section, I'll show you how to implement unary and binary operators and a special kind of operator, a *conversion operator*, that allows you to control implicit and explicit conversions to and from your classes.

Creating Custom Unary Operators

Unary operators work on one instance of a type. The most commonly used are the postfix increment and decrement operators (++ and --). Listing 8-17 demonstrates a custom unary operator applied to a custom type.

Listing 8-17. Defining a Custom Unary Operator

```
class Product {
    public string Name { get; set; }
    public int ItemsInStock { get; set; }
    public double PricePerItem { get; set; }


    public static Product operator ++(Product p) {
        p.ItemsInStock++;
        return p;
    }
}
```

There are eight parts to the custom unary operator in Listing 8-17, but many of them we have seen before when we covered properties and indexers. The parts of the operator are illustrated in Figure 8-3.

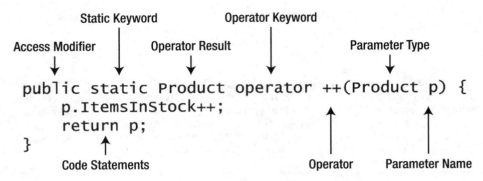

Figure 8-3. The anatomy of a custom unary operator

Unary operators work on a single object, which means that custom unary operators must have the same parameter type and operator result. In the case of the example, this is the Product class. All operators must be static and must use the operator keyword. Access modifiers for operators are the same as for properties and are described in the "Using Access Modifiers" section earlier in the chapter.

Instead of a name, a custom operator declares the operation that is being implemented. The operator in Listing 8-17 is the unary increment operator, ++.

In a custom operator, the code statements allow you to perform whatever tasks are required to implement the operator in the context of the type it operates on. In the case of Listing 8-17, I have decided that incrementing an instance of Product means incrementing the value of the ItemsInStock, but it is whatever makes sense for your classes. The code statements can access the original object using the parameter name (p in the example) and must return an instance of the operator result. This can be a new object or the parameter value, modified to reflect the operation.

The following code demonstrates how to use the operator in Listing 8-17:

```
using System;

class Listing_17_Test {

    static void Main(string[] args) {

        // create a new product
        Product p = new Product() {
            Name = "oranges",
            ItemsInStock = 10,
            PricePerItem = 20
        };

        // use the increment operator
        p++;

        // print out the number of items in stock
        Console.WriteLine("Items in stock: {0}", p.ItemsInStock);

        // wait for input before exiting
        Console.WriteLine("Press enter to finish");
        Console.ReadLine();
```

```
    }
}
```

The previous code creates a new instance of the Product class and then uses the ++ operator to increment the value, which actually increments the value of one of the fields. Compiling and running this code and Listing 8-17 produces the following results:

```
Items in stock: 11
Press enter to finish
```

Table 8-3 lists and describes the unary operators.

Table 8-3. Unary Operators

Operator	Description
+	Unary plus operator; changes the sign of the object to positive.
-	Unary negative operator; changes the sign of the object to negative.
!	Unary negation operator; if the object is considered true, returns false. If the object is considered false, then returns true.
~	Unary NOT operator.
++	Unary increment (can be used post-fix or prefix).
--	Unary decrement (can be used post-fix or prefix).

You don't have to implement all of the operators. You can just implement the ones that make sense for your objects. The unary operators are less widely used than the binary operators that I describe in the next section. My advice is that if there is no sensible and obvious meaning for an operator, then you should not implement it. Using an operator to perform a nonobvious function leads to confusion when someone else uses your class. If in doubt, use a method instead.

Creating Custom Binary Operators

Binary operators work on two objects. Listing 8-18 contains an example.

Listing 8-18. A Custom Binary Operator

```
class Product {
    public string Name { get; set; }
    public int ItemsInStock { get; set; }
    public double PricePerItem { get; set; }
```

```
    public static Product operator +(Product p1, Product p2) {
        return new Product() {
            Name = p1.Name,
            ItemsInStock = p1.ItemsInStock + p2.ItemsInStock,
            PricePerItem = p1.PricePerItem
        };
    }
}
```

The binary operator in Listing 8-18 is illustrated in Figure 8-4. There are seven main parts, but they are closely related to what we have seen in previous sections.

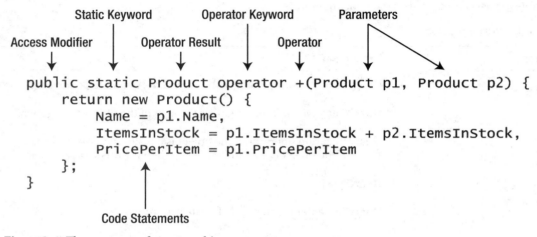

Figure 8-4. The anatomy of a custom binary operator

Binary operators must always be static and must have two parameters. The operator in Listing 8-18 implements binary addition for the Product class, meaning that we can add two Product objects together, like this:

```
using System;

class Listing_18_Test {

    static void Main(string[] args) {

        // create a new product
        Product p1 = new Product() {
            Name = "oranges",
            ItemsInStock = 10,
            PricePerItem = 20
        };

        // create a second product instance
        Product p2 = new Product() {
```

```
            Name = "oranges",
            ItemsInStock = 5,
            PricePerItem = 20
        };

        // use the postfix increment operator
        Product sum = p1 + p2;

        // print out the number of items in stock
        Console.WriteLine("Items in stock: {0}", sum.ItemsInStock);

        // wait for input before exiting
        Console.WriteLine("Press enter to finish");
        Console.ReadLine();
    }
}
```

These statements create two instances of Product and then add them together using the binary addition operator (+). This statement is shown in bold. The operator creates a new Product object with the Name and PricePerItem values from the first parameter and sets the ItemsInStock value of the result to be the sum of the ItemsInStock values from the two parameters. As with unary operators, the code statements in a binary operator can do whatever you need to make sense for your object.

You can implement operators that add different types together. Listing 8-19 provides an example.

Listing 8-19. A Binary Operator That Works on Different Types

```
class Product {
    public string Name { get; set; }
    public int ItemsInStock { get; set; }
    public double PricePerItem { get; set; }


    public static Product operator +(Product p1, int number) {
        return new Product() {
            Name = p1.Name,
            ItemsInStock = p1.ItemsInStock + number,
            PricePerItem = p1.PricePerItem
        };
    }
}
```

The operator in Listing 8-19 allows us to add an integer value to a Product object. This is done by adding the int to the ItemsInStock property. The following statements demonstrate how to use this operator:

```
class Listing_19_Test {

    static void Main(string[] args) {

        // create a new product
        Product p1 = new Product() {
```

```
            Name = "oranges",
            ItemsInStock = 10,
            PricePerItem = 20
        };

        // use the postfix increment operator
        Product sum = p1 + 20;

        // print out the number of items in stock
        Console.WriteLine("Items in stock: {0}", sum.ItemsInStock);

        // wait for input before exiting
        Console.WriteLine("Press enter to finish");
        Console.ReadLine();
    }
}
```

These statements create a Product object and use the addition operator to add a numeric literal value of 20 to it. Compiling and running this code produces the following results:

```
Items in stock: 30
Press enter to finish
```

The result of a binary operator can be an entirely different type to the parameters, as demonstrated by Listing 8-20.

Listing 8-20. Returning Another Object Type from a Binary Operator

```
class Product {
    public string Name { get; set; }
    public int ItemsInStock { get; set; }
    public double PricePerItem { get; set; }


    public static int operator +(Product p1, string str) {
        return p1.ItemsInStock + int.Parse(str);
    }
}
```

This operator lets us sum a Product object and a string. The string is parsed into an int, which is then added to the value of the Product.ItemsInStock property and returned as an int result. This is a pretty useless operator, but it does illustrate the flexibility of the custom operator feature, which gives you the freedom to implement as many different operators as you need to, each of which you can tailor to make sense for your objects.

Creating Custom Conversion Operators

Conversion operators allow you to specify how one type is converted to another. Listing 8-21 demonstrates a class that uses custom conversion operators.

Listing 8-21. Using Custom Conversion Operators

```
class Product {
    public string Name { get; set; }
    public int ItemsInStock { get; set; }
    public double PricePerItem { get; set; }


    public static implicit operator string(Product p) {
        return p.Name;
    }
}
```

The parts that make up the operator in Listing 8-21 are illustrated in Figure 8-5.

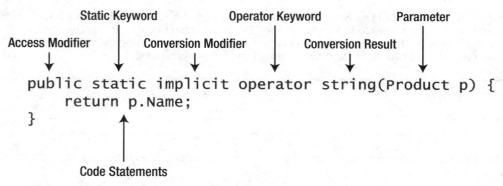

Figure 8-5. The anatomy of a custom conversion operator

Conversion operators are always static and require the operator keyword. The conversion modifier must be either implicit or explicit (we'll come to the difference in a moment). The conversion result is the type that the parameter type will be converted to by this operator. In Listing 8-21, the operator converts a Product into a string.

The code statements can perform any tasks that are required to convert the parameter type to the conversion result type and must use the return keyword to return an instance of this type.

When you use the implicit conversion modifier, the conversion between the parameter and result types will be performed implicitly, that is, without the need to make a type cast. The following statements demonstrate how to perform an implicit conversion with the class defined in Listing 8-21:

```
using System;

class Listing_21_Test {
```

```
static void Main(string[] args) {

    // create a new product
    Product p1 = new Product() {
        Name = "oranges",
        ItemsInStock = 10,
        PricePerItem = 20
    };

    // assign the product to a string variable
    string str = p1;

    // print out the local variable
    Console.WriteLine("String result: {0}", str);

    // wait for input before exiting
    Console.WriteLine("Press enter to finish");
    Console.ReadLine();
}
}
```

The statement marked in bold assigns the Product object to a string local variable. This is an implicit conversion, and the operator defined in Listing 8-21 will be used to generate the string. The code statements in the Listing 8-21 operator convert a Product to a string by returning the value of the Name property. If we compile and run these statements, we get the following results:

```
String result: oranges
Int result: 10
Press enter to finish
```

Explicit conversion operators require one type to be deliberately cast to another. Listing 8-22 contains an example.

Listing 8-22. An Explicit Conversion Operator

```
class Product {
    public string Name { get; set; }
    public int ItemsInStock { get; set; }
    public double PricePerItem { get; set; }

    public static explicit operator int(Product p) {
        return p.ItemsInStock;
    }
}
```

This operator works in just the same way as the implicit operator in Listing 8-21, but the use of the explicit keyword changes the way that it is used. The following statements demonstrate this:

```
using System;
```

```
class Listing_22_Test {

    static void Main(string[] args) {

        // create a new product
        Product p1 = new Product() {
            Name = "oranges",
            ItemsInStock = 10,
            PricePerItem = 20
        };

        // assign the product to an int variable
        int i = (int)p1;

        // print out the local variable
        Console.WriteLine("Int result: {0}", i);

        // wait for input before exiting
        Console.WriteLine("Press enter to finish");
        Console.ReadLine();
    }
}
```

This time, when assigning the Product object to a local variable of the target type (an int in this example), I need to perform a cast operation, as shown in bold.

Implicit conversions are usually used when all of the significant data contained in one type can be captured in the other so that it doesn't matter if an object is inadvertently converted. Explicit conversions are usually used when there is some loss of data; requiring an explicit cast operation is intended to make the programmer think about the impact of the conversion process.

Summary

In this chapter, we explored the flexible property, indexer, and custom operator features to look at the different ways they can be used. If you have come to C# from a language that doesn't have an equivalent to these features, you might be asking, why not just use methods? You can certainly do that, but these are powerful and expressive convenience features that reduce code clutter and make working with C# objects more natural. You can certainly write C# programs without using properties, indexers, and operators, but I suggest you keep them in mind. They tend to grow on you as you begin to use them.

CHAPTER 9

■ ■ ■

Methods

A method is a member that implements an action that can be performed by an object. In this chapter, we will explore C# methods and see how they form the essential core of a C# program. In short, without methods, there could be no C# programs, and understanding how to define and use methods is essential to becoming an effective and productive C# programmer.

This chapter is relatively long because methods are such an important topic and there are many language features that relate to their use. To make it easier to understand methods, I start with a quick tour of the basic features and then dig down into the detail of each. Toward the end of the chapter, I describe some special kinds of method, the most important of which is the constructor. You will use some of these special method types in every program you create, so an understanding of what they are and how they work can be very important.

There are a lot of examples in this chapter, and you may want to download the source code that accompanies this book so that you don't have to type them all in. The source code is available for free at Apress.com. Table 9-1 provides the summary for this chapter.

Table 9-1. Quick Problem/Solution Reference for Chapter 9

Problem	Solution	Listings
Create and use a simple method.	Follow the pattern illustrated in Figure 9-1.	9-1 through 9-8
Pass data in and out of a method.	Use value, reference, or output parameters.	9-9 through 9-14
Process an unknown number of method parameters.	Use a parameter array.	9-15, 9-16
Provide default values for parameters.	Use optional parameters.	9-17, 9-18
Provide parameter values in a different order to which they were defined.	Use named parameters.	9-19
Temporarily store values and references in a method.	Define and use local variables.	9-20 through 9-22

Problem	Solution	Listings
Return a result from a method.	Use the `return` keyword.	9-23
Create a method which belongs to the class instead of an object.	Use the `static` keyword.	9-24
Create a method that can be overridden in a derived class.	Use the `virtual` keyword.	9-25
Create a method that cannot be overridden in a derived class	Omit the `virtual` keyword or use the `sealed` keyword.	9-26, 9-36
Create a method that must be implemented in a derived class.	Use the `abstract` keyword.	9-27, 9-61 through 9-63
Create different versions of the same method in a class.	Overload a method.	9-28, 9-29
Implement a new version of a method from a base class in a derived class.	Use the `override` or `new` keyword.	9-30 through 9-35, 9-37
Define the entry point for a program.	Implement a `Main` method.	9-38 through 9-40
Differentiate an object as it is created.	Implement a constructor.	9-41 through 9-47
Call a base class constructor.	Use the `base` keyword.	9-48, 9-49
Restrict access to a constructor.	Apply an access modifier.	9-50
Create an object by copying another object of the same type.	Implement a copy constructor.	9-51, 9-52
Initialize static members of a class.	Implement a static constructor.	9-53
Control the construction of objects.	Implement a factory method.	9-54
Enable enumeration of object data.	Use an iterator block.	9-55 through 9-59

Problem	Solution	Listings
Split methods across multiple class definitions.	Use partial methods.	9-60, 9-61
Extend the functionality of a class without modifying it.	Create an extension method.	9-64 through 9-66

Creating and Using a Simple Method

The best place to start with methods is to see an example. Listing 9-1 shows a class that has one method. This method computes the product of two integer values.

Listing 9-1. A Class with a Simple Method

```
class MyClass {

    public int CalculateProduct(int num1, int num2) {
        // compute the product
        return num1 * num2;
    }
}
```

There are a lot of parts to a method, even for one as simple as this. For the first part of this chapter, we'll take apart the method in Listing 9-1 and look at each part in turn. Figure 9-1 shows the five parts that make up the example method.

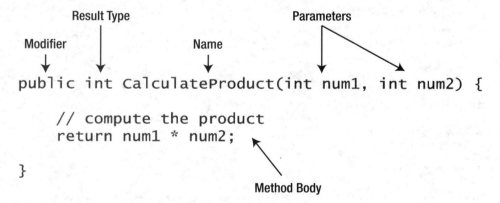

Figure 9-1. The anatomy of a simple method

Each of the following sections describes one part of the method, and then we turn our attention to how to use the method now that we know how the pieces fit together. The rest of the chapter covers different kinds of methods and the ways in which you can tailor the way your method works and is used.

Defining the Method Name

The first thing to decide when you are creating a new method is what to call it. You should pick a name that makes it clear what the method does. Bear in mind that other developers may not know what cryptic names mean when they come to use your class. In general, method names should be verbs or phrases that relate to verbs, for example Add, CopyTo, and Convert. The convention for C# methods is to use Pascal case, meaning that one or more words are combined together and each, including the first, is capitalized; you can see this convention in the name of the example method, CalculateProduct.

Each method in a class must have a unique *signature*, which is the combination of the method name and the types and order of the parameters. You can have several methods that have the same name if the parameters are different. This is called *overloading a method* and is discussed in the "Overloading Methods" section later in this chapter.

Defining the Result Type

Methods perform a calculation or action, and this often generates a result. The result for the method in Listing 9-1 is the product of two integers, which is itself an integer. When defining a method, you must specify the result type; in this case, it is int. A method is said to *return* the type of the result, so, for example, we would say that the method in Listing 9-1 returns an int. You can return any type from a method, including custom types you have created yourself. Listing 9-2 contains a method that returns a custom type.

Listing 9-2. Returning a Custom Type

```
class ProductResult {
    public int FirstParam { get; set; }
    public int SecondParam { get; set; }
    public int Result { get; set; }
}

class MyClass {

    public ProductResult CalculateProduct(int num1, int num2) {
        // compute the product
        return new ProductResult() {
            FirstParam = num1,
            SecondParam = num2,
            Result = num1 * num2
        };
    }
}
```

Listing 9-2 contains a custom type named ProductResult, which represents the result of integer multiplication. It contains three properties—one for each of the two numbers that were multiplied and one for the result of the multiplication. You can find out more about properties, including the automatically implemented kind used here in Chapter 8. The `CalculateProduct` method in `MyClass` returns an instance of `ProductResult`. I have highlighted the return type for the method in bold.

■ **Note** Methods that return a result must use the `return` keyword; see the "Defining the Method Body" section for more information.

You don't have to return a result from your method. You can use the void keyword in place of a return type to indicate that your method doesn't return a result. Listing 9-3 contains an example of a method that doesn't return a value.

Listing 9-3. Using the void Keyword

```
class MyClass {

    public void CalculateProduct(int num1, int num2) {
        // compute the product and print the result
        System.Console.WriteLine("Product: {0}", num1 * num2);
    }
}
```

The method in Listing 9-3 computes the product of two integers and then uses the `Console` class to write out the result. The method doesn't return a result, so the void keyword has been used. You don't need to use the return keyword if your method doesn't return a result, but doing so allows us to terminate the execution of a method early.

Defining the Parameters

The *parameters*, also known as the *arguments*, allow the caller of your method to supply objects or values for processing by your method. In the case of the method in Listing 9-1, the parameters are the two int values that are to be multiplied together. Each parameter is given a name unique to that method. For the example, I used `num1` and `num2`. You can use any name for your parameters, but the convention is to use descriptive names to make using your method simpler. C# parameters names use *camel case*, where the first letter of the name is lowercase, but the first letters of any subsequent words are uppercase, for example, `firstNumber`. Parameters are a common cause of confusion for programmers new to C#. There are a lot of different options and features available; see the "Understanding Parameters" section later in this chapter for more information.

Methods are not required to have parameters. You can omit them entirely if your method doesn't need to receive objects to process. Listing 9-4 contains a method that doesn't have any parameters.

Listing 9-4. A Method Without Parameters

```
class MyClass {

    public void PrintMessage() {
        // print a message
```

```
        System.Console.WriteLine("Hello World");
    }
}
```

Defining the Modifiers

You can use a number of modifier keywords in a method definition to change the behavior. The modifier that you will use most frequently is an *access modifier*, which determines how your method can be used. Table 9-2 lists the access modifiers for methods. For information on the other kinds of modifier available, see the "Using Method Modifiers" section later in the chapter.

Table 9-2. Access Modifiers for Methods

Access Modifier	Description
public	The method can be accessed anywhere.
protected	The method can be accessed only by the containing class or derived classes.
internal	The method can accessed by any member of the current assembly, but not other assemblies.
protected internal	The method can be accessed by any member in the current assembly or any class in any assembly that derives from the containing class.
private	The member can be accessed only by the containing class.

Access modifiers take on a special importance in methods because they are the most common way to expose functionality from your class for other types to use. If you make a change to any part of your method, you run the risk of breaking all of the types that depended on the original version, and you won't always have access to the code that needs to be fixed. Careful thought about which methods you want anyone to use, which methods you want subclasses to use, and which should not be used outside of your class can save a lot of trouble later.

The default access level for a method is private, meaning that not using one of the access modifier keywords when you define a method is the same as using the private modifier. One of the most common reasons for using private or protected methods is to avoid having to repeat the same code in several methods that you don't want to be accessible to other types. Listing 9-5 shows a class that has methods repeating the same code.

Listing 9-5. A Class with Repeating Code in Methods

```
using System;

class MyClass {

    public int CalculateProduct(int num1, int num2) {
        // check that the parameters are valid
```

```
            if (num1 > 0 && num1 < 100 && num2 > 0 && num2 < 100) {
                // number is valid - perform calculation
                return num1 * num2;
            } else {
                // throw an exception - the arguments are not valid
                throw new ArgumentOutOfRangeException();
            }
        }

        public int CalculateSum(int num1, int num2) {
            // check that the parameters are valid
            if (num1 > 0 && num1 < 100 && num2 > 0 && num2 < 100) {
                // number is valid - perform calculation
                return num1 + num2;
            } else {
                // throw an exception - the arguments are not valid
                throw new ArgumentOutOfRangeException();
            }
        }

        public double CalculateRatio(int num1, int num2) {
            // check that the parameters are valid
            if (num1 > 0 && num1 < 100 && num2 > 0 && num2 < 100) {
                // number is valid - perform calculation
                return num1 / num2;
            } else {
                // throw an exception - the arguments are not valid
                throw new ArgumentOutOfRangeException();
            }
        }
    }
```

The class in Listing 9-5 contains three methods, each of which calculates a result from two `int` arguments. We want to make sure that the argument values are within a certain range, so each method performs a range check and throws an exception if they are not. (Exceptions are the C# way of handling errors; you can find more details in Chapter 14.) This kind of code duplication in Listing 9-5 is a maintenance risk. If the acceptable range needs to be altered, I have to make three sets of changes—one for each method. I may forget to change one or make an incorrect change. We can address this by moving the range validation into a private or protected method, as shown by Listing 9-6.

Listing 9-6. Consolidating the Range Validation Logic

```
using System;

class MyClass {

    public int CalculateProduct(int num1, int num2) {
        // check that the parameters are valid
        if (CheckRange(num1, num2)) {
            // number is valid - perform calculation
            return num1 * num2;
```

```
            } else {
                // throw an exception - the arguments are not valid
                throw new ArgumentOutOfRangeException();
            }
        }

        public int CalculateSum(int num1, int num2) {
            // check that the parameters are valid
            if (CheckRange(num1, num2)) {
                // number is valid - perform calculation
                return num1 + num2;
            } else {
                // throw an exception - the arguments are not valid
                throw new ArgumentOutOfRangeException();
            }
        }

        public double CalculateRatio(int num1, int num2) {
            // check that the parameters are valid
            if (CheckRange(num1, num2)) {
                // number is valid - perform calculation
                return num1 / num2;
            } else {
                // throw an exception - the arguments are not valid
                throw new ArgumentOutOfRangeException();
            }
        }

        private bool CheckRange(int num1, int num2) {
            return num1 > 0 && num1 < 100 && num2 > 0 && num2 < 100;
        }
}
```

The class in Listing 9-6 contains a private method called CheckRange, which is called by the other methods. Since this a private method, no other type can use the CheckRange functionality, meaning that I can make changes without breaking other code that depends on MyClass. We can go further and include the exception into the CheckRange method to further reduce duplication, as shown in Listing 9-7.

Listing 9-7. Combining Validation and Exception Generation in a private Method

```
using System;

class MyClass {

    public int CalculateProduct(int num1, int num2) {
        // check that the parameters are valid
        CheckRange(num1, num2);

        // perform calculation
        return num1 * num2;
    }
```

```
public int CalculateSum(int num1, int num2) {
    // check that the parameters are valid
    CheckRange(num1, num2);

    // perform calculation
    return num1 + num2;
}

public double CalculateRatio(int num1, int num2) {
    // check that the parameters are valid
    CheckRange(num1, num2);

    // perform calculation
    return num1 / num2;
}

private void CheckRange(int num1, int num2) {
    if (!(num1 > 0 && num1 < 100 && num2 > 0 && num2 < 100)) {
        throw new ArgumentOutOfRangeException();
    }
}
}
```

Now we have the range validation and the exception generation in a single `private` method, allowing us to make changes in one place and affect all the `public` methods. For more information about the `protected` keyword, see the "Hiding and Overriding Methods" section later in the chapter. For information on the other kinds of modifier available, see the "Using Method Modifiers" section later in the chapter.

Defining the Method Body

The statements in a method body are responsible for taking any arguments that have been provided, performing the action described by the method name, producing the method result, and updating the state of your object along the way. The body of a method consists of zero or more code statements.

CONVENTION: DOING WHAT THE METHOD NAME SUGGESTS

A powerful convention is that method bodies do what is implied by the method name. If you have a method called `CalculateProduct`, programmers using your class are going to expect that the method result is the product of the method parameters. If the method does nothing or produces a result that has nothing to do with calculating the product, then you are going to cause problems and confusion.

If a method doesn't return a result (that is, it is defined using the `void` keyword), then the simplest method is one that has no parameters, no modifiers, and no code statements, like this:

```
void MyMethod() {
}
```

If a method does return a result, then the simplest method requires one code statement, which must use the return keyword with an instance of the specified result type or a statement that produces an instance of the result type, such as the following:

```
int MyMethod() {
    return 2+2;
}
```

These are the simplest methods possible, and, of course, they are not especially useful. You can see some more realistic examples of method bodies when we dig into the detail in the "Understanding Method Bodies" section, later in the chapter.

Using the Methods

Having defined a set of methods in Listing 9-7, we can begin to use them. First, we need to create a new instance of the type that contains the methods we want to use and assign it a name, like this:

```
MyClass mc = new MyClass();
```

This statement creates a new instance of MyClass with the name mc. We then use one of the methods, known as *invoking* or *calling* the method, by using the dot operator (.) followed by the name of the method, like this:

```
mc.CalculateProduct(10, 50);
```

Following the method name, we have to provide the parameters. We do this by using the open parenthesis ((), the parameters separated by commas (,), and then the close parenthesis ()). Since this is a single statement, I have added a semicolon at the end. The previous statement calls the CalculateProduct method of the MyClass instance called mc, using parameters of 10 and 50. This is a request to multiply the values 10 and 50, and this method returns a result. We can assign the result to a local variable like this:

```
int result = mc.CalculateProduct(10, 50);
```

We'll look more at local variable in the "Understanding Method Bodies" section later in the chapter. In the previous statement, I specify the parameters using the numeric literals feature, which is discussed in Chapter 5. Listing 9-8 demonstrates using the methods we defined in Listing 9-7.

Listing 9-8. Using Methods

```
class Listing_08 {

    static void Main(string[] args) {

        // create a new instance of my class
        MyClass mc = new MyClass();

        // call the methods in the MyClass instance
        int result1 = mc.CalculateProduct(10, 50);
```

```
        int result2 = mc.CalculateSum(10, 50);
        int result3 = mc.CalculateProduct(10, 50);

        // print out the results
        Console.WriteLine("Product: {0}", result1);
        Console.WriteLine("Sum: {0}", result2);
        Console.WriteLine("Ratio: {0}", result3);

        // wait for input before exiting
        Console.WriteLine("Press enter to finish");
        Console.ReadLine();
    }
}
```

Ignore the method called Main for the moment. This is a special method that I explain in the "Special Methods" section later in the chapter. Focus instead on the statements in bold, which demonstrate using the methods we created in context. After creating a new instance of MyClass, I call each of the three public methods in turn, the result of which I assign to a local variable. When I have made all the calls, I print out the results. Compiling and running the code in Listing 9-8 produces the following results:

```
Product: 500
Sum: 60
Ratio: 500
Press enter to finish
```

There are a couple of points to note about this example. First, I am unable to call the CheckRange method from the Listing_08 class because we used the private access modifier. Second, I didn't check to see whether any of the methods threw exceptions to indicate errors, which they would have done had I specified values outside the expected range. I did this to keep the example simple, and you can find full details of exceptions and how to detect and deal with them in Chapter 14.

Understanding Parameters

Parameters allow the caller of your method to provide data to assist in the calculation or action that you undertake. In the examples in the previous section, the parameters were the numeric values to be used in the computation that each method provided. The significance of a parameter is up to you. You can use them in any way that makes sense in your program. In this section, I'll show you how C# parameters work and how you can use different parameter features.

Using Value Parameters

You define the parameters you want your method to have by specifying the type of the parameter and the identifier you want to assign to it. If your method has more than one parameter, then they should be separated by commas (,). Parameters can be of any type you choose, and parameter identifiers must be unique for that parameter. Each parameter in a method must have a different name, but different methods can have parameters of the same name. You can see where parameters should be placed in a method in Figure 9-1. Listing 9-9 shows a simple example.

Listing 9-9. A Simple Method with Three Parameters

```
using System;

class MyData {
    // ...class members ...
}

class MyClass {

    public void MyMethod(MyData md, int count, bool enableOption) {
        // method body goes here
    }
}
```

The `MyClass.MyMethod` method has three parameters. The first is a custom reference type that is defined in the example. The second and third are value types—an `int` and a `bool`, respectively. Table 9-3 summarizes the types and identifiers of these three parameters.

Table 9-3. The MyMethod Parameters from Listing 9-9

Parameter Type	Parameter Identifier
MyData	md
Int	count
Bool	enableOption

In the method body, you can refer to the parameters using the names you have assigned them. For example, to print out the value of the `int` parameter with the identifier of count, we might do this:

```
public void MyMethod(MyData md, int count, bool enableoption) {
    Console.WriteLine("Int value: {0}", count);
}
```

In the following sections, I'll cover the modifiers you can apply to parameters. Parameters without modifiers, like the ones in Listing 9-9, are called *value parameters*. If a value parameter is a value type, then a new copy is created. If a value parameter is of a reference type, then a new reference is created. The terminology here is confusing, but it is vitally important that you get a grasp of this. A value parameter can be a value type or reference type (the word *value* is being used to describe two different characteristics). The first is the kind of type, and the second is the kind of parameters, which is unrelated to the kind of type. This is best explained with an example, contained in Listing 9-10.

Listing 9-10. Understanding Value Parameters

```
using System;

class Person {
```

```
    public Person(string name) {
        Name = name;
    }

    public string Name { get; set; }
}

class MyClass {

    public void MyMethod(Person employee, int count) {
        // print out the values of the parameters
        Console.WriteLine("MyMethod - parameter values: {0}, {1}",
            employee.Name, count);

        // modify the parameters
        employee = new Person("Joe Smith");
        count = 20;

        // print out the values again
        Console.WriteLine("MyMethod - modified parameter values: {0}, {1}",
            employee.Name, count);
    }
}

class Listing_10 {

    static void Main(string[] args) {

        // define local variables to use as parameters
        Person myperson = new Person("John Doe");
        int mycount = 10;

        // print out the values of the variables
        Console.WriteLine("Main Method - variable values before: {0}, {1}",
            myperson.Name, mycount);

        // create a new instance of MyClass and call the method
        MyClass mc = new MyClass();
        mc.MyMethod(myperson, mycount);

        // print out the value of the variables again
        Console.WriteLine("Main Method - variable values after: {0}, {1}",
            myperson.Name, mycount);

        // wait for input before exiting
        Console.WriteLine("Press enter to finish");
        Console.ReadLine();
    }
}
```

In this example, the class MyClass contains a method called MyMethod. This method has two value parameters, a custom reference type Person and a value type int. In the Main method of the Listing_10 class, I create a Person instance and an int and pass as parameters to MyMethod. In MyMethod, I assign a new instance of Person to the employee parameter and a new value to the count parameter. As all of this happens, I print out the Name property from the Person type and the value of the int. Compiling and running the code in Listing 9-10 produces the following results:

```
Main Method - variable values before: John Doe, 10
MyMethod - parameter values: John Doe, 10
MyMethod - modified parameter values: Joe Smith, 20
Main Method - variable values after: John Doe, 10
Press enter to finish
```

Let's deal with the value type first, the int. When a value type is used as a value parameter, a new instance of the type is made that is entirely independent of the original. When I assigned a new value to the int parameter in MyMethod, the value was assigned to the new copy, and it left the original unchanged. This is why the value in the Main method was 10 before and after I called MyMethod, even though I set the parameter to 20 inside the method.

When a reference type is used as a value parameter, a new reference to the object is created. When I assigned a new instance of Person to the parameter, I was changing the object that the new reference pointed at. This did not change the original reference, which still pointed at the instance of Person I created before calling the method. Nor did it do anything to change the Person object that existed before the method was called. I created a whole new instance of Person and assigned it to the parameter.

Even though a new reference is created, it still points to the same object as the original reference, meaning that you can use the parameter to change the object and those changes persist after the method has been called. Listing 9-11 contains an example.

Listing 9-11. Using a Value Parameter to Modify a Reference Type

```
class MyClass {

    public void MyMethod(Person employee, int count) {
        // print out the values of the parameters
        Console.WriteLine("MyMethod - parameter values: {0}, {1}",
            employee.Name, count);

        // modify the parameters
        employee.Name = "Joe Smith";
        count = 20;

        // print out the values again
        Console.WriteLine("MyMethod - modified parameter values: {0}, {1}",
            employee.Name, count);
    }
}

class Listing_11 {

    static void Main(string[] args) {
```

```
        // define local variables to use as parameters
        Person myperson = new Person("John Doe");
        int mycount = 10;

        // print out the values of the variables
        Console.WriteLine("Main Method - variable values before: {0}, {1}",
            myperson.Name, mycount);

        // create a new instance of MyClass and call the method
        MyClass mc = new MyClass();
        mc.MyMethod(myperson, mycount);

        // print out the value of the variables again
        Console.WriteLine("Main Method - variable values after: {0}, {1}",
            myperson.Name, mycount);

        // wait for input before exiting
        Console.WriteLine("Press enter to finish");
        Console.ReadLine();
    }
}
```

This example contains one change, which is shown in bold. Rather than assign a new object to the value parameter reference, I used the reference to change the value of the Name property in the Person object it points to. Because the employee parameter in the MyMethod method and the myperson variable in the Listing_11.Main method both point to the same Person object, the change I make to the Name property in the method is reflected when I print out the value of the same property after the method has been called. Compiling and running the code in Listing 9-11 produces the following results:

```
Main Method - variable values before: John Doe, 10
MyMethod - parameter values: John Doe, 10
MyMethod - modified parameter values: Joe Smith, 20
Main Method - variable values after: Joe Smith, 10
Press enter to finish
```

I recommend that you spend some time working through this behavior by defining methods with value parameters that are value types and reference types and understanding the effect that modifying them has. A lot of programmers new to C# or object programming in general struggle with the behavior of parameters . You might find that reading the following section about reference parameters helps put things in context.

Using Reference Parameters

When you apply the ref modifier to a parameter, you create a reference parameter. Unlike a value parameter, a reference parameter doesn't create new a new copy of a value or object reference. Making a change to the parameter also changes the original type. Listing 9-12 contains a demonstration.

Listing 9-12. Using Reference Parameters

```
using System;

class Person {

    public Person(string name) {
        Name = name;
    }

    public string Name { get; set; }
}

class MyClass {

    public void MyMethod(ref Person employee, ref int count) {
        // print out the values of the parameters
        Console.WriteLine("MyMethod - parameter values: {0}, {1}",
            employee.Name, count);

        // modify the parameters
        employee = new Person("Joe Smith");
        count = 20;

        // print out the values again
        Console.WriteLine("MyMethod - modified parameter values: {0}, {1}",
            employee.Name, count);
    }
}

class Listing_12 {

    static void Main(string[] args) {

        // define local variables to use as parameters
        Person myperson = new Person("John Doe");
        int mycount = 10;

        // print out the values of the variables
        Console.WriteLine("Main Method - variable values before: {0}, {1}",
            myperson.Name, mycount);

        // create a new instance of MyClass and call the method
        MyClass mc = new MyClass();
        mc.MyMethod(ref myperson, ref mycount);

        // print out the value of the variables again
        Console.WriteLine("Main Method - variable values after: {0}, {1}",
            myperson.Name, mycount);

        // wait for input before exiting
```

```
        Console.WriteLine("Press enter to finish");
        Console.ReadLine();
    }
}
```

In this example, I have used the ref modifier to make both parameters of the MyMethod method reference parameters, like this:

```
public void MyMethod(ref Person employee, ref int count) {
```

You can mix and match reference and value parameters in the same method. I have made both parameters into reference parameters to contrast against the results from the examples in the previous section.

You must also use the ref modifier when calling a method that has reference parameters, like this:

```
mc.MyMethod(ref myperson, ref mycount);
```

Compiling and running the code in Listing 9-12 produces the following results:

```
Main Method - variable values before: John Doe, 10
MyMethod - parameter values: John Doe, 10
MyMethod - modified parameter values: Joe Smith, 20
Main Method - variable values after: Joe Smith, 20
Press enter to finish
```

You can see from the results that the changes made in the MyMethod method have affected the local variables passed as reference parameters from the Main method. If you have been struggling to follow the difference between reference types, reference parameters, value types, and value parameters, comparing the results from Listing 9-12 to the results from Listings 9-10 and 9-11 may help put things in context.

Using Output Parameters

Output parameters are used to return multiple results from a method and are created with the out modifier. Variables don't need to be initialized before they are used as output parameters, but output parameters need to be initialized before the method returns. The most common use of output parameters in C# is with the TryXXX pattern. Imagine that we have class that contains a method that can throw an exception, like this one:

```
class Calculator {

    public int PerformCalculation(int x, int y) {
        if (x > 10 || y > 10) {
            throw new ArgumentOutOfRangeException();
        } else {
            return x * 10;
        }
    }
}
```

When we call the `PerformCalculation` method, we have to be careful to catch and handle the exception that will be thrown if the parameter is out of range. As a convenience, we can use the TryXXX pattern to create an additional method that acts as a wrapper around `PerformCalculation` and takes care of the exception for us, using the method result to tell us whether the calculation succeeded and an output parameter to give us the result. Listing 9-13 demonstrates how this can be done.

Listing 9-13. Using an Output Parameters as Part of the TryXXX Pattern

```
class Calculator {

    public int PerformCalculation(int x, int y) {
        if (x > 10 || y > 10) {
            throw new ArgumentOutOfRangeException();
        } else {
            return x * 10;
        }
    }

    public bool TryPerformCalculation(int x, int y, out int result) {
        try {
            result = PerformCalculation(x, y);
            return true;
        } catch (ArgumentOutOfRangeException) {
            result = -1;
            return false;
        }
    }
}
```

The naming convention for this kind of method is to prepend the word Try to the name of the method that it mediates access to. In this example, since the original method is called `PerformCalculation`, the additional method is called `TryPerformCalculation`.

You can see that the `TryPerformCalculation` method has an additional parameter that has been modified with the out keyword, indicating that this is an output parameter. The method body uses a try statement to call the `PerformCalculation` method, assigns the result to the output parameter, and returns true. If the `PerformCalculation` method throws an exception, the catch clause of the try statement sets the value of the output parameter to -1 and return false. (Exceptions, try statements, and catch clauses are all covered in Chapter 14.)

So, if the `TryPerformCalculation` method returns true, we know that the underlying calculation was performed without a problem and that the output parameter contains the result. If the `TryPerformCalculation` method returns false, we know that the calculation didn't succeed, and we should ignore the value of the output parameter. Listing 9-14 shows the `TryPerformCalculation` method in use.

Listing 9-14. Calling a TryXXX Method

```
class Listing_14 {

    static void Main(string[] args) {

        // create a new instance of Calculator
```

```
    Calculator calc = new Calculator();

    // use the perform calc method directly
    int result = calc.PerformCalculation(5, 5);
    Console.WriteLine("Direct result: {0}", result);

    // use the tryXXX method
    int result2;
    bool success = calc.TryPerformCalculation(5, 5, out result2);
    Console.WriteLine("TryXXX first result: {0}, {1}", success, result2);

    success = calc.TryPerformCalculation(20, 5, out result2);
    Console.WriteLine("TryXXX second result: {0}, {1}", success, result2);

    // wait for input before exiting
    Console.WriteLine("Press enter to finish");
    Console.ReadLine();
  }
}
```

The code in Listing 9-14 creates a new instance of the Calculator class and first calls the PerformCalculation method directly. Our TryXXX method doesn't replace the original but is available alongside as an optional convenience. I then call the TryPerformCalculation method, once with parameter values that will produce a good result and then again with parameters that will cause the PerformCalculation method to throw an exception. When calling a method that has an output parameter, you must use the out keyword before the parameter value, as shown in bold. If you do not, the C# compiler will report an error. This is to avoid inadvertently allowing a method to change the value of a variable via an output parameter. Compiling and running the code in Listings 9-13 and 9-14 produces the following result:

```
Direct result: 50
TryXXX first result: True, 50
TryXXX second result: False, -1
Press enter to finish
```

Using Parameter Arrays

Parameter arrays are a convenient feature that lets you create methods that can be called with different numbers of arguments without the caller having to use arrays or collection classes. (Arrays are discussed in Chapter 13 and collections in Chapter 19.) You can have only one parameter array in a method, and it must be the last parameter. Listing 9-15 contains an example.

Listing 9-15. Creating a Parameter Array with the params Modifier

```
class Calculator {

    public int CalculateSum(params int[] numbers) {
        int result = 0;
        foreach (int i in numbers) {
```

```
            result += i;
        }
        return result;
    }
}
```

You create a parameter array by using the params modifier, as shown in bold. You can apply the params keyword only to parameters that are arrays. In the method body, you treat the parameter as you would any other value parameter that is an array. In the example, I enumerate the contents of the array and add each value to a running total, which I then return as the result.

The effect of the params keyword comes when you use the method. Listing 9-16 shows how this is done.

Listing 9-16. Using a Parameter Array

```
class Listing_16 {

    static void Main(string[] args) {

        // create a new instance of Calculator
        Calculator calc = new Calculator();

        // create an array of int values and pass them
        // as a parameter to the CalculateSum method
        int[] data = { 10, 34, 54, 124, 23 };
        int result = calc.CalculateSum(data);
        Console.WriteLine("First result: {0}", result);

        // call the CalculateSum method with one argument
        result = calc.CalculateSum(10);
        Console.WriteLine("Second result: {0}", result);

        // call with two arguments
        result = calc.CalculateSum(10, 34);
        Console.WriteLine("Third result: {0}", result);

        // call with the same values that were in the array
        result = calc.CalculateSum(10, 34, 54, 124, 23);
        Console.WriteLine("Fourth result: {0}", result);

        // wait for input before exiting
        Console.WriteLine("Press enter to finish");
        Console.ReadLine();
    }
}
```

You can treat a parameter array just like a regular array, and that is what I have done first of all in Listing 9-16—defined an array of int values and then passed the array as a parameter to the CalculateSum method.

But you can also provide an arbitrary number of parameters, which you can see I have done for one, two, and five int values. C# takes care of packaging up the int values into an array for me, making my method easier to use. Compiling and running the code in Listing 9-16 produces the following results:

```
First result: 245
Second result: 10
Third result: 44
Fourth result: 245
Press enter to finish
```

Using Optional Parameters

A common technique in C# and similar programming languages is to define a series of methods, where each provides some default parameters for the next. Listing 9-17 contains an example.

Listing 9-17. Related Methods with Default Parameter Values

```
class Calculator {

    public int PerformCalculation(int x, int y, int divisor) {
        return (x * y) / divisor;
    }

    public int PerformCalculation(int x, int y) {
        return PerformCalculation(x, y, 2);
    }

    public int PerformCalculation(int x) {
        return PerformCalculation(x, 10);
    }
}
```

If you call the version of the method that has two arguments, then a default value is used for the divisor parameter. If you call the version that has only one parameter, then default values are used for the y and divisor parameters. This is a nice way of providing consistent default values, but it does tend to clutter up a class file with largely redundant method definitions. You can get the same effect without the clutter using the optional parameters feature. Listing 9-18 contains an example.

Listing 9-18. Using an Optional Parameter

```
class Calculator {

    public int PerformCalculation(int x, int y = 10, int divisor = 2) {
        return (x * y) / divisor;
    }
}
```

To make a parameter optional, you provide a default value for the parameter. You can see in Listing 9-17 that I have provided a default value for y of 10 and for divisor of 2. Optional parameters must appear after any mandatory parameters. The mandatory parameter in Listing 9-17 is the int called x. When using the method, you can elect to provide values for optional parameters or to rely on the defaults, like this:

```
// call the method with three arguments
int result1 = calc.PerformCalculation(5, 10, 2);
// call the method with two arguments
int result2 = calc.PerformCalculation(5, 10);
// call the method with one argument
int result3 = calc.PerformCalculation(5);
```

Using Named Parameters

The named parameter feature allows you provide arguments to a method out of the order in which they have been specified. Listing 9-19 contains an example.

Listing 9-19. Using Named Parameters

```
using System;

class Calculator {

    public int PerformCalculation(int x, int y = 10, int divisor = 2) {
        return (x * y) / divisor;
    }
}

class Listing_19 {

    static void Main(string[] args) {

        // create a new instance of Calculator
        Calculator calc = new Calculator();

        int result = calc.PerformCalculation(y: 10, x: 120, divisor: 5);
        Console.WriteLine("Result: {0}", result);

        // wait for input before exiting
        Console.WriteLine("Press enter to finish");
        Console.ReadLine();
    }
}
```

The important part of this example is the call to the PerformCalculation method from the Listing_19.Main method. In this statement, I have changed the order in which I supply the parameter values by using the parameter name, followed by a colon (:), followed by the value I want to pass as a parameter. This may seem like a very odd thing to do, but it becomes quite useful when combined with optional parameters. In the Calculator class in Listing 9-19, the PerformCalculation method has two optional parameters, y and divisor. If I want to provide a value x and y and rely on the default for divisor, I can just make a call like the ones we saw in the previous section:

```
int result = calc.PerformCalculation(5, 10);
```

But what do I do if I want to provide a value for x and divisor but not y? Well, I use a named parameter, like this:

```
int result = calc.PerformCalculation(120, divisor: 5);
```

Notice that I am able to mix regular and named parameters in a single method call. The value I have passed to x is 120, the value to divisor is 5, and I have relied on the default value for the optional parameter y.

Understanding Method Bodies

Method bodies are where the logic that makes your program work reside—a collection of code statements that perform some kind of task that moves the execution of your program forward by performing a calculation or undertaking an action of some kind. If this sounds vague, it is because the details are unique to each program. As long as you use properly formed C# code statements, you can have your method bodies do just about anything, including the following:

- Read and modify parameter values

- Read and modify object fields and properties

- Return a result value

- Create, read, and modify local variables

- Call methods within the same object

- Call methods within other objects

- Throw exceptions

In fact, much of this book is filled with examples of things you can do in method bodies, such as creating user interfaces, opening network connections, querying data, and so on. In the following sections, I'll cover the things you can do that relate to methods and objects in a general sense so that when we come to the more specific topics (databases, networks, interfaces, and so on), the examples will make more sense.

Using Local Variables

You can create variables inside of methods and assign values or references to them. These variables are limited in scope to the method body, although you can pass them as parameters to other methods. Listing 9-20 contains a simple example.

Listing 9-20. Defining a Local Variable

```
class Calculator {

    public int PerformCalculation(int x, int y) {

        // create a local variable
        int product = x * y;

        // return the local variable
        return product;
    }
}
```

The local variable in Listing 9-20 is shown in bold. You can see that defining a local variable is similar to defining a field, which we covered in Chapter 7, and in fact, when you define a field or local variable, you are creating a new storage location to which you assign a value or a reference. You can define a local variable and assign a value, as I did in Listing 9-20. Or you can define the variable in one statement and assign a value in another, like this:

```
int product;
product = x * y;
```

You can assign new values to a variable (which is why they are called *variables*; the value or reference they represent can change), like this:

```
int product;
product = x * y;
product = 100;
```

Local variables can be used of any type, such as the value types I have demonstrated so far, or reference types, such as string, and you can have many local variables in a single method:

```
public int PerformCalculation(int x, int y) {

    // create a local variable
    int product = x * y;

    // create another local variable
    string str = "Hello World";

    // return the local variable
    return product;
}
```

You can assign parameters to local variables and use the new keyword to create new objects and assign a reference to a local variable:

```
class Calculator {
```

```
public int PerformCalculation(int x, int y) {

    // create a local variable
    int product = x * y;

    // create a local variable of the current type
    Calculator calc = new Calculator();

    // create a local variable and assign the
    // value of one of the parameters
    int localVar = x;

    // return the local variable
    return product;
    }
}
```

And, of course, you can create a local variable and assign it the value of another local variable or a field or property from the enclosing object:

```
class Calculator {
    private int myField = 20;

    public int PerformCalculation(int x, int y) {

        // create a local variable
        int product = x * y;

        // create a new variable and assign it
        // the value of the product variable
        int localVar = product;

        // assign the value of the field to the variable
        localVar = myField;

        // return the local variable
        return product;
        }
}
```

The list of things that you can do with a local variable just goes on and on. Once you have defined a local variable, you can assign it any value or reference of the correct type, either by using a literal (such as the numeric literals discussed in Chapter 5), by using the result of any C# operator, or by using the result of any C# statement, such as a call to other methods.

Naming Variables

The naming convention for local variables is camel case, meaning the first letter is lowercase, multiple words are concatenated together, and the first letter of each subsequent word is uppercase, for example, myVariable.

You can't use a name that is already assigned to a parameter, but you can use a name that is already assigned to a field in the enclosing object. Listing 9-21 contains an example.

Listing 9-21. Hiding a Field with a Local Variable

```
class Calculator {
    private int divisor = 20;

    public int PerformCalculation(int x, int y) {

        // create a local variable with the same name
        // as used for the class field
        int divisor = 100;

        // perform a calculation and return the result
        return x * y / divisor;
    }
}
```

In Listing 9-21, the local variable divisor has the same name as a field. The variable is said to be *hiding* the field. When the last statement in the method refers to divisor, the value that will be used is the one from the local variable, not the field.

If you want to access the field, you use the this keyword, as follows:

```
return x * y / this.divisor;
```

The keyword this refers to the current object instance. It means "the instance of the object that contains this method." For example, to call a method that has a parameter of the type that contains the method you are writing, you can use this as the parameter value, like this:

```
class Calculator {
    public int PerformCalculation(int x, int y) {

        // create a local variable with the same name
        // as used for the class field
        int divisor = 100;

        ManageCalculator(this);

        // perform a calculation and return the result
        return x * y / divisor;
    }

    public void ManageCalculator(Calculator calc) {
        // ... method body
    }
}
```

The .NET runtime interprets the this keyword to mean the object on which the current method has been called. The ManageCalculator method takes a Calculator object as a parameter. The PerformCalculation method calls the ManageCalculator method, using this to refer to the current instance of Calculator.

Understanding Variable Scope and Lifetime

Local variables can be used only within the code block that defines them. They are not accessible to other methods within the same class or to other classes. When the last statement in the method has been executed, the local variables are destroyed.

For value types, this means that the value assigned to the local variable is also destroyed. For reference types, this means that the reference to the object is destroyed. The object that was referred to is *not* destroyed. There may be other references to it elsewhere in the program. If there are no other references, then the garbage collector will ultimately destroy the object; see Chapter 18 for details of garbage collection.

You can pass local variables as parameters to other methods. This may cause new references to objects and new values types to be created, but these are local to the method you are calling, the exceptions being reference and output parameters, which I discussed earlier in the chapter. But even then, if you have used local variables as reference or output parameters, then these will be destroyed when the runtime has finished executing the statements in the method.

Local variables that are defined inside a nested code block, for example, within a try statement, cannot be used in the outer code block. Listing 9-22 contains an example.

Listing 9-22. Defining Local Variables Inside of Nested Code Blocks

```
class Calculator {

    public void PerformCalculation(int x, int y) {

        try {
            int result = x * y;
        } catch (Exception) {
            // handle exception...
        }

        Console.WriteLine("Result: {0}", result);
    }
}
```

This example will not compile because the local variable result, defined in the nested code block of the try statement, is not available to be used as a parameter for the Console.WriteLine method call in the outer code block, the method body. You can address this by defining the variable in the outer block and assigning a value in the nested block, like this:

```
public void PerformCalculation(int x, int y) {

    int result = 0;

    try {
        result = x * y;
    } catch (Exception) {
        // handle exception...
    }

    Console.WriteLine("Result: {0}", result);
}
```

Alternatively, you can group all of the statements that use a local variable inside the same code block, like this:

```
public void PerformCalculation(int x, int y) {

    try {
        int result = x * y;
        Console.WriteLine("Result: {0}", result);
    } catch (Exception) {
        // handle exception...
    }
}
```

Using Method Results

Methods can return a result. The statement that called the method can assign this result as to a local variable, perform further operations on it, or pass it as a parameter to another method. Returning a result is a two-part process. First, you have to declare the type of the result in the method definition, as illustrated by Figure 9-1. Second, you return an instance of that type by using the return keyword in your method body. Listing 9-23 contains a demonstration.

Listing 9-23. Returning a Result from a Method

```
class Calculator {

    public int PerformCalculation(bool calcProduct, int x, int y) {

        if (calcProduct) {
            return x * y;
        } else {
            return x + y;
        }
    }
}
```

The Calculator class in Listing 9-23 contains a method called PerformCalaculation that returns an int value as its result. In the method body, the value of the calcProduct parameter is checked using an if statement. If the parameter value is true, the return keyword is used to return the result of the multiplication operator (*) on the two other parameters. If the calcProduct parameter value is false, then the return keyword is used to return the result of using the addition operator (+) on the two other parameters.

As soon as the runtime encounters the return keyword, no further statements in the method will be executed. (An exception to this is if the return keyword is used inside a try statement that has a finally clause, in which cause the statements in the clause will be executed; see Chapter 14 for details of try statements.)

As you can see in Listing 9-23, a method can have more than one return statement. If a method has defined a return type, then all the paths through the method body must return a result. If this is not the case, then the code will not compile. If the return type of a method is a reference type, then you can return the default value null, although this may cause an exception in the calling code if it is not expected.

You can use the void keyword in your method definition if you do not need to return a result. You can use output parameters to return more than one value from a method; see the "Using Output Parameters" section earlier in this chapter for details.

Understanding Method Modifiers

You can apply modifiers to methods to change the way that they behave or can be used. The following sections discuss the set of C# method modifiers.

Using Access Modifiers

The most commonly used modifiers for methods are the access modifiers, which control where your method can be called from. Several modifiers are available, and they allow you to restrict your method so that it can be called only from within the containing class and so they make it available to any other class and a few settings in between. We covered the access modifiers earlier in the chapter. You can see the list of modifiers described in Table 9-2 and some demonstrations of their use in Listings 5-7.

Creating Static Methods

Most of the methods in the examples so far in this chapter have been *instance methods*, meaning that you create an instance of a class and then use the dot (.) operator on the name of the object reference and the name of the method that you want to invoke, as follows:

```
MyClass mc = new MyClass();
mc.MyMethod("Hello", "World");
```

You can also create *static methods*, which you access using the type name instead of the instance name. Static methods are related to static fields and properties, which we saw in Chapters 7 and 8. In fact, in a static method, you can access *only* static members of this enclosing class—static fields, static properties, and other static methods. A class that has only static members can be made into a *static class*, which is described in Chapter 6. Listing 9-24 contains an example of a static method.

Listing 9-24. A Static Method

```
class Calculator {

    public static int PerformCalculation(int x, int y) {
        return x * y;
    }
}
```

You create a static method by using the static keyword, as shown in bold in the listing. To access a static method, you would use a statement like this:

```
int result = Calculator.PerformCalculation(10, 10);
```

Notice that the method is accessed through the class name and not the name of an instance of the class. You don't need to create a new instance of the `Calculator` class to be able to call the static `PerformCalculation` method.

Creating Virtual Methods

The virtual keyword can be applied to a method to allow it to be overridden by a derived class. Listing 9-25 contains an example of a virtual method.

Listing 9-25. A Virtual Method

```
class Calculator {

    public virtual int PerformCalculation(int x, int y) {
        return x * y;
    }
}
```

The virtual keyword is marked in bold in Listing 9-25. Applying this keyword as a modifier to this method means that classes that derive from the `Calculator` class can override the `PerformCalculation` method. Virtual methods and method overriding are explained in the "Hiding and Overriding Methods" section later in this chapter.

Creating Sealed Methods

The sealed modifier is applied to an overridden method and prevents further overriding in derived classes. See the "Hiding and Overriding Methods" section later in the chapter for details of virtual methods and overriding methods. Listing 9-26 contains a simple example.

Listing 9-26. Sealing a Method

```
class Calculator {

    public virtual int CalculateSum(int x, int y) {
        return x + y;
    }

    public virtual int CalculateProduct(int x, int y) {
        return x * y;
    }
}

class DerivedCalc : Calculator {

    public sealed override int CalculateSum(int x, int y) {
        // more specialized implementation of method action/calculation
    }

    public override int CalculateProduct(int x, int y) {
```

```
        // more specialized implementation of method action/calculation
    }
}
```

In this example, the Calculator class contains two virtual methods, CalculateSum and CalculateProduct. The DerivedCalc class is derived from Calculator and overrides both methods, but the DerivedCalc implementation of the CalculateSum method has been modified with the sealed keyword. Any class that derives from DerivedCalc will be able to further override the CalculateProduct method but not the CalculateSum method.

Creating Abstract Methods

The abstract modifier can be used to declare a method that has no method body and that must be implemented in a derived class. Abstract methods can exist only in classes that have also been modified by the abstract keyword, as shown in Listing 9-27.

Listing 9-27. Defining and Implementing Abstract Methods

```
abstract class AbstractCalculator {

    public abstract int CalculateSum(int x, int y);

    public abstract int CalculateProduct(int x, int y);

}

class Calculator : AbstractCalculator {

    public override int CalculateSum(int x, int y) {
        return x + y;
    }

    public override int CalculateProduct(int x, int y) {
        return x * y;
    }

}
```

In this example, the abstract class AbstractCalculator has two abstract methods, CalculateSum and CalculateProduct. Any class that derives from AbstractCalculator has to implement bodies for these methods or be modified as abstract itself.

The Calculator class is derived from AbstractCalculator and, since it is not an abstract class, must override the abstract methods. Overriding methods is described in the "Hiding and Overriding Methods" section later in the chapter.

Overloading Methods

You can define many different methods with the same name in a class. This is called *method overloading* and is usually used to make using a class more convenient. Each overloaded method must have a different sequence of parameter types, and they can return the same type or different types as the method result. Listing 9-28 contains an example.

Listing 9-28. Overriding Methods

```
class Calculator {

    public int CalculateSum(int x, int y) {
        return x + y;
    }

    public int CalculateSum(string x, string y) {
        return CalculateSum(int.Parse(x), int.Parse(y));
    }

    public float CalculateSum(float x, float y) {
        return x + y;
    }
}
```

The Calculator class in this example contains three methods, all of which are called CalculateSum. Each of these methods has a different sequence of parameter types. The first version takes two int parameters. The second version is a convenience method that takes two string parameters, parses them to int values, and then calls the first method, sparing the caller of the method the need convert the types. The third method takes two float values as parameters and returns a float as a result. This method doesn't call either of the others.

The reason that overloaded methods must have different parameter types is so that the runtime can figure out which version of a method is being called. Overloaded methods can have the same parameters types, just as long as they are in a different order, like this, for example:

```
public int CalculateSum(int x, string y) {
    //...
}

public int CalculateSum(string x, int y) {
    // ...
}
```

When overloading methods, you must be careful of the effect that type inference can have. Listing 9-29 has a simple example.

Listing 9-29. Numeric Literal Type Inference for Overloaded Methods

```
using System;

class Calculator {

    public int PerformCalculation(int x, int y) {
        return x + y;
    }
```

```
        public long PerformCalculation(long x, long y) {
            return x * y;
        }
}

class Listing_29 {

    static void Main(string[] args) {

        // create a new instance of Calculator
        Calculator calc = new Calculator();

        // call the PerformCalculation method
        long res = calc.PerformCalculation(10, 10);

        // print the results
        Console.WriteLine("Result: {0}", res);

        // wait for input before exiting
        Console.WriteLine("Press enter to finish");
        Console.ReadLine();
    }
}
```

The types for the parameters and results in the overloaded methods in the Calculator class can be converted implicitly, and that can cause problems when the runtime infers the type, such as when numeric literals are used. Details of numeric literals and how types are inferred from them are in Chapter 5. The Main method in the Listing_29 class calls the PerformCalculaton method with two numeric literal parameters like this:

```
long res = calc.PerformCalculation(10, 10);
```

Which version of the method is being called? The .NET runtime looks at the parameter types to figure this out, and since numeric literals are inferred to the smallest possible numeric type, we have effectively provided two int parameters. Therefore, we get the first version of the method, which sums the numeric values. If we wanted the second method version, we would have had to override the numeric type inference with a type suffix, like this:

```
long res = calc.PerformCalculation(10L, 10L);
```

This kind of overloading leads to surprising results when you come to use your class; it is important to select parameters types that mean it is always obvious which overloaded version is going to be called.

■ **Tip** In many languages, it is common practice to overload methods to provide default values for parameters. You don't need to do this in C#; see the "Using Optional Parameters" section earlier in this chapter for details.

Hiding and Overriding Methods

When you derive one class from another, you can provide your own implementations of the methods in the base class. You do this to provide an implementation of the action that the method performs, which is specialized to the derived type. If you are new to object programming and you don't know why you would want to do this, then I give some examples in the "Understanding Method Specialization" section after I have explained the related C# features. Listing 9-30 contains a simple example.

Listing 9-30. Implementing a Base Class Method in a Derived Class

```
using System;

class BaseClass {

    public void PrintMessage() {
        Console.WriteLine("Base class message");
    }
}

class DerivedClass : BaseClass {

    public void PrintMessage() {
        Console.WriteLine("Derived class message");
    }
}

class Listing_30 {

    static void Main(string[] args) {

        // create a new instance of the base class
        BaseClass bClass = new BaseClass();

        // print out the message
        bClass.PrintMessage();

        // create a new instance of the derived class
        DerivedClass dClass = new DerivedClass();

        // print out the message
        dClass.PrintMessage();

        // create a new instance of DerivedClass but
        // assign it to a BaseClass local variable
        bClass = dClass;

        // print the message
        bClass.PrintMessage();

        // wait for input before exiting
        Console.WriteLine("Press enter to finish");
```

```
        Console.ReadLine();
    }
}
```

In this example, the class `DerivedClass` derives from `BaseClass` and implements its own `PrintMessage` method. We create an instance of `BaseClass` and call the `PrintMessage` method. We then create an instance of `DerivedClass` and call the `PrintMessage` method. Finally, we assign the `DerivedClass` to the `BaseClass` local variable and then call `PrintMessage` again. Compiling and running the code in Listing 9-30 produces the following results:

```
Base class message
Derived class message
Base class message
Press enter to finish
```

The first and second lines of the output are what we might expect, but the third line is often a surprise to programmers who are new to C#. The `PrintMessage` method we added to `DerivedClass` doesn't replace the method of the same name in the base class; it adds a new, distinct method. In the following sections, I'll explain why this happens, how to make use of this feature, and how to get the behavior that you might have been expecting.

Hiding Methods

If we create a new instance of `DerivedClass` and call `PrintMessage`, we are calling the version of `PrintMessage` in `DerivedClass`, like this:

```
(new DerivedClass()).PrintMessage();
```

But when we create an instance of `DerivedClass`, cast it to `BaseClass` (or assign it to a local variable that is of the type `BaseClass`) and call the `PrintMessage` method, we are calling the version in the base class, like this:

```
((BaseClass)new DerivedClass()).PrintMessage();
```

This behavior is called *method hiding*; the `PrintMessage` method in `DerivedClass` hides the `PrintMessage` method in `BaseClass`. There is nothing wrong with method hiding other than it can cause unexpected results and so requires careful use. See Chapter 6 for details of polymorphism and the effect of upcasting on hidden members. To help prevent inadvertent method hiding, the C# compiler will generate a warning if you hide methods as I have done in Listing 9-30. To avoid this error, you must make your method hiding explicit by using the new keyword as a modifier to the method in the derived class, as shown in Listing 9-31.

Listing 9-31. Using the **new** *Modifier to Explicitly Hide a Method*

```
class BaseClass {

    public void PrintMessage() {
        Console.WriteLine("Base class message");
    }
```

```
}

class DerivedClass : BaseClass {

    public new void PrintMessage() {
        Console.WriteLine("Derived class message");
    }
}
```

Using the new keyword like this indicates that you want to hide the base method. If you want to call the hidden method from the new method, you can do so using the base keyword and the dot (.) operator with the method name, as shown in Listing 9-32.

Listing 9-32. Calling the Hidden Method in the Base Class

```
using System;

class BaseClass {

    public void PrintMessage() {
        Console.WriteLine("Base class message");
    }
}

class DerivedClass : BaseClass {

    public new void PrintMessage() {
        base.PrintMessage();
        Console.WriteLine("Derived class message");
    }
}

class Listing_32 {

    static void Main(string[] args) {

        // create a new instance of the derived class
        DerivedClass dClass = new DerivedClass();

        // print out the message
        dClass.PrintMessage();

        // wait for input before exiting
        Console.WriteLine("Press enter to finish");
        Console.ReadLine();
    }
}
```

You can see the call to the hidden method in the DerivedClass.PrintMessage method. Compiling and running the code in Listing 9-32 produces the following results:

```
Base class message
Derived class message
Press enter to finish
```

Overriding Methods

The alternative to hiding a base class method is to override it. If we override a method, then our new version is always used, irrespective of whether we are referring to an object as the base class or the derived class. Listing 9-33 contains an example.

Listing 9-33. Overriding a Method

```
using System;

class BaseClass {

    public virtual void PrintMessage() {
        Console.WriteLine("Base class message");
    }
}

class DerivedClass : BaseClass {

    public override void PrintMessage() {
        Console.WriteLine("Derived class message");
    }
}

class Listing_33 {

    static void Main(string[] args) {

        // create a new instance of the derived class
        DerivedClass dClass = new DerivedClass();

        // print out the message
        dClass.PrintMessage();

        // create a new instance of DerivedClass but
        // assign it to a BaseClass local variable
        BaseClass bClass = dClass;

        // print the message
        bClass.PrintMessage();

        // wait for input before exiting
        Console.WriteLine("Press enter to finish");
        Console.ReadLine();
    }
```

```
}
```

We override a base method by using the override modifier on the derived method. The base method must be modified with the virtual keyword before it can be overridden. Both keywords are marked in bold in the listing. When we compile and run the code in Listing 9-33, we get the following results:

```
Derived class message
Derived class message
Press enter to finish
```

You can see from the results that the derived version of the method is used even when we refer to the object as an instance of the base class. An overridden method can be overridden itself, as Listing 9-34 demonstrates.

Listing 9-34. Overriding an Already Overridden Method

```
class BaseClass {

    public virtual void PrintMessage() {
        Console.WriteLine("Base class message");
    }
}

class DerivedClass : BaseClass {

    public override void PrintMessage() {
        Console.WriteLine("Derived class message");
    }
}

class FurtherDerivedClass : DerivedClass {

    public override void PrintMessage() {
        Console.WriteLine("Further derived class message");
    }
}
```

If you have used another object-oriented language, this is probably the behavior you are expecting and will use most frequently. In fact, hiding, rather than overriding methods, is a pretty unusual thing. Often you will want to override a method but do so in a way that manipulates the result of the base method. You can access the base method through the base keyword and the dot (.) operator. Listing 9-35 contains an example.

Listing 9-35. Calling an Overridden Method

```
class Calculator {

    public virtual int CalculateSum(int x, int y) {
```

```
        return x + y;
    }
}

class DoubleResultCalc : Calculator {

    public override int CalculateSum(int x, int y) {
        // call the base implementation of this method
        int interimResult = base.CalculateSum(x, y);

        // return twice the result we got from the base class
        return interimResult * 2;
    }
}
```

In this example, the DoubleResultCalc class overrides the CalculateSum method with an implementation that uses the base keyword to call the original method version and returns doubles the result.

Sealing Methods

If you are writing a base class and you don't want anyone to override your method, you can simply omit the virtual modifier. Derived classes can still hide your method, but they can't override it (you saw an example of this in Listing 9-30). Methods that override other methods can themselves be overridden by default. In other words, if you have used the override modifier on a method, then classes that derive from your class can also use the override keyword. You can prevent this by using the sealed modifier, as demonstrated by Listing 9-36.

Listing 9-36. Sealing a Method

```
class Calculator {

    public virtual int CalculateSum(int x, int y) {
        return x + y;
    }
}

class DoubleResultCalc : Calculator {

    public sealed override int CalculateSum(int x, int y) {
        // call the base implementation of this method
        int interimResult = base.CalculateSum(x, y);

        // return twice the result we got from the base class
        return interimResult * 2;
    }
}
```

In this example, the DoubleResultCalc class has sealed the CalculateSum method, which it has overridden from the base class. Classes that derived from DoubleResultCalc will not be able to further override this method.

Understanding Method Specialization

If you have not used an object language before, you might be wondering what the point of overriding a method is. As I said at the start of the chapter, a method implements an action that an object can perform. Overriding a method allows you to provide an implementation that performs that action in a way which is specialized to your class. Usually, this means replying on the features of your class to do the action more efficiently or effectively. Let's look at a simple example of increased effectiveness, shown in Listing 9-37.

Listing 9-37. Providing More Information in an Overridden Method

```
class Person {
    public string Name { get; set; }
    public string Age { get; set; }
    public string City { get; set; }

    public virtual void PrintInformation() {
        Console.WriteLine("--- Information ---");
        Console.WriteLine("Name: {0}", Name);
        Console.WriteLine("Age: {0}", Age);
        Console.WriteLine("City: {0}", City);
    }
}

class Employee : Person {
    public string Employer { get; set; }
    public int HourlyRate { get; set; }

    public override void PrintInformation() {
        // have the base class print out the basic info
        base.PrintInformation();

        // print out the additional information we have
        Console.WriteLine("Employer: {0}", Employer);
        Console.WriteLine("Rate: ${0}/hr", HourlyRate);
    }
}
```

In this example, the base class, Person, has a number of automatically implemented properties and a PrintInformation method that writes this information to the console window. The derived class, Employee, is a specialized version of Person that has additional information about employment. We can override the PrintInformation method to build on the functionality of the base method and include the additional information we have in the Employee class. You can see this is exactly what I have done.

In the same way that Employee is a specialization of Person, the new version of the PrintInformation method is a specialization of the base implementation. We have taken advantage of the additional features we have added to the Employee class to make the action performed by the method more useful and relevant.

As a rule of thumb, you should override a method if you can use the additional features that a derived class has added to improve the value or efficiency of the action performed by base class method. There are some situations in which you will have no choice but to override a method—a good example is when you are deriving from an abstract class, which requires you to provide implementations for methods. See the "Creating Abstract Methods" and "Special Methods" sections in this chapter for more information on abstract methods.

Special Methods

There are some methods that C# treats differently from the ones we have seen so far in this chapter. In the following sections, I'll show you each of them and demonstrate their use. These are not arcane features; you will use some of these special methods in every C# program you create.

The Main Method

You have seen the Main method used in most of the examples. The Main method is the entry point for most kinds of C# program, meaning that this is where the runtime starts to execute your program statements. Code library projects don't need a Main method, for example. Listing 9-38 demonstrates the Main method.

Listing 9-38. The C# Main Method

```
using System;

class Listing_38 {

    static void Main() {

        Console.WriteLine("Main method");

        // wait for input before exiting
        Console.WriteLine("Press enter to finish");
        Console.ReadLine();
    }
}
```

There can be only one Main method in a C# program. The Main method is always static, and it can return void or an int value. (A value of zero is usually used to indicate that a program ran successfully, and a value of one represents an error; this is convention, but you can use any values you like.)

The .NET runtime runs your program by calling your Main method and executing the statements it contains. For the simple example in Listing 9-38, the only statements are a series of calls to the System.Console class. Compiling and running the code in Listing 9-38 produces the following output:

```
Main method
Press enter to finish
```

The Main method is the first thing that is called in your program, with one exception. If the class that contains your Main method also contains a static constructor, this will be called before the Main method. See the "Constructors" section later in this chapter for details of static constructors.

Because the Main method is static, you cannot call any instance members without creating an instance of the enclosing type, as shown in Listing 9-39.

Listing 9-39. Creating an Instance of the Type That Encloses a Main Method

```
using System;

class Listing_39 {
    private string message { get; set; }

    static void Main(string[] args) {

        // in order to be able to read and write the
        // message property, we need to create a new
        // instance of this class and access the property
        // using the reference and the dot operator
        Listing_39 l39 = new Listing_39();
        l39.message = "Hello";

        // print out the value of the property
        Console.WriteLine("Instance Property: {0}", l39.message);

        // wait for input before exiting
        Console.WriteLine("Press enter to finish");
        Console.ReadLine();
    }
}
```

In this example, the Listing_39 class has an instance property called message. To access this property when the runtime starts executing code statements in the static Main method, we have to create an instance of Listing_39 and use the dot operator to access the property. Notice that the property has the private access modifier but can still be accessed by the Main method. This is because the property and the Main method are enclosed by the same class. Compiling and running the code in Listing 9-39 produces the following results:

```
Instance Property: Hello
Press enter to finish
```

The Main method can be specified with an optional string array. This is the format of Main method that you will usually see in the examples in this book, because it is the one used by Visual Studio when you create a new Console Application project. The contents of the string array are the argument passed to the executable when your application was started. You can use the command-line arguments to change the way that your program runs. Listing 9-40 contains a demonstration.

Listing 9-40. Working with Command-Line Arguments

```csharp
using System;

class Listing_40 {

    static void Main(string[] args) {

        // print out the number of arguments
        Console.WriteLine("There are {0} arguments", args.Length);

        // enumerate the arguments
        foreach (string s in args) {
            Console.WriteLine("Argument: {0}", s);
        }

        // wait for input before exiting
        Console.WriteLine("Press enter to finish");
        Console.ReadLine();
    }
}
```

If you compile and run this program by selecting Start Without Debugging from the Debug menu in Visual Studio, you will get the following output:

```
There are 0 arguments
Press enter to finish
```

Open a command prompt, and change the directory to where the compiled program resides. This will be in the bin\Debug or bin\Release directory relative to where you saved your Visual Studio project. The name of the program file will depend on the name of your project; for me, the name is Listing_40.exe. We can run the program and supply some command-line arguments, like this:

```
Listing_40.exe hello world 1 2 3
```

Starting the program with those arguments produces the following results:

```
There are 5 arguments
Argument: hello
Argument: world
Argument: 1
Argument: 2
Argument: 3
Press enter to finish
```

Constructors

As we have discussed, a class is the blueprint for a type, and an object represents an instance of that type. We use the properties and fields defined in a class to differentiate the different instances. For example, if our class described people, we might have properties representing a person's name, age, and city of residence. A constructor is a special method that lets you prepare an object before it is used, providing initial values for properties and fields. Listing 9-41 contains an example.

Listing 9-41. Using a Constructor

```
using System;

class Person {
    public string Name { get; set; }
    public int Age { get; set; }
    public string City { get; set; }

    public Person(string name, int age, string city) {
        Name = name;
        Age = age;
        City = city;
    }
}
```

The constructor in Listing 9-41 is shown in bold. There are four parts to a basic constructor like the one in the listing, and they are described in Figure 9-2.

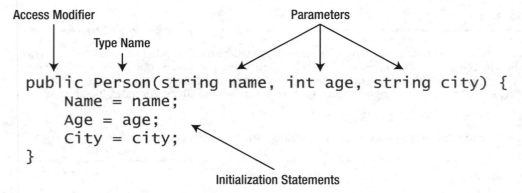

Figure 9-2. The anatomy of a basic constructor

It is important to keep in mind that a constructor is a special kind of method and that most of the C# features that apply to regular methods also apply to constructors. That said, you can see from Figure 9-2 that although a constructor does look like a method, there are some differences.

The two main differences are that the method name must match the type name, so in the case of our example, the constructor name is Person because it is a constructor for the Person class. The second difference is that there is no return type. The modifiers applied to a constructor (in this case, the public access modifier) are followed immediately by the constructor name.

Constructor parameters work in the same way as they do for normal methods. You can use all the features described in the "Understanding Parameters" section earlier in this chapter.

The body of a constructor consists of code statements. You can perform any actions you want to in a constructor, but there is a strong convention that constructors should contain only the statements that are essential to initialize and configure an instance of your type. There is no hard-and-fast rule about what kinds of actions are essential, but as a rule of thumb, any statements that are not assigning values to fields and properties are candidates to be moved out of the constructor and into regular methods. The statements in the example assign the parameter values to the instance properties.

When you have defined a constructor for a class, you can use it to create new instances of that class. So, to complete our simple example, Listing 9-42 contains a demonstration of creating an instance of the Person class.

Listing 9-42. Using a Constructor to Create a New Instance of a Class

```
class Listing_42 {

    static void Main(string[] args) {

        // create a new person instance
        Person person = new Person(
            "Adam Freeman",
            38,
            "London");

        // print out the details of the person object
        Console.WriteLine("--- Person ---");
        Console.WriteLine("Name: {0}", person.Name);
        Console.WriteLine("Age: {0}", person.Age);
        Console.WriteLine("City: {0}", person.City);

        // wait for input before exiting
        Console.WriteLine("Press enter to finish");
        Console.ReadLine();
    }
}
```

The statement that uses the constructor is shown in bold. I create the new instance by using the new keyword, followed by the class name, and then supply parameter values as I would for a regular method. The result of the new operation is an instance of the Person class that has been populated with the parameters values, which I then print out to the console. Compiling and running the code in Listings 9-41 and 9-42 produces the following results:

```
--- Person ---
Name: Adam Freeman
Age: 38
City: London
Press enter to finish
```

Using the Default Constructor

The *default constructor* is one that has no parameters. If you don't specify a constructor in your class, the C# compiler will add a default constructor automatically when you compile your project. The constructor that is added will have no parameters and no code statements. I have been relying on this automatically added constructor so far in this book to keep the code samples simple. Here is a class that doesn't contain a constructor:

```
class Person {
    public string Name { get; set; }
    public int Age { get; set; }
    public string City { get; set; }
}
```

When we compile this class, the C# compiler adds a default constructor for us, meaning that the previous class is equivalent to this one:

```
class Person {
    public string Name { get; set; }
    public int Age { get; set; }
    public string City { get; set; }

    public Person() {
    }
}
```

You create instances of a class with the default constructor in the same way, even if the C# compiler has created it for you, by using the new keyword and the name of the class. Because the constructor has no parameters, we use the open and close parentheses, like this:

```
Person p = new Person();
```

The automatic creation of the default constructor reduces code clutter in classes that don't require initialization. There are times when you will want to explicitly define the default constructor. The most obvious is that you want to include code statements to initialize your class, most often to assign initial values to properties and fields. You will also want to explicitly add the default constructor to change the access modifier (default constructors are always created with the public modifier) or control which constructor is called in the base class (see the "Calling Base Class Constructors" section).

Initializing Properties and Fields at Construction

If your class defines public fields or properties, you can assign them values outside the constructor when you create a new instance of a class. This is known as *object initialization*. Listing 9-43 provides a demonstration. Properties are explained in Chapter 8, and fields are explained in Chapter 7.

Listing 9-43. Setting Values for Public Properties at Construction

```
using System;

class Person {
```

```
        public string Name { get; set; }
        public int Age { get; set; }
        public string City { get; set; }
}

class Listing_43 {

    static void Main(string[] args) {

        // create a new instance of Person and
        // provide values for the public properties
        Person person = new Person() {
            Name = "Adam Freeman",
            Age = 38,
            City = "London"
        };

        // wait for input before exiting
        Console.WriteLine("Press enter to finish");
        Console.ReadLine();
    }
}
```

The Person class in Listing 9-43 uses the implicit default constructor feature, meaning that initial values for an instance of Person cannot be provided as constructor parameters. Instead, I have supplied the values for the public properties in a code block that follows the constructor. For each property, I made an assignment using the assignment operator (=), and each assignment is separated by a comma (,). In Listing 9-43, I have included the open and closed parentheses characters, but you can omit them if there are no constructor parameters, like this:

```
Person person = new Person {
    Name = "Adam Freeman",
    Age = 38,
    City = "London"
};
```

This is a nice feature, but it should be used with caution. In effect, you are relying on the person creating an instance of your class to ensure public fields are initialized with useful values. You should write your classes so that property setters check for valid values and your methods so that you check to ensure that values have been assigned. (You can use this feature with fields as well as properties, but it is generally better practice to use public properties to expose the value of your fields, as explained in Chapter 7.)

Overloading Constructors

You can overload constructors just as you can regular methods. You can have as many constructors as you like in a class, as long as the sequence of parameters types is unique. Overloaded constructors are usually provided as a convenience to simplify creating new instances of a class. Listing 9-44 contains an example.

Listing 9-44. Overloading a Constructor

```
class Person {
    public string Name { get; set; }
    public int Age { get; set; }
    public string City { get; set; }

    public Person(string name, int age, string city) {
        Name = name;
        Age = age;
        City = city;
    }

    public Person(string name, string age, string city) {
        Name = name;
        Age = int.Parse(age);
        City = city;
    }
}
```

The Person class in Listing 9-44 contains two constructors. The second constructor allows me to specify the age parameter as a `string`, rather than the `int` that is required by the first constructor. If the Person class is created at different places in a program, providing the second constructor means that I don't have to duplicate the code that parses the string to get an integer value, which is always a good thing, not least because I can change the way that the parsing is done in a single place.

Calling One Constructor from Another

In fact, the only difference between the two constructors in Listing 9-44 is the type of the age parameter. I can reduce the duplication in the Person class by having the second constructor make use of the first one. I do this with the `this` keyword. Listing 9-45 contains a demonstration.

Listing 9-45. Calling One Constructor from Another

```
class Person {
    public string Name { get; set; }
    public int Age { get; set; }
    public string City { get; set; }

    public Person(string name, int age, string city) {
        Name = name;
        Age = age;
        City = city;
    }

    public Person(string name, string age, string city)
        : this(name, int.Parse(age), city) {
    }
}
```

To have one constructor call another, you place a colon (:) after the parameter list and then use the this keyword, which is illustrated in Figure 9-3.

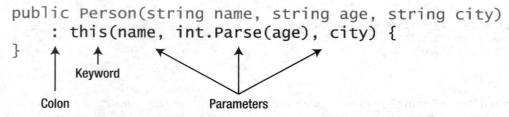

Figure 9-3. *The use of the this keyword*

The open parenthesis (() follows this, and you define the set of parameters you want to pass to the other constructor version (if any), followed by the close parenthesis ()). You cannot call other constructors in your constructor body as you can with other languages. The only way to call another constructor is with the this keyword, as shown in Figure 9-3.

When creating instances of a class with overloaded constructors, you provide parameters values that match the signature of the constructor signature that is most convenient. Here are two statements that use the two constructor versions of the Person class in Listing 9-45:

```
Person p1 = new Person("Adam Freeman", 38, "London");
Person p2 = new Person("Adam Freeman", "38", "London");
```

You can pass on the parameters values by name, as I have done for the name and city parameters, or by using literals (you can see an example of using a literal in Listing 9-46). You can also perform operations on parameters. This is what I have done for the age parameter, calling the int.Parse method to obtain an int value from a string.

You can include only one statement when calling another constructor, but there is a lot of flexibility in what that statement can do. For example, if we wanted to ensure that we don't send any negative values, we could do something like this:

```
public Person(string name, string age, string city)
    : this(name, age[0] == '-' ? 0 : int.Parse(age), city) {
}
```

A neater way to deal with this kind of thing is to define a static method that transforms a parameter value and then call this method when using this:

```
class Person {
    public string Name { get; set; }
    public int Age { get; set; }
    public string City { get; set; }

    public Person(string name, int age, string city) {
        Name = name;
        Age = age;
        City = city;
    }
```

```
    public Person(string name, string age, string city)
        : this(name, ConvertAge(age), city) {
    }

    static int ConvertAge(string str) {
        int age = int.Parse(str);
        return age < 0 ? 0 : age;
    }
}
```

If the method you are calling is in the same class as the constructor, you must ensure the method is static. You can't call an instance method from a constructor because the instance hasn't been created yet. If you need to call an instance method from another class, you can create an instance and call the method in a single statement, like this:

```
public Person(string name, string age, string city)
    : this(name, new AgeFormatter().ConvertAge(age), city) {
}
```

Overloaded constructors can contain their own code statements. You can use this feature to handle transforming parameters, but some care is required. Listing 9-46 contains a demonstration.

Listing 9-46. Using Overloaded Constructor Statements to Format Parameters

```
class Person {
    public string Name { get; set; }
    public int Age { get; set; }
    public string City { get; set; }

    public Person(string name, int age, string city) {
        Name = name;
        Age = age;
        City = city;
    }

    public Person(string name, string age, string city)
        : this(name, 0, city) {

        // perform some complex formatting operation on
        // the age string and set the field value
        Age = int.Parse(age);
    }
}
```

In Listing 9-46, the constructor version that takes three string parameters calls the other version, providing a literal value of zero for the age parameter. The constructor body contains a statement that parses the string parameter and uses the result to set the value for the Age property. This works because the constructor you are calling is executed before the constructor that you are calling from, so the first constructor version assigns values to the properties, including assigning zero to Age. Then the calling constructor is executed, which assigns a new value to Age, derived from the string parameter.

This is not an ideal technique. You must be sure that no values are set based on the value of the age parameter in the first constructor version. Or, if there are, then you must take to replicate this in the overloaded version. Here is an example of the problem:

```
class Person {
    public string Name { get; set; }
    public int Age { get; set; }
    public string City { get; set; }
    public bool IsOver18 { get; set; }

    public Person(string name, int age, string city) {
        Name = name;
        Age = age;
        City = city;
        IsOver18 = age > 18;
    }

    public Person(string name, string age, string city)
        : this(name, 0, city) {

        // perform some complex formatting operation on
        // the age string and set the field value
        Age = int.Parse(age);
    }
}
```

In the first constructor, the value of the IsOver18 property is set based on the age parameter. The second constructor calls the first with a value of zero, meaning that any instance of Person created using the second constructor will have a property value of false for IsOver18.

Using Optional Parameters in a Constructor

A common pattern in other programming languages is to overload constructors to provide default values, like this:

```
class Person {
    public string Name { get; set; }
    public int Age { get; set; }
    public string City { get; set; }

    public Person(string name, int age, string city) {
        Name = name;
        Age = age;
        City = city;
    }

    public Person(string name, int age)
        : this(name, age, "London") { }

    public Person(string name)
        : this(name, 38) { }
```

279

```
}
```

With this example, when you call a constructor with fewer parameters, default values are used to call other constructor versions. The following statements create instances of Person that are equivalent:

```
Person p1 = new Person("Adam Freeman");
Person p2 = new Person("Adam Freeman", 38);
Person p3 = new Person("Adam Freeman", 38, "London");
```

You can use the C# optional parameter feature to reduce code clutter, as demonstrated in Listing 9-47. The optional parameter feature is explained in the "Using Optional Parameters" section earlier in this chapter.

Listing 9-47. Using Optional Parameters in Constructors

```
class Person {
    public string Name { get; set; }
    public int Age { get; set; }
    public string City { get; set; }

    public Person(string name, int age = 38, string city = "London") {
        Name = name;
        Age = age;
        City = city;
    }
}
```

Calling Base Class Constructors

When you derive from a base class, your constructors must call one of the base constructors to ensure that the base class fields and properties are correctly initialized. Listing 9-48 contains a demonstration.

Listing 9-48. Calling a Base Constructor

```
class Person {
    public string Name { get; set; }
    public int Age { get; set; }
    public string City { get; set; }

    public Person(string name, int age = 38, string city = "London") {
        Console.WriteLine("Person constructor called");
        Name = name;
        Age = age;
        City = city;
    }
}

class Employee : Person {
    public string Company { get; set; }
```

```
    public Employee(string name, string company)
        : base(name) {
        Console.WriteLine("Employee constructor called");
        Company = company;
    }
}
```

In this example, the Employee class is derived from the Person class. The constructor in Employee calls the constructor in the Person class. This is done using the base keyword, illustrated in Figure 9-4.

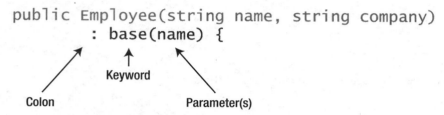

Figure 9-4. The base keyword

The parameters of a constructor are followed by a colon (:), which is followed by the base keyword, the open parenthesis character ((), the parameters to pass to the base constructor, and the close parenthesis character ()). In the example, I pass only one parameter value, taking advantage of the optional parameters feature used by the Person constructor. You cannot call base constructors from the body of your constructor as you can in other programming languages. The only way to call a base constructor is by using the base keyword, as shown in Figure 9-4.

You can do the same kinds of things with parameters when using the base keyword as you can when using the this keyword; see the "Overloading Constructors" section for details and an example.

The body of the base class constructor is executed before the derived class constructor. If we were to create an instance of Employee using the following statement:

```
Employee e = new Employee("Adam Freeman", "BigCorp");
```

we would see the following output:

```
Person constructor called
Employee constructor called
```

If a base class has overloaded constructors, you can specify which one is called through the parameters you pass to the base keyword. If you want to call the default constructor, you can either use the base keyword with no parameters or omit it entirely, which means this constructor:

```
public Employee(string name, string company)
        : base() {
```

is equivalent to this one:

```
public Employee(string name, string company) {
```

Creating Instances of a Derived Type

When you implement a constructor in a derived class, you are effectively replacing the base constructors. To create an instance of the derived type, you must use a constructor from the derived type; even if you are assigning the instance, you create to a local variable that is of the base type. Listing 9-49 contains a demonstration.

Listing 9-49. Creating a Derived Type with a Derived Constructor

```
using System;

class Person {
    public string Name { get; set; }
    public int Age { get; set; }
    public string City { get; set; }

    public Person(string name, int age = 38, string city = "London") {
        Name = name;
        Age = age;
        City = city;
    }
}

class Employee : Person {
    public string Company { get; set; }

    public Employee(string name, string company)
        : base(name) {

        Company = company;
    }
}

class Listing_49 {

    static void Main(string[] args) {

        // create a new instance of Employee
        Person p = new Employee("Adam Freeman", "BigCorp");

        Console.WriteLine("--- Person ---");
        Console.WriteLine("Name: {0}", p.Name);
        Console.WriteLine("Age: {0}", p.Age);
        Console.WriteLine("City: {0}", p.City);

        // wait for input before exiting
        Console.WriteLine("Press enter to finish");
        Console.ReadLine();
    }
}
```

In this example, I create an instance of the Employee class, which is derived from the Person class. I have to use the constructor from the Employee class, even though I am assigning the object I create to a variable that is of the type Person.

Controlling Access to Constructors

You can control access to constructors using the same set of modifiers as used by other members. The access level applied to constructors can be more restrictive than has been applied to the containing class, and overloaded constructors can have different access levels. Table 9-4 describes the access modifiers available and the effect they have on constructors.

Table 9-4. Access Modifiers and Their Effect on Constructors

Access Modifier	Description
public	The constructor can be accessed anywhere.
protected	The constructor can be accessed only by the containing class or derived classes.
internal	The constructor can be accessed by any code in the current assembly but not other assemblies.
protected internal	The constructor can be accessed by any code in the current assembly or by any class in any assembly that derives from the containing class.
private	The constructor can be accessed only by the containing class.

The main reason for restricting access to constructors is to limit the way that new instances can be created. For example, if all your class constructors are modified with the protected keyword, then you can only create instances of derived class or using a factory method (described later in this chapter). Listing 9-50 contains an example of using the protected keyword to limit direct creation of new base objects.

Listing 9-50. Restricting Directly Created Instances

```
using System;

class Person {
    public string Name { get; set; }
    public int Age { get; set; }
    public string City { get; set; }

    protected Person(string name, int age = 38, string city = "London") {
        Name = name; Age = age; City = city;
    }
}
```

```
class Employee : Person {
    public string Company { get; set; }

    public Employee(string name, string company)
        : base(name) {

        Company = company;
    }
}

class Listing_50 {

    static void Main(string[] args) {

        Person p = new Employee("Adam Freeman", "BigCo");

        // wait for input before exiting
        Console.WriteLine("Press enter to finish");
        Console.ReadLine();
    }
}
```

In Listing 9-50, the protected constructor in the Person class means that it can be called only from within the Person class (from another constructor, for example) or by a derived class. The only way to create instances of the Person class is to create instances of Employee, as shown in the Main method of the Listing_50 class.

Creating Copy Constructors

If you want to create one instance of a class that has the same field and property values as another instance of the same class, then you need to implement a copy constructor. There are two approaches to creating copy constructors, the first of which is shown in Listing 9-51.

Listing 9-51. Creating and Using a Copy Constructor

```
using System;

class Person {
    public string Name { get; set; }
    public int Age { get; set; }
    public string City { get; set; }

    public Person(string name, int age = 38, string city = "London") {
        Name = name; Age = age; City = city;
    }

    public Person(Person originalPerson) {
        Name = originalPerson.Name;
        Age = originalPerson.Age;
        City = originalPerson.City;
```

```
        }
}

class Listing_51 {

    static void Main(string[] args) {

        // create a new instance of Person
        Person orig = new Person("Joe Smith", 50, "New York");

        // create an instance of Person
        // using the copy constructor
        Person copy = new Person(orig);

        // print out the details of the copied Person
        Console.WriteLine("--- Person ---");
        Console.WriteLine("Name: {0}", copy.Name);
        Console.WriteLine("Age: {0}", copy.Age);
        Console.WriteLine("City: {0}", copy.City);

        // wait for input before exiting
        Console.WriteLine("Press enter to finish");
        Console.ReadLine();
    }

}
```

The Person class in the example contains a copy constructor, marked in bold. Copy constructors have a single parameter that is of the same type as the enclosing class. In this case, the parameter is an instance of Person. The copy constructor sets the value of each property to be the value in the parameter instance of Person. The Main method in the example creates an instance of Person and then creates a second instance using the copy constructor. Compiling and running the code in Listing 9-51 produces the following output:

```
--- Person ---
Name: Joe Smith
Age: 50
City: New York
Press enter to finish
```

The second approach is to have the copy constructor call another constructor. Here is an example:

```
class Person {
    public string Name { get; set; }
    public int Age { get; set; }
    public string City { get; set; }

    public Person(string name, int age = 38, string city = "London") {
        Name = name; Age = age; City = city;
    }
```

```
    public Person(Person originalPerson)
        : this(originalPerson.Name, originalPerson.Age, originalPerson.City) {
    }
}
```

The change is shown in bold, and this technique produces the same result as the approach in Listing 9-51; it is simply a matter of personal preference.

Copy constructors are usually simple to use as long as you realize that when you copy a reference, the object it points to is still referred to by the original object. Listing 9-52 contains an example.

Listing 9-52. Copying References in a Copy Constructor

```
using System;

class Company {
    public string Name { get; set; }
    public string City { get; set; }
}

class Employee {
    public string Name { get; set; }
    public Company Employer { get; set; }

    public Employee(string personName, string companyName, string city) {
        Name = personName;
        Employer = new Company() { Name = companyName, City = city };
    }

    public Employee(Employee originalEmployee) {
        Name = originalEmployee.Name;
        Employer = originalEmployee.Employer;
    }
}

class Listing_52 {

    static void Main(string[] args) {

        // create an Employee object
        Employee original = new Employee("Adam Freeman", "BigCo", "Boston");

        // create a copy Employee using the copy constructor
        Employee copy = new Employee(original);

        // print out the employer city from the copy
        Console.WriteLine("City: {0}", copy.Employer.City);

        // modify the original company name
        original.Employer.City = "Paris";

        // print out the employer city from the copy
```

```
        Console.WriteLine("City: {0}", copy.Employer.City);

        // wait for input before exiting
        Console.WriteLine("Press enter to finish");
        Console.ReadLine();
    }
}
```

The Employee class in Listing 9-52 has a property that is of the reference type Company. The Employee copy constructor copies the reference from the original instance of Employee to the copy Employee. Since we are copying the reference, the property value in both objects now point to the same instance of Company, and when I make a change to the City property via the original Employee, the change affects the copied Employee object as well. Compiling and running the code in Listing 9-52 produces the following results:

```
City: Boston
City: Paris
Press enter to finish
```

If you want to create truly distinct copies, then you need to either implement copy constructors in all the types used by the class you want to copy or create new instances using the underlying value types. For Listing 9-52, we could do this by changing the copy constructor as follows:

```
public Employee(Employee originalEmployee) {
    Name = originalEmployee.Name;
    Employer = new Company() {
        Name = originalEmployee.Employer.Name,
        City = originalEmployee.Employer.City};
}
```

Rather than copying the reference to the Company object, a new instance is created using the value types that make up a Company instance. The sharing of references in a copy constructor is easy to fix in a simple example like this one but can be much more difficult to address in more complex classes or where you don't have access to the source code of all the classes.

Using Static Constructors

A static constructor can be used to initialize static properties and fields. You do not need to call a static constructor—the .NET runtime does this automatically for you. Static fields and properties are shared between all instances of a class, so a static constructor is called only the first time that the enclosing class is used in an application domain (and since most programs have only one application domain, this means that constructors are called only once each time a program is run). Listing 9-53 demonstrates a class with a static constructor.

Listing 9-53. Using a Static Constructor

```
using System;

class Calculator {
    public static int Multiplier;

    static Calculator() {
        Console.WriteLine("Static constructor called");
        Multiplier = 2;
    }

    public Calculator() {
        Console.WriteLine("Instance constructor called");
    }

    public int PerformCalculation(int x, int y) {
        return x * y * Multiplier;
    }
}

class Listing_53 {

    static void Main(string[] args) {

        // create 5 instances of Calculator
        for (int i = 0; i < 5; i++) {
            Calculator calc = new Calculator();
        }

        // wait for input before exiting
        Console.WriteLine("Press enter to finish");
        Console.ReadLine();
    }
}
```

The static constructor in Listing 9-53 is shown in bold. Static constructors are modified with the static keyword and have no parameters. Classes can have only one static constructor. The Main method in Listing 9-53 creates five instances of the Calculator class. Compiling and running the code in Listing 9-53 produces the following results:

```
Static constructor called
Instance constructor called
Instance constructor called
Instance constructor called
Instance constructor called
Instance constructor called
Press enter to finish
```

You can see from the results that the static constructor is called only once. Static constructors can only use static fields and properties in the containing class and call static methods, although you can create instances of other classes and assign these to static fields and properties. You don't have to call the base static constructor from a derived class. The static constructors are all executed automatically.

The code statements in a static constructor are executed when a static member is called. This includes static methods, meaning that the static constructor is called before the code statements in a Main method; see "The Main Method" section earlier in the chapter for details of this special method.

Creating Factory Methods

A factory method is a static member that used to create new instances of a class, usually used when there are constraints on how many instances can be created. For example, there may be limited connections available to a database. Factory methods are used with private or protected constructors to prevent new instances being created directly. Listing 9-54 contains an example.

Listing 9-54. A Simple Factory Method

```
using System;

class Person {
    public string Name { get; set; }
    public int Age { get; set; }
    public string City { get; set; }
    private static int instanceCount;
    private static int instanceLimit;

    static Person() {
        instanceCount = 0;
        instanceLimit = 3;
    }

    private Person(string name, int age, string city) {
        Name = name; Age = age; City = city;
    }

    public static Person CreatePerson(string name, int age, string city) {
        // check to see if we have reached the limit
        if (instanceCount >= instanceLimit) {
            throw new InvalidOperationException("Instance limit reached");
        } else {
            // create a new instance of the class
            Person p = new Person(name, age, city);
            // increment the counter
            instanceCount++;
            // return the newly created instance
            return p;
        }
    }
}
```

```
class Listing_54 {

    static void Main(string[] args) {

        for (int i = 1; i < 5; i++) {
            try {
                Person p = Person.CreatePerson("Adam Freeman", 38, "London");
                Console.WriteLine("Successfully Created Instance Number: {0}", i);
            } catch (InvalidOperationException) {
                Console.WriteLine("Exception thrown while creating instance {0}", i);
                break;
            }
        }

        // wait for input before exiting
        Console.WriteLine("Press enter to finish");
        Console.ReadLine();
    }
}
```

The factory method in Listing 9-54 is shown in bold. The Person class has a static instructor that initializes two static fields used to track and limit the number of Person instances that can be created. A private constructor is used by the factory method to create new instances of Person. When the number of instances created exceeds the limit, further requests to the factory method result in an exception being thrown. (Exceptions and the try statement used in the Main method are discussed in Chapter 14.) Compiling and running the code in Listing 9-54 produces the following results:

```
Successfully Created Instance Number: 1
Successfully Created Instance Number: 2
Successfully Created Instance Number: 3
Exception thrown while creating instance 4
Press enter to finish
```

This is a very simple demonstration of a factory method, and there are a couple of problems with it. The first is that it is not safe for use with programs that use parallel programming techniques. These techniques, and the features you can use to make code like Listing 9-54 safe, are discussed later in this book. The second problem is that there is no way to restore the limited supply of Person instances. Once a certain number have been created, further requests result in an exception. A technique called *object pooling* can be used to avoid this permanent exhaustion. This technique is beyond the scope of an introductory book like this one, but there are a number of good descriptions of object pooling available online, starting with the one at Wikipedia.

Destructors

Destructors are methods that are called when an object is no longer referenced but before it is deleted from memory. Destructors are part of the .NET memory management system and are discussed fully in Chapter 18.

Iterator Blocks

An iterator block is a special method that allows you to easily implement iterators in your code. The simplest way of creating an iterator block is to implement a method with the name GetEnumerator, which returns System.Collections.Generic.IEnumerator<T>, where T is the type of object you are going to provide for enumeration. Listing 9-55 contains an example.

Listing 9-55. Creating an Iterator Block

```
using System.Collections.Generic;

class Counter {

    public IEnumerator<int> GetEnumerator() {
        for (int i = 0; i < 5; i++) {
            yield return i;
        }
    }
}
```

An iterator block is identified by the presence of the yield keyword. When the C# compiler detects an iterator block, it rewrites your class so that it implements the System.Collections.Generic.IEnumerator<T> and System.Collections.IEnumerator interfaces. Interfaces are described in Chapter 12, and the System.Collections namespaces are described later in the book.

You don't have to worry about the changes that are made, just the effect that they have. When you put an iterator block in your class, you can then use an instance of that class as though it were an IEnumerator<T>, where T is the type of data that your iterator block returns. Here is a simple example using the Counter class in Listing 9-55:

```
using System;

class Listing_55_Test {

    static void Main(string[] args) {

        // create a new instance of the Counter class
        Counter count = new Counter();

        // use the counter instance as the source for a foreach loop
        foreach (int i in count) {
            Console.WriteLine("Value: {0}", i);
        }

        // wait for input before exiting
        Console.WriteLine("Press enter to finish");
        Console.ReadLine();
    }
}
```

I create an instance of the Counter class and then use it as the source in a foreach loop, printing out each value that the loop generates. Compiling and running the previous code and the code in Listing 9-55 produces the following results:

```
Value: 0
Value: 1
Value: 2
Value: 3
Value: 4
Press enter to finish
```

Using the yield Keyword

The magic in Listing 9-55 comes from the yield keyword. When yield is followed by the return keyword, the value that follows will be exposed to the iterator. This is what happened in Listing 9-55:

```
public IEnumerator<int> GetEnumerator() {
    for (int i = 0; i < 5; i++) {
        yield return i;
    }
}
```

I placed the yield return statement in a for loop. Each time the loop body was executed, the yield return produced a value for the iterator output, which is the source of the incrementing results shown in the previous section.

The alternative use of the yield keyword is with the break keyword. This indicates that no more values are available. This is useful if you are using a loop of some kind and want to end execution prematurely. Listing 9-56 contains an example.

Listing 9-56. Using a yield break Statement

```
using System;
using System.Collections.Generic;

class Counter {

    public IEnumerator<int> GetEnumerator() {
        int resultCount = 0;
        int result = 0;
        while (true) {
            if (resultCount < 5) {
                resultCount++;
                yield return result++;
            } else {
                yield break;
            }
        }
    }
}
```

```
class Listing_56 {

    static void Main(string[] args) {

        // create a new instance of the Counter class
        Counter count = new Counter();

        // use the counter instance as the source for a foreach loop
        foreach (int i in count) {
            Console.WriteLine("Value: {0}", i);
        }

        // wait for input before exiting
        Console.WriteLine("Press enter to finish");
        Console.ReadLine();
    }
}
```

In this example, the iterator block uses an infinite while loop to generate iterator values. When a certain number of values has been generated, the yield break statement is used.

Exposing Field Iterators

The two iterator blocks that I have demonstrated so far have generated their values through calculation. Often, however, you will want to provide iteration over the contents of one of your fields. Listing 9-57 provides a demonstration.

Listing 9-57. Exposing a Field to Iteration

```
using System;
using System.Collections.Generic;

class Counter {
    private int[] arrData = {2, 4, 6, 8, 10};

    public IEnumerator<int> GetEnumerator() {
        foreach (int i in arrData) {
            yield return i;
        }
    }
}

class Listing_57 {

    static void Main(string[] args) {

        // create a new instance of Counter
        Counter count = new Counter();
```

```
        // enumerate the contents of the counter
        foreach (int i in count) {
            Console.WriteLine("Value: {0}", i);
        }

        // wait for input before exiting
        Console.WriteLine("Press enter to finish");
        Console.ReadLine();
    }
}
```

In this example, the Counter class has a private field that is an array of int values. The iterator block uses a foreach loop to enumerate the contents of the loop and the yield return statement to return each value. Compiling and running the code in Listing 9-57 produces the following results:

```
Value: 2
Value: 4
Value: 6
Value: 8
Value: 10
Press enter to finish
```

If the field you want to expose through an iterator block is a collection or an array, as was the case in the previous example, then there is an alternative approach. Collection classes (described in a later part of this book) and arrays (described in Chapter 13) implement their own iterator blocks, which means that we can simply return the result of their implementation of the GetEnumerator method. There is a small wrinkle when using arrays in this way, in that in order to get a strongly typed IEnumerator<T>, we have to cast the array to an IList<T>, as follows:

```
using System.Collections.Generic;

class Counter {
    private int[] arrData = {2, 4, 6, 8, 10};

    public IEnumerator<int> GetEnumerator() {
        return ((IList<int>)arrData).GetEnumerator();
    }
}
```

Using Multiple yield Statements

An iterator block can contain more than one yield return statements, which means that you need not generate all your values in a single loop or as a result of a single calculation. Listing 9-58 contains a simple demonstration.

Listing 9-58. Using Multiple yield return Statements in an Iterator Block

```
using System.Collections.Generic;
```

```
class Counter {
    private int[] arrDataOdd  = { 1, 3, 5 };
    private int[] arrDataEven = { 2, 4, 6 };

    public IEnumerator<int> GetEnumerator() {
        for (int i = 0; i < arrDataEven.Length; i++) {
            yield return arrDataOdd[i];
            yield return arrDataEven[i];
            yield return arrDataEven[i] + arrDataOdd[i];
        }
        yield return 100;
        yield return 500;
    }
}
```

The iterator block in Listing 9-58 abounds with yield return statements. The for loop yields values from two arrays and a calculation based on values from those arrays. When the for loop has run its course, two numeric literal values are yielded as well (see Chapter 5 for details of numeric literals). Using an instance of the Counter class in Listing 9-58 in a foreach loop, like this:

```
// create a new instance of Counter
Counter count = new Counter();

// use the Counter instance in a foreach loop
foreach (int i in count) {
    Console.WriteLine("Value: {0}", i);
}
```

produces the following results:

```
Value: 1
Value: 2
Value: 3
Value: 3
Value: 4
Value: 7
Value: 5
Value: 6
Value: 11
Value: 100
Value: 500
Press enter to finish
```

Using Named Iterator Blocks

The iterator blocks in the previous examples have been *unnamed*, meaning that you use an instance of the class as the iteration source. You can also add *named iterator* blocks to a class. Listing 9-59 contains an example.

Listing 9-59. A Named Iterator Block

```
using System.Collections.Generic;

class Counter {

    public IEnumerable<int> SumSequence(int start, int max) {
        for (int i = start; i < max; i++) {
            yield return i;
        }
    }
}
```

A named iterator block returns a `System.Collections.Generic.IEnumerable<T>` and, unlike an unnamed block, can have any name you choose and can have parameters. In Listing 9-59, the named iterator block is called `SumSequence` and takes parameters that are used in the generation of the iterator values. The `yield` keyword is used in the same way as for an unnamed block. To use a named iterator, you call the method name, as follows:

```
using System;

class Listing_59_Test {

    static void Main(string[] args) {

        // create a new instance of Counter
        Counter count = new Counter();

        // use the named iterator block
        foreach (int i in count.SumSequence(5, 10)) {
            Console.WriteLine("Value: {0}", i);
        }

        // wait for input before exiting
        Console.WriteLine("Press enter to finish");
        Console.ReadLine();
    }
}
```

You can see the call to the named iterator block marked in bold. The ability to pass in parameters makes named iterator blocks more flexible to work with; in this example, the parameters are used to dictate the start and end of the iterator values. A class can contain multiple named iterator blocks, and named blocks can exist in a class that also contains an unnamed block.

Partial Methods

Partial methods are a feature of partial types, introduced in Chapter 6. A partial type is split into different sections, typically across different source code files. Usually, part of a partial class is generated automatically (from a database schema for example), and part is written by the programmer. A partial method is defined in one part of a partial type and implemented in another. Listing 9-60 contains a partial class.

Listing 9-60. A Simple Partial Class

```
partial class Calculator {

    partial void ValidateNumbers(int x, int y);
    partial void ValidateResult(int result);

    public int PerformCalculation(int x, int y) {
        // call the validation partial method
        ValidateNumbers(x, y);

        // perform the calculation
        int result = x * y;

        // call the validation partial method
        ValidateResult(result);

        // return the result
        return result;
    }
}
```

Notice that the Calculator class in Listing 9-60 is defined using the partial keyword. Partial methods can exist only in classes that have been declared as partial. The Calculator class contains the definitions for two partial methods: ValidateNumbers and ValidateResult. Partial methods must return void and cannot have an access modifier (partial methods are implicitly private; see Table 9-2 for details of the private modifier).

The nonpartial method PerformCalculation calls the partial methods before and after performing a simple calculation. When you compile a partial class and there are no implementations of the partial methods that have been defined, the C# compiler removes all references to the methods so that if we compiled the class in Listing 9-60 on its own, it would be equivalent to the following:

```
partial class Calculator {

    public int PerformCalculation(int x, int y) {
        // perform the calculation
        int result = x * y;

        // return the result
        return result;
    }
}
```

This means that there is no performance overhead in defining, but not implementing, a partial method. We can use the class in Listing 9-60 quite happily without providing implementations of the partial methods. For example, if we were to use the following statements:

```
// create a new instance of Calculator
```

```
Calculator calc = new Calculator();

// perform a calculation
int result = calc.PerformCalculation(10, 20);

// print out the result
Console.WriteLine("Result: {0}", result);
```

we would get the following results:

```
Result: 200
Press enter to finish
```

To implement the partial methods, we create a class with the same name and provide implementations for the methods defined in the first partial class. Listing 9-61 contains an example.

■ **Tip** The class that defines the partial methods and the class or classes that implement them must be in the same namespace (although they can still be in different files). See Chapter 11 for details and examples of namespaces.

Listing 9-61. Implementing a Partial Method

```
partial class Calculator {

    partial void ValidateNumbers(int x, int y) {
        Console.WriteLine("ValidateNumbers: {0}, {1}", x, y);
    }
}
```

The partial class in Listing 9-61 implements one of the two partial classes defined in Listing 9-60. The two partial classes in Listings 9-60 and 9-61 can be in the same file or different files in the Visual Studio project. When the project is compiled, a single combined class is created that combines all the methods from the partial classes.

There can be only one implementation of each partial method in a project, but the methods can be spread across several partial classes. We can introduce a third partial Calculator class that implements the remaining partial method from Listing 9-60, as follows:

```
partial class Calculator {

    partial void ValidateResult(int result) {
        Console.WriteLine("Validate Result: {0}", result);
    }
}
```

If we compile the project containing the three partial `Calculator` classes, create a new instance of the class, and call the `PerformCalculation` method with parameters of 10 and 20 (as we did previously), we get the following results:

```
ValidateNumbers: 10, 20
Validate Result: 200
Result: 200
Press enter to finish
```

Abstract Methods

Abstract methods are part of abstract classes and are methods that must be implemented in derived classes. Abstract classes are described in Chapter 6. Listing 9-62 contains an example of an abstract method.

Listing 9-62. An Abstract Method

```
abstract class BaseCalculator {

    protected abstract int CalculateProduct(int x, int y);
    protected abstract int CalculateSum(int x, int y);

    public int PerformCalculation(int x, int y, bool calcProduct) {
        if (calcProduct) {
            return CalculateProduct(x, y);
        } else {
            return CalculateSum(x, y);
        }
    }
}
```

The `BaseCalculator` class in Listing 9-62 contains two abstract methods, shown in bold. Abstract methods can be added only to an abstract class (which is a class modified by the `abstract` keyword). Abstract methods are created by applying the `abstract` keyword as a modifier. Abstract methods are like virtual methods, except that the base class doesn't provide an implementation.

Abstract classes can contain regular methods, and these methods can call abstract methods, as demonstrated by the `PerformCalculation` method, which uses one of the two abstract methods based on a parameter value. You can't create an instance of an abstract class, only a derived class that implements all the abstract methods. Listing 9-63 shows a class that does just this.

Listing 9-63. Providing Implementations of Abstract Methods

```
class CalcImpl : BaseCalculator {

    protected override int CalculateProduct(int x, int y) {
        return x * y;
    }
```

```
    protected override int CalculateSum(int x, int y) {
        return x + y;
    }
}
```

Implementing an abstract method is just like overriding a virtual method. You use the override keyword, match the signature of the method, and provide an implementation of the method. (When you implement an abstract method, you can't use the base keyword to call the base class implementation of the method; there isn't one, of course, and the C# compiler will generate an error.)

The class in Listing 9-63 provides implementations of both of the abstract methods in the base class. We can create instances of this derived class and treat it either as an instance of the base class or as an instance of the derived class, like this:

```
// create an new CalcImpl
BaseCalculator calc = new CalcImpl();

// perform some calculations
int result1 = calc.PerformCalculation(10, 20, true);
int result2 = calc.PerformCalculation(10, 20, false);

// print out the results
Console.WriteLine("Result1: {0}", result1);
Console.WriteLine("Result2: {0}", result2);
```

Compiling and running the two classes from Listings 9-61 and 9-62, and these statements produce the following results:

```
Result1: 200
Result2: 30
Press enter to finish
```

If a derived class doesn't implement all the abstract methods in a base class, then the derived class must also be declared as abstract. Derived classes can choose to implement some of the abstract methods and even seal them so that further derived classes cannot provide their own implementations. Listing 9-64 contains an example.

Listing 9-64. Selectively Implementing Abstract Methods

```
abstract class SelectiveImpl : BaseCalculator {

    protected sealed override int CalculateProduct(int x, int y) {
        return x * y;
    }
}

class FinalCalculator : SelectiveImpl {

    protected override int CalculateSum(int x, int y) {
        return x + y;
```

```
    }
}
```

The first class, SelectiveImpl, in Listing 9-64 implements just one of the abstract methods that we defined in Listing 9-62, but it also uses the sealed modifier, meaning that derived classes cannot provide their own implementations of this method. Since this class doesn't implement all the abstract methods of its base class, it is an abstract class, too.

The second class, FinalCalculator, is derived from SelectiveImpl. If we want to create a class that we can create instances of, we must implement the remaining abstract method, but we can't implement the sealed method. We have to accept the implementation of the SelectiveImpl class.

Extension Methods

Extension methods allow you to seemingly add methods to classes without modifying them. I say *seemingly*, because extension methods are a clever feature that makes it appear as though a method has been added to a class when it hasn't really. Let's start with the class we are going to extend:

```
class Person {
    public string Name { get; set; }
    public int Age { get; set; }
    public string City { get; set; }

    public Person(string name, int age, string city) {
        Name = name; Age = age; City = city;
    }
}
```

We have seen this class in previous examples. It has three public properties and a constructor. Listing 9-65 contains an extension method that operates on this class.

Listing 9-65. Defining an Extension Method

```
using System;

static class ExtensionMethods {

    public static void PrintInformation(this Person p) {
        Console.WriteLine("--- Person ---");
        Console.WriteLine("Name: {0}", p.Name);
        Console.WriteLine("Age: {0}", p.Age);
        Console.WriteLine("City: {0}", p.City);
    }
}
```

Extension methods must be static and can exist only inside a static class (static classes are described in Chapter 6). Unlike partial methods, the name of the class that contains the extension methods doesn't matter. The first parameter in an extension method must have the this modifier, and the type of the parameter is the type on which the extension method will operate. Using an extension method is like using a regular method. Listing 9-66 demonstrates using the extension method in Listing 9-65.

Listing 9-66. Using an Extension Method

```
using System;

class Listing_66 {

    static void Main(string[] args) {

        // create a new instance of Person
        Person p = new Person("Adam Freeman", 38, "London");

        // call the extension method
        p.PrintInformation();

        // wait for input before exiting
        Console.WriteLine("Press enter to finish");
        Console.ReadLine();
    }
}
```

In Listing 9-66, I create an instance of the Person class and then call the PrintInformation extension method as though it were a regular method. Compiling and running the Person class and Listings 9-65 and 9-66 produces the following results:

```
--- Person ---
Name: Adam Freeman
Age: 38
City: London
Press enter to finish
```

You don't need to provide a value for the first parameter in an extension method (the one modified with this). It is implicit from the object that you have called the method on. Inside an extension method, you can refer to this parameter to access the members of the object. Extension methods don't have any special access to the members of an object, so you can only use those members to which you have access. This will typically be those that are modified using the public or internal keywords.

This is what I meant when I said that extension methods seem to extend classes. In fact, we have defined an entirely method in an entirely separate class, but the magic of the C# compiler allows us to use it as though it were part of the original Person class.

Extension methods are a syntax convenience. I could have achieved the same effect by creating a method with a Person parameter, such as this one:

```
private static void PrintPersonInformation(Person p) {
    Console.WriteLine("--- Person ---");
    Console.WriteLine("Name: {0}", p.Name);
    Console.WriteLine("Age: {0}", p.Age);
    Console.WriteLine("City: {0}", p.City);
}
```

This is functionally equivalent to the extension method in Listing 9-65, but there is something pleasing and natural about the way that extension methods appear as regular methods in code files. Extension methods are most useful when you don't have access to the source code of the class you want to work with. Listing 9-67 provides an example.

Listing 9-67. Using an Extension Method on a Library Class

```
static class ExtensionMethods {

    public static bool ContainsLetter(this string s, char c) {
        // enumerate the characters in the string
        // and see if we have a match
        foreach (char ch in s) {
            if (ch == c) {
                return true;
            }
        }
        // we have finished checking all of the characters
        // in the string, meaning that there is no match
        return false;
    }
}
```

The type of the first parameter in the extension method in Listing 9-67 is string, meaning that this method can be called on instances of string. This class checks each of the characters in a string to see whether one of them matches a character value provided as a parameter. If there is a match, then extension method returns true. If there is no match, false is returned.

■ **Tip** There is a better implementation of this feature available in the System.String class. I just need a simple example to demonstrate extension methods in this chapter. See Chapter 16 for details and examples of strings and characters in C#.

The following code applies the extension method defined in Listing 9-67 to an instance of string:

```
class Listing_67_Test {

    static void Main(string[] args) {

        // define a string
        string str = "Hello World";

        // use the extension method on the string
        bool containsCharX = str.ContainsLetter('x');
        bool containsCharE = str.ContainsLetter('e');

        Console.WriteLine("String contains X: {0}", containsCharX);
```

```
        Console.WriteLine("String contains E: {0}", containsCharE);

        // wait for input before exiting
        Console.WriteLine("Press enter to finish");
        Console.ReadLine();
    }
}
```

Once again, we can see that the extension method is used just like a regular method and that we don't have to provide a value for the first parameter. We don't have access to the source code for the string class, but we have been able to neatly extend the functionality of the class by creating an extension method. Compiling and running the previous code produces the following output:

```
String contains X: False
String contains E: True
Press enter to finish
```

Summary

In this chapter, we have taken a detailed look at defining, implementing, and using methods. Methods are the muscles of a C# program. The code statements contained in a method are executed to perform actions and calculations, and the definitions and modifiers define how those methods can be connected together. Without methods, there is no C# program.

We looked at the different types of parameter that can be used in methods, and we learned that parameters are how we pass data around a program. We explored overloading and overriding methods, which are two of the key concepts in object-oriented programming. Finally, we looked at some special kinds of methods: the Main method, the constructor, and so on. These special methods shape the way that programs are executed and objects are differentiated. Along the way, we saw several convenience features, ranging from optional parameters to compiler-generated iterator blocks. There was a lot of information to learn in this chapter, but a good understanding of methods is an essential foundation for effective C# programming.

CHAPTER 10

■ ■ ■

Delegates, Events, and Anonymous Methods

Delegates are special types that encapsulate a method, similar to function pointers found in other programming languages. Delegates have a number of uses in C#, but you are most likely to encounter a special type of delegate—the *event*. Events make notifying interested parties simple and flexible, and I'll explain the convention for their use later in the chapter.

I'll also explain the Func and Action types that let you use delegates in a more convenient form and that are used extensively in some of the latest C# language features, such as parallel programming.

We'll finish up this chapter with a look at anonymous methods and lambda expressions, two C# features that let us implement delegates without having to define methods in our classes. Table 10-1 provides the summary for this chapter

Table 10-1. Quick Problem/Solution Reference for Chapter 10

Problem	Solution	Listings
Define a delegate.	Use the delegate keyword to define a new delegate type and to define a delegate field. Assign a method to the delegate.	10-1 through 10-3
Notify an object when something interesting happens.	Use a delegate to perform a callback or use an event.	10-4, 10-8 through 10-15
Use a single delegate to invoke multiple methods.	Combine methods using the delegate += operator. Remove methods using the -= operator.	10-5
Create delegated methods based on parameter values.	Select methods to delegate at runtime.	10-6
Discover the methods that will be called by a delegate.	Use the GetInvocationList method to get a list of the methods, and use the Target and Method properties to obtain details of each method.	10-7
Override a base class event to implement custom code.	Override the OnXXX method; do not override the event field.	10-16

Problem	Solution	Listings
Use delegates without defining custom delegate types.	Use the System.Func and System.Action types.	10-17 through 10-20
Implement a delegate without defining a method.	Use an anonymous method or a lambda expression.	10-21 through 10-25

Using Delegates

A *delegate* is a special C# type that represents a method signature. Methods are discussed in Chapter 9, and the signature is the combination of the return type and the type and order of the method parameters. Listing 10-1 contains an example of a delegate.

Listing 10-1. Defining a Delegate Type

```
public delegate int PerformCalc(int x, int y);
```

There are five parts to the delegate in Listing 10-1, and they are illustrated in Figure 10-1.

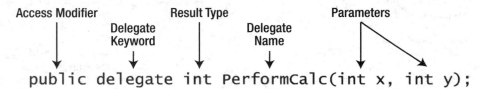

Figure 10-1. The anatomy of a delegate

The first two parts of a delegate are simple. First, all delegates require the delegate keyword. Second, delegates, like all types, can have access modifiers. See Chapter 6 for a description of how these modifiers apply to classes; they have the same effect on delegates.

The delegate name is the name by which we will refer to the type we have created. This is equivalent to the class name. The name of the delegate type in Listing 10-1 is PerformCalc.

The remaining parts of the delegate specify the kind of method that instances of this delegate can represent. In Listing 10-1, instances of the delegate can represent methods that return an int and that have two int parameters.

As we look at each part of the delegate in Listing 10-1, it is important to bear in mind that when we define a new delegate, we are defining a new type. What we are saying is, "Here is a new type that can be used to refer to a specific kind of method." Delegates can be hard to understand, and if you find yourself getting lost in this chapter, you should come back to the previous sentence. You can define a new delegate type in the same places as you can create a new class—in a namespace, class, or struct.

Once we have defined a new delegate type, we can create an instance of it and initialize it with a value. Listing 10-2 contains a demonstration.

Listing 10-2. Defining a Delegate Field

```
public delegate int PerformCalc(int x, int y);

class Calculator {
    PerformCalc perfCalc;

    public Calculator() {
        perfCalc = CalculateProduct;
    }

    public PerformCalc CalcDelegate {
        get { return perfCalc; }
    }

    private int CalculateProduct(int num1, int num2) {
        return num1 * num2;
    }
}
```

The Calculator class in Listing 10-2 has a field called perfCalc that is of the type of delegate we defined in Listing 10-1. This has created a field that can be used to represent a method that matches the delegate, in other words, a method that returns an int and has two int parameters. The Calculator class contains a method called CalculateProduct that matches that description, and in the Calculator constructor, I assign a value to the delegate field by using the name of the matching method. The definition of the field and the assignment of a value are shown in bold.

The Calculator class in Listing 10-2 also contains a public property that returns an instance of the delegate type. The accessor in the property returns the value assigned to the delegate field.

Now we have a new delegate type, PerformCalc, instances of it can be used to represent methods that return an int and that have two int parameters. We have a Calculator class that has a private field of the PerformCalc type and that has been assigned the CalculateMethod and a public property that returns the value of the delegate field. Listing 10-3 demonstrates how to use the delegate.

Listing 10-3. Using a Delegate Obtained Through a Property

```
class Listing_03 {

    static void Main(string[] args) {

        Calculator calc = new Calculator();

        // get the delegate
        PerformCalc del = calc.CalcDelegate;

        // invoke the delegate to get a result
        int result = del(10, 20);

        // print out the result
        Console.WriteLine("Result: {0}", result);
```

```
        // wait for input before exiting
        Console.WriteLine("Press enter to finish");
        Console.ReadLine();
    }
}
```

A new instance of the Calculator class is created, and the CalcDelegate property is used to assign a value to a local variable of the PerformCalc delegate type; this means that the del variable contains a reference to the CalculateProduct method in the Calculator object. I invoke the delegate with the following statement:

```
int result = del(10, 20);
```

This statement passes the parameters 10 and 20 to the method assigned to the del variable, which means that the CalculateProduct method in the Calculator object is called. The result from the delegated method is assigned to the local result variable, just as would happen with a regular method call.

The reason that I created a new Calculator object is that I wanted to delegate an instance method, and you can do that only once you have an instance to work with. If you want to delegate a static method, then you can do so by using the class name; you can see an example of delegating a static method in Listing 10-4 later in the chapter.

You can also use generic types with delegates. If we wanted a generic version of the delegate type defined in Listing 10-1, we could define the following:

```
public delegate T PerformCalc<T>(T x, T y);
```

Then to create the delegate field in the Calculator class, we would use the following:

```
class Calculator {
    PerformCalc<int> perfCalc;
    ...
```

In this way, we can define a general-purpose delegate and provide the type parameters as needed when we define the delegate fields or variables. Generic types are described in Chapter 15.

There are a couple of points to note about all the examples so far. The first is that we passed around a method as we would a regular variable, invoking it only when we needed. The other is that the class that called the delegated method had no direct relationship to the method being invoked. We delegated a private method hidden away inside the Calculator class that the Listing_03 class wouldn't otherwise be able to access.

The examples have shown *how* to use delegates but didn't really explain *why* you might find them useful. In the following sections, I'll show you ways to use delegates that simplify common coding patterns and demonstrate some useful C# features.

Using Delegates for Callbacks

You can use delegates to create *callbacks,* where one object is notified when something of interest happens in another object. Listing 10-4 contains an example of a simple callback to notify an interested class when a calculation is performed.

Listing 10-4. Using a Delegate for a Callback

```
using System;

delegate void NotifyCalculation(int x, int y, int result);

class Calculator {
    NotifyCalculation calcListener;

    public Calculator(NotifyCalculation listener) {
        calcListener = listener;
    }

    public int CalculateProduct(int num1, int num2) {
        // perform the calculation
        int result = num1 * num2;

        // notify the delegate that we have performed a calc
        calcListener(num1, num2, result);

        // return the result
        return result;
    }
}

class CalculationListener {
    public static void CalculationPrinter(int x, int y, int result) {
        Console.WriteLine("Calculation Notification: {0} x {1} = {2}",
            x, y, result);
    }
}

class Listing_04 {

    static void Main(string[] args) {

        // create a new Calculator, passing in the printer method
        Calculator calc = new Calculator(CalculationListener.CalculationPrinter);

        // perform some calculations
        calc.CalculateProduct(10, 20);
        calc.CalculateProduct(2, 3);
        calc.CalculateProduct(20, 1);

        // wait for input before exiting
        Console.WriteLine("Press enter to finish");
        Console.ReadLine();
    }
}
```

The delegate type in this example is called NotifyCalculation and has parameters for the two numbers that have been used for the calculation and the result that was computed. The Calculator class in this example has a constructor argument that takes an instance of the delegate type, which is then invoked inside the CalculateProduct method.

The Listing_04 class creates a new instance of Calculator and passes a reference to the static CalculationListener.CalculationPrinter method as the constructor parameter. The delegate is called each time the Calculator.CalculateProduct method is invoked, printing out a notification of the calculation that has been performed. Compiling and running the code in Listing 10-4 produces the following result:

```
Calculation Notification: 10 x 20 = 200
Calculation Notification: 2 x 3 = 6
Calculation Notification: 20 x 1 = 20
Press enter to finish
```

Using delegates in callbacks means that the source of the notifications doesn't need to know anything about the class that receives them, allowing the notification receiver to be refactored or replaced without the source having to be modified at all. As you'll see in the "Delegating Selectively" section later in the chapter, we can select a delegate at runtime, which provides us with even greater flexibility.

Multicasting with Delegates

When performing callbacks, you will often need to cater for multiple listeners, rather than the single listener shown in Listing 10-4. The delegate type uses custom + and – operators that let you combine several method references together into a single delegate and invoke them in one go, known as *multicasting*. Custom operators are discussed in Chapter 8. Listing 10-5 contains an example of a multicasting delegate callback.

Listing 10-5. Using Delegate Multicasting

```
using System;

delegate void NotifyCalculation(int x, int y, int result);

class Calculator {
    NotifyCalculation calcListener;

    public void AddListener(NotifyCalculation listener) {
        calcListener += listener;
    }

    public void RemoveListener(NotifyCalculation listener) {
        calcListener -= listener;
    }

    public int CalculateProduct(int num1, int num2) {
        // perform the calculation
```

```
        int result = num1 * num2;

        // notify the delegate that we have performed a calc
        calcListener(num1, num2, result);

        // return the result
        return result;
    }
}

class CalculationListener {
    private string idString;

    public CalculationListener(string id) {
        idString = id;
    }

    public void CalculationPrinter(int x, int y, int result) {
        Console.WriteLine("{0}: Notification: {1} x {2} = {3}",
            idString, x, y, result);
    }
}

class AlternateListener {

    public static void CalculationCallback(int x, int y, int result) {
        Console.WriteLine("Callback: {0} x {1} = {2}",
            x, y, result);
    }
}

class Listing_05 {

    static void Main(string[] args) {

        // create a new Calculator
        Calculator calc = new Calculator();

        // create and add listeners
        calc.AddListener(new CalculationListener("List1").CalculationPrinter);
        calc.AddListener(new CalculationListener("List2").CalculationPrinter);
        calc.AddListener(AlternateListener.CalculationCallback);

        // perform a calculation
        calc.CalculateProduct(10, 20);

        // remove a listener
        calc.RemoveListener(AlternateListener.CalculationCallback);

        // perform a calculation
        calc.CalculateProduct(10, 30);
```

```
        // wait for input before exiting
        Console.WriteLine("Press enter to finish");
        Console.ReadLine();
    }
}
```

The Calculator class in this example defines two methods that register and unregister callback delegates using the += and -= operators. There are two classes that contain methods that match the delegate signature, CalculationListener and AlternateListener, and the Listing_05 class registers and unregisters the methods as delegates with the Calculator object. You can see that you use a multicast delegate just as you would a single delegate. Compiling and running the code in Listing 10-5 produces the following results:

```
List1: Notification: 10 x 20 = 200
List2: Notification: 10 x 20 = 200
Callback: 10 x 20 = 200
List1: Notification: 10 x 30 = 300
List2: Notification: 10 x 30 = 300
Press enter to finish
```

Delegating Selectively

One of the benefits of being able to pass delegates around as variables is to apply delegates selectively, such that we create a delegate that is tailored to a given situation. Listing 10-6 contains a simple example.

Listing 10-6. Creating Anonymous Delegates Based on Parameter Value

```
using System;

delegate int PerformCalc(int x, int y);

class Calculator {
    public enum Modes {
        Normal,
        Iterative
    };

    public PerformCalc GetDelegate(Modes mode) {
        if (mode == Modes.Normal) {
            return CalculateNormally;
        } else {
            return CalculateIteratively;
        }
    }

    private int CalculateNormally(int x, int y) {
        return x * y;
    }
```

```
    private int CalculateIteratively(int x, int y) {
        int result = 0;
        for (int i = 0; i < x; i++) {
            result += y;
        }
        return result;
    }
}

class Listing_06 {

    static void Main(string[] args) {

        // create a new Calculator
        Calculator calc = new Calculator();

        // get a delegate
        PerformCalc del = calc.GetDelegate(Calculator.Modes.Normal);

        // use the delegate
        Console.WriteLine("Normal product: {0}", del(10, 20));

        // get a delegate
        del = calc.GetDelegate(Calculator.Modes.Iterative);

        // use the delegate
        Console.WriteLine("Iterative product: {0}", del(10, 20));

        // wait for input before exiting
        Console.WriteLine("Press enter to finish");
        Console.ReadLine();
    }
}
```

The Calculator class in Listing 10-6 has a GetDelegate method that returns an delegate based on the parameter value, selected from an enum. If the parameter is the Normal enum value, the delegate returned by the method uses the standard C# multiplication operator, but if the value is Iterative, then the method returns a delegate that performs multiplication as an iterative series of additions.

Interrogating Delegates

The base type for all delegates is System.Delegate, and we can use the members of this class to find out which methods a delegate will invoke on our behalf. Listing 10-7 contains an example.

Listing 10-7. Interrogating Delegate Types

```
using System;

delegate int PerformCalc(int x, int y);
```

```
class Calculator {

    public int CalculateSum(int x, int y) {
        return x + y;
    }
}

class AlternateCalculator {

    public int CalculateProduct(int x, int y) {
        return x * y;
    }
}

class Listing_07 {

    static void Main(string[] args) {

        // create a delegate variable
        PerformCalc del = new Calculator().CalculateSum;

        // combine with another method
        del += new AlternateCalculator().CalculateProduct;

        // Interrogate the delegate
        Delegate[] inlist = del.GetInvocationList();
        foreach (Delegate d in inlist) {
            Console.WriteLine("Target: {0}", d.Target);
            Console.WriteLine("Method: {0}", d.Method);
        }

        // wait for input before exiting
        Console.WriteLine("Press enter to finish");
        Console.ReadLine();
    }
}
```

The Listing_07 class creates a new delegate variable and uses it to combine methods from the Calculator and AlternateCalculator classes. I use the GetInvocationList method on the delegate variable, which returns an array of System.Delegate objects. I enumerate the contents of the array with a foreach loop and print out the value of the Target and Method properties for each Delegate object. (C# arrays are described in Chapter 13.) Table 10-2 describes the Target and Method properties.

Table 10-2. The System.Delegate Properties

Property	Description
Target	Returns the object that the delegate will use to invoke the method or null if the delegate method is static.
Method	Returns a System.Reflection.MethodInfo that describes the method that will be invoked by the delegate.

Compiling and running the code in Listing 10-7 produces the following results:

```
Target: Calculator
Method: Int32 CalculateSum(Int32, Int32)
Target: AlternateCalculator
Method: Int32 CalculateProduct(Int32, Int32)
Press enter to finish
```

Using Events

Events are specialized delegates designed to simplify the callback model we saw earlier in the chapter. There can be a problem when you use a delegate type as a field, where one object interferes with another. Listing 10-8 contains a demonstration.

Listing 10-8. One Type Modifying a Delegate Supplied by Another Type

```csharp
using System;

delegate void NotifyCalculation(int x, int y, int result);

class Calculator {
    public static NotifyCalculation CalculationPerformed;

    public static int CalculateProduct(int num1, int num2) {
        // perform the calculation
        int result = num1 * num2;

        // notify any listeners
        CalculationPerformed(num1, num2, result);

        // return the result
        return result;
    }
}
```

```
class NefariousClass {
    private NotifyCalculation orig;

    public NefariousClass() {
        // get a reference to the existing listener
        orig = Calculator.CalculationPerformed;

        // set a new listener for Calculator
        Calculator.CalculationPerformed = HandleNotifyCalculation;
    }

    public void HandleNotifyCalculation(int x, int y, int result) {
        // lie to the original listener
        orig(x, y, x + y);

        // print out the details of the real calculation
        Console.WriteLine("NefariousClass: {0} x {1} = {2}",
            x, y, result);
    }
}

class Listing_08 {

    static void Main(string[] args) {

        // set a listener for the Calculator class
        Calculator.CalculationPerformed = StandardHandleResult;

        // create an instance of the Nefarious class
        NefariousClass nc = new NefariousClass();

        // perform a calculation
        Calculator.CalculateProduct(20, 72);

        // wait for input before exiting
        Console.WriteLine("Press enter to finish");
        Console.ReadLine();
    }

    private static void StandardHandleResult(int x, int y, int result) {
        Console.WriteLine("Good Class: {0} x {1} = {2}", x, y, result);
    }
}
```

In this example, the Listing_08 class contains a method that matches the delegate type used for the Calculator.CalculationPerformed field. This method is used to process callbacks from the Calculator class. The idea is that the anonymous method will be called each time a calculation is performed by the Calculator class, just as in some of the earlier examples.

The Listing_08 class also creates a new NefariousClass object, and the fun begins. The NefariousClass constructor assigns a new method to the Calculator delegate field, displacing the original. This method then feeds bad information to the original value of the delegate field. If we compile and run the code in Listing 10-9, we get the following results:

```
Good Class: 20 x 72 = 92
NefariousClass: 20 x 72 = 1440
Press enter to finish
```

The original method is invoked each time a calculation is performed, but NefariousClass has inserted itself in the way and changes the details of the calculation that is reported. And the problems don't stop there—because the delegate field is public, any object can invoke the delegate as it wants, simulating callbacks even though no calculation has been performed.

This example demonstrates deliberate interference, but most of the problems with public delegate fields arise because of sloppy programming, where an object makes an explicit assignment using = to set the value of the delegate field instead of using += to combine delegates. You could take steps to avoid this problem—make the delegate field private and implement methods that enforce checks to ensure that objects are not interfering with each other—but the C# event feature takes care of this for you.

Defining an event is just like defining a delegate field, with the addition of the event keyword. So, here's our delegate field from Listing 10-9:

```
class Calculator {
    public static NotifyCalculation CalculationPerformed;
```

becomes the following:

```
class Calculator {
    public static event NotifyCalculation CalculationPerformed;
```

When you make a delegate into an event, the class that contains the field can still invoke the delegate and make full use of the type members and operators. Every other object can use only the += and -= operators to add and subtract methods. It is no longer possible to interrogate the delegate or replace the methods assigned to the delegate as I did in Listing 10-8. Although you can make any delegate into an event, there is strong convention in C# to use a certain pattern for events known as the EventHandler pattern, which makes it easier for others to use your events in their code. I describe the pattern in the following sections.

Defining and Publishing EventHandler Pattern Events

The first step in defining an event is to derive a class from the System.EventArgs class, which contains properties and fields to contain any custom data that you want to pass when you invoke the event delegate; the name of this class should end with EventArgs. Listing 10-9 contains an example for the calculation notification from earlier examples.

Listing 10-9. A Custom EventArgs Implementation

```
class CalculationEventArgs : EventArgs {
    private int x, y, result;

    public CalculationEventArgs(int num1, int num2, int resultVal) {
        x = num1;
        y = num2;
        result = resultVal;
```

```
    }

    public int X {
        get { return x; }
    }

    public int Y {
        get { return y; }
    }

    public int Result {
        get { return result; }
    }
}
```

You can include any fields and properties that you need to express information about your event, but you should make sure that the fields cannot be modified. This is because the same EventArgs object will be passed to each of the subscribers of your event, and a poorly or maliciously coded recipient could change the information that subsequent listeners receive. The CalculationEventArgs class derives from EventArgs and defines fields for the details of our calculation and a set of read-only properties to provide access to the field values. You can get more information about properties in Chapter 8 and more information about fields in Chapter 7.

The next step is to define an event in your class. You don't have to define a delegate for events (although as I showed earlier you certainly can), because you can use the generic EventHandler delegate, which is part of the System namespace. Listing 10-10 demonstrates the definition of an event.

Listing 10-10. Defining an Event Using the Genetic EventHandler Delegate

```
class Calculator {
    public event EventHandler<CalculationEventArgs> CalculationPerformedEvent;
    ...
}
```

To define the event using the generic EventHandler delegate, you use your custom EventArgs class as the type parameter, as shown in the listing. The convention is that the name of the event should end with the word Event. You can learn more about generic types and generic type parameters in Chapter 15.

The convention dictates that you put the code to invoke your event delegate in a method whose name starts with On concatenated with the event name, less the word event. So, for example, since we have defined an event called CalculationPerformedEvent, the method would be called OnCalculationPerformed. This method should make a copy of the event to avoid a race condition (race conditions arise in parallel programming and are explained in later in this book) and ensure that the event has subscribers by ensuring that the event field is not null. Listing 10-11 shows the Calculator class updated to use the event pattern fully.

Listing 10-11. Implementing the EventArgs Pattern

```
class Calculator {
    public event EventHandler<CalculationEventArgs> CalculationPerformedEvent;

    public int CalculateProduct(int num1, int num2) {
        // perform the calculation
```

```
        int result = num1 * num2;

        // publish the event
        OnCalculationPerformed(new CalculationEventArgs(num1, num2, result));

        // return the result
        return result;
    }

    private void OnCalculationPerformed(CalculationEventArgs args) {
        // make a copy of the event
        EventHandler<CalculationEventArgs> handler = CalculationPerformedEvent;

        // check to see we have subscribers
        if (handler != null) {
            handler(this, args);
        }
    }
}
```

You can see that the `CalculateProduct` method creates a new instance of the `CalculationEventArgs` class and uses it to call the `OnCalculationPerformed` method, which then copies the event, checks to see that it isn't `null`, and invokes it.

Subscribing to events is just like using a delegate, with the exception that the subscriber is limited to using the `+=` and `-=` operators. Listing 10-12 shows a class that uses the events defined in the previous examples.

Listing 10-12. Subscribing to Events

```
class Listing_12 {

    static void Main(string[] args) {

        // create a new instance of the Calculator class
        Calculator calc = new Calculator();

        // subscribe to the event in the calaculator class
        calc.CalculationPerformedEvent += HandleEvent;

        // perform a calculation
        calc.CalculateProduct(20, 72);

        // wait for input before exiting
        Console.WriteLine("Press enter to finish");
        Console.ReadLine();
    }

    static void HandleEvent(object sender, CalculationEventArgs e) {
        Console.WriteLine("Good Class: {0} x {1} = {2}", e.X, e.Y, e.Result);
    }
}
```

You must ensure that the method you are going to use to handle events is not publically accessible; otherwise, you are still liable to encounter problems with other classes, as demonstrated by Listing 10-13.

Listing 10-13. Removing Another Delegate from an Event

```
using System;

class CalculationEventArgs : EventArgs {
    private int x, y, result;

    public CalculationEventArgs(int num1, int num2, int resultVal) {
        x = num1;
        y = num2;
        result = resultVal;
    }

    public int X {
        get { return x; }
    }

    public int Y {
        get { return y; }
    }

    public int Result {
        get { return result; }
    }
}

class Calculator {
    public event EventHandler<CalculationEventArgs> CalculationPerformedEvent;

    public int CalculateProduct(int num1, int num2) {
        // perform the calculation
        int result = num1 * num2;

        // publish the event
        OnCalculationPerformed(new CalculationEventArgs(num1, num2, result));

        // return the result
        return result;
    }

    private void OnCalculationPerformed(CalculationEventArgs args) {
        // make a copy of the event
        EventHandler<CalculationEventArgs> handler = CalculationPerformedEvent;

        // check to see we have subscribers
        if (handler != null) {
            handler(this, args);
        }
```

```
    }
}

class NefariousClass {

    public NefariousClass(Calculator calc) {
        // add a new listener for Calculator
        calc.CalculationPerformedEvent += HandleNotifyCalculation;

        // unsubscribe someone else's event handler
        calc.CalculationPerformedEvent -= Listing_13.HandleEvent;
    }

    public void HandleNotifyCalculation(object sender, CalculationEventArgs e) {
        // print out the details of the real calculation
        Console.WriteLine("NefariousClass: {0} x {1} = {2}",
            e.X, e.Y, e.Result);
    }
}

class Listing_13 {

    static void Main(string[] args) {

        // create a new instance of the Calculator class
        Calculator calc = new Calculator();

        // subscribe to the event in the calaculator class
        calc.CalculationPerformedEvent += HandleEvent;

        // create an instance of NefariousClass
        NefariousClass nef = new NefariousClass(calc);

        // perform a calculation
        calc.CalculateProduct(20, 72);

        // wait for input before exiting
        Console.WriteLine("Press enter to finish");
        Console.ReadLine();
    }

    public static void HandleEvent(object sender, CalculationEventArgs e) {
        Console.WriteLine("Good Class: {0} x {1} = {2}", e.X, e.Y, e.Result);
    }
}
```

The NefariousClass constructor in the example adds a new listener to the Calculator event, but it also removes the listener added by the Listing_13 class. It can do this because the Listing_13.HandleEvent method is public and therefore can be accessed outside of its containing class. Changing the access modifier on the HandleEvent class to a more restrictive setting would prevent this from happening.

Creating Nongeneric Events

Another approach to events is to use the nongeneric version of EventHandler. This is more like using a delegate in that you have to define the event/delegate type. This approach predates the introduction of generic types in C#, but I have included it because it is still widely used. Listing 10-14 shows the Calculator example implemented without generic support.

Listing 10-14. Implementing Events Without Generic Types

```
using System;

delegate void CalculationPerformedEventHandler(object sender, CalculationEventArgs args);

class CalculationEventArgs : EventArgs {
    private int x, y, result;

    public CalculationEventArgs(int num1, int num2, int resultVal) {
        x = num1;
        y = num2;
        result = resultVal;
    }

    public int X {
        get { return x; }
    }

    public int Y {
        get { return y; }
    }

    public int Result {
        get { return result; }
    }
}

class Calculator {
    public event CalculationPerformedEventHandler CalculationPerformedEvent;

    public int CalculateProduct(int num1, int num2) {
        // perform the calculation
        int result = num1 * num2;

        // publish the event
        OnCalculationPerformed(new CalculationEventArgs(num1, num2, result));

        // return the result
        return result;
    }

    private void OnCalculationPerformed(CalculationEventArgs args) {
        // make a copy of the event
```

```
        CalculationPerformedEventHandler handler = CalculationPerformedEvent;

        // check to see we have subscribers
        if (handler != null) {
            handler(this, args);
        }
    }
}

class Listing_14 {

    static void Main(string[] args) {

        // create a new instance of the Calculator class
        Calculator calc = new Calculator();

        // subscribe to the event in the calaculator class
        calc.CalculationPerformedEvent += HandleEvent;

        // perform a calculation
        calc.CalculateProduct(20, 72);

        // wait for input before exiting
        Console.WriteLine("Press enter to finish");
        Console.ReadLine();
    }

    static void HandleEvent(object sender, CalculationEventArgs e) {
        Console.WriteLine("Good Class: {0} x {1} = {2}", e.X, e.Y, e.Result);
    }
}
```

There isn't much to say about this example; it is very similar to the generic event listings but has an additional delegate definition.

Creating Events Without Custom Data

If you don't need to pass custom data as part of your event, then you can use EventArgs directly, as shown in Listing 10-15.

Listing 10-15. Creating and Using Events with No Custom Data

```
using System;

class Calculator {
    public event EventHandler CalculationPerformedEvent;

    public int CalculateProduct(int num1, int num2) {
        // perform the calculation
        int result = num1 * num2;
```

```
        // publish the event
        OnCalculationPerformed();

        // return the result
        return result;
    }

    private void OnCalculationPerformed() {
        // make a copy of the event
        EventHandler handler = CalculationPerformedEvent;

        // check to see we have subscribers
        if (handler != null) {
            handler(this, EventArgs.Empty);
        }
    }
}

class Listing_15 {

    static void Main(string[] args) {

        // create a new instance of the Calculator class
        Calculator calc = new Calculator();

        // subscribe to the event in the calaculator class
        calc.CalculationPerformedEvent += HandleEvent;

        // perform a calculation
        calc.CalculateProduct(20, 72);

        // wait for input before exiting
        Console.WriteLine("Press enter to finish");
        Console.ReadLine();
    }

    static void HandleEvent(object sender, EventArgs e) {
        Console.WriteLine("Event Received");
    }
}
```

There is no need to define a custom delegate if you don't need custom data. When defining the event, you simply use the EventHandler type, as follows:

```
public event EventHandler CalculationPerformedEvent;
```

The event still requires two arguments to invoke it, but you can use the static EventArgs.Empty property to get a reference to a ready-made EventArgs instance that has no custom data. You can see this in the OnCalculationPerformed method of the Calculator class, which has been updated to remove the method parameters.

Applying Modifiers to Events

You can control access to your events using the public, protected, internal, and private keywords. See Chapter 7 for details of these keywords and the effect they have on fields.

You should not use the virtual modifier on events. If you do, it is possible that your events will not be delivered properly. If you want to override an event from a base class, then you should mark the OnXXX method as virtual and override the method in the derived class. Listing 10-16 provides a demonstration. You can find more details and examples of overriding methods in Chapter 9.

Listing 10-16. Deriving Event Implementations

```
class Calculator {
    public event EventHandler<CalculationEventArgs> CalculationPerformedEvent;

    public int CalculateProduct(int num1, int num2) {
        // perform the calculation
        int result = num1 * num2;

        // publish the event
        OnCalculationPerformed(new CalculationEventArgs(num1, num2, result));

        // return the result
        return result;
    }

    protected virtual void OnCalculationPerformed(CalculationEventArgs args) {
        // make a copy of the event
        EventHandler<CalculationEventArgs> handler = CalculationPerformedEvent;

        // check to see we have subscribers
        if (handler != null) {
            handler(this, args);
        }
    }
}

class DerivedCalc : Calculator {

    protected override void OnCalculationPerformed(CalculationEventArgs args) {
        // perform custom logic here

        // call the base method
        base.OnCalculationPerformed(args);
    }
}
```

In this example, the DerivedCalc class overrides the OnCalculationPerformed method, which has been marked as virtual in the base Calculator class. The overridden method can perform modifications to the custom EventArgs implementation (or perform any other required task) before calling the base OnCalculationPerformed method to publish the event.

Using Action and Func Delegates

The Func and Action classes are special types that allow you to use delegates without having to specify a custom delegate type. They are used throughout the .NET Framework. For example, you will see examples of both when we look at parallel programming.

Using Action Delegates

Action delegates encapsulate methods that do not return results. In other words, they can be used only with methods that are defined with the void keyword. The simplest Action delegate is the System.Action class, which is used for methods that have no parameters (and no results). Listing 10-17 contains an example.

Listing 10-17. Using the Basic Action Delegate

```
using System;

class Calculator {

    public void CalculateProduct() {
        // perform the calculation
        int result = 10 * 20;

        // print out a message with the result
        Console.WriteLine("Result: {0}", result);
    }
}

class Listing_17 {

    static void Main(string[] args) {

        // create a new instance of Calculator
        Calculator calc = new Calculator();

        // create an action and assign a method
        Action act = calc.CalculateProduct;

        // invoke the method via the Action
        act();

        // wait for input before exiting
        Console.WriteLine("Press enter to finish");
        Console.ReadLine();
    }
}
```

The key statement in Listing 10-17 is shown in bold; it creates a new local Action variable and assigns the CalculateProduct method from an instance of Calculator as the value. The Action is then invoked, just as a regular delegate would be. Compiling and running the code in Listing 10-17 products the following results:

```
Result: 200
Press enter to finish
```

We didn't have to define a custom delegate in this example. The System.Action type handled everything for us. There are 17 different Action implementations available. Starting with the one used in Listing 10-17, each adds a new generic parameter. This is not as confusing as it may sound; you just create the generic implementation that matches the number of parameters the target method required. Listing 10-18 contains an example that uses two parameters.

Listing 10-18. Using a Generic Action Delegate

```
using System;

class Calculator {

    public void CalculateProduct(int x, int y) {
        // perform the calculation
        int result = x * y;

        // print out a message with the result
        Console.WriteLine("Result: {0}", result);
    }
}

class Listing_18 {

    static void Main(string[] args) {

        // create a new instance of Calculator
        Calculator calc = new Calculator();

        // create an action and assign a method
        Action<int, int> act = calc.CalculateProduct;

        // invoke the method via the Action
        act(10, 20);

        // wait for input before exiting
        Console.WriteLine("Press enter to finish");
        Console.ReadLine();
    }
}
```

In this example, the method I want to delegate has two int parameters, so I used the Action<int, int> delegate (the parameter types for an Action need not all be the same). If I had wanted to delegate a method with five parameters, then I would have used the Action<T1, T2, T3, T4, T5> type and filled in the type parameters of the Action type to match the parameter types of the delegated method.

Using Func Delegates

System.Func delegates are just like Action delegates, except that they can return results. The simplest Func implementation has no parameters. Listing 10-19 contains an example; you can see the similarities to the Action examples.

Listing 10-19. A Simple Func Example

```
using System;

class Calculator {

    public int CalculateProduct() {
        // perform the calculation
        return 10 * 20;
    }
}

class Listing_19 {

    static void Main(string[] args) {

        // create a new instance of Calculator
        Calculator calc = new Calculator();

        // create a Func and assign a method
        Func<int> act = calc.CalculateProduct;

        // invoke the method via the Action
        int result = act();

        // print out the result
        Console.WriteLine("Result: {0}", result);

        // wait for input before exiting
        Console.WriteLine("Press enter to finish");
        Console.ReadLine();
    }
}
```

The last generic type for System.Func is the result type for the delegate. So, in Listing 10-19, the Func<int> I used had no parameters but returned an int. Just like Action, there are 17 Func implementations with an increasing number of parameters, each of which can be of a different type. Listing 10-20 demonstrates using Func with two int parameters.

Listing 10-20. Using a Func with Parameters

```
using System;

class Calculator {

    public int CalculateProduct(int x, int y) {
        // perform the calculation
        return x * y;
    }
}

class Listing_20 {

    static void Main(string[] args) {

        // create a new instance of Calculator
        Calculator calc = new Calculator();

        // create a Func and assign a method
        Func<int, int, int> act = calc.CalculateProduct;

        // invoke the method via the Action
        int result = act(10, 20);

        // print out the result
        Console.WriteLine("Result: {0}", result);

        // wait for input before exiting
        Console.WriteLine("Press enter to finish");
        Console.ReadLine();
    }
}
```

Anonymous Methods

All of the examples so far in this chapter have used *named methods,* that is, methods that exist in classes and have a method identifier. C# also supports anonymous methods, which allow you to implement a delegate without defining a method. Listing 10-21 contains an anonymous method.

Listing 10-21. An Anonymous Method

```
using System;

class Listing_21 {

    static void Main(string[] args) {

        // create a new Calculator
```

```
Calculator calc = new Calculator();

// create a delegate with an anonymous method
calc.CalculationPerformedEvent += delegate(object sender, CalculationEventArgs e) {
    Console.WriteLine("Anonymous Calc: {0} x {1} = {2}", e.X, e.Y, e.Result);
};

// perform a calculation
calc.CalculateProduct(20, 40);

// wait for input before exiting
Console.WriteLine("Press enter to finish");
Console.ReadLine();
    }
}
```

The class in Listing 10-21 works with the Calculator and CalculationEventArgs classes defining in Listing 10-9. I have omitted them from this listing for brevity. You can see the anonymous method in bold; it is also illustrated in Figure 10-2.

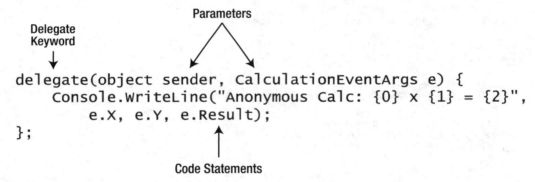

Figure 10-2. The anatomy of an anonymous method

An anonymous method has a number of similarities to a named method. You can see the parameters and code block in Figure 10-2 are just like those you would get in a regular method. There is no method identifier (because there is no method name), and you must use the delegate keyword when defining an anonymous method.

Using an anonymous method as a delegate is just like using a named method, as you can see from Listing 10-21. I used the += operator to add the anonymous method to the event in the Calculator class. When the event invokes the delegate, the statements in the anonymous method body are executed, just as would happen for a regular method.

If we compile and run the code in Listing 10-21, we get the following results:

```
Anonymous Calc: 20 x 40 = 800
Press enter to finish
```

Anonymous methods work very well with Func and Action delegates, allowing you to define a delegate without needing to create a delegate type or implement a named method. When implementing a delegate that returns a result, simply use the return keyword as you would for a named method, as demonstrated by Listing 10-22.

Listing 10-22. An Anonymous Method That Returns a Result

```
using System;

class Listing_22 {

    static void Main(string[] args) {

        // define a func and implement it with an anonymous method
        Func<int, int, int> productFunction = delegate(int x, int y) {
            return x * y;
        };

        // invoke the func and get a result
        int result = productFunction(10, 20);

        // print out the result
        Console.WriteLine("Result: {0}", result);

        // wait for input before exiting
        Console.WriteLine("Press enter to finish");
        Console.ReadLine();
    }
}
```

The bold statement in Listing 10-22 defines a Func that returns an int result and that has two int parameters. The implementation of this delegate is provided by an anonymous method that returns the product of the two parameters values. You invoke the delegate in the normal way, as though it were a method. Compiling and running the code in Listing 10-22 produces the following results:

```
Result: 200
Press enter to finish
```

Capturing Outer Variables

Anonymous methods do more than reduce the number of methods in your class; they are also able to access the local variables that are defined in the containing methods, known as *outer variables*. Listing 10-23 provides a demonstration.

Listing 10-23. Accessing Outer Variables

```
using System;
```

```
class Calculator {
    Func<int, int, int> calcFunction;

    public Calculator(Func<int, int, int> function) {
        calcFunction = function;
    }

    public int PerformCalculation(int x, int y) {
        return calcFunction(x, y);
    }
}

class Listing_23 {

    static void Main(string[] args) {

        // define a local variable
        int calculationCount = 0;

        // define and implement a Func
        Func<int, int, int> productFunc = delegate(int x, int y) {
            // increment the outer variables
            calculationCount++;

            // calculate and return the result
            return x * y;
        };

        // create a new instance of Calculator
        Calculator calc = new Calculator(productFunc);

        // perform several calculations
        for (int i = 0; i < 5; i++) {
            Console.WriteLine("Result {0} = {1}", i, calc.PerformCalculation(i, i));
        }

        // print out the value of the outer variable
        Console.WriteLine("calculationCount: {0}", calculationCount);

        // wait for input before exiting
        Console.WriteLine("Press enter to finish");
        Console.ReadLine();
    }
}
```

The Calculator class in this example takes a Func<int, int, int> as a constructor parameter and invokes the delegate when the PerformCalculation method is called. The Listing_23 class defines a matching Func using an anonymous method. This is passed to the constructor of the Calculator instance.

The anonymous method increments the calculationCount variable each time that it is invoked, even though the variable is defined outside of the anonymous method and even though the Func is invoked by an entirely different method in an entirely different object. Compiling and running the code in Listing 10-23 produces the following result:

```
Result 0 = 0
Result 1 = 1
Result 2 = 4
Result 3 = 9
Result 4 = 16
calculationCount: 5
Press enter to finish
```

Variables that are accessed outside the anonymous method are called *captured* variables. The calculationCount variable in Listing 10-23 was captured by the anonymous method. An anonymous method that captures variables is called a *closure*.

Captured variables are evaluated when the delegate is invoked, which means that you should take care when making assumptions about the value of a variable. Listing 10-24 provides a demonstration.

Listing 10-24. Evaluating Captured Variables

```
using System;

class Listing_24 {

    static void Main(string[] args) {

        // define a variable that will be captured
        string message = "Hello World";

        // define an anonymous method that will capture
        // the local variables
        Action printMessage = delegate() {
            Console.WriteLine("Message: {0}", message);
        };

        // modify one of the local vaiables
        message = "Howdy!";

        // invoke the delegate
        printMessage();

        // wait for input before exiting
        Console.WriteLine("Press enter to finish");
        Console.ReadLine();
    }
}
```

When the anonymous method is defined, the value of the message variable is Hello World. But defining an anonymous method doesn't capture the variables it references—that doesn't happen until the delegate is invoked, by which time the value of the message variable has changed. Compiling and running the code in Listing 10-24 produces the following result:

```
Message: Howdy!
Press enter to finish
```

Lambda Expressions

Lambda expressions have largely replaced anonymous methods since they were introduced in C# 3.0. They have much the same functionality as an anonymous method but are slightly more convenient to use. Listing 10-25 contains an anonymous method and an equivalent lambda expression.

Listing 10-25. Comparing an Anonymous Method with a Lambda Expression

```
using System;

class Listing_25 {

    static void Main(string[] args) {

        // implement an anonymous method that multiplies ints
        Func<int, int, int> anonFunc = delegate(int x, int y) {
            return x * y;
        };

        // do the same thing with a lambda expression
        Func<int, int, int> lambaFunc = (x, y) => {
            return x * y;
        };

        // invoke the delegates
        Console.WriteLine("Anonymous Method Result: {0}", anonFunc(10, 10));
        Console.WriteLine("Lambda Expression Result: {0}", lambaFunc(10, 10));

        // wait for input before exiting
        Console.WriteLine("Press enter to finish");
        Console.ReadLine();
    }
}
```

The lambda expression in Listing 10-25 is shown in bold. There are only three parts to a lambda expression, and they are illustrated in Figure 10-3.

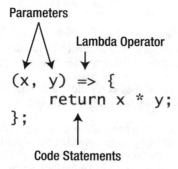

Figure 10-3. *The anatomy of a lambda expression*

Although the format of a lambda expression looks a little odd, the basic premise is the same as for anonymous methods. Parameters in a lambda expression are specified without their types—the types are inferred.

The code statements are just like for a method, named or anonymous. You access the parameters by the names they have been specified by. In the case of Listing 10-25, the parameters x and y are multiplied together, and the result is returned.

You can omit the braces and the return keyword if there is a single operation in a lambda expression so that the lambda expression in Listing 10-25 can also be written as follows:

```
(x, y) => x * y;
```

The lambda operator (=>) is, as you might expect, required for lambda operators. It is often described as the *goes to* operator. For the expression in Listing 10-25, we can say that the parameters x and y *go to* the product of x and y.

Compiling and running the code in Listing 10-25 produces the following results:

```
Anonymous Method Result: 100
Lambda Expression Result: 100
Press enter to finish
```

The C# compiler is pretty good at inferring the types of parameters for lambda expressions, but on occasion the compiler won't be able to work it out, and you will you need to explicitly tell the compiler what they are. Here is an example:

```
(int x, int y) => x * y;
```

I have used lambda expressions extensively in software projects and for other C# books, and I have found only a small number of instances where the compiler couldn't figure things out implicitly, but when you do encounter one of those situations (or if you just prefer explicit typing), then it is good to know how to do it.

Summary

In this chapter, you have how delegates can be used to encapsulate references to static and instance methods and passed around like regular types. You have seen the limitations of delegates when they are shared between objects and how events address this shortcoming.

The convention for using events is widely adopted, and I recommend that you follow it in your own code. Not only does it make your code easier for other programmers to use, but it also helps you create events that can be overridden reliably in derived classes.

We looked briefly at the System.Func and System.Action types, both of which allow us to work with delegates without creating custom delegate types, and we looked at anonymous methods and lambda expressions, which allow us to implement delegates without having to define methods. We learned how anonymous methods and lambda expressions capture local variables and when those variables are evaluated. We'll see a lot more of Func, Action, and lambda expressions when we explore some of the advanced C# language features such as LINQ and parallel programming.

■ ■ ■

CHAPTER 11

Namespaces

Namespaces allow related classes to be grouped together. You can use them in your program to add some structure to your projects. The .NET Framework uses namespaces to organize the thousands of classes in the class library to make them easier to use. In this chapter, we'll explore how to use namespaces to access the library classes, how to create custom namespaces to organize your own classes, and how to address the problems of ambiguity and collision in type names. Table 11-1 provides the problem/solution summary for this chapter.

Table 11-1. *Quick Problem/Solution Reference for Chapter 11*

Problem	Solution	Listings
Access a type contained in a namespace.	Use the fully qualified name of the type.	11-1, 11-2
Import a namespace.	Use the using keyword.	11-3
Create a namespace or add types to an existing namespace.	Use the namespace keyword.	11-4, 11-10
Create a nested namespace.	Declare one namespace inside of another or create a namespace whose name contains periods.	11-5 through 11-7
Create a namespace that spans multiple code files.	Define the namespace in each file.	11-8, 11-9
Disambiguate types with the same unqualified name.	Use fully qualified names, alias a type, alias an entire namespace, or use the global:: prefix.	11-13 through 11-18

Consuming Namespaces

The best place to start with namespaces is the .NET Framework class library. There are thousands of classes in the library, and these classes provide capabilities that range from the common (the ability to print a message to the console) to the highly specialized (the ability to read metadata from SQL Server 2008) and cover just about everything in between.

So many classes are available that Microsoft has used namespaces to group related parts of the library together. There are two ways to use namespaces to refer to the classes in the library.

Using Fully Qualified Names

One of the classes that you'll see used in examples throughout this book is the System.Console class, which can write messages and read from the keyboard in console applications. This is the *fully qualified name* of the class, which comes in two parts: the namespace identifier (System) and the class identifier (Console). We combine the two parts using the dot operator (.) to get the fully qualified name.

If we want to call the static WriteLine method of the System.Console class (which prints a message to the console), we use the dot operator to append the method name to the fully qualified class and call System.Console.WriteLine. Remember that static methods are accessed through the class that contains them and not through an instance of this class; see Chapter 9 for details. Listing 11-1 contains a simple example of a console application that uses the System.Console class.

Listing 11-1. Using the System.Console Class

```
class MyClass {

    static void Main(string[] args) {

        // print out a simple message
        System.Console.WriteLine("Hello World");

        // wait for input before exiting
        System.Console.WriteLine("Press enter to finish");
        System.Console.ReadLine();
    }
}
```

Figure 11-1 shows the fully qualified call to the WriteLine method in Listing 11-1.

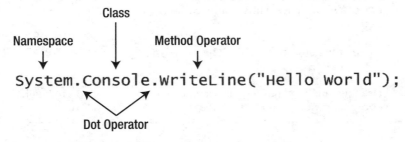

Figure 11-1. The anatomy of a fully qualified static method call

Listing 11-1 uses the System.Console class three times. The first time, the WriteLine method is called to display Hello World. The second time, the WriteLine method is called to display Press enter to finish. The final time, the ReadLine method is called; this method waits until the user hits the Enter key.

You can use a similar approach when you want to create a variable using a type that is in a namespace. Here is an example that uses the StringBuilder class in the System.Text namespace:

```
System.Text.StringBuilder myBuilder = new System.Text.StringBuilder("Hello");
myBuilder.Append(" World");
```

The first statement in the previous code creates a new instance of the StringBuilder class and assigns it to a StringBuilder variable, both of which have been specified using the fully qualified name for the class. In the second statement, I call a method using the variable. Notice that I don't need to use the fully qualified name once I have created the object and assigned it to a variable; I can just call the methods and other members using the variable name.

As you can see from the fully qualified class name, the namespace has two parts: System and Text. Namespaces can contain other namespaces, as you will see when we come to create our own. We use the dot operator to join the individual elements of the namespace together with the class name to get the fully qualified name System.Text.StringBuilder.

This is the default way of referring to classes (and other types) in the .NET Framework class library, but it is hardly ever used because it requires endless typing and results in some unreadable code. But, it is important to understand that classes have a fully qualified name that incorporates the namespace and that you can refer to classes in this manner.

Importing Namespaces

The classes I used in the previous examples had relatively short names, but namespaces can be nested very deeply, resulting in some very fully qualified names. For example, there is a class called BinaryFormatter in the System.Runtime.Serialization.Formatters.Binary namespace. Listing 11-2 demonstrates defining a variable of this type.

Listing 11-2. Using a Class with a Long Namespace Identifier

```
class MyClass {

    static void Main(string[] args) {

        // define a variable using a type with a long namespace
        System.Runtime.Serialization.Formatters.Binary.BinaryFormatter binaryFormatter;

        // print out a simple message
        System.Console.WriteLine("Hello World!");

        // wait for input before exiting
        System.Console.WriteLine("Press enter to finish");
        System.Console.ReadLine();
    }
}
```

You can see that referring to this class becomes unwieldy. To make things easier, C# has the using keyword, which lets you *import* a namespace, allowing you to refer to the classes in that namespace without having to use their fully qualified names. Listing 11-3 demonstrates the using keyword.

Listing 11-3. The using keyword

```
using System;
using System.Runtime.Serialization.Formatters.Binary;
```

```
class MyClass {

    static void Main(string[] args) {

        // define an object with a long namespace
        BinaryFormatter binaryFormatter;

        // print out a simple message
        Console.WriteLine("Hello World!");

        // wait for input before exiting
        Console.WriteLine("Press enter to finish");
        Console.ReadLine();
    }
}
```

You put the namespace you want to import (but not the individual classes) after the using keyword and finish the line with a semicolon. The using keyword makes all the classes in the specified namespace available for use without having to provide the fully qualified class name. You can see in the example that importing the System namespace has allowed me to refer to the System.Console class as just Console, for example, and to refer to the System.Runtime.Serialization.Formatters.Binary.BinaryFormatter class simply as BinaryFormatter. This reduces the amount of typing you have to do and, much more importantly, makes the code easier to read. If you want to know the namespace that a type belongs to, you can move the pointer over the type name in Visual Studio, and a pop-up will provide the details, as shown in Figure 11-2.

```
// define an object with a long namespace
BinaryFormatter binaryFormatter;
```
```
class System.Runtime.Serialization.Formatters.Binary.BinaryFormatter
Serializes and deserializes an object, or an entire graph of connected objects, in binary format.
```
```
// wait for input before exiting
```

Figure 11-2. Displaying the namespace associated with a type

Creating Namespaces

You don't have to create namespaces for your own C# types. Almost all the examples I have used in this book have not used the namespaces feature. If you don't explicitly define your class within a namespace, it is assigned to the default namespace, known as the *global namespace*. Usually, though, you would use a namespace in your project; when you create a new Visual Studio project, a namespace is created with the same name as the project. Listing 11-4 demonstrates putting the example class from the previous section into a namespace called MyNamespace.

Listing 11-4. Creating a Simple Namespace

```
using System;
using System.Runtime.Serialization.Formatters.Binary;

namespace MyNamespace {

    class MyClass {

        static void Main(string[] args) {

            // define an object with a long namespace
            BinaryFormatter binaryFormatter;

            // print out a simple message
            Console.WriteLine("Hello World!");

            // wait for input before exiting
            Console.WriteLine("Press enter to finish");
            Console.ReadLine();
        }
    }
}
```

Creating a namespace is pretty simple. You use the namespace keyword, followed by the name you want your namespace to be known by. A namespace has a body, which can contain a range of types, including classes, structs, and other namespaces. Putting the MyClass type into the namespace has changed the fully qualified name for the class to be MyNamespace.MyClass. The common convention is that using statements appear at the top of your code file, as shown in Listing 11-4, but you can place them inside your namespace declaration, like this:

```
namespace MyNamespace {

    using System;
    using System.Runtime.Serialization.Formatters.Binary;

    class MyClass {

        static void Main(string[] args) {

            // define an object with a long namespace
            BinaryFormatter binaryFormatter;

            // print out a simple message
            Console.WriteLine("Hello World!");

            // wait for input before exiting
            Console.WriteLine("Press enter to finish");
            Console.ReadLine();
        }
```

```
        }
}
```

■ **Tip** The naming convention for namespaces is Pascal format, just as for type names. This convention capitalizes the first letter of each word in a namespace identifier and combines words without punctuation, for example MyNamespace.

Nesting Namespaces

One of the things you can put in a namespace body is another namespace, which in turn can contain all the same things as the first namespace, including classes. Listing 11-5 gives an example.

Listing 11-5. Nesting a Namespace

```csharp
using System;

namespace MyNamespace {

    class MyClass {

        static void Main(string[] args) {

            int result = new NestedNamespace. AdditionHelper().AddIntegers(10, 20);
            Console.WriteLine("Result: {0}", result);

            // wait for input before exiting
            Console.WriteLine("Press enter to finish");
            Console.ReadLine();
        }
    }

    namespace NestedNamespace {

        class AdditionHelper {

            internal int AddIntegers(int x, int y) {
                return x + y;
            }
        }
    }
}
```

In Listing 11-5, we have the namespace called MyNamespace that contains a class called MyClass and a nested namespace called NestedNamespace. In turn, NestedNamespace contains a class called AdditionHelper, which is a simple class whose single member adds two numbers together. The fully qualified name of `MyClass` is `MyNamespace.MyClass`. The fully qualified name of the other class is `MyNamespace.NestedNamespace.AdditionHelper`.

Notice that when I refer to the `AdditionHelper` class from within `MyClass`, I can use the partially qualified name `NestedNamespace.AdditionHelper` because the C# compiler infers the local namespace automatically. If I want to be able to refer to the class simply as `AdditionHelper`, I have to add a using statement, even though the classes are defined in the same code file. This is demonstrated by Listing 11-6.

Listing 11-6. A using Statement to Import a Namespace Defined in the Same Code File

```
using System;
using MyNamespace.NestedNamespace;

namespace MyNamespace {

    class MyClass {

        static void Main(string[] args) {

            int result = new AdditionHelper().AddIntegers(10, 20);
            Console.WriteLine("Result: {0}", result);

            // wait for input before exiting
            Console.WriteLine("Press enter to finish");
            Console.ReadLine();
        }
    }

    namespace NestedNamespace {

        class AdditionHelper {

            internal int AddIntegers(int x, int y) {
                return x + y;
            }
        }
    }
}
```

Logically Nesting Namespaces

You can create a nested namespace without having to nest the namespace declarations. Listing 11-7 demonstrates this feature.

Listing 11-7. Creating Logically Nested Namespace

```
using System;
using MyNamespace.NestedNamespace;

namespace MyNamespace {

    class MyClass {

        static void Main(string[] args) {

            int result = new AdditionHelper().AddIntegers(10, 20);
            Console.WriteLine("Result: {0}", result);

            // wait for input before exiting
            Console.WriteLine("Press enter to finish");
            Console.ReadLine();
        }
    }
}

namespace MyNamespace.NestedNamespace {

    class AdditionHelper {

        internal int AddIntegers(int x, int y) {
            return x + y;
        }
    }
}
```

The namespace called `MyNamespace.NestedNamespace` is defined at the same level in the code file as `MyNamespace`. I have marked the name of the nested namespace in bold. Even though the nested namespace was declared outside the parent namespace, the result is the same as in Listing 11-6.

Spreading Namespaces Across Files

The contents of a namespace don't need to be defined in a single code file. They can be spread out across multiple files and even multiple assemblies. This allows you to apply two levels of organization to your program; you can group related types into namespaces based on functionality and organize the individual code files to make development and maintenance easier. If you download the code samples for this book, you'll see that the Visual Studio solution for this chapter contains a project called `Listing_08-09`. In this project are two code files, `Listing_08.cs` and `Listing_09.cs`. Listing 11-8 shows the contents of the `Listing_08.cs` file, which contains the `MyClass` type from earlier examples.

Listing 11-8. A Class That Relies on the Contents of a Nested Namespace in Another File

```
using System;
using MyNamespace.NestedNamespace;
```

```
namespace MyNamespace {

    class MyClass {

        static void Main(string[] args) {

            int result = new AdditionHelper().AddIntegers(10, 20);
            Console.WriteLine("Result: {0}", result);

            // wait for input before exiting
            Console.WriteLine("Press enter to finish");
            Console.ReadLine();
        }
    }
}
```

You can see that this class is using the AdditionHelper class from the nested namespace, even though neither the class nor the namespace is defined in this file. Listing 11-9 shows the contents of the Listing_09.cs file.

■ **Tip** Although you can spread a namespace across multiple code files, the fully qualified name of each type must be unique. If you define two types in the same namespace with the same name (even in different code files), the compiler will generate an error.

Listing 11-9. A Nested Namespace Defined in Its Own Class

```
namespace MyNamespace.NestedNamespace {

    class AdditionHelper {

        internal int AddIntegers(int x, int y) {
            return x + y;
        }
    }
}
```

This is one of the nice features of namespaces. I can put the types in any of the files in my project using a convention that suits my needs, spreading the contents of a namespace across multiple files and multiple assemblies...whatever makes the most sense for organizing the contents of my program.

Adding Types to Existing Namespaces

There are no access modifiers for namespaces—anyone can add types to any namespace. You just put the definition in your code file, and your types become part of the specified namespace. Listing 11-10 contains an example.

Listing 11-10. Adding a Type to an Existing Namespace

```
namespace System {

    class MyConsoleHelper {

        internal void PrintMessages() {
            Console.WriteLine("Hello World");
            Console.WriteLine("Press enter to finish");
        }

    }

}

class Listing_10 {

    static void Main(string[] args) {

        // use the MyConsoelHelper class
        new System.MyConsoleHelper().PrintMessages();

        // wait for input before exiting
        System.Console.ReadLine();
    }
}
```

Listing 11-10 relies on the fact that namespaces can be spread across many assemblies to extend the System namespace, which is the home of the Console class. I have added a new class, called MyConsolerHelper, which has a helpful method that prints some messages to the console for me.

Notice that because my new type is part of the System namespace, I can refer to the Console class using an unqualified name, in other words, without any part of the namespace. This is because the namespace that contains your type is implicitly imported as though you had used a using statement. Listing 11-10 also includes a class that uses the System.MyConsoleHelper type; you can see that there is no real different between using the Console class that Microsoft put into the System namespace and using the class that I added.

Although you can add types to any namespace, there really isn't any benefit in adding your types to the namespaces defined by the .NET Framework class library. There are no protections to stop types from being added to namespaces because it doesn't grant you any special access or language features. In practical terms, you may as well define your own namespaces for your own types.

Disambiguating Namespaces and Types

Namespaces are important because they allow classes to exist with the same name. If two programmers are working on related projects, there is a highly probability that they are going to end up creating classes with the same name. Pretty much every big program ends up with a class called User or Product. And that's fine; namespaces allow those programmers to bring their code together into a single program without any problems as long as each programmer has been using their own namespace. In essence, namespaces and the fully qualified names that they impart on types disambiguate names. The system knows that my code wants to use the Product class in my namespace and not the Product class in your namespace. Listing 11-11 shows how this works.

Listing 11-11. Two Classes with the Same Unqualified Name, Disambiguated by Namespace

```
namespace BillingSystem {

    class Product {
        // class body
    }

    class Bill {
        // class body
    }

}

namespace OrderSystem {

    class Product {
        // class body
    }

    class Order {
        // class body
    }

}
```

The fully qualified names of the two Product classes in Listing 11-11 are BillingSystem.Product and OrderSystem.Product. Since C# implicitly imports the types for the namespace in which class has been defined, any class in the BillingSystem namespace that uses the unqualified type name Product will use BillingSystem.Product and not OrderSystem.Product.

The ability for classes like this to coexist is very convenient, but we hit a problem when we need to use types from both namespaces. Perhaps we need to build an audit system that checks the output for orders and bills. Listing 11-12 shows the problem.

Listing 11-12. Type Name Ambiguity

```
using BillingSystem;
using OrderSystem;
```

```
namespace AuditSystem {

    class Audit {

        public static void Main(string[] args) {

            // create a new instance of a type from
            // the BillingSystem namespace
            Bill b = new Bill();

            // create a new instance of a type from
            // the OrderSystem namespace
            Order o = new Order();

            // create a new instance of the Product class
            Product p = new Product();
        }
    }
}
```

In Listing 11-12, I have imported the BillingSystem and OrderSystem namespaces with the using statement. Of course, this imports *all* the types in each namespace, including the two Product classes.

I create an instance of the Bill class. That works fine, because there is only one class with that name—the one with the fully qualified name of BillingSystem.Bill. The same is true when I create an instance of the Order class. There is only one class with that name, OrderSystem.Order. But when I create an instance of Product, which of the two classes with that name should the C# compiler assume that I am using, OrderSystem.Product or BillingSystem.Product? Visual Studio can't work it out, and you'll see the error that is displayed in Figure 11-3.

Figure 11-3. Visual Studio 2010 highlighting type ambiguity

We have a problem known as *type ambiguity* or *type name collision*. Fortunately, we can address this in a number of ways.

Disambiguation with Fully Qualified Names

The obvious way to disambiguate is to use the fully qualified names for the classes, as shown in Listing 11-13. This solves the problem but creates code that can be difficult to read, especially when you are using namespaces with lengthy names.

Listing 11-13. Disambiguating Classes Using Fully Qualified Names

```
using BillingSystem;
using OrderSystem;

namespace AuditSystem {

    class Audit {

        public static void Main(string[] args) {

            // create a new instance of a type from
            // the BillingSystem namespace
            Bill b = new Bill();

            // create a new instance of a type from
            // the OrderSystem namespace
            Order o = new Order();

            // create instances of each of the Product classes
            BillingSystem.Product p1 = new BillingSystem.Product();
            OrderSystem.Product p2 = new OrderSystem.Product();
        }
    }
}
```

Disambiguating with Aliases

A more elegant solution to type ambiguity is to use the C# namespace alias feature. This allows you to assign a new name to a type in a namespace—one that doesn't collide with a type in another namespace. Listing 11-14 provides a demonstration, with the namespace alias statements shown in bold.

Listing 11-14. Disambiguating with Namespace Aliases

```
using BillingSystem;
using OrderSystem;
using BillingProduct = BillingSystem.Product;
using OrderProduct = OrderSystem.Product;
```

```
namespace AuditSystem {

    class Audit {

        public static void Main(string[] args) {

            // create a new instance of a type from
            // the BillingSystem namespace
            Bill b = new Bill();

            // create a new instance of a type from
            // the OrderSystem namespace
            Order o = new Order();

            // create instances of each of the Product classes
            BillingProduct p1 = new BillingProduct();
            OrderProduct p2 = new OrderProduct();
        }
    }
}
```

You use the using keyword, but instead of importing a namespace, you specify the new name you want to use for a type, followed by the equals sign and then the name of the type you want to alias. So, the following statement:

```
using BillingProduct = BillingSystem.Product;
```

creates a new alias for the BillingSystem.Product type called BillingProduct. You can then create new instances of BillingProduct, and the C# system knows to translate that back to BillingSystem.Product. I have created two aliases in Listing 11-14, one for each of the types called Product. I could have just created one alias to avoid the name conflict, but it is good practice to alias all of the conflicting types so you don't inadvertently use the original name.

Aliasing Namespaces

Another way of disambiguating types is to use the fully qualified names but alias those names to a shorter name. This has the benefit of applying to all the types in a namespace, rather than just one type as we saw in the previous section. Listing 11-15 demonstrates how to alias an entire namespace, with the alias statements shown in bold.

Listing 11-15. Disambiguating by Aliasing an Entire Namespace

```
using B = BillingSystem;
using O = OrderSystem;

namespace AuditSystem {

    class Audit {

        public static void Main(string[] args) {
```

```
        // create a new instance of a type from
        // the BillingSystem namespace
        B.Bill b = new B.Bill();

        // create a new instance of a type from
        // the OrderSystem namespace
        O.Order o = new O.Order();

        // create instances of each of the Product classes
        B.Product p1 = new B.Product();
        O.Product p2 = new O.Product();
    }
  }
}
```

You can see from the listing that aliasing an entire namespace is very similar to aliasing a single type. You use the using keyword, followed by the alias you want to use, an equals sign, and, finally, the name of the namespace you want to alias. The following statement:

```
using B = BillingSystem;
```

creates an alias called B for the BillingSystem namespace. Once you have created an alias like this, you can refer to any of the types in the BillingSystem namespace via the alias, like this:

```
B.Bill b = new B.Bill();
```

I have used the aliases O and B throughout the example in Listing 11-14. The aliased using statement doesn't let you use the real name of the namespace—although you can import it with a second, regular using statement, that can just lead you back to the original problem unless you are careful.

Resolving Type or Namespace Hiding

There is a variation of the ambiguity problem where a type can hide another type, known as *type hiding*. Listing 11-16 contains an example.

Listing 11-16. The Hidden Type Problem

```
using System;

namespace AuditSystem {

    class Audit {

        public static void Main(string[] args) {

            System.Console.WriteLine("Hello World");
            System.Console.WriteLine("Press enter to finish");
            System.Console.ReadLine();

        }
    }
```

}

The code in Listing 11-16 looks good. But it if you open the example project for this chapter, you'll see that the code won't compile. Figure 11-4 shows you the Visual Studio screen where one of the errors has been flagged.

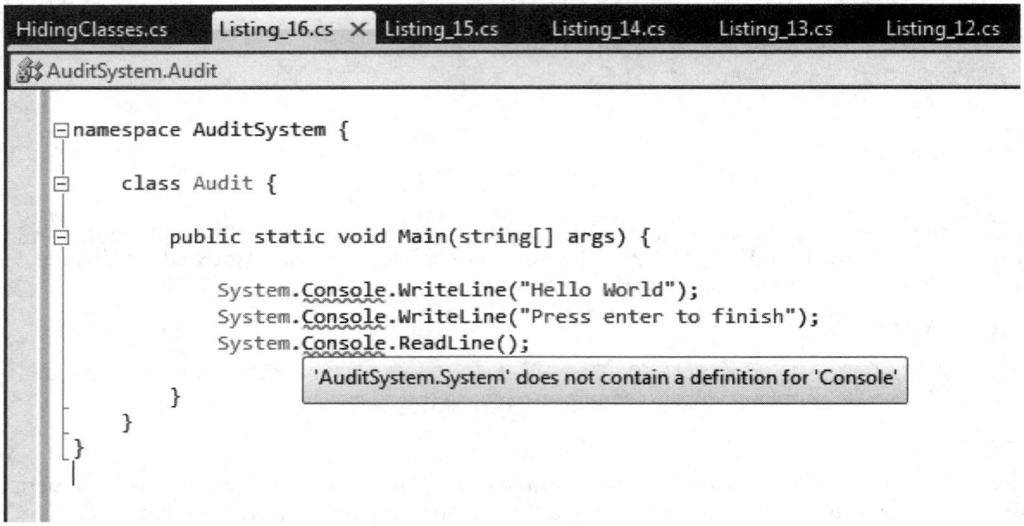

```
HidingClasses.cs    Listing_16.cs  X  Listing_15.cs    Listing_14.cs    Listing_13.cs    Listing_12.cs

AuditSystem.Audit

namespace AuditSystem {

    class Audit {

        public static void Main(string[] args) {

            System.Console.WriteLine("Hello World");
            System.Console.WriteLine("Press enter to finish");
            System.Console.ReadLine();
                        'AuditSystem.System' does not contain a definition for 'Console'
        }
    }
}
```

Figure 11-4. *Visual Studio highlighting the hiding problem*

At first glance, the Visual Studio error doesn't make any sense, and it can take a while to figure out what is happening the first time that you come across this problem. Somewhere else in your namespace is a class called System. In my example project, there is a second code file that contains the code in Listing 11-17.

Listing 11-17. The Problematic Code

```
namespace AuditSystem {

    class System {
        // class body
    }
}
```

The problem here is that C# looks in the local namespace for your type before looking elsewhere. The AuditSystem namespace contains a class called System, so my calls to the System.Console class are assumed to relate to the AuditSystem.System class, and the error arises because there is no member in the AuditSystem.System class called Console. You can sort this out by using the alias techniques or by using fully qualified names as covered in the previous sections, but there is another way, which is to use the global keyword. If you prefix your statement with global::, you tell the C# compiler not to look for a local type that matches the name but to start with the global namespace and go from there. Listing 11-18 shows how this keyword can be used to fix the problems in the previous example.

Listing 11-18. Unhiding a Class by Using the global Keyword

```
namespace AuditSystem {

    class Audit {

        public static void Main(string[] args) {

            global::System.Console.WriteLine("Hello World");
            global::System.Console.WriteLine("Press enter to finish");
            global::System.Console.ReadLine();

        }
    }
}
```

Summary

Namespaces are a flexible way of grouping types together to help organize your program. You don't *have* to use namespaces in your code, but you do have to know how they work so that you can take full advantage of the .NET Framework class library, which contains thousands of useful types.

The flexibility of namespaces can lead to some problems, especially when it comes to ambiguity of type names. We saw how to use different techniques to work around name conflicts and name ambiguity, and although most programmers don't encounter these problems regularly, it is good to know that they can be resolved when the need arises.

CHAPTER 12

■ ■ ■

Interfaces, Structs, and Enums

The previous chapters have been focused on classes, but C# supports other categories of types, three of which are the subject of this chapter: interfaces, structs, and enums.

Must C# programmers won't use these types as frequently as classes, but each of these three has its place in the programming tool set, and a working knowledge of them is useful, not least because you will find examples of each when you come to use the .NET Framework. Table 12-1 provides the summary for this chapter.

Table 12-1. *Quick Problem/Solution Reference for Chapter 12*

Problem	Solution	Listings
Impose consistent features on types that are otherwise unrelated.	Define and implement an interface.	12-1 through 6, 12-10, 12-11, 12-14, 12-15
Extend the set of members that an interface defines.	Derive one interface from another.	12-7, 12-8
Define an interface across multiple code files.	Define a partial interface.	12-9
Avoid member ambiguity when implementing interfaces that specify the same members.	Explicitly implement an interface.	12-12, 12-13
Create a custom value type.	Define a struct.	12-16 through 12-20
Duplicate the values of a struct.	Copy a struct value.	12-21
Work with a defined range of values.	Define and use an enum.	12-22 through 12-25
Combine enum values.	Use the Flags attribute and assign explicit numeric values that increment in powers of two.	12-26, 12-27

Using Interfaces

Interfaces contain a set of specifications for methods and other members. A class is said to *implement* an interface when it contains implementations for all the members defined in an interface. In the following sections, I'll show you how to define, implement, and use interfaces and explain how they differ from other C# features such as abstract classes.

WHEN TO USE INTERFACES AND BASE CLASSES

Base classes allow you to create shared behavior in derived classes, which is useful when all the classes that you want to have the same features are related to one another. You can see examples of this in Chapter 6.

Interfaces allow you to create common behavior across classes that do not share common ancestors, meaning that you can upcast any object whose class implements a given interface and handle them using the same code.

Defining and Using a Simple Interface

In this section, we'll look at a simple interface, define a class that implements it, and demonstrate how the class can be used.

Defining an Interface

Listing 12-1 contains a simple interface.

Listing 12-1. A Simple Interface

```
public interface IBasicCalculator {

    int CalculateSum(int x, int y);

    int CalculateProduct(int x, int y);

}
```

The interface in Listing 12-1 is called `IBasicCalculator`. The convention for naming interfaces in C# is that they follow Pascal case and start with the letter I. You can see a fully list of naming conventions for C# in Chapter 4. Figure 12-1 illustrates the `IBasicCalculator` interface.

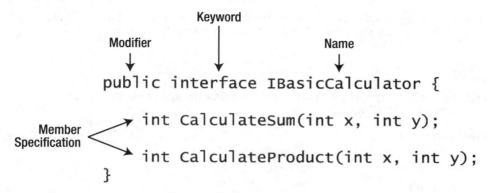

Figure 12-1. *The anatomy of a simple interface*

Interfaces are defined using the interface keyword. You can apply the standard access modifiers to interfaces, and they operate as for classes; see Chapter 6 for details.

The most important parts of an interface are the member specifications. In Listing 12-1, two methods are specified: CalculateSum and CalculateProduct. These specifications define methods that take two int parameters and return an int result. Interfaces can include specifications for other kinds of members, which are covered later in the chapter.

All interface member specifications are implicitly public, meaning that you cannot use access modifiers to restrict access.

Implementing an Interface

Once an interface has been defined, you can create classes that implement the interface. Listing 12-2 contains an example of a class that implements the interface defined in Listing 12-1.

Listing 12-2. Implementing an Interface

```
class Calculator : IBasicCalculator {

    public int CalculateSum(int x, int y) {
        return x + y;
    }

    public int CalculateProduct(int x, int y) {
        return x * y;
    }
}
```

Implementing an interface is like deriving from a base class. You place a colon (:) after the name of your class and add the name of the interface that you want to implement.

You must provide an implementation of each member in the interface in your class. In the example, the Calculator class has to provide implementations of the CalculatorSum and CalculateProduct methods in order to implement the IBasicCalculator interface. Your class can implement additional members but must, at a minimum, implement all the members in the interface. You don't need to use the override keyword when implementing methods defined in an interface.

Using an Interface

When a class has implemented an interface, objects created from that class can be upcast to the interface type, as demonstrated by Listing 12-3.

Listing 12-3. Using an Interface

```
class Listing_03 {

    static void Main(string[] args) {

        // create an object and upcast it to the interface type
        IBasicCalculator calc = new Calculator();

        // perform some calculations using the interface members
        int sumresult = calc.CalculateSum(100, 100);
        int productresult = calc.CalculateProduct(100, 100);

        // print out the results
        Console.WriteLine("Sum Result: {0}", sumresult);
        Console.WriteLine("Product Result: {0}", productresult);

        // wait for input before exiting
        Console.WriteLine("Press enter to finish");
        Console.ReadLine();
    }
}
```

In this example, a new Calculator object is created and upcast by being assigned to an IBasicCalculator local variable. Once an object has been upcast to an interface type, only the members specified in the interface can be used. In the example, the CalculateSum and CalculateProduct methods are called, and the results are printed out.

Using an interface confers the same set of benefits as deriving from a base class. Your code can work with objects at a given level of abstraction, and new classes can be defined without having to modify existing code. And, as you may have noticed, we could have achieved the same effect as the code in Listings 1-3 by using an abstract class (abstract classes are described in Chapter 6).

The main advantage in using interfaces is that classes can implement more than one of them, as opposed to being able to derive from a single base class (abstract or otherwise). In fact, as we shall see in the following sections, a class can have a base class *and* implement multiple interfaces.

Specifying Interface Members

An interface can specify methods, properties, events, and indexers for classes to implement. In this section, I'll show you the format for each of them and demonstrate their implementation.

Specifying Methods

Listing 12-1 demonstrated specifying a method in an interface. Figure 12-2 illustrates the first of these method specifications. You can learn more about methods in Chapter 6.

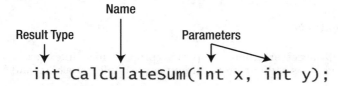

Figure 12-2. *The anatomy of a method specification*

When you specify a method, you provide the result type (or use the void keyword if your method doesn't return a result), the name of the method you are specifying, and, optionally, the parameters for the method.

All interface member specifications are implicitly abstract, implicitly virtual, and implicitly public. These keywords are all explained in Chapter 6.

When a class implements an interface that specifies a method, the return type, name, and parameters of the implemented method must match those specified by the interface. The method implementation must be public. You do not need to use the override keyword to implement a method specified by an interface. Listing 12-2 demonstrates a class that implements the method specified in Figure 12-2.

Specifying Properties

Interfaces can specify properties, obliging a class that implements the interface to provide implementations for one or both accessors. Properties are described in Chapter 8. Listing 12-4 contains an interface that specifies a property.

Listing 12-4. Specifying a Property in an Interface

```
public interface IBasicCalculator {

    int CalculationsPerformedCounter { get; set; }

    int CalculateSum(int x, int y);

    int CalculateProduct(int x, int y);
}
```

The property specification in the interface is shown in bold and illustrated by Figure 12-3.

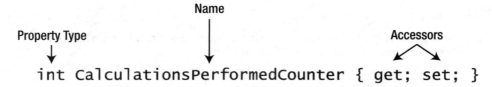

Figure 12-3. The anatomy of a property specification

You don't provide implementations for the accessors when you specify a property in an interface, but nor do you need to use the abstract keyword. As with methods, properties are implicitly public, and you may not use an access modifier keyword.

You can choose to specify only one of the accessors, but whatever accessors you specify will have to be implemented by a class that implements the interface itself. Here is a class that implements the interface in Listing 12-4:

```
public class Calculator : IBasicCalculator {
    private int calcCounter = 0;

    public int CalculationsPerformedCounter {
        get {
            return calcCounter;
        }
        set {
            calcCounter = value;
        }
    }

    public int CalculateSum(int x, int y) {
        // increment the calculation counter
        CalculationsPerformedCounter++;
        // perofrm the calculation and return the result
        return x + y;
    }

    public int CalculateProduct(int x, int y) {
        // increment the calculation counter
        CalculationsPerformedCounter++;
        // perform the calculation and return the result
        return x * y;
    }
}
```

The implementation of the property specified in Listing 12-4 is shown in bold. I have implemented this property using a backing field, but I could have used an automatically implemented property instead. Properties that are implemented for interfaces must be public. Classes that implement a property specified in an interface are free to add whatever code they like to the property accessors, so you can use all the techniques that are discussed in Chapter 8.

Specifying an Event

Interfaces can specify events; the specification of an event in an interface and the corresponding implementation in a class are surprisingly similar. Listing 12-5 demonstrates an interface that specifies an event. You can read more about events in Chapter 10.

Listing 12-5. Specifying an Event in an Interface

```
public interface IBasicCalculator {

    event EventHandler<EventArgs> CalculationPerformedEvent;

    int CalculateSum(int x, int y);
}
```

The event specified by the interface is shown in bold and is illustrated by Figure 12-4.

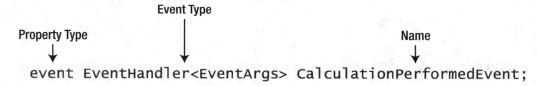

Figure 12-4. The anatomy of an event specification

As with the other members that you can specify in an interface, events are implicitly public, and you do not use an access modifier in the specification. Here is a class that implements the interface in Listing 12-5:

```
class Calculator : IBasicCalculator {

    public event EventHandler<EventArgs> CalculationPerformedEvent;

    public int CalculateSum(int x, int y) {
        // calculate the result
        int result = x + y;

        // invoke the event
        CalculationPerformedEvent(this, EventArgs.Empty);
        // return the result
        return result;
    }
}
```

The implementation of the event in the class is the same as the specification in the interface, with the addition of the public access modifier.

Specifying an Indexer

The remaining kind of member you can implement in an interface is an indexer. Listing 12-6 contains an example.

Listing 12-6. Specifying an Indexer in an Interface

```
public interface IBasicCalculator {

    int this[int x, int y] { get; set; }
}
```

The indexer in Listing 12-6 has two `int` parameters and returns an `int`. You can choose to specify one or both of the accessors; the specification in Listing 12-6 contains both. Figure 12-5 illustrates the indexer specification.

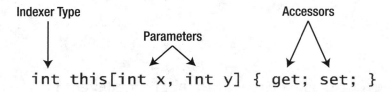

Figure 12-5. The anatomy of an indexer specification

As with the other member specifications, indexers are `implicitly` abstract and implicitly `public`, although you do not use either keyword. Here is a class that implements the interface in Listing 12-6:

```
class Calculator : IBasicCalculator {

    public int this[int x, int y] {
        get {
            return x + y;
        }
        set {
            throw new NotImplementedException();
        }
    }
}
```

This class uses the getter to perform calculations and will throw an exception if the setter is used. You can read about indexers in Chapter 8 and about exceptions in Chapter 14.

Deriving Interfaces

Interfaces can be derived from other interfaces, in the same way that classes can be derived from other classes. Listing 12-7 contains a base interface and a derived interface.

Listing 12-7. Deriving an Interface

```
interface IBaseCalculator {

    int CalculateSum(int x, int y);
}

interface IDerivedCalculator : IBaseCalculator {

    int CalculateProduct(int x, int y);
}
```

The IDerivedCalculator interface derives from the IBaseCalculator; you derive an interface by placing a colon (:) after the name of your interface and specifying the name of the base interface.

A derived interface inherits all the member specifications of the base interface. A class that implements IDerivedCalculator must implement the CalculateProduct method it specifies as well as the CalculateSum method specified by the base interface. Here is a class that implements the interface:

```
class Calculator : IDerivedCalculator {

    public int CalculateProduct(int x, int y) {
        return x * y;
    }

    public int CalculateSum(int x, int y) {
        return x + y;
    }
}
```

Objects created from classes that implement derived interfaces can be upcast to the derived and base interface types, like this:

```
// create an instance of Calculator and upcast it
IDerivedCalculator derivedCalc = new Calculator();

// upcast the derived interface to the base interface
IBaseCalculator baseCalc = derivedCalc;
```

When you upcast to a base interface, you can only access the members specified by that interface, just as for upcasting to base classes.

Deriving from Multiple Base Interfaces

Unlike classes, interfaces can have more than one base interface. Listing 12-8 contains an example.

Listing 12-8. Multiple Inheritance in Interfaces

```
interface IProductCalculator {
```

```
    int CalculateProduct(int x, int y);
}

interface ISumCalculator {

    int CalculateSum(int x, int y);
}

interface ISubtractionCalculator {

    int CalculateSubtraction(int x, int y);
}

interface ICombinedCalculator : IProductCalculator, ISumCalculator, ISubtractionCalculator {

    int CalculateDivision(int x, int y);
}
```

The first three interfaces, IProductCalculator, ISumCalculator, and ISubtractionCalculator, in Listing 12-8 are unrelated to one another; each specifies a single method. The final interface is derived from all three of the others, meaning that the derived interface specifies the members specified by each of the other three plus the member that it specifies itself.

To derive from multiple base interfaces, simply separate the name of each base interface with a comma, as shown by the bold statement in Listing 12-8. A class that implements the ICombinedCalculator interface must implement all four methods, like this:

```
class Calculator : ICombinedCalculator {

    public int CalculateDivision(int x, int y) {
        return x / y;
    }

    public int CalculateProduct(int x, int y) {
        return x * y;
    }

    public int CalculateSum(int x, int y) {
        return x + y;
    }

    public int CalculateSubtraction(int x, int y) {
        return x - y;
    }
}
```

When a class implements an interface that has multiple base interfaces, objects created from that class can be upcast to any of the base interface types. When this is done, only the members specified in the base interface can be accessed, like this:

```
// create an object and upcast it to the combined interface
ICombinedCalculator calc = new Calculator();
```

```
// upcast to the base interfaces and call the method that each defines
IProductCalculator prodCalc = calc;
int prodResult = prodCalc.CalculateProduct(10, 10);
ISumCalculator sumCalc = calc;
int calcResult = sumCalc.CalculateSum(10, 10);
ISubtractionCalculator subCalc = calc;
int subResult = subCalc.CalculateSubtraction(10, 2);
```

You can also explicitly cast from one base interface to another (but only if you are sure that the object you are casting implements both interfaces), like this:

```
// explicitly cast from one base interface to another
prodCalc = (IProductCalculator)subCalc;
```

Defining a Partial Interface

Interfaces can be modified with the partial keyword and defined in several places. Just as with partial classes (discussed in Chapter 6), the compiler will combine the partial elements to create a unified interface definition. Member specifications must be unique across all the parts of a partial interface. Listing 12-9 demonstrates a partial interface.

Listing 12-9. Defining a Partial Interface

```
partial interface ICalculator {

    int CalculateProduct(int x, int y);
}

partial interface ICalculator {

    int CalculateSum(int x, int y);
}
```

The two parts of this partial interface are defined in the same code file to make a convenient example, but normally they would be in separate code files. Each part of the partial interface must be defined with the partial keyword and must have the same fully qualified name (see Chapter 11 for details of namespaces and fully qualified names).

Implementing Interfaces

Classes can implement an interface in addition to being derived from a base class. Listing 12-10 contains an example.

Listing 12-10. Deriving from a Base Class and Implementing an Interface

```
interface ICalculator {

    int CalculateSum(int x, int y);
}
```

```
class BaseCalculator {

    public virtual int CalculateProduct(int x, int y) {
        return x * y;
    }
}

class DerivedCalculator : BaseCalculator, ICalculator {

    public int CalculateSum(int x, int y) {
        return x + y;
    }
}
```

In this example, the DerivedCalculator class is derived from the BaseCalculator class *and* implements the ICalculator interface. In the declaration for the class, the base class must be specified first, followed by the interface that a class is implementing, separated by a comma.

■ **Tip** If you right-click the interface name in your class declaration in Visual Studio 2010, you will see the Implement Interface menu. There are two submenu items available. The Implement Interface menu will create all the members you need to implement the interface you selected. The Implement Interface Explicitly menu will do the same for an explicit interface implementation, discussed later in this chapter.

Implementing Multiple Interfaces

Classes can be derived from only a single class, but they can implement multiple interfaces. In such cases, the interfaces that are implemented appear after the base class, separated by commas. Listing 12-11 contains an example.

Listing 12-11. Implementing Multiple Interfaces

```
interface IProductCalculator {

    int CalculateProduct(int x, int y);
}

interface ISumCalculator {

    int CalculateSum(int x, int y);
}

interface ISubtractionCalculator {

    int CalculateSubtraction(int x, int y);
```

```
}

class Calculator : IProductCalculator, ISumCalculator, ISubtractionCalculator {

    public int CalculateProduct(int x, int y) {
        return x * y;
    }

    public int CalculateSum(int x, int y) {
        return x + y;
    }

    public int CalculateSubtraction(int x, int y) {
        return x - y;
    }
}
```

In this example, the Calculator class doesn't have an explicit base class but does implement three interfaces. As you might expect, the class must implement all the members specified by each of the interfaces.

Explicitly Implementing an Interface

Implementing multiple interfaces is a simple process until you want to implement interfaces that specify identical members. Listing 12-12 contains an example.

Listing 12-12. Interfaces with Identical Member Specifications

```
interface ISumCalculator {

    int PerformCalculation(int x, int y);

}

interface IProductCalculator {

    int PerformCalculation(int x, int y);

}
```

Classes that want to implement both of the interfaces in Listing 12-12 face a problem. Here is a class that implements the ISumCalculator and IProductCalculator interfaces:

```
class Calculator : ISumCalculator, IProductCalculator {

    public int PerformCalculation(int x, int y) {
        // ???
    }
}
```

The problem is knowing which interface the PerformCalculation method should be implemented for. When a Calculator object is upcast to ISumCalculator, calls to the PerformCalculation method are expecting a different result than if the same method was called when the object is upcast to IProductCalculator.

To get around this, you can use explicit interface implementations, where you specify which interface a member implementation relates to. Listing 12-13 demonstrates a class that explicitly implements the interfaces in Listing 12-12.

Listing 12-13. Explicitly Implementing Multiple Interfaces

```
class Calculator : ISumCalculator, IProductCalculator {


    int ISumCalculator.PerformCalculation(int x, int y) {
        Console.WriteLine("ISumCalculator.PerformCalculation was called");
        return x + y;
    }

    int IProductCalculator.PerformCalculation(int x, int y) {
        Console.WriteLine("IProductCalculator.PerformCalculation was called");
        return x * y;
    }
}
```

When you explicitly implement a member specified by an interface, you prefix the implementation with the name of the interface it relates to, as illustrated by Figure 12-6.

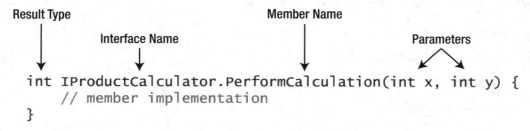

Figure 12-6. The anatomy of an explicit interface member implementation

When an object of a class that uses explicit interface implementation is upcast to one of the interface types, the .NET runtime ensures that the correct member implementation is invoked. Here are some statements that upcast and call the PerformCalculation method:

```
class Listing_13_Test {

    static void Main(string[] args) {

        // create an instance of the Calculator object
        Calculator calc = new Calculator();

        // upcast to IProductCalculator and call the method
```

```
        IProductCalculator pcalc = calc;
        int productResult = pcalc.PerformCalculation(10, 10);

        // upcast to ISumCalculator and call the method
        ISumCalculator scalc = calc;
        int sumResult = scalc.PerformCalculation(10, 10);

        // print the result
        Console.WriteLine("Product result: {0}", productResult);
        Console.WriteLine("Sum Result: {0}", sumResult);

        // wait for input before exiting
        Console.WriteLine("Press enter to finish");
        Console.ReadLine();
    }
}
```

Each explicit implementation of the PerformCalculation method contains a statement that prints out which interface it relates to. Compiling and running the previous statements produces the following results:

```
IProductCalculator.PerformCalculation was called
ISumCalculator.PerformCalculation was called
Product result: 100
Sum Result: 20
Press enter to finish
```

The explicit implementations of an interface member are available only when an object is upcast to that interface type. This means, for example, that you cannot call the PerformCalculation method on objects created from the class in Listing 12-13 until they are upcast, and this means that the Calculator class appears to have no members until it is upcast to one of the explicitly implemented interfaces.

Inheriting Interface Implementations

When a base class implements an interface, derived classes also implement the interface, and, if the base class uses the virtual keyword on the members used to implement the interface, the derived class can provide its own versions of those methods. Listing 12-14 provides a demonstration.

Listing 12-14. Inheriting and Overriding Interface Implementations

```
interface ICalculator {

    int CalculateSum(int x, int y);

}

class BaseCalc : ICalculator {
```

```
    public virtual int CalculateSum(int x, int y) {
        return x + y;
    }
}

class DerivedCalc : BaseCalc {

    public override int CalculateSum(int x, int y) {
        return base.CalculateSum(x, y) * 2;
    }
}
```

In this example, the BaseCalc class implements the ICalculator interface, modifying the implementation of the CalculateSum method with the virtual keyword. The DerivedCalc class is derived from BaseCalc and uses the override keyword to override the base implementation of the CalculateSum method.

Because derived classes inherit the base class interface implementations, DerivedCalc implicitly implements the ICalculator interface. Here are some statements that create a DerivedCalc object and upcast to both the base type and the interface type:

```
class Listing_14_Test {

    static void Main(string[] args) {

        // create an instance of the derived class
        DerivedCalc calc = new DerivedCalc();

        // upcast to the base type
        BaseCalc bCalc = calc;

        // upcast the dervied type to the interface type
        ICalculator iCalc = calc;

        // call the method defined by the interface and
        // print out the results
        int result = iCalc.CalculateSum(10, 10);
        Console.WriteLine("Result: {0}", result);

        // wait for input before exiting
        Console.WriteLine("Press enter to finish");
        Console.ReadLine();
    }
}
```

Implementing an Interface in an Abstract Class

An abstract class can implement an interface but force derived classes to provide an implementation of the members that the interface specifies. Listing 12-15 contains a demonstration.

Listing 12-15. Implementing an Interface in an Abstract Class

```
interface ICalculator {

    int CalculateSum(int x, int y);
    int CalculateProduct(int x, int y);
}

abstract class AbstractCalculator : ICalculator {

    public abstract int CalculateSum(int x, int y);


    public int CalculateProduct(int x, int y) {
        return x * y;
    }
}
```

To force a derived class to provide an implementation for an interface member, you simple restate the member specification, adding the public access modifier and the abstract keyword. The AbstractCalculator class in the example implements one of the members from the ICalculator interface directly and defines the other as abstract. Classes that are derived from the AbstractCalculator class must provide an implementation for the abstract method, like this:

```
class Calculator : AbstractCalculator {

    public override int CalculateSum(int x, int y) {
        return x + y;
    }
}
```

When an abstract class implements an interface, classes derived from the abstract class implicitly implement the interface as well, and objects created from the derived class can be upcast to the interface type.

Using Structs

Most of the chapters in this part of the book have been focused on classes, one use of which is to create custom reference types. The C# struct feature allows you to create your own value types. Structs can use many of the same features as classes but have some special constraints and demonstrate value-type behavior. In this section, I'll show you how to create and use structs and explain how they differ from classes.

Defining and Instantiating a Struct

Structs are defined using the struct keyword. Listing 12-16 defines a simple struct.

Listing 12-16. Defining a Simple Struct

```
public struct Product {
    public int CasesInStock;
    public int ItemsPerCase;

    public Product(int cases, int itemspc) {
        CasesInStock = cases;
        ItemsPerCase = itemspc;
    }
}
```

Defining a simple struct is similar to defining a class. Figure 12-7 illustrates the struct defined in Listing 12-16.

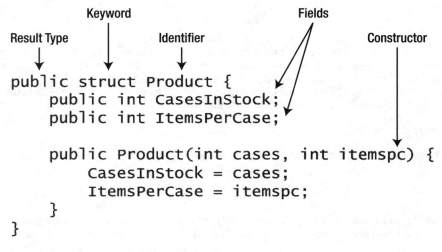

Figure 12-7. *The anatomy of a simple struct*

As you can see from the listing, structs and classes have a lot in common. In fact, the Product struct defined in Listing 12-16 looks very much like a class, aside from using a different keyword.

Structs are value types, so when we use the new keyword, we create a struct value. The following statement creates a Product value, using the struct defined in Listing 12-16 and assigns the value to a local variable of the same type:

```
Product prod = new Product(100, 10);
```

As you can see from Figure 12-7, structs can have constructors and fields. We have used the constructor to create the new Product value, and we can use the fields as we would if we were working with a class, like this:

```
// get and print out the value of one of the fields
Console.WriteLine("Cases in Stock: {0}", prod.CasesInStock);
```

```
// set the value of one of the fields
prod.CasesInStock = 75;
```

Structs can contain the same set of members as classes, including methods, properties, events, indexers, and custom operators. See the earlier chapters in this book for details of each of them. They are applied to structs just as to classes. For example, Listing 12-17 builds on Listing 12-16 to define a struct that contains a constructor, fields, properties, and a method.

Listing 12-17. Adding Members to a Struct

```
public struct Product {
    private int casesInStock;
    private int itemsPerCase;

    public Product(int cases, int itemspc) {
        casesInStock = cases;
        itemsPerCase = itemspc;
    }

    public int CasesInStock {
        get {
            return casesInStock;
        }
        set {
            casesInStock = value;
        }
    }

    public int ItemsPerCase {
        get {
            return itemsPerCase;
        }
        set {
            itemsPerCase = value;
        }
    }

    public void PrintDetails() {
        Console.WriteLine("--- Product Details ---");
        Console.WriteLine("Cases In Stock: {0}", CasesInStock);
        Console.WriteLine("Items per Case: {0}", ItemsPerCase);
    }
}
```

Access modifiers for structs work in the same was as for classes; see Chapter 6 for details.

Implementing Interfaces

Structs can implement interfaces and, like classes, can implement more than one interface. Listing 12-18 demonstrates a simple struct that implements an interface.

Listing 12-18. Implementing an Interface in a Struct

```
interface ISalesItem {

    int PricePerItem();

}

public struct Product : ISalesItem {
    public int CasesInStock;
    public int ItemsPerCase;

    public Product(int cases, int itemspc) {
        CasesInStock = cases;
        ItemsPerCase = itemspc;
    }

    public int PricePerItem() {
        return 100;
    }
}
```

You can upcast a struct value to the interface type, like this:

```
class Listing_18_Test {

    static void Main(string[] args) {

        // create a new struct value and upcast to the interface type
        ISalesItem salesItem = new Product(10, 10);

        // call the method specified in the interface
        int price = salesItem.PricePerItem();
        Console.WriteLine("Price per item: {0}", price);

        // wait for input before exiting
        Console.WriteLine("Press enter to finish");
        Console.ReadLine();
    }
}
```

As with classes, when you upcast a struct value, you can only access the members specified by the interface and not any additional members that the struct has introduced.

Differences Between Structs and Classes

The previous examples give the impression that structs look and behave like classes, and this is true to an extent. But there are significant differences, which I describe in the following sections.

Base Structs and Inheritance

Structs are implicitly derived from the System.ValueType class and are also implicitly sealed. This means that a struct cannot be derived from another struct (or class), and a struct cannot act as the base for another struct (or class).

Because there can be no base or derived structs, the C# compiler will report an error if you use the virtual, override, sealed, or abstract keywords on methods and other members in a struct.

Defining Fields

When defining fields in a constructor, you may not initialize a field with a value. For example, this struct will not compile:

```
public struct Product {
    public int CasesInStock = 20;
}
```

You must either create a constructor that assigns a value to this field (see the next section) or assign a value to the field after the struct value has been created, like this:

```
Product p = new Product();
p.CasesInStock = 20;
```

Defining a Struct Constructor

All structs have an implicit parameterless constructor that cannot be override by the struct. If you create a struct value using the default constructor, all of the fields and properties will be initialized to the default value for their type. For the built-in numeric types, this will be zero and null for reference types. Listing 12-19 demonstrates defining a struct that has only the default constructor and creating a value from it.

Listing 12-19. Creating a Struct Value Using the Default Constructor

```
using System;

public struct Product {
    public int CasesInStock;
    public int ItemsPerCase;
}

class Listing_19 {

    static void Main(string[] args) {

        // create a new struct value
        Product prod = new Product();

        // print out the value of the fields
        Console.WriteLine("Cases In Stock: {0}", prod.CasesInStock);
```

```
        Console.WriteLine("Items Per Case: {0}", prod.ItemsPerCase);

        // wait for input before exiting
        Console.WriteLine("Press enter to finish");
        Console.ReadLine();
    }
}
```

In the listing, the default constructor is used to create a new Product value. The values of the fields are written to the console. Compiling and running the code in Listing 12-19 produces the following results, confirming the default field values:

```
Cases In Stock: 0
Items Per Case: 0
Press enter to finish
```

If you define a custom constructor, you must initialize all the fields and properties that your struct defines. You can do this by using literal values or passing parameters to the constructor, but if you don't assign a value to each and every field and property, the C# compiler will report an error. Listing 12-20 contains a struct that uses a custom constructor.

Listing 12-20. Defining a Custom Constructor for a Struct

```
public struct Product {
    public int CasesInStock;
    public int ItemsPerCase;

    public Product(int cases, int items) {
        CasesInStock = cases;
        ItemsPerCase = items;
    }
}
```

Implementing a custom constructor doesn't stop the default constructor being used. The struct in Listing 12-20 can be used to create values by providing parameters values, like this:

```
Product prod = new Product(20, 20);
```

Or it can be done through the default constructor, like this:

```
Product prod = new Product();
```

Copying a Struct

The biggest difference between a struct and a class comes when you copy a struct. Since a struct is a value type, a new and distinct copy of the struct is created. Remember from Chapter 4 that value types contain their data directly. This means that when we create a new value from the struct in Listing 12-20 like this:

```
Product prod = new Product(20, 20);
```

we create something that is self-contained in memory, as illustrated by Figure 12-8.

Type:	Product
Name:	prod
CasesInStock:	20
ItemsPerCase:	20

Figure 12-8. A struct value in memory

The following statement assigns the struct value to a new variable:

```
Product prod2 = prod;
```

When we do this, we create a new struct value, just as we saw in Chapter 4. We how have two Product values, as illustrated by Figure 12-9.

Type:	Product
Name:	prod
CasesInStock:	20
ItemsPerCase:	20

Type:	Product
Name:	**prod2**
CasesInStock:	20
ItemsPerCase:	20

Figure 12-9. Copying a struct value

The second struct value is a copy of the first, but once the copy has been created, a change applied to one of the values doesn't affect the other. However, if your struct has a reference type as a field, then you end up with a slightly different effect. Listing 12-21 defines a struct that has a class field, that is, a field that is a reference type.

Listing 12-21. A Struct with a Reference Type Field

```
using System.Text;

public struct Product {
    public int CasesInStock;
    public int ItemsPerCase;
    public StringBuilder SupplierName;

    public Product(int cases, int items, StringBuilder name) {
        CasesInStock = cases;
        ItemsPerCase = items;
```

```
        SupplierName = name;
    }
}
```

The struct in Listing 12-21 has a `StringBuilder` field; this class can be found in the `System.Text` namespace and is described in Chapter 16. The following statement creates a new value from the struct in Listing 12-21:

```
// create a StringBuilder object
StringBuilder sb = new StringBuilder("BigCo Supplies");

// create a struct value
Product prod = new Product(20, 20, sb);
```

Figure 12-10 illustrates the value as it will be created in memory.

Type:	Product
Name:	prod
CasesInStock:	20
ItemsPerCase:	20
SupplierName:	●

Type:	StringBuilder
Data:	BigCo Supplies

Figure 12-10. A struct value with a reference-type field

We can copy the value to a new local variable like this:

```
Product prod2 = prod;
```

And this is where the behavior becomes more complicated. The value-type fields in the struct value are copied, but only the reference to the object is copied, as illustrated in Figure 12-11.

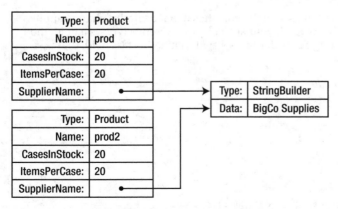

Figure 12-11. Copying a struct value that has a reference-type field

When you modify one of the value-type fields in one of the values, the other value is unaffected. But if you modify the object that is referred to by the reference-type field, then the change will be reflected through the reference to the same object contained in the second struct value. The following statements demonstrate this:

```
using System;
using System.Text;

class Listing_21_Test {

    static void Main(string[] args) {

        // create a StringBuilder object
        StringBuilder sb = new StringBuilder("BigCo Supplies");

        // create a struct value
        Product prod = new Product(20, 20, sb);

        // create a copy of the struct value
        Product prod2 = prod;

        // make a change to a value-type field in the original struct value
        prod.ItemsPerCase = 30;

        // write out both copies of the same field
        Console.WriteLine("Original Value ItemsPerCase: {0}", prod.ItemsPerCase);
        Console.WriteLine("Copy Value ItemsPerCase: {0}", prod2.ItemsPerCase);

        // make a change to the reference-type field in the original struct value
        prod.SupplierName.Append(" Inc");

        // print out both values for the reference-type field
        Console.WriteLine("Original Value Supplier: {0}", prod.SupplierName);
        Console.WriteLine("Copy Value Supplier: {0}", prod2.SupplierName);

        // wait for input before exiting
        Console.WriteLine("Press enter to finish");
        Console.ReadLine();
    }
}
```

These statements create a value from the struct in Listing 12-21 and assign a copy to another local variable. A change is made to both a value-type field and the reference-type field, and the values of those fields in both struct values are printed out. Compiling and running the code produces the following results:

```
Original Value ItemsPerCase: 30
Copy Value ItemsPerCase: 20
Original Value Supplier: BigCo Supplies Inc
Copy Value Supplier: BigCo Supplies Inc
```

```
Press enter to finish
```

You can see that the two struct values are related through their reference to a single object. Structs are value types, but you need to be careful that you understand the mix of behaviors when you use reference types as fields.

Using an Enum

An *enum* is a value type that defines a set of named constant values and that can be incredibly useful when you need to express a fixed range of available options. If you look back at Chapter 6, many of the examples were based around cars, especially this class:

```
public class VolvoC30 {
    public string CarOwner;
    public string PaintColor;

    public VolvoC30(string newOwner, string paintColor) {
        CarOwner = newOwner;
        PaintColor = paintColor;
    }
}
```

You will see that I defined the color of a car using a string. This is reasonable enough, but it does create scope for errors because I have to be careful how I treat the string values to recognize that are intended to be the same; capitalization issues (Black vs. black), additional information (Green vs. Matt Green), and simple errors (mistyping rde for red) all have the potential to give unexpected results. As we'll see in the following sections, using an enum can help reduce the likelihood of problems.

Defining an Enum

Enum are defined using the enum keyword; Listing 12-22 contains an example.

Listing 12-22. Defining an Enum

```
public enum PaintColor {
    Black,
    Red,
    Green,
    Silver,
}
```

The enum in Listing 12-22 defines constant values for a range of paint colors and is illustrated in Figure 12-12.

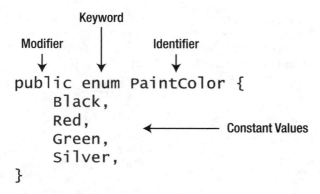

Figure 12-12. The anatomy of an enum

The modifiers for an enum are limited to the access modifiers (public, private, and so on) and new, which is used when you want to hide an enum defined in a base class. See Chapters 6 and 9 for details of member hiding. The identifier for your enum is the name of the type and works just as the name for a class, struct, or interface.

The base type allows you to specify the underlying type used to create the numeration; we'll return to this later in this section.

The constant values are all given name, each separated by a comma (,). The names must be unique but can be any name that makes sense in your program. The convention for enumeration types and values is to use Pascal case; see Chapter 4 for details.

Using an Enum

Once we have defined an enum type, we can create variables of that type and assign values from the range of named constants. Listing 12-23 updates the car class from a previous chapter to use the enum defined in Listing 12-22.

Listing 12-23. Using an Enum

```
public class VolvoC30 {
    public string CarOwner;
    public PaintColor Color;

    public VolvoC30(string newOwner, PaintColor paintColor) {
        CarOwner = newOwner;
        Color = paintColor;
    }
}
```

This class now has a field of the enum type PaintColor and a constructor parameter of the same type. We specify one of the constant values by using the name of the enum type and the constant we want, joined together using the dot operator (.), like this:

```
VolvoC30 myCar = new VolvoC30("Adam Freeman", PaintColor.Black);
```

We do the same thing when assigning a value to a local variable:

```
PaintColor color = PaintColor.Green;
```

C# supports using enum values in switch statements, as shown in Listing 12-24.

Listing 12-24. Using Enum Values in a switch Statement

```
PaintColor color = PaintColor.Black;

switch (color) {
    case PaintColor.Black:
        Console.WriteLine("Paint Color is black");
        break;

    case PaintColor.Green:
        Console.WriteLine("Paint Color is green");
        break;

    case PaintColor.Red:
    case PaintColor.Silver:
        Console.WriteLine("Paint Color is red or silver");
        break;
}
```

You can also use enum values in expressions and statements, like this:

```
if (color == PaintColor.Black) {
    Console.WriteLine("Paint color is black");
}
```

Using Underlying Types and Numeric Values

When you specify constant values in an enum, the values are assigned a number. By default, this starts at zero and is incremented for each constant. You can explicitly assign the numeric values when you create your enum, as shown in Listing 12-25.

Listing 12-25. Explicitly Assigning Numeric Values

```
public enum PaintColor {
    Black = 10,
    Red,
    Green = 15,
    Silver
}
```

As you can see from the listing, you don't have to assign numeric values to all the constants. Values are assigned automatically by incrementing the previous value so that the numeric value of Red is 11 and the numeric value of Silver will be 16. You can assign the same value to multiple constants. You can obtain the numeric value for a constant by casting to a numeric type, like this:

```
Console.WriteLine("Numeric Value of Red: {0}", (int)PaintColor.Red);
```

The result of this statement is as follows:

```
Numeric Value of Red: 11
```

When you define an enum, you can specify the underlying numeric type that will be used to assign numeric values to your constants. For example, if you need to assign especially large numeric values, then you can specify that the enum should be based on the long numeric type. If you do not specify an underlying type, then int will be used. Details of the numeric types available (including the range of values they can represent) can be found in Chapter 5. Listing 12-26 demonstrates defining an enum that is based on the long type.

Listing 12-26. Specifying an Underlying Type for an Enum

```
public enum PaintColor : long {
    Black = 10,
    Red,
    Green = 15,
    Silver
}
```

As the listing shows, specifying an underlying type for an enum follows the same format as specifying a base for a class or interface.

Combining Enum Values

You can combine the values of an enum by using the C# logical operators that were described in Chapter 5. To do this, you create an enum where the numeric values assigned to each constant increase in powers of two, as shown in Listing 12-27.

Listing 12-27. A Combinable Enum

```
[Flags]
public enum CarOptions {
    AlloyWheels = 1,
    CDPlayer = 2,
    SatNav = 4,
    Bluetooth = 8
}
```

You should apply the Flags attribute when you define an enum like this; attributes are described in Chapter 17. Once you have created your enum, you can use the logical operators to combine and test enum values, as shown in Listing 12-28.

Listing 12-28. Combining Enum Values

```
class Listing_27 {

    static void Main(string[] args) {

        // combine two of the values together
        CarOptions ops = CarOptions.AlloyWheels | CarOptions.SatNav;

        // test to see if the combined value contains SatNav
        bool hasSatNav = (ops & CarOptions.SatNav) == CarOptions.SatNav;

        // wait for input before exiting
        Console.WriteLine("Press enter to finish");
        Console.ReadLine();
    }
}
```

Summary

In this chapter, we have looked at three categories of C# type: the interface, the struct, and the enum. Most C# programmers spend most of their time working on classes, but these types have their place and can be very useful in certain circumstances: interfaces are useful when you want to impose consistency on classes and structs that are not otherwise related, structs are useful when you want to create custom value types, and enums are useful when you need to work with a fixed range of values.

CHAPTER 13

■ ■ ■

Arrays

Arrays are special types that let you gather objects of the same type together conveniently and efficiently. Imagine you have a simple program that keeps track of a list of product names; Listing 13-1 gives an example.

Listing 13-1. A Program with Multiple Instances of the Same Type

```
using System;

class Listing_01 {

    static void Main(string[] args) {

        // define the product names
        string product1 = "oranges";
        string product2 = "apples";
        string product3 = "guava";
        string product4 = "cherry";
        string product5 = "strawberry";

        // select the product names > six chars
        CheckLengthAndPrintName(product1);
        CheckLengthAndPrintName(product2);
        CheckLengthAndPrintName(product3);
        CheckLengthAndPrintName(product4);
        CheckLengthAndPrintName(product5);

        // wait for input before exiting
        Console.WriteLine("Press enter to finish");
        Console.ReadLine();
    }

    static void CheckLengthAndPrintName(string name) {
        if (name.Length > 5) {
            Console.WriteLine("Item: {0}", name);
        }
    }
}
```

The example shows five product names. Defining and working with the names quickly becomes verbose and tiresome. I want to use the CheckLengthAndPrintName method, so I call this method for each of the product names in turn. Working with five items is bad enough and error-prone. In writing that simple example, I made two typos with the variable names as I cut and pasted the code statements; imagine how painful this would become with dozens or even hundreds of items.

Arrays let us group objects together, and once we have created an array, we can pass it around as a single object, enumerate the contents, and take advantage of some very useful convenience features that C# includes. As a quick demonstration, Listing 13-2 shows the product name program written using an array.

Listing 13-2. Using an Array to Group Related Items Together

```
using System;

class Listing_02 {

    static void Main(string[] args) {

        // define the product names in an array
        string[] names = { "oranges", "apples", "guava", "cherry", "strawberry" };

        // select the product names > six chars
        CheckLengthAndPrintNames(names);

        // wait for input before exiting
        Console.WriteLine("Press enter to finish");
        Console.ReadLine();
    }

    static void CheckLengthAndPrintNames(string[] names) {
        foreach (string name in names) {
            if (name.Length > 5) {
                Console.WriteLine("Item: {0}", name);
            }
        }
    }
}
```

When dealing with five items, the code is slightly more concise than for the previous example, but it scales a lot better. We make only one call to the CheckLengthAndPrintNames method irrespective of how many items we are working with because we are passing the array as the parameter, and not the individual items, allowing the method to enumerate the contents. In this chapter, I'll show you how to create, populate, and work with the different kinds of array that are available in C#. Table 13-1 provides the summary for this chapter.

Table 13-1. Quick Problem/Solution Reference for Chapter 13

Problem	Solution	Listings
Define an array to contain objects of a given type and get and set values in the array.	Use the array notation ([ ]).	13-1 through 13-5
Define and populate an array in a single statement.	Use the array initializer feature.	13-6, 13-7
Enumerate the contents of an array.	Use a for loop, a foreach loop or work directly with the IEnumerator<T> interface.	13-8 through 13-14
Sort the contents of an array.	Use the static System.Array.Sort method.	13-15
Process all of the items in an array.	Use the static System.Array.ForEach method.	13-16, 13-17
Determine the capacity of an array.	Use the Length property.	13-18
Copy the contents of one array to another.	Use the static System.Array.Copy method.	13-19
Change the capacity of an array.	Use the static System.Array.Resize method.	13-20
Find items in an array.	Use the static System.Array.Find or FindAll methods or use LINQ.	13-21 through 13-23
Treat arrays as collections.	Cast the array to one of the collection interfaces.	13-24
Create and use a multidimensional array.	Use the [,] array notation to create a rectangular array.	13-25 through 13-31
Create a multidimensional array where the capacity of each dimension can differ.	Use the [ ][ ] array notation to create a jagged array.	13-32 through 13-35

Defining and Initializing Arrays

The simplest way to defining and initializing arrays is to look at a C# statement. Listing 13-3 shows such a statement.

Listing 13-3. Defining Array Variables

```
string[] nameArray = new string[5];
```

A statement to define and initialize an array has five parts: the array type, the array notation, the new keyword, and the capacity of the array. These parts are illustrated in Figure 13-1.

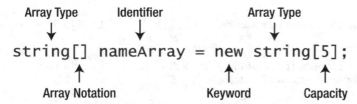

Figure 13-1. The anatomy of an array statement

The array type defines the type of object that the array will hold; all of the items in an array must be of the same type. The statement in Listing 13-3 uses the string type, meaning that the array will only hold instances of string. An array of a given type is often referred to as a *type array*; for example, an array of strings is a *string array*, and an array of ints is an *int array*.

The array notation is the open and close square brackets ([ ]). This indicates that the variable or field you are defining is an array. More specifically, the statement in Listing 13-3 has created a single-dimensional array. Other types of arrays are available, and these are described in the "Using Multidimensional Arrays" section later in the chapter.

The identifier is the name by which your field or variable will be known. The naming convention for arrays is the same as for other kinds of field or local variable.

The new keyword specifies that you are initializing the array. You can omit new if you are using the array initializer feature, described later in this section.

Arrays have a fixed capacity that must be defined when the array is initialized. This means that you have to decide the capacity you want to allocate to the array prior to its use and specify that capacity between the open and close square brackets, as shown in Figure 13-1. The capacity is specified using one of the C# integer types, such as int or long. You can find more information on C# integers in Chapter 5. The statement in Figure 13-1 creates an array with a capacity of five objects.

Arrays are like a row of slots; each of which can hold a reference or value of the type you have specified for the array. The number of slots is the capacity you have assigned to your array. This is illustrated by Figure 13-2, which shows an array with a capacity for four items.

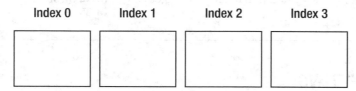

Figure 13-2. An array is like a row of slots.

When you initialize an array, it is populated with the default value for the array type. This is zero for numeric types, false for bool, and null for reference types. The array created in Listing 13-3 has five slots, each of which will be initialized with null since string is a reference type.

■ **Tip** The .NET Framework Library contains classes that you can use to gather together items without having to allocate capacity in advance. See Chapter 19 for more details.

You will notice that the array type in Listing 13-3 is repeated on the left and right sides of the statement. In Listing 13-3, both of these types are string, meaning that I have created a local variable that is a string array and assigned it a reference that is also a string array. However, you can vary the types so that you assign an array of a derived type to a variable or field that is an array of a base type. Listing 13-4 contains a simple example.

Listing 13-4. Initializing Arrays

```
object[] nameArray = new string[5];
```

The statement in Listing 13-4 has assigned a string array with a capacity for five objects to a variable called nameArray, which has been defined as an array of objects. This is an example of upcasting, which is explained in Chapter 6.

Getting and Setting Array Values

Each value in an array is given a position index, starting at zero and counting upward. You can see the sequence of indices in Figure 13-1. You access the value at a given index by using the array notation. For example, if I want to get the value at the first index of an array, I use the following statement:

```
string str = nameArray[0];
```

If I want to get the value in the third element, I use the following statement:

```
string str = nameArray[2];
```

Assigning values to positions in the array is very similar. The following statement assigns a value to the fourth position in an array:

```
nameArray[3] = "bananas";
```

The range of indexes available in an array is determined by the capacity you have allocated. Because the first index is always zero, the maximum valid index for an array is one less than the allocated capacity. The range between zero and the last index is called the *bounds* of the array. If you try to get or set an index outside this range, you are said to be *out of bounds*, and an instance of System.IndexOutOfRangeException will be thrown. See Chapter 14 for details of exceptions and exception handling.

■ **Tip** C# allows you to define array-like indexers for your custom types. See Chapter 8 for details.

Listing 13-5 contains a series of statements that get and set array values, including one that causes an exception by trying to get the value of an index that is outside the bounds of the array.

Listing 13-5. Getting and Setting Index Value

```
using System;

namespace Listing_05 {
    class Listing_05 {

        static void Main(string[] args) {

            // create an initialize an array
            string[] nameArray = new string[3];

            // set 2 of the array values
            nameArray[0] = "bananas";
            nameArray[1] = "cherries";

            // get the array values
            string value = nameArray[0];
            Console.WriteLine("Item: {0}", value);

            // get an array value that has not been set
            // and so will still be null
            value = nameArray[2];
            Console.WriteLine("Item: {0}", value == null);

            try {
                // try to get an index that is out of bounds
                value = nameArray[10];
            } catch (IndexOutOfRangeException ex) {
                Console.WriteLine("Exception: {0}", ex);
            }

            // wait for input before exiting
            Console.WriteLine("Press enter to finish");
            Console.ReadLine();
        }
    }
}
```

Compiling and running the code in Listing 13-5 produces the following results:

```
Item: bananas
```

```
Item: True
Exception: System.IndexOutOfRangeException: Index was outside the bounds of the array.
   at Listing_05.Listing_05.Main(String[] args) in C:\Listing_05\Listing_05.cs:line 25
Press enter to finish
```

The type of object you get or set in an array is the type of the variable, not the array you assigned to the variable. For example, in the previous section, I assigned a string array to an object array variable like this:

```
object[] nameArray = new string[5];
```

When I get from an index in the array, I will get an object and not a string, like this:

```
object obj = nameArray[0];
```

If I want to work with strings, then I have to cast each object I retrieve, as follows:

```
string str = (string)nameArray[0];
```

Using Array Initializers

When you initialize an array, it is filled with the default value of the type that the array contains. Sometimes, you already know what objects are going to go into the array, and in these cases, you can initialize the array so that it is populated with the data you want, rather than the default value for the array type.

To do this, you must define and populate the array in a single statement. The format to populate the array is an open brace ({), followed by the list of items you want to add, followed by a close brace (}). Each of the items in the list is separated by a comma. For example, the following statement:

```
string[] names = { "oranges", "apples", "guava" };
```

creates a string array with three items. This statement is equivalent to the following:

```
string[] names = new string[3];
names[0] = "oranges";
names[1] = "apples";
names[2] = "guava";
```

When defining and populating an array in a single statement, the size of the array is inferred by the number of items you have supplied in the list. There are a couple of variations of the syntax you can use, which are shown in Listing 13-6.

Listing 13-6. Using Array Initializers

```
using System;

namespace Listing_06 {
    class Listing_06 {

        static void Main(string[] args) {
```

```
        // define, initialize and populate a string array in one go
        string[] names1 = { "oranges", "apples", "guava" };

        // define, initialize and populate a string array in one go
        string[] names2 = new string[] { "oranges", "apples", "guava" };

        // define, initialize and populate a string array in one go
        string[] names3 = new string[3] { "oranges", "apples", "guava" };

        // wait for input before exiting
        Console.WriteLine("Press enter to finish");
        Console.ReadLine();
      }
    }
}
```

You can specify a capacity, as I have done in the statement marked in bold, but if you do this, the number of items between the braces must match the capacity. The first form is the simplest because it allowed you to omit the new keyword, the type, and the capacity. The format for populating the array is the same for custom types, as demonstrated by Listing 13-7.

Listing 13-7. Using Array Initializers with Custom Reference Types

```
using System;

class Product {
    private string name;

    public Product(string namearg) {
        name = namearg;
    }

    public string Name {
        get { return name; }
    }
}

class Listing_07 {

    static void Main(string[] args) {

        // create and initialize a new array
        Product[] prods = {
                        new Product("oranges"),
                        new Product("apples"),
                        new Product("guava")
                };

        // wait for input before exiting
        Console.WriteLine("Press enter to finish");
        Console.ReadLine();
```

```
        }
}
```

Enumerating Arrays

You can enumerate the contents of an array using foreach and for statements that are described in more detail in Chapter 4.

Enumerating with a for Loop

Listing 13-8 contains a simple example of a for statement to enumerate the contents of a three-item string array.

Listing 13-8. Enumerating with a for Statement

```csharp
using System;

class Listing_08 {

    static void Main(string[] args) {

        string[] names = { "oranges", "apples", "guava" };

        for (int i = 0; i < 3; i++) {
            Console.WriteLine("Item: {0}", names[i]);
        }

        // wait for input before exiting
        Console.WriteLine("Press enter to finish");
        Console.ReadLine();
    }
}
```

A for statement, also known as a for loop, has five parts: the for keyword, the initializer, the condition, the iterator, and the code statements. These parts are illustrated in Figure 13-3.

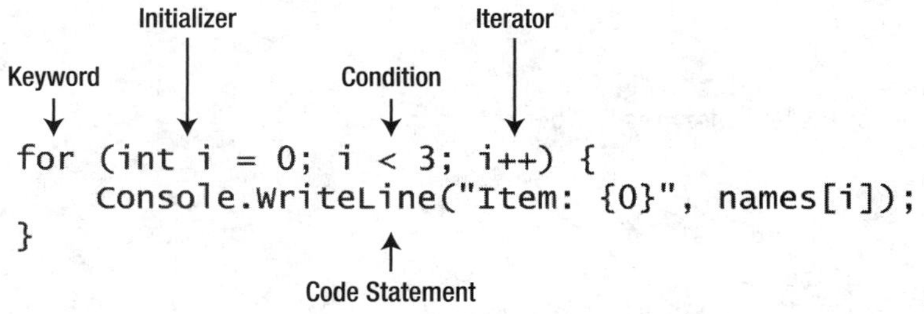

Figure 13-3. The anatomy of a for loop

A for loop evaluates the condition before anything else happens. If the condition doesn't evaluate to true, the code statements are not executed, and the for loop finishes. If the condition does evaluate to true, then the code statements are performed.

In the example, the condition is i < 3, so the loop checks the condition, and if the variable i has a value less than 3, the code statement is executed.

After the code statement has been executed, the for loop evaluates the condition again, and the cycle continues—check, execute, check, execute—until the condition evaluates to false, at which point the for loop finishes.

After each time the code statement is executed, the for loop executes the iterator statement. This is how you can stop the condition check/code statement cycle from repeating forever. In the example, I increment the variable i. Before any of this happens, the initializer is executed once, which gives you an opportunity to define and initialize the variables you are going to use in the condition and iterator. In the example, I define the variable i and assign it a value of zero. The result of this loop is that the code statement will be executed three times, with the variable i having a value of 0, 1, and then 2. These are the index values for a three-item array, so we can use variable value with the array index notation ([ ]) to access the elements in the array in turn.

Compiling the code in Listing 13-8 produces the following output:

```
Item: oranges
Item: apples
Item: guava
Press enter to finish
```

You can use a for loop to enumerate part of an array by using the initializer to assign a start index to the local variable that is greater than zero and use a condition that is satisfied sooner than the end of the array. You can get more details about for loops in Chapter 4.

If you don't know the capacity of an array you want to enumerate, then you can use the Length property that all arrays inherit from the System.Array class (see the "Using Array Members" section later in the chapter for details of other available members). Listing 13-9 demonstrates the use of the Length property.

Listing 13-9. Using the Array Length Property

```
using System;

class Listing_09 {

    static void Main(string[] args) {

        string[] names1 = { "oranges", "apples", "guava" };
        string[] names2 = { "pineapples", "cherries", "pears", "apricots" };

        printArrayContents(names1);
        printArrayContents(names2);

        // wait for input before exiting
        Console.WriteLine("Press enter to finish");
        Console.ReadLine();
    }
```

```
static void printArrayContents(string[] arr) {
    for (int i = 0; i < arr.Length; i++) {
        Console.WriteLine("Array Item {0}: {1}", i, arr[i]);
    }
}
}
```

The listing includes a `printArrayContents` method that uses the `Length` property in a `for` loop condition to enumerate the contents of arrays that are passed as method parameters. The `Length` property returns the capacity allocated to the array when it was defined, meaning that there may be default values for the array type in the array, including `null` for reference types.

Enumerating with a foreach Loop

Listing 13-10 contains a simple example of a `foreach` loop that enumerates the contents of a three-item string array.

Listing 13-10. Using a foreach Loop to Enumerate an Array

```
using System;

class Listing_10 {

    static void Main(string[] args) {

        string[] names = { "oranges", "apples", "guava" };

        foreach (string str in names) {
            Console.WriteLine("Item: {0}", str);
        }

        // wait for input before exiting
        Console.WriteLine("Press enter to finish");
        Console.ReadLine();
    }
}
```

The `foreach` loop, also known as the `foreach` statement, has five parts: the `foreach` keyword, the variable, the `in` keyword, the array to enumerate, and the code statements. Figure 13-4 illustrates these five parts.

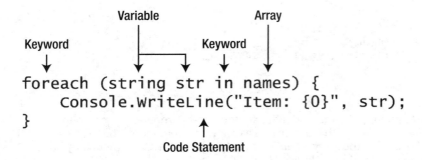

Figure 13-4. *The anatomy of a foreach loop*

When using a foreach loop, your code statements are executed once for each item in the array you have specified. Each time the code statements are executed, one item from the array is assigned to the loop variable, using the name that you have specified. In the example, the variable is called str, so I can refer to the current array item using this variable name in the code statement. The items in the array are processed in order, starting with index zero. The code statements will be executed for each array index in turn, including those to which you have not assigned a value, so your code should check for null values if you are working with an array of reference types.

The benefit of foreach loops is simplicity if you want to process every item in an array. You don't have to worry about the initializer, condition, and iterator as you do with a for loop. The drawback is that you can't tell the index of the item being processed without tracking it yourself.

Enumerating Using IEnumerator and IEnumerator<T>

The for and foreach loops work using the System.Collections.IEnumerator interface and its generic equivalent, System.Collections.IEnumerator<T>, both of which are implemented by arrays through the GetEnumerator method. Generic types are explained in Chapter 15, and interfaces are explained in Chapter 12. You can use these interfaces directly to enumerate the contents of an array. Listing 13-11 demonstrates the use of IEnumerator.

Listing 13-11. Using the Nongeneric IEnumerator Interface to Enumerate an Array

```
using System;
using System.Collections;

class Listing_11 {

    static void Main(string[] args) {

        string[] names = { "oranges", "apples", "guava" };

        IEnumerator e = names.GetEnumerator();

        while (e.MoveNext()) {
            string str = (string)e.Current;
            Console.WriteLine("Item: {0}", str);
```

```
        }

        // wait for input before exiting
        Console.WriteLine("Press enter to finish");
        Console.ReadLine();
    }
}
```

Calling the GetEnumerator method on an array returns an implementation of the nongeneric IEnumerator interface, which has two key members, MoveNext and Current. These methods are described in Table 13-2.

Table 13-2. *The Members of the IEnumerator and IEnumerator<T> Interface*

Member	Description
MoveNext()	Increments the index of the item from the array that will be returned by the Current property. Returns true if there is an item available via Current or false if all the items in the array have been enumerated. This method must be called once before Current will return the first item in the array.
Current	Returns an item from the array; this will be of type object for the IEnumerator interface and of type T for the IEnumerator<T> interface.

The members of the IEnumerator interface are typically used with a while loop. The MoveNext method must be called before the Current property will return the first item in the array, and so you use calls to MoveNext as the condition in the while loop, as shown in Listing 13-11.

If you are using the nongeneric IEnumerator interface, the type returned by the Current property will be object, irrespective of the type of your array. To emphasize this, I have assigned the result from Current to a local variable in the example, explicitly casting to string.

You don't have to perform the cast if you use the strongly typed IEnumerator<T> generic interface. But there is wrinkle; although arrays implement the strongly typed enumeration interfaces, the support is added by the compiler, and these features are not directly available. But you can use a feature of LINQ that lets you create a strongly typed enumerator from a weakly typed one. Listing 13-12 contains an example.

Listing 13-12. Using the Generic IEnumerator<T> Interface to Enumerate an Array

```
using System;
using System.Collections.Generic;
using System.Linq;

class Listing_12 {

    static void Main(string[] args) {

        string[] names = { "oranges", "apples", "guava" };

        IEnumerator<string> e = names.AsEnumerable<string>().GetEnumerator();
```

```
        while (e.MoveNext()) {
            string str = e.Current;
            Console.WriteLine("Item: {0}", str);
        }

        // wait for input before exiting
        Console.WriteLine("Press enter to finish");
        Console.ReadLine();
    }
}
```

If you import the System.Linq namespace, you can use the AsEnumerable<T> extension method that casts a weakly typed IEnumerator into a strongly typed IEnumerator<T>. There are references here that relate to other chapters; namespaces are explained in Chapter 11, extension methods are covered in Chapter 9, and LINQ itself is covered in Chapters 27 through 31. The important statement in Listing 13-12 is shown in bold. Once you have a generic IEnumerator<T> to work with, the Current property will return objects of the type T. In the example, this means that Current returns string objects.

You might be tempted to try to explicitly cast from a weakly typed IEnumerator to a strongly typed one, like this:

```
IEnumerator<string> e = (IEnumerator<string>)names.GetEnumerator();
```

This statement will compile but throw an exception at runtime, so you should avoid casting in this way.

Breaking from Enumerations

One common reason for enumerating the contents of an array is to find the first item that matches some kind of criteria. Listing 13-13 demonstrates a simple example of this.

Listing 13-13. Searching for the First Matching Item in an Array

```
using System;

class Listing_13 {

    static void Main(string[] args) {

        string[] names = { "oranges", "apples", "guava", "peaches", "bananas", "grapes" };

        foreach (string s in names) {
            Console.WriteLine("Checking...{0}", s);
            if (s.StartsWith("p")) {
                Console.WriteLine("Match! {0}", s);
            }
        }

        // wait for input before exiting
        Console.WriteLine("Press enter to finish");
        Console.ReadLine();
```

```
    }
}
```

In this example, I am looking for the first item in a string array that begins with the letter p. I use a foreach loop and print out message for each item that I check and a message when I make a match. Compiling and running the code in Listing 13-13 produces the following results:

```
Checking...oranges
Checking...apples
Checking...guava
Checking...peaches
Match! peaches
Checking...bananas
Checking...grapes
Press enter to finish
```

The problem with the code in the example is that it keeps checking items in the array even when I have made a match. The items bananas and grapes are still processed, even after I have successfully found peaches. We can fix this problem by using the break keyword when we find the array element we are looking for, as demonstrated by Listing 13-14.

Listing 13-14. Using break When Finding a Matching Array Item

```
using System;

class Listing_14 {

    static void Main(string[] args) {

        string[] names = { "oranges", "apples", "guava", "peaches", "bananas", "grapes" };

        foreach (string s in names) {
            Console.WriteLine("Checking...{0}", s);
            if (s.StartsWith("p")) {
                Console.WriteLine("Match! {0}", s);
                break;
            }
        }

        // wait for input before exiting
        Console.WriteLine("Press enter to finish");
        Console.ReadLine();
    }
}
```

When the break keyword is executed, it prevents further elements from the array being enumerated. You can use break with any of the enumeration techniques described in this chapter.

Using System.Array Members

C# arrays are implemented using the System.Array class. You can't create new instances of this class or derive new types from it. You must use the C# array syntax described at the start of this chapter. But C# arrays do inherit members from the System.Array class, and you can use these, and additional static methods, to make working with arrays simpler and easier. In this section, I describe some of the more commonly used members, and you can get additional information in Chapter 19, when I explain the use of the .NET collection classes.

Sorting Arrays

You can sort the contents of an array using the static System.Array.Sort method. Listing 13-15 contains a demonstration of this method.

Listing 13-15. Sorting an Array

```
using System;

class Listing_15 {

    static void Main(string[] args) {

        // define and populate the array
        string[] names = { "oranges", "apples", "guava", "peaches", "bananas", "grapes" };

        // sort the array
        Array.Sort(names);

        // enumerate the contents of the (now sorted) array
        foreach (string s in names) {
            Console.WriteLine("Item: {0}", s);
        }

        // wait for input before exiting
        Console.WriteLine("Press enter to finish");
        Console.ReadLine();
    }
}
```

The static Array.Sort method takes the array you want to sort as a parameter. Compiling and running the code in Listing 13-15 produces the following results:

```
Item: apples
Item: bananas
Item: grapes
Item: guava
Item: oranges
Item: peaches
```

Press enter to finish

There are overloaded versions of this method that let you specify how the items will be sorted. You can get more information on sorting in the Chapter 19.

Processing All of the Elements in an Array

The static Array.ForEach method lets you specify an Action delegate that will be applied to each element in the array in turn. This is another way of enumerating the array but allows you to use delegates. You can find more information about the Action class and delegates in general in Chapter 10. Listing 13-16 contains an example of using the ForEach method to enumerate an array.

Listing 13-16. Using the Array.ForEach Method

```
using System;

class Listing_16 {

    static void Main(string[] args) {

        // define and populate the array
        string[] names = { "oranges", "apples", "guava", "peaches", "bananas", "grapes" };

        // define an Action delegate
        Action<string> act = new Action<string>(printItem);

        // enumerate the contents of the array using the delegate
        Array.ForEach(names, act);

        // wait for input before exiting
        Console.WriteLine("Press enter to finish");
        Console.ReadLine();
    }

    static void printItem(string param) {
        Console.WriteLine("Item: {0}", param);
    }
}
```

In the example, I define an Action delegate that references the static printItem method. This method simply prints a message. I then pass the array I want to process and the delegate as parameters to the Array.ForEach method. Compiling and running the code in Listing 13-16 produces the following results:

```
Item: oranges
Item: apples
Item: guava
```

```
Item: peaches
Item: bananas
Item: grapes
Press enter to finish
```

You can use anonymous methods and delegates with the ForEach method. Listing 13-17 shows the same code using a lambda expression. However, if you end up using anonymous methods with the Array.ForEach method, you should consider using a regular foreach loop as described in the "Enumerating Arrays" section earlier in the chapter.

Listing 13-17. Using the Array.ForEach Method with a Lambda Expression

```
using System;

class Listing_17 {

    static void Main(string[] args) {

        // define and populate the array
        string[] names = { "oranges", "apples", "guava", "peaches", "bananas", "grapes" };

        // enumerate the contents of the array using the delegate
        Array.ForEach(names, s => {
            Console.WriteLine("Item: {0}", s);
        });

        // wait for input before exiting
        Console.WriteLine("Press enter to finish");
        Console.ReadLine();
    }
}
```

Resizing and Copying an Array

Arrays have a fixed capacity that is specified when they are initialized. If you don't know how many items you will be working with in advance, you can use one of the collection classes (described in Chapter 19) or resize your array to ensure that it always has sufficient capacity to hold your data. Resizing an array manually is a process of creating a new array of the increased capacity and populating it with the data from the original array, as demonstrated in Listing 13-18.

Listing 13-18. Determining Array Capacity Using the LongLength Property

```
using System;

class Listing_18 {

    static void Main(string[] args) {

        // define and populate an array
```

```
        string[] names = { "oranges", "apples", "guava", "peaches", "bananas", "grapes" };

        // print out the details of the array
        printArrayDetails(names);

        // create a larger array
        string[] biggerNames = new string[names.Length + 2];

        // copy the data from the original array to the new array
        for (int i = 0; i < names.Length; i++) {
            biggerNames[i] = names[i];
        }

        // assign the new array to the old array variable
        names = biggerNames;

        // print out the details of the array
        Console.WriteLine("\nFinished resizing array");
        printArrayDetails(names);

        // wait for input before exiting
        Console.WriteLine("Press enter to finish");
        Console.ReadLine();
    }

    static void printArrayDetails(string[] arr) {
        // report the size of the array
        Console.WriteLine("Array Length: {0}", arr.Length);

        // report on the contents of the array
        foreach (string s in arr) {
            if (s == null) {
                Console.WriteLine("Item: null");
            } else {
                Console.WriteLine("Item: {0}", s);
            }
        }
    }
}
```

The code in Listing 13-18 resizes an array with capacity for six items to one with eight items. It creates a new array, copies the data from the old array, and assigns the new array to the local variable that previously referenced the old array. The additional capacity will be initialized with the default value for the array type, which will be null for the example since string is a reference type. Compiling and running the code in Listing 13-18 produces the following output:

```
Array Length: 6
Item: oranges
Item: apples
```

```
Item: guava
Item: peaches
Item: bananas
Item: grapes

Finished resizing array
Array Length: 8
Item: oranges
Item: apples
Item: guava
Item: peaches
Item: bananas
Item: grapes
Item: null
Item: null
Press enter to finish
```

The members of the static System.Array class can help us simplify this process in two ways. The first is with the Copy method, which you can use to copy the contents of one array to another. Listing 13-19 contains an example of using this method to resize the arrays from the previous listing.

Listing 13-19. Using the Array.Copy Method

```csharp
using System;

class Listing_19 {

    static void Main(string[] args) {

        // define and populate an array
        string[] names = { "oranges", "apples", "guava", "peaches", "bananas", "grapes" };

        // print out the details of the array
        printArrayDetails(names);

        // create a larger array
        string[] biggerNames = new string[names.Length + 2];

        // copy the data from the original array to the new array
        Array.Copy(names, biggerNames, names.Length);

        // assign the new array to the old array variable
        names = biggerNames;

        // print out the details of the array
        Console.WriteLine("\nFinished resizing array");
        printArrayDetails(names);

        // wait for input before exiting
        Console.WriteLine("Press enter to finish");
```

```
        Console.ReadLine();
    }

    static void printArrayDetails(string[] arr) {
        // report the size of the array
        Console.WriteLine("Array Length: {0}", arr.Length);

        // report on the contents of the array
        foreach (string s in arr) {
            if (s == null) {
                Console.WriteLine("Item: null");
            } else {
                Console.WriteLine("Item: {0}", s);
            }
        }
    }
}
```

The Copy method takes the source array, the destination array, and the number of items to copy as parameters. There are overloaded versions of the Copy method available that allow you to be more selective about the data that is copied. Arrays inherit the instance method CopyTo, which copies all the items in the array to another array. I could have replaced the Copy statement in bold in the listing with the following, where the parameters are the array to copy the data into and the index to start the copy from:

```
names.CopyTo(biggerNames, 0);
```

The second way that the System.Array members can help us is with the static Resize method, which handles all the steps of resizing an array in one method call. Listing 13-20 contains an example.

Listing 13-20. Using the System.Array.Resize Method

```
using System;

class Listing_20 {

    static void Main(string[] args) {

        // define and populate an array
        string[] names = { "oranges", "apples", "guava", "peaches", "bananas", "grapes" };

        // print out the details of the array
        printArrayDetails(names);

        // resize the array
        Array.Resize(ref names, 8);

        // print out the details of the array
        Console.WriteLine("\nFinished resizing array");
        printArrayDetails(names);

        // wait for input before exiting
```

```
        Console.WriteLine("Press enter to finish");
        Console.ReadLine();
    }

    static void printArrayDetails(string[] arr) {
        // report the size of the array
        Console.WriteLine("Array Length: {0}", arr.Length);

        // report on the contents of the array
        foreach (string s in arr) {
            if (s == null) {
                Console.WriteLine("Item: null");
            } else {
                Console.WriteLine("Item: {0}", s);
            }
        }
    }
}
```

The Resize method requires a ref parameter of the array you want to resize and the required size. See Chapter 9 for details of ref parameters.

Finding Items in an Array

In the "Enumerating Arrays" section, I demonstrated the break keyword as a way to efficiently find the first element in an array that matches a given condition. The System.Array class contains some static methods that can simplify this process, as shown in Listing 13-21.

Listing 13-21. Using the Find Method

```
using System;

class Listing_21 {

    static void Main(string[] args) {

        // define and populate an array
        string[] names = { "oranges", "apples", "guava", "peaches", "bananas", "grapes" };

        // define the predicate
        Predicate<string> pred = new Predicate<string>(CheckString);

        // search for a match
        string match = Array.Find(names, pred);

        // print the result
        Console.WriteLine("Match: {0}", match);

        // wait for input before exiting
        Console.WriteLine("Press enter to finish");
        Console.ReadLine();
```

```
        }

    static bool CheckString(string s) {
        return s.StartsWith("p");
    }
}
```

The static `System.Array.Find` method takes the array in which you want to find a matching item and an instance of the `System.Predicate<T>` delegate, where `T` is the type that the array contains. The Predicate delegate is passed an object of type `T` and returns `true` if the object matches your search criteria. You can assign the delegate to a named method (as I have done in the example) or to an anonymous method or lambda expression. For example, I could have written the statement that calls the Find method like this:

```
string match = Array.Find(names, s => s.StartsWith("p"));
```

You can find full details of delegates in Chapter 10. The Find method returns the first object in the array that causes the predicate delegate to return `true`. Compiling and running the code in Listing 13-21 produces the following results:

```
Match: peaches
Press enter to finish
```

A useful variation is the static `Array.FindAll` method that returns a new array containing only the items that satisfy the criteria in a predicate delegate. This can be an easy way to shrink an array and remove any `null` values, as demonstrated by Listing 13-22.

Listing 13-22. Using the FindAll Method to Shrink an Array

```csharp
using System;

class Listing_21 {

    static void Main(string[] args) {

        // define and populate an array including some null values
        string[] names = { "oranges", "apples", null, "guava", "peaches", null};

        // shrink the array by finding all of the items which are not null
        string[] shrinkNames = Array.FindAll(names, s => s != null);

        // print out the details of the array
        Console.WriteLine("Array length: {0}", shrinkNames.Length);
        foreach (string s in shrinkNames) {
            Console.WriteLine("Item: {0}", s);
        }

        // wait for input before exiting
        Console.WriteLine("Press enter to finish");
        Console.ReadLine();
```

```
    }
}
```

The code in the listing defines an array that has two null items, which we are going to remove. We call the static `Array.FindAll` method, which takes the array we want to work with and a `System.Predicate` delegate as parameters. The `FindAll` method returns an array containing only the items that cause the predicate delegate to return true. In this case, that's every item that it not null. Compiling and running the code in Listing 13-22 produces the following results:

```
Array length: 4
Item: oranges
Item: apples
Item: guava
Item: peaches
Press enter to finish
```

Using Arrays with LINQ

You can use arrays as the data source in LINQ queries. LINQ is detailed fully later in this book but allows you to perform SQL-like queries on a range of data sources, including arrays. I am not going to go into any details for LINQ in this chapter, but Listing 13-23 demonstrates how to use LINQ to shrink an array and remove null values, just like the code in Listing 13-22.

Listing 13-23. Using LINQ to Shrink an Array

```
using System;
using System.Collections.Generic;
using System.Linq;

class Listing_21 {

    static void Main(string[] args) {

        // define and populate an array including some null values
        string[] names = { "oranges", "apples", null, "guava", "peaches", null };

        IEnumerable<string> filtered = from s in names
                                       where s != null
                                       select s;

        string[] shrinkNames = filtered.ToArray();

        // print out the details of the array
        Console.WriteLine("Array length: {0}", shrinkNames.Length);
        foreach (string s in shrinkNames) {
            Console.WriteLine("Item: {0}", s);
        }
```

```
        // wait for input before exiting
        Console.WriteLine("Press enter to finish");
        Console.ReadLine();
    }
}
```

Using Arrays as Collections

C# arrays implicitly implement interfaces from the Sytem.Collections and System.Collections.Generic namespaces. I cover collections in a later chapter and won't go into the detail in this chapter. Listing 13-24 demonstrates using the IList<T> generic interface from the System.Collections.Generic namespace.

Listing 13-24. Using an Array as a Collection

```
using System;
using System.Collections.Generic;

class Listing_24 {

    static void Main(string[] args) {

        // define and populate an array
        string[] names = { "oranges", "apples", "guava", "peaches", "bananas", "grapes" };

        // implicitly cast the array to an IList<T>
        IList<string> ilist = names;

        // access the array through the IList<T> members
        int index = ilist.IndexOf("apples");

        // print out the result
        Console.WriteLine("Index: {0}", index);

        // wait for input before exiting
        Console.WriteLine("Press enter to finish");
        Console.ReadLine();
    }
}
```

Using Multidimensional Arrays

All the arrays so far in this chapter have been *single-dimensional* arrays, meaning that the arrays are like a long row of slots, where the allocated capacity determines how many slots there are. This was illustrated by Figure 13-2, which showed a single-dimensional array a capacity to hold four objects.

Single-dimensional arrays are the type that programmers use most frequently. This is the simplest kind of array and allows you to collect related objects in a neat and efficient way. But C# also supports two kinds of multidimensional array, which allows you to capture more complex relationships between objects.

Using Rectangular Arrays

A rectangular array is more like a table, with rows and columns. Figure 13-5 illustrates a rectangular array that has three rows and four columns; the indices for both rows and columns start with zero, just as for a single-dimensional array.

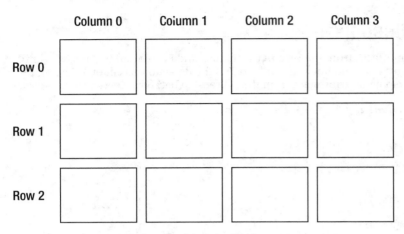

Figure 13-5. *A rectangular multidimensional array*

Defining a rectangular array requires a slight variation on the array syntax we have used so far in this chapter. Listing 13-25 demonstrates creating a rectangular array.

Listing 13-25. Creating a Rectangular Array

```
int[,] rectArray = new int[3, 4];
```

There are some differences in the notation, which are illustrated by Figure 13-6.

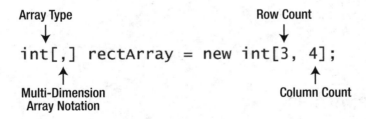

Figure 13-6. Defining a rectangular array

The most obvious difference is the addition of the comma in the array notation on the left of the statement. Adding one comma creates a two-dimensional array (with rows and columns), and you can add additional commas to create arrays with three and more dimensions; see the "Creating Rectangular Arrays with Additional Dimensions" section later in this chapter for some examples.

Getting and Setting Rectangular Array Values

To get and set values in a rectangular array, you specify the row and column indices for the position in the table you want to work with, separated by a comma. Listing 13-26 contains a demonstration.

Listing 13-26. Getting and Setting Values in a Two-Dimensional Rectangular Array

```
using System;

class Listing_26 {

    static void Main(string[] args) {

        // define a rectangular array of strings
        string[,] namesArray = new string[5, 5];

        // set values in the array
        namesArray[2, 3] = "Oranges";
        namesArray[2, 4] = "Apples";

        // get a value from the array
        string val = namesArray[2, 4];

        // wait for input before exiting
        Console.WriteLine("Press enter to finish");
        Console.ReadLine();
    }
}
```

Using Rectangular Array Initializers

As with single-dimensional arrays, you can define and populate an array in one statement. This is very useful if you know in advance what data you want to put into the array. Listing 13-27 contains an example.

Listing 13-27. Populating a Two-Dimensional String Array

```
using System;

class Listing_27 {

    static void Main(string[] args) {

        // define and populate a rectangular array of strings
        string[,] namesArray = {
            {"apples", "oranges", "grapes", "pears"},
            {"green", "orange", "red", "green"}
        };

        // get a value from the array
```

```
            string val = namesArray[1, 3];

            Console.WriteLine("Value: {0}", val);

            // wait for input before exiting
            Console.WriteLine("Press enter to finish");
            Console.ReadLine();
        }
}
```

To populate a rectangular array, you define the contents of each row, separated by a comma. The content of each row consists of the content for each column in that row, also separated by a column. The code in the listing creates an array with two rows and four columns.

Enumerating a Rectangular Array

Enumerating the contents of a rectangular array is just like enumerating a single-dimensional array. The simplest approach is to use a foreach loop, which hides the complexity caused by the extra dimensions. Listing 13-28 contains an example.

Listing 13-28. Enumerating the Contents of a Rectangular Array

```
using System;

class Listing_28 {

    static void Main(string[] args) {

        // define and populate a rectangular array of strings
        string[,] namesArray = {
            {"apples", "oranges", "grapes", "pears"},
            {"green", "orange", "red", "green"}
        };

        Console.WriteLine("Enumerating using a foreach loop");
        foreach (string s in namesArray) {
            Console.WriteLine("Item: {0}", s);
        }

        // wait for input before exiting
        Console.WriteLine("Press enter to finish");
        Console.ReadLine();
    }
}
```

Compiling and running the code in Listing 13-28 produces the following results:

```
Enumerating using a foreach
Item: apples
Item: oranges
```

```
Item: grapes
Item: pears
Item: green
Item: orange
Item: red
Item: green
Press enter to finish
```

You can see from the results that the content of each row is enumerated in turn. Things are more complicated if you want to enumerate a rectangular array using a for loop. You have to use the GetLength method, which all arrays inherit from System.Array. This method returns the number of slots in a given dimension, and you pass the dimension you are interested in as a parameter to the method. Listing 13-29 contains an example.

Listing 13-29. Enumerating the Contents of a Rectangular Array Using a for Loop

```
using System;

class Listing_29 {

    static void Main(string[] args) {

        // define and populate a rectangular array of strings
        string[,] namesArray = {
            {"apples", "oranges", "grapes", "pears"},
            {"green", "orange", "red", "green"}
        };

        Console.WriteLine("Enumerating using a for loop");
        int dim0Len = namesArray.GetLength(0);
        int dim1Len = namesArray.GetLength(1);

        for (int row = 0; row < dim0Len; row++) {
            for (int column = 0; column < dim1Len; column++) {
                Console.WriteLine("Row: {0}, Col: {1}, Value: {2}",
                    row, column, namesArray[row, column]);
            }
        }

        // wait for input before exiting
        Console.WriteLine("Press enter to finish");
        Console.ReadLine();
    }
}
```

I get the number of slots in dimension 0, which equates to the number of rows. The number of slots in dimension 1 equates to the number of columns. I then use a pair of for loops to enumerate the contents of each column in each row. Compiling and running the code in Listing 13-29 produces the following results:

```
Enumerating using a for loop
Row: 0, Col: 0, Value: apples
Row: 0, Col: 1, Value: oranges
Row: 0, Col: 2, Value: grapes
Row: 0, Col: 3, Value: pears
Row: 1, Col: 0, Value: green
Row: 1, Col: 1, Value: orange
Row: 1, Col: 2, Value: red
Row: 1, Col: 3, Value: green
Press enter to finish
```

Creating Rectangular Arrays with Additional Dimensions

You can create arrays with more than two dimensions by adding additional commas to the array definition. Listing 13-30 contains an example of a three-dimensional array, which transforms the table format of our previous example into a cube.

Listing 13-30. Creating a Three-Dimensional Array

```csharp
using System;

class Listing_30 {

    static void Main(string[] args) {

        string[, ,] namesArray = new string[3, 3, 3];

        // set some values in the array
        namesArray[1, 2, 2] = "oranges";
        namesArray[0, 0, 1] = "apples";

        // get a value from the array
        string val = namesArray[0, 0, 1];

        Console.WriteLine("Value: {0}", val);

        // wait for input before exiting
        Console.WriteLine("Press enter to finish");
        Console.ReadLine();
    }
}
```

You can see that to get or set values in the array, you must specify three index values, and using the array initializer feature requires a similar change, as demonstrated by Listing 13-31.

Listing 13-31. Creating and Populating a Three-Dimensional Array

```csharp
using System;
```

```
class Listing_31 {

    static void Main(string[] args) {

        string[, ,] namesArray = {
            {
                {"apples", "oranges", "bananas"}
            },
            {
                {"green", "orange", "yellow"}
            },
            {
                {"round", "round", "curved"}
            }
        };

        // get a value from the array
        string val = namesArray[0, 0, 1];

        Console.WriteLine("Value: {0}", val);

        // wait for input before exiting
        Console.WriteLine("Press enter to finish");
        Console.ReadLine();
    }
}
```

The code required to initialize arrays with three or more dimensions becomes complex and error-prone.

Using Jagged Arrays

The arrays in the previous section are known as rectangular arrays because each dimension has the same capacity. You can also create jagged arrays that have irregular capacity. Listing 13-32 contains an example of defining a jagged array.

Listing 13-32. Creating a Jagged Array

```
string[][] jaggedArray = new string[3][];

jaggedArray[0] = new string[2];
jaggedArray[1] = new string[1];
jaggedArray[2] = new string[3];
```

Jagged arrays are also known as *arrays of arrays,* and you can see why this is from the code statements in Listing 13-32. The variable jaggedArray is an array of string arrays, each of which has to be initialized separately. The array in the example is illustrated in Figure 13-7.

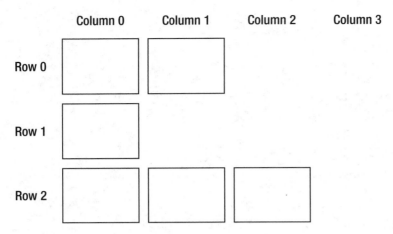

Figure 13-7. A jagged array

You can see where the term *jagged* comes from when looking at Figure 13-7. The first row in the array contains two slots, the second contains one slot, and the third row contains three slots.

Getting and Setting Jagged Array Values

Getting and setting values in a jagged array is similar to doing so for a rectangular array, but you need to pay more attention to the bounds for each row because they can have an irregular capacity. Listing 13-33 contains some example statements for getting and setting with a jagged array.

Listing 13-33. Getting and Setting Jagged Array Values

```
using System;

class Listing_33 {

    static void Main(string[] args) {

        string[][] jaggedArray = new string[3][];

        jaggedArray[0] = new string[2];
        jaggedArray[1] = new string[1];
        jaggedArray[2] = new string[3];

        // set some values in the array
        jaggedArray[0][1] = "oranges";
        jaggedArray[2][2] = "apples";

        // get a value from the array
        string value = jaggedArray[2][2];
        Console.WriteLine("Value: {0}", value);
```

```
        // wait for input before exiting
        Console.WriteLine("Press enter to finish");
        Console.ReadLine();
    }
}
```

You can see that I have to specify the index for each dimension between a set of square brackets, such as jaggedArray[0][1].

Using Jagged Array Initializers

You can initialize each individual array in a jagged array using the standard initializers used for single-dimensional arrays, as demonstrated by Listing 13-34.

Listing 13-34. Initializing a Jagged Array

```
using System;

class Listing_34 {

    static void Main(string[] args) {

        string[][] jaggedArray = new string[3][];

        jaggedArray[0] = new string[] {"apples", "oranges"};
        jaggedArray[1] = new string[] {"bananas"};
        jaggedArray[2] = new string[] { "guavas", "pears", "cherries" };

        // wait for input before exiting
        Console.WriteLine("Press enter to finish");
        Console.ReadLine();
    }
}
```

Enumerating a Jagged Array

When enumerating a jagged array, you work on the basis that it is an array of arrays and use a pair of for loops to enumerate the contents. You can also use a pair for foreach loops, one to enumerate the individual arrays and one to enumerate the individual elements. Listing 13-35 demonstrates using both kinds of loop.

Listing 13-35. Enumerating the Contents of a Jagged Array

```
using System;

class Listing_35 {

    static void Main(string[] args) {
```

```
string[][] jaggedArray = new string[3][];

jaggedArray[0] = new string[] { "apples", "oranges" };
jaggedArray[1] = new string[] { "bananas" };
jaggedArray[2] = new string[] { "guavas", "pears", "cherries" };

foreach (string[] outer in jaggedArray) {
    foreach (string s in outer) {
        Console.WriteLine("Item: {0}", s);
    }
}

for (int i = 0; i < jaggedArray.Length; i++) {
    for (int j = 0; j < jaggedArray[i].Length; j++) {
        Console.WriteLine("Row: {0}, Col: {1}, Value: {2}",
            i, j, jaggedArray[i][j]);
    }
}

// wait for input before exiting
Console.WriteLine("Press enter to finish");
Console.ReadLine();
    }
}
```

Summary

In this chapter, we explored the different kinds of arrays that C# supports and the features that each kind has to offer. The most commonly used is the single-dimensional array that dominates this chapter. This kind of array allows you group together related objects in a simple and efficient way. We also looked at multidimensional arrays, which can be used to express more complex relationships between objects. They are less frequently used and can become complex and confusing to use as the number of dimensions increases. We saw how arrays of all types can be used, enumerated, and populated, as well as how to use the members inherited from the System.Array class to perform common array-related tasks.

■ ■ ■

CHAPTER 14

Exceptions

Exceptions are the way that errors are handled in C#. If you have used C++ or Java, you will already be familiar with the idea of exceptions. In C#, all exceptions are runtime exceptions, meaning that methods do not have to declare the exceptions they will throw (for example, there is no equivalent to the Java throws keyword in method definitions). This can take a while to get used to, not least because any method you call can throw any kind of exception. Careful testing and a considered approach to handling runtime exceptions are essential in C# programs. In this chapter, I'll show you how to handle exceptions, throw exceptions, create custom exceptions, and aggregate multiple exceptions. Table 14-1 provides the summary for this chapter.

Table 14-1. Quick Problem/Solution Reference for Chapter 14

Problem	Solution	Listings
Catch and handle an exception.	Use a try statement with a catch clause.	14-1 through 14-3
Handle exceptions based on type.	Use a try statement with multiple catch clauses.	14-4 through 14-6
Catch exceptions that are not handled by other catch clauses.	Use a general catch clause or nest try statements.	14-7, 14-8
Obtain details about an exception you have caught.	Use the members of the System.Exception type.	14-9, 14-10
Define code statements that will be performed whether or not an exception is thrown.	Use a try statement with a finally clause.	14-11, 14-12
Throw an exception to indicate an error condition in your code.	Use the throw keyword.	14-13 through 14-16
Define custom exceptions for your program.	Derive from the System.Exception class.	14-17, 14-18

Problem	Solution	Listings
Throw an exception that maps a system error condition to a program-specific condition.	Use a try statement with a catch clause that throws a custom exception type.	14-19, 14-20
Create a chain of exceptions.	Use the standard constructor that accepts another exception as a parameter.	14-21, 14-22
Aggregate an exception to represent multiple simultaneous problems.	Use the System.AggregateException class.	14-23, 14-24

Handling Exceptions

The best place to start with exceptions is to see one at work. Listing 14-1 shows the kind of exception that you are likely to see most often as you start working with C#.

Listing 14-1. The NullReferenceException

```
using System;

class Listing_01 {

    static void Main(string[] args) {

        // define a loval variable
        string myLocalVar = null;

        // try to so something with the local variable
        Console.WriteLine("First letter: {0}", myLocalVar[0]);

        // wait for input before exiting
        Console.WriteLine("Press enter to finish");
        Console.ReadLine();
    }
}
```

The code in Listing 14-1 creates a local reference-type variable but doesn't assign a reference to it, so it remains null. The local reference is then used as if it *were* assigned to an object, which produces the following result:

```
Unhandled Exception: System.NullReferenceException: Object reference not set to
an instance of an object.
    at Listing_01.Main(String[] args) in C:\\Listing_01\Listing_01.cs:line 11
Press any key to continue . . .
```

Exceptions are used to express errors. In this case, the error was caused by trying to make a method call to a null reference. The C# code inside the runtime detected what we were trying to do and *threw* or *raised* an exception. When an exception is *thrown*, the runtime tries to find a handler for the exception. There wasn't a handler in Listing 14-1, so the default was used. The default handler in C# console applications prints out a message and then terminates the program, which is why we got the output shown previously.

Using try Statements and catch Clauses

I could have avoided the exception in Listing 14-1 by checking whether the local variable was null. Although such checks are good practice, they are rarely applied consistently throughout a program, and not all exceptions are as easily avoided. There comes a point where you need to know how to deal with exceptions when they arise, and you do this using a try statement. Listing 14-2 demonstrates a simple use of a try statement.

Listing 14-2. A Simple try Statement

```
try {

    // try to so something with the local variable
    Console.WriteLine("First letter: {0}", myLocalVar[0]);

} catch (NullReferenceException ex) {
    Console.WriteLine("Exception: {0}", ex.Message);
}
```

There are six parts to a basic try statement: the try keyword, the code statements, the catch keyword, the exception type, the exception identifier, and the handler statements. These six parts are illustrated in Figure 14-1.

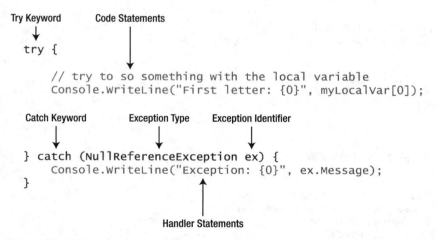

Figure 14-1. The anatomy of a try statement

A try statement affects code statements that appear between the try and catch keywords. Each code statement is executed in turn. If the statement doesn't throw an exception, then control moves to the next statement. If all the code statements have been executed, then control moves to the first code statement after the try block, skipping over the handler statements.

If any of the statements does throw an exception, no further code statements are executed from the try statement, and the runtime looks for a handler that can deal with the exception. A handler can deal with an exception if the exception type declared in the catch clause is of the type of the exception that has been thrown or is a base type of the exception that has been thrown. In Listing 14-2, there is a handler for the NullReferenceException type. Exceptions of this type can be handled, but the runtime will have to continue looking for a handler for other exception types.

When an exception is thrown, the runtime looks to see whether the current statement is enclosed by a try statement. If it is and there is a matching catch clause that will handle the exception, the handler statements are executed. The idea is that you use this opportunity to return your program to a state that will allow it to continue despite the exception.

If the statement that caused the exception is not enclosed by a try statement or is enclosed by a try block that doesn't have a matching catch clause, then the method that called the current method is searched to see whether it contains an enclosing try statement with a matching catch clause. This process continues up the call stack until a match is found. If there is no match, then the default handler is used, which terminates the program. You can see how this works in Listing 14-3.

Listing 14-3. Exception Handling

```csharp
using System;

class Listing_03 {

    static void Main(string[] args) {

        try {

            MethodOne();

        } catch (NullReferenceException ex) {
            Console.WriteLine("Exception: {0}", ex.Message);
        }

        // wait for input before exiting
        Console.WriteLine("Press enter to finish");
        Console.ReadLine();
    }

    static void MethodOne() {
        Console.WriteLine("Start of MethodOne");
        MethodTwo();

        // print out a message - this statement will not
        // be reached because the previous statement calls
        // a method that throws an exception
        Console.WriteLine("End of MethodOne");
    }
```

```
static void MethodTwo() {
    try {
        Console.WriteLine("Start of MethodTwo");
        MethodThree();

        // print out a message - this statement will not
        // be reached because the previous statement calls
        // a method that throws an exception
        Console.WriteLine("End of MethodTwo");

    } catch (ArgumentOutOfRangeException ex) {
        // handle this kind of exception
    }
}

static void MethodThree() {
    Console.WriteLine("Start of MethodThree");

    // define a loval variable
    string myLocalVar = null;

    // try to so something with the local variable
    Console.WriteLine("First letter: {0}", myLocalVar[0]);

    // print out a message - this statement will not
    // be reached because the previous statement will
    // throw an exception
    Console.WriteLine("End of MethodThree");
}
}
```

The sequence of method calls in Listing 14-3 is shown in Figure 14-2. I have made all the methods in this example static for simplicity. The Main method calls MethodOne, which calls MethodTwo, which calls MethodThree.

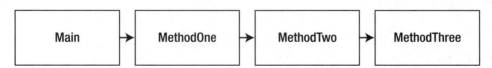

Figure 14-2. *Call stack for Listing 14-3*

The sequence of method calls is called the *call stack*. In the listing, the exception is thrown in MethodThree (this is the same exception we saw previously), which is an instance of System.NullReferenceException. When the exception is thrown, the search for a handler begins.

First, the runtime looks at the statement in MethodThree that caused the exception and checks to see whether it is enclosed by a try statement. In this example, it is not.

Next, the runtime looks at the statement that called MethodThree. This is contained in MethodTwo. You can see that we are moving back up the call stack. The call in MethodTwo is enclosed in a try statement, so the runtime looks at the catch clause to see whether it can handle a NullReferenceException. It doesn't—the catch clause in MethodTwo is only able to handle an ArgumentOutOfRangeException, so the search continues.

The runtime moves up the stack again to MethodOne and checks to see whether the statement that called MethodTwo is enclosed in a try statement. No luck there. The runtime moves up the call stack again, this time to the Main method. The statement that invoked MethodOne *is* enclosed in a try statement, and this time, there is a catch clause that can handle a NullReferenceException. The runtime executes the statements in the catch clause. In this example, a single statement prints out the value of the Message property.

Compiling and running the code in Listing 14-3 produces the following results:

```
Start of MethodOne
Start of MethodTwo
Start of MethodThree
Exception: Object reference not set to an instance of an object.
Press enter to finish
```

Execution of the program continues from the next statement after the catch clause that has handled the exception. You can see from the output that the statements that print out a message at the end of each method are not performed, but the statements that follow the try statement in the Main method are, starting with this one:

```
Console.WriteLine("Press enter to finish");
```

Understanding which statements are executed when an exception occurs and has been handled is essential to using exceptions effectively, as well as understanding how the runtime searches for a handler to process the exception.

Handling Different Exception Types

A try statement can have more than one catch clause, and each catch clause can handle a different kind of exception. Listing 14-4 contains an example.

Listing 14-4. catch Clauses in a try Statement

```
try {

    // statements likely to cause exceptions

} catch (NullReferenceException ex) {

    // code which handles a NullReferenceException

} catch (ArgumentOutOfRangeException ex) {

    // code which handles an ArgumentOutOfRangeException

} catch {
    // code which handles all exception types not handled
    // in the clauses above
```

}

There are three catch clauses in Listing 14-4. The first will be used to handle a NullReferenceException, and the second will be used to handle an ArgumentOutOfRangeException. These are both *specific catch clauses*, in that they deal with a specific exception type. The third catch clause is a *general catch clause* and deals with any exception type that has not been handled by one of the other clauses.

Using Specific catch Clauses

A specific catch clause is defined with an exception type and, optionally, an identifier for the exception. If a try statement has more than one catch clauses, the runtime looks at them in the order in which they are defined to find a match. A specific catch clause is considered a match if the clause exception type is the same as the type of the exception that has been thrown *or* the clause exception type is a base class of the exception that has been thrown.

The root for all exceptions in .NET is the System.Exception class, so you can catch every kind of exception by specifying this as the type in the catch clause—although you can achieve a similar effect using a general catch clause, described in the next section. If you define a catch clause using System.Exception, it must be the last clause in the try statement, because it will always make a match for an exception and any subsequent clauses will not be checked and used.

A catch clause for System.Exception is most frequently used as a backstop to ensure that all exceptions are handled, preventing the exception from being pushed up the call stack and potentially triggering the default exception handler. Listing 14-5 demonstrates a try statement that uses this approach.

Listing 14-5. Catching System.Exception as a Backstop

```
try {

    // statements likely to cause exceptions

} catch (NullReferenceException ex) {

    // code which handles a NullReferenceException

} catch (ArgumentOutOfRangeException ex) {

    // code which handles an ArgumentOutOfRangeException

} catch (Exception ex) {

    // code which handles all exception types not handled
    // in the clauses above

}
```

The try statement in Listing 14-5 includes catch clauses that will be used for two specific exception types and then a clause that catches everything else.

The identifier for the exception in a catch clause is optional, but if you omit the identifier, then you are unable to access the members of the exception that is being handled. Listing 14-6 demonstrates a try statement with two catch clauses, one of which omits the exception identifier.

Listing 14-6. Omitting the Exception Identifier in a Specific catch Clause

```
try {

    // statements likely to cause exceptions

} catch (NullReferenceException ex) {

    Console.WriteLine("Message: {0}", ex.Message);

} catch (ArgumentOutOfRangeException) {

    // code which handles an ArgumentOutOfRangeException

}
```

The first catch clause defines an identifier, ex, for the exception. This allows the handler statements to refer to the exception using this identifier—for example, reading the Message property from the exception by calling ex.Message. The second catch clause doesn't define an identifier and so cannot make such a reference.

Using General catch Clauses

A try statement can have at most one general catch clause, and it must be the last catch clause in the list. General catch clauses can be used as an effective backstop to prevent exceptions from propagating up the call stack to the default handler. Despite this, general clauses are rarely used, because they don't allow you to access the exception that is being thrown, which is a severe limitation. A more common solution is to use a specific catch clause for the System.Exception type; see the previous section for details.

Omitting catch Clauses

All the examples in this chapter so far have included at least one catch clause, but in fact, you can define try statements that don't have any catch clauses at all. Listing 14-7 demonstrates such a try statement, which has no catch clauses but does have a finally clause, which I describe later in the chapter.

Listing 14-7. Omitting catch Clauses from a try Statement

```
try {

    // statements likely to cause exceptions
```

```
} finally {

    // finally statements go here...
}
```

Any exceptions caused by the code statements enclosed by the try statement will go unhandled, and the runtime will have to search further up the call stack, as discussed earlier in the chapter. This is a very uncommon use of the try statement, which usually includes at least one catch clause.

Nesting try Statements

You can define one try statement so that it is enclosed by another. In the event of an exception, the runtime will look first at the inner try statement and then work its way out, trying to find a match for a catch clause. Listing 14-8 contains an example.

Listing 14-8. Nesting try Statements

```
try {

    try {

        // statements likely to cause exceptions

    } catch (Exception) {

        // handler statements for the inner try statement
    }

    // more code statements

} catch (Exception) {

    // handler statements for the outer try statement
}
```

The effect of this example is to define a set of catch clauses for one group of code statements and a different set for others. In Listing 14-8, both try statements have catch clauses for the same exception type, but this need not be the case, and if an exception is unhandled by the inner catch clause, the runtime will examine the outer try statement and use any matching catch clauses it can find.

Using Exception Members

When you include an exception identifier in a catch clause, you can refer to the members of the exception using that identifier, just as you would any local variable. Table 14-2 describes the most useful properties of the System.Exception class. Some of these members are demonstrated here and others in the following sections.

Table 14-2. *Useful Members of the System. Exception Class*

Member	Description
Data	Returns an IDictionary that can be used to get and set name/value pairs.
InnerException	Returns the exception that caused this exception, or null if there is no exception
Message	Returns a message that describes the current exception
Source	Gets or sets the name of the object that caused the exception
StackTrace	Gets a string representation of the call stack
TargetSite	Gets the details of the method that caused the exception
GetBaseException()	Returns the root exception in a chain of exceptions
ToString()	Returns details of the type message and stack trace of the exception

When you are debugging an application, the most useful member is the ToString method, which returns a helpful string that contains pretty much all you need to know from the exception. Listing 14-9 contains an example of using this method.

Listing 14-9. Using the Exception. ToString Method

```
using System;

class Listing_09 {

    static void Main(string[] args) {

        try {
            // define a loval variable
            string myLocalVar = null;

            // try to so something with the local variable
            Console.WriteLine("First letter: {0}", myLocalVar[0]);

        } catch (Exception ex) {
            Console.WriteLine("---Start of ToString() output---");
            Console.WriteLine(ex);
            Console.WriteLine("---End of ToString() output---");
        }

        // wait for input before exiting
```

```
        Console.WriteLine("Press enter to finish");
        Console.ReadLine();
    }
}
```

In this exception, I cause an exception and then call the ToString method. I have printed out statements before and after the result of the ToString method. Compiling and running the code in Listing 14-9 produces the following results:

```
---Start of ToString() output---
System.NullReferenceException: Object reference not set to an instance of an object.
   at Listing_09.Main(String[] args) in C:\Listing_09\Listing_09.cs:line 12
---End of ToString() output---
Press enter to finish
```

This may not look like much, but it contains a wealth of information. First, it contains the type of the exception. In this example, it is NullReferenceException, and this is reported even though my catch clause is for System.Exception. Second, it contains a helpful descriptive message that tells me what may have caused the exception. Finally, it contains the stack trace. This isn't very long in such an example, but it does tell me that the problem occurred in line 12 of the Listing_09.cs file and within the Main method.

We can get the individual parts of this string using the individual members of the Exception class. Listing 14-10 provides a demonstration. This can be more useful than calling ToString if you want to selectively log information about an exception, rather than performing debugging.

Listing 14-10. Using the Members of the System.Exception Class

```
using System;

class Listing_10 {

    static void Main(string[] args) {

        try {
            // define a loval variable
            string myLocalVar = null;

            // try to so something with the local variable
            Console.WriteLine("First letter: {0}", myLocalVar[0]);

        } catch (Exception ex) {

            Console.WriteLine("Type: {0}", ex.GetType());
            Console.WriteLine("Message: {0}", ex.Message);
            Console.WriteLine("Stack: {0}", ex.StackTrace);
        }

        // wait for input before exiting
        Console.WriteLine("Press enter to finish");
```

```
            Console.ReadLine();
    }
}
```

Compiling and running the code in Listing 14-10 produces the following output:

```
Type: System.NullReferenceException
Message: Object reference not set to an instance of an object.
Stack:    at Listing_10.Main(String[] args) in C:\Listing_10\Listing_10.cs:line 12
Press enter to finish
```

Using finally Clauses

The way that control can jump around in a try statement can cause problems for some programs. This is especially true if you need to release resources or reset the state of your program whether an exception is thrown and handled. You can do this by adding a finally clause to your try statement, as shown in Listing 14-11.

Listing 14-11. Using a finally Clause in a try Statement

```
using System;

class Listing_11 {

    static void Main(string[] args) {

        // allocate the resources
        AllocateResources();

        try {

            // statements which uses the resources
            // and which may cause an exception
            Console.WriteLine("Perform work...");

            // define a loval variable
            string myLocalVar = null;

            if (true) {
                // try to so something with the local variable
                Console.WriteLine("First letter: {0}", myLocalVar[0]);
            }

        } catch (NullReferenceException ex) {

            // handle this kind of exception
            Console.WriteLine("Exception: {0}", ex.GetType());

        } finally {
```

```
            Console.WriteLine("Finally clause executed");

            // release the resources
            ReleaseResources();
        }

        // wait for input before exiting
        Console.WriteLine("Press enter to finish");
        Console.ReadLine();
    }

    static void AllocateResources() {
        Console.WriteLine("Allocated Resources");
    }

    static void ReleaseResources() {
        Console.WriteLine("Release Resources");
    }
}
```

In this example, there are two methods that represent allocating and releasing resources: AllocateResources and ReleaseResources. There are lots of scenarios where you need to make sure to release a resource whether or not an exception is thrown. One of the most common is opening and closing a connection to a database.

The AllocateResources method is called before the try statement, which would usually contain statements that use the allocated resources and that may throw an exception. In my example, I have defined, but not initialized, a local variable called myLocalVar. When the condition in the if statement is true, a statement is executed that causes a NullReferenceException to be thrown. Compiling and running the code in Listing 14-11 produces the following results:

```
Allocated Resources
Perform work...
Exception: System.NullReferenceException
Finally clause executed
Release Resources
Press enter to finish
```

You can see that when the exception is thrown the statements in the catch clause are executed, followed by those in the finally clause. In the example, this means calling the ReleaseResources method so that any allocated resources can be released promptly for use by others. We can change the condition of the if statement to false like this:

```
if (false) {
    // try to so something with the local variable
    Console.WriteLine("First letter: {0}", myLocalVar[0]);
}
```

The change prevents the statement that causes the exception from being executed. Compiling and running the modified code produces the following results:

```
Allocated Resources
Perform work...
Finally clause executed
Release Resources
Press enter to finish
```

The statements in the finally clause are executed, even though no exception has been thrown, ensuring that we can release resource (or perform any other actions) whatever happens.

A try statement can have only one finally clause, and it must be the last clause defined in the statement. You do not define an exception or identifier because the code statements will be executed even if there is no exception. You can use a finally clause on a try statement that doesn't have any catch clauses; this is shown in Listing 14-12.

Listing 14-12. A try Statement with a finally Clause but No catch Clauses

```
try {

    // statements which uses the resources
    // and which may cause an exception
    Console.WriteLine("Perform work...");

    // define a loval variable
    string myLocalVar = null;

    // try to so something with the local variable
    Console.WriteLine("First letter: {0}", myLocalVar[0]);

} finally {

    Console.WriteLine("Finally clause executed");

    // release the resources
    ReleaseResources();
}
```

This example won't handle an exceptions that are thrown, but the statements in the finally clause will be executed whether an exception is thrown by one of the code statements.

Throwing Exceptions

Handling exception is only half of the story. You also need to throw them in your code when errors occur. This is done using the throw keyword, as demonstrated by Listing 14-13.

Listing 14-13. Using the throw Keyword

```
using System;

class Listing_13 {
```

```
static void Main(string[] args) {

    // define a string array
    string[] array = { "orange", "apple", "pear" };

    try {
        // make a call to the GetStringLength method
        int result = GetStringLength(array, 2);
        Console.WriteLine("Result: {0}", result);

        // make a call that will cause an exception
        result = GetStringLength(array, 100);

    } catch (Exception ex) {
        Console.WriteLine(ex.ToString());
    }

    // wait for input before exiting
    Console.WriteLine("Press enter to finish");
    Console.ReadLine();
}

static int GetStringLength(string[] array, int index) {
    if (index < array.Length) {
        return array[index].Length;
    } else {
        throw new Exception();
    }
}
}
```

In this example, the static GetStringLength method throws an exception if the index parameter is greater or equal to the length of the array parameter. The throw statement is marked in bold and must always be followed by an instance of System.Exception or of a class that derives from System.Exception. You can create and throw a new exception in a single statement as shown in the example, or you can create and throw on separate statements; you can see an example of this in Listing 14-14.

Execution of your code statements stops when you throw an exception. The runtime will begin searching for a handler to process your exception.

The throw statement in the example throws a new instance of the base exception class. This is not especially helpful to anyone using this method because it contains no useful information about what went wrong. If we compile and run the code in Listing 14-13, we get the following results:

```
Result: 4
System.Exception: Exception of type 'System.Exception' was thrown.
   at Listing_13.GetStringLength(String[] array, Int32 index) in C:\Listing_13\Listing
_13.cs:line 31
   at Listing_13.Main(String[] args) in C:\Listing_13\Listing_13.cs:line 16
Press enter to finish
```

The convention in C# is that the type of the exception class that is used illustrates the nature of the exception that has been thrown and that as much information as possible is provided in the exception so that it can be handled as effectively as possible.

To make this process easier, the .NET class library contains a selection of exceptions that are derived from System.Exception that you can use for commonly occurring problems. Some of these exceptions are described in Table 14-3; all of these classes are in the System namespace. See Chapter 11 for details of namespaces and how to use them.

Table 14-3. Convenience Exceptions from the .NET Framework Class Library

Exception	Description
ArgumentNullException	Use when an argument passed to a method is null.
ArgumentOutOfRangeException	Use when an argument passed to a method is outside the supported range.
IndexOfOufRangeException	Use when an attempt is made to access an index that is out of the supported range.
NotImplementedException	Use when a method is not implemented—for example when an interface method has no relevance for a given implementation or when a derived class is expected to implement an overridden version of the method.
NotSupportedException	Use when a method is not supported. Usually used when a derived class is expected to implement the method.

There are a lot of exception classes in the .NET, but the five in the table are the ones that you'll throw (and catch) most often. For a program of any significant complexity, you'll also need to define custom exceptions, which are described later in the chapter. Exceptions classes can contain additional members that can provide more information about what caused the exception to occur. As an example, the ArgumentOutOfRangeException class has two useful properties, described in Table 14-4.

Table 14-4. The Additional Members of the ArgumentOutOfRangeException Class

Member	Description
ParamName	The name of the parameter that caused the exception
ActualValue	The value of the parameter that caused the exception

You can provide values that will be returned by these properties through the constructor for the ArgumentOutOfRangeException class. You don't have to provide values (there are override constructors that don't require them), but it is good practice and makes your exception much more informative. Listing 14-14 demonstrates providing values in this way.

Listing 14-14. Populating and Throwing an Exception

```csharp
using System;

class Listing_14 {

    static void Main(string[] args) {

        // define a string array
        string[] array = { "orange", "apple", "pear" };

        try {
            // make a call to the GetStringLength method
            int result = GetStringLength(array, 2);
            Console.WriteLine("Result: {0}", result);

            // make a call that will cause an exception
            result = GetStringLength(array, 100);

        } catch (ArgumentOutOfRangeException ex) {
            Console.WriteLine(ex.ToString());
        }

        // wait for input before exiting
        Console.WriteLine("Press enter to finish");
        Console.ReadLine();
    }

    static int GetStringLength(string[] array, int index) {
        if (index < array.Length) {
            return array[index].Length;
        } else {
            // create a new exception
            ArgumentOutOfRangeException ex = new ArgumentOutOfRangeException(
                "index",
                index,
                "Index is greather than array length");

            // throw the exception
            throw ex;
        }
    }
}
```

This listing throws an exception under the same circumstances as the previous example, but rather than throwing the generic System.Exception, it uses an exception type that is representative of the problem and uses a constructor that allows additional information to be provided. Compiling and running the code in Listing 14-14 produces the following, much more informative, results:

```
Result: 4
System.ArgumentOutOfRangeException: Index is greather than array length
Parameter name: index
Actual value was 100.
   at Listing_14.GetStringLength(String[] array, Int32 index) in C:\Listing_14\Listing
_14.cs:line 37
   at Listing_14.Main(String[] args) in C:\Listing_14\Listing_14.cs:line 16
Press enter to finish
```

Rethrowing Exceptions

You can use the throw keyword on its own in a catch clause to *rethrow* the exception that caused the catch clause to be invoked. This is useful if you want to log the exception, but otherwise rely on the runtime to find another clause to handle the exception. Listing 14-15 demonstrates this technique.

Listing 14-15. Rethrowing an Exception

```
using System;

class Listing_15 {

    static void Main(string[] args) {

        try {

            try {

                // throw an exception
                throw new NullReferenceException();

            } catch (NullReferenceException ex) {
                Console.WriteLine("Inner try statement - Exception logged: {0}",
                    ex.GetType());
                throw;
            }

        } catch (NullReferenceException ex) {
            // handle the exception
            Console.WriteLine("Outer try statement - Exception handled: {0}",
                ex.GetType());
        }

        // wait for input before exiting
        Console.WriteLine("Press enter to finish");
        Console.ReadLine();
    }
}
```

The key statement is shown in bold; it is simply the throw keyword on its own. You don't need to use the exception identifier, even if you have defined one in your catch clause. The example shows a pair of nested try statements, each with a catch clause for NullReferenceException. The code statement in the inner try statement throws an exception of this type, which is then passed to the inner catch clause for handling.

Usually, this would be the end of the story, but the inner catch clause uses the throw keyword, which marks the exception has being unhandled again and causes the runtime to begin searching for another handler. No statements will be executed once a throw statement is encountered, so they are generally the last statement in a catch clause. In the example, the outer try statement also has a catch clause for NullReferenceException, and so the exception that has been rethrown by the inner statement is handled by the outer statement. Compiling and running the code in Listing 14-15 produces the following output:

```
Inner try statement - Exception logged: System.NullReferenceException
Outer try statement - Exception handled: System.NullReferenceException
Press enter to finish
```

You can also rethrow an exception after adding additional data. Every exception class inherits the Data property from the System.Exception class, which returns an IDictionary in which you can place name/value pairs. Listing 14-16 contains an example. You can get more information about dictionaries in Chapter 19.

Listing 14-16. Adding Data to an Exception

```csharp
using System;
using System.Collections;

class Listing_16 {

    static void Main(string[] args) {

        try {

            try {

                // throw an exception
                throw new NullReferenceException();

            } catch (NullReferenceException ex) {
                // get the dictionary from the exception
                IDictionary d = ex.Data;
                // add some additional information to the exception
                d.Add("Additional Information", "This is some helpful state info");
                d.Add("More Information", "This is some extra helpful state info");

                // rethrow the exception
                throw;
            }

        } catch (NullReferenceException ex) {
            // handle the exception
            Console.WriteLine("Outer try statement - Exception handled: {0}", ex.GetType());
```

437

```
            // get the additional info
            IDictionary d = ex.Data;
            foreach (object o in d.Keys) {
                Console.WriteLine("Info: {0} = {1}", o, d[o]);
            }
        }
    }

    // wait for input before exiting
    Console.WriteLine("Press enter to finish");
    Console.ReadLine();
    }
}
```

The catch clause of the inner try statement in the example handles a NullReferenceException, adds some additional data, and rethrows the exception. The modified exception is then handled by the outer try statement, which also has a handler for NullReferenceException and which prints out the additional data.

There is no convention for the use of the name/value pairs, but you should try to provide information useful to someone trying to figure out why the exception was thrown. The IDictionary returned by the Data property can be modified by exception handlers, so you should not rely on the contents being secure or immutable. Compiling and running the code in Listing 14-16 produces the following results:

```
Outer try statement - Exception handled: System.NullReferenceException
Info: Additional Information = This is some helpful state info
Info: More Information = This is some extra helpful state info
Press enter to finish
```

Creating and Throwing Custom Exceptions

There are a lot of ready-made exception classes in the .NET class library, but sometimes you will need to create an exception class that is specific to your program. You can easily do this by deriving from System.Exception.

WHAT HAPPENED TO SYSTEM.APPLICATIONEXCEPTION AND SYSTEM.SYSTEMEXCEPTION?

Earlier versions of .NET included a convention that the exception classes included in the System namespace would derive from System.SystemException, while non-Microsoft programmers would derive their exceptions from System.ApplicationException. This convention has been dropped, and you should derive your exceptions directly from System.Exception or from another custom exception type.

You can still see the earlier convention in the way that some of the built-in exceptions use SystemException, but this is for compatibility only.

Listing 14-17 demonstrates a custom exception class.

Listing 14-17. Defining a Custom Exception Class

```
class CustomException : Exception {

    public CustomException()
        : base() {
    }

    public CustomException(string message)
        : base(message) {
    }

    public CustomException(string message, Exception inner)
        : base(message, inner) {
    }
}
```

This is the simplest custom exception possible. It doesn't define any additional program-specific members. The value in this exception comes from the convention to use different exception types to represent different exception conditions. It follows the convention for a custom exception, which is a name that ends with Exception and the set of constructors shown. You can define additional constructors as required, but you should always include the three that are shown in the listing.

Throwing a custom exception is just like throwing one of the system exceptions. You create a new instance and then use the throw keyword. catch clauses can be defined to handle your exception as normal; this is shown in Listing 14-18.

Listing 14-18. Throwing and Catching a Custom Exception

```
using System;

class CalculationException : Exception {
    private int param1, param2;

    public CalculationException()
        : base() {
    }

    public CalculationException(string message)
        : base(message) {
    }

    public CalculationException(string message, Exception inner)
        : base(message, inner) {
    }

    public CalculationException(string message, int p1, int p2)
        : base(message) {
            param1 = p1;
            param2 = p2;
```

```
        }

    public int Param1 {
        get { return param1; }
    }

    public int Param2 {
        get { return param2; }
    }
}

class Calculator {

    public static int PerformCalculation(int param1, int param2) {
        if (param1 > 0 && param2 > 0) {
            // perform the calculation and return the results
            return param1 * param2;
        } else {
            // one or more of the params are a problem
            throw new CalculationException("One of parameters is too small",
                param1, param2);
        }
    }
}

class Listing_18 {

    static void Main(string[] args) {

        try {

            // perform a calculation that we know will cause an exception
            Calculator.PerformCalculation(0, 100);

        } catch (CalculationException ex) {
            Console.WriteLine("Caught exception of type: {0}", ex.GetType());
            Console.WriteLine("Message: {0}", ex.Message);
            Console.WriteLine("Param1: {0}", ex.Param1);
            Console.WriteLine("Param2: {0}", ex.Param2);
        }

        // wait for input before exiting
        Console.WriteLine("Press enter to finish");
        Console.ReadLine();
    }
}
```

The custom exception class in the listing, named CalculationException, goes beyond the basics of a custom exception to include two additional properties. This exception will be used when there is a problem in the Calculator class and the two properties relate to the two numbers the calculation was requested for.

The Calculator class contains a single static method that calculates the product of two int values but that throws an exception if either parameter is less than or equal to zero. You can see that the CalculationException class includes an additional constructor that sets the values for the properties and that this is used when the PerformCalculation method creates a new instance of the exception class.

The Listing_18 class calls the PerformCalculation method using parameters that we know will cause an exception. The try statement has a catch clause that will handle the custom CalculationException and prints out the details of the property values. Compiling and running the code in Listing 14-18 produces the following results:

```
Caught exception of type: CalculationException
Message: One of parameters is too small
Param1: 0
Param2: 100
Press enter to finish
```

You can derive custom exceptions from other custom exceptions. The convention is to make the derived exception more specific than the base class. So, for example, our CalaculationException class may represent general problems with a calculation, but a derived class will represent some specific problem, such as division by zero.

Throwing Meaningful Exceptions

Exceptions should be meaningful, which means that you will often need to be selective about allowing exceptions caused by your code to be handled outside your code. Listing 14-19 demonstrates a simple exception dilemma.

Listing 14-19. Throwing a Meaningless Exception

```csharp
using System;

class Calculator {
    private int[,] resultsData;

    public Calculator() {
        // initialize and populate the results data
        resultsData = new int[10, 10];
        for (int i = 0; i < 10; i++) {
            for (int j = 0; j < 10; j++) {
                resultsData[i, j] = i * j;
            }
        }
    }

    public int PerformCalculation(int num1, int num2) {
        return resultsData[num1, num2];
    }
}
```

```
class Listing_19 {

    static void Main(string[] args) {

        // create a new instance of the Calculator class
        Calculator calc = new Calculator();

        try {

            // make a call to the Calculator.PerformCalculation method
            // which we know will cause an exception
            calc.PerformCalculation(100, 10);

        } catch (Exception ex) {
            Console.WriteLine("Handled exception of type: {0}", ex.GetType());
            Console.WriteLine(ex.ToString());
        }

        // wait for input before exiting
        Console.WriteLine("Press enter to finish");
        Console.ReadLine();
    }
}
```

Listing 14-19 contains a Calculator class that uses a rectangular multidimensional array to hold a set of results that are computed in the constructor. You can learn more about arrays of all kinds in Chapter 13. When the PerformCalculation method is called, the parameter values are used as indices into the results array to return a result.

This works fine unless the parameter values are not valid indices for the array, which is what the code in the Main method of the Listing_19 class relies on to cause an exception. Compiling and running the code in the listing produces the following results:

```
Handled exception of type: System.IndexOutOfRangeException
System.IndexOutOfRangeException: Index was outside the bounds of the array.
   at Calculator.PerformCalculation(Int32 num1, Int32 num2) in
      C:\Listing_19\Listing_19.cs:line 21
   at Listing_19.Main(String[] args) in C:\Listing_19\Listing_19.cs:line 36
Press enter to finish
```

The results show a problem. We have thrown an exception that makes no sense to anyone using the Calculator class. They asked for a calculation to be performed, and they got back details of a problem relating to an array. In essence, we have exposed the inner workings of our class and have done so in a way that doesn't help debug the problem.

Mapping One Exception Type to Another

We can make exceptions more useful by catching and handling one kind of exception and then throwing another, more meaningful kind in the catch clause. Listing 14-20 contains an example.

Listing 14-20. Mapping from One Exception Type to Another

```csharp
using System;

class Calculator {
    private int[,] resultsData;

    public Calculator() {
        // initialize and populate the results data
        resultsData = new int[10, 10];
        for (int i = 0; i < 10; i++) {
            for (int j = 0; j < 10; j++) {
                resultsData[i, j] = i * j;
            }
        }
    }

    public int PerformCalculation(int num1, int num2) {
        try {
            return resultsData[num1, num2];
        } catch (IndexOutOfRangeException) {
            // throw a more useful exception
            throw new CalculationParameterRangeException();
        }
    }
}

class CalculationParameterRangeException : Exception {
    public CalculationParameterRangeException() : base() { }
    public CalculationParameterRangeException(string message) : base(message) { }
    public CalculationParameterRangeException(string message, Exception inner)
        : base(message, inner) { }
}

class Listing_20 {

    static void Main(string[] args) {

        // create a new instance of the Calculator class
        Calculator calc = new Calculator();

        try {

            // make a call to the Calculator.PerformCalculation method
            // which we know will cause an exception
            calc.PerformCalculation(100, 10);

        } catch (Exception ex) {
            Console.WriteLine("Handled exception of type: {0}", ex.GetType());
            Console.WriteLine(ex.ToString());
        }
```

```
        // wait for input before exiting
        Console.WriteLine("Press enter to finish");
        Console.ReadLine();
    }
}
```

In this example, the PerformCalaculation exception catches IndexOutOfRange exceptions and throws a corresponding CalaculationParameterRangeException. We could add some fields to the custom exception to provide additional information, but just by having a basic custom exception, we have provided some useful information about what went wrong. The name of the custom exception, CalaculationParameterRangeException, makes it clear that the was a problem performing the calculation, and that problem was caused by one or more of the parameters being outside of an expected range. Compiling and running the code in Listing 14-20 produces the following results:

```
Handled exception of type: CalculationParameterRangeException
CalculationParameterRangeException: Exception of type 'CalculationParameterRange
Exception' was thrown.
    at Calculator.PerformCalculation(Int32 num1, Int32 num2) in
        C:\Listing_20\Listing_20.cs:line 21
    at Listing_20.Main(String[] args) in C:\ Listing_20\Listing_20.cs:line 43
Press enter to finish
```

Creating Exception Chains

There is a problem mapping one kind of exception to another, which is that details of what caused the original problem are lost. We can address this by using the original exception as a constructor argument when creating the replacement exception, as demonstrated by Listing 14-21.

Listing 14-21. Creating an Exception That Has an Inner Exception

```
public int PerformCalculation(int num1, int num2) {
    try {
        return resultsData[num1, num2];
    } catch (IndexOutOfRangeException ex) {
        // throw a more useful exception
        throw new CalculationParameterRangeException("Parameter out of range", ex);
    }
}
```

You can see that I have used the exception constructor that takes another exception as a parameter. This is how you can associate one exception as the cause of another. In effect, the IndexOutOfRange exception directly led to the CalculationParameterRangeException.

You can chain as many exceptions as you need together to capture the sequence of problems, and, of course, programmers who catch your exceptions can wrap them in their own. Listing 14-22 demonstrates how to create an exception chain and how the details of each exception can be read.

Listing 14-22. Creating an Exception Chain

```
using System;

class CustomException : Exception {
    public CustomException() : base() { }
    public CustomException(string message) : base(message) { }
    public CustomException(string message, Exception inner) : base(message, inner) { }
}

class Listing_22 {

    static void Main(string[] args) {

        try {
            // create a chain of exceptions
            ArgumentOutOfRangeException ex1
                = new ArgumentOutOfRangeException("This is the original exception");
            NullReferenceException ex2
                = new NullReferenceException("This is the 2nd exception", ex1);
            CustomException ex3
                = new CustomException("This is the 3rd exception", ex2);
            IndexOutOfRangeException ex4
                = new IndexOutOfRangeException("This is the outer exception", ex3);
            // throw the outermost exception
            throw ex4;

        } catch (IndexOutOfRangeException ex) {

            // print the details of the exception we have caught
            Console.WriteLine("---Outer Exception---");
            Console.WriteLine("Type: {0}", ex.GetType());
            Console.WriteLine("Message: {0}", ex.Message);

            // define a local variable for the inner exception
            Exception inner = ex;
            // work our way along the chain
            while ((inner = inner.InnerException) != null) {
                Console.WriteLine("---Inner Exception---");
                Console.WriteLine("Type: {0}", inner.GetType());
                Console.WriteLine("Message: {0}", inner.Message);
            }
            Console.WriteLine("---End of Inner Exception Chain");
        }

        // wait for input before exiting
        Console.WriteLine("Press enter to finish");
        Console.ReadLine();
    }
}
```

The code statements in the try statement create a series of four exceptions, each one being used as a constructor argument for the next. The final, or outermost, exception is then thrown. The try statement contains a catch clause for the outermost type, which then uses a while loop to work its way down the chain to the innermost exception, printing out the details of each exception in turn. This is done using the InnerException property, which returns an instance of Exception or a class derived from Exception (if there is an inner exception available) or null (if the exception was created without an inner exception). Compiling and running the code in Listing 14-22 produces the following output:

```
---Outer Exception---
Type: System.IndexOutOfRangeException
Message: This is the outer exception
---Inner Exception---
Type: CustomException
Message: This is the 3rd exception
---Inner Exception---
Type: System.NullReferenceException
Message: This is the 2nd exception
---Inner Exception---
Type: System.ArgumentOutOfRangeException
Message: Specified argument was out of the range of valid values.
Parameter name: This is the original exception
---End of Inner Exception Chain
Press enter to finish
```

You can see from the results that the chain of exceptions preserves both the original exception and the exceptions that have been wrapped around it to give contextual meaning. When dealing with a chain of exceptions, you can get the original, inner exception from any of the exceptions in the chain by calling the GetBaseException method.

Aggregating Exceptions

Exceptions typically represent a single problem. This works because most code statements are executed in sequence, and when a problem arises, you throw an exception that represents that problem. Sometimes, however, you want to show that more than one thing went wrong, and you can do this using the System.AggregateException class.

AggregateException is a wrapper around instances of other exceptions. Listing 14-23 contains an example of using this class. In the listing, I create a List<Exception> to contain the exceptions I am going to aggregate. The List<T> class is a collection, and you can get full details of this class and other collection types in Chapter 19. For this example, it is enough to know that calling the Add method allows me to add an exception to my collection. In the Calculator.PerformCalculation method, I perform a series of checks on the parameters. I add an exception to the collection if either of the int parameters are less than 1 or if the object parameter is null. When I have performed the parameter checks, I use the Count property of the List<Exception> to see whether I need to throw any exceptions. If there are any exceptions, I will throw an AggregateException. You might be tempted to throw an exception directly if there is only one, but this forces the handler of your exception to be able to cope with AggregateException and all of the individual types in their try statement.

I use the AggregateException constructor that allows me to provide an IEnumerable<Exception>, which is an interface implemented by the List<Exception> class, and then use the throw keyword to throw the aggregated exceptions.

Listing 14-23. Aggregating Exceptions

```
using System;
using System.Collections.Generic;

class Calculator {

    public static int PerformCalculation(int param1, int param2, object context) {

        // define a collection to store exceptions
        List<Exception> list = new List<Exception>();

        // check the parameters
        if (param1 < 1) {
            list.Add(new ArgumentOutOfRangeException("param1",
                param1, "Param1 is out of range"));
        }
        if (param2 < 1) {
            list.Add(new ArgumentOutOfRangeException("param2",
                param2, "Param2 is out of range"));
        }
        if (context == null) {
            list.Add(new NullReferenceException("Context parameter is null"));
        }

        // check to see if we have any exceptions
        if (list.Count > 0) {
            throw new AggregateException(list);
        } else {
            // perform the calculation and return the result
            return param1 * param2;
        }
    }
}

class Listing_23 {

    static void Main(string[] args) {

        try {

            // call the PerformCalculation method to cause all of
            // the indivual exceptions to be aggregated
            Calculator.PerformCalculation(-1, -1, null);

        } catch (AggregateException ex) {

            // get the aggregated exceptions
```

```
        foreach (Exception e in ex.InnerExceptions) {
            Console.WriteLine("--- Aggregated Exception ---");
            Console.WriteLine("Type: {0}", e.GetType());
            Console.WriteLine("Message: {0}", e.Message);
        }
    }

    // wait for input before exiting
    Console.WriteLine("Press enter to finish");
    Console.ReadLine();
}
}
```

In the Main method in the Listing_23 class, the try statement has a catch clause that handles
AggregateException. You can get the set of aggregated exceptions through the InnerExceptions property.
In the example, I use a foreach loop to enumerate the exceptions and print information about each one.
Compiling and running the code in Listing 14-23 produces the following results:

```
--- Aggregated Exception ---
Type: System.ArgumentOutOfRangeException
Message: Param1 is out of range
Parameter name: param1
Actual value was -1.
--- Aggregated Exception ---
Type: System.ArgumentOutOfRangeException
Message: Param2 is out of range
Parameter name: param2
Actual value was -1.
--- Aggregated Exception ---
Type: System.NullReferenceException
Message: Context parameter is null
Press enter to finish
```

Selectively Handling Aggregated Exceptions

You can selectively handle aggregated exceptions by using the Handle method of the AggregateException
class. This method takes a System.Predicate parameter, which in turn takes an Exception as the sole
parameter and returns true if the exception has been handled. The System.Predicate class is a special
form of delegate. You can learn more about delegates in Chapter 10. Listing 14-24 demonstrates how to
selectively handle exceptions in this way.

Listing 14-24. Selectively Handling Aggregated Exeptions

```
using System;
using System.Collections.Generic;

class Calculator {

    public static int PerformCalculation(int param1, int param2, object context) {
```

```
        // define a collection to store exceptions
        List<Exception> list = new List<Exception>();

        // check the parameters
        if (param1 < 1) {
            list.Add(new ArgumentOutOfRangeException("param1",
                param1, "Param1 is out of range"));
        }
        if (param2 < 1) {
            list.Add(new ArgumentOutOfRangeException("param2",
                param2, "Param2 is out of range"));
        }
        if (context == null) {
            list.Add(new NullReferenceException("Context parameter is null"));
        }

        // check to see if we have any exceptions
        if (list.Count > 0) {
            throw new AggregateException(list);
        } else {
            // perform the calculation and return the result
            return param1 * param2;
        }
    }
}

class Listing_24 {

    static void Main(string[] args) {

        try {

            try {

                // call the PerformCalculation method to cause all of
                // the indivual exceptions to be aggregated
                Calculator.PerformCalculation(-1, -1, null);

            } catch (AggregateException ex) {

                ex.Handle(agg => {
                    if (agg is ArgumentOutOfRangeException) {
                        Console.WriteLine("--- Selectively Handled Exception ---");
                        Console.WriteLine("Type: {0}", agg.GetType());
                        Console.WriteLine("Message: {0}", agg.Message);
                        return true;
                    } else {
                        return false;
                    }
                });
```

```
                    // rethrow the aggregate exception if there are
                    // any unhandled exceptions left
                    if (ex.InnerExceptions.Count > 0) {
                        throw ex;
                    }
                }
            } catch (AggregateException ex) {
                // enumerate the unhandled exceptions
                // get the aggregated exceptions
                foreach (Exception e in ex.InnerExceptions) {
                    Console.WriteLine("--- Unhandled Exception ---");
                    Console.WriteLine("Type: {0}", e.GetType());
                    Console.WriteLine("Message: {0}", e.Message);
                }
            }

            // wait for input before exiting
            Console.WriteLine("Press enter to finish");
            Console.ReadLine();
    }
}
```

In this example, I have used a lambda expression with the Handle method in the catch clause of the inner try statement. The Handle method invokes the Predicate for each aggregated exception. I return true for each exception that is an instance of ArgumentOutOfRangeException. Each time that I handle an exception, it is removed from the set of aggregated exceptions. I then check to see whether there are any remaining exceptions (which are the ones for which the Predicate has returned false) and rethrow the AggregateException if there are. The outer try statement has a catch clause that handles AggregateException and enumerates all the remaining exceptions. Compiling and running the code in Listing 14-24 produces the following results:

```
--- Selectively Handled Exception ---
Type: System.ArgumentOutOfRangeException
Message: Param1 is out of range
Parameter name: param1
Actual value was -1.
--- Selectively Handled Exception ---
Type: System.ArgumentOutOfRangeException
Message: Param2 is out of range
Parameter name: param2
Actual value was -1.
--- Unhandled Exception ---
Type: System.NullReferenceException
Message: Context parameter is null
Press enter to finish
```

This technique of using a predicate delegate to handle aggregated exceptions is widely used in the Task Parallel Library and in Parallel LINQ, both of which are explained in later chapters. You should be careful when using AggregateException because it makes more work for the programmer dealing with the problems that have arisen in your code. You should consider whether the potential confusion you will cause is justified by the ability to show that multiple things went wrong. My advice is to avoid using this type unless using a single exception would cause *more* confusion than using `AggregateException`.

Summary

In this chapter, we have explored the mechanism that C# uses to express and process error conditions. We have thrown, caught, and handled the built-in exceptions that the .NET Framework includes for common problems and derived custom types that can be used for application-specific issues.

We have also covered the need to throw meaningful exceptions that are useful to other programmers and the importance of including as much relevant information as possible when throwing an exception. We have seen the convention of differentiating between different problems by throwing instances of different classes derived from `System.Exception`. Finally, we looked at aggregating exceptions when it is essential to indicate multiple, simultaneous issues—something that we will revisit when we come to look at parallel programming techniques later in this book.

■ ■ ■

CHAPTER 15

Generic and Anonymous Types

In this chapter, we will look at the C# support for generic and anonymous types. Anonymous types are relatively simple, so most of this chapter is dedicated to the much more complex and involved topic of generic types.

Understanding generic types requires a good understanding of regular C# types, so if you have skipped over the chapters before this one, I suggest you go back and read more closely. Chapters 1, 3, and 9 have particular bearing on this chapter, which is summarized in Table 15-1.

Table 15-1. *Quick Problem/Solution Reference for Chapter 15*

Problem	Solution	Listings
Create a class, struct, or interface that works with a type that is selected at instantiation.	Create and instantiate a generic class, struct, or interface.	15-1 through 10, 15-21, 15-22
Cast a parameterized type.	Use the as operator.	15-11
Constrain the available choices for a parameterized type.	Apply one of the six kinds of C# type parameter constraint.	15-12 through 15-14
Define a type parameter for a specific method.	Use the method-specific deferred type feature.	15-15, 15-16
Derive from a generic class.	Elect to inherit the deferred types or implement the derived class for a specific type.	15-17 through 15-20
Cast a parameterized type.	Use covariant or contravariant types.	15-23 through 15-27
Obtain the default value for a parameterized type.	Use the default keyword.	15-28
Combine a set of read-only properties in a single object without defining a type.	Create an anonymous type.	15-29

Using Generic Types

The C# *generic type* feature, also known as the *strong type* feature, allows you to write code that can be reused to work with different types. Imagine that we want to write a stack that can hold int values (this would be a pretty strange thing to do, but it makes a nice example; you can see details of a real stack class in Chapter 19). Listing 15-1 shows a simple stack.

Listing 15-1. A Simple Stack Class

```
class IntStack{
    int[] dataArray = new int[10];
    int currentPos = 0;

    public void Push(int value) {
        dataArray[currentPos++] = value;
    }

    public int Pop() {
        return dataArray[--currentPos];
    }
}
```

A stack lets you store and retrieve objects values. When you store a value in a stack, you are said to have *pushed* the value. When you retrieve a value, you are said to have *popped* the value. When you pop an object from a stack, you get the most recently pushed object. Here is a simple demonstration of popping and pushing using the Push and Pop methods in the IntStack class from Listing 15-1:

```
// create a new IntStack
IntStack stack = new IntStack();

// push some values into the stack
stack.Push(2);
stack.Push(4);
stack.Push(8);

// pop values from the stack
for (int i = 0; i < 3; i++) {
    Console.WriteLine("Pop value: {0}", stack.Pop());
}
```

The output from these statements is as follows:

```
Pop value: 8
Pop value: 4
Pop value: 2
```

So, we have a stack that handles int values. And we can quickly copy and modify the IntStack class if we want to handle, say, string objects. But if we want to deal with a lot of different types, then we end up copying and modifying a lot of code, which goes against the idea of object-oriented programming.

So, then we realize that everything in C# is derived from object, so we rewrite our stack to work with the System.Object type, as shown in Listing 15-2.

Listing 15-2. A Stack That Uses System.Object

```
class ObjectStack {
    object[] dataArray = new object[10];
    int currentPos = 0;

    public void Push(object value) {
        dataArray[currentPos++] = value;
    }

    public object Pop() {
        return dataArray[--currentPos];
    }
}
```

We fixed the code duplication issue, but we created another problem. We wanted a stack that held values of a *specified type*, but we have ended up with a stack that can hold values of *any type*. Here's a demonstration:

```
ObjectStack stack = new ObjectStack();

stack.Push(2);
stack.Push("apple");
stack.Push(8);
```

These statements create an ObjectStack object and then proceed to push a mix of string and int values. When we pop the values, we can't assume that they are of any given type, so, if we try to cast to int, we will get an exception.

This is the problem that generic types fix. We can use the C# generic type feature to create classes that work with values of other types, and only those types, but we don't need to know what types they will be when we write our code. Listing 15-3 contains our simple stack, implemented using the generic type feature.

Listing 15-3. A Generic Stack

```
class GenericStack<T> {
    T[] dataArray = new T[10];
    int currentPos = 0;

    public void Push(T value) {
        dataArray[currentPos++] = value;
    }

    public T Pop() {
        return dataArray[--currentPos];
    }
}
```

Generic type notation can look a little odd when you first see it. A class that is defined using generic type notation is called a *generic class*. To dig into the details of generic classes, I am going to jump between explaining how to define and how to use a generic class.

Defining a Generic Class

The easiest way to explain a generic type is to look first at the class definition. The definition for the generic class in Listing 15-3 is illustrated in Figure 15-1.

Type Parameter
↓

```
class GenericStack<T> {
    // class body
}
```

Figure 15-1. *The anatomy of a generic class definition*

You already know how to define a regular class from Chapter 6. The difference in defining a generic class is the addition of a *type parameter*. The <T> added after the class name. T is also known as the *parameterized type*. The type parameter is a placeholder for the type our stack will store. We know we only want to work with one type; we just don't know which one yet. For this reason, T is sometimes referred to as the *deferred type*, because the decision about which type T really represents is deferred until the generic class is used to create an object.

The letter T allows us to refer to this type in our class. The convention is to use the letter T in generic classes when there is one generic type parameter and to start the type parameter with the letter T when there is more than one type parameter. (We'll see some examples of multiple parameters later in this chapter.)

Another convention is to refer to generic types using the name and the type parameter, so the class in Listing 15-3 is GenericStack<T>. This convention makes it clear when a class is generic. We'll return to the rest of our generic class after we have seen how to create objects from it.

■ **Note** Although I focus on classes in this section, the same features and rules apply to structs.

Creating Objects from Generic Classes

It is not until we create an object from our generic class that we have to specify which type of object the stack will hold. We do this by specifying a type in place of the T in the type parameter. The statement in Listing 15-4 provides a demonstration.

Listing 15-4. Creating an Object from a Generic Class

```
GenericStack<int> intStack = new GenericStack<int>();
```

The statement in Listing 15-4 creates an instance of GenericStack<T>, which stores int values and assigns the object to a local variable. The type of the object that has been created and the variable to which the object has been assigned is GenericStack<int>.

This is an important point—not all objects created from the GenericStack<T> class are of the same type. I can create an object to work with string values, like this:

```
GenericStack<string> stringStack = new GenericStack<string>();
```

I have created an object that is a different type from the one that I created in Listing 15-4. The intStack object is a GenericStack<int>, and the stringStack object is a GenericStack<string>. See the "Deriving from a Generic Base Class" section later in this chapter for more details of how to work with the types created from using the generics feature.

Implementing and Using Generic Class Members

Now that we've seen how the type parameter is transformed to a specific type, we can look at how to implement members in a generic class. Listing 15-5 contains the Push method from our GenericStack<T> class.

Listing 15-5. A Generic Class Member

```
public void Push(T value) {
    dataArray[currentPos++] = value;
}
```

We can refer to the generic type by using the name we gave to the type parameter, in this case T. The Push method takes an object of the generic type and adds it to the array called dataArray. As you can see in Listing 15-3, dataArray is defined using the type parameter name as well:

```
T[] dataArray = new T[10];
```

By using the type parameter in this way, we are saying that we don't know what the specific type will be, but that when an object is created from the generic class, we want an array that contains ten objects of that type should be created and a method called Push that will take an object of that type should exist. When we create an instance of GenericStack<int>, the method in Listing 15-5 will be transformed so that it takes an int parameter and the dataArray array will be created as an int[]. This transformation will occur at each place in the class where we have used the placeholder T.

We cannot call any members of the generic type T other than those defined by object. This is because we don't know what type it is when we write the generic class, and all the C# compiler can be sure of is that every type has to be derived from object. The most commonly used examples of generic classes in .NET are the collection classes, which are described in Chapter 16.

You can use the generic type in any class member. Listing 15-3 contains methods and fields that use the generic type. Listing 15-6 adds an indexer to our simple stack class.

Listing 15-6. Adding Members to a Generic Class

```
class GenericStack<T> {
    T[] dataArray = new T[10];
    int currentPos = 0;

    public void Push(T value) {
```

457

```
            dataArray[currentPos++] = value;
        }

        public T Pop() {
            return dataArray[--currentPos];
        }

        public T this[int index] {
            get {
                return dataArray[index];
            }
        }
    }
}
```

Not all the members in a generic class have to use the type parameter. As an example, the stack shown in Listing 15-7 adds a read-only property that uses regular types.

Listing 15-7. Adding a Regular Member to a Generic Class

```
class GenericStack<T> {
    T[] dataArray = new T[10];
    int currentPos = 0;

    public void Push(T value) {
        dataArray[currentPos++] = value;
    }

    public T Pop() {
        return dataArray[--currentPos];
    }

    public T this[int index] {
        get {
            return dataArray[index];
        }
    }

    public int CurrentPosition {
        get {
            return currentPos;
        }
    }
}
```

When we create an object from a generic class, the transformation to substitute the type parameter in the class definition to the type we have requested is performed throughout the class. So, if we create an instance of GenericStack<int> from the GenericStack<T> class shown in Listing 15-7, every T in the class is replaced with int. This means that to use, say, the Pop method, we have to provide an int parameter. Listing 15-8 contains a demonstration of using a GenericStack<int> object.

Listing 15-8. Using an Object Created from a Generic Class

```
using System;

class Listing_08 {

    static void Main(string[] args) {

        GenericStack<int> intStack = new GenericStack<int>();

        intStack.Push(2);
        intStack.Push(4);
        intStack.Push(8);

        for (int i = 0; i < 3; i++) {
            Console.WriteLine("Pop value: {0}", intStack.Pop());
        }

        // wait for input before exiting
        Console.WriteLine("Press enter to finish");
        Console.ReadLine();
    }
}
```

As you can see from the listing, once we have specified the type for the generic class, we use the members as normal. Compiling and running the code in Listing 15-8 produces the following output:

```
Pop value: 8
Pop value: 4
Pop value: 2
Press enter to finish
```

If you look back to the start of the chapter, you will see that this is the same output that we got from Listing 15-1. However, the benefit of generics is that we can use the same class defined in Listing 15-7 to work with string values (or any other object) without making any changes to the generic class. Here is an example of using GenericStack<T> with strings:

```
GenericStack<string> stringStack = new GenericStack<string>();
stringStack.Push("C#");
stringStack.Push("to");
stringStack.Push("Introduction");

for (int i = 0; i < 3; i++) {
    Console.WriteLine("Pop value: {0}", stringStack.Pop());
}
```

Compiling and running these statements produces the following output:

```
Pop value: Introduction
Pop value: to
Pop value: C#
```

You don't need to use the type parameter notation when you define a constructor for a generic class. Even though the class is GenericStack<T>, the constructor is named GenericStack, as shown in Listing 15-9.

Listing 15-9. Implementing a Constructor for a Generic Class

```
class GenericStack<T> {
    T[] dataArray;
    int currentPos;

    public GenericStack(int capacity) {
        dataArray = new T[capacity];
        currentPos = 0;
    }

    public void Push(T value) {
        dataArray[currentPos++] = value;
    }

    public T Pop() {
        return dataArray[--currentPos];
    }
}
```

The constructor in the generic class in Listing 15-9 is shown in bold. I have taken the opportunity to initialize the fields in the constructor, but that is not a requirement. I just wanted to demonstrate that you can refer to the parameterized type even in the constructor. We create objects from this class as we did previously. Here is an example:

```
GenericStack<int> structStack = new GenericStack<int>(10);
```

Defining Multiple Parameter Types

You are not limited to one parameterized type when you define a generic class. You can create as many as you need. Listing 15-10 contains an example of a generic class that has two deferred types.

Listing 15-10. A Class with Two Parameterized Types

```
using System;

class KeyStack<TKey, TVal> {
    TKey[] keysArray = new TKey[5];
    TVal[] valsArray = new TVal[5];
    int currentPos = 0;
```

```
    public void Push(TKey newKey, TVal newVal) {
        keysArray[currentPos] = newKey;
        valsArray[currentPos] = newVal;
        currentPos++;
    }

    public Tuple<TKey, TVal> Pop() {
        currentPos -= 1;
        return new Tuple<TKey, TVal>(keysArray[currentPos], valsArray[currentPos]);
    }
}
```

Listing 15-10 defines a class called KeyStack<TKey, TVal>, which enhances our previous example to perform stack operations on key/value pairs. The KeyStack class has two type parameters, TKey and TVal. Multiple parameters types are declared in a similar way to a single parameter type and are separated by commas (,).

When we create an object from this class, we have to decide what the types will be for the keys and values that we work with, and since we have two parameterized types, we can have keys and values of different types. Here is a statement that creates a KeyStack<string, int>:

```
KeyStack<string, int> stack = new KeyStack<string, int>();
```

We create an object following the same approach as for a generic type with a single deferred type and separate each type using a comma (,). Here are some example statements that create and use a KeyStack<TKey, TVal> object:

```
// create a new stack
KeyStack<string, int> stack = new KeyStack<string, int>();

// push in some data
stack.Push("One", 1);
stack.Push("Two", 2);
stack.Push("Three", 3);

// pop data from the stack
for (int i = 0; i < 3; i++) {
    Tuple<string, int> item = stack.Pop();
    Console.WriteLine("Key: {0}, Value: {1}", item.Item1, item.Item2);
}
```

In the Push method of the KeyStack<TKey, TVal> class, I accept the key and value as separate method parameters. In the Pop method, I have used the handy System.Tuple class, which lets you create a simple wrapper around two objects and so pass them back as the result of a method. I could also have used out parameters; see Chapter 9 for details.

Casting from Parameterized Types

You can't do a great deal with a parameterized type object. All that the C# compiler knows for sure is that the type must be derived from object, so you are allowed to call the members that System.Object defines. If you really need to convert from the parameterized type to a specific type, then you can use the as operator, as demonstrated by Listing 15-11.

Listing 15-11. Using the as Operator to Cast a Parameterized Type

```
using System;

class GenericStack<T> {
    T[] dataArray = new T[10];
    int currentPos = 0;

    public void Push(T value) {
        string str = value as string;
        if (str != null) {
            Console.WriteLine("Value is a string: {0}", value);
        }

        dataArray[currentPos++] = value;
    }

    public T Pop() {
        return dataArray[--currentPos];
    }
}
```

The class in Listing 15-11 modifies our basic GenericStack<T> class to use the as operator to convert the parameterized type to a string. You should not assume that the conversion will be successful, since the actual type could be very different from what you were expecting.

Constraining Parameterized Types

You can limit the range of types that a generic class is prepared to work with by using type parameter constraints. Listing 15-12 demonstrates the use of one such constraint.

Listing 15-12. Applying a Parameterized Type Constraint

```
using System;

class GenericStack<T> where T : IComparable<T> {
    T[] dataArray = new T[10];
    int currentPos = 0;

    public void Push(T value) {
        dataArray[currentPos++] = value;
    }

    public T Pop() {
        return dataArray[--currentPos];
    }

    public bool Contains(T value) {
        for (int i = 0; i < currentPos; i++) {
            if (value.CompareTo(dataArray[i]) == 0) {
```

```
            return true;
        }
    }
    return false;
    }
}
```

Figure 15-2 illustrates the constraint applied to the generic class in Listing 15-12.

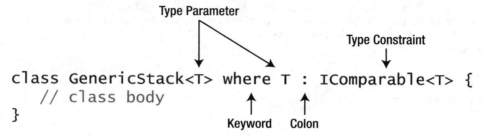

Figure 15-2. The anatomy of a generic type constraint

Type constraints follow the standard generic class declaration and consist of the where keyword followed by the type parameters, a colon (:), and the constraint that you want to apply. The constraint shown in Listing 15-12 will allow the GenericStack<T> class to be created only if the parameterized type implements the IComparable<T> interface.

The IComparable<T> interface lets you compare one object to another and is implemented by all the built-in types. This type constraint means that I can create stack objects from these types, like this:

```
GenericStack<string> stack = new GenericStack<string>();
```

But if I try to specify a type that doesn't implement the interface in the constraint, then the compiler will generate an error. There are six different types of constraint you can apply to parameterized types, and they are described in Table 15-2.

Table 15-2. The Six Kinds of Type Constraint

Constraint	Description
where T : *interface*	Allow types that implement the named interface.
where T : *base-class*	Allow types that are derived from the named class.
where T : class	Allow reference types.
where T : struct	Allow value types.
where T : new()	Allow types which implement a parameterless constructor.

Constraint	Description
where X : T	Allow types that are derived from another parameterized type in the same class; in this case, the type X must be derived from T.

When you constrain a parameterized type by naming a class or interface, you can access the members of that class or interface through the parameterized type values. For example, in Listing 15-12, I constrained the parameterized type to classes that implement the IComparable<T> interface. This interface contains a CompareTo method that compares two values and returns 0 if they are the same. I can use this method to compare two values of the parameterized type, which is why I added the Contains method, shown again here:

```
public bool Contains(T value) {
    for (int i = 0; i < currentPos; i++) {
        if (value.CompareTo(dataArray[i]) == 0) {
            return true;
        }
    }
    return false;
}
```

I call the CompareTo method on the value parameter in order to make comparisons with the data items that have been pushed into the stack. You can do the same thing when you specify a class rather than an interface.

The class and struct constraints speak for themselves. You can only create an object from the generic class if the deferred type you have provided is defined using the class or struct keyword. You can learn more about classes in Chapter 6 and structs in Chapter 12.

The new() constraint restricts the use of the generic class to deferred types that implement a parameterless constructor. This is usually applied when your generic class expects to create new instances of the deferred type.

The final constraint applies only to generic classes that define more than one parameterized types. The first type named in the constraint must be derived from the second named type. You can see an example of this in the next section.

Applying Multiple Constrains to a Parameterized Type

You can apply more than one constraint to a single parameterized type. When doing so, you simply separate the constraints using a comma. Not all the constraints can be combined. For example, you cannot specify that a type be a class and a struct; you have to pick one or the other. The class and struct constraints must be placed before named classes and interfaces. Listing 15-13 demonstrates applying two constraints to the GenericStack<T> class so that T must be a struct that implements the IComparable<T> interface.

Listing 15-13. Applying Multiple Constraints to a Parameterized Type

```
using System;

class GenericStack<T> where T : class, IComparable<T> {
```

```
    T[] dataArray = new T[10];
    int currentPos = 0;

    public void Push(T value) {
        dataArray[currentPos++] = value;
    }

    public T Pop() {
        return dataArray[--currentPos];
    }
}
```

Constraining Multiple Parameterized Types

You can apply different constraints to each parameterized type when a generic class defines more than one. Listing 15-14 contains an example.

Listing 15-14. Constraining More Than One Parameterized Type

```
using System;

class KeyStack<TKey, TVal> where TKey : class, IComparable<TKey> where TVal : struct {
    TKey[] keysArray = new TKey[5];
    TVal[] valsArray = new TVal[5];
    int currentPos = 0;

    public void Push(TKey newKey, TVal newVal) {
        keysArray[currentPos] = newKey;
        valsArray[currentPos] = newVal;
        currentPos++;
    }

    public Tuple<TKey, TVal> Pop() {
        currentPos -= 1;
        return new Tuple<TKey, TVal>(keysArray[currentPos], valsArray[currentPos]);
    }
}
```

In this example, TKey is constrained to being a class that implements IComparable<T> and TVal is constrained to being a struct. To define the second and subsequent constraints, you use the where keyword immediately after the previous constraint and declare the constraint you require.

Defining a Method-Specific Parameterized Type

So far, all the examples in this chapter have defined parameterized types for the entire class. C# also lets you define parameterized types for individual members; Listing 15-15 is a class that defines a parameterized type for a single method.

Listing 15-15. A Generic Method in a Regular Class

```
using System;

class Calculator {

    public int CalculateSum(int x, int y) {
        return x + y;
    }

    public T GreatestValue<T>(T left, T right) where T : IComparable<T> {
        if (left.CompareTo(right) <= 0) {
            return right;
        } else {
            return left;
        }
    }
}
```

The class in Listing 15-15 contains a method called GreatestValue<T>. As you can see, this method has a type parameter, T, which is constrained to types that implement the IComparable<T> interface. There are no other parameterized types in this class. You can create an instance of the class as you would normally and use the regular methods as, well, regular methods, like this:

```
// create a new instance of Calculator
Calculator calc = new Calculator();

// use the non-generic method
int result = calc.CalculateSum(10, 20);
Console.WriteLine("Result: {0}", result);
```

When we want to call the method with the type parameter, we have to decide what type we want to use. We can call the method repeatedly and use a different type each time, like this:

```
// call the generic method with int values
int biggestInt = calc.GreatestValue<int>(20, 30);
Console.WriteLine("Biggest: {0}", biggestInt);

// call the generic method with string values
string biggestString = calc.GreatestValue<string>("Hello", "World");
Console.WriteLine("Biggest: {0}", biggestString);
```

You can omit the type parameter, and the C# compiler will try to infer the type from the parameters you have provided, like this:

```
result = calc.GreatestValue(c, d);
```

A parameterized type can be used only in the method that defines it. This feature is usually used in conjunction with class-wide parameterized types and a generic type constraint. Listing 15-16 contains an example.

Listing 15-16. Combining Class-wide and Method-wide Parameterized Types

```
using System;

class GenericStack<T> {
    T[] dataArray = new T[10];
    int currentPos = 0;

    public void Push(T value) {
        dataArray[currentPos++] = value;
    }

    public T Pop() {
        return dataArray[--currentPos];
    }

    public GenericStack<U> FilterStack<U>() where U : T {
        GenericStack<U> resultStack = new GenericStack<U>();

        for (int i = 0; i < currentPos; i++) {
            if (dataArray[i] is U) {
                resultStack.Push((U)dataArray[i]);
            }
        }
        return resultStack;
    }

    public int Count {
        get {
            return currentPos;
        }
    }
}
```

In this example, the FilterStack<U> method filters the contents of the stack and returns a stack that contains only U objects, where U is constrained to be derived from T, which is the parameterized type defined for the class as a whole.

Deriving from a Generic Base Class

When you create a class that is derived from a generic class, you have a choice about how to handle the parameterized types. In this section, I'll show you the two approaches and explain when you are likely to want to use each of them.

Inheriting Type Deferral

The first option is to make you derived class a generic class as well, inheriting the parameterized types from the base class. Listing 15-17 provides a demonstration.

Listing 15-17. Inheriting Parameterized Types

```
using System;

class GenericStack<T> {
    T[] dataArray = new T[10];
    int currentPos = 0;

    public void Push(T value) {
        dataArray[currentPos++] = value;
    }

    public virtual T Pop() {
        return dataArray[--currentPos];
    }
}

class EventStack<T> : GenericStack<T> {
    public event EventHandler<EventArgs> PoppedEvent;

    public override T Pop() {
        // invoke the event
        PoppedEvent(this, EventArgs.Empty);
        // call the base implementation of the method
        return base.Pop();
    }
}
```

In this example, the EventStack<T> class is derived from GenericStack<T> and preserves the deferred type. The Pop method in the base class has been modified with the virtual keyword, and the EventStack<T> class has overridden this method so that an event is invoked each time the method is called.

You can upcast an instance of the derived class to an instance of the base class as long as the parameterized types are the same. Here is an example:

```
// create an instance from the derived type
EventStack<int> eStack = new EventStack<int>();

// upcast to the base generic class
GenericStack<int> gSTack = eStack;
```

Applying Further Constraints on an Inherited Type Parameter

You can use a derived class to place constraints on the parameterized types defined in the base class, as demonstrated by Listing 15-18 where the parameterized type T defined by the base class is constrained so that only struct types can be used.

Listing 15-18. Constraining Parameterized Types in a Derived Class

```
class EventStack<T> : GenericStack<T> where T : struct {
    public event EventHandler<EventArgs> PoppedEvent;

    public override T Pop() {
        // invoke the event
        PoppedEvent(this, EventArgs.Empty);
        // call the base implementation of the method
        return base.Pop();
    }
}
```

You can also define new parameterized types in addition to those defined in the base class. Listing 15-19 provides a demonstration.

Listing 15-19. Defining New Parameterized Types in a Derived Generic Class

```
using System;

class GenericStack<T> {
    protected T[] dataArray = new T[10];
    protected int currentPos = 0;

    public void Push(T value) {
        dataArray[currentPos++] = value;
    }

    public T Pop() {
        return dataArray[--currentPos];
    }
}

class EventStack<T> : GenericStack<T> {

    public GenericStack<U> FilterStack<U>() where U : T {
        // create a stack using the more derived type
        GenericStack<U> resultStack = new GenericStack<U>();

        // run through the contents of this stack and
        // add those items which are of the derived type
        for (int i = 0; i < currentPos; i++) {
            if (dataArray[i] is U) {
                resultStack.Push((U)dataArray[i]);
            }
        }

        // return the result stack
        return resultStack;
    }
```

```
}
```

I have added a method-specific parameterized type in this example, but you can define class-wide types, like this:

```
class EventStack<T, U> : GenericStack<T> {
    // class body
}
```

Specifying Parameterized Types

The alternative when deriving from a generic type is to specify types for each of the type parameters, thereby creating a non-generic-derived class from a generic base class. Listing 15-20 contains an example.

Listing 15-20. Specifying Parameterized Types in a Derived Class

```
using System;

class GenericStack<T> {
    protected T[] dataArray = new T[10];
    protected int currentPos = 0;

    public void Push(T value) {
        dataArray[currentPos++] = value;
    }

    public T Pop() {
        return dataArray[--currentPos];
    }
}

class IntStack : GenericStack<int> {

    public bool Contains(int value) {
        for (int i = 0; i < currentPos; i++) {
            if (value == dataArray[i]) {
                return true;
            }
        }
        return false;
    }
}
```

In Listing 15-20, the IntStack class is derived from GenericStack<int>. Specifying the base class with a type rather than a type parameter creates a derived class that is tied to a single type. Here is a statement that shows how to create an instance of the derived class:

```
IntStack intStack = new IntStack();
```

The IntStack class is no longer a generic class. It can be created and used as a normal class. You can upcast an object created from a type like this, as follows:

```
// create an instance from the derived type
IntStack intStack = new IntStack();

// upcast to the base type
GenericStack<int> gStack = intStack;
```

You can even treat the type parameter variables in the base class as the specified type. In Listing 15-20 I have added the Contains method that treats the dataArray field as an int[ ] rather than a T[ ].

Creating Generic Interfaces

Interfaces can also be generic. The same approach is taken for using a generic interface as for a generic class. Listing 15-21 contains a simple generic interface.

Listing 15-21. A Generic Interface

```
interface IStack<T> {

    void Push(T value);

    T Pop();
}
```

You have the same choice when implementing a generic interface as you do when deriving from a generic class. You can defer the generic type selection or implement using a specific type. As an example, here is a generic class that implements the IStack<T> interface from Listing 15-21:

```
class GenericStack<T> : IStack<T> {
    T[] dataArray = new T[10];
    int currentPos = 0;

    public void Push(T value) {
        dataArray[currentPos++] = value;
    }

    public T Pop() {
        return dataArray[--currentPos];
    }
}
```

As an alternative, the following class implements the interface specifically for int values:

```
class IntStack : IStack<int> {
    int[] dataArray = new int[10];
    int currentPos = 0;

    public void Push(int value) {
```

```
        dataArray[currentPos++] = value;
    }

    public int Pop() {
        return dataArray[--currentPos];
    }
}
```

Creating Generic Structs

There isn't much to say about generic structs. All of the same features and rules apply as for generic classes, but the structs maintain value-type behaviors. Listing 15-22 contains a generic struct implementation of the stack example.

Listing 15-22. A Generic Struct

```
struct GenericStack<T> where T: struct {
    T[] dataArray;
    int currentPos;

    public GenericStack(int capacity) {
        dataArray = new T[capacity];
        currentPos = 0;
    }

    public void Push(T value) {
        dataArray[currentPos++] = value;
    }

    public T Pop() {
        return dataArray[--currentPos];
    }
}
```

Type Variance

In the section on deriving from a generic base class, I showed you how to upcast to the base generic type. If the base type is called BaseType<T> and is derived to create DerivedType<T>, you can upcast like this:

```
DerivedType<int> myDerivedObject = new DerivedType<int>();
BaseClass<int> myUpcastObject = myDerivedObject;
```

What you can't do is cast the parameterized type; you'll get a compiler error if you try this:

```
DerivedType<object> myBaseObject = myDerivedObject;
```

This is an error in C# even though the parameterized type of the original object (int) is derived from the parameterized type of the target object (object). There is a good reason for C# preventing this kind of conversion. Listing 15-23 defines three simple classes and a generic stack class.

Listing 15-23. Three Classes and a Stack

```
class Car {
    // no members defined in this class
}

class VolvoC30 : Car {
    // no members defined in this class
}

class FordFiesta : Car {
    // no members defined in this class
}

class GenericStack<T> {
    T[] dataArray = new T[10];
    int currentPos = 0;

    public void Push(T value) {
        dataArray[currentPos++] = value;
    }

    public T Pop() {
        return dataArray[--currentPos];
    }
}
```

The Car class is derived to create the VolvoC30 and FordFiesta classes. None of the three classes defines any members. We only need these classes to demonstrate type conversion.

If we *could* upcast based on the parameter type, then we could legally define and compile the following statements:

```
// create a GenericStack<T> using the derived type
GenericStack<VolvoC30> volvoStack = new GenericStack<VolvoC30>();

// upcast the paramterized type
GenericStack<Car> carStack = volvoStack;    // this won't compile

// push in a data item via the upcast instance
carStack.Push(new FordFiesta());
```

The statement that causes the problem is marked in bold. If we were able to cast from a GenericStack<VolvoC30> to a GenericStack<Car>, then we could use the Push method on the converted object to store a FordFiest object in the stack, as shown earlier.

When we come to use the Pop method to retrieve an object from the GenericStack<VolvoC30>, we would expect to get one type but receive something else entirely:

```
// CAUTION - this would cause an exception because
// although we are expecting a VolvoC30 object, we
// are actually going to get a FordFiesta instead
VolvoC30 dataItem = volvoStack.Pop();
```

You can see that C# is protecting us from a type-safety issue when we call VolvoC30 specific members on a FordFiesta object. But this becomes an inflexible barrier when we want to create classes that operate generic objects with a certain parameterized type value. Listing 15-24 contains such a class.

Listing 15-24. A Class That Operates on Generic Objects with a Specific Parameterized Type

```
class CarPrinter {

    public static void PrintFirstCarDetails(GenericStack<Car> carStack) {
        Car myCar = carStack.Pop();
        Console.WriteLine("Car value popped: {0}", myCar);
    }
}
```

The CarPrinter class has a single static method that calls the Pop method on a GenericStack<Car> and prints out some information on the popped Car object. But we have a problem. We can't convert from a GenericStack<VolvoC30> to a GenericStack<Car>, even though the CarPrinter class doesn't prevent any risks to us. Here is an example of the problem:

```
// create a GenericStack<T> using the derived type
GenericStack<VolvoC30> volvoStack = new GenericStack<VolvoC30>();

// push a data item into the stack
volvoStack.Push(new VolvoC30());

// print the details of the first item in the stack
CarPrinter.PrintFirstCarDetails(volvoStack);    // this statement won't compile
```

The last statement won't compile. We have three choices at this point. We can redefine the PrintFirstCarDetails method in the CarPrinter class so that there is an implementation that works with each and every class that we derive from Car, but this requires us to modify the CarPrinter class each time we derive a new class, thereby defeating one of the main benefits of object programming.

A better solution would be to make CarPrinter a generic class and use a parameterized type constraint, like this:

```
class CarPrinter {

    public static void PrintFirstCarDetails<T>(GenericStack<T> carStack) where T : Car {
        Car myCar = carStack.Pop();
        Console.WriteLine("Car value popped: {0}", myCar);
    }
}
```

There is a third solution; it is known as *type variance*.

■ **Note** Type variance is an advanced topic that confuses even the most experienced programmers. You can skip this section and refer to it later if you ever need to perform the kind of cast I showed earlier.

Type variance is performed through generic interfaces that use the in or out keyword. It is a slightly convoluted technique, but it does give a lot of flexibility when implemented correctly. Type variance is broken down into contravariance and covariance.

Covariance

Covariance allows us to upcast the parameterized type, allowing us to solve the CarPrinter dilemma from the previous section. We do this by defining a covariant generic interface by using the out keyword. Listing 15-25 contains an example of a covariant generic interface.

Listing 15-25. A Covariant Generic Interface

```
interface IPop<out T> {

    T Pop();
}
```

As you can see from Listing 15-25, the out keyword is placed before the parameterized type. When you use the out keyword like this, it creates a restriction on how you use the parameterized type in the interface. It can be used only for outputs, meaning that it can only be used as the return type for methods, properties, and so on. In Listing 15-25, the parameterized type T is used only as the result of the Pop method. You cannot use T in any other way. See the next section for details of contravariance, which allows the opposite behavior.

Once you have defined your covariant interface, you implement it in the generic class. Here is the GenericStack<T> class, updated to implement the IPop<T> interface:

```
class GenericStack<T> : IPop<T> {
    T[] dataArray = new T[10];
    int currentPos = 0;

    public void Push(T value) {
        dataArray[currentPos++] = value;
    }

    public T Pop() {
        return dataArray[--currentPos];
    }
}
```

The only change to the GenericStack<T> class is the implementation of the interface, which maps to the preexisting Pop method. To solve the PrintCar problem, we have to update the PrintFirstCarDetails method to work on the IPop<T> interface, rather than the generic class, like this:

```
class CarPrinter {

    public static void PrintFirstCarDetails(IPop<Car> carStack) {
        Car myCar = carStack.Pop();
        Console.WriteLine("Car value popped: {0}", myCar);
    }
}
```

To use covariant, we have to cast the GenericStack<VolvoC30> to IPop<Car> and pass it to the CarPrinter.PrintFirstCarDetails method, like this:

```
// create a GenericStack<T> using the derived type
GenericStack<VolvoC30> volvoStack = new GenericStack<VolvoC30>();

// push a data item into the stack
volvoStack.Push(new VolvoC30());

// cast the stack to the contravariant interface
IPop<Car> carPop = volvoStack;

// print the details of the first item in the stack
CarPrinter.PrintFirstCarDetails(carPop);
```

I have made each step explicit in the previous statements, but if you pass the instance of the generic class to the PrintFirstCarDetails method, the conversion to the covariant interface is handled implicitly, like this:

```
CarPrinter.PrintFirstCarDetails(volvoStack);
```

Covariance is type-safe because you can only get base type objects out of the interface, which is why the out keyword is used. Every instance of the derived type is also an instance of the base type as well, so there are no possible issues in performing the conversion.

Contravariance

Contravariance is the counterpart to covariance and allows us to use derived types in place of base types for parameters in interfaces. Listing 15-26 contains a contravariant interface.

Listing 15-26. A Contravariant Interface

```
interface IPush<in T> {

    void Push(T value);
}
```

Contravariance is enabled using the in keyword, placed immediately before the parameterized type in the interface declaration. When you use the in keyword, it restricts the use of the parameterized type to method parameters. You cannot return T from methods as a result. You need a covariant interface for this, as described in the previous section. Here is the GenericStack<T> class, updated to implement the contravariant interface:

```
class GenericStack<T> : IPush<T> {
    T[] dataArray = new T[10];
    int currentPos = 0;

    public void Push(T value) {
        dataArray[currentPos++] = value;
    }
```

```
    public T Pop() {
        return dataArray[--currentPos];
    }
}
```

This is the same pattern as for covariance. We can now cast the GenericStack<Car> to an IPush<VolvoC30>, like this:

```
// create a GenericStack<T> using the base type
GenericStack<Car> carStack = new GenericStack<Car>();

// convert to the contravariant interface
IPush<VolvoC30> volvoPush = carStack;

// push in a value via the contravariant inteface
volvoPush.Push(new VolvoC30());
```

This is type safe because we can only use the contravariant type to input derived objects via the interface, and the derived objects are also instances of the base type.

Combining Contravariance and Covariance

A single generic class can implement covariant and contravariant interfaces for the same type, as shown in Listing 15-27. An instance of this class can be cast to either variant interface.

Listing 15-27. A Generic Type That Implements Covariant and Contravariant Interfaces

```
class GenericStack<T> : IPush<T>, IPop<T> {
    T[] dataArray = new T[10];
    int currentPos = 0;

    public void Push(T value) {
        dataArray[currentPos++] = value;
    }

    public T Pop() {
        return dataArray[--currentPos];
    }
}
```

Using the default Keyword

The last aspect of generic types we will look at is the use of the default keyword. As we know, C# requires you to assign a value to a variable before it is used, but how do you do this when you don't know whether the parameterized type will be an object, a built-in reference type, or some other kind of struct? The answer is to the use the default keyword. Listing 15-28 contains an example.

Listing 15-28. Using the default Keyword in a Generic Class

```
using System;

class GenericStack<T> {
    T[] dataArray = new T[10];
    int currentPos = 0;

    public void Push(T value) {
        dataArray[currentPos++] = value;
    }

    public T Pop() {
        return dataArray[--currentPos];
    }

    public U PopAndConvert<U>() where U : T {

        U result = default(U);

        // pop the value
        T popped = Pop();
        if (popped is U) {
            result = (U)popped;
        }

        // return the result
        return result;
    }
}
```

In this example, the GenericStack<T> class has been enhanced with the PopAndConvertMethod, which will pop an item from the stack and return it if it matches the deferred type specified when the method is called. This method will return the default value if the popped item isn't a base class for the deferred type.

The default keyword will return null for objects, 0 for built-in numeric types, and an instance of a struct with all the members initialized to the default values for their types.

Using Anonymous Types

Anonymous types are a C# feature that lets you combine a set of read-only properties in a single object without having to define a class or struct beforehand. Listing 15-29 contains a demonstration of an anonymous type.

Listing 15-29. An Anonymous Type

```
using System;

class Listing_29 {
```

```
static void Main(string[] args) {

    // create a new anonymous type
    var myObject = new {
        Name = "Adam Freeman",
        Age = 38,
        City = "London"
    };

    // access the properties of the anonymous type
    Console.WriteLine("Name: {0}", myObject.Name);
    Console.WriteLine("Age: {0}", myObject.Age);
    Console.WriteLine("City: {0}", myObject.City);

    // wait for input before exiting
    Console.WriteLine("Press enter to finish");
    Console.ReadLine();
    }
}
```

The anonymous type in Listing 15-29 is shown in bold and is illustrated by Figure 15-3.

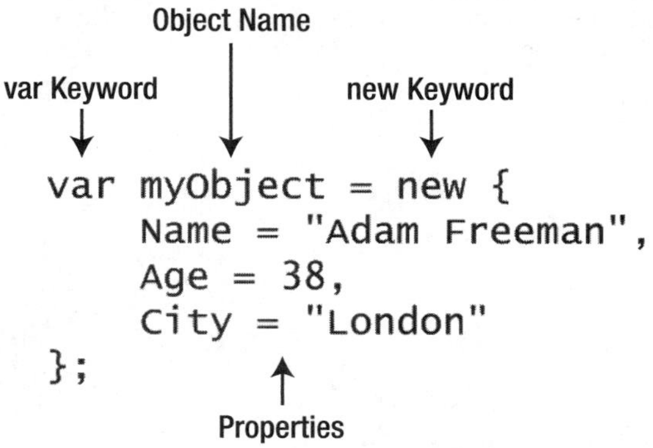

Figure 15-3. *The anatomy of an anonymous type*

Anonymous types have to be assigned using the var keyword. We'll see more of this keyword when we come to the LINQ chapters in Part IV of this book. The object name can be anything you like. The anonymous type itself is defined using the new keyword, followed by the open brace ({). The read-only properties are defined and assigned, and if there is more than one, they are separated by commas (,). The close brace character (}) finishes the type definition, and a semicolon completes the statement.

The anonymous type in Listing 15-29 is assigned to a variable called myObject and has properties called Name, Age, and City. The values assigned to these properties cannot be changed, but they can be read like regular properties, as shown by the set of Console.WriteLine statements.

Compiling and running the code in Listing 15-29 produces the following output:

```
Name: Adam Freeman
Age: 38
City: London
Press enter to finish
```

An anonymous type cannot be passed to other methods, which restricts their utility significantly. You can only use an anonymous type in the scope of the method in which it is defined. They are most frequently used with LINQ, which is in Part IV of this book.

Summary

In this chapter, we examined generic and anonymous types. Generic types let us constrain the types that a class will work with but do so in a flexible way. Generics can take a while to get used to, but they can be invaluable, especially when it comes to collection classes, which are discussed in Part III of this book. We also looked at the advanced topic of generic covariance and contravariance. Don't worry if these topics make no sense. This is a feature that causes even the best programmers to scratch their heads. If that section made little sense, then my advice is to ignore it for the moment, returning to only when the need arises. Most programs do not require covariant or contravariant generic classes to function.

At the end of this chapter, we took a brief look at anonymous types. Our examination was brief because they have such limited functionality. But don't dismiss them. We will see them again in the LINQ chapter, where their power and flexibility will become apparent.

CHAPTER 16

■ ■ ■

Strings and Characters

This chapter describes the C# support for characters and strings. We start with the char type, which represents a single character, before moving on to strings, which represent a sequence of characters. We will see how literals can be used to define char and string values, how to perform operations on both types, and the members that are available in the char struct and the string class to make working with these types simpler.

We will finish this chapter by looking at the composite formatting feature, which allows you to embed format items into strings that are later replaced with string representations of objects and values. This is a powerful feature that you will use in almost every program you write using C#. Table 16-1 provides the summary for this chapter.

Table 16-1. Quick Problem/Solution Reference for Chapter 16

Problem	Solution	Listings
Define a char value.	Use a char literal.	16-1, 16-2
Compare char or string values.	Use the comparison operator.	16-3, 16-7, 16-8
Determine the nature of a char.	Use the members of the System.Char struct.	16-4
Define a string value.	Use a string literal.	16-5, 16-6
Combine string values.	Use the addition operator.	16-9
Read or enumerate characters from a string.	Use the string indexer.	16-10, 16-11
Selective perform statements based on string values.	Use a switch statement.	16-12
Use regular expressions.	Use the System.Text.RegularExpressions.Regex class.	16-13
Manipulate the contents of a string.	Use the members of the System.String class.	16-14, 16-16
Search the contents of a string.	Use the members of the System.String class.	16-15

Problem	Solution	Listings
Create mutable strings.	Use the System.Text.StringBuilder class.	16-17 through 16-19
Format strings.	Use composite formatting.	16-20 through 16-25
Define string representations of custom types.	Override the ToString method.	16-26, 16-27
Define custom formatting.	Use the IFormatProvider interface.	16-28, 16-29

Working with Characters

The built-in **char** type represents a single Unicode character. Unicode is a widely used standard for encoding text. It supports nearly 200,000 different characters in 91 different scripts. C# stores each character using two bytes. The char keyword is an alias to the System.Char struct.

Expressing Characters Using Literals

To make using char easier, C# supports character literals, an example of which is shown in Listing 16-1.

Listing 16-1. A Character Literal

```
char myChar = 'a';
```

The statement in Listing 16-1 uses a character literal to assign the lowercase a character to a char variable called myChar. Character literals are expressed between single quotes, as illustrated by Figure 16-1.

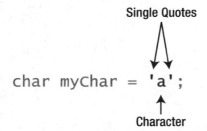

Figure 16-1. *The anatomy of a simple character literal*

Some special characters cannot be expressed directly, and so character literals can be expressed using an escape sequence or a Unicode encoding. For example, the single quote character cannot be expressed directly since it is used to define other character literals. Listing 16-2 demonstrates how to express this character using an escape sequence and a Unicode encoding.

Listing 16-2. Expressing a Character Through an Escape Sequence

```
char myEscapedQuote = '\'';
char myUnicodeQuote = '\u0027';
char myHexQuote = '\x0027';
```

Character literal escape sequences start with a backslash character (\) and can be a *simple escape* sequence or a Unicode encoding, expressed either in decimal (prefixed with a u) or in hexadecimal (prefixed with an x). Table 16-2 shows some of the most frequently used character literal escape sequences.

Table 16-2. Selected Character Literal Escape Sequences

Description	Simple Escape Sequence	Numeric Value
Single quote	\'	0x0027
Double quote	\"	0x0022
Backslash	\\	0x005C
New line	\n	0x000A
Carriage return	\r	0x000D
Tab	\t	0x0009

Performing Operations on Characters

You can perform operations on chars as you would with other built-in types, and for the most part, you will get expected results. For example, the assignment operator used in Listing 16-1 assigns the character represented by the literal value a to a char variable. You can compare two characters using the comparison operator, as illustrated by Listing 16-3.

Listing 16-3. Using the Comparison Operator on char Values

```
using System;

class Listing_03 {

    static void Main(string[] args) {

        char myChar = 'a';

        if (myChar == 'b') {
```

```
            Console.WriteLine("Characters are the same");
        } else {
            Console.WriteLine("Characters are different");
        }

        switch (myChar) {
            case 'a':
                Console.WriteLine("Char is a");
                break;
            case 'b':
            case 'c':
                Console.WriteLine("Char is b or c");
                break;
            default:
                Console.WriteLine("Char is not a, b or c");
                break;
        }

        // wait for input before exiting
        Console.WriteLine("Press enter to finish");
        Console.ReadLine();
    }
}
```

You can see in Listing 16-3 that you can mix character literal values and char variables freely in comparison operations. This listing also demonstrates that, because character literals are constant values, you can use them in switch statements. Compiling and running the code in Listing 16-3 produces the following results:

```
Characters are different
Char is a
Press enter to finish
```

The only thing to be aware of is when using the addition operator, with statements like these:

```
char myChar = 'a';
myChar += 'b';
```

Adding characters like this doesn't combine them to create ab. Instead, it converts the characters to their underlying numeric type and adds the numeric value together. In the previous statements, the result of the addition is to assign the character with a numeric value of 195 to the myChar variable. The char type can represent only a single character. If you want to create sequences of characters, then you need to use the string type, which is discussed later in this chapter.

Using Struct Members

The char keyword is an alias to the System.Char struct, which contains a number of static methods to aid in working with characters. The most useful are described in Table 16-3.

Table 16-3. Useful Members of the System.Char Struct

Method	Description
GetNumericValue(char)	Converts a char to a number (for example, the char 3 is converted to a numeric value of 3). Returns -1 if the char is not a number.
IsDigit(char)	Returns true if the char parameter is a decimal digit.
IsLetter(char)	Returns true if the char parameter is a letter.
IsLetterOrDigit(char)	Returns true if the char parameter is a letter or decimal digit.
IsLower(char) IsUpper(char)	Returns true if the char parameter is of the specific case.
IsPunctuation(char) IsSeparator(char) IsSymbol(char) IsWhiteSpace(char)	Returns true if the char parameter is classified as Unicode punctuation, a separator, a symbol, or whitespace.
ToLower(char) ToUpper(char)	Convert the char parameter to the specified case.

Listing 16-4 demonstrates the use of the static members described in Table 16-3.

Listing 16-4. Using Members of the System.Char Struct

```
using System;

class Listing_04 {

    static void Main(string[] args) {

        char myChar = 'x';

        Console.WriteLine("Numeric Value: {0}", Char.GetNumericValue(myChar));
        Console.WriteLine("Is Digit? {0}", Char.IsDigit(myChar));
        Console.WriteLine("Is Letter? {0}", Char.IsLetter(myChar));
        Console.WriteLine("Is Letter Or Digit? {0}", Char.IsLetterOrDigit(myChar));
        Console.WriteLine("IsLower? {0}", Char.IsLower(myChar));
        Console.WriteLine("IsUpper? {0}", Char.IsUpper(myChar));
        Console.WriteLine("Is Punctuation? {0}", Char.IsPunctuation(myChar));
        Console.WriteLine("Is Separator? {0}", Char.IsSeparator(myChar));
        Console.WriteLine("Is Symbol ? {0}", Char.IsSymbol(myChar));
        Console.WriteLine("Is White space? {0}", Char.IsWhiteSpace(myChar));
        Console.WriteLine("Convert to Upper: {0}", Char.ToUpper(myChar));
        Console.WriteLine("Convert to Lower: {0}", Char.ToLower(myChar));
```

```
        // wait for input before exiting
        Console.WriteLine("Press enter to finish");
        Console.ReadLine();
    }
}
```

Compiling and running the code in Listing 16-4 produces the following results:

```
Numeric Value: -1
Is Digit? False
Is Letter? True
Is Letter Or Digit? True
IsLower? True
IsUpper? False
Is Punctuation? False
Is Separator? False
Is Symbol ? False
Is White space? False
Convert to Upper: X
Convert to Lower: x
Press enter to finish
```

Using Strings

A string object represents a read-only sequence of Unicode characters. The string keyword is an alias for the System.String class, and like all the other built-in type aliases, you can choose to use either the keyword or the class name or switch between them freely.

Expressing Strings Using String Literals

As with the other C# built-in types, you can define string values using literals, as demonstrated by Listing 16-5.

Listing 16-5. Using a String Literal

```
string myString = "Introduction to C#";
```

String literals are defined by placing a sequence of characters between a pair of double quotes ("), as illustrated by Figure 16-2.

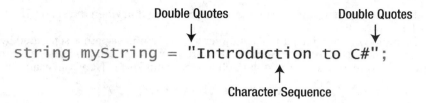

Figure 16-2. *The anatomy of a string literal*

The statement in Listing 16-5 uses a string literal to create a string object with the value of "Introduction of C#" and assigns it to a string variable called myString.

Using String Escape Sequences and Verbatim Literals

Strings can contain the same escape sequences that are available for characters, examples of which were described in Table 16-2. Escape sequences can be mixed in with regular characters, as demonstrated by Listing 16-6.

Listing 16-6. String Escape Sequences and Verbatim String Literals

```
using System;

class Listing_06 {

    static void Main(string[] args) {

        // define a string using a literal that contains escape sequences
        string myString = "Introduction\nto\nC#";

        // print out the string
        Console.WriteLine(myString);

        // define a sample file path
        string myFilePath = "c:\\Books\\Intro to C#\\Manuscript\\Chapter 16";

        // print out the file path
        Console.WriteLine("File path: {0}", myFilePath);

        // define the file path as a veratim string literal
        myFilePath = @"c:\Books\Intro to C#\Manuscript\Chapter 16";
        Console.WriteLine("Verbatim path: {0}", myFilePath);

        // wait for input before exiting
        Console.WriteLine("Press enter to finish");
        Console.ReadLine();
    }
}
```

The first `string` literal includes the new line escape sequence, meaning that when the `string` is displayed, it will be spread over three lines.

The second literal is a sample Windows file path. Each directory in a Windows path is separated by a backslash, which, as we have seen, is used by C# to indicate the start of an escape sequence. We have to use a two backslash characters (\\) to get a single backslash character in our string. Here's an example:

```
string myFilePath = "c:\\Books\\Intro to C#\\Manuscript\\Chapter 16";
```

This is messy and difficult to read. Fortunately, C# supports *verbatim string literals*, where the literal value is not scanned for escape sequences. A verbatim literal is defined by placing an at sign in front of the literal value, like this:

```
string myFilePath = @"c:\Books\Intro to C#\Manuscript\Chapter 16";
```

Listing 16-6 includes this file path expressed in both literal forms. Compiling and running the listing produces the following output:

```
Introduction
to
C#
File path: c:\Books\Intro to C#\Manuscript\Chapter 16
Verbatim path: c:\Books\Intro to C#\Manuscript\Chapter 16
Press enter to finish
```

Verbatim `string` values can be very useful, but you can use them only if you are sure there are no escape sequences to be processed. For example, consider the following statements:

```
string myString = @"Introduction\nto\nC#";
Console.WriteLine(myString);
```

I have defined a verbatim `string` literal that contains escape sequences. When the `string` variable is printed out, we can see that the escape sequences have not been interpreted, and I end up with an unreadable message:

```
Introduction\nto\nC#
```

Verbatim literals can include any characters, including new lines. Here is an example of such a literal `string` value, which spans three lines and includes two new line characters:

```
string myString = @"Introduction
to
C#";
```

Performing Operations on Strings

The following sections demonstrate how to perform common operations on `string` objects.

Comparing Strings

C# lets you compare strings directly using the comparison operators (== and !=). There is no need to use a comparison method, such as the Java equals method. Listing 16-7 demonstrates the use of these operators on string objects.

Listing 16-7. Using the Relational Operators on string Objects

```
using System;

class Listing_07 {

    static void Main(string[] args) {

        string firstString = "Introduction";
        string secondString = "to C#";

        if (firstString == secondString) {
            Console.WriteLine("Result of == operator: strings are the same");
        } else {
            Console.WriteLine("Result of == operator: strings are not the same");
        }

        if (firstString != secondString) {
            Console.WriteLine("Result of != operator: strings are different");
        } else {
            Console.WriteLine("Result of != operator: strings are not different");
        }

        // wait for input before exiting
        Console.WriteLine("Press enter to finish");
        Console.ReadLine();
    }
}
```

Compiling and running Listing 16-7 produces the following results:

```
Result of == operator: strings are not the same
Result of != operator: strings are different
Press enter to finish
```

These operators are case sensitive so that the string Introduction is not the same as the string introduction.

Strings in C# can be empty, meaning that they represent a sequence of zero characters. This is more useful that it might appear. If you present the user with a text entry box and they don't enter any text, you will end up dealing with an empty string. You can check to see whether a string is empty by comparing it with another empty string (the literal value "") or by using the string.Empty field. The latter of these techniques is shown in Listing 16-8.

Listing 16-8. Using the string.Empty Field

```
using System;

class Listing_08 {

    static void Main(string[] args) {

        // print a message to the console
        Console.WriteLine("Enter a line of text and press enter");
        Console.WriteLine("Enter 'x' and press enter to quit");

        while (true) {
            string userString = Console.ReadLine();

            if (userString == string.Empty) {
                Console.WriteLine("String is empty");
            } else {
                Console.WriteLine("Read line: {0}", userString);
                if (userString == "x") {
                    break;
                }
            }
        }

        // wait for input before exiting
        Console.WriteLine("Press enter to finish");
        Console.ReadLine();
    }
}
```

This example reads strings entered by the user and compares them to the string.Empty field.
Compiling and running the code in Listing 16-8 with a few sample values produces the following results:

```
Enter a line of text and press enter
Enter 'x' and press enter to quit
Hello, World!
Read line: Hello, World!

String is empty
x
Read line: x
Press enter to finish
```

■ **Tip** When working with strings, it is important to remember that they are reference types and that string field and variables can be null.

Combining Strings

Strings can be combined using the addition operator (+), as demonstrated by Listing 16-9.

Listing 16-9. Combining Strings

```
using System;

class Listing_09 {

    static void Main(string[] args) {

        // define two local string variables
        string firstString = "Hello";
        string secondString = "World";

        // combine the strings with a string literal value
        // using the addition operator
        string combinedString = firstString + " " + secondString;

        // write the combined string to the console
        Console.WriteLine("Combined string: {0}", combinedString);

        // wait for input before exiting
        Console.WriteLine("Press enter to finish");
        Console.ReadLine();
    }
}
```

Compiling and running Listing 16-9 produces the following results:

```
Combined string: Hello World
Press enter to finish
```

Strings are read-only sequences of characters, so when you add two strings together using the addition operator, C# has to create a new string that contains the result of the addition. You won't care that this happens most of the time, but you do need to be careful when using the addition operator on a string object, which has multiple references to it. Consider the following statements:

```
// create a new string object
string firstString = "Hello";
string secondString = firstString;

// combine a new string using the addition assignment operator
secondString += " World";

// print out the string values
Console.WriteLine("firstString value: {0}", firstString);
Console.WriteLine("secondString value: {0}", secondString);
```

The first pair of statements creates two `string` local variables that reference a single `string` object. I then use the addition assignment operator (+=) to combine a `string` with the one of the local variables. I finish by writing the value of both local variables to the console. The output of these statements is as follows:

```
firstString value: Hello
secondString value: Hello World
Press enter to finish
```

When I used the addition assignment operator, a new `string` object was created, and the local variable was updated so that it referred to the new object. Although C# strings are objects, their read-only nature does lead to some unexpected behavior.

■ **Tip** Combining strings using the addition operator (+) or the addition assignment operator (+=) is less efficient than using the `StringBuilder` class. See the "Using the StringBuilder Class" section later in this chapter for more details.

Reading Individual Characters

The `string` class implements an indexer that allows you to access individual characters. You can't use the indexer to modify the characters since strings are read-only. You learn more about indexers in Chapter 8. Listing 16-10 demonstrates using the indexer, along with the `Length` property, in a for loop to enumerate the contents of a string. The `string.Length` property is described in Table 16-6 in this chapter; for loops are described in Chapter 4.

Listing 16-10. Using a String Indexer

```
using System;

class Listing_10 {

    static void Main(string[] args) {

        // define a new string
        string myString = "Hello World";

        // use the string indexer and the Length property
        // to enumerate the contents of the string
        for (int i = 0; i < myString.Length; i++) {
            Console.WriteLine("Character at position {0}: {1}", i ,myString[i]);
        }

        // wait for input before exiting
        Console.WriteLine("Press enter to finish");
```

```
            Console.ReadLine();
        }
}
```

Compiling and running the code in Listing 16-10 produces the following results:

```
Character at position 0: H
Character at position 1: e
Character at position 2: l
Character at position 3: l
Character at position 4: o
Character at position 5:
Character at position 6: W
Character at position 7: o
Character at position 8: r
Character at position 9: l
Character at position 10: d
Press enter to finish
```

Enumerating a String

The string class implements the IEnumerable<char> interface, which means you can use a foreach loop to enumerate the characters in a string. Listing 16-11 provides a demonstration.

Listing 16-11. Using a foreach Loop to Enumerate the Characters in a String

```
using System;

class Listing_11 {

    static void Main(string[] args) {

        // define a new string
        string myString = "Hello World";

        // enumerate the contents of the string with a foreach loop
        foreach (char c in myString) {
            Console.WriteLine("Character: {0}", c);
        }

        // wait for input before exiting
        Console.WriteLine("Press enter to finish");
        Console.ReadLine();
    }
}
```

Compiling and running Listing 16-11 produces the following results:

```
Character: H
Character: e
Character: l
Character: l
Character: o
Character:
Character: W
Character: o
Character: r
Character: l
Character: d
Press enter to finish
```

Using Strings in a switch Statement

You can use string literals as the case labels in switch statements (switch statements are described in Chapter 4). Listing 16-12 provides an example of using strings and switch statements.

Listing 16-12. Switching on Strings

```
using System;

class Listing_12 {

    static void Main(string[] args) {

        string myBook = "Introduction to C#";

        switch (myBook) {
            case "Pro .NET Parallel Programming":
                Console.WriteLine("This is a parallel programming book");
                break;
            case "Pro LINQ":
                Console.WriteLine("This is a LINQ book");
                break;
            case "Introduction to C#":
                Console.WriteLine("This is a C# introduction book");
                break;
        }

        // wait for input before exiting
        Console.WriteLine("Press enter to finish");
        Console.ReadLine();
    }
}
```

Using Regular Expressions

You can use regular expressions to search and manipulate strings using the
System.Text.RegularExpressions.Regex class. Regular expressions are an advanced topic that is beyond
the scope of this book, but I have included a simple example in this chapter so that you know the feature
exists. You can find details of C# regular expressions at the following URL:
http://msdn.microsoft.com/en-us/library/hs600312.aspx. Listing 16-13 contains an example of using
regular expressions to search strings.

Listing 16-13. Using a Simple Regular Expression

```
using System;
using System.Text.RegularExpressions;

class Listing_13 {

    static void Main(string[] args) {

        // define an array of strings
        string[] bookTitles = { "Introduction to C#",
                                "Visual C# Recipes",
                                "Pro .NET Parallel Programming",
                                "Pro LINQ" };

        // define the term we will search for
        string searchTerm = "pro";

        // enumerate through the title strings and look for the search term
        foreach (string title in bookTitles) {
            Console.WriteLine("--- Title ---");
            Console.WriteLine("Book title: {0}", title);
            if (Regex.IsMatch(title, searchTerm, RegexOptions.IgnoreCase)) {
                Console.WriteLine("Title contains search term!");
            } else {
                Console.WriteLine("No match found");
            }
        }

        // wait for input before exiting
        Console.WriteLine("Press enter to finish");
        Console.ReadLine();
    }
}
```

The example in Listing 16-13 searches a set of book titles for the term pro, looking for matches
irrespective of case (that is, pro, Pro, PRo and pr0 would all be considered matches). Compiling and
running Listing 16-13 produces the following results:

```
--- Title ---
Book title: Introduction to C#
```

```
No match found
--- Title ---
Book title: Visual C# Recipes
No match found
--- Title ---
Book title: Pro .NET Parallel Programming
Title contains search term!
--- Title ---
Book title: Pro LINQ
Title contains search term!
Press enter to finish
```

Using Class Members

The System.String class defines a wide range of methods that can be used to work with string values. The following sections describe the most commonly used, broken down by category.

Manipulating Strings

Table 16-4 describes the method available for manipulating strings. As previously mentioned, string values are read-only, and so those methods that seem to edit the value of a string are in fact creating new string values. See the "Combining Strings" section earlier in this chapter for a demonstration of the effect this can have.

Table 16-4. Members of the System.String Class for Manipulating Strings

Method	Description
Concat(string, params string)	Concatenates string values. Overloaded versions of this method are available to concatenate string arrays and string representations of objects.
Format(string, object)	Applies formatting to a string; see the "Formatting Strings" section later in this chapter for details. There are several overloaded versions of this method available.
Insert(int, string)	Inserts the string parameter into the current string instance at the specified int index.
Join(string, IEnumerable<string>)	Creates a new string by concatenating the elements of the IEnumerable<string> using the string parameter as a separator. There are several overloaded versions of this method available.
PadLeft(int) PadRight(int)	Aligns a string by adding spaces to the left or right of the current string instance to reach the total number of characters specified by the parameter value. Overridden versions of this method allow you to specify the padding character.

Method	Description
Remove(int) Remove(int, int)	Creates a new string by removing characters from the current string instance. The first version of this method deletes characters from the index specified by the int parameter through to the end of the string. The second version deletes the number of characters specified by the second int parameter, starting at the index specified by the first int parameter.
Replace(char, char) Replace(string, string)	The first version of this method replaces every instance of the first char parameter with the second char parameter. The second version of this method does the same thing, but for the sequences of characters contains in the string parameters.
Split(params char[])	Returns a string array that contains the substrings of the current string that are delimited by any of the parameter characters. Overridden versions of this method are available that allow strings to be split using different criteria.
Substring(int) Substring(int, int)	Retrieves a subrange of characters from the current string. The first version retrieves the characters from the index specified by the Int parameter to the end of the string. The second version retrieves the number of characters specified by the second parameter starting from the index specified by the first parameter.
ToUpper() ToLower()	Converts the current string instance to uppercase or lowercase.
TrimStart() TrimEnd() Trim()	Removes any whitespace characters from the start (TrimStart), end (TrimEnd), or start and end (Trim) of the current string instance.

Listing 16-14 contains a demonstration of some of these methods.

Listing 16-14. Using System.String Methods to Manipulate Strings

```
using System;

class Listing_14 {

    static void Main(string[] args) {

        // define some strings
        string firstString = "Introduction";
        string secondString = "to";
        string thirdString = "C#";

        // concat the strings
        string concatString = String.Concat(firstString, secondString, thirdString);
        // write out the concatenated value
```

```
        Console.WriteLine("Concat: {0}", concatString);

        // insert some spaces into the string
        string insertString = concatString.Insert(12, " ");
        insertString = insertString.Insert(15, " ");
        // write out the modified string
        Console.WriteLine("Insert: {0}", insertString);

        // define an array of strings
        string[] strArray = {"Introduction", "to", "C#"};
        // join the strings together using space as a separator
        string joinString = String.Join(" ", strArray);
        // write out the modified string
        Console.WriteLine("Join: {0}", joinString);

        // pad the string
        string padString = joinString.PadLeft(25);
        // write out the modified string
        Console.WriteLine("Pad: -{0}-", padString);

        // remove some characters
        string removeString = joinString.Remove(12);
        // write out the modified string
        Console.WriteLine("Remove: {0}", removeString);

        // replace some characters
        string replaceString = removeString.Replace('o', 'O');
        // write out the modified string
        Console.WriteLine("Replace: {0}", replaceString);

        // split a string an enumerate the contents
        string splitString = "Introduction to C#";
        string[] strElements = splitString.Split(' ');
        foreach (string s in strElements) {
            Console.WriteLine("Element: {0}", s);
        }

        // force a string into uppoer and lowe case
        string upperString = splitString.ToUpper();
        string lowerString = splitString.ToLower();
        // write out the modified strings
        Console.WriteLine("Upper: {0}", upperString);
        Console.WriteLine("Lower: {0}", lowerString);

        // wait for input before exiting
        Console.WriteLine("Press enter to finish");
        Console.ReadLine();
    }
}
```

Compiling and running Listing 16-14 produces the following results:

```
Concat: IntroductiontoC#
Insert: Introduction to C#
Join: Introduction to C#
Pad: -          Introduction to C#-
Remove: Introduction
Replace: Intr0ducti0n
Element: Introduction
Element: to
Element: C#
Upper: INTRODUCTION TO C#
Lower: introduction to c#
Press enter to finish
```

Searching Strings

The string class defines several methods to search strings. These are in addition to the support for regular expressions that was described earlier in this chapter. Table 16-5 describes the most commonly used search methods in the string class.

Table 16-5. Members of the System.String Class for Searching Strings

Method	Description
Contains(string)	Returns true if the current string contains the substring specified by the parameter and false otherwise.
StartsWith(string) EndsWith(string)	Returns true if the current string starts with or ends with the string specified by the parameter and false otherwise.
IndexOf(char) IndexOf(string)	Returns the index of the first occurrence of the character or substring in the current string specified by the parameter. Overridden versions of this method allow you to specify a start index for the search. Returns -1 if no match is found.
LastIndexOf(char) LastIndexOf(string)	Returns the index of the last occurrence of the character or substring in the current string specified by the parameter. Returns -1 if no match is found.
IndexOfAny(char[]) LastIndexOfAny(char[])	Returns the first or last index of any individual character in the array of characters specified in the parameter. Returns -1 if no match is found.

Listing 16-15 demonstrates the use of some of the methods described in Table 16-5.

Listing 16-15. Searching Strings

```
using System;

class Listing_15 {

    static void Main(string[] args) {

        // define a string to work with
        string myString = "Introduction to C#";

        // use the Contains method
        bool contains = myString.Contains("duct");
        Console.WriteLine("Contains: {0}", contains);

        // use the StartsWith and EndsWith methods
        bool startsWith = myString.StartsWith("Intro");
        bool endsWith = myString.EndsWith("Intro");
        Console.WriteLine("StartsWith: {0}", startsWith);
        Console.WriteLine("EndsWith: {0}", endsWith);

        // use the IndexOf and LastIndexOf methods
        int indexOf = myString.IndexOf('o');
        int lastIndexOf = myString.LastIndexOf('o');
        Console.WriteLine("IndexOf: {0}", indexOf);
        Console.WriteLine("LastIndexOf: {0}", lastIndexOf);

        // wait for input before exiting
        Console.WriteLine("Press enter to finish");
        Console.ReadLine();
    }
}
```

Compiling and running the code in Listing 16-15 produces the following results:

```
Contains: True
StartsWith: True
EndsWith: False
IndexOf: 4
LastIndexOf: 14
Press enter to finish
```

Other Class Members

Two other members of the string class are worth mentioning but do not fit into the manipulating or searching strings categories. They are described in Table 16-6.

Table 16-6. *Other Members of the System.String Class*

Method	Description
Length	This property returns the number of characters in the current string.
ToCharArray()	This property copies the contents of the current string to a char array.

Listing 16-16 demonstrates the use of these two members.

Listing 16-16. Using the Length and ToCharArray Members

```
using System;

class Listing_16 {

    static void Main(string[] args) {

        // define a string using a literal
        string myString = "Hello World";

        // get the length of the string
        int len = myString.Length;
        Console.WriteLine("Length: {0}", len);

        // get the characters from the string
        char[] charArray = myString.ToCharArray();
        // enumerate the character array
        foreach (char c in charArray) {
            Console.WriteLine("Char: {0}", c);
        }

        // wait for input before exiting
        Console.WriteLine("Press enter to finish");
        Console.ReadLine();
    }
}
```

Compiling and running the code in Listing 16-16 produces the following results:

```
Length: 11
Char: H
Char: e
Char: l
Char: l
Char: o
Char:
Char: W
Char: o
```

501

```
Char: r
Char: l
Char: d
Press enter to finish
```

Using the StringBuilder Class

The StringBuilder class, contained in the System.Text namespace, is the mutable companion to the read-only string class. You can edit the contents of a string represented by a StringBuilder object and perform operations that are faster and more efficient than working with strings directly. The main use of the StringBuilder class is to build strings through multiple append operations.

Creating a StringBuilder Object

There is no equivalent to the string literal to define StringBuilder values. You must instead use one of the class constructors, the simplest of which has no parameters, like this:

```
StringBuilder myBuilder = new StringBuilder();
```

A StringBuilder object uses a char array to store the characters of the string it represents. This array will be resized as needed to accommodate the effect of building a string by adding characters. You can recommend an initial size of array for a StringBuilder object to allocate by providing an int constructor parameter, like this:

```
StringBuilder myBuilder = new StringBuilder(10);
```

Suggesting an array capacity that is large enough to hold the string you intend to build can avoid the time-consuming operation of creating a larger array and copying the contents of the StringBuilder to it.

If you already have the foundation for the string that you want to build, you can provide this as the basis of the StringBuilder, like this:

```
StringBuilder myBuilder = new StringBuilder("Introduction to");
```

Using a StringBuilder Object

The StringBuilder class includes a range of members that help you manipulate the contents of strings. These are summarized in Table 16-7.

Table 16-7. Members of the System.Text.StringBuilder Class

Method	Description
Append(string)	Appends a string to the current StringBuilder object. See the "Using the Append and Insert Methods" section later in this chapter.
AppendFormat(string, object) AppendFormat(string,params object)	See the "Formatting Strings" section later in this chapter
Capacity	Gets or sets the maximum number of characters that the current StringBuilder object can represent.
AppendLine() AppendLine(string)	AppendLine() appends a line terminator character to the current StringBuilder object. AppendLine(string) appends a copy of the string parameter followed by a line terminator to the current StringBuilder object.
Clear()	Removes all the characters from the current StringBuilder object.
EnsureCapacity(int)	Ensures that the underlying char array used by the current StringBuilder object can hold at least the number of characters specified by the int parameter.
Insert(int, string)	Inserts a string into the current StringBuilder object at the specified index. See the "Using the Append and Insert Methods" section later in this chapter.
Remove(int, int)	Removes a range of characters starting at the index specified by the first parameter. The number of characters to remove is specified by the second parameter.
Replace(char, char) Replace(string, string)	Replace all the instances of the char or string specified by the first parameter with the char or string specified by the second parameter.
ToString()	Convert the contents of the current StringBuilder object to a string.

Listing 16-17 demonstrates using some of the methods from Table 16-7. The Append method, the Insert method, and the class indexer are described in the following sections.

Listing 16-17. Using the Members of the System.Text.StringBuilder Class

```
using System;
using System.Text;

class Listing_17 {

    static void Main(string[] args) {

        // create a StringBuilder object
        StringBuilder myBuilder = new StringBuilder("Introduction to C#");

        // report the capacity of the StringBuilder
        Console.WriteLine("Capacity: {0}", myBuilder.Capacity);

        // remove some characters
        myBuilder.Remove(12, 6);
        Console.WriteLine("Remove: {0}", myBuilder);

        // replace some characters
        myBuilder.Replace('o', 'O');
        Console.WriteLine("Replace: {0}", myBuilder);

        // convert to and assign to a string
        string myString = myBuilder.ToString();
        Console.WriteLine("ToString: {0}", myString);

        // clear the contents of the StringBuilder
        myBuilder.Clear();
        Console.WriteLine("Cleared: {0}", myBuilder);

        // wait for input before exiting
        Console.WriteLine("Press enter to finish");
        Console.ReadLine();
    }
}
```

Compiling and running the code in Listing 16-17 produces the following results:

```
Capacity: 18
Remove: Introduction
Replace: IntrOductiOn
ToString: IntrOductiOn
Cleared:
Press enter to finish
```

Using the Append and Insert Methods

The Append and Insert methods are the heart of the StringBuilder class. They allow you to quickly build strings by concatenating smaller strings together and inserting fragments of strings into larger ones.

There are 19 versions of the Append method and 18 versions of the Insert method. Don't be put off by the number of different versions. The most commonly used version of each method is the one that takes a string parameter. Listing 16-18 demonstrates using the versions of the Append and Insert method that have a string parameter.

Listing 16-18. Using the StringBuilder Append and Insert Methods

```
using System;
using System.Text;

class Listing_18 {

    static void Main(string[] args) {

        // create an empty StringBuilder object
        StringBuilder myBuilder = new StringBuilder();

        // append a string to the StringBuilder
        myBuilder.Append(" to C#");

        // insert a string into the StringBuilder
        myBuilder.Insert(0, "Introduction");

        // write out the StringBuilder
        Console.WriteLine("Contents: {0}", myBuilder);

        // wait for input before exiting
        Console.WriteLine("Press enter to finish");
        Console.ReadLine();
    }
}
```

Compiling and running the code in Listing 16-18 produces the following results:

```
Contents: Introduction to C#
Press enter to finish
```

All the other versions of the Append and Insert methods are a convenience so that you can add or insert instances of the built-in types without having to convert them to strings by calling the ToString method. This means that an Append statement like this:

```
bool myBool = true;
myBuilder.Append(myBool);
```

is equivalent to this one:

```
myBuilder.Append(myBool.ToString());
```

The ToString method is covered in the "Formatting Strings" section later in this chapter.

Using the StringBuilder Indexer

The last point of note for the StringBuilder class is that you can read and modify characters using a custom indexer. (By contrast, you can only read characters using the indexer implemented in the string class.) Listing 16-19 contains a simple demonstration.

Listing 16-19. Reading and Writing Characters via the StringBuilder Indexer

```csharp
using System;
using System.Text;

class Listing_19 {

    static void Main(string[] args) {

        // create a string builder
        StringBuilder myBuilder = new StringBuilder("Introduction to C#");

        // read some chars using the indexer
        for (int i = 0; i < 5; i++) {
            Console.WriteLine("Char at index {0}: {1}", i, myBuilder[i]);
        }

        // change a character
        myBuilder[0] = 'Z';

        // write out the contents of the StringBuilder object
        Console.WriteLine("Modified: {0}", myBuilder);

        // wait for input before exiting
        Console.WriteLine("Press enter to finish");
        Console.ReadLine();
    }
}
```

Compiling and running Listing 16-19 produces the following results:

```
Char at index 0: I
Char at index 1: n
Char at index 2: t
Char at index 3: r
Char at index 4: o
Modified: Zntroduction to C#
Press enter to finish
```

Formatting Strings

C# has comprehensive support for formatting strings through a feature called *composite formatting*. The following sections demonstrate how to use this feature to format strings in a range of different ways.

Using Composite Formatting

The composite formatting feature is one that I have used in many of the examples in this book. You specify a `string` that contains one or more *format items* and an object or value for each of those items. The C# composite formatting feature will create a `string` representation for each object, which is used to replace the corresponding format item. Listing 16-20 contains an example of using the composite formatting feature.

Listing 16-20. Using Composite Formatting

```
using System;

class Listing_20 {

    static void Main(string[] args) {

        string formatString = "My name is {0} and I live in {1}";

        Console.WriteLine(formatString, "Adam", "London");
        Console.WriteLine(formatString, "Jane", "New York");

        // wait for input before exiting
        Console.WriteLine("Press enter to finish");
        Console.ReadLine();
    }
}
```

Listing 16-20 is a basic composite formatting example. The `string` that contains the format items is illustrated in Figure 16-3.

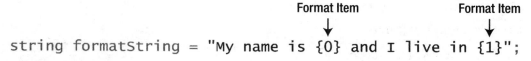

Figure 16-3. The anatomy of a basic format item string

A format item is wrapped in brace characters ({ and }) and are numbered from zero onward. There are two format items contained in the `string` assigned to the `formatString` local variable in Listing 16-20, numbered 0 and 1.

The static `Console.WriteLine` method supports the composite formatting feature and will accept a number of parameters. The first parameter to follow the `string` will be used for format item zero, the next for format item one, and so on. Consider the following statement taken from Listing 16-20:

```
Console.WriteLine(formatString, "Adam", "London");
```

In this statement, the string Adam is used for formatting item zero, and the string London is used to replace format item one, to produce the following composited string:

```
My name is Adam and I live in London
```

The string that contains the format items can be used with different parameters, which is demonstrated in Listing 16-20. Compiling and running Listing 16-20 produces the following results:

```
My name is Adam and I live in London
My name is Jane and I live in New York
Press enter to finish
```

Format items don't have to appear in sequence and can be used more than once. Here is an example:

```
string myString = "{1} is the home city of {0}. {0} is {2} years old.";
Console.WriteLine(myString, "Adam", "London", 38);
```

The output from these statements is as follows:

```
London is the home city of Adam. Adam is 38 years old.
```

Other Composite Formatting Methods

The Console.WriteLine method isn't the only one that supports the composite formatting feature. The static string.Format and StringBuilder.AppendFormat instance method will also process a string for format items, as demonstrated by Listing 16-21.

Listing 16-21. Using Other Composite Formatting Methods

```
using System;
using System.Text;

class Listing_21 {

    static void Main(string[] args) {

        // define a string with format items
        string formatString = "My name is: {0}";

        // use the static string.Format method
        string outputString = string.Format(formatString, "Adam");
        Console.WriteLine("String.Format: {0}", outputString);

        // create an empty StringBuilder
        StringBuilder myBuilder = new StringBuilder();
```

```
        // append and format the string in one step
        myBuilder.AppendFormat(formatString, "Jane");
        Console.WriteLine("StringBuilder.AppendFormat: {0}", myBuilder);

        // wait for input before exiting
        Console.WriteLine("Press enter to finish");
        Console.ReadLine();
    }
}
```

Compiling and running the code in Listing 16-21 produces the following results:

```
String.Format: My name is: Adam
StringBuilder.AppendFormat: My name is: Jane
Press enter to finish
```

Specifying Alignment

You can specify that the result of substituting a value for a format item be a minimum number of characters by providing an alignment component to the format item. Listing 16-22 contains an example.

Listing 16-22. Using a Format Item with an Alignment Component

```
using System;

class Listing_22 {

    static void Main(string[] args) {

        // specify the a string with a format item
        string formatString = "The cost of item {0} is {1, 3}";

        // use the composite formatting feature
        Console.WriteLine(formatString, 1, 100);
        Console.WriteLine(formatString, 2, 23);
        Console.WriteLine(formatString, 3, 1);

        // wait for input before exiting
        Console.WriteLine("Press enter to finish");
        Console.ReadLine();
    }
}
```

An alignment component is specified by following the format item index with a comma and the minimum number of characters that should be used, as illustrated by Figure 16-4.

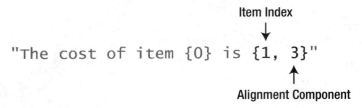

Figure 16-4. *The anatomy of a format item with an alignment component*

If the item that is going to be substituted has fewer characters than specified by the alignment component, then additional spaces will be added to increase the length. The alignment component in Listing 16-22 specifies a minimum of three characters, so when a value of 1 is provided, two spaces will be added to pad out the value. The results of compiling and running Listing 16-22 are as follows:

```
The cost of item 1 is 100
The cost of item 2 is  23
The cost of item 3 is   1
Press enter to finish
```

If the alignment component is a positive value, as in Listing 16-22, then the padding characters will be added to the left of the value. If the alignment component is a negative value, then the padding characters will be added to the right of the value. Here is the code from Listing 16-22 but with a negative alignment component value:

```
// specify the a string with a format item
string formatString = "The cost of item {0} is {1, -3}";

// use the composite formatting feature
Console.WriteLine(formatString, 1, 100);
Console.WriteLine(formatString, 2, 23);
Console.WriteLine(formatString, 3, 1);
```

The output from this code is as follows:

```
The cost of item 1 is 100
The cost of item 2 is 23
The cost of item 3 is 1
```

Escaping Braces

If you want to display brace characters in a `string` that you will use for composite formatting, then you must use an escape sequence. Two open brace characters ({{) will be interpreted as a single open brace character ({), and two close brace characters (}}) will be interpreted as a single close brace character (}). Listing 16-23 contains an example of mixing brace escape sequences and format items.

Listing 16-23. Escaping Brace Characters in a Composite Format String

```
using System;

class Listing_23 {

    static void Main(string[] args) {

        // create a string that has format items and
        // escape sequences for brace characters
        string formatString = "My name is {{{0}}}";

        // use composite formatting
        Console.WriteLine(formatString, "Adam");

        // wait for input before exiting
        Console.WriteLine("Press enter to finish");
        Console.ReadLine();
    }
}
```

Compiling and running Listing 16-23 produces the following results:

```
My name is {Adam}
Press enter to finish
```

Formatting Types

When you use composite formatting, you can specify any object or value you want to include in the composited `string`. The composite formatting system creates a string representation of the object or value by calling the `ToString` method, which is defined in `System.Object` and so is inherited by all reference and value types. When you use composite formatting, there are some options to control how an object or value is represented as a string.

Using a Format Component

A format component is an optional part of a format item that specifies how an object or value should be displayed. Listing 16-24 contains an example.

Listing 16-24. Using a Format Component

```
using System;

class Listing_24 {

    static void Main(string[] args) {
```

```
float itemsPerCase = 3f;
float costPerCase = 10f;

// work out the cost per item
float costPerItem = costPerCase / itemsPerCase;

// define a format string
string formatString1 = "Cost per item: {0}";
// define a format string with a format string component
string formatString2 = "Cost per item: {0:F2}";

// use composite formatting
Console.WriteLine(formatString1, costPerItem);
Console.WriteLine(formatString2, costPerItem);

// wait for input before exiting
Console.WriteLine("Press enter to finish");
Console.ReadLine();
    }
}
```

The statement that contains the format item with the format component is shown in bold. The format string is illustrated by Figure 16-5.

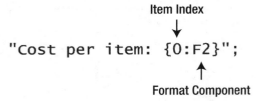

Figure 16-5. The anatomy of a format item with a format component

A format component consists of a single character and an optional numeric value. The character specifies the kind of formatting that should be applied, and the numeric value specifies the precision. In the case of Listing 16-24, the format component specifies that the fixed-point formatting should be used and that the prevision should be two decimal places. Compiling and running Listing 16-24 produces the following output:

```
Cost per item: 3.333333
Cost per item: 3.33
Press enter to finish
```

You can see from the output that when there is no format component, the float value passed to the composite formatting method is displayed to six decimal places but that when I apply the F2 format component, the value is displayed to two decimal places.

You can mix format components and alignment components in a single format item. Here is a simple example, based on Listing 16-24:

```
// define a format string with a format string component
string formatString2 = "Cost per item: {0,8:F2}";
// use composite formatting
Console.WriteLine(formatString2, costPerItem);
```

Format components are available for the built-in numeric types and date and time types. The most useful numeric format components are described in Table 16-8 and dates and times are covered in Chapter 22. Details of the built-in numeric types can be found in Chapter 5.

Table 16-8. Selected Format Components for Built-in Numeric Types

Format Component	Description	Meaning of Precision Digits
C	Formats a currency value	Number of decimal digits
D	Formats an integer value	Minimum number of digits
E	Formats an exponential (scientific) value	Minimum number of digits
F	Formats integer and real number values	Number of decimal digits
N	Formats integer or real number values with group separators (for example, commas every three digits) and a decimal place	Number of decimal places
P	Formats a percentage value where 1.0 is equivalent to 100 percent	The number of decimal places.
X	Formats a hexadecimal value	The number of digits

Listing 16-25 demonstrates how to use the format components in Table 16-8.

Listing 16-25. Using Format Components on Built-in Numeric Types

```
using System;

class Listing_25 {

    static void Main(string[] args) {

        // use the C format component
        Console.WriteLine("Currency: {0:C2}", 123.456f);

        // use the D format component
        Console.WriteLine("Decimal: {0:D5}", 123);

        // use the E format component
```

```
        Console.WriteLine("Exponential: {0:E5}", 123456);

        // use the F format component
        Console.WriteLine("Fixed-point: {0:F5}", 123.456f);

        // use the P format component
        Console.WriteLine("Percentage: {0:P2}", 0.123f);

        // use the X format component
        Console.WriteLine("Hex: {0:X6}", 123456);

        // wait for input before exiting
        Console.WriteLine("Press enter to finish");
        Console.ReadLine();
    }
}
```

Compiling and running Listing 16-25 produces the following results:

```
Currency: $123.46
Decimal: 00123
Exponential: 1.23456E+005
Fixed-point: 123.45600
Percentage: 12.30 %
Hex: 01E240
Press enter to finish
```

Some of the format components include culturally specified details. For example, the C format component creates a currency format and includes the currency symbol of the default locale. You should take into account that the result of using format components will change based on the settings of the machine running the code.

Creating String Representations of Custom Types

The composite formatting feature relies on creating string representations of objects and values by calling the ToString method, which is defined in the System.Object class and inherited by all types. Unfortunately, the default implementation of this method simply returns the name of the type that contains it, which is pretty much useless. Listing 16-26 demonstrates the problem.

Listing 16-26. Using the Default String Representations of a Custom Type

```
using System;

class Car {
    public string Manufacturer { get; set; }
    public string Model { get; set; }
    public string Color { get; set; }
}
```

```
class Listing_26 {

    static void Main(string[] args) {

        // create two Car objects
        Car myVolvo = new Car() { Manufacturer = "Volvo", Model = "C30", Color = "Black" };
        Car myFord = new Car() { Manufacturer = "Ford", Model = "Fiesta", Color = "Green" };

        // write out the string representations of the Car objects
        Console.WriteLine("Volvo Object: {0}", myVolvo);
        Console.WriteLine("Ford Object: {0}", myFord);

        // wait for input before exiting
        Console.WriteLine("Press enter to finish");
        Console.ReadLine();
    }
}
```

In Listing 16-26, I create two objects from the Car class, representing a Volvo and a Ford. I then pass the objects to the Console.WriteLine method, using the composite formatting feature. The result of compiling and running Listing 16-26 is as follows:

```
Volvo Object: Car
Ford Object: Car
Press enter to finish
```

The string representation for both of these objects is the same, Car. If we want something more meaningful, then we need to create a custom implementation of the ToString method that knows about the details of our type. Listing 16-27 extends the Car class to include a more useful implementation of the ToString method.

Listing 16-27. A Custom ToString Implementation

```
using System;
using System.Text;

class Car {
    public string Manufacturer { get; set; }
    public string Model { get; set; }
    public string Color { get; set; }

    public override string ToString() {
        // use the composite formatting feature to create
        // a meaningful string representation of this object
        return string.Format("Manufacturer: {0}, Model: {1}, Color: {2}",
            Manufacturer, Model, Color);
    }
}
```

```
class Listing_27 {

    static void Main(string[] args) {

        // create two Car objects
        Car myVolvo = new Car() { Manufacturer = "Volvo", Model = "C30", Color = "Black" };
        Car myFord = new Car() { Manufacturer = "Ford", Model = "Fiesta", Color = "Green" };

        // write out the string representations of the Car objects
        Console.WriteLine("Volvo Object: {0}", myVolvo);
        Console.WriteLine("Ford Object: {0}", myFord);

        // wait for input before exiting
        Console.WriteLine("Press enter to finish");
        Console.ReadLine();
    }
}
```

The overridden version of the ToString method in the Car class uses the composite formatting feature to create a meaningful representation of the object by using the object's property values. When we compile and run Listing 16-27, we get the following (more useful) results:

```
Volvo Object: Manufacturer: Volvo, Model: C30, Color: Black
Ford Object: Manufacturer: Ford, Model: Fiesta, Color: Green
Press enter to finish
```

Your custom types can override the ToString method to return string values that are meaningful in whatever way makes sense, but bear in mind that the ToString method is public, and so you should be careful if including the values of private fields and properties that you would not want exposed.

Performing Custom Composite Formatting

You can define custom format components and implement support for them using the System.IFormatProvider and System.ICustomFormatter interfaces. Let's imagine that we want to create a custom format component that we will use to format the string representation of Car objects. We want format component to be a combination of three characters: M to represent the manufacturer, O for the model, and C for the color. We want to be able to exclude one or more of the characters and be able to change the order of the characters to change the order of the information in the string representation of the Car.

The first step is to create an implementation of the IFormatProvider interface. Listing 16-28 contains an implementation suitable for our example.

Listing 16-28. An Implementation of the IFormatProvider Interface

```
class CarFormatProvider : IFormatProvider {

    public object GetFormat(Type formatType) {
        if (formatType == typeof(System.ICustomFormatter)) {
```

```
            return new CarFormatter();
        } else {
            return null;
        }
    }
}
```

The IFormatProvider interface defines one method, called GetFormat. When this method is called, the composite formatting system is checking to see whether our custom formatting support is able to format a specific kind of object. We only want to support custom formatting, so we return null unless the parameter to the method is the ICustomFormatter type. If the parameter is the ICustomFormatter type, when we create and return a new instance of the CarFormatter class, which is an implementation of the ICustomFormatter interface and is shown in Listing 16-29.

Listing 16-29. An Implementation of the ICustomFormatter Interface

```
class CarFormatter : ICustomFormatter {

    public string Format(string format, object arg, IFormatProvider formatProvider) {
        // cast the object to a car
        Car myCar = (Car) arg;
        // create a string builder so we can compose the string
        StringBuilder myBuilder = new StringBuilder();
        // switch on each character in the format component
        foreach (char c in format.ToUpper()) {
            switch (c) {
                case 'M':
                    myBuilder.AppendFormat(" Manufacturer: {0}", myCar.Manufacturer);
                    break;
                case 'O':
                    myBuilder.AppendFormat(" Model: {0}", myCar.Model);
                    break;
                case 'C':
                    myBuilder.AppendFormat(" Color: {0}", myCar.Color);
                    break;
            }
        }
        // return the contents of the StringBuilder as a string
        return myBuilder.ToString().Trim();
    }
}
```

The ICustomFormatter class also has just one method, this time called Format. This method is called to format an object using a custom format component. The format component is passed as the format parameter, the object to format is passed as the object parameter, and the IFormatProvider that referred the composite formatting system to this implementation is passed as the formatProvider parameter.

You have complete freedom in how you translate the custom format component into a string representation of the object. In Listing 16-29, the CarFormatter class looks for the three characters described at the start of this section and appends a sequence of characters to a StringBuilder, the contents of which are returned as the representation of the object at the end of the Format method.

The last step is to use our custom format component support. Some of the methods that support composite formatting also allow you to provide an implementation of the IFormatProvider interface as a parameter. The following code demonstrates doing this with the string.Format method:

```
using System;

class CustomFormatTest {

    static void Main(string[] args) {

        // create two Car objects
        Car myVolvo = new Car() { Manufacturer = "Volvo", Model = "C30", Color = "Black" };

        // create a custom formatter
        CarFormatProvider formatProvider = new CarFormatProvider();

        // use the custom formatter to format the object
        string outputString = string.Format(formatProvider, "Car Details: {0:CMO}",
            myVolvo);

        // write out the formatted string
        Console.WriteLine(outputString);

        // wait for input before exiting
        Console.WriteLine("Press enter to finish");
        Console.ReadLine();
    }
}
```

The custom format component is shown in bold. I can omit or change the order of the characters in the format component to change the string representation of the Car object. Compiling and running this code produces the following output:

```
Car Details: Color: Black Manufacturer: Volvo Model: C30
Press enter to finish
```

Summary

Strings are important in any programming language, and C# is no exception. In this chapter, we looked at the C# support for individual characters and for strings, which represent sequences of characters. We saw how to use literal values to define character and string values and how to perform operations on both types.

We explored the range of class members and operators available to make working with strings easier and looked at the System.Text.StringBuilder class, which is a mutable companion to the read-only System.String class.

We finished the chapter by looking at the composite formatting feature, which allows strings to be composed by embedding format items in strings, which become placeholders for string representations of other objects. We saw how to format the built-in numeric types and how to create custom format components.

CHAPTER 17

■■■

Attributes

You have seen how modifiers like public and abstract can be applied to classes, interfaces, and other types to change how they behave. The .NET attribute feature allows you to create and apply your own modifiers without having to add keywords to the C# language.

In this chapter, I'll show you two of the many dozens of attributes that are included in the .NET Framework Class Library, how to test for the presence of an attribute, and how to create and apply custom attributes. Table 17-1 provides the summary for this chapter.

Table 17-1. *Quick Problem/Solution Reference for Chapter 17*

Problem	Solution	Listings
Modify the behavior of a C# code element.	Apply an attribute.	17-1, 17-2
Test to see whether an attribute has been applied to a type or a member of a type.	Use reflection and the System.Attribute class.	17-3 through 17-6, 17-8
Create a custom attribute.	Derive from the System.Attribute class.	17-7, 17-9
Restrict where a custom attribute can be applied.	Apply the AttributeUsage attribute to your custom attribute class.	17-10
Control whether a custom attribute applied to a type is inherited by a derived type.	Set the Inherited property of the AttributeUsage attribute.	17-11

Using Attributes

To use an attribute, you apply it to a C# program element, such as a class or method. Attributes are applied immediately before the element that they refer to. Listing 17-1 contains an example of using a standard .NET attribute.

Listing 17-1. Using an Attribute

```
using System;
```

```
[Flags]
enum MyProducts {
    Apples = 2,
    Bananas = 4,
    Cherries = 8
}
```

The attribute in Listing 17-1 is shown in bold and has been applied to an enum; it is illustrated in Figure 17-1.

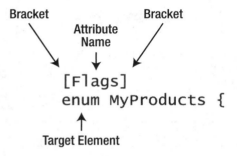

Figure 17-1. *The anatomy of a simple attribute*

The name of the attribute is placed between square brackets ([ ]). The attribute shown in Listing 17-1 applies the Flags attribute to the MyProducts enum. The name of the attribute maps to a class derived from System.Attribute. The convention for attributes is that the name of the attribute class ends with the word Attribute. The .NET runtime looks for an attribute class by appending Attribute to the name you have specified. In the case of the attribute in Listing 17-1, the name Flags relates to the System.FlagsAttribute class. If you prefer, you can specify the name fully like this:

```
[FlagsAttribute]
enum MyProducts {
```

You can also use the fully qualified name of the attribute class (with or without Attribute in the name), like this:

```
[System.Flags]
enum MyProducts {
...
[System.FlagsAttribute]
enum MyProducts {
```

An attribute can have any meaning, as we will see when we come to implement a custom attribute later in the chapter. When the Flags attribute is applied to an emum, it means that the string representation of an enum value should show which individual values have been combined. Here is some code that provides a demonstration:

```
using System;
```

```
class FlagsTest {

    static void Main(string[] args) {

        // combine enum values to represent a mix of products
        MyProducts productMix = MyProducts.Apples | MyProducts.Bananas;

        // print out the product mix
        Console.WriteLine("Products: {0}", productMix);

        // wait for input before exiting
        Console.WriteLine("Press enter to finish");
        Console.ReadLine();
    }
}
```

This example uses the logical OR operator to combine values from the enum defined in Listing 17-1 and print out a string representation to the console. You can find more information about combining enum values in Chapter 9. The output from this code is as follows:

```
Products: Apples, Bananas
Press enter to finish
```

If I remove the attribute from the enum and run the previous code again, I get the following results:

```
Products: 6
Press enter to finish
```

You can see that the Flags attribute changes the string representation created by the ToString method. You can learn more about string representations of objects and values, and how to format them, in Chapter 16.

Applying Attributes with Parameters

Some attributes can be configured with parameters. A good example is System.ObsoleteAttribute, which you can use to warn other programmers (or yourself) that a type member, such as a method or property, has been superseded and should not be used. Listing 17-2 provides a demonstration.

Listing 17-2. Using an Attribute That Takes Arguments

```
using System;

class Calculator {

    [Obsolete("Don't use this method", true)]
    public int CalculateProduct(int x, int y) {
        return x + y;
```

```
    }
}
```

Listing 17-2 applies the Obsolete attribute to the CalculateProduct method. There are two parameters to this attribute. The first is a message to explain why the method is obsolete, and the second controls whether using the method constitutes a compiler warning or a compiler error. A value of true means an error and any code that tries to access the obsolete method won't compile.

The parameters you specify when applying an attribute are used as constructor parameters to create a new instance of the attribute type. We'll see more of this when we create a custom attribute later in the chapter.

Using parameters with attributes allows you to flexibly apply the same attribute differently based on the circumstances. The parameters to the Obsolete attribute can be varied to give different error messages and to control the behavior of the C# compiler.

Notice that, like the previous attribute, Obsolete has no meaning until it is interpreted by some other piece of code. In the case of the Flags attribute, the interpretation is found in the ToString method of the System.Enum class, which is the base for all enums. For the Obsolete attribute, the interpretation is found in the C# compiler.

There are dozens of attributes included in the .NET Framework Library, but since each is interpreted and given meaning by another part of the .NET Framework, it is impossible and meaningless to catalog them out of their individual contexts. We will see some of the most commonly used attributes in other chapters in this book, including Chapter 23, where we cover the serialization of object.

Testing for an Attribute

Checking for an attribute is a lot more complex than applying an attribute and relies upon a technique known as *reflection*. I don't want to get into the details of reflection in this chapter, so I have included here the code that you need to check for an attribute that you can use verbatim in your projects with the detail explained later in this book.

Attributes can be applied to any type or type member. In the following sections, I'll demonstrate testing for the Obsolete attribute applied to a class, a method, a field, and a property. The goal in each case is to end up with an object of the attribute type. Since I am using the Obsolete attribute, my goal is to obtain an instance of the System.ObsoleteAttribute class.

Testing for an Attribute Applied to a Class

The simplest test is for an attribute that has been applied to a class (or other type). Here is an example:

```
using System;

[Obsolete("Don't use this class")]
class Calculator {

    public int CalculateProduct(int x, int y) {
        return x + y;
    }
}
```

The Obsolete attribute has been applied to the entire Calculator class. Listing 17-3 shows a class that you can use to test whether an attribute has been applied to a class.

Listing 17-3. Testing for an Attribute Applied to a Class

```
using System;

class AttributeTester<T> where T : Attribute {

    public bool TestForClassAttribute(Type classType) {
        return Attribute.IsDefined(classType, typeof(T));
    }

    public T GetClassAttribute(Type classType) {
        return Attribute.GetCustomAttribute(classType, typeof(T)) as T;
    }

    public bool TestForClassAttribute(object obj) {
        return TestForClassAttribute(obj.GetType());
    }

    public T GetClassAttribute(object obj) {
        return GetClassAttribute(obj.GetType());
    }
}
```

To check whether a class has had an attribute applied, create a new instance of the AttributeTester<T> class where T is the attribute you are interested in. Here's an example:

```
// create an Attribute Tester for the attribute we are interested in
AttributeTester<ObsoleteAttribute> attrTester = new AttributeTester<ObsoleteAttribute>();
```

Once you have created an AttributeTester<T> object, you can use it to check for and retrieve attributes. If you just want to check to see whether an attribute has been applied, you can use the TestForClassAttribute method. There are overloaded versions of this method that let you test using an object or a System.Type. Here is an example of testing for the Obsolete attribute using an object:

```
using System;

class ObjectTest {

    static void Main(string[] args) {

        // create an Attribute Tester for the attribute we are interested in
        AttributeTester<ObsoleteAttribute> attrTester
            = new AttributeTester<ObsoleteAttribute>();

        // create an instance of the Calculator class
        Calculator calc = new Calculator();

        // check to see whether the attribute has been defined using the class name
```

```
                bool classTest = attrTester.TestForClassAttribute(calc);
                if (classTest) {
                    // the attribute is defined - get the instance of the attribute
                    ObsoleteAttribute attr = attrTester.GetClassAttribute(calc);
                    // write out the properties of the attribute
                    Console.WriteLine("Attribute: message: {0}, error: {1}",
                        attr.Message, attr.IsError);
                }

                // wait for input before exiting
                Console.WriteLine("Press enter to finish");
                Console.ReadLine();
            }
        }
```

The previous example creates a Calculator object and assigns it to a local variable called calc. The local variable is then passed as a parameter to the TestForClassAttribute method (shown in bold), which returns true if the class that the object was created from has been modified with the attribute.

This example also demonstrates the use of the GetClassAttribute method, which allows you to retrieve the attribute and read the properties it defines. These expose the values that were provided as constructor arguments. The GetClassAttribute method will return an instance of the attribute class (in this case a System.ObsoleteAttribute object) if the attribute has been applied or null if it has not. Once you have obtained an attribute object, you can read the properties it contains, as demonstrated in the example.

If you want to test to see whether a class has been modified with an attribute but you don't have an object created from that class to work with, then you can use the versions of the TestForClassAttribute and GetClassAttribute methods that accept System.Type parameters. You use the typeof operator to get a System.Type, providing the name of the class you are interested in as a parameter. Here is an example of using typeof:

```
using System;

class TypeTest {

    static void Main(string[] args) {

        // create an Attribute Tester for the attribute we are interested in
        AttributeTester<ObsoleteAttribute> attrTester
            = new AttributeTester<ObsoleteAttribute>();

        // check to see whether the attribute has been defined using the class type
        bool classTest = attrTester.TestForClassAttribute(typeof(Calculator));
        if (classTest) {
            // the attribute is defined - get the instance of the attribute
            ObsoleteAttribute attr = attrTester.GetClassAttribute(typeof(Calculator));
            // write out the properties of the attribute
            Console.WriteLine("Attribute: message: {0}, error: {1}",
                attr.Message, attr.IsError);
        }

        // wait for input before exiting
```

```
        Console.WriteLine("Press enter to finish");
        Console.ReadLine();
    }
}
```

You can see that to get attributes in this way for the Calculator class, we must use typeof(Calculator) and pass the result as a parameter to the AttributeTester class methods. The result of both of these approaches is the same and is as follows:

```
Attribute: message: Don't use this class, error: False
Press enter to finish
```

Testing for an Attribute Applied to a Field

Testing for attributes applied to fields is a little more complicated because a class can have multiple fields. Here is an example of the Calculator class updated so that one of two fields has been modified with the Obsolete attribute:

```
using System;

class Calculator {
    [Obsolete("Don't use this field")]
    public const int MultiplierField = 20;
    public int OtherField;

    public int CalculateProduct(int x, int y) {
        return x + y;
    }
}
```

Listing 17-4 contains an AttributeTester<T> class that can test for attributes applied to a field.

Listing 17-4. Testing for Attributes Applied to a Field

```
using System;
using System.Collections.Generic;
using System.Linq;
using System.Reflection;

class AttributeTester<T> where T : Attribute {

    public bool TestForFieldAttribute(Type classType, string fieldName) {
        FieldInfo fieldInfo = classType.GetField(fieldName);
        return Attribute.IsDefined(fieldInfo, typeof(T));
    }

    public T GetFieldAttribute(Type classType, string fieldName) {
        FieldInfo fieldInfo = classType.GetField(fieldName);
        return Attribute.GetCustomAttribute(fieldInfo, typeof(T)) as T;
```

```
    }

    public string[] GetModifiedFields(Type classType) {
        IList<string> resultList = new List<string>();
        FieldInfo[] fields = classType.GetFields();
        foreach (FieldInfo fi in fields) {
            if (Attribute.IsDefined(fi, typeof(T))) {
                resultList.Add(fi.Name);
            }
        }
        return resultList.ToArray();
    }

    public bool TestForFieldAttribute(object obj, string fieldName) {
        return TestForFieldAttribute(obj.GetType(), fieldName);
    }

    public T GetFieldAttribute(object obj, string fieldName) {
        return GetFieldAttribute(obj.GetType(), fieldName);
    }

    public string[] GetModifiedFields(object obj) {
        return GetModifiedFields(obj.GetType());
    }
}
```

You need to know the name of the field that you want to test for, which you specify as a string parameter. Once again, I have included versions of the methods that work with object as well as System.Type parameters. Here is an example of testing for the Obsolete attribute on the field called MultiplierField:

```
using System;

class FieldTest {

    static void Main(string[] args) {

        // create an Attribute Tester for the attribute we are interested in
        AttributeTester<ObsoleteAttribute> attrTester
            = new AttributeTester<ObsoleteAttribute>();

        // check to see whether the attribute has been applied to a field
        bool fieldTest
            = attrTester.TestForFieldAttribute(typeof(Calculator), "MultiplierField");

        if (fieldTest) {
            // the attribute is defined - get the instance of the attribute
            ObsoleteAttribute attr
                = attrTester.GetFieldAttribute(typeof(Calculator), "MultiplierField");

            // write out the properties of the attribute
            Console.WriteLine("Attribute: message: {0}, error: {1}",
```

```
                attr.Message, attr.IsError);
        }

        // wait for input before exiting
        Console.WriteLine("Press enter to finish");
        Console.ReadLine();
    }
}
```

The output from this test is as follows:

```
Attribute: message: Don't use this field, error: False
Press enter to finish
```

You can use the `AttributeTester.GetModifiedFields` method if you want to get a list of names of fields that have been modified by a parameter. Here is an example:

```
using System;

class FieldTest {

    static void Main(string[] args) {

        // create an Attribute Tester for the attribute we are interested in
        AttributeTester<ObsoleteAttribute> attrTester
            = new AttributeTester<ObsoleteAttribute>();

        // get a list of the names of the fields that have been modified
        string[] modifiedFieldNames = attrTester.GetModifiedFields(typeof(Calculator));
        foreach (string s in modifiedFieldNames) {
            Console.WriteLine("Modified field: {0}", s);
        }

        // wait for input before exiting
        Console.WriteLine("Press enter to finish");
        Console.ReadLine();
    }
}
```

The output from this example is as follows:

```
Modified field: MultiplierField
Press enter to finish
```

You can see that the unmodified field called `OtherField` is omitted from the results, whereas the `MultiplierField`, which has been modified with the `Obsolete` attribute, is included.

Testing for an Attribute Applied to a Property

Testing for attributes applied to properties is very similar to testing for attributes applied to fields. Here is an example of the Obsolete attribute applied to a property:

```
using System;

class Calculator {

    [Obsolete("Don't use this property")]
    public int MyProperty {
        get;
        set;
    }

    public int CalculateProduct(int x, int y) {
        return x + y;
    }
}
```

Listing 17-5 contains an implementation of the AttributeTester<T> class, which lets you test for and retrieve attributes applied to properties and get a list of names of properties to which an attribute has been applied.

Listing 17-5. Testing for Attributes Applied to Properties

```
using System;
using System.Collections.Generic;
using System.Linq;
using System.Reflection;

class AttributeTester<T> where T : Attribute {

    public bool TestForPropertyAttribute(Type classType, string propertyName) {
        PropertyInfo propInfo = classType.GetProperty(propertyName);
        return Attribute.IsDefined(propInfo, typeof(T));
    }

    public T GetPropertyAttribute(Type classType, string propertyName) {
        PropertyInfo propInfo = classType.GetProperty(propertyName);
        return Attribute.GetCustomAttribute(propInfo, typeof(T)) as T;
    }

    public string[] GetModifiedProperties(Type classType) {
        IList<string> resultList = new List<string>();
        PropertyInfo[] props = classType.GetProperties();
        foreach (PropertyInfo pi in props) {
            if (Attribute.IsDefined(pi, typeof(T))) {
                resultList.Add(pi.Name);
            }
        }
```

```
        return resultList.ToArray();
    }
}
```

You need to know the name of the property you want to check, or you can use the
GetModifiedProperties method to get a list of names of properties to which the attribute has been
applied. Here is an example of using testing properties for attributes:

```
using System;

class Listing_03 {

    static void Main(string[] args) {

        // create an Attribute Tester for the attribute we are interested in
        AttributeTester<ObsoleteAttribute> attrTester
            = new AttributeTester<ObsoleteAttribute>();

        // check to see whether the attribute has been applied to a property
        bool propTest = attrTester.TestForPropertyAttribute(typeof(Calculator),
            "MyProperty");

        if (propTest) {
            // the attribute is defined - get the instance of the attribute
            ObsoleteAttribute attr = attrTester.GetPropertyAttribute(typeof(Calculator),
                "MyProperty");
            // write out the properties of the attribute
            Console.WriteLine("Attribute: message: {0}, error: {1}",
                attr.Message, attr.IsError);
        }

        // get a list of the names of the properties that have been modified
        string[] modifiedFieldNames = attrTester.GetModifiedProperties(typeof(Calculator));
        foreach (string s in modifiedFieldNames) {
            Console.WriteLine("Modified property: {0}", s);
        }

        // wait for input before exiting
        Console.WriteLine("Press enter to finish");
        Console.ReadLine();
    }
}
```

The output from this example is as follows:

```
Attribute: message: Don't use this property, error: False
Modified property: MyProperty
Press enter to finish
```

Testing for an Attribute Applied to a Method

Testing whether an attribute has been applied to a method is more complicated because there can be overloaded versions of a method, some of which have the attribute and some that don't. Here is an example of such a class:

```
using System;

class Calculator {

    [Obsolete("Don't use this method")]
    public int CalculateProduct(int x, int y) {
        return x + y;
    }

    public int CalculateProduct(params int[] values) {
        int result = 0;
        foreach (int i in values) {
            result += i;
        }
        return result;
    }
}
```

Listing 17-6 contains an implementation of the AttributeTester<T> class that you can use to test for attributes applied to methods. Listing 17-6 also contains a struct used to report on methods and their attributes.

Listing 17-6. Testing for Attributes Applied to Methods

```
using System;
using System.Collections.Generic;
using System.Linq;
using System.Reflection;

struct MethodAttributePair<T> {
    public string MethodSignature;
    public T Attribute;
}

class AttributeTester<T> where T : Attribute {

    public bool TestForMethodAttribute(Type classType, string methodName) {
        MethodInfo[] methods = classType.GetMethods();
        foreach (MethodInfo mi in methods) {
            if (mi.Name == methodName && Attribute.IsDefined(mi, typeof(T))) {
                return true;
            }
        }
        return false;
    }
```

```
public string[] GetModifiedMethodNames(Type classType) {
    IList<string> resultList = new List<string>();
    MethodInfo[] methods = classType.GetMethods();
    foreach (MethodInfo mi in methods) {
        if (Attribute.IsDefined(mi, typeof(T))) {
            resultList.Add(mi.ToString());
        }
    }
    return resultList.ToArray();
}

public MethodAttributePair<T>[] GetModifiedMethods(Type classType) {
    IList<MethodAttributePair<T>> resultList = new List<MethodAttributePair<T>>();
    MethodInfo[] methods = classType.GetMethods();
    foreach (MethodInfo mi in methods) {
        T attr = Attribute.GetCustomAttribute(mi, typeof(T)) as T;
        if (attr != null) {
            resultList.Add(new MethodAttributePair<T>() { Attribute = attr,
                MethodSignature = mi.ToString() });
        }
    }
    return resultList.ToArray();
}
}
```

Using this class to test methods for attributes is slightly different from testing other class members. The TestForMethodAttribute method will return true if any overloaded version of the method whose name you specify as the string parameter has been modified using the target attribute. The GetModifiedMethodNames method will return an array of strings describing the signature of any method in the class that has been modified with the target parameter. The GetModifiedMethods method returns an array of MethodAttributePair<T> struct values, each of which contains an attribute and the signature of the method it has been applied to. You can use this method to read the properties from the attributes. Here is an example of using the class in Listing 17-6:

```
using System;

class MethodTest {

    static void Main(string[] args) {

        // create an Attribute Tester for the attribute we are interested in
        AttributeTester<ObsoleteAttribute> attrTester
            = new AttributeTester<ObsoleteAttribute>();

        // check to see whether the attribute has been applied to a property
        bool methodTest = attrTester.TestForMethodAttribute(typeof(Calculator),
            "CalculateProduct");
        Console.WriteLine("At least one overloaded method has attribute: {0}", methodTest);

        // get a list of the names of the properties that have been modified
        string[] modifiedMethods = attrTester.GetModifiedMethodNames(typeof(Calculator));
        foreach (string s in modifiedMethods) {
```

```
                Console.WriteLine("Modified method: {0}", s);
            }

            // get a series of structs representing modified methods and their attributes
            MethodAttributePair<ObsoleteAttribute>[] mods
                = attrTester.GetModifiedMethods(typeof(Calculator));

            foreach (MethodAttributePair<ObsoleteAttribute> mp in mods) {
                Console.WriteLine("--- Method with Obsolete Attribute ---");
                Console.WriteLine("Method signature: {0}", mp.MethodSignature);
                Console.WriteLine("Attribute message: {0}", mp.Attribute.Message);
                Console.WriteLine("Attribute error: {0}", mp.Attribute.IsError);
            }

            // wait for input before exiting
            Console.WriteLine("Press enter to finish");
            Console.ReadLine();
        }
}
```

The output of this code is as follows:

```
At least one overloaded method has attribute: True
Modified method: Int32 CalculateProduct(Int32, Int32)
--- Method with Obsolete Attribute ---
Method signature: Int32 CalculateProduct(Int32, Int32)
Attribute message: Don't use this method
Attribute error: False
Press enter to finish
```

Creating a Custom Attribute

To create a new custom attribute, we create a class that is derived from System.Attribute. Listing 17-7 provides a demonstration.

Listing 17-7. Creating a Custom Attribute

```
using System;

public class DetailLevelAttribute : Attribute {

    public DetailLevelAttribute(bool useDetailed) {
        UseDetailed = useDetailed;
    }

    public bool UseDetailed {
        get;
        private set;
    }
```

}

We are going to create an attribute that will modify the way that a class creates string representations of itself. This is similar to the way that the Flags attribute works, but we are going to apply it to a custom class.

The attribute is called DetailLevel, and the class that implements the attribute is called DetailLevelAttribute. There is a constructor parameter that is used to set a public property called UseDetailed.

Using a Custom Attribute

We can apply the custom attribute to any class, but it only makes sense to do so for classes that understand the meaning of the attribute. Other classes will simply ignore it. Listing 17-8 contains a class that tests for the presence of the attribute.

Listing 17-8. Using a Custom Attribute in a Class

```
using System;

class Car {
    public string Manufacturer {get; set;}
    public string Model {get; set;}
    public string Color {get; set;}

    public Car(string manufacturer, string model, string color) {
        Manufacturer = manufacturer;
        Model = model;
        Color = color;
    }

    public sealed override string ToString() {
        // see whether the attribute has been applied to this class
        DetailLevelAttribute attr = Attribute.GetCustomAttribute(
            this.GetType(), typeof(DetailLevelAttribute)) as DetailLevelAttribute;

        if (attr != null && attr.UseDetailed) {
            // we need to provide a detailed string representation
            return string.Format("Manufacturer: {0}, Model: {1}, Color: {2}",
                Manufacturer, Model, Color);
        }
        // we don't have an attribute, or we do have an attribute, but the
        // UseDetailed property is set to false - call the base implementation
        // of this method
        return base.ToString();
    }
}
```

This class overrides the ToString method defined in the base class (System.Object). The derived version checks to see whether the attribute has been applied, and if it has and the constructor parameter has been set to true, then a more detailed string representation of the current Car object will be created.

If the attribute has not been applied or if it has been applied but the constructor argument is set to false, then the base class implementation of the ToString method is used.

We don't have to apply the attribute to the Car class, even though this is the class that knows the meaning of it. We can as easily apply it to a class derived from Car and get the desired result. Here is an example of a derived class that has been modified with the DetailLevel attribute:

```
[DetailLevel(true)]
class VolvoCar : Car {

    public VolvoCar(string model, string color) : base("Volvo", model, color) {
        // do nothing
    }
}
```

This class implements only a constructor. Note that it cannot override the base implementation of the ToString method. This is because I have modified the base implementation with the sealed keyword, which is described in Chapter 6. If the VolvoCar class were able to implement a new version of ToString, then we could end up with a base class that understands the meaning of the DetailLevel attribute and a derived class that ignores it. The following statements create an instance of the VolvoCar object and writes out a string representation of it:

```
using System;

class CustomAttributeTest {

    static void Main(string[] args) {

        VolvoCar myCar = new VolvoCar("C30", "Black");

        Console.WriteLine("Car: {0}", myCar);

        // wait for input before exiting
        Console.WriteLine("Press enter to finish");
        Console.ReadLine();
    }
}
```

The output from these statements is as follows:

```
Car: Manufacturer: Volvo, Model: C30, Color: Black
Press enter to finish
```

If I remove the attribute from the VolvoCar class and rerun the previous statements, I get the following results:

```
Car: VolvoCar
Press enter to finish
```

You can see the effect of the attribute in the string representations of the VolvoCar objects. When the attribute is present and the constructor argument is set to true, we get a string representation that contains more detail than when the attribute is not present.

Defining Properties in a Custom Attribute

When you create custom attributes, you also have to create the code that can detect them and read the values you have provided as constructor parameters. The normal way to do this is to create properties that are set using the constructor parameter values. This is what I did with the DetailLevel attribute in Listing 17-8.

It is important that the properties be read-only. If the value of the properties can be changed, then the meaning assigned to the class by the attribute will also be changed, leading to inconsistent and unexpected results. You can either make the set accessor of an automatically implemented property private so that it can be used only within the attribute class or use field-backed properties, which is demonstrated in Listing 17-9.

Listing 17-9. Using Field-Backed Properties in a Custom Attribute Class

```
using System;

public class DetailLevelAttribute : Attribute {
    private bool useDetailed;

    public DetailLevelAttribute(bool useDetailedParam) {
        useDetailed = useDetailedParam;
    }

    public bool UseDetailed {
        get { return useDetailed; }
    }
}
```

It doesn't matter which approach you use, just as long as the value of the properties cannot be modified.

Controlling How a Custom Attribute Can Be Used

As it stands, our custom attribute can be applied anywhere—to classes, to fields, to methods, and so on. The meaning of our attribute is limited to classes, and we can restrict where our attribute can be used by applying attributes to it, specifically, the AttributeUsage attribute. It may seem odd to apply attributes to attributes, but it works rather well in practice. Listing 17-10 contains a demonstration of restricting the use of our custom attribute to classes.

Listing 17-10. Restricting the Use of a Custom Attribute

```
using System;

[AttributeUsage(AttributeTargets.Class)]
public class DetailLevelAttribute : Attribute {
```

```
    private bool useDetailed;

    public DetailLevelAttribute(bool useDetailedParam) {
        useDetailed = useDetailedParam;
    }

    public bool UseDetailed {
        get { return useDetailed; }
    }
}
```

To restrict where an attribute can be used, you pass values from the System.AttributeTarget enum. The Class value restricts the use of the DetailLevel attribute to classes. Table 17-2 describes the most commonly used values available for controlling attribute use.

Table 17-2. Values from the AttributeTarget Enum

Value	Description
Class	Attribute can be applied to classes
Struct	Attribute can be applied to structs
Enum	Attribute can be applied to enums
Constructor	Attribute can be applied to constructors
Method	Attributes can be applied to methods
Property	Attribute can be applied to properties
Field	Attribute can be applied to fields
Event	Attribute can be applied to events
Interface	Attribute can be applied to interfaces
Parameter	Attribute can be applied to parameters
Delegate	Attribute can be applied to delegates
Return Value	Attribute can be applied to return values
GenericParameter	Attribute can be applied to generic parameters
All	Attribute can be applied anywhere (this is the default)

You can combine values together using the logical OR operator (|). So, for example, if you wanted to be able to apply the DetailLevel attribute to classes and structs (but nowhere else), then you would use the following:

```
[AttributeUsage(AttributeTargets.Class | AttributeTargets.Struct)]
public class DetailLevelAttribute : Attribute {
...
```

Controlling Attribute Inheritance

When you define a custom attribute, you can control whether a derived class inherits the application of that attribute from a base class. This is done by setting the Inherited property on the AttributeUsage attribute to true. Listing 17-11 contains a demonstration.

Listing 17-11. Controlling Attribute Application Inheritance

```
using System;

[AttributeUsage(AttributeTargets.Class, Inherited=true ) ]
public class DetailLevelAttribute : Attribute {
    private bool useDetailed;

    public DetailLevelAttribute(bool useDetailedParam) {
        useDetailed = useDetailedParam;
    }

    public bool UseDetailed {
        get { return useDetailed; }
    }
}
```

When Inherited is set to true, base classes pass on their DetailLevel attribute to derived classes. Here is an example of two classes, where the base class has the DetailLevel attribute applied:

```
[DetailLevel(true)]
class VolvoCar : Car {

    public VolvoCar(string model, string color)
        : base("Volvo", model, color) {
        // do nothing
    }
}

class VolvoC30 : VolvoCar {

    public VolvoC30(string color)
        : base("C30", color) {
        // do nothing
    }
}
```

Even though the VolvoC30 class doesn't have the DetailLevel attribute, we still get results as though it had. Here is a simple test:

```
using System;

class CustomAttributeTest {

    static void Main(string[] args) {

        VolvoC30 myCar = new VolvoC30("Black");

        Console.WriteLine("Car: {0}", myCar);

        // wait for input before exiting
        Console.WriteLine("Press enter to finish");
        Console.ReadLine();
    }
}
```

The result of this test is as follows:

```
Car: Manufacturer: Volvo, Model: C30, Color: Black
Press enter to finish
```

If we change the value of Inherited to false and run the test again, we get the following results:

```
Car: VolvoC30
Press enter to finish
```

As you can see, changing the specification of the custom attribute causes the derived class to revert to the base string representation, just as though the attribute had not been applied.

Summary

In this chapter, we saw how the .NET attribute system allows you to apply modifiers to your custom types without having to add new keywords to C#. We started by looking at two of the built-in attributes, and I described how an attribute doesn't have value until some other part of the system gives it meaning. In the examples we looked at, the meaning was provided by a method in a base class and the C# compiler.

We saw how to create and apply custom attributes and how to use reflection techniques to test to see whether attributes have been applied. This introduced topics that are covered fully in Chapter 23. The .NET Framework contains dozens of attributes, but they need to be described in context. We'll see some of the most useful when we come to Chapter 23, and others are used in LINQ, the Entity Framework, and other applied .NET technologies.

Garbage Collection

One of the most useful features of C# (and .NET more generally) is automatic memory management. When you create a new object, the memory required to store it is allocated automatically. You don't need to do anything specific when you have finished working with the object. The .NET runtime takes care of releasing the memory that the object was using for you.

The part of the .NET runtime that handles releasing memory is called the *garbage collector* (GC), and it generally works without you being aware that it is there and without you having to intervene in its operation. There are times, however, when an understanding of garbage collection can be useful, and there are some explicit steps you can take to help the garbage collector work more effectively.

In this chapter, we look at how you modify your classes to work with the garbage collector. The garbage collector runs as part of your program within the .NET runtime. You don't need to enable it, and you don't need to configure it; it is enabled automatically when you start your program.

When the garbage collector is in operation, it is said to be performing a *run*. It only runs periodically. The rest of the time it waits until it needs to run again. When it runs, the garbage collector looks for objects that you have created that are no longer used and deletes them from memory. An object is no longer used if there are no references to it, meaning that there are no local variables or fields that refer to the object.

The garbage collector runs when the amount of free memory is low, when your program exits, or when you explicitly tell it to run. I'll show you how to do this later in the chapter.

Except for the specific features in this chapter, you don't need to worry about the details of garbage collection. The internals of garbage collection are an advanced topic and beyond the scope of this book, but, for the most part, you are unlikely to need to know anything more about the garbage collector than it exists for most C# projects. Part of the magic of the garbage collector is that it is almost entirely invisible and frees you from having to manage memory yourself. Table 18-1 provides the summary for this chapter.

Table 18-1. Quick Problem/Solution Reference for Chapter 18

Problem	Solution	Listings
Explicitly run the garbage collector.	Call the `System.GC.Collect` method	18-1
Release resources or generally tidy up an object before it is destroyed by the garbage collector.	Implement a destructor or implement the `System.IDisposable` interface.	18-2, 18-3

Problem	Solution	Listings
Force the Dispose method of an object that implements the IDisposable interface to be called when the object is no longer required.	Use the using keyword.	18-4
Create a reference that is invisible to the garbage collector and that will not prevent an object from being destroyed.	Use a weak reference.	18-5

Explicitly Running the Garbage Collector

You can run the garbage collector manually by calling the static System.GC.Collect method. I recommend that you don't do this in your projects, relying instead on the garbage collector to decide when it needs to run. For the examples in this chapter, I want to be able to demonstrate the effect of garbage collection without having to wait for it to occur naturally, so I will be using this method. Listing 18-1 contains a simple demonstration of calling the Collect method.

Listing 18-1. Explicitly Running the Garbage Collector

```
using System;

class Listing_01 {

    static void Main(string[] args) {

        // run the garbage collector
        GC.Collect();

        // wait for input before exiting
        Console.WriteLine("Press enter to finish");
        Console.ReadLine();
    }
}
```

You might be tempted to run the garbage collector like this yourself. I really recommend that you don't, but if you believe you have no choice, you should take the time to understand how the collector works and what the impact of manual collection will be on your program.

Implementing a Destructor

Some objects need to perform actions before they can be safely destroyed; the most common examples are where connections to databases and other servers need to be explicitly closed. The actions you take will depend on your object, but whatever it is you need to do can be included in a *destructor*.

A destructor is a special method that is called after the garbage collector has identified an object as being unused but before it is deleted from memory. Listing 18-2 contains a class with a destructor.

Listing 18-2. Defining a Class Destructor

```
using System;

class MyClass {

    public MyClass() {
        // constructor statements
        Console.WriteLine("Constructor called");
    }

    ~MyClass() {
        // destructor statements
        Console.WriteLine("Destructor called");
    }
}
```

A class destructor is a special method that is named after the class that it destructs, prepended with a tilde character (~), as illustrated by Figure 18-1.

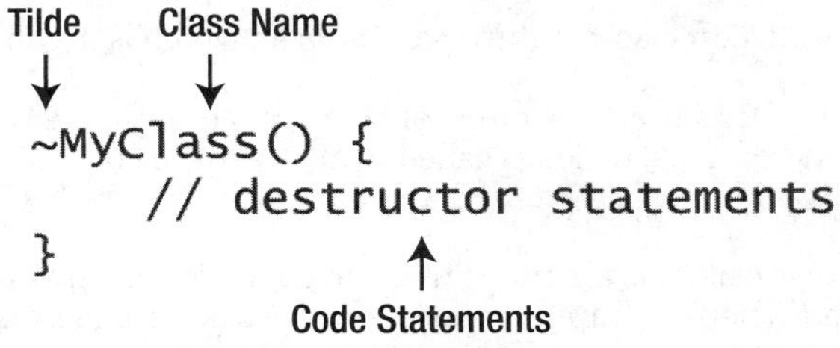

Figure 18-1. The anatomy of a destructor

When you define a destructor, you must not use an access modifier or add parameters to the method. In the code statement block, you can add statements to release any resources and generally tidy up prior to the destruction of your object.

Here is a simple example that causes the destructor to be called:

```
using System;

class DestructorTest {

    static void Main(string[] args) {
```

```
        // create a new MyClass object, but don't assign
        // it to a variable or field
        new MyClass();

        // manually invoke the GC
        GC.Collect();

        // wait for input before exiting
        Console.WriteLine("Press enter to finish");
        Console.ReadLine();
    }
}
```

This code creates a new MyClass object but doesn't assign it to a local variable or field. This means that there are no references to the object, and it will be identified as a candidate for destruction by the garbage collector, which I explicitly call. The results of compiling and running these statements are as follows:

```
Constructor called
Press enter to finish
Destructor called
```

The garbage collector runs in the background of a .NET process, which is why the output from the destructor method comes after the Press enter to finish output.

Destructors vs. Finalizers

If you read the C# and .NET documentation, you will come across the term *finalizer*, which is used in much the same way as the term *destructor*.

The confusion arises because .NET objects can be written in a range of languages (C#, VB.NET, and so on). All of these objects inherit a method called Finalize, which is called by the garbage collector immediately prior to an object's destruction. This is known as *finalizing* an object. This is a .NET feature that applies to all .NET languages.

C# implements finalization using destructors. C# objects are not allowed to override the Finalize method and must implement a destructor instead. The C# compiler interprets a destructor and uses the code statements it contains to create a Finalize method for your class automatically. As an example, when the C# compiler sees a destructor like this:

```
~MyClass() {
    // destructor statements
    Console.WriteLine("Destructor called");
}
```

it converts it to a Finalize method like this:

```
protected override void Finalize() {
    try {
        // destructor statements
```

```
        Console.WriteLine("Destructor called");
    } finally {
        base.Finalize()
    }
}
```

You can see from this that your destructor doesn't need to call the Finalize method and that you can ignore the directive in the documentation to call the base class implementation of the Finalize method (because this is done for you when your destructor is compiled).

Problems with Destructors

Destructors must be used with care; there are some important considerations explained in the following sections.

Performance Impact

The first problem with destructors is that they have an impact on the performance of the garbage collector, which has to stop and perform the code statements your constructor contains. For this reason, you should not use destructors that are empty (that is, that do not contain code statements) and should use destructors only when they are essential.

Uncertain Execution

For most programs, the garbage collector is invisible. It decides when it needs to run, and it does so without your code being aware that collection is taking place. When you are using destructors, this uncertainty means you don't know when the statements in your destructor will be performed. Worse, if your program doesn't exit properly, the statements in the destructors won't be performed at all.

There are no guarantees available for destructors. The .NET Framework will make a good faith attempt to execute them, but you cannot rely on this or predict when it might happen. Taking matters into your own hands by explicitly invoking a collection will generally make things worse and kill the performance of your program.

If you have cleanup statements that you need performed at a specific moment, then you should consider implementing a disposal method, which is described in the "Using Disposal" section later in this chapter.

Uncertain Ordering

The garbage collector doesn't call the destructors in any particular order, so you cannot rely on objects being destroyed in the order in which they were created. You must write your destructors defensively, making no assumptions about the state of other objects.

Using Disposal

You can avoid some of the uncertainty of finalization by using a slightly different technique called *disposal*. To use disposal, your class must implement the System.IDisposable interface. Listing 18-3 demonstrates a class that implements this interface.

Listing 18-3. Implementing the IDisposable Interface

```
using System;

class MyClass : IDisposable {

    public MyClass() {
        // constructor statements
        Console.WriteLine("Constructor called");
    }

    public void DoSomeWork() {
        Console.WriteLine("Doing some work...");
    }

    public void Dispose() {
        // disposal statements
        Console.WriteLine("Dispose method called");
    }
}
```

The System.IDisposable interface defines a single method, called Dispose. When we are done with an object created from the MyClass class, we can call the Dispose method to release any resources that the object has been using. Here is an example:

```
using System;

class DisposalTest {

    static void Main(string[] args) {

        // create a new MyClass object
        MyClass myClass = new MyClass();

        // do some work with the object we created
        myClass.DoSomeWork();

        // call the dispose method
        myClass.Dispose();

        // wait for input before exiting
        Console.WriteLine("Press enter to finish");
        Console.ReadLine();
    }
}
```

In this example, I create an object from the MyClass class, I do some work with it, and, when I no longer want to use the object, I call the Dispose method. Here is the output from compiling and running these statements:

```
Constructor called
Doing some work...
Dispose method called
Press enter to finish
```

Instead of manually calling the Dispose method, you can use the using keyword to define the scope in which you will use an object. Listing 18-4 contains a demonstration.

Listing 18-4. Limiting Scope with the using Keyword

```csharp
using System;

class Listing_04 {

    static void Main(string[] args) {

        // create a new MyClass object
        MyClass myClass = new MyClass();

        using (myClass) {

            // do some work with the object we created
            myClass.DoSomeWork();

        }

        // wait for input before exiting
        Console.WriteLine("Press enter to finish");
        Console.ReadLine();
    }
}
```

The using keyword is shown in bold in Listing 18-4. When the .NET runtime reaches the end of the using statement code block, the Dispose method is called on the object that we provided as a parameter, in this case, the object created from the MyClass class. Here are the results of compiling and running Listing 18-4:

```
Constructor called
Doing some work...
Dispose method called
Press enter to finish
```

Using Weak References

The garbage collector will only destroy objects if there are no references to it, meaning that no local variable or field refers to that object. Sometimes, it can be useful to use references that are effectively invisible to the garbage collector, which means that the objects they refer to will *always* be candidates to be destroyed. Such references are called *weak references*, while regular references are called *strong references*.

A common use of weak references is in a data cache. A cache is a temporary store of data that can be obtained or generated again but that is stored because generating it takes time (or incurs some other cost) and that we expect to need again (typically because we expect another user to request the same data items that we have cached). We want the performance benefits that a cache can bring, but we don't want it to tie up all of our system memory, so rather than have to actively manage the data in the cache, we can use weak references. Listing 18-5 contains a demonstration of using a weak reference.

Listing 18-5. Using a Weak Reference

```
using System;

class MyClass {

    public MyClass() {
        // constructor statements
        Console.WriteLine("Constructor called");
    }

    ~MyClass() {
        // destructor statement
        Console.WriteLine("Destructor called");
    }

    public void DoSomeWork() {
        Console.WriteLine("Doing some work...");
    }
}

class Listing_05 {

    static void Main(string[] args) {

        // create a weak reference
        WeakReference weakRef = new WeakReference(new MyClass());

        // use the weak reference to access the object and so some work
        if (weakRef.IsAlive) {
            ((MyClass)weakRef.Target).DoSomeWork();
        }

        // run the garbage collector
        GC.Collect();

        // test to see if the weak reference is still alive
```

```
        Console.WriteLine("Still alive? {0}", weakRef.IsAlive);

        // wait for input before exiting
        Console.WriteLine("Press enter to finish");
        Console.ReadLine();
    }
}
```

Weak references are created using the System.WeakReference class. You create a new instance and pass the object you want a weak reference to as the constructor parameter. You must be careful to ensure that there are no strong references to the object. If there is, the strong reference will prevent the garbage collector from destroying the object when it runs, making the use of the weak reference meaningless.

Because you cannot tell when the garbage collector has destroyed your weak references object, you must test to see whether it is available using the WeakReference.IsAlive property, which will return true if the object still exists and false if it has been destroyed.

You can access the object through the Target property. You will need to cast the result to a derived type, as demonstrated by Listing 18-5. Once again, you must be careful not to create any strong references to the object. Compiling and running Listing 18-5 produces the following results:

```
Constructor called
Doing some work...
Still alive? False
Press enter to finish
Destructor called
```

Summary

In this short chapter, we looked at how you can modify your classes to ensure that resources are released properly and that objects have a chance to tidy themselves up before they are destroyed by the garbage collector. We also looked at weak references, which allow you to create objects that are always candidates for destruction by the garbage collector.

PART 3

■ ■ ■

The .NET Class Library

The libraries of a new programming language are the means by which you build useful applications. You need to understand the language, but if you don't know the libraries, then you have to write every feature you require from scratch. C# relies on the .NET Framework Class Library, which contains thousands of classes that support everything from networking to data management and from parallel programming to databases. In this part of the book, I will show you some of the most useful parts of the library and demonstrate how they can be used to solve common problems.

In Chapter 19, we tour the collection classes, which are a consistent way to group related C# objects; there are very few C# programs written that don't involve at least one collection. In Chapter 20, I show you the support that .NET provides for working with the file system and all things I/O. This leads nicely into Chapter 21, where I demonstrate some of the networking facilities that are available.

In Chapter 22, we'll look at measuring, expressing, and working with periods of time. Chapter 23 shows you how you can persist your C# objects so that they can continue to exist when your program isn't running.

Chapters 24 and 25 cover one of my two favorite C#/.NET features—parallel programming. Using the features described in this chapter will let you take advantage of the additional cores and processors in your computers and servers.

The final chapter in this part of the book, Chapter 26, contains some features and classes that are useful but that don't really fit anywhere else. Every programmer builds up a list of handy features and shortcuts that make life easier, and in this chapter I demonstrate some of mine.

CHAPTER 19

■ ■ ■

Collections

You will find that you have more and more objects to deal with as your program gets bigger and more complex. And, to make things worse, you will find that as you write increasingly complex code, the number of things you can take for granted starts to diminish. In a simple application, you can create arrays to keep track of objects. You know that there will be exactly ten products to track, so you create an array with ten slots. You know which product object will be in each slot, because there are only ten objects. You'll probably have a sticky note on your desk that has the list. Index 0 is this product, index 1 is that product, and so on.

And that's great—until one day you have to deal with 11 products, or 1,000. Or, much more likely, you won't know how many products there will be when you write the code. The classes I describe in this chapter can help you. They're called the *collection classes* or just *collections*, and they allow you gather together related objects. There are two main advantages to using collection classes. The first is that you don't need to know how many items you are dealing with when you create them. The second is that different types of collection store data in different ways; some are just like arrays, while others impose some kind of ordering on the items that have been collected, or map one object to another, so that you can store key/value pairs. As we go through this chapter, I'll show you each of the collection classes in turn.

The collection classes rely on the C# generic types feature that I described in Chapter 15. If you haven't read that chapter yet, you should do so now. It will help you make sense of the <T> notation that is used throughout this chapter.

■ **Note** The classes I describe in this chapter are not safe for parallel programming. See Chapter 24 for details of how to use the concurrent collection classes (which have been specifically designed for parallel programming) or the steps you can take to use the classes in this chapter safely.

Table 19-1 provides the problem/solution summary for this chapter. I'll show you the most important members and how to use them for each of the main collection interfaces and classes. Collections are exceptionally useful, and you will find yourself using them frequently. This is a chapter that is worth reading carefully to ensure you understand how each of the collection types differs and where they can best be used in your programs.

Table 19-1. Quick Problem/Solution Reference for Chapter 19

Problem	Solution	Listings
Replace an array with as few changes as possible.	Use the `List<T>` class.	19-1 through 19-15
Create a linked list.	Use the `LinkedList<T>` class.	19-16 through 19-18
Create a list where the items are stored in a sorted order.	Use the `SortedList<T>` class.	19-19, 19-20
Work with key/value pairs.	Use the `Dictionary<TKey, TVal>` class.	19-21 through 19-23
Work with key/value pairs where the keys are stored in a sorted order.	Use the `SortedDictionary<TKey, TVal>` class.	19-24
Compare collections as sets.	Use the `ISet<T>` interface, which is implemented by the `HashSet<T>` and `SortedSet<T>` classes.	19-25 through 19-27
Create queues and stacks.	Use the `Queue<T>` and `Stack<T>` classes.	19-28, 19-29
Implement custom sorting and equality checking.	Implement the `IComparer<T>` or `IEqualityComparer<T>` interfaces.	19-30, 19-31
Treat arrays as collections.	Use the static members of the `System.Array` class.	19-32, 19-33
Creating read-only collections.	Use the `List<T>.AsReadOnly` method or create a custom wrapper around another collection class.	19-34, 19-35
Create a collection that can hold all types of object.	Create a collection that is strongly typed to object. For example, use `List<object>` or use one of the legacy collections in the `System.Collections` namespace.	19-36

The classes that are the main focus of this chapter are collectively called the *generic collections.* Generic collections are strongly typed, meaning that they contain a collection of objects, all of which are the same type. If you want to be able to collect objects of different types, you can either create a collection that works on instance of object or use the legacy collection classes that were created before the generics feature was added to C#. The legacy collections are described later in this chapter.

The generic collections are the ones that you are likely to use most often. They are simple, they are fast, and the strong typing makes them easy to use because you don't have to check the type of the items you are adding and removing from the collections. There are a range of classes available for different collection types, and there are a set of interfaces that let you work with collections without needing to know which specific class has been created.

My focus in this chapter is the collection classes themselves, but the Language Integrated Query to Objects (LINQ to Objects) feature lets you perform complex queries using collections as the data source. See Chapter 27 for more information on LINQ to Objects. Unless otherwise noted, all classes and interfaces are found in the System.Collections.Generic namespace, which is part of the mscorlib assembly.

The ICollection<T> Interface

All the generic collection classes implement the ICollection<T> interface, which defines the basic methods that you need to work with a collection irrespective of the implementation class. Table 19-2 summarizes the members of ICollection<T>.

Table 19-2. The Members of the ICollection<T> Interface

Member	Description
Add(T)	Adds an instance of T to the collection
Clear()	Removes all the items from the collection
Contains(T)	Returns true if the collection contains a given instance of T
CopyTo(T[], int)	Copies the contents of the collection to an array starting at the specified index
Count	Returns the number of items in the collection
GetEnumerator()	Returns an IEnumerator<T> that yields the collected items
IsReadOnly	Returns true if the collection is read-only and false if modifications can be made
Remove(T)	Removes an instance of T from the collection

The ICollection<T> contains the core functionality shared by all the generic collections, allowing you to work with a collection without knowing (or caring) what specific implementation is being used. Listing 19-1 shows the ICollection<T> interface being used to manipulate a List<T>, a class that we'll come to in the next section.

Listing 19-1. Using the ICollection<T> Interface

```
using System;
using System.Collections.Generic;

namespace Listing_01 {
```

```
class Listing_01 {
    static void Main(string[] args) {

        // create a new collection
        ICollection<string> coll = new List<string>();

        // add some items
        coll.Add("apple");
        coll.Add("orange");

        // check to see if a value is in the collection
        Console.WriteLine("Contains 'apple': {0}", coll.Contains("apple"));
        Console.WriteLine("Contains 'cherry': {0}", coll.Contains("cherry"));

        // copy to an array
        string[] arr = new string[coll.Count];
        coll.CopyTo(arr, 0);

        // enumerate the collection contents
        foreach (string str in coll) {
            Console.WriteLine("Collection item: {0}", str);
        }

        // print out the collection count
        Console.WriteLine("Count: {0}", coll.Count);

        // clear the contents of the collection
        coll.Clear();

        // wait for input before exiting
        Console.WriteLine("Press enter to finish");
        Console.ReadLine();
    }
}
}
```

The ICollection<T> has limited functionality because it contains only those functions that are common to all the generic collections. In effect, it trades features in favor of flexibility. If you require more specific functionality, you can work directly with a collection class or, as you'll see shortly, with the intermediate interface classes that bridge the gap between ICollection<T> and the collections themselves, such as the IList<T> interface that we discuss in the next section.

Generic Lists

When you enumerate the contents of a list, the items are returned in the order in which they are added. This is because lists are first-in, first-out (FIFO) collections. In fact, working with lists is very similar to working with an array, with the benefit that you don't have to decide in advance how many elements there will be. Lists are widely used because of their similarity to arrays, a form of collecting data that most programmers are familiar with.

The IList<T> Interface

IList<T> is derived from ICollection<T> and is one of the intermediate interfaces I mentioned earlier. It contains additional members that are common to working with lists. There still isn't access to all the features of the collection class, but it does manage to maintain a degree of abstraction, which can be a good balance. The members of the IList<T> interface are summarized in Table 19-3.

Table 19-3. *The Members of the IList<T> Interface*

Member	Description
Item	An indexer that gets or sets values at a given index. Throws an exception if the index is out of range for the collection.
IndexOf(T)	Returns an int for the index of a specific instance of T if it is in the collection or -1 if the instance is not part of the collection.
Insert(int, T)	Inserts an instance of T into the collection at a given index, represented by an int.
RemoveAt(int)	Removes the element at the specific index from the collection.

As you can see from the table, the members of the IList<T> interface are designed to make using a list just as easy as using an array. Listing 19-2 shows how to use the interface to work with a list. The example uses the List<T> class, but the point of the IList<T> interface is that you can work with any of the generic lists without caring which implementation you are using.

Listing 19-2. Using the IList<T> Interface to Work with Generic Lists

```
using System;
using System.Collections.Generic;

namespace Listing_02 {
    class Listing_02 {
        static void Main(string[] args) {

            // create a new list
            IList<string> list = new List<string>();

            // add new items with the Add method
            list.Add("apple");
            list.Add("orange");
            list.Add("cherry");

            // use the indexer to set the third value
            list[2] = "mango";

            // insert an item at the head of the list
            list.Insert(0, "banana");
```

```
                // remove an item
                list.RemoveAt(2);

                // enumerate the items in the list
                foreach (string str in list) {
                    Console.WriteLine("List item: {0}", str);
                }

                // check for items in the list
                Console.WriteLine("Index of {0}: {1}", "apple",
                    list.IndexOf("apple"));
                Console.WriteLine("Index of {0}: {1}", "apricot",
                    list.IndexOf("apricot"));

                // wait for input before exiting
                Console.WriteLine("Press enter to finish");
                Console.ReadLine();
            }
        }
    }
```

The code in Listing 19-2 is pretty simple. We create a new instance of the List<string> class (which I describe later in this section), assign it to a variable of the type IList<string>, and then use the Add method to put three items in the collection.

We then use the indexer to change the value of the item at index 2. Note that the list is really like an array; you can't use the indexer to get or set index values that don't exist. If I had tried to set the item in location 10, I would have gotten an exception because there are only four items in the collection.

We then use the Insert method to place an item at the first position in the list. This has the effect of pushing all the other items back so that the item that was at index 0 is now at index 1, for example.

Using the Remove method, we remove the item at index 2. Because IList<T> implements the IEnumerable<T> interface, we can enumerate the contents using the foreach loop, which is what we do.

Finally, we use the IndexOf method to get the position of two data elements—one that exists and one that doesn't. Compiling and running the code in Listing 19-1 gives the following result:

```
List item: banana
List item: apple
List item: mango
Index of apple: 1
Index of apricot: -1
Press enter to finish
```

The List<T> Collection

The List<T> class is the most commonly used of the generic collection classes. The data items are contained in an array, which is resized as needed to accommodate the collected data. The class has three constructors, which are described in Table 19-4.

Table 19-4. Constructors for List<T>

Constructor	Description
List<T>()	Creates a new instance with no initial capacity. That is, the array used to collect the data starts as a zero-length array and is resized when the first item is added.
List<T>(IEnumerable<T>)	Creates a new instance that is populated with the items in the IEnumerable<T>.
List<T>(int)	Creates a new instance with a specified initial capacity.

If you have an idea of how many elements will be in the collection, you can improve the performance of using the collection by using the constructor that lets you specify an initial capacity. Each time the number of data elements in the collection exceeds the size of the internal array, a larger array has to be created, and the contents of the collection are copied to it.

In the previous section, we saw the IList<T> interface can be used to work with a list without knowing what kind of list it is. The disadvantage of using the interface is that you can't use the implementation-specific features, and when it comes to the List<T> class, there is so much functionality available that you may want to consider working with the type directly. So many features are available that I have broken them down into sections based on the kind of activity they support.

Adding, Retrieving, and Removing Items

List<T> adds a number of convenience methods for adding and removing items and extracting ranges of items from the collection. Table 19-5 summarizes these methods.

Table 19-5. Members for Adding, Retrieving and Removing Items

Member	Description
AddRange(IEnumerable<string>)	Appends the contents of an IEnumerable<T> to the collection
GetRange(int, int)	Returns a List<T> containing a subset of the items in the collection
InsertRange(int, IEnumerable<string>)	Inserts the contents of an IEnumerable<T> into the collection at a specified index
RemoveRange(int, int)	Removes a subset of items from the collection

Listing 19-3 demonstrates using these methods to add, obtain, and remove items. These methods exist in addition to those of the IList<T> and ICollection<T> interfaces, so you can still use the Add and Insert methods and get and set values using the indexer, for example.

Listing 19-3. Adding, Getting, and Removing List<T> Items

```
using System;
using System.Collections.Generic;

namespace Listing_03 {
    class Listing_03 {
        static void Main(string[] args) {

            // create two lists, specifying the initial elements
            List<string> list1 = new List<string>() { "apple", "orange"};
            List<string> list2 = new List<string>() { "cherry", "mango"};

            // use the add range method to add the
            // contents of one list to the other
            list1.AddRange(list2);

            // enumerate the contents of the list
            writeList("Combined List", list1);

            // use the GetRange method
            List<string> rangelist = list1.GetRange(1, 2);
            writeList("GetRange List", rangelist);

            // use the InsertRange method
            list1.InsertRange(1, rangelist);
            writeList("InsertRange List", list1);

            // remove a specific item
            list1.Remove("orange");
            writeList("Removed value orange", list1);

            // use RemoveRange
            list1.RemoveRange(0, 3);
            writeList("RemoveRange List", list1);

            // wait for input before exiting
            Console.WriteLine("Press enter to finish");
            Console.ReadLine();
        }

        private static void writeList(string msg, List<string> list) {
            Console.WriteLine(msg);
            foreach (string str in list) {
                Console.WriteLine("List item: {0}", str);
            }
        }
    }
}
```

Listing 19-3 demonstrates how to specify the initial data elements for the collection at construction. You can see this when I create the List<T> instances list1 and list2. This is a very useful feature for small sets of data, such as we will use in the examples in this chapter. Compiling and running the code in Listing 19-3 gives us the following results:

```
Combined List
List item: apple
List item: orange
List item: cherry
List item: mango
GetRange List
List item: orange
List item: cherry
InsertRange List
List item: apple
List item: orange
List item: cherry
List item: orange
List item: cherry
List item: mango
Removed value orange
List item: apple
List item: cherry
List item: orange
List item: cherry
List item: mango
RemoveRange List
List item: cherry
List item: mango
Press enter to finish
```

Finding List Items

The List<T> class has a number of methods that help you find data in the collection. I tend not to use these methods, preferring to use LINQ to Objects, which you can learn more about in Chapter 27. Nonetheless, these methods can be useful and, because they are tailored to the implementation of the List<T> class, offer a high-performance alternative to LINQ. The methods are summarized in Table 19-6.

Table 19-6. Members for Finding List Items

Member	Description
BinarySearch(T) BinarySearch(T, IComparer(T)) BinarySearch(int, int, T, IComparer(T))	Uses a binary search algorithm to return the index of a specified item in the list

Member	Description
Exists(Predicate(<T>)	Returns true if there is at least one element in the list for which the predicate returns true
Find(Predicate<T>)	Returns the first item in the list for which the predicate returns true
FindAll(Predicate<T>)	Returns a List<T> containing all the items in the list for which the specified predicate returns true
FindIndex(Predicate<T>)) FindIndex(int, Predicate<T>) FindIndex(int, int, Predicate<T>)	Returns the index of the first element in the list for which the predicate returns true
FindLast(Predicate<T>)	Returns the last item in the list for which the predicate returns true
FindLastIndex(Predicate<T>) FindLastIndex(int, Predicate<T>) FindLastIndex(int, int, Predicate<T>)	Returns the index of the last item in the list for which the predicate returns true
LastIndexOf(T) LastIndexOf(T, int) LastIndexOf(T, int, int)	Returns the index of the last occurrence of a given item in the list

Finding Items Using Binary Searches

Using the BinarySearch method is a very efficient way of finding an element in the list, but it requires that the elements in the collection are in order. You can either insert the elements in order as you create or build the collection, or you can collect the items in any order and then use the Sort method, which I describe in the following section. Listing 19-4 shows the BinarySearch method in action.

Listing 19-4. Using the BinarySearch Method

```
using System;
using System.Collections.Generic;

namespace Listing_04 {
    class Listing_04 {

        static void Main(string[] args) {
```

```
List<string> list = new List<string>() {
    "apple", "apricot", "banana", "cherry",
    "mango", "orange", "pear"};

int index1 = list.BinarySearch("orange");
Console.WriteLine("Index 1: {0}", index1);

int index2 = list.BinarySearch("papaya");
Console.WriteLine("Index 2 : {0} {1}", index2, ~index2);

// wait for input before exiting
Console.WriteLine("Press enter to finish");
Console.ReadLine();
        }
    }
}
```

The BinarySearch method depends on the IComparer<T> interface, which I describe later in this chapter. The BinarySearch overload that takes one argument uses the default IComparer<T>, while the other two overloads let you specify the comparer to use. Compiling and running the code in Listing 19-4 gives the following results:

```
Index 1: 5
Index 2 : -7 6
Press enter to finish
```

If the value you are looking for is in the collection, the BinarySearch method returns the index it occupies in the list. You can see this when I search for orange, which gives me a result of 5, indicating that orange is the sixth element in the list (the index is zero-based).

If the value you are looking for is not in the collection, then the result will be negative. If you NOT the result with the NOT operator (~), you will get the index of the first element in the list, which is greater than the item you were looking for. You can use this value to insert the item you searched for and preserve the ordering of the list. In the listing, I search for papaya, which is not in the collection. The result I receive is negative (-7), and the NOT result of this value is 6, meaning that if I call this:

```
list.Insert(6, "papaya");
```

the order of the list will be preserved, and I can conduct further binary searches without having to sort the data. The BinarySearch method will return unpredictable results if you use it on unsorted data.

The data in the example is sorted alphabetically, but you can search data that has been sorted using a different approach by providing an implementation of the IComparer<T> interface as an argument to the BinarySearch method. I show you how to sort and search using this interface in the "Sorting List Items" section later in the chapter.

Finding Items Using Predicates

Many of the List<T> methods for finding items use predicates, so you can provide arbitrary conditions for your searches. As a reminder, a Predicate<T> is a specialized form of delegate that receives an instance of T as an argument and returns true if the conditions defined by the predicate are met. You can create predicates explicitly or use a lambda expression to get the same effect. Listing 19-5 demonstrates both approaches used on the Exists method.

Listing 19-5. Using Predicates with the Exists Method

```
using System;
using System.Collections.Generic;

namespace Listing_05 {
    class Listing_05 {

        static void Main(string[] args) {

            // create the list collection
            List<string> list = new List<string>() {
                "apple", "apricot", "banana", "cherry",
                "mango", "orange", "pear"};

            // create a predicate that uses the
            // PredicateExample method
            Predicate<string> p = new Predicate<string>(PredicateExample);

            // use the Exists method with the predicate
            bool result1 = list.Exists(p);

            // use the Exists method with a lambda expression

            bool result2 = list.Exists(s => s.Length == 6 && s[0] == 'b');

            // write out the results
            Console.WriteLine("Result1: {0}, Result2: {1}", result1, result2);

            // wait for input before exiting
            Console.WriteLine("Press enter to finish");
            Console.ReadLine();
        }

        static bool PredicateExample(string str) {
            return str.Length == 6 && str[0] == 'b';
        }
    }
}
```

In this example, I create a List<string> and populate it with the names of seven different fruits. I create a Predicate<string>, which uses the PredicateExample method. This method takes a string and returns true if there are six characters in the string and the first character is b.

The Exists method returns true if any of the elements in the list match the conditions in the predicate. This means that the predicate method is called for each element in the list until one of them returns true. In our example, this happens when we get to banana. I repeat this again using a lambda expression. Compiling and running the code in Listing 19-5 gives the following results:

```
Result1: True, Result2: True
Press enter to finish
```

The Find, FindAll, FindIndex, FindLast, and FindLastIndex methods all require predicates as arguments and do what their name suggests. Listing 19-6 shows these methods being used.

Listing 19-6. Using Other Predicate Methods

```csharp
using System;
using System.Collections.Generic;

namespace Listing_06 {
    class Listing_06 {

        static void Main(string[] args) {

            // create the list collection
            List<string> list = new List<string>() {
                "apple", "apricot", "banana", "cherry",
                "mango", "orange", "pear"};

            // create a predicate so we can resuse the
            // same instance in multiple method calls
            Predicate<string> p = new Predicate<string>(s => s[0] == 'a');

            // find the first matches with the predicate
            string item1 = list.Find(p);
            int index1 = list.FindIndex(p);

            // find the last matches with the predicate
            string item2 = list.FindLast(p);
            int index2 = list.FindLastIndex(p);

            // print out the results
            Console.WriteLine("Find: {0}, FindIndex: {1}", item1, index1);
            Console.WriteLine("FindLast: {0}, FindLastIndex: {1}", item2, index2);

            List<string> sublist = list.FindAll(p);
            // enumerate the sub-list
            foreach (string str in sublist) {
                Console.WriteLine("Sublist Item: {0}", str);
            }

            // wait for input before exiting
            Console.WriteLine("Press enter to finish");
            Console.ReadLine();
        }
    }
}
```

I've used the same predicate in all the searches. Unlike BinarySearch, the methods that use predicates don't require the list items to be sorted. Each item in the list is evaluated by the predicate in turn until a match is found. The odd-one-out method is FindAll, which returns a List<T> of items that match the predicate, rather than a single item or index. Compiling and running the code in Listing 19-6 gives the following results:

```
Find: apple, FindIndex: 0
FindLast: apricot, FindLastIndex: 1
Sublist Item: apple
Sublist Item: apricot
Press enter to finish
```

Finding Items with LastIndexOf

The final List<T> method for finding items is LastIndexOf, which is the complement to the IndexOf method defined in the IList<T> interface. The difference is that LastIndexOf works backward starting from the end of the list. Listing 19-7 demonstrates the use of this method.

Listing 19-7. Using the LastIndexOf Method

```
using System;
using System.Collections.Generic;

namespace Listing_07 {
    class Listing_07 {

        static void Main(string[] args) {

            // create the list collection
            List<string> list = new List<string>() {
                "apple", "apricot", "banana", "cherry",
                "mango", "orange", "apricot", "pear"};

            // find an item using IndexOf and LastIndexOf
            int index1 = list.IndexOf("apricot");
            int index2 = list.LastIndexOf("apricot");

            // write the results
            Console.WriteLine("IndexOf: {0}", index1);
            Console.WriteLine("LastIndexOf: {0}", index2);

            // wait for input before exiting
            Console.WriteLine("Press enter to finish");
            Console.ReadLine();
        }
    }
}
```

In this example, I have duplicated the apricot list item so that IndexOf and LastIndexOf will generate different results. Compiling and running the code in Listing 19-7 produces the following results:

```
IndexOf: 1
LastIndexOf: 6
```

Sorting List Items

The List<T> class includes two methods for changing the order of the items in the collection. These methods are described in Table 19-7.

Table 19-7. Members for Sorting List Items

Member	Description
Reverse() Reverse(int, int)	Reverses the order of the entire list or a specified region of the list
Sort() Sort(Comparison<T>) Sort(IComparer<T>) Sort(int, int, IComparer<T>)	Sorts the entire list or a region of the list, either using the default item comparer or using a custom comparer

The Reverse method simply reverses the order for all the items in the list or for a region that you specify. Listing 19-8 shows both overloads of the Reverse method.

Listing 19-8. Using the Reverse Method

```
using System;
using System.Collections.Generic;

namespace Listing_08 {
    class Listing_08 {

        static void Main(string[] args) {

            // create the list collection
            List<string> list = new List<string>() {
                "apple", "apricot", "banana", "cherry",
                "mango", "orange", "pear"};

            // reverse the order of the list
            list.Reverse();

            // enumerate the contents of the list
            Console.WriteLine("---Complete Reverse---");
            foreach (string s in list) {
```

```
                    Console.WriteLine("List item: {0}", s);
                }

                // reverse a part of the list
                list.Reverse(1, 5);

                // enumerate the contents of the list again
                Console.WriteLine("---Range Reverse---");
                foreach (string s in list) {
                    Console.WriteLine("List item: {0}", s);
                }

                // wait for input before exiting
                Console.WriteLine("Press enter to finish");
                Console.ReadLine();
            }
        }
    }
```

Using the Reverse method is very simple. The code in the example reverses all the items in the list and reverses a subset. Compiling and running the code in Listing 19-8 produces the following results:

```
---Complete Reverse---
List item: pear
List item: orange
List item: mango
List item: cherry
List item: banana
List item: apricot
List item: apple
---Range Reverse---
List item: pear
List item: apricot
List item: banana
List item: cherry
List item: mango
List item: orange
List item: apple
Press enter to finish
```

The Sort method places the items in the list in order. You can supply the code that will compare items so that can be sorted, or you can rely on the default comparison. When you rely on the default comparison, the Sort method uses Comparer<T>.Default as the comparer. This is the built-in comparison mechanism that supports the core .NET types. Listing 19-9 demonstrates using the default comparison implicitly and explicitly to demonstrate that they are the same.

Listing 19-9. Implicitly and Explicitly Using the Default Comparer

```
using System;
using System.Collections.Generic;
```

```
namespace Listing_09 {
    class Listing_09 {

        static void Main(string[] args) {

            // create the first list collection
            List<string> list1 = new List<string>() {
                "mango", "cherry", "apricot", "banana",
                "apple", "pear", "orange"};

            // create the second list
            List<string> list2 = new List<string>() {
                "mango", "cherry", "apricot", "banana",
                "apple", "pear", "orange"};

            // call the Sort() method on the first list
            list1.Sort();

            // explicitly use the default Comparer on the second list
            list2.Sort(Comparer<string>.Default);

            // enumerate the contents of the lists
            foreach (string s in list1) {
                Console.WriteLine("List 1 item: {0}", s);
            }
            foreach (string s in list2) {
                Console.WriteLine("List 2 item: {0}", s);
            }

            // wait for input before exiting
            Console.WriteLine("Press enter to finish");
            Console.ReadLine();
        }
    }
}
```

Compiling and running the code in Listing 19-9 gives the following results:

```
List 1 item: apple
List 1 item: apricot
List 1 item: banana
List 1 item: cherry
List 1 item: mango
List 1 item: orange
List 1 item: pear
List 2 item: apple
List 2 item: apricot
List 2 item: banana
List 2 item: cherry
List 2 item: mango
```

```
List 2 item: orange
List 2 item: pear
Press enter to finish
```

As you can see, Comparer<string>.Default compares strings such that the list is sorted alphabetically, and both lists have been sorted identically. If we want to sort the list using a different characteristic of the contents, say, the length of the string, we have to provide a custom comparison. We can do that by providing an implementation of either the IComparer<T> interface or the System.Comparison<T> delegate. I explain the IComparer<T> interface fully later in the chapter, but Listing 19-10 shows both techniques used to sort the strings in my fruit collection by length.

Listing 19-10. Custom List Sorting

```
using System;
using System.Collections.Generic;

namespace Listing_10 {
    class Listing_10 {

        static void Main(string[] args) {

            // create the first list collection
            List<string> list1 = new List<string>() {
                "mango", "cherry", "apricot", "banana",
                "apple", "pear", "orange"};

            // sort using a lambda expression
            list1.Sort(new Comparison<string>(
                (s1, s2) =>
                Comparer<int>.Default.Compare(s1.Length, s2.Length)));

            // enumerate the contents of the list
            foreach (string s in list1) {
                Console.WriteLine("List 1 item: {0}", s);
            }

            // create the second list collection
            List<string> list2 = new List<string>() {
                "mango", "cherry", "apricot", "banana",
                "apple", "pear", "orange"};

            // sort using an implementation of IComparer<T>
            list2.Sort(new StringLengthComparer());

            // enumerate the contents of the list
            foreach (string s in list2) {
                Console.WriteLine("List 2 item: {0}", s);
            }

            // wait for input before exiting
```

```
            Console.WriteLine("Press enter to finish");
            Console.ReadLine();
        }
    }

    class StringLengthComparer : IComparer<string> {
        public int Compare(string x, string y) {
            return Comparer<int>.Default.Compare(x.Length, y.Length);
        }
    }
}
```

System.Comparison<T> is useful because it provides allows us to use lambda expressions to perform comparison.

I've also created a class that implements IComparer<string> so that you can see both approaches to providing custom comparisons when sorting. I have used the same comparison logic in both, such that I call the default comparer for the int type and use it to compare the length of each string. Compiling and running the code in Listing 19-10 gives us the following output, in which you can see that the length of each string has been used to place them in order, shortest first:

```
List 1 item: pear
List 1 item: apple
List 1 item: mango
List 1 item: orange
List 1 item: cherry
List 1 item: banana
List 1 item: apricot
List 2 item: pear
List 2 item: apple
List 2 item: mango
List 2 item: orange
List 2 item: cherry
List 2 item: banana
List 2 item: apricot
Press enter to finish
```

The only wrinkle when using custom comparers for sorting is if you want to use the BinarySearch method to find an item efficiently. You need to provide the same custom comparer to the BinarySearch method. Listing 19-11 demonstrates this and shows you what happens if you forget to do so.

Listing 19-11. Using Binary Searching on a Custom Sorted List

```
using System;
using System.Collections.Generic;

namespace Listing_11 {
    class Listing_11 {

        static void Main(string[] args) {
```

```
            // create the first list collection
            List<string> list = new List<string>() {
                "mango", "cherry", "apricot", "banana",
                "apple", "pear", "orange"};

            // create the comparer
            StringLengthComparer slc = new StringLengthComparer();

            // sort the list
            list.Sort(slc);

            // perform the binary searches
            int index1 = list.BinarySearch("cherry", slc);
            int index2 = list.BinarySearch("cherry");

            // write out the results
            Console.WriteLine("Result 1: {0}", index1);
            Console.WriteLine("Result 2: {0}", index2);

            // wait for input before exiting
            Console.WriteLine("Press enter to finish");
            Console.ReadLine();
        }
    }

    class StringLengthComparer : IComparer<string> {
        public int Compare(string x, string y) {
            return Comparer<int>.Default.Compare(x.Length, y.Length);
        }
    }
}
```

You can see that I sort the data using the StringLengthComparer class, which I then reuse for the first call to the BinarySearch method. BinarySearch doesn't have an overload that accepts an instance of System.Comparison and so can't accept a lambda expression directly. The second call to BinarySearch doesn't specify an implementation of IComparer<string>, so the default is used. This second search therefore works on the basis that the contents of the list have been sorted alphabetically and, since they are actually sorted by length, gives us an unexpected result. Compiling and running the code in Listing 19-11 gives us the following results:

```
Result 1: 3
Result 2: -3
Press enter to finish
```

The message here is that if you use custom logic to sort the contents of a list, you must use the same logic to perform binary searches.

Processing Items

The List<T> class provides two methods that perform operations on all the items in the collection. These methods are described in Table 19-8.

Table 19-8. *Members for Sorting List Items*

Member	Description
ForEach(Action<T>)	Performs the specified Action<T> on each item in the collection
TrueForAll(Predicate<T>)	Returns true if every item in the list matches the conditions in the predicate

The ForEach method is just like using a foreach loop. It doesn't provide any additional functionality. The TrueForAll method returns true if all the elements in the List<T> match a given predicate. Listing 19-12 demonstrates the use of both methods.

Listing 19-12. *Using the ForEach and TrueForAll Methods*

```
using System;
using System.Collections.Generic;

namespace Listing_12 {
    class Listing_12 {

        static void Main(string[] args) {

            // create the first list collection
            List<string> list = new List<string>() {
                "mango", "cherry", "apricot", "banana",
                "apple", "pear", "orange"};

            // use the ForEach method
            list.ForEach(s => Console.WriteLine("List Item: {0}", s));

            // use the TrueForAll method
            bool result = list.TrueForAll(s => s.Length > 2);

            Console.WriteLine("Result: {0}", result);

            // wait for input before exiting
            Console.WriteLine("Press enter to finish");
            Console.ReadLine();
        }
    }
}
```

In Listing 19-12, I use the ForEach method to print out the value of each element using Console.WriteLine and the TrueForAll method to check that the length of each string is greater than two characters. Compiling and running the code in Listing 19-12 gives the following results:

```
List Item: mango
List Item: cherry
List Item: apricot
List Item: banana
List Item: apple
List Item: pear
List Item: orange
Result: True
Press enter to finish
```

Other List<T> Members

The remaining methods in the List<T> class are described in Table 19-9.

Table 19-9. Other List<T> Members

Member	Description
AsReadOnly()	Returns a ReadOnlyCollection<T> that does not allow the elements in the list to be changed
Capacity	Gets or sets the number of elements that the list can contain before the underlying array is resized
ConvertAll(Converter<T, TOut>>	Converts each item in the list to type TOut and returns a List<TOut> containing the results
CopyTo(T[]) CopyTo(T[], int) CopyTo(T[], int, int)	Copies the elements of the list into an array
Count	Gets the number of elements in the list
TrimExcess()	Removes excess capacity from the underlying array so that it matches the number of items presently in the list

The List<T> class dynamically resizes the array it uses to store the collected data items, but because array resizing can be an expensive operation to perform, List<T> tries to minimize overhead by allocating more storage than is required. If you have finished adding data to a List<T> and want to release the unused storage, you can call the TrimExcess method. If the underlying array is less than 90 percent full, TrimExcess will shrink it. Listing 19-13 demonstrates the TrimExcess method, as well as the Count and Capacity properties.

Listing 19-13. Managing List<T> Capacity

```
using System;
using System.Collections.Generic;

namespace Listing_13 {
    class Listing_13 {

        static void Main(string[] args) {

            // create the collection
            List<string> list = new List<string>(100) {
                "mango", "cherry", "apricot", "banana",
                "apple", "pear", "orange"};

            // write out the element count and the capacity
            Console.WriteLine("Count: {0}, Capacity: {1}", list.Count, list.Capacity);

            // trim the excess capacity
            list.TrimExcess();

            // write out the element count and the capacity again
            Console.WriteLine("Count: {0}, Capacity: {1}", list.Count, list.Capacity);

            // wait for input before exiting
            Console.WriteLine("Press enter to finish");
            Console.ReadLine();
        }
    }
}
```

This example creates a List<string> with an initial capacity of 100 items but only adds seven items. You can see the effect of the TrimExcess method from the values of the Count and Capacity properties in the following results:

```
Count: 7, Capacity: 100
Count: 7, Capacity: 7
Press enter to finish
```

The ConvertAll method lets you convert each element in a list to another type. The results are returned in a List<TOut> where TOut is the type you have converted to. Listing 19-14 demonstrates using this method to create a List<int> where each item is the length of a string from the source list.

Listing 19-14. Using the ConvertAll Method

```
using System;
using System.Collections.Generic;

namespace Listing_14 {
```

```
class Listing_14 {

    static void Main(string[] args) {

        // create the collection
        List<string> list = new List<string>(100) {
            "mango", "cherry", "apricot", "banana",
            "apple", "pear", "orange"};

        // convert the list
        List<int> convertedList = list.ConvertAll(s => s.Length);

        // enumerate the results
        foreach (int i in convertedList) {
            Console.WriteLine("Converted List Item: {0}", i);
        }

        // wait for input before exiting
        Console.WriteLine("Press enter to finish");
        Console.ReadLine();
    }
}
}
```

Compiling and running the code in Listing 19-14 produces the following results:

```
Converted List Item: 5
Converted List Item: 6
Converted List Item: 7
Converted List Item: 6
Converted List Item: 5
Converted List Item: 4
Converted List Item: 6
Press enter to finish
```

The CopyTo method copies the contents of a List<T> to an array of T. You have to create the array and pass it as an argument to the CopyTo method, and you must ensure that there is enough capacity for the array to hold the contents of the collection. You can use the overloaded versions of the method to copy only some of the elements. Listing 19-15 demonstrates the use of the CopyTo method.

Listing 19-15. Using the CopyTo Method

```
using System;
using System.Collections.Generic;

namespace Listing_15 {
    class Listing_15 {

        static void Main(string[] args) {
```

```
        // create the collection
        List<string> list = new List<string>(100) {
            "mango", "cherry", "apricot", "banana",
            "apple", "pear", "orange"};

        // create the array
        string[] array = new string[list.Count];

        // copy the contents of the list to the array
        list.CopyTo(array);

        // enumerate the contents of the array
        foreach (string s in array) {
            Console.WriteLine("Array Item: {0}", s);
        }

        // wait for input before exiting
        Console.WriteLine("Press enter to finish");
        Console.ReadLine();
    }
  }
}
```

Compiling and running the code in Listing 19-15 produces the following output:

```
Array Item: mango
Array Item: cherry
Array Item: apricot
Array Item: banana
Array Item: apple
Array Item: pear
Array Item: orange
Press enter to finish
```

The AsReadOnly method returns a version of the collection that cannot be modified; see the "Creating Constrained Collections" section for more details of read-only collections and how to use this method.

The LinkedList<T> Collection

As the name suggests, the LinkedList<T> class collects data using a linked list, rather than the array used by the List<T> class. This approach offers improved performance for some operations but comes at the cost in reduced convenience, as we'll see when we dig into the detail. The constructors for the LinkedList<T> class are described in Table 19-10.

Table 19-10. *Constructors for* LinkedList<T>

Constructor	Description
LinkedList<T>()	Creates a new LinkedList<T> with no data items
LinkedList<T>(IEnumerable<T>)	Creates a new LinkedList<T> and populates it with the contents of the IEnumerable<T>

A LinkedList<T> is like a chain; each link in the chain is an instance of the LinkedListNode<T> class, which has four properties, summarized in Table 19-11. When you add a new item of type T to the collection, it is wrapped in an instance of LinkedListNode<T>, and the Next and Previous properties are set to the neighbors in the collection.

Table 19-11. *Properties of the* LinkedListNode<T> *Class*

Property	Description
List	Returns the LinkedList<T> that this node is associated with
Next	Returns the next LinkedListNode<T> in the chain or null if this is the last item in the list
Previous	Returns the previous LinkedListNode<T> in the chain or null if this is the first item in the list
Value	Returns the value for this node

A LinkedList<T> has no indexer. It can't because the collection class keeps references only to the first and last items in the chain. And that's it. If you want to find the tenth item, for example, you go to the first item (often called the *head*) and get the reference to the Next item. You repeat until you get the item you are looking for or you get to the last item in the chain (often called the *tail*). The collection can't support an index to give you direct access, because there is no underlying array.

■ **Note** The LinkedList<T> class does not implement the List<T> interface. This is because there is no indexer support. The ICollection<T> interface is implemented, so you can rely on the members defined there for basic functionality.

Adding, Retrieving, and Removing Items

The operations to add, get, and remove items from a LinkedList<T> are based around accessing the first and last items in the chain. Table 19-12 describes the members of the LinkedList<T> class that you can use to access or modify the data.

Table 19-12. Members for Adding, Retrieving, and Removing Items

Member	Description
AddAfter(LinkedListNode<T>, T)	Inserts a new item into the collection after the specified LinkedListNode<T>
AddBefore(LinkedListNode<T>, T)	Inserts a new item into the collection before the specified LinkedListNode<T>
AddFirst(T)	Inserts a new item into the collection at the head of the list
AddLast(T)	Inserts a new item into the collection at the tail of the list
RemoveFirst()	Removes the first item from the list
RemoveLast()	Removes the last item from the list
First	Returns the head item from the list
Last	Returns the tail item from the list

Adding and removing items is just as you would expect. Listing 19-16 demonstrates the use of the key methods. Notice that when we add new values to the LinkedList<T>, we receive the LinkedListNode<T> instance that is used to wrap the value for inclusion in the collection. You can use that to perform subsequent operations, such as the AddAfter and AddBefore calls in Listing 19-16, which use the results from the AddFirst and AddLast method calls.

Listing 19-16. Adding and Removing Items from a LinkedList<T>

```
using System;
using System.Collections.Generic;

namespace Listing_16 {
    class Listing_16 {

        static void Main(string[] args) {

            // create and populate the collection
            LinkedList<string> list = new LinkedList<string>(
                new string[] {
                    "mango", "cherry", "apricot", "banana",
                });

            // add new first and last items
            LinkedListNode<string> newfirst = list.AddFirst("apple");
            LinkedListNode<string> newlast = list.AddLast("guava");
```

```
            // print out the contents of the list
            EnumerateList("Added new first and last items", list);

            // insert items using the LinkedListNodes we got
            // back when we added new first and last items
            list.AddAfter(newfirst, "papaya");
            list.AddBefore(newlast, "peach");

            // print out the contents of the list
            EnumerateList("Inserted new items", list);

            // remove the first and last items
            list.RemoveFirst();
            list.RemoveLast();

            // print out the contents of the list
            EnumerateList("Removed first and last items", list);

            // wait for input before exiting
            Console.WriteLine("Press enter to finish");
            Console.ReadLine();
        }

        static void EnumerateList(string message, LinkedList<string> list) {
            Console.WriteLine(message);
            foreach (string s in list) {
                Console.WriteLine("List Item: {0}", s);
            }
            Console.WriteLine();
        }
    }
}
```

The LinkedList<T> class doesn't have an Add method, which means that we can't use the handy collection population feature when we create a new instance. Instead, I have placed the initial values for the collection in a string array and passed that as a constructor argument. Arrays implement the IEnumerable<T> interface so that LinkedList<T> will be populated with my sample data. Compiling and running the code in Listing 19-16 gives the following results:

```
Added new first and last items
List Item: apple
List Item: mango
List Item: cherry
List Item: apricot
List Item: banana
List Item: guava

Inserted new items
List Item: apple
List Item: papaya
List Item: mango
```

```
List Item: cherry
List Item: apricot
List Item: banana
List Item: peach
List Item: guava

Removed first and last items
List Item: papaya
List Item: mango
List Item: cherry
List Item: apricot
List Item: banana
List Item: peach

Press enter to finish
```

You can see that I have enumerated the contents of the LinkedList<T> using a normal foreach loop in Listing 19-16. The alternative approach is to work directly with the LinkedListNodes<T> contained in the collection. Listing 19-17 demonstrates enumerating in this manner.

Listing 19-17. Enumerating a Linked List via the Chain of Nodes

```
using System;
using System.Collections.Generic;

namespace Listing_17 {
    class Listing_17 {

        static void Main(string[] args) {

            // create and populate the collection
            LinkedList<string> list = new LinkedList<string>(
                new string[] {
                    "mango", "cherry", "apricot", "banana",
                });

            LinkedListNode<string> currentNode = list.First;

            do {
                Console.WriteLine("List Item: {0}", currentNode.Value);
                currentNode = currentNode.Next;
            } while (currentNode.Next != null);

            // wait for input before exiting
            Console.WriteLine("Press enter to finish");
            Console.ReadLine();
        }
    }
}
```

We start with the LinkedListNode<T> returned by the First property and then work our way along the chain by using the Next property. We know that we have reached the end of the chain when Next returns null. For each LinkedListNode<T> that we find in the chain, we print out the data element by using the Value property.

Finding List Items

The LinkedList<T> class provides two methods that find items in the list. These methods are described in Table 19-13.

Table 19-13. Members for Finding List Items

Member	Description
Find(T)	Returns the first LinkedListNode<T> that contains the specified value
FindLast(T)	Returns the last LinkedListNode<T> that contains the specified value

These methods return an instance of LinkedListNode<T>. You can use this value to work your way up and down the list by using the Next and Previous properties. Listing 19-18 contains an example of using the Find method and prints out the value of the found node and the values of its neighbors.

Listing 19-18. Finding Nodes in a LinkedList<T>

```
using System;
using System.Collections.Generic;

namespace Listing_18 {
    class Listing_18 {

        static void Main(string[] args) {

            // create and populate the collection
            LinkedList<string> list = new LinkedList<string>(
                new string[] {
                    "mango", "cherry", "apricot", "banana",
                });

            // find a value in the list
            LinkedListNode<string> node = list.Find("cherry");

            // print out the details of the node we found
            Console.WriteLine("Node Value: {0}", node.Value);
            Console.WriteLine("Node Next: {0}", node.Next.Value);
            Console.WriteLine("Node Previous: {0}", node.Previous.Value);

            // wait for input before exiting
            Console.WriteLine("Press enter to finish");
            Console.ReadLine();
```

```
        }
      }
}
```

Compiling and running the code in Listing 19-18 produces the following results:

```
Node Value: cherry
Node Next: apricot
Node Previous: mango
Press enter to finish
```

The SortedList<TKey, TVal> Collection

The last of the generic list collection classes is SortedList<TKey, TVal>. However, oddly, this class isn't a list at all. It implements the IDictionary<TKey, TVal> interface, which we'll see more of when we get to the "Generic Dictionaries" section of this chapter. In fact, this class is a kind of cross-over between a list and a dictionary. The difference from List<T> is that the items are sorted as they are added. This is different from List<T> where the items are stored in the sequence they are added until the Sort method is used. The SortedList<TKey, TVal> class has six constructors, which are listed in Table 19-14.

Table 19-14. Constructors for SortedList<TKey, TVal>

Constructor	Description
SortedList<TKey, TVal>()	Creates a new list with the default initial capacity, sorted using the default comparer for TKey
SortedList<TKey, TVal>(IComparer<TKey>)	Creates a new list with the default initial capacity, sorted using the specified IComparer<TKey>
SortedList<TKey, TVal>(IDictionary<TKey, TVal>)	Creates a new list sorted using the default comparer for TKey, and populated with the contents of the IDictionary<TKey, TVal>
SortedList<TKey, TVal>(int)	Creates a new list with the specified initial capacity, sorted using the default comparer for TKey
SortedList<TKey, TVal>(int, IComparer<TKey>)	Creates a new list with the specified initial capacity, sorted using the specified IComparer<TKey>
SortedList<TKey, TVal>(IDictionary<TKey, TVal>, IComparer<TKey>)	Creates a new list sorted using the specified comparer and populated with the contents of the IDictionary<TKey, TVal>

You can see that the SortedList<TKey, TVal> class is strongly typed with a key and a value type—TKey and TVal, respectively. When you add data to the collection, you supply both a key and a value, much as you do with a dictionary collection, which we'll come to in the next section. The list is sorted using the keys. The SortedList<TKey, TVal> class requires that the keys are unique. Since you can supply your own sorting logic, this means that there should be no key for which the IComparer<TKey> used to sort the collection contents returns zero; see the IComparer<T> section later in this chapter for more details about IComparer<T>.

Adding, Retrieving, and Removing Items

You can really see the mix between the list and dictionary functionality of the SortedList<TKey, TVal> class when it comes to the members used to add, retrieve and remove items. We will see some members, such as Keys and Values, again when we come to look at the dictionary collections later in the chapter. Others, such as IndexOfKey and IndexOfValue, are characteristic of a conventional list. The members are described in Table 19-15.

Table 19-15. Members for Adding, Retrieving, and Removing Items

Member	Description
Add(TKey, TVal)	Add a new key/value pair to the list
IndexOfKey(TKey)	Returns the index of the specified key or -1 if there is no matching key in the list
IndexOfValue(TVal)	Returns the index of the specified value or -1 if there is no matching value in the list
RemoveAt(int)	Remove the key/value pair at the specified index
Item	An indexer that takes a TKey and returns the associated TVal
Keys	Returns an IList<TKey> containing all of the keys, in sorted order
Values	Returns an IList<TVal> containing all of the values, in sorted order
TryGetValue(TKey, out TVal)	Returns true and sets the out TVal to the value associated with a given key or returns false and sets the out TVal to the default value for the TVal type if there is no match

Listing 19-19 demonstrates some of the collection members. I create an instance of SortedList<string, string>, meaning that the type of the keys and the type of the values are both string. Since I have not supplied an IComparer<T> to sort the data, the default will be used. For strings, this means that the keys will be sorted alphabetically. I add some data to the list using the Add method. I have used the names of fruit and their usual color since this collection requires keys and values.

```csharp
using System;
using System.Collections.Generic;

namespace Listing_19 {
    class Listing_19 {

        static void Main(string[] args) {

            // create a sorted list
            SortedList<string, string> slist
                = new SortedList<string, string>();

            // add some data to the list
            slist.Add("apple",  "green");
            slist.Add("pear",   "green");
            slist.Add("banana", "yellow");
            slist.Add("cherry", "red");

            // get the list of keys
            IList<string> keys = slist.Keys;
            // enumerate the keys
            foreach (string s in keys) {
                Console.WriteLine("Key value: {0}", s);
            }

            // use the indexer
            string value1 = slist["apple"];
            string value2 = slist["cherry"];
            Console.WriteLine("Value for 'apple': {0}", value1);
            Console.WriteLine("Value for 'cherry': {0}", value2);

            // get some indices
            int index1 = slist.IndexOfKey("apple");
            int index2 = slist.IndexOfValue("red");
            Console.WriteLine("Index of key 'apple': {0}", index1);
            Console.WriteLine("Index of value 'red': {0}", index2);

            // wait for input before exiting
            Console.WriteLine("Press enter to finish");
            Console.ReadLine();
        }
    }
}
```

I use the Keys property to get an IList<string> of the keys. These are returned to me in their sorted order, which you can see when I enumerate them. I then use the indexer to get values for keys and finish by using the IndexOfKey and IndexOfValue to demonstrate the list-like nature of this collection. Compiling and running the code in Listing 19-19 gives the following output:

```
Key value: apple
Key value: banana
Key value: cherry
Key value: pear
Value for 'apple': green
Value for 'cherry': red
Index of key 'apple': 0
Index of value 'red': 2
Press enter to finish
```

The TryGetValue deserves special mention because it works in a different way to the other collection members. You provide the key you want to retrieve and an out parameter.

If the key exists in the collection, the out parameter will be set to the associated value. If the key doesn't exist in the collection, the out parameter will be set to the default value for the value type. The TryGetValue method returns true if the key exists in the collection and false if not. Listing 19-20 demonstrates the use of this method.

Listing 19-20. Using the TryGetValue Method

```
using System;
using System.Collections.Generic;

namespace Listing_20 {
    class Listing_20 {

        static void Main(string[] args) {

            // create a sorted list
            SortedList<string, string> slist
                = new SortedList<string, string>();

            // add some data to the list
            slist.Add("apple", "green");

            // define the strings that will hold the results
            string result1;
            string result2;

            // call the TryGetValue method
            bool found1 = slist.TryGetValue("apple", out result1);
            bool found2 = slist.TryGetValue("guava", out result2);

            // print out the result
            Console.WriteLine("Result: {0}, Value: {1}", found1, result1);
            Console.WriteLine("Result: {0}, Value: {1}", found2, result2);
```

```
        // wait for input before exiting
        Console.WriteLine("Press enter to finish");
        Console.ReadLine();
    }
  }
}
```

In the example, I create a SortedList<string, string> and add one key and value. I then call TryGetValue using the key I have inserted into the collection and again using a key that doesn't exist. Compiling and running the code in Listing 19-20 gives the following result:

```
Result: True, Value: green
Result: False, Value:
Press enter to finish
```

For the key that exists, the TryGetValue method returns true, and the out parameter is set to the associated value, in this case, green. For the key that doesn't exist, the TryGetValue method returns false, and the out parameter is set to the empty string, which is the default value for the string type.

Other SortedList<TKey, TVal> Members

The remaining members of the SortedList<TKey, TVal> class are described in Table 19-16.

Table 19-16. Other SortedList<TKey, TVal> Members

Member	Description
ContainsKey(TKey)	Returns true if the list contains the specified key
ContainsValue(TVal)	Returns true if the list contains the specified value
TrimExcess	Removes unused space from the underlying array (see List<T> for an example that uses this method)
Count	Returns the number of keys contained in the list
Capacity	Returns the capacity of the array used to store the data

Generic Dictionaries

A dictionary stores key/value pairs, just like we saw when using SortedList<TKey, TVal> in the previous section. If you have used a hash table in another programming language, then you'll already understand the model used by a dictionary. The types TKey and TVal can differ, such that you can have int values and string keys.

The IDictionary<TKey, TVal> Interface

The IDictionary<TKey, TVal> interface defines the behavior for a dictionary that uses keys of type TKey to store values of type TVal. Much like the IList<T> interface, IDictionary<TKey, TVal> allows you to work with a dictionary without worrying about what implementation you are using. The members of the interfaces are described in Table 19-17.

Table 19-17. The Members of the IDictionary<TKey, TVal> Interface

Member	Description
Add(TKey, TVal)	Adds a new key and value to the dictionary.
ContainsKey(TKey)	Returns true if the dictionary contains a specified key.
Remove(TKey)	Removes a key (and its associated value) from the dictionary.
TryGetValue(TKey, out TVal)	Returns true and sets the out TVal to the value associated with a given key or returns false and sets the out TVal to the default value for the TVal type if there is no match. See the SortedList<TKey, TVal> section of this chapter for an example of using this method.
Item	An indexer that gets or sets the value associated with a specified key.
Keys	Returns an ICollection<TKey> containing all the keys.
Values	Returns an ICollection<TVal> containing all the values.

Listing 19-21 demonstrates using some of the member of the IDictionary<TKey, TVal> interface. The implementation in this example is the Dictionary<TKey, TVal> class, which we explore fully later in the chapter. In this example, I create a dictionary and use the members of the interface to add data, enumerate the contents of the dictionary in different ways, modify the data, and check that a given key exists.

Listing 19-21. Using the IDictionary<TKey, TVal> Interface

```
using System;
using System.Collections.Generic;

namespace Listing_21 {
    class Listing_21 {

        static void Main(string[] args) {

            // create the IDictionary instance
            IDictionary<string, string> dict = new Dictionary<string, string>();

            // add some data to the dictionary
            dict.Add("apple", "red");
```

```
            dict.Add("cherry", "red");
            dict.Add("banana", "yellow");

            // use the indexer
            dict["apple"] = "green";

            // enumerate the contents of the dictionary
            Console.WriteLine("Enumerating dictionary items");
            foreach (KeyValuePair<string, string> kvp in dict) {
                Console.WriteLine("Dictionary Item. Key: {0}, Value: {1}",
                    kvp.Key, kvp.Value);
            }

            // enumerate just the keys
            Console.WriteLine("\nEnumerating dictionary keys");
            foreach (string key in dict.Keys) {
                Console.WriteLine("Dictionary Key: {0}", key);
            }

            // enumerate just the values
            Console.WriteLine("\nEnumerating dictionary values");
            foreach (string value in dict.Values) {
                Console.WriteLine("Dictionary Value: {0}", value);
            }

            // check to see if a key exists
            bool keyexists = dict.ContainsKey("cherry");
            Console.WriteLine("\nIDictionary contains key 'cherry': {0}", keyexists);

            // wait for input before exiting
            Console.WriteLine("Press enter to finish");
            Console.ReadLine();
        }
    }
}
```

Compiling and running the code in Listing 19-21 gives the following output:

```
Enumerating dictionary items
Dictionary Item. Key: apple, Value: green
Dictionary Item. Key: cherry, Value: red
Dictionary Item. Key: banana, Value: yellow

Enumerating dictionary keys
Dictionary Key: apple
Dictionary Key: cherry
Dictionary Key: banana

Enumerating dictionary values
Dictionary Value: green
Dictionary Value: red
```

```
Dictionary Value: yellow

IDictionary contains key 'cherry': True
Press enter to finish
```

You'll notice that when I enumerated the keys and values separately using the Keys and Values properties, I received an ICollection<TKey> and an ICollection<TVal> to work with. In the example, these were both ICollection<string>. But when I enumerated the dictionary directly, I had to work with KeyValuePair<string, string>. I'll describe this useful structure in the next section.

The KeyValuePair<TKey, TVal> Structure

The KeyValuePair<TKey, TVal> structure is a wrapper that contains, not surprisingly, a key and a value. IDictionary<TKey, TVal> does something clever with this structure, which is to use it to extend ICollection<KeyValuePair<TKey, TVal>>. This means that all the members of the ICollection<T> interface are available through the IDictionary<TKey, TVal> interface, where T is KeyValuePair<TKey, TVal>. Table 19-18 describes the members of KeyValuePair<TKey, TVal>.

Table 19-18. The Members of the KeyValuePair<TKey, TVal> Class

Member	Description
KeyValuePair<TKey, TVal>(TKey, TVal)	Creates a new instance with the specified key and value
Key	Gets the key
Value	Gets the value

An example will make this clearer. Listing 19-22 shows you how to manipulate a Dictionary<string, string> using only the KeyValuePair structure and the ICollection<KeyValuePair<string, string>> interface.

Listing 19-22. Using Key/Value Pairs

```
using System;
using System.Collections.Generic;

namespace Listing_22 {
    class Listing_22 {

        static void Main(string[] args) {

            // create the ICollection instance
            ICollection<KeyValuePair<string, string>> coll
                = new Dictionary<string, string>();
```

```
            // add some data to the dictionary
            coll.Add(new KeyValuePair<string, string>("apple", "green"));
            coll.Add(new KeyValuePair<string, string>("cherry", "red"));
            coll.Add(new KeyValuePair<string, string>("banana", "yellow"));

            // see if the collection contains specific key value pairs
            bool result1 = coll.Contains(
                new KeyValuePair<string, string>("apple", "green"));
            bool result2 = coll.Contains(
                new KeyValuePair<string, string>("apple", "blue"));

            Console.WriteLine("Collection contains apple/green: {0}", result1);
            Console.WriteLine("Collection contains apple/blue: {0}", result2);

            // remove an item from the collection
            coll.Remove(new KeyValuePair<string, string>("apple", "green"));

            // enumerate the results
            foreach (KeyValuePair<string, string> kvp in coll) {
                Console.WriteLine("Collection item: {0}/{1}", kvp.Key, kvp.Value);
            }

            // wait for input before exiting
            Console.WriteLine("Press enter to finish");
            Console.ReadLine();
        }
    }
}
```

The KeyValuePair structure is acting as an adapter, allowing a class that works with two types (TKey and TVal) to work with one (KeyValuePair<TKey,TVal>). In the example, I am able to add data to the dictionary, check to see whether particular values are present, remove data, and enumerate the collection contents, solely through the ICollection<T> interface. Compiling and running the code in Listing 19-22 gives the following results:

```
Collection contains apple/green: True
Collection contains apple/blue: False
Collection item: cherry/red
Collection item: banana/yellow
Press enter to finish
```

The Dictionary<TKey, TVal> Collection

The Dictionary<TKey, TVal> class is the implementation I used to describe the IDictionary<TKey, TVal> interface and the KeyValuePair<TKey, TVal> structures in the previous sections. It provides a standard hash table, much as you would encounter in any modern programming language. The Dictionary<TKey, TVal> class has six constructors, which are described in Table 19-19.

Table 19-19. Constructors for Dictionary<TKey, TVal>

Constructor	Description
Dictionary<TKey,TVal>()	Creates a dictionary with the default initial capacity and using the default equality comparer for TKey
Dictionary<TKey, TVal>(IDictionary<TKey, TVal>)	Creates a dictionary with the default initial capacity and using the default equality comparer for TKey, populated with the contents of the IDictionary<TKey, TVal>
Dictionary<TKey, TVal>(IEqualityComparer>TKey>)	Creates a dictionary with the default initial capacity and using the specified IEqualityComparer<TKey>
Dictionary<TKey, TVal>(int)	Creates a dictionary with the specified initial capacity
Dictionary<TKey, TVal>(IDictionary<TKey, TVal>, IEqualityComparer<TKey, TVal>)	Creates a dictionary using the specified IEqualityComparer<TKey>, populated with the contents of the IDictionary<TKey, TVal>
Dictionary<TKey, TVal>(int, IEqualityComparer<TKey>)	Creates a dictionary with the specified initial capacity and using the IEqualityComparer<TKey>

The three options you can set when creating a Dictionary<TKey, TVal> are the initial capacity for the collection, the initial content for the collection, and the implementation of IEqualityComparer<TKey> that will be used to determine whether two keys are equal. Keys in dictionaries are unique. When you add a new key/value pair, the IEqualityComparer<TKey> is used to see whether there is already a matching key in the collection. If the key doesn't already exist, the key/value pair is added to the collection, but if there is, then an exception is thrown. I describe the IEqualityComparer<T> interface later in the chapter.

Adding, Retrieving, and Removing Items

Manipulating the contents of a Dictionary<TKey, TVal> is, as you might expect, just like working with the IDictionary<TKey, TVal> interface. Table 19-20 summarizes the methods that let you add, retrieve and remove items from the collection.

Table 19-20. Members for Adding, Retrieving, and Removing Items

Member	Description
Add(TKey, TVal)	Adds a new key/value pair to the dictionary or changes the value associated with the key if there is already a matching key/value pair in the collection.
Remove(TKey)	Removes a key/value pair from a dictionary.
TryGetValue(Tkey, out TVal)	Returns true and sets the out TVal to the value associated with a given key or returns false and sets the out TVal to

Member	Description
	the default value for the TVal type if there is no match. See the SortedList<TKey, TVal> section of this chapter for an example of using this method.
Item	An indexer that gets or sets the value associated with a key.
Keys	Returns an ICollection<TKey>, which can be used to enumerate the keys.
Values	Returns an ICollection<TVal>, which can be used to enumerate the values.

Listing 19-23 refactors the example that used the IDictionary<TKey, TVal> interface to work directly with Dictionary<TKey, TVal>. The only difference between these examples is that I have populated the collection as part of the constructor call.

Listing 19-23. Using the Dictionary<TKey, TVal> Class

```
using System;
using System.Collections.Generic;

namespace Listing_23 {
    class Listing_23 {

        static void Main(string[] args) {

            // create the Dictionary instance
            Dictionary<string, string> dict = new Dictionary<string, string>() {
                { "apple", "red" },
                { "cherry", "red" },
                { "banana", "yellow" }
            };

            // use the indexer
            dict["apple"] = "green";

            // enumerate the contents of the dictionary
            Console.WriteLine("Enumerating dictionary items");
            foreach (KeyValuePair<string, string> kvp in dict) {
                Console.WriteLine("Dictionary Item. Key: {0}, Value: {1}",
                    kvp.Key, kvp.Value);
            }

            // enumerate just the keys
            Console.WriteLine("\nEnumerating dictionary keys");
            foreach (string key in dict.Keys) {
                Console.WriteLine("Dictionary Key: {0}", key);
            }
```

```
        // enumerate just the values
        Console.WriteLine("\nEnumerating dictionary values");
        foreach (string value in dict.Values) {
            Console.WriteLine("Dictionary Value: {0}", value);
        }

        // check to see if a key exists
        bool keyexists = dict.ContainsKey("cherry");
        Console.WriteLine("\nIDictionary contains key 'cherry': {0}", keyexists);

        // wait for input before exiting
        Console.WriteLine("Press enter to finish");
        Console.ReadLine();
    }
  }
}
```

Compiling and running the code in Listing 19-23 gives the following results:

```
Enumerating dictionary items
Dictionary Item. Key: apple, Value: green
Dictionary Item. Key: cherry, Value: red
Dictionary Item. Key: banana, Value: yellow

Enumerating dictionary keys
Dictionary Key: apple
Dictionary Key: cherry
Dictionary Key: banana

Enumerating dictionary values
Dictionary Value: green
Dictionary Value: red
Dictionary Value: yellow

IDictionary contains key 'cherry': True
Press enter to finish
```

Other Dictionary<TKey, TVal> Members

The remaining members of Dictionary<TKey, TVal> are described in Table 19-21. You can see the ContainsKey member used in Listing 19-23.

Table 19-21. Other Dictionary<TKey, TVal> Members

Member	Description
ContainsKey(TKey)	Returns true if the collection contains the specified key
ContainsValue(TKey>	Returns true if the collection contains the specified value
Comparer	Gets the IEqualityComparer<T>
Count	Returns the number of key/value pairs in the collection

The SortedDictionary<TKey, TVal> Collection

The SortedDictionary<TKey, TVal> collection is just like the regular Dictionary<TKey, TVal>, except that the key/value pairs are sorted based on the key. Listing 19-24 compares the two kinds of collection.

Listing 19-24. Comparing Dictionary<TKey, TVal> and SortedDictionary<TKey, TVal>

```
using System;
using System.Collections.Generic;

namespace Listing_24 {
    class Listing_24 {

        static void Main(string[] args) {

            // create the Dictionary instance
            Dictionary<string, string> dict = new Dictionary<string, string>() {
                { "apple", "green" },
                { "cherry", "red" },
                { "mango", "green"},
                { "banana", "yellow" },
                { "strawberry", "red" }
            };

            // enumerate the contents of the Dictionary
            Console.WriteLine("Enumerating Dictionary");
            foreach (KeyValuePair<string, string> kvp in dict) {
                Console.WriteLine("Dictionary Key: {0}, Value: {1}",
                    kvp.Key, kvp.Value);
            }

            // create the SortedDictionary
            SortedDictionary<string, string> sdict
                = new SortedDictionary<string, string>(dict);
```

```
        // enumerate the contents of the Dictionary
        Console.WriteLine("\nEnumerating SortedDictionary");
        foreach (KeyValuePair<string, string> kvp in sdict) {
            Console.WriteLine("SortedDictionary Key: {0}, Value: {1}",
                kvp.Key, kvp.Value);
        }

        // wait for input before exiting
        Console.WriteLine("Press enter to finish");
        Console.ReadLine();
    }
  }
}
```

In the listing, I create a regular Dictionary<TKey, TVal> and use a foreach loop to enumerate the contents of the collection. I then use a SortedDictionary<TKey, TVal>, which I populate using the contents of the regular collection, and use another foreach to enumerate the contents. Compiling and running the code in Listing 19-24 produces the following output:

```
Enumerating Dictionary
Dictionary Key: apple, Value: green
Dictionary Key: cherry, Value: red
Dictionary Key: mango, Value: green
Dictionary Key: banana, Value: yellow
Dictionary Key: strawberry, Value: red

Enumerating SortedDictionary
SortedDictionary Key: apple, Value: green
SortedDictionary Key: banana, Value: yellow
SortedDictionary Key: cherry, Value: red
SortedDictionary Key: mango, Value: green
SortedDictionary Key: strawberry, Value: red
Press enter to finish
```

You can see that the keys are in order when I enumerate the SortedDictionary<TKey, TVal>. Aside from this feature, using SortedDictionary<TKey, TVal> is just like using Dictionary<TKey, TVal>. The two classes have the same members, although SortedDictionary<TKey, TVal> does have different constructors to allow you to specify a custom sorting approach. These constructors are described in Table 19-22. The SortedDictionary<TKey, TVal> class relies on the IComparer<T> interface for sorting, which I describe later in this chapter.

Table 19-22. Constructors for SortedDictionary<TKey, TVal>

Constructor	Description
SortedDictionary<TKey, TVal>()	Creates a SortedDictionary<TKey, TVal> using the default IComparer<TKey> to sort the keys
SortedDictionary<TKey, TVal>(IComparer(TKey)	Creates a SortedDictionary<TKey, TVal> using the specified IComparer<TKey> to sort the keys

Constructor	Description
SortedDictionary<TKey, TVal>(IDictionary<TKey, TVal>)	Creates a SortedDictionary<TKey, TVal> using the default IComparer<TKey> and populated with the contents of the IDictionary<TKey, TVal>
SortedDictionary<TKey, TVal>(IDictionary<TKey, TVal>, IComparer<TKey>)	Creates a SortedDictionary<TKey, TVal> using the specified IComparer<TKey> and populated with the contents of the IDictionary<TKey, TVal>

Generic Sets

Sets are collections that have no duplicate items, and in general, the items are in no particular order. As a programming tool, the .NET generic sets are most useful because they allow you to compare one collection of objects with another. You can determine which elements two collections have in common, if one collection is a superset or subset of another collection, and which elements are unique to one of the collections. Sets are not as widely used as some of the generic collections, but they can be a real time-saver when you need them.

The ISet<T> Interface

The ISet<T> interface allows you to work with different set collection implementations in a consistent manner. The members of the ISet<T> interface are described in Table 19-23.

Table 19-23. The Members of the ISet<T> Interface

Member	Description
Add(T)	Adds an item to the set
ExceptWith(IEnumerable<T>)	Removes all the items in the IEnumerable<T> from the set
IntersetWith(IEnumerable<T>)	Modifies the set so that it contains only the elements that are also in the IEnumerable<T>
IsProperSubsetOf(IEnumerable<T>)	Returns true if the IEnumerable<T> contains one or more items that are not in the set
IsProperSupersetOf(IEnumerable<T>)	Returns true if the set has at least one item that is not in the IEnumerable<T>
IsSubsetOf(IEnumerable<T>)	Returns true if the IEnumerable<T> contains zero or more items that are not in the set

Member	Description
IsSupersetOf(IEnumerable<T>)	Returns true if the set contains zero or more items that are not in the IEnumerable<T>
Overlaps(IEnumerable<T>)	Returns true if the set and the IEnumerable<T> contain one or more items in common
SetEquals(IEnumerable<T>)	Returns true if the set and the IEnumerable<T> contain the same elements
SymmetricExceptWith(IEnumerable<T>)	Modifies the set so that it contains items that are in the set and in the IEnumerable<T> but not those items that are in both
UnionWith<IEnumerable<T>>	Modifies the set so that it contains the elements that are in both the set and the IEnumerable<T>

Using ISet<T> is pretty straightforward. Listing 19-25 demonstrates some of the more useful members, using the HashSet<T> collection class (which I describe in the next section of this chapter).

Listing 19-25. Working with the ISet<T> Interface

```
using System;
using System.Collections.Generic;

namespace Listing_25 {
    class Listing_25 {

        static void Main(string[] args) {

            // create the ISet<T>
            ISet<string> set = new HashSet<string>() {
                "apple", "banana", "cherry"
            };

            // create the other collection
            IEnumerable<string> otherCollection
                = new string[] { "banana", "strawberry", "pear", "cherry", "apple" };

            // use the proper superset and subset methods
            bool result1 = set.IsProperSubsetOf(otherCollection);
            bool result2 = set.IsProperSupersetOf(otherCollection);
            // write out the results
            Console.WriteLine("IsProperSubset: {0}, IsProperSuperset: {1}",
                result1, result2);

            // use the regular superset and subset methods
            bool result3 = set.IsSubsetOf(otherCollection);
```

```
            bool result4 = set.IsSupersetOf(otherCollection);
            // write out the results
            Console.WriteLine("IsSubset: {0}, IsSuperset: {1}", result3, result4);

            // use the overlaps methods
            bool result5 = set.Overlaps(otherCollection);
            Console.WriteLine("Overlaps: {0}", result5);

            // get the interset
            set.IntersectWith(otherCollection);

            // enumerate the (intersected) set
            foreach (string s in set) {
                Console.WriteLine("Set Item: {0}", s);
            }

            // wait for input before exiting
            Console.WriteLine("Press enter to finish");
            Console.ReadLine();
        }
    }
}
```

Compiling and running the code in Listing 19-25 gives the following results:

```
IsProperSubset: True, IsProperSuperset: False
IsSubset: True, IsSuperset: False
Overlaps: True
Set Item: apple
Set Item: banana
Set Item: cherry
Press enter to finish
```

The HashSet<T> Collection

The HashSet<T> class is the standard implementation of the ISet<T> interface. The constructors for HashSet<T> are described in Table 19-24. Sets don't contain duplicate items, so HashSet<T> uses the IEqualityComparer<T> interface to determine equality between collections items. If you don't provide an implementation of IEqualityComparer<T>, then the default is used for the collection item type. I describe the IEqualityComparer<T> interface later in the chapter.

Table 19-24. Constructors for HashSet<T>

Constructor	Description
HashSet<T>()	Creates a set using the default IEqualityComparer<T> for the type T
HashSet<T>(IEnumerable<T>)	Creates a set using the default IEqualityComparer<T>, populated with the contents of the IEnumerable<T>
HashSet<T>(IEqualityComparer<T>)	Creates a set using the specified IEqualityComparer<T> for item comparison
HashSet<T>(IEnumerable<T>, IEqualityComparer<T>)	Creates a set using the specified IEqualityComparer<T> for item comparisons and populated with the contents of the IEnumerable<T>

I tend to use HashSet<T> when I want to compare, merge, or deduplicate a pair of other collections. The constructor that takes an IEnumerable<T> is especially useful for this because it allows me to create a set that is populated with the contents of one of the collections I want to work with. Listing 19-26 demonstrates some examples of using HashSet<T>.

Listing 19-26. Working with the HashSet<T> Collection

```
using System;
using System.Collections.Generic;

namespace Listing_26 {
    class Listing_26 {

        static void Main(string[] args) {

            // create the two collections we want to work with
            List<string> list1 = new List<string>() { "cherry", "apple", "cherry" };
            List<string> list2 = new List<string>() { "apple", "banana", "orange" };

            // create the HashSet, using one of the collections
            HashSet<string> set = new HashSet<string>(list1);

            // enumerate the set
            Console.WriteLine("Enumerating the HashSet");
            foreach (string s in set) {
                Console.WriteLine("Set Item: {0}", s);
            }

            // modify the set so that it contains only the items
            // which existed in both source collections
            set.UnionWith(list2);
```

```
            // create a new list that contains the contents of the set
            List<string> result = new List<string>(set);

            // enumerate the result list
            Console.WriteLine("\nEnumerating the result set");
            foreach (string s in result) {
                Console.WriteLine("Result List Item: {0}", s);
            }

            // wait for input before exiting
            Console.WriteLine("Press enter to finish");
            Console.ReadLine();
        }
    }
}
```

In the example, I create two List<string> and use the first of them as the source for a HashSet<string>. You can see when I enumerate the contents of the set that the duplicate items in the list have been removed during the construction of the HashSet<string>. I then call the UnionWith method to modify the set so that it contains only those items that were in both the set and the second List<string>. I then take the HashSet<string> and use it to populate a new List<string> containing the deduplicated union of my two original List<string> instances, which I then enumerate. Compiling and running the code in Listing 19-26 gives the following results:

```
Enumerating the HashSet
Set Item: cherry
Set Item: apple

Enumerating the result set
Result List Item: cherry
Result List Item: apple
Result List Item: banana
Result List Item: orange
Press enter to finish
```

The SortedSet<T> Collection

The SortedSet<T> class implements the ISet<T> interface but stores the items in sorted order. This is different from HashSet<T>, which doesn't maintain any special order for the collection items. The constructors for SortedSet<T> are described in Table 19-25.

Table 19-25. Constructors for SortedSet<T>

Constructor	Description
SortedSet<T>()	Creates a set that uses the default comparer for T
SortedSet<T>(IComparer<T>)	Creates a set that uses the specified comparer for T
SortedSet<T>(IEnumerable<T>)	Creates a set that uses the default comparer for T and that is populated with the contents of the IEnumerable<T>
SortedSet<T>(IEnumerable<T>, IComparer<T>)	Creates a set that uses the specified comparer and that is populated with the contents of the IEnumerable<T>

The SortedSet<T> class uses the IComparer<T> interface to compare items when sorting them. I describe this interface later in the chapter. Using the SortedSet<T> collection is just like using HashSet<T>, although storing the items in a sorted order does allow SortedSet<T> to define offer additional features. Listing 19-27 demonstrates the use of the SortedSet<T> class.

Listing 19-27. Using the SortedSet<T> Class

```
using System;
using System.Collections.Generic;

namespace Listing_27 {
    class Listing_27 {

        static void Main(string[] args) {

            SortedSet<string> set = new SortedSet<string>() {
                "banana", "apple", "cherry", "strawberry", "mango"
            };

            // enumerate the contents of the sorted set
            Console.WriteLine("Enumerating SortedSet");
            foreach (string s in set) {
                Console.WriteLine("SortedSet Item: {0}", s);
            }

            // get a view of part of the set
            SortedSet<string> view = set.GetViewBetween("banana", "mango");
            // enumerate the view
            Console.WriteLine("\nEnumerating View");
            foreach (string s in view) {
                Console.WriteLine("View Item: {0}", s);
            }

            // remove some items from the set
```

```
        set.RemoveWhere(s => s.Length < 6);

        // enumerate the set now we have removed some items
        Console.WriteLine("\nEnumerating SortedSet");
        foreach (string s in set) {
            Console.WriteLine("SortedSet Item: {0}", s);
        }

        // enumerate the view
        Console.WriteLine("\nEnumerating View");
        foreach (string s in view) {
            Console.WriteLine("View Item: {0}", s);
        }

        // wait for input before exiting
        Console.WriteLine("Press enter to finish");
        Console.ReadLine();
        }
    }
}
```

The additional methods offered by SortedSet<T> are described in Table 19-26.

Table 19-26. The Additional Members of the SortedSet<T> Class

Member	Description
GetViewBetween(T, T)	Returns a SortedSet<T> that contains only the items between two specified values
RemoveWhere(Predicate<T>)	Removes items that meet the conditions defined by the Predicate<T>
Reverse()	Returns an IEnumerator<T> that enumerates the content of the set in reverse

In the listing, I create a new SortedSet<T> and enumerate the contents. You can see from the results shown next that the items are sorted. Since I have not specified an IComparer<T>, the default sorting has been applied, which is alphabetical order for the string type. Having enumerated the set, I then create and enumerate a view, which returns a SortedSet<string> containing a subset of the items.

```
Enumerating SortedSet
SortedSet Item: apple
SortedSet Item: banana
SortedSet Item: cherry
SortedSet Item: mango
SortedSet Item: strawberry

Enumerating View
```

```
View Item: banana
View Item: cherry
View Item: mango

Enumerating SortedSet
SortedSet Item: banana
SortedSet Item: cherry
SortedSet Item: strawberry

Enumerating View
View Item: banana
View Item: cherry
Press enter to finish
```

I call the RemoveWhere method using a lambda expression that selects items with fewer than six characters and then enumerate the set again. The final step is to enumerate the view once more. You will notice from the results that the view is linked to the SortedSet<T> and that removing items from the SortedSet<T> also removes them from the SortedSet<T> returned by the GetViewBetween method.

Generic Queues and Stacks

The last two collection classes to describe are used to create queues and stacks. Both types of collection constrain access to the collected items. Queues allow you to add items to the end of the queue and take items from the head of the queue. The items are returned in the order in which they are added. A stack, by contrast, allows you to retrieve only the item you added most recently.

The Queue<T> Collection

As the class name suggests, this collection is just like the queue at a bank. The people in a queue are ordered as they arrive, so the first person to arrive is at the head of the queue, and the most recently arrived person is at the back of the queue. This is known as a first-in, first-out (FIFO) collection and sometimes known as *temporal* ordering, since the items in the collection are ordered by arrival time. Queues are most often used to collect messages from one part of a program to another, for example, log messages. The constructors for Queue<T> are described in Table 19-27.

Table 19-27. Constructors for Queue<T>

Constructor	Description
Queue<T>()	Creates an empty queue with the default initial capacity
Queue<T>(IEnumerable<T>)	Creates a queue populated with the content of the IEnumerable<T>
Queue<T>(int)	Creates an empty queue with the specified capacity

You'll notice that there are no constructors that take IEqualityComparer<T> or IComparer<T> implementations. This is because Queue<T> will collect duplicate items. Table 19-28 describes the key members of the Queue<T> class.

Table 19-28. Queue<T> Members

Member	Description
Enqueue(T)	Adds an item to the end of the queue
Dequeue()	Removes and returns the item at the beginning of the queue
Peek()	Returns the item at the beginning of the queue without removing it
Count	Returns the number of items in the queue

When using Queue<T>, you can work only with the head and tail of the queue. You must use the Enqueue, Dequeue, and Peek methods to modify the contents of a Queue<T>. There is no indexer, for example, so you can't jump in and modify the second element. Listing 19-28 demonstrates the use of the Queue<T> class.

Listing 19-28. Using the Queue<T> Class

```
using System;
using System.Collections.Generic;

namespace Listing_28 {
    class Listing_28 {

        static void Main(string[] args) {

            // create the Queue<T>
            Queue<string> queue = new Queue<string>();

            // enqueue some items
            queue.Enqueue("apple");
            queue.Enqueue("cherry");
            queue.Enqueue("banana");

            // peek at the first item
            string peekItem = queue.Peek();
            Console.WriteLine("Peeked: {0}", peekItem);

            // dequeue an item
            string dequeueItem = queue.Dequeue();
            Console.WriteLine("Dequeued: {0}", dequeueItem);

            // enumerate the remaining items
            foreach (string s in queue) {
```

```
                    Console.WriteLine("Queue Item: {0}", s);
                }

                // wait for input before exiting
                Console.WriteLine("Press enter to finish");
                Console.ReadLine();
            }
        }
}
```

In the listing, I create a Queue<string> and Enqueue a number of items. I Peek at the first item and then Dequeue it before enumerating the remaining items in the collection. Compiling and running the code in Listing 19-28 gives the following results:

```
Peeked: apple
Dequeued: apple
Queue Item: cherry
Queue Item: banana
Press enter to finish
```

The Stack<T> Collection

Stacks are last-in, first-out (LIFO) collections. Adding an item to a stack is called *pushing*, and retrieving an item is called *popping*. The item most recently pushed onto a stack is the one that is returned when an item is popped. The constructors for Stack<T> are described in Table 19-29.

Table 19-29. Constructors for Stack<T>

Constructor	Description
Stack<T>()	Creates an empty stack with the default initial capacity
Stack<T>(IEnumerable<T>)	Creates a stack populated with the content of the IEnumerable<T>
Stack<T>(int)	Creates an empty stack with the specified capacity

The remaining key members of Stack<T> are shown in Table 19-30. When working with Stack<T>, you only get access to the end of the collection. You can add a new item using the Push method, get and remove the most recently added item using the Pop method, and look at the most recently added item without removing it using the Peek method.

Table 19-30. Stack<T> Members

Member	Description
Push(T)	Adds a new item to the stack
Pop()	Removes and return the most recently added item from the stack
Peek()	Returns the most recently added item without removing it
Count	Returns the number of items in the stack

Listing 19-29 demonstrates the use of the Stack<T> class.

Listing 19-29. Using the Stack<T> Class

```
using System;
using System.Collections.Generic;

namespace Listing_29 {
    class Listing_29 {

        static void Main(string[] args) {

            // create the Stack<T>
            Stack<string> stack = new Stack<string>();

            // push some items
            stack.Push("apple");
            stack.Push("cherry");
            stack.Push("banana");

            // peek at the first item
            string peekItem = stack.Peek();
            Console.WriteLine("Peeked: {0}", peekItem);

            // pop an item
            string poppedItem = stack.Pop();
            Console.WriteLine("Popped: {0}", poppedItem);

            // enumerate the remaining items
            foreach (string s in stack) {
                Console.WriteLine("Stack Item: {0}", s);
            }

            // wait for input before exiting
            Console.WriteLine("Press enter to finish");
            Console.ReadLine();
        }
```

```
        }
}
```

If you compile and run the code in Listing 19-29, you get the following results. You can see that the order of the items as they are added and removed differs in a Stack<T> from a Queue<T>.

```
Peeked: banana
Popped: banana
Stack Item: cherry
Stack Item: apple
Press enter to finish
```

Other Generic Collection Interfaces

Two interfaces are used to compare and sort collection items. We have seen them in the constructors of many of the collection classes, and for the most part, I have ignored them and used the default implementations. In this section, we'll look at the interfaces in detail and see how to implement custom comparison and equality code.

The IComparer<T> Interface

We saw IComparer<T> interface in the constructor of the collection classes that sort data. This is the interface you use to specify custom sorting. The interface has one method, which is described in Table 19-31.

Table 19-31. The Single Method of the IComparer<T> Interface

Member	Description
Compare(T, T)	Compares two instance of T

Your implementation of the Compare method is passed two instances of the type T, T1 and T2. If T1 has a lower value that T2, return -1. If T1 and T2 are of equal value, then return 0. If T1 has a greater value than T2, return 1. Listing 19-30 demonstrates an implementation of IComparer<T> used with SortedSet<T>.

Listing 19-30. Using the IComparer<T> Interface

```
using System;
using System.Collections.Generic;

namespace Listing_30 {
    class Listing_30 {

        static void Main(string[] args) {
```

```
        // create and populate the collection
        SortedSet<string> set = new SortedSet<string>(
            new StringLengthComparer()) {
                "banana", "mango", "cherry", "apple", "guava"
        };

        // enumerate the contents of the set
        foreach (string s in set) {
            Console.WriteLine("Set Item: {0}", s);
        }

        // wait for input before exiting
        Console.WriteLine("Press enter to finish");
        Console.ReadLine();
    }

    class StringLengthComparer : IComparer<string> {
        public int Compare(string T1, string T2) {
            return Comparer<int>.Default.Compare(T1.Length, T2.Length);
        }
    }
}
}
```

The StringLengthComparer class in the listing, shown in bold, implements the IComparer<string> interface and compares instances of string based on their length. I used the default comparer for the int type by calling Comparer<int>.Default. This returns an instance of IComparer<int>. You can use the default comparer for any type that implements the System.IComparable<T> interface, which includes many of the C# intrinsic types.

Of course, I could have implemented the comparer without relying on the default, in which case the Compare method would have looked something like this:

```
public int Compare(string T1, string T2) {
    if (T1.Length == T2.Length) {
        return 0;
    } else if (T1.Length > T2.Length) {
        return 1;
    } else {
        return -1;
    }
}
```

Using the default comparer is a convenience but far from essential. Compiling and running the code in Listing 19-30 gives the following output:

```
Set Item: mango
Set Item: banana
Press enter to finish
```

You will notice that some of the items I put into the SortedSet<string> at construction are missing. This happens because the SortedSet<T> class doesn't accept duplicate entries and uses the IComparer<T> to determine which items have the same value. Since my implementation of IComparer<string> works on the length of the string, any strings that have the same number of characters are assumed to be equal. You have to be a little careful when providing your own IComparer<T> that you understand how the collection class performs comparisons.

The IEqualityComparer<T> Interface

The IEqualityComparer<T> interface is used by the Dictionary<TKey, TVal> class to determine if keys are equal. The interface has two methods, which are described in Table 19-32.

Table 19-32. The Methods of the IEqualityComparer<T> Interface

Member	Description
Equals(T, T)	Compares two instance of T for quality; returns true if they are equal, false otherwise.
GetHashCode(T)	Returns an int hash code for an instance of T. The hash code must be consistent with the Equals method so that if two instances of T are reported as equal, the GetHashCode method should return the same hash code for both of them.

Your implementation of the Equals method returns true if the two instances are equal in your custom policy. You must make sure that the GetHashCode implementation and the Equals method are consistent so that two instances that the Equals method reports as being equal should return the same hash code. Listing 19-31 demonstrates implementing a custom equality policy using the IEqualityComparer<T> interface and the Dictionary<TKey, TVal> class.

Listing 19-31. Using the IEqualityComparer<T> Interface

```
using System;
using System.Collections.Generic;

namespace Listing_31 {
    class Listing_31 {

        static void Main(string[] args) {

            // create the Dictionary
            Dictionary<string, string> dict = new Dictionary<string, string>
                (new StringLengthEqualityComparer()) {
                    {"apple", "green"},
                    {"banana", "yellow"},
            };

            bool containsKey = dict.ContainsKey("mango");
            Console.WriteLine("Dictionary contains key 'mango': {0}",
```

```
            containsKey);

        // enumerate the keys
        foreach (string key in dict.Keys) {
            Console.WriteLine("Key: {0}", key);
        }

        // wait for input before exiting
        Console.WriteLine("Press enter to finish");
        Console.ReadLine();
    }
}

class StringLengthEqualityComparer : IEqualityComparer<string> {

    public bool Equals(string x, string y) {
        return x.Length == y.Length;
    }

    public int GetHashCode(string x) {
        return x.Length;
    }
}
}
```

The StringLengthEqualityComparer class in the example, shown in bold, implements the IEqualityComparer<string> interface, using the string length to determine equality. This class also uses the length as the hash code so that strings with the same number of characters produce the same result. Compiling and running the code in Listing 19-31 produces the following result:

```
Dictionary contains key 'mango': True
Key: apple
Key: banana
Press enter to finish
```

Default implementations for IEqualityComparer<T> are available through the Default property of the EqualityComparer class.

Treating Arrays as Collections

System.Array is the base class used to support arrays. You can't derive from the System.Array class. You must use the C# language features to work with arrays, as we saw in Chapter 13. But you *can* take advantage of the feature of the System.Array class, and one of the most useful of those features is that System.Array implements the IList<T>, ICollection<T>, and IEnumerable<T> interfaces. This means that arrays are also collections and can be used alongside the other generic collection classes. Listing 19-32 gives a simple demonstration of using an array as a collection.

Listing 19-32. Using an Array as a Collection

```csharp
using System;
using System.Collections.Generic;

namespace Listing_32 {
    class Listing_32 {

        static void Main(string[] args) {

            // create an array
            string[] strArray = new string[] { "apple", "orange",
                "banana", "cherry", "guava" };

            // use the implicit interface implementations
            // to populate a List<T>
            List<string> list = new List<string>(strArray);

            // filter the items in the array
            string[] filterArray = Array.FindAll(strArray, s => s.Length == 6);
            // enumerate the filter results
            Console.WriteLine("Enumerating filter results");
            foreach (string s in filterArray) {
                Console.WriteLine("Filtered item: {0}", s);
            }

            // sort the array
            Array.Sort(strArray);

            // enumerate the (sorted) array
            Console.WriteLine("\nEnumerating sorted array");
            foreach (string s in strArray) {
                Console.WriteLine("Array item: {0}", s);
            }

            // wait for input before exiting
            Console.WriteLine("Press enter to finish");
            Console.ReadLine();
        }
    }
}
```

I use the standard C# language features to create and populate a string array. The next step is to use this array to populate a List<string>. We can do this because the List<T> class has a constructor that allows the list to be populated by an IEnumberable<T>, which System.Array implements.

I then use some of the static methods of the System.Array class to work with my string array. First, I use the FindAll method to filter the contents of the array using a predicate. In this case, I want all the items that have six characters. I get the results of the filter as another string array, which I then enumerate. Next, I use the Sort method to arrange the items in the array into alphabetical order and enumerate the results. Compiling and running the code in Listing 19-32 gives the following results:

```
Enumerating filter results
Filtered item: orange
Filtered item: banana
Filtered item: cherry

Enumerating sorted array
Array item: apple
Array item: banana
Array item: cherry
Array item: guava
Array item: orange
Press enter to finish
```

The syntax for using these features is clumsy (needing to mix array syntax and static methods), but the result is pretty good. Being able to treat arrays as collections is an exceptionally useful feature. Table 19-33 describes some useful members of the System.Array class.

Table 19-33. Useful Members of the System.Array Class

Member	Description
BinarySearch(T[], T] BinarySearch(T[], T, IComparer<T>)	Searches an array for a value, either using the default IComparer<T> or using a custom IComparer<T>
ConvertAll(TIn[], TOut[], Converter<TIn, TOut>)	Converts the items in an array to a different type
Copy(T[], T[])	Copies the items in one array to a different array of the same type
Exists(T[], Predicate<T>)	Returns true if at least one item in the array meets the predicate conditions
Find(T[], Predicate<T>) FindLast(T[], Predicate<T>)	Finds the first or last item in the array that meets the predicate conditions
FindAll(T[], Pridcate<T>)	Returns all the items in the array that meet the predicate conditions as a new array of the type T
FindIndex(T[], Predicate<T>) FindLastIndex(T[], Predicate<T>)	Returns the index of the first or last item in the array to match the predicate conditions
Sort(T[]) Sort(T[], IComparer<T>)	Sorts the array in place, using either the default comparer for T or the specified IComparer<T>
TrueForAll(T[], Predicate<T>)	Returns true if all the items in the array meet the predicate conditions

In all cases, you need to have created an array using the normal array language features and pass the array as an argument to the static System.Array method you want to use. One method that warrants particular attention is ConvertAll, which lets you convert an array of one type into an array of an entirely different type. Listing 19-33 demonstrates the use of this method to convert a string array to an int array.

Listing 19-33. Converting an Array of One Type to an Array of Another Type

```
using System;

namespace Listing_33 {
    class Listing_33 {

        static void Main(string[] args) {

            // create the source array
            string[] strArray = new string[] {
                "apple", "orange", "banana",
                "cherry", "guava" };

            // convert the string[] to an int[]
            int[] intArray = Array.ConvertAll(
                strArray,
                new Converter<string, int>(s => s.Length)
            );

            // enumerate the int[]
            foreach (int i in intArray) {
                Console.WriteLine("Int Array Item: {0}", i);
            }

            // wait for input before exiting
            Console.WriteLine("Press enter to finish");
            Console.ReadLine();
        }
    }
}
```

The two arguments to the ConvertAll method are the array you want to covert and an instance of the System.Converter class, which you can use as a wrapper around a lambda expression to handle the conversion. In the example listing, I create a new Converter<string, int>, which means that my lambda expression will be passed an instance of a string and required to return an instance of an int.

The result from the ConvertAll method is an array of the type you are converting to. In the case of the example, this is an int array. Compiling and running the code in the listing gives the following result:

```
Int Array Item: 5
Int Array Item: 6
Int Array Item: 6
Int Array Item: 6
Int Array Item: 5
Press enter to finish
```

Creating Constrained Collections

For a lot of the time, you will use the collection classes to maintain a view of the state of your program. Your collection items will be the list of current users of the system or the list of sales made in a region for the last week. The set of items in these collections will continue to change as your program runs or the collections themselves will be short-lived, because the entire collection is discarded at the end of a task.

Sometimes, you'll want something a little different. In this section, I'll show you how to create read-only collections and to create new types of collection that selectively expose functionality.

Read-Only Lists

Read-only collections are useful when you have collected all related data items and need to ensure that this set of items cannot be modified. If you are working with the List<T> class, there is built-in support for creating a read-only version of the collection, as shown by Listing 19-34.

Listing 19-34. Creating a Read-Only List<T>

```
using System;
using System.Collections.Generic;

namespace Listing_34 {
    class Listing_34 {

        static void Main(string[] args) {

            // create a normal List<T> and populate it
            List<string> normalList = new List<string>() { "apple", "orange", "banana" };

            // create a readonly list from the normal list
            IList<string> readonlyList = normalList.AsReadOnly();

            // report on Read-Only state of each list
            Console.WriteLine("normalList is read-only: {0}",
                ((IList<string>)normalList).IsReadOnly);
            Console.WriteLine("readonlyList is read-only: {0}",
                readonlyList.IsReadOnly);

            // try to modify the read-only collection
            Console.WriteLine("\nTrying to remove an item from the read-only list");
            try {
                readonlyList.Add("guava");
            } catch (Exception ex) {
                Console.WriteLine("Exception: {0}", ex.GetType());
            }

            // remove an item from the normal List<T>
            normalList.Remove("orange");

            // enumerate the contents of the read-only list
            Console.WriteLine("\nEnumerating readonly list");
```

```
            foreach (string s in readonlyList) {
                Console.WriteLine("Readonly List Item: {0}", s);
            }

            // wait for input before exiting
            Console.WriteLine("Press enter to finish");
            Console.ReadLine();
        }
    }
}
```

In the example, I create a regular List<T> and populate it with three string items. I then call the AsReadOnly method to create a read-only version of the collection. I assign the result of calling the AsReadOnly method to an IList<string>, but the underlying class that is returned is System.Collections.ObjectModel.ReadOnlyCollection, which also implements IList<T>, ICollection<T>, and IEnumerable<T> interfaces.

You can determine whether a collection is read-only by using the IsReadOnly property of the ICollection<T> interface. In the example, I have written out the result of this property for both of the lists. Using a read-only IList<T> is just like using a regular list, unless you try to modify the contents, in which case an instance of System.NotSupportedException is thrown. You can see this in the listing when I try to add guava to the collection. Compiling and running the code in Listing 19-34 produces the following results:

```
normalList is read-only: False
readonlyList is read-only: True

Trying to remove an item from the read-only list
Exception: System.NotSupportedException

Enumerating readonly list
Readonly List Item: apple
Readonly List Item: banana
Press enter to finish
```

Toward the end of the listing, I remove an item from the regular list and then enumerate the read-only list. You can see from the results that the item I removed is gone from both lists. As you can see, some care if required to ensure that you don't pass around references to the regular list since it can be used to modify both collections and so undermine the purpose of using a read-only collection in the first place. If you want to disassociate the read-only list from the regular list, then you can create an intermediate collection that will be used by the read-only list as follows:

```
IList<string> readonlyList =  new List<string>(normalList).AsReadOnly();
```

Other Read-Only Collections

Although List<T> is the only collection class that includes built-in support for creating read-only instances, you can achieve the same effect by creating an implementation of one of the collection interfaces and writing a wrapper around a regular collection instance. Methods that you want to support are mapped to the underlying collection, while the ones that you don't want to support throw a

NotSupportedException. Listing 19-35 demonstrates creating such a read-only wrapper for
Dictionary<TKey, TVal>.

Listing 19-35. Creating a Read-Only Collection

```
using System;
using System.Collections.Generic;

namespace Listing_35 {
    class Listing_35 {

        static void Main(string[] args) {

            // create a regular dictionary
            Dictionary<string, string> dict = new Dictionary<string, string>() {
                {"apple", "green"}, {"orange", "orange"}, {"cherry", "red"}};

            // create the read-only wrapper
            ReadOnlyDictionary<string, string> readOnlyDict
                = new ReadOnlyDictionary<string,string>(dict);

            // enumerate the keys
            foreach (string s in readOnlyDict.Keys) {
                Console.WriteLine("Key: {0}", s);
            }

            // try to add an item to the read-only collection
            try {
                readOnlyDict.Add("pear", "green");
            } catch (Exception ex) {
                Console.WriteLine("Exception: {0}", ex.GetType());
            }

            // wait for input before exiting
            Console.WriteLine("Press enter to finish");
            Console.ReadLine();
        }
    }

    class ReadOnlyDictionary<TKey, TVal> : IDictionary<TKey, TVal> {
        IDictionary<TKey, TVal> readwriteDict;

        public ReadOnlyDictionary(IDictionary<TKey, TVal> rwdict) {
            readwriteDict = rwdict;
        }

        public void Add(TKey key, TVal value) {
            throw new NotSupportedException();
        }

        public bool ContainsKey(TKey key) {
```

```
        return readwriteDict.ContainsKey(key);
    }

    public ICollection<TKey> Keys {
        get { return readwriteDict.Keys; }
    }

    public bool Remove(TKey key) {
        throw new NotSupportedException();
    }

    public bool TryGetValue(TKey key, out TVal value) {
        return readwriteDict.TryGetValue(key, out value);
    }

    public ICollection<TVal> Values {
        get { return readwriteDict.Values; }
    }

    public TVal this[TKey key] {
        get {
            return readwriteDict[key];
        }
        set {
            throw new NotSupportedException();
        }
    }

    public void Add(KeyValuePair<TKey, TVal> item) {
        throw new NotSupportedException();
    }

    public void Clear() {
        throw new NotSupportedException();
    }

    public bool Contains(KeyValuePair<TKey, TVal> item) {
        return readwriteDict.Contains(item);
    }

    public void CopyTo(KeyValuePair<TKey, TVal>[] array, int arrayIndex) {
        throw new NotSupportedException();
    }

    public int Count {
        get { return readwriteDict.Count; }
    }

    public bool IsReadOnly {
        get { return true; }
    }
```

```
        public bool Remove(KeyValuePair<TKey, TVal> item) {
            throw new NotSupportedException();
        }

        public IEnumerator<KeyValuePair<TKey, TVal>> GetEnumerator() {
            return readwriteDict.GetEnumerator() ;
        }

        System.Collections.IEnumerator System.Collections.IEnumerable.GetEnumerator() {
            return readwriteDict.GetEnumerator();
        }
    }
}
```

Compiling and running the code in Listing 19-35 gives the following results:

```
Key: apple
Key: orange
Key: cherry
Exception: System.NotSupportedException
Press enter to finish
```

Legacy Collections

The System.Collections and System.Collections.Specialized namespaces contain collection classes from before C# supported strongly typed classes. I am not going to cover these classes in any detail, because there is little point in using them in preference to the generic collections, but it can be useful to know how the legacy classes relate to the generic classes, especially if you are working with an old code base.

When working with the legacy classes, you are responsible for ensuring that the objects that you add and retrieve from the collection are of the type you are expecting. Otherwise, using a legacy class is very similar to using the equivalent generic replacement. Listing 19-36 demonstrates the use of the System.Collections.ArrayList class, which is the legacy equivalent of List<T> in the System.Collections.Generic namespace.

Listing 19-36. Using the Legacy ArrayList Class

```
using System;
using System.Collections;

namespace Listing_36 {
    class Listing_36 {

        static void Main(string[] args) {

            // create the legacy list
            ArrayList list = new ArrayList() { "apple", 3, "banana", "cherry" };
```

```
        // enumerate the contents of the list
        foreach (object o in list) {
            string s = o as string;
            if (s != null) {
                Console.WriteLine("List item - string: {0}", s);
            } else {
                Console.WriteLine("List item - {0}: {1}",
                    o.GetType().Name, o.ToString());
            }
        }

        // wait for input before exiting
        Console.WriteLine("Press enter to finish");
        Console.ReadLine();
    }
  }
}
```

When populating the ArrayList, I am able to add any object as an item to the collection. In this example, I have added three strings and an int. When I come to enumerate the contents of the ArrayList, I get a sequence of object instances, which I have to cast to another type to work with; I check the type using the as keyword.

```
List item - string: apple
List item - Int32: 3
List item - string: banana
List item - string: cherry
Press enter to finish
```

Prior to C# generic support, most bugs relating to collections were caused by unexpected items being retrieved from a collection and not properly checked before being cast. The strongly typed collections are a significant step forward in this regard. You can still work at the highest level of abstraction by creating a List<object>, for example, and so there is really very little reason to use the legacy collection classes. My advice is to stick with the generic collections. Table 19-34 shows the main legacy collections and their equivalent generic replacement.

Table 19-34. Legacy Collection Classes and Their Generic Replacements

Legacy Collection	Generic Collection Replacement
ArrayList	List<T>,
Hashtable	Dictionary<TKey, TVal>, SortedDictionary<TKey, TVal>
Queue	Queue<T>
SortedList	SortedList<TKey, TVal>
Stack	Stack<T>

Summary

In this chapter, we took a tour of the generic collection classes, looking at lists, dictionaries, sets, queues, and stacks. These are classes that you will use day-in, day-out in your projects. You'll probably use List<T> most often to begin with, because it can be used as a direct replacement for an array, which most programmers are already comfortable with. But the other collection classes are worth your attention also, so I suggest you take the time to understand them all.

We also looked at how to apply some collection-like features to arrays using the System.Array class. This is a very useful feature that doesn't get as much attention as it deserves. Collections are a complement to arrays, not a replacement, and being able to treat an array as you would a collection can be a great time-saver.

Finally, we looked at how to create read-only collections and touched upon the legacy collections that have been part of the .NET class library since before C# supported generics. I strongly recommend that you stick to the generic classes, which have more features and where strong typing will help eliminate runtime exceptions.

CHAPTER 20

■ ■ ■

Files, Streams, and IO

In this chapter, we will look at how C# supports files and IO. These two areas are related because the mechanism that C# uses for reading and writing files is usually accessed through the classes that are used to find files and directories in the first place. All the classes in this directory can be found in the `System.IO` and `System.IO.Compression` namespaces. Table 20-1 provides the summary for this chapter.

Table 20-1. *Quick Problem/Solution Reference for Chapter 20*

Problem	Solution	Listings
Find the files and directories within a given directory.	Use the `Directory` or `DirectoryInfo` classes.	20-1 through 20-3, 20-9
Get detailed information about a file or directory.	Use the `Directory`, `FileInfo`, or `DirectoryInfo` classes.	20-4, 20-6, 20-7, 20-8, 20-10
Get or set the current working directory of the current process.	Use the `GetCurrentDirectory` and `SetCurrentDirectory` methods of the `Directory` class.	20-5
Read and write data without using streams.	Use the convenience methods in the `File` class.	20-11
Create and manipulate path strings.	Use the `Path` class.	20-12
Monitor a directory for changes.	Use the `FileSystemWatcher` class.	20-13 through 20-15
Read and write sequential data in a consistent way from a range of data sources.	Use `Stream` objects.	20-16
Stream data in memory.	Use the `MemoryStream` class.	20-17
Stream data in files.	Use the `FileStream` class.	20-18

Problem	Solution	Listings
Manipulate data as it is read from or written to streams.	Use a pass-through stream.	20-19, 20-20
Read and write binary representations of C# built-in types.	Use the BinaryReader and BinaryWriter classes.	20-21
Read and write string representations of C# types.	Use the StreamReader and StreamWriter classes.	20-22, 20-23

Working with Files and Directories

We will start this chapter by looking at the facilities C# provides for working with files and directories. As you will see, there is a lot of duplication in the available classes, and the ones that you choose for use in your program are a matter of personal preference.

Using the System.IO.Directory Class

The System.IO.Directory class has a range of static methods that you can use to interrogate and manipulate files and directories. In the following sections, I'll demonstrate some of the most commonly used methods.

Enumerating Files and Directories

The Directory class contains a set of methods that let you enumerate the contents of a directory. These methods are described in Table 20-2.

Table 20-2. Enumeration Methods of System.IO.Directory

Method	Description
GetDirectories(string) GetDirectories(string, string) GetDirectories(string, string, SearchOption)	Returns a string[] containing the names of the directories contained within the directory specified by the first string parameter. If the second string parameter is used, then the contents are filtered to those that contain the parameter value. The third parameter control whether the results should include the contents of subdirectories.
GetFiles(string) GetFiles(string, string) GetFiles(string, string, SearchOption)	Like the GetDirectories method but returns a string array containing file names.

Method	Description
GetFileSystemEntries(string) GetFileSystemEntries(string, string) GetFileSystemEntries(string, string, SearchOption)	Like the GetDirectories method but returns a string array containing file and directory names.

Listing 20-1 demonstrates using the basic version of each of the methods described in Table 20-2 to get details of the files and directories of my C:\ directory.

Listing 20-1. Getting Information Using the Directory Class

```
using System;
using System.IO;

class Listing_01 {

    static void Main(string[] args) {

        string[] filesArray = Directory.GetFiles(@"C:\");
        Console.WriteLine("--- GetFiles Results ---");
        foreach (string name in filesArray) {
            Console.WriteLine("File name: {0}", name);
        }

        string[] dirsArray = Directory.GetDirectories(@"C:\");
        Console.WriteLine("\n--- GetDirectories Results ---");
        foreach (string name in dirsArray) {
            Console.WriteLine("Directory name: {0}", name);
        }

        string[] allArray = Directory.GetFileSystemEntries(@"C:\");
        Console.WriteLine("\n--- GetFileSystemEntries Results ---");
        foreach (string name in allArray) {
            Console.WriteLine("FileSystemEntry name: {0}", name);
        }

        // wait for input before exiting
        Console.WriteLine("Press enter to finish");
        Console.ReadLine();
    }
}
```

Notice that I have prefixed each path name parameter with the @ symbol. This is to denote the path string as a verbatim literal so that the backslash character (\) in the path parameter is not interpreted as the start of a string escape sequence. You will learn more about verbatim string literals and escape sequences in Chapter 16. Compiling and running Listing 20-1 produces the following results on my computer:

```
--- GetFiles Results ---
File name: C:\hiberfil.sys
File name: C:\pagefile.sys

--- GetDirectories Results ---
Directory name: C:\$Recycle.Bin
Directory name: C:\Config.Msi
Directory name: C:\Documents and Settings
Directory name: C:\MSOCache
Directory name: C:\Northwind Database
Directory name: C:\PerfLogs
Directory name: C:\Program Files
Directory name: C:\Program Files (x86)
Directory name: C:\ProgramData
Directory name: C:\Recovery
Directory name: C:\System Volume Information
Directory name: C:\Users
Directory name: C:\Windows

--- GetFileSystemEntries Results ---
FileSystemEntry name: C:\$Recycle.Bin
FileSystemEntry name: C:\Config.Msi
FileSystemEntry name: C:\Documents and Settings
FileSystemEntry name: C:\hiberfil.sys
FileSystemEntry name: C:\MSOCache
FileSystemEntry name: C:\Northwind Database
FileSystemEntry name: C:\pagefile.sys
FileSystemEntry name: C:\PerfLogs
FileSystemEntry name: C:\Program Files
FileSystemEntry name: C:\Program Files (x86)
FileSystemEntry name: C:\ProgramData
FileSystemEntry name: C:\Recovery
FileSystemEntry name: C:\System Volume Information
FileSystemEntry name: C:\Users
FileSystemEntry name: C:\Windows
Press enter to finish
```

You can see from the results that the path I specified for the search is prepended to the name of each file and directory name. If I had specified a relative path, then this would also have been prepended to the results. Here is an example of using a relative path:

```csharp
string[] filesArray = Directory.GetFiles(@".");
Console.WriteLine("--- GetFiles Results ---");
foreach (string name in filesArray) {
    Console.WriteLine("File name: {0}", name);
}
```

```
--- GetFiles Results ---
File name: .\Listing_01.exe
```

```
File name: .\Listing_01.pdb
File name: .\Listing_01.vshost.exe
File name: .\Listing_01.vshost.exe.manifest
```

Filtering File and Directory Results

The overloaded versions of the methods described in Table 20-2 allow you to apply a filter so that only files or directories that match a search string are included in the results. Listing 20-2 contains an example.

Listing 20-2. Filtering Results with a Search String

```csharp
using System;
using System.IO;

class Listing_02 {

    static void Main(string[] args) {

        string[] filteredNames = Directory.GetFiles(@"C:\", "page*");

        foreach (string name in filteredNames) {
            Console.WriteLine("Name: {0}", name);
        }

        // wait for input before exiting
        Console.WriteLine("Press enter to finish");
        Console.ReadLine();
    }
}
```

There are two special characters you can use when specifying a search filter. An asterisk (*) will match zero or more characters, and a question mark (?) will match any one character. In Listing 20-2, the search filter is page*, which will match any result that starts with page. Compiling and running Listing 20-2 produces the following result:

```
Name: C:\pagefile.sys
Press enter to finish
```

The file pagefile.sys is a match for the search filter because it begins with the string page. Here is an example of using the ? character in a search filter:

```csharp
string[] filteredNames = Directory.GetFiles(@"C:\", "pagefile.???");

foreach (string name in filteredNames) {
    Console.WriteLine("Name: {0}", name);
}
```

The search filter in this example will match any filename that starts with pagefile. (including the period) and that has any three characters as the file extension. The output from these statements on my machine is the same as the previous example:

```
Name: C:\pagefile.sys
Press enter to finish
```

The examples so far have only listed the files and directories at the root level of the directory we have specified. You can use values from the System.IO.SearchOption enumeration to control whether the search will include subdirectories. Table 20-3 describes the two values of SearchOption.

Table 20-3. Values from the System.IO.SearchOption Enumeration

Value	Description
TopDirectoryOnly	The results will include only files and directories in the top directory.
AllDirectories	The results will include files and directories in subdirectories.

Listing 20-3 contains a demonstration of searching subdirectories by using the AllDirectories value from the SearchOption enumeration.

Listing 20-3. Including Subdirectories in a File System Search

```csharp
using System;
using System.IO;

class Listing_03 {

    static void Main(string[] args) {

        string[] filteredNames = Directory.GetFiles(@"C:\Program Files",
            "*.exe",
            SearchOption.AllDirectories);

        foreach (string name in filteredNames) {
            Console.WriteLine("Name: {0}", name);
        }

        // wait for input before exiting
        Console.WriteLine("Press enter to finish");
        Console.ReadLine();
    }
}
```

Listing 20-3 uses the `Directory.GetFiles` method to create a list of all the `.exe` files that are in the `C:\Program Files` directory and any of its subdirectories. Compiling and running Listing 20-3 produces the following results, which I have edited for length; there are a lot of executable files:

```
Name: C:\Program Files\7-Zip\7z.exe
Name: C:\Program Files\7-Zip\7zFM.exe
Name: C:\Program Files\7-Zip\7zG.exe
Name: C:\Program Files\Common Files\Microsoft Shared\DW\DW20.EXE
Name: C:\Program Files\Common Files\Microsoft Shared\DW\DWTRIG20.EXE
Name: C:\Program Files\Common Files\Microsoft Shared\EQUATION\EQNEDT32.EXE
Name: C:\Program Files\Common Files\Microsoft Shared\ink\ConvertInkStore.exe
...
Name: C:\Program Files\Windows Media Player\WMPSideShowGadget.exe
Name: C:\Program Files\Windows NT\Accessories\wordpad.exe
Name: C:\Program Files\Windows Photo Viewer\ImagingDevices.exe
Name: C:\Program Files\Windows Sidebar\sidebar.exe
Press enter to finish
```

You must be careful when using the `GetFiles`, `GetDirectories`, and `GetFileSystemEntries` methods to ensure that you have the required permissions to view all the files and directories that are in the directory parameter you pass to the method and its subdirectories. If you do not, then you will encounter an exception. Here is a demonstration:

```
string[] filteredNames = Directory.GetFiles(@"C:\Windows",
    "*.exe", SearchOption.AllDirectories);

foreach (string name in filteredNames) {
    Console.WriteLine("Name: {0}", name);
}
```

This example searches for all executable files in the `C:\Windows` directory and its subdirectories. If I compile and run these statements without administration privileges, I get the following exception:

```
Unhandled Exception: System.UnauthorizedAccessException: Access to the path
'C:\Windows\AppCompat\Programs\' is denied.
   at System.IO.__Error.WinIOError(Int32 errorCode, String maybeFullPath)
   at System.IO.FileSystemEnumerableIterator`1.AddSearchableDirsToStack(SearchData
localSearchData)
   at System.IO.FileSystemEnumerableIterator`1.MoveNext()
   at System.Collections.Generic.List`1..ctor(IEnumerable`1 collection)
   at System.IO.Directory.GetFiles(String path, String searchPattern, SearchOption
searchOption)
   at Listing_03.Main(String[] args) in C:\Listing_03\Listing_03.cs:line 9
Press any key to continue . . .
```

Getting and Setting Information for a File or Directory

The System.IO.Directory class contains a set of static methods that allow you to get and set detailed information about a single file or directory. Table 20-4 describes these methods.

Table 20-4. System.IO.Directory Methods to Get or Set File and Directory Information

Method	Description
GetCreationTime(string)	Gets a DateTime describing the creation time of the file or directory specified in the parameter
GetLastAccessTime(string)	Gets a DateTime describing the last time the file or directory specified in the parameter was accessed
GetLastWriteTime(string)	Gets a DateTime describing the last time the file or directory specified in the parameter was modified
SetCreationTime(string, DateTime)	Changes the creation time of the file or directory specified in the parameter to the DateTime parameter
SetLastAccessTime(string, DateTime)	Changes the last access time of the file or directory specified in the parameter to the DateTime parameter
SetLastWriteTime(string, DateTime)	Changes the modification time of the file or directory specified in the parameter to the DateTime parameter

The System.DateTime struct is used to represent a moment in time. This struct is discussed in detail in Chapter 22. I don't want to get into the detail of DateTime in this chapter, so Listing 20-4 demonstrates how to read information from a file and prints it out using the default string representation of DateTime.

Listing 20-4. Reading Information About a File

```
using System;
using System.IO;

class Listing_04 {

    static void Main(string[] args) {

        string[] fileNames = Directory.GetFiles(@"C:\");

        // print out information for each file
        foreach (string name in fileNames) {
            Console.WriteLine("---");
            Console.WriteLine("File name: {0}", name);
            Console.WriteLine("Created: {0}", Directory.GetCreationTime(name));
            Console.WriteLine("Accessed: {0}", Directory.GetLastAccessTime(name));
            Console.WriteLine("Modified: {0}", Directory.GetLastWriteTime(name));
```

```
        }

        // wait for input before exiting
        Console.WriteLine("Press enter to finish");
        Console.ReadLine();
    }
}
```

Compiling and running Listing 20-4 produces the following results:

```
---
File name: C:\hiberfil.sys
Created: 04/29/2010 15:32:42
Accessed: 04/29/2010 15:32:42
Modified: 07/12/2010 08:10:09
---
File name: C:\pagefile.sys
Created: 04/29/2010 15:32:42
Accessed: 07/03/2010 15:07:12
Modified: 07/12/2010 08:10:09
Press enter to finish
```

Changing the Current Working Directory

The current working directory is used when you list the files using a relative path (that is, without specifying a drive or starting the path with a backslash character (\)). The Directory class provides methods to get and set the working directory for your program, which are described in Table 20-5.

Table 20-5. System.IO.Directory Methods to Get or Set the Current Working Directory

Method	Description
GetCurrentDirectory()	Gets the name of the current working directory, which is used for relative file and directory requests
SetCurrentDirectory(string)	Sets the current working directory to the value specified by the parameter

Listing 20-5 provides a simple demonstration of using and changing the working directory.

Listing 20-5. Using and Changing the Working Directory

```
using System;
using System.IO;

class Listing_05 {

    static void Main(string[] args) {
```

```
        // get the current working directory
        string currentDir = Directory.GetCurrentDirectory();
        Console.WriteLine("Current directory: {0}", currentDir);

        // get the files in this directory
        string[] fileNames = Directory.GetFiles(".");
        foreach (string name in fileNames) {
            Console.WriteLine("File: {0}", name);
        }

        // change the working directory
        Directory.SetCurrentDirectory(@"C:\");

        // get the files in this directory
        fileNames = Directory.GetFiles(".");
        Console.WriteLine("--- New Working Directory ---");
        foreach (string name in fileNames) {
            Console.WriteLine("File: {0}", name);
        }

        // wait for input before exiting
        Console.WriteLine("Press enter to finish");
        Console.ReadLine();
    }
}
```

Compiling and running Listing 20-5 produces the following results:

```
Current directory: C:\Listing_05\bin\Debug
File: .\Listing_05.exe
File: .\Listing_05.pdb
File: .\Listing_05.vshost.exe
File: .\Listing_05.vshost.exe.manifest
--- New Working Directory ---
File: .\hiberfil.sys
File: .\pagefile.sys
Press enter to finish
```

Using the FileInfo and DirectoryInfo Classes

The static methods of the System.IO.Directory class are useful for searching directories and getting basic information about files and directories, but performing more advanced operations on file and directories requires creating an object from the FileInfo or DirectoryInfo classes, both of which are in the System.IO namespace.

Using the FileInfo Class

The FileInfo class has a constructor that takes a string parameter specifying the path of the file you want to work with. This path can be fully qualified, part-qualified, or relative, as demonstrated by Listing 20-6.

Listing 20-6. Creating FileInfo Objects

```
using System;
using System.IO;

class Listing_06 {

    static void Main(string[] args) {

        // set the working directory for the program
        Directory.SetCurrentDirectory(@"C:\");

        // create a FileInfo object using a drive letter
        FileInfo fqInfo = new FileInfo(@"C:\pagefile.sys");

        // create a FileInfo object with a path starting with a backslash
        FileInfo pqInfo = new FileInfo(@"\pagefile.sys");

        // create a FileInfo object with a relative path
        FileInfo relativeInfo = new FileInfo("pagefile.sys");

        // wait for input before exiting
        Console.WriteLine("Press enter to finish");
        Console.ReadLine();
    }
}
```

Listing 20-6 creates three FileInfo objects, all of which reference the same file. You can create FileInfo objects for files that do not exist and then call the appropriate methods to create the file; see the later Table 20-7 for a summary of the methods that do this and the "Working with Streams, Readers, and Writers" section for details of how to use them.

Once you have created a FileInfo object, there are a range of instance methods and properties that you can use to work with the file; these are summarized in Table 20-6.

Table 20-6. System.IO.FileInfo Members

Member	Description
CopyTo(string) CopyTo(string, bool)	Copies the file represented by the FileInfo object to the new file specified by the string parameter. If the bool parameter is used, a true value will overwrite any existing file.
CreationTime	Returns the time that the file was created.

631

Member	Description
Delete()	Deletes the file.
Directory	Returns a DirectoryInfo representing the directory that contains this file.
DirectoryName	Returns the full path of the parent directory.
Encrypt() Decrypt()	Encrypts or decrypts the file using the standard windows disk encryption.
Exists	Returns true if the file exists or false if it does not exist or is a directory.
Extension	Returns the extension part of the filename, including the period.
FullPath	The fully qualified path of the file.
IsReadOnly	Gets or sets the read-only status of the file.
LastAccessTime	Returns the time that the file was last accessed.
LastWriteTime	Returns the time that the file was last modified.
Length	Returns the length of the file in bytes as a long value.
MoveTo(string)	Moves the file to the destination specified by the string parameter.
Name	Returns the name of the file.
OriginalPath	Returns the path specified by the constructor parameter.
Refresh()	Rereads the information about the file from the file system. This is useful if you suspect another program may have modified the file.
Replace(string, string)	Replaces the file named in the first parameter with the contents of current file and backs up the original file to the destination specified by the second parameter.

Listing 20-7 demonstrates using some of the FileInfo methods and properties.

Listing 20-7. Using a FileInfo Object

```
using System;
using System.IO;

class Listing_07 {

    static void Main(string[] args) {

        FileInfo myFile = new FileInfo(@"C:\pagefile.sys");

        // does the file exist?
        bool fileExists = myFile.Exists;
        Console.WriteLine("File Exists? {0}", fileExists);

        // get the file extension
        string fileExtension = myFile.Extension;
        Console.WriteLine("File Extension: {0}", fileExtension);

        // get the size of the file
        long fileSize = myFile.Length;
        Console.WriteLine("File length: {0} bytes", fileSize);

        // get the name of the directory
        string directoryName = myFile.DirectoryName;
        Console.WriteLine("Directory name: {0}", directoryName);

        // wait for input before exiting
        Console.WriteLine("Press enter to finish");
        Console.ReadLine();
    }
}
```

Compiling and running Listing 20-7 gives us the following results:

```
File Exists? True
File Extension: .sys
File length: 4283621376 bytes
Directory name: C:\
Press enter to finish
```

In addition to the members in Table 20-6, the FileInfo class also contains a set of methods that return stream, reader, or writer objects, described in Table 20-7. These are used to read the contents of the file or to write new content. I describe stream, reader, and writer objects in the "Working with Streams, Readers, and Writers section" later in this chapter.

Table 20-7. System.IO.FileInfo Stream, Reader, and Writer Members

Method	Description
AppendText()	Returns a StreamWriter that will append text to the file.
Create()	Returns a FileSteam that can be used to read from and write to the file. If the file already exists, it will be overwritten.
CreateText()	Returns a StreamWriter that can be used to write to the file.
Open(FileMode) Open(FileMode, FileAccess)	Returns a FileStream in the modes specified by the FileMode and FileAccess enumeration parameters.
OpenRead()	Returns a read-only FileStream that can be used to read the contents of the file.
OpenText()	Opens a StreamReader that can be used to read the contents of a text file.
OpenWrite()	Opens a write-only FileStream to the file.

Using the DirectoryInfo Class

The DirectoryInfo class shares some common traits with FileInfo but works on directories. In addition to working with specific directories, the DirectoryInfo class can be used to search for files and subdirectories.

The constructor for the DirectoryInfo class takes a single string parameter containing the path to the directory you want to work with. Here is an example:

```
DirectoryInfo myDir = new DirectoryInfo(@"C:\");
```

You can create DirectoryInfo objects for directories that do not exist and then use the object methods to create the directory. I have split the members of the DirectoryInfo class into two sections. Table 20-8 summarized the methods and properties of the DirectoryInfo class that operate on the current directory.

Table 20-8. System.IO.DirectoryInfo Members That Operate on the Current Directory

Members	Description
Create()	Creates the directory specified in the constructor; does nothing if the directory already exists.
CreateSubDirectory(string)	Creates a directory with the specified name inside the current directory.
CreationTime	Returns the time that the directory was created.
Delete() Delete(bool)	The first version of this method will delete the directory if it is empty. The second version will delete the files and subdirectories if the parameter value is true.
Exists	Returns true if the directory specified by the constructor parameter exists and is a directory.
LastAccessTime	Returns the time that the directory was last accessed.
LastWriteTime	Returns the time that the directory was last modified.
MoveTo(string)	Moves the directory (and its contents) to the path specified by the string parameter.
Name	Returns the name of the directory.
Parent	Returns a DirectoryInfo object representing the parent directory
Refresh()	Rereads the information about the directory from the file system.
Root	Returns a DirectoryInfo object representing the root directory.

Listing 20-8 demonstrates the use of some of these methods and properties.

Listing 20-8. Using the Basic Members of the DirectoryInfo Class

```
using System;
using System.IO;

class Listing_08 {
```

```
static void Main(string[] args) {

    DirectoryInfo myDir = new DirectoryInfo(@"C:\Program Files");

    // does the directory exist
    bool dirExists = myDir.Exists;
    Console.WriteLine("Directory exists? {0}", dirExists);

    // what is the name of the directory
    string dirName = myDir.Name;
    Console.WriteLine("Directory name: {0}", dirName);

    // what is the parent directory name
    string parentName = myDir.Parent.Name;
    Console.WriteLine("Parent name: {0}", parentName);

    // what is the root name
    string rootName = myDir.Root.Name;
    Console.WriteLine("Root name: {0}", rootName);

    // wait for input before exiting
    Console.WriteLine("Press enter to finish");
    Console.ReadLine();
    }
}
```

Compiling and running Listing 20-8 gives the following results:

```
Directory exists? True
Directory name: Program Files
Parent name: C:\
Root name: C:\
Press enter to finish
```

The remaining methods in the DirectoryInfo class can be used to search for files and directories. These methods work much like their equivalents in the Directory class, except that the results are instances of DirectoryInfo and FileInfo and the search is always relative to the directory specified by the constructor parameter. These methods are described in Table 20-9.

Table 20-9. System.IO.DirectoryInfo Search Members

Method	Description
GetDirectories() GetDirectories(string) GetDirectories(string, SearchOption)	Returns an array of DirectoryInfo objects representing the subdirectories of the current directory. The overloaded versions of this method allow you to filter the results and specify whether the subdirectories themselves should be searched.

Method	Description
GetFiles() GetFiles(string) GetFiles(string, SearchOption)	Returns an array of FileInfo objects representing the files in the current directory. The overloaded versions of this method allow you to filter the results and specify whether subdirectories should be searched as well.
GetFileSystemInfos() GetFileSystemInfos(string) GetFileSystemInfos(string, SearchOption)	Returns an array of FileSystemInfo objects representing the files and directories in the current directory. The overloaded versions of this method allow you to filter the results and specify if subdirectories should be searched as well.

These methods use the same special characters as the equivalent methods in the Directory class; see Listing 20-2 for an example of filtering.

The base class of both FileInfo and DirectoryInfo is FileSystemInfo. You can use the GetFileSystemInfos method in the DirectoryInfo class to get an array that contains FileSystemInfo objects representing both files and directories. Some of the key members of the FileSystemInfo class are more restricted than the derived classes and are summarized in Table 20-10.

Table 20-10. Selected System.IO.FileSystemInfo Members

Member	Description
CreationTime	Returns the time that the file or directory was created
Delete()	Deletes the file or directory
FullName	Returns the fully qualified name of the file or directory
LastAccessTime	Returns the time that the file or directory was last accessed
LastWriteTime	Returns the time that the file or directory was last modified
Name	Returns the name of the file or directory
Refresh()	Refreshes the information about the file or directory from the file system

You can use the members of the FileSystemInfo class or explicitly cast to either FileInfo or DirectoryInfo, as demonstrated by Listing 20-9.

Listing 20-9. Working with the FileSystemInfo Class

```
using System;
using System.IO;

class Listing_09 {

    static void Main(string[] args) {

        // create the DirectoryInfo object
        DirectoryInfo myDir = new DirectoryInfo(@"C:\");

        // get the FileSystemInfo objects for the directory
        FileSystemInfo[] fsiArray = myDir.GetFileSystemInfos();

        // process each FileSystemInfo
        foreach (FileSystemInfo fsi in fsiArray) {
            string fileOrDir = fsi is FileInfo ? "file" : "directory";
            Console.WriteLine("{0} is a {1}", fsi.Name, fileOrDir);
        }

        // wait for input before exiting
        Console.WriteLine("Press enter to finish");
        Console.ReadLine();
    }
}
```

Compiling and running Listing 20-9 produces the following results on my machine:

```
$Recycle.Bin is a directory
Config.Msi is a directory
Documents and Settings is a directory
hiberfil.sys is a file
MSOCache is a directory
Northwind Database is a directory
pagefile.sys is a file
PerfLogs is a directory
Program Files is a directory
Program Files (x86) is a directory
ProgramData is a directory
Recovery is a directory
System Volume Information is a directory
Users is a directory
Windows is a directory
Press enter to finish
```

Using the System.IO.File Class

The File class is the counterpart to the Directory class that we looked at earlier. I have left this class to last in this section because it contains some useful convenience methods that can be used to read and write files. The File class also contains a set of static methods that can be used to get information about and make other changes to files; I will start with these methods and then detail the more interesting convenience methods afterward. The basic File methods are listed in Table 20-11.

Table 20-11. Basic System.IO.File Members

Method	Description
Copy(string, string)	Copies the file specified by the first parameter to a new file specified by the second parameter.
Delete(string)	Deletes the file specified by the parameter.
Encrypt(string) Decrypt(string)	Encrypts or decrypts a file.
Exists(string)	Returns true if the file exists.
GetCreationTime(string) GetLastAccessTime(string) GetLastWriteTime(string)	Returns the creation/access/modification time of the file specified by the parameter.
Move(string, string)	Moves the file specified by the first parameter to the new file specified by the second parameter.
Replace(string, string, string)	Replaces the contents of a file with the contents of another file.
SetCreationTime(string, DateTime) SetLastAccessTime(string, DateTime) SetLastWriteTime(string, DateTime)	Sets the creation/access/modification time of the file specified by the parameter. The use of the DateTime class is explained in Chapter 22.

Listing 20-10 demonstrates the use of some of these static methods.

Listing 20-10. Using the Basic Methods of the File Class

```
using System;
using System.IO;

class Listing_10 {

    static void Main(string[] args) {

        // create a string variable for the file name
        string fileName = @"C:\pagefile.sys";
```

```
        // does the file exist?
        bool fileExists = File.Exists(fileName);
        Console.WriteLine("File exists: {0}", fileExists);

        // get the creation, accessed and modified times
        DateTime createdTime = File.GetCreationTime(fileName);
        DateTime accessedTime = File.GetLastAccessTime(fileName);
        DateTime writeTime = File.GetLastWriteTime(fileName);
        Console.WriteLine("Created: {0}", createdTime);
        Console.WriteLine("Accessed: {0}", accessedTime);
        Console.WriteLine("Modified: {0}", writeTime);

        // wait for input before exiting
        Console.WriteLine("Press enter to finish");
        Console.ReadLine();
    }
}
```

Compiling and running Listing 20-10 gives the following results:

```
File exists: True
Created: 29/04/2010 15:32:42
Accessed: 03/07/2010 15:07:12
Modified: 12/07/2010 08:10:09
Press enter to finish
```

Using the File Convenience Methods

The convenience methods in the File class allow simple file operations to be performed without needing to use streams (streams are covered later in this chapter and can be relatively complex and fiddly). Table 20-12 describes these convenience methods.

Table 20-12. System.IO.File Convenience Members

Method	Description
AppendAllLines(string, IEnumerable<string>)	Appends the strings contained in the IEnumerable<string> to the file, each on a separate line
AppendAllText(string, string)	Appends the string in the second parameter to the file specified in the first parameter
ReadAllBytes(string)	Reads the contents of a binary file and returns them as a byte array

Method	Description
ReadAllLines(string)	Reads the contents of a text file and returns a string array containing the lines of text
ReadAllText(string)	Reads the contents of a text file and returns a string containing the contents
ReadLines(string)	Reads the contents of a text file and returns an IEnumerable<string>, which enumerates the individual lines
WriteAllBytes(string, byte[])	Writes the byte array to the specified file; if the file exists, it is overwritten with the new content
WriteAllLines(string, string[]) WriteAllLines(string, IEnumberable<string>)	Writes the collection of strings to the specified file; if the file already exists, it is overwritten with the new content
WriteAllText(string, string)	Writes the string to the specified file, replacing any existing content if the file already exists

Listing 20-11 demonstrates using some of the convenience methods.

Listing 20-11. Using the System.IO.File Convenience Methods

```
using System;
using System.IO;

class Listing_11 {

    static void Main(string[] args) {

        // create a unique temporary filename
        string fileName = Path.GetTempFileName();
        Console.WriteLine("File name is: {0}", fileName);

        // define a string array that we'll use for the file contents
        string[] lineArray = new string[] { "apple", "banana", "apricot", "cherry" };

        // write the string array to the temporary file
        File.WriteAllLines(fileName, lineArray);

        // read the contents of the file
        foreach (string str in File.ReadAllLines(fileName)) {
            Console.WriteLine("Read line: {0}", str);
        }

        // wait for input before exiting
```

```
        Console.WriteLine("Press enter to finish");
        Console.ReadLine();
    }
}
```

Listing 20-11 creates a temporary file using the Path class, which is covered in the next section. A string array is written as lines to the file and then read back; both of these operations are performed using File convenience methods. Compiling and running Listing 20-11 produces the following results:

```
File name is: C:\Users\Adam\AppData\Local\Temp\tmpEAOA.tmp
Read line: apple
Read line: banana
Read line: apricot
Read line: cherry
Press enter to finish
```

Using the Stream, Reader, and Writer Methods

The File class also defines a set of methods that return stream, reader, or writer objects. I explain how to use these objects in the "Working with Streams, Readers, and Writers" section later in this chapter. Table 20-13 describes these methods for reference.

Table 20-13. System.IO.File Stream, Reader, and Writer Members

Method	Description
AppendText(string)	Returns a StreamWriter that can be used to append text to the file
Create(string)	Creates or overwrites the specified file and returns a FileStream that can be used to read from and write to the file
CreateText(string)	Creates or overwrites the specified file and returns a StreamWriter that can be used to write to the file
Open(string, FileMode)	Returns a FileStream that can be used to read and write to the specified file, which must already exist
OpenRead(string)	Returns a FileStream that can be used to read the specified file, which must already exist
OpenWrite(string)	Returns a FileStream that can be used to write to the specified file, which must already exist

Using the System.IO.Path Class

The Path class simplifies working with path strings and does so in a platform-independent way. This means that you don't have to hard-code separator characters, for example. Table 20-14 summarizes the members of the Path class.

Table 20-14. System.IO.Path Members

Member	Description
ChangeExtension(string, string)	Changes the extension component of a path string
Combine(string[]) Combine(string, string) Combine(string, string, string) Combine(string, string, string)	Combines the parameters (or the elements in the array parameter) to form a properly separated path string, which is returned as a result
GetDirectoryName(string)	Returns the directory part of a path string
GetFileName(string) GetFileNameWithoutExtension(string)	Returns the name of the file from a path string, with or without the file extension component
GetFullPath(string)	Returns a fully qualified path from a relative path
GetInvalidFileNameChars() GetInvalidPathNameChars()	Returns a char array that contains the characters that cannot be used in file names or paths
GetPathRoot(string)	Returns the root component of a path string
GetRandomeFileName()	Returns a random string that can be used as a file or directory name.
GetTempFileName()	Creates a uniquely named temporary file on disk and returns the name of it.
GetTempPath()	Returns the path for the current user's temporary folder
HasExtension(string)	Returns true if the specified path has an extension component
PathSeparator	Returns the platform specific path separator character

Listing 20-12 demonstrates using some of the members of the Path class. These methods do not modify the files or directories that the path strings refer to; they only help manipulate the strings themselves.

Listing 20-12. Using the Path Class

```
using System;
using System.IO;

class Listing_12 {

    static void Main(string[] args) {

        // combine strings to make a path
        string[] strComponents = new string[] { @"C:\", "pagefile.sys" };
        string combinedPath = Path.Combine(strComponents);
        Console.WriteLine("Combined path: {0}", combinedPath);

        // does the path have an extension?
        bool hasExtension = Path.HasExtension(combinedPath);
        Console.WriteLine("Has extension: {0}", hasExtension);

        // change the extension part of the path
        string extensionMod = Path.ChangeExtension(combinedPath, "dat");
        Console.WriteLine("Modified path: {0}", extensionMod);

        // get the file name (with and without the extension)
        string fileName = Path.GetFileName(combinedPath);
        string fileNameNoExt = Path.GetFileNameWithoutExtension(combinedPath);
        Console.WriteLine("File name: {0}", fileName);
        Console.WriteLine("File name (no extension): {0}", fileNameNoExt);

        // get the user's temp directory
        string tempDir = Path.GetTempPath();
        Console.WriteLine("Temp dir: {0}", tempDir);

        // wait for input before exiting
        Console.WriteLine("Press enter to finish");
        Console.ReadLine();
    }
}
```

Compiling and running Listing 20-12 produces the following output:

```
Combined path: C:\pagefile.sys
Has extension: True
Modified path: C:\pagefile.dat
File name: pagefile.sys
File name (no extension): pagefile
Temp dir: C:\Users\Adam\AppData\Local\Temp\
Press enter to finish
```

Monitoring for Changes

The System.IO.FileSystemWatcher class can be used to monitor a directory for changes. The class defines a set of events, which are invoked when different kinds of change are detected. Chapter 10 describes C# events. Listing 20-13 demonstrates using a FileSystemWatcher to monitor a directory.

Listing 20-13. Monitoring a Directory for Changes

```
using System;
using System.IO;

class Listing_13 {

    static void Main(string[] args) {

        // create temporary directory
        string tempDirPath = Path.Combine(Path.GetTempPath(), Path.GetRandomFileName());

        // create the directory specified by the path
        Directory.CreateDirectory(tempDirPath);

        // create a FileSystemWatcher to look for changes
        FileSystemWatcher fsWatcher = new FileSystemWatcher(tempDirPath);

        // register handlers with the events of the watcher
        fsWatcher.Changed += new FileSystemEventHandler(HandleFileSystemChangeEvent);
        fsWatcher.Created += new FileSystemEventHandler(HandleFileSystemChangeEvent);
        fsWatcher.Deleted += new FileSystemEventHandler(HandleFileSystemChangeEvent);

        // start watching for events
        fsWatcher.EnableRaisingEvents = true;

        // create a file name that we will use in the temp directory
        string tempFilePath = Path.Combine(tempDirPath, Path.GetRandomFileName());
        Console.WriteLine("Temp file name is: {0}", tempFilePath);

        // create a new file in the temp directory
        File.WriteAllText(tempFilePath, "Hello World");

        // replace the contents of the file
        File.WriteAllText(tempFilePath, "Introduction to C#");

        // delete the file
        File.Delete(tempFilePath);

        // wait for input before exiting
        Console.WriteLine("Press enter to finish");
        Console.ReadLine();
    }

    static void HandleFileSystemChangeEvent(object sender, FileSystemEventArgs arg) {
```

```
        Console.WriteLine("--- Change Event ---");
        Console.WriteLine("Affected File Name: {0}", arg.Name);
        Console.WriteLine("Change type: {0}", arg.ChangeType);
    }
}
```

Listing 20-13 creates a new FileSystemWatcher, providing the directory that will be monitored as a constructor parameter. In this example, a temporary directory is created so that only the changes that the example creates will trigger the events. The FileSystemWatcher class defines four events, which are described in Table 20-15.

Table 20-15. System.IO.FileSystemWatcher Events

Event	Description
Changed	This event is raised when a monitored file or directory is changed; this includes the content and attributes of the file.
Created	This event is raised when a new file or directory is created.
Deleted	This event is raised when a file or directory is deleted.
Renamed	The event is raised when a file or directory is renamed.

Listing 20-13 registers for three of the four events in the FileSystemWatcher class, using the same method as a handler. In keeping with the standard pattern for C# events (see Chapter 10 for details), the handler method is passed an object representing the source of the event (in this case the FileSystemWatcher object) and a derived EventArgs class containing the event details. The FileSystemWatcher events use the FileSystemEventArgs class, whose properties are described in Table 20-16.

Table 20-16. Properties of the System.IO.FileSystemEventArgs Class

Property	Description
ChangeType	A value from the WatcherChangeTypes enumeration indicating which type of change has been detected
FullPath	Returns the fully qualified name of the file or directory that the event relates to
Name	Returns the name of the changed file or directory, relative to the directory being monitored

The Renamed event uses the RenamedEventArgs class, which is derived from FileSysemEventArgs and adds two properties: the OldName returns the previous name following a rename event. The OldFullPath returns the previous fully qualified name. The values of the WatcherChangeTypes enumeration are listed in Table 20-17.

Table 20-17. *Values from the* WatcherChangeTypes *Enumeration*

Value	Description
Created	The creation of a file or directory
Deleted	The deletion of a file or directory
Changed	The modification of a file or directory
Renamed	The renaming of a file or directory
All	A combination of all of the other values

So, returning to Listing 20-13, we can see that once the event handlers have been registered, a series of changes are made to the directory using the convenience methods of the File class. Compiling and running Listing 20-13 gives the following results:

```
Temp file name is: C:\Users\Adam\AppData\Local\Temp\cjw2vwg1.uOr\wqgetm5w.crb
Press enter to finish
--- Change Event ---
Affected File Name: wqgetm5w.crb
Change type: Created
--- Change Event ---
Affected File Name: wqgetm5w.crb
Change type: Changed
--- Change Event ---
Affected File Name: wqgetm5w.crb
Change type: Changed
--- Change Event ---
Affected File Name: wqgetm5w.crb
Change type: Changed
--- Change Event ---
Affected File Name: wqgetm5w.crb
Change type: Deleted
```

You will see that there are more events than there are calls to the File methods. This is because the methods encapsulate several file operations as a convenience. Also notice that in Listing 20-13, I had to explicitly enable raising events as follows:

```
fsWatcher.EnableRaisingEvents = true;
```

Until the EnableRaisingEvents property is set to true, the FileSystemWatcher object will ignore changes to the directory. Table 20-18 describes other members of the FileSystemWatcher class.

Table 20-18. Members of the `System.IO.FileSystemWatcher` *Class*

Member	Description
EnableRaisingEvents	When set to `true`, events will be raised when changes are detected. When set to `false` (which is the initial setting for a new `FileSystemWatcher` object), changes will be ignored.
Filter	Gets or sets a string that filters which files are monitored. The default is *.*.
IncludeSubdirectories	When set to `true`, the subdirectories of the monitored directory will also be watched. The default value for a new `FileSystemWatcher` object is `false`.
NotifyFilter	Gets or sets the changes that will cause the `Changed` event to be raised.

The following sections demonstrate how to use the `Filter` and `NotifyFilter` properties to restrict the flow of events from a `FileSystemWatcher` object.

Filtering the Monitored Files and Directories

You can apply a filter to the `FileSystemMonitor` so that only changes affecting files and directories whose names match the filter cause events to be raised. The default filter is *.*, which means that changes to any file or folder will result in a change. Listing 20-14 demonstrates applying a filter.

Listing 20-14. Filtering the Files That Are Monitored by a `FileSystemWatcher`

```
using System;
using System.IO;

class Listing_14 {

    static void Main(string[] args) {

        // create temporary directory
        string tempDirPath = Path.Combine(Path.GetTempPath(), Path.GetRandomFileName());

        // create the directory specified by the path
        Directory.CreateDirectory(tempDirPath);

        // create a FileSystemWatcher to look for changes
        FileSystemWatcher fsWatcher = new FileSystemWatcher(tempDirPath);

        // filter the files we are interested in
        fsWatcher.Filter = "*.txt";
        Console.WriteLine("Filter: {0}", fsWatcher.Filter);

        // start watching for events
        fsWatcher.EnableRaisingEvents = true;
```

```
        // wait for input before exiting
        Console.WriteLine("Press enter to finish");
        Console.ReadLine();
    }
}
```

The `FileSystemWatcher` in Listing 20-14 is set to only report on changes to files with the `.txt` extension. The statement that sets the `Filter` property is shown in bold.

Filtering the Triggers for a Change Event

The `FileSystemWatcher.NotifyFilter` property allows you to restrict the kinds of changes that will cause the `Changed` event to be raised. Listing 20-15 provides a demonstration.

Listing 20-15. Using the `FileSystemWatcher.NotifyFilter` Property

```
using System;
using System.IO;

class Listing_14 {

    static void Main(string[] args) {

        // create temporary directory
        string tempDirPath = Path.Combine(Path.GetTempPath(), Path.GetRandomFileName());

        // create the directory specified by the path
        Directory.CreateDirectory(tempDirPath);

        // create a FileSystemWatcher to look for changes
        FileSystemWatcher fsWatcher = new FileSystemWatcher(tempDirPath);

        // filter the changes that will raise the event
        fsWatcher.NotifyFilter = NotifyFilters.FileName | NotifyFilters.LastWrite;

        // start watching for events
        fsWatcher.EnableRaisingEvents = true;

        // wait for input before exiting
        Console.WriteLine("Press enter to finish");
        Console.ReadLine();
    }
}
```

You specify the kinds of changes you are interested in by setting the `NotifyFilter` property to one or more values from the `NotifyFilters` enumeration; multiple values can be specified using the logical OR operator (|). Table 20-19 lists the values of the `NotifyFilters` enum.

Table 20-19. *Values of the NotifyFilters Enum*

Value	Description
FileName	The name of the file
DirectoryName	The name of the directory
Attributes	The attributes of the file or directory
Size	The size of the file or directory
LastWrite	The date that the file or directory was last written to
LastAccess	The date that the file or directory was last accessed
CreationTime	The date that the file or directory was created
Security	The security settings of the file or directory

Working with Streams, Readers, and Writers

You can perform simple read and write operations using the convenience methods in the System.IO.File class. For anything more complex, you need to use streams, readers, and writers. In this section, I'll explain the role of each of these type categories and demonstrate how they are used.

Using Streams

Streams allow you to read and write data from a range of data sources in a consistent way. For example, you can work with data that is stored in memory, data that is stored in a file, or data that has been sent over a network in the same way. The only difference when working with these different data source is the way that you get a steam object to operate on.

The base class for all streams is System.IO.Stream. This is an abstract class, but it provides the core members that all streams implement. The Stream class supports reading and writing sequential byte values using a cursor. Figure 20-1 illustrates the basic nature of a stream and the underlying sequence of data.

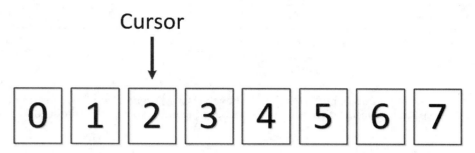

Figure 20-1. The anatomy of a stream

The cursor marks the position you have reached in the stream. When you create a new stream, the cursor usually starts at position zero. When you read a byte from the stream, the value marked by the cursor is the one that is retrieved. When you write a byte to the cursor, the new value replaces the one that the cursor has marked. Whenever you read or write a byte, the cursor automatically moves to the next position in the data sequence so that the next read or write operation affects the next data item.

Streams are a low-level abstraction that allow you to work with different types of data source using the same approach (and often the same code). You usually won't want to work with byte values; I'll show you how to work with more useful data types when we come to look at readers and writers later in this chapter.

Being able to work with different kinds of data source means that all streams support the same features. For example, some streams are read-only, some are write-only, some allow you to reposition the cursor, and others don't. It all depends on the kind of data source you are working with and, in some cases, how you obtained the Stream object. This will become clearer as we start to look at some examples.

The Stream class is abstract. You do not create instances of Stream but obtain Stream objects from your data sources. We'll see some examples of obtaining Stream objects in the next section. The Stream class defines a set of members that allow you to read and write byte data and find out some basic information about the capabilities that the current Stream object supports. The most commonly used Stream members are summarized in Table 20-20.

Table 20-20. System.IO.Stream Members

Member	Description
CanRead CanSeek CanWrite	The value of these properties specifies the capabilities of the current stream implementation.
Close()	Closes the stream.
CopyTo(Stream)	Copies the contents of the current stream to the stream specified by the parameter.
Flush()	Forces any buffered data to be written to the backing store.

Member	Description
Length	Gets the number of bytes in the stream.
Position	Returns the position of the cursor.
Read(byte[], int, int)	Reads the number of bytes specified by the last parameter into the byte array specified by the first parameter, starting at the index specified by the second parameter.
ReadByte()	Reads a single byte.
Seek(long, SeekOrigin)	Moves the cursor to the specified position relative to the SeekOrigin value.
SetLength(long)	Sets the length of the current stream.
Write(byte[], int, int)	Writes the number of bytes specified by the last parameter from the byte array parameter, starting at the index specified by the second parameter.
WriteByte(byte)	Writes a single byte to the stream.

Listing 20-16 gives a simple demonstration of using a Stream. Ignore how the Stream object is obtained in this example. I'll go into more details about this in the next section.

Listing 20-16. Using a Stream Object

```
using System;
using System.IO;

class Listing_16 {

    static void Main(string[] args) {

        // create the stream object
        Stream myStream = File.Create(Path.GetTempFileName());

        // check the capabilities of the Stream
        Console.WriteLine("CanRead: {0}", myStream.CanRead);
        Console.WriteLine("CanWrite: {0}", myStream.CanWrite);
        Console.WriteLine("CanSeek: {0}", myStream.CanSeek);

        // write a series of bytes to the stream
        for (int i = 0; i < 5; i++) {
            Console.WriteLine("Writing value: {0}", i);
            myStream.WriteByte((byte)i);
        }

        // flush the stream
        myStream.Flush();
```

```
        // reposition the cursor to the start of the stream
        myStream.Seek(0, SeekOrigin.Begin);

        // read in a series of bytes
        for (int i = 0; i < 5; i++) {
            Console.WriteLine("Read value: {0}", myStream.ReadByte());
        }

        // reposition the cursor to the start of the stream
        myStream.Seek(0, SeekOrigin.Begin);

        // write a series of bytes to the stream
        for (int i = 10; i < 15; i++) {
            Console.WriteLine("Writing value: {0}", i);
            myStream.WriteByte((byte)i);
        }

        // flush the stream
        myStream.Flush();

        // close the stream
        myStream.Close();

        // wait for input before exiting
        Console.WriteLine("Press enter to finish");
        Console.ReadLine();
    }
}
```

Streams are such an important concept that I am going to work through the code in the listing and explain each phase of the example. You may want to skip over the next section if you have already used streams in another programming language.

Using the System.IO.Stream Class (in Detail)

The first part of Listing 20-16 obtains a Stream object using the File.Create method:

```
Stream myStream = File.Create(Path.GetTempFileName());
```

The Create method in the File class returns a FileStream class, but since I want to demonstrate using the base class, I have upcast to Stream. We'll return to FileStream later in the chapter.

The next set of statements prints out the values of the CanRead, CanWrite, and CanSeek properties:

```
Console.WriteLine("CanRead: {0}", myStream.CanRead);
Console.WriteLine("CanWrite: {0}", myStream.CanWrite);
Console.WriteLine("CanSeek: {0}", myStream.CanSeek);
```

The features that a Stream object supports will change based on the data source and the way that you obtained the object. For example, when working with a network connection, you will usually obtain two Stream objects. The first will be read-only and allows you to read the data sent to you, and the second will be write-only and allow you to send data. When working a file, as we are in this example, the features depend how you opened the file. It is possible to create Stream objects that are read-only, that are write-only, or that can be used to both read and write. The Stream object that we get back from the File.Create method can be used to read from and write to the file.

The CanSeek property tells you whether the Stream object explicitly supports repositioning the cursor to a different point in the data sequence. Once again, the ability to do this depends on what data store you are working with. You can typically do this with files, because all the data is always available on the disk, but this feature has no meaning when working with network connections where data is arriving over time.

At this point in the code, we have created a Stream object that is using a newly created temporary file as its backing store. The cursor is positioned at the start of the file, but there is no data (since the file is empty). Figure 20-2 illustrates what we have so far.

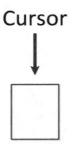

Figure 20-2. Opening a Stream to a newly created temporary file

Writing to a Stream

The next set of statements writes a sequence of byte values to the stream:

```
for (int i = 0; i < 5; i++) {
    Console.WriteLine("Writing value: {0}", i);
    myStream.WriteByte((byte)i);
}
```

I have used incrementing int values and converted them to byte values for this example. Each time I write a byte value, it is appended to the data sequence, and the cursor is moved to the end of the stream. After the five write operations, I have five byte values in my file, as illustrated by Figure 20-3.

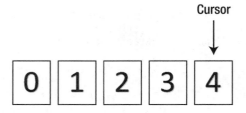

Figure 20-3. Writing data to a stream

Some Stream objects don't write a byte to the data store immediately. They buffer the data to improve performance or to conform to the model of the data store. You can request that the Stream object write all the buffered data to the data store by using the Flush method, which is what I do after I have written the five byte values to the Stream:

```
myStream.Flush();
```

Seeking Within a Stream

Having ensured that all my data has been written, I explicitly change the position of the cursor so that it is back at the start of the file, using the Seek method:

```
myStream.Seek(0, SeekOrigin.Begin);
```

The Seek method takes two parameters. The first is a long value that is applied relative to the position specified by the second parameter—a value from the System.IO.SeekOrigin enumeration. Table 20-21 shows the SeekOrigin values.

Table 20-21. SeekOrigin Values

Value	Description
Begin	Specifies the start of the stream
Current	Specifies the current cursor position
Emd	Specifies the end of the stream

The long parameter is combined with the SeekOrigin value to determine the new position of the cursor. In Listing 20-16, I specified a long value of 0 and a SeekOrigin value of Begin, which positions the cursor at the start of the stream. Positive long values will advance the cursor relative to the SeekOrigin value, and negative long values will retard the cursor. For example, if I wanted to move the cursor back by one position, I would call this:

```
myStream.Seek(-1, SeekOrigin.Current);
```

When you move the cursor, you must ensure that you don't try to move it too far. You will cause an exception if you try to move it to a position that doesn't exist. Following the Seek call, I have five byte values in my stream, and the cursor is at the start of the stream, as illustrated by Figure 20-4.

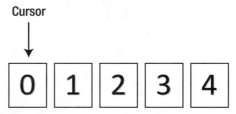

Figure 20-4. The Stream following the Seek call

Reading from a Stream

I called the Seek method in Listing 20-16 because I wanted to reposition the cursor at the start of the stream so that I can read the values that I have previously written. The following statements read the data in the stream, one byte value at a time:

```
for (int i = 0; i < 5; i++) {
    Console.WriteLine("Read value: {0}", myStream.ReadByte());

}
```

As each value is read, the cursor is moved to the next position in the data sequence, which means that at the end of the for loop, the cursor is back at the end of the Stream, in the same position as shown by Figure 20-3. When you read data using the ReadByte method, the result will be the next value in the stream or -1 if you have reached the end of the stream.

Replacing Data in a Stream

Having read the data, I reposition the cursor back at the start of the Stream and write new values:

```
myStream.Seek(0, SeekOrigin.Begin);

for (int i = 10; i < 15; i++) {
    Console.WriteLine("Writing value: {0}", i);
    myStream.WriteByte((byte)i);
}

myStream.Flush();
```

As each value is written, the cursor is advanced to the next position, and the existing values are overwritten by the new values. When the write operations have completed (and the Flush method has been called to ensure that the data is not buffered), the Stream is as shown in Figure 20-5.

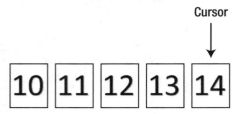

Figure 20-5. The Stream after overwriting the data

The last Stream-related statement in the example calls the Close method:

```
myStream.Close();
```

It is important to call the Close method when you have finished with a Stream. This ensures that the resources that have been tied up in the data store are released and can be used again. Compiling and running Listing 20-16 produces the following results:

```
CanRead: True
CanWrite: True
CanSeek: True
Writing value: 0
Writing value: 1
Writing value: 2
Writing value: 3
Writing value: 4
Read value: 0
Read value: 1
Read value: 2
Read value: 3
Read value: 4
Writing value: 10
Writing value: 11
Writing value: 12
Writing value: 13
Writing value: 14
Press enter to finish
```

Using Base Streams

The .NET Framework Class Library contains a number of base streams, each of which works with a different kind of data store. In this section, we'll look at two in detail. They work with an in-memory store and files on disk, and we'll see examples of another kind in Chapter 21 when we come to look at networking.

Streams that have data stores are called *base streams*, and they are said to be *backed* by that store. For example, a FileStream object has a file as its data store, so a FileStream is said to be backed by a file. FileStream is one of the backing stream classes we will look at in this section. The other is MemoryStream, which is backed by an array of bytes held in memory.

Using the MemoryStream Class

The MemoryStream class is backed by a byte array held in memory. This means that the data you write to the stream is not persistent and will be lost when your program finishes or the MemoryStream object is destroyed by the garbage collector. You obtain MemoryStream objects by using the MemoryStream class constructor. Table 20-22 describes the constructors for this class.

Table 20-22. MemoryStream Constructors

Constructor	Description
MemoryStream()	Creates an automatically resizing MemoryBuffer with no initial content.
MemoryStream(int)	Creates an automatically resizing MemoryBuffer with no initial content and an initial capacity specified by the parameter value.
MemoryStream(byte[])	Creates a fixed-capacity MemoryBuffer using the byte array as the initial content. The capacity is fixed to the size of the array.

If you create a MemoryStream using the default constructor or the version that takes an int parameter, then the byte array that backs the stream will be resized to accommodate any data that you write. If you use the constructor that takes a byte array, then the capacity of the stream is fixed, but the initial content of the stream is set to be the content of the array. In addition to the members defined by the Stream class, MemoryStream has some additional members that are specific to a memory-backed stream. You can't use these members if you have upcast to the base class, but they can be helpful if you are working with the MemoryStream type directly. The additional members introduced by the MemoryStream class are described in Table 20-23.

Table 20-23. Additional MemoryStream Members

Member	Description
Capacity	Gets or sets the size of the byte array that backs the MemoryStream.
ToArray()	Returns a byte array containing the contents of the stream. Bytes that have been allocated in the array but that have not been assigned a value are omitted.
WriteTo(Stream)	Writes the contents of the MemoryStream to another Stream object.

Listing 20-17 demonstrates the use of the MemoryStream class.

Listing 20-17. Using the MemoryStream Class

```
using System;
using System.IO;

class Listing_17 {

    static void Main(string[] args) {
```

```
        // create an empty MemoryStream
        MemoryStream myStream = new MemoryStream();

        // write a series of bytes to the stream
        for (int i = 0; i < 5; i++) {
            myStream.WriteByte((byte)i);
        }

        // reposition the cursor to the start of the stream
        myStream.Seek(0, SeekOrigin.Begin);

        // read back the byte values
        for (int value; (value = myStream.ReadByte()) > -1; ) {
            Console.WriteLine("Read value: {0}", value);
        }

        // get the data in the stream as an array
        byte[] dataArray = myStream.ToArray();

        // create a new memory stream using the dataArray
        MemoryStream myOtherStream = new MemoryStream(dataArray);

        // write out the capacity of the stream
        Console.WriteLine("Capacity: {0}", myOtherStream.Capacity);

        // read the data back from the stream
        // read back the byte values
        for (int i = 0; i < 5; i++) {
            Console.WriteLine("Read value from second stream: {0}",
                myOtherStream.ReadByte());
        }

        // wait for input before exiting
        Console.WriteLine("Press enter to finish");
        Console.ReadLine();
    }
}
```

Listing 20-17 creates a MemoryStream and writes a series of byte values to it. These values are then read back, converted to a byte array, and used as the basis for a second MemoryStream. When reading the data from the first MemoryStream, I read all the available data by detecting the -1 value that is returned when the end of the stream is reached (as opposed to reading a fixed number of bytes as in the previous example):

```
for (int value; (value = myStream.ReadByte()) > -1; ) {
    Console.WriteLine("Read value: {0}", value);
}
```

I have used a for loop where the condition reads a byte, assigns it to a variable, and checks for the -1 value in a single statement. This is possible in C# because the result of the assignment operator (=) is the value that is being assigned. In the example, this means that the value of assigning a byte value to the value variable is the byte value. Compiling and running Listing 20-17 produces the following results:

```
Read value: 0
Read value: 1
Read value: 2
Read value: 3
Read value: 4
Capacity: 5
Read value from second stream: 0
Read value from second stream: 1
Read value from second stream: 2
Read value from second stream: 3
Read value from second stream: 4
Press enter to finish
```

Using the FileStream Class

The FileStream class is backed by a file on a disk. This means that your data will continue to exist (persist) after your program has finished. You can get FileStream objects in a range of ways. The most common are using the methods defined in the File class (which are listed in Table 20-13) or the FileInfo class (Table 20-7) or using the constructor to create an object directly from the class. There are a number of constructor versions in the FileStream class, but the one you will typically use is this one:

```
FileStream(string, FileMode, FileAccess)
```

The string parameter is the path of the file you want to work with. The FileMode enumeration defines how you want the file to be opened; these values are described in Table 20-24.

Table 20-24. FileMode Values

Values	Description
CreateNew	A new file will be created. If the file specified by the string parameter exists, an IOException will be thrown.
Create	If the specified file exists, it will be overwritten. If it does not exist, it will be created.
Open	If the file exists, it will be opened. If it does not exist, a FileNotFoundException is thrown.
OpenOrCreate	If the file exists, it is opened (and not overwritten). If the file does not exist, it is created.
Truncate	The file is opened and truncated so that the size is zero and any previous data is deleted.
Append	If the file exists, it will be opened, and the cursor moved to the end of the file.

The FileAccess enumeration allows you specify whether you want to read and/or write to the FileStream that is created. The FileAccess values are described in Table 20-25.

Table 20-25. FileAccess Values

Values	Description
Read	The stream will allow data to be read.
Write	The stream will allow data to be written.
ReadWrite	The stream will allow data to be read and written.

In addition to the members defined by the Stream class, FileStream defines methods that are helpful for working with files; these are described in Table 20-26.

Table 20-26. FileStream Methods

Method	Description
Flush(bool)	Flushes any cached data. If the parameter value is true, any intermediate buffers (such as those maintained by the operating system) will also be flushed so that the data is written to disk.
Lock(long, long)	Locks a region of the file so that other processes cannot read or write to that part of the file. The first parameter defines the start of the region to lock. The second parameter defines the length of the region.
Unlock(long, long)	Unlocks a previously locked region of the file.

Listing 20-18 provides a demonstration of using the FileStream class.

Listing 20-18. Using the FileStream Class

```
using System;
using System.IO;

class Listing_18 {

    static void Main(string[] args) {

        // create a file stream to an existing file
        FileStream myStream = new FileStream("tempfile.txt",
            FileMode.Create, FileAccess.ReadWrite);

        // write some data to the file
        for (int i = 0; i < 5; i++) {
            Console.WriteLine("Writing value: {0}", i);
            myStream.WriteByte((byte)i);
```

```
        }

        // flush the data, including any intermediate buffers
        myStream.Flush(true);

        // close the file
        myStream.Close();

        // create a new Stream to the same file
        FileStream myOtherStream = new FileStream("tempfile.txt",
            FileMode.Open, FileAccess.Read);

        // read the data from the stream
        for (int value; (value = myOtherStream.ReadByte()) > -1; ) {
            Console.WriteLine("Read Value: {0}", value);
        }

        // close the file
        myOtherStream.Close();

        // delete the file
        File.Delete("tempfile.txt");

        // wait for input before exiting
        Console.WriteLine("Press enter to finish");
        Console.ReadLine();
    }
}
```

Listing 20-18 opens a FileStream that creates a new file and writes a series of byte values to it. The data is flushed to the disk, and the FileStream is closed. A second FileStream opens the file in a read-only mode and reads the data back in again. The file is deleted so that the example can be run repeatedly. Compiling and running Listing 20-18 produces the following results:

```
Writing value: 0
Writing value: 1
Writing value: 2
Writing value: 3
Writing value: 4
Read Value: 0
Read Value: 1
Read Value: 2
Read Value: 3
Read Value: 4
Press enter to finish
```

Using Pass-Through Streams

Some streams are backed by other streams; these are called *pass-through streams*. When you write data to a pass-through stream, it is processed in some way and then passed to the backing stream, which in turn passes it to the actual data store. When you read data from a pass-through stream, data is obtained from the backing stream, which gets it from the actual data store, processed in some way and then returned to you. This is illustrated by Figure 20-6.

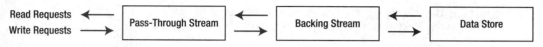

Figure 20-6. Using a pass-through stream

A pass-through stream can be used to perform any kind of operation on a backing stream. The most commonly used pass-through streams in the .NET Framework Library are used to compress data before writing it to the stream and to buffer data.

Using a Buffered Pass-Through Stream

The BufferedStream class allows you to add a layer of buffering to your stream. The buffer is used to reduce the number of read and write operations that are passed through to the backing stream; this is typically done to improve performance. You create BufferedStream objects by using the following constructor:

BufferedReader(Stream, int)

The Stream parameter is the Stream that you want to apply buffering to, and the int parameter is the size of the buffer you want in bytes. The size of the buffer is important; it should be larger than the number of bytes you will read or write in a single operation. If it is smaller, the buffer will not be used. Once you have created a BufferedStream, you can use it as you would any other Stream object. This class doesn't define any members that are specific to working with a buffer. Listing 20-19 provides a simple demonstration of using the BufferedStream class.

Listing 20-19. Using the BufferedStream Class

```
using System;
using System.IO;

class Listing_19 {

    static void Main(string[] args) {

        // create the stream
        FileStream myBaseStream = new FileStream(Path.GetTempFileName(),
            FileMode.OpenOrCreate, FileAccess.ReadWrite);

        // create the BufferedStream
        BufferedStream myBufferedStream = new BufferedStream(myBaseStream, 10 * 1024);
```

```
        // write some data to the buffered stream
        for (int i = 0; i < 5; i++) {
            Console.WriteLine("Writing value: {0}", i);
            myBufferedStream.WriteByte((byte)i);
        }

        // flush so that the buffer is cleared
        myBufferedStream.Flush();

        // reposition the cursor to the start of the buffer
        myBufferedStream.Seek(0, SeekOrigin.Begin);

        // read the data back
        for (int value; (value = myBufferedStream.ReadByte()) > -1;) {
            Console.WriteLine("Read value: {0}", value);
        }

        // close the stream
        myBufferedStream.Close();

        // wait for input before exiting
        Console.WriteLine("Press enter to finish");
        Console.ReadLine();
    }
}
```

You don't have to worry about the backing stream when working with a pass-through stream. For example, calling Flush or Close on the pass-through stream will cause the same method to be called on the backing stream as well. Compiling and running Listing 20-19 produces the following output:

```
Writing value: 0
Writing value: 1
Writing value: 2
Writing value: 3
Writing value: 4
Read value: 0
Read value: 1
Read value: 2
Read value: 3
Read value: 4
Press enter to finish
```

Compressing Data with Pass-Through Streams

The System.IO.Compression namespace contains two pass-through streams that can be used to compress and decompress data. The DeflateStream class uses the deflate compression algorithm, while the GZipStream class uses gzip. I'll focus on the GZipStream in this section, but both classes operate in the same way, other than for the compression algorithm they employ. You create GZipStream objects directly using the constructor:

GZipStream(Stream, CompressionMode)

The Stream parameter is the backing stream. The CompressionMode parameter is a value from the CompressionMode enumeration, which contains the two values described in Table 20-27.

Table 20-27. CompressionMode Values

Value	Description
Decompress	Decompresses the data read from the backing stream
Compress	Compresses the data written to the backing stream

You can combine the values from the CompressionMode enumeration, but these streams don't allow you to reposition the cursor, so you really need to create one GZipStream object when you want to compress data and another GZipStream object when you want to read and decompress the data. Listing 20-20 provides an example.

Listing 20-20. Using the GZipStream Class

```
using System;
using System.IO;
using System.IO.Compression;

class Listing_20 {

    static void Main(string[] args) {

        // create a path for a temporary file with the gzip extension
        string filePath = Path.ChangeExtension(Path.GetRandomFileName(), ".gzip");

        // open a write-only file stream using the file path
        FileStream writeFileStream = new FileStream(filePath,
            FileMode.OpenOrCreate, FileAccess.Write);

        // create the compression stream, backed using the file stream
        GZipStream compressStream = new GZipStream(writeFileStream,
            CompressionMode.Compress);

        // write some data to the compression stream
        for (int i = 0; i < 5; i++) {
            Console.WriteLine("Writing value: {0}", i);
            compressStream.WriteByte((byte)i);
        }

        // flush and close the stream
        compressStream.Flush();
        compressStream.Close();

        // open the file again, this time as read-only
        FileStream readFileStream = new FileStream(filePath,
```

```
            FileMode.Open, FileAccess.Read);

        // create a decompression stream, backed by the read-only file stream
        GZipStream decompressStream = new GZipStream(readFileStream,
            CompressionMode.Decompress);

        // read the compressed data back
        for (int value; (value = decompressStream.ReadByte()) > -1; ) {
            Console.WriteLine("Read value: {0}", value);
        }

        // close the stream
        decompressStream.Close();

        // wait for input before exiting
        Console.WriteLine("Press enter to finish");
        Console.ReadLine();
    }
}
```

Listing 20-20 creates a file with the .gzip extension and uses a GZipStream to compress some data values that are written to a FileStream and then to the file. Another FileStream object is created and used as the backing stream for a decompressing GZipStream, which then reads the previously compressed data from the file. Compiling and running Listing 20-20 produces the following results:

```
Writing value: 0
Writing value: 1
Writing value: 2
Writing value: 3
Writing value: 4
Read value: 0
Read value: 1
Read value: 2
Read value: 3
Read value: 4
Press enter to finish
```

Using Readers and Writers

Streams are a low-level feature, which works on data at the level of individual bytes. All data can be reduced to bytes, but it is often inconvenient to do so. The System.IO namespace contains a set of classes, known as *readers* and *writers*, that work at a higher level, allowing you to get all the benefits of streams but using native C# data types. Reader classes are used to read data from a stream. Writer classes are used to write data to a stream.

Reading and Writing Binary Data

The BinaryWriter class defines a set of methods that allow you to write C# built-in type values to a stream. The BinaryReader class defines a set of methods that allow you to read C# built-in types from a stream. Readers and writers are backed by a Stream object, which can be a pass-through stream or a base stream. To create a BinaryWriter object, you use the following constructor:

BinaryWriter(Stream)

Once you have created a BinaryWriter object, you can use the methods described in Table 20-28 to write values to the underlying Stream.

Table 20-28. *BinaryWriter Methods for Writing Built-in Values*

Methods	Description
Write(bool)	Writes a bool value
Write(byte) Write(sbyte)	Writes a byte or sbyte value
Write(byte[]) Write(byte[], int, int)	Writes all of a byte array or a region of a byte array
Write(char)	Writes a char value
Write(char[]) Write(char[], int, int)	Writes all or a region or a char array
Write(decimal)	Writes a decimal value
Write(double)	Writes a double value
Write(short) Write(ushort)	Writes a short or ushort value
Write(int) Write(uint)	Writes a int or uint value
Write(long) Write(ulong)	Writes a long or ulong value
Write(string)	Writes a string

Listing 20-21 demonstrates using a BinaryWriter to write built-in values to a MemoryStream.

Listing 20-21. *Using the* BinaryWriter *and* BinaryWriter *Classes*

```
using System;
using System.IO;

class Listing_21 {

    static void Main(string[] args) {

        // create the backing stream
        MemoryStream backingStream = new MemoryStream();

        // create the BinaryWriter object, backed by the MemoryStream
        BinaryWriter myWriter = new BinaryWriter(backingStream);

        // write a sequence of values to the stream
        myWriter.Write(true);
        myWriter.Write(23.2D);
        myWriter.Write("Hello World");
        myWriter.Write(20172);

        // reset the cursor on the backing stream
        backingStream.Seek(0, SeekOrigin.Begin);

        // create a BinaryReader object, backed by the memory stream
        BinaryReader myReader = new BinaryReader(backingStream);

        // read the data sequence from the reader
        Console.WriteLine("Read bool value: {0}", myReader.ReadBoolean());
        Console.WriteLine("Read float value: {0}", myReader.ReadDouble());
        Console.WriteLine("Read string value: {0}", myReader.ReadString());
        Console.WriteLine("Read int value: {0}", myReader.ReadInt32());

        // wait for input before exiting
        Console.WriteLine("Press enter to finish");
        Console.ReadLine();
    }
}
```

Listing 20-21 also demonstrates the use of the BinaryReader, which is the complement to the BinaryWriter class and which can be used to read built-in values from an underlying Stream object. When you use BinaryWriter to write values to a stream, the values are converted to bytes; there is no information about which types have been written included in the stream.

When you read values back using a BinaryReader, you need to know which methods to call to get the right sequence of data values. The methods available for doing this are described in Table 20-29.

Table 20-29. BinaryReader Methods for Reading Built-in Values

Methods	Description
Read()	Reads a single byte from the underlying stream
Read(byte[], int, int)	Reads a number of bytes from the stream into the array parameter
Read(char[], int, int)	Reads a number of characters from the stream into the array parameter
ReadBoolean()	Reads a bool value
ReadByte()	Reads a byte value
ReadBytes(int)	Reads the specified number of bytes; these are returned in a byte array
ReadChar()	Reads a single char value
ReadChars(int)	Reads the specified number of characters; these are returned in a char array
ReadDecimal()	Reads a decimal value
ReadDouble()	Reads a double value
ReadInt16() ReadInt32() ReadInt64()	Reads a short, int, or long value
ReadUInt16() ReadUUnt32() ReadUInt64()	Reads a ushort, uint, or ulong value
ReadString()	Reads a string from the underlying stream

Compiling and running Listing 20-21 produces the following results:

```
Read bool value: True
Read float value: 23.2
Read string value: Hello World
Read int value: 20172
Press enter to finish
```

Reading and Writing Textual Data

The StreamWriter and StreamReader classes are similar to BinaryWriter and BinaryReader, except they write text representations of values to the underlying stream, rather than binary representations. The StreamWriter class has a number of constructors, the most useful of which are shown in Table 20-30.

Table 20-30. StreamWriter Constructors

Constructor	Description
StreamWriter(Stream)	Creates a StreamWriter backed by the Stream parameter.
StreamWriter(string)	Creates a StreamWriter that writes to the file specified by the string parameter.
StreamWriter(string, bool)	Creates a StreamWriter that writes to the specified file. If the bool parameter is true, new data is appended to the end of the file; if it is false, any existing data will be overwritten.

Once you have created a StreamWriter, you can use the methods described in Table 20-31 to write data.

Table 20-31. StreamWriter WriteLine Methods

Method	Description
WriteLine()	Writes an empty line to the stream.
WriteLine(bool)	Writes a bool, followed by a line terminator, to the stream.
WriteLine(char)	Writes a char, followed by a line terminator, to the stream.
WriteLine(char[])	Writes a char array, followed by a line terminator, to the stream.
WriteLine(double) WriteLine(decimal)	Writes a double or decimal value, followed by a line terminator, to the stream.
WriteLine(Int32) WriteLine(Int64) WriteLine(UInt32) WriteLine(UInt64)	Writes an int, long, uint, or ulong value to the stream, followed by a line terminator.
WriteLine(object)	Writes the string representation of the object parameter to the stream, followed by a line terminator.
WriteLine(string)	Writes a string to the stream, followed by a line terminator.

Method	Description
WriteLine(string, object)	Uses composite formatting to format the string and writes the result to the stream, followed by a line terminator. See Chapter 16 for details of composite formatting.

When you use one of these methods, the value and a line terminator character are written to the stream. If you are writing to a text file, this means that there is one string written to each line in the file. Listing 20-22 provides an example.

Listing 20-22. Using a StreamWriter

```
using System;
using System.IO;

class Listing_22 {

    static void Main(string[] args) {

        // create a temporary file name
        string path = Path.GetRandomFileName();

        // create a StreamWriter
        StreamWriter myWriter = new StreamWriter(path);

        // write some values to the stream
        myWriter.WriteLine("Hello, World");
        myWriter.WriteLine(true);
        myWriter.WriteLine(20172);
        myWriter.WriteLine(12.345D);

        // flush and close the writer
        myWriter.Flush();
        myWriter.Close();

        // wait for input before exiting
        Console.WriteLine("Press enter to finish");
        Console.ReadLine();
    }
}
```

Compiling and running Listing 20-22 produces a text file that has the following contents:

```
Hello, World
True
20172
12.345
```

Listing 20-23 demonstrates using the StreamReader class.

Listing 20-23. Using the StreamReader Class

```
using System;
using System.IO;

class Listing_23 {

    static void Main(string[] args) {

        // create a backing stream
        MemoryStream memStream = new MemoryStream();

        // create a StreamWriter
        StreamWriter myWriter = new StreamWriter(memStream);

        // write some values to the stream
        myWriter.WriteLine("Hello, World");
        myWriter.WriteLine(true);
        myWriter.WriteLine(20172);
        myWriter.WriteLine(12.345D);

        // flush the data
        myWriter.Flush();

        // reposition the cursor in the backing stream
        memStream.Seek(0, SeekOrigin.Begin);

        // create a stream reader
        StreamReader myReader = new StreamReader(memStream);

        // read the strings
        string value;
        while ((value = myReader.ReadLine()) != null) {
            Console.WriteLine("Read Line: {0}", value);
        }

        // wait for input before exiting
        Console.WriteLine("Press enter to finish");
        Console.ReadLine();


    }
}
```

Listing 20-23 uses the StreamReader class to read back the string values written by the StreamWriter class. The ReadLine method returns the next string in the underlying stream or null if the end of the stream has been reached. Compiling and running Listing 20-23 produces the following results:

```
Read Line: Hello, World
```

```
Read Line: True
Read Line: 20172
Read Line: 12.345
Press enter to finish
```

The StreamReader class has a small number of methods that can read a single string from the underlying stream (such as ReadLine, used in Listing 20-23) or read multiple lines. These methods are described by Table 20-32.

Table 20-32. StreamReader Methods

Method	Description
ReadLine()	Reads a single string from the underlying stream. Returns null if the end of the stream has been reached.
ReadToEnd()	Reads the stream from the current cursor to the end of the stream and returns the result as a single string.
ReadBlock(char[], int, int)	Reads a block of characters into the char array.

Some care must be taken when reading string values from a StreamReader, especially when using the ReadToEnd method. The amount of data that is read from the Stream can be exceed the amount of memory available and cause an exception.

Summary

In this chapter, we looked at how C# supports working with files and directories, using either the File and Directory or FileInfo and DirectoryInfo classes. We saw how to compose and manipulate file paths using the Path class and how to monitor a directory for changes and how to specify which changes we are interested in.

We also explored the support for streams, which are a general-purpose feature for reading and writing sequential byte data to a range of backing stores in a consistent way. Because working with byte values can be very tedious, we also looked at the reader and writer classes that make working with binary and textual representations of built-in type values a breeze.

■ ■ ■

Networking & WCF

The .NET Framework Class Library contains extensive support for network programming. Classes range from the convenient (allowing you to retrieve data from HTTP servers simply and easily) to the low-level (creating custom network protocols) to the feature-rich (creating web-services and service-oriented protocol). To get the most from this chapter, you will need a basic understanding of networking—in particular, an appreciation of the Internet Protocol (IP) and associated protocols, such as TCP, UDP and HTTP. Table 21-1 provides the summary for this chapter.

Table 21-1. Quick Problem/Solution Reference for Chapter 21

Problem	Solution	Listings
Retrieve data from a server.	Use the WebClient class.	21-1 through 21-5
Create a simple TCP server.	Use the TcpListener class.	21-6, 21-7
Implement a simple TCP client.	Use the TcpClient class.	21-8, 21-9
Create a web service.	Use the Windows Communications Foundation.	21-10 through 21-12
Consume a web service.	Use the Windows Communications Foundation.	21-13, 21-14
Create an HTTP server.	Use the HttpListener class.	21-15
Create a UDP client.	Use the UdpClient class.	21-16, 21-17
Query the Domain Name System.	Use the Dns class.	21-18

Requesting Data

One of the most common network programing activities is requesting data from a remote server—most typically, a web server. The System.Net.WebClient provides a simple and convenient means of doing just that, as demonstrated by Listing 21-1.

Listing 21-1. Requesting Server Data Using the WebClient Class

```
using System;
using System.IO;
using System.Net;

class Listing_01 {

    static void Main(string[] args) {

        // create a Webclient object
        WebClient myWebClient = new WebClient();

        // open a stream to the target URL
        Stream dataStream = myWebClient.OpenRead("http://microsoft.com");

        // create a StreamReader around the Stream
        StreamReader dataReader = new StreamReader(dataStream);

        // read the contents of the URL as a single string
        string dataLine = dataReader.ReadToEnd();

        // write out the received data
        Console.WriteLine(dataLine);

        // close the reader
        dataReader.Close();

        // wait for input before exiting
        Console.WriteLine("Press enter to finish");
        Console.ReadLine();
    }
}
```

In Listing 21-1, you create new instance of the WebClient class using the default constructor and then call the OpenRead method, passing a string value representing the URL you want to download. The OpenRead method returns a Stream object which is backed by the network connection. Wrap this in a StreamReader object so that you can read the entire response from the server as a single string using the ReadToEnd method. The WebClient class really makes it easy to handle simple network requests. Compiling and running Listing 21-1 produces the following output:

```
<html><head><title>Microsoft Corporation</title><meta http-equiv="X-UA-Compatibl
e" content="IE=EmulateIE7"></meta><meta http-equiv="Content-Type" content="text/
html; charset=utf-8"></meta><meta name="SearchTitle" content="Microsoft.com" sch
eme=""></meta><meta name="Description" content="Get product information, support
, and news from Microsoft." scheme=""></meta><meta name="Title" content="Microso
ft.com Home Page" scheme=""></meta><meta name="Keywords" content="Microsoft, pro
duct, support, help, training, Office, Windows, software, download, trial, previ
ew, demo, business, security, update, free, computer, PC, server, search, downl
oad, install, news" scheme=""></meta><meta name="SearchDescription" content="Mic
```

```
rosoft.com Homepage" scheme=""></meta></head><body><p>Your current User-Agent st
ring appears to be from an automated process, if this is incorrect, please click
 this link:<a href="http://www.microsoft.com/en/us/default.aspx?redir=true">Unit
ed States English Microsoft Homepage</a></p></body></html>
Press enter to finish
```

Listing 21-1 demonstrates how to make a simple request, but the WebClient class has features to give you control over how your request is made and how you get the data. I'll show you how to use the members to configure a request, to retrieve the data from the server in different ways, and to use events to be notified when data is available.

Using WebClient Members to Configure a Request

The WebClient class defines a set of properties that you can use to configure the request. The most commonly used properties are described in Table 21-2.

Table 21.2. WebClient Configuration Properties

Property	Description
BaseAddress	Sets a base address that is combined with relative addresses to make multiple queries from the same WebClient object.
Headers	Gets and sets a collection of name value pairs that are sent as headers in the request.
QueryString	Gets or sets a name value pairs that will be appended to the URL preceded by a question mark (?).

Listing 21-2 demonstrates using some of these properties. In particular, notice how the BaseAddress property is used to create a common basis on which multiple relative requests can be made using the same WebClient object.

Listing 21-2. Using the Configuration Properties of the WebClient Class

```
using System;
using System.Collections.Specialized;
using System.IO;
using System.Net;

class Listing_02 {

    static void Main(string[] args) {

        // create a WebClient object
        WebClient myWebClient = new WebClient();
```

```
        // use the BaseAddress property
        myWebClient.BaseAddress = "http://www.microsoft.com";

        // get the headers collection
        NameValueCollection headersCollection = myWebClient.Headers;

        // add a header to the collection
        headersCollection.Add("MyHeader", "MyHeaderValue");

        // get the data for the US english home page
        Console.WriteLine("--- First result ---");
        Stream dataStream = myWebClient.OpenRead("en/us/default.aspx");
        Console.WriteLine(ReadFirstString(dataStream));

        // reuse the same web request to get the UK englsh page
        Console.WriteLine("--- Second Result ---");
        dataStream = myWebClient.OpenRead("en/gb/default.aspx");
        Console.WriteLine(ReadFirstString(dataStream));

        // wait for input before exiting
        Console.WriteLine("Press enter to finish");
        Console.ReadLine();
    }

    static string ReadFirstString(Stream dataStream) {
        // create a reader around the stream
        StreamReader myReader = new StreamReader(dataStream);
        // read the first line from the stream
        string firstString = myReader.ReadLine().Substring(0, 80);
        // close the reader (and therefore the stream as well)
        myReader.Close();
        // return the string
        return firstString;
    }
}
```

The Headers and QueryString properties store name/value pairs using the
System.Collections.Specialized.NameValueCollection class. The most important method in this class is
Add, which allows you to add a new name/value pair to the collection by specifying two string
parameters, as demonstrated in Listing 21-2. The same headers and query string information will be
used for each request made using the WebClient object, meaning that you can provide this information
once and get the benefit of it on all subsequent requests.

The two web pages requested in Listing 21-2 are the US and UK home pages from the Microsoft site.
The pages are quite lengthy, so the responses have been trimmed to 80 characters. Compiling and
running Listing 21-2 produces the following results:

```
--- First result ---
<!DOCTYPE html PUBLIC "-//W3C//DTD XHTML 1.0 Transitional//EN" "http://www.w3.or

--- Second Result ---
<!DOCTYPE html PUBLIC "-//W3C//DTD XHTML 1.0 Transitional//EN" "http://www.w3.or
```

```
Press enter to finish
```

Using WebClient Members to Retrieve Data

The previous two examples used the OpenRead method to obtain a Stream object from which you could read the data – either byte-by-byte or by using a StreamReader to read string values. The WebClient class defines other methods that are generally more convenient, depending on the kind of data that you have requested. Table 21-3 describes these methods.

Table 21-3. WebClient *Data Methods*

Method	Description
DownloadData(string)	Downloads the data available at the specified URL as a byte array.
DownloadFile(string, string)	Downloads the data at the URL specified by the first parameter and saves it in a file whose path is specified by the second parameter.
DownloadString(string)	Downloads the data at the specified URL and returns it as a single string.
OpenRead(string)	Returns a Stream that can be used to read the data at the specified URL.
OpenWrite(string)	Returns a Stream that can be used to write data to the specified URL.
UploadData(string, byte[])	Uploads the data in the byte array to the specified URL.
UploadFile(string, string)	Uploads the contents of the file whose path is specified by the second parameter to the URL specified by the first parameter.
UploadString(string, string)	Uploads the content of the second parameter to the URL specified by the first parameter.

Listing 21-3 demonstrates using some of the methods from Table 21-3.

Listing 21-3. Using the WebClient *Data Convenience Methods*

```
using System;
using System.Net;

class Listing_03 {
```

```
static void Main(string[] args) {

    // create a new WebClient object
    WebClient myWebClient = new WebClient();

    // set a base address
    myWebClient.BaseAddress = "http://www.microsoft.com";

    // download a URL to a byte array
    byte[] byteData = myWebClient.DownloadData("en/us/default.aspx");
    // print out the first few byte values
    Console.WriteLine("--- Byte Data ---");
    for (int i = 0; i < 20 && i < byteData.Length; i++) {
        Console.Write("{0},", byteData[i]);
    }
    Console.WriteLine();

    // download the data to a string
    string dataString = myWebClient.DownloadString("en/us/default.aspx");
    // print the first few characters of the string
    Console.WriteLine("--- String Data ---");
    Console.WriteLine(dataString.Substring(0, 80));

    // wait for input before exiting
    Console.WriteLine("Press enter to finish");
    Console.ReadLine();
    }
}
```

Listing 21-3 retrieves the data from the same URL using the DownloadData and DownloadString methods. The DownloadData method is most useful when you are expecting binary data, and the DownloadString method is most useful when you are expecting text. Compiling and running Listing 21-3 produces the following results:

```
--- Byte Data ---
239,187,191,60,33,68,79,67,84,89,80,69,32,104,116,109,108,32,80,85,
--- String Data ---
<!DOCTYPE html PUBLIC "-//W3C//DTD XHTML 1.0 Transitional//EN" "http://www.w3.or

Press enter to finish
```

Getting the WebClient Response Headers

The WebClient class includes a property called ResponseHeaders that provides access to the headers included by the server in the response to your request. This property returns a System.Collections.Specialized.NameValueCollection object; this is the same type you use when using the Headers and QueryString properties. Listing 21-4 demonstrates how to use the ResponseHeaders property.

Listing 21-4. Using the WebClient.ResponseHeaders Property

```
using System;
using System.Collections.Specialized;
using System.Net;

class Listing_04 {

    static void Main(string[] args) {

        // create a new WebClient object
        WebClient myWebClient = new WebClient();

        // download a URL as a string
        string dataString = myWebClient.DownloadString("http://www.microsoft.com");

        // get the headers
        NameValueCollection headers = myWebClient.ResponseHeaders;

        foreach (string key in headers.AllKeys) {
            Console.WriteLine("Header: {0}, Value: {1}", key, headers[key]);
        }

        // wait for input before exiting
        Console.WriteLine("Press enter to finish");
        Console.ReadLine();
    }
}
```

You get the set of headers from the NameValueCollection object using the AllKeys property. This returns a string array that you use in a foreach loop to get the value for each header using the class indexer. Compiling and running Listing 21-4 produces the following results:

```
Header: VTag, Value: 279369612500000000
Header: Accept-Ranges, Value: bytes
Header: Content-Length, Value: 1020
Header: Cache-Control, Value: no-cache
Header: Content-Type, Value: text/html
Header: Date, Value: Sun, 18 Jul 2010 09:40:35 GMT
Header: ETag, Value: "67991fbd76a6c91:0"
Header: Last-Modified, Value: Mon, 16 Mar 2009 20:35:26 GMT
Header: P3P, Value: CP="ALL IND DSP COR ADM CONo CUR CUSo IVAo IVDo PSA PSD TAI
TELo OUR SAMo CNT COM INT NAV ONL PHY PRE PUR UNI"
Header: Server, Value: Microsoft-IIS/7.5
Header: X-Powered-By, Value: ASP.NET
Press enter to finish
```

Using WebClient Events

All of the WebClient examples so far in this section have been *synchronous,* meaning that the code doesn't continue executing until the request to the server has been completed. WebClient also supports asynchronous requests where you are notified that a request is completed through an event. Listing 21-5 contains an example.

Listing 21-5. Using WebClient to Asynchronously Request Data

```
using System;
using System.Net;

class Listing_05 {

    static void Main(string[] args) {

        // create a new WebClient objecty
        WebClient myWebClient = new WebClient();

        // subscribe to an event
        myWebClient.DownloadStringCompleted += (sender, eventArgs) => {
            // write out the first part of the string
            Console.WriteLine("--- Async Result ---");
            Console.WriteLine(eventArgs.Result.Substring(0, 50));
        };

        // make an asynchronous request
        myWebClient.DownloadStringAsync(new Uri("http://www.microsoft.com"));

        // do some other work while the request is being performed in the background
        for (int i = 0; i < 10; i++) {
            Console.WriteLine("Doing other work...{0}", i);
        }

        // wait for input before exiting
        Console.WriteLine("Press enter to finish");
        Console.ReadLine();
    }
}
```

Listing 21-5 uses a lambda expression to subscribe to the DownloadStringCompleted event in the WebClient object before calling the DownloadStringAsync method.

The DownloadStringAsync method takes a System.Uri parameter. The simplest way to create an Uri is to use the constructor that takes a string parameter whose value is the URL you want to retrieve.

The DownloadStringAsync method returns immediately, and the request is performed in the background. In Listing 21-5, a for loop simulates a program doing other work while the request is being handled.

When the request has been completed and the result converted into a string, the lambda expression is called. The parameters passed to the lambda expression are the WebClient that has performed the request and a DownloadStringCompletedEventArgs object; the Result property returns the string that has been retrieved from the server. Compiling the running Listing 21-5 produces the following results:

```
Doing other work...0
Doing other work...1
Doing other work...2
Doing other work...3
Doing other work...4
Doing other work...5
Doing other work...6
Doing other work...7
Doing other work...8
Doing other work...9
Press enter to finish
--- Async Result ---
<html><head><title>Microsoft Corporation</title><m
```

Table 21-4 contains a list of the asynchronous methods and the corresponding events and event argument classes defined by the `WebClient` class.

Table 21-4. WebClient Asynchronous Methods and Events

Method	Event	EventArgs Class
DownloadDataAsync(Uri)	DownloadDataCompleted	DownloadDataCompletedEventArgs
DownloadFileAsync(Uri)	DownloadFileCompleted	AsyncCompletedEventArgs
DownloadStringAsync(Uri)	DownloadStringCompleted	DownloadStringCompletedEventArgs
OpenReadAsync(Uri)	OpenReadCompleted	OpenReadCompletedEventArgs
OpenWriteAsync(Uri)	OpenWriteCompleted	OpenWriteCompletedEventArgs
UploadDataAsync(Uri)	UploadDataCompleted	UploadDataCompletedEventArgs
UploadFileAsync(Uri)	UploadFileCompleted	UploadFileCompletedEventArgs
UpLoadStringAsync(Uri)	UploadStringCompleted	UploadStringCompletedEventArgs

The base class for the event argument classes is `AsyncCompletedEventArgs` from the `System.ComponentModel` namespace; this is also the class used by the `DownloadFileCompleted` event. `AsyncCompletedEventArgs` has two helpful properties that you can use to find out how your asynchronous request went. These properties are described in Table 21-5.

Table 21-5. AsyncCompletedEventArgs Properties

Property	Description
Cancelled	Returns true if the request was cancelled using the WebClient.CancelAsync method.
Error	If an error occurred while the request was being performed, this property will return the corresponding Exception. If no error has occurred, then null will be returned.

It is good practice to check the Error property when handling an event before reading any other property. The classes derived from AsyncCompletedEventArgs define an additional property called Result, which returns an object of the type most suited to the asynchronous methods that was called. Table 21-6 lists the derived classes and the types that their Result property returns.

Table 21-6. Derived EventArgs Classes and the Type of the Result Property

Derived Class	Result Property Type
DownloadDataCompletedEventArgs	byte[]
DownloadStringCompletedEventArgs	string
OpenReadCompletedEventArgs	Stream
OpenWriteCompletedEventArgs	Stream
UploadDataCompletedEventArgs	byte[]
UploadFileCompletedEventArgs	byte[]
UploadStringCompletedEventArgs	string

Programming with Sockets

Sockets are a low-level network programming feature that allows you to create custom network protocols that your client and server programs can use to communicate or to provide your own implementation of standard network protocols. In general, socket programming is an advanced and complex topic, but simple socket programming can be performed using some C# helper classes.

Creating a Simple TCP Client & Server

Now let's look at two helper classes, TcpListener and TcpClient. These classes allow the programmer to use the Transmission Control Protocol (TCP) to communicate between a client and server. I'm not going to go into any detail about TCP, other than to say that if you are new to networking, you probably want to use this protocol as opposed to UDP, which is covered in a later section in this chapter.

The purpose of the TcpListener and TcpClient classes is to provide a facility to create a pair of Stream objects, as illustrated by Figure 21-1.

Figure 21-1. Streams and networks

When the client writes data to the first Stream object, it can be read by the server using a corresponding Stream object; equally, when the server writes data to its Stream object, it can be read by the client. The entire point of the TcpClient and TcpListener classes is to create those Stream objects and connect them together. Once you have the Stream objects, you can read and write any data you like, using the methods and techniques described in Chapter 20.

Creating the Server

The TcpListener class can be used to listen for connections on a specific port, which can then be used to create the Stream object that will be used to send and receive data from the client. Listing 21-6 demonstrates a simple network server.

Listing 21-6. A Simple TCP Server

```
using System;
using System.IO;
using System.Net;
using System.Net.Sockets;

class Listing_06 {

    static void Main(string[] args) {

        // create a new TcpListener object
        TcpListener myListener = new TcpListener(IPAddress.Any, 12000);

        // start accepting connections
        myListener.Start();

        // define a bool that will determine if we keep accepting connections
        bool acceptConnections = true;

        while (acceptConnections) {

            // wait for a connection
            Console.WriteLine("Waiting for connection");
```

```
        TcpClient theClient = myListener.AcceptTcpClient();
        Console.WriteLine("Connection accepted");

        // get the Stream object
        Stream netStream = theClient.GetStream();

        // handle the connection - use the result to
        // determine if we continue to accept connections
        acceptConnections = HandleClientStream(netStream);

        // close the stream
        netStream.Close();
        // close the network connection
        theClient.Close();
    }

    // stop listening on the port
    myListener.Stop();

    // wait for input before exiting
    Console.WriteLine("Press enter to finish");
    Console.ReadLine();
}

private static bool HandleClientStream(Stream clientStream) {
    // ...
    // implement code to handle client here
    // ...
    // return true if you want to accept further connections, false otherwise
    return false;

}
}
```

Listing 21-6 demonstrates how to create a server, but the server doesn't do anything useful at the moment. I'll come back to that later, after I have walked through each of the major steps in creating a server.

The first step is to create a new instance of TcpClient, specifying which port should be used to listen for client connections. The TcpClient class can be found in the System.Net.Sockets namespace, and the constructor takes a System.Net.IPAddress object and an int value. The IPAddress object specifies which network interface the server will use to listen for client connections. Unless you are building especially complex networks, the IPAddress.Any property will give you what you want; it indicates that all interfaces should be used. The int value is the port that will be used to listen for connections. This can be any port, but unless you are providing your own implementation of a well-known protocol, this should be a high number that you are not using for anything else. A port cannot be shared between processes. I have selected 12000 as the port for this demonstration, for no other reason than it is a nice round number that I am not using elsewhere. Here is the statement that performs the first step in Listing 21-6:

```
TcpListener myListener = new TcpListener(IPAddress.Any, 12000);
```

The second step is to call the Start method. The TcpListener object has been created, but until you call the Start method, you won't get any client connections. Here is the relevant statement from Listing 21-6:

```
myListener.Start();
```

The next step is to wait for clients to connect to the server. You do that by calling the AcceptTcpClient method. This method will block until a client connects (i.e. execution of the code statements in the method that calls AcceptTcpClient will not continue until a client connects). When a client does connect, the AcceptTcpClient method will return a new TcpClient object. The AcceptTcpClient method is usually called in a loop, so that when you have finished dealing with one client, you begin waiting for the next. Here is the accept statement from Listing 21-6:

```
TcpClient theClient = myListener.AcceptTcpClient();
```

You want to get a Stream object that you can use to communicate with the client. You do this by calling the GetStream method on the TcpClient object that was returned by the AcceptTcpClient method, like this:

```
Stream netStream = theClient.GetStream();
```

Writing to that Stream object will send data to the client. Data that the client has sent to your server can be accessed by reading from the Stream. In Listing 21-6, you call the HandleClientStream method, which is where you will implement a custom network protocol later in this section. Note that it is the HandleClientStream method that you will want to modify if you are using this example as a template in your own program:

```
acceptConnections = HandleClientStream(netStream);
```

After the HandleClientStream method has completed, you call the Close method on the Stream object and the TcpClient object; this closes the underlying network connection:

```
netStream.Close();
theClient.Close();
```

The return type of the HandleClientStream method is set to be a bool, which you then use as the condition of the while loop that accepts connections from the TcpListener object. This means that returning false from the HandleClientStream method will close down the server, while returning true will have the server wait for another connection. Next, stop the server by calling the Stop method on the TcpListener object:

```
myListener.Stop();
```

In a nutshell, that is a simple TCP server. You can add statements to the HandleClientStream method to communicate with the client. For this example, let's implement a calculator function. The client will send the server two integer values, separated by a space character, and the server will add those numbers together and return the result. Listing 21-7 shows how to implement this.

Listing 21-7. Implementing a Network Protocol

```
private static bool HandleClientStream(Stream clientStream) {

    // create StreamReader and StreamWriter objects around the Stream
    StreamReader myReader = new StreamReader(clientStream);
```

```
StreamWriter myWriter = new StreamWriter(clientStream);

// define a string that will be used to read from the StreamReader
string dataLine;
// enter a loop to read lines from the client
while ((dataLine = myReader.ReadLine()) != null) {

    // read a string from the StreamReader and split it on the space character
    string[] stringElements = dataLine.Split(' ');

    // parse the two integer values
    int firstInt = int.Parse(stringElements[0]),
        secondInt = int.Parse(stringElements[1]);

    // compute the result
    int result = firstInt + secondInt;

    // print out the information locally
    Console.WriteLine("Server processed request: {0} + {1} = {2}",
        firstInt, secondInt, result);

    // return the result of the calculation to the cliebt
    myWriter.WriteLine(result);
    // flush the writer to make sure that the data is flushed
    myWriter.Flush();
}
// return true if you want to accept further connections, false otherwise
return false;
}
```

The method in Listing 21-7 uses the features seen in Chapter 20 to work with streams, Chapter 16 for splitting strings, and Chapter 5 for parsing numeric values. The StreamReader is used to read a sequence of text lines from the client, which are then broken down and parsed to obtain the two int values. The StreamWriter class is used to return the result to the client.

When you are testing a network client, the built-in Windows firewall might ask you if you want to allow the program to accept connections, as illustrated by Figure 21-2.

The simplest way of making sure that your server program can accept connections is to check the boxes for both private and public networks, as shown in the figure. However, you should be aware that this will allow any client program, not just the one you create, to connect to your server.

Figure 21-2. Allowing the server to accept connections

Creating the Client

Creating the client for this example requires the use of the TcpClient class. Listing 21-8 demonstrates a client that works with the calculator server defined in Listing 21-7.

Listing 21-8. Creating a Simple Client

```
using System;
using System.IO;
using System.Net;
using System.Net.Sockets;

class Listing_08 {

    static void Main(string[] args) {

        // create the TcpClient object
        TcpClient myClient = new TcpClient(IPAddress.Loopback.ToString(), 12000);

        // get the Stream object from the client
        Stream dataStream = myClient.GetStream();

        // call the HandleServerStream method
        HandleServerStream(dataStream);
```

```
        // close the stream
        dataStream.Close();
        // close the connection
        myClient.Close();

        // wait for input before exiting
        Console.WriteLine("Press enter to finish");
        Console.ReadLine();
    }

    public static void HandleServerStream(Stream serverStream) {

        // create a StreamReader and StreamWriter around the Stream
        StreamReader myReader = new StreamReader(serverStream);
        StreamWriter myWriter = new StreamWriter(serverStream);

        int[] firstSet = { 10, 20, 30, 40, 50 };
        int[] secondSet = { 3, 6, 9, 3, 4 };

        for (int i = 0; i < 5; i++) {
            // write a message
            Console.WriteLine("Writing message: {0} {1}", firstSet[i], secondSet[i]);
            myWriter.WriteLine("{0} {1}", firstSet[i], secondSet[i]);
            myWriter.Flush();
            // read a message
            string responseString = myReader.ReadLine();
            Console.WriteLine("Got response: {0}", responseString);
        }
    }
}
```

Creating a client is generally simpler than creating a server. In Listing 21-8, the first step is to create a TcpClient object that has the name of the server and the port that you want to connect to. You want to run the client and the server on the same machine, so use the loopback address, obtained using the Loopback property of the IPAddress class. The port number must match the one that the server is listening to for connections—in this case, 12000. Here is the relevant statement from Listing 21-8:

```
TcpClient myClient = new TcpClient(IPAddress.Loopback.ToString(), 12000);
```

To get the Stream that you will use to communicate with the server by calling the GetStream method, do this:

```
Stream dataStream = myClient.GetStream();
```

You have followed the same pattern as for the server and separated the statements that communicate with the server into a separate method called HandleServerStream. You call this method, passing the Stream object that connects you to the server as a parameter:

```
HandleServerStream(dataStream);
```

When the HandleServerStream method returns, call the Close method on the Stream object and the TcpClient object:

```
dataStream.Close();
myClient.Close();
```

All that remains for the client is the implementation of the `HandleServerStream` method, which will make use of the server calculator function. In Listing 21-8 you define two integer arrays, and you use a for loop to send a sequence of number pairs to the server using the `StreamWriter` and use the `StreamReader` to read the calculation results. To test these examples, you must first start the server and then the client. Here is the output from the server:

```
Waiting for connection
Connection accepted
Server processed request: 10 + 3 = 13
Server processed request: 20 + 6 = 26
Server processed request: 30 + 9 = 39
Server processed request: 40 + 3 = 43
Server processed request: 50 + 4 = 54
Press enter to finish
```

And here is the output from the client:

```
Writing message: 10 3
Got response: 13
Writing message: 20 6
Got response: 26
Writing message: 30 9
Got response: 39
Writing message: 40 3
Got response: 43
Writing message: 50 4
Got response: 54
Press enter to finish
```

Writing a Parallel Server

A serious limitation with the server in the previous section is that it only processes one client request at a time. One way of dealing with this is to use the Task Parallel Library, which is the topic of a later chapter. As a taste of things to come, Listing 21-9 demonstrates a parallel version of the calculator server which can provide service to multiple clients simultaneously.

Listing 21-9. A Parallel Server

```
using System;
using System.IO;
using System.Net;
using System.Net.Sockets;
using System.Threading.Tasks;
```

```
class Listing_07 {

    static void Main(string[] args) {

        // create a new TcpListener object
        TcpListener myListener = new TcpListener(IPAddress.Any, 12000);

        // start accepting connections
        myListener.Start();

        while (true) {

            // wait for a connection
            Console.WriteLine("Waiting for connection");
            TcpClient theClient = myListener.AcceptTcpClient();
            Console.WriteLine("Connection accepted");

            Task.Factory.StartNew(() => {

                // get the Stream object
                Stream netStream = theClient.GetStream();

                // handle the connection - use the result to
                // determine if we continue to accept connections
                HandleClientStream(netStream);

                // close the stream
                netStream.Close();
                // close the network connection
                theClient.Close();
            });
        }

        // wait for input before exiting
        Console.WriteLine("Press enter to finish");
        Console.ReadLine();
    }

    private static bool HandleClientStream(Stream clientStream) {

        // create StreamReader and StreamWriter objects around the Stream
        StreamReader myReader = new StreamReader(clientStream);
        StreamWriter myWriter = new StreamWriter(clientStream);

        // define a string that will be used to read from the StreamReader
        string dataLine;
        // enter a loop to read lines from the client
        while ((dataLine = myReader.ReadLine()) != null) {
            // read a string from the StreamReader and split it on the space character
            string[] stringElements = dataLine.Split(' ');

            // parse the two integer values
```

```
        int firstInt = int.Parse(stringElements[0]),
            secondInt = int.Parse(stringElements[1]);

        // compute the result
        int result = firstInt + secondInt;
        // print out the information locally
        Console.WriteLine("Task {3}: Server processed request: {0} + {1} = {2}",
            firstInt, secondInt, result, Task.CurrentId);

        // return the result of the calculation to the cliebt
        myWriter.WriteLine(result);
        // flush the writer to make sure that the data is flushed
        myWriter.Flush();
    }
    // return true if you want to accept further connections, false otherwise
    return false;
    }
}
```

Be sure to read the Parallel Programming chapter before you use this example as the basis for your own programs. In particular, you should read the section on synchronization to avoid a frequently encountered set of problems associated with parallel programming.

The Windows Communication Foundation

The calculator client/server example in the previous example demonstrated how to use the TcpListener and TcpClient classes, but the result didn't really take advantage of the C# language features. The client could send any message to the server, not just the int values that the server was expecting. Extending the protocol between the client and the server is certainly possible but potentially troublesome, and you'd still need to write some code to check for errors in processing messages from the client.

An alternative approach is to use the *Windows Commination Foundation* (WCF), which is the .NET programming model for creating service-oriented applications, informally known as web services. The benefit of using WCF is that you get to work with C# objects, giving you the benefits of type safety, exception handling, and everything else that Part I of this book covered. The drawback of using WCF is complexity; WCF supports many different options and configurations. Getting started with WCF is reasonably simple, but mastering WCF—especially for large-scale applications—requires time and patience.

There isn't space in this book to get deeply into WCF, but in the following sections I'll show you how to create basic a basic WCF server and client and demonstrate how to implement the simple calculator example from earlier in the chapter.

■ **Note** To use WCF you must add a reference to the System.ServiceModel assembly to your project. In the Visual Studio Solution Explorer, right click on the References folder, select the .NET tab, select System.ServiceModel from the list, and click OK.

Creating the WCF Server

Before you can create a WCF server, you must give your user account the required permissions. As administrator, issue the following command, using your domain and user name instead of mine:

```
netsh http add urlacl url=http://+:13000/ user=SHUTTLE\adam
```

This command gives permission to create WCF servers that will listen on port 13000; if you want to use another port, you will have to edit the command.

Creating the Service Contract

A service contract is the set of methods that your server will support and is defined using a C# interface. For your calculator example, you will define four methods to handle addition, multiplication, division, and subtraction, as shown by Listing 21-10.

Listing 21-10. A Simple WCF Service Contract

```
using System.ServiceModel;

[ServiceContract]
public interface ICalculatorServer {

    [OperationContract]
    int PerformAddition(int x, int y);

    [OperationContract]
    int PerformMultiplcation(int x, int y);

    [OperationContract]
    int PerformSubtraction(int x, int y);

    [OperationContract]
    float PerformDivision(int x, int y);
}
```

To create a service contract from an interface, you must apply the ServiceContract attribute to the entire interface and the OperationContract attribute to each method in the interface that you want to make available to clients. Both attributes are found in the System.ServiceModel namespace. Applying the OperationContract to every method can be tedious, but it does allow you to create a service contract from an interface that already exists in your program, selecting only some methods to be published to clients. Having created a service contract, you need to create an implementation class. This is just like implementing a regular C# interface. The example implementation is shown in Listing 21-11.

Listing 21-11. Implementing a Service Contract

```
using System;

class CalculatorImpl : ICalculatorServer {
```

```
    public int PerformAddition(int x, int y) {
        int result = x + y;
        Console.WriteLine("Addition Request: {0} + {1} = {2}",
            x, y, result);
        return result;
    }

    public int PerformMultiplcation(int x, int y) {
        int result = x * y;
        Console.WriteLine("Multiplcation Request: {0} * {1} = {2}",
            x, y, result);
        return result;
    }

    public int PerformSubtraction(int x, int y) {
        int result = x - y;
        Console.WriteLine("Subtraction Request: {0} - {1} = {2}",
            x, y, result);
        return result;
    }

    public float PerformDivision(int x, int y) {
        float result = ((float)x) / ((float)y);
        Console.WriteLine("Division Request: {0} / {1} = {2}",
            x, y, result);
        return result;
    }
}
```

There is nothing special to note here. Each method performs a simple calculation and returns the result. Details of each calculation are printed out using the Console.WriteLine method.

The final step is to publish your WCF service; this means that the methods of your implementation class will be available for clients to call. Most of the functionality of WCF allows you to control how and where your methods are published and under what circumstances they can be used. Listing 21-12 publishes your calculation service using some of the basic WCF features.

Listing 21-12. Publishing the WCF Service

```
using System;
using System.ServiceModel;
using System.ServiceModel.Description;

class PublishServer {

    static void Main(string[] args) {

        // define the URI that will be used to publish the service
        Uri serviceAddress = new Uri("http://localhost:13000/WCF");

        // create the ServiceHost object
        ServiceHost myServiceHost = new ServiceHost(typeof(CalculatorImpl), serviceAddress);
```

```
                // add the end point with the HTTP binding
                myServiceHost.AddServiceEndpoint(typeof(ICalculatorServer),
                    new WSHttpBinding(), "CalculatorServer");

                // add support for getting the meta-data via HTTP
                ServiceMetadataBehavior smb = new ServiceMetadataBehavior();
                 smb.HttpGetEnabled = true;
                myServiceHost.Description.Behaviors.Add(smb);

                // start receiving requests from clients
                myServiceHost.Open();
                Console.WriteLine("Calculator Server ready");

                // wait for input before exiting
                Console.WriteLine("Press enter to finish");
                Console.ReadLine();
            }
        }
```

The first step is to create and configure a ServiceHost object; this will take care of publishing your methods. The two parameters for the ServiceHost constructor are the type of the class that implements the service contract and a Uri object. The Uri object specifies the port that will be used to listen for client events and a prefix that will be put in front of each service name; the prefix is useful when you want to run related services together. The port for this example is 13000, which is the same port you enabled using the netsh command at the start of this section. Here are the relevant statements from Listing 21-10:

```
Uri serviceAddress = new Uri("http://localhost:13000/WCF");
ServiceHost myServiceHost = new ServiceHost(typeof(CalculatorImpl), serviceAddress);
```

You need to tell the ServiceHost that your CalculatorImpl class is an implementation of the service contract defined by the ICalculatorServer interface. There are a lot of options available for doing this. Here is the statement from Listing 21-10 that creates the association between the class and the contract:

```
myServiceHost.AddServiceEndpoint(typeof(ICalculatorServer),
    new WSHttpBinding(), "CalculatorServer");
```

Clients of your service need to be able to get information about the methods your service publishes; in this case, the methods in the ICalculatorServer interface. Here are the statements from Listing 21-10 that enable this feature:

```
ServiceMetadataBehavior smb = new ServiceMetadataBehavior();
smb.HttpGetEnabled = true;
myServiceHost.Description.Behaviors.Add(smb);
```

The key part here is setting the HttpGetEnabled property of the ServiceMetadataBehavior object to true. This allows clients to get the information about your service from the service itself. You'll use this to create the client in a moment. The very last thing you need to do is call the Open method on the ServiceHost object. Once you have done this, the server will start to listen for client requests on the port that you specified.

Creating the WCF Client

Visual Studio provides special features for implementing WCF clients. To create a client for the WCF service created in the previous section, you need to start by creating a regular C# console application project, as described in Chapter 2. My client project is called Listing_13 and has been created using the template for all of the examples in the book. Listing 21-13 shows the (almost) empty code file, Listing_13.cs.

Listing 21-13. The Empty Code File

```
using System;

class WCFClient {

    static void Main(string[] args) {

        // wait for input before exiting
        Console.WriteLine("Press enter to finish");
        Console.ReadLine();
    }
}
```

Listing 21-13 shows my stripped down examples template which I use to reduce unnecessary code clutter. You code file may look slightly different—you may have a namespace and a different set of using statements, for example.

The next step is to have Visual Studio create a C# object that you can use to communicate with the server. There are different ways to do this, but you are going to have Visual Studio get the information from your WCF service.

■ **Important** The WCF server created in the previous section must be running before you can create the client. Switch to the project that contains the PublishServer class and select Start Without Debugging from the Visual Studio Debug menu.

Right click on the References folder for your client project in the Solution Explorer window and select Add Service Reference. Enter http://localhost:13000/WCF in the address box and press the Go button. The details of your server will be shown, as illustrated in Figure 21-3.

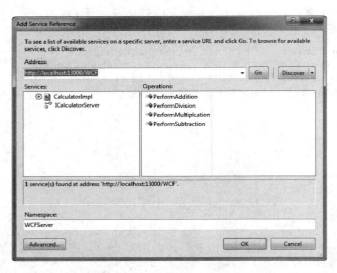

Figure 21-3. *Adding a service reference*

On the left hand side of the dialog, you will see an item representing the `CalculatorImpl` class. Expand this to see the set of service contracts that the class has implemented. In your case, there is only one contract, `ICalculatorService`. The methods defined by the service contract are shown on the right side of the dialog box. Change the text in the Namespace box to `WCFServer`, as shown in Figure 21-3, and press the `OK` button.

Visual Studio will add a set of assembly references to your client project and create a `Service References` folder that contains a `WCFServer` item, as shown in Figure 21-4.

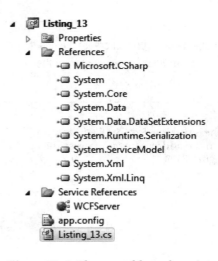

Figure 21-4. *The assembly and service references added by Visual Studio*

The final step is to make use of the WCF service. The first change you have to make is to add a using statement for the namespace that Visual Studio has just created for your service reference. This namespace will be the name of your project and the name you entered into the Namespace area in the Add Service Reference dialog box combined with the dot operator; in this case, it will be Listing_13.WCFServer. Listing 21-14 demonstrates the modified class.

Listing 21-14. Implementing the WCF Client

```
using System;
using Listing_13.WCFServer;

class WCFClient {

    static void Main(string[] args) {

        // create a new client object
        CalculatorServerClient calcClient = new CalculatorServerClient();

        // perform some calculations
        int result = calcClient.PerformAddition(10, 20);
        Console.WriteLine("Addition result: {0}", result);

        result = calcClient.PerformMultiplcation(20, 30);
        Console.WriteLine("Multiplication result: {0}", result);

        result = calcClient.PerformSubtraction(30, 40);
        Console.WriteLine("Subtraction result: {0}", result);

        float divisionResult = calcClient.PerformDivision(40, 50);
        Console.WriteLine("Division result: {0}", divisionResult);

        // wait for input before exiting
        Console.WriteLine("Press enter to finish");
        Console.ReadLine();
    }
}
```

In the service reference namespace will be an object named after the service you published, with the word Client appended. In the case of this example, you called the service CalculatorService, so the class will be CalculatorServerClient. To use the service, create an object from this class using the default constructor and call the methods that the class contains; these map to the methods of your service contract. The details of creating the network connection, converting your C# values to network data, and parsing messages is taken care of for you.

Compiling and running the client produces the following output:

```
Addition result: 30
Multiplication result: 600
Subtraction result: -10
Division result: 0.8
Press enter to finish
```

Running the client also produces output from the server:

```
Calculator Server ready
Press enter to finish
Addition Request: 10 + 20 = 30
Multiplcation Request: 20 * 30 = 600
Subtraction Request: 30 - 40 = -10
Division Request: 40 / 50 = 0.8
```

As you can see, with very little effort you have been able to create a server that publishes capabilities using C# interfaces, methods, and attributes and a client that can communicate with the server using C# objects and values without having to worry about the details of the network plumbing. This has been a crash course in WCF, but I hope that it demonstrates the basic capabilities and encourages you to look deeper into the functionality on offer.

Other Useful Network Classes

The .NET Framework class library contains a wide range of classes that can be used to perform many different kinds of network activity. In this section, I'll demonstrate three useful classes that can be used to create a simple web server, use connectionless IP networking, and perform lookups in the Domain Name System.

Writing a Simple Web Server

At the start of the chapter, I showed you how to make requests using the WebClient class, which is a useful convenience class for making HTTP requests. The .NET Framework library also provides support for implementing a simple HTTP server which you can use to deliver content to your clients. This support comes in the form of the System.Net.HttpListener class.

There was a point back in the mid-1990s where every programmer wrote their own web server. I ended up writing about a dozen different ones to be embedded in different projects. Things are different now. The quality of the off-the-shelf servers has improved significantly and we have all realized that writing our own server can expose our projects to all kinds of security problems. That said, if you are going to write a simple web server, this is how you do it. Listing 21-15 provides a demonstration of using the HttpListener class.

Listing 21-15. A simple Web Server

```
using System;
using System.IO;
using System.Net;

class Listing_15 {

    static void Main(string[] args) {

        // define the directory that will be used to load the images
        string baseDir = @"..\..\images\";
```

```
    // create a new listener
    HttpListener myListener = new HttpListener();

    // add the prefixes we will listen for
    myListener.Prefixes.Add("http://+:14000/demo/");

    // start listening for client requests
    myListener.Start();

    while (true) {

        // wait for a client request to arrive
        Console.WriteLine("Waiting for client request");
        HttpListenerContext reqContext = myListener.GetContext();

        // get the request and response objects from the context
        HttpListenerRequest clientRequest = reqContext.Request;
        HttpListenerResponse clientResponse = reqContext.Response;

        // get the file component from the URL
        string filename = clientRequest.Url.LocalPath;
        filename = string.Format("{0}{1}{2}", baseDir, '\\',
            filename.Substring(filename.LastIndexOf('/') + 1));

        // see if the file exists
        if (File.Exists(filename)) {
            Console.WriteLine("Request for file: {0}", filename);
            // open a stream to the file and copy the contents to the response stream
            Stream filestream = File.Open(filename, FileMode.Open, FileAccess.Read);
            filestream.CopyTo(clientResponse.OutputStream);
            // close the input stream
            filestream.Close();
        } else {
            // the file does not exist
            Console.WriteLine("Request for nonexistent file: {0}", filename);
            // set an error code for the client
            clientResponse.StatusCode = 404;
        }

        // close the response
        clientResponse.Close();

    }

    // wait for input before exiting
    Console.WriteLine("Press enter to finish");
    Console.ReadLine();
    }
}
```

Listing 21-15 will serve files contained in a directory specified by the baseDir variable, set to be the images directory in the project directory (this is defined using a relative path from where the program will be started, which is either the bin\Debug or bin\Release directories). Requests for files which do not exist in this directory, or requests for anything else, will return a "not found" message to the client.

Start by creating an HttpListener object and telling it what prefixes it should listen for. Here are the relevant statements from the example:

```
HttpListener myListener = new HttpListener();
myListener.Prefixes.Add("http://+:14000/demo/");
```

The prefix used in the example tells the HttpListener object to listen to port 14000 and requests that start with /demo/. The plus sign (+) means that it should accept requests that contain any hostname. A single HttpListener can support more than one prefix, but let's keep things simple for this example. When you have added the prefixes you require to the HttpListener, you can start listening for requests by calling the Start method, like this:

```
myListener.Start();
```

Using HttpListener is very similar to using TcpListener, albeit HttpListener takes care of parsing client requests so that you get an HTTP-centric view of what is happening. You accept a request from a client by calling the GetContext method, which blocks until a client connects and returns an HttpListenerContext object when one does. The HttpListenerContext class defines a pair of properties that let you get details of the request from the client and the object used to return a response. These properties are described in Table 21-7.

Table 21-7. HttpListenerContext *Properties*

Property	Description
Request	Returns an HttpListenerRequest object that represents the request from the client.
Response	Returns an HttpListenerResponse object that is used to create the reply to the client.

In this simple example, you only want to know which file the client has requested, so you use the Url property of the HttpListenerRequest class and manipulate it to work out what the local file path would be:

```
HttpListenerRequest clientRequest = reqContext.Request;

string filename = clientRequest.Url.LocalPath;
filename = string.Format("{0}{1}{2}", baseDir, '\\',
    filename.Substring(filename.LastIndexOf('/') + 1));
```

The HttpListenerRequest class has a set of properties that provide access to details about the query. The most useful of these are described in Table 21-8.

Table 21-8. *HttpListenerRequest Properties*

Property	Description
Headers	Returns a collection of name/value pairs containing the headers that the client included in the request.
HttpMethod	Returns a string representing the HTTP method that the client used in the request, typically GET or POST.
InputStream	Returns a Stream that can be used to read data sent by the client.
IsLocal	Returns true if the request has been sent from the same computer that the HttpListener object is running on and false otherwise.
ProtocolVersion	Returns the version of HTTP that the client has used in the request.
QueryString	Returns a collection of name/value pairs containing the query parts of the request URL.
Url	Returns an Uri object representing the URL that the client requested.
UserAgent	Returns the string that the client used to identify itself in the request.

In Listing 21-15, you check to see if there is a file in the source directory. If there is, then you open a Stream to read from the file and copy the file contents to the client using the HttpListenerResponse.OutputStream property and the Stream.CopyTo method:

```
HttpListenerResponse clientResponse = reqContext.Response;

Stream filestream = File.Open(filename, FileMode.Open, FileAccess.Read);
filestream.CopyTo(clientResponse.OutputStream);
```

If the requested file doesn't exist, you use the HttpListenerResponse.StatusCode property to set an error result that will be passed to the client:

```
clientResponse.StatusCode = 404;
```

Whether or not the request can be serviced, you must call the Close method on the HttpListenerResponse. Until you do this, the response will not be sent back to the client:

```
clientResponse.Close();
```

The HttpListenerResponse class contains a range of members that you can use to build the response to the client. Table 21-9 describes some of the most frequently used members.

Table 21-9. *HttpListenerResponse Members*

Member	Description
Abort()	Closes the connection to the client without sending a response.
AddHeader(string, string)	Adds a header to the response; the first parameter is the header name and the second is the header value.
Close()	Sends the response to the client and closes the connection.
ContentType	Gets or sets the MIME type for the response to the client.
ContentLength64	Gets or sets the number of bytes in the response to the client.
Redirect(string)	Redirects the client to the URL specified by the string parameter.
OutputStream	Returns a Stream object that can be used to write data to the client.
StatusCode	Gets or sets the status code that will be returned to the client. This property defaults to 200.
StatusDesdcription	Gets or sets the status description message that will be returned to the client.

You will need administration rights to run the simple server defined in Listing 21-15. Open the Windows Start menu and type cmd. Right click on the cmd.exe item in the list and click Run as administrator. Change to your project directory and then to bin\Debug or bin\Release. Run Listing_15.exe to start the server.

Using a web browser, navigate to the following URL:

http://localhost:14000/demo/cherry.jpg

You should see an image of some cherries. If you change cherry.jpg in the URL to apple.jpg or orange.jpg, you will see the other images included in the project. If you ask for any other file, or remove the demo part of the URL, you will see an error.

Using Connectionless Networking

All of the examples so far in this chapter have used connection-oriented networking. A client communicates with the server to establish a connection, data flows in both directions, and the connection is closed. All of this is done using the Transmission Control Protocol (TCP) behind the scenes. Internet Protocol (IP) networking doesn't guarantee that data is delivered across the network, but when you use TCP, it watches out for missing data and ensures that it is resent.

The complement to TCP is the *User Datagram Protocol* (UDP). UDP allows you to send data across the network without creating a connection, but doesn't provide any protections against data loss, so you must ensure that your programs are able to detect when messages are missing and provide a mechanism that will permit some kind of recovery. In this section, I'll show you how to use the System.Net.Sockets.UdpClient class to create a connectionless network program. Listing 21-16 demonstrates using the UdpClient class.

Listing 21-16. Using the UdpClient Class

```
using System;
using System.Net;
using System.Net.Sockets;
using System.Text;
using System.Threading.Tasks;

class UdpReceiver {

    public void Start() {
        Task.Factory.StartNew(() => ReceiveAndPrintMessages());
    }

    private void ReceiveAndPrintMessages() {

        // create the UdpClient object
        UdpClient myUdpClient = new UdpClient(15000);

        // create the end point
        IPEndPoint endPoint = new IPEndPoint(IPAddress.Any, 0);

        while (true) {
            Console.WriteLine("Receiver: Waiting for a message");
            // wait to receive data
            byte[] data = myUdpClient.Receive(ref endPoint);
            // convert the byte data to a string
            string message = Encoding.Default.GetString(data);
            // print out the details of the received message
            Console.WriteLine("Receiver: Message from {0} on port {1}",
                endPoint.Address, endPoint.Port);
            Console.WriteLine("Receiver: Message is: {0}", message);
        }
    }
}
```

The Start method in Listing 21-16 uses the Task Parallel Library (TPL) to perform work in the background. I won't go into details about the TPL or the Task class here, so see Chapter 25 for full details. For the purposes of this chapter, the ReceiveAndPrintMessages method contains all the action.

The ReceiveAndPrintMessages method creates a new UdpClient object; the constructor parameter indicates which port the UdpClient should use to listen for messages—in this case, port 15000:

```
UdpClient myUdpClient = new UdpClient(15000);
```

The next step in code is to create an IPEndPoint object. You have to pass this object as a reference parameter to the Receive message (see Chapter 9 for details of reference parameters). When you receive a network message, the IPEndPoint object will be modified to give us details about where the message originated.

To wait for a message to arrive, you call the UdpClient.Receive method, which blocks until a message arrived and returns a byte array when one does. The array contains the message, which you convert to a string using the System.Text.Encoding class (details of which can be found in Chapter 26). The message and details about the sender obtained from the IPEndPoint object and printed to the console. Listing 21-17 demonstrates using the UdpClient class to send messages across the network.

Listing 21-17. Sending Messages with the UdpClient Class

```
using System;
using System.Net;
using System.Net.Sockets;
using System.Text;

class UdpSender {

    public void SendMessages() {

        // create the UdpClient object
        UdpClient myUdpClient = new UdpClient();

        // specify where we want to send our messages
        myUdpClient.Connect(IPAddress.Loopback, 15000);

        // enter a loop to send messages
        for (int i = 0; i < 5; i++) {
            // create the string we will send
            string messageString = string.Format("{0} x {0} = {1}", i, i * i);
            // write out a message to the console
            Console.WriteLine("Sender: sending message: {0}", messageString);
            // convert the string to bytes
            byte[] dataArray = Encoding.Default.GetBytes(messageString);
            // send the bytes
            myUdpClient.Send(dataArray, dataArray.Length);
        }

        // close the UdpClient object
        myUdpClient.Close();
    }
}
```

The SendMessages method in this class creates a new UdpClient and uses the connect method to detail where messages should be send. In this case, it is to port 15000 on the local machine. A for loop is then used to create a sequence of message strings, each of which is converted to a byte array using the Encoding class. The byte array is then passed to the UdpClient.Send method, which takes care of sending the data. The following code uses the classes in Listings 21-16 and 21-17 together:

```
class UdpTest {

    static void Main(string[] args) {

        // create the UdpReceiver object and start listening
```

```
        new UdpReceiver().Start();

        // create the UdpSender and send the messages
        new UdpSender().SendMessages();

        // wait for input before exiting
        Console.WriteLine("Press enter to finish");
        Console.ReadLine();
    }
}
```

Compiling all three classes and running the UdpTest class produces the following results:

```
Receiver: Waiting for a message
Sender: sending message: 0 x 0 = 0
Sender: sending message: 1 x 1 = 1
Sender: sending message: 2 x 2 = 4
Receiver: Message from 127.0.0.1 on port 57636
Receiver: Message is: 0 x 0 = 0
Receiver: Waiting for a message
Receiver: Message from 127.0.0.1 on port 57636
Receiver: Message is: 1 x 1 = 1
Receiver: Waiting for a message
Sender: sending message: 3 x 3 = 9
Sender: sending message: 4 x 4 = 16
Receiver: Message from 127.0.0.1 on port 57636
Receiver: Message is: 2 x 2 = 4
Receiver: Waiting for a message
Receiver: Message from 127.0.0.1 on port 57636
Receiver: Message is: 3 x 3 = 9
Receiver: Waiting for a message
Receiver: Message from 127.0.0.1 on port 57636
Receiver: Message is: 4 x 4 = 16
Receiver: Waiting for a message
Press enter to finish
```

■ **Tip** You may be prompted by the Windows firewall when you first run this example. You should ensure that access to private networks in enabled, as shown in Figure 21-2.

Using the Domain Name System

The Domain Name System (DNS) is used to convert between user-friendly host names (such as www.microsoft.com) and IP addresses (such as 207.46.170.123). The System.Net.Dns class provides static methods that let you make queries of the DNS. Listing 21-18 provides a simple demonstration.

Listing 21-18. Using the Dns Class

```csharp
using System;
using System.Net;

class Listing_18 {

    static void Main(string[] args) {

        // perform a DNS lookup on www.microsoft.com
        IPHostEntry myEntry = Dns.GetHostEntry("www.microsoft.com");

        // print out the host name
        Console.WriteLine("Hostname: {0}", myEntry.HostName);

        // enumerate the addresses for this host
        foreach (IPAddress addr in myEntry.AddressList) {
            Console.WriteLine("Address: {0}", addr);
        }

        if (myEntry.Aliases.Length > 0) {
            // enumerate the strings for this host
            foreach (string str in myEntry.Aliases) {
                Console.WriteLine("Alias: {0}", str);
            }
        } else {
            Console.WriteLine("There are no aliases");
        }

        // wait for input before exiting
        Console.WriteLine("Press enter to finish");
        Console.ReadLine();
    }
}
```

The Dns class provides two methods, which are shown in Table 21-10.

Table 21-10. Dns Methods

Methods	Description
GetHostEntry(string)	Returns an IPHostEntry object representing the host name or IP address specified by the parameter.
GetHostName()	Returns the name of the local computer.

The GetHostEntry method takes string parameter containing either a host name or an IP address and returns an IPHostEntry object that contains the details of the corresponding DNS record. The properties of the IPHostEntry class are described in Table 21-11.

Table 21-11. IPHostEntry Properties

Property	Description
AddressList	Returns an array of IPAddress objects.
Aliases	Returns an array of string values representing names that resolve to the IP addresses in the AddressList property.
HostName	Returns a string representing the primary hostname

Compiling and running Listing 21-17 produces the information available for the hostname www.microsoft.com, which is as follows:

```
Hostname: lb1.www.ms.akadns.net
Address: 207.46.170.123
Address: 207.46.170.10
There are no aliases
Press enter to finish
```

You can see that the hostname belongs to Akamai, a company that provides content distribution services for high-traffic domains. Note that your results will almost certainly be different because content distribution networks (CDNs) localize their infrastructure to individual internet service providers.

Summary

In this chapter you looked at the .NET Framework class library facilities for networking. You learned how to use the WebClient class to retrieve data from HTTP servers, how to use the TcpListener, TcpClient, and UdpClient classes to perform connection-oriented and connectionless networking, how to use the Dns class to retrieve DNS information, and how to use the HttpListener class to create a simple web server.

You also took a quick tour of the Windows Communications Foundation, which supports C# object and value semantics across networks—something that requires a little more work, but makes the resulting program more robust and natural to work with.

CHAPTER 22

■ ■ ■

Time & Dates

Working with times and dates is a common task. You may want to check if a file has changed since last you looked, test how long an operation takes to complete, or work out some kind of schedule for future activities. C# and the .NET Framework Class Library have extensive support for measuring and managing time and dates. This chapter starts with support for measuring small amounts of time very accurately and moves on to the mainstays of time representation, the System.TimeSpan and System.DateTime structures. Table 22-1 provides the summary for this chapter.

Table 22-1. Quick Problem/Solution Reference for Chapter 22

Problem	Solution	Listings
Measure how long an activity takes.	Use the StopWatch class.	22-1, 22-2
Represent a period of time.	Use the TimeSpan struct.	22-3, 22-4
Combine, subtract or compare periods of time.	Use the TimeSpan custom operators.	22-5
Format periods of time as strings.	Use the built-in TimeSpan format components or create a custom string using the TimeSpan format specifiers.	22-6 through 22-8
Represent a moment in time.	Use the DateTime struct.	22-9 through 22-11
Combine, subtract or compare moments in time and periods of time.	Use the DateTime custom operators.	22-12, 22-13
Format moments in time as strings.	Use the built-in DateTime format components or create a custom string using the DateTime format specifiers.	22-14, 22-15

Measuring Small Amounts of Time

Programmers often need to measure how long an operation takes to complete, especially if the code isn't performing as well as it should. Visual Studio offers performance analysis tools, but for simpler problems, adding time measuring statements to your code can be exceptionally helpful.

The System.Diagnostics.StopWatch class provides support for accurately measuring periods of time down to the *tick*, which is the smallest amount of time a specific machine can measure. (Note that this measurement can vary with hardware and operating system versions.) Listing 22-1 provides a demonstration of using the StopWatch class.

Listing 22-1. Using the StopWatch Class

```
using System;
using System.Diagnostics;

class Listing_01 {

    static void Main(string[] args) {

        // create a new StopWatch object
        Stopwatch myTimer = new Stopwatch();

        // start timing
        myTimer.Start();

        // perform the task we want to measure
        long total = 0;
        for (int i = 0; i < int.MaxValue; i++) {
            total += i;
        }

        // stop the timer
        myTimer.Stop();

        // print out the result
        Console.WriteLine("Result: {0}", total);

        // print out how long the operation took
        long elapsedMs = myTimer.ElapsedMilliseconds;
        Console.WriteLine("Operation took: {0}", elapsedMs);

        // wait for input before exiting
        Console.WriteLine("Press enter to finish");
        Console.ReadLine();
    }
}
```

Once you have created a StopWatch object, you can start timing by calling the Start method. Timing is stopped by calling the Stop method. The number of milliseconds that has passed between the calls to Start and Stop is available through the ElapsedMilliseconds property. Listing 22-1 uses the StopWatch class to time how long it takes to add up all of the positive values that the int type can represent.

Compiling and running Listing 22-1 produces the following results, which shows that it takes 7,662 milliseconds to run on my computer:

```
Result: 23058430005992468481
Operation took: 7662
Press enter to finish
```

The members of the StopWatch class are described in Table 22-2.

Table 22-2. Members of the StopWatch Class

Member	Description
Frequency	Static field that returns the number of ticks per second recorded by the time.
Elapsed	Returns the elapsed time as a TimeSpan object (details of the TimeSpan struct appear later in this chapter).
ElapsedMilliseconds	Returns a long value representing the elapsed time in milliseconds.
ElapsedTicks	Returns a long value representing the elapsed time in timer ticks.
GetTimestamp()	Returns a long value representing the current system timer counter.
IsHighResolution	Static field that returns true if the StopWatch class is able to use a high-resolution performance counter, and false if timing will be based on the standard system timer.
IsRunning	Returns true if the StopWatch object is currently measuring time and false otherwise.
Reset()	Stops measuring time and resets the elapsed time to zero.
Restart()	Stops measuring time, resets the elapsed time to zero, and starts measuring time again.
Start()	Starts or resumes measuring elapsed time.
StartNew()	Static method that creates a new StopWatch object and calls the Start method.
Stop()	Stops measuring time.

The StopWatch class works by reading the value of a system counter. If your operating system and hardware support a high-resolution counter, the StopWatch class will use this automatically. If not, the standard system counter will be used instead. These counters don't measure absolute time; they start at zero when the system starts and are incremented several thousand times per second. To measure elapsed time, the StopWatch class records the counter value when you call the Start method and deducts the number from the counter value when you call the Stop method. Different system counters are incremented at different frequencies, so the number of elapsed ticks has to be divided by the frequency to get the time in seconds. You can use the members of the StopWatch class to work with the tick counter directly, as Listing 22-2 shows.

Listing 22-2. Using Ticks Directly to Measure Time

```
using System;
using System.Diagnostics;

class Listing_02 {

    static void Main(string[] args) {

        // print out details of the timing resolution and frequency
        Console.WriteLine("Frequency: {0}", Stopwatch.Frequency);
        Console.WriteLine("High Resolution: {0}", Stopwatch.IsHighResolution);

        // get the tick value
        long initialCounterValue = Stopwatch.GetTimestamp();

        // perform the task we want to measure
        long total = 0;
        for (int i = 0; i < int.MaxValue; i++) {
            total += i;
        }

        // get the tick value again
        long finalCounterValue = Stopwatch.GetTimestamp();

        // get the elapsed number of ticks by deducting the
        // initial value from the final value
        long elapsedCount = finalCounterValue - initialCounterValue;

        // work out how many milliseconds have elapsed by using the
        // counter frequency
        float milliSecondsElapsed = (elapsedCount / ((float)Stopwatch.Frequency)) * 1000;
        Console.WriteLine("Operation took: {0:F0}ms", milliSecondsElapsed);

        // wait for input before exiting
        Console.WriteLine("Press enter to finish");
        Console.ReadLine();
    }
}
```

The first thing that Listing 22-2 does is write the frequency and resolution information for the current system to the console. The static GetTimestamp method is used to get the counter value before and after the operation you want to time (which is adding together the positive int values again). You can then use the counter frequency information to work out how the number of counter ticks relates to seconds passed, and multiple the result by 1,000 to get the number of milliseconds (just for consistency with Listing 22-1). Compiling and running Listing 22-2 on my system produces the following results:

```
Frequency: 2613212
High Resolution: True
Operation took: 7667ms
Press enter to finish
```

Your results will differ depending on the configuration and capability of your system. There is usually no need to work directly with the tick values, but I find it helps to understand how the timing is being performed.

Working with Periods of Time

Working with milliseconds or ticks is only convenient for the smallest periods of time. A more flexible approach is to use the System.TimeSpan struct. You can create TimeSpan instances directly, get them from other classes (such as the StopWatch class), or get them as a result of operations on other date and time types (see the section on the DateTime struct for examples).

■ **Tip** One confusing aspect of the TimeSpan struct is that it has a different concept of ticks than the StopWatch class. When using StopWatch, the duration of a tick is defined by the highest resolution timer that the system supports. TimeSpan, however, defines a tick as 100 nanoseconds, always. (There are 10,000,000 nanoseconds in a second).

Creating and Using TimeSpan Values

You can create TimeSpan values using the different versions of the constructor shown in Table 22-3. TimeSpan values represent a period of time; see the section covering the DateTime struct if you want to represent a point in time (such as January 20, 2012).

Table 22-3. TimeSpan Constructors

Constructor	Description
TimeSpan()	Creates a TimeSpan that represents no time.
TimeSpan(long)	Creates a TimeSpan that represents the number of 100-nanosecond ticks specified by the parameter value.
TimeSpan(int, int, int)	Creates a TimeSpan that represents the number of hours, minutes, and seconds specified by the parameters (in that order).

Constructor	Description
TimeSpan(int, int, int, int)	Creates a TimeSpan that represents the number of days, hours, minutes, and seconds specified by the parameters (in that order).
TimeSpan(int, int. int. int. int)	Creates a TimeSpan that represents the number of days, hours, minutes, seconds, and milliseconds specified by the parameters (in that order).

Once you have created a TimeSpan value, you can use a set of properties that provides information about the duration that the value represents. These properties are described in Table 22-4.

Table 22-4. TimeSpan Informational Properties

Property	Description
Days	The days component of the duration that the struct represents.
Hours	The hours component of the duration that the struct represents.
Minutes	The minutes component of the duration that the struct represents.
Seconds	The seconds component of the duration that the struct represents.
Milliseconds	The milliseconds component of the duration that the struct represents.
Ticks	The ticks component of the duration that the struct represents.
TotalDays	The duration expressed in days.
TotalHours	The duration expressed in hours.
TotalMinutes	The duration expressed in minutes.
TotalSeconds	The duration expressed in seconds.
TotalMilliseconds	The duration expressed in milliseconds.

The properties whose names begin with Total (TotalDays, TotalHours, etc.) return a double value representing the entire duration expressed in the relevant units and can be used on their own. The other properties (the ones whose names don't start with Total) return only the whole number of those units and are usually used in conjunction with other properties. Listing 22-3 demonstrates creating TimeSpan values and using the properties.

Listing 22-3. Creating and Using TimeSpan Values

```
using System;

class Listing_03 {

    static void Main(string[] args) {

        // create a TimeSpan value
        TimeSpan myDuration = new TimeSpan(24, 30, 0);

        // print out the value of some of the TotalXXX properties
        Console.WriteLine("Total days: {0}", myDuration.TotalDays);
        Console.WriteLine("Total hours: {0}", myDuration.TotalHours);
        Console.WriteLine("Total minutes: {0}", myDuration.TotalMinutes);
        Console.WriteLine("Total seconds: {0}", myDuration.TotalSeconds);

        // print out the value of some of the other properties
        Console.WriteLine("Days: {0}", myDuration.Days);
        Console.WriteLine("Hours: {0}", myDuration.Hours);
        Console.WriteLine("Mins: {0}", myDuration.Minutes);
        Console.WriteLine("Seconds: {0}", myDuration.Seconds);

        // wait for input before exiting
        Console.WriteLine("Press enter to finish");
        Console.ReadLine();
    }
}
```

Compiling and running Listing 22-3 produces the following results:

```
Total days: 1.02083333333333
Total hours: 24.5
Total minutes: 1470
Total seconds: 88200
Days: 1
Hours: 0
Mins: 30
Seconds: 0
Press enter to finish
```

You can also create TimeSpan values using static methods defined by the struct. These methods take a double value representing a number of a given unit, which is translated into a TimeSpan value. Table 22-5 describes these methods.

Table 22-5. *Static TimeSpan Creation Methods*

Method	Description
FromDays(double)	Creates a TimeSpan value from the specified number of days.
FromHours(double)	Creates a TimeSpan value from the specified number of hours.
FromMinutes(double)	Creates a TimeSpan value from the specified number of minutes.
FromSeconds(double)	Creates a TimeSpan value from the specified number of seconds.
FromMilliseconds(double)	Creates a TimeSpan value from the specified number of milliseconds.
FromTicks(double)	Creates a TimeSpan value from the specified number of ticks.

Listing 22-4 provides a demonstration of using some of these methods to create TimeSpan values. Listing 22-4 uses the FromXXX methods shown in Table 22-5 to create TimeSpan values from the output of Listing 22-3.

Listing 22-4. Using the TimeSpan FromXXX Methods

```
using System;

class Listing_04 {

    static void Main(string[] args) {

        TimeSpan value1 = TimeSpan.FromDays(1.02083333333333d);
        Console.WriteLine("Timespan 1: {0}", value1);

        TimeSpan value2 = TimeSpan.FromHours(24.5);
        Console.WriteLine("Timespan 2: {0}", value2);

        TimeSpan value3 = TimeSpan.FromMinutes(1470);
        Console.WriteLine("Timespan 3: {0}", value3);

        TimeSpan value4 = TimeSpan.FromSeconds(88200);
        Console.WriteLine("Timespan 3: {0}", value4);

        // wait for input before exiting
        Console.WriteLine("Press enter to finish");
        Console.ReadLine();
    }
}
```

Compiling and running Listing 22-4 produces the following results:

```
Timespan 1: 1.00:30:00
Timespan 2: 1.00:30:00
Timespan 3: 1.00:30:00
Timespan 3: 1.00:30:00
Press enter to finish
```

Performing Operations on TimeSpan Values

The TimeSpan **struct defines a set of operators that lets you combine, subtract, and compare** TimeSpan values. The set of operators is described in Table 22-6.

Table 22-6. TimeSpan Operators

Operator	Description
+	Addition – add two TimeSpan values together.
-	Subtraction – subtract one TimeSpan from another.
==	Equality – returns true if two TimeSpan values are equal.
!=	Inequality – returns true if two TimeSpan values are different.
>	Greater Than – returns true if the TimeSpan on the left of the operator is longer than the TimeSpan on the right of the operator.
>=	Greater Than Or Equal – returns true if the TimeSpan on the left of the operator is longer or the same as the TimeSpan on the right of the operator.
<	Less Than – returns true if the TimeSpan on the left of the operator is shorter than the TimeSpan on the right of the operator.
<=	Less Than Or Equal – returns true if the TimeSpan on the left of the operator is shorter or the same as the TimeSpan on the right of the operator.

Listing 22-5 demonstrates using some of the TimeSpan operators.

Listing 22-5. Using TimeSpan Operators

```
using System;

class Listing_05 {

    static void Main(string[] args) {
```

```
            // create two TimeSpan values
            TimeSpan ts1 = new TimeSpan(4, 0, 0);
            TimeSpan ts2 = new TimeSpan(2, 30, 0);

            // test for equality
            Console.WriteLine("TimeSpan values are equal: {0}", ts1 == ts2);
            Console.WriteLine("TimeSpan values are unequal: {0}", ts1 != ts2);

            // use the addition and subtraction operators
            TimeSpan addResult = ts1 + ts2;
            Console.WriteLine("TimeSpan addition result: {0}", addResult);
            TimeSpan subtractionResult = ts1 - ts2;
            Console.WriteLine("TimeSpan subtraction result: {0}", subtractionResult);

            // compare the values
            Console.WriteLine("TS1 > TS2? {0}", ts1 > ts2);
            Console.WriteLine("TS1 < TS2? {0}", ts1 < ts2);

            // wait for input before exiting
            Console.WriteLine("Press enter to finish");
            Console.ReadLine();
    }
}
```

Compiling and running Listing 22-5 produces the following results:

```
TimeSpan values are equal: False
TimeSpan values are unequal: True
TimeSpan addition result: 06:30:00
TimeSpan subtraction result: 01:30:00
TS1 > TS2? True
TS1 < TS2? False
Press enter to finish
```

Formatting TimeSpan Strings

The TimeSpan struct supports composite formatting, allowing format strings to be used to control the way a string representation of a TimeSpan value is created. There are three built-in formats available, accessible through the c, g, and G format components. Listing 22-6 shows the use of these components. See Chapter 16 for more information about composite formatting and formatting components.

Listing 22-6. Using the Standard TimeSpan Format Components

```
using System;

class Listing_06 {

    static void Main(string[] args) {
```

```
        // create a TimeSpan value
        TimeSpan myDuration = new TimeSpan(14, 23, 12, 20);

        // write the value to the console using the standard formatting elements
        Console.WriteLine("Constant format: {0:c}", myDuration);
        Console.WriteLine("General short format: {0:g}", myDuration);
        Console.WriteLine("General long format: {0:G}", myDuration);

        // wait for input before exiting
        Console.WriteLine("Press enter to finish");
        Console.ReadLine();
    }
}
```

Compiling and running Listing 22-6 produces the following results:

```
Constant format: 14.23:12:20
General short format: 14:23:12:20
General long format: 14:23:12:20.0000000
Press enter to finish
```

The long and short general formats are culture-sensitive, meaning that the result of the formatting operation will change based on the regional settings of the machine on which the program is running. If you were to compile and run Listing 22-6 on a machine set to the French/France locale, you would see the following results:

```
Constant format: 14.23:12:20
General short format: 14:23:12:20
General long format: 14:23:12:20,0000000
Press enter to finish
```

If you look closely, you will see that a comma (,) is used instead of a period (.) in the general long format. This is because different grouping characters are used in different locales. The constant format doesn't change; it will produce a consistent result irrespective of culture settings.

Creating Custom TimeSpan Format Strings

You can create your own formats for string representations of TimeSpan values by passing a format string to the TimeSpan.ToString method. Listing 22-7 provides a simple demonstration.

Listing 22-7. Creating a Custom TimeSpan String Representation

```
using System;

class Listing_07 {
```

```
static void Main(string[] args) {

    // create a TimeSpan value
    TimeSpan myDuration = new TimeSpan(14, 23, 12, 20);

    string customRep = myDuration.ToString("d' days, 'h' hours and 'm' minutes'");

    // write the custom representaion to the console
    Console.WriteLine("Custom format: {0}", customRep);

    // wait for input before exiting
    Console.WriteLine("Press enter to finish");
    Console.ReadLine();
  }
}
```

Listing 22-7 uses a custom format string as a parameter to the TimeSpan.ToString method; the letters d, h and m are detected by the composite formatting system and converted into the number of days, hours, and minutes that the TimeSpan represents. Compiling and running Listing 22-7 produces the following results:

```
Custom format: 14 days, 23 hours and 12 minutes
Press enter to finish
```

Table 22-7 describes the most commonly used components for a custom TimeSpan formatting string.

Table 22-7. TimeSpan Custom Format Components

Format Component	Description
D	The number of whole days in the interval.
H	The number of whole hours in the interval.
M	The number of whole minutes in the interval.
s	The number of whole seconds in the interval.
'string'	A literal string (see Listing 22-7 for an example).
\	The escape character.

The components can be repeated to introduce leading zeros as padding. Listing 22-8 contains a demonstration.

Listing 22-8. Repeating Format Components

```
using System;
```

```
class Listing_08 {

    static void Main(string[] args) {

        // create a TimeSpan value
        TimeSpan myDuration = new TimeSpan(14, 3, 2, 0);

        string customRep = myDuration.ToString("ddd' days, 'hh' hours and 'mm' minutes'");

        // write the custom representaion to the console
        Console.WriteLine("Custom format: {0}", customRep);

        // wait for input before exiting
        Console.WriteLine("Press enter to finish");
        Console.ReadLine();
    }
}
```

The format string contains a sequence of three d characters, two h characters, and two m characters. This will ensure that the numbers of days will be represented using at least three digits and the hours and minutes will be represented using two digits. Leading zeros will be added to ensure that these minimums are met, as demonstrated by the results produced by compiling and running Listing 22-8:

```
Custom format: 014 days, 03 hours and 02 minutes
Press enter to finish
```

Working with Particular Dates and Times

The System.DateTime struct is used to represent a specific moment in time, as opposed to a period of time—for example, 9AM on the 20th of January 2010. Listing 22-9 demonstrates how to create a DateTime value that represents that time.

Listing 22-9. Creating a DateTime Value

```
using System;

class Listing_09 {

    static void Main(string[] args) {

        // create a DateTime value
        DateTime myTime = new DateTime(2010, 1, 20, 9, 0, 0, 0);

        // print out the value
        Console.WriteLine("DateTime: {0}", myTime);

        // wait for input before exiting
```

```
            Console.WriteLine("Press enter to finish");
            Console.ReadLine();
        }
}
```

Listing 22-9 creates a DateTime and then uses the Console.WriteLine method to print out a string representation of the value. Compiling and running Listing 22-9 produces the following result:

```
DateTime: 01/20/2010 09:00:00
Press enter to finish
```

Creating and Using DateTime Values

You can obtain DateTime values from a range of other .NET classes; for example, the File and FileInfo classes that are described in Chapter 20. Alternatively, you can create your own DateTime values to represent particular times using one of the struct constructors, as I did in Listing 22-9. The most commonly used DateTime constructors are described in Table 22-8.

Table 22-8. DateTime Constructors

Constructor	Description
DateTime()	Creates a DateTime value representing midnight on January 1st of the year 1.
DateTime(int, int, int)	Creates a DateTime value representing the year, month, and day specified (in that order) by the parameters.
DateTime(int, int, int, int, int, int)	Creates a DateTime value representing the year, month, day, hour, minute, and second specified (in that order) by the parameters.
DateTime(int, int, int, int, int, int, int)	Creates a DateTime value representing the year, month, day, hour, minute, second, and millisecond specified (in that order) by the parameters.

The constructors create DateTime values with differing levels of detail, ranging from a day to a moment in time measured by a millisecond. You can create a DateTime value representing the current moment by using the static Now property and representing today's date (with the time component set to midnight) by using the static Today property. Both of these properties are demonstrated in Listing 22-10.

Listing 22-10. Using the DateTime.Now Property

```
using System;

class Listing_10 {
```

```
static void Main(string[] args) {

    // use the Now property
    DateTime nowValue = DateTime.Now;
    // print out the value
    Console.WriteLine("Now: {0}", nowValue);

    // use the Today property
    DateTime todayValue = DateTime.Today;
    // print out the value
    Console.WriteLine("Today: {0}", todayValue);

    // wait for input before exiting
    Console.WriteLine("Press enter to finish");
    Console.ReadLine();
  }
}
```

Compiling and running Listing 22-10 produces the following result:

```
Now: 7/23/2010 9:48:25 AM
Today: 7/23/2010 12:00:00 AM
Press enter to finish
```

Once you have created a DateTime value, you can use a set of properties that provides information about the duration that the value represents. These properties are described in Table 22-9.

Table 22-9. DateTime Informational Properties

Property	Description
Date	Returns a DateTime value that contains only the date component of the current value; the time component is set to midnight.
DayOfWeek	Returns a value from the System.DayOfWeek enum representing the day component of the DateTime value; the values in the enum range from DayOfWeek.Sunday to DayOfWeek.Saturday.
DayOfYear	Returns the day of the year as an int between 1 and 366.
TimeOfDay	Returns a TimeSpan representing the time passed since midnight.
Millisecond	Returns the millisecond component as an int between 0 and 000.
Second	Returns the seconds component as an int between 0 and 59.
Minute	Returns the minute component as an int between 0 and 59.

Property	Description
Hour	Returns the hour component as an int between 0 and 23.
Day	Returns the day component of the value as an int between 1 and 31.
Month	Returns the month component as an int between 1 and 12.
Year	Returns the year component as an int between 0 and 9999.

Listing 22-11 demonstrates the use of some of these properties.

Listing 22-11. Using the DateTime Informational Properties

```
using System;

class Listing_11 {

    static void Main(string[] args) {

        // use the Now property
        DateTime nowValue = DateTime.Now;

        // use the informational properties to print out details
        Console.WriteLine("Day of week: {0}", nowValue.DayOfWeek);
        Console.WriteLine("Day of year: {0}", nowValue.DayOfYear);
        Console.WriteLine("Time of day: {0}", nowValue.TimeOfDay);
        Console.WriteLine("Year: {0}", nowValue.Year);
        Console.WriteLine("Month: {0}", nowValue.Month);
        Console.WriteLine("Day: {0}", nowValue.Day);
        Console.WriteLine("Hour: {0}", nowValue.Hour);
        Console.WriteLine("Minutes: {0}", nowValue.Minute);

        // wait for input before exiting
        Console.WriteLine("Press enter to finish");
        Console.ReadLine();
    }
}
```

Compiling and running Listing 22-11 produces the following results:

```
Day of week: Friday
Day of year: 204
Time of day: 09:53:22.3595401
Year: 2010
Month: 7
Day: 23
Hour: 9
```

```
Minutes: 53
Press enter to finish
```

Performing Operations on DateTime Values

The DateTime struct defines a set of operators that lets you combine, subtract, and compare DateTime and TimeSpan values. The set of operators is described in Table 22-10.

Table 22-10. DateTime Operators

Operator	Description
+	Addition – add a DateTime and a TimeSpan together to create a new DateTime value.
-	Subtraction — there are two versions of this operator. The first creates a new TimeSpan by subtracting one DateTime value from another. The second version creates a new DateTime by subtracting a TimeSpan from a DateTime value.
==	Equality – returns true if two DateTime values are equal.
!=	Inequality – returns true if two DateTime values are different.
>	Greater Than – returns true if the DateTime on the left of the operator is after the DateTime on the right of the operator.
>=	Greater Than Or Equal – returns true if the DateTime on the left of the operator is after or the same as the DateTime on the right of the operator.
<	Less Than – returns true if the DateTime on the left of the operator is before the DateTime on the right of the operator.
<=	Less Than Or Equal – returns true if the DateTime on the left of the operator is before or the same as the DateTime on the right of the operator.

Listing 22-12 demonstrates the use of some of these operators.

Listing 22-12. Using DateTime Operators

```
using System;

class Listing_12 {
```

```
static void Main(string[] args) {

    // create future and past DateTime values
    DateTime futureValue = new DateTime(2012, 1, 20);
    DateTime pastValue = new DateTime(2008, 1, 20);

    // use the addition operator
    TimeSpan ts = new TimeSpan(5, 0, 0, 0);
    DateTime additionResult = futureValue + ts;
    Console.WriteLine("Addition: {0}", additionResult);

    // use both subtraction operators
    TimeSpan difference = futureValue - pastValue;
    Console.WriteLine("Subtraction 1: {0}", difference);
    DateTime subDate = futureValue - ts;
    Console.WriteLine("Subtraction 2: {0}", subDate);

    // use the quality and inequality operators
    Console.WriteLine("Values are equal: {0}", futureValue == pastValue);
    Console.WriteLine("Values are unequal: {0}", futureValue != pastValue);

    // use the comparison operators
    Console.WriteLine("Future > Past: {0}", futureValue > pastValue);
    Console.WriteLine("Future < Past: {0}", futureValue < pastValue);

    // wait for input before exiting
    Console.WriteLine("Press enter to finish");
    Console.ReadLine();
  }
}
```

Compiling and running Listing 22-12 produces the following results:

```
Addition: 1/25/2012 12:00:00 AM
Subtraction 1: 1461.00:00:00
Subtraction 2: 1/15/2012 12:00:00 AM
Values are equal: False
Values are unequal: True
Future > Past: True
Future < Past: False
Press enter to finish
```

The DateTime structure also defines a set of methods that allow you add to the individual components of a DateTime value. These methods are described in Table 22-11.

Table 22-11. DateTime Addition Methods

Method	Description
Add(TimeSpan)	Add a TimeSpan to the current DateTime value.
AddYears(int)	Add the specified number of years to the current DateTime value.
AddMonths(int)	Add the specified number of months to the current DateTime value.
AddDays(double)	Add the specified number of days to the current DateTime value.
AddHours(double)	Add the specified number of hours to the current DateTime value.
AddMinutes(double)	Add the specified number of minutes to the current DateTime value.
AddSeconds(double)	Add the specified number of seconds to the current DateTime value.
AddMilliseconds(double)	Add the specified number of milliseconds to the current DateTime value.
AddTicks(long)	Add the specified number of ticks to the current DateTime value.

These methods return new DateTime values which include the addition; the original value is not modified. Listing 22-13 demonstrates the use of this kind of method.

Listing 22-13. Using the DateTime.AddXXX methods

```
using System;

class Listing_13 {

    static void Main(string[] args) {

        // create a DateTime value
        DateTime dateTime = new DateTime(2000, 1, 1);
        Console.WriteLine("Initial value: {0}", dateTime);

        // perform some additions
        Console.WriteLine("Add 5 years: {0}", dateTime.AddYears(5));
        Console.WriteLine("Add 5 months: {0}", dateTime.AddMonths(5));
        Console.WriteLine("Add 5 days: {0}", dateTime.AddDays(5));

        // use a double value to change two components
        Console.WriteLine("Add 1.5 hours: {0}", dateTime.AddHours(1.5d));

        // wait for input before exiting
        Console.WriteLine("Press enter to finish");
        Console.ReadLine();
```

```
    }
}
```

Compiling and running Listing 22-13 produces the following result:

```
Initial value: 1/1/2000 12:00:00 AM
Add 5 years: 1/1/2005 12:00:00 AM
Add 5 months: 6/1/2000 12:00:00 AM
Add 5 days: 1/6/2000 12:00:00 AM
Add 1.5 hours: 1/1/2000 1:30:00 AM
Press enter to finish
```

Formatting DateTime Strings

The DateTime struct supports a range of composite format specifiers that you can use to create string representations of DateTime values. Table 22-12 describes the most commonly used specifiers.

Table 22-12. DateTime Format Specifiers

Specifier	Description	Example
D	Short date format	1/20/2012
D	Long date format	Friday, January 20, 2012
F	Full date/time format with short time	Friday, January 20, 2012 9:50 AM
F	Full date/time format with long time	Friday, January 20, 2012 9:50:32 AM
G	General format with short time	1/20/2012 9:50 AM
G	General format with long time	1/20/2012 9:50:32 AM
M	Month/day format	January 20
T	Short time pattern	9:50 AM
T	Long time pattern	9:50:32 AM
Y	Year/month pattern	January, 2012

Listing 22-14 demonstrates using some of these format specifiers.

Listing 22-14. Using the DateTime Format Specifiers

```
using System;

class Listing_14 {

    static void Main(string[] args) {

        // create a DateTime value
        DateTime myDateTime = new DateTime(2012, 1, 20, 9, 50, 32);

        // print out the short date format
        Console.WriteLine("Short date format: {0:d}", myDateTime);
        // print out the full format with the long time option
        Console.WriteLine("Full format (long time): {0:F}", myDateTime);

        // wait for input before exiting
        Console.WriteLine("Press enter to finish");
        Console.ReadLine();
    }
}
```

Compiling and running Listing 22-14 produces the following output:

```
Short date format: 1/20/2012
Full format (long time): Friday, January 20, 2012 9:50:32 AM
Press enter to finish
```

The format specifiers are culturally sensitive. The results from Listing 22-14 above and the examples in Table 22-12 are what you would expect to see in the US. If you ran Listing 22-14 in the UK, where the day precedes the month in dates, you would see the following:

```
Short date format: 20/01/2012
Full format (long time): 20 January 2012 09:50:32
Press enter to finish
```

Creating Custom DateTime Format Strings

You can create your own formats for string representations of DateTime values by passing a format string to the DateTime.ToString method. Listing 22-15 provides a simple demonstration.

Listing 22-15. Creating a Custom DateTime String Representation

```
using System;

class Listing_15 {
```

```
static void Main(string[] args) {

    // create a DateTime value
    DateTime myDateTime = new DateTime(2012, 1, 20, 9, 50, 32);

    string customRep = "'Month: 'MMM', Year: 'yyyy";

    // write the custom representation to the console
    Console.WriteLine("Custom format: {0}", myDateTime.ToString(customRep));

    // wait for input before exiting
    Console.WriteLine("Press enter to finish");
    Console.ReadLine();
  }
}
```

In the custom format string, the sequences MMM and yyyy are interpreted and replaced with the abbreviated month name and the year in four digits. Compiling and running Listing 22-15 produces the following results:

```
Custom format: Month: Jan, Year: 2012
Press enter to finish
```

Table 22-13 describes the most commonly-used components for custom DateTime formatting strings.

Table 22-13. DateTime Custom Format Components

Format Component	Description
d dd	The day of the month, 1 through 31 or 01 through 31.
ddd dddd	The abbreviated or full name of the day of the week.
h hh	The hour using a 12-hour clock, 1 through 12 or 01 through 12.
H HH	The hour using a 24-hour clock, 1 through 23 or 01 through 23.
m mm	The minute, 1 through 59 or 01 through 59.
M MM	The month, 1 through 12, or 01 through 12.

Format Component	Description
MMM MMMM	The abbreviated or full name of the month.
tt	The AM/PM designator.
yy yyyy	The year in two- or four-digit format.

Summary

In this chapter you have seen how to use the .NET Framework class library to measure small amounts of time, represent periods of time, and represent moments in time. These are features that most programmers use frequently. One of the features I like most in the way that .NET and C# represent times and dates is the custom operators, which make comparing and combining dates and periods simple and elegant.

CHAPTER 23

■ ■ ■

Serialization

Serialization is the process of taking a C# object or value and creating a stream of bytes or an XML document. *Deserialization* is the opposite process: taking the previously generate bytes or XML and using them to recreate the serialized object or value.

Serialization can create long-lived objects, which are serialized and stored, typically to disk, when a program exits and are then retrieved from storage and deserialized the next time they are required. The other main use for serialization is to transmit copies of objects across a network to a remote application. You unknowingly took advantage of this feature when you looked at the Windows Communication Foundation in Chapter 21.

The .NET Framework contains four separate serialization systems. Each serialization system has its own benefits and drawbacks. In this chapter, I'll show you how to use each of them to serialize and deserialized C# objects and values.

As a general rule, binary serialization offers the best performance when you intend to serialize objects for use only within .NET programs, but that performance comes with a lack of compatibility with other languages and systems. If you need to create serialized data that you can share with non-.NET systems, the I recommend using the Data Contract Serializer, particularly because you can choose to emit JSON data, which is simple and very widely supported. Table 23-1 provides the summary for this chapter.

Table 23-1. Quick Problem/Solution Reference for Chapter 23

Problem	Solution	Listings
Prepare an object for serialization for binary or SOAP serialization.	Use the Serializable attribute.	23-1
Prepare an object for serialization with the Data Contract Serializer.	Use the DataContract and DataMember attributes or use the Serializable attribute.	23-17
Serialize or deserialize objects to a binary stream or a SOAP message.	Use the BinaryFormatter or SoapFormatter classes.	23-2 through 23-6, 23-12
Selectively omit fields from binary or SOAP serialization.	Use the NonSerialized attribute.	23-7
Participate in the serialization process.	Use the serialization callback attributes.	23-8

Problem	Solution	Listings
Use strict version checking and version tolerance.	Enable the full assembly format option and apply the OptionalField attribute when making changes.	23-9 through 23-11
Serialize or deserialize objects to XML.	Use the XmlSerializer or the Data Contract Serializer.	23-13
Selectively omit fields when using the XmlSerializer class.	Use the XmlIgnore attribute.	23-14
Write a field as an attribute of change the name that a field is mapped to in the XML when using the XmlSerializer class.	Use the XmlAttribute and XmlElement attributes.	23-15, 23-16
Create portable XML serialization data.	Use the DataContractSerializer class.	23-18
Create .NET specific XML serialization data.	Use the NetDataContractSerializer class.	23-19
Create JSON serialization data.	Use the DataContractJsonSerializer class.	23-20

Using Binary Serialization

Binary serialization generates a stream of bytes to represent your serialized objects. This technique is fast and creates the most compact output, but it specific to the .NET Framework. In other words, you can't share the serialization data with system created with other programming languages and platforms. Serialization is a two-step process. The first step is to prepare your class with the Serializable attribute, as demonstrated in Listing 23-1.

Listing 23-1. Using the Serializable Attribute

```
using System;

[Serializable]
class Person {
    private string name;
    private string city;

    public Person(string nameParam, string cityParam) {
        name = nameParam;
        city = cityParam;
    }
```

```
    public string Name {
        get { return name; }
        set { name = value; }
    }

    public string City {
        get { return city;}
        set { city = value; }
    }
}
```

Listing 23-1 contains a simple class called Person that has two string fields. The class has been annotated with the Serializable attribute, which can be found in the System namespace. Applying this attribute enables serialization for your class. The second step in serialization is to create an object from the class and serialize it. Listing 23-2 provides a demonstration using the Person class defined in Listing 23-1.

Listing 23-2. Serializing an Object

```
using System;
using System.IO;
using System.Runtime.Serialization;
using System.Runtime.Serialization.Formatters.Binary;

class SerializeTest {

    static void Main(string[] args) {

        // create a new Person object
        Person myPerson = new Person("Adam Freeman", "London");

        // create an output stream to the file
        Stream outputStream = File.OpenWrite("person.bin");

        // create a new binary formatter
        IFormatter serializer = new BinaryFormatter();

        // serialize the object
        serializer.Serialize(outputStream, myPerson);

        // close the stream
        outputStream.Close();

        // wait for input before exiting
        Console.WriteLine("Press enter to finish");
        Console.ReadLine();
    }
}
```

In Listing 23-2, you create a new Person object. This is the object that you are going to serialize. You're going to store the serialized object in a file, so you create a new Stream object that allows you to write to a file called person.bin. (Streams and files are explained in Chapter 20.)

Once you have the object to serialize and the Stream ready to write to the file, you can create a BinaryFormatter object. This is the class that will perform the serialization process. The convention in C# is to refer to a BinaryFormatter object using the IFormatter interface; this allows you to switch between serialization engines more easily, as you will see when you come to XML serialization later in the chapter. The IFormatter interface can be found in the System.Runtime.Serialization namespace, and the BinaryFormatter class can be found in the System.Runtime.Serialization.Binary namespace.

To serialize your object, you call the Serialize method of the IFormatter interface and pass the object to serialize and the Stream to write the serialized data to as parameters:

```
serializer.Serialize(outputStream, myPerson);
```

This method creates a sequence of bytes that contain the Person object and write it to the Stream. All that remains to do is Close the stream to make sure that the data is properly written to the disk. Listing 21-2 creates a machine-readable file, which is efficient and compact, but not readable by programmers.

Deserializing an object is a very similar process, as demonstrated by Listing 21-3.

Listing 21-3. Deserializing the Object

```csharp
using System;
using System.IO;
using System.Runtime.Serialization;
using System.Runtime.Serialization.Formatters.Binary;

class DeSerializeTest {

    static void Main(string[] args) {

        // create a formatter
        IFormatter deserializer = new BinaryFormatter();

        // open the stream to the file
        Stream inputStream = File.OpenRead("person.bin");

        // deserialize the object
        Person deserializedPerson = (Person)deserializer.Deserialize(inputStream);

        // print out the value of the fields of the deserialized object
        Console.WriteLine("Deserialized name: {0}", deserializedPerson.Name);
        Console.WriteLine("Deserialized city: {0}", deserializedPerson.City);

        // wait for input before exiting
        Console.WriteLine("Press enter to finish");
        Console.ReadLine();
    }
}
```

To deserialize the object, you open a Stream from the file that contains the binary serialization data and pass it as a parameter to the Deserialize method of the BinaryFormatter object through the

IFormatter interface. Notice that this method returns an object, which has been cast to Person. It is the responsibility of the programmer to ensure that the object that is returned by the Deserialize method is of a specific type.

Compiling and running Listing 23-3 produces the following output (you will need to have compiled and run Listing 23-2 to create the serialized object that Listing 23-3 deserializes):

```
Deserialized name: Adam Freeman
Deserialized city: London
Press enter to finish
```

Serializing an object makes a copy of its state at the moment it is serialized. This means that you can make changes to the original object after the serialized copy has been made, but those changes will not be reflected in the serialized data and will not be available when you later deserialize the copy of the object.

Serializing Graphs of Objects

If a class that has been annotated with the Serializable attribute has fields that are custom classes, then these must also be marked with the Serializable attribute. This is because the serialization engine tries to capture the entire state of an object, including the state of other objects that are referenced. Listing 23-4 contains a version of the Person class that relies on another class for its state.

Listing 23-4. Related Serializable Objects

```
using System;
using System.IO;

[Serializable]
class Person {
    private string name;
    private string city;
    private Company employer;

    public Person(String nameParam, String cityParam, Company companyParam) {
        name = nameParam;
        city = cityParam;
        employer = companyParam;
    }

    public String Name {
        get { return name; }
        set { name = value; }
    }

    public String City {
        get { return city; }
        set { city = value; }
    }
```

```
        public Company Employer {
            get { return employer; }
            set { employer = value; }
        }
    }

    [Serializable]
    class Company {
        private string name;
        private string city;

        public Company(string nameParam, string cityParam) {
            name = nameParam;
            city = cityParam;
        }

        public string Name {
            get { return name; }
        }

        public string City {
            get { return city; }
        }
    }
```

In Listing 23-4, the Person class relies on the Company class, so both have been annotated with the Serializable attribute. There are no special steps required when serializing objects that have this kind of relationship. In this example, you would serialize a Person object and the associated Company object would be serialized (and deserialized) automatically. Here is an example of doing this:

```
using System;
using System.IO;
using System.Runtime.Serialization;
using System.Runtime.Serialization.Formatters.Binary;

class SerializeTest {

    static void Main(string[] args) {

        // create a new company
        Company myCompany = new Company("BigCorp", "Paris");

        // create a new Person object
        Person myPerson = new Person("Adam Freeman", "London", myCompany);

        // create an output stream to the file
        Stream outputStream = File.OpenWrite("person.bin");

        // create a new binary formatter
        IFormatter serializer = new BinaryFormatter();

        // serialize the object
        serializer.Serialize(outputStream, myPerson);
```

```
        // close the stream
        outputStream.Close();

        // create a formatter
        IFormatter deserializer = new BinaryFormatter();
        // open the stream to the file
        Stream inputStream = File.OpenRead("person.bin");
        // deserialize the object
        Person deserializedPerson = (Person)deserializer.Deserialize(inputStream);

        // print out the value of the fields of the deserialized object
        Console.WriteLine("Deserialized name: {0}", deserializedPerson.Name);
        Console.WriteLine("Deserialized city: {0}", deserializedPerson.City);
        Console.WriteLine("Deserialized company name: {0}",
            deserializedPerson.Employer.Name);
        Console.WriteLine("Deserialized company city: {0}",
            deserializedPerson.Employer.City);

        // wait for input before exiting
        Console.WriteLine("Press enter to finish");
        Console.ReadLine();
    }
}
```

Compiling and running this code produces the following results:

```
Deserialized name: Adam Freeman
Deserialized city: London
Deserialized company name: BigCorp
Deserialized company city: Paris
Press enter to finish
```

You will get an exception if you try to serialize an object that isn't marked as serializable (either directly or as part of an object graph). It is therefore important to ensure that the Serializable attribute is applied to all of your classes that are likely to be serialized. Alternatively, you can exclude individual fields from serialization (see the "Selectively Serializing Fields" section later in this chapter).

Serializing Multiple Objects to a Single Stream

The previous examples have all serialized a single object or object graph to a file, but the serialization system supports reading and writing multiple objects, as demonstrated by Listing 23-5.

Listing 23-5. Using the Same Stream for Multiple Objects

```
using System;
using System.IO;
using System.Runtime.Serialization;
using System.Runtime.Serialization.Formatters.Binary;
```

```
[Serializable]
class Person {
    private string name;
    private string city;

    public Person(String nameParam, String cityParam) {
        name = nameParam;
        city = cityParam;
    }

    public String Name {
        get { return name; }
        set { name = value; }
    }

    public String City {
        get { return city; }
        set { city = value; }
    }
}

class Listing_05 {

    static void Main(string[] args) {

        // create a number of Person objects
        Person person1 = new Person("Adam Freeman", "London");
        Person person2 = new Person("Joe Smith", "New York");
        Person person3 = new Person("Angela Peters", "Hong Kong");

        // create the binary formatter
        IFormatter formatter = new BinaryFormatter();

        // create a stream to hold the serialized data
        Stream fileStream = File.Open("people.bin", FileMode.Create);

        // serialize the Person objects
        foreach (Person p in new Person[] {person1, person2, person3}) {
            formatter.Serialize(fileStream, p);
        }

        // reposition the stream cursor so we can read the data back
        fileStream.Seek(0, SeekOrigin.Begin);

        // deserialize the Person objects from the Stream
        for (int i = 0; i < 3; i++) {
            Person p = (Person)formatter.Deserialize(fileStream);
            Console.WriteLine("--- Deserialized Person ---");
            Console.WriteLine("Name: {0}", p.Name);
            Console.WriteLine("City: {0}", p.City);
        }
```

```
        // wait for input before exiting
        Console.WriteLine("Press enter to finish");
        Console.ReadLine();
    }
}
```

In Listing 23-5, you use the same Stream to write the serialized data and then read it back. Compiling and running Listing 23-5 produces the following results:

```
--- Deserialized Person ---
Name: Adam Freeman
City: London
--- Deserialized Person ---
Name: Joe Smith
City: New York
--- Deserialized Person ---
Name: Angela Peters
City: Hong Kong
Press enter to finish
```

Almost all of the commonly-used .NET types can be serialized, which means that an alternative approach to serializing multiple objects is to place them in a collection and serialize that. Listing 23-6 contains a demonstration of serializing a List<T> containing multiple Person objects.

Listing 23-6. Serializing a Collection of Objects

```
using System;
using System.Collections.Generic;
using System.IO;
using System.Runtime.Serialization;
using System.Runtime.Serialization.Formatters.Binary;

class Listing_06 {

    static void Main(string[] args) {

        // create the collection
        List<Person> listCollection = new List<Person>();

        // create a number of Person objects
        listCollection.Add(new Person("Adam Freeman", "London"));
        listCollection.Add(new Person("Joe Smith", "New York"));
        listCollection.Add(new Person("Angela Peters", "Hong Kong"));

        // create the binary formatter
        IFormatter formatter = new BinaryFormatter();

        // create a stream to hold the serialized data
        Stream fileStream = File.Open("peopleCollection.bin", FileMode.Create);
```

```
        // serialize the collection
        formatter.Serialize(fileStream, listCollection);

        // reposition the stream cursor so we can read the data back
        fileStream.Seek(0, SeekOrigin.Begin);

        // deserialize the collection from the stream
        List<Person> deserializedCollection =
            (List<Person>)formatter.Deserialize(fileStream);

        foreach (Person p in deserializedCollection) {
            Console.WriteLine("--- Deserialized List Person ---");
            Console.WriteLine("Name: {0}", p.Name);
            Console.WriteLine("City: {0}", p.City);
        }

        // wait for input before exiting
        Console.WriteLine("Press enter to finish");
        Console.ReadLine();
    }
}
```

Compiling and running Listing 23-6 produces the following results:

```
--- Deserialized List Person ---
Name: Adam Freeman
City: London
--- Deserialized List Person ---
Name: Joe Smith
City: New York
--- Deserialized List Person ---
Name: Angela Peters
City: Hong Kong
Press enter to finish
```

Selectively Serializing Fields

Not all fields of an object are suitable to be serialized. This can be because they are of a type that is not serializable or because the data the field contains is ephemeral and would have no sensible meaning when the object was deserialized. You can specify that a field not be serialized with its containing object by using the NonSerialized attribute. Listing 23-7 provides an example.

Listing 23-7. Selectively Omitting Fields from Serialization

```
using System;

[Serializable]
class Person {
```

```
    private string name;
    [NonSerialized]
    private string city;

    public Person(String nameParam, String cityParam) {
        name = nameParam;
        city = cityParam;
    }

    public String Name {
        get { return name; }
        set { name = value; }
    }

    public String City {
        get { return city; }
        set { city = value; }
    }
}
```

The Person class in Listing 23-7 is annotated with the Serializable attribute, but its city field is annotated with the NonSerialized attribute. This means that Person objects can be serialized, but that the serialized data will omit the value assigned to the city field.

You don't have to take any special steps when serializing a class that has NonSerialized fields, but you must be careful when deserializing the object because the NonSerialized fields will not be assigned values; they will default to null for reference types and the default for value types.

Using Serialization Callbacks

You can tailor the way that your objects are serialized and deserialized by applying one of four attributes to methods in your class. Listing 23-8 contains an example of using one of these attributes.

Listing 23-8. Using a Serialization Callback Attribute

```
using System;

[Serializable]
class Person {
    private string name;
    [NonSerialized]
    private string city;

    public Person(String nameParam, String cityParam) {
        name = nameParam;
        city = cityParam;
    }

    public String Name {
        get { return name; }
        set { name = value; }
```

```
        }

        public String City {
            get { return city; }
            set { city = value; }
        }

        [OnDeserializing]
        public void OnDeserializing(StreamingContext context) {
            Console.WriteLine("OnDeserializing method called");
            city = "London";
        }
    }
}
```

The city field in the Person class in Listing 23-8 has been annotated with the NonSerialized attribute, meaning that no value for this field will be included in the serialized data. Note the method called OnDeserializing that is annotated with the OnDeserializing attribute; this method is called when the object is being deserialized. You can use this opportunity to set a value for the city field so that all deserialized Person objects will have a value of London for this field (even if this was not the value of the field in the original object prior to it being serialized). The following code provides a demonstration of serializing and deserializing the Person class in Listing 23-8:

```
using System;
using System.IO;
using System.Runtime.Serialization;
using System.Runtime.Serialization.Formatters.Binary;

class Listing_08_Test {

    static void Main(string[] args) {

        // create a new Person object
        Person myPerson = new Person("Adam Freeman", "Paris");

        // create an output stream to the file
        Stream outputStream = File.OpenWrite("person.bin");

        // create a new binary formatter
        IFormatter serializer = new BinaryFormatter();

        // serialize the object
        serializer.Serialize(outputStream, myPerson);

        // close the stream
        outputStream.Close();

        // create a formatter
        IFormatter deserializer = new BinaryFormatter();
        // open the stream to the file
        Stream inputStream = File.OpenRead("person.bin");
        // deserialize the object
        Person deserializedPerson = (Person)deserializer.Deserialize(inputStream);
```

```
        // print out the value of the fields of the deserialized object
        Console.WriteLine("Deserialized name: {0}", deserializedPerson.Name);
        Console.WriteLine("Deserialized name: {0}", deserializedPerson.City);

        // wait for input before exiting
        Console.WriteLine("Press enter to finish");
        Console.ReadLine();
    }
}
```

Compiling and running this code produces the following results (note that the value of the city field in the original object was Paris, but the value in the deserialized object is London):

```
OnDeserializing method called
Deserialized name: Adam Freeman
Deserialized name: London
Press enter to finish
```

Table 23-2 describes the four attributes that you can use to have a method called in a serializable class.

Table 23-2. Serialization Callback Attributes

Attribute	Description
OnSerializing	Called before an object is serialized; it can be used to prepare field values, for example.
OnSerialized	Called after an object has been serialized; it can be used to log events relating to serialization.
OnDeserializing	Called before deserialization; it can be used to initialize field values, especially for those fields whose values are not included in the serialized data.
OnDeserialized	Called after deserialization; it can be used to set field values based on other field values.

Each of these attributes can be applied to only one method in the serializable class. Furthermore, the methods that these attributes are applied to must declare no return type (by using the void keyword) and must have a single parameter of the StreamingContext struct from the System.Runtime.Serialization namespace. (The StreamingContext struct is an advanced type outside of the scope of this book).

Version Tolerance

When you serialize an object, the serialized data can be stored indefinitely, which means that it can outlive the current version of your program or project. The BinaryFormatter class is very tolerant of changes between classes and serialized data.

If you serialize a class and then add or remove fields from the class definition, the BinaryFormatter will still deserialize the serialized object, even though the class has changed. If you have added fields to the class, they will not be initialized when the old data is deserialized. If you have removed fields, the serialized values for these fields will be quietly discarded.

This isn't always desirable behavior. You might want to reject serialized objects if they were created from a previous version of your class, for example. Fortunately, you can make the BinaryFormatter behave much more strictly when it detects changes. This section will walk you through the process of enabling strict change checking and how to manage versioning when it is in use. Listing 23-9 demonstrates serializing an object, just as you have seen in previous examples.

Listing 23-9. Serializing an Object

```
using System;
using System.IO;
using System.Runtime.Serialization;
using System.Runtime.Serialization.Formatters.Binary;

[Serializable]
class Person {
    private string name;
    private string city;

    public Person(String nameParam, String cityParam) {
        name = nameParam;
        city = cityParam;
    }

    public String Name {
        get { return name; }
        set { name = value; }
    }

    public String City {
        get { return city; }
        set { city = value; }
    }
}

class Listing_09 {

    static void Main(string[] args) {

        // create a new Person object
        Person myPerson = new Person("Adam Freeman", "London");

        // create an output stream to the file
```

```
        Stream outputStream = File.OpenWrite("person.bin");

        // create a new binary formatter
        IFormatter serializer = new BinaryFormatter();

        // serialize the object
        serializer.Serialize(outputStream, myPerson);

        // close the stream
        outputStream.Close();

        // wait for input before exiting
        Console.WriteLine("Press enter to finish");
        Console.ReadLine();
    }
}
```

If you compile and run Listing 23-9, you produce a file called person.bin that contains binary serialization data for a Person object. Imagine now that time passes and you need to add a new field to your Person class. Listing 23-10 demonstrates this change and includes code to deserialize the data you created in Listing 23-9.

Listing 23-10. Deserializing with a Version of the Person Class

```
using System;
using System.IO;
using System.Runtime.Serialization;
using System.Runtime.Serialization.Formatters;
using System.Runtime.Serialization.Formatters.Binary;

[Serializable]
class Person {
    private string name;
    private string city;
    private int age;

    public Person(String nameParam, String cityParam, int ageParam) {
        name = nameParam;
        city = cityParam;
        age = ageParam;
    }

    public String Name {
        get { return name; }
        set { name = value; }
    }

    public String City {
        get { return city; }
        set { city = value; }
    }
```

```
    public int Age {
        get { return age; }
        set { age = value; }
    }
}

class Listing_10 {

    static void Main(string[] args) {

        // create a formatter
        IFormatter deserializer
            = new BinaryFormatter() { AssemblyFormat = FormatterAssemblyStyle.Full };

        // open the stream to the file
        Stream inputStream = File.OpenRead("person.bin");
        // deserialize the object
        Person deserializedPerson = (Person)deserializer.Deserialize(inputStream);

        // print out the value of the fields of the deserialized object
        Console.WriteLine("Deserialized name: {0}", deserializedPerson.Name);
        Console.WriteLine("Deserialized city: {0}", deserializedPerson.City);
        Console.WriteLine("Deserialized age: {0}", deserializedPerson.Age);

        // wait for input before exiting
        Console.WriteLine("Press enter to finish");
        Console.ReadLine();
    }
}
```

Version 2 of your Person class introduces a field called age. When you create the BinaryFormatter object in preparation for deserialization, you enable the strict change checking by setting the value of the AssemblyFormat property to the Full value from the FormatterAssemblyStyle enumeration (this enumeration can be found in the System.Runtime.Serialization.Formatters namespace). The AssemblyFormat.Full value enables strict change checking. The other value defined in the enumeration (Simple) is the default, which is tolerant to changes. Compiling and running Listing 23-10 to deserialize the data created in Listing 23-9 produces the following exception, which has been edited for brevity:

```
Unhandled Exception: System.Runtime.Serialization.SerializationException: Member
 'age' in class 'Person' is not present in the serialized stream and is not ma
rked with System.Runtime.Serialization.OptionalFieldAttribute.
    at System.Runtime.Serialization.Formatters.Binary.BinaryFormatter.Deserialize
(Stream serializationStream)
    at Listing_09.Main(String[] args) in C:\Listing_09\Listing_09.cs:line 64
```

As you can see from the exception message, the deserialization process has discovered that the serialized data doesn't contain any reference to the age field introduced in Version 2 of the Person class.

Adding Tolerance for Specific Changes

You can use strict change checking and introduce version tolerance by using the OptionalField attribute, which tells the BinaryFormatter class that objects that were serialized before the annotated field was added can still be safely deserialized. Listing 23-11 demonstrates the application of the OptionalField attribute to the Person class.

Listing 23-11. Applying the OptionalField Attribute

```
using System;
using System.IO;
using System.Runtime.Serialization;
using System.Runtime.Serialization.Formatters;
using System.Runtime.Serialization.Formatters.Binary;

[Serializable]
class Person {
    private string name;
    private string city;
    [OptionalField(VersionAdded=2)]
    private int age;

    public Person(String nameParam, String cityParam, int ageParam) {
        name = nameParam;
        city = cityParam;
        age = ageParam;
    }

    public String Name {
        get { return name; }
        set { name = value; }
    }

    public String City {
        get { return city; }
        set { city = value; }
    }

    public int Age {
        get { return age; }
        set { age = value; }
    }
}

class Listing_11 {

    static void Main(string[] args) {

        // create a formatter
        IFormatter deserializer
            = new BinaryFormatter() { AssemblyFormat = FormatterAssemblyStyle.Full };
```

```
        // open the stream to the file
        Stream inputStream = File.OpenRead("person.bin");
        // deserialize the object
        Person deserializedPerson = (Person)deserializer.Deserialize(inputStream);

        // print out the value of the fields of the deserialized object
        Console.WriteLine("Deserialized name: {0}", deserializedPerson.Name);
        Console.WriteLine("Deserialized city: {0}", deserializedPerson.City);
        Console.WriteLine("Deserialized age: {0}", deserializedPerson.Age);

        // wait for input before exiting
        Console.WriteLine("Press enter to finish");
        Console.ReadLine();
    }
}
```

The `OptionalField` attribute is in bold. The `VersionAdded` property is optional, but it can help you keep track of when you made which changes to serializable classes. With this attribute applied to the new field, the `BinaryFormatter` deserializes the Version 1 `Person` class and assigns the age field its default value; since the field is an int, the default value is 0. Compiling and running Listing 23-11 produces the following output:

```
Deserialized name: Adam Freeman
Deserialized city: London
Deserialized age: 0
Press enter to finish
```

Using SOAP Serialization

SOAP, the Simple Object Access Protocol, is an XML format used for the exchange of structured information, and one of the serialization options supported by the .NET Framework is to serialize an object using this format. SOAP is a more verbose format than the binary output you produced in the previous section, but is more portable between different types of systems and somewhat more human readable. Here is an example of the output from serializing an object using SOAP:

```
<SOAP-ENV:Envelope xmlns:xsi="http://www.w3.org/2001/XMLSchema-instance"
xmlns:xsd="http://www.w3.org/2001/XMLSchema" xmlns:SOAP-
ENC="http://schemas.xmlsoap.org/soap/encoding/" xmlns:SOAP-
ENV="http://schemas.xmlsoap.org/soap/envelope/"
xmlns:clr="http://schemas.microsoft.com/soap/encoding/clr/1.0" SOAP-
ENV:encodingStyle="http://schemas.xmlsoap.org/soap/encoding/">
<SOAP-ENV:Body>
<a1:Person id="ref-1"
xmlns:a1="http://schemas.microsoft.com/clr/assem/Listing_09%2C%20Version%3D1.0.0.0%2C%20Cultur
e%3Dneutral%2C%20PublicKeyToken%3Dnull">
<name id="ref-3">Adam Freeman</name>
```

```
<city id="ref-4">London</city>
</a1:Person>
</SOAP-ENV:Body>
</SOAP-ENV:Envelope>
```

A lot of the output is information that the recipient of the serialized data can use to figure out the content of the SOAP message, but you can also see the type information for the serialized object (it was a Person object) and the field values (for the fields name and city) highlighted in bold.

■ **Note** The classes for SOAP serialization are in the System.Runtime.Serialization.Formatters.Soap assembly that must be added to your project before you can compile the examples in this section. Right-click on your project in the Solution Explorer window and select Add Reference. Click on the .NET tab of the Add Reference dialog box, scroll down until you find the System.Runtime.Serialization.Formatters.Soap assembly, and click OK.

Using SOAP serialization is very similar to using binary serialization, as demonstrated in Listing 23-12. The Serializable attribute that you used for binary serialization is used in the same way for SOAP serialization.

Listing 23-12. Using SOAP Serialization

```
using System;
using System.IO;
using System.Runtime.Serialization;
using System.Runtime.Serialization.Formatters.Soap;

[Serializable]
class Person {
    private string name;
    private string city;

    public Person(String nameParam, String cityParam) {
        name = nameParam;
        city = cityParam;
    }

    public String Name {
        get { return name; }
        set { name = value; }
    }

    public String City {
        get { return city; }
        set { city = value; }
    }
}
```

```
class Listing_12 {

    static void Main(string[] args) {

        // create a new Person object
        Person myPerson = new Person("Adam Freeman", "London");

        // create an output stream to the file
        Stream outputStream = File.OpenWrite("person.soap");

        // create a new binary formatter
        IFormatter serializer = new SoapFormatter();

        // serialize the object
        serializer.Serialize(outputStream, myPerson);

        // close the stream
        outputStream.Close();

        // create a formatter
        IFormatter deserializer = new SoapFormatter();
        // open the stream to the file
        Stream inputStream = File.OpenRead("person.soap");
        // deserialize the object
        Person deserializedPerson = (Person)deserializer.Deserialize(inputStream);

        // print out the value of the fields of the deserialized object
        Console.WriteLine("Deserialized name: {0}", deserializedPerson.Name);
        Console.WriteLine("Deserialized city: {0}", deserializedPerson.City);

        // wait for input before exiting
        Console.WriteLine("Press enter to finish");
        Console.ReadLine();
    }
}
```

The only change here is that you create a SoapFormatter object instead of a BinaryFormatter object. Both classes implement the IFormatter interface, which means that you can switch between them with very few code changes. However, as the following sections explain, there are some important differences between the capabilities of the SoapFormatter and BinaryFormatter class.

Version Tolerance

The SoapFormatter class doesn't support the default version tolerance that BinaryFormatter uses. An exception will be thrown if a new field has been added to a class since the object was serialized and the field hasn't been annotated with the OptionalField attribute.

Serializing Generic Objects

The SoapFormatter class does not support serializing generic objects. This can be a critical limitation, most frequently if you want to serialize collections as demonstrated by Listing 23-6.

Using XML Serialization

The third serialization option is known as *XML Serialization* and is performed using the System.Xml.Serialization.XmlSerializer class. The XmlSerializer produces XML, but it only includes the values of an object's public fields and properties in the serialization data. The values of private fields and properties are omitted.

You do not need to apply any attributes to make a class serializable by XmlSerializer, but the class must be public and must have a parameterless constructor. Listing 23-13 demonstrates using the XmlSerializer class.

Listing 23-13. Serializing Using the XmlSerializer Class

```
using System;
using System.Xml.Serialization;
using System.IO;

public class Person {
    private string name;
    private string city;

    public Person() {
        // do nothing
    }

    public Person(String nameParam, String cityParam) {
        name = nameParam;
        city = cityParam;
    }

    public String Name {
        get { return name; }
        set { name = value; }
    }

    public String City {
        get { return city; }
        set { city = value; }
    }
}

class Listing_13 {

    static void Main(string[] args) {

        // create a new Person object
```

```
        Person myPerson = new Person("Adam Freeman", "London");

        // open the stream to the file we want to store the data in
        Stream outputStream = File.OpenWrite("person.xml");

        // create the XMLSerializer
        XmlSerializer serializer = new XmlSerializer(typeof(Person));
        // serialize the object
        serializer.Serialize(outputStream, myPerson);
        // close the stream to the file
        outputStream.Close();

        // wait for input before exiting
        Console.WriteLine("Press enter to finish");
        Console.ReadLine();
    }
}
```

Listing 23-13 contains a Person class that has three changes from previous examples: the class is public, it contains a parameterless constructor, and the Serializable attribute has not been applied.

When creating an XmlSerializer object, you must pass the type of the object that you are going to serialize. You can get this using the typeof keyword or by calling the GetType method on the object itself, like this:

```
XmlSerializer serializer = new XmlSerializer(myPerson.GetType());
```

Once you have created an XmlSerializer object, you can call the Serialize method, passing in the Stream you want the XML written to and the object to serialize. Here is the content of the file created by compiling and running Listing 23-13:

```
<?xml version="1.0"?>
<Person xmlns:xsi="http://www.w3.org/2001/XMLSchema-instance"
xmlns:xsd="http://www.w3.org/2001/XMLSchema">
  <Name>Adam Freeman</Name>
  <City>London</City>
</Person>
```

The process for deserializing is very similar, except that you call the Deserialize method, passing the Stream from which the serialized data is to be read. Here is an example:

```
// open a stream so we can read the file
Stream inputStream = File.OpenRead("person.xml");
// create an XmlSerializer object
XmlSerializer deserializer = new XmlSerializer(typeof(Person));
// deserialize the object from the stream
Person myDeserializedPerson = (Person)deserializer.Deserialize(inputStream);

// print out details from the deserialized person object
Console.WriteLine("Name: {0}", myDeserializedPerson.Name);
Console.WriteLine("City: {0}", myDeserializedPerson.City);
```

Selectively Serializing Fields

If you want to prevent a field or property from being serialized, you can apply the XmlIgnore attribute. This attribute should only be applied to public fields or properties; other fields and properties are automatically excluded. Listing 23-14 provides a demonstration of applying this attribute.

Listing 23-14. Applying the XmlIgnore Attribute

```
using System;
using System.Xml.Serialization;

public class Person {
    private string name;
    private string city;

    public Person() {
        // do nothing
    }

    public Person(String nameParam, String cityParam) {
        name = nameParam;
        city = cityParam;
    }

    public String Name {
        get { return name; }
        set { name = value; }
    }

    [XmlIgnore]
    public String City {
        get { return city; }
        set { city = value; }
    }
}
```

The XmlIgnore attribute (which is part of the System.Xml.Serialization namespace) has been applied to the City property of the Person class. Serializing an object created from this class with an XmlSerializer produces the following XML:

```
<?xml version="1.0"?>
<Person xmlns:xsi="http://www.w3.org/2001/XMLSchema-instance" xmlns:xsd="http://
www.w3.org/2001/XMLSchema">
  <Name>Adam Freeman</Name>
</Person>
```

If you compare the output from Listing 23-14 with the output from Listing 23-13, you will see that the XmlIgnore attribute has caused the value of the City property to be omitted from the serialized XML.

Mapping Members to Elements and Attributes

The XmlSerializer class represents fields and properties as XML elements, but you can choose to have individual fields or properties expressed at XML attributes instead by applying the XmlAttribute attribute. Listing 23-15 contains an example.

Listing 23-15. Applying the XmlAttribute Attribute

```
using System;
using System.Xml.Serialization;

public class Person {
    private string name;
    private string city;

    public Person() {
        // do nothing
    }

    public Person(String nameParam, String cityParam) {
        name = nameParam;
        city = cityParam;
    }

    public String Name {
        get { return name; }
        set { name = value; }
    }

    [XmlAttribute]
    public String City {
        get { return city; }
        set { city = value; }
    }
}
```

In Listing 23-15, you have applied the XmlAttribute attribute to the City property. Serializing an object created from this class with an XmlSerializer produces the following XML:

```
<?xml version="1.0"?>
<Person xmlns:xsi="http://www.w3.org/2001/XMLSchema-instance" xmlns:xsd="http://
www.w3.org/2001/XMLSchema" City="London">
  <Name>Adam Freeman</Name>
</Person>
```

You can see that the City property and its value (London) are now attributes of the Person node, whereas the Name property and it value remain as XML elements.

Changing the Name for Attributes and Elements

The XmlSerializer will create elements and attributes in the XML output to match the name of the corresponding fields and properties. You can override the these names and provide your own by using the XmlAttribute and XmlElement attributes and specifying the name you want to appear in the serialized XML as a parameter to each attribute. Listing 23-16 contains an example of using both attributes in this way.

Listing 23-16. Using the XmlAttribute and XmlElement Attributes to Change Names

```
using System;
using System.Xml.Serialization;

public class Person {
    private string name;
    private string city;

    public Person() {
        // do nothing
    }

    public Person(String nameParam, String cityParam) {
        name = nameParam;
        city = cityParam;
    }

    [XmlElement("FullName")]
    public String Name {
        get { return name; }
        set { name = value; }
    }

    [XmlAttribute("PlaceOfResidence")]
    public String City {
        get { return city; }
        set { city = value; }
    }
}
```

In Listing 23-16, you have applied the XmlElement attribute to the Name property and the XmlAttribute attribute to the City property. Serializing an object created from this class with an XmlSerializer produces the following XML:

```
<?xml version="1.0"?>
<Person xmlns:xsi="http://www.w3.org/2001/XMLSchema-instance" xmlns:xsd="http://
www.w3.org/2001/XMLSchema" PlaceOfResidence="London">
  <FullName>Adam Freeman</FullName>
</Person>
```

You can see from the serialized output that the names of the properties have been changed to match the parameters passed to the XmlElement and XmlAttribute attributes.

Using Data Contract Serialization

The final serialization option is the Data Contract Serializer, which was introduced to support the Windows Communication Foundation (this was touched on briefly in Chapter 21). The Data Contract Serializer has a number of classes that can be used to produce serialized data with differing levels of interoperability.

Preparing a Class for Data Contract Serialization

The DataContract attribute prepares a class for serialization using the Data Contract Serializer system, and the DataMember attribute indicates which properties and fields should be serialized. Listing 23-17 provides a demonstration.

■ **Note** The classes for Data Contract serialization are in the System.Runtime.Serialization assembly, which must be added to your project before you can compile the examples in this section. Right-click on your project in the Solution Explorer window and select Add Reference. Click on the .NET tab of the Add Reference dialog box, scroll down until you find the System.Runtime.Serialization assembly, and click OK.

Listing 23-17. Using the DataContract and DataMember Attributes

```
using System.Runtime.Serialization;

[DataContract]
public class Person {
    private string name;
    private string city;

    public Person(string nameParam, string cityParam) {
        name = nameParam;
        city = cityParam;
    }

    [DataMember]
    public string Name {
        get { return name; }
        set { name = value; }
    }

    [DataMember]
    public string City {
```

```
            get { return city; }
            set { city = value; }
        }
}
```

The DataContract attribute is applied to the entire class, and the DataMember attribute is applied to those members that you want to include in the serialized data. To omit a property or field, simple don't apply the DataMember attribute.

Alternatively, if you want to serialize every field and property in an object, you can apply the Serializable attribute to the class, as you did for binary serialization at the start of the chapter. Here is an example, which is equivalent to Listing 23-17:

```
[Serializable]
public class Person {
    private string name;
    private string city;

    public Person(string nameParam, string cityParam) {
        name = nameParam;
        city = cityParam;
    }

    public string Name {
        get { return name; }
        set { name = value; }
    }

    public string City {
        get { return city; }
        set { city = value; }
    }
}
```

Generating Portable XML

The most portable XML available from the Data Contact serialization system comes from using the DataContractSerializer class, which is in the System.Runetime.Serialization namespace. Listing 23-18 demonstrates how to use this class to serialize the Person class in Listing 23-17.

Listing 23-18. Using the DataContractSerializer Class

```
using System;
using System.IO;
using System.Runtime.Serialization;

class Listing_18 {

    static void Main(string[] args) {

        // create a new Person object
```

```
        Person myPerson = new Person("Adam Freeman", "London");

        // open the stream to the file we want to store the data in
        Stream myStream = new MemoryStream();

        // create the serialize
        DataContractSerializer serializer = new DataContractSerializer(typeof(Person));

        // serialize the Person object
        serializer.WriteObject(myStream, myPerson);

        // reset the cursor and deserialize the object
        myStream.Seek(0, SeekOrigin.Begin);
        Person myDeserializedPerson = (Person)serializer.ReadObject(myStream);

        // wait for input before exiting
        Console.WriteLine("Press enter to finish");
        Console.ReadLine();
    }
}
```

To create a DataContractSerializer object, you must pass the type that you want to serialize as a constructor parameter, either by using the typeof keyword and the class name (as in the example) or by calling the GetType method on the object you want to serialize. Once you have a DataContractSerializer, you can call the WriteObject method, passing in the Stream you want the serialized data to be written to and the object that you want to be serialized as parameters:

```
serializer.WriteObject(myStream, myPerson);
```

In Listing 23-18, you have sent the serialized data to a MemoryStream so that the XML is stored in memory. Here is the XML result of serializing the Person object:

```
<Person xmlns="http://schemas.datacontract.org/2004/07/"
xmlns:i="http://www.w3.org/2001/XMLSchema-instance">
    <City>London</City>
    <Name>Adam Freeman</Name>
</Person>
```

To deserialize an object, you call the ReadObject method of the DataContractSerializer class, passing in the Stream from which the serialized data will be read as a parameter:

```
Person myDeserializedPerson = (Person)serializer.ReadObject(myStream);
```

Generating .NET-specific XML

You can generate XML that contains more information about .NET assemblies and types by using the NetDataContractSerializer. Listing 23-19 provides a demonstration of using this serializer.

Listing 23-19. Using the NetDataContractSerializer Class

```
using System;
using System.IO;
using System.Runtime.Serialization;

class Listing_19 {

    static void Main(string[] args) {

        // create a new Person object
        Person myPerson = new Person("Adam Freeman", "London");

        // open the stream to the file we want to store the data in
        Stream myStream = new MemoryStream();

        // create the serialize
        NetDataContractSerializer serializer = new NetDataContractSerializer();
        // serialize the Person object
        serializer.WriteObject(myStream, myPerson);

        // reset the cursor and deserialize the object
        myStream.Seek(0, SeekOrigin.Begin);
        Person myDeserializedPerson = (Person)serializer.ReadObject(myStream);

        // wait for input before exiting
        Console.WriteLine("Press enter to finish");
        Console.ReadLine();
    }
}
```

The only difference in this example compared with Listing 23-18 is that you have created a NetDataContractSerializer object rather than a DataContractSerializer object. The NetDataContractSerializer class doesn't require a constructor argument. Here is the XML that this serializer generates:

```
<Person z:Id="1" z:Type="Person" z:Assembly="Listing_19, Version=1.0.0.0, Culture=neutral,
PublicKeyToken=null" xmlns="http://schemas.datacontract.org/2004/07/"
xmlns:i="http://www.w3.org/2001/XMLSchema-instance"
xmlns:z="http://schemas.microsoft.com/2003/10/Serialization/">
    <City z:Id="2">London</City>
    <Name z:Id="3">Adam Freeman</Name>
</Person>
```

As you can see, this serialized data contains more .NET-specific information, including details of the assembly.

Generating JSON

The JavaScript Object Notation (JSON) is a lightweight data exchange format that has gained popularity for its compact nature and simplicity to process. If you want to exchange data with a system that understands JSON, then you can use the DataContractJsonSerializer class in the System.Runtime.Serialization.Json namespace. Listing 23-20 provides a demonstration.

Listing 23-20. Using the DataContractJsonSerializer Class

```
using System;
using System.IO;
using System.Runtime.Serialization;
using System.Runtime.Serialization.Json;

class Listing_20 {

    static void Main(string[] args) {

        // create a new Person object
        Person myPerson = new Person("Adam Freeman", "London");

        // open the stream to the file we want to store the data in
        Stream myStream = new MemoryStream();

        // create the serialize
        DataContractJsonSerializer serializer
            = new DataContractJsonSerializer(typeof(Person));

        // serialize the Person object
        serializer.WriteObject(myStream, myPerson);

        // reset the cursor and deserialize the object
        myStream.Seek(0, SeekOrigin.Begin);
        Person myDeserializedPerson = (Person)serializer.ReadObject(myStream);

        // wait for input before exiting
        Console.WriteLine("Press enter to finish");
        Console.ReadLine();
    }
}
```

As you can see, the change in this Listing is to create a DataContractJsonSerializer object, which takes the type of the object you want to serialize as a constructor argument. Here is the JSON data generated by Listing 23-20:

```
{"City":"London","Name":"Adam Freeman"}
```

Summary

This chapter showed the four different approaches available for serializing objects. If you want to serialize data for use within or between .NET programs, the binary serializer offers the best performance and feature set. The Data Contract Serializer can be used to generate the most portable XML or JSON, both of which are suitable for creating data you can share with non-.NET programs and systems.

CHAPTER 24

Parallel Programming

One of the newest additions to the .NET Framework Library is the Task Parallel Library (TPL), a set of classes that makes parallel programming simpler and easier than ever before. This chapter covers what parallel programming is and how to use some of the core features of the TPL. Table 24-1 provides the summary for this chapter.

Producing simple parallel programs is easy using the TPL, but more complex programs require more in-depth knowledge of parallel programing concepts and the features of the TPL. In addition to this book, I have also written *Pro .NET 4 Parallel Programming in C#* (Apress), which is dedicated to parallel programming using C# and the TPL; it includes much more in-depth coverage than I can provide in this chapter.

Table 24-1. Quick Problem/Solution Reference for Chapter 24

Problem	Solution	Listings
Perform two or more items of work at the same time.	Use the Task class.	24-1 through 24-4
Wait for a Task to complete.	Call the Wait method.	24-5
Wait for more than one Task to complete.	Use the static Task.WaitAll method.	24-6
Return a result from a Task.	Use the derived Task<T> class.	24-7, 24-8
Pass state information to a Task.	Pass a parameter when creating the Task.	24-9
Get the status of a Task.	Read the value of the Status property or the value of one of the IsXXX properties.	24-10
Cancel a Task.	Use a CancellationTokenSource.	24-11 through 24-13
Deal with Task exceptions.	Deal with the exception in the Task body, catch the exception from a trigger member or implement a custom escalation property.	24-14 through 24-18

Problem	Solution	Listings
Create a chain of Tasks.	Use the ContinueWith method.	24-19 through 24-22
Create a chain of Tasks which will executed selectively.	Use the ContinueWith method and a value from the TaskContinuationOptions enumeration.	24-23
Create a critical region.	Use the lock keyword.	24-25
Use collections without encountering race conditions.	Use the concurrent collection classes.	24-27, 24-28

Understanding Single- and Multi-Threaded Execution

A *thread* is the part of the .NET Framework that performs the statements in your code. By default, the .NET Framework creates one thread to execute your C# programs. This thread starts its work by executing the first statement in your Main method. When that statement has been executed, it moves on to the next line of code and executes that—and then the next and the next. When these statements call other methods or methods in other objects, the thread doggedly executes the code statements that have been called before returning to the Main method and carrying on as before. The job of the thread is to execute every statement it encounters in sequence until the final statement of your Main method has been executed and your program can finish.

You don't have to do anything to create the main thread; it is done for you by the .NET framework. This model of programming is sometimes called *sequential execution* or *sequential programming* because each code statement is executed strictly in sequence. It is also called single-threaded execution because there is one thread doing all the work.

The advantage of sequential programming is that it is familiar and predictable. It is the technique used by 95% of programmers to solve 95% of programming problems. Listing 24-1 contains a simple example of a sequential program.

Listing 24-1. Sequential Execution

```
using System;
using System.Diagnostics;

class Listing_01 {

    static void Main(string[] args) {

        // create and start a new StopWatch
        Stopwatch timer = Stopwatch.StartNew();

        // add up all the positive values that int can represent
        long posTotal = 0;
        for (int i = 0; i < int.MaxValue; i++) {
            posTotal += i;
        }
```

```
    // add up all the negative values that int can represent
    long negTotal = 0;
    for (int i = 0; i > int.MinValue; i--) {
        negTotal += i;
    }

    // add the result values together
    long combinedTotal = posTotal + negTotal;

    // stop the timer
    timer.Stop();

    // print out the total time
    Console.WriteLine("Elapsed time: {0}", timer.Elapsed);
    Console.WriteLine("Positive total {0}", posTotal);
    Console.WriteLine("Negative total {0}", negTotal);
    Console.WriteLine("Combined total {0}", combinedTotal);

    // wait for input before exiting
    Console.WriteLine("Press enter to finish");
    Console.ReadLine();
    }
}
```

There are two for loops in Listing 24-1. The first sums a series of positives integer values and the second sums a series of negative integer values. When both for loops have completed, the individual results are combined to produce an overall result. I have used the StopWatch class, described in Chapter 22, to measure how long it takes to complete these tasks. Because this is a sequentially executed program, each step will be performed in order, as illustrated by Figure 24-1.

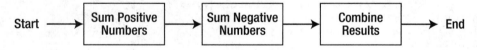

Figure 24-1. Sequential execution, visually

Compiling and running Listing 24-1 produces the following output:

```
Elapsed time: 00:00:15.3397309
Positive total 2305843005992468481
Negative total -2305843008139952128
Combined total -2147483647
Press enter to finish
```

The disadvantage of sequential programming is that you cannot make use of the ability of modern hardware to execute more than one thread at a time, and this limits the performance of your application. Multi-core/multi-processor hardware is very common these days, and sequential programming is unable to take advantage of this sharp increase in computing power.

The alternative to sequential execution is *parallel execution*. The program starts with one thread doing all the work, but you use the TPL to create additional threads to take on some of the work and speed things up. The terms *parallel execution* or *parallel programming* are used because more than one code statement is executed at a time. The term *multi-threaded* programming is used because there is more than one thread at work in your program. Listing 24-2 demonstrates the application of the TPL to your int summing example.

Listing 24-2. Parallel Execution

```
using System;
using System.Diagnostics;
using System.Threading.Tasks;

class Listing_02 {

    static void Main(string[] args) {

        // create and start a new StopWatch
        Stopwatch timer = Stopwatch.StartNew();

        // add up all the positive values that int can represent
        Task<long> positiveTask = Task<long>.Factory.StartNew(() => {
            long posTotal = 0;

            for (int i = 0; i < int.MaxValue; i++) {
                posTotal += i;
            }
            return posTotal;
        });

        // add up all the negative values that int can represent
        Task<long> negativeTask = Task<long>.Factory.StartNew(() => {
            long negTotal = 0;
            for (int i = 0; i > int.MinValue; i--) {
                negTotal += i;
            }
            return negTotal;
        });

        // add the result values together
        long combinedTotal = positiveTask.Result + negativeTask.Result;

        // stop the timer
        timer.Stop();

        // print out the total time
        Console.WriteLine("Elapsed time: {0}", timer.Elapsed);
        Console.WriteLine("Positive total {0}", positiveTask.Result);
        Console.WriteLine("Negative total {0}", negativeTask.Result);
        Console.WriteLine("Combined total {0}", combinedTotal);
```

```
        // wait for input before exiting
        Console.WriteLine("Press enter to finish");
        Console.ReadLine();
    }
}
```

There are eight changes required to Listing 24-1 to create Listing 24-2—and some of those changes are very small, such as a new using statement. Don't worry about the meaning of those changes for the moment; I'll explain how to use the Task class you see in Listing 24-2 as you proceed through the chapter. For the moment, it is enough to know that the Task class represents a new thread of execution—an additional worker to speed things up.

When Listing 24-2 is compiled and executed, it starts off as a regular sequentially executed program. But rather than execute the for loops itself, the single thread creates Task objects to handle the work on its behalf. These Task objects execute the for loops simultaneously, as illustrated by Figure 24-2.

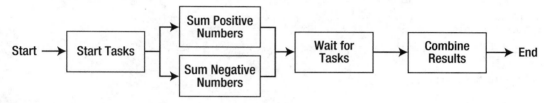

Figure 24-2. *Parallel execution, visually*

The calculations to determine the positive total happen at the same time as the calculations to determine the negative total. The initial thread waits for the Task objects to complete their work and then combines the individual results to create the overall total. As Figure 24-2 demonstrates, you have added additional steps to the program, but because two of those steps are performed at the same time, the overall performance will improve. Compiling and running Listing 24-2 produces the following results:

```
Elapsed time: 00:00:07.7404294
Positive total 2305843005992468481
Negative total -2305843008139952128
Combined total -2147483647
Press enter to finish
```

Listing 24-2 completed in less than 8 seconds, as opposed to the 15 seconds it took for Listing 24-1 to complete. With a few small changes, the performance has almost doubled. These results come from a four-core Windows 7 machine; your results will vary based on the hardware and software configuration of your computer(s).

Getting Started with Tasks

The basic building block of the TPL is the Task class, which is part of the System.Threading.Tasks namespace. There are three basic steps to using Task object: create the Task, start the Task working, and wait for the Task to complete. The following sections show you how to perform each of these steps.

Creating a Task

You create a Task using the class constructor. If you want the Task to perform some work that doesn't produce a result, use the Task class and pass an Action as the constructor parameter. Listing 24-3 contains an example.

Listing 24-3. Creating a Task

```
using System;
using System.Threading.Tasks;

class Listing_03 {

    static void Main(string[] args) {

        // create the action
        Action myAction = new Action(DoSomeWork);

        // create the Task using the Action
        Task myActionTask = new Task(myAction);

        // create an equivilent Task using a lambda expression
        Task myLambdaTask = new Task(() => {
            long total = 0;
            for (int i = 0; i < int.MaxValue; i++) {
                total += i;
            }
            Console.WriteLine("Total from method: {0}", total);
        });

        // wait for input before exiting
        Console.WriteLine("Press enter to finish");
        Console.ReadLine();
    }

    public static void DoSomeWork() {
        long total = 0;
        for (int i = 0; i < int.MaxValue; i++) {
            total += i;
        }
        Console.WriteLine("Total from method: {0}", total);
    }
}
```

In Listing 24-3, the Task called myActionTask is created using an Action which will invoke the DoSomeWork method. This has the effect of creating a Task that, once started, will call the DoSomeWork method in parallel with whatever other Task objects are running.

A common approach is to replace the Action with a lambda expression, which has been done for the myLambdaTask in Listing 24-3. The Task objects myLambdaTask and myActionTask are equivalent. You can read more about using the Action class and lambda expressions in Chapter 10. However they are specified, the code statements that a Task performs in parallel are referred to as the *Task body*.

Starting a Task

Once you have created a Task, you can start it working by calling the Start method. This requests that the Task begins processing its workload. I say "requests" because the TPL will manage the set of Task objects you have started to ensure that optimum performance is achieved. This can mean that a Task is not started immediately.

You can create and start a Task in a single step by using the Task.Factory.StartNew method. This method creates a new Task using the Action that you have provided as a parameter, calls Start on the Task, and then returns it as a result. Listing 24-4 demonstrates both ways of starting Task objects.

Listing 24-4. Starting Tasks

```
using System;
using System.Threading.Tasks;

class Listing_04 {

    static void Main(string[] args) {

        // create the action
        Action myAction = new Action(DoSomeWork);

        // create the Task using the Action
        Task manuallyStartedTask = new Task(myAction);

        // manually start the task
        manuallyStartedTask.Start();

        // create and start a Task in a single step
        Task autoStartTask = Task.Factory.StartNew(myAction);

        // wait for input before exiting
        Console.WriteLine("Press enter to finish");
        Console.ReadLine();
    }

    public static void DoSomeWork() {
        long total = 0;
        for (int i = 0; i < int.MaxValue; i++) {
            total += i;
        }
        Console.WriteLine("Total from method: {0}", total);
```

```
    }
}
```

Compiling and running Listing 24-4 produces the following output:

```
Press enter to finish
Total from method: 2305843005992468481
Total from method: 2305843005992468481
```

Notice that the Press enter to finish message appears before the results from the tasks. This happens because the single thread that was created by the .NET Framework for sequential execution reaches the end of the Main method before the two Task objects reach the end of their calculation and print out their results—the program exits and the Tasks are killed.

Waiting for a Task

You can change the order of the results from Listing 24-4 by asking the main thread to wait for the two Task objects to complete their work before continuing to print the Press enter to finish message. To wait for a Task to complete, you simply call the Wait method. This method will not return until the Task object on which you have called the method has finished its work. Listing 24-5 provides a demonstration.

Listing 24-5. Waiting for Tasks to Complete

```
using System;
using System.Threading.Tasks;

class Listing_05 {

    static void Main(string[] args) {

        // create the action
        Action myAction = new Action(DoSomeWork);

        // create the Task using the Action
        Task manuallyStartedTask = new Task(myAction);
        // manually start the task
        manuallyStartedTask.Start();

        // create and start a Task in a single step
        Task autoStartTask = Task.Factory.StartNew(myAction);

        // wait for both Tasks to complete
        manuallyStartedTask.Wait();
        autoStartTask.Wait();

        // wait for input before exiting
        Console.WriteLine("Press enter to finish");
```

```
        Console.ReadLine();
    }

    public static void DoSomeWork() {
        long total = 0;
        for (int i = 0; i < int.MaxValue; i++) {
            total += i;
        }
        Console.WriteLine("Total from method: {0}", total);
    }
}
```

The Wait calls are marked in bold. In Listing 24-5, you call Wait on one method and then the other. If a Task has completed its work before you call Wait, then the method returns immediately. If you have a lot of Tasks, it can be more convenient to use the static Task.WaitAll method, which will wait for a set of Tasks in a single method call. Listing 24-6 contains an example.

Listing 24-6. Waiting for a Set of Tasks

```
using System;
using System.Threading.Tasks;

class Listing_06 {

    static void Main(string[] args) {

        // create the action
        Action myAction = new Action(DoSomeWork);

        // create the Task using the Action
        Task manuallyStartedTask = new Task(myAction);
        // manually start the task
        manuallyStartedTask.Start();

        // create and start a Task in a single step
        Task autoStartTask = Task.Factory.StartNew(myAction);

        // wait for both Tasks to complete
        Task.WaitAll(manuallyStartedTask, autoStartTask);

        // wait for input before exiting
        Console.WriteLine("Press enter to finish");
        Console.ReadLine();
    }

    public static void DoSomeWork() {
        long total = 0;
        for (int i = 0; i < int.MaxValue; i++) {
            total += i;
        }
        Console.WriteLine("Total from method: {0}", total);
```

```
    }
}
```

The WaitAll method does not return until all of the Task objects passed as parameters have completed their work. The WaitAll method takes a parameter array, meaning that you can pass a list of Task objects separated by commas or an array of Task objects. Compiling and running Listing 24-6 produces the following results:

```
Total from method: 23058430059922468481
Total from method: 23058430059922468481
Press enter to finish
```

As you can see, the main thread doesn't reach the Console.WriteLine statement that prints out Press enter to finish until after the two Task objects have written out their results.

Getting Results from Tasks

The Tasks in the previous examples don't produce a result. Instead, they call a method that performs some work and then prints the result to the console. You can specify a result from parallel work by using the Task<T> class, where T is the type of result that will be returned. So, for example, if you create and run a Task<int> object, then the result that the work produces will be an int. The Task<T> class is an example of a generic type, which is explained in Chapter 15.

Instead of an Action as the constructor parameter, you must use a Func<T> where T matches the result type that you have specified for the Task<T>. Listing 24-7 demonstrates how to use the Task<T>, Func<T> combination in this way.

Listing 24-7. Getting a Result from a Task

```
using System;
using System.Threading.Tasks;

class Listing_07 {

    static void Main(string[] args) {

        // create the Func
        Func<long> myFunc = new Func<long>(DoSomeWork);

        // create and start a Task using the Func
        Task<long> myTask = Task<long>.Factory.StartNew(myFunc);

        // get the result from the Task
        long result = myTask.Result;

        // print out the result
        Console.WriteLine("Result: {0}", result);

        // wait for input before exiting
```

```
        Console.WriteLine("Press enter to finish");
        Console.ReadLine();
    }

    public static long DoSomeWork() {
        long total = 0;
        for (int i = 0; i < int.MaxValue; i++) {
            total += i;
        }
        return total;
    }
}
```

The Task<T> class has a Result property that you can use to read the output of the parallel work that was performed. The Result method will block until the Task<T> has finished its work, meaning that you don't need to use the Wait method before reading the result. The Task<T> class has a static Factory property that you can use to create and start a Task<T> in a single step, just as you did for the Task class.

Compiling and running Listing 24-7 produces the following result:

```
Result: 2305843005992468481
Press enter to finish
```

■ **Tip** The Task<T> class is derived from Task. A common mistake is to create a Task<T> but assign the object to a Task variable. This means that you will not have access to the Result property. You must take care to assign Task<T> objects to Task<T> variables if you want to read results.

Listing 24-7 creates each of the required objects explicitly and uses a Func<T> rather than a lambda expression. Listing 24-8 demonstrates the same example, but written in a more compact manner using a lambda expression.

Listing 24-8. Reading a Result of a Task<T> that has a Lambda Expression

```
using System;
using System.Threading.Tasks;

class Listing_08 {

    static void Main(string[] args) {

        // create the Task<T> using a lambda expression
        Task<long> myTask = Task<long>.Factory.StartNew(() => {
            long total = 0;
            for (int i = 0; i < int.MaxValue; i++) {
                total += i;
            }
```

```
            return total;
        });

        // get the result from the Task
        long result = myTask.Result;

        // print out the result
        Console.WriteLine("Result: {0}", result);

        // wait for input before exiting
        Console.WriteLine("Press enter to finish");
        Console.ReadLine();
    }
}
```

Passing Parameters to a Task

You can pass a parameter to a Task or Task<T> to provide some external state information. The mechanism for doing this is a bit clumsy because you can only pass an object. You need to downcast that object to another type to work with its derived members. Listing 24-9 provides a demonstration of using a parameter.

Listing 24-9. Passing a State Object to a Task

```
using System;
using System.Threading.Tasks;

class Listing_09 {

    static void Main(string[] args) {

        // create the array of int values we will pass as parameters to the Tasks
        int[] maxValues = new int[] { int.MaxValue, int.MaxValue / 2, int.MaxValue / 4 };

        // create an array to make tracking the Task objects easier
        Task<long>[] tasks = new Task<long>[maxValues.Length];

        // define the Func we will use for all of the Tasks
        Func<object, long> myFunction = DoSomeWork;

        for (int i = 0; i < maxValues.Length; i++) {
            tasks[i] = Task<long>.Factory.StartNew(myFunction, maxValues[i]);
        }

        // wait for all the Tasks to complete
        Task.WaitAll(tasks);

        // print out the results from each Task
        foreach (Task<long> t in tasks) {
            Console.WriteLine("Result: {0}", t.Result);
```

```
    }

    // wait for input before exiting
    Console.WriteLine("Press enter to finish");
    Console.ReadLine();
}

public static long DoSomeWork(object objectParam) {
    int maxValue = (int)objectParam;
    long total = 0;
    for (int i = 0; i < maxValue; i++) {
        total += i;
    }
    return total;
}
}
```

Listing 24-9 demonstrates creating three Tasks that use a for loop. Note that the code to create each Task uses the same Func each time—only the parameter value changes. The parameter is passed to the Task constructor or the Factory.StartNew method, like this:

```
tasks[i] = Task<long>.Factory.StartNew(myFunction, maxValues[i]);
```

This statement creates a Task<long> which will pass the parameter maxValues[i] to the Func<object, long> called myFunction. You can only pass objects as Task parameters. If you are calling a method directly in a lambda expression, you would use a statement like this:

```
tasks[i] = Task<long>.Factory.StartNew((stateObject) =>
DoSomeWork((int)stateObject), maxValues[i]);
```

The name stateObject will be given to the parameter for the lambda expression. As shown in the statement, this will be cast to an int value and passed as a parameter to the DoSomeWork method. The value that will be assigned to stateObject is maxValues[i].

The third permutation is to do away with the method call entirely and put the for loop directly into the lambda expression, like this:

```
tasks[i] = Task<long>.Factory.StartNew(stateObject => {
    int maxValue = (int)stateObject;
    long total = 0;
    for (int j = 0; j < maxValue; j++) {
        total += j;
    }
    return total;
}, maxValues[i]);
```

Once again, the parameter is called stateObject and the value that will be assigned to it is passed to the StartNew method as the second parameter value, after the lambda expression. Compiling and running Listing 24-9 (or either of the alternative approaches) produces the following results:

```
Result: 2305843005992468481
Result: 576460750692810753
```

```
Result: 144115187270549505
Press enter to finish
```

Getting the Status of a Task

The Status property returns the status of a Task using a value from the System.Threading.Tasks.TaskStatus enumeration. Table 24-2 describes the most commonly used values from the TaskStatus enumeration.

Table 24-2. TaskStatus Enumeration Values

Value	Description
Created	The task has been initialized but not yet scheduled.
WaitingToRun	The task is awaiting execution.
Running	The task is running.
RanToCompletion	The task completed without being cancelled and without an exception being thrown.
Canceled	The task was cancelled (see the "Cancelling Tasks" section in this chapter).
Faulted	The task threw an exception (see the "Handling Task Exceptions" section in this chapter).

Listing 24-10 demonstrates the use of the Status property.

Listing 24-10. Using the Task.Status Property

```
using System;
using System.Threading.Tasks;

class Listing_10 {

    static void Main(string[] args) {

        // create (but don't start) a Task<long>
        Task<long> myTask = new Task<long>(() => {
            long total = 0;
            for (int i = 0; i < int.MaxValue; i++) {
                total += i;
            }
            return total;
```

```
        });

        // print the Task status
        Console.WriteLine("Task status: {0}", myTask.Status);

        // start the Task
        myTask.Start();

        // print the Task status
        Console.WriteLine("Task status: {0}", myTask.Status);

        // wait for the Task to complete
        myTask.Wait();

        // print the Task status
        Console.WriteLine("Task status: {0}", myTask.Status);

        // print out the result from the Task
        Console.WriteLine("Result: {0}", myTask.Result);

        // wait for input before exiting
        Console.WriteLine("Press enter to finish");
        Console.ReadLine();
    }
}
```

Listing 24-10 creates a Task<long> and prints out the value of the Status property as the Task goes through its life. Compiling and running Listing 24-10 produces the following results:

```
Task status: Created
Task status: Running
Task status: RanToCompletion
Result: 2305843005992468481
Press enter to finish
```

These results show the Task moving from the Created status to Running and finally to RanToCompletion. When you run this example, you might see slightly different results, like this:

```
Task status: Created
Task status: WaitingToRun
Task status: RanToCompletion
Result: 2305843005992468481
Press enter to finish
```

You can see the WaitingToRun status if the TPL has not started execution of your Task before the Status property is read.

Using the Status Properties

The Task and Task<T> classes define three properties that let you check for three specific status conditions. These properties are described in Table 24-3.

Table 24-3. Task Status Properties

Property	Description
IsCanceled	Returns true if the Task has been cancelled (see the "Cancelling Tasks" section later in this chapter).
IsCompleted	Returns true if the Task has competed.
IsFaulted	Returns true if the Task has encountered an exception (see the "Handling Task Exceptions" section later in this chapter for more details).

The IsCompleted property will return true if the Task has completed, even if the reason for its completion is because the Task was cancelled or because it encountered an Exception. See the relevant sections later in this chapter for details of cancelling Tasks and handling exceptions in Tasks.

Canceling Tasks

Occasionally, you will want to stop a Task without waiting for it to complete its work; for example, in response to the user clicking a Cancel button. The TPL has a mechanism for supporting Task cancellation using a technique called *cooperative cancelation*—meaning that your Task body has to be written so that it checks to see if the Task has been cancelled. Listing 24-11 shows how to cancel a Task.

Listing 24-11. Canceling a Task

```
using System;
using System.Threading;
using System.Threading.Tasks;

class Listing_11 {

    static void Main(string[] args) {

        // create a token source
        CancellationTokenSource cancelTS = new CancellationTokenSource();

        // create and start a Task using the Token
        Task myTask = Task.Factory.StartNew(() => {

            long total = 0;

            // do some work
```

```
            Console.WriteLine("Doing first chunk of work...");
            for (int i = 0; i < int.MaxValue; i++) {
                total += i;
            }

            // check to see if we have been canceled
            if (cancelTS.Token.IsCancellationRequested) {
                Console.WriteLine("Cancellation detected");
                // we can perform any tidying up here - closing streams, etc
                // throw an exception to show that we have canceled properly
                throw new OperationCanceledException(cancelTS.Token);
            }

            // do some more work
            Console.WriteLine("Doing second chunk of work...");
            for (int i = 0; i > int.MinValue; i--) {
                total += i;
            }

            // print out the total
            Console.WriteLine("Total: {0}", total);

        }, cancelTS.Token);

        // read a line from the Console
        Console.WriteLine("Press enter to cancel token");
        Console.ReadLine();

        // cancel the token
        Console.WriteLine("Token canceled");
        cancelTS.Cancel();

        // wait for input before exiting
        Console.WriteLine("Press enter to finish");
        Console.ReadLine();
    }
}
```

The first step in creating a cancelable Task is to create an instance of the CancellationTokenSource class which can be found in the System.Threading namespace. The Token property of this class returns a CancellationToken object that can be used by the TPL and the Task body to monitor for cancellation.

The second step is to create a Task object using the result of the CancellationToken.Token property as a constructor argument. Listing 24-11 uses the StartNew method to create and start the Task in a single statement; the first parameter is the lambda expression containing the Task body, and the second parameter is the result of the Token property.

The Task body has to cooperate with the cancellation, which it does by checking the IsCancellationRequested property of the CancellationToken obtained through the Token property of the CancellationToken source, like this:

```
if (cancelTS.Token.IsCancellationRequested) {
```

If the IsCancellationRequested property returns true, the Task should release any resources it is holding and throw an OperationCanceledException exception, created by passing the CancellationToken as a constructor parameter, like this:

```
throw new OperationCanceledException(cancelTS.Token);
```

Throwing the exception shows the TPL that your Task has acknowledged the cancelation. You can simply return from the Task body, but then the Task.Status property won't return the Canceled value.

When you want to cancel a Task, call the Cancel method on the CancellationTokenSource. This sets the result of the Token.IsCancellationRequested property to true:

```
cancelTS.Cancel();
```

In Listing 24-11, the Task performs some work, checks for cancellation and continues to a second piece of work. If the Task has been canceled, the OperationCanceledException is thrown. The Task is canceled when the user presses the Enter key.

Cooperative cancellation allows the programmer to decide when and how often to check for cancellation. In Listing 24-11, only one check is performed, which means that the user has to press the Enter key during the first block of work to prevent the second block being performed, as illustrated by Figure 24-3.

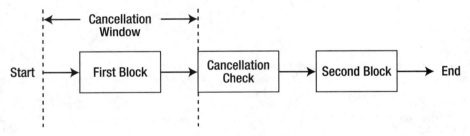

Figure 24-3. *The cancellation window for Listing 24-11*

In Listing 24-11, there is no way for the user to interrupt the first block of work so she must press the Enter key during the first block to cancel the Task before the second block of work commences. This creates a relatively narrow window for canceling the Task. There is a balance to be struck between checking too frequently (and compromising performance) and checking too infrequently (reducing the opportunities the user has to cancel a Task). The appropriate balance will be different for each program (and often differ for different kinds of Task in the same program).

Checking and Throwing in a Single Statement

Listing 24-11 checks the IsCancelationRequested property and separately throws the OperationCanceledException. This provides an opportunity to release any resources or generally tidy up before execution of the Task body ceases.

If you don't need such an opportunity, you can handle cancelation in a single statement by using the CancellationToken.ThrowIfCancellationRequested method. This method will create and throw the OperationCanceledException for you if the value of the IsCancellationRequested property is true. Listing 24-12 demonstrates the use of this method.

Listing 24-12. Checking and Throwing in a Single Statement

```
using System;
using System.Threading;
using System.Threading.Tasks;

class Listing_12 {

    static void Main(string[] args) {

        // create a token source
        CancellationTokenSource cancelTS = new CancellationTokenSource();

        // create and start a Task using the Token
        Task myTask = Task.Factory.StartNew(() => {

            long total = 0;

            // do some work
            Console.WriteLine("Doing first chunk of work...");
            for (int i = 0; i < int.MaxValue; i++) {
                total += i;
            }

            // check to see if we have been canceled
            cancelTS.Token.ThrowIfCancellationRequested();

            // do some more work
            Console.WriteLine("Doing second chunk of work...");
            for (int i = 0; i > int.MinValue; i--) {
                total += i;
            }

            // print out the total
            Console.WriteLine("Total: {0}", total);

        }, cancelTS.Token);

        // read a line from the Console
        Console.WriteLine("Press enter to cancel token");
        Console.ReadLine();

        // cancel the token
        Console.WriteLine("Token canceled");
        cancelTS.Cancel();

        // wait for input before exiting
        Console.WriteLine("Press enter to finish");
        Console.ReadLine();
    }
}
```

The change from Listing 24-11 is shown in bold. There is no change in the way that the cancellation request is handled; this is just a convenience method that allows you to reduce code clutter.

Cancelling Multiple Tasks

The CancellationToken from a single CancellationTokenSource can be used to cancel several Tasks in one go if the token is passed as a parameter when each Task is created. This can be more convenient if the Tasks are related in some way. Listing 24-13 demonstrates cancelling several Tasks together.

Listing 24-13. Cancelling Multiple Tasks

```
using System;
using System.Threading;
using System.Threading.Tasks;

class Listing_13 {

    static void Main(string[] args) {

        // create a token source
        CancellationTokenSource cancelTS = new CancellationTokenSource();

        for (int i = 0; i < 4; i++) {
            // create a Task
            Task.Factory.StartNew(stateObject => {
                Console.WriteLine("Task {0} started", stateObject);
                long total = 0;
                for (int j = 0; j < int.MaxValue; j++) {
                    total += j;
                    if (cancelTS.Token.IsCancellationRequested) {
                        Console.WriteLine("Task {0} canceled", stateObject);
                        throw new OperationCanceledException(cancelTS.Token);
                    }
                }

                Console.WriteLine("Task {0} completed", stateObject);
            }, i, cancelTS.Token);
        }

        // read a line from the Console
        Console.WriteLine("Press enter to cancel token");
        Console.ReadLine();

        // cancel the token
        Console.WriteLine("Token canceled");
        cancelTS.Cancel();

        // wait for input before exiting
        Console.WriteLine("Press enter to finish");
        Console.ReadLine();
```

```
    }
}
```

Listing 24-13 creates a set of Tasks which all monitor the same CancellationToken. The Cancel method is called on the CancellationTokenSource when the user presses the Enter key and this has the effect of cancelling all of the Tasks. Compiling and running Listing 24-13 (and pressing the Enter key) produces the following results:

```
Press enter to cancel token
Task 2 started
Task 0 started
Task 1 started
Task 3 started

Token canceled
Press enter to finish
Task 3 canceled
Task 1 canceled
Task 2 canceled
Task 0 canceled
```

In Listing 24-13, the Task body (which is common to all of the Tasks created) checks for cancellation after every calculation, which means that the Tasks stop execution almost immediately once the Enter key is pressed.

Handling Task Exceptions

When you run a sequential program, exceptions will stop your program from running. If you have used a try statement, you can handle the exception, and the execution of your program will continue. If you don't handle the exception, it is propagated up until it causes your program to be terminated. Things are more complicated in parallel programs because the .NET Framework can't make an assessment of the impact of the exception if it occurs in a Task body that is being executed in parallel with other Task bodies. As a consequence, handling exceptions encountered by Tasks is slightly complicated. The following sections show you the ways in which exceptions are thrown and how you can handle them.

Handling an Exception in a Task Body

The first approach to handling an exception is with a try statement in the Task body. This is just like using a try statement in a sequentially executed program and means that the Task itself handles the problem represented by the exception. Listing 24-14 provides a demonstration.

Listing 24-14. Handling an Exception Inside of a Task Body

```
using System;
using System.Threading.Tasks;

class Listing_14 {
```

```csharp
static void Main(string[] args) {

    Task<long> myTask = Task.Factory.StartNew<long>(() => {
        long total = 0;
        for (int i = 0; i < int.MaxValue; i++) {
            try {

                total = CalculateSum(i, total);

            } catch (ArgumentOutOfRangeException ex) {
                Console.WriteLine("---- Exception Caught In Task Body ---");
                Console.WriteLine("---- Exception type: {0}", ex.GetType());
            }
        }
        return total;
    });

    // Get the result from the Task
    long taskResult = myTask.Result;
    // write out the result
    Console.WriteLine("Result: {0}", taskResult);

    // wait for input before exiting
    Console.WriteLine("Press enter to finish");
    Console.ReadLine();
}

public static long CalculateSum(int x, long y) {
    if (x == 1000) {
        throw new ArgumentOutOfRangeException();
    } else {
        return x + y;
    }
}
}
```

In Listing 24-14, the Task body calls the CalculateSum method to add a new int value to the running total. This method throws an ArgumentOutOfRange exception if the value of the first parameter is 1000 for the purposes of providing an example.

The Task body is prepared for this exception and wraps the call to the CalculateSum method in a try statement with a catch clause than can handle the ArgumentOutOfRange exception type. The try statement is inside of the for loop, meaning that the Task body continues iterating through its work when the exception has been caught and handled. Compiling and running Listing 24-14 produces the following results:

```
---- Exception Caught In Task Body ---
---- Exception type: System.ArgumentOutOfRangeException
Result: 2305843005992467481
Press enter to finish
```

Handling an Exception from a Trigger Method

The TPL stores any exceptions that a Task encounters that are not handled in the Task body. These exceptions are then re-thrown when you access a *trigger-member;* this includes the Result property, the Wait method, and the static Task.WaitAll method. Listing 24-15 provides a demonstration.

Listing 24-15. Handling an Exception Thrown by a Trigger Method

```
using System;
using System.Threading.Tasks;

class Listing_15 {

    static void Main(string[] args) {

        Task<long> myTask = Task.Factory.StartNew<long>(() => {
            long total = 0;
            for (int i = 0; i < int.MaxValue; i++) {
                total = CalculateSum(i, total);
            }
            return total;
        });

        try {
            // Get the result from the Task
            long taskResult = myTask.Result;

            // write out the result
            Console.WriteLine("Result: {0}", taskResult);
        } catch (AggregateException aggEx) {
            Console.WriteLine("---- Exception Caught From Trigger Member ---");
            Console.WriteLine("---- Exception type: {0}", aggEx.GetType());
        }

        // wait for input before exiting
        Console.WriteLine("Press enter to finish");
        Console.ReadLine();
    }

    public static long CalculateSum(int x, long y) {
        if (x == 1000) {
            throw new ArgumentOutOfRangeException();
        } else {
            return x + y;
        }
    }
}
```

In this example, the ArgumentOutOfRange exception isn't handled in the Task body. The TPL stores the exception until one of the trigger members is called; in this case, it is the Result property. Instead of returning a result value, the exception is re-thrown. Here are the results of compiling and running Listing 24-15:

```
---- Exception Caught From Trigger Member ---
---- Exception type: System.AggregateException
Press enter to finish
```

Notice that the exception that was thrown by the CalculateSum method is wrapped in an AggregateException, which is a special kind of exception that can be used to bundle multiple exceptions together. The InnerExceptions property returns a collection of exceptions that you can use to get details of the exceptions thrown in the Task body. Here is an example applied to the catch clause in Listing 24-15:

```
try {

    long taskResult = myTask.Result;
    Console.WriteLine("Result: {0}", taskResult);

} catch (AggregateException aggEx) {
    // get the inner exceptions
    foreach (Exception innerEx in aggEx.InnerExceptions) {
        Console.WriteLine("Inner Exception type: {0}", innerEx.GetType());
        Console.WriteLine("Inner Exception message: {0}", innerEx.Message);
    }
}
```

Handling Exceptions from Multiple Tasks

If you are working with multiple Tasks and you have called the WaitAll method, any AggregateException that may be thrown will contain all of the exceptions that the individual Tasks have encountered. Iterating through the InnerExceptions collection will give you access to each original exception in turn, as demonstrated by Listing 24-16.

Listing 24-16. Unpacking Exceptions from Multiple Tasks

```
using System;
using System.Threading.Tasks;

class Listing_16 {

    static void Main(string[] args) {

        // create a collection to contain the Tasks
        Task<long>[] tasksArray = new Task<long>[4];

        // create the tasks
        for (int i = 0; i < tasksArray.Length; i++) {
            tasksArray[i] = Task<long>.Factory.StartNew((stateObject) => {
```

```
            int taskID = (int)stateObject;
            long total = 0;
            for (int j = 0; j < int.MaxValue; j++) {
                total = CalculateSum(taskID, j, total);
            }
            return total;
        }, i);
    }

    try {

        // wait for all of the tasks to complete
        Task.WaitAll(tasksArray);

    } catch (AggregateException aggEx) {
        // enumerate the exceptions
        foreach (Exception innerEx in aggEx.InnerExceptions) {
            Console.WriteLine("Inner exception: {0} - {1}",
                innerEx.GetType(), innerEx.Message);
        }
    }

    // wait for input before exiting
    Console.WriteLine("Press enter to finish");
    Console.ReadLine();
}

public static long CalculateSum(int taskID, int x, long y) {
    if (taskID % 2 == 0 && x == 1000) {
        throw new ArgumentOutOfRangeException(
            string.Format("Exception for taskID {0}", taskID));
    } else {
        return x + y;
    }
}
}
```

This is a slightly more complicated example where the state object passed to each Task when it is created is used by the CalculateSum method to selectively throw exceptions. This means that of the four Tasks that are created in Listing 24-16, two of them will run to completion and two will cause exceptions to be thrown.

The trigger member in Listing 24-16 is the WaitAll method, which means that the AggregateException that is re-thrown will contain two exceptions. Compiling and running Listing 24-16 produces the following results:

```
Inner exception: System.ArgumentOutOfRangeException - Specified argument was out
 of the range of valid values.
Parameter name: Exception for taskID 2
Inner exception: System.ArgumentOutOfRangeException - Specified argument was out
 of the range of valid values.
Parameter name: Exception for taskID 0
```

Press enter to finish

Dealing with Exceptions using Task Properties

In the previous section, you used the state parameter to differentiate exceptions so that it was obvious which aggregated exception originated from which of the Tasks. This is not always possible (since you won't be able to insert the state object value into the message of exceptions thrown by other programmer's code) or desirable (because you will want to use the state object to pass more useful information to the Task body). An alternative way of processing exceptions is to use a trigger member to re-throw the exceptions, but use the individual Task properties to work out what went wrong, as illustrated by Listing 24-17.

Listing 24-17. Dealing with Exceptions Using Properties

```
using System;
using System.Threading.Tasks;

class Listing_17 {

    static void Main(string[] args) {

        // create a collection to contain the Tasks
        Task<long>[] tasksArray = new Task<long>[4];

        // create the tasks
        for (int i = 0; i < tasksArray.Length; i++) {
            tasksArray[i] = Task<long>.Factory.StartNew((stateObject) => {
                int taskID = (int)stateObject;
                long total = 0;
                for (int j = 0; j < int.MaxValue; j++) {
                    total = CalculateSum(taskID, j, total);
                }
                return total;
            }, i);
        }

        try {

            // wait for all of the tasks to complete
            Task.WaitAll(tasksArray);

        } catch (AggregateException) {
            // work through the set of Tasks and use the properties
            // to determine what happened
            for (int i = 0; i < tasksArray.Length; i++) {
                // get the exception at the current index
                Task<long> currentTask = tasksArray[i];
                if (currentTask.IsFaulted) {
                    Console.WriteLine("Task {0} encountered an exception", i);
```

```
                // enumerate the exceptions for this Task
                foreach (Exception innerException in
                    currentTask.Exception.InnerExceptions) {

                    Console.WriteLine("Exception type for Task {0}: {1}",
                        i, innerException.GetType());
                    Console.WriteLine("Exception message for Task {0}: {1}",
                        i, innerException.Message);
                }
            } else {
                Console.WriteLine("Task {0} ran to completion", i);
                Console.WriteLine("Result for Task {0}: {1}", i, currentTask.Result);
            }
        }
    }

    // wait for input before exiting
    Console.WriteLine("Press enter to finish");
    Console.ReadLine();
}

public static long CalculateSum(int taskID, int x, long y) {
    if (taskID % 2 == 0 && x == 1000) {
        throw new ArgumentOutOfRangeException(
            string.Format("Exception for taskID {0}", taskID));
    } else {
        return x + y;
    }
}
}
```

In Listing 24-17, the catch clause of the try statement is used to read the IsFaulted property of each Task that has been created. You know that there has been at least one exception, because otherwise the catch clause wouldn't be invoked. You can then interrogate the Task objects to find out which ones have had problems.

As you saw in Table 24-3, the IsFaulted property returns true if a Task has encountered an exception. You can get details by using the Exception property, which returns an AggregateException that you can process just as you did previously. Compiling and running Listing 24-17 produces the following results:

```
Task 0 encountered an exception
Exception type for Task 0: System.ArgumentOutOfRangeException
Exception message for Task 0: Specified argument was out of the range of valid values.
Parameter name: Exception for taskID 0
Task 1 ran to completion
Result for Task 1: 2305843005992468481
Task 2 encountered an exception
Exception type for Task 2: System.ArgumentOutOfRangeException
Exception message for Task 2: Specified argument was out of the range of valid values.
Parameter name: Exception for taskID 2
Task 3 ran to completion
```

```
Result for Task 3: 2305843005992468481
Press enter to finish
```

From these results, you can see that the first and third Tasks you created encountered ArgumentOutOfRange exceptions and the second and fourth Tasks were able to run to completion and return results.

Using a Custom Exception Escalation Policy

If you don't handle an exception in the Task body or by calling a trigger member and handling the resulting AggregateException, the exception is escalated. By default, this escalation results in the unhandled exceptions being thrown when your Task objects are finalized by the garbage collector (see Chapter 18 for details of finalization). Since you can't predict when the garbage collector will finalize a given Task, this means that an unhandled exception can cause your program to terminate unexpectedly.

You can change the way unhandled exceptions are dealt with by implementing a custom escalation policy. You do this by subscribing to the static TaskScheduler.UnobservedTaskException event. The TaskScheduler class is in the System.Threading namespace; the other members of this class are for advanced Task management and not within the scope of this book. Listing 24-18 demonstrates implementing a custom exception escalation policy.

Listing 24-18. Implementing a Custom Task Exception Escalation Policy

```
using System;
using System.Threading.Tasks;

class Listing_18 {

    static void Main(string[] args) {

        TaskScheduler.UnobservedTaskException +=
            (object sender, UnobservedTaskExceptionEventArgs eventArgs) => {

                // mark the exception as being handled
                eventArgs.SetObserved();

                // get the aggregate exception
                AggregateException aggEx = (AggregateException)eventArgs.Exception;

                // enumerate the exceptions
                Console.WriteLine("--- Exceptions handled by custom policy ---");
                foreach (Exception innerEx in aggEx.InnerExceptions) {
                    Console.WriteLine("Inner exception: {0} - {1}",
                        innerEx.GetType(), innerEx.Message);
                }
            };

        // create the tasks
        for (int i = 0; i < 4; i++) {
```

```
        Task.Factory.StartNew((stateObject) => {
            int taskID = (int)stateObject;
            long total = 0;
            for (int j = 0; j < int.MaxValue; j++) {
                total = CalculateSum(taskID, j, total);
            }
            Console.WriteLine("Task {0} ran to completion", taskID);
        }, i);
    }

    // prompt the user to press enter to run the GC
    Console.WriteLine("Press enter to run GC");
    Console.ReadLine();

    // run the GC
    GC.Collect();

    // wait for input before exiting
    Console.WriteLine("Press enter to finish");
    Console.ReadLine();
}

public static long CalculateSum(int taskID, int x, long y) {
    if (taskID % 2 == 0 && x == 1000) {
        Console.WriteLine("Throwing an exception for Task {0}", taskID);
        throw new Exception(string.Format("Exception for taskID {0}", taskID));
    } else {
        return x + y;
    }
}
}
```

The custom policy in Listing 24-18 is shown in bold. You register with the UnobservedTaskException event; when exceptions are not handled using the other techniques, your policy will be used by invoking your event handler. You can learn more about events and event handling in Chapter 10.

The UnobservedTaskExceptionEventArgs class (from the System.Threading.Tasks namespace) is used to pass details of the unhandled exceptions to your policy code. The Exception property returns an AggregateException containing the unhandled exceptions, although you will need to cast to the AggregateException type before you can access the inner exceptions.

The SetObserved method tells the TPL that your custom policy has handled the exception and that no further action is required. The default escalation policy will be used if you don't call the SetObserved method in your custom policy, allowing you to decide to selectively handle exceptions. The custom policy shown in Listing 24-18 calls the SetObserved method and enumerates the aggregated exceptions.

The rest of Listing 24-18 creates a set of Tasks, some of which run to completion and some of which encounter exceptions. When the user presses the Enter key, the garbage collector is explicitly called, which causes the Task objects to be finalized (this assumes that the user doesn't press the Enter key until all of the Tasks have finished). The finalization of the Task objects causes the unhandled exceptions to be escalated to the custom policy. Compiling and running Listing 24-18 produces the following results:

```
Press enter to run GC
```

```
Throwing an exception for Task 0
Throwing an exception for Task 2
Task 1 ran to completion
Task 3 ran to completion

Press enter to finish
--- Exceptions handled by custom policy ---
Inner exception: System.Exception - Exception for taskID 0
--- Exceptions handled by custom policy ---
Inner exception: System.Exception - Exception for taskID 2
```

Chaining Tasks Together

You can create Tasks that will be started when another Task finishes. These are called *continuations*. You can create different kinds of continuations to achieve different arrangements of related Tasks.

Creating a Simple Continuation

The simplest kind of continuation can be created using the Task.ContinueWith method. You create the first Task as normal, and then use the ContinueWith method to pass an Action parameter that will be invoked when the first task has completed. Listing 24-19 provides an example.

Listing 24-19. Creating a Simple Continuation

```
using System;
using System.Threading.Tasks;

class Listing_19 {

    static void Main(string[] args) {

        Task firstTask = new Task(() => {
            Console.WriteLine("First task starting");
            long result = 0;
            for (int i = 0; i < int.MaxValue; i++) {
                result += i;
            }
            Console.WriteLine("First task result: {0}", result);
            Console.WriteLine("First task complete");
        });

        Task secondTask = firstTask.ContinueWith((Task antecedent) => {
            Console.WriteLine("Second task starting");
            long result = 0;
            for (int i = 0; i > int.MinValue; i--) {
                result += i;
            }
```

```
            Console.WriteLine("Second task result: {0}", result);
            Console.WriteLine("Second task complete");
        });

        // start the first task
        firstTask.Start();

        // wait for both tasks to complete
        Task.WaitAll(firstTask, secondTask);

        // wait for input before exiting
        Console.WriteLine("Press enter to finish");
        Console.ReadLine();
    }
}
```

The ContinueWith method is called on the first Task that is created in Listing 24-19. The parameter for the ContinueWith method is a lambda expression used in place of an Action. The parameter called antecedent is the original Task (which is called the *antecedent*), which allows you to check the status of the continuation Task. The result of the ContinueWith method is the newly created Task. You don't have to explicitly start the continuation Task; it will be started automatically when the antecedent has finished. Compiling and running Listing 24-19 produces the following results:

```
First task starting
First task result: 2305843005992468481
First task complete
Second task starting
Second task result: -2305843008139952128
Second task complete
Press enter to finish
```

Getting Details of the Antecedent

You can get details of the status of the antecedent by using the Status property or one of the three informational properties. If your antecedent is a Task<T>, then you can use the Result property to get the result value. Listing 24-20 provides a demonstration of using the antecedent parameter to get details of the antecedent Task.

Listing 24-20. Getting Antecedent Details

```
using System;
using System.Threading.Tasks;

class Listing_20 {

    static void Main(string[] args) {

        Task<long> firstTask = new Task<long>(() => {
            Console.WriteLine("First task starting");
```

```
        long result = 0;
        for (int i = 0; i < int.MaxValue; i++) {
            result += i;
        }
        Console.WriteLine("First task complete");
        return result;
    });

    Task secondTask = firstTask.ContinueWith((Task<long> antecedent) => {
        Console.WriteLine("Second task starting");
        // get the result and status from the antecedent task
        Console.WriteLine("Result from antecedent: {0}", antecedent.Result);
        Console.WriteLine("Status from antecedent: {0}", antecedent.Status);
        Console.WriteLine("Second task complete");
    });

    // start the first task
    firstTask.Start();

    // wait for both tasks to complete
    Task.WaitAll(firstTask, secondTask);

    // wait for input before exiting
    Console.WriteLine("Press enter to finish");
    Console.ReadLine();
    }
}
```

When the antecedent is a Task<T> object, then the parameter to the lambda expression or Action is a Task<T> also, as you can see from the bold statement in Listing 24-20. The continuation task in Listing 24-20 reads the Status and Result properties from the antecedent Task<long>. Compiling and running this example produces the following results:

```
First task starting
First task complete
Second task starting
Result from antecedent: 2305843005992468481
Status from antecedent: RanToCompletion
Second task complete
Press enter to finish
```

Providing a Continuation Result

If you want your continuation Task to produce a result, you can use the ContinueWith<T> method, where T is the result type. The antecedent Task can produce a different type of result or no result at all. Listing 24-21 shows a continuation producing a different type of result to its antecedent.

Listing 24-21. Returning a Result from a Continuation

```csharp
using System;
using System.Threading.Tasks;

class Listing_21 {

    static void Main(string[] args) {

        Task<long> firstTask = new Task<long>(() => {
            Console.WriteLine("First task starting");
            long result = 0;
            for (int i = 0; i < int.MaxValue; i++) {
                result += i;
            }
            Console.WriteLine("First task complete");
            return result;
        });

        Task<int> secondTask = firstTask.ContinueWith<int>((Task<long> antecedent) => {
            Console.WriteLine("Second task starting");
            // get the result and status from the antecedent task
            Console.WriteLine("Result from antecedent: {0}", antecedent.Result);
            Console.WriteLine("Status from antecedent: {0}", antecedent.Status);
            // perform the work
            long result = 0;
            for (int i = 0; i > int.MinValue; i--) {
                result += i;
            }
            Console.WriteLine("Second task complete");
            return (int)(result + antecedent.Result);
        });

        // start the first task
        firstTask.Start();

        // wait for both tasks to complete
        Task.WaitAll(firstTask, secondTask);

        // print out the result from the continuation Task
        Console.WriteLine("Continuation result: {0}", secondTask.Result);

        // wait for input before exiting
        Console.WriteLine("Press enter to finish");
        Console.ReadLine();
    }
}
```

The antecedent in Listing 24-21 is a Task<long> and the continuation is a Task<int>, created by calling ContinueWith<int>. The continuation takes the long result from the antecedent and combines it with the output of its own work to create an int result. Compiling and running Listing 24-21 produces the following output:

```
First task starting
First task complete
Second task starting
Result from antecedent: 2305843005992468481
Status from antecedent: RanToCompletion
Second task complete
Continuation result: -2147483647
Press enter to finish
```

Creating Chains of Continuations

You can chain together more than two Tasks. In fact, you can chain together as many as you want simply by calling the ContinueWith method. Listing 24-22 shows you how to do this.

Listing 24-22. Creating a Longer Chain of Tasks

```csharp
using System;
using System.Threading.Tasks;

class Listing_22 {

    static void Main(string[] args) {

        // create the first task
        Task<int> firstTask = new Task<int>(() => {
            Console.WriteLine("First Task Started");
            // do some simple work and return the result
            return 10 + 20;
        });

        // create the second task
        Task<int> secondTask =  firstTask.ContinueWith<int>((Task<int> antecedent) => {
            Console.WriteLine("Second Task Started");
            // do some simple work and combine with the antecdent result
            return 30 + antecedent.Result;
        });

        // create the third task
        Task<int> thirdTask = secondTask.ContinueWith<int>((Task<int> antecedent) => {
            Console.WriteLine("Third Task Started");
            // do some simple work and combine with the antecedent result
            return 40 + antecedent.Result;
        });

        // create the fourth task
        Task finalTask = thirdTask.ContinueWith((Task<int> antecedent) => {
```

```
            Console.WriteLine("Final Task Started");
            // do some simple work and combine with the antecedent result
            int finalResult = antecedent.Result * 10;
            Console.WriteLine("Final Task Finished");
        });

        // start the first Task
        firstTask.Start();

        // wait for the final Task to complete
        finalTask.Wait();

        // wait for input before exiting
        Console.WriteLine("Press enter to finish");
        Console.ReadLine();
    }
}
```

Listing 24-22 creates a chain of four Tasks. Most of them are Task<int> objects, but the last one is a plain Task (I did this just for variety; there are no restrictions on what kinds of Task you can chain together). Once you have created the continuation chain, start the first Task; each Task is started as its antecedent finishes. The result of compiling and running Listing 24-22 is as follows:

```
First Task Started
Second Task Started
Third Task Started
Final Task Started
Final Task Finished
Press enter to finish
```

Creating Selective Continuations

The ContinueWith method creates a continuation that will be performed regardless of what happens to the antecedent Task, even if the antecedent is canceled or encounters an exception. Listing 24-23 provides a demonstration.

Listing 24-23. Using a Selective Continuation

```
using System;
using System.Threading;
using System.Threading.Tasks;

class Listing_23 {

    static void Main(string[] args) {

        // create a token source for cancellation
        CancellationTokenSource tokenSource = new CancellationTokenSource();
```

```
            // create a Task
            Task<long> firstTask = new Task<long>(() => {
                Console.WriteLine("First task started");
                long result = 0;
                for (int i = 0; i < int.MaxValue; i++) {
                    result += i;
                    if (tokenSource.Token.IsCancellationRequested) {
                        Console.WriteLine("Task cancelled");
                        tokenSource.Token.ThrowIfCancellationRequested();
                    }
                }
                return result;
            }, tokenSource.Token);

            firstTask.ContinueWith((Task<long> antecedent) => {
                Console.WriteLine("Ran to completion continuation - antecedent result is: {0}",
                    antecedent.Result);
            }, TaskContinuationOptions.OnlyOnRanToCompletion);

            firstTask.ContinueWith((Task<long> antecedent) => {
                Console.WriteLine("Canceled continuation");
            }, TaskContinuationOptions.OnlyOnCanceled);

            // start the first task
            firstTask.Start();

            // prompt the user to cancel the token
            Console.WriteLine("Press enter to cancel");
            Console.ReadLine();
            // cancel the token
            tokenSource.Cancel();

            // wait for input before exiting
            Console.WriteLine("Press enter to finish");
            Console.ReadLine();
        }
    }
}
```

Selective continuations are created by providing a value from the TaskContinuationOptions enumeration as a parameter to the Task.ContinueWith method. In Listing 24-23, there are two selective continuations. The first uses the OnlyRanToCompletion enum value; this means that the continuation will only run if the antecedent completes without being cancelled or encountering an unhandled exception. The second continuation uses the OnlyOnCanceled value; this means that the continuation Task will run only if the antecedent has been canceled. The values from the TaskContinuationOptions enum are described in Table 24-4.

Table 24-4. `TaskContinuationOptions` *Values*

Value	Description
`NotOnRanToCompletion`	The continuation will run if the antecedent has been canceled or has encountered an unhandled exception.
`NotOnFaulted`	The continuation will run if the antecedent has not encountered an unhandled exception.
`NotOnCanceled`	The continuation will run if the antecedent has not been canceled.
`OnlyOnRanToCompletion`	The continuation will run if the antecedent has not been canceled or has not encountered an unhandled exception.
`OnlyOnFaulted`	The continuation will run if the antecedent has encountered an unhandled exception
`OnlyOnCanceled`	The continuation will run if the antecedent has been canceled

Using one of these values when you use the `ContinueWith` method allows you to limit the conditions under which a continuation will be run or, as in the case of Listing 24-23, create different continuations to be run under different circumstances. If the user presses the Enter key while Listing 24-23 is running, the antecedent Task will be cancelled and the following output will be displayed:

```
Press enter to cancel
First task started

Task cancelled
Press enter to finish
Canceled continuation
```

If the user doesn't press the Enter key, the antecedent will run to competition and the other continuation Task will be run instead. This produces different results:

```
Press enter to cancel
First task started
Ran to completion continuation - antecedent result is: 23058429812964066
```

Sharing Data between Tasks

The Tasks in the examples so far in this chapter have worked in isolation. This is ideal for demonstrating the features of the TPL, but not at all realistic. Most of the time, you will need to share data between

Tasks, and this can be troublesome unless you take the time to coordinate the way that the Tasks operate. Listing 24-24 shows the kind of problem that can arise when Tasks share data in an uncoordinated way.

Listing 24-24. Problems Arising when Sharing Data Between Tasks

```
using System;
using System.Threading.Tasks;

class Listing_24 {

    static void Main(string[] args) {

        // define a shared counter
        int counter = 0;

        // create an array of Tasks
        Task[] taskArray = new Task[10];

        // create and start a series of Tasks that will share the counter
        for (int i = 0; i < taskArray.Length; i++) {
            taskArray[i] = Task.Factory.StartNew(() => {
                // enter a loop and increment the counter
                for (int j = 0; j < 1000; j++) {
                    // increment the shared counter
                    counter++;
                }
            });
        }

        // wait for all of the Tasks to complete
        Task.WaitAll(taskArray);

        // print out the value of the shared counter
        Console.WriteLine("Counter value: {0}", counter);

        // wait for input before exiting
        Console.WriteLine("Press enter to finish");
        Console.ReadLine();
    }
}
```

In Listing 24-24, ten Tasks are created. Each enters a for loop that increments a shared int variable 1,000 times. The main thread waits for all of the Tasks to finish and then prints out the value of the shared variable. If you have ten Tasks and each of them increments the int 1,000 times, then you would expect the value of the counter to be 10,000.

And that's the result you get—well, sometimes. When I compiled and ran Listing 24-24 on my PC, I got a result of 10,000 about 50% of the time. The result of the time, I got a different result, like this one:

```
Counter value: 9132
```

```
Press enter to finish
```

The problem is caused by the statement that increments the shared counter:

```
counter++;
```

The unary increment operator (++) is short-hand for a statement like this:

```
counter = counter + 1;
```

This statement breaks down into the following steps.

1. Read the current value of the counter variable.
2. Calculate the sum of the value and 1.
3. Assign the result of the value back to the counter variable.

You see the range of results from Listing 24-24 because there are slight variations in the timing of the ten Tasks, as shown in Figure 24-4.

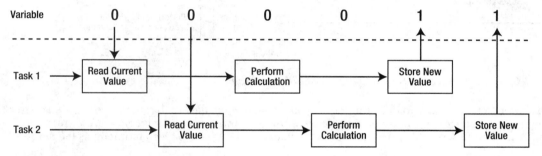

Figure 24-4. *The problem with shared data*

Figure 24-4 shows what can happen when two Tasks from Listing 24-24 are slightly out of phase with one another. Both Tasks read the current value of the variable and get the initial value of zero. Both Tasks add one to the value to produce a result of 1. Both Tasks store the result in the variable. The result produced by the second Task overwrites the result produced by the first Task and you end up missing an increment. This is how you end up with a range of results from Listing 24-24.

This kind of issue is called a *race condition*, also known as a *data race* or a *race hazard*. Race conditions are a major cause of problems in parallel programming. Every time you share data between two or more Tasks, you must ask yourself if there is a chance that a race condition will arise. If there is such a chance, there are a range of different techniques you can employ to prevent unexpected results. These techniques are collectively called *synchronization*.

The next section shows you how to use one of the most basic types of synchronization, known as a *critical region*. See my book on C# parallel programming for details of more advanced techniques.

Understanding a Critical Region

A critical region is a group of statements that only one Task at a time can execute. If Tasks were people, a critical region would be a room with a guard outside. When a Task tries to enter the room, the guard checks to see if anyone is already inside. If the room is empty, the Task is allowed in. If there is another Task already in the room, the guard makes the Task wait outside until the room is empty again. At any time, there can be zero or one Tasks in the room.

To stop race conditions, you put the statements that access shared data inside of a critical region. This means that only one Task will be able to access the shared data at a time, as illustrated by Figure 24-5.

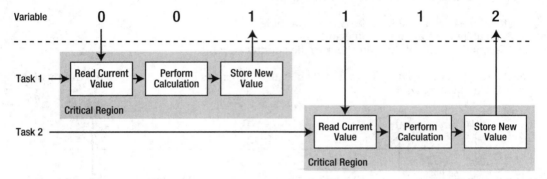

Figure 24-5. *Applying a critical region to prevent a race condition*

To prevent a race condition in Listing 24-24, you would need to ensure that the three steps taken to read, increment, and store the counter variable were contained within a critical region. Were you to do this, then only one Task would be able to access the shared variable at any given moment, as the figure shows.

Creating a Critical Region

Listing 24-25 demonstrates applying a critical region to the previous example.

Listing 24-25. Creating a Critical Region

```
using System;
using System.Threading.Tasks;

class Listing_25 {

    static void Main(string[] args) {

        // define a shared counter
        int counter = 0;

        // create an object to use in the critical region
        object myLock = new object();
```

```
        // create an array of Tasks
        Task[] taskArray = new Task[10];

        // create and start a series of Tasks that will share the counter
        for (int i = 0; i < taskArray.Length; i++) {
            taskArray[i] = Task.Factory.StartNew(() => {
                // enter a loop and increment the counter
                for (int j = 0; j < 1000; j++) {
                    lock (myLock) {
                        // increment the shared counter
                        counter++;
                    }
                }
            });
        }

        // wait for all of the Tasks to complete
        Task.WaitAll(taskArray);

        // print out the value of the shared counter
        Console.WriteLine("Counter value: {0}", counter);

        // wait for input before exiting
        Console.WriteLine("Press enter to finish");
        Console.ReadLine();
    }
}
```

Critical regions are created using the lock keyword, as illustrated by Figure 24-6.

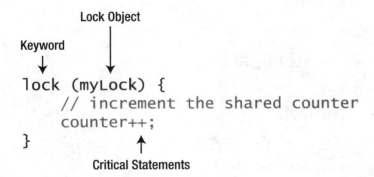

Figure 24-6. The anatomy of a critical region

A lock statement consists of the lock keyword and a parameter that is used to control access to the critical region. The parameter must be shared by all of the Tasks that will use the critical region, and the convention is to create an object specifically for use in the lock statement, like this:

```
object myLock = new object();
```

The statements contained inside of the lock statement code block are the ones that will be protected by the critical region, and only one Task at a time will be able to enter the critical region to execute those statements. Compiling and running Listing 24-25 consistently produces the following results:

```
Counter value: 10000
Press enter to finish
```

Avoiding Synchronization

A critical region will help prevent a race condition, but it can have a huge impact on performance because it introduces sequential execution to parts of your program. Using synchronization effectively is a process of ensuring that only the smallest number of critical regions exist; you will end up with a race condition if you have too few and a sluggishly performing program if you have too many.

It is good practice to review your solution to the problem you are trying to solve and see if there is a way to get the same results without sharing data between Tasks. As a simple example, if you look back at Listing 24-25, you can see that the Tasks do not need to store the results of their calculations after each iteration. The same effect could be achieved by the Tasks working independently and then combining the individual Task results at the end, as demonstrated by Listing 24-26.

Listing 24-26. Avoiding the Use of Synchronization

```
using System;
using System.Threading.Tasks;

class Listing_26 {

    static void Main(string[] args) {

        // define a shared counter
        int counter = 0;

        // create an object to use in the critical region
        object myLock = new object();

        // create an array of Tasks
        Task<int>[] taskArray = new Task<int>[10];

        // create and start a series of Tasks that will share the counter
        for (int i = 0; i < taskArray.Length; i++) {
            taskArray[i] = Task<int>.Factory.StartNew(() => {

                // create a local counter to work with
                int localCounter = 0;

                // enter a loop and increment the counter
                for (int j = 0; j < 1000; j++) {
                    // increment the shared counter
                    localCounter++;
```

```
                }

                // return the local counter
                return localCounter;
            });
        }

        // wait for all of the Tasks to complete
        Task.WaitAll(taskArray);

        // combine the individual results of each Task
        foreach (Task<int> t in taskArray) {
            counter += t.Result;
        }

        // print out the value of the shared counter
        Console.WriteLine("Counter value: {0}", counter);

        // wait for input before exiting
        Console.WriteLine("Press enter to finish");
        Console.ReadLine();
    }
}
```

This is a trivial adaptation of a trivial example, but the point to bear in mind is that when you get deeply entangled in trying to balance performance against the need to avoid race conditions, it can often be worthwhile to review your overall approach. Reducing the amount of data that is shared between Tasks is often a more useful technique than trying to squeeze performance out of critical regions.

Using Concurrent Collections

Collections are amongst the most commonly used classes in the .NET Framework class library. Unfortunately, the standard collection classes are prone to race conditions, as demonstrated by Listing 24-27.

Listing 24-27. A Race Condition with a Collection Class

```
using System;
using System.Collections.Generic;
using System.Threading.Tasks;

class Listing_27 {
    private static object lockObject = new object();
    private static int counter = 0;

    static void Main(string[] args) {

        // create a queue and fill it with data
        Queue<int> myQueue = new Queue<int>();
        for (int i = 0; i < 10000; i++) {
```

```
            myQueue.Enqueue(i);
        }

        // create an array to make tracking the Tasks simpler
        Task[] taskArray = new Task[10];

        // create and start the Tasks
        for (int i = 0; i < taskArray.Length; i++) {
            taskArray[i] = Task.Factory.StartNew(() => {
                while (myQueue.Count > 0) {
                    // take an item from the queue
                    int item = myQueue.Dequeue();
                    // increment the counter to report that we have taken an item
                    IncrementCounter();
                }
            });
        }

        // wait for all of the Tasks to finish
        Task.WaitAll(taskArray);

        // print out the value of the counter
        Console.WriteLine("Items Processed: {0}", counter);

        // wait for input before exiting
        Console.WriteLine("Press enter to finish");
        Console.ReadLine();
    }

    private static void IncrementCounter() {
        lock (lockObject) {
            counter++;
        }
    }
}
```

Listing 24-27 creates a Queue<int> collection and populates it with 10,000 int values. Ten Tasks are created, the bodies of which enter a while loop whose condition is that the Queue<int> contains some items. On each loop iteration, the Dequeue method is called to remove an item from the collection. Each time a Task removes an item, it calls the IncrementCounter method that contains a critical region that safely updates a shared counter. When all of the Tasks have finished, the value of the shared counter is written to the console. If there are 10,000 items in the Queue<int>, you would hope that the counter value is also 10,000, showing that all of the items were removed by the Tasks.

Of course, that isn't what you see. There are three possible outcomes and if you run Listing 24-27 over and over, you will quickly see them all. The first is the hoped-for result: there are 10,000 items in the collection and the counter value is 10,000. Here is the output of this outcome:

```
Items Processed: 10000
Press enter to finish
```

The next kind of outcome is where the value of the shared counter doesn't match the number of items in the collection. The output from this outcome is as follows:

```
Items Processed: 10001
Press enter to finish
```

The difference is usually quite small—one or two items—but something has definitely gone wrong. The third kind of outcome is an exception, like this:

```
Unhandled Exception: System.AggregateException: One or more errors occurred. ---
> System.InvalidOperationException: Queue empty.
   at System.ThrowHelper.ThrowInvalidOperationException(ExceptionResource resource)
   at System.Collections.Generic.Queue`1.Dequeue()
   at Listing_27.<>c__DisplayClass2.<Main>b__0() in C:\Listing_27\Listing_27.cs:line 26
   at System.Threading.Tasks.Task.InnerInvoke()
   at System.Threading.Tasks.Task.Execute()
   --- End of inner exception stack trace ---
   at System.Threading.Tasks.Task.WaitAll(Task[] tasks, Int32 millisecondsTimeout,
CancellationToken cancellationToken)
   at System.Threading.Tasks.Task.WaitAll(Task[] tasks, Int32 millisecondsTimeout)
   at System.Threading.Tasks.Task.WaitAll(Task[] tasks)
   at Listing_27.Main(String[] args) in C: \Listing_27\Listing_27.cs:line 34
Press any key to continue . . .
```

The cause of the second and third outcomes is a race condition; between the time that a Task calls the Count property to check if there are still items in the collection and the time that the Dequeue method is called to get an item, another Task has changed the state of the Queue<int>. You see a different shared counter value because two Tasks called Dequeue and got the same item from the Queue<int>. You get the exception because two Tasks tried to get the last item from the collection, but only one succeeded. Of course, you could use a critical region to protect access to the collection, but that would have a serious impact on performance for a program which makes such intensive use of the shared data.

The collection classes in the System.Collections.Generic namespace are designed to be convenient, but they are not suitable for using with Tasks. However, the collection classes in the System.Collections.Concurrent namespace are designed to work with Tasks, although they are not particularly convenient to use. The concurrent collection classes use sophisticated synchronization techniques to avoid race conditions without incurring the performance problems that critical regions incur. Table 25-5 describes the most useful concurrent collection classes.

Table 25-5. Concurrent Collection Classes

Class	Description
ConcurrentQueue	Collect items on a first-in, first-out basis
ConcurrentStack	Collect items on a first-in, last-out basis
ConcurrentDictionary	Collect name/value pairs

You can see that the concurrent classes are replacements for some of the important generic collection classes (you can learn more about the generic collections in Chapter 19). Listing 24-28 shows the use of the ConcurrentQueue class to solve the race condition present in Listing 24-27.

Listing 24-28. Using a ConcurrentQueue

```
using System;
using System.Collections.Concurrent;
using System.Threading.Tasks;

class Listing_28 {
    private static object lockObject = new object();
    private static int counter = 0;

    static void Main(string[] args) {

        // create a queue and fill it with data
        ConcurrentQueue<int> myQueue = new ConcurrentQueue<int>();
        for (int i = 0; i < 10000; i++) {
            myQueue.Enqueue(i);
        }

        // create an array to make tracking the Tasks simpler
        Task[] taskArray = new Task[10];

        // create and start the Tasks
        for (int i = 0; i < taskArray.Length; i++) {
            taskArray[i] = Task.Factory.StartNew(() => {
                while (myQueue.Count > 0) {
                    // take an item from the queue
                    int item;
                    bool gotItem = myQueue.TryDequeue(out item);
                    if (gotItem) {
                        // increment the counter to report that we have taken an item
                        IncrementCounter();
                    }
                }
            });
        }
```

```
        // wait for all of the Tasks to finish
        Task.WaitAll(taskArray);

        // print out the value of the counter
        Console.WriteLine("Items Processed: {0}", counter);

        // wait for input before exiting
        Console.WriteLine("Press enter to finish");
        Console.ReadLine();
    }

    private static void IncrementCounter() {
        lock (lockObject) {
            counter++;
        }
    }
}
```

The key statement in Listing 24-28 is shown in bold. The concurrent collection classes implement methods that start with Try, take an out parameter, and return a bool result. The result indicates whether the operation was successful. In the case of the ConcurrentQueue.TryDequeue method, a result of true means that an item was de-queued and its value assigned to the out parameter (you can learn more about out parameters in Chapter 9). A result of false indicates that the operation failed and no item was available. In Listing 24-28, a true result leads to calling the IncrementCounter method and a false result leads to the condition of the enclosing while loop being evaluated again.

What this means is that some of the requests you make of a concurrent collection will fail if satisfying the request would lead to a race condition. All of the concurrent collection classes take a similar approach, which can take a while to get used to, but when mastered will provide a good balance between performance and avoiding race conditions.

Summary

This chapter explored one of my favorite C# topics—parallel programming using the Task Parallel Library (the other is LINQ, in case you were wondering). Parallel programming has remained a niche skill in recent years, despite the emergence of multi-core and multi-processor machines. Once reason for the niche status is the complexity in writing parallel programs, something which I think the TPL does a good job of addressing.

Effective parallel programing still requires an investment of time and patience because it requires a new approach to breaking down your problems and working out which data must be shared (and how it will be protected), but it is an investment that pays dividends—you can do more work with less equipment and at lower cost.

■ ■ ■

Asynchronous Methods and Parallel Loops

This chapter covers two features sets that are related to the Task Parallel Library discussed in Chapter 24. Asynchronous methods existed before the TPL was added to the .NET Framework and offer a simple alternative (albeit with less robust features) to using Tasks. This chapter will also cover parallel loops, which are built on top of the TPL and create parallel versions of for and foreach loops. Table 25-1 provides the summary for this chapter.

Table 25-1. Quick Problem/Solution Reference for Chapter 25

Problem	Solution	Listings
Perform an asynchronous operation on a library class that supports asynchronous methods.	Use the Begin and End methods.	25-1, 25-2
Call any method asynchronously.	Create a delegate and use the BeginInvoke and EndInvoke methods.	25-3
Wait for an asynchronous method to complete.	Call the AsyncWaitHandle.WaitOne method on the IAsyncResult that was returned from the Begin method or call the End method.	25-4, 25-5
Create a Task from an asynchronous method.	Use the static Task.Factory.FromAsync method.	25-6
Create a parallel foreach loop.	Use the static Parallel.ForEach method.	25-7
Create a parallel for loop.	Use the static Parallel.For method.	25-8
Terminate the execution of a parallel loop.	Use the Break or Stop methods in the ParallelLoopState class.	25-9, 25-10

Using Asynchronous Methods

Asynchronous methods are a convenient way to perform certain activities in parallel without needing to create and manage Tasks – although asynchronous methods don't have anywhere near the range of features and options that Tasks include. Classes throughout the .NET Framework Class Library support asynchronous methods, especially those classes which relate to networking and I/O. And, with a little more work, you can use delegates to call any method asynchronously. The following sections show you how to do both.

Using Pre-Built Asynchronous Methods

The simplest way to understand asynchronous methods is to see an example of the problem they solve. Chapter 21 showed you how to use the System.Net.Dns class to query the Domain Name System. Now imagine that you have a number of queries to make. Listing 25-1 demonstrates how to use regular methods to do this.

Listing 25-1. Querying the DNS

```
using System;
using System.Net;

class Listing_01 {

    static void Main(string[] args) {

        string[] hostNames = new string[] { "www.microsoft.com", "www.apple.com",
            "www.google.com", "www.ibm.com" };

        for (int i = 0; i < hostNames.Length; i++) {
            // perform a DNS lookup using a name from the array
            IPHostEntry myHostEntry = Dns.GetHostEntry(hostNames[i]);

            // print out the hostname component of the host entry
            Console.WriteLine("Result for {0} is {1}", hostNames[i], myHostEntry.HostName);
        }

        // wait for input before exiting
        Console.WriteLine("Press enter to finish");
        Console.ReadLine();
    }
}
```

Regular methods are also called *synchronous methods* because the main thread that calls the method must wait until the statements inside the method body are performed and the result is produced. For Listing 25-1, this means that the main thread calls the Dns.GetHostEntry method for each value in the hostNames array and must wait until the request has been completed before moving on to the next value. This process is shown in Figure 25-1.

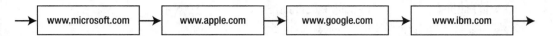

Figure 25-1. *Sequential DNS lookups*

The Dns class supports asynchronous methods, meaning that you can perform your queries in parallel, as demonstrated by Listing 25-2.

Listing 25-2. Asynchronously Querying the DNS

```
using System;
using System.Net;

class Listing_02 {

    static void Main(string[] args) {

        string[] hostNames = new string[] { "www.microsoft.com", "www.apple.com",
            "www.google.com", "www.ibm.com" };

        for (int i = 0; i < hostNames.Length; i++) {
            Dns.BeginGetHostEntry(hostNames[i], GetHostEntryCallback, hostNames[i]);
        }

        // wait for input before exiting
        Console.WriteLine("Press enter to finish");
        Console.ReadLine();
    }

    static void GetHostEntryCallback(IAsyncResult result) {
        // get the result of the async method call
        IPHostEntry hostEntry = Dns.EndGetHostEntry(result);

        // print out the host name
        Console.WriteLine("Result for {0} is {1}", result.AsyncState, hostEntry.HostName);
    }
}
```

When the main thread calls an asynchronous method, it doesn't have to wait until the method has completed. Asynchronous methods come in pairs, and the names of these methods are the same as the synchronous equivalent, prefixed with Begin and End. So, for the example in Listing 25-2, the asynchronous counterparts to the GetHostEntry are BeginGetHostEntry and EndGetHostEntry. Start by using the Begin method; this method takes the same parameters as the synchronous equivalent, plus a *callback method* and a *state object*, as illustrated by Figure 25-2.

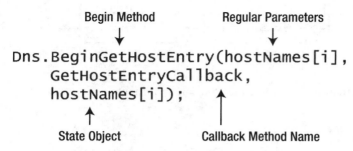

Figure 25-2. *The anatomy of an asynchronous* Begin *method*

When you call a Begin method, the statements in the method are executed in parallel, just as though you had created a Task. When the statements have been executed and the result is ready, the method that you named as the callback will be called. The callback method can have any name, but must return void and take an IAsyncResult as its sole parameter. The callback method in Listing 25-2 is GetHostEntryCallback, which has the following definition:

```
static void GetHostEntryCallback(IAsyncResult result) {
```

The state object you provided when calling the Begin method is available through the IAsyncResult.AsyncState property. In Listing 25-2, I set the state object to be the name that I wanted to look up in DNS, but you can set the state object to any value which will help you differentiate between the queries you have started.

To get the result of the asynchronous method, you call the End method; in this example, the End method is EndGetHostEntry. The return type of the End method is the same type as you would have received had you called the synchronous equivalent; in the case of the EndGetHostEntry method, the return is an IPHost entry. The IAsyncResult that was passed as a parameter to the callback method must be used to call the End method.

The callback method in Listing 25-2 uses the state object and the result of the End method to print out the original name and the result from the DNS. The benefit of making queries in this way is that they happen in parallel, as illustrated by Figure 25-3.

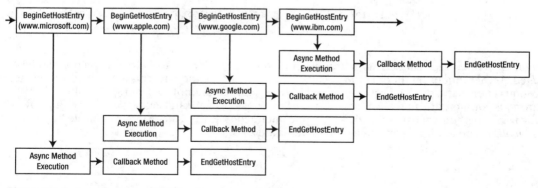

Figure 25-3. *Asynchronous DNS lookups*

Compiling and running Listing 25-2 produces the following results:

```
Result for www.microsoft.com is lb1.www.ms.akadns.net
Result for www.apple.com is e3191.c.akamaiedge.net
Result for www.google.com is www-tmmdi.l.google.com
Result for www.ibm.com is www.ibm.com.cs186.net
Press enter to finish
```

You could get the same effect using Tasks to perform the lookups, but asynchronous methods offer an alternative approach that you might prefer.

Asynchronously Calling Any Method

The Dns class isn't the only one that supports asynchronous methods; you will find them available for a range of operations in the Stream and TcpListener classes, for example (these classes were discussed in Chapters 20 and 21, respectively). But eventually you will want to call a one of your own methods asynchronously or a method in a library class that doesn't have Begin and End methods. This section shows you how to use delegates to call any method asynchronously. Listing 25-3 provides a demonstration.

Listing 25-3. Using an Asynchronous Delegate

```
using System;

class Listing_03 {
    public delegate long PerformCalc(int start, int end, int increment);

    static void Main(string[] args) {

        // assign the deleate
        PerformCalc myDelegate = PerformCalcMethod;

        // call the method several times
        myDelegate.BeginInvoke(0, int.MaxValue, 1, AsyncMethodCallback, myDelegate);
        myDelegate.BeginInvoke(0, int.MaxValue/2, 1, AsyncMethodCallback, myDelegate);
        myDelegate.BeginInvoke(0, int.MaxValue/4, 4, AsyncMethodCallback, myDelegate);

        Console.WriteLine("Async methods are running...");

        // wait for input before exiting
        Console.WriteLine("Press enter to finish");
        Console.ReadLine();
    }

    static void AsyncMethodCallback(IAsyncResult asyncResult) {
        // get the delegate that is being called from the result
        long result = ((PerformCalc)asyncResult.AsyncState).EndInvoke(asyncResult);
```

```
        // write out the result
        Console.WriteLine("Result: {0}", result);
    }

    static long PerformCalcMethod(int start, int end, int increment) {
        long result = 0;
        for (int i = start; i < end; i += increment) {
            result += i;
        }
        return result;
    }
}
```

Listing 25-3 defines a delegate called PerformCalc which takes three parameters and returns a long result. The PerformCalcMethod matches the delegate signature and performs a calculation based on the parameter values. The Main method creates a delegate and calls the BeginInvoke method, which is the Begin method for delegate types. As before, you pass in the normal parameters plus a callback method and a state object.

The callback method is AsyncMethodCallback. This example uses the delegate instance as the state object, so the callback casts to the correct type and calls the EndInvoke method; this is the End method for delegates. The EndInvoke method returns the result type of the delegate—in this example, a long value. Listing 25-3 starts three asynchronous calls using the delegate. Compiling and running Listing 25-3 produces the following results:

```
Async methods are running...
Press enter to finish
Result: 36028796750528512
Result: 576460750692810753
Result: 2305843005992468481
```

Waiting for an Asynchronous Method to Complete

The result produced by calling a Begin method is an IAsyncResult. I have discarded these in the previous examples, but you can use them to wait for an asynchronous method to complete. This is similar to the Task.Wait method seen in Chapter 24. Listing 25-4 demonstrates waiting for asynchronous method.

Listing 25-4. Waiting for an Asynchronous Method to Complete

```
using System;

class Listing_04 {
    public delegate long PerformCalc(int start, int end, int increment);

    static void Main(string[] args) {

        // assign the deleate
        PerformCalc myDelegate = PerformCalcMethod;

        // call the method several times
```

```
        IAsyncResult res1 = myDelegate.BeginInvoke(0, int.MaxValue, 1,
            AsyncMethodCallback, myDelegate);
        IAsyncResult res2 = myDelegate.BeginInvoke(0, int.MaxValue / 2, 1,
            AsyncMethodCallback, myDelegate);
        IAsyncResult res3 = myDelegate.BeginInvoke(0, int.MaxValue / 4, 4,
            AsyncMethodCallback, myDelegate);

        Console.WriteLine("Async methods are running...");

        // wait for each of the async methods to complete
        res1.AsyncWaitHandle.WaitOne();
        res2.AsyncWaitHandle.WaitOne();
        res3.AsyncWaitHandle.WaitOne();

        Console.WriteLine("Async methods have all completed");

        // wait for input before exiting
        Console.WriteLine("Press enter to finish");
        Console.ReadLine();
    }

    static void AsyncMethodCallback(IAsyncResult asyncResult) {
        // get the delegate that is being called from the result
        long result = ((PerformCalc)asyncResult.AsyncState).EndInvoke(asyncResult);
        // write out the result
        Console.WriteLine("Result: {0}", result);
    }

    static long PerformCalcMethod(int start, int end, int increment) {
        long result = 0;
        for (int i = start; i < end; i += increment) {
            result += i;
        }
        return result;
    }
}
```

The IAsyncResult.WaitHandle method returns a System.Threading.WaitHandle object and if you call the WaitOne method, the main thread or current Task will block until the asynchronous method that the IAsyncResult relates to has completed. In Listing 25-4, the WaitOne method is called for each of the IAsyncResults that were created from the BeginInvoke method calls. Here is the result of compiling and running Listing 25-4:

```
Async methods are running...
Result: 36028796750528512
Result: 576460750692810753
Result: 2305843005992468481
Async methods have all completed
Press enter to finish
```

You can make waiting for an asynchronous method more like waiting for a Task by using the IAsyncResult returned from BeginInvoke to call the EndInvoke method. This may seem a little odd, but when you do this, the EndInvoke method blocks until the asynchronous method has finished executing. When using this technique, you do not need to provide a callback method, as demonstrated in Listing 25-5.

Listing 25-5. Using EndInvoke to Wait for an Asynchronous Method

```
using System;

class Listing_05 {
    public delegate long PerformCalc(int start, int end, int increment);

    static void Main(string[] args) {

        // assign the deleate
        PerformCalc myDelegate = PerformCalcMethod;

        // call the method several times
        IAsyncResult res1 = myDelegate.BeginInvoke(0, int.MaxValue, 1,
            null, myDelegate);
        IAsyncResult res2 = myDelegate.BeginInvoke(0, int.MaxValue / 2, 1,
            null, myDelegate);
        IAsyncResult res3 = myDelegate.BeginInvoke(0, int.MaxValue / 4, 4,
            null, myDelegate);

        Console.WriteLine("Async methods are running...");

        foreach (IAsyncResult res in new IAsyncResult[] { res1, res2, res3 }) {
            long result = myDelegate.EndInvoke(res);
            Console.WriteLine("Result: {0}", result);
        }

        Console.WriteLine("Async methods have all completed");

        // wait for input before exiting
        Console.WriteLine("Press enter to finish");
        Console.ReadLine();
    }

    static long PerformCalcMethod(int start, int end, int increment) {
        long result = 0;
        for (int i = start; i < end; i += increment) {
            result += i;
        }
        return result;
    }
}
```

Compiling and running Listing 25-5 produces the following output:

```
Async methods are running...
Result: 2305843005992468481
Result: 576460750692810753
Result: 36028796750528512
Async methods have all completed
Press enter to finish
```

Mixing Asynchronous Methods and Tasks

The TPL provides support for mixing Tasks and asynchronous methods. The advantage of doing this is to include existing code based on asynchronous methods (which pre-date Tasks in .NET) in a continuation chain of Tasks. Listing 25-6 provides a demonstration of creating a Task that uses asynchronous methods.

Listing 25-6. Creating a Task for Asynchronous Methods

```
using System;
using System.Net;
using System.Threading.Tasks;

class Listing_06 {

    static void Main(string[] args) {

        // create a Task that will asychronously perform a DNS lookup
        Task<IPHostEntry> dnsTask = Task<IPHostEntry>.Factory.FromAsync(
            Dns.BeginGetHostEntry,
            Dns.EndGetHostEntry,
            "www.microsoft.com",
            null);

        // create a continuation that consumes the result from the DNS query
        Task continuationTask = dnsTask.ContinueWith(antecedent => {
            Console.WriteLine("Result from DNS Task is: {0}", antecedent.Result.HostName);
        });

        // wait for the continuation to complete
        continuationTask.Wait();

        // wait for input before exiting
        Console.WriteLine("Press enter to finish");
        Console.ReadLine();
    }
}
```

You use the Task<T>.Factory.FromAsync method to create a Task from an asynchronous method; the parameters are the Begin method, the End method, the parameters to pass to the Begin method, and a state object. There are overloaded versions with different numbers of parameters to accommodate different Begin method signatures. The result from the FromAsync call in Listing 25-6 is a Task<IPHostEntry>. This Task is used as the antecedent for a continuation Task that consumes the IPHostEntry result from the Task and writes the name of the HostName property to the console.

■ **Tip** The Task that is created when you use the FromAsync method is automatically started. If you call the Start method yourself, you will see an exception complaining that the Task body is null.

Compiling and running Listing 25-6 produces the following results:

```
Result from DNS Task is: lb1.www.ms.akadns.net
Press enter to finish
```

Using Parallel Loops

Parallel loops are another convenience that you can use instead of Tasks. In fact, the parallel loops feature is built using the Task classes seen in Chapter 24. Parallel loops don't contain any features that you couldn't implement yourself using the TPL, but they are a convenient way of solving a particular kind of problem without having to reinvent the wheel. The problem they solve is the sequential nature of regular loops, like the foreach loop. When you perform a foreach loop, each element in the data source is processed in sequence, as illustrated by Figure 25-4.

Figure 25-4. Sequentially processing items in a loop

Creating a Parallel ForEach Loop

The foreach loop is an ideal candidate for parallel execution because the loop executes the same code block for each item in the data source. Parallel loops are created through the System.Threading.Tasks.Parallel class; Listing 25-7 provides a demonstration of a simple parallel foreach loop.

Listing 25-7. A Simple Parallel Foreach Loop

```
using System;
using System.Threading.Tasks;

class Listing_07 {
```

```
static void Main(string[] args) {

    // create a datasource
    string[] fruits = new string[] {"apple", "plum", "cherry",
        "grape", "banana", "pear", "mango"};

    // create a parallel foreach to process each item
    Parallel.ForEach<string>(fruits, dataItem => {
        Console.WriteLine("{0} has {1} characters", dataItem, dataItem.Length);
    });

    // wait for input before exiting
    Console.WriteLine("Press enter to finish");
    Console.ReadLine();
}
}
```

The static `Parallel.ForEach<T>` method creates a parallel foreach loop where each item that will be processed is of type T. In Listing 25-7, the data source is a `string` array, so I have used `Parallel.ForEach<string>`. The parameters for a basic parallel foreach loop are the data source and an `Action` or lambda expression that will be used to process each item, as illustrated by Figure 25-5.

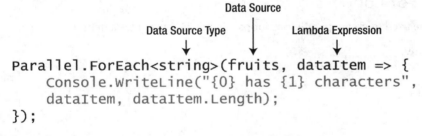

Figure 25-5. The anatomy of a parallel foreach loop

You won't usually need to provide the generic type when creating a parallel loop because the C# will infer the required type from your data source. A parallel foreach loop takes the data source you have provided and breaks it into *chunks*, also known as *partitions* or *regions*. These chunks are then passed to a group of `Task`s which apply the lambda expression or `Action` to each item in their chunk. This process, known as *chunked execution*, is illustrated by Figure 25-6.

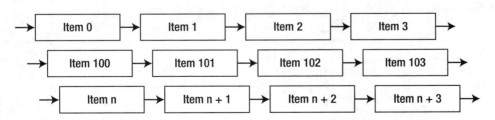

Figure 25-6. Parallel loops and chunked execution

The number of chunks that are created and how many items are in each chunk is determined by the TPL and is intended to take into account the capabilities of the hardware on which the program that created the parallel loop is running. Future versions might be more sophisticated, but as of .NET 4.0, the number of chunks is equal to the number of processors or cores installed. Compiling and running Listing 25-7 produces the following results:

```
apple has 5 characters
cherry has 6 characters
plum has 4 characters
grape has 5 characters
banana has 6 characters
pear has 4 characters
mango has 5 characters
Press enter to finish
```

Notice that the order of the fruit names in the results do not match the order in which they appear in the source array. This is because the chunking means that the first item that some Tasks will process will be part way into the data.

Creating a Parallel For Loop

The Parallel class can also be used to create parallel for loops. Listing 25-8 provides a demonstration.

Listing 25-8. A Parallel For Loop

```csharp
using System;
using System.Threading.Tasks;

class Listing_08 {

    static void Main(string[] args) {

        // create a datasource
        string[] fruits = new string[] { "apple", "plum", "cherry", "grape",
            "banana", "pear", "mango" };

        // create a paralell for loop to process each item
        Parallel.For(0, fruits.Length, dataIndex => {
            Console.WriteLine("{0} has {1} characters", fruits[dataIndex],
                fruits[dataIndex].Length);
        });

        // wait for input before exiting
        Console.WriteLine("Press enter to finish");
        Console.ReadLine();
    }
}
```

The static `Parallel.For` method is used to create a parallel for loop. The parameters are the start index, the (inclusive) end index, and a lambda expression or `Action` that takes an int parameter.

The `Parallel.For` method generates a sequence of int values to cover the range between the start and end parameter values. These are broken into chunks and passed to a set of Tasks. The Tasks then call the lambda expression of `Action` for each of the values in their chunk. A parallel for loop is much like a parallel foreach loop, except that instead of items from a data source, your `Action` is passed an int value as the parameters. This is often used as an index into an array, as demonstrated in Listing 25-8.

Compiling and running Listing 25-8 produces the following output:

```
apple has 5 characters
grape has 5 characters
cherry has 6 characters
banana has 6 characters
plum has 4 characters
mango has 5 characters
pear has 4 characters
Press enter to finish
```

Breaking and Stopping Parallel Loops

In a sequential loop you can choose to terminate early by using the break keyword; the current item or index will be the last that is processed. You can achieve the same effect with parallel loops, although the technique is slightly more complicated than using break.

The `Parallel.For` and `Parallel.ForEach` methods both have overloaded versions in which an instance of `System.Threading.Tasks.ParallelLoopState` is passed to the lambda expression or `Action`. Here is the signature for `Parallel.For`:

```
Parallel.For(0, 100, (int dataIndex, ParallelLoopState loopState) => {
    // ...loop body...
});
```

And here is the corresponding signature for `Parallel.ForEach` (assuming a string array as the data source):

```
string[] dataItems = new string[] { "apple", "plum", "cherry", "grape" };

Parallel.ForEach(dataItems, (string dataItem, ParallelLoopState loopState) => {
    // ...loop body...
}
```

The `ParallelLoopState` class has three members that help terminate loops; these members are described in Table 25-2.

Table 25-2. Selected `ParallelLoopState` *Members*

Member	Description
Stop()	Request that the loop stop execution as soon as possible.
Break()	Request that the loop be stopped as soon as all of the items in the data source up to the current item are processed (foreach loops) or the index values to the current index are processed (for loops).
ShouldExitCurrentIteration	Returns true if the current item or index should be abandoned.

The Stop method is useful when you are looking for a specific result, such as any fruit name in the data source that begins with the letter b. When you call Stop, the Parallel class doesn't start processing any new chunks, but chunks that are already being processed may run to completion, so some items or index values may still be processed after you call the Stop method.

You can reduce the amount of data that is processed following a call to Stop by checking the ShouldExistCurrentIteration property, which will return true if the Stop or Break methods have been called. Listing 25-9 demonstrates stopping a parallel foreach loop.

Listing 25-9. Stopping a Parallel Foreach Loop

```
using System;
using System.Threading.Tasks;

class Listing_09 {

    static void Main(string[] args) {

        // create a datasource
        string[] fruits = new string[] { "apple", "plum", "cherry", "grape",
            "banana", "pear", "mango" , "persimmon", "lemon", "lime", "coconut",
            "pineapple", "orange"};

        // create a parallel loop to process each item
        Parallel.ForEach<string>(fruits, (dataItem, loopstate) => {
            if (dataItem[0] == 'b' || loopstate.ShouldExitCurrentIteration) {
                Console.WriteLine("Found match: {0}", dataItem);
                loopstate.Stop();
            } else {
                Console.WriteLine("{0} has {1} characters", dataItem, dataItem.Length);
            }
        });

        // wait for input before exiting
        Console.WriteLine("Press enter to finish");
        Console.ReadLine();
    }
}
```

The lambda expression used in the foreach loop calls Stop when the current fruit name begins with b or if the ShouldExitCurrentIteration property returns true. Compiling and running Listing 25-9 produces the following result:

```
grape has 5 characters
Found match: banana
mango has 5 characters
apple has 5 characters
Press enter to finish
```

The results show that the grape, mango, and apple items were being processed in parallel with the banana item, which triggered a call to the Stop method. The lambda expression checks the ShouldExitCurrentIteration property frequently, which minimizes the amount of needlessly processed data. To change the lambda expression so that it doesn't check this property, do this:

```
Parallel.ForEach<string>(fruits, (dataItem, loopstate) => {
    if (dataItem[0] == 'b') {
        Console.WriteLine("Found match: {0}", dataItem);
        loopstate.Stop();
    } else {
        Console.WriteLine("{0} has {1} characters", dataItem, dataItem.Length);
    }
});
```

Compiling and running this revised version of Listing 25-9 produces the following output, which shows that more items are processed following the Stop method being called:

```
apple has 5 characters
grape has 5 characters
mango has 5 characters
plum has 4 characters
Found match: banana
persimmon has 9 characters
lime has 4 characters
cherry has 6 characters
orange has 6 characters
Press enter to finish
```

The Break method ensures that at least all of the items that precede the current item are processed—the key term is *at least*, because more data than is required to achieve that goal may be processed. Once again, the use of the ShouldExitCurrentIteration property can help reduce unneeded processing. Listing 25-10 demonstrates the use of the Break method.

Listing 25-10. Breaking a Parallel Foreach Loop

```
using System;
using System.Threading.Tasks;

class Listing_09 {

    static void Main(string[] args) {

        // create a datasource
        string[] fruits = new string[] { "apple", "plum", "cherry", "grape", "banana",
            "pear", "mango" ,"persimmon", "lemon", "lime", "coconut", "pineapple",
            "orange"};

        // create a parallel loop to process each item
        Parallel.ForEach<string>(fruits, (dataItem, loopstate) => {
            if (dataItem[0] == 'b' || loopstate.ShouldExitCurrentIteration) {
                Console.WriteLine("Found match: {0}", dataItem);
                loopstate.Break();
            } else {
                Console.WriteLine("{0} has {1} characters", dataItem, dataItem.Length);
            }
        });

        // wait for input before exiting
        Console.WriteLine("Press enter to finish");
        Console.ReadLine();
    }
}
```

The Break method is called when the banana item is processed (it is the only one that begins with the letter b). This means that all of the items that precede banana in the data source should be processed, even if that means processing chunks that have yet to be started. The output from Listing 25-9 should show that at least the apple, plum, cherry, and grape items should be processed. Compiling and running Listing 25-9 produces the following results:

```
apple has 5 characters
orange has 6 characters
grape has 5 characters
lime has 4 characters
mango has 5 characters
plum has 4 characters
Found match: banana
persimmon has 9 characters
coconut has 7 characters
cherry has 6 characters
Press enter to finish
```

You can see from the output that all of the required items are indeed processed, as well as some additional items that were not required.

Summary

In this chapter, you have learned about two simple alternatives to the Task-based parallel programming seen in Chapter 24. You first looked at asynchronous methods, which pre-date the Task Parallel Library. These methods can be used with library classes that implement Begin and End methods and, via delegates, with any method you are interested in. You also saw how to create a Task from an asynchronous method so that it can be used as the foundation for a continuation chain (see Chapter 24 for details of Task chains).

You also looked at parallel loops, which are built on the TPL and allow you to create parallel versions of the for and foreach loop. These loops can deliver significant performance increases over their sequentially-executed counterparts and are quick and simple to implement.

CHAPTER 26

■ ■ ■

Other Useful Features and Classes

In this chapter, we will cover some C# features and classes that don't really fit into any of the previous chapters but that are worth knowing about nonetheless. There is no common thread that connects these topics, and they are in no particular order. The only common characteristic is that they can save you a lot of time and effort when the need for them arises.

As you become familiar with the thousands of classes in the .NET Framework Class Library, you will find little gems like the ones described in this chapter. In the following sections, I have listed some of those that I have found. Many are widely known and used, but there are a couple that few people seem to know of and employ. Table 26-1 provides the summary for this chapter.

Table 26-1. *Quick Problem/Solution Reference for Chapter 26*

Problem	Solution	Listings
Convert between base types.	Use the Convert class.	26-1
Return multiple results from a method.	Use the Tuple class.	26-2
Make generic type names easier to use.	Alias the generic type with a using statement.	26-3
Create nullable types.	Use the Nullable<T> struct or the T? syntax.	26-4, 26-5
Select a default value when a nullable type is null.	Use the null coalescing operator.	26-6
Read input from the keyboard.	Use the Console class.	26-7
Make a beep noise.	Use the Console class.	26-8
Modify the appearance of the command window.	Use the Console class.	26-9
Generate a nonsecure random number.	Use the Random class.	26-10

Problem	Solution	Listings
Convert strings to bytes and bytes to strings.	Use the Encoding class.	26-11
Get information about the environment a program is running in.	Use the Environment class.	26-12
Perform mathematic operations.	Use the Math class.	26-13
Conditionally include and exclude code statements during compilation.	Use preprocessor symbols and directives.	26-14, 26-15
Check network connectivity.	Use the NetworkInterface class.	26-16
Monitor changes in network connectivity.	Use the NetworkChange class.	26-17

Converting Between Types

The System.Convert class provides convenient support for converting between types and parsing string values to obtain type values. These are tasks that you can do in other ways—implicit and explicit casting, using Parse or TryParse methods, and so on—but the Convert class does all of this in one place and has the benefit of performing overflow checking on numeric types, which means you don't have to remember to do it each time you perform a conversion. The Convert class contains a set of methods that take the form ToXXX, with overloaded versions that take different parameter types for conversion. For example, there is a ToInt32 method with overload versions with different types:

```
ToInt32(bool)
ToInt32(byte)
ToInt32(char)
ToInt32(int)
ToInt32(long)
```

The method names use the name of the type in the System namespace, so to convert a value to an int, you use the ToInt32 method; to convert a value to a long, you use the ToInt64 method; and so on. The set of supported types (and their System namespace equivalents) is as follows: bool (Boolean), char (Char), sbyte (SByte), byte (Byte), short (Int16), int (Int32), long (Int64), ushort (UInt16), uint (UInt32), ulong (UInt64), float (Single), double (Double), decimal (Decimal), DateTime, and string (String).

■ **Tip** If a custom object implements the System.IConvertible interface, it can be converted to one of the base C# types using the Convert class as well.

For each target type, there is a set of overloaded ToXXX methods, with different parameter types for each source type, as illustrated for the ToInt64 method in Figure 26-1.

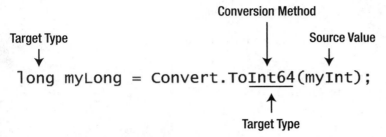

Figure 26-1. The anatomy of a Convert ToXXX method

Listing 26-1 provides a demonstration of using some of these methods.

Listing 26-1. Using the System.Convert Class

```
using System;

class Listing_01 {

    static void Main(string[] args) {

        // define an int value
        int myInt = int.MaxValue;

        // convert the int to a long
        long myLong = Convert.ToInt64(myInt);
        Console.WriteLine("Long value: {0}", myLong);

        // try to represent the int as a byte - this
        // won't work because the value is too large
        try {
            byte myByte = Convert.ToByte(myInt);
        } catch (OverflowException) {
            Console.WriteLine("Got an OverflowException converting to a byte");
        }

        // define a string that contains a numeric value
        string myString = "23";

        // convert the string to an int
        int myParsedInt = Convert.ToInt32(myString);
        Console.WriteLine("Int value: {0}", myParsedInt);

        // convert the string to a float
        float myParsedFloat = Convert.ToSingle(myString);
        Console.WriteLine("Float value: {0}", myParsedFloat);
```

```
        // try to parse a string that doesn't contain a numeric value
        string myBadString = "Hello";
        try {
            int myBadInt = Convert.ToInt32(myBadString);
        } catch (FormatException) {
            Console.WriteLine("Cannot parse {0} to an int", myBadString);
        }

        // wait for input before exiting
        Console.WriteLine("Press enter to finish");
        Console.ReadLine();
    }
}
```

In Listing 26-1, I perform a series of different type conversions using the Convert class. If a conversion can be performed, the ToXXX method returns the value specified by the parameter by using the target type. You can see this happening when I convert from an int to a long:

```
long myLong = Convert.ToInt64(myInt);
```

If the value cannot be represented using the target type, then a System.OverflowException will be thrown, just as we saw with manual overflow checking in Chapter 5. You can see this when I try to convert an int value that is too large to represent as a byte:

```
try {
    byte myByte = Convert.ToByte(myInt);
} catch (OverflowException) {
    Console.WriteLine("Got an OverflowException converting to a byte");
}
```

When you pass a string value to a ToXXX method, the Convert class parses the string to create a value using the target type. If the string can't be parsed, then a System.FormatException is thrown. You can see successful and unsuccessful attempts to parse a string to a float and an int, respectively, in Listing 26-1. Compiling and running Listing 26-1 produces the following output:

```
Long value: 2147483647
Got an OverflowException converting to a byte
Int value: 23
Float value: 23
Cannot parse Hello to an int
Press enter to finish
```

Returning Multiple Results from Methods Using Tuples

There are times where you want to return multiple objects or values as results from a method. We covered creating output parameters using the out keyword in Chapter 9, which would let us create a method like this:

```
public void PerformCalculation(int firstValue,
        int secondValue,
        out int sumResult,
        out int productResult) {

    // calculate the sum
    int sum = firstValue + secondValue;
    // calculate the product
    int product = firstValue * secondValue;
    // pass the results back via the out parameters
    sumResult = sum;
    productResult = product;
}
```

Output parameters work very nicely, but they require a slightly odd syntax when they are called. The variables that will be used to hold the results have to be defined in advance, and the output parameters have to be marked with the out keyword in the method call as well, like this:

```
int sum, product;
PerformCalculation(10, 20, out sum, out product);
```

Another approach would be to create a custom type to contain the various objects or values. We could do this using a struct or class, like this:

```
public struct CalculationResult {
    public int SumResult;
    public int ProductResult;
}

public CalculationResult PerformCalculation(int firstValue, int secondValue) {

    // calculate the sum
    int sum = firstValue + secondValue;
    // calculate the product
    int product = firstValue * secondValue;

    // pass the results back via the struct
    return new CalculationResult() {
        SumResult = sum,
        ProductResult = product
    };
}
```

This feels more natural to me. Using parameters to get results always feels...wrong. It is a very effective technique, but parameters will forever be inputs to me. By creating a struct to contain the results, we avoided using output parameters and got to the same solution. Here's how you would call a method like this:

```
CalculationResult result = PerformCalculation(10, 20);
```

If you want to get this effect but don't want to create a custom type for each result like this you need to return, you can use the System.Tuple class. This is a handy little class that you can use to create generic Tuple objects that contain multiple objects or values. Listing 26-2 provides a demonstration.

Listing 26-2. Using the Tuple Class

```
using System;

class Calculator {

    public Tuple<int, int> PerformCalculation(int firstValue, int secondValue) {

        // calculate the sum
        int sum = firstValue + secondValue;
        // calculate the product
        int product = firstValue * secondValue;

        // create and return a tuple<T, T> to contain the result
        return Tuple.Create(sum, product);
    }
}

class Listing_02 {

    static void Main(string[] args) {

        Tuple<int, int> result = new Calculator().PerformCalculation(10, 20);

        Console.WriteLine("Sum result: {0}, Product result: {1}",
            result.Item1, result.Item2);

        // wait for input before exiting
        Console.WriteLine("Press enter to finish");
        Console.ReadLine();
    }
}
```

You create tuples using the static Create method of the Tuple class. There are overloaded versions that take from one to eight parameters. The Create method returns a generic Tuple object that is strongly typed based on the parameters you passed to the Create method. For example, when I called the Create method with two int values, the result was a Tuple<int, int>, which you can see is the result type from the PerformCalculation method in Listing 26-2.

You can access the objects or values in the tuple using the properties called Item1, Item2, Item3, and so on, where the number of properties corresponds to the number of parameters you passed to the Tuple.Create method.

I tend to use the Tuple class when I am quickly prototyping a solution and don't yet have a firm idea of how the results will be passed around. They are a quick and convenient way of compositing complex results. I avoid using them in methods that other programmers will use, preferring to define a custom type instead.

Aliasing Generic Types

Code can become unwieldy when using generic types. Imagine that we wanted to create a dictionary containing the results from the calculations in Listing 26-2. If we used Tuples<int, int> to store the inputs and the results, we would end up dealing with statements like this:

```
Dictionary<Tuple<int, int>, Tuple<int, int>> myDict
    = new Dictionary<Tuple<int, int>, Tuple<int, int>>();
```

This may seem contrived, but you will find that this kind of nested generic typing is required more often than you'd expect. One way of dealing with this is to use the alias feature of the using keyword. Listing 26-3 contains a demonstration.

Listing 26-3. Aliasing a Complex Generic Type with a using Statement

```
using System;
using System.Collections.Generic;
using ResultCache =
    System.Collections.Generic.Dictionary<System.Tuple<int, int>, System.Tuple<int, int>>;
using ResultTuple = System.Tuple<int, int>;

class Calculator {
    public Tuple<int, int> PerformCalculation(int firstValue, int secondValue) {
        // calculator the sum
        int sum = firstValue + secondValue;
        // calculate the product
        int product = firstValue * secondValue;
        // create and return a tuple<T, T> to contain the result
        return Tuple.Create(sum, product);
    }
}

class Listing_03 {

    static void Main(string[] args) {

        // create the calculator object
        Calculator calc = new Calculator();

        // create the cache using the aliased generic type
        ResultCache myCache = new ResultCache();

        // add some entries to the cache
        myCache.Add(Tuple.Create(10, 20), calc.PerformCalculation(10, 20));
        myCache.Add(Tuple.Create(20, 30), calc.PerformCalculation(20, 30));
        myCache.Add(Tuple.Create(30, 40), calc.PerformCalculation(30, 40));

        // print out the contents of the cache
        foreach (ResultTuple key in myCache.Keys) {
            // get the entry associated with the key
            ResultTuple result = myCache[key];
```

```
            // print out the details
            Console.WriteLine("First value: {0}, Second value: {1}, Sum: {2}, Product: {3}",
                key.Item1, key.Item2, result.Item1, result.Item2);
        }

        // wait for input before exiting
        Console.WriteLine("Press enter to finish");
        Console.ReadLine();
    }
}
```

In Listing 26-3 I have aliased two generic types so that I can refer to them with more convenient names. Once the names are defined, I can use the aliases as substitutes in my code. Compiling and running Listing 26-3 produces the following output:

```
First value: 10, Second value: 20, Sum: 30, Product: 200
First value: 20, Second value: 30, Sum: 50, Product: 600
First value: 30, Second value: 40, Sum: 70, Product: 1200
Press enter to finish
```

In Listing 26-3, I had to specify the fully qualified generic class names when creating the aliases. You can use partially qualified names if you define the alias inside a namespace that is defined after using statements that import the classes you want to use, like this:

```
using System;
using System.Collections.Generic;

namespace MyNameSpace {

    using ResultCache = Dictionary<Tuple<int, int>, Tuple<int, int>>;
    using ResultTuple = Tuple<int, int>;

    class Calculator {
        public Tuple<int, int> PerformCalculation(int firstValue, int secondValue) {
            // calculator the sum
            int sum = firstValue + secondValue;
            // calculate the product
            int product = firstValue * secondValue;
            // create and return a tuple<T, T> to contain the result
            return Tuple.Create(sum, product);
        }
    }
...
```

This is a nice way of tidying up the aliases and making them easier to read if you are using namespaces in your project (and most programmers do).

Using Nullable Types

Nullable types are a wrapper around a base type (such as int, long, or bool) that can represent all the values of a base type or the value null. The null value is usually associated with reference types, but sometimes it can be useful to assign null to a value type. The most common example of this is when you are dealing with a column in a database table that contains a numeric type but that accepts the SQL value NULL. When you read such a value from the database, you need some means of indicating that there is no value available.

You can work with nullable types by creating instances of the System.Nullable<T> struct, as Listing 26-4 demonstrates.

Listing 26-4. Using Nullable<T>

```
using System;

class Listing_04 {

    static void Main(string[] args) {

        Nullable<int> myNullableInt = null;

        // no value has been assigned so far
        Console.WriteLine("Nullable variable - has value: {0}", myNullableInt.HasValue);

        // assign a value
        myNullableInt = 34;
        Console.WriteLine("Nullable variable - has value: {0}, value: {1}",
            myNullableInt.HasValue, myNullableInt.Value );

        // wait for input before exiting
        Console.WriteLine("Press enter to finish");
        Console.ReadLine();
    }
}
```

The Nullable<T>.HasValue property will return true if a non-null value has been assigned and false otherwise. The assigned value can be read using the Value property, but if you try to read this property while the HasValue property returns false, an exception will be thrown. Compiling and running Listing 26-4 produces the following results:

```
Nullable variable - has value: False
Nullable variable - has value: True, value: 34
Press enter to finish
```

You can also refer to nullable properties using the form T?, where T is the base type to be used. For example, a Nullable<int> can be referred to as int?. Listing 26-5 shows the use of this alternative form to rewrite Listing 26-4.

Listing 26-5. Using the T? nullable Form

```
using System;

class Listing_05 {

    static void Main(string[] args) {

        // define some nullable types using T? syntax
        int? myNullableInt = null;

        // no value has been assigned so far
        Console.WriteLine("Nullable variable - has value: {0}", myNullableInt.HasValue);

        // assign a value
        myNullableInt = 34;
        Console.WriteLine("Nullable variable - has value: {0}, value: {1}",
            myNullableInt.HasValue, myNullableInt.Value);

        // wait for input before exiting
        Console.WriteLine("Press enter to finish");
        Console.ReadLine();
    }
}
```

Using the Null-Coalescing Operator

One issue that arises with nullable types is when you come to assign their value to non-nullable type variables, like this:

```
int? myNullable = null;
int myRegularInt = myNullable.Value;
```

The Nullable<int> hasn't been assigned a value that the regular int can represent, so the second statement throws a System.InvalidOperationException. We could address this by testing to see whether a value has been assigned and, if not, assign a value that int can represent, like this:

```
int myRegularInt;
if (myNullable.HasValue) {
    myRegularInt = myNullable.Value;
} else {
    myRegularInt = 0;
}
```

A neater way of achieving the same effect is to use the null-coalescing operator (??), as demonstrated in Listing 26-6.

Listing 26-6. Using the Null-Coalescing Operator

```
using System;

class Listing_06 {

    static void Main(string[] args) {

        int? myNullable = null;

        int myRegularInt = myNullable ?? 0;

        Console.WriteLine("Int value: {0}", myRegularInt);

        // wait for input before exiting
        Console.WriteLine("Press enter to finish");
        Console.ReadLine();
    }
}
```

The null-coalescing operator is used in conjunction with a nullable type, as shown in bold in Listing 26-6. If the nullable type has been assigned a non-null value, then this will be assigned to the int. If the nullable type has been assigned null, then the value to the right of the operator (??) will be assigned to the int instead. In Listing 26-6, the nullable int has been assigned null, so the value to the right is used instead (0). Compiling and running Listing 26-6 produces the following results:

```
Int value: 0
Press enter to finish
```

Working with the Console

Almost every code listing in this book uses the System.Console class at the end of the Main method, like this:

```
Console.WriteLine("Press enter to finish");
Console.ReadLine();
```

But the Console class has more features, as the following sections demonstrate.

Reading from and Writing to the Console

When you create a console application in Visual Studio, the Console class can be exceptionally useful, as the two previous statements demonstrate. The first writes a message for the user to see, and the second reads a line of input from the user. Table 26-2 describes the set of related static methods in the Console class that you can use to read from and write to the console.

Table 26-2. Methods for Reading from and Writing to the Console

Method	Description
Read() ReadLine()	Reads the next input character or the entire line
ReadKey(), ReadKey(bool)	Reads a single key press
Write(bool), Write(char), Write(int), and so on	Writes a string representation of value or object to the console
WriteLine(bool), WriteLine(char), WriteLine(int), and so on	Writes a string representation of value or object, followed by the line terminator, to the console

The Write and WriteLine methods have overloaded versions that accept all the built-in C# types, as well as versions that accept objects and that support composite string formatting. You can read how to create string representations of custom objects and find details of composite formatting in Chapter 16.

The Read and ReadLine methods don't return any data until the user presses the Enter key, at which point the ReadLine method returns the data entered as a string, and the Read method returns a single character. You can call the Read method repeatedly to get the characters entered one by one.

The ReadKey method reads single key press. You don't have to wait until the user presses Enter to get the data. The result of calling the ReadKey method is a ConsoleKeyInfo object, which contains details of the key pressed and any modifier keys that were used (Shift, Ctrl, or Alt). Listing 26-7 provides a demonstration.

Listing 26-7. Using the ReadKey Method

```csharp
using System;

class Listing_07 {

    static void Main(string[] args) {

        Console.WriteLine("Start pressing keys - press 'x' key to stop");

        while (true) {
            // read a key press using the Console class
            ConsoleKeyInfo keyInfo = Console.ReadKey(true);

            // print out the details of the key we have read
            Console.Write("You pressed: ");
            if ((keyInfo.Modifiers & ConsoleModifiers.Alt) != 0) {
                Console.Write("ALT+");
            }
            if ((keyInfo.Modifiers & ConsoleModifiers.Control) != 0) {
```

```
            Console.Write("CONTROL+");
        }
        if ((keyInfo.Modifiers & ConsoleModifiers.Shift) != 0) {
            Console.Write("SHIFT+");
        }
        Console.WriteLine(keyInfo.Key);

        // see if we have to break the loop
        if (keyInfo.KeyChar == 'x') {
            Console.WriteLine("Stoppping");
            break;
        }
    }

    // wait for input before exiting
    Console.WriteLine("Press enter to finish");
    Console.ReadLine();
    }
}
```

I have used the version of the ReadKey method that takes a bool parameter. If the parameter is true, the key press is not echoed to the console screen.

I read the modifiers from the ConsoleKeyInfo struct and check to see whether each of the modifiers defined in the ConsoleModifiers enumeration has been pressed—more than one can be pressed at once, of course, so it is important to test for each value. The ConsoleModifiers enum contains the values Alt, Shift, and Control.

I use the Console.Write method to build up a line of text to display to the user, starting with the modifier keys that have been pressed. I use the ConsoleKeyInfo.Key property to get details of the key that has been pressed. This property returns a value from the ConsoleKey enum, which has values defined for every possible key press and has the nice touch of printing a description of the key pressed when converted to a string, so, for example, the left arrow is described as LeftArrow.

Finally, I check to see whether the x key has been pressed, and if it has, then I break out of the while loop that has been reading key presses. Compiling and running Listing 26-7 (and pressing some keys) produces the following output:

```
Start pressing keys - press 'x' key to stop
You pressed: H
You pressed: E
You pressed: L
You pressed: L
You pressed: O
You pressed: CONTROL+SHIFT+H
You pressed: CONTROL+SHIFT+E
You pressed: CONTROL+SHIFT+L
You pressed: CONTROL+SHIFT+L
You pressed: CONTROL+SHIFT+O
You pressed: X
Stoppping
Press enter to finish
```

Making the Console Beep

You can make a beeping noise using the Console.Beep method. There are two forms of this method, described in Table 26-3.

Table 26-3. Methods for Making Beep Noises

Method	Description
Beep()	Makes a single beep at 800 hertz for 200 milliseconds
Beep(int, int)	Makes a single beep at the specified frequency and duration

Listing 26-8 provides a demonstration of using both forms of the Beep method.

Listing 26-8. Making the Console Beep

```
using System;

class Listing_08 {

    static void Main(string[] args) {

        Console.Beep();

        Console.Beep(850, 200);
        Console.Beep(900, 200);
        Console.Beep(950, 200);

        // wait for input before exiting
        Console.WriteLine("Press enter to finish");
        Console.ReadLine();
    }
}
```

Modifying the Appearance of the Console

The Console class has a number of members that let you control the appearance of the command window that the user sees. Table 26-4 describes some of these members.

Table 26-4. Console Members That Control Command Window Appearance

Member	Description
BackgroundColor	Gets or sets the background color for the console
CursorVisible	Gets or sets whether the console cursor is visible

Member	Description
ForegroundColor	Gets or sets the foreground color for the console
ResetColor()	Resets the foreground and background colors
Title	Sets the title for the console window
WindowHeight	Gets or sets the height of the console window on the screen
WindowLeft	Gets or sets the left position of the console window on the screen
WindowTop	Gets or sets the top position of the console window on the screen
WindowWidth	Gets or sets the width of the console window on the screen

The BackgroundColor and ForegroundColor properties use values from the System.ConsoleColor enum, which defines values for 16 colors: Black, White, Red, and so on. Listing 26-9 demonstrates changing the appearance of the console and then restoring it again.

Listing 26-9. Modifying the Appearance of the Command Window

```
using System;

class Listing_09 {

    static void Main(string[] args) {

        Console.WriteLine("Press Enter to change appearance");
        Console.ReadLine();

        // get the settings that we want to restore to
        int originalWidth = Console.WindowWidth;
        string originalTitle = Console.Title;

        // change the appearance of the console
        Console.BackgroundColor = ConsoleColor.White;
        Console.ForegroundColor = ConsoleColor.Black;
        Console.WindowWidth = 40;
        Console.Title = "Introduction to C#";

        // prompt the user to change things back
        Console.WriteLine("Press Enter to restore appearance");
        Console.ReadLine();

        // reset the appearance
        Console.ResetColor();
```

```
            Console.WindowWidth = originalWidth;
            Console.Title = originalTitle;

            // wait for input before exiting
            Console.WriteLine("Press enter to finish");
            Console.ReadLine();
        }
    }
```

Figure 26-2 shows the result of compiling and running Listing 26-9.

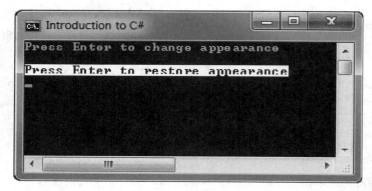

Figure 26-2. A modified command window

Generating Random Numbers

The System.Random class can be used to generate pseudorandom numbers. These are suitable for use in everyday programming but should not be used for cryptographic operations; see Chapter 37 for details of generating secure random numbers. Listing 26-10 demonstrates using the Random class to generate a sequence of numbers.

Listing 26-10. Generating Random Numbers

```
using System;

class Listing_10 {

    static void Main(string[] args) {

        // create a new Random object
        Random myRNG = new Random();

        for (int i = 0; i < 5; i++) {
            Console.WriteLine("Value: {0}", myRNG.Next(100));
        }
```

```
        // wait for input before exiting
        Console.WriteLine("Press enter to finish");
        Console.ReadLine();
    }
}
```

The Random class has a number of methods that you can use to get random numbers in different formats. These methods are described in Table 26-5.

Table 26-5. System.Random Methods

Method	Description
Next()	Returns an int value between 0 and int.MaxValue
Next(int)	Returns an int value between 0 and the specified value
Next(int, int)	Returns an int value between the two specified values
NextBytes(byte[])	Fills the byte array parameter with random values
NextDouble()	Returns a double value between 0 and 1.0

Compiling and running Listing 26-10 produces the following output; obviously the results differ each time the program is run:

```
Value: 73
Value: 12
Value: 13
Value: 86
Value: 64
Press enter to finish
```

Converting Strings to and from Bytes

The System.Text.Encoding class is very useful for converting strings to bytes and back again. Listing 26-11 provides a simple demonstration.

Listing 26-11. Converting a String to Bytes and Back Again

```
using System;
using System.Text;

class Listing_11 {

    static void Main(string[] args) {
```

```
        // get the bytes from the string
        byte[] myBytes = Encoding.ASCII.GetBytes("Hello World");

        // get the string from the bytes
        string myString = Encoding.ASCII.GetString(myBytes);

        Console.WriteLine("String value: {0}", myString);

        // wait for input before exiting
        Console.WriteLine("Press enter to finish");
        Console.ReadLine();
    }
}
```

The Encoding class provides access to a range of text encoding styles. I used ASCII encoding by calling the ASCII property in Listing 26-11 (although there are other encodings available through other Encoding properties). Once you have selected an encoding, the GetBytes method will return the bytes contained in a string, and the GetString will convert the bytes back into a string value. Compiling and running Listing 26-11 produces the following results:

```
String value: Hello World
Press enter to finish
```

Getting Environment Information

The System.Environment class contains members that provide access to the environment in which your program is running. Table 26-6 describes some of the most useful of these members.

Table 26-6. Selected Members of the Environment Class

Member	Description
CurrentDirectory	Gets or sets the current working directory for the program
Exit(int)	Terminates this program and gives the specified exit code to the operating system
GetCommandLineArgs()	Returns a string array containing the command-line arguments used to start the current program
GetEnvironmentVariable(string)	Returns the value for a specified environment variable
GetEnvironmentVariables()	Returns an IDictionary containing all the environment variables

Member	Description
Is64BitOperatingSystem	Returns true if the program is running on a 64-bit version of Windows
Is64BitProcess	Returns true if the current program is a 64-bit program
MachineName	Returns the name of the computer that the program is running on
OSVersion	Returns details of the operating system version the program is running on
ProcessorCount	Returns the number of processors in the computer that the program is running on
User	Returns the name of the user account under which the program is running
SetEnvironmentVariable(string, string)	Sets the environment variable specified by the first parameter to the value specified by the second parameter
Version	Returns details of the version of the .NET runtime that the program is running on

Listing 26-12 demonstrates using some of these members.

Listing 26-12. Using the System.Environment Class

```
using System;

class Listing_12 {

    static void Main(string[] args) {

        Console.WriteLine("64 bit OS? {0}", Environment.Is64BitOperatingSystem);
        Console.WriteLine("64 bit program? {0}", Environment.Is64BitProcess);
        Console.WriteLine("Machine name: {0}", Environment.MachineName);
        Console.WriteLine("Processor count: {0}", Environment.ProcessorCount);
        Console.WriteLine("User: {0}", Environment.UserName);
        Console.WriteLine("Version: {0}", Environment.Version);

        // wait for input before exiting
        Console.WriteLine("Press enter to finish");
        Console.ReadLine();
    }
}
```

Compiling and running Listing 26-12 on my computer produces the following results:

```
64 bit OS? True
64 bit program? True
Machine name: SHUTTLE
Processor count: 4
User: Adam
Version: 4.0.30319.1
Press enter to finish
```

Performing Math Operations

I showed you how to perform simple calculations in Chapter 5, but for more advanced math functions, we can use the System.Math class. The most useful members are described in Table 26-7.

Table 26-7. Selected Members of the System.Math Class

Member	Description
E	Returns the natural logarithmic base as a double.
PI	Returns the value of pi as a double.
Ceiling(double)	Returns the smallest integer larger than the specified value.
Cos(double)	Returns the cosine of the specified angle, expressed in radians.
Exp(double)	Returns e raised to the specified power.
Floor(double)	Returns the largest integer smaller than the specified value.
Log(double)	Returns the natural logarithm of the specified value.
Log10(double)	Returns the base 10 logarithm of the specified value.
Max(int, int)	Returns the larger of the two specified values. There are overloaded versions of this method that accept all the built-in numeric types.
Min(int, int)	Returns the smaller of the two specified values. There are overloaded versions of this method that accept all the built-in numeric types.
Round(double)	Rounds the specified number to the nearest integer
Sin(double)	Returns the sine of the specified angle, expressed in radians.
Tan(double)	Returns the tangent of the specified angle, expressed in radians.

Member	Description
Truncate(double)	Discards any fractional digits and returns the integer component of the specified value.

Listing 26-13 demonstrates the use of some of these methods.

Listing 26-13. Using the Math Class

```
using System;

class Listing_13 {

    static void Main(string[] args) {

        double myDouble = 123.456;

        Console.WriteLine("Ceiling: {0}", Math.Ceiling(myDouble));
        Console.WriteLine("Floor: {0}", Math.Floor(myDouble));
        Console.WriteLine("Max from {0}, {1}: {2}", 10, 20, Math.Max(10, 20));
        Console.WriteLine("Min from {0}, {1}: {2}", 10, 20, Math.Min(10, 20));
        Console.WriteLine("Round: {0}", Math.Round(myDouble));
        Console.WriteLine("Truncate: {0}", Math.Truncate(myDouble));

        // wait for input before exiting
        Console.WriteLine("Press enter to finish");
        Console.ReadLine();
    }
}
```

Compiling and running Listing 26-13 produces the following results:

```
Ceiling: 124
Floor: 123
Max from 10, 20: 20
Min from 10, 20: 10
Round: 123
Truncate: 123
Press enter to finish
```

Using Conditional Compilation

The C# compiler supports a set of preprocessor directives that you can use to include or exclude methods or individual code statements from the compiled output of your program. Listing 26-14 provides a demonstration.

Listing 26-14. Using Preprocessor Directives

```csharp
#define PRINT_CALC_DETAILS

using System;

class Listing_14 {

    static void Main(string[] args) {

        // perform some calculations
        int sumResult = CalculateSum(10, 20);
        Console.WriteLine("Sum result: {0}", sumResult);

        // wait for input before exiting
        Console.WriteLine("Press enter to finish");
        Console.ReadLine();
    }

    public static int CalculateSum(int firstValue, int secondValue) {
#if PRINT_CALC_DETAILS
        PrintOutCalculationDetails("sum", firstValue, secondValue);
#endif
        return firstValue + secondValue;
    }

    private static void PrintOutCalculationDetails(string calcType, params int[] values) {
        Console.Write("Calculation type: {0} ", calcType);
        foreach (int value in values) {
            Console.Write("{0} ", value);
        }
        Console.WriteLine();
    }
}
```

The first line in Listing 26-14 is a preprocessor directive, in this case #define. All preprocessor directives begin with a number symbol (#). The #define directive defines a symbol, which allows us to define conditions for the compiler to evaluate. This symbol is called PRINT_CALC_DETAILS. You can call your symbols whatever makes sense in the context of your program, but the convention is that they be uppercase. The #define symbol must be used before regular code statements in your code file.

You can see some more directives in the CalculateSum method: #if and #endif. The code statements between these two directives will be included in the compiled output if the symbol named next to the #if directive has been defined. If we compile and run Listing 26-14, we get the following results:

```
Calculation type: sum 10 20
Sum result: 30
Press enter to finish
```

You can see that the call to the `PrintOutCalculationDetails` method is performed. This is because the `PRINT_CALC_DETAILS` symbol is defined. We can change the behavior of the `#if` directive by commenting out the `#define` directive, like this:

```
//#define PRINT_CALC_DETAILS
```

Compiling and running the example without the `#define` directive produces the following result:

```
Sum result: 30
Press enter to finish
```

You can see that the call to the `PrintOutCalculationDetails` method has been ignored by the compiler. Our code file isn't modified; the call still exists in the C# file, but as long as the `#define` directive is commented out, the `#if` and `#endif` directives will prevent the method call from being included in the compiled output.

Using Visual Studio to Define Symbols

The `#define` directive only affects the code file in which it is used. You can use the Visual Studio project settings to define symbols that will affect all the code files in your project. In the Solution Explorer window, right-click your project, and select the Properties item from the pop-up menu. Click the Build table on the left side of the display, as shown in Figure 26-3.

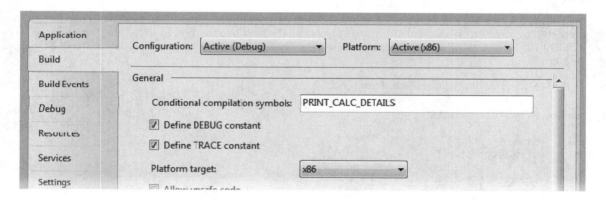

Figure 26-3. Defining a project-wide preprocessor symbol

Enter the name of the symbol that you want to define in the text box, and save the changes. When you compile and run the project, the symbol you have defined will be applied to all the code files in the project. If you don't want to define the symbol, then simply remove it from the text box and recompile.

You can see from Figure 26-3 that Visual Studio has check boxes that allow you to define the `DEBUG` and `TRACE` symbols. We'll have more to say about these in Chapter 38, but for the moment, it is helpful to know that you can use these in your code. When you switch the build configuration from Debug to

Release (see the drop-down menu at the top of Figure 26-3), the check box for the DEBUG symbol is unchecked, as shown by Figure 26-4.

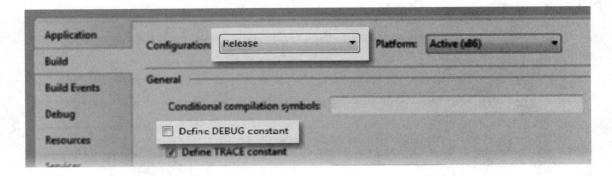

Figure 26-4. *The disabled DEBUG symbol*

You can use this feature to include and exclude statements depending on your build configuration by using the #if DEBUG directive.

Conditionally Compiling Methods

In Listing 26-14, I used a directive to control conditional compilation of a call to a method. It can be pretty tedious and error-prone to apply directives to all the calls of a method in a real program. A more efficient way of achieving the same effect is to use the Conditional attribute, as demonstrated by Listing 26-15.

Listing 26-15. Using the Conditional Attribute

```
#define PRINT_CALC_DETAILS

using System;
using System.Diagnostics;

class Listing_15 {

    static void Main(string[] args) {

        // perform some calculations
        int sumResult = CalculateSum(10, 20);
        Console.WriteLine("Sum result: {0}", sumResult);
        int productResult = CalculateProduct(10, 20);
        Console.WriteLine("Product result: {0}", productResult);

        // wait for input before exiting
        Console.WriteLine("Press enter to finish");
        Console.ReadLine();
```

```
    }

    public static int CalculateSum(int firstValue, int secondValue) {
        PrintOutCalculationDetails("sum", firstValue, secondValue);
        return firstValue + secondValue;
    }

    public static int CalculateProduct(int firstValue, int secondValue) {
        PrintOutCalculationDetails("product", firstValue, secondValue);
        return firstValue * secondValue;
    }

    [Conditional("PRINT_CALC_DETAILS")]
    private static void PrintOutCalculationDetails(string calcType, params int[] values) {
        Console.Write("Calculation type: {0} ", calcType);
        foreach (int value in values) {
            Console.Write("{0} ", value);
        }
        Console.WriteLine();
    }
}
```

The Conditional attribute can be found in the System.Diagnostics namespace and can be applied only to methods. The parameter for the attribute is the name of the symbol that you want to check for, expressed as a string. In Listing 26-15, the use of the PrintOutCalculationDetails method is contingent on the PRINT_CALC_DETAILS symbol being defined. If the symbol is not defined, then the method will not be called, and references to the method will be ignored. You can only apply the Conditional attribute to methods that don't return a result, that is, methods that are defined using the void keyword. If we compile and run Listing 26-15 with the symbol defined (as shown earlier), we get the following results:

```
Calculation type: sum 10 20
Sum result: 30
Calculation type: product 10 20
Product result: 200
Press enter to finish
```

If we comment out the #define directive and compile and run Listing 26-15 again, we get different results:

```
Sum result: 30
Product result: 200
Press enter to finish
```

Checking Network Connectivity

A useful feature when using the network programming techniques we covered in Chapter 21 is to be able to determine whether there is network connectivity available before starting a network operation. We can do this using the NetworkInterface class in the System.Net.NetInformation namespace, as demonstrated by Listing 26-16.

Listing 26-16. Obtaining Connectivity Information

```
using System;
using System.Net.NetworkInformation;

class Listing_16 {

    static void Main(string[] args) {

        // check the overall connectivity
        bool isNetworkAvailable = NetworkInterface.GetIsNetworkAvailable();

        // enumerate the status of individual interfaces
        NetworkInterface[] myInterfaces = NetworkInterface.GetAllNetworkInterfaces();
        foreach (NetworkInterface networkInterface in myInterfaces) {
            if (networkInterface.OperationalStatus == OperationalStatus.Up) {
                Console.WriteLine("Name: {0}, Type: {1}, Avalable: {2}",
                    networkInterface.Name,
                    networkInterface.NetworkInterfaceType,
                    networkInterface.OperationalStatus);
            }
        }

        // wait for input before exiting
        Console.WriteLine("Press enter to finish");
        Console.ReadLine();
    }
}
```

If you care that there is network connectivity but don't care about which interfaces are operational, then the static GetIsNetworkAvailable method can be of great use. It returns true if there is at least one operational network interface and false if there is not. If you care about specific interfaces being available, then you can obtain an array of NetworkInterface objects by calling the static GetAllNetworkInterfaces method. The array contains one NetworkInterface object for each of the network interfaces on the current machine. The NetworkInteface class contains a number of useful properties that can be used to get information about an interface. The most useful of these is described in Table 26-8.

Table 26-8. Selected Properties of the NetworkInterface Class

Property	Description
Description	Returns a string that describes the current interface
Name	Returns the name assigned to the current interface
NetworkInterfaceType	Returns a value from the NetworkInterfaceType enumeration that describes the type of the current interface
OperationalStatus	Returns a value from the OperationalStatus enumeration that describes the state of the current interface
Speed	Returns the speed of the current interface as a long, representing the number of bits per second

The OperationalStatus enumeration defines values for different status conditions. The most useful for this example are Up and Down, which we can use to determine the overall state of each interface. Compiling and running Listing 26-16 produces the following output, which reports on the overall connectivity and prints out a list of the active interfaces on my computer:

```
Name: StrongVPN, Type: Ppp, Avalable: Up
Name: Local Area Connection, Type: Ethernet, Avalable: Up
Name: Loopback Pseudo-Interface 1, Type: Loopback, Available: Up
Name: Local Area Connection* 9, Type: Tunnel, Available: Up
Name: 6TO4 Adapter, Type: Tunnel, Avalable: Up
Press enter to finish
```

Some of the interfaces returned by the GetAllNetworkInterfaces method are logical or software interfaces. For example, you can see from the first line of the results of running Listing 26-16 that I use a commercial VPN service, which is reported as a Ppp interface. The NetworkInterfaceType enumeration contains values for a wide range of interface types. The most commonly encountered are Ethernet, Ppp, and Tunnel, but many more are defined.

Listening for Connectivity Changes

You can use the NetworkChange class if you need to be notified when there is a change in network connectivity. This class defines the NetworkAvailabilityChanged event, which is triggered when the overall connectivity status changes, as demonstrated by Listing 26-17.

Listing 26-17. Listening for Connectivity Changes

```
using System;
using System.Net.NetworkInformation;

class Listing_17 {

    static void Main(string[] args) {

        // register a handler with the connectivity change event
        NetworkChange.NetworkAvailabilityChanged += (sender, e) => {
            Console.WriteLine("Connectivity Changed - network available? {0}",
                e.IsAvailable);
        };

        // wait for input before exiting
        Console.WriteLine("Press enter to finish");
        Console.ReadLine();
    }
}
```

The event information is passed to your handler using a `NetworkAvailabilityEventArgs` object, which has a property called `IsAvailable`. This property returns `true` if there is at least one connected network interface and `false` otherwise. Compiling and running Listing 26-17 (and disabling and enabling my Ethernet interface) produces the following result:

```
Press enter to finish
Connectivity Changed - network available? False
Connectivity Changed - network available? True
```

Summary

In this chapter, we covered a wide range of topics that don't really fit into the previous chapter. Sometimes, there is a poor fit because the technique or class mixes different techniques or because the feature is slightly too advanced for an introduction, but what all of these topics have in common is that they can be exceptionally useful under the right circumstances. Every programmer has their collection of favorite language tricks; in this chapter, I have shown you some of mine.

PART 4

■ ■ ■

Data and Databases

One of my favorite .NET features is the Language Integrated Query (LINQ) support, which provides a system for performing queries on a wide range of different data sources. There are special keywords in C# to support LINQ to make the queries similar to SQL, which is a bonus if you have done any previous work on relational database.

A big part of the value of LINQ is the way you can use the same kinds of queries on different types of data, including C# objects, XML documents, and databases. Once you have mastered the basic features of LINQ, you can apply them again and again to handle different types of data from different data sources.

In this part of the book, we will use LINQ as the platform for exploring techniques for working with different sources of data. In Chapter 27, I introduce LINQ and demonstrate how it can be used to process groups of C# objects, such as arrays and collection classes. In Chapter 28, I will show you how to use some of the features of the Task Parallel Library we saw in Chapter 24 in order to perform parallel LINQ queries (known as PLINQ). In Chapter 29, you will see how LINQ can be used to make processing and creating XML data simple and fast. In Chapters 30 and 31, I demonstrate how to use LINQ two different database technologies. .NET has a number of different approaches for working with databases, and I'll show you how to set up and use two of these: the Entity Framework and DataSets.

CHAPTER 27

■ ■ ■

LINQ to Objects

LINQ—which stands for *Language Integrated Query* and is pronounced as "link"—allows you to query almost any data using SQL-like syntax, even if the data isn't in a database. This may not sound like a particularly useful idea at first, but once you start using LINQ, you won't know how you managed without it. LINQ is one of my two favorite features of C# (the other being the parallel programming features covered in Chapter 24), and I find it endlessly useful.

LINQ can operate on a range of different data sources. When LINQ operates on a specific kind of data source, the term LINQ is joined to the data source type with the word *to*, so when LINQ is applied to objects in your program, you are using *LINQ to Objects*. When querying XML data, you are using *LINQ to XML*, and so on.

In this chapter, I'll introduce you to the basics of LINQ syntax and introduce you to LINQ to Objects, that is, performing LINQ queries on collections of objects in your program. In the following chapters, you'll see how LINQ can be used to query XML data and, as you might expect, databases.

LINQ is a big topic, and I can only scratch the surface in this book. In fact, LINQ has so many features that Joe Rattz and I have written an 800-page book just on LINQ. It is called *Pro LINQ in C# 2010* and is also published by Apress.

Table 27-1 provides the summary for this chapter.

Table 27-1. Quick Problem/Solution Reference for Chapter 27

Problem	Solution	Listings
Query a set of objects.	Use LINQ to query an IEnumerable<T> implementation and enumerate the results.	27-1 through 27-5
Cast the items contained in a data source to a different type.	Declare an explicit type for the query range variable.	27-6
Let the compiler infer the types in a LINQ query.	Use the var keyword in place of specific type names.	27-7
Filter data.	Use a where clause.	27-8, 27-9
Project data.	Use a select clause.	27-10 through 27-13
Sort data.	Use an orderby clause.	27-14 through 27-17

Problem	Solution	Listings
Group data.	Use a groupby clause.	27-18 through 27-21
Use LINQ features for which there are no keywords.	Use method syntax.	27-22, 27-23
Reuse a query.	Enumerate the results each time you want the query to be performed.	27-24, 27-25
Force a query to execute immediately.	Use an extension method that requires the results to be enumerated in order to produce a result; for example, use an aggregation method.	27-26, 27-27
Convert the results to a collection or an array.	Use a conversion extension method.	27-28
Use a legacy collection as a data source.	Explicitly type the query range variable, or use the Cast or OfType extension methods.	27-29 through 27-31
Aggregate data.	Use one of the aggregation extension methods.	27-32 through 27-33
Join data.	Use a join clause.	27-34
Combine data sources.	Define an additional range variable.	27-35, 27-36

Performing a Simple LINQ Query

The best place to start with LINQ is with an example. Listing 27-1 demonstrates the simplest LINQ query, which is to select all the items in a data source. To use LINQ in a project, you will need to import the System.Linq and System.Collections.Generic namespaces.

Listing 27-1. Performing a LINQ Query

```
using System;
using System.Collections.Generic;
using System.Linq;

class Listing_01 {

    static void Main(string[] args) {

        string[] fruits = new string[] { "apple", "plum", "cherry",
            "grape", "banana", "pear", "mango" , "persimmon", "lemon",
            "lime", "coconut", "pineapple", "orange"};
```

```
IEnumerable<string> results = from e in fruits
                             select e;

foreach (string str in results) {
    Console.WriteLine("Result item: {0}", str);
}

// wait for input before exiting
Console.WriteLine("Press enter to finish");
Console.ReadLine();
    }
}
```

Basic LINQ queries follow a standard format; there are three keywords (from, in, and select), which are used to delineate the data source, a range variable, and a selection, as well as to create a result. Figure 27-1 illustrates these elements.

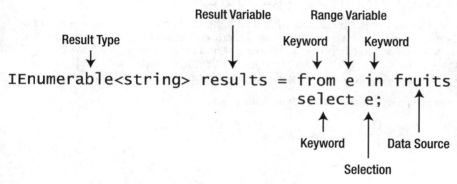

Figure 27-1. *The anatomy of a basic LINQ query*

The from keyword tells the C# compiler that this is the start of LINQ query. The *range variable* is similar to the variable in a foreach loop and will be assigned each item in the data source in turn as the query is executed. You can use any name for the range variable, but the convention is to use a single letter. The in keyword is followed by the data source that you want to query. In Listing 27-1, this is a string array called fruits.

LINQ will work its way through the items in the data source and assign each item in turn to the range variable e. The select keyword specifies what should be added to the result for that item. In the example, I have selected e, which tells LINQ that each value of e should be added to the results.

The result of a LINQ query is an IEnumerable<T>, where T is the data type of whatever you select in the query (we'll come to selecting different things later). In Listing 27-1, the result is an IEnumerable<string> because I am selecting e, which is a string (because the data source is a string array).

After defining the query, I use a foreach loop to print out the results. Since I have selected each value assigned to the range variable, the names of all the fruits in the data source should be printed out. Compiling and running Listing 27-1 produces the following results; you can see that each item in the data source is represented in the same order in which they are defined in the data source:

```
Result item: apple
Result item: plum
Result item: cherry
Result item: grape
Result item: banana
Result item: pear
Result item: mango
Result item: persimmon
Result item: lemon
Result item: lime
Result item: coconut
Result item: pineapple
Result item: orange
Press enter to finish
```

Understanding LINQ to Objects Data Sources

LINQ to Objects can work with any data source that implements the IEnumerable<T> interface from the System.Collections.Generic namespace. This includes the generic collection classes (discussed in Chapter 19) and C# arrays (discussed in Chapter 13). (We will see other data sources, such XML documents and databases in the following chapters.) Listing 27-1 demonstrated using a string array as a data source; Listing 27-2 shows the same query but with the data elements contained in a List<string>.

Listing 27-2. Using a Collection as a LINQ to Object Data Source

```
using System;
using System.Collections.Generic;
using System.Linq;

class Listing_02 {

    static void Main(string[] args) {

        List<string> myFruitList = new List<string>() {
            "apple", "plum", "cherry", "grape", "banana", "pear", "mango" ,
            "persimmon", "lemon", "lime", "coconut", "pineapple", "orange"};

        IEnumerable<string> results = from e in myFruitList
                                      select e;

        foreach (string str in results) {
            Console.WriteLine("Result item: {0}", str);
        }

        // wait for input before exiting
        Console.WriteLine("Press enter to finish");
        Console.ReadLine();
    }
}
```

Listing 27-2 is equivalent to Listing 27-1. The List<T> class keeps a set of items in sequence that produces the same effect as using an array. The generic collection classes provide a wide range of implementations of IEnumerable<T>, either directly through collection classes that implement this interface (such as List<T>) or through members that return objects that implement IEnumerable<T> (such as the Keys and Values properties of the Dictionary<Key, Value> class).

The generic type named in the IEnumerable<T> used as the data source determines the type of the range variable. If you use an IEnumerable<MyObject>, then the range variable will be of the type MyObject as well, and you can refer to the members of MyObject when referring to the range variable in your query; see the "Performing LINQ Operations" section for examples of using range variable type members in queries.

■ **Tip** You can use the nongeneric legacy collection classes as data sources with just a little preparatory work to help tell LINQ what data type is contained in the collection. See the "Using Legacy Collections as LINQ Data Sources" section later in this chapter.

Understanding Query Results

The IEnumerable<T> interface contains a single method called GetEnumerator, which returns an implementation of the IEnumerator<T> interface. The most common use of IEnumerable<T> is with a foreach loop (as you have seen in the examples so far in this chapter).

■ **Tip** Most queries are not executed until you start to enumerate the results. See "Understanding Deferred Execution" later in this chapter for more information.

Enumerating Results Manually

You can work directly with the IEnumerator<T> implementation if you prefer. The members of the IEnumerator<T> interface are described in Table 27-2.

Table 27-2. Members of the IEnumerator<T> Interface

Member	Description
Current	Returns the current item
MoveNext()	Moves to the next position in the sequence and returns true if there is another item to be read, false if the end of the sequence has been reached
Reset()	Resets the enumeration to its original state

Listing 27-3 demonstrates using GetEnumerator method of the IEnumerable<T> interface to get an implementation of IEnumerator<T> and enumerating the contents manually. This is an unusual thing to do, but I have included it for completeness.

Listing 27-3. Manually Enumerating Query Results

```
using System;
using System.Collections.Generic;
using System.Linq;

class Listing_03 {

    static void Main(string[] args) {

        List<string> myFruitList = new List<string>() {
            "apple", "plum", "cherry", "grape", "banana", "pear", "mango" ,
            "persimmon", "lemon", "lime", "coconut", "pineapple", "orange"};

        IEnumerable<string> results = from string e in myFruitList
                                      select e;

        // get the IEnumerator<T> from the IEnumerable<T>
        IEnumerator<string> myEnumerator = results.GetEnumerator();

        while (myEnumerator.MoveNext()) {
            Console.WriteLine("Result item: {0}", myEnumerator.Current);
        }

        // wait for input before exiting
        Console.WriteLine("Press enter to finish");
        Console.ReadLine();
    }
}
```

You can see the manual enumeration statements marked in bold in Listing 27-3. The MoveNext method moves a cursor through the sequence of items in the results. The cursor starts immediately before the first item, meaning that you must call the MoveNext method before you read the Current property.

Using Results as Data Sources

You can use any implementation of IEnumerable<T> as a data source, and since the result of a LINQ query is an IEnumerable<T>, you can use the results produced by one query as the data source for another. Listing 27-4 provides a demonstration.

Listing 27-4. Using the Results of One Query as the Data Source for Another

```
using System;
using System.Collections.Generic;
using System.Linq;
```

```
class Listing_04 {

    static void Main(string[] args) {

        List<string> myFruitList = new List<string>() {
            "apple", "plum", "cherry", "grape", "banana", "pear", "mango" ,
            "persimmon", "lemon", "lime", "coconut", "pineapple", "orange"};

        // define the first query
        IEnumerable<string> results = from e in myFruitList
                                      select e;

        // define a second query using the results from the
        // first query as the data source
        IEnumerable<string> results2 = from e in results
                                       select e;

        // enumerate the results
        foreach (string str in results2) {
            Console.WriteLine("Result item: {0}", str);
        }

        // wait for input before exiting
        Console.WriteLine("Press enter to finish");
        Console.ReadLine();
    }
}
```

The first query selects all the items in the myFruitList data source. The second query selects all the items in the results from the first query (which, admittedly, is the same thing; we'll come onto some more interesting operations later in the chapter). Compiling and running Listing 27-3 produces the following results:

```
Result item: apple
Result item: plum
Result item: cherry
Result item: grape
Result item: banana
Result item: pear
Result item: mango
Result item: persimmon
Result item: lemon
Result item: lime
Result item: coconut
Result item: pineapple
Result item: orange
Press enter to finish
```

Understanding Query Types

One of the most confusing aspects of LINQ to programmers new to the topic is the relationship between the different C# types used in a LINQ query. In this section, I'll show you how LINQ infers types from a query.

The Range Variable Type

LINQ infers the type of the range variable from the generic type of the data source. In Listing 27-4, for example, I used a `List<string>` as the data source, so LINQ infers from this that the range variable must also be a string. This is illustrated in Figure 27-2.

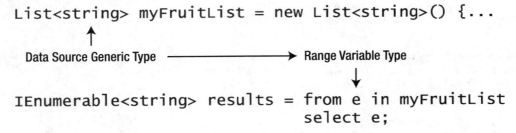

Figure 27-2. The relationship between the data source generic type and the range variable type

If you are unsure of the inferred type for the range variable, you can place the mouse pointer above the range variable, and a pop-up window will tell you what the type is, as demonstrated by Figure 27-3.

```
// define the first query
IEnumerable<string> results = from e in myFruitList
                              selec┌─────────────────────────┐
                                   │ (range variable) string e │
                                   └─────────────────────────┘
// define a second query using the results from the
// first query as the data source
```

Figure 27-3. Seeing the inferred type in Visual Studio 2010

The Result Type

The generic type of the result `IEnumerable<T>` is determined by the `select` clause in a LINQ query. In all the examples so far in this chapter, my `select` clause has been `select e`, which selects the object assigned to the range variable. This has meant that when my data source has been an `IEnumerable<string>` or `IEnumerable<MyClass>`, my results have also been `IEnumerable<string>` or `IEnumerable<MyClass>`. However, as we will see when we look at LINQ operations, you can be more specific in what you select (also known as *projecting*). Listing 27-5 contains an example that projects the first character from each fruit name.

Listing 27-5. Selecting a Character from a String

```
using System;
using System.Collections.Generic;
using System.Linq;

class Listing_05 {

    static void Main(string[] args) {

        // define the collection
        string[] fruits = new string[] { "apple", "plum", "cherry",
            "grape", "banana", "pear", "mango" , "persimmon", "lemon",
            "lime", "coconut", "pineapple", "orange"};

        // define the query
        IEnumerable<char> results = from e in fruits
                                    select e[0];

        // enumerate the results
        foreach (char c in results) {
            Console.WriteLine("Result item: {0}", c);
        }

        // wait for input before exiting
        Console.WriteLine("Press enter to finish");
        Console.ReadLine();
    }
}
```

You can see that the select clause in the query in Listing 27-5 is select e[0]. We know that the data source contains string values, which means that the result of using an indexer will be a char. Hence, the result type for the query will be an IEnumerable<char>. The relationship between the select clause and the generic type of the result enumeration is shown in Figure 27-4.

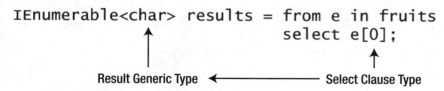

Figure 27-4. The relationship between the select type and the result enumeration generic type

Compiling and running Listing 27-5 produces the following results:

```
Result item: a
Result item: p
```

```
Result item: c
Result item: g
Result item: b
Result item: p
Result item: m
Result item: p
Result item: l
Result item: l
Result item: c
Result item: p
Result item: o
Press enter to finish
```

Explicitly Specifying the Range Variable Type

There will be occasions when you don't want the range variable to be inferred from the data source—for example, when you know that a collection whose generic type is a base class of the type that it actually contains. In these situations, you can explicitly specify the type of the range variable, and LINQ will try to cast each item in the data source to the type you have specified. Listing 27-6 contains a demonstration.

Listing 27-6. Explicitly Specifying a Range Variable Type

```
using System;
using System.Collections.Generic;
using System.Linq;

public class Fruit {

    public Fruit(string name) {
        Name = name;
    }

    public string Name { get; set; }
}

public class RedFruit : Fruit {

    public RedFruit(string name, string size)
        : base(name) {
        Size = size;
    }

    public string Size { get; set; }

    public override string ToString() {
        return string.Format("Name: {0}, Size: {0}", Name, Size);
    }
}
```

```
class Listing_06 {

    static void Main(string[] args) {

        // create a collection of RedFruits, but assign them to a Fruit collection
        List<Fruit> myFruitList = new List<Fruit> {
            new RedFruit("cherry", "small"),
            new RedFruit("apple", "large"),
            new RedFruit("plum", "medium")
        };

        // define the query, explicitly specifying the range variable type
        IEnumerable<RedFruit> results = from RedFruit e in myFruitList
                                        select e;

        // enumerate the results
        foreach (RedFruit rf in results) {
            Console.WriteLine("Result: {0}", rf);
        }

        // wait for input before exiting
        Console.WriteLine("Press enter to finish");
        Console.ReadLine();
    }
}
```

In Listing 27-6, the RedFruit class is derived from the Fruit class. I create a List<Fruit> but populate it with RedFruit objects. In the LINQ query, I explicitly specify the type for the range variable by putting the type in front of the variable name. This is marked in bold in the listing. When the query is executed, LINQ will cast each Fruit object it gets from the data source to a RedFruit and assign the object to the range variable. When using this technique, you must ensure that all the objects in the data source can be cast to the type you have specified. If not, an exception will be thrown when the query is executed.

Letting the Compiler Infer Types

You can let the C# compiler infer the types for the data source and result generic types by using the var keyword. Listing 27-7 shows you how this is done.

Listing 27-7. Using Compiler-Inferred Types

```
using System;
using System.Collections.Generic;
using System.Linq;

class Listing_07 {

    static void Main(string[] args) {
```

```
        // define the collection
        var fruits = new string[] { "apple", "plum", "cherry",
            "grape", "banana", "pear", "mango" , "persimmon", "lemon",
            "lime", "coconut", "pineapple", "orange"};

        // define the query
        var results = from e in fruits
                        select e[0];

        // enumerate the results
        foreach (char c in results) {
            Console.WriteLine("Result item: {0}", c);
        }

        // wait for input before exiting
        Console.WriteLine("Press enter to finish");
        Console.ReadLine();
    }
}
```

The var keyword is used in place of a C# local variable type. It doesn't change the type of the object that is assigned to the variable; it just asks the compiler to infer the type for you. If you position the mouse pointer over var in Visual Studio, the type that has been inferred will be shown, as illustrated by Figure 27-5.

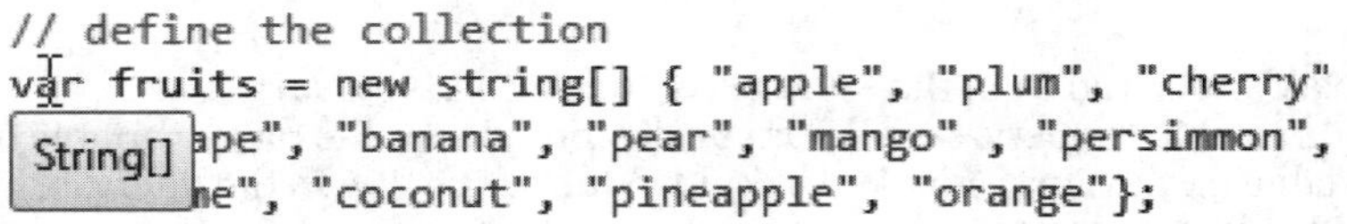

```
// define the collection
var fruits = new string[] { "apple", "plum", "cherry"
  String[] ape", "banana", "pear", "mango" , "persimmon",
        me", "coconut", "pineapple", "orange"};
```

Figure 27-5. Seeing the inferred type in Visual Studio 2010

I have used var for both the data source and the results in Listing 27-7. Compiling and running this listing produces the same results as when I had defined the variable types explicitly. You can see further examples of using var in Chapter 15 and later in this chapter when we look at LINQ operations.

Performing LINQ Operations

In the previous sections, we saw how a very basic LINQ query is a constructor, how types are inferred (or specified if you prefer), and the role of the data source and the results. The query we looked at was pretty useless. It simply copied each element from the data source to the results. In this section, we will see how to perform some more useful queries and start to see the power and flexibility of LINQ.

Filtering Data

You can filter the items in a data source by using the where keyword and specifying a condition defined using the range variable. Each element in the data source is assigned to the range variable in turn and evaluated using the where clause condition. Those that return true are added to the results. Listing 27-8 provides a demonstration.

Listing 27-8. Filtering Data

```
using System;
using System.Collections.Generic;
using System.Linq;

class Listing_08 {

    static void Main(string[] args) {

        List<string> myFruitList = new List<string>() {
            "apple", "plum", "cherry", "grape", "banana", "pear", "mango" ,
            "persimmon", "lemon", "lime", "coconut", "pineapple", "orange"};

        IEnumerable<string> results = from e in myFruitList
                                      where e[0] == 'p'
                                      select e;

        foreach (string str in results) {
            Console.WriteLine("Result item: {0}", str);
        }

        // wait for input before exiting
        Console.WriteLine("Press enter to finish");
        Console.ReadLine();
    }
}
```

The where clause in the query in Listing 27-8 filters the data items so that only those whose first character is p are added to the results. Notice that the condition is defined using the range variable. The range variable type in this example is string, so the indexer can be used to access individual characters in the string value. Compiling and running Listing 27-8 produces the following output:

```
Result item: plum
Result item: pear
Result item: persimmon
Result item: pineapple
Press enter to finish
```

You can see from the results that only those fruits whose name begins with the letter p have been added to the results. You can use the AND (&&) and OR (||) operators to create more complex conditions, as demonstrated by Listing 27-9.

Listing 27-9. Creating a More Complex Condition in a where Clause

```
using System;
using System.Collections.Generic;
using System.Linq;

class Listing_09 {

    static void Main(string[] args) {

        List<string> myFruitList = new List<string>() {
            "apple", "plum", "cherry", "grape", "banana", "pear", "mango" ,
            "persimmon", "lemon", "lime", "coconut", "pineapple", "orange"};

        IEnumerable<string> results = from e in myFruitList
                                      where e[0] == 'p' && e[1] == 'e' && e.Length > 4
                                      select e;

        foreach (string str in results) {
            Console.WriteLine("Result item: {0}", str);
        }

        // wait for input before exiting
        Console.WriteLine("Press enter to finish");
        Console.ReadLine();
    }
}
```

The query in Listing 27-9 filters the data elements, allowing only those whose first letter is p, whose second letter is e, and whose Length is greater than four characters. Compiling and running Listing 27-9 produces the following results:

```
Result item: persimmon
Press enter to finish
```

Projecting Data

Projecting data, also known as *selecting data*, is performed by the select clause of a LINQ query. When you project data, you select what will be placed into the results for each item that is being processed. The projected data can be the same as the source data, values from one or more members of the source data, or different data entirely. You have already seen how to project the same data as in the results (Listing 27-9, for example). Almost all LINQ queries end with a select clause. In the following sections, I'll show you how to do some other kinds of projection.

Projecting a Single Member

You can project the value of a single member of a data type into the results by selecting that value in the select clause of your LINQ query. We already saw this when we selected the first character of a string value using an indexer, but Listing 27-10 provides another example.

Listing 27-10. Projecting a Single Member

```
using System;
using System.Collections.Generic;
using System.Linq;

class Listing_10 {

    static void Main(string[] args) {

        List<string> myFruitList = new List<string>() {
            "apple", "plum", "cherry", "grape", "banana", "pear", "mango" ,
            "persimmon", "lemon", "lime", "coconut", "pineapple", "orange"};

        IEnumerable<int> results = from e in myFruitList
                                   where e[0] == 'p'
                                   select e.Length;

        foreach (int i in results) {
            Console.WriteLine("Result item: {0}", i);
        }

        // wait for input before exiting
        Console.WriteLine("Press enter to finish");
        Console.ReadLine();
    }
}
```

The generic type of the data source is string in Listing 27-10, and the select clause in projects the value of the Length member, which is an int. Notice that the generic type of the results has changed to int as well. The result from this query will be a sequence of int values representing the number of characters in the fruit names.

The LINQ query in Listing 27-10 has a where clause as well. I have included this to demonstrate that you can combine the various LINQ operations to create more complex queries. In this query, the where clause filters the data items so only those that start with the letter p are passed to the select clause, which then projects the Length value. Compiling and running Listing 27-10 produces the following results:

```
Result item: 4
Result item: 4
Result item: 9
Result item: 9
Press enter to finish
```

877

Projecting Anonymous Types

You can select more than one member from a data type by projecting an anonymous type (anonymous types are explained in Chapter 15). Listing 27-11 provides an example.

Listing 27-11. Projecting an Anonymous Type

```
using System;
using System.Collections.Generic;
using System.Linq;

class Listing_11 {

    static void Main(string[] args) {

        List<string> myFruitList = new List<string>() {
            "apple", "plum", "cherry", "grape", "banana", "pear", "mango" ,
            "persimmon", "lemon", "lime", "coconut", "pineapple", "orange"};

        var results = from e in myFruitList
                        select new {
                            Length = e.Length,
                            FirstChar = e[0]
                        };

        foreach (var item in results) {
            Console.WriteLine("Result item -  Length: {0}, FirstChar: {1}",
                item.Length, item.FirstChar);
        }

        // wait for input before exiting
        Console.WriteLine("Press enter to finish");
        Console.ReadLine();
    }
}
```

The anonymous type in Listing 27-11 contains two properties. The Length property contains the number of characters in the fruit name, and the FirstChar property contains the first character in the name. You must use the var keyword for the result generic type when you project an anonymous type and when you enumerate the results, as shown in the listing. Compiling and running Listing 27-11 produces the following results:

```
Result item -  Length: 5, FirstChar: a
Result item -  Length: 4, FirstChar: p
Result item -  Length: 6, FirstChar: c
Result item -  Length: 5, FirstChar: g
Result item -  Length: 6, FirstChar: b
Result item -  Length: 4, FirstChar: p
Result item -  Length: 5, FirstChar: m
```

```
Result item -  Length: 9, FirstChar: p
Result item -  Length: 5, FirstChar: l

Result item -  Length: 4, FirstChar: l
Result item -  Length: 7, FirstChar: c
Result item -  Length: 9, FirstChar: p
Result item -  Length: 6, FirstChar: o
Press enter to finish
```

Anonymous types are very useful, but you cannot pass them as parameters to other methods. See the following section for a related example that shows you how to use the select clause to create a project a new object, the results from which can be passed to other methods.

Projecting Derived Data

You can project any data you like into the results, including data that you have derived from a characteristic of a data item. Listing 27-12 provides a demonstration that projects bool values.

Listing 27-12. Projecting Derived Data

```
using System;
using System.Collections.Generic;
using System.Linq;

class Listing_12 {

    static void Main(string[] args) {

        List<string> myFruitList = new List<string>() {
            "apple", "plum", "cherry", "grape", "banana", "pear", "mango" ,
            "persimmon", "lemon", "lime", "coconut", "pineapple", "orange"};

        IEnumerable<bool> results = from e in myFruitList
                        select e.Length > 5;

        foreach (bool item in results) {
            Console.WriteLine("Result item: {0}", item);
        }

        // wait for input before exiting
        Console.WriteLine("Press enter to finish");
        Console.ReadLine();
    }
}
```

The select clause in this query projects true if the number of characters in the value assigned to the range variable is greater than 5 and false otherwise. Compiling and running Listing 27-12 produces the following results:

```
Result item: False
Result item: False
Result item: True
Result item: False
Result item: True
Result item: False
Result item: False
Result item: True
Result item: False
Result item: False
Result item: True
Result item: True
Result item: True
Press enter to finish
```

You can also project new objects, as demonstrated by Listing 27-13, which uses characteristics of the value assigned to the range value to create a new object that is projected into the results.

Listing 27-13. Projecting a New Object

```csharp
using System;
using System.Collections.Generic;
using System.Linq;

class NameInfo {

    public NameInfo(char charParam, int lenParam) {
        FirstChar = charParam;
        Length = lenParam;
    }

    public char FirstChar { get; set; }
    public int Length { get; set; }

}

class Listing_12 {

    static void Main(string[] args) {

        List<string> myFruitList = new List<string>() {
            "apple", "plum", "cherry", "grape", "banana", "pear", "mango" ,
            "persimmon", "lemon", "lime", "coconut", "pineapple", "orange"};

        IEnumerable<NameInfo> results = from e in myFruitList
                                        select new NameInfo(e[0], e.Length);

        foreach (NameInfo item in results) {
            Console.WriteLine("Result item - FirstChar: {0}, Length: {1}",
                item.FirstChar, item.Length);
```

```
        }

        // wait for input before exiting
        Console.WriteLine("Press enter to finish");
        Console.ReadLine();
    }
}
```

The select clause in Listing 27-13 creates and projects NameInfo objects. This example may appear similar to using anonymous types but has the advantage of allowing you to pass the query results as parameters to other methods, which you can't do when you use anonymous types. Compiling and running Listing 27-13 produces the following results:

```
Result item - FirstChar: a, Length: 5
Result item - FirstChar: p, Length: 4
Result item - FirstChar: c, Length: 6
Result item - FirstChar: g, Length: 5
Result item - FirstChar: b, Length: 6
Result item - FirstChar: p, Length: 4
Result item - FirstChar: m, Length: 5
Result item - FirstChar: p, Length: 9
Result item - FirstChar: l, Length: 5
Result item - FirstChar: l, Length: 4
Result item - FirstChar: c, Length: 7
Result item - FirstChar: p, Length: 9
Result item - FirstChar: o, Length: 6
Press enter to finish
```

Ordering Data

You can order data using the orderby clause. Listing 27-14 shows how this can be done.

Listing 27-14. Ordering Data

```
using System;
using System.Collections.Generic;
using System.Linq;

class Listing_14 {

    static void Main(string[] args) {

        List<string> myFruitList = new List<string>() {
            "apple", "plum", "cherry", "grape", "banana", "pear", "mango" ,
            "persimmon", "lemon", "lime", "coconut", "pineapple", "orange"};

        IEnumerable<string> results = from e in myFruitList
                                      orderby e[0]
                                      select e;
```

```
        foreach (string item in results) {
            Console.WriteLine("Result item: {0}", item);
        }

        // wait for input before exiting
        Console.WriteLine("Press enter to finish");
        Console.ReadLine();
    }
}
```

In Listing 27-14, the results are sorted by the first letter of each string value in the data source. Compiling and running Listing 27-14 produces the following results:

```
Result item: apple
Result item: banana
Result item: cherry
Result item: coconut
Result item: grape
Result item: lemon
Result item: lime
Result item: mango
Result item: orange
Result item: plum
Result item: pear
Result item: persimmon
Result item: pineapple
Press enter to finish
```

By default, the orderby clause will sort in ascending value. You can sort in descending value by appending descending to the clause, as shown in Listing 27-15.

Listing 27-15. Using the descending Keyword

```
using System;
using System.Collections.Generic;
using System.Linq;

class Listing_15 {

    static void Main(string[] args) {

        List<string> myFruitList = new List<string>() {
            "apple", "plum", "cherry", "grape", "banana", "pear", "mango" ,
            "persimmon", "lemon", "lime", "coconut", "pineapple", "orange"};

        IEnumerable<string> results = from e in myFruitList
                            orderby e[0] descending
                                select e;
```

```
        foreach (string item in results) {
            Console.WriteLine("Result item: {0}", item);
        }

        // wait for input before exiting
        Console.WriteLine("Press enter to finish");
        Console.ReadLine();
    }
}
```

Compiling and running Listing 27-15 produces the following results:

```
Result item: plum
Result item: pear
Result item: persimmon
Result item: pineapple
Result item: orange
Result item: mango
Result item: lemon
Result item: lime
Result item: grape
Result item: cherry
Result item: coconut
Result item: banana
Result item: apple
Press enter to finish
```

You can see that the results are sorted in descending order by the first letter. If all you need to do is sort a sequence of data items, you may find that using sorting features of the collection classes or of the Array class is faster; see Chapter 19 for details. The power of the LINQ orderby clause comes when you combine it with other LINQ features so that the ordering is done as part of a larger query. Listing 27-16 demonstrates ordering data, which is also filtered and projected as an anonymous type.

Listing 27-16. A More Complex Ordering Operation

```
using System;
using System.Collections.Generic;
using System.Linq;

class Listing_16 {

    static void Main(string[] args) {

        List<string> myFruitList = new List<string>() {
            "apple", "plum", "cherry", "grape", "banana", "pear", "mango" ,
            "persimmon", "lemon", "lime", "coconut", "pineapple", "orange"};

        var results = from e in myFruitList
                    where e[0] == 'p' && e.Length > 3
                    orderby e.Length
```

```
                      select new {
                          Name = e,
                          FirstChar = e[0],
                          Length = e.Length,
                      };

          foreach (var item in results) {
              Console.WriteLine("Result item - Name: {0}, First Char: {1}, Length: {2}",
                  item.Name, item.FirstChar, item.Length);
          }

          // wait for input before exiting
          Console.WriteLine("Press enter to finish");
          Console.ReadLine();
      }
}
```

Compiling and running Listing 27-16 produces the following results:

```
Result item - Name: plum, First Char: p, Length: 4
Result item - Name: pear, First Char: p, Length: 4
Result item - Name: persimmon, First Char: p, Length: 9
Result item - Name: pineapple, First Char: p, Length: 9
Press enter to finish
```

You can apply additional sorting operations in an orderby clause by separating the characteristics to sort by with a comma (,), as demonstrated by Listing 27-17.

Listing 27-17. Applying Multiple Sorts

```
using System;
using System.Collections.Generic;
using System.Linq;

class Listing_17 {

    static void Main(string[] args) {

        List<string> myFruitList = new List<string>() {
            "apple", "plum", "cherry", "grape", "banana", "pear", "mango" ,
            "persimmon", "lemon", "lime", "coconut", "pineapple", "orange"};

        var results = from e in myFruitList
                      orderby e.Length descending, e[1] , e[2]
                      select e;

        foreach (var item in results) {
            Console.WriteLine("Result item: {0}", item);
        }
```

```
        // wait for input before exiting
        Console.WriteLine("Press enter to finish");
        Console.ReadLine();
    }
}
```

The orderby clause in Listing 27-17 first sorts the data items by the value of their Length properties in descending order and then performs a secondary sort using the second character of the name and then a tertiary sort using the third character of the name. Compiling and running Listing 27-17 produces the following results:

```
Result item: persimmon
Result item: pineapple
Result item: coconut
Result item: banana
Result item: cherry
Result item: orange
Result item: mango
Result item: lemon
Result item: apple
Result item: grape
Result item: pear
Result item: lime
Result item: plum
Press enter to finish
```

Grouping Data

The group clause allows you to group items together based on a key you specify. Listing 27-18 demonstrates grouping string values based on their first character.

Listing 27-18. Grouping Items

```
using System;
using System.Collections.Generic;
using System.Linq;

class Listing_18 {

    static void Main(string[] args) {

        List<string> myFruitList = new List<string>() {
            "apple", "plum", "cherry", "grape", "banana", "pear", "mango" ,
            "persimmon", "lemon", "lime", "coconut", "pineapple", "orange"};

        IEnumerable<IGrouping<char, string>> results = from e in myFruitList
                                            group e by e[0];

        foreach (IGrouping<char, string> group in results) {
```

```
            Console.WriteLine("Group key: {0}", group.Key);
            foreach (string value in group) {
                Console.WriteLine("Group item: {0}", value);
            }
        }

        // wait for input before exiting
        Console.WriteLine("Press enter to finish");
        Console.ReadLine();
    }
}
```

A group clause replaces the select clause, as demonstrated by the query in Listing 27-18. The group clause in Listing 27-18 groups the string values in the data source by their first letter, as illustrated in Figure 27-6.

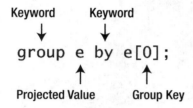

Figure 27-6. *The anatomy of a group clause*

The group keyword is followed by the value you want projected for the current range variable. In the example, I project the entire string value, but you can project anything that you can do in a select clause. The projected value is followed by the by keyword, after which you specify the key by which the projected values will be grouped.

The result of a group clause is an IEnumerable<IGrouping<TKey, TValue>>, where TKey is the type of the group key and TValue is the type of the projected value. This relationship is illustrated in Figure 27-7.

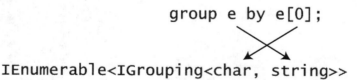

Figure 27-7. *The type relationship in a group query result*

The IGrouping<TKey, TValue> interface is derived from IEnumerable<TValue> and defines the additional property Key, which returns the TKey value used to group the enumerable values together. In the case of Listing 27-18, the Key property for each IGrouping<char, string> will return a single character, and the collected values will be the fruit names that start with that character. The result from a group clause is an IEnumerable<T>, where T is IGrouping<TKey, TValue>, so a pair of nested foreach loops can be used to process the data, like this:

```
foreach (IGrouping<char, string> group in results) {
    Console.WriteLine("Group key: {0}", group.Key);
    foreach (string value in group) {
        Console.WriteLine("Group item: {0}", value);
    }
}
```

Compiling and running Listing 27-18 produces the following results:

```
Group key: a
Group item: apple
Group key: p
Group item: plum
Group item: pear
Group item: persimmon
Group item: pineapple
Group key: c
Group item: cherry
Group item: coconut
Group key: g
Group item: grape
Group key: b
Group item: banana
Group key: m
Group item: mango
Group key: l
Group item: lemon
Group item: lime
Group key: o
Group item: orange
Press enter to finish
```

You can see that the result of a group operation is essentially a list of lists; each list contains a list of items that are grouped together using a common key.

Grouping Using a Boolean Value

One of the most common uses of the group clause is to separate the items in a data source into two groups—one containing the items that meet some criteria and one containing those items that don't. Listing 27-19 provides a demonstration, grouping the fruit names into those whose names are longer than five characters and those whose names are not.

Listing 27-19. Grouping into Boolean Groups

```
using System;
using System.Collections.Generic;
using System.Linq;
```

```
class Listing_19 {

    static void Main(string[] args) {

        List<string> myFruitList = new List<string>() {
            "apple", "plum", "cherry", "grape", "banana", "pear", "mango" ,
            "persimmon", "lemon", "lime", "coconut", "pineapple", "orange"};

        IEnumerable<IGrouping<bool, string>> results = from e in myFruitList
                                            group e by e.Length > 5;

        foreach (IGrouping<bool, string> group in results) {
            if (group.Key) {
                Console.WriteLine("--- Names longer than 5 chars ---");
            } else {
                Console.WriteLine("--- Names 5 chars or less long ---");
            }

            foreach (string value in group) {
                Console.WriteLine("Item: {0}", value);
            }
        }

        // wait for input before exiting
        Console.WriteLine("Press enter to finish");
        Console.ReadLine();
    }
}
```

In this example, the key values for the grouping are true and false. The true group contains those items whose name is longer than five characters. Compiling and running Listing 27-19 produces the following results:

```
--- Names 5 chars or less long ---
Item: apple
Item: plum
Item: grape
Item: pear
Item: mango
Item: lemon
Item: lime
--- Names longer than 5 chars ---
Item: cherry
Item: banana
Item: persimmon
Item: coconut
Item: pineapple
Item: orange
Press enter to finish
```

Grouping Using an Anonymous Type

You can group using more than one characteristic by using an anonymous type as the group key. Each permutation of property values in the anonymous type will lead to a new group being created in the results. Listing 27-20 demonstrates this technique, grouping on first letter and a Boolean representing whether the length of the string value is greater than five characters.

Listing 27-20. Grouping Using an Anonymous Type

```
using System;
using System.Collections.Generic;
using System.Linq;

class Listing_20 {

    static void Main(string[] args) {

        List<string> myFruitList = new List<string>() {
            "apple", "plum", "cherry", "grape", "banana", "pear", "mango" ,
            "persimmon", "lemon", "lime", "coconut", "pineapple", "orange"};

        var results = from e in myFruitList
                      where e[0] == 'p' || e[0] == 'l'
                      group e by new {
                          FirstChar = e[0],
                          LengthGt5 = e.Length > 5
                      };

        foreach (var group in results) {
            Console.WriteLine("---Group Key - FirstChar: {0}, LengthGt5: {1}",
                group.Key.FirstChar, group.Key.LengthGt5);

            foreach (string value in group) {
                Console.WriteLine("Item: {0}", value);
            }
        }

        // wait for input before exiting
        Console.WriteLine("Press enter to finish");
        Console.ReadLine();
    }
}
```

The query in Listing 27-20 uses a where clause to filter out items that don't start with the letter p or l. Those that do are then grouped using an anonymous type. Compiling and running Listing 27-20 produces the following results:

```
---Group Key - FirstChar: p, LengthGt5: False
Item: plum
Item: pear
```

```
---Group Key - FirstChar: p, LengthGt5: True
Item: persimmon
Item: pineapple
---Group Key - FirstChar: l, LengthGt5: False
Item: lemon
Item: lime
Press enter to finish
```

You can see from the results that there are three groups in the results. Only groups that contain items are included in results. The fourth group that might exist in the results is omitted because there are no items that meet the group criteria (names that begin with l and have more than five characters).

Querying Grouped Data

You can use the into keyword in your group clause to create a *group range variable* that will be assigned each group that is created. You can then use other kinds of clauses to filter, sort, and project those groups, as demonstrated by Listing 27-21.

Listing 27-21. Projecting from Grouped Data

```
using System;
using System.Collections.Generic;
using System.Linq;

class Listing_21 {

    static void Main(string[] args) {

        List<string> myFruitList = new List<string>() {
            "apple", "plum", "cherry", "grape", "banana", "pear", "mango" ,
            "persimmon", "lemon", "lime", "coconut", "pineapple", "orange"};

        var results = from e in myFruitList
                    group e by e[0] into fruitGroup
                    where fruitGroup.Count() > 1
                    orderby fruitGroup.Key
                    select fruitGroup;

        foreach (var group in results) {
            Console.WriteLine("--- Group Key: {0}", group.Key);
            foreach (string value in group) {
                Console.WriteLine("Item: {0}", value);
            }
        }

        // wait for input before exiting
        Console.WriteLine("Press enter to finish");
        Console.ReadLine();
    }
```

}

The query in Listing 27-21 groups data items by their first letter and uses the `into` keyword to create a group range variable called `fruitGroup`:

```
group e by e[0] into fruitGroup
```

I then use a `where` clause to filter out groups that have only one member, an `order` clause to sort the groups by their Key values, and a `select` statement to project the group into the results. Compiling and running Listing 27-20 produces the following results:

```
--- Group Key: c
Item: cherry
Item: coconut
--- Group Key: l
Item: lemon
Item: lime
--- Group Key: p
Item: plum
Item: pear
Item: persimmon
Item: pineapple
Press enter to finish
```

Using Method Syntax

The queries in the examples so far in this chapter have been performed using C# keywords, like `from`, `in`, and `select`. This is known as *query syntax*, but there is another way to define LINQ queries that some programmers find more natural, called *method syntax*. Each of the C# keywords for LINQ is translated into a call to an extension method defined in the `System.Linq.Enumerable` class. In fact, this class contains some LINQ extension methods for which there are no equivalent C# keywords. As an alternative to using query syntax, you can call the extension methods directly. Listing 27-22 contains an example. You can find more about extension methods in general in Chapter 9.

Listing 27-22. Using Method Syntax to Perform LINQ Queries

```
using System;
using System.Collections.Generic;
using System.Linq;

class Listing_22 {

    static void Main(string[] args) {

        // create the data source
        List<string> myFruitList = new List<string>() {
            "apple", "plum", "cherry", "grape", "banana", "pear", "mango" ,
            "persimmon", "lemon", "lime", "coconut", "pineapple", "orange"};

        // define the LINQ query
        IEnumerable<string> results = myFruitList
                                    .Where(e => e[0] == 'p')
                                    .Select(e => e);

        // enumerate the results
        foreach (string str in results) {
            Console.WriteLine("Result: {0}", str);
        }

        // wait for input before exiting
        Console.WriteLine("Press enter to finish");
        Console.ReadLine();
    }
}
```

Method syntax uses lambda expressions or Funcs to process items in the data source; see Chapter 10 for details of Funcs. In this chapter, I'll use lambda expressions when I demonstrate method syntax, since that is the more common practice. The method syntax lambda expressions are passed a parameter of the same type as the data source items. In the case of Listing 27-22, this means the parameter e for the Where and Select methods is a string. Different LINQ extension methods return different kinds of result; for example, the Where method returns a bool value, which is true if you want to include the value in the query and false if you don't. When using the Select method, you return whatever it is you want to project into the result. In the case of Listing 27-22, the Select method projects the entire item.

In the listing, I have placed each method call on a separate line for clarity, but you can write the same expression on a single line, like this:

```
IEnumerable<string> results = myFruitList.Where(e => e[0] == 'p').Select(e => e);
```

Table 27-3 lists the query keywords we have seen so far in the chapter and their extension method equivalents.

Table 27-3. Selected C# LINQ Keywords and the Corresponding Extension Methods

Keyword	Extension Method	Description
where	Where	Filters items from the IEnumerable<T> data source, returning true to include the item and false otherwise
select	Select	Projects a member or value from the IEnumerable<T> data source into the results
group	GroupBy	Returns a member or value for an item from the IEnumerable<T> data source that will be used to group the item
orderby	OrderBy	Returns a member or value for an item from the IEnumerable<T> data source that will be used to sort the item

As a rule, the name of the extension method that corresponds to a C# query keyword is very similar to the keyword. For example, the select keyword corresponds to the Select extension method. See the documentation for the System.Linq.Enumerable class for a full list of the available extension methods.

■ **Tip** You can mix method and query syntax in the same query. You can see examples of this in Chapter 28 where the AsParallel extension method in used in a query expressed using C# keywords.

I find myself using query syntax for simple LINQ queries and method syntax for more complex queries when I want to access features that are available only as extension methods. I also use method syntax when I want to use lambda expressions, often because this allows me to debug my queries more readily. Listing 27-23 contains an example.

Listing 27-23. Debugging a LINQ Query Using Method Syntax

```
using System;
using System.Collections.Generic;
using System.Linq;

class Listing_23 {

    static void Main(string[] args) {

        // create the data source
        List<string> myFruitList = new List<string>() {
            "apple", "plum", "cherry", "grape", "banana", "pear", "mango" ,
            "persimmon", "lemon", "lime", "coconut", "pineapple", "orange"};
```

```
        // define the LINQ query
        IEnumerable<string> results = myFruitList
                                    .Where(e => {
                                        bool res = e[0] == 'p';
                                        Console.WriteLine("Filter: {0} is included: {1}",
                                            e, res);
                                        return res;
                                    })
                                    .Select(e => e);

        // enumerate the results
        foreach (string str in results) {
            Console.WriteLine("Result: {0}", str);
        }

        // wait for input before exiting
        Console.WriteLine("Press enter to finish");
        Console.ReadLine();
    }
}
```

In Listing 27-23, I perform the filter check (does the name begin with the letter *p*?) but print out the data item and the outcome before returning the result in the lambda expression. This is a simple example, but I find this technique can be helpful when dealing with complex queries. Compiling and running Listing 27-23 produces the following results:

```
Filter: apple is included: False
Filter: plum is included: True
Result: plum
Filter: cherry is included: False
Filter: grape is included: False
Filter: banana is included: False
Filter: pear is included: True
Result: pear
Filter: mango is included: False
Filter: persimmon is included: True
Result: persimmon
Filter: lemon is included: False
Filter: lime is included: False
Filter: coconut is included: False
Filter: pineapple is included: True
Result: pineapple
Filter: orange is included: False
Press enter to finish
```

Understanding Deferred Execution

LINQ queries are not performed when they are defined. Nothing happens until you enumerate the results. If you define a query and don't enumerate the results, the query will never be performed. There are some benefits to this approach and some things to be wary of, as explained in the following sections.

Reusing Queries

You can reuse a query by enumerating the result more than once. Each time you do this, the query is executed again. Changes will be reflected in the results if you have modified the source data between enumerations, as Listing 27-24 demonstrates.

Listing 27-24. Reusing a Query

```
using System;
using System.Collections.Generic;
using System.Linq;

class Listing_24 {

    static void Main(string[] args) {

        // create the data source
        List<string> myFruitNames =
            new List<string>() { "apple", "plum", "cherry", "grape" };

        // define the LINQ query
        IEnumerable<string> results = from e in myFruitNames
                                      where e[0] == 'a'
                                      select e;

        // enumerate the results
        Console.WriteLine("--- First iteration ---");
        foreach (string str in results) {
            Console.WriteLine("Result: {0}", str);
        }

        // modify the collection
        myFruitNames.Add("apricot");

        // enumerate the results again
        Console.WriteLine("--- Second iteration ---");
        foreach (string str in results) {
            Console.WriteLine("Result: {0}", str);
        }

        // wait for input before exiting
        Console.WriteLine("Press enter to finish");
        Console.ReadLine();
    }
```

}

The query in Listing 27-24 filters the data source for items that start with the letter a and selects the entire item. The query is performed when the results are first enumerated, at which point there is only one matching item in the data source. I then add an item to the data source and enumerate again, and this time there are two results, confirmed by the result of compiling and running Listing 27-24:

```
--- First iteration ---
Result: apple
--- Second iteration ---
Result: apple
Result: apricot
Press enter to finish
```

Referring to Variables

Variables that you refer to from your LINQ query are evaluated when the query results are enumerated. This can be useful (if you want to change an external condition between enumerations) or confusing (if the value of your variable changes unexpectedly). Listing 27-25 provides a demonstration.

Listing 27-25. Referring to a Variable from Within a LINQ Query

```
using System;
using System.Collections.Generic;
using System.Linq;

class Listing_25 {

    static void Main(string[] args) {

        // create the data source
        List<string> myFruitNames
            = new List<string>() { "apple", "plum", "cherry", "grape" };

        // define a variable that will be captured by the query
        char firstLetter = 'a';

        // define the LINQ query
        IEnumerable<string> results = from e in myFruitNames
                                      where e[0] == firstLetter
                                      select e;

        // enumerate the results
        Console.WriteLine("--- First iteration ---");
        foreach (string str in results) {
            Console.WriteLine("Result: {0}", str);
        }

        // change the value assigned to the variable
```

```
        firstLetter = 'c';

        // enumerate the results again
        Console.WriteLine("--- Second iteration ---");
        foreach (string str in results) {
            Console.WriteLine("Result: {0}", str);
        }

        // wait for input before exiting
        Console.WriteLine("Press enter to finish");
        Console.ReadLine();
    }
}
```

The LINQ query in Listing 27-25 makes use of a local variable for filtering in the where clause. This value assigned to the variable changes between the first time that the results are enumerated and the second time, producing a different set of results from the same query. If you want to take advantage of this flexibility, it can be very useful, but if you are relying on a value that is shared by other code, you need to be sure the value doesn't change unexpectedly. The best way of doing this is to make a copy of the variable just for use in the LINQ query.

Forcing Immediate Execution

There are some LINQ extension methods that force immediate execution; these are typically methods that aggregate the source data in some way. Listing 27-26 provides a demonstration using the Count method, which returns the number of results. You can see further examples of aggregation in the "Aggregating Data" section later in this chapter.

Listing 27-26. Forcing Immediate Query Execution

```
using System;
using System.Collections.Generic;
using System.Linq;

class Listing_26 {

    static void Main(string[] args) {

        // create the data source
        List<string> myFruitList = new List<string>() {
            "apple", "plum", "cherry", "grape", "banana", "pear", "mango" ,
            "persimmon", "lemon", "lime", "coconut", "pineapple", "orange"};

        // define a variable that will be captured by the query
        char firstLetter = 'p';

        // define the LINQ query
        int resultCount = myFruitList
                        .Where(e => e[0] == firstLetter)
                        .Select(e => e).Count();
```

```
            // print out the results
            Console.WriteLine("Result count: {0}", resultCount);

            // wait for input before exiting
            Console.WriteLine("Press enter to finish");
            Console.ReadLine();
    }
}
```

The LINQ query in Listing 27-26 is performed when it is defined so that a value can be assigned to the resultCount local variable. Deferred execution applies only when the result of a query is an IEnumerable<T>. If you aggregate or convert the results, the query will be executed immediately. Compiling and running Listing 27-25 produces the following results:

```
Result count: 4
Press enter to finish
```

If you want to define an aggregated query (by using the Count method, for example) but you don't want to perform it immediately, you can split the query into the regular part and the immediate execution part. Listing 27-27 shows you how this is done.

Listing 27-27. Splitting Out the Immediate Execution Element from a LINQ Query

```
using System;
using System.Collections.Generic;
using System.Linq;

class Listing_27 {

    static void Main(string[] args) {

        // create the data source
        List<string> myFruitList = new List<string>() {
            "apple", "plum", "cherry", "grape", "banana", "pear", "mango" ,
            "persimmon", "lemon", "lime", "coconut", "pineapple", "orange"};

        // define a variable that will be captured by the query
        char firstLetter = 'p';

        // define the LINQ query - leave out the aggregation part
        IEnumerable<string> results = myFruitList
                        .Where(e => e[0] == firstLetter)
                        .Select(e => e);

        //
        // do some other things....
        //

        // aggregate the results from the LINQ query by applying the Count
```

```
        // extension method to the query results - this will cause the query
        // to be performed
        int resultCount = results.Count();

        // print out the results
        Console.WriteLine("Result count: {0}", resultCount);

        // we can reuse the deferred part of the query again
        foreach (string str in results) {
            Console.WriteLine("Item: {0}", str);
        }

        // wait for input before exiting
        Console.WriteLine("Press enter to finish");
        Console.ReadLine();
    }
}
```

In Listing 27-27, the Count method is applied to the IEnumerable<string> result from the query only as a value is required. The deferred part of the query can be reused as enumerating the results (which is all that the Count method is doing to generate a result). Compiling and running Listing 27-27 produces the following output:

```
Result count: 4
Item: plum
Item: pear
Item: persimmon
Item: pineapple
Press enter to finish
```

Converting Query Results

Getting the results of a query as an IEnumerable<T> isn't always convenient. The System.Linq.Enumerable class contains some convenience extension methods that can be applied to IEnumerable<T> to convert the results of a query into a different form.

■ **Tip** Using the methods described in this section forces immediate execution of a LINQ query. See the "Understanding Deferred Execution" section earlier in the chapter for more details of deferred and immediate execution.

Table 27-4 describes the methods you can use to transform the results.

Table 27-4. System.Linq.Enumerable Methods Used to Convert Results

Method	Description
ToArray()	Returns an array of T from the IEnumerable<T> results
ToList()	Returns a List<T> from the IEnumerable<T> results
ToDictionary(Func(T))	Returns a Dictionary<TKey, T> from the IEnumerable<T> results, using the Func to create the key for each item

These methods are demonstrated in Listing 27-28.

Listing 27-28. Using the Result Conversion Extension Methods

```
using System;
using System.Collections.Generic;
using System.Linq;

class Listing_28 {

    static void Main(string[] args) {

        // create the data source
        List<string> myFruitList = new List<string>() {
            "apple", "plum", "cherry", "grape", "banana", "pear", "mango" ,
            "persimmon", "lemon", "lime", "coconut", "pineapple", "orange"};

        // define the LINQ query - leave out the aggregation part
        IEnumerable<string> results = myFruitList
                        .Where(e => e[0] == 'p' || e[0] == 'l')
                        .Select(e => e);

        // convert the results to an array
        string[] resultArray = results.ToArray();

        // print out the contents of the array
        foreach (string str in resultArray) {
            Console.WriteLine("Array result: {0}", str);
        }

        // convert the results to a List<T>
        List<string> resultList = results.ToList();

        // print out the contents of the List<string>
        foreach (string str in resultList) {
            Console.WriteLine("List result: {0}", str);
        }
```

```
        // group the results based on first letter
        IEnumerable<IGrouping<char, string>> groupResults = results.GroupBy(e => e[0]);

        // convert the results to a Dictionary<TKey, TVal>
        Dictionary<char, IGrouping<char, string>> resultDict
            = groupResults.ToDictionary(e => e.Key);

        // print out the contents of the dictionary
        foreach (char key in resultDict.Keys) {
            Console.WriteLine("Dictionary Key: {0}", key);
            // get the IGrouping associated with the key
            IEnumerable<string> groupEnum = resultDict[key];
            foreach (string str in groupEnum) {
                Console.WriteLine("Dictionary entry: {0}", str);
            }
        }

        // wait for input before exiting
        Console.WriteLine("Press enter to finish");
        Console.ReadLine();
    }
}
```

The results from the query in Listing 27-28 are converted into an array, a List<T>, and a Dictionary<TKey, TVal>. You can find out more about arrays in Chapter 13 and about the List<T> and Dictionary<TKey, TVal> classes in Chapter 19. Compiling and running Listing 27-28 produces the following results:

```
Array result: plum
Array result: pear
Array result: persimmon
Array result: lemon
Array result: lime
Array result: pineapple
List result: plum
List result: pear
List result: persimmon
List result: lemon
List result: lime
List result: pineapple
Dictionary Key: p
Dictionary entry: plum
Dictionary entry: pear
Dictionary entry: persimmon
Dictionary entry: pineapple
Dictionary Key: l
Dictionary entry: lemon
Dictionary entry: lime
Press enter to finish
```

Using Legacy Collections as LINQ Data Sources

The legacy collection classes contained in the System.Collections namespace implement the nongeneric IEnumerable interface, rather than IEnumerable<T>. This means that LINQ can't infer the type of the range variable from the type of the data contained in the collection. LINQ provides three different approaches to addressing this, which is useful for when you want to use LINQ to query data created by legacy code.

Explicitly Specifying the Range Variable Type

The first approach you can take is to explicitly specify the type of the range variable in the LINQ query so that LINQ doesn't need to infer it for you. Listing 27-29 provides a demonstration using the legacy ArrayList class.

Listing 27-29. Explicitly Specifying the Range Variable Type

```
using System;
using System.Collections;
using System.Collections.Generic;
using System.Linq;

class Listing_29 {

    static void Main(string[] args) {

        ArrayList myFruitList = new ArrayList() {
            "apple", "plum", "cherry", "grape", "banana", "pear", "mango" ,
            "persimmon", "lemon", "lime", "coconut", "pineapple", "orange"};

        // define the first query
        IEnumerable<string> results = from string e in myFruitList
                                      select e;

        // enumerate the results
        foreach (string str in results) {
            Console.WriteLine("Result item: {0}", str);
        }

        // wait for input before exiting
        Console.WriteLine("Press enter to finish");
        Console.ReadLine();
    }
}
```

In Listing 27-29 I have created an ArrayList that contains the fruit names. In the LINQ query, I have told LINQ that the ArrayList contains string values by preceding the range variable with the string type. This works if you are sure of the contents of the collection, but if any of the items in the ArrayList are not strings, then a System.InvalidCastException will be thrown.

Using Cast and OfType Extension Methods

The second approach is to convert the nongeneric collection class to a generic IEnumerable<T> using the Cast extension method, which can be applied to IEnumerable implementations. Listing 27-30 contains a demonstration.

Listing 27-30. Using the Cast Method

```
using System;
using System.Collections;
using System.Collections.Generic;
using System.Linq;

class Listing_30 {

    static void Main(string[] args) {

        ArrayList myFruitList = new ArrayList() {
            "apple", "plum", "cherry", "grape", "banana", "pear", "mango" ,
            "persimmon", "lemon", "lime", "coconut", "pineapple", "orange"};

        // use the Cast extension method to create an IEnumerable<string>
        IEnumerable<string> myEnum = myFruitList.Cast<string>();

        // define the query
        IEnumerable<string> results = from e in myEnum
                                      select e;

        // enumerate the results
        foreach (string str in results) {
            Console.WriteLine("Result item: {0}", str);
        }

        // wait for input before exiting
        Console.WriteLine("Press enter to finish");
        Console.ReadLine();
    }
}
```

Much like providing an explicit type for the range variable, using the Cast extension method requires that all the objects in the source collection can be converted to the type you have specified, string values in the example. An exception will be thrown in an object cannot be converted to the target type. Compiling and running Listing 27-30 produces the following results:

```
Result item: apple
Result item: plum
Result item: cherry
Result item: grape
Result item: banana
Result item: pear
```

```
Result item: mango
Result item: persimmon
Result item: lemon
Result item: lime
Result item: coconut
Result item: pineapple
Result item: orange
Press enter to finish
```

The third way of dealing with legacy collections is to use the OfType extension method. This is a more tolerant version of Cast and simply discards any object that cannot be cast to the target type, as demonstrated by Listing 27-31.

Listing 27-31. Using the OfType Extension Method

```csharp
using System;
using System.Collections;
using System.Collections.Generic;
using System.Linq;

class Listing_31 {

    static void Main(string[] args) {

        ArrayList myNumbers = new ArrayList() {10, 20, 30, 40, "apple"};

        // use the Cast extension method to create an IEnumerable<string>
        IEnumerable<int> myEnum = myNumbers.OfType<int>();

        // define the query
        IEnumerable<int> results = from e in myEnum
                                    select e;

        // enumerate the results
        foreach (int val in results) {
            Console.WriteLine("Result item: {0}", val);
        }

        // wait for input before exiting
        Console.WriteLine("Press enter to finish");
        Console.ReadLine();
    }
}
```

The ArrayList in Listing 27-31 contains an item that can't be cast to the target type, so the OfType method simply excludes it from the IEnumerble<int>. Compiling and running Listing 27-31 produces the following results:

```
Result item: 10
Result item: 20
Result item: 30
Result item: 40
Press enter to finish
```

Performing Advanced LINQ Operations

For the last part of this chapter, we will look at some more advanced LINQ operations. There are a lot of things you can do with LINQ, and some of the most interesting are demonstrated in the following sections. For further information about LINQ to Objects and its features, I recommend the MSDN LINQ portal (http://msdn.microsoft.com/en-us/library/dd264799.aspx) or, of course, my *Apress Pro LINQ* book.

Aggregating Data

A number of LINQ methods can be used to aggregate data into a single value. These methods are described in Table 27-5.

Table 27-5. System.Linq.Enumerable Methods Used to Aggregate Results

Method	Description
Average()	Returns the average of the data values.
Count() LongCount()	Returns the number of items in the results. The LongCount method can be used where the number of items is expected to be a value greater than an int can represent.
Max()	Returns the largest of the data values.
Min()	Returns the smallest of the data values.
Sum()	Calculates the sum of the data values.

These methods are demonstrated in Listing 27-32.

Listing 27-32. Aggregating Data Values

```
using System;
using System.Collections;
using System.Collections.Generic;
using System.Linq;

class Listing_32 {
```

```
static void Main(string[] args) {

    int[] dataValues = new int[] { 10, 20, 30, 40, 50, 60};

    // use the Average method
    double aveResult = dataValues
                        .Where(e => e > 10)
                        .Average();

    // use the Count method
    int countResult = dataValues
                        .Where(e => e > 10)
                        .Count();

    // use the Max and Min methods
    int maxResult = dataValues.Where(e => e > 10).Max();
    int minResult = dataValues.Where(e => e > 10).Min();

    // use the Sum method
    int sumResult = dataValues.Where(e => e > 10).Sum();

    // print out the results
    Console.WriteLine("Average: {0}", aveResult);
    Console.WriteLine("Count: {0}", countResult);
    Console.WriteLine("Max: {0}", maxResult);
    Console.WriteLine("Min: {0}", minResult);
    Console.WriteLine("Sum: {0}", sumResult);

    // wait for input before exiting
    Console.WriteLine("Press enter to finish");
    Console.ReadLine();
    }
}
```

Compiling and running Listing 27-32 produces the following results:

```
Average: 40
Count: 5
Max: 60
Min: 20
Sum: 200
Press enter to finish
```

■ **Tip** The aggregation methods all cause the LINQ query to be executed immediately. See the "Understanding Deferred Execution" section for details of immediate and deferred execution of LINQ queries.

If you want to aggregate some aspect of non-numeric data, you can either use the Select method to project the numeric characteristic you are interested in or use the overloaded versions of the aggregation methods, which take a Func parameter or lambda expression to convert the source data type into an value that can be aggregated. Listing 27-33 demonstrates using both techniques to aggregate the length of string values.

Listing 27-33. Aggregating a Characteristic of a Non-numeric Type

```
using System;
using System.Collections;
using System.Collections.Generic;
using System.Linq;

class Listing_33 {

    static void Main(string[] args) {

        List<string> myFruitList = new List<string>() {
            "apple", "plum", "cherry", "grape", "banana", "pear", "mango" ,
            "persimmon", "lemon", "lime", "coconut", "pineapple", "orange"};


        // project a numeric type and then aggregate
        double projectResult = myFruitList.Select(e => e.Length).Average();

        // use the version of the Average method which selects inline
        double extensionResult = myFruitList.Average(e => e.Length);

        // print out the results
        Console.WriteLine("Projected Result: {0}", projectResult);
        Console.WriteLine("Extension Result: {0}", extensionResult);

        // wait for input before exiting
        Console.WriteLine("Press enter to finish");
        Console.ReadLine();
    }
}
```

Compiling and running Listing 27-33 produces the following output:

```
Projected Result: 5.76923076923077
Extension Result: 5.76923076923077
Press enter to finish
```

Joining Data

When you *join* two data sources, you associate two objects that share a common characteristic. If you have used SQL, the chances are that you have performed a join. You can do something similar when with

LINQ to Objects using the join query keyword or the Join extension method. Listing 27-34 provides a demonstration.

Listing 27-34. Performing a LINQ Join

```
using System;
using System.Collections;
using System.Collections.Generic;
using System.Linq;

class Fruit {

    public Fruit(string nameParam, int codeParam) {
        Name = nameParam;
        StockCode = codeParam;
    }

    public string Name { get; set; }
    public int StockCode { get; set; }
}

class StockRecord {

    public StockRecord(int codeParam, int stockParam) {
        StockCode = codeParam;
        ItemsInStock = stockParam;
    }

    public int StockCode { get; set; }
    public int ItemsInStock { get; set; }
}

class Listing_34 {

    static void Main(string[] args) {

        // create an array of Fruit objects
        Fruit[] fruitArray = new Fruit[] {
            new Fruit("apple", 100), new Fruit("plum", 101), new Fruit("cherry", 102)};

        // create an array of StockRecords
        StockRecord[] stockRecords = new StockRecord[] {
            new StockRecord(100, 50), new StockRecord(101, 10), new StockRecord(102, 500)};

        // define the query
        var results = from fruit in fruitArray
                    join stock in stockRecords on fruit.StockCode equals stock.StockCode
                    select new {
                        Name = fruit.Name,
                        StockCode = fruit.StockCode,
                        ItemsInStock = stock.ItemsInStock
                    };
```

```
    // enumerate the results
    foreach (var item in results) {
        Console.WriteLine("Name: {0}, Code: {1} Stock Level: {2}",
            item.Name, item.StockCode, item.ItemsInStock);
    }

    // wait for input before exiting
    Console.WriteLine("Press enter to finish");
    Console.ReadLine();
    }
}
```

The join keyword introduces a second range variable and creates the association between the two data sources by identifying the common characteristic, as illustrated by Figure 27-8.

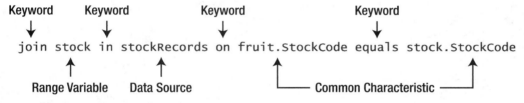

Figure 27-8. *The anatomy of a join clause*

When a query containing a join clause, like the one in Listing 27-33, is executed, the select clause is called for each occurrence of the same value appearing in the common characteristic. In Listing 27-34, this means that the select clause will be called when the StockCode property for the fruit range value has the same value as a StockCode property of an object in the stockRecords data source. You can refer to both range values in the select clause, a feature that I use to create a new anonymous type containing values from both. Compiling and running Listing 27-34 produces the following results:

```
Name: apple, Code: 100 Stock Level: 50
Name: plum, Code: 101 Stock Level: 10
Name: cherry, Code: 102 Stock Level: 500
Press enter to finish
```

The method syntax equivalent of the join keyword is the Join method, which is unusual among the extension methods because it combines its function and projection in a single method. This is because the input to the projection is two variables (one from each data source). Here is Listing 27-34 rewritten using method syntax:

```
var results = fruitArray.Join(
    stockRecords,
    fruit => fruit.StockCode,
    stock => stock.StockCode,
    (fruit, stock) => new {
        Name = fruit.Name,
```

```
        StockCode = fruit.StockCode,
        ItemsInStock = stock.ItemsInStock
});
```

The parameters to the Join method are the second data source, a key selector function for the first data source, a key selector function for the second data source, and a function that receives a parameter from each data source and projects the result.

Creating Combinations of Data

You can define more than one range value in a LINQ query, and when the query is executed, the select clause will be called for each combination of range values from both data sources. Listing 27-35 provides a demonstration.

Listing 27-35. Creating Combinations of Data

```
using System;
using System.Collections;
using System.Collections.Generic;
using System.Linq;

class Listing_35 {

    static void Main(string[] args) {

        List<string> myFruitList
            = new List<string>() {"apple", "plum", "cherry"};

        string[] mySizes = new string[] { "small", "medium", "large" };

        // define a LINQ query that has two range values
        var results = from fruit in myFruitList
                      from size in mySizes
                      select new {
                          Name = fruit,
                          Size = size
                      };

        // enumerate the results
        foreach (var item in results) {
            Console.WriteLine("Result - Name: {0}, Size: {1}",
                item.Name, item.Size);
        }

        // wait for input before exiting
        Console.WriteLine("Press enter to finish");
        Console.ReadLine();
    }
}
```

In this example, I create a range variable for two data sources and use them in a LINQ query that uses a select clause to create an anonymous type. A new object will be created for each combination of values from the data sources. Compiling and running Listing 27-35 produces the following output:

```
Result - Name: apple, Size: small
Result - Name: apple, Size: medium
Result - Name: apple, Size: large
Result - Name: plum, Size: small
Result - Name: plum, Size: medium
Result - Name: plum, Size: large
Result - Name: cherry, Size: small
Result - Name: cherry, Size: medium
Result - Name: cherry, Size: large
Press enter to finish
```

Creating Additional Range Variables

As you can see from the join and combination operations, having additional range variables can be useful. You can create your own and assign any value you want to it by using the let keyword. Listing 27-36 provides a demonstration.

Listing 27-36. Creating a arrange Variable with the let Keyword

```csharp
using System;
using System.Collections.Generic;
using System.Linq;

class Fruit {

    public Fruit(string nameParam, string colorParam, int stockParam) {
        Name = nameParam;
        Color = colorParam;
        ItemsInStock = stockParam;
    }

    public string Name { get; set; }
    public string Color { get; set; }
    public int ItemsInStock { get; set; }
}

class Listing_36 {

    static void Main(string[] args) {

        // create a data source containing Fruit objects
        List<Fruit> myFruitList = new List<Fruit>() {
            new Fruit("Cherry", "Red", 500),
            new Fruit("Apple", "Green", 230),
            new Fruit("Plum", "Red", 300),
```

```
        new Fruit("Banana", "Yellow", 100),
        new Fruit("Grape", "Green", 400)
    };

    // perform the query
    IEnumerable<string> results = from e in myFruitList
                                  let nameLength = e.Name.Length
                                  let lowStock = e.ItemsInStock < 200
                                  where nameLength > 4 && lowStock
                                  select e.Name;

    // enumerate the results
    foreach (string str in results) {
        Console.WriteLine("Result: {0}", str);
    }

    // wait for input before exiting
    Console.WriteLine("Press enter to finish");
    Console.ReadLine();
    }
}
```

The query in Listing 27-36 defines two additional range variables using the let keyword, and both are derived from the main range variable e. The nameLength range variable is assigned the length of the Name property of the current Fruit object. The lowStock range variable is assigned true if the ItemsInStock property of the current Fruit object is lower than 200 and false otherwise. Figure 27-9 illustrates the use of the let keyword to create additional range variables.

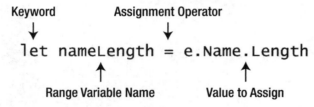

Figure 27-9. The anatomy of the let keyword

When you assign a new range variable a value that is derived from the main range variable, a new value will be calculated for each item in the data source. In the case of Listing 27-36, that means the length of the Name property and the value of the ItemsInStock property will be used to create new values for the nameLength and lowStock range variables each time the Fruit assigned to e, the main range variable, changes.

■ **Tip** Range variables apply only when you are using query syntax. When using method syntax, you can create local variables within your lambda expressions.

Summary

In this chapter, you were introduced to the world of LINQ and saw some demonstrations of using LINQ to Objects. LINQ can take a little while to get used to, but the flexibility and elegance that it can bring to a program is worth the investment in time. One of the best features of LINQ is consistency. As you will see the chapters that follow, everything that you have learned about to LINQ to Objects can be applied to LINQ to XML, LINQ to Entities, and so on. There are differences, but they are not as great as you might expect.

I have lost count of the number of times that I have been able to perform complex data transformations using LINQ to reduce complex legacy programs to a handful of simple queries. I encourage you to dig further into the details of LINQ and take the time to master of the best features available in C#.

CHAPTER 28

■ ■ ■

Parallel LINQ

Parallel LINQ (known as PLINQ and pronounced *pee-link*) is LINQ to Objects enabled for parallel processing using the features of the Task Parallel Library (TPL). You can learn more about C# parallel programming in Chapter 24, although you don't need to know anything about the TPL in order to use PLINQ.

PLINQ divides up the items in your query data source and processes the resulting chunks of data in parallel. This can deliver a significant performance improvement over regular LINQ queries, although the use of PLINQ is limited to LINQ to Objects; you can't use PLINQ on the data sources such as databases and XML data that are described in the following chapters.

This is a short chapter. PLINQ builds heavily on the LINQ knowledge from the previous chapter and is very simple to use. In fact, most of the functionality is available by using a single extension method. Table 28-1 provides the summary for this chapter.

Table 28-1. Quick Problem/Solution Reference for Chapter 28

Problem	Solution	Listings
Perform a LINQ to Objects query using parallel processing	Use the AsParallel extension method	28-1,28-2
Preserve the ordering of PLINQ results	Use the AsOrdered extension method	28-3
Force PLINQ to use parallel execution	Use the WithExecutionMode extension method	28-4
Create a query that doesn't produce a result	Use the ForAll extension method	28-5

Performing a Parallel LINQ Query

The key to using PLINQ is the AsParallel extension method in the System.Linq.ParallelEnumerable class. Calling this method on a data source transforms a LINQ query into a PLINQ one. Listing 28-1 provides a demonstration.

Listing 28-1. A Simple PLINQ Query

```
using System;
using System.Collections.Generic;
using System.Linq;

class Listing_01 {

    static void Main(string[] args) {

        string[] fruits = new string[] { "apple", "plum", "cherry",
            "grape", "banana", "pear", "mango" , "persimmon", "lemon",
            "lime", "coconut", "pineapple", "orange"};

        // define a regular LINQ to Objects query
        var regularResults = from e in fruits
                                where e[0] == 'p'
                                select new {
                                    Name = e,
                                    Length = e.Length
                                };

        // enumerate the regular results
        Console.WriteLine("--- Regular LINQ Results ---");
        foreach (var item in regularResults) {
            Console.WriteLine("Result - Name: {0}, Length: {1}",
                item.Name, item.Length);
        }

        // define the same query using PLINQ
        var parallelResults = from e in fruits.AsParallel()
                                where e[0] == 'p'
                                select new {
                                    Name = e,
                                    Length = e.Length
                                };

        // enumerate the parallel results
        Console.WriteLine("--- Parallel LINQ Results ---");
        foreach (var item in parallelResults) {
            Console.WriteLine("Result - Name: {0}, Length: {1}",
                item.Name, item.Length);
        }

        // wait for input before exiting
        Console.WriteLine("Press enter to finish");
        Console.ReadLine();
    }
}
```

The first query in Listing 28-1 filters for items that start with the letter p and projects an anonymous type containing the value and the length of the value. The second query does exactly the same thing, but applies the AsParallel method to the data source (as illustrated by Figure 28-1), meaning that the second query is performed in parallel using PLINQ.

PLINQ Enabler Method
↓

```
var parallelResults = from e in fruits.AsParallel()
                      where e[0] == 'p'
```

Figure 28-1. The anatomy of a PLINQ query

When you use regular LINQ, each item is taken from the data source and processed sequentially. When you use PLINQ, the items in the data source are divided into chunks and the chunks are processed in parallel using Tasks. This is similar to the difference between a regular loop and a parallel loop as described in Chapter 25. You can find out more about Tasks and parallel programming in Chapter 24. Compiling and running Listing 28-1 produces the following results:

```
--- Regular LINQ Results ---
Result - Name: plum, Length: 4
Result - Name: pear, Length: 4
Result - Name: persimmon, Length: 9
Result - Name: pineapple, Length: 9
--- Parallel LINQ Results ---
Result - Name: persimmon, Length: 9
Result - Name: pineapple, Length: 9
Result - Name: plum, Length: 4
Result - Name: pear, Length: 4
Press enter to finish
```

And that's all it takes to get started with PLINQ: you call the AsParallel method on your data source. There is no C# keyword available for AsParallel, which means that you must mix query and method syntax, or use just method syntax. Listing 28-2 demonstrates the parallel query from Listing 28-1 written using method syntax.

Listing 28-2. A Parallel Query Written in Method Syntax

```
using System;
using System.Collections.Generic;
using System.Linq;

class Listing_02 {

    static void Main(string[] args) {

        string[] fruits = new string[] { "apple", "plum", "cherry",
```

```
                    "grape", "banana", "pear", "mango" , "persimmon", "lemon",
                    "lime", "coconut", "pineapple", "orange"};

            // define a parallel query using method syntax
            var parallelResults = fruits.AsParallel()
                                    .Where(e => e[0] == 'p')
                                    .Select(e => new {
                                        Name = e,
                                        Length = e.Length
                                    });

            // enumerate the results
            foreach (var item in parallelResults) {
                Console.WriteLine("Result - Name: {0}, Length: {1}",
                    item.Name, item.Length);
            }

            // wait for input before exiting
            Console.WriteLine("Press enter to finish");
            Console.ReadLine();
        }
    }
```

Understanding PLINQ Result Ordering

If you are particularly observant, you will have noticed that the output of the PLINQ query in Listing 28-1 was different from the output of the sequential LINQ query—the order of the items was different.

When you use regular, sequential LINQ, the order of the results depends on the order of the items in the data source. The first item that passes the filter in a where clause, for example, will be the first item projected into the results by a select clause, as illustrated by Figure 28-2.

Data Source

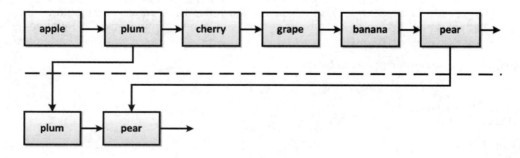

Results

Figure 28-2. Result ordering in a sequential LINQ query

As the sequential query in Listing 28-1 works its way through the items in the data source, the where clause excludes any that don't begin with the letter p. The first value, apple, is rejected but the second, plum, is passed to the select clause and projected into the results. The sequence continues; cherry, grape and banana are all filtered out, but pear is included. You can look at the items in the data source and tell in advance what sequence of results will be produced: plum will always generate the first result, pear will always generate the second, and so on.

This implicit ordering is lost when you use PLINQ because the individual chunks of the data source are processed in parallel and the Task processing the first chunk may not find a result until after other Tasks have done so, as illustrated by Figure 28-3.

Data Source Chunks

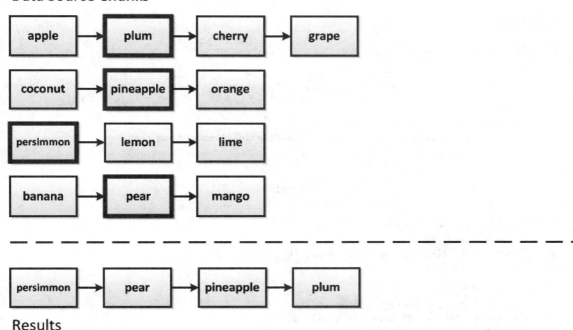

Results

Figure 28-3. Parallel processing data source chunks

You can see from the figure that the third chunk contains a matching item right at the start. This usually means that this item will be used to generate the first result. However, you can't rely on this. There can also be variations in result ordering when you run the same PLINQ query multiple times, caused by the Tasks being started at slightly different times and running at slightly different speeds. In short, you should not make any assumptions about the order of results in a standard PLINQ query. If you simply cannot do without the order of the results of your query being linked to the order of the data items, then you can force order to be preserved. This is described in the following section.

Preserving Order in a PLINQ query

If result ordering is essential to your program, you can use the AsOrdered extension method to instruct PLINQ to order the results to match the order of the data source items that generated them. Doing this can have a significant performance impact and may negate the benefits of using a parallel query at all. Listing 28-3 demonstrates preserving order in a PLINQ query.

Listing 28-3. Preserving PLINQ Result Order

```
using System;
using System.Collections.Generic;
using System.Linq;

class Listing_03 {

    static void Main(string[] args) {

        string[] fruits = new string[] { "apple", "plum", "cherry",
            "grape", "banana", "pear", "mango" , "persimmon", "lemon",
            "lime", "coconut", "pineapple", "orange"};

        // define an ordered PLINQ query
        var parallelResults = from e in fruits.AsParallel().AsOrdered()
                              where e[0] == 'p'
                              select new {
                                  Name = e,
                                  Length = e.Length
                              };

        // enumerate the results
        foreach (var item in parallelResults) {
            Console.WriteLine("Result - Name: {0}, Length: {1}",
                item.Name, item.Length);
        }

        // wait for input before exiting
        Console.WriteLine("Press enter to finish");
        Console.ReadLine();
    }
}
```

The AsOrdered method is applied after the AsParallel method, as illustrated by Figure 28-4.

PLINQ Enabler Method   Result Ordering Method
         ↓   ↓

```
var parallelResults = from e in fruits.AsParallel().AsOrdered()
                      where e[0] == 'p'
```

Figure 28-4. The anatomy of an ordered PLINQ query

Compiling and running Listing 28-3 produces the following results:

```
Result - Name: plum, Length: 4
Result - Name: pear, Length: 4
Result - Name: persimmon, Length: 9
Result - Name: pineapple, Length: 9
Press enter to finish
```

You can see from the results that the order has been preserved to match the order that the items appeared in the data source.

Forcing Parallel Execution

A query that contains a call to the AsParallel method won't always be executed in parallel. The PLINQ engine will revert to sequential execution if its analysis suggests that sequential performance will exceed parallel performance. If you want to force parallel execution, even when PLINQ would usually perform a query sequentially, then you can use the WithExecutionMode method, passing the ForceParallelism value of the ParallelExecutionMode enumeration as a parameter. Listing 28-4 demonstrates how this is done.

Listing 28-4. Forcing Parallel Query Execution

```
using System;
using System.Collections.Generic;
using System.Linq;

class Listing_04 {

    static void Main(string[] args) {

        string[] fruits = new string[] { "apple", "plum", "cherry",
            "grape", "banana", "pear", "mango" , "persimmon", "lemon",
            "lime", "coconut", "pineapple", "orange"};

        // define an ordered PLINQ query
        var parallelResults = from e in fruits.AsParallel()
                        .AsOrdered()
                        .WithExecutionMode(ParallelExecutionMode.ForceParallelism)
                    where e[0] == 'p'
                    select new {
                        Name = e,
                        Length = e.Length
                    };

        // enumerate the results
        foreach (var item in parallelResults) {
            Console.WriteLine("Result - Name: {0}, Length: {1}",
                item.Name, item.Length);
        }
```

```
            // wait for input before exiting
            Console.WriteLine("Press enter to finish");
            Console.ReadLine();
        }
    }
```

Unfortunately, you can't determine in advance if PLINQ will run your query in parallel or sequential mode; its decision is based on the complexity of the query, the number of items in the data source, and the parallel capabilities of the hardware on which the query will be executed. Therefore, you can only decide to leave the decision to PLINQ or to force parallel execution in advance.

Performing Queries without Results

PLINQ has a useful feature in the ForAll extension method, which performs an Action on each item in a data source. The items in the data source are broken into chunks, and the chunks are processed in parallel using Tasks. This is like a parallel loop (see Chapter 25), but it allows you to apply LINQ ordering and filtering to the data before it is processed. Listing 28-5 contains a demonstration.

Listing 28-5. Using the PLINQ ForAll Method

```
using System;
using System.Collections.Generic;
using System.Linq;

class Listing_05 {

    static void Main(string[] args) {

        string[] fruits = new string[] { "apple", "plum", "cherry",
            "grape", "banana", "pear", "mango" , "persimmon", "lemon",
            "lime", "coconut", "pineapple", "orange"};

        // use the ForAll extension method
        fruits.AsParallel()
            .Where(e => e[0] == 'p')
            .ForAll(e => Console.WriteLine("Result: {0}", e));

        // wait for input before exiting
        Console.WriteLine("Press enter to finish");
        Console.ReadLine();
    }
}
```

The ForAll method can only be used in a query where the AsParallel method has been applied to the data source, as is the case in the example. The query in Listing 28-5 uses the Where method to filter the items to exclude any that don't start with the letter p. The ForAll method simply prints out the value, but you could perform any operation here. Compiling and running Listing 28-5 produces the following results:

```
Result: persimmon
Result: plum
Result: pineapple
Result: pear
Press enter to finish
```

Summary

In this chapter, you have taken a brief tour of the parallel version of LINQ to Objects—PLINQ. PLINQ lets you use the power of parallel processing on your LINQ queries with one method call. Depending on your query and data, the performance benefits can be enormous. You can use PLINQ without any reference to the Task class, which underpins the performance improvements. PLINQ is really a simple and powerful addition to LINQ.

CHAPTER 29

LINQ to XML

LINQ to XML lets you apply the LINQ query style that we saw in Chapter 27 to XML data. This is done through a set of classes that represent XML data in a way that is designed to accommodate LINQ to Objects queries. These classes are in the System.Xml.Linq namespace, and they make it easy to work with XML. Once you understand how these classes work and relate to one another, you can use LINQ queries to create powerful and simple XML handlers.

The LINQ to XML classes read all the XML data into memory. This is similar to the Document Object Model (DOM) approach, which you may have used in other programming languages. C# does provide support for DOM, but it has been eclipsed by the more flexible and expressive LINQ to XML features.

The first part of this chapter shows you how to create and work with XML documents using the classes in the System.Xml.Linq namespace. The second part of this chapter shows you how to use LINQ queries to create and manipulate objects using the classes covered in the first part. We've already done the hard work understanding LINQ in Chapter 27. In this chapter, the heavy lifting is all about the System.Xml.Linq classes. Table 29-1 provides the summary for this chapter.

Table 29-1. Quick Problem/Solution Reference for Chapter 29

Problem	Solution	Listings
Create an object to represent an XML element.	Use the XElement class.	29-1
Create an XML fragment.	Use the XElement class, and pass other XElement objects as constructor parameters.	29-2 through 4, 29-7
Create different types of XML node.	Use other classes in the System.Linq.Xml namespace, such as XAttribute and XComment.	29-5
Create a valid XML document.	Use the XDocument class.	29-6
Read and write XML files.	Use the XElement.Load, XElement.Save, XDocument.Load, or XDocument.Save methods.	29-8, 29-9
Process an XElement.	Use the Attributes, Descendants, or Elements methods or the Name and Value properties.	29-10 through 29-12
Modify an XElement.	Use XElement class modification methods described in Table 29-5.	29-13, 29-14

Problem	Solution	Listings
Query an XML fragment.	Use the Elements or Descendants methods to get an IEnumerble<XElement> suitable for use as a query data source.	29-15
Create XML from a query.	Project new XElement objects.	29-16, 29-17
Create objects from XML.	Project new objects whose fields and properties are set using XElement values.	29-18
Transform XML data.	Use the standard LINQ query operators with IEnumerable<XElement> data sources.	29-19 through 29-25
Use a query to modify the XML objects in the query data source.	Use Parallel LINQ and the ForAll extension method.	29-26, 29-27

Using the LINQ XML Classes

The System.Xml.Linq namespace contains a set of classes that you can use to create or modify XML. LINQ to XML relies heavily on these classes, and we need to understand how they function before we can move on to XML-related LINQ queries.

Creating XML Declaratively

At the heart of LINQ to XML is the XElement class from the System.Xml.Linq namespace. We will use this class, or one of its close relations, in most of our LINQ to XML operations. We can use this class directly to create XML, as Listing 29-1 demonstrates; this is known as *declarative* or *functional* XML creation.

Listing 29-1. Using the XElement Directly

```
using System;
using System.Xml.Linq;

class Listing_01 {

    static void Main(string[] args) {

        // create XElements
        XElement myNameElement = new XElement("Name", "Orange");
        XElement mySizeElement = new XElement("Size", "Large");

        // print out the XElement objects
        Console.WriteLine(myNameElement);
        Console.WriteLine(mySizeElement);
```

```
        // wait for input before exiting
        Console.WriteLine("Press enter to finish");
        Console.ReadLine();
    }
}
```

In Listing 29-1, I create two XElement objects using a constructor that takes two parameters: the name of the element and the value of the element. I then use the `Console.WriteLine` method to write the XElement objects out, producing the following output:

```
<Name>Orange</Name>
<Size>Large</Size>
Press enter to finish
```

You can see that the XElement objects produce fragments of XML. There is another XElement constructor that we can use to create a hierarchy of XML fragments, which is demonstrated in Listing 29-2.

Listing 29-2. Creating an XML Hierarchy

```
using System;
using System.Xml.Linq;

class Listing_02 {

    static void Main(string[] args) {

        // create XElements
        XElement myNameElement = new XElement("Name", "Orange");
        XElement mySizeElement = new XElement("Size", "Large");

        // create a hierarchy of XElements
        XElement myFruit = new XElement("Fruit", myNameElement, mySizeElement);

        // print out the XElement object
        Console.WriteLine(myFruit);

        // wait for input before exiting
        Console.WriteLine("Press enter to finish");
        Console.ReadLine();
    }
}
```

The second constructor takes a `string` parameter and a variable number of XElements (it is a parameter array, which is described in Chapter 9). The `string` is the name of the XML element, and the XElements are the children for this element. The output from compiling and running Listing 29-2 is as follows:

```
<Fruit>
  <Name>Orange</Name>
  <Size>Large</Size>
</Fruit>
Press enter to finish
```

We have created the parent XElement and added two children, and with very little effort we have a simple XML document. I have created the children and then added them to the parent, but I could have done everything in a single statement, like this:

```
XElement myFruit = new XElement("Fruit",
    new XElement("Name", "Orange"),
    new XElement("Size", "Large"));
```

This way of creating elements is very important when we start to use LINQ queries to generate XML in the "Creating XML from LINQ Queries" section later in this chapter.

Using Arbitrary Types to Create XElements

In Listings 29-1 and 29-2, I created the child XElements by passing two string parameters to the constructor: the name of the element and the value. In fact, you can pass any object as the second parameter, and a string representation of the object will be included in the XML data. Listing 29-3 demonstrates this using an enum and a custom class.

Listing 29-3. Using String Representations of Objects in XElements

```
using System;
using System.Xml.Linq;

enum FruitSize {
    Small, Medium, Large
}

class Fruit {

    public Fruit(string nameParam, int stockParam) {
        Name = nameParam;
        ItemsInStock = stockParam;
    }

    public string Name { get; set; }
    public int ItemsInStock { get; set; }

    public override string ToString() {
        return Name;
    }
}

class Listing_03 {
```

```
static void Main(string[] args) {

    // create a Fruit object
    Fruit myFruitObject = new Fruit("Orange", 200);

    // create XElements using the Fruit object
    XElement myNameElement = new XElement("Name", myFruitObject);
    XElement mySizeElement = new XElement("Size", FruitSize.Large);

    // create a hierarchy of XElements
    XElement myFruitElement = new XElement("Fruit", myNameElement, mySizeElement);

    // print out the XElement object
    Console.WriteLine(myFruitElement);

    // wait for input before exiting
    Console.WriteLine("Press enter to finish");
    Console.ReadLine();
    }
}
```

In Listing 29-3, I pass a Fruit object as the parameter to create one XElement, which includes the result of the ToString method in the XML. The other XElement is created using a value from an enum, which is expressed as a helpful string value. Compiling and running Listing 29-3 produces the following output:

```
<Fruit>
  <Name>Orange</Name>
  <Size>Large</Size>
</Fruit>
Press enter to finish
```

Notice that only the result from the ToString method of the Fruit object is included in the XML. The Fruit class defines a property called ItemsInStock that is ignored. If you pass an object to the constructor of XElement like this, you must be sure that the ToString method returns all the information you need included in the XML. As an alternative, you can create XElements to express the value or result of individual members, as demonstrated in Listing 29-4.

Listing 29-4. Creating Multiple XElements from the Members of an Object

```
using System;
using System.Xml.Linq;

class Listing_04 {

    static void Main(string[] args) {

        // create a Fruit object
        Fruit myFruitObject = new Fruit("Orange", 200);
```

```
        // create XElements using the Fruit object
        XElement myNameElement = new XElement("Name", myFruitObject.Name);
        XElement myStockElement = new XElement("ItemsInStock", myFruitObject.ItemsInStock);
        XElement mySizeElement = new XElement("Size", FruitSize.Large);

        // create a hierarchy of XElements
        XElement myFruitElement = new XElement("Fruit",
            myNameElement, myStockElement, mySizeElement);

        // print out the XElement object
        Console.WriteLine(myFruitElement);

        // wait for input before exiting
        Console.WriteLine("Press enter to finish");
        Console.ReadLine();
    }
}
```

Listing 29-4 explicitly creates XElements for both of the properties of the Fruit object. Compiling and running Listing 29-4 produces the following result:

```
<Fruit>
  <Name>Orange</Name>
  <ItemsInStock>200</ItemsInStock>
  <Size>Large</Size>
</Fruit>
Press enter to finish
```

Creating Other XML Node Types

XElement isn't the only kind of XML node available. There are classes that you can use to create different node types. Listing 29-5 provides an example.

Listing 29-5. Creating Different XML Node Types

```
using System;
using System.Xml.Linq;

class Listing_05 {

    static void Main(string[] args) {

        // create an XElement
        XElement myElement = new XElement("ElementName", "ElementValue");

        // create an attribute
        XAttribute myAttribute = new XAttribute("AttributeName", "AttributeValue");
```

```
        // create a comment
        XComment myComment = new XComment("This is a comment");

        // add the nodes to a parent element
        XElement myParentElement = new XElement("ParentElement",
            myElement, myAttribute, myComment);

        // write out the contents of the parent element
        Console.WriteLine(myParentElement);

        // wait for input before exiting
        Console.WriteLine("Press enter to finish");
        Console.ReadLine();
    }
}
```

Listing 29-5 demonstrates the use of the XAttribute and XComment classes, which create XML attributes and comments, respectively. These nodes are added to a parent XElement as in the previous examples, producing the following output when the listing is compiled and run:

```
<ParentElement AttributeName="AttributeValue">
  <ElementName>ElementValue</ElementName>
  <!--This is a comment-->
</ParentElement>
Press enter to finish
```

Table 29-2 describes the classes used to create the most commonly used types of XML node.

Table 29-2. Classes Used to Create Common XML Nodes

Class	Description
XElement	Creates an XML element
XText	Creates a text block
XCData	Creates a CDATA block
XAttribute	Creates an XML attribute, which is expressed as part of the parent element
XComment	Creates an XML comment
XDocument	Creates a valid XML document
XDeclaration	Used with XDocument to provide a declaration specifying the version and encoding information for an XML document and to specify whether the XML document stands alone

Class	Description
XDocumentType	Used with XDocument to specify the Document Type Definition (DTD)

Creating Valid XML Documents

The XDocument class provides features for creating a valid XML document, as opposed to the XML fragments we have created so far. Listing 29-6 provides a demonstration of creating a valid XML document.

Listing 29-6. Using the XDocument Class

```
using System;
using System.Xml.Linq;

class Listing_06 {

    static void Main(string[] args) {

        XDeclaration myDeclaration = new XDeclaration("1.0", "utf-8", "yes");
        XDocumentType myDocType = new XDocumentType("FruitList", null, null, null);

        // create XElements
        XElement myNameElement = new XElement("Name", "Orange");
        XElement mySizeElement = new XElement("Size", "Large");

        // create my root element
        XElement myRootElement = new XElement("Fruit", myNameElement, mySizeElement);

        // create the XML document
        XDocument myDoc = new XDocument(
            myDeclaration,
            myDocType,
            myRootElement);

        // print out the XElement object
        Console.WriteLine(myDoc);

        // wait for input before exiting
        Console.WriteLine("Press enter to finish");
        Console.ReadLine();
    }
}
```

The XDeclaration and XDocumentType classes are used to specify the version and encoding information and to provide details of the DTD. In Listing 29-6, I have used basic values to create these objects, but there are a lot of options for the information they can represent. Compiling and running Listing 29-6 produces the following results:

```
<!DOCTYPE FruitList >
<Fruit>
  <Name>Orange</Name>
  <Size>Large</Size>
</Fruit>
Press enter to finish
```

You can see that the DTD information has been included but that the XML declaration has not. This is an oddity of using the XDocument.ToString method, which Console.WriteLine calls to create a string representation of the XML. If we serialize the XML to a file and examine its content, we can see the declaration as follows:

```
<?xml version="1.0" encoding="utf-8" standalone="yes"?>
<!DOCTYPE FruitList >
<Fruit>
  <Name>Orange</Name>
  <Size>Large</Size>
</Fruit>
```

You can learn how to write XML data to a file in the "Reading and Writing XML Files" section later in the chapter.

Populating an XElement or XDocument with an IEnumerable

If you create an XElement or an XDocument and pass in an implementation of IEnumerable or IEnumerable<T> containing XML node objects, these objects will be added to the newly created element. This means you can use collections and arrays of XML node objects and pass them directly to the constructor, as demonstrated by Listing 29-7.

Listing 29-7. Populating an XElement with a Collection

```
using System;
using System.Collections.Generic;
using System.Xml.Linq;

class Listing_07 {

    static void Main(string[] args) {

        // create an array of XElements
        List<XElement> myElements = new List<XElement>() {
            new XElement("Name", "Orange"),
            new XElement("Size", "Large"),
            new XElement("ItemsInStock", 250),
```

```
        };

        // create an element using the array
        XElement myFruit = new XElement("Fruit", myElements);

        // print out the XElement object
        Console.WriteLine(myFruit);

        // wait for input before exiting
        Console.WriteLine("Press enter to finish");
        Console.ReadLine();
    }
}
```

Compiling and running Listing 29-7 produces the following output:

```
<Fruit>
  <Name>Orange</Name>
  <Size>Large</Size>
  <ItemsInStock>250</ItemsInStock>
</Fruit>
Press enter to finish
```

As we'll see when we come to generating XML from queries, the ability to populate an XElement or XDocument from an IEnumerable<T> allows us to project results from a query that will generate XML fragments and documents.

Reading and Writing XML Files

Being able to create XML isn't very useful if we can't create files and read them back later. The following sections demonstrate how to save and load XML. This can be done from a file or a Stream or TextReader/TextWriter; see Chapters 20 and 21 for examples of different kinds of Streams, readers, and writers.

Saving XML

Having created an XML fragment or document, we often need to save it. We can do this using the Save method of the XElement or XDocument classes, as demonstrated by Listing 29-8.

Listing 29-8. Saving an XML Fragment

```
using System;
using System.Collections.Generic;
using System.Xml.Linq;

class Listing_08 {
```

```
static void Main(string[] args) {

    // create an array of XElements
    List<XElement> myElements = new List<XElement>() {
        new XElement("Name", "Orange"),
        new XElement("Size", "Large"),
        new XElement("ItemsInStock", 250),
    };

    // create an element using the array
    XElement myFruit = new XElement("Fruit", myElements);

    // save the XML fragment to a file
    myFruit.Save("fragment.xml");

    // wait for input before exiting
    Console.WriteLine("Press enter to finish");
    Console.ReadLine();
    }
}
```

In Listing 29-8, I call the Save method on an XElement object and provide the name of the file I want to write to as a string parameter. This saves the XML to the specified file. The contents of the file are as follows:

```
<?xml version="1.0" encoding="utf-8"?>
<Fruit>
  <Name>Orange</Name>
  <Size>Large</Size>
  <ItemsInStock>250</ItemsInStock>
</Fruit>
```

Notice that the XML declaration is added even though I wrote a fragment to the file. There are overloaded versions of the Save method, which are described in Table 29-3.

Table 29-3. *Overloaded versions of the Save Method*

Method Version	Description
Save(string) Save(string, SaveOptions)	Saves the XML to the file specified in the string parameter, using the default or specified options
Save(Stream) Save(Stream, SaveOptions)	Saves the XML to a Stream using the default or specified options (see Chapter 20 for details of streams)
Save(TextWriter) Save(TextWriter, SaveOptions)	Saves the XML to a TextWriter using the default or specified options (see Chapter 20 for details of the TextWriter class)

The SaveOptions parameter is a value from the System.Xml.Linq.SaveOptions enum. If you provide the value DisableFormatting, then the whitespace structure will be omitted from the XML output. The default value is None, which is the same as omitting the parameter entirely.

Loading XML

The counterpart to the Save method is the static Load method, which reads XML from a file, Stream, or TextReader and returns an XElement representing the root node. Listing 29-9 demonstrates reading the fragment.xml file generated in the previous section.

Listing 29-9. Reading an XML File

```
using System;
using System.Collections.Generic;
using System.Linq;
using System.Xml.Linq;

class Listing_09 {

    static void Main(string[] args) {

        // load the XML file using the static Load method
        XElement myRootElement = XElement.Load(@"..\..\fragment.xml");

        // print out the XElement
        Console.WriteLine(myRootElement);

        // wait for input before exiting
        Console.WriteLine("Press enter to finish");
        Console.ReadLine();
    }
}
```

The output of compiling and running Listing 29-9 is as follows. Note that the XML declaration has been read from the file but is not displayed when you write out the XElement to the Console:

```
<Fruit>
  <Name>Orange</Name>
  <Size>Large</Size>
  <ItemsInStock>250</ItemsInStock>
</Fruit>
Press enter to finish
```

Processing XML Declaratively

Once you have read or created an XElement object, you can easily process the data by using the various properties defined in the XElement class. Listing 29-10 provides an example.

Listing 29-10. Processing an XElement

```
using System;
using System.Collections.Generic;
using System.Xml.Linq;

class Listing_10 {

    static void Main(string[] args) {

        // load the XML file using the static Load method
        XElement myRootElement = XElement.Load(@"..\..\fragment.xml");

        // print out the name of the root node
        Console.WriteLine("Root node name: {0}", myRootElement.Name);

        // get the child elements
        IEnumerable<XElement> elementsEnum = myRootElement.Elements();

        foreach (XElement elem in elementsEnum) {
            Console.WriteLine("Name: {0}, Value: {1}",
                elem.Name, elem.Value);
        }

        // wait for input before exiting
        Console.WriteLine("Press enter to finish");
        Console.ReadLine();
    }
}
```

Listing 29-10 loads an XML file to create an XElement representing the root element, prints out the name of the element, and then obtains the set of descendent elements as an IEnumerable<XElement> by using the Descendants method. A foreach loop is used to enumerate the XElements, and the Name and Value properties for each XElement are printed to the console. The result of compiling and running Listing 29-10 is as follows:

```
Root node name: Fruit
Name: Name, Value: Orange
Name: Size, Value: Large
Name: ItemsInStock, Value: 250
Press enter to finish
```

You can see from the results that this is the XML file that was created in Listing 29-8. Table 29-4 describes the members of the XElement class that can be used to process XML

Table 29-4. XElement Members

Member	Description
Name	Returns the name of the current element.
Value	Returns the value assigned to the current element
Attributes() Attributes(string)	Returns an IEnumerable<XAttribute> containing all the attributes of the current element or just the attributes that match the specified string parameter.
Descendants() Descendants(string)	Returns an IEnumerable<XElement> containing all the descendant elements for the current element or just the attributes that match the string parameter
Elements() Elements(string)	Returns an IEnumerable<XElement> containing all the immediate (that is, just one level down and no further) descendant elements for the current element

Filtering Elements by Name

Some of the methods in Table 29-4 have string parameters. In fact, they really take an instance of the XName class, but you create the XName by providing a string, and the conversion is performed implicitly. These versions of the methods return only those elements that match the name you have provided, as demonstrated by Listing 29-11.

Listing 29-11. Filtering Elements with a Name

```
using System;
using System.Collections.Generic;
using System.Xml.Linq;

class Listing_11 {

    static void Main(string[] args) {

        // load the XML file using the static Load method
        XElement myRootElement = XElement.Load(@"..\..\fragment.xml");

        // get the child elements
        IEnumerable<XElement> elementsEnum = myRootElement.Elements("Size");

        foreach (XElement elem in elementsEnum) {
            Console.WriteLine("Name: {0}, Value: {1}",
                elem.Name, elem.Value);
        }
```

```
        // wait for input before exiting
        Console.WriteLine("Press enter to finish");
        Console.ReadLine();
    }
}
```

In Listing 29-11, I pass the string value Size to the Elements method, which filters the result to contain only those elements called Size. Compiling and running Listing 29-11 produces the following results:

```
Name: Size, Value: Large
Press enter to finish
```

Finding All Descendants

The Elements method returns those XElements that are immediate children of the current node. If you want to get all the XElements, including children of children, then you can use the Descendants method. Listing 29-12 provides a demonstration, using the following XML file, which is saved in the project directory:

```xml
<?xml version="1.0" encoding="utf-8"?>
<Fruit>
  <Name>Orange</Name>
  <Size>Large</Size>
  <ItemsInStock>250</ItemsInStock>
  <Description>
    <Color>Orange</Color>
    <Flavor>Citrus</Flavor>
  </Description>
</Fruit>
```

I have added some new elements to the XML in this file, some of which are not children of the root node.

Listing 29-12. Finding Immediate and All Descendants

```csharp
using System;
using System.Collections.Generic;
using System.Xml.Linq;

class Listing_11 {

    static void Main(string[] args) {

        // load the XML file using the static Load method
        XElement myRootElement = XElement.Load(@"..\..\fragment.xml");

        // get the child elements
        IEnumerable<XElement> elementsEnum = myRootElement.Elements();
```

```
        foreach (XElement elem in elementsEnum) {
            Console.WriteLine("Element - Name: {0}, Value: {1}",
                elem.Name, elem.Value);
        }

        // get the descendant elements
        IEnumerable<XElement> descendantEnum = myRootElement.Descendants();

        foreach (XElement elem in descendantEnum) {
            Console.WriteLine("Descendant - Name: {0}, Value: {1}",
                elem.Name, elem.Value);
        }

        // wait for input before exiting
        Console.WriteLine("Press enter to finish");
        Console.ReadLine();
    }
}
```

Compiling and running Listing 29-12 produces the following results:

```
Element - Name: Name, Value: Orange
Element - Name: Size, Value: Large
Element - Name: ItemsInStock, Value: 250
Element - Name: Description, Value: OrangeCitrus
Descendant - Name: Name, Value: Orange
Descendant - Name: Size, Value: Large
Descendant - Name: ItemsInStock, Value: 250
Descendant - Name: Description, Value: OrangeCitrus
Descendant - Name: Color, Value: Orange
Descendant - Name: Flavor, Value: Citrus
Press enter to finish
```

You can see from the results that the call to the Elements method includes all the immediate descendants from the root node but excludes the children of the Description element. The Descendants method includes all the descendants of the root node, including the Description children, Color and Flavor.

Modifying XML

The System.Linq.Xml classes provide methods that allow you to change their content and descendants once they have been created. Listing 29-13 provides a demonstration using the following XML file, saved in the project directory as data.xml:

```
<?xml version="1.0" encoding="utf-8" ?>
<Fruits>
  <Fruit>
    <Name>Cherry</Name>
```

```
    <Color>Red</Color>
    <StockLevel>500</StockLevel>
  </Fruit>
  <Fruit>
    <Name>Apple</Name>
    <Color>Green</Color>
    <StockLevel>230</StockLevel>
  </Fruit>
  <Fruit>
    <Name>Plum</Name>
    <Color>Red</Color>
    <StockLevel>300</StockLevel>
  </Fruit>
</Fruits>
```

Listing 29-13 uses the XElement Add and Remove methods to change the structure of the XML.

Listing 29-13. Modifying the Structure of XML Data

```
using System;
using System.Xml.Linq;

class Listing_13 {

    static void Main(string[] args) {

        // load the XML data
        XElement rootNode = XElement.Load(@"..\..\data.xml");

        // define the name of the elements we are going to make into attributes
        string[] elementNames = new string[] { "Name", "Color", "StockLevel" };

        // enumerate each element that belongs to the child node
        foreach (XElement elem in rootNode.Elements()) {
            // process each of the defined element names in turn
            foreach (string name in elementNames) {
                // get the element by name
                XElement subElement = elem.Element(name);
                // add an attribute to the parent element
                elem.Add(new XAttribute(subElement.Name, subElement.Value));
                // remove the sub element
                subElement.Remove();
            }
        }

        // print out the XML to the Console
        Console.WriteLine(rootNode);

        // wait for input before exiting
        Console.WriteLine("Press enter to finish");
        Console.ReadLine();
    }
```

```
}
```

I enumerate the XElements that are direct descendants of the root node of the XML data—the first-level elements. From each first-level XElement, I obtain the Name, Color, and StockLevel second-level XElement objects by using the Element method. I create a new XAttribute object using the name and value of each second-level XElement and call the Add method to add it to the first-level XElement. Finally, I have the second-level XElements remove themselves from their first-level parent by calling the Remove method. Compiling and running Listing 29-13 produces the following XML output, which demonstrates that I have converted the elements to attributes:

```
<Fruits>
  <Fruit Name="Cherry" Color="Red" StockLevel="500" />
  <Fruit Name="Apple" Color="Green" StockLevel="230" />
  <Fruit Name="Plum" Color="Red" StockLevel="300" />
</Fruits>
Press enter to finish
```

There are several methods you can use to manipulate XElements, the most useful of which are described in Table 29-5.

Table 29-5. XElement Modification Members

Member	Description
Add(object)	Adds an XML object to the current XElement
AddFirst(object)	Adds an XML object as the first child of the current XElement
Remove()	Removes the current XElement from its parent
RemoveAll()	Removes all the nodes and attributes from the current XElement
RemoveAttributes()	Removes all the attributes from the current XElement
ReplaceAll(object[])	Removes all the attributes and nodes from the current XElement and replaces them with the XML objects provided as parameters
ReplaceAttributes(object[])	Removes all the attributes from the current XElement and replaces them with the attributes provided as parameters
Name Value	Gets or sets the name and value of the current XElement

You can use these methods to manipulate XML data in any way you need to, changing the structure of the XML as well as the name and value of any attribute. Once you have retrieved an XElement from your root node (either by enumeration or using a method such as Element), you can then use the methods described in Table 29-5 to change the content. Listing 29-14 provides a demonstration of changing the name of an element, using the same source XML as Listing 29-13.

Listing 29-14. Changing the Name of an Element

```
using System;
using System.Collections.Generic;
using System.Xml.Linq;

class Listing_14 {

    static void Main(string[] args) {

        // load the XML data
        XElement rootNode = XElement.Load(@"..\..\data.xml");

        // get all of the nodes called StockLevel anywhere in the XML
        IEnumerable<XElement> stockElements = rootNode.Descendants("StockLevel");

        // enumerate the elements and change the name of each
        foreach (XElement elem in stockElements) {
            elem.Name = "ItemCount";
        }

        // print out the XML to the Console
        Console.WriteLine(rootNode);

        // wait for input before exiting
        Console.WriteLine("Press enter to finish");
        Console.ReadLine();
    }
}
```

I use the Descendants method to obtain an enumeration of all the elements with the name StockLevel and then assign a new value to the Name property. This has the effect of changing the name of these elements, as the following output demonstrates:

```
<Fruits>
  <Fruit>
    <Name>Cherry</Name>
    <Color>Red</Color>
    <ItemCount>500</ItemCount>
  </Fruit>
  <Fruit>
    <Name>Apple</Name>
    <Color>Green</Color>
    <ItemCount>230</ItemCount>
  </Fruit>
  <Fruit>
    <Name>Plum</Name>
    <Color>Red</Color>
```

```
    <ItemCount>300</ItemCount>
  </Fruit>
</Fruits>
Press enter to finish
```

Using LINQ to XML Queries

You can use the System.Xml.Linq namespace classes on their own. These classes can stand on their own, and there are no additional features that come from using these classes with LINQ queries. But to use these classes without LINQ queries is to miss out on the flexibility and simplicity that combining them can bring. In the following sections, I'll show you some different techniques for using queries on XML data. All of these examples could be achieved without the query, but the code required would be more verbose and more error-prone.

Most of the examples in this section use the following XML file:

```xml
<?xml version="1.0" encoding="utf-8" ?>
<Fruits>
  <Fruit>
    <Name>Cherry</Name>
    <Color>Red</Color>
    <StockLevel>500</StockLevel>
  </Fruit>
  <Fruit>
    <Name>Apple</Name>
    <Color>Green</Color>
    <StockLevel>230</StockLevel>
  </Fruit>
  <Fruit>
    <Name>Plum</Name>
    <Color>Red</Color>
    <StockLevel>300</StockLevel>
  </Fruit>
  <Fruit>
    <Name>Banana</Name>
    <Color>Yellow</Color>
    <StockLevel>100</StockLevel>
  </Fruit>
  <Fruit>
    <Name>Grape</Name>
    <Color>Green</Color>
    <StockLevel>400</StockLevel>
  </Fruit>
</Fruits>
```

This file is included in the Visual Studio projects as data.xml and loaded at the start of each example that uses it.

Querying XML for Data

A good place to start is to query an XML document to extract data that matches something we are interested in. Listing 29-15 provides a very simple example.

Listing 29-15. Performing a Query on XML Data

```
using System;
using System.Collections.Generic;
using System.Linq;
using System.Xml.Linq;

class Listing_15 {

    static void Main(string[] args) {

        // load the XML data
        XElement rootNode = XElement.Load(@"..\..\data.xml");

        // perform a query on the XML
        var results = from fruit in rootNode.Elements()
                      let stockLevel = int.Parse(fruit.Element("StockLevel").Value)
                      where stockLevel < 250
                      select new {
                          Name = fruit.Element("Name").Value,
                          Count = stockLevel
                      };

        // write out the results
        Console.WriteLine("Fruits that are low on stock:");
        foreach (var item in results) {
            Console.WriteLine("Name: {0}, Current Stock: {1}",
                item.Name, item.Count);
        }

        // wait for input before exiting
        Console.WriteLine("Press enter to finish");
        Console.ReadLine();
    }
}
```

This query enumerates the elements that are immediate descendants of the root node. An int range variable is defined using the let keyword and assigned the value of parsing the Value property of the StockLevel element. A where clause filters for items that have a low stock level, and the select clause projects an anonymous type containing the Value property of the first-level element and the value of the int range variable. With a simple query, we have created a stock reorder report. Compiling and running Listing 29-15 produces the following results:

```
Fruits that are low on stock:
Name: Apple, Current Stock: 230
```

```
Name: Banana, Current Stock: 100
Press enter to finish
```

Creating XML from LINQ Queries

LINQ to XML makes it very easy to create XML from a set of objects. Listing 29-16 provides a demonstration.

Listing 29-16. Creating XML Using a LINQ Query

```csharp
using System;
using System.Collections.Generic;
using System.Linq;
using System.Xml.Linq;

class Fruit {

    public Fruit(string nameParam, string colorParam, int stockParam) {
        Name = nameParam;
        Color = colorParam;
        ItemsInStock = stockParam;
    }

    public string Name { get; set; }
    public string Color { get; set; }
    public int ItemsInStock { get; set; }
}

class Listing_16 {

    static void Main(string[] args) {

        // create a data source containing Fruit objects
        List<Fruit> myFruitList = new List<Fruit>() {
            new Fruit("Cherry", "Red", 500),
            new Fruit("Apple", "Green", 230),
            new Fruit("Plum", "Red", 300),
            new Fruit("Banana", "Yellow", 100),
            new Fruit("Grape", "Green", 400)
        };

        // perform a query to generate XElements
        IEnumerable<XElement> elements = from e in myFruitList
                                    select new XElement("Fruit",
                                        new XAttribute("Name", e.Name),
                                        new XAttribute("Color", e.Color),
                                        new XAttribute("StockLevel", e.ItemsInStock)
                                    );
```

```
        // create a root node to contain the query results
        XElement rootNode = new XElement("Fruits", elements);

        // print out the XML data
        Console.WriteLine(rootNode);

        // wait for input before exiting
        Console.WriteLine("Press enter to finish");
        Console.ReadLine();
    }
}
```

Listing 29-16 defines the Fruit class, which has three attributes. In the Main method, I create a List<Fruit> and populate it with some Fruit objects. I then perform a LINQ query and use the select clause to project an XElement object for each Fruit object in the data source. I use the constructor parameter array of the XElement class to supply a set of three attributes for the XElement objects, each of which corresponds to a property value from the Fruit range variable.

The result from my LINQ query is an IEnumerable<XElement> containing one XElement for each Fruit in the data source. At the moment, these are independent of one another. To create a hierarchy, I create a new XElement object to be the root node and pass the IEnumerable<XElement> query results as a constructor argument. I then print out the contents of the root node to the console, producing the following XML output:

```
<Fruits>
  <Fruit Name="Cherry" Color="Red" StockLevel="500" />
  <Fruit Name="Apple" Color="Green" StockLevel="230" />
  <Fruit Name="Plum" Color="Red" StockLevel="300" />
  <Fruit Name="Banana" Color="Yellow" StockLevel="100" />
  <Fruit Name="Grape" Color="Green" StockLevel="400" />
</Fruits>
Press enter to finish
```

You'll appreciate how simple it is to use LINQ to create XML like this if you've ever tried to do the same thing using another language or using another C# XML API. Combining LINQ queries with the System.Xml.Linq classes make generating XML simple and quick.

In Listing 29-16, I made each Fruit property into an attribute, but I could as easily have created nested elements, comments, text blocks, and so on, by creating different objects when projecting the XElement for the range variable. Listing 29-17 provides an example.

Listing 29-17. Creating Different Kinds of XML Element in a LINQ Query

```
using System;
using System.Collections.Generic;
using System.Linq;
using System.Xml.Linq;

class Listing_17 {

    static void Main(string[] args) {
```

```
        // create a data source containing Fruit objects
        List<Fruit> myFruitList = new List<Fruit>() {
            new Fruit("Cherry", "Red", 500),
            new Fruit("Apple", "Green", 230),
            new Fruit("Plum", "Red", 300),
            new Fruit("Banana", "Yellow", 100),
            new Fruit("Grape", "Green", 400)
        };

        // perform a query to generate XElements
        IEnumerable<XElement> elements = from e in myFruitList
                                where e.Color == "Red"
                                select new XElement("Fruit",
                                    new XElement("Name", e.Name),
                                    new XElement("Details",
                                        new XElement("Color", e.Color),
                                        new XElement("StockLevel", e.ItemsInStock)
                                    )
                                );

        // create a root node to contain the query results
        XElement rootNode = new XElement("Fruits", elements);

        // print out the XML data
        Console.WriteLine(rootNode);

        // wait for input before exiting
        Console.WriteLine("Press enter to finish");
        Console.ReadLine();
    }
}
```

In this example, I have created some additional structure and used the Fruit properties values to create nested XElement objects. Here is the XML that compiling and running Listing 29-17 produces:

```
<Fruits>
  <Fruit>
    <Name>Cherry</Name>
    <Details>
      <Color>Red</Color>
      <StockLevel>500</StockLevel>
    </Details>
  </Fruit>
  <Fruit>
    <Name>Plum</Name>
    <Details>
      <Color>Red</Color>
      <StockLevel>300</StockLevel>
    </Details>
  </Fruit>
```

```
</Fruits>
Press enter to finish
```

Making changes to the XElement that is projected by the select clause in the query allows us to create whatever XML we need. If you look at the results from Listing 29-17, you'll notice that there are only two fruits listed in the XML. This is because I added a where clause to the query in Listing 29-17 to filter out any Fruit whose Color property isn't Red. Not only can you readily create XML from objects, but you can also use all the LINQ features for filtering, grouping, and sorting features that we learned about in Chapter 27.

Create Objects from XML

As the complement to creating XML from objects, you can also use a LINQ query to create objects from XML, as shown by Listing 29-18.

Listing 29-18. Querying XML to Create Objects

```
using System;
using System.Collections.Generic;
using System.Linq;
using System.Xml.Linq;

class Fruit {

    public Fruit(string nameParam, string colorParam, int stockParam) {
        Name = nameParam;
        Color = colorParam;
        ItemsInStock = stockParam;
    }

    public string Name { get; set; }
    public string Color { get; set; }
    public int ItemsInStock { get; set; }
}

class Listing_18 {

    static void Main(string[] args) {

        // load the XML to create an XElement
        XElement rootNode = XElement.Load(@"..\..\data.xml");

        // query the XML
        IEnumerable<Fruit> results =
                from e in rootNode.Elements()
                select new Fruit(
                    e.Element("Name").Value,
                    e.Element("Color").Value,
                    int.Parse(e.Element("StockLevel").Value)
```

```
            );

        // enumerate the results
        foreach (Fruit f in results) {
            Console.WriteLine("Name: {0}, Color: {1}, Stock: {2}",
                f.Name, f.Color, f.ItemsInStock);
        }

        // wait for input before exiting
        Console.WriteLine("Press enter to finish");
        Console.ReadLine();
    }
}
```

The data source for the query in Listing 29-18 is the IEnumerable<XElement> obtained by calling the Elements method on the root node. I then use the Element method that allows me to search for XElements by name to get the values I need to call the constructor of the Fruit class. I project new Fruit objects for each Fruit node in the XML data. Compiling and running Listing 29-15 produces the following results:

```
Name: Cherry, Color: Red, Stock: 500
Name: Apple, Color: Green, Stock: 230
Name: Plum, Color: Red, Stock: 300
Name: Banana, Color: Yellow, Stock: 100
Name: Grape, Color: Green, Stock: 400
Press enter to finish
```

Modifying and Transforming XML Data

The classes in the System.Xml.Linq namespace make it easy to use LINQ queries to modify or transform XML data. There is any number of different ways to do this, but I'll show you some common examples to provide a starting place.

Adding Elements to XML

A common problem is adding information to XML data. One of the most powerful ways to do this is using a LINQ join operation, as demonstrated by Listing 29-19.

Listing 29-19. Using a Join to Add Attributes to XML

```
using System;
using System.Collections.Generic;
using System.Linq;
using System.Xml.Linq;

class WeightInformation {

    public WeightInformation(string nameParam, float weightParam) {
```

```
                FruitName = nameParam; WeightInOunces = weightParam;
        }
        public string FruitName { get; set; }
        public float WeightInOunces { get; set; }
}

class Listing_19 {

    static void Main(string[] args) {

        // load the XML data
        XElement rootNode = XElement.Load(@"..\..\data.xml");

        // create a data source
        List<WeightInformation> weightList = new List<WeightInformation>() {
            new WeightInformation("Plum", 2.3f),
            new WeightInformation("Cherry", 0.3f)
        };

        IEnumerable<XElement> results = rootNode.Elements().Join(
            // define the second data source
            weightList,
            // select the key from the XML data
            e => e.Element("Name").Value,
            // select the key from the object data
            e => e.FruitName,
            // project a result
            (e, f) => {
                // duplicate the XElement so we don't modify the source data
                XElement duplicateElement = new XElement(e);
                // add an attribute for the weight
                duplicateElement.Add(new XAttribute("Weight", f.WeightInOunces));
                // return the duplicated and modified element
                return duplicateElement;
            });

        // create a structure around the query results
        XElement newRootNode = new XElement("Fruits", results);

        // print out the new XML
        Console.WriteLine(newRootNode);

        // wait for input before exiting
        Console.WriteLine("Press enter to finish");
        Console.ReadLine();
    }

}
```

The query in Listing 29-19 is based around a join operation, which is very similar to what we saw in the previous chapter. There are two XML-specific aspects to the query. The first is that one of the keys for matching items is the value of the Name element of an XElement object; that is to say, we are using a value in the XML data as a key for matching items in the data sources.

The second XML-specific aspect is in the projection. I don't want to modify the source XML data, so I used the XElement constructor that takes another XElement as the parameter, like this:

```
XElement duplicateElement = new XElement(e);
```

This constructor creates a copy of the parameter object, allowing me to make changes without affecting the source XElement. I then create a new XAttribute object and use the XElement.Add method to add it to the duplicate XElement. In this way, I am able to duplicate, modify, and then project the XElement using the joined data from the object data source. Compiling and running Listing 29-19 produces the following output:

```
<Fruits>
  <Fruit Weight="0.3">
    <Name>Cherry</Name>
    <Details>
      <Color>Red</Color>
      <StockLevel>500</StockLevel>
    </Details>
  </Fruit>
  <Fruit Weight="2.3">
    <Name>Plum</Name>
    <Details>
      <Color>Red</Color>
      <StockLevel>300</StockLevel>
    </Details>
  </Fruit>
</Fruits>
Press enter to finish
```

There are only details of two fruits in the XML result because the join operation only projects data items for which there is a common key in both data sources, and in Listing 29-19, there is only average weight information available for plums and cherries.

Creating a CSV File from XML

A common problem is to create a text file for a legacy system from XML. Listing 29-20 provides a simple demonstration of how to do this.

Listing 29-20. Creating a Text File from XML

```
using System;
using System.Collections.Generic;
using System.Linq;
using System.Xml.Linq;

class Listing_20 {

    static void Main(string[] args) {
```

```
        // load the XML data
        XElement rootNode = XElement.Load(@"..\..\data.xml");

        IEnumerable<string> results = from e in rootNode.Elements()
                                      select string.Format("{0},{1},{2}",
                                          e.Element("Name").Value,
                                          e.Element("Color").Value,
                                          e.Element("StockLevel").Value);

        // enumerate the strings
        foreach (string str in results) {
            Console.WriteLine(str);
        }

        // wait for input before exiting
        Console.WriteLine("Press enter to finish");
        Console.ReadLine();
    }
}
```

The query in Listing 29-20 uses the composite formatting feature to project a series of strings that contain the details of each XML node in comma-separated form. Compiling and running Listing 29-20 produces the following output:

```
Cherry,Red,500
Apple,Green,230
Plum,Red,300
Banana,Yellow,100
Grape,Green,400
Press enter to finish
```

Creating XML from CSV Data

The complement to the previous example is to create XML from legacy CSV data. Listing 29-21 provides an example.

Listing 29-21. Creating XML from CSV Data

```
using System;
using System.Collections.Generic;
using System.Linq;
using System.Xml.Linq;

class Listing_20 {

    static void Main(string[] args) {

        // define the CSV data
        string[] csvData = new string[] {
```

```
                    "Cherry,Red,500",
                    "Apple,Green,230",
                    "Plum,Red,300",
                    "Banana,Yellow,100",
                    "Grape,Green,400"
            };

            IEnumerable<XElement> results = from e in csvData
                                            let elements = e.Split(',')
                                            where elements[1] == "Red"
                                            select new XElement("Fruit",
                                                new XElement("Name", elements[0]),
                                                new XElement("Color", elements[1]),
                                                new XElement("ItemsInStock", elements[2])
                                                );

        // assign the results to a root node
        XElement rootNode = new XElement("Fruits", results);

        // write the XML to the console
        Console.WriteLine(rootNode);

        // wait for input before exiting
        Console.WriteLine("Press enter to finish");
        Console.ReadLine();
    }
}
```

The query in Listing 29-21 uses the Split method of the string class (described in Chapter 16) to extract the individual elements from the CSV data and project new XElements for each CSV data line. I have also used a where clause to filter out any CSV data line where the second element isn't Red. Compiling and running Listing 29-20 produces the following output:

```
<Fruits>
  <Fruit>
    <Name>Cherry</Name>
    <Color>Red</Color>
    <ItemsInStock>500</ItemsInStock>
  </Fruit>
  <Fruit>
    <Name>Plum</Name>
    <Color>Red</Color>
    <ItemsInStock>300</ItemsInStock>
  </Fruit>
</Fruits>
Press enter to finish
```

Changing and Deleting Elements

In this section, I will show you how to re-create the examples in the "Modifying XML" section from the first part of the chapter but using queries instead of declarative programming. We start with converting elements to attributes, as demonstrated by Listing 29-22.

Listing 29-22. Converting Elements to Attributes

```
using System;
using System.Collections.Generic;
using System.Linq;
using System.Xml.Linq;

class Listing_22 {

    static void Main(string[] args) {

        // load the XML data
        XElement rootNode = XElement.Load(@"..\..\data.xml");

        IEnumerable<XElement> results = from e in rootNode.Elements()
                    select new XElement(e.Name,
                        new XAttribute("Name", e.Element("Name").Value),
                        new XAttribute("Color", e.Element("Color").Value),
                        new XAttribute("StockLevel", e.Element("StockLevel").Value));

        // assign to a root node and print out the XML to the console
        Console.WriteLine(new XElement("Fruits", results));

        // wait for input before exiting
        Console.WriteLine("Press enter to finish");
        Console.ReadLine();
    }
}
```

Listing 29-22 uses the Element method to extract information from the range variable and project a new XElement containing the same information but expressed as attributes instead of elements. Compiling and running Listing 29-22 produces the following results:

```
<Fruits>
  <Fruit Name="Cherry" Color="Red" StockLevel="500" />
  <Fruit Name="Apple" Color="Green" StockLevel="230" />
  <Fruit Name="Plum" Color="Red" StockLevel="300" />
  <Fruit Name="Banana" Color="Yellow" StockLevel="100" />
  <Fruit Name="Grape" Color="Green" StockLevel="400" />
</Fruits>
Press enter to finish
```

Listing 29-23 changes the name of an element.

Listing 29-23. Changing the Name of an Element

```
using System;
using System.Collections.Generic;
using System.Linq;
using System.Xml.Linq;

class Listing_23 {

    static void Main(string[] args) {

        // load the XML data
        XElement rootNode = XElement.Load(@"..\..\data.xml");

        XElement newRoot = new XElement("Fruits",
            rootNode.Elements()
            .Where(e => e.Element("Color").Value == "Red")
            .Select(e => {
                XElement duplicateElem = new XElement(e);
                duplicateElem.Element("StockLevel").Name = "ItemCount";
                return duplicateElem;
            }));

        // print out the XML to the console
        Console.WriteLine(newRoot);

        // wait for input before exiting
        Console.WriteLine("Press enter to finish");
        Console.ReadLine();
    }
}
```

The query in Listing 29-23 is more verbose than the declarative approach shown in Listing 29-14 but has the advantage of allowing me to use some of the other LINQ features. In this case, I have filtered the content so that only red fruits are projected into the results. Note also that I have embedded the LINQ query into the constructor of the root node of the projected data. Compiling and running Listing 29-23 produces the following output:

```
<Fruits>
  <Fruit>
    <Name>Cherry</Name>
    <Color>Red</Color>
    <ItemCount>500</ItemCount>
  </Fruit>
  <Fruit>
    <Name>Plum</Name>
    <Color>Red</Color>
    <ItemCount>300</ItemCount>
  </Fruit>
</Fruits>
```

Press enter to finish

Sorting XML

Controlling the order of elements in the XML projected from a query is very simple. Listing 29-24 demonstrates ordering the data based on the number of items in stock.

Listing 29-24. Sorting XML Data

```
using System;
using System.Collections.Generic;
using System.Linq;
using System.Xml.Linq;

class Listing_24 {

    static void Main(string[] args) {

        // load the XML data
        XElement rootNode = XElement.Load(@"..\..\data.xml");

        // sort the XML data
        IEnumerable<XElement> results = from e in rootNode.Elements()
                                        orderby int.Parse(e.Element("StockLevel").Value)
                                        select e;

        // create a new root node
        XElement newRoot = new XElement("Fruits",
            new XAttribute("SortedBy", "StockLevel"),
            results);

        // print out the XML to the console
        Console.WriteLine(newRoot);

        // wait for input before exiting
        Console.WriteLine("Press enter to finish");
        Console.ReadLine();
    }
}
```

Notice that I parse the StockLevel value as an int before using it for ordering the data. If I had sorted on the string values, I would have problems with values with a leading zero, such as 0500, being ordered incorrectly. Compiling and running Listing 29-24 produces the following results:

```
<Fruits SortedBy="StockLevel">
  <Fruit>
    <Name>Banana</Name>
    <Color>Yellow</Color>
```

```
    <StockLevel>100</StockLevel>
  </Fruit>
  <Fruit>
    <Name>Apple</Name>
    <Color>Green</Color>
    <StockLevel>230</StockLevel>
  </Fruit>
  <Fruit>
    <Name>Plum</Name>
    <Color>Red</Color>
    <StockLevel>300</StockLevel>
  </Fruit>
  <Fruit>
    <Name>Grape</Name>
    <Color>Green</Color>
    <StockLevel>400</StockLevel>
  </Fruit>
  <Fruit>
    <Name>Cherry</Name>
    <Color>Red</Color>
    <StockLevel>500</StockLevel>
  </Fruit>
</Fruits>
Press enter to finish
```

Grouping XML

The next operation we will look at is transforming XML by using grouping, as demonstrated by Listing 29-25.

Listing 29-25. Grouping XML Elements

```
using System;
using System.Collections.Generic;
using System.Linq;
using System.Xml.Linq;

class Listing_25 {

    static void Main(string[] args) {

        // load the XML data
        XElement rootNode = XElement.Load(@"..\..\data.xml");

        // sort the XML data
        IEnumerable<IGrouping<string, XElement>> results =
            from e in rootNode.Elements()
            group e by e.Element("Color").Value;
```

```
        // define a new root node
        XElement newRoot = new XElement("Fruits");

        foreach (IGrouping<string, XElement> group in results) {
            newRoot.Add(new XElement(string.Format("{0}Fruits", group.Key), group));
        }

        // print out the XML to the console
        Console.WriteLine(newRoot);

        // wait for input before exiting
        Console.WriteLine("Press enter to finish");
        Console.ReadLine();
    }
}
```

The query in Listing 29-25 uses a group clause to group Fruit elements by the value of the Color element. The projected group Key value is then used to create a new degree of structure that contains all the Fruit elements of a given Color value. Compiling and running Listing 29-25 produces the following results:

```
<Fruits>
  <RedFruits>
    <Fruit>
      <Name>Cherry</Name>
      <Color>Red</Color>
      <StockLevel>500</StockLevel>
    </Fruit>
    <Fruit>
      <Name>Plum</Name>
      <Color>Red</Color>
      <StockLevel>300</StockLevel>
    </Fruit>
  </RedFruits>
  <GreenFruits>
    <Fruit>
      <Name>Apple</Name>
      <Color>Green</Color>
      <StockLevel>230</StockLevel>
    </Fruit>
    <Fruit>
      <Name>Grape</Name>
      <Color>Green</Color>
      <StockLevel>400</StockLevel>
    </Fruit>
  </GreenFruits>
  <YellowFruits>
    <Fruit>
      <Name>Banana</Name>
      <Color>Yellow</Color>
      <StockLevel>100</StockLevel>
```

```
    </Fruit>
  </YellowFruits>
</Fruits>
Press enter to finish
```

Using Parallel LINQ to Process XML

LINQ to XML is essentially a set of classes that are designed to accommodate LINQ to Objects queries. The support for getting elements as an IEnumerable<XElement> and the ability to pass IEnumerable<XElement>s to constructors are good examples of how these classes are designed to support the inputs and outputs of LINQ queries. A side benefit of this approach is that you can use Parallel LINQ (PLINQ) to process XML. We covered PLINQ in Chapter 28, and I don't intend to repeat what is there, but there is one aspect of PLINQ in particular that bears attention when using the LINQ to XML classes, and that is the ForAll method. All the queries in the second part of this chapter have projected new XML, leaving the source data unmodified. This is the nature of LINQ. You project new results using a select or group clause, but the ForAll method can be used to modify the source data. Listing 29-26 provides a demonstration.

Listing 29-26. Modifying the Source XML in a Query

```
using System;
using System.Collections.Generic;
using System.Linq;
using System.Xml.Linq;

class Listing_26 {

    static void Main(string[] args) {

        // load the XML data
        XElement rootNode = XElement.Load(@"..\..\data.xml");

        // change the name of the StockLevel element to ItemsInStock
        rootNode.Descendants("StockLevel")
            .AsParallel()
            .ForAll(e => e.Name = "ItemsInStock");

        // print out the XML to the console
        Console.WriteLine(rootNode);

        // wait for input before exiting
        Console.WriteLine("Press enter to finish");
        Console.ReadLine();
    }
}
```

The parallel query in Listing 29-26 changes the name of all the StockLevel elements to ItemsInStock. There is no new XML data projected. The original XML objects created when the data.xml file was loaded were modified. Compiling and running Listing 29-26 produces the following result:

```
<Fruits>
  <Fruit>
    <Name>Cherry</Name>
    <Color>Red</Color>
    <ItemsInStock>500</ItemsInStock>
  </Fruit>
  <Fruit>
    <Name>Apple</Name>
    <Color>Green</Color>
    <ItemsInStock>230</ItemsInStock>
  </Fruit>
  <Fruit>
    <Name>Plum</Name>
    <Color>Red</Color>
    <ItemsInStock>300</ItemsInStock>
  </Fruit>
  <Fruit>
    <Name>Banana</Name>
    <Color>Yellow</Color>
    <ItemsInStock>100</ItemsInStock>
  </Fruit>
  <Fruit>
    <Name>Grape</Name>
    <Color>Green</Color>
    <ItemsInStock>400</ItemsInStock>
  </Fruit>
</Fruits>
Press enter to finish
```

As with other PLINQ queries, the order of the results may not match the order of the source data, but this is an effective way of modifying or transforming XML without having to create duplicate objects in memory. Listing 29-27 provides a more complex transformation.

Listing 29-27. Modifying XML Structure in Situ

```
using System;
using System.Collections.Generic;
using System.Linq;
using System.Xml.Linq;

class Listing_27 {

    static void Main(string[] args) {

        // load the XML data
        XElement rootNode = XElement.Load(@"..\..\data.xml");

        // process the XML elements
        rootNode.Elements()
            .AsParallel()
```

961

```
            .Where(e => e.Element("Color").Value == "Red")
            .ForAll(e => {
                // remove the StockLevel element
                e.Element("StockLevel").Remove();
                // move the Color element to be an attribute
                XElement colorElem = e.Element("Color");
                e.Element("Name").Add(new XAttribute("Color", colorElem.Value));
                colorElem.Remove();
            });

        // print out the XML to the console
        Console.WriteLine(rootNode);

        // wait for input before exiting
        Console.WriteLine("Press enter to finish");
        Console.ReadLine();
    }
}
```

The query in Listing 29-27 removes the StockLevel element and changes the Color element into an attribute. The Where method filters the source data so that only Fruit elements that have a Color element with the value Red are affected. Note that since we are modifying the source data, this means that non-Red Fruits are left in the source XML and are unchanged by the statements in the ForAll method. Compiling and running Listing 29-27 produces the following result:

```
<Fruits>
  <Fruit>
    <Name Color="Red">Cherry</Name>
  </Fruit>
  <Fruit>
    <Name>Apple</Name>
    <Color>Green</Color>
    <StockLevel>230</StockLevel>
  </Fruit>
  <Fruit>
    <Name Color="Red">Plum</Name>
  </Fruit>
  <Fruit>
    <Name>Banana</Name>
    <Color>Yellow</Color>
    <StockLevel>100</StockLevel>
  </Fruit>
  <Fruit>
    <Name>Grape</Name>
    <Color>Green</Color>
    <StockLevel>400</StockLevel>
  </Fruit>
</Fruits>
Press enter to finish
```

Summary

In this chapter, we saw how the classes in the System.Xml.Linq namespace can be used to create and represent XML data and how they have been designed to work well with LINQ queries. We saw how to work with XML data declaratively and how to do the same using LINQ queries. If you have used other XML processing APIs, such as SAX and DOM, then you will appreciate the flexibility and ease of use that LINQ to XML offers, and the ability to use LINQ queries and PLINQ queries is exceptionally useful.

CHAPTER 30

■ ■ ■

LINQ to Entities

The Entity Framework is an *object-relational mapping* (ORM) system that allows us to work with data in a relational database using normal C# data types and without needing to use SQL. LINQ to Entities is just one part of the Entity Framework, and it allows us to use standard LINQ queries to search for and retrieve data from the underlying database using a data model that maps C# objects to database tables and rows. The Entity Framework is part of ADO.NET, which is the part of .NET responsible for data access and which contains several major areas of functionality.

The Entity Framework can create very complex data models, and objects can be created from multiple tables and even multiple databases. The Entity Framework supports a wide range of database servers, including Oracle, DB2, MySQL, SQLite, and Microsoft SQL Server. We'll be using SQL Server in this chapter and creating only a very simple data model. Even so, you'll be able to get a good sense of what the Entity Framework is about and how to use LINQ to Entities.

Although LINQ to Entities allows you to query a database without using SQL, that doesn't mean you can ignore the database entirely. When using LINQ to Entities, you are using a data model that is usually generated from a database, and the names, properties, and relationships of the objects are closely related to the database schema. That said, for most programming tasks, I would much rather use LINQ to Entities than use SQL directly, and I am sure that you will start to feel the same way as we work through this chapter.

■ **Tip** LINQ to Entities is the successor to LINQ to SQL, which was a simpler ORM system based on LINQ. It had fewer features than the Entity Framework and couldn't represent complex database relationships very well, but it was simpler to use and very popular. Microsoft has announced that no further enhancements will be made for LINQ to SQL and that programmers should use LINQ to SQL from now on.

Table 30-1 provides the summary for this chapter.

Table 30-1. *Quick Problem/Solution Reference for Chapter 30*

Problem	Solution	Listings
Query a database using LINQ to Entities.	Create a data model context, and use one of the properties as the data source for a LINQ query.	30-1
Work with data related through a foreign-key relationship.	Use the navigation properties created for each entity class.	30-2 through 30-4
Avoid separate queries for related data when processing LINQ query results.	Use the Include extension method to eagerly load associated data.	30-5, 30-6
Create a parameterized LINQ query that can be reused.	Create a compiled query.	30-7
Query a database view.	Use one of the data model context object view properties as the data source for a LINQ query.	30-8
Use a stored procedure.	Import the procedure into the data model, and then use the method that is added to the data model context object as a data source for a LINQ query.	30-9
Insert data into the database.	Create a new entity object, populate it, and add it to one of the object collections maintained by the data model context. Call the SaveChanges method to perform the insert.	30-10, 30-11
Update data in the database.	Modify the property values of one or more entity objects, and call the SaveChanges method.	30-12
Delete data from the database.	Use the context object DeleteObject method, and call the SaveChanges method.	30-13

Getting Ready

Before we can use LINQ to Entities, we have to create the Entity Framework data model for the database we want to use. This is the heart of any ORM system and provides the mapping between the database and C# objects we will use, meaning that we can work using C# classes, objects, and other language features and not have to worry too much about SQL queries and SQL data types. In this section, I'll show you how to prepare the database and create the data model. Fortunately, we can use Visual Studio to do the heavy lifting for us.

Preparing the Database

The first step we need to perform is to copy the database files to an easy-to-find location. I have included the database files in the source code download for this book, which you can get from Apress.com. There are two files—Northwind.mdf and Northwind_log.LDF—and I have copied them to the C:\Northwind directory on my machine. You can place them anywhere convenient, but you'll have to remember to adjust for a different location as you follow the instructions in this chapter.

■ **Caution** There are different versions of the Northwind database available online. Use only the extended version that I have included in the source code download available from Apress.com. Other versions may produce different results than the ones shown in this chapter.

Creating the Model

We start creating the model by adding a new item to a Visual Studio project. Right-click the project item in the Solution Explorer window, and select ADO.NET Entity Data Model from the list of templates, as shown by Figure 30-1. The set of templates that you see in this dialog box will depend on the version of Visual Studio you installed and the language options you checked during the installation.

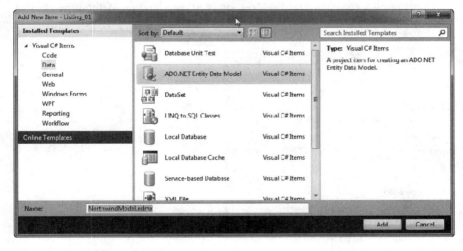

Figure 30-1. Adding a new item

In the Name text box, we enter the name we want to give to the model. I will use the name NorthwindModel.edmx for the examples in this chapter. Click the Add button to move to the next stage in the process, which is to launch the Entity Data Model Wizard. Figure 30-2 shows the first screen from the wizard.

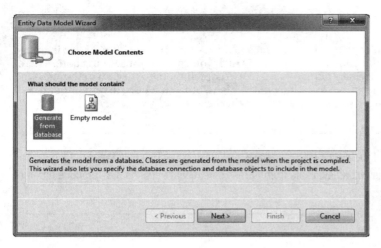

Figure 30-2. *Selecting the source for the data model*

You can create an EF data model from scratch or generate one from a preexisting database. We are going to do the latter, so select the "Generate from database" item and click the Next button.

The next step is to select the connection that will be used to communicate with the database. There are no connections at the moment, so we will have to create one. Click the New Connection button in the dialog box, as illustrated by Figure 30-3. The wizard will present you with a range of different connection types, as shown in Figure 30-4.

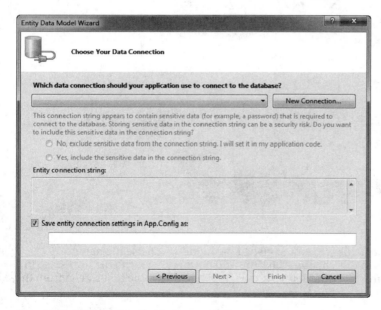

Figure 30-3. *Choosing the data connection*

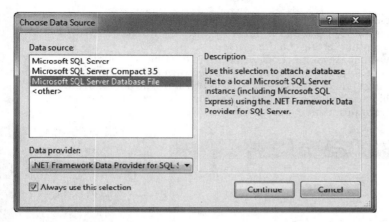

Figure 30-4. *Selecting the data source*

We are going to use a SQL Server database file, so select Microsoft SQL Server Database File from the list, and click the Continue button. The Connection Properties dialog box will be shown, as in Figure 30-5.

Figure 30-5. *Selecting the database file*

Click the Browse button, and select the `Northwind.mdf` file from the location to which you copied it. In my case, I copied the database files to the `C:\Northwind` directory. Click OK when you have selected the file; there is no need to change the other settings on this screen.

Now that we have created a new database connection, we return to the Choose Your Data Connection screen, as shown by Figure 30-6, which has been populated with the details we need. Ensure that the "Save entity connection settings" check box is checked. This will store the details of our connection in our project, which will make things easier for us to change if we want to connect to a different database, for example, a test or production system. Click the Next button.

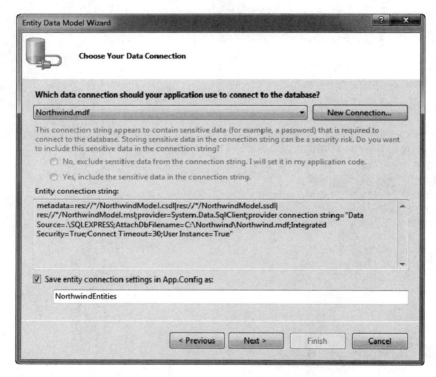

Figure 30-6. *The populated data connection dialog box*

You will be presented with a dialog box offering to copy the database files into the Visual Studio project directory, as shown in Figure 30-7. Select No if you are following the examples in this chapter; otherwise, each project will have a duplicate copy of the data. In real-world projects, it can be useful to copy the file locally because it will be in scope for change management/version control.

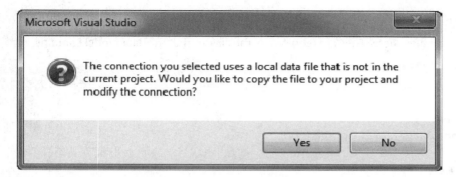

Figure 30-7. Copying the database file

The Entity Data Model Wizard will connect to the database and read the schema, which contains details of all the tables, views, and stored procedures. You will see a dialog box like the one in Figure 30-8. Ensure that the database objects options are selected (Tables, Views, and Stored Procedures) and that "Pluralize or singularize generated object names" and "Include foreign key columns in the model" are also selected. Ensure that Model Namespace has been set to NorthwindModel. Click Finish to generate the data model.

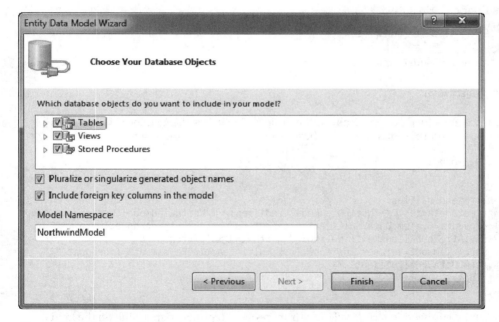

Figure 30-8. Selecting the contents of the model

Visual Studio will use the schema from the database to create the data model. As part of this process, your project will have some new references automatically added, as shown by Figure 30-9. It is important that you don't remove these. They are required by the classes that the data model contains.

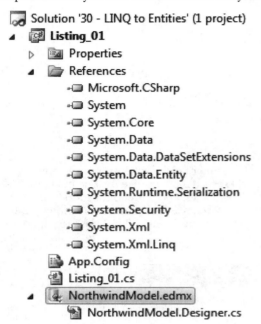

Figure 30-9. *New project items*

Two other entries are added automatically to the project. The first is the App.Config file, which contains the connection information for our database. The contents will look something like this:

```
<?xml version="1.0" encoding="utf-8"?>
<configuration>
  <connectionStrings>
    <add name="NorthwindEntities"
connectionString="metadata=res://*/NorthwindModel.csdl|res://*/NorthwindModel.ssdl|res://*/Nor
thwindModel.msl;provider=System.Data.SqlClient;provider connection string=&quot;Data
Source=.\SQLEXPRESS;AttachDbFilename=C:\Northwind\Northwind.mdf;Integrated
Security=True;Connect Timeout=30;User Instance=True;MultipleActiveResultSets=True&quot;"
providerName="System.Data.EntityClient" />
  </connectionStrings>
</configuration>
```

The contents of the connection string will differ from project to project depending on the kind of database you are using and how you are connecting to it. We don't need to go into the details of the connection string for this example; it is enough to know that it contains the details that will be used to make the connection.

The second new item is the data model. There are two parts to this new item. The first has a suffix of .edmx; if you double-click this part, you will see a graphical representation of the data model, showing the objects that have been created and the relationship between them, as illustrated by Figure 30-10.

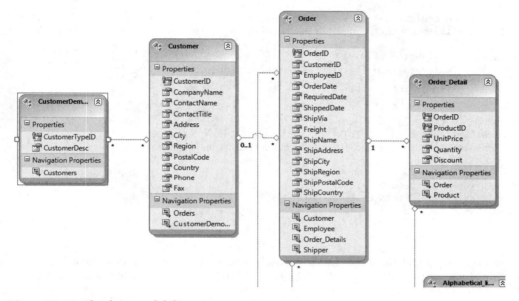

Figure 30-10. The data model diagram

The second part of the data model is a C# code file that contains the classes we will use to work with the data in the database.

■ **Tip** Don't change the code that has been generated by Visual Studio to create the data model. You can regenerate the database to reflect schema changes, and when this happens, your changes will be lost.

Using LINQ to Entities

Now that we have created the model, we can start to use it. The main purpose of LINQ to Entities is to allow us to work with the database using C# language features and data types. Listing 30-1 provides an example that performs a query on a table in the database, and, as you can see, there is no SQL in sight.

Listing 30-1. A Simple LINQ to Entities Query

```
using System;
using System.Linq;
using NorthwindModel;
```

```
class Listing_01 {

    static void Main(string[] args) {

        // create the context
        NorthwindEntities context = new NorthwindEntities();

        // query the database
        IQueryable<Employee> result = from e in context.Employees
                                      where e.City == "London"
                                      select e;

        // enumerate the results
        foreach (Employee e in result) {
            Console.WriteLine("Name: {0} {1}", e.FirstName, e.LastName);
        }

        // wait for input before exiting
        Console.WriteLine("Press enter to finish");
        Console.ReadLine();
    }
}
```

Listing 30-1 is quite simple, but it contains some useful information about how we use an Entity Framework data model. In the following sections, I'll walk through the various elements and explain what is happening.

Using the Data Model Context

The first important statement creates the *context* for our data model:

```
NorthwindEntities context = new NorthwindEntities();
```

The context is our access point into the data model; it takes care of managing the connections to the database, and it takes care of tracking changes we have made to the data and writing them back to the database. It is also the class that provides access to the data types that have been created to represent tables and rows in the database.

The name of the context class depends on the name of the database. Since we are using the Northwind database, our context class is called NorthwindEntities. Visual Studio places the context and all the other types in the data model into a namespace, which has the same name as your project. My data model is contained in a project called NorthwindModel, which has been added as a reference to the Listing_01 project. This means my model is contained with a namespace also called NorthwindModel, which you can see imported into my code file with a using statement. If I had created the model inside the Listing_01 project, the namespace containing all the entity classes would have been called Listing_01. Before you can use the data model, you must create a context. The simplest way is to use the default constructor, as I have done.

Using Table Properties and Row Objects

The context class is created with a property for each of the tables in the database. For example, the Northwind context contains a property called Employees that relates to the Employees table in the database. You can see that I read the value of this property in the LINQ query in Listing 30-1 to get the data source query:

```
from e in context.Employees
```

The property returns a collection of Employee objects, created to represent rows in the Employees table. The collection is a System.Data.Objects.ObjectSet<T> where T is the model class for items in the table you have referred to, ObjectSet<Employee> in this example. You don't have to work with the ObjectSet<T> class directly. It implements the IEnumerable<T> interface, which allows us to use a foreach loop to enumerate the objects in the collection.

The class that has been created to represent a row in a table has a property for each table column. If you look at the data model diagram in Visual Studio (double-click NorthwindModel.edmx in the Solution Explorer window), you will be able to find the Employee object, as illustrated by Figure 30-11.

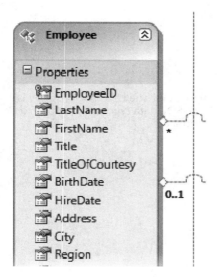

Figure 30-11. *The Employee object diagram*

You can see that there are many properties available, each of which corresponds to a column in the Employees database table. If you right-click one of the properties and select Properties from the pop-up menu, you can see some important details. Figure 30-12 shows some of the properties for the LastName property of the Employee class.

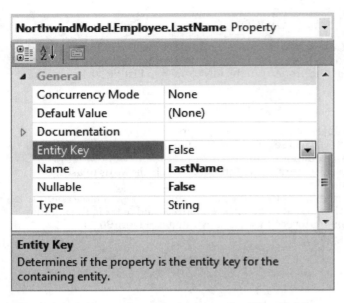

Figure 30-12. Properties of the Employee LastName field

The most important information for us at this point is that we can tell the LastName property is represented using a C# string. When the data model is created, the SQL data types are mapped to C# types. Table 30-2 shows you how some common SQL types are mapped.

Table 30-2. SQL to C# Type Mappings

SQL Type	C# Type
id int	int
bigint	long
char nchar ntext nvarchar text varchar xml	string
date	DateTime
decimal	decimal

SQL Type	C# Type
numeric	
float	double
real	float

Understanding the IQueryable<T> Interface

We now know that the context Employees property returns an IEnumerable<Employee>, where each Employee represents a row in the table. We also know that an Employee object has properties representing each column in the table. Put these together, and we can understand what the query in Listing 30-1 does:

```
IQueryable<Employee> result = from e in context.Employees
                              where e.City == "London"
                              select e;
```

The data source for the query is the set of data rows in the Employees database table. The where clause filters those rows so that only those whose City property has the value London are included. The select clause projects the Employee object into the results.

Notice that the result is an IQueryable<Employee>. This is an interface that is derived from IEnumerable<T> and is used by the query provider to translate LINQ queries into database queries. We don't need to use this interface directly. We can upcast to IEnumerable<T> for consistency with other LINQ queries, but when you see this used in code, you can tell that an external data source will be queried for data.

There is one interesting thing that we can do with this interface, and that is to display the SQL query that a LINQ query results in. This can be used to fine-tune the SQL so that we only request the data we need and don't generate unnecessary load on the database server. The technique for getting the SQL string relies on a class that is beyond the scope of this book, so I'll just show you how to achieve it without explaining how it works. Here is the statement that creates a string showing the SQL for Listing 30-1 and prints it to the console:

```
Console.WriteLine(((System.Data.Objects.ObjectQuery)result).ToTraceString());
```

You can only do this when you are performing LINQ to Entities queries. Adding this statement to Listing 30-1 shows us what SQL was generated to satisfy the LINQ query:

```
SELECT
[Extent1].[EmployeeID] AS [EmployeeID],
[Extent1].[LastName] AS [LastName],
[Extent1].[FirstName] AS [FirstName],
[Extent1].[Title] AS [Title],
[Extent1].[TitleOfCourtesy] AS [TitleOfCourtesy],
[Extent1].[BirthDate] AS [BirthDate],
[Extent1].[HireDate] AS [HireDate],
[Extent1].[Address] AS [Address],
[Extent1].[City] AS [City],
```

```
[Extent1].[Region] AS [Region],
[Extent1].[PostalCode] AS [PostalCode],

[Extent1].[Country] AS [Country],
[Extent1].[HomePhone] AS [HomePhone],
[Extent1].[Extension] AS [Extension],
[Extent1].[Photo] AS [Photo],
[Extent1].[Notes] AS [Notes],
[Extent1].[ReportsTo] AS [ReportsTo],
[Extent1].[PhotoPath] AS [PhotoPath]
FROM [dbo].[Employees] AS [Extent1]
WHERE N'London' = [Extent1].[City]
```

The select clause in the query in Listing 30-1 projects the entire Employee object into the results for the LINQ query, which creates SQL query that retrieves all the columns in the Employees table. Given that we only print out the value of the FirstName and LastName properties, we can reduce the amount of data we request from the database by limiting what we project. Here is a modified query that selects only the data we want:

```
var result = from e in context.Employees
             where e.City == "London"
             select new {
                 FirstName = e.FirstName,
                 LastName = e.LastName
             };
```

The SQL query generated to satisfy this query is as follows:

```
SELECT
1 AS [C1],
[Extent1].[FirstName] AS [FirstName],
[Extent1].[LastName] AS [LastName]
FROM [dbo].[Employees] AS [Extent1]
WHERE N'London' = [Extent1].[City]
```

As a general rule, it is good practice to avoid retrieving data from the database if you don't need to use it in your program. You can see that projecting only the fields we need in our LINQ select clause makes for a much simpler SQL query.

Enumerating the Results

The last part of Listing 30-1 is enumerating the results. In keeping with other forms of LINQ, LINQ to Entities doesn't execute the query until you enumerate the result. In Listing 30-1, I enumerate the results using a foreach loop and print the value of the FirstName and LastName properties to the console:

```
foreach (Employee e in result) {
    Console.WriteLine("Name: {0} {1}", e.FirstName, e.LastName);
}
```

Compiling and running Listing 30-1 produces the following results:

```
Name: Steven Buchanan
Name: Michael Suyama
Name: Robert King
Name: Anne Dodsworth
Press enter to finish
```

Navigating Using Foreign Key Relationships

When there is a foreign-key relationship between database tables, the Entity Framework data model is created with a navigation property between the two classes used to represent rows from the related tables. If you look at the bottom of the Employee object in the data model diagram, for example, you'll see some entries "Navigation Properties" section, as illustrated by Figure 30-13.

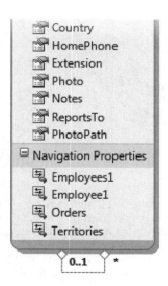

Figure 30-13. Navigation properties in the Employee data model object

There are navigation properties for Orders and Territories and Employee1 and Employee1. Each of these properties exists because there is a relationship between the Employees table and another table—the Orders and Territories tables, in this case—or between fields in the same table, which is the case for the Employee1 and Employees1 properties, where the supervisor relationship is expressed between rows in the same table. We can use these tables to effortless navigate between related tables, as demonstrated by Listing 30-2.

Listing 30-2. Using the Navigation Properties of the Employee Entity Class

```
using System;
using System.Data.Objects.DataClasses;
using System.Linq;
using NorthwindModel;

class Listing_02 {

    static void Main(string[] args) {

        // create the context
        NorthwindEntities context = new NorthwindEntities();

        // get the first Employee using the First extension method
        Employee myEmployee = context.Employees.First();

        // get the orders associated with the employee
        EntityCollection<Order> myOrders = myEmployee.Orders;

        // enumerate the orders
        Console.WriteLine("There are {0} orders for employee: {1} {2}",
            myOrders.Count, myEmployee.FirstName, myEmployee.LastName);

        foreach (Order myOrder in myOrders) {
            Console.WriteLine("Order number: {0}", myOrder.OrderID);
        }

        // wait for input before exiting
        Console.WriteLine("Press enter to finish");
        Console.ReadLine();
    }
}
```

In this example, I use the LINQ First extension method, which returns the first item in an IEnumerable<T>. This allows me to obtain an Employee object from the Employees context property. I then use the Orders navigation property, which returns an EntityCollection<Order> containing all the orders that share the same foreign-key value as my Employee key.

The EntityCollection<T> class is in the System.Data.Objects.DataClasses namespace. The type T will be the data model class used to represent rows in the related table. In the case of the example, this is the Order class, which is used to represent rows in the Orders table. The EntityCollection<T> class implements the IEnumerable<T> interface, so you can ignore the class altogether if you just want to enumerate the Order objects. I have used the Count property defined by the class, which returns the number of objects in the EntityCollection<T>.

Notice that I didn't have to deal with the foreign-key relationship in any way. The data model took care of this for me. By accessing the Orders property, I get the set of Orders that are associated with my Employee, because the results of compiling and running Listing 30-2 show (I have edited these results; there are more than 100 lines of output produced by this example):

```
There are 123 orders for employee: Nancy Davolio
```

```
Order number: 10258
Order number: 10270

Order number: 10275

Order number: 10285
Order number: 10292
Order number: 10293
Order number: 10304
Order number: 10306
Press enter to finish
```

The relationships work both ways. We can start with an Order object and get the Employee object that contains the details of the person that created the order, as demonstrated by Listing 30-3.

Listing 30-3. Following the Relationship Between Orders and Employees

```
using System;
using System.Linq;
using NorthwindModel;

class Listing_03 {

    static void Main(string[] args) {

        // create the context
        NorthwindEntities context = new NorthwindEntities();

        // get the first Order
        Order myOrder = context.Orders.First();

        // get the Employee associated with this order
        Employee myEmployee = myOrder.Employee;

        // print the details of the relationship
        Console.WriteLine("The order with ID {0} was created by {1} {2}",
            myOrder.OrderID, myEmployee.FirstName, myEmployee.LastName);

        // wait for input before exiting
        Console.WriteLine("Press enter to finish");
        Console.ReadLine();
    }
}
```

This time I use the First extension method to get an Order object. I then use the Employee navigation property to get the associated Employee object. Notice that there is no EntityCollection<T> this time. This is because the relationship between Order and Employee is one-to-one (that is, there is only one Employee associated with each Order), but the relationship between Employee and Order is one-to-many (that is, there can be more than one Order associated with each Employee). Compiling and running Listing 30-3 produces the following results:

```
The order with ID 10248 was created by Steven Buchanan
Press enter to finish
```

Querying Using Navigation Properties

We can use navigation properties with queries. This allows us to start with one kind of object that we care about and then suck in data from related tables. Listing 30-4 contains an example.

Listing 30-4. Using Navigation Properties in a LINQ Query

```
using System;
using System.Linq;
using NorthwindModel;

class Listing_04 {

    static void Main(string[] args) {

        // create the context
        NorthwindEntities context = new NorthwindEntities();

        // perform a LINQ query that uses navigation properties
        var results = from e in context.Orders
                      where e.Employee.City == "London" && e.Customer.Country == "UK"
                      select new {
                          OrderID = e.OrderID,
                          EmployeeLastName = e.Employee.LastName,
                          CustomerName = e.Customer.CompanyName
                      };

        // enumerate the results
        foreach (var item in results) {
            Console.WriteLine("ID: {0} Name: {1} Customer: {2}",
                item.OrderID, item.EmployeeLastName, item.CustomerName);
        }

        // wait for input before exiting
        Console.WriteLine("Press enter to finish");
        Console.ReadLine();
    }
}
```

The query in Listing 30-4 uses the collection of Orders as the data source, but the where clause filters based on columns from the Employees and Customers tables, and the select clause projects an anonymous type that contains properties from all three tables. Compiling and running Listing 30-4 produces the following results:

```
ID: 10289 Name: King Customer: B's Beverages
ID: 10355 Name: Suyama Customer: Around the Horn

ID: 10359 Name: Buchanan Customer: Seven Seas Imports

ID: 10523 Name: King Customer: Seven Seas Imports
ID: 10532 Name: King Customer: Eastern Connection
ID: 10538 Name: Dodsworth Customer: B's Beverages
ID: 10539 Name: Suyama Customer: B's Beverages
ID: 10599 Name: Suyama Customer: B's Beverages
ID: 10804 Name: Suyama Customer: Seven Seas Imports
ID: 10829 Name: Dodsworth Customer: Island Trading
ID: 10848 Name: King Customer: Consolidated Holdings
ID: 10869 Name: Buchanan Customer: Seven Seas Imports
ID: 10933 Name: Suyama Customer: Island Trading
ID: 10953 Name: Dodsworth Customer: Around the Horn
ID: 11016 Name: Dodsworth Customer: Around the Horn
ID: 11047 Name: King Customer: Eastern Connection
Press enter to finish
```

Using Navigation Data Efficiently

When you use navigation properties in a query like the one in Listing 30-4, the SQL statement that is generated to query the database includes joins to get the required data as efficiently as possible. The same is not true if you access the navigation properties as you enumerate the results from a query, as demonstrated in Listing 30-5.

Listing 30-5. Using Navigation Properties When Enumerating Results

```
using System;
using System.Collections.Generic;
using System.Linq;
using NorthwindModel;

class Listing_05 {

    static void Main(string[] args) {

        // create the context
        NorthwindEntities context = new NorthwindEntities();

        // perform a query
        IEnumerable<Order> results = from e in context.Orders
                                     where e.Customer.Country == "UK"
                                     select e;

        // enumerate the results
        foreach (Order myOrder in results) {
            // print out the name of the order
            Console.WriteLine("Order ID: {0}, Customer Name: {1}",
```

```
            myOrder.OrderID, myOrder.Customer.CompanyName);

        // use the navgiation properties to get the employee
        Employee myEmployee = myOrder.Employee;
        Console.WriteLine("Order created by: {0} {1}",
            myEmployee.FirstName, myEmployee.LastName);
    }

    // wait for input before exiting
    Console.WriteLine("Press enter to finish");
    Console.ReadLine();
    }
}
```

In Listing 30-5, I perform a LINQ query to get all the Orders whose associated Customer object has a Country value of UK. Because I used the navigation property to get the Customer object inside the LINQ query, a single query containing a join operation was sent to the database.

However, when I enumerate the results, I use the Employee and Customer navigation properties to read related data. This wasn't in the original query, and it results in a new database request each time I read the related data. This causes a higher load on the database that we would like. Database queries are relatively expensive to perform, and it is good practice to perform a few as possible to do the work at hand. This is known as *lazy data loading*. The data we want isn't loaded from the database until the last moment, which reduces the potential for loading data that isn't used but increases the number of queries overall.

We can make this much more efficient if we tell LINQ to Entities that we want some related data in advance. We do this using the Include extension method, as demonstrated in Listing 30-6.

Listing 30-6. Using the Include Extension Method to Eagerly Load Data

```
using System;
using System.Collections.Generic;
using System.Linq;
using NorthwindModel;

class Listing_06 {

    static void Main(string[] args) {

        // create the context
        NorthwindEntities context = new NorthwindEntities();

        // perform a query
        IEnumerable<Order> results = from e in context.Orders
                                        .Include("Employee")
                                        .Include("Customer")
                                     where e.Customer.Country == "UK"
                                     select e;

        // enumerate the results
        foreach (Order myOrder in results) {
            // print out the name of the order
```

```
        Console.WriteLine("Order ID: {0}, Customer Name: {1}",
            myOrder.OrderID, myOrder.Customer.CompanyName);

        // use the navgiation properties to get the employee
        Employee myEmployee = myOrder.Employee;
        Console.WriteLine("Order created by: {0} {1}",
            myEmployee.FirstName, myEmployee.LastName);
    }

    // wait for input before exiting
    Console.WriteLine("Press enter to finish");
    Console.ReadLine();
    }
}
```

This is known as *eager data loading*. The data we have specified is loaded, even though we don't need it for the LINQ query itself. In Listing 30-6, I have applied the Include extension method to the query data source and specified that the Employee and Customer navigation properties be included in the query. You specify each navigation property to load in a separate call to the Include method. The additional data is included in the SQL query generated by the LINQ query, and the data is cached by the Entity Framework so that no further queries are required when we use the navigation properties on the LINQ query results.

Performing Common Database Operations

Now that we understand how the entity classes are mapped to the database and how we use the navigation properties to take advantage of foreign-key relationships, we can move on to performing the most common types of database operations. In the following sections, I'll show you how to perform different types of query, insert data into the database, modify existing data, and delete data.

Querying Data

Almost all the examples so far in this chapter have demonstrated using a LINQ query to retrieve data using the entity model. The benefits of this approach are that you can use the standard LINQ syntax and features, you can work in C# data types, you don't have to express your query using SQL, and you can use navigation properties to traverse foreign-key relationships between tables. In this section, I'll show you some different kinds of query that are slightly different from the ones we have used so far.

Compiling Queries

You can create parameterized compiled queries that you can reuse with different parameter values. Listing 30-7 provides a demonstration.

Listing 30-7. Creating a Compiled Parameterized Query

```
using System;
using System.Collections.Generic;
using System.Data.Objects;
```

```
using System.Linq;
using NorthwindModel;

class Listing_07 {

    static void Main(string[] args) {

        // create the compiled LINQ query
        Func<NorthwindEntities, string, IEnumerable<Employee>> compiledQuery =
            CompiledQuery.Compile(
            (NorthwindEntities contextParam, string cityParam) =>
                from e in contextParam.Employees
                where e.City == cityParam
                select e);

        // create a context
        NorthwindEntities context = new NorthwindEntities();

        // define the set of cities we are interested in
        string[] cityNames = new string[] { "London", "Redmond", "Seattle" };

        // use the compiled query with each of the city names as parameters
        foreach (string city in cityNames) {
            IEnumerable<Employee> employees = compiledQuery(context, city);

            // print out the results
            Console.WriteLine("--- Employees in city: {0} ---", city);
            foreach (Employee emp in employees) {
                Console.WriteLine("{0} {1}", emp.FirstName, emp.LastName);
            }
        }

        // wait for input before exiting
        Console.WriteLine("Press enter to finish");
        Console.ReadLine();
    }
}
```

The CompiledQuery class in the System.Data.Objects namespace contains a method called Compile. You can use this to create a reusable parameterized LINQ query, like the one in Listing 30-7. The result of the method call is a Func that takes an Entity Framework context and your values as parameters and that returns the result type from your query. In the case of Listing 30-7, I pass in a string representing the name of a city, and the result is an IEnumerable<Employee>. This is illustrated by Figure 30-14. You can learn more about Funcs in Chapter 10.

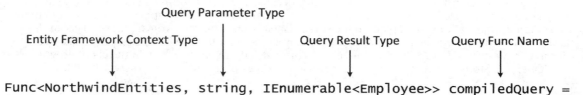

Figure 30-14. *The anatomy of a compiled query Func*

To define the function, you pass a lambda express to the Compile method that returns a LINQ expression. This is illustrated by Figure 30-15.

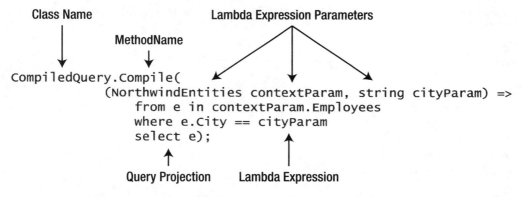

Figure 30-15. *The anatomy of a compiled LINQ to Entities expression*

Once you have defined a Func and assigned it a compiled LINQ expression, you can pass different parameter values and execute the expression. In Listing 30-7, I pass in three different city names and query for the Employee objects whose City property matches each of the names. Compiling and running Listing 30-7 produces the following output:

```
--- Employees in city: London ---
Steven Buchanan
Michael Suyama
Robert King
Anne Dodsworth
--- Employees in city: Redmond ---
Margaret Peacock
--- Employees in city: Seattle ---
Nancy Davolio
Laura Callahan
Press enter to finish
```

Compiling a query improves the performance because the query doesn't have to be analyzed and translated into SQL each time. You can specify up to 16 parameters in a compiled query, but note that you cannot project anonymous types in the select clause (this is because you are using a Func and anonymous types cannot be passed as method parameters). Compiling a LINQ expression like this doesn't create a stored procedure on the server. This is strictly an optimization in the client program. See the "Querying Stored Procedures" section for an alternative optimization that *is* server-based.

Querying Views

When we created the Entity Framework data model, we check the options to include views and stored procedures from the database. These options were shown in Figure 30-8.

You can see the views available by using the Entity Data Model Browser windows in Visual Studio. Double-click the NorthwindModel.edmx entry in the Solution Explorer, and then select Entity Data Model Browser from the View ➤ Other Windows menu. There will be a list of the tables and views available under the NorthwindModel.Store entry, as shown by Figure 30-16.

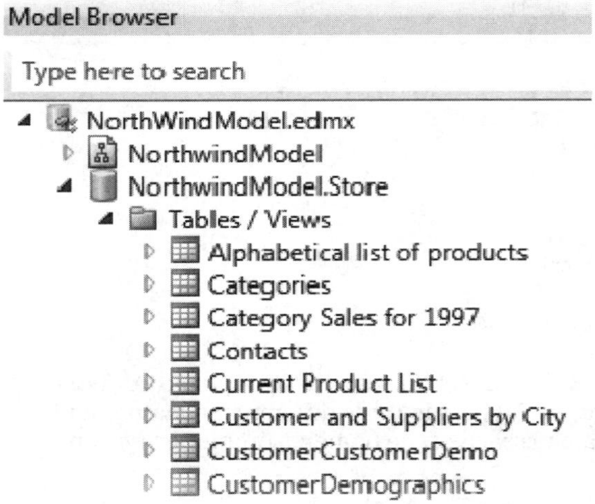

Figure 30-16. The list of views and tables in the Model Browser window

The data model doesn't distinguish between views and models, and you query them in the same way. You can see from the Figure 30-16 that there is a view called Customer and Suppliers by City. Listing 30-8 demonstrates using LINQ to query this view.

Listing 30-8. Querying a View

```
using System;
using System.Collections.Generic;
using System.Linq;
using NorthwindModel;
```

```
class Listing_08 {

    static void Main(string[] args) {

        // create a context
        NorthwindEntities context = new NorthwindEntities();

        // query the view
        IEnumerable<Customer_and_Suppliers_by_City> results
            = from e in context.Customer_and_Suppliers_by_Cities
              where e.City == "London" || e.City == "Paris"
              select e;

        // enumerate the results
        foreach (Customer_and_Suppliers_by_City item in results) {
            Console.WriteLine("Name: {0}, City: {1}",
                item.CompanyName,
                item.City);
        }

        // wait for input before exiting
        Console.WriteLine("Press enter to finish");
        Console.ReadLine();
    }
}
```

The entity object names can become cumbersome, as you can see in Listing 30-8 where the entity objects are of the Customer_and_Suppliers_by_City type, but otherwise working with views is just like working with tables. Compiling and running Listing 30-8 produces the following results:

```
Name: Around the Horn, City: London
Name: B's Beverages, City: London
Name: Consolidated Holdings, City: London
Name: Eastern Connection, City: London
Name: Exotic Liquids, City: London
Name: North/South, City: London
Name: Seven Seas Imports, City: London
Name: Aux joyeux ecclésiastiques, City: Paris
Name: Paris spécialités, City: Paris
Name: Spécialités du monde, City: Paris
Press enter to finish
```

Querying Stored Procedures

Using stored procedures is more complicated than using views. Even though we included the stored procedures available in the database when we created the Northwind data model, we have to explicitly enable the ones we want before we can use them.

You can see which stored procedures are available in the Entity Data Model Browser window, which has a section for stored procedures immediately after the section for tables and views that we saw in the previous section. Figure 30-17 shows the stored procedures available in the Northwind model.

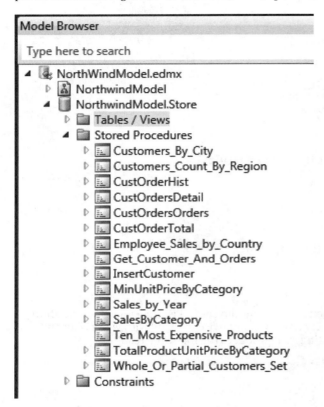

Figure 30-17. The list of available stored procedures in the Northwind model

To enable a stored procedure, right-click the one that you want, and select Add Function Import from the menu. This will display the Add Function Import dialog box, as illustrated by Figure 30-18, which shows result of selecting the Customers_By_City stored procedure.

Figure 30-18. *Importing a stored procedure*

The text in the Function Import Name text box is used for the property that will be added to the data model context. We will stick with the default value for this example. The most important thing to do in this dialog box is to specify the stored procedure return type. If the stored procedure returns a SQL type that easily maps to a built-in C# type, then you can select from the Scalars menu. If the stored procedure returns a type that matches one of the other classes created in the data model, you can select from the Entities menu. The stored procedure I have selected doesn't map readily to either of those categories, so I need to create a new class.

First, click the Get Column Information button. This obtains the details of the columns returned by the stored procedure. Then click the Create New Complex Type button. This adds a new C# type to the data model to represent the result created by the selected stored procedure. You will see that a name is suggested in the Complex text box. Accept the suggestion, and click the OK button. The imported stored procedure is added to the Function Imports section of the Model Browser window, as shown in Figure 30-19.

Figure 30-19. The imported stored procedure

When we import a stored procedure, a new method is added to the data model context object. This method takes parameters that will be used to execute the procedure. In the case of the Customers_By_City stored procedure, the method takes a single parameter that is the name of the city we want customer information for. Listing 30-9 demonstrates using the stored procedure in a LINQ query.

Listing 30-9. Querying a Stored Procedure

```
using System;
using System.Collections.Generic;
using System.Linq;
using NorthwindModel;

class Listing_09 {

    static void Main(string[] args) {

        // create a context
        NorthwindEntities context = new NorthwindEntities();

        // query the stored procedure
        IEnumerable<Customers_By_City_Result> results =
            from e in context.Customers_By_City("London")
            where !e.ContactName.Contains("Hardy")
            select e;

        foreach (Customers_By_City_Result item in results) {
            Console.WriteLine("Name: {0}", item.CompanyName);
        }

        // wait for input before exiting
        Console.WriteLine("Press enter to finish");
        Console.ReadLine();
    }
}
```

As with views, the names of the result types and the name of the context member can be unwieldy, but you can edit the data model and change these if it is a problem. It is a little awkward having to import each stored procedure before it can be used, but once this is done, you can take advantage of the significant performance improvements that stored procedures offer, especially for complex queries. Compiling and running Listing 30-9 produces the following results:

```
Name: B's Beverages
Name: Consolidated Holdings
Name: Eastern Connection
Name: North/South
Name: Seven Seas Imports
Press enter to finish
```

Inserting Data into the Database

There are four steps to inserting new data into the database using the data model. The first is to create a new instance of one of the entity classes. If we were adding a new row to the Employees table, for example, we would create a new Employee object.

Once we have an object, we assign values to its properties that represent the columns of the table we want to insert the record into. At the very least, we have to assign values to those properties that relate to table columns that cannot be null.

The third step is to add tell the data model context object that we want to add the object by calling the AddObject method on the appropriate ObjectSet<T> property.

The final step is to call the SaveChanges method on the data model context object. This writes our changes to the database. Listing 30-10 demonstrates these steps to create a new row in the Employees table.

Listing 30-10. Inserting New Data

```
using System;
using System.Collections.Generic;
using System.Linq;
using NorthwindModel;

class Listing_10 {

    static void Main(string[] args) {

        // create a context
        NorthwindEntities context = new NorthwindEntities();

        // STEP 1 - create the new Employee object
        Employee myNewEmployee = Employee.CreateEmployee(12345, "Freeman", "Adam");

        // STEP 2 - fill in some of the other details of the new object
        myNewEmployee.City = "London";
        myNewEmployee.Country = "UK";
```

```
        // STEP 3 - add the new object to the context collection for that type
        context.Employees.AddObject(myNewEmployee);

        // STEP 4 - save the changes to the database
        context.SaveChanges();

        // wait for input before exiting
        Console.WriteLine("Press enter to finish");
        Console.ReadLine();
    }
}
```

In Listing 30-10, I have created the new Employee object using the static CreateXXX method that every entity type has. The Employee class has the CreateEmployee method, the Customer class has the CreateCustomer method, and so on. These methods have parameters for the properties that cannot be left null. Using these methods is good practice because it avoids a database error when you inadvertently leave a required field empty. For the Employee entity type, the required fields are for the employee ID and the person's first and last name.

If we compile and run Listing 30-10, we can see a new record has been added to the Employees table. We can do this by opening the Database Explorer windows in Visual Studio Express and the Server Explorer in other editions of Visual Studio. Expand the Data Connections item, then the Northwind.mdf item, and then Tables. You will see the list of tables that the database contains, as illustrated by Figure 30-20.

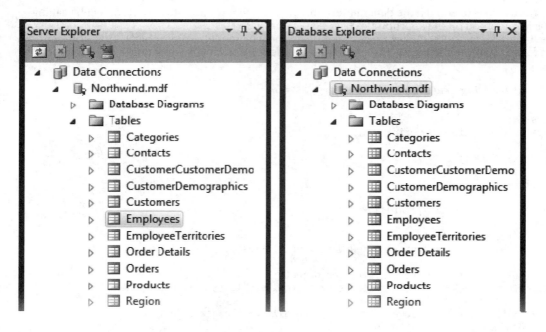

Figure 30-20. The Server Explorer and Database Explorer

Right-click the Employees table entry, and select Show Table Data. This will open a new window that contains the data currently in the Employees table, as shown in Figure 30-21. You can see that my new record has been created.

EmployeeID	LastName	FirstName	Title	TitleO...	BirthDate	HireDate	Address	City
1	Davolio	Nancy	Sales Represent...	Ms.	08/12/1948 ...	01/05/1992...	507 - 20th Av...	Seattle
2	Fuller	Andrew	Vice President, ...	Dr.	19/02/1952 ...	14/08/1992...	908 W. Capita...	Tacoma
3	Leverling	Janet	Sales Represent...	Ms.	30/08/1963 ...	01/04/1992...	722 Moss Bay ...	Kirkland
4	Peacock	Margaret	Sales Represent...	Mrs.	19/09/1937 ...	03/05/1993...	4110 Old Red...	Redmond
5	Buchanan	Steven	Sales Manager	Mr.	04/03/1955 ...	17/10/1993...	14 Garrett Hill	London
6	Suyama	Michael	Sales Represent...	Mr.	02/07/1963 ...	17/10/1993...	Coventry Hou...	London
7	King	Robert	Sales Represent...	Mr.	29/05/1960 ...	02/01/1994...	Edgeham Hol...	London
8	Callahan	Laura	Inside Sales Co...	Ms.	09/01/1958 ...	05/03/1994...	4726 - 11th A...	Seattle
9	Dodsworth	Anne	Sales Represent...	Ms.	27/01/1966 ...	15/11/1994...	7 Houndstoot...	London
11	Freeman	Adam	NULL	NULL	NULL	NULL	NULL	London
NULL	NULL	NULL	NULL	NULL	NULL	NULL	NULL	NULL

Figure 30-21. A newly inserted row

Inserting Attached Objects

We can use the navigation properties to create associated objects and write them to the database. The Entity Framework will detect the relationship between the entity objects and insert them into the database together. Listing 30-11 provides an example.

Listing 30-11. Inserting Attached Objects

```
using System;
using System.Collections.Generic;
using System.Linq;
using NorthwindModel;

class Listing_11 {

    static void Main(string[] args) {

        // create a context
        NorthwindEntities context = new NorthwindEntities();

        // create the new customer
        Customer cust = new Customer {
            CustomerID = "LAWN",
            CompanyName = "Lawn Wranglers",
            ContactName = "Mr. Abe Henry",
            ContactTitle = "Owner",
            Address = "1017 Maple Leaf Way",
            City = "Ft. Worth",
            Region = "TX",
```

```
                PostalCode = "76104",
                Country = "USA",
                Phone = "(800) MOW-LAWN",
                Fax = "(800) MOW-LAWO"
            };

            // create the new order
            Order ord = new Order {
                CustomerID = "LAWN",
                EmployeeID = 4,
                OrderDate = DateTime.Now,
                RequiredDate = DateTime.Now.AddDays(7),
                ShipVia = 3,
                Freight = new Decimal(24.66),
                ShipName = "Lawn Wranglers",
                ShipAddress = "1017 Maple Leaf Way",
                ShipCity = "Ft. Worth",
                ShipRegion = "TX",
                ShipPostalCode = "76104",
                ShipCountry = "USA"
            };

            // attach the order to the customer
            cust.Orders.Add(ord);

            // add the new Customer
            context.Customers.AddObject(cust);

            // save the changes
            context.SaveChanges();

            // wait for input before exiting
            Console.WriteLine("Press enter to finish");
            Console.ReadLine();
        }
    }
```

Listing 30-11 creates a new Customer object and populated the fields. This time I have used the default constructor for the entity class, as opposed to the static CreateXXX method of the previous listing.

I then create a new Order object. Also, using the default class constructor, I then attach to the Customer object using the Add method of the navigation property. I tell the context about the new Customer by using the AddObject method on the Customers property and then call the SaveChanges method. The context detects the newly added Order and writes the details of both objects to the database tables in a single step.

Updating Data in the Database

To update data, you simply change the value assigned to properties of the entity objects that interest you and call SaveChanges. Listing 30-12 contains a demonstration, modifying the Employee record that I created in Listing 30-10 (if you are following these examples, you will need to compile and run Listing 30-10 to create the record before this listing will work).

Listing 30-12. Updating a Database Record Through an Entity Object

```
using System;
using System.Collections.Generic;
using System.Linq;
using NorthwindModel;

class Listing_12 {

    static void Main(string[] args) {

        // create a context
        NorthwindEntities context = new NorthwindEntities();

        // query to find the empoyee record we are looking for
        IEnumerable<Employee> results = from e in context.Employees
                                        where e.LastName == "Freeman"
                                        select e;

        // enumerate the results and make changes
        foreach (Employee emp in results) {
            emp.City = "Boston";
            emp.Country = "USA";
            emp.Title = "Sales Representative";
            emp.ReportsTo = 2;
        }


        // save the changes
        context.SaveChanges();

        // wait for input before exiting
        Console.WriteLine("Press enter to finish");
        Console.ReadLine();
    }
}
```

Listing 30-12 uses LINQ to query the database for the data we want and then assigns new values to the Employee object. When all the changes are made, I call the SaveChanges method, and the database is updated. If we inspect the Employee table data, we can see that the changes have been made, as illustrated by Figure 30-22.

EmployeeID	LastName	FirstName	Title	TitleO...	BirthDate	HireDate	Address	City
1	Davolio	Nancy	Sales Represent...	Ms.	08/12/1948 ...	01/05/1992...	507 - 20th Av...	Seattle
2	Fuller	Andrew	Vice President, ...	Dr.	19/02/1952 ...	14/08/1992...	908 W. Capita...	Tacoma
3	Leverling	Janet	Sales Represent...	Ms.	30/08/1963 ...	01/04/1992...	722 Moss Bay ...	Kirkland
4	Peacock	Margaret	Sales Represent...	Mrs.	19/09/1937 ...	03/05/1993...	4110 Old Red...	Redmond
5	Buchanan	Steven	Sales Manager	Mr.	04/03/1955 ...	17/10/1993...	14 Garrett Hill	London
6	Suyama	Michael	Sales Represent...	Mr.	02/07/1963 ...	17/10/1993...	Coventry Hou...	London
7	King	Robert	Sales Represent...	Mr.	29/05/1960 ...	02/01/1994...	Edgeham Hol...	London
8	Callahan	Laura	Inside Sales Co...	Ms.	09/01/1958 ...	05/03/1994...	4726 - 11th A...	Seattle
9	Dodsworth	Anne	Sales Represent...	Ms.	27/01/1966 ...	15/11/1994...	7 Houndstoot...	London
11	Freeman	Adam	Sales Represent...	NULL	NULL	NULL	NULL	Boston
* NULL	NULL	NULL	NULL	NULL	NULL	NULL	NULL	NULL

Figure 30-22. The modified Employee data

Deleting Data

To delete data from the database, you simple call the DeleteObject method of the context object and pass in the entity object that you want to delete as the parameter. Then you call the SaveChanges method. Listing 30-13 provides a demonstration, which deletes the row in the Employee table that I created in Listing 30-10.

Listing 30-13. Deleting Data from the Database

```
using System;
using System.Collections.Generic;
using System.Linq;
using NorthwindModel;

class Listing_13 {

    static void Main(string[] args) {

        // create a context
        NorthwindEntities context = new NorthwindEntities();

        // query to find the empoyee record we are looking for
        IEnumerable<Employee> results = from e in context.Employees
                                        where e.LastName == "Freeman"
                                        select e;

        // enumerate the results and delete them
        foreach (Employee emp in results) {
            context.DeleteObject(emp);
        }

        // save the changes
        context.SaveChanges();
```

```
        // wait for input before exiting
        Console.WriteLine("Press enter to finish");
        Console.ReadLine();
    }
}
```

Compiling and running Listing 30-13 removes the row from the database and restores it to its original state.

Enabling Concurrency Checking

The Entity Framework uses an *optimistic concurrency model* by default. Optimism in this case means that we cross our fingers and hope that we don't get a data race between clients using the same database. You can learn more about data races in Chapter 24. The essence for this chapter is that two client programs read the same data from the database at roughly the same time. The first client makes a change to the data and updates the database. A moment later, the second client makes a different change to the same data and performs an update. When the second update is applied, the original set of changes are lost.

You can enable concurrency checking on individual fields in the data model. This is still optimistic concurrency because no data is locked in the database, but it does mean that you will know when someone else has made changes to data that you intend to modify.

In the section, I'll demonstrate how to apply concurrency checking to a single field, the LastName property in the Employee entity object. Open the data model diagram by double-clicking the NorthwindModel.edmx entry in the Solution Explorer window. Scroll down until you see the Employee diagram, right-click the LastName property, and select Properties. Find the Concurrency Mode property, and change the setting to Fixed, as illustrated by Figure 30-23.

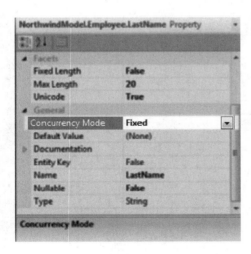

Figure 30-23. Setting the Concurrency Mode property

Select Save from the File menu to save the change to the data model. This has enabled concurrency checking for one field. If you want this feature enable for fields, you must repeat these steps for each and every one. There is no facility for changing all of the fields in one go. If we try to update the `LastName` field when someone else has modified since we read it from the database, the Entity Framework will throw an `OptimisticConcurrencyException` when we call the `SaveChanges` method. We can catch this method and prevent overwriting changes made by others.

Summary

In this chapter, we saw now the Entity Framework can be used to create a data model that lets us work with a database using C# data types and LINQ queries. Features such as navigation properties make working with the data much more like working with regular C# objects, and we don't need to break out the SQL at any point. The Entity Framework can be used to create incredibly complex and sophisticated data models, and we have only scratched the surface with the model we used in this chapter, but even so, you can see how object-relational mapping can be performing using the Entity Framework and how LINQ to Entities can be used in place of SQL to query the underlying data.

CHAPTER 31

LINQ to DataSet

The last of our chapters on LINQ relates to the `System.Data.DataSet` class, which can be used to create an in-memory cache of data from a database and which can be used as the data source for LINQ queries.

The `DataSet` class is part of ADO.NET—just like the Entity Framework that we saw in the previous chapter. ADO.NET is big; it allows you to access a wide range of data sources in a wide range of ways. In this chapter, we'll be looking at working with databases more directly than with the Entity Framework. We won't be using data models or C# objects that represent tables and rows. In fact, if you have been waiting for a chance to break out your SQL skills, then this is the chapter for you.

ADO.NET supports all the major databases and quite a few of the minor ones. We won't be going into the details of setting up and configuring a database, and our examples will all be based on SQL Server Express. That said, everything you learn in this chapter can be transferred to other database servers because of the way that ADO.NET provides consistent access to data and databases. Table 31-1 provides the summary for this chapter.

Table 31-1. *Quick Problem/Solution Reference for Chapter 31*

Problem	Solution	Listings
Connect to a database.	Use the `SqlConnection` class.	31-1, 31-2
Store connection strings outside of code files.	Use an `App.config` file, and read the contents using the `ConfigurationManager` class.	31-3
Execute a SQL query.	Use the `SqlCommand` class.	31-4
Creating an in-memory result cache.	Use the `DataSet` class, and fill it using a `SqlDataAdapter`.	31-5, 31-6
Use LINQ to query a `DataSet`.	Call the `AsEnumerable` method on `Data` objects to make them suitable LINQ data sources, and then perform LINQ queries as usual.	31-7 through 31-10
Using cached `DataSet` data to modify an underlying database.	Make changes to the `DataRow` objects contained in the `DataSet` `DataTables`, and call the `SqlDataAdapter.Update` method to update the database.	31-11 through 31-13

Connecting to and Querying a Database

We have to do some groundwork in order to get to the point where we can use a `DataSet` object as the data source for a LINQ query. That groundwork starts with creating a database that we can use for the examples in this chapter.

Setting Up the Database

Before we can begin, we have to create a database that we can use in our code examples. Unlike the previous chapter, we don't have to create a database model, but we do have to load the database file in Visual Studio so that we can connect to it and make queries. In this section, I'll walk you through the steps required to get set up using the extended `Northwind` database that I included in the source code download for this book, which you can download freely from Apress.com. For this chapter, I have copied the files `Northwind.mdf` and `Northwind_log.LDF` to the `C:\Northwind` directory on my computer. You can copy them anywhere, but remember to change the path to the files when following the examples if you pick a different location.

If you followed the examples in the previous chapter, Visual Studio will already have created the database for you. If not, then you'll need to perform the following steps.

To create the database, open the Server Explorer window in Visual Studio. You can find it under the View ➤ Other Windows menu. If you are using Visual Studio Express, then you will need the Database Explorer window instead. For our purposes, both windows work in the same way.

Right-click the Data Connections item in the Server Explorer/Database Explorer window, and select Add Connection from the pop-up menu, as illustrated in Figure 31-1. The figure shows Visual Studio Express, but the appearance of the other editions is very similar.

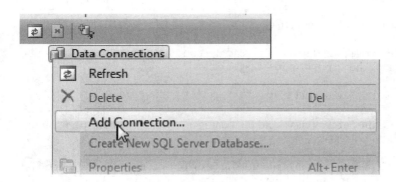

Figure 31-1. *Creating a new connection*

You will be presented with a choice of data sources. The number of possible sources depends on the edition of Visual Studio you are using. Figure 31-2 shows the reduced list available in the Express edition. For this chapter, we are going to work with a database file, so select the Microsoft SQL Server Database File option, and click the Continue button.

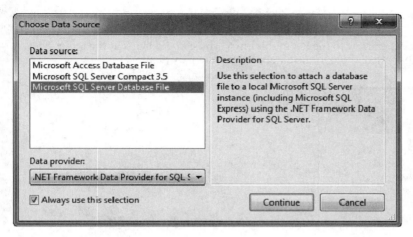

Figure 31-2. Selecting the data source type

The next step is to select the database file, as shown in Figure 31-3. Click the Browse button, and select the Northwind.mdf file from wherever you copied it to. The full path for my file is C:\Northwind\Northwind.mdf, as shown in the figure.

Figure 31-3. Selecting the database file

There is no need to change any of the options. Just click the OK button when you have selected the database file. You'll see that a new entry has appeared in the Server Explorer/Database Explorer window called Northwind.mdf. If you click the arrow to the left of this entry, you can then look at the tables, views, stored procedures, and so on, that are defined in the database, as shown by Figure 31-4.

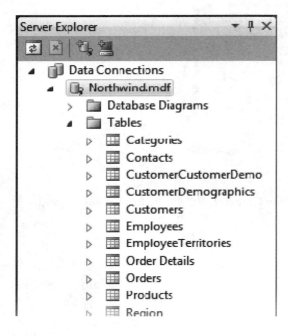

Figure 31-4. Viewing the tables in the Northwind database

The final thing we need to do is to make a note of the connection details. We'll need these in the next section. Right-click the Northwind.mdf entry, and select Properties from the pop-up menu. One of the properties displayed will be the connection string; mine has the following value:

```
Data Source=.\SQLEXPRESS;AttachDbFilename=C:\Northwind\Northwind.mdf;Integrated
Security=True;Connect Timeout=30;User Instance=True
```

Creating a Connection to the Database

Now that we have used Visual Studio to load the database file, we can connect to the database in our code. We have to manage the connections manually in this approach. This is not as bad as it seems, although it does require us to do more work in the code file. Listing 31-1 provides a demonstration of creating a connection.

Listing 31-1. Creating a Connection to the Database

```csharp
using System;
using System.Data;
using System.Data.SqlClient;

class Listing_01 {

    static void Main(string[] args) {

        // create a connection object
        SqlConnection myConnection = new SqlConnection();

        // set the connection string
        myConnection.ConnectionString = @"Data
Source=.\SQLEXPRESS;AttachDbFilename=C:\Northwind\Northwind.mdf;Integrated
Security=True;Connect Timeout=30;User Instance=True";

        // open the connection to the database
        myConnection.Open();

        // display the connection state
        if (myConnection.State == ConnectionState.Open) {
            Console.WriteLine("Connection is open");
        } else {
            Console.WriteLine("Connection didn't open properly");
        }

        // close the connection
        myConnection.Close();

        // wait for input before exiting
        Console.WriteLine("Press enter to finish");
        Console.ReadLine();
    }
}
```

Quite a few things happen in Listing 31-1, so I will walk through the steps involved. The first thing I did was create a new System.Data.SqlClient.SqlConnection object using the default constructor:

```csharp
SqlConnection myConnection = new SqlConnection();
```

This is the object that will manage our connection to the database. It doesn't connect when we create the object, not least because we have yet to provide it with the details of our database, which is what I do next using the ConnectionString property:

```csharp
myConnection.ConnectionString = @"Data
Source=.\SQLEXPRESS;AttachDbFilename=C:\Northwind\Northwind.mdf;Integrated
Security=True;Connect Timeout=30;User Instance=True";
```

The connection string is what we copied from the Properties window in Visual Studio. It contains all the information that the SqlConnection object will need to make a connection to our database. When including the string directly in the code file like this, it is important to make the string a verbatim literal using the @ symbol. See Chapter 16 for details of verbatim literals.

I am not going to go into what the individual parts of the connection string are. First, they vary from database to database, and second, you can always copy what you need from Visual Studio, as we did in the previous section. For larger projects, your DBA will usually provide a connection string for you to use.

It is important to copy the string carefully; small changes can cause connections to fail. Working with connection strings in the code like this is pretty inflexible. See the next section for a more programmer-friendly technique.

■ **Tip** In this chapter, the classes for the examples are contained in two namespaces. The System.Data namespace contains the classes that are common across all databases, while the System.Data.SqlClient namespace contains classes with functionality specific to Microsoft SQL Server. If you were using a different database, you would use a different namespace; for example, the System.Data.OracleClient namespace provides support for using Oracle databases.

My next step is to open the connection by calling the Open method:

```
myConnection.Open();
```

This establishes the connection to the database but doesn't do anything else. We can check to see whether our connection works by testing the value of the State property, which returns a value from the System.Data.ConnectionState enumeration. The Open value is the one we are looking for, but the enumeration defines a range of values, which are described in Table 31-2.

Table 31-2. Values from the ConnectionState Enum

Value	Description
Open	The connection is open.
Closed	The connection is closed.
Broken	The connection was opened but has since been closed for some reason.
Connecting Executing Fetching	These values are defined but reserved for use in the future.

It is important to check that the connection to the database is Open before issuing commands or queries. You run the risk of raising exceptions otherwise:

```
if (myConnection.State == ConnectionState.Open) {
    Console.WriteLine("Connection is open");
} else {
    Console.WriteLine("Connection didn't open properly");
}
```

The last step in the code is to close the connection when I am finished with it, using the Close method:

```
myConnection.Close();
```

It is important to ensure that connections are closed. Most database servers will support a finite amount of connections, and your program will tie up all the server resources if you create a new one for each operation and don't close them afterward. Compiling and running Listing 31-1 produces the following results:

```
Connection is open
Press enter to finish
```

The need to call the Close method on a connection is so important that you will often see SqlConnection objects created and used inside a using code block, as shown in Listing 31-2.

Listing 31-2. Using a SqlConnection Object in a using Block

```
using System;
using System.Data;
using System.Data.SqlClient;

class Listing_02 {

    static void Main(string[] args) {

        using (SqlConnection myConnection = new SqlConnection()) {

            // set the connection string
            myConnection.ConnectionString = @"Data
Source=.\SQLEXPRESS;AttachDbFilename=C:\Northwind\Northwind.mdf;Integrated
Security=True;Connect Timeout=30;User Instance=True";

            // open the connection to the database
            myConnection.Open();

            // display the connection state
            if (myConnection.State == ConnectionState.Open) {
                Console.WriteLine("Connection is open");
            } else {
                Console.WriteLine("Connection didn't open properly");
            }
        }
```

```
        // wait for input before exiting
        Console.WriteLine("Press enter to finish");
        Console.ReadLine();
    }
}
```

Listing 31-2 creates the SqlConnection within a using block. When we reach the end of the using statement code block, the SqlConnection object will go out of scope, and the Dispose method will be called, which in turn calls the Close method for us. You can learn more about using statements in Chapter 18.

■ **Note** Applying using statements with database connections is good practice, and I recommend that you do it in your own code. However, in this chapter I am not going to do so because it makes the code harder to read.

Storing Connection Strings

It doesn't matter if you use a monolithic string or build one, keeping the connection string in the code can be unwieldy, not least because changing the string requires a recompile. A better technique is to store the connection string in a configuration file. The simplest way to do this is to use the built-in support for configuration files and a handy feature of Visual Studio.

The first step is to add an item to our project. Right-click your project in the Solution Explorer window, select Add from the pop-up menu, and then select New Item. Select Application Configuration File from the list of templates, and ensure that the name for the new item is App.config, as shown in Figure 31-5.

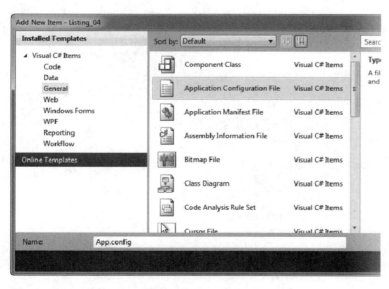

Figure 31-5. Adding an application configuration file

Click the Add button, and the new item will be added to your project. Open the `App.config` file, and change the content so that it matches the following:

```
<?xml version="1.0" encoding="utf-8"?>
<configuration>
  <connectionStrings>
    <add name="NorthwindConnection" connectionString="Data
Source=.\SQLEXPRESS;AttachDbFilename=C:\Northwind\Northwind.mdf;Integrated
Security=True;Connect Timeout=30;User Instance=True" />
  </connectionStrings>
</configuration>
```

We have created an application configuration file, into which we have placed our connection string. There are predefined regions for different kinds of configuration information, one of which is specific to connection strings. You can see that I have given the connection a string—`NorthwindConnection`. This is so I can refer to it later.

The useful Visual Studio feature I mentioned is that when you compile your program, Visual Studio copies your `App.config` file into the output directory and renames it so that it will be found by the .NET configuration management classes, which look for configuration information in the same place as the executable for the program. If your project output was called `MyProgram.exe`, then the `App.config` file would be copied to `MyProgram.exe.config` in the bin/Debug or bin/Release directory of your project.

We now need to read the connection string from the configuration file. To do this, we need to add a reference to another assembly. Right-click your project in the Solution Explorer window, and select Add Reference from the pop-up menu. Then select System.Configuration from the .NET tab of the Add Reference dialog box, as shown by Figure 31-6.

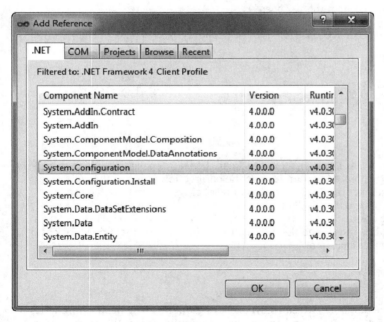

Figure 31-6. Adding a new assembly reference

The assembly contains the ConfigurationManager class in the System.Configuration namespace, which we can use to read our configuration file quickly and easily. Listing 31-3 provides a demonstration.

Listing 31-3. Reading a Connection String from a Configuration File

```
using System;
using System.Configuration;
using System.Data;
using System.Data.SqlClient;

class Listing_03 {

    static void Main(string[] args) {

        ConnectionStringSettings connStringSettings
            = ConfigurationManager.ConnectionStrings["NorthwindConnection"];

        using (SqlConnection myConnection
            = new SqlConnection(connStringSettings.ConnectionString)) {

            // open the connection to the database
            myConnection.Open();

            // display the connection state
            if (myConnection.State == ConnectionState.Open) {
                Console.WriteLine("Connection is open");
            } else {
                Console.WriteLine("Connection didn't open properly");
            }
        }

        // wait for input before exiting
        Console.WriteLine("Press enter to finish");
        Console.ReadLine();
    }
}
```

To read the connection string from the configuration file, I call the static ConnectionStrings indexer of the ConfigurationManager class, specifying the name I gave the connection string in the configuration file, NorthwindConnection. The indexer returns a ConnectionStringSettings object, which contains details of the connection string we put into the file. The property we care about in this example is ConnectionString, which returns the connection string in a form that we can use to pass to the SqlConnection constructor. You'll notice that I read the connection string outside the using block and pass it as a constructor parameter in this example.

Executing a SQL Query

Now that we have a connection to the database, we can start executing queries. The basic approach is to follow the traditional path of sending a SQL query and processing the results. This is the most approach to using databases that most programmers will be familiar with, which is why I have included it a demonstration. I won't go into the classes in any depth, but I wanted to include this example so you can see how it differs from the LINQ to DataSet approach that we are building toward. Listing 31-4 shows how to perform a basic query.

Listing 31-4. Executing a SQL Query

```
using System;
using System.Configuration;
using System.Data;
using System.Data.SqlClient;

class Listing_04 {

    static void Main(string[] args) {

        ConnectionStringSettings connStringSettings
            = ConfigurationManager.ConnectionStrings["NorthwindConnection"];

        // create the connection object
        SqlConnection myConnection = new SqlConnection(connStringSettings.ConnectionString);

        // create a SQL command object
        SqlCommand myCommand = myConnection.CreateCommand();
        myCommand.CommandText = "SELECT * FROM Employees WHERE City='London'";

        // open the connection to the database
        myConnection.Open();

        // execute the command
        SqlDataReader myReader = myCommand.ExecuteReader();

        // process the data
        while (myReader.Read()) {
            // get the fields for this current row
            string firstName = (string) myReader["FirstName"];
            string lastName = (string) myReader["LastName"];
            string city = (string) myReader["City"];
            // print out the information for this record
            Console.WriteLine("Name: {0} {1}, City: {2}",
                firstName, lastName, city);
        }

        // close the database connection
        myConnection.Close();

        // wait for input before exiting
        Console.WriteLine("Press enter to finish");
        Console.ReadLine();
    }
}
```

There are several stages to executing a query in this way. Once I have created the `SqlConnection` object, I call the `CreateCommand` method to create a `SqlCommand` object. This is the object that will represent our query. I provide the SQL itself using the `CommandText` property. In the case of this example, I am querying for all columns in the `Employees` table for rows where the `City` column has the value London:

```
myCommand.CommandText = "SELECT * FROM Employees WHERE City='London'";
```

I then open the connection using the `Open` method, at which point I am ready to execute my query. I do this by calling the `ExecuteReader` method on the `SqlCommand` object:

```
SqlDataReader myReader = myCommand.ExecuteReader();
```

This method returns a `SqlDataReader`, which contains the rows of data that our query generated. The `Read` method moves a cursor through the rows, and I access the columns I am interested in by providing the column name as an indexer. I am making this process look more basic than it really is. There are methods in the `SqlDataReader` class that allow you to specify the SQL data type that a column contains and have the result mapped to a corresponding C# type, whereas in the example I use the indexer and cast the `object` that is returned to a `string`. Compiling and running Listing 31-4 produces the following results:

```
Name: Steven Buchanan, City: London
Name: Michael Suyama, City: London
Name: Robert King, City: London
Name: Anne Dodsworth, City: London
Press enter to finish
```

Understanding the DataSet Class

The approach taken in Listing 31-4 is a very manual one, and we get the data in a very raw state. This means that if we want to perform sophisticated operations on the data, we need to collect and organize it ourselves. If we want to modify data or add or delete records based on the outcome of a query, we have to handle that manually in our code and generate follow-on statements to perform the required operations.

That said, although the process is manual, it is workable, and it is the approach that many programmers use every day, including me, on occasion. If I have a particularly simple query to make, I'll tend to use the classes shown in Listing 31-4 even though easier-to-use alternatives are available. There are two reasons for doing this. The first is habit: people tend to approach similar problems in similar ways, and I am so used to this model of database programming that I'll sometimes use it without thinking. The second reason is resource efficiency: by working at a low level, we can consume fewer system resources and take particular care to retrieve only the data we need from the database. This is in contrast to the Entity Framework, which we saw in Chapter 30, where we give up efficiency for ease of use. There are times where LINQ to Entities is perfect for the job at hand, but that isn't always the case, and a simple approach is desirable.

There is a nice middle ground, and it is the central topic of this chapter, of course. The `System.Data.DataSet` class is an in-memory cache of data generated by a SQL query, and it allows us to process and modify the data simple and easily without inducing the complexity of something like the Entity Framework. Listing 31-5 contains a demonstration of creating a `DataSet` and filling it with data from a SQL query.

Listing 31-5. Creating and Filling a DataSet

```
using System;
using System.Configuration;
using System.Data;
using System.Data.SqlClient;

class Listing_05 {

    static void Main(string[] args) {

        // get the connection string from the config file
        ConnectionStringSettings connStringSettings
            = ConfigurationManager.ConnectionStrings["NorthwindConnection"];

        // create the connection object
        SqlConnection myConnection
            = new SqlConnection(connStringSettings.ConnectionString);

        // create the SQL command object
        SqlCommand myCommand = myConnection.CreateCommand();
        myCommand.CommandText = "SELECT * FROM Employees WHERE City='London'";

        // create the SqlDataAdapter
        SqlDataAdapter myAdapter = new SqlDataAdapter(myCommand);

        // create the DataSet object
        DataSet myDataSet = new DataSet();

        // fill the dataset into the named table
        myAdapter.Fill(myDataSet, "Employees");

        // close the database connection
        myConnection.Close();

        // wait for input before exiting
        Console.WriteLine("Press enter to finish");
        Console.ReadLine();
    }
}
```

When working with the DataSet class, we begin as we have in the previous examples. We read the connection string for the database from the configuration file and use it to create a SqlConnection object. From the SqlConnection, we create a SqlCommand, but we use a SqlDataAdapter rather than the SqlDataReader that we saw in the previous example. The SqlDataAdapter class is capable of taking the data that is returned from a SQL query and creating an in-memory cache using the DataSet class. Here are the key statements:

```
SqlDataAdapter myAdapter = new SqlDataAdapter(myCommand);
DataSet myDataSet = new DataSet();
myAdapter.Fill(myDataSet, "Employees");
```

The first statement creates the SqlDataAdapter object, taking the SqlCommand as the single constructor parameter. The SqlCommand contains details of the query to execute and the connection to use to talk to the database. The second statement creates an empty DataSet object. The third statement calls the Fill method of the SqlDataAdapter class, passing the DataSet object and the name of the table that the data originated from as parameters. We'll come back to that later.

And that's it—the DataSet object we created now contains the data that was retrieved using our SQL query. This may not seem very different from querying the database manually, but the power of the DataSet class comes from what you can do once you have some data in there.

Enumerating Results with DataTable and DataRow Objects

When we called the Fill method in the previous example, our DataSet object was populated with the data that resulted in our query. To access that data, we use the DataTable and DataRow classes, instances of which we obtain from our DataSet. The DataSet.Tables property returns a DataTable collection that contains one item for each table in the result set. In the case of our example query, there is one DataTable, which contains the data we retrieved from the Employees table. Each DataTable object has a collection of DataRow objects that are accessible through the Rows property. By using the DataTable and DataRow classes, we can enumerate the data that we got back from the query, as demonstrated by Listing 31-6.

Listing 31-6. Enumerating the Data in a DataSet Object

```
using System;
using System.Configuration;
using System.Data;
using System.Data.SqlClient;

class Listing_06 {

    static void Main(string[] args) {

        // get the connection string from the config file
        ConnectionStringSettings connStringSettings
            = ConfigurationManager.ConnectionStrings["NorthwindConnection"];

        // create the connection object
        SqlConnection myConnection
            = new SqlConnection(connStringSettings.ConnectionString);

        // create the SqlDataAdapter
        SqlDataAdapter myAdapter = new SqlDataAdapter(
            "SELECT * FROM Employees WHERE City='London'",
            myConnection);

        // create the DataSet object
        DataSet myDataSet = new DataSet();

        // fill the dataset into the named table
        myAdapter.Fill(myDataSet, "Employees");
```

```
        // get the DataTable
        DataTable employeeResultTable = myDataSet.Tables["Employees"];

        // report the number of rows in the table
        Console.WriteLine("There are {0} DataRows in the DataTable",
            employeeResultTable.Rows.Count);

        // enumerate the rows in the table
        foreach (DataRow row in employeeResultTable.Rows) {
            // extract the fields we want
            string firstName = (string) row["FirstName"];
            string lastName = (string) row["Lastname"];
            string city = (string) row["City"];

            // print out the results
            Console.WriteLine("Result - Name: {0} {1}, City: {2}",
                firstName, lastName, city);
        }

        // close the database connection
        myConnection.Close();

        // wait for input before exiting
        Console.WriteLine("Press enter to finish");
        Console.ReadLine();
    }
}
```

■ **Tip** Notice that I have used a more convenient constructor for the `SqlDataAdapter`—one that takes the query and the `SqlConnection` object and so doesn't require me to create a `SqlCommand`. There are a lot of classes available in the `System.Data` and `System.Data.SqlClient` namespaces and lots of convenience constructors to help you put them together in different ways.

To obtain a `DataTable` from the `DataSet`, I use an indexer into the collection returned by the `Tables` property, like this:

```
DataTable employeeResultTable = myDataSet.Tables["Employees"];
```

The indexer parameter is the name that I used in the `Fill` method. This name need not correspond to the source table in the database, but I will keep things consistent in these examples. Once I have the `DataTable` with my data, I write the number of rows available and use a `foreach` loop to enumerate through the set of `DataRows` returned by calling the `DataTable.Rows` property.

To get the value for a column in a `DataRow`, you use an indexer where the parameter is the name of the column whose value you require. This returns an object that you can cast to a more useful C# type, as I have done here:

```
string firstName = (string) row["FirstName"];
```

```
string lastName = (string) row["LastName"];
string city = (string) row["City"];
```

You can see that I have obtained the values of the FirstName, LastName, and City columns and cast the results to string values. As an alternative, you can take advantage of the Field<T> extension method in the System.Data.DataRowExtensions methods class to get strongly typed access to row values, like this:

```
string firstName = row.Field<string>("FirstName");
```

When using the Field<T> extension method, T is the type you want the value to be cast to. That's why I use Field<string> to get the FirstName value. Compiling and running Listing 31-6 produces the following results:

```
There are 4 DataRows in the DataTable
Result - Name: Steven Buchanan, City: London
Result - Name: Michael Suyama, City: London
Result - Name: Robert King, City: London
Result - Name: Anne Dodsworth, City: London
Press enter to finish
```

Querying DataSets with LINQ

As you might have guessed from the title of this chapter, you can query the contents of a DataSet using LINQ. This means you can execute the SQL query on the database and then use LINQ to query the results in different ways on your computer. Listing 31-7 provides a demonstration.

Listing 31-7. Querying a DataSet Using LINQ

```
using System;
using System.Collections.Generic;
using System.Configuration;
using System.Data;
using System.Data.SqlClient;

class Listing_07 {

    static void Main(string[] args) {

        // get the connection string from the config file
        ConnectionStringSettings connStringSettings
            = ConfigurationManager.ConnectionStrings["NorthwindConnection"];

        // create the connection object
        SqlConnection myConnection
            = new SqlConnection(connStringSettings.ConnectionString);

        // create the SqlDataAdapter
        SqlDataAdapter myAdapter = new SqlDataAdapter(
            "SELECT * FROM Employees", myConnection);
```

```csharp
    // create the DataSet object
    DataSet myDataSet = new DataSet();

    // fill the dataset into the named table
    myAdapter.Fill(myDataSet, "Employees");

    // query the results with LINQ
    IEnumerable<DataRow> cityResults
        = from row in myDataSet.Tables["Employees"].AsEnumerable()
          where row.Field<string>("City") == "London"
          select row;

    // enumerate the results
    foreach (DataRow row in cityResults) {
        Console.WriteLine("City Result: {0} {1}",
            row.Field<string>("FirstName"),
            row.Field<string>("Lastname"));
    }

    // use LINQ to perform a different query on the same data
    var titleResults
        = from row in myDataSet.Tables["Employees"].AsEnumerable()
          where row.Field<string>("Title") == "Sales Representative"
          select new {
              Firstname = row.Field<string>("FirstName"),
              LastName = row.Field<string>("Lastname")
          };

    // enumerate the second set of results
    foreach (var item in titleResults) {
        Console.WriteLine("Title Result: {0} {1}",
            item.Firstname,
            item.LastName);
    }

    // close the database connection
    myConnection.Close();

    // wait for input before exiting
    Console.WriteLine("Press enter to finish");
    Console.ReadLine();
    }
}
```

In this example, I execute a SQL query that selects all the rows in the Employees table in the database. I then use the DataTable object as a data source for a LINQ query:

```csharp
IEnumerable<DataRow> cityResults
    = from row in myDataSet.Tables["Employees"].AsEnumerable()
      where row.Field<string>("City") == "London"
      select row;
```

Notice that I have to call the AsEnumerable() extension method on the DataTable object. This converts the DataTable into a strongly typed collection of DataRow objects, which is a suitable data source for a LINQ query. Inside the query, I project only those DataRow objects whose value for the City field is London. In essence, I have used LINQ to further filter the data I got back from the database.

I then create a second LINQ query using the same DataTable as the data source. I am able to do this without making a second SQL query because the DataSet is an in-memory cache of result data from the database. The query I perform projects an anonymous type that contains the FirstName and LastName fields of the DataRow objects in the DataTable whose value for the Title field is Sales Representative. I enumerate the results from both queries, and compiling and running Listing 31-7 produces the following output:

```
City Result: Steven Buchanan
City Result: Michael Suyama
City Result: Robert King
City Result: Anne Dodsworth
Title Result: Nancy Davolio
Title Result: Janet Leverling
Title Result: Margaret Peacock
Title Result: Michael Suyama
Title Result: Robert King
Title Result: Anne Dodsworth
Press enter to finish
```

It is important to realize that when you use LINQ to query a DataSet, you are only querying the data that was returned from the SQL query used to populate it. Unlike the Entity Framework, a LINQ to DataSet query won't query the database for additional data. If you populated a DataSet for rows in the Employees table that have a City value of London, using LINQ to query for rows that have a value of Seattle won't return any results, even though there are such rows in the database.

Perform Joins on a DataSet

A DataSet can contain the results of multiple queries—for example, the result of querying to tables of the same database. In fact, the DataSet class doesn't care where the data comes from, so it can be very handy when you need to work with data from two different databases. You can see an example of using results from queries of two tables in the same database in Listing 31-8, which creates two SqlDataAdapter objects, each with a different SQL query, and calls the Fill method on each of them to populate a single DataSet item.

Listing 31-8. Combining and Querying Results in a DataSet

```
using System;
using System.Configuration;
using System.Data;
using System.Data.SqlClient;
using System.Linq;

class Listing_08 {
```

```csharp
static void Main(string[] args) {

    // get the connection string from the config file
    ConnectionStringSettings connStringSettings
        = ConfigurationManager.ConnectionStrings["NorthwindConnection"];

    // create the connection object
    SqlConnection myConnection
        = new SqlConnection(connStringSettings.ConnectionString);

    // create the SqlDataAdapters
    SqlDataAdapter myEmployeesAdapter = new SqlDataAdapter(
        "SELECT * FROM Employees", myConnection);
    SqlDataAdapter myOrdersAdapter = new SqlDataAdapter(
        "SELECT * FROM Orders", myConnection);

    // create the DataSet object
    DataSet myDataSet = new DataSet();

    // fill the dataset into the named tables
    myEmployeesAdapter.Fill(myDataSet, "Employees");
    myOrdersAdapter.Fill(myDataSet, "Orders");

    // perform the LINQ query
    var results
        = from employee in myDataSet.Tables["Employees"].AsEnumerable()
          where employee.Field<string>("City") == "London"
          join order in myDataSet.Tables["Orders"].AsEnumerable()
              on employee.Field<int>("EmployeeID") equals order.Field<int>("EmployeeID")
          select new {
              OrderID = order.Field<int>("OrderID"),
              EmployeeName = string.Format("{0} {1}",
                  employee.Field<string>("FirstName"),
                  employee.Field<string>("LastName")),
          } into interimresult
          group interimresult by interimresult.EmployeeName;

    // enumerate the results
    foreach (var group in results) {
        Console.WriteLine("Employee: {0}", group.Key);
        // print out the first five orders for this employee
        foreach (var order in group.Take(2)) {
            Console.WriteLine("Order ID: {0}", order.OrderID);
        }
        Console.WriteLine("------------");
    }

    // close the database connection
    myConnection.Close();

    // wait for input before exiting
    Console.WriteLine("Press enter to finish");
```

```
        Console.ReadLine();
    }
}
```

When I call the Fill method, I specify the name I want assigned to the DataTable object that will be created to hold the data. To keep things consistent, I use the same names as the SQL Server tables from which the data was obtained. The main reason for putting multiple sets of data into a DataSet in this way is to perform a LINQ join operation, which is what I have done in Listing 31-8. This query looks more complicated than it really is because of the verbose syntax for accessing fields in the DataRow objects, but the query just joins orders and employees that share a common ID and are in London and projects an anonymous type that is then grouped using one of the type properties. The result is that the orders are grouped by the name of the employee who created them.

There are a lot of orders in the Northwind database, so to reduce the size of the output, I have used the Take extension method, which retrieves only the specified number of items from the data source:

```
foreach (var order in group.Take(2)) {
    Console.WriteLine("Order ID: {0}", order.OrderID);
}
```

A parameter value of 2 means that my foreach loop receives only the first two orders for each employee. One of the features of the LINQ extension methods is that you can use them outside of LINQ queries like this. Compiling and running Listing 31-8 produces the following results:

```
Employee: Steven Buchanan
Order ID: 10248
Order ID: 10254
------------
Employee: Michael Suyama
Order ID: 10249
Order ID: 10264
------------
Employee: Robert King
Order ID: 10289
Order ID: 10303
------------
Employee: Anne Dodsworth
Order ID: 10255
Order ID: 10263
------------
Press enter to finish
```

Of course, we could have performed the same join operation using a SQL statement, but the benefit of having an in-memory cache like DataSet is that we can perform *different* queries on the data returned from a single SQL query and avoid putting additional load on the database. The decision as to which approach should be used can often be finely balanced and will vary from project to project.

Comparing Data

You can use LINQ to compare the contents of two DataTable objects. I tend to find this most useful when comparing snapshots generated by the same query at two different times. This is something that isn't often set up in production databases but that can be useful for tracking down data-related bugs.

Querying for Data Intersects

The first kind of comparison we will look at is an intersection, which is the set of DataRow objects that two DataTables have in common. Listing 31-9 provides a demonstration.

Listing 31-9. Using the Intersect Extension Method to Find Common Data Rows

```
using System;
using System.Collections.Generic;
using System.Configuration;
using System.Data;
using System.Data.SqlClient;
using System.Linq;
class Listing_09 {

    static void Main(string[] args) {

        // get the connection string from the config file
        ConnectionStringSettings connStringSettings
            = ConfigurationManager.ConnectionStrings["NorthwindConnection"];

        // create the connection object
        SqlConnection myConnection
            = new SqlConnection(connStringSettings.ConnectionString);

        // create the SqlDataAdapters
        SqlDataAdapter adapter1 = new SqlDataAdapter(
            "SELECT * FROM Employees WHERE City='London' OR City = 'Seattle'",
            myConnection);
        SqlDataAdapter adapter2 = new SqlDataAdapter(
            "SELECT * FROM Employees WHERE City='London' OR City = 'Redmond'",
            myConnection);

        // create the DataSet object
        DataSet myDataSet = new DataSet();

        // fill the dataset into the named tables
        adapter1.Fill(myDataSet, "LondonOrSeattle");
        adapter2.Fill(myDataSet, "LondonOrRedmond");

        // find the intersection of the data
        IEnumerable<DataRow> results
            = myDataSet.Tables["LondonOrSeattle"].AsEnumerable()
              .Intersect(myDataSet.Tables["LondonOrRedmond"].AsEnumerable(),
```

```
        DataRowComparer.Default);

        // enumerate the common data
        foreach (DataRow row in results) {
            Console.WriteLine("Common Item - Name: {0} {1}, City: {2}",
                row.Field<string>("FirstName"),
                row.Field<string>("LastName"),
                row.Field<string>("City"));
        }

        // close the database connection
        myConnection.Close();

        // wait for input before exiting
        Console.WriteLine("Press enter to finish");
        Console.ReadLine();
    }
}
```

I can't easily demonstrate time-lapsed queries for this book, so in Listing 31-9 I have made two slightly different queries from the same Northwind table. The first query selects the rows that have a City value of London or Seattle, and the second selects the rows that have a City value of London or Redmond. I place the results of both queries into the same DataSet using the Fill method of the SqlDataAdapter class.

I use the Intersect extension method to find the DataRows, which are common to both sets of results. This method operates on one IEnumerable<T> and takes another IEnumerable<T> as a parameter to use for comparison. We have to be careful here. The extension methods checks to see whether the objects are the same, but we want to compare the row data inside the object. To address this, we pass a parameter that contains an object that is capable of comparing DataRow objects, and we get this using the static DataRowComparer.Default property. So, we end up with the following statement to perform the comparison:

```
IEnumerable<DataRow> results
    = myDataSet.Tables["LondonOrSeattle"].AsEnumerable()
        .Intersect(myDataSet.Tables["LondonOrRedmond"].AsEnumerable(),
        DataRowComparer.Default);
```

The result of the Intersect method is an IEnumerable<T> where T is DataRow in our example. That is to say, we get a collection of the DataRows that are common to both queries. Compiling and running Listing 31-9 produces a list of employees who are based in London:

```
Common Item - Name: Steven Buchanan, City: London
Common Item - Name: Michael Suyama, City: London
Common Item - Name: Robert King, City: London
Common Item - Name: Anne Dodsworth, City: London
Press enter to finish
```

Subtracting Results

You can use the Except extension method to remove any rows in one DataTable, which also exist in another DataTable. Listing 31-10 provides a demonstration.

Listing 31-10. Querying for Distinct Data Rows

```
using System;
using System.Configuration;
using System.Data;
using System.Data.SqlClient;
using System.Linq;
using System.Collections.Generic;

class Listing_10 {

    static void Main(string[] args) {

        // get the connection string from the config file
        ConnectionStringSettings connStringSettings
            = ConfigurationManager.ConnectionStrings["NorthwindConnection"];

        // create the connection object
        SqlConnection myConnection
            = new SqlConnection(connStringSettings.ConnectionString);

        // create the SqlDataAdapters
        SqlDataAdapter adapter1 = new SqlDataAdapter(
            "SELECT * FROM Employees WHERE City='London' OR City = 'Seattle'",
            myConnection);
        SqlDataAdapter adapter2 = new SqlDataAdapter(
            "SELECT * FROM Employees WHERE City='London' OR City = 'Redmond'",
            myConnection);

        // create the DataSet object
        DataSet myDataSet = new DataSet();

        // fill the dataset into the named tables
        adapter1.Fill(myDataSet, "LondonOrSeattle");
        adapter2.Fill(myDataSet, "LondonOrRedmond");

        // find the exception of the data
        IEnumerable<DataRow> results
            = myDataSet.Tables["LondonOrSeattle"].AsEnumerable()
                .Except(myDataSet.Tables["LondonOrRedmond"].AsEnumerable(),
                DataRowComparer.Default);

        // enumerate the common data
        foreach (DataRow row in results) {
            Console.WriteLine("Item - Name: {0} {1}, City: {2}",
                row.Field<string>("FirstName"),
```

```
                row.Field<string>("LastName"),
                row.Field<string>("City"));
        }

        // close the database connection
        myConnection.Close();

        // wait for input before exiting
        Console.WriteLine("Press enter to finish");
        Console.ReadLine();
    }
}
```

The Except method is applied to one DataTable and takes the other DataTable as a parameter. And, as with the Interset operator, we have to provide the value of the static DataRowComparer.Default property so that the Except method will be able to compare DataRow objects properly. The effect of using the Except method on the data returned by my queries in Listing 31-10 is to create a list of the employees who are based in Seattle. Here is the output from compiling and running the listing:

```
Item - Name: Nancy Davolio, City: Seattle
Item - Name: Laura Callahan, City: Seattle
Press enter to finish
```

Performing Database Operations Using Cached Data

We have seen how the DataSet class can be used to cache data in memory, and we've seen how we can use LINQ to query the cached data in different ways. All of this is good, but we have yet to see how we can insert, update, or delete data. These are the features that elevate DataSet from being an interesting idea to a useful programming feature.

The key to generating database changes from changes made to a DataSet is the SqlCommandBuilder class. If you create an instance of this class and associate it with your SqlDataAdapter, it will be able to generate the SQL commands you will need when you want to reflect changes made to cached data in the database. The following sections demonstrate how to insert, update, and delete data in this way.

Inserting Data

The process for inserting new data begins with creating a new DataRow object. This DataRow is then added to a DataTable and populated with the field values you required. The update to the database is performed using the SqlDataAdapter.Update method. Listing 31-11 provides a demonstration.

Listing 31-11. Inserting New Data

```
using System;
using System.Collections.Generic;
using System.Configuration;
using System.Data;
using System.Data.SqlClient;
```

```
class Listing_11 {

    static void Main(string[] args) {

        // get the connection string from the config file
        ConnectionStringSettings connStringSettings
            = ConfigurationManager.ConnectionStrings["NorthwindConnection"];

        // create the connection object
        SqlConnection myConnection
            = new SqlConnection(connStringSettings.ConnectionString);

        // create the SqlDataAdapter
        SqlDataAdapter myAdapter = new SqlDataAdapter(
            "SELECT * FROM Employees", myConnection);

        // create the command builder
        SqlCommandBuilder myCommandBuilder = new SqlCommandBuilder(myAdapter);

        // create the DataSet object
        DataSet myDataSet = new DataSet();

        // fill the dataset into the named table
        myAdapter.Fill(myDataSet, "Employees");

        // create a new DataRow
        DataRow newRow = myDataSet.Tables["Employees"].NewRow();

        // set some field values for the new DataRow
        newRow["FirstName"] = "Adam";
        newRow["LastName"] = "Freeman";
        newRow["City"] = "London";

        // add the new row to the table
        myDataSet.Tables["Employees"].Rows.Add(newRow);

        // update the database
        int updatedRows = myAdapter.Update(myDataSet, "Employees");
        Console.WriteLine("There were {0} updated rows", updatedRows);

        // close the database connection
        myConnection.Close();

        // wait for input before exiting
        Console.WriteLine("Press enter to finish");
        Console.ReadLine();
    }
}
```

First, notice that I have created a SqlCommandBuilder object and passed my SqlDataAdapter object as a constructor parameter. I don't have to do anything with the SqlCommandBuilder other than to create it.

It will configure the SqlAdapter object so that it has valid SQL commands to use when we come to modify the database later.

To insert new data, we must begin by creating a new DataRow object. We do this by calling the NewRow method on the DataTable that you want to add data to. In my example, this is the Employees table:

```
DataRow newRow = myDataSet.Tables["Employees"].NewRow();
```

We then set values for the fields we want to include. For this demonstration, I am going create a new employee record that contains values for just the FirstName, LastName, and City fields, like this:

```
newRow["FirstName"] = "Adam";
newRow["LastName"] = "Freeman";
newRow["City"] = "London";
```

We now have to add the DataRow object to the DataTable, even though we used the DataTable to create the DataRow in the first place. A common mistake is to forget this step, which means that the new data won't be written to the database. We use the Add method on the collection returned by the Rows property, as follows:

```
myDataSet.Tables["Employees"].Rows.Add(newRow);
```

The last step is to perform the update by calling the Update method on the SqlDataAdapter object. We pass in the DataSet that contains the new data and the name of the database table to which the update applies:

```
int updatedRows = myAdapter.Update(myDataSet, "Employees");
```

The Update method returns the number of changed rows that resulted from the update. In the example, this should be 1 since we have inserted one new row. If we compile and run Listing 31-11, we get the following output:

```
There were 1 updated rows
Press enter to finish
```

We can examine the contents of the Employees table in the database by expanding the Data Connections item in the Server Explorer or Data Explorer window, right-clicking the Employees table entry, and selecting Show Table Data. After running Listing 31-11, the database reflects the new addition, as shown in Figure 31-7.

6	Suyama	Michael	Sales Represent...	Mr.
7	King	Robert	Sales Represent...	Mr.
8	Callahan	Laura	Inside Sales Co...	Ms.
9	Dodsworth	Anne	Sales Represent...	Ms.
13	Freeman	Adam	NULL	NULL
NULL	NULL	NULL	NULL	NULL

Figure 31-7. Data inserted into the database

Modifying Data

Modifying data works in much the same way. To modify rows, you simply provide new values for the fields of the DataRow objects you want to change. LINQ can be useful for selecting rows for modification, as demonstrated by Listing 31-12.

Listing 31-12. Modifying Data Using LINQ to DataSet

```
using System;
using System.Collections.Generic;
using System.Configuration;
using System.Data;
using System.Data.SqlClient;

class Listing_12 {

    static void Main(string[] args) {

        // get the connection string from the config file
        ConnectionStringSettings connStringSettings
            = ConfigurationManager.ConnectionStrings["NorthwindConnection"];

        // create the connection object
        SqlConnection myConnection
            = new SqlConnection(connStringSettings.ConnectionString);

        // create the SqlDataAdapter
        SqlDataAdapter myAdapter = new SqlDataAdapter(
            "SELECT * FROM Employees", myConnection);

        // create the command builder
        SqlCommandBuilder myCommandBuilder = new SqlCommandBuilder(myAdapter);

        // create the DataSet object
        DataSet myDataSet = new DataSet();

        // fill the dataset into the named table
        myAdapter.Fill(myDataSet, "Employees");

        // query the DataSet using LINQ
        IEnumerable<DataRow> results
            = from row in myDataSet.Tables["Employees"].AsEnumerable()
              where row.Field<string>("Title") == "Sales Representative"
              select row;

        // enumerate through the results and modify the Title field
        foreach (DataRow row in results) {
            row["Title"] = "Client Liaison";
        }

        // update the database
```

```
        int updatedRows = myAdapter.Update(myDataSet, "Employees");
        Console.WriteLine("There were {0} updated rows", updatedRows);

        // close the database connection
        myConnection.Close();

        // wait for input before exiting
        Console.WriteLine("Press enter to finish");
        Console.ReadLine();
    }
}
```

In this example, I use LINQ to select all the DataRow objects that have a Title value of Sales Representative from the Employees data cached in the DataSet object. I then change the value of the Title field for the selected rows to Client Liaison and call the SqlDataAdapter.Update method to update the changes in the database. Compiling and running Listing 31-12 produces the following output, reporting the number of changes that were made:

```
There were 6 updated rows
Press enter to finish
```

If we look at the data contained in the database table, we can see that the changes have been made, as shown in Figure 31-8.

	Employ...	LastName	FirstName	Title	TitleOfC...
	1	Davolio	Nancy	Client Liaison	Ms.
	2	Fuller	Andrew	Vice President, Sales	Dr.
▶	3	Leverling	Janet	Client Liaison	Ms.
	4	Peacock	Margaret	Client Liaison	Mrs.
	5	Buchanan	Steven	Sales Manager	Mr.
	6	Suyama	Michael	Client Liaison	Mr.
	7	King	Robert	Client Liaison	Mr.
	8	Callahan	Laura	Inside Sales Coordinator	Ms.
	9	Dodsworth	Anne	Client Liaison	Ms.
*	NULL	NULL	NULL	NULL	NULL

Figure 31-8. Modified data in the database

Deleting Data

The last operation we will look at is deleting data, which is done by calling the Delete method on each DataRow object that you want removed and then calling the SqlDataAdapter.Update method, as shown in Listing 31-13.

Listing 31-13. Deleting Data from a DataSet

```csharp
using System;
using System.Collections.Generic;
using System.Configuration;
using System.Data;
using System.Data.SqlClient;

class Listing_13 {

    static void Main(string[] args) {

        // get the connection string from the config file
        ConnectionStringSettings connStringSettings
            = ConfigurationManager.ConnectionStrings["NorthwindConnection"];

        // create the connection object
        SqlConnection myConnection
            = new SqlConnection(connStringSettings.ConnectionString);

        // create the SqlDataAdapter
        SqlDataAdapter myAdapter = new SqlDataAdapter(
            "SELECT * FROM Employees", myConnection);

        // create the command builder
        SqlCommandBuilder myCommandBuilder = new SqlCommandBuilder(myAdapter);

        // create the DataSet object
        DataSet myDataSet = new DataSet();

        // fill the dataset into the named table
        myAdapter.Fill(myDataSet, "Employees");

        // query the DataSet using LINQ
        IEnumerable<DataRow> results
            = from row in myDataSet.Tables["Employees"].AsEnumerable()
              where row.Field<string>("LastName") == "Freeman"
              select row;

        // enumerate through the results and delete the rows
        foreach (DataRow row in results) {
            row.Delete();
        }

        // update the database
```

```
        int updatedRows = myAdapter.Update(myDataSet, "Employees");
        Console.WriteLine("There were {0} updated rows", updatedRows);

        // close the database connection
        myConnection.Close();

        // wait for input before exiting
        Console.WriteLine("Press enter to finish");
        Console.ReadLine();
    }
}
```

Listing 31-13 deletes the row created in Listing 31-11, which means that if you want to see Listing 31-13 at work, you'll need to compile and run Listing 31-11 first. Compiling and running Listing 31-13 produces the following output:

```
There were 1 updated rows
Press enter to finish
```

Summary

In this chapter, we looked at the DataSet class and its relationship with LINQ. If you want some of the convenience of a managed data environment but don't want the overhead of the Entity Framework, then the DataSet functionality may be of use, especially given the support for in-memory queries that comes with LINQ to DataSet.

When using DataSet, you have to be much more aware of the structure and content of the database than when using an entity model, but in return you gain finer-grained control over the operations and queries that are performed. The approach that a project demands will depend on individual circumstances, but as you have seen from this and the preceding chapter, C# and .NET give you a lot of flexibility when it comes to working with databases.

PART 5
■ ■ ■
User Interfaces

The .NET Framework contains a suite of technologies for creating programs with graphical user interfaces, as opposed to the text-based console programs we have used in most of the examples. These technologies can be used to create traditional Windows programs or web-based applications.

In this part of the book, we look at five different .NET user interface technologies. In an introductory book like this one, I can only give you a flavor of the facilities and features of each technology. User interface toolkits are rich and complex, and details of each of the five could easily fill a book. I will demonstrate two sample programs in each chapter. The first is entirely self-contained, which will allow me to demonstrate the process for using and configuring the design tools in Visual Studio and to highlight the differences and similarities between individual each technology. The second example will display data from the Northwind sample database used in the LINQ chapters; displaying data is one of the most common user interface tasks. These two examples provide a solid foundation for creating user interfaces and for you to explore and discover more on your own.

The first chapter in this part of the book, Chapter 32, deals with Windows Forms, which has been part of the .NET Framework since version 1.0. In Chapter 33, we look at the Windows Presentation Foundation, a relative new addition to .NET that has particularly strong support for working with different media types. Chapter 34 shows you how to use two different ASP.NET technologies: Web Forms and Dynamic Data. We finish, in Chapter 35, with Silverlight. This is the .NET competitor to Adobe Flash and is used to create richly interactive web applications.

As we look at each technology, you'll see some common design features. Two of the most important are the use of properties to configure user interfaces and the use of events to respond to actions performed by the user. These techniques, combined with a consistent approach in the Visual Studio design tools, means that a basic knowledge of one technology can be used to create interfaces in one of the others.

CHAPTER 32

Windows Forms

Windows Forms was the original Windows client user interface toolkit that shipped with .NET version 1.0. There have been many enhancements and additions since then, but the basic design approach has remained the same. You can use Windows Forms to quickly create programs that match the look and feel of Windows, and there is an extensive market in third-party add-ons that enrich the overall feature set.

Windows Forms has lost some programmer mind share since the Windows Presentation Foundation (WPF), which is covered in Chapter 33, was released. WPF doesn't replace Windows Forms, but many programmers have moved to it because it is a new technology and because it has richer support for multimedia. This is a shame, because Windows Forms are ideally suited to building line-of-business applications, which is what most programmers spend their days doing. WPF has some super features, but that doesn't mean you shouldn't give Windows Forms serious consideration when planning a project.

In this chapter, we'll start by creating a stand-alone program that solves a simple real-life problem I faced recently. This will introduce you to some of the user interface controls that are available and the property/event model that is used to configure and consume the control features. We will then move on to integrating data from a database into a Windows Form application. This is a process that is painless and simple and demonstrates one of the features that makes Windows Forms so eminently suitable for business applications. We will finish by looking at the add-on support Microsoft provides for accessing features that are specific to Windows 7 and Vista, and I'll demonstrate one of those features—the much loved Aero Glass.

Building a Stand-Alone Window Forms Program

We will start by building a self-contained Window Forms program. Although simple, this program solves a real-life problem—for me, at least. As I write this, I am training for my first triathlon, and being something of a stats geek, I keep detailed records of my training sessions. I record my running and cycling distances in miles, but when I do my swim training, it is in a pool that is measured in meters. I also like to keep a rough count of the calories I burn while training so that I can balance my diet. I use a heart-rate monitor when I run or cycle, but it doesn't work in the pool. I record the number of pool lengths I complete and the time that it has taken me, and from this I want to know the distance in miles, the number of calories I have burned, and my average pace. We are going to use Windows Forms to build a converter to solve my problem. Figure 32-1 shows the completed program.

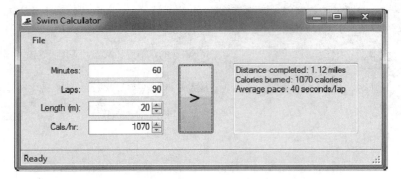

Figure 32-1. *The completed Swim Calculator program*

In the following sections, I'll demonstrate how to create this program and explain some of the characteristics of Windows Forms along the way.

Creating the Project

The first step is to create the Windows Forms project. Select New ➤ Project from the Visual Studio File menu, and select Windows Forms Application from the list of templates, as shown in Figure 32-2. The set of templates available will depend on which edition of Visual Studio you have installed and which options you selected during installation.

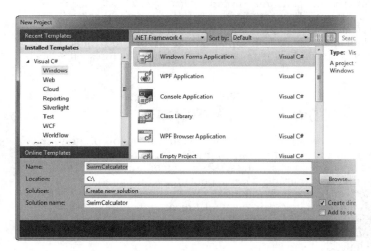

Figure 32-2. *Selecting the Windows Forms Application template*

Give your project a name, and click the OK button. The new project will contain two key files. The first is Program.cs. This is the code file that contains the Main method for your program. It will have contents similar to Listing 32-1.

Listing 32-1. The Contents of Program.cs

```
using System;
using System.Collections.Generic;
using System.Linq;
using System.Windows.Forms;

namespace SwimCalc {
    static class Program {
        /// <summary>
        /// The main entry point for the application.
        /// </summary>
        [STAThread]
        static void Main() {
            Application.EnableVisualStyles();
            Application.SetCompatibleTextRenderingDefault(false);
            Application.Run(new Form1());
        }
    }
}
```

We don't need to edit this file, but you can see that a Windows Forms program has class and a Main method like any other C# program. The code statements in the Main method call members of the Application class in the System.Windows.Forms namespace, which contains most of the Windows Forms classes. The most important statement is this one:

```
Application.Run(new Form1());
```

This statement creates a new Form1 object and passes it to the Application.Run method. The Form1 class is contained in the Form1.cs code file in the project. If you double-click this file in the Solution Explorer, you will see the Windows Forms *design surface*. All that is on the design surface at the moment is the main Windows Form for our program, as shown in Figure 32-3.

Figure 32-3. *The empty design surface*

All the user interface technologies that .NET supports have visual designers, where you drag *controls* you require to the design surface and arrange them as you want them to appear. Controls are the elements of a user interface. They range from basic items (such as buttons and labels) to complex components (date pickers and data grids), and they include items that can help you with the function of your program but that are invisible to the user (data sources and LINQ queries). The design surface in Figure 32-3 is a blank gray window because we have not yet put any controls in place. We get some basic functions for free, even though we haven't done any design work. If you compile and run the project, you will see the same empty window. Note that the icon in the taskbar and the button at the top right of the window works as it should.

Adding the Controls

The list of Widows Forms controls is available in the Toolbox window, which you can open from Visual Studio's View menu. The controls are grouped together—common controls, containers, data, and so on, as shown in Figure 32-4.

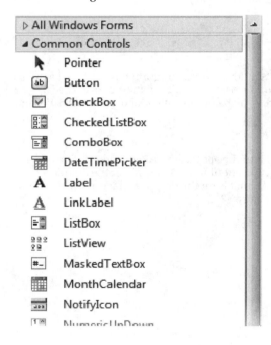

Figure 32-4. The Windows Forms controls Toolbox

You can see from the Toolbox window that there are a wide range of components, but there is also an active market for third-party controls that are either more functional versions of the standard controls or that do not exist in the standard set. Prices and quality vary, but there are some very impressive add-on control libraries available if you can't do what you need using the standard controls.

We can build the example program using the standard controls. You drag a control from the Toolbox window to the design surface to add it to your program. Some of the controls in the Toolbox can help you lay out other controls. These are helpful for building complex programs, not least because they help the interface adjust properly when the user resizes the window. In this example, however, we are going to use *absolute positioning*, where we drag the control to the position we want, and it won't move when the window is resized.

As a demonstration, drag a Button control from the Toolbox to the design surface, and let go. It doesn't matter where you place it for the moment. You'll see that a button placeholder has been added to the project. Using the Solution Explorer window, expand the Form1.cs item, and double-click the Form1.Designer.cs code file. If you click the plus sign in the left margin next to the line that says Windows Form Designer generated code, you can see what happened when you added the Button control. There will be some statements like these:

```
this.button1.Location = new System.Drawing.Point(83, 91);
this.button1.Name = "button1";
this.button1.Size = new System.Drawing.Size(75, 23);
this.button1.TabIndex = 0;
this.button1.Text = "button1";
this.button1.UseVisualStyleBackColor = true;
```

These were generated automatically when you dragged the button onto the design surface. Go back to the design window, and move the button to the top-left corner by dragging the placeholder around. If you go back to the Form1.Designer.cs tab, you'll see that the first statement has changed to something like this:

```
this.button1.Location = new System.Drawing.Point(3, 3);
```

The Windows Form designer is generating C# code for us based on what we add to the design surface. When you moved the button placeholder, the generated code was updated to reflect the change. If you delete the button placeholder, all the code that was generated for it will be removed. Similarly, you can change the dimensions by dragging one or more of the grab handles, and you can align or distribute controls by selecting two or more and using the Visual Studio Format menu. There are menu items for alignment, spacing, and so on. The main window on the design surface also has grab handles, which you can use to change the initial size of the main program window. You don't have to use the Windows Forms designer at all; you could just create the C# statements yourself, but this is a repetitive and error-prone approach for all but the most experienced programmers, and I recommend you use the designer for your projects.

For our project, drag controls onto your design surface, and arrange and resize them so that they match Figure 32-5. The type of each control is shown in the figure.

Make sure you leave a generous gap at the top and bottom. We'll need this space when we add the menu and status bar later. As you move controls around and resize them, you'll see guidelines appear that show you size and position relative to other controls to help you align controls neatly.

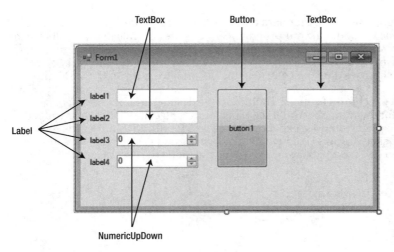

Figure 32-5. Dragging controls to the design surface

Setting the Control Properties

Each control on the design surface has a set of properties. These properties determine the appearance and layout. Each of the statements we saw when we looked at the generated C# code earlier set the value for a control property. In this section, we'll change the properties of our controls so that they behave and appear the way we want.

To start with, select the form itself. You can do this by clicking the top of the window. Open the Properties window, and you will see the set of properties. Scroll down until you see the Text property; it will have a value of Form1. Change this name to Swim Calculator. Notice that the name of the window has changed in the design surface.

Let's do a more complex example. On the design surface, select the TextBox, which is on its own on the right side of the display. Find the Multiline property in the Properties window, and change the value to True. You will see additional grab handles have appeared on the control placeholder to allow you to resize it. By default, the TextBox control will display only one line of text, but when you enable the Multiline property, we can display multiple lines. Use the grab handles so the TextBox is the same height as the Button it is next to.

Configuring the Labels

The only property we need to change for the Label controls is the Text property. This sets what the label will display in the window. Starting with the topmost Label, change the value of the Text properties to Minutes:, Laps:, Length (m):, and Cals/hr:. Select each Label on the design surface in turn, locate the Text property, and set the required value. You may need to shuffle your controls around to make sure everything fits. When you have finished, your design surface should look like Figure 32-6.

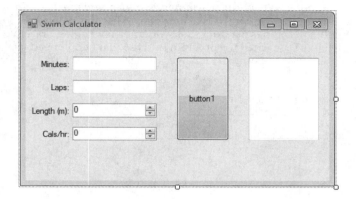

Figure 32-6. The design surface with configured Label *controls*

Configuring the TextBoxes and NumericUpDowns

We want the two TextBox controls on the left of the window to display an initial value of zero and to align their text to the right of the display. When you want to apply the same changes to more than one control, you can select the controls on the design surface and edit the properties. The changes will affect all the controls you selected. Apply the changes shown in Table 32-1.

Table 32-1. Property Changes for TextBox Controls

Property	Value
Text	0
TextAlign	Right

As you select each property, a short message describing what effect the property has is shown at the bottom of the Properties window, as illustrated by Figure 32-7 for the TextAlign property of the TextBox control. There are too many controls and properties for me to describe in this chapter, but these messages are one of the best ways of finding the property that has the effect you are looking for.

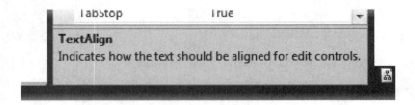

Figure 32-7. Discovering the meaning of control properties

The NumericUpDown control is like a TextBox, but it will only display numeric values, and the user can change the value using the scroll buttons on the right of the control. We are going to use this type of control for the length of the pool and the number of calories per hour that swimming consumes. I rarely change these values, so we will display the defaults I use when the program starts so that I don't need to type them in each time I go swimming. Table 32-2 lists the property changes to make to the NumericUpDown controls.

Table 32-2. Property Changes for NumericUpDown Controls

Property	Value
TextAlign	Right
Minimum	1
Maximum	2000
Value	20 (for the top control) 1070 (for the bottom control)

For the second NumericUpDown control, you must be sure to set the Maximum property before the Value property. Otherwise, the value of 1070 will exceed the default upper limit for the control. For the large TextBox on the right of the screen, change the ReadOnly property to True. This is where we are going to display the results of the calculations, and we don't want the user to be able to type text in this area. When you have configured these controls, your design surface should look like Figure 32-8.

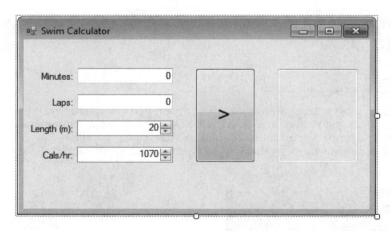

Figure 32-8. The design surface with configured TextBox and NumericUpDown controls

Configuring the Button

We need to make two changes to the Button control. The first is to change the value of the Text property to the > character. The second is to change the font size. If you click the value for the Font property, you'll see an ellipsis button appear. Click this, and a Font selection dialog box will pop up, as shown in Figure 32-9.

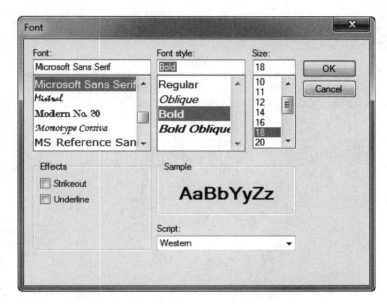

Figure 32-9. The Font dialog box

Use the Font dialog box to select 18-point bold text. Click the OK button to dismiss the dialog box and change the property value.

Adding the MenuStrip and StatusStrip

Most of the controls work in a similar way to the ones covered in the previous section. We need to use two controls that are slightly different, however. The first is the MenuStrip, which will provide the standard menu across the top of the program window.

Start by dragging a MenuStrip control to the top left of the main Form on the design surface (you may have to expand some of the other control groups to find this control). The MenuStrip will expand to fill the window horizontally, as shown in Figure 32-10.

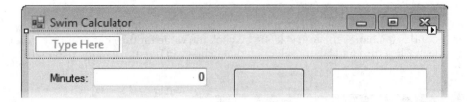

Figure 32-10. Adding a MenuStrip to the main window

Enter **File** in the Type Here box. This creates a standard File menu. As you type, additional boxes will pop up below and to the right so that you add items to the current menu or add a new menu to the MenuStrip. We only want a Quit item on a File menu, so enter **Quit** in the lowest box, as shown in Figure 32-11.

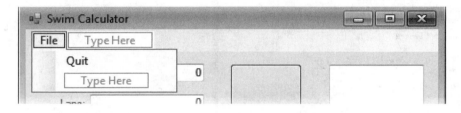

Figure 32-11. Defining the menus

■ **Tip** You can create a more complete (and more standard) set of menus by clicking the menu strip and then clicking the small arrow on the top right of the control. Select Insert Standard Menus from the pop-up menu, and a complete set of menu items will be created automatically.

The StatusStrip control provides the status bar at the bottom of the window. Drag a StatusStrip control into the design surface so that it is positioned at the bottom of the main window. Click the drop-down arrow icon on the control, and select StatusLabel from the pop-up menu, as shown by Figure 32-12.

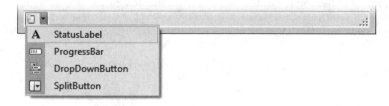

Figure 32-12. Selecting a status label in a StatusStrip

The StatusStrip control can display different kinds of information. We only need a simple text label, so that's why you select the StatusLabel option. Click the label when it has been added, and change the Text property to Ready. When you have added these items and changed the property, your design surface should look similar to Figure 32-13.

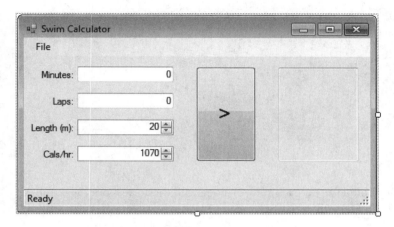

Figure 32-13. *The design surface with all the controls added*

Setting the Control Names

A member name is generated automatically for each control that is added to the design surface. We need to be able to refer to the controls when we write some code later in this chapter, and the names that are created automatically don't refer to the control type rather than the purpose of the control. For example, the TextBox controls are named textbox1, tetxBox2, and so on. In this section, we are going to assign meaningful names for the controls that we want to refer to later.

As an example, to change the name used for the Button control, select the Button in the design surface, and change the (Name) property, which is in the Design property group, to convertButton. If you look at the code statement that defines the member in the Form1.Designer.cs file, you will be able to see that the name has been changed, as follows:

```
private System.Windows.Forms.Button convertButton;
```

When we come to refer to this control in our code later, we can use this more meaningful name. Figure 32-14 shows the controls whose names need to be changed, and each has been assigned a number.

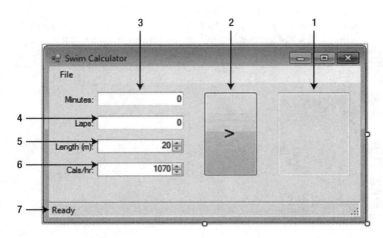

Figure 32-14. *The numbered controls*

Table 32-3 shows the name you should use for each control along with the corresponding number from Figure 32-14.

Table 32-3. *Control Names*

Number	Type	Name
1	TextBox	resultsTextBox
2	Button	convertButton
3	TextBox	minutesTextBox
4	TextBox	lapsTextBox
5	NumericUpDown	poolLength
6	NumericUpDown	calsPerHour
7	ToolStripStatusLabel	statusLabel

You don't have the change the names, but I find that I tend to create bugs in my code when I come to use the control names. I end up forgetting that textBox32 does this and textBox37 does that. Changing the names the names of the controls you need to access in your code takes only a moment, but it can save hours of painful debugging later.

Setting the Tab Order

The next step is to ensure that the tab order for the controls will make sense to the user. The tab order specifies which control will be selected (known as *focused*) when the tab key is pressed. By default the tab order is the same order in which you added the controls. When a control is focused (also known as *having the focus*), user input, such as key presses, is directed to that control rather than any of the others. The Tab key is used to move the focus from control to control. For our sample, I want to be able to tab through the three controls that I will use the most: the TextBox for entering the number of minutes of exercise, the TextBox for entering the number of laps, and the Button that, when clicked, will lead to the calculations being performed. I don't want to tab to the NumericUpDown controls. The default values for these will be correct most of the time. To view the current order, select the Tab Order menu item from the View menu. You'll see a series of numbered blue boxes showing the order in which using the Tab key will select controls. To change the order, click the blue boxes in the sequence you require. As you click each one, the color will change to white, and the new order number will appear, as shown in Figure 32-15.

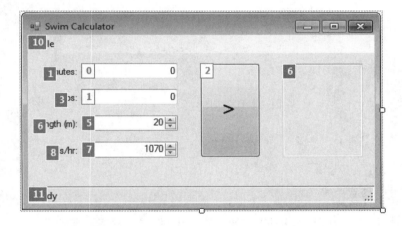

Figure 32-15. Changing the tab order

As you can see from Figure 32-15, I have clicked the controls in the order I want to use them. Click the three controls in the order shown in the figure and then disable the tab order overlay by selecting the Tab View item from the View menu again. You can stop a control from being selected by the Tab key by changing the TabStop property to False. I have done this for the large TextBox and NumericUpDown controls in the project. You don't have to change the tab order, but a surprising number of users use the Tab key to navigate through forms, and you can make your program easier and reduce frustration by using a tab order that follows the natural order a user will want to take through the information.

Wiring the Controls

If you start the program by selecting Start without Debugging from the Debug menu, you can see how far we have come. We have something that looks like a proper Windows program. We can set values in the text boxes, we can tab between controls, and we can click the button. In this section, we'll connect the controls to the code that will validate the data entered by the user and perform the calculations to give us the results we want.

All controls have events. These events are triggered when something about the control changes—such as mouse movement, a key press, a button being pressed, and so on. Each control implements the events that make sense for that kind of control. To see the events that a control implements, select the control in the design surface, and then click the icon that looks like a lightning strike in the Properties window. Figure 32-16 illustrates some of the events that the Button control implements.

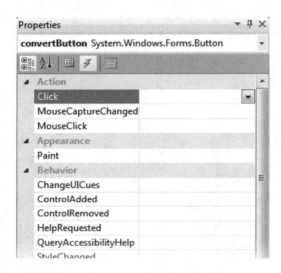

Figure 32-16. Events implement by the Button control

Events are explained fully in Chapter 10. If you skipped ahead to get to this chapter, you should consider going back and reading that chapter now. In the following sections, we'll add code to respond to different events from the various controls we are using. The code statements go into what is called a *code-behind* file. There is a partial class in the Form1.cs file. To see the code, right-click Form1.cs in the Solution Explorer, and select View Code from the pop-up menu. At the moment, there is nothing there aside from a call to the InitializeComponent method inside the Form1 constructor. The process of connecting code in the code-behind file to the events from the controls is known as *wiring the controls* or *wiring the events*. In the following sections, I'll show you how to wire up the controls we need for our example program.

Wiring the Quit Menu

We will start with the Quit menu we added to the MenuStrip earlier. On the design surface, click the File item and then the Quit item. New Type Here boxes will appear to let you add new menu items, but you can ignore them. Click the Events button in the Properties window to display the events that the menu item supports. Click the empty space next to the Click event, and once the event name has been highlighted, double-click in the same space, as shown in Figure 32-17.

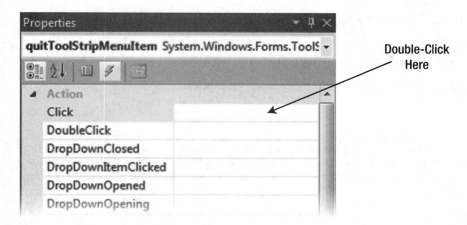

Figure 32-17. Double-clicking the Click event

The first mouse click selects the event, and the double-click tells Visual Studio that you want it to automatically generate an event handler in the code-behind file for you. The code-view of the Form1.cs file will appear, and a new method will have been added, as shown in Listing 32-2.

Listing 32-2. An Automatically Generated Control Event Handler

```
using System;
using System.Collections.Generic;
using System.ComponentModel;
using System.Data;
using System.Drawing;
using System.Linq;
using System.Text;
using System.Windows.Forms;

namespace Creating_the_Project {
    public partial class Form1 : Form {
        public Form1() {
            InitializeComponent();
        }

        private void quitToolStripMenuItem_Click(object sender, EventArgs e) {

        }
    }
}
```

The name of the method is derived from the name of the control and the name of the event. We didn't change the name of this menu item control, so the default was used and combined with the event name using an underscore. You can see that the parameters for the method are consistent with the C# event pattern that we saw in Chapter 10. This method will be called when the user selects the Quit menu item in our program. That doesn't happen automatically, so we have to perform that action in this method.

The Application class in the System.Windows.Forms namespace has a static method called Exit that is used to exit a Windows Forms program, so our method becomes as follows:

```
private void quitToolStripMenuItem_Click(object sender, EventArgs e) {
    Application.Exit();
}
```

If you compile and run the program and then select the Quit menu, you will be able to see the effect of the change. If you return to the design surface and look at the Click event for the menu item, you will see that the name of our generated event-handling method has been added alongside the event name. And a matching statement has been added to the Form1.Designer.cs code file, although it can be hard to find because there is a lot of code:

```
this.quitToolStripMenuItem.Click += new
System.EventHandler(this.quitToolStripMenuItem_Click);
```

Wiring the TextBoxes

Generating event handlers automatically is very useful, but when you want an event from multiple components handled in the same way, it makes more sense to define a single event handler and associate it with the controls afterward. This is what we will do for the TextBoxes in which I enter the duration of my swim and the number of laps.

I want to filter the key presses when either of the TextBox controls is focused so that only numeric values can be added. All controls inherit a set of standard events from the System.Windows.Forms.Control class, one of which is KeyDown, triggered when the user presses a key on the keyboard. The KeyDown event is a System.Windows.Forms.KeyEventHandler delegate, which has the following signature:

```
public delegate void KeyEventHandler(object sender, KeyEventArgs e)
```

We must implement a method with the same signature in the Form1.cs code-behind file, as shown by Listing 32-3.

Listing 32-3. Handling the Event

```
using System;
using System.Collections.Generic;
using System.ComponentModel;
using System.Data;
using System.Drawing;
using System.Linq;
using System.Text;
using System.Windows.Forms;

namespace Creating_the_Project {
    public partial class Form1 : Form {
        public Form1() {
            InitializeComponent();
        }
```

```
        private void ValidateKeyPress(object sender, KeyEventArgs e) {

        }

        private void quitToolStripMenuItem_Click(object sender, EventArgs e) {
            Application.Exit();
        }
    }
}
```

The new method is shown in bold. Return to the design surface, and select both of the small TextBox controls. View the control events in the Properties window, find the KeyDown event in the list, and click in the space to the right of the event name. A drop-down arrow will appear, and if you click it, the list of methods that match the delegate signature for the event will be displayed, as shown by Figure 32-18.

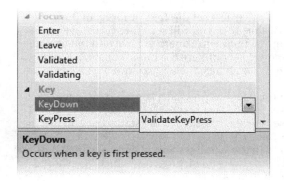

Figure 32-18. *Selecting a method as an event handler*

There is only one item in this list because there is only one method in the code-behind file that matches the delegate signature for the event. Select the method name. This will assign the method we added as the handler for the KeyDown event for both TextBox controls.

We want to ignore most key presses. We need to respond only to numeric keys—those on the main keypad and the number pad—and to the Delete key. The KeyEventArgs object that is passed to method has a property called KeyCode, which we can compare to values in the Keys enum to work out what key has been pressed to trigger the event. Here are three statements that test for each kind of key we are interested in:

```
bool isNumberKey = e.KeyCode >= Keys.D0 && e.KeyCode <= Keys.D9;
bool isNumberPadKey = e.KeyCode >= Keys.NumPad0 && e.KeyCode <= Keys.NumPad9;
bool isDeleteKey = e.KeyCode == Keys.Delete || e.KeyCode == Keys.Back;
```

The 0 key is known as D0 on the main keyboard and NumPad0 on the numeric keypad. The 9 key is D9 on the main keyboard and NumPad9 on the numeric keypad. The values in the Keys are arranged in sequence, so we can test for the number keys by ensuring that the pressed key falls inside a specific range. One of first two bool values, isNumberKey and isNumberPadKey, will be set to true if a numeric key has been pressed.

The last statement checks to see whether either the Delete or Backspace key has been pressed. If we didn't check for these keys, the TextBox controls wouldn't allow errors to be corrected. We can use these bool values to test for the keys we are interested in, like this:

```
if (isNumberKey || isNumberPadKey || isDeleteKey) {
    // this is a key we want to support
    statusLabel.Text = "Ready";
} else {
    // this is not a key we want to support
    // - suppress the key event
    e.SuppressKeyPress = true;
    // send a message to the status bar
    statusLabel.Text = string.Format("Ignored: {0}", e. KeyCode);
    // play an alert sound
    SystemSounds.Beep.Play();
 }
```

I start by testing the bool values. If any of them evaluate to true, I set the Text property of the statusLabel object to the value Ready. If you look back at Table 32-3, you will see that statusLabel is the name of the status label control in the StatusStrip. By setting the Text property, I have told the control to display Ready. Setting the properties at design time is how you configure the initial state of a Windows Forms control, and changing the values of properties is how we change the appearance and behavior at runtime.

If none of the bool values is true, then we know that the user has pressed a key we want to ignore. I present the key press being displayed by the control by setting the SuppressKeyPress property to true. I want to tell the user that something has happened, so I set the text message in the status bar and use the SystemSounds class to play the standard Windows Beep sound. This class is in the System.Media namespace and plays the sounds that the user has selected in the Windows Sound control panel. Putting these statements together gives us the key validation method shown in Listing 32-4, which you should add to your code-behind file if you are following along with the example.

Listing 32-4. The Complete Key Validation Method

```
private void ValidateKeyPress(object sender, KeyEventArgs e) {
    // we want to allow numbers, the left and right cursor keys and the delete key
    bool isNumberKey = e.KeyCode >= Keys.D0 && e.KeyCode <= Keys.D9;
    bool isNumberPadKey = e.KeyCode >= Keys.NumPad0 && e.KeyCode <= Keys.NumPad9;
    bool isDeleteKey = e.KeyCode == Keys.Delete || e.KeyCode == Keys.Back;

    if (isNumberKey || isNumberPadKey || isDeleteKey) {
        // this is a key we want to support
        statusLabel.Text = "Ready";
    } else {
        // this is not a key we want to support
        // - suppress the key event
        e.SuppressKeyPress = true;
        // send a message to the status bar
        statusLabel.Text = string.Format("Ignored: {0}", e.KeyCode);
        // play an alert sound
        SystemSounds.Beep.Play();
    }
```

```
}
```

You can see the effect of this filtering if you compile and run the project. Numeric key values can be added and the Delete key can be used, but any other key press will be rejected. In real projects, you will need to be more sophisticated about the key strokes you ignore. For example, in the example we have ignored the arrow keys, which a user might use to move the caret position to correct an error. But for a simple example, our filtering will work just fine.

Wiring the Button

The final control for us to wire up is the button. Clicking this will read the values from the TexBox and NumericUpDown controls and perform the calculations. We need to handle the Click event for the button. To create an empty handler method, click and then double-click as we did earlier for the Quit menu item. This will create an empty method as follows:

```
private void convertButton_Click(object sender, EventArgs e) {

}
```

We can now add the statements that contain bulk of the logic for the program. Listing 32-5 shows the completed method.

Listing 32-5. The Event Handler Method for the Button Control

```
private void convertButton_Click(object sender, EventArgs e) {

    // define the variables that will hold the control values
    int minutesCompleted, lapsCompleted, lapLength, caloriesPerHour;

    // parse the control contents into the variables
    try {
        // extract the values entered by the user from the form controls
        minutesCompleted = int.Parse(minutesTextBox.Text);
        lapsCompleted = int.Parse(lapsTextBox.Text);
        lapLength = (int)poolLength.Value;
        caloriesPerHour = (int)calsPerHour.Value;

    } catch (Exception) {
        statusLabel.Text = "Cannot parse values";
        SystemSounds.Beep.Play();
        // return from this method
        return;
    }

    // ensure that we have values which are greater than zero
    if (minutesCompleted <= 0 || lapsCompleted <= 0
        || lapLength <= 0 || caloriesPerHour <= 0) {

        // we cannot proceed - we have one or more bad values
        statusLabel.Text = "Cannot calculate - use values greater than zero";
```

```
        // alert the user to the error
        SystemSounds.Beep.Play();
        return;
    }

    // perform the calculations we need for the results
    float distance = (lapsCompleted * lapLength) * 0.00062137119223733f;
    float caloriesBurned = (minutesCompleted / 60f) * caloriesPerHour;
    float pace = (minutesCompleted * 60) / lapsCompleted;

    // compose and set the results
    resultsTextBox.Lines = new string[] {
        string.Format("Distance completed: {0:F2} miles", distance),
        string.Format("Calories burned: {0:F0} calories", caloriesBurned),
        string.Format("Average pace: {0:F0} seconds/lap", pace),
    };
}
```

I start off by defining local variables that will hold the input from the controls. I have specified the int type because I don't need any floating-point accuracy or to deal with very large values. The next step is to read the values from the TextBox controls and parse them to int values:

```
minutesCompleted = int.Parse(minutesTextBox.Text);
lapsCompleted = int.Parse(lapsTextBox.Text);
```

The TextBox control will accept any keyboard input by default and returns its content via the Text property as a string. We parse this to an int value before we can perform our calculations. You can learn about parsing numeric values in Chapter 5.

The next step is to cast the values from the NumericUpDown controls (which are returned as float values from the Value property) to int values:

```
lapLength = (int)poolLength.Value;
caloriesPerHour = (int)calsPerHour.Value;
```

If there is a problem parsing or casting the input values, I display a message on the status bar and play the system beep sound, as follows:

```
statusLabel.Text = "Cannot parse values";
SystemSounds.Beep.Play();
```

Having obtained and converted the values, I want to make sure that none of them is zero, and if they are, I display a message, play the system beep, and return from the method. If the values are OK, then we can finally perform the calculations:

```
float distance = (lapsCompleted * lapLength) * 0.00062137119223733f;
float caloriesBurned = (minutesCompleted / 60f) * caloriesPerHour;
float pace = (minutesCompleted * 60) / lapsCompleted;
```

There are three results generated from the input data. The first is the distance in miles, which I obtain by multiplying the overall distance in meters by a constant value. The other two values, caloriesBurned and pace, are obtained directly from the input values. All that remains is to display the results in the large TextBox, which I do like this:

```
resultsTextBox.Lines = new string[] {
    string.Format("Distance completed: {0:F2} miles", distance),
    string.Format("Calories burned: {0:F0} calories", caloriesBurned),
    string.Format("Average pace: {0:F0} seconds/lap", pace),
};
```

The Lines property is used to set the content of a TextBox that has the MultiLine property enabled. This property takes a string array, and each string in the array is displayed on its own line. I use the composite formatting feature (discussed in Chapter 16) to format the results.

Setting the Icon

The last step is to set the icon that will be displayed on the taskbar and at the top of the program window. This may seem like a trivial thing, but it is one of the questions most asked by programmers when they build Windows programs. The generic icon is not widely liked. Click somewhere where there isn't a control (or click the menu of the main form window) on the design surface, and scroll down the list of properties until you see Icon. Click the value, and an ellipsis (...) button will appear. If you click this button, you will be able to select an .ico file to use for your program. The .ico file format is supported by many graphics programs. I tend to use the free (and excellent) Paint.NET, for which you can obtain a plug-in that will save files in the required format.

Testing the Program

All that remains is to compile, run, and test the program. There are many improvements that you can make to this simple program, such as better key press filtering, a window that resizes elegantly, the pool length and calorie settings now in a separate dialog box—the list is endless. But as you play around with this program, take a moment to realize how the controls were added and configured using properties and then wired together using events. Features that are core to the C# language turn out to be core to Windows Forms as well.

Using Windows Forms Data Binding

One of the most common programming tasks is to display and edit data from a database, and in this section I'll show you how Windows Forms makes this a simple task. Our goal will be to create a program that can display, update, and edit the contents of the Employee table from the sample Northwind database. In doing this, we'll use the Entity Framework and LINQ. If you have skipped ahead to this chapter, you may want to return to Chapters 27 and 30 before reading this rest of this chapter.

Creating the Project and Creating the Data Model

As you might expect, the first step is to create a new Visual Studio 2010 project. Select the Windows Forms Application template from the list, and call the project **DataApp**. The project will be created and open a design surface containing the main window for our program, just as with the previous example.

We need to create an Entity Framework data model so that we can read and write the data to the database using C# objects.

Prepare the database, and create the data model following the steps in the "Getting Ready" section of Chapter 30. I am not going to repeat the steps here because they are identical to those we followed when exploring LINQ to Entities.

Creating and Using the Object Data Source

Once we have created the data model, we need to tell the Windows Forms system that we want to display data using one of the C# classes created by the Entity Framework. In our case, we want the Employee class, since that is used to represent rows in the Northwind Employees table.

Select the Add New Data Source item from the Data menu. This will open the Data Source Configuration Wizard. Select the Object option, as shown in Figure 32-19, and click the Next button.

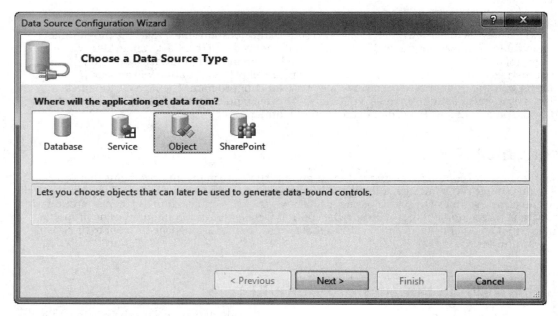

Figure 32-19. Selecting the object data source

In the next dialog box, expand the items until you see the list of C# classes created by the Entity Framework, and check the Employee item, as shown in Figure 32-20.

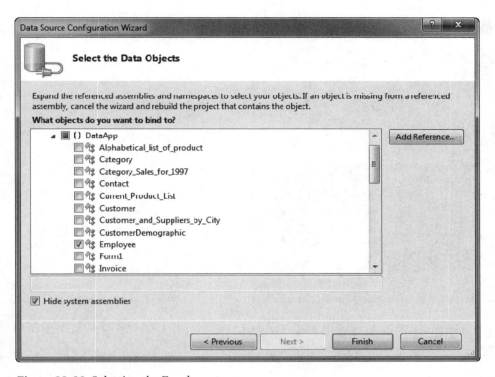

Figure 32-20. Selecting the Employee type

Click the Finish button, and then select the Show Data Sources item from the Data menu. This will open a window that will list the available data in the project, which will include the data model we created and the Employee class we just added. Select the Employee item (the one that is at the top of the list, not the one under the NorthwindEntities item), drag it to the Form window on the design surface, and drop it. A series of controls will be added to the surface, as shown in Figure 32-21.

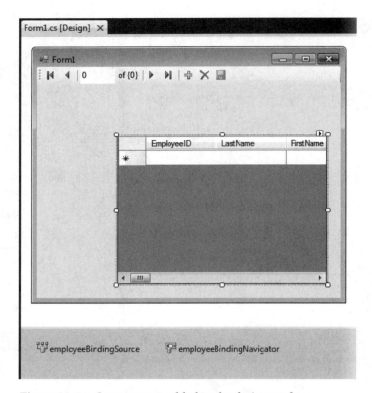

Figure 32-21. *Components added to the design surface*

The gray area at the bottom of the design surface has been added to contain two controls that we will rely on but that are not displayed to the user. The employeeBindingSource is an instance of the BindingSource control, which will associate our data with the grid control (which is the large control added to the main window). The employeeBindingNavigator is an instance of the BindingNavigator control that lets us page through our data. This is done by the toolbar that has been added to the top of the screen.

Formatting the Grid Control

The large control added to the design surface is a DataGridView control, and it will display our data in a table. The control automatically adds columns for each public property in the data type it will display. You can see that ours has added columns for each of the properties of the Employee class, starting with EmployeeID, LastName, and so on. In this section, we are going to format the control to change the columns it displays and the order in which it displays them.

But first, we are going to resize the control. Click the smart tab icon (the small arrow at the top right of the control), and open the pop-up menu, as shown in Figure 32-22.

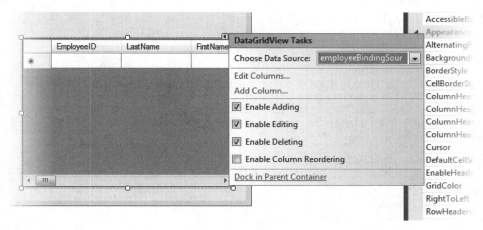

Figure 32-22. *Opening the smart tab menu*

Click the Dock in Parent Container link at the bottom of the menu. This will expand the control so that it fills the window. We also want to change the way that the columns are displayed so that they are resized to fill the display. Do this by changing the value of the AutoSizeColumnsMode to Fill in the Properties window. Don't worry that the display shows all of the columns packed in tightly. Our next step is to remove the columns we don't want.

Click the smart tab arrow again, and select Edit Columns. This will open the Edit Columns dialog box. Use the Remove button to remove columns from the list, and use the up and down arrow buttons to change the order until you have the same columns in the same orders as in Figure 32-23.

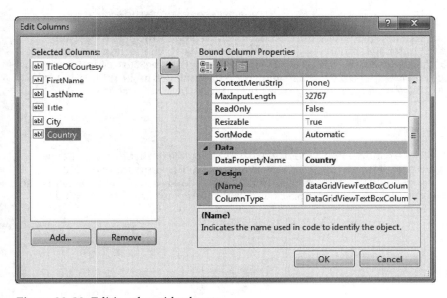

Figure 32-23. *Editing the grid columns*

Click OK to dismiss the dialog box and change the columns.

Loading the Data

When we dragged the Employee class from the list of data sources onto the design surface, we told the Windows Forms systems what kind of data we wanted to display. Now we need to specify how to get the data itself. We do this in the code-behind file, which you can access by right-clicking Form1.cs in your project and selecting View Code from the pop-up menu. Listing 32-6 demonstrates the changes we need to make, which are shown in bold.

Listing 32-6. Loading the Data in the Code-Behind File

```
using System.Windows.Forms;

namespace DataApp {
    public partial class Form1 : Form {

        // define the EntityFramework context field
        NorthwindEntities entityContext = new NorthwindEntities();

        public Form1() {
            InitializeComponent();

            // set the data source for the data binding
            employeeBindingSource.DataSource = entityContext.Employees;
        }
    }
}
```

The first statement defines a new field using the context object created by the data model and creates a new instance; see Chapter 30 for more details of the context object. The second statement sets the DataSource property of the employeeBindingSource object. This is the BindingSource control that was added to the design surface and is responsible for managing the data displayed in the grid. I want to display all the Employee records, so I set the property to be the Employees field of the context object.

Wiring the Save Button

The DataGridView control will let us add, modify, and delete data in the table itself, but these changes won't be passed to the database until we call the SaveChanges method on the entity framework data context object. To do this, we are going to wire up the button that was added to the toolbar earlier in the process. The button, which is highlighted in Figure 32-24, is disabled by default when it is created.

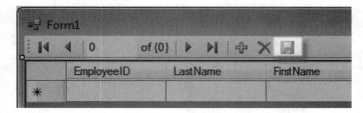

Figure 32-24. *The disabled Save button*

To enable the button, select it and change the value of the Enabled property to True. You'll see it brighten on the design surface. Now double-click the button to create an event handler for the Click event. The display will switch to the code-behind file, and you will see a new method has been added. Add a statement to save the changes in the Entity Framework data, as shown in Listing 32-7.

Listing 32-7. Saving Data in the Code-Behind File

```
using System.Windows.Forms;

namespace DataApp {
    public partial class Form1 : Form {

        // define the EntityFramework context field
        NorthwindEntities entityContext = new NorthwindEntities();

        public Form1() {
            InitializeComponent();

            // set the data source for the data binding
            employeeBindingSource.DataSource = entityContext.Employees;
        }

        private void employeeBindingNavigatorSaveItem_Click(object sender,
            System.EventArgs e) {

            entityContext.SaveChanges();
        }
    }
}
```

The name of your method may be slightly different from mine, but the statement you must add is the same and is shown in bold in the listing. Wiring up the button like this means that any changes we made are saved when we click the button.

Testing the Program

All that remains is to compile and run the program. The data will be loaded automatically from the database and displayed in the window, as shown by Figure 32-25.

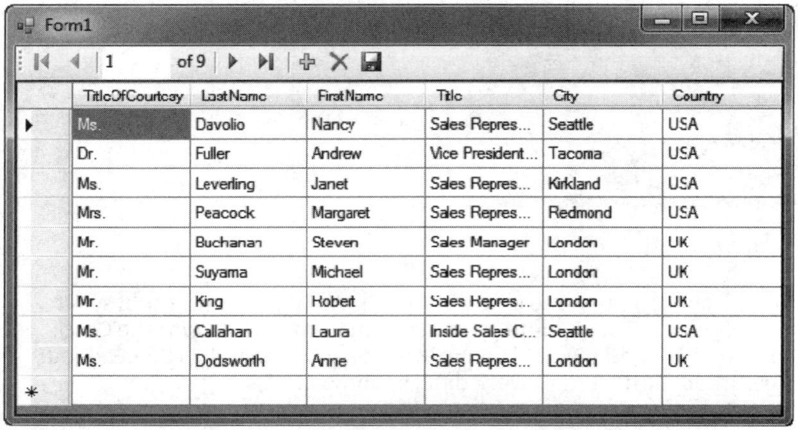

Figure 32-25. The data-driven Windows Forms program

We get a lot of functionality for very little effort. You can move through the data using the backward and forward arrows, and if there is more data than can be fit on the screen, it will be automatically grouped into pages that you can move through.

We can add records by clicking the plus button and delete the current records by clicking the cross button. We can modify any field by double-clicking it and entering a new value. And all of these changes can be saved to the database by clicking the Save button that we wired up. In fact, we can build a simple but functional data-driven program in about ten minutes. Most of which is spent setting up the database and creating the data model.

Two Program Variations

In the following sections, I show you two simple variations that widen the possibilities offered by the data support in Windows Forms, and even then, we are still only skimming the surface. The way that controls can display data is very rich indeed, and I recommend exploring further.

Filtering the Data with LINQ

In the sample, we displayed all the rows in the Employee database, but we can easily filter the data by using a LINQ query as the data source for the BindingSource control. Listing 32-8 demonstrates this, applied to the code-behind file.

Listing 32-8. Using a LINQ Query to Filter Data

```
using System.Windows.Forms;
using System.Linq;

namespace DataApp {
    public partial class Form1 : Form {

        // define the EntityFramework context field
```

```
NorthwindEntities entityContext = new NorthwindEntities();

public Form1() {
    InitializeComponent();

    // set the data source for the data binding
    employeeBindingSource.DataSource
        = entityContext.Employees
            .Where(e => e.City == "London")
            .Select(e => e);
}

private void employeeBindingNavigatorSaveItem_Click(object sender,
    System.EventArgs e) {

    entityContext.SaveChanges();
}
}
}
```

The LINQ query in the listing filters the Employee objects so that only those with a City value of London will be selected. The effect of using this query is shown in Figure 32-26. You can use any LINQ to Entities query as the data source, but you must be careful to match the data type projected by your query to the one that you used to create and populate the grid columns.

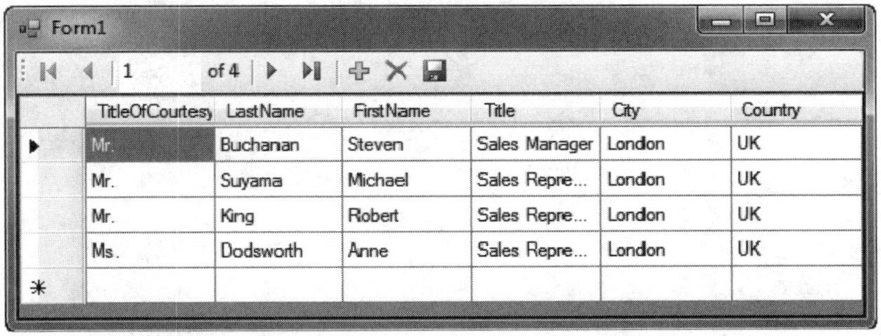

Figure 32-26. *Filtering the data*

Displaying Data Fields

We created the data grid in the previous examples by dragging the Employee data source to the data surface, but there is another way to display the data using the same technique. Select the Show Data Sources item from the Data menu, select the Employee item on the list, and then click the arrow button that appears. This will display the menu shown in Figure 32-27.

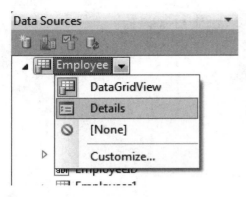

Figure 32-27. *The data source menu*

Select the Details item from the menu, and then drag the Employee item onto an empty drawing surface. This will create a series of controls that display the details of each record individually. Loading the data and wiring up the Save button are done in the same way; the resulting program is shown in Figure 32-28.

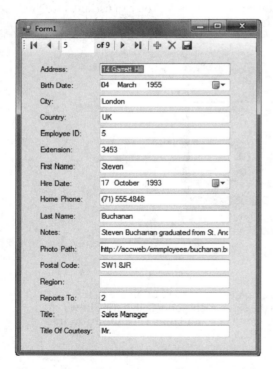

Figure 32-28. *The automatically generated details view*

Windows 7 UI Integration

One area of weakness for Windows Forms is built-in integration with the new interface features with Windows 7, such as jump lists, taskbar menus, and Aero transparency. To remedy this shortfall, Microsoft publishes the free-of-charge Windows API Code Pack, which provides .NET classes that allow you to access some Windows features, including those of the Windows 7 interface, such as taskbar jump lists and Aero transparency. You can download the code pack from http://code.msdn.microsoft.com/WindowsAPICodePack. The code pack contains the C# source code for all the classes, and you build it yourself using Visual Studio and then include the assemblies into your own project. I have included the current version as of writing this book in the downloadable samples, available from Apress.com, but you should check for newer releases.

The code pack comes with an extensive collection of examples that demonstrate how to use each feature. In the following section, I'll show you how to use just one of these features, which is *Aero Glass*. This is an unashamed eye-candy effect that makes a window transparent so that you can see the windows that are underneath. Enabling Aero Glass on your program doesn't change its functionality but does make it fit with other programs the user may be running and is very popular with users.

Using Aero Glass

Before we start, we must compile the code pack. Open the WindowsAPICodePack.sln file using Visual Studio, and select Build Solution from the Build menu. The code pack version that is current as I write this chapter was created using an earlier version of Visual Studio, and this causes a conversion wizard to appear when opening the solution to upgrade the project files.

The System.Windows.Form class is the one that provides the base window that you see on the design surface when you create a new Windows Forms project. This class doesn't provide support for the Aero transparency feature, so we need to replace it with one that does. The replacement class is contained within the code pack.

To start, create a new Windows Forms project, as we did for the previous two examples. You will see a new design surface with the standard window displayed.

We need to add references to two assemblies that were created when we compiled the Windows API Code Pack. Select your project in the Solution Explorer window, and select Add Reference from the pop-up menu. Select the Browse tab, and navigate to the Shell project inside the Windows API Code Pack directory. In either the bin\Debug or bin\Release directory, you will see the Microsoft.WindowsAPICodePack.dll and Microsoft.WindowsAPICodePack.Shell.dll assembly files, as shown in Figure 32-29. Select both of them, and click OK to dismiss the dialog box.

■ **Tip** You don't need to copy the Windows API Code Pack assemblies to your project. Visual Studio will do this for you automatically when you compile your project.

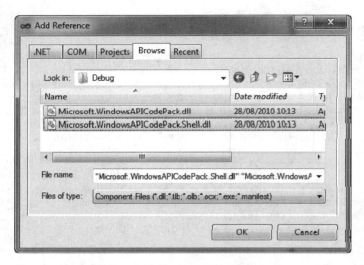

Figure 32-29. *Adding the Windows API Code Pack assemblies*

Open the code-behind file by right-clicking the Form1.cs file in the Visual Studio Solution Explorer window and selecting View Code from the pop-up menu. We are going to change the base class to the GlassForm class that is included in the Microsoft.WindowsAPICodePack.Shell namespace. Listing 32-9 demonstrates this change.

Listing 32-9. Changing the Base Class for a Windows Forms Project

```csharp
using System;
using System.Collections.Generic;
using System.ComponentModel;
using System.Data;
using System.Drawing;
using System.Linq;
using System.Text;
using System.Windows.Forms;

namespace Listing_09 {
    public partial class Form1 : Microsoft.WindowsAPICodePack.Shell.GlassForm {
        public Form1() {
            InitializeComponent();
        }
    }
}
```

The change is shown in bold. You won't see any differences on the design surface, and you can add and use controls as we have done elsewhere in this chapter. But when you compile and run the project, you will see the effect this change has, as illustrated by Figure 32-30.

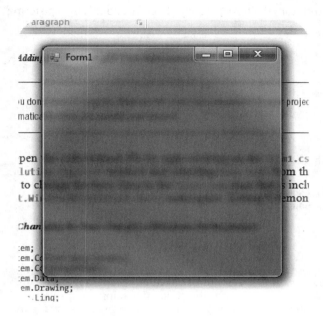

Figure 32-30. A transparent form

There is a wrinkle in using Aero Glass with Windows Forms, which is that it makes all of the controls transparent. If we change the base class for our swimming calculator example, we get a very strange result, as shown by Figure 32-31.

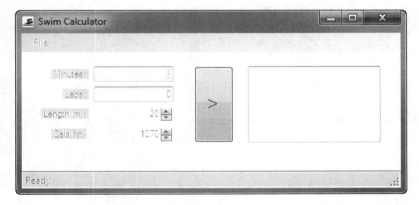

Figure 32-31. A side effect of using Aero Glass

To avoid this, we have to add a Panel control to the main window and then drag our individual controls (such as Buttons and TextBox controls) into the panel. We then need to tell the GlassForm control that we want to exclude the Panel control from the transparency effect. We do this by registering a handler for a specific event, as shown here:

```
using System;
using System.Media;
using System.Windows.Forms;
using Microsoft.WindowsAPICodePack.Shell;

namespace Calculator {

    public partial class Form1 : GlassForm {
        public Form1() {
            InitializeComponent();

            AeroGlassCompositionChanged += (source, args) => {
                ExcludeControlFromAeroGlass(panel1);
            };
        }
    }
...
```

The event handler calls the ExcludeControlFromAeroGlass method, to which you pass the name of the panel control (panel1 in this example) as a parameter. This has the effect of making the window border transparent but leaving the Panel and all the controls inside opaque, as demonstrated by Figure 32-32.

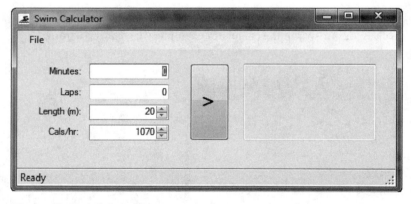

Figure 32-32. Mixing transparent and opaque controls

Summary

In this chapter, we took a whistle-stop tour of Windows Forms, the oldest and most mature of the .NET user interface technologies. You have seen how the properties and events model are used to configure and wire up controls to create traditional Windows clients and how easy it is to integrate external data into such a program. We also looked at using the Windows API Code Pack, which provides support for accessing Windows 7/Vista-specific features such as jump lists and windows transparency.

Windows Forms has fallen out of favor since WPF arrived on the scene. This is a shame, because Windows Forms is rich in features and incredibly widely used. It lacks some of the flashy features that WPF supports, since these are rarely used in business programs. I recommend you don't dismiss Windows Forms and consider it seriously for your interface projects.

■ ■ ■

CHAPTER 33

Windows Presentation Foundation

The Windows Presentation Foundation (WPF) is a relatively new addition to .NET and is an alternative to Windows Forms for creating user interfaces. WPF and Windows Forms both continue to be developed and supported by Microsoft, but WPF receives more of Microsoft's love and attention.

On one hand, there is nothing you can do with WPF that you can't also do with Windows Forms. On the other, WPF is clearly the future of .NET user interface development, and my belief is that, over time, Microsoft will place less emphasis on Windows Forms until it eventually becomes a legacy technology (I suspect that this would already have happened were it not for the fact that many corporate customers have a deep commitment to Windows Forms in their business applications).

That said, there is a lot to like in WPF—better design tools, some nice support for flashy display transitions and animations, and built-in support for Windows 7 user interface features, for example. In this chapter, I'll start by showing you how to construct the same two applications we built using Windows Forms. This will let us explore the similarities and differences. We'll then take a look at some of the features that make WPF interesting and useful to work with. We will see more of WPF when we come to look at Silverlight in Chapter 35 because WPF is used to provide the user interface elements of Silverlight applications as well.

WPF, much like Windows Forms, is full of features and controls, and I can only give you a flavor of what is possible in an introductory book like this one. For more details on WPF, I recommend Matthew MacDonald's book *Pro WPF in C# 2010*, also published by Apress. It is a very detailed and thorough guide to the inner workings of WPF.

Building a Stand-Alone WPF Program

We will start by creating the same basic swimming calculator that we built using Windows Forms. This is a nice way of showing you what WPF and Windows Forms have in common and to start to highlight some of the key differences. In this chapter, I am going to assume that you have read the Windows Forms chapter and that you are familiar with dragging controls to the design surface, setting properties and events, and so on. I won't break out the instructions with quite as much detail as in the previous chapter.

Creating the Project

The first step is to create a new project. Select New and then Project from the Visual Studio File menu, and select the WPF Application template, as shown in Figure 33-1.

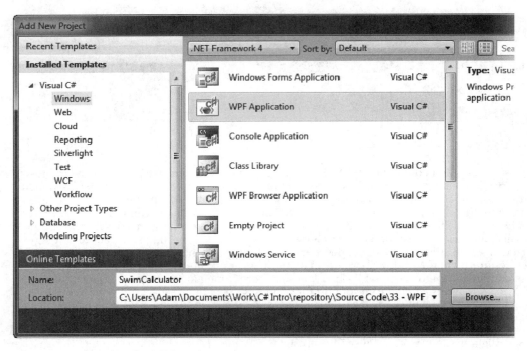

Figure 33-1. *Creating the WPF project*

Set the name of the project to **SwimCalculator**, and click the OK button to create the project. Once the project is created, the WPF design surface will open. You can see that it looks loosely similar to the Windows Forms equivalent, but there are some key differences.

First, if you open the Toolbox window, you will see that WPF has its own controls—WPF and Windows Forms don't share controls. There isn't a one-to-one match between controls, either. WPF has more controls, but, as we will see, some of Windows Forms controls that we used in the previous chapters don't have direct equivalents.

But the big difference is that the design view is split. The design surface is at the top of the display, and some XML is displayed at the bottom, as shown by Figure 33-2.

Figure 33-2. The WPF split view

WPF uses XML to describe a user interface. The XML dialect is called XAML (which is pronounced *zammel*). When we drag a control onto the design surface of our Windows Forms project, the designer adds new C# statements to our code file. When you drag a component onto the WPF surface, XML elements are added to our XAML document. Here is the default XAML document that was created as part of our new project:

```
<Window x:Class="SwimCalculator.MainWindow"
        xmlns="http://schemas.microsoft.com/winfx/2006/xaml/presentation"
        xmlns:x="http://schemas.microsoft.com/winfx/2006/xaml"
        Title="MainWindow" Height="350" Width="525">
    <Grid>

    </Grid>
</Window>
```

If I drag a Button control onto the design surface, the XAML is updated to reflect the change:

```
<Window x:Class="SwimCalculator.MainWindow"
        xmlns="http://schemas.microsoft.com/winfx/2006/xaml/presentation"
        xmlns:x="http://schemas.microsoft.com/winfx/2006/xaml"
```

```
        Title="MainWindow" Height="350" Width="525">
    <Grid>
        <Button Content="Button" Height="23" HorizontalAlignment="Left" Margin="132,94,0,0"
            Name="button1" VerticalAlignment="Top" Width="75" />
    </Grid>
</Window>
```

The new element specifies that a Button control has been added and includes details of the text on the button (the Content attribute), the size of the button (the Width and Height button), and so on. You can design your program by editing the XAML directly or by using the property editor. Changing the Height attribute in the XAML has the same effect as changing the Height property in the editor.

Using an XML layout document has some benefits over the code-based approach of other user interface toolkits, but they apply mostly to the producers of design and testing tools. Processing XML is a lot easier and less error-prone than processing C# code files. As an example, Microsoft has produced Expression Blend, which is a WPF-based design tool that allows designers to create WPF interfaces without having to use Visual Studio and generate code files. Whether you focus on the design view or the XAML view is a matter of personal choice rather than of need.

Adding the Controls

Not all the controls we used in Windows Forms have equivalent WPF controls. For example, there is no NumericUpDown control. You could remedy this by purchasing a third-party control library, by using one of the free replacements available, or, as we shall do, by using the closest match. Figure 33-3 shows the controls that you should add to the design WPF surface to create the interface for our swimming calculator.

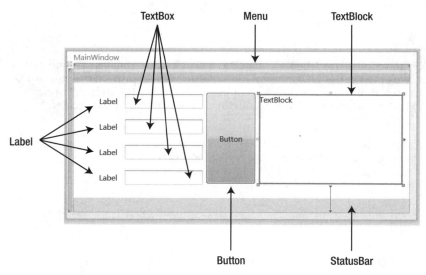

Figure 33-3. Laying out the WPF components

You can see from the figure that I have used TextBox controls in place of the Windows Forms NumericUpDown controls. Another change is that I have used a TextBlock, which is a convenient way of displaying a paragraph of text. The TextBlock control is selected in Figure 33-3 because you can't see its borders when it is not selected.

When you drag controls around the design surface, you'll see red lines appear that indicate how the current position relates to other controls. You can use these lines to guide your alignment, or you can edit the XAML document to position your controls precisely. WPF provides a good selection of layout controls that will position other controls based on some kind of policy. We are using the Grid layout that is added to new projects by default, but there are others available if you want a more sophisticated approach. Even the Grid control allows you to position controls manually or to create rows and columns that you can use to add structure to your layout.

When you click a control, you will see that there are lines that reach out from the control to the edge of the Grid control. If you click the small arrow at the control end of the line, the line will disappear. If you click the small circle, the line will reappear. Figure 33-4 shows what the design surface looks like when all four lines have been created.

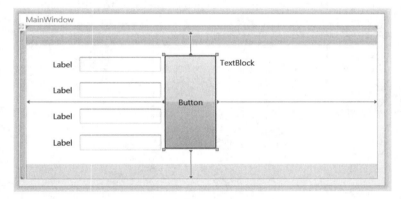

Figure 33-4. *Anchoring a control*

These lines tell the WPF layout system what to do with the control when the containing control is resized. A line means that the control should maintain its distance from the edge of the parent, even if that means resizing itself. For the Button in Figure 33-4, the four lines mean that the button will resize itself in all four directions. Compiling and running the example and resizing the window will resize the Button, as shown in Figure 33-5.

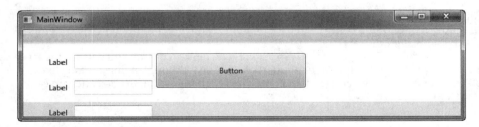

Figure 33-5. *The resized button*

You can see that the Button control has been resized to accommodate the long, thin shape of the window. You can also see that the Label and TextBox controls have started to disappear off the bottom of the screen. It can take a while to get the hang of using this feature, but it does a nice job of maintaining the layout of your controls as the underlying window is resized.

Setting the Control Properties

In the following sections, we will set the properties for each of the controls. The basic approach to this is the same in WPF as we saw in the previous chapter, although you will see some differences in the designer interface.

Configuring the Label Controls

The only configuration we need for the Label controls is to change the text they display, which is controlled by the Content property. Change the Content property for each of the Labels on the design surface so that they match those shown in Figure 33-6.

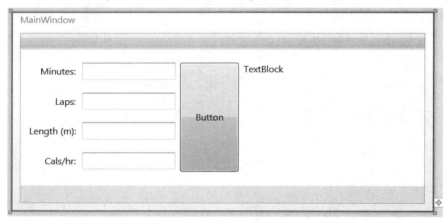

Figure 33-6. The configured labels

Configuring the TextBox Controls

Because there is no NumericUpDown control in WPF, we have four TextBox controls to configure in this example. We want to set the names of the controls so we can more readily refer to them in the code, set the default content values, and align the text.

Setting the name of a control is slightly differently in WPF. If you click a control, you will see the type of the control and the current name at the top of the Properties window. Although it doesn't look like it at first, when you roll your mouse over the current name, the display changes to a text box and you can type in a new value, as shown in Figure 33-7.

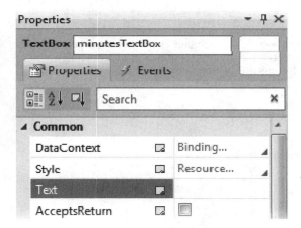

Figure 33-7. *Changing the name of a control*

Change the name of each control in sequence to `minutesTextBox`, `lapsTextBox`, `lengthTextBox`, and `caloriesTextBox`. Select the topmost pair of TextBox controls, and set the Text property to 0. This will set the default value when the program starts. Select the `lengthTextBox`, and set the Text property to 20. Select the `caloriesTextBox`, and set the Text property to 1070.

Finally, select all the TextBox controls together, and scroll down the Properties window until you find the Text properties group. Click the right-alignment button, as shown in Figure 33-8.

Figure 33-8. *Configuring the Text properties*

Configuring the TextBlock Control

We only want to change the Name property (to `resultsTextBlock`) and clear the Text property for the TextBlock control. When we clear the Text property, the control will display a thin border so we can see it on the design surface.

Configuring the Button

To configure the Button control, change the name to convertButton, change the Content property to the > character, and change the text font so that the > character fills the button area. I made mine 40 points. If you have been following along, you should have a design surface that is similar to the one shown in Figure 33-9.

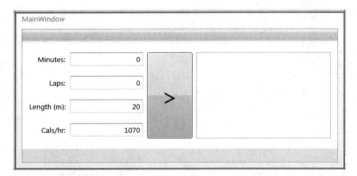

Figure 33-9. *The configured controls on the design surface*

Adding the StatusBar Item

The WPF StatusBar control works differently than its Windows Forms counterpart. It is more flexible and can be used to display a wider range of data. For our example, we only need a simple text label that we can update with messages for the user. To get started, click the StatusBar item on the design surface, find the Items property in the Properties window, and click the ellipsis (...) button. This will open the Collection Editor dialog box, which lets us add items to the StatusBar control.

Click the Add button to add a StatusBarItem to the StatusBar control. A new item will appear in the list on the left side of the dialog box, and a set of properties appears on the right side, as shown in Figure 33-10.

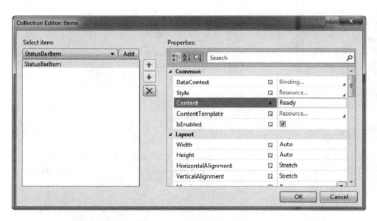

Figure 33-10. *Adding a StatusBarItem to a StatusBar control*

Change the value of the Content property to Ready, which is the default value we want displayed. Click OK to dismiss the dialog box. Click the word *Ready* that has now appeared on the StatusBar, and you will see that the Properties window shows the details for the StatusBarItem we added. Change the name of the StatusBarItem control to statusLabel.

Adding the Menu Item

Adding a MenuItem for quitting the program is a similar process to adding the StatusBarItem. Click the Menu control in the design surface, and click the ellipsis button for the Items property. This will being up a dialog box very similar to the one shown in Figure 33-10. Click the Add button to create a new MenuItem control. The new item will appear in the list on the left side of the dialog box, and its properties will appear on the right side. Change the value of the Header property to File. Click the OK button to dismiss the dialog box. You will see that a File item has appeared on the Menu control, as shown by Figure 33-11.

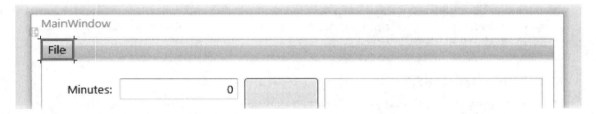

Figure 33-11. The File MenuItem on the Menu control

Click the File MenuItem, and then click the ellipsis button in its Items property. WPF allows controls to contain a wide range of other controls, which is why the names of the properties we are editing keep changing (Header, Items, Content, and so on). It is very useful in advanced applications, but it does mean that we have to build up the hierarchy of controls in a series of steps.

Click the Add button to add a new MenuItem to the File MenuItem, and change the Header property value to Quit. Click the OK button to dismiss the dialog box. If you compile and run the program now, you'll see that we have the File menu, and it contains a Quit item.

Setting the Tab Order

There is no visual overlay for setting the tab order of WPF controls. By default, the tab order is determined by the order in which controls appear in the XAML for your program, so one approach is to rearrange the XAML elements to get the effect you require. This is fine for simple programs but quickly becomes a problem with complex projects.

We can achieve a better effect by setting the values of the TabIndex and IsTabStop properties. Tab order is determined by the ascending order of the TabIndex property and controls whose IsTabStop property is set to false and won't be included in the tab order at all.

For our simple program, I want the Tab key to move from the minutesTextBox to the lapsTextBox to the convertButton controls and to exclude all other controls. Table 33-1 shows the properties that have to be set for this to happen.

Table 33-1. Property Changes for Tab Ordering

Control	Property	Value
minutesTextBox	TabIndex	1
lapsTextBox	TabIndex	2
lengthTextBox	IsTabStop	False
caloriesTextBox	IsTabStop	False
convertButton	TabIndex	3

In addition, select the MenuItem control at the top of the design surface, and uncheck the IsTabStop property. If you compile and run the program now, you will see that the Tab key cycles between the top two TextBox controls and the Button.

Wiring the Controls

The process for wiring up WPF controls is similar to the approach we saw in the previous chapter. You select a control, switch to the Events view in the Properties window, and then double-click to create a handler for the event you want to process.

■ **Tip** WPF commands offer an alternative way of wiring controls; see the "Using WPF Commands" section later in this chapter.

Wiring the Quit Menu

To select the Quit MenuItem, right-click the Menu control on the design surface, and select Document Outline from the pop-up menu. A new window will open, which will show you the hierarchy of controls in the program. You can see that the Menu control has a single MenuItem, which in turn contains a single MenuItem. If you roll your mouse over the items in the Document Outline view, you will see that a picture of the control pops up, as shown in Figure 33-12.

The Document View is very useful for finding and selecting controls. Select the Quit menu item, switch to the Event view in the Properties window, and double-click the Click event. The view will switch to the code-behind file, and a handler for the event will be added. Exiting a WPF program is done through the System.Windows.Application class, which has a static property called Current. We read the value of this property to get an Application object that represents this program, and we call the Shutdown method to exit. Listing 33-1 shows the event handler method. I have removed the using statements that were added automatically but that are unused in our program.

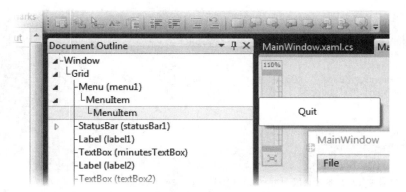

Figure 33-12. *Using the Document Outline view*

Listing 33-1. Adding a Handler to Exit the Program

```
using System.Windows;

namespace SwimCalculator {

    public partial class MainWindow : Window {

        public MainWindow() {
            InitializeComponent();
        }

        private void MenuItem_Click(object sender, RoutedEventArgs e) {
            Application.Current.Shutdown();
        }
    }
}
```

If you compile and run the program and select the Quit menu item, the program will exit.

Wiring the TextBox Controls

We want to filter the key presses that the TextBox controls receive to ensure that they contain only numeric values. We need to do this for all four TextBox controls, because we can't rely on the implied filtering that comes with a NumericUpDown control. Listing 33-2 shows the method I have added to the MainWindow.xaml.cs code-behind file that we will use to process key presses. This is very similar to the code that we used for the Windows Forms example.

Listing 33-2. The ValidateKeyPress Method

```
private void ValidateKeyPress(object sender, KeyEventArgs e) {

    // define the keys we want
```

```
        bool isNumberKey = e.Key >= Key.D0 && e.Key <= Key.D9;
        bool isNumberPadKey = e.Key >= Key.NumPad0 && e.Key <= Key.NumPad9;
        bool isDeleteKey = e.Key == Key.Delete || e.Key == Key.Back;
        bool isTab = e.Key == Key.Tab;

        if (isNumberKey || isNumberPadKey || isDeleteKey || isTab) {
            // this is a key we want to support
            statusLabel.Content = "Ready";
        } else {
            // this is not a key we want to support
            // - supclick the key event
            e.Handled = true;
            // send a message to the status bar
            statusLabel.Content = string.Format("Ignored: {0}", e.Key);
            // play an alert sound
            SystemSounds.Beep.Play();
        }
    }
}
```

The main difference for WPF is that the events are described using different `EventArgs` classes, and so we access the key that was pressed using the Key property of the `KeyEventArgs` class, which is in the `System.Windows.Input` namespace. The other changes reflect the different property names that the WPF controls use. For example, we set the text that will be displayed on the status bar using the `Content` property, rather than the Text property we used for the equivalent Windows Forms control.

Select all four TextBox controls on the design surface, switch to the Event view in the Properties window, and scroll down until you find the KeyDown event. Click the arrow, and select `ValidateKeyClick` from the list. This assigns the `ValidateKeyPress` method as the handler for `KeyDown` events. If you compile and run the program, you will find that you can only enter numeric values in the TextBox controls and that pressing any other key will display a message on the status bar. The call to the `SystemSounds.Beep.Play` method is the same one that we used in the Windows Forms chapter and required the `System.Media` namespace.

Wiring the Button

The last event we have to handle is the Button press. Double-click the Button control on the design surface, and a new handler will be added to the code-behind file for the Click event. Listing 33-3 shows the code that must be added to complete this method.

Listing 33-3. Handling the Button Click Event

```
private void convertButton_Click(object sender, RoutedEventArgs e) {
    // extract the values from the controls
    int minutesCompleted = int.Parse(minutesTextBox.Text);
    int lapsCompleted = int.Parse(lapsTextBox.Text);
    int lapLength = int.Parse(lengthTextBox.Text);
    int caloriesPerHour = int.Parse(caloriesTextBox.Text);

    // ensure that we have values that are greater than zero
    if (minutesCompleted <= 0 || lapsCompleted <= 0 ||
        lapLength <= 0 || caloriesPerHour <= 0) {
```

```
        // we cannot proceed - we have one or more bad values
        statusLabel.Content = "Cannot calculate - use values greater than zero";
        // alert the user to the erro
        SystemSounds.Beep.Play();
        return;
    }

    // perform the calculations we need for the results
    float distance = (lapsCompleted * lapLength) * 0.00062137119223733f;
    float caloriesBurned = (minutesCompleted / 60f) * caloriesPerHour;
    float pace = (minutesCompleted * 60) / lapsCompleted;

    StringBuilder resultBuilder = new StringBuilder();
    resultBuilder.AppendFormat("Distance completed: {0:F2} miles\n", distance);
    resultBuilder.AppendFormat("Calories burned: {0:F0} calories\n", caloriesBurned);
    resultBuilder.AppendFormat("Average pace: {0:F0} seconds/lap", pace);

    // compose and set the results
    resultsTextBlock.Text = resultBuilder.ToString();
}
```

This is identical to the logic we used for the Windows Forms example, updated to reflect the different property names used by the WPF controls.

Managing the Focus

Two minor WPF annoyances are that the first control in the tab order isn't passed the focus automatically and that when a TextBox control does get the focus, the text it contains isn't selected. We can fix this by adding two small event handlers.

Focusing on the First Control

We will add a handler for the Loaded event of the main WPF window in our program. This event is called when the program is loaded and all the controls have been created and configured. In this method, we will call the Focus method of the minutesTextBox object, which is the topmost in our program layout.

Select the Window control in the design surface by clicking the title bar, and double-click the Loaded event in the Event view Properties window. This will create a handler method for the event. Add a statement to the method so that it matches the one in Listing 33-4.

Listing 33-4. Adding a Focus Command to the Loaded Event Handler

```
private void Window_Loaded(object sender, RoutedEventArgs e) {
    minutesTextBox.Focus();
}
```

With this change, the focus will be passed to the control when the program starts.

Selecting the TextBox Text on Focus

Select the topmost pair of TextBox controls, and double-click the GotFocus event. This will create a new method handler. Add the statements shown in Listing 33-5 so that when one of the TextBox controls gets the focus, all of the text that it contains is selected.

Listing 33-5. The GetFocus Event Handler Method

```
private void caloriesTextBox_GotFocus(object sender, RoutedEventArgs e) {
    if (e.Source is TextBox) {
        ((TextBox)e.Source).SelectAll();
    }
}
```

These statements in this method check that the source of the event is really a TextBox control and, if it is, then calls the SelectAll method. Notice that the name given to the event is derived from only one control name. To avoid confusion later, we can change the name to something that doesn't imply that the method relates to a single control. Click the name of the method, right-click, and select Refactor and then Rename from the pop-up menus. Enter the new name for the method, and click OK. You'll see a preview of the changes, and if you click Apply, the method and all of the references to it in the XAML will be renamed. If you compile and run the program now, you will see that the focus starts on the topmost TextBox and that as you tab between controls, the text is selected each time.

Setting the Program Icon and Window Name

The final steps to finish our program are to set the name that is displayed on the Window and to set the icon. Both of these can be done by setting properties for the Window control in the design surface. To set the name, change the Title property to Swim Calculator. To change the icon, click the ellipsis button in the Icon property area, and select the .ico file you want.

Testing the Program

If you compile and test the program, you should see something similar to Figure 33-13.

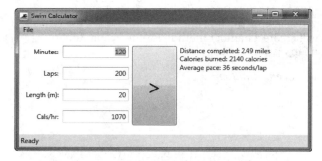

Figure 33-13. The completed WPF program

In our quick tour of building a stand-alone WPF application, we have seen some of the common traits that are shared with Windows Forms (drag-and-drop design, properties, and events) and some of the differences (XAML documents, different sets of controls). One difference that may not be apparent is that WPF has much better support for Windows 7 interface features. The window in Figure 33-13, for example, supports Aero Glass without requiring any additional downloads or code changes, and there is built-in support for other features such as jump lists and task bar menus. All of these things are possible to achieve when using Windows Forms, but WPF makes them simpler and easier.

Using WPF Data Binding

Creating a simple data-centric WPF program is very similar to the technique we used to create the equivalent Windows Forms program. To begin, create a new Visual Studio WPF project, and follow the instructions in Chapter 30 to create an entity data model. Then follow the instructions in Chapter 32 to create an Employee object data source.

Drag the Employee object data source from the Data Sources window to the design surface and release (you may have to build the project before this will work). When you release the object, a DataGrid control will be created, and the XAML for your project will be updated with details of the columns that are required to display the properties of the Employee object.

At the bottom left of the design surface, a small icon will have appeared. This is the object that will connect our Entity Framework data to the DataGrid control. Clicking this icon will display the name that has been assigned to the object, as shown by Figure 33-14. This object is an instance of the CollectionViewSource class.

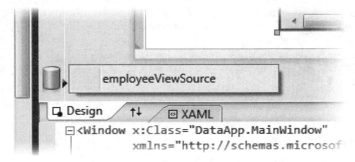

Figure 33-14. The name of the nondisplay control

Position the DataGrid in the display, add a Button control below the grid, and change the value of the Content property to be Save. Your design surface should look similar to the one in Figure 33-15.

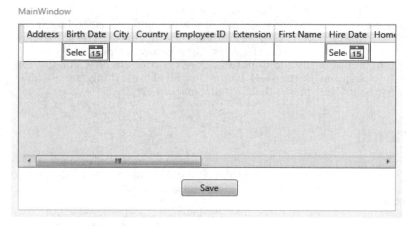

Figure 33-15. The data program design surface

Formatting the DataGrid Control

The only formatting we need to do on the DataGrid is reduce the number of columns to omit the data we don't want to see and to change the column widths so that the data we do want fits properly.

Click the DataGrid control, and click the ellipsis button in the Columns property value area. This will open the Collection Editor dialog box, which you can use to remove and reorder the columns that will be displayed. Edit your columns so that they match the set and order shown in Figure 33-16.

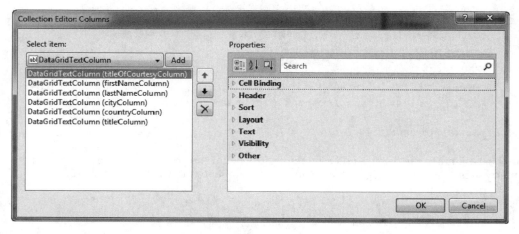

Figure 33-16. Changing the columns and their order

Click each of the columns in the list, and change the Width property to Auto. You can find the Width property in the Layout group. This value ensures that the columns are wide enough to display the data value. By default the column width is derived from the length of the column header, which truncates our Employee data. Click the OK button when you are done.

Loading the Data

We add the data to the DataGrid in the handler for the Loaded event for the Window control. If you look at the code-behind file, you will see that this method already exists and that there is a helpful code comment explaining how to set the data source. We also need to define a NorthwindEntities field and instantiate it in the class constructor. Listing 33-6 shows the changes to the code-behind file.

Listing 33-6. Loading Data in the Code-Behind File

```
using System.Windows;

namespace DataApp {

    public partial class MainWindow : Window {

        NorthwindEntities myContext;

        public MainWindow() {
            InitializeComponent();

            // create the data model context
            myContext = new NorthwindEntities();
        }

        private void Window_Loaded(object sender, RoutedEventArgs e) {

            System.Windows.Data.CollectionViewSource employeeViewSource
                = ((System.Windows.Data.CollectionViewSource)
                  (this.FindResource("employeeViewSource")));

            // Load data by setting the CollectionViewSource.Source property:
            // employeeViewSource.Source = [generic data source]
            employeeViewSource.Source = myContext.Employees;
        }
    }
}
```

The additions that I have made are shown in bold.

Wiring the Button

The final step is to wire the Button control so that we save changes to the database. Double-click the Button in the design view, and add the following statement to the event handler method that is created:

```
myContext.SaveChanges();
```

Testing the Program

If you compile and run the program, you should see the DataGrid is populated with the data from the Employees table of the Northwind database, as shown in Figure 33-17.

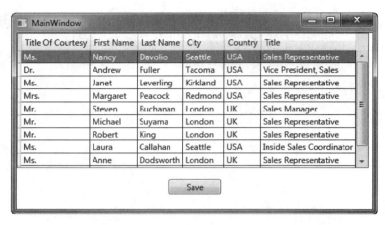

Figure 33-17. *The completed WPF data program*

WPF doesn't provide the paging and editing control that we got with Windows Forms, but you can still create, modify, and delete records using the DataGrid. To add a new record, scroll to the bottom of the grid, and fill in the fields for the empty row you will see there. To modify a record, double-click a field, and edit the contents. To delete a row, click the Delete key. To save the changes you have made to the database, click the Save button.

Using WPF-Specific Features

The previous sections have given you a flavor of how to use WPF, and there are a lot of similarities between creating a WPF program and creating a Windows Forms program. And that's a good thing—the property and event model is well-established and well-understood, and the commonality between the two UI technologies means that you can leverage your knowledge of one system to build programs using either approach.

That said, WPF has a set of features go beyond what can conveniently be done with Windows Forms. I say *conveniently*, because if you had the time and the patience, you could achieve the same functionality using Windows Forms, but one of the strengths of WPF is that these features already exist and are ready to go. I only have the space in this chapter to quickly demonstrate two of these features, but I recommend that you explore them further if you adopt WPF for your Windows client development.

Using WPF Animations

WPF provides support for animating almost any aspect of the interface. Controls can be made to appear, disappear, and change size using animations. When used carefully, animations can enhance user interactions with a program, drawing the user's eye to a change in state or emphasizing the available actions. Animations are also used in Silverlight applications where users have higher expectations of the gloss and polish given to an interface. We'll see more of Silverlight in Chapter 35.

The WPF animation capabilities are very comprehensive, but in this section, I'll just show you some very simple animations that change the size of a button. You can define WPF animations entirely in XAML, but we'll use the more compact C# alternative.

Creating the Project

Create a new WPF project in Visual Studio, and drag a Button control onto the design surface. The position of the button doesn't matter, but you should end up with a design surface that looks like the one in Figure 33-18.

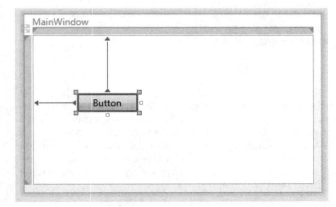

Figure 33-18. *The project design surface*

Adding the Animation

Double-click the Button in the design surface to create a method that will handle the Click event. Listing 33-7 shows the updated code file, including the animation. I have removed the using statements that we don't need, and I added one for the System.Windows.Media.Animation namespace, which contains the classes that support animation.

Listing 33-7. Using a WPF Animation

```
using System;
using System.Windows;
using System.Windows.Controls;
using System.Windows.Media.Animation;

namespace AnimationDemo {

    public partial class MainWindow : Window {
```

```
public MainWindow() {
    InitializeComponent();
}

private void button1_Click(object sender, RoutedEventArgs e) {

    // create the animation class
    DoubleAnimation myAnimation = new DoubleAnimation();
    // set the value to start with
    myAnimation.From = button1.Width;
    // set the value to finish with
    myAnimation.To = button1.Width + 50;
    // set the duration of the animation
    myAnimation.Duration = TimeSpan.FromSeconds(1);

    // have the button perform the animation on its width
    button1.BeginAnimation(Button.WidthProperty, myAnimation);
}
}
}
```

The animation in Listing 33-7 will increase the width of the Button control by 50 pixels every time it is clicked. Animation in WPF works on control properties, meaning if you want to animate the width of a button, you create an animation that increases the value of Width property over a period of time.

To start, we have to select an animation class to use. There are more than 40 different animation classes available, and, in general, the one that you choose is driven by the data type of the property you want to animate. In our case, the Width property of a Button control is a double value, so we need to use the DoubleAnimation class. We create one using the default constructor:

```
DoubleAnimation myAnimation = new DoubleAnimation();
```

The next step is to specify the value we want for the property at the start and finish of the animation, which we do using the From and To properties. We want the Button control to grow by 50 pixels from its current size, so we set the value of From and To using values taken from the Button control, like this:

```
myAnimation.From = button1.Width;
myAnimation.To = button1.Width + 50;
```

We need to tell the animation how long it should take to move between the values we assigned to the From and To properties. We do this using the Duration property, as follows:

```
myAnimation.Duration = TimeSpan.FromSeconds(1);
```

The easiest way to set the Duration property is to use the TimeSpan structure that we looked at in Chapter 22. The earlier statement sets the Duration to one second. The last step is to ask the Button control to use the animation to change its width:

```
button1.BeginAnimation(Button.WidthProperty, myAnimation);
```

Almost all WPF controls have the BeginAnimation method, and the parameters are the property that should be changed by the animation and the animation itself. WPF has a different approach to properties, called *dependency properties*. This is an advanced topic, but for our purposes it means that you specify the property you want to animate using a static property that belongs to the control class. We want to animate the Width of a Button control, so we specify Button.WidthProperty as a parameter to the BeginAnimation method.

Testing the Animation

If we compile and run the WPF program, we can see the effect of the animation. Each time you click the Button, it becomes 50 pixels wider, as shown by Figure 33-19.

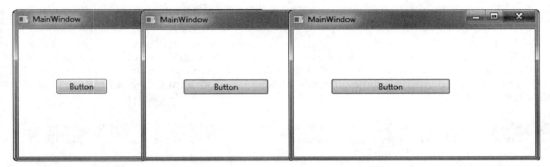

Figure 33-19. *The effect of a WPF animation*

Combining Multiple Animations

You can perform multiple simultaneous animations, even animating two different properties of the same control. Listing 33-8 provides a demonstration.

Listing 33-8. Performing Simultaneous Animations

```
using System;
using System.Windows;
using System.Windows.Controls;
using System.Windows.Media.Animation;

namespace AnimationDemo {

    public partial class MainWindow : Window {

        public MainWindow() {
            InitializeComponent();
        }

        private void button1_Click(object sender, RoutedEventArgs e) {

            DoubleAnimation myWidthAnimation = new DoubleAnimation();
            myWidthAnimation.From = button1.Width;
            myWidthAnimation.To = button1.Width + 50;
            myWidthAnimation.Duration = TimeSpan.FromSeconds(1);
```

```
        DoubleAnimation myHeightAnimation = new DoubleAnimation();
        myHeightAnimation.From = button1.Height;
        myHeightAnimation.To = button1.Height + 20;
        myHeightAnimation.Duration = TimeSpan.FromSeconds(2);

        button1.BeginAnimation(Button.WidthProperty, myWidthAnimation);
        button1.BeginAnimation(Button.HeightProperty, myHeightAnimation);
    }
  }
}
```

In this listing, I define two animations—one that is applied to the width of the Button and one that is applied to the height. The height animation takes twice as long as the width one but increases the property value by a smaller amount. Compiling and running the example shows that the animations start together, although the height animation continues after the width animation has finished. Figure 33-20 illustrates the final effect.

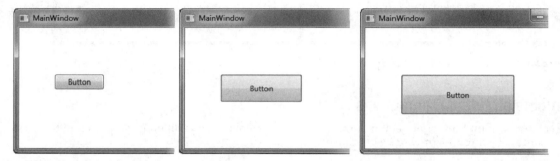

Figure 33-20. The effect of simultaneous animations

Using WPF Commands

WPF has a nice feature known as *commands*. There are various uses for commands; one that I find the most useful is coordinating controls that have the same function. In complex projects, it is common to have multiple controls that all have the same purpose. For example, you might be able to create a new document by selecting a New menu item, clicking a New button in the main window, and pressing a New button in an options dialog box. The WPF command feature lets us wire them together in an interesting way.

Creating the Project

We will start by creating a new Visual Studio WPF project. Drag a Menu control and two Button controls to the design surface so that you have something similar to Figure 33-21.

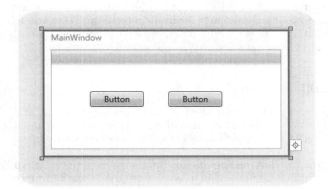

Figure 33-21. *The new design surface*

We are going to see how a command works by having all three controls be responsible for the New function in our program. These three controls will simulate three different controls in a more complex program where the user might see a New button or menu item.

Configuring the Button Controls

Select both Button controls on the design surface, and then click the value area of the Command property in the Properties window. Click the arrow that appears, and take a look at the drop-down list. This is shown in Figure 33-22.

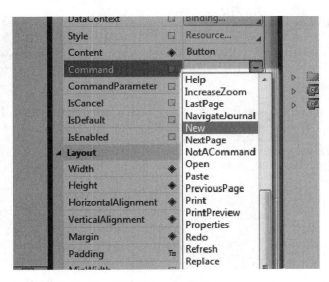

Figure 33-22. *The WPF Command list*

WPF includes a number of predefined commands, and the list contains their names. You can define custom commands for actions that are specific to your program, but the built-in commands are enough for most projects. Select New from the Command list. We have told WPF that these Button controls are both related to the New feature in our program; we don't have a New feature yet, but we will add one soon.

Adding and Configuring the MenuItem Control

Click the Menu control in the design surface, and select the Items property. Click the ellipsis button, and add a new MenuItem with a Header property value of File, just as you did when you created the swimming calculator example. Add a nested MenuItem to the File item, but instead of setting a Header value, select New from the Command property list.

If you compile and run the program, you will see that the File menu contains a New item that has a shortcut key defined. The name and the key combination have been inferred from the Command property value you set, as shown in Figure 33-23.

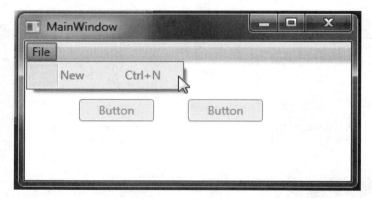

Figure 33-23. The command-driven menu item

Binding the Command

We have now created three controls and associated them with the WPF New command. We now have to bind the command to our program code and decide what we want to do when the command is executed.

Double-click the main Window control on the design surface to create a handler method for the Loaded event. Listing 33-9 shows the changes that we need to make to the code file.

Listing 33-9. Binding a Command

```
using System.Windows;
using System.Windows.Input;

namespace CommandsDemo {

    public partial class MainWindow : Window {
```

```
public MainWindow() {
    InitializeComponent();
}

private void Window_Loaded(object sender, RoutedEventArgs e) {

    // create a command binding
    CommandBinding myBinding = new CommandBinding(ApplicationCommands.New);

    myBinding.Executed += (source, eventArgs) => {
        MessageBox.Show("New command has been executed");
    };

    // add the binding to the set for this program
    CommandBindings.Add(myBinding);
    }
  }
}
```

The statements to add are shown in bold in the listing. There are three steps to activating a command. The first is to create a CommandBinding object. This is the object that you use to activate a command for your program. When there is no binding for a command, the controls that are associated with the command are disabled, which is why our menu and buttons were grayed out when we selected New from the Command property list. Here is the statement that creates the binding object:

```
CommandBinding myBinding = new CommandBinding(ApplicationCommands.New);
```

The parameter to the CommandBinding constructor is the command that you want to use. Commands are defined as static properties in the ApplicationCommands, NavigationCommands, EditingCommands, ComponentCommands, and MediaCommands classes, all of which are in the System.Windows.Input namespace. The New command is a property of the ApplicationCommands class, so I use ApplicationCommands.New as the constructor argument. There is no easy way of working out which class contains which command. You have to look at each class in turn until you find the entry you selected from the properties list.

The next step is to add a handler to the Executed event, which is triggered when one of the controls associated with the event is activated. For our example, this means that when one of the Buttons is clicked or when the MenuItem is selected. I have used a lambda expression that uses the static MessageBox.Show method to display a simple dialog box.

The last step is to add the command binding object to the set of commands that WPF is keeping track of. We do this through the Add method of the CommandBindings property, like this:

```
CommandBindings.Add(myBinding);
```

If we compile and run our program now, we will see that the controls are all activated and that using any of them causes the dialog box to appear, as shown in Figure 33-24.

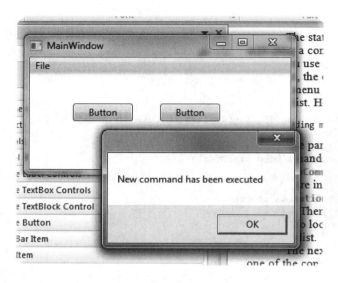

Figure 33-24. *The activated command controls*

Selectively Activating the Command

If you have been following the examples in this chapter, you'll have realized that using a WPF command hasn't really given us anything substantial. We could have achieved the same effect by creating an event handler method for the controls and performing our New action there. So, let's take a look at the first of two features that make commands interesting, selective activation.

Add a CheckBox control to the design surface, and change the Content property to Command Active and the IsChecked property to True. Your design surface should look like the one in Figure 33-25.

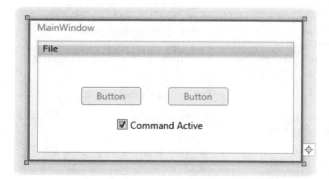

Figure 33-25. *Adding a CheckBox control to the project*

Switch to the code-behind file, and make the change that is shown in Listing 33-10.

Listing 33-10. Adding a CanExecute Handler

```
using System.Windows;
using System.Windows.Input;

namespace CommandsDemo {

    public partial class MainWindow : Window {

        public MainWindow() {
            InitializeComponent();
        }

        private void Window_Loaded(object sender, RoutedEventArgs e) {

            // create a command binding
            CommandBinding myBinding = new CommandBinding(ApplicationCommands.New);

            myBinding.Executed += (source, eventArgs) => {
                MessageBox.Show("New command has been executed");
            };

            myBinding.CanExecute += (source, eventArgs) => {
                eventArgs.CanExecute = checkBox1.IsChecked ?? false;
            };

            // add the binding to the set for this program
            CommandBindings.Add(myBinding);
        }
    }
}
```

The addition is a lambda expression that handles the CanExecute event defined by the
CommandBinding class. This event is used to determine whether a command is active. You specify this by
setting a bool value for the CanExecute property of the event argument class, like this:

```
eventArgs.CanExecute = checkBox1.IsChecked ?? false;
```

The state of the command is controlled by whether the CheckBox control is checked, which is
reported through the IsChecked property. This property can return true, false, or null, so I have used
the null coalescing operator (??) that I described in Chapter 26 to map a null value to false. If we
compile and run the program, you will see that toggling the CheckBox enables and disables the WPF
command, which in turn enables and disables the controls that are associated with the commands. This
is illustrated by Figure 33-26.

Figure 33-26. Enabling and disabling the WPF command

I am using a CheckBox to demonstrate this feature, but you can enable and disable commands based on the internal state of your program. Imagine your program is in the middle of a save operation and isn't able to perform a New command. Rather than have to keep track of all the controls that relate to the New operation, you just disable the command, and WPF takes care of the rest. When you finish the save, you enable the command again, and everything returns to normal. Being able to selectively enable and disable commands is a very handy feature that I find myself using more and more.

Using Commands to Set Control Content

When we added a MenuItem and associated it with the New command, WPF automatically set the text that the MenuItem displays and created a keyboard shortcut so that the menu can be selected using Ctrl+N. We can get the same effect for our buttons by reading the Text property of the WPF command, as demonstrated by Listing 33-11.

Listing 33-11. Programmatically Setting Button Content from a WPF Command

```
using System.Windows;
using System.Windows.Input;

namespace CommandsDemo {

    public partial class MainWindow : Window {

        public MainWindow() {
            InitializeComponent();
        }

        private void Window_Loaded(object sender, RoutedEventArgs e) {

            // create a command binding
            CommandBinding myBinding = new CommandBinding(ApplicationCommands.New);

            myBinding.Executed += (source, eventArgs) => {
                MessageBox.Show("New command has been executed");
            };
```

```
        myBinding.CanExecute += (source, eventArgs) => {
            eventArgs.CanExecute = checkBox1.IsChecked ?? false;
        };

        // add the binding to the set for this program
        CommandBindings.Add(myBinding);

        // set the Content property for the Button controls
        button1.Content = ApplicationCommands.New.Text;
        button2.Content = ApplicationCommands.New.Text;
    }
  }
}
```

The additions to the code file are shown in bold. If you compile and run the program, you'll see that the Button controls now display New, as illustrated by Figure 33-27.

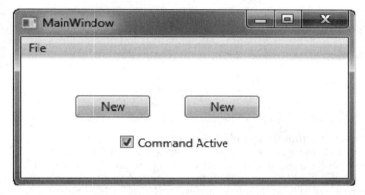

Figure 33-27. *Deriving control content from a WPF command*

That's a modest convenience, but it gets better. If you assign a new value to the Text property of a command in the constructor of your Window object, you can change the value displayed by any control that depends on the command for its content. In our case, that is the MenuItem and both Button controls. Here is an example of a statement that changes the value:

```
ApplicationCommands.New.Text = "Hello";
```

If you place this statement in the MainWindow constructor and then compile and run the program, you'll see that the MenuItem and the Buttons display the new value, as shown in Figure 33-28.

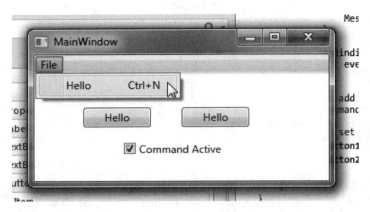

Figure 33-28. Changing the Text property of a WPF command

This can be useful if you need to universally change the term associated with a command, but the real value comes when your users run your program on a machine configured for another language. WPF automatically changes the Text property to a localized value so that Spanish-language users see Spanish terms for the commands, French-language users see French terms for the commands, and so on.

Summary

In this chapter, we used WPF to create the same stand-alone and data-centric programs we used Windows Forms for. There is a lot in common between these two technologies when building basic programs—a similar approach to properties and events, a drag-and-drop designer, and so on. But for every similarity, there is an important difference—XAML layout documents, control sets that don't overlap exactly, and slightly different approaches to bind data to controls.

We also saw two features that are unique to WPF. The first was animations, which allows you to create rich interaction models by changing the characteristics of controls over periods of time. The second was the command feature, which lets you group controls by the functionality they add to your program and enable, disable, and work them as a single group.

WPF may lack some of the robustness and maturity of Windows Forms, but it has a much more modern foundation and some interaction features that can be used to add pleasing richness to interfaces. It is easy to understand why WPF is starting to gain ground.

■ ■ ■

CHAPTER 34

ASP.NET

ASP.NET is the .NET platform for building web applications. ASP.NET is a huge and feature-rich technology—it is so big that the book *Pro ASP.NET 4 in C# 2010*, the Apress book about ASP.NET that I wrote with Matthew MacDonald, is more than 1,500 pages. In this chapter, we are going to look at two of the user interface technologies that ASP.NET supports: Web Forms and Dynamic Data.

ASP.NET relies on Internet Information Services (IIS), which is an application server that has been enhanced to deliver ASP.NET applications to clients. IIS 7 is available as part of Windows and works particularly well on Windows Server. The latest version is IIS 7.5, which is supported on Windows 7 and Windows Server 2008 R2. You can get details of IIS, including instructions for deploying ASP.NET applications, at the Microsoft IIS site: www.iis.net. We won't be using IIS in this chapter. Instead, we will rely on the server that is built into Visual Studio and that can be used to test and debug projects.

If you are using the Express edition of Visual Studio 2010, you will need to use the Web Developer version for this chapter. You can install Web Developer alongside the C# Express version, and the two will coexist quite happily. This chapter will follow the same approach as the previous two, in that we will create a web-based version of the swim calculator program and then look at how we can access data from the Northwind database.

Building a Web Forms Program

In this section, we will re-create the swim calculator program using ASP.NET Web Forms. I have referred to this as a stand-alone program in the Windows Forms and WPF chapters, but I am not sure that we could count any Web Forms program as being truly stand-alone. After all, we are talking about a web program that involves a browser and a server. Web Forms is, as the name suggests, the web counterpart to Windows Forms, and you will see the now-familiar properties and events model has been used again here.

Creating the Project

To create the project for this section, go to the Add New Project dialog box, select the ASP.NET Empty Web Application template, change the name to **SwimCalculator**, and click the OK button, as illustrated by Figure 34-1.

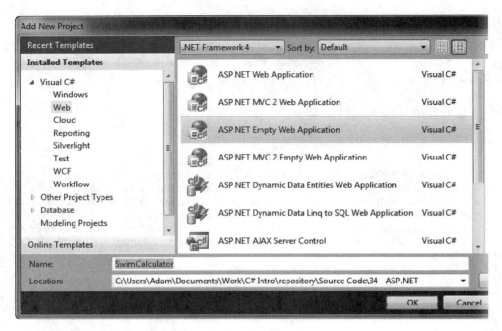

Figure 34-1. *Creating the Web Forms project*

You will find the template under the Web category. Make sure you select the C# version if you are using Visual Studio Express because this edition includes Visual Basic templates with the same name.

Select the project in the Solution Explorer window, right-click, and choose Add and Add New Item from the pop-up menus. Under the Web category, you will see the Web Form template; click this, and set the name of the item to **Default.aspx**.

A web form is a special file that will be translated into an HTML page that will be displayed in a browser and a C# assembly that contains your program logic for processing the web page. This is similar to WPF, where XAML and C# are combined to provide the layout and the logic for a program window.

Click the Add button to dismiss the dialog box, and add the item to your project. The editor for the `Default.aspx` file will open. Click the Split button at the bottom of the window, as shown in Figure 34-2.

Figure 34-2. *Selecting the split view*

The split view is similar to the one we used for WPF, except that we are working with HTML rather than XAML. Open the Toolbox window, and drag a `Button` control to the design surface. The `Button` control will appear on the surface, and the HTML will be updated in the other part of the split view. The tag that has been added to the HTML will be `<asp:Button>`, which is one that you probably haven't seen before. These tags are the secret sauce of ASP.NET Web Forms. When you compile a Web Forms application, there are two outputs: the assembly that contains your C# code and the `.aspx` file that contains the HTML with the special <asp> tags. The <asp> tags are the glue between the HTML that the client sees and the logic of your C# code.

Web Forms applications are deployed to Internet Information Services, which is Microsoft's web application server. When IIS receives a request from a browser for your .aspx file, it returns regular HTML to the browser, having translated your <asp> tags into regular HTML controls and hidden state information.

We won't be using IIS in this chapter. We can use the development ASP.NET server that is included with Visual Studio 2010 instead. To see how this works, select Start Without Debugging from the Visual Studio Debug menu. The development server will start automatically, and you'll see a notification on your Windows task base, similar to the one shown in Figure 34-3.

Figure 34-3. Starting the ASP.NET development server

Your default web browser will be started, and the URL for your ASP.NET Web Forms page will be loaded. The URL for the page will be the combination of the server URL (which is shown when the ASP.NET server is loaded; you can see from Figure 34-3 that mine has started on http://localhost:2083) and the name you gave your web form (Default.aspx), so the browser will load http://localhost:2083/Default.aspx on my machine (you may get a slightly different URL).

Because our web form contains only a single Button control, that is what we see in the browser, as Figure 34-4 shows. My favorite browser is Google Chrome, and you can see that Web Forms applications work just as well in Chrome as in Internet Explorer. In fact, Web Forms applications work in every modern browser.

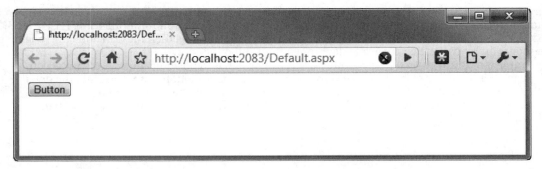

Figure 34-4. Viewing an ASP.NET Web Forms application in Chrome

If we look at the HTML source for the web page that the browser has displayed, the <asp> tag that we see in Visual Studio looks like this:

```
<asp:Button ID="Button1" runat="server" Text="Button" />
```

This has been translated into regular HTML like this:

```
<input type="submit" name="Button1" value="Button" id="Button1" />
```

You will also see some additions to the HTML like this one:

```
<input type="hidden" name="__VIEWSTATE" id="__VIEWSTATE"
value="/wEPDwUKMjAOOTM4MTAwNGRkbpBHRr2koJt27jitjyifSDFWTs1+Jbf9fKjzfBMozOU=" />
```

These long data strings are how Web Forms keeps track of the state of the application. We don't need to edit or work with these directly, but it helps to understand how our actions on the design surface result in HTML that browsers can understand and display.

■ **Note** The transmission of state data can become an area of weakness for the Web Forms technology. As we build more complex Web Forms application, the amount of data that has to be sent between the browser and the server increases sharply, presenting problems for users with slower network connections. For this reason, Web Forms has gained wide adoption for corporate intranet applications but has struggled to gain ground in the Internet applications space. ASP.NET has two other technologies that don't have this problem. The first is Silverlight, which is the .NET rival to Adobe Flash; we will look at Silverlight in Chapter 35. The second technology is MVC (which stands for Model View Controller). MVC is an advanced technology that is beyond the scope of this book, but if you want more details, I suggest the book that I wrote with Steven Sanderson entitled *Pro ASP.NET MVC Framework*, also published by Apress.

Adding the Controls

There are two approaches to laying out controls on an ASP.NET web form. The first approach is to use HTML tags to create a page structure that contains the controls. This is commonly done using HTML tables, CSS, or some of the ASP.NET controls that group other controls together; these include the Panel and View controls, both of which are available through the Toolbox window.

For simplicity, we are going to use the other approach, which is to position controls absolutely on the web page. This allows us to focus on the workings of web forms without having to get into the detail of HTML structure. To enable absolute positioning, select Options from the Visual Studio Tools menu, expand the HTML Designer group, select CSS Styling, and select the last item in the list, as shown in Figure 34-5.

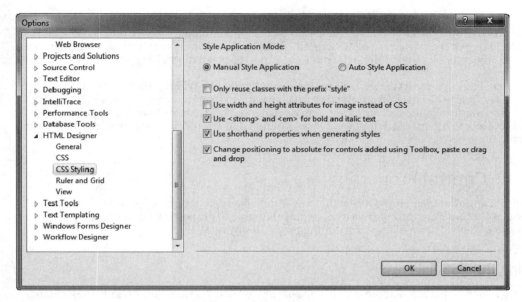

Figure 34-5. *Enabling absolute positioning for web forms*

Click the OK button to dismiss the Options dialog box. Now you can place or move controls on the design surface, and their position will remain fixed when displayed in the browser. Adding the controls is similar to using the design surfaces we saw in the Windows Forms and WPF chapters. Drag the controls on to the surface, and position them so that they are arranged similarly to those shown in Figure 34-6. The Web Forms design surface has some wrinkles. For example, you can't always reposition a control until there are at least two controls on the surface, and the Shift key doesn't select multiple controls. You need to use the Ctrl key to do that. Aside from these minor oddities, you should have little trouble re-creating Figure 34-6. If you are having trouble moving a control, try selecting the Set Position – Absolute menu item from the Format menu.

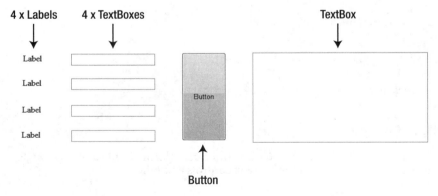

Figure 34-6. *The web forms controls for the swim calculator*

You can position and align controls using the Format menu. Web Forms uses a slightly different set of controls from Windows Forms and WPF. The controls tend to be simpler because they have to be converted to HTML that the browser can understand, and there is a definite emphasis on web page–like objects, such as images, links, and tables, which is to be expected given the web page model that Web Forms follows.

You'll notice that there are fewer controls in this example than the Widows Forms and WPF equivalents. This is partly because we are creating a web page and the browser provides some of the windowing infrastructure for us, such as a Quit item on a menu. We also have fewer components because the feedback to the user for input validation is handled differently in web forms, as you'll see in the "Wiring the Controls" section later in the chapter.

Setting the Control Properties

One of the nice features of Web Forms is that the now-familiar system of properties and events is used. In this section, we'll configure the controls by changing the value of properties. I'll be briefer in my instructions since you will be an old hand at editing properties by now.

Configuring the Labels

We need to change the labels so that the significance of each related `TextBox` control is obvious. Change the `Text` property for the labels so that the values are (from the topmost control to the bottom) `Minutes:`, `Laps:`, `Length (m):`, `Cals/hr:`.

Notice that the HTML changes each time you edit a control. Some programmers prefer to write the HTML directly and avoid using the design tools. This can be a quicker way to create a program but also tends to create more errors. Once you have made the changes, your design surface should look similar to Figure 34-7.

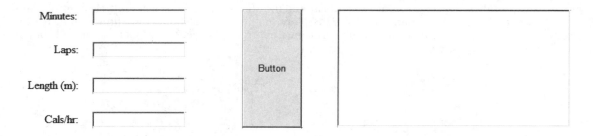

Figure 34-7. *Configuring the label controls*

Configuring the TextBox Controls

There are five `TextBox` controls in this example. The `TextBox` control can perform double duty as a single- or multiple-line display. Figure 34-8 assigns each of the `TextBox` controls a number.

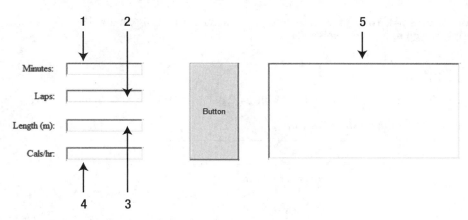

Figure 34-8. *Numbering the* TextBox *controls*

Table 34-1 details the property values that must be set for each of the TextBox controls, identified using the numbers from Figure 34-8.

Table 34-1. *Property Changes for* TextBox *Controls*

Control	Property	Value
1	ID	minutesTextBox
2	ID	lapsTextBox
3	ID	lengthTextBox
4	ID	caloriesTextBox
5	ID	resultsTextBox
1, 2	Text	0
3	Text	20
4	Text	1070
5	TextMode	MultiLine
5	ReadOnly	True

The changes detailed in Table 34-1 set the name by which we will refer to each control in our C# code and configure the display of text. The text alignment of the TextBox control can't be set using the Properties window. To do this, you must select the control and use the Format ➤ Justify menu. Select the

Right menu item for controls 1–4. You will need to do this for each control individually. The designer doesn't correctly apply the changes when you select multiple controls.

Configuring the Button

The final control we have to configure is the Button. Table 34-2 details the changes we need to make.

Table 34-2. Property Changes for the Button Control

Property	Value
ID	convertButton
Font	X-Large, Bold
Text	>

The Font settings are contained within their own group, which you have to expand by clicking the arrow to the left of the property name. Your design surface should look like Figure 34-9 once you have made the changes in this and the previous section.

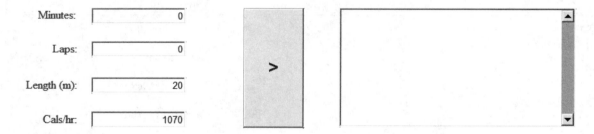

Figure 34-9. Configuring the TextBox controls

Setting the Tab Order

The tab order for Web Forms controls is set using the TabIndex property. Focus moves to the control with the lowest TabIndex value. A TabIndex value of -1 for a control means that the tab key doesn't select the control at all. To set the tab order for our example, give the minutesTextBox control a TabIndex value of 1, the lapsTextBox a value of 2, and the Button control a value of 3. The other TextBox controls should have a TaxIndex value of -1. The Label controls are not selected and can be left unchanged. If you select Start Without Debugging from the Visual Studio Debug menu and click the Tab key, you will see the focus cycle through the first two TextBox controls and the Button. The focus may also cycle to include the area of the browser where you enter the URL to view. This depends on your browser and cannot be easily controlled using Web Forms.

Wiring the Button Control

To wire the Button, double-click the Button in the design surface to create a method that will be used to handle the Click event. Visual Studio will display the code-behind file so that we can add our program logic. We've already done the groundwork by naming the properties, so all we have to do is add the code that will read the values from the controls and perform the calculation, as shown in Listing 34-1.

Listing 34-1. Wiring the Button Control

```
using System;
using System.Text;

namespace SwimCalculator {
    public partial class Default : System.Web.UI.Page {

        protected void convertButton_Click(object sender, EventArgs e) {

            // get the values from the controls
            int minutesCompleted = int.Parse(minutesTextBox.Text);
            int lapsCompleted = int.Parse(lapsTextBox.Text);
            int lapLength = int.Parse(lengthTextBox.Text);
            int caloriesPerHour = int.Parse(caloriesTextBox.Text);

            // perform the calculations we need for the results
            float distance = (lapsCompleted * lapLength) * 0.00062137119223733f;
            float calsBurned = (minutesCompleted / 60f) * caloriesPerHour;
            float pace = (minutesCompleted * 60) / lapsCompleted;

            StringBuilder resultBuilder = new StringBuilder();
            resultBuilder.AppendFormat("Distance completed: {0:F2} miles\n", distance);
            resultBuilder.AppendFormat("Calories burned: {0:F0} calories\n", calsBurned);
            resultBuilder.AppendFormat("Average pace: {0:F0} seconds/lap", pace);

            // compose and set the results
            resultsTextBox.Text = resultBuilder.ToString();
        }
    }
}
```

The Text property gets or sets the contents of a Web Forms TextBox control. You can see this used when I read the values from the four leftmost TextBoxes and again when I set the same property to display the results.

Setting the Focus

The last change we need to make is to set the default focus so that the minutesTextBox is focused automatically when the web page loads. To do this, click any of the controls on the design surface, and then select form#form1 from the bottom of the screen, as illustrated by Figure 34-10.

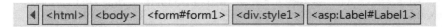

Figure 34-10. *Selecting the form*

When you click a control, the bottom of the window displays the hierarchy of HTML elements from the HTML tag at the top of the document to the control you have selected, and clicking an item in the hierarchy selects that element. Once you have selected the `form#form1` element, change the value of the `DefaultFocus` property to `minutesTextBox`. This will ensure that the control is focused automatically.

Testing the Program

If you compile and run the project, your browser will load the web page and display the application. You can enter values in the `TextBox` controls and click the button to perform the calculation, as shown in Figure 34-11.

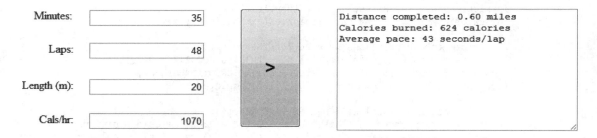

Figure 34-11. *Testing the program*

You can see how much similarity there is between Web Forms and Windows Forms/WPF. The logic of our Web Forms program is expressed as a series of event-handling methods, much like the other user interface technologies we have looked at. This consistency between the different user interface tool kits is very convenient. It means that a little knowledge can go a long way when you switch between technologies. Of course, there are differences between Web Forms and Windows Forms. How can there not be? After all, one is used to create web applications, and the other is used to create Windows programs. But the consistency of the underlying design and coding approach emphasizes the similarity and plays down the differences.

Using Web Forms Data Binding

In this section, we will look at the first of two approaches to developing data-centric ASP.NET applications—using the Web Forms data features. The steps taken to create a Web Forms data application are strikingly similar to the approach taken by Windows Forms and WPF, and since the previous section introduced you to the basics of Web Form controls, I am not going to spend too much time on the details.

Create the Project and the Entity Data Model

We start by creating a new project using the same ASP.NET Empty Web Application template that we used in the previous section. I have named my project **DataApp** in the code samples download that accompanies this book.

We will use an Entity Framework Data Model as the bridge between our program and the database. To do this, follow the steps set out in the "Creating the Model" section of Chapter 30. You must compile your project after you have added the data model. If you don't, then the Web Forms controls won't be able to read the connection information and metadata properly.

Adding the Web Form

Because we selected the empty ASP.NET template, we must add a web form to develop with. Select your project in the Solution Explorer, right-click, and select Add ➤ New Item from the pop-up menu. Find the Web Form template in the Web section, set the name to `Default.aspx`, and click Add to create the item in the project. The HTML Source view will be opened, showing you the basic page structure.

Creating the Web Forms Data Source

We need to create a bridge between the data model and web forms. To do this, switch to the split view, and drag an `EntityDataSource` control onto the design surface. You can find this control in the Data section of the Toolbox window. When you drop the `EntityDataSource` control, a smart tag menu appears. Click the Configure Data Source link, as shown in Figure 34-12.

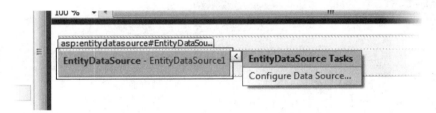

Figure 34-12. *Adding and configuring the data source*

The Configure Data Source dialog box will appear. Select the NorthwindEntities item from the Named Connection list, and ensure that the DefaultContainer name is set to NorthwindEntities as well, as shown by Figure 34-13.

Figure 34-13. *The Configure Data Source dialog box*

Click the Next button to move to the next configuration section. This is where we can select the classes that we want from the data model. We display the contents of the **Employees** table, so ensure that Employees is selected for the EntitySetName item and Employee is selected for the EntityTypeFilter item. Also ensure that the Select All option is selected in the main part of the dialog box and that the three options to enable automatic inserts, updates, and deletes are all selected, as shown in Figure 34-14.

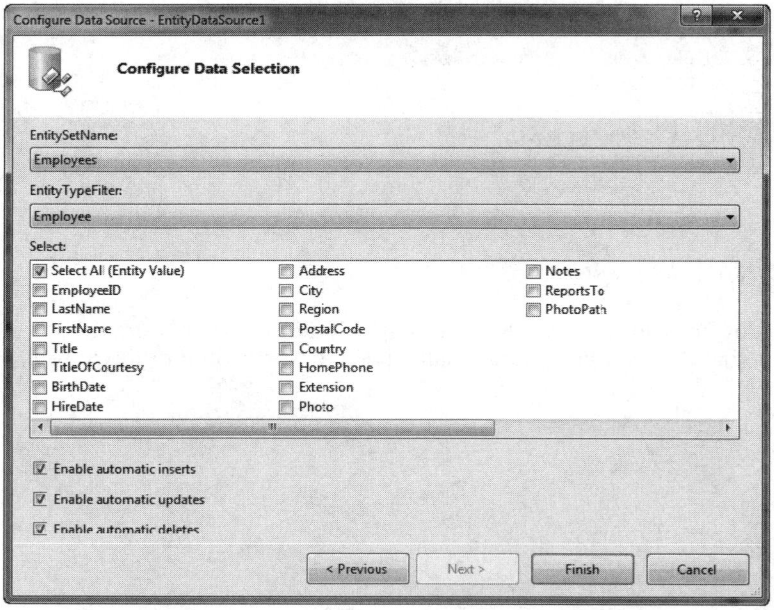

Figure 34-14. *Selecting the entity data model types*

Click the Finish button to dismiss the dialog box. If you have the split view open, you'll see that details are added to the tab that declares the `EntityDataSource` control, specifying the types we selected.

Adding the GridView Control

The last step is to add a control that will display the data being managed by the `EntityDataSource`. Drag a `GridView` control from the Toolbox window, and drop it onto the design surface. Click the Smart Tag arrow to open the pop-up GridView Tasks menu, as shown in Figure 34-15.

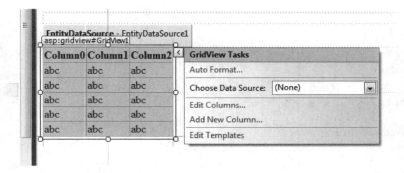

Figure 34-15. Configuring the `GridView`

Select EntityDataSource1 from the Choose Data Source drop-down list; this creates the relationship with the `EntityDataSource` control, which in turn is related to our data model. When you make the selection, columns will be added to the `DataGrid` for each of the properties of the `Employee` entity class.

From the GridView Tasks menu, select Edit Columns to open the Fields dialog box, which we can use to remove and reorder columns in the table view. Edit the columns so that they match those shown in Figure 34-16.

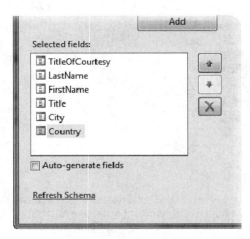

Figure 34-16. Editing the columns displayed in the `GridView` *control*

Click the OK button to close the Fields dialog box. Finally, select all the Enable options (Enable Paging, Enable Sorting, and so on), as shown in Figure 34-17. This changes the display from being static to allow the user to sort and edit the data.

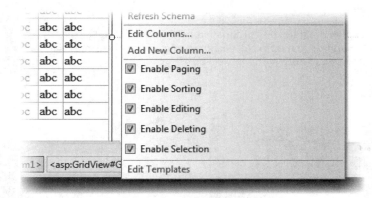

Figure 34-17. Enabling the GridView control features

Testing the Program

All that remains is to test the program. Select Start Without Debugging from the Visual Studio Debug menu, and our data-centric application will be displayed in your browser. If you have followed all the instructions, you should have something that looks similar to Figure 34-18.

	TitleOfCourtesy	**LastName**	**FirstName**	
Edit Delete Select	Ms.	Davolio	Nancy	S
Update Cancel	Dr.	Fuller	Andrew	[
Edit Delete Select	Ms.	Leverling	Janet	S
Edit Delete Select	Mrs.	Peacock	Margaret	S
Edit Delete Select	Mr.	Buchanan	Steven	S
Edit Delete Select	Mr.	Suyama	Michael	S
Edit Delete Select	Mr.	King	Robert	S
Edit Delete Select	Ms.	Callahan	Laura	I
Edit Delete Select	Ms.	Dodsworth	Anne	S

Figure 34-18. The Web Forms data application

The application we have produced is pretty crude. The layout is very basic, and the user interactions feel slightly dated, although this can be improved somewhat by using the formatting options available (click the DataGrid smart tag, and select AutoFormat to get an idea of what is available). Even though the result is basic, you can still page through content and select, edit, and delete records, which is not bad for a few moments of work.

Using ASP.NET Dynamic Data

If you got the impression that I sort of ran through the data binding for web forms rather quickly, well, you'd be right. Web forms can be used to build robust and reliable data-centric applications, but there is only so much space available in each chapter, and I wanted to get onto the topic of this section: ASP.NET Dynamic Data.

ASP.NET Dynamic Data lets you build data-centric web applications exceptionally quickly. It is a feature that doesn't get as much attention as it deserves, given that it can be used to deliver basic data applications with virtually no effort at all. In this section, you'll get to see just how quickly it can be done and just how little effort we need.

Creating the Project

As always, we need a new project. In this case, we need to use the ASP.NET Dynamic Data Entities Web Application template, as shown in Figure 34-19. There is another Dynamic Data project template, which you can use if you are working with LINQ to SQL, which is the predecessor to LINQ to Entities; see Chapter 30 for more details.

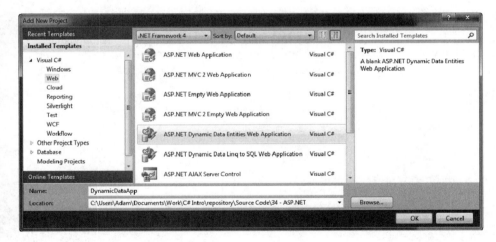

Figure 34-19. *Creating the ASP.NET Dynamic Data project*

The project is created with all sorts of files. These contain templates and logic for generating our program. In using ASP.NET Dynamic Data, we are taking advantage of a database user interface toolkit. We simply point the project at our data model, and it creates everything we need. We can customize the result, but we don't have to create the program itself.

Creating the Entity Data Model

Once again, we will use an Entity Framework data model as the bridge between our program and the database. To do this, follow the steps set out in the "Creating the Model" section of Chapter 30.

Registering the Data Model

The final step (yes, we are on the final step already) is to register the data model we created with the ASP.NET Dynamic Data system, which we do by editing the `Global.asax.cs` file and, in particular, this statement, which is commented out in a new project:

```
//DefaultModel.RegisterContext(typeof(YourDataContextType), new
ContextConfiguration() { ScaffoldAllTables = false });
```

You'll find this statement in the `RegisterRoutes` method. It comes at the end of the first block of comments. We need to make three changes: uncomment the statement, replace `YourDataContextType` with `NorthwindEntities`, and change the value of the `ScaffoldAllTables` property to `true`. The edited statement looks like this:

```
DefaultModel.RegisterContext(typeof(NorthwindEntities), new ContextConfiguration()
{ ScaffoldAllTables = true});
```

Testing the Program

That's all we need to do. We can see the result by selecting Start Without Debugging from the Visual Studio Debug menu. What you see in your browser should look similar to Figure 34-20.

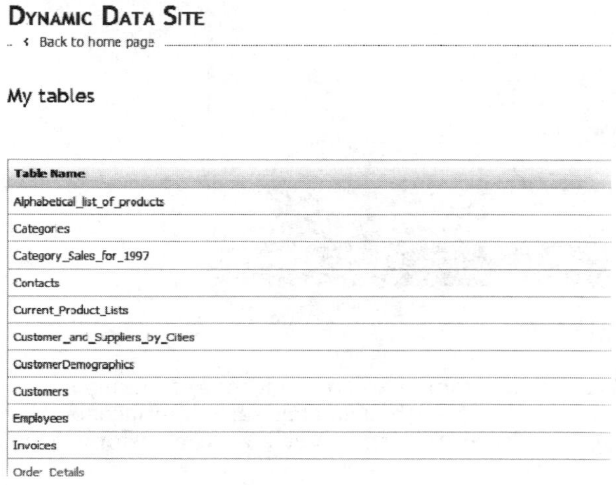

DYNAMIC DATA SITE
‹ Back to home page

My tables

Table Name
Alphabetical_list_of_products
Categories
Category_Sales_for_1997
Contacts
Current_Product_Lists
Customer_and_Suppliers_by_Cities
CustomerDemographics
Customers
Employees
Invoices
Order Details

Figure 34-20. The ASP.NET Dynamic Data application

We have a page that contains links for every table and view we created in the data model. If you click one of the links, the data it refers to will be displayed. Figure 34-21 illustrates the `Employees` table.

DYNAMIC DATA SITE
‹ Back to home page

Employees

Employee1 All

			LastName	FirstName	Title	TitleOfCourtesy	BirthDate	Hir
Edit	Delete	Details	Davolio	Nancy	Sales Representative	Ms.	08/12/1948 00:00:00	01/(
Fdit	Delete	Details	Fuller	Andrew	Vice President, Sales	Dr.	19/02/1952 00:00:00	14/(
Edit	Delete	Details	Leverling	Janet	Sales Representative	Ms.	30/08/1963 00:00:00	01/(
Edit	Delete	Details	Peacock	Margaret	Sales Representative	Mrs.	19/09/1937 00:00:00	03/(
Edit	Delete	Details	Buchanan	Steven	Sales Manager	Mr.	04/03/1955 00:00:00	17/
Edit	Delete	Details	Suyama	Michael	Sales Representative	Mr.	02/07/1963 00:00:00	17/
Edit	Delete	Details	King	Robert	Sales Representative	Mr.	29/05/1960 00:00:00	02/(
Edit	Delete	Details	Callahan	Laura	Inside Sales Coordinator	Ms.	09/01/1958 00:00:00	05/(
Edit	Delete	Details	Dodsworth	Anne	Sales Representative	Ms.	27/01/1966 00:00:00	15/

+ Insert new item

Figure 34-21. Displaying the Employees table

Notice the link at the bottom of the page to insert a new item and the Edit, Delete, and Details links in each of the table rows. The ASP.NET Dynamic Data system has created a framework not only for displaying our data but also for editing it as well. If you click an Edit link, you'll be presented with a page where you can change the value of the fields for the selected record, as shown in Figure 34-22.

DYNAMIC DATA SITE
‹ Back to home page

Edit entry from table Employees

LastName	Fuller
FirstName	Andrew
Title	Vice President, Sales
TitleOfCourtesy	Dr.
BirthDate	19/02/1952 00:00:00
HireDate	14/08/1992 00:00:00
Address	908 W. Capital Way

Figure 34-22. Editing a record using ASP.NET Dynamic Data

1115

Return to the Employees data page, and scroll to the right of the screen. You'll see that the ASP.NET Dynamic Data system has created links to other data views related to each record. For example, the Orders column contains a link that displays all the orders for a given employee. Click one of the View Orders links, and you'll see something similar to Figure 34-23.

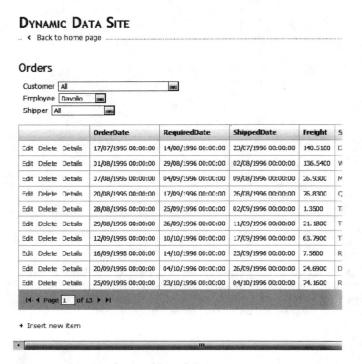

DYNAMIC DATA SITE

... ‹ Back to home page

Orders

Customer [All]
Employee [Davolio]
Shipper [All]

	OrderDate	RequiredDate	ShippedDate	Freight	S
Edit Delete Details	17/07/1996 00:00:00	14/08/1996 00:00:00	23/07/1996 00:00:00	140.5100	C
Edit Delete Details	01/08/1996 00:00:00	29/08/1996 00:00:00	02/08/1996 00:00:00	136.5400	W
Edit Delete Details	07/08/1996 00:00:00	04/09/1996 00:00:00	09/08/1996 00:00:00	26.9300	M
Edit Delete Details	20/08/1996 00:00:00	17/09/1996 00:00:00	26/08/1996 00:00:00	76.8300	C
Edit Delete Details	28/08/1996 00:00:00	25/09/1996 00:00:00	02/09/1996 00:00:00	1.3500	T
Edit Delete Details	29/08/1996 00:00:00	26/09/1996 00:00:00	11/09/1996 00:00:00	21.1800	T
Edit Delete Details	12/09/1996 00:00:00	10/10/1996 00:00:00	17/09/1996 00:00:00	63.7900	T
Edit Delete Details	16/09/1996 00:00:00	14/10/1996 00:00:00	23/09/1996 00:00:00	7.5600	R
Edit Delete Details	20/09/1996 00:00:00	04/10/1996 00:00:00	26/09/1996 00:00:00	24.6900	D
Edit Delete Details	25/09/1996 00:00:00	23/10/1996 00:00:00	04/10/1996 00:00:00	74.1600	R

I◄ ◄ Page [1] of 13 ► ►I

◆ Insert new item

Figure 34-23. Displaying filtered data

The data in Figure 34-23 is the set of orders associated with the employee Davolio, but look at the top of the page. The ASP.NET Dynamic Data system has included drop-down lists that we can use to filter the data in different ways, including seeing the data for other employees. Notice also that page controls are added when there are too many records to display in a single list. Figure 34-23 shows the first of 13 pages of Davolio orders, for example. And, of course, the links to insert or modify records are there as well.

From this example, I hope you will understand why I wanted to make room in this chapter for the ASP.NET Dynamic Data system. It is quick to use, it is well-designed, and it offers creates a comprehensively functional database application with minimal effort.

Customizing a Dynamic Data Application

Although I love the speed with which we were able to create our ASP.NET Dynamic Data application, I have to admit that it has a few rough edges. For example, all our tables and views are displayed, and we get all the columns from every table; neither of these is ideal. In this section, I'll show you how to address both of these issues and how to customize some other aspects of an ASP.NET Dynamic Data application.

Changing the Name of a Table

The ASP.NET Dynamic Data system uses the name of the table or view when it creates the home page for our application. That name is used again when we click the link to view the data. So, the Employees table is displayed using the name Employees. This can be a problem if the name that has been assigned to the table makes sense in the database but not when displayed to the user or when the name isn't especially user friendly, such as Order_Details.

Customizations to the way that ASP.NET Dynamic Data works with the data model are applied using a metadata file. This is a C# code file that has classes annotated with attributes that the Dynamic Data system looks for when it creates its views.

To add a metadata file, simply right-click your project in the Solution Explorer, and select Add ➤ New Item from the pop-up menu. Select Code File from the list of templates, and give your file a name. You can use any name that appeals to you, and I have called my file MetaData.cs. Open the code file, and edit the contents so that they match Listing 34-2.

Listing 34-2. Creating the Metadata File

```
using System.ComponentModel;
using System.ComponentModel.DataAnnotations;

namespace DynamicDataApp {

    [DisplayName("Sales Staff")]
    public class EmployeeMetaData {
    }

    [MetadataType(typeof(EmployeeMetaData))]
    public partial class Employee {
    }
}
```

ASP.NET Dynamic Data metadata classes work using partial classes, which we covered in Chapter 6. For this reason, it is essential that the namespace in your metadata file matches the namespace in your data model. If you are doubt, expand the .edmx entry in the Solution Explorer, right-click the .Designer.cs file, select View Code, and copy the namespace statement. The attributes we need are in the System.ComponentModel and System.ComponentModel.DataAnnotations namespaces. I find it simpler to import these namespaces with using statements, as shown in Listing 34-2.

We must create a class that we want to use to apply metadata to a table or view and then apply attributes to it. Here is the class that I have defined to use with the Employee table in Listing 34-2:

```
[DisplayName("Sales Staff")]
public class EmployeeMetaData {
}
```

The convention is to give the class a name that combines the name of the table or view and the term MetaData. I have called my class EmployeeMetaData.

When the `DisplayName` attribute is applied to the metadata class for a table, it specifies the name that will be used to display it. The argument to the attribute provides the name to use—`Sales Staff`, in this example.

The final step is to tell the ASP.NET Dynamic Data system that our `EmployeeMetaData` class should be used as a source of metadata for the `Employee` table. We do this by using a partial class, as follows:

```
[MetadataType(typeof(EmployeeMetaData))]
public partial class Employee {
}
```

We create a partial class that matches the Entity Data Model class that is associated with the table and then apply the `MetadataType` attribute, passing the type of our metadata class (using `typeof(EmployessMetaData)` in this case) as a parameter.

If you run the application, you will see that the `Employees` entry has been replaced by a `Sales Staff` entry on the home page, as illustrated by Figure 34-24.

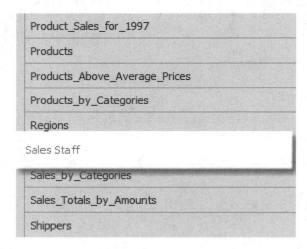

Figure 34-24. Renaming a table

The new name is applied throughout the application. If you click the Sales Staff link on the home page, you'll see that the title for the detailed page and the data filter have also been updated. The change is even applied to associated data. Look at the details for the `Orders` table, and you will see that the column of links to `Employee` records has also been renamed, as shown in Figure 34-25.

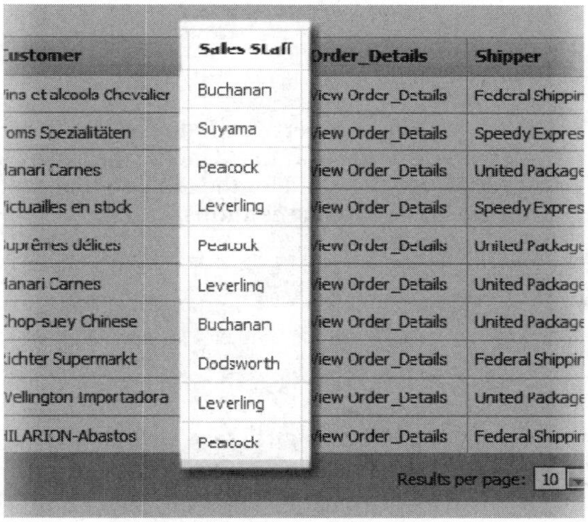

Figure 34-25. *Renamed foreign-key relationships*

Changing the Name and Visibility of a Column

We can use the metadata technique to rename or hide individual columns in a table. By default, the ASP.NET Dynamic Data system displays all the columns in a table and uses the names that are obtained from the data model. For the `Employees` data, this means that we see unfriendly column names such as `LastName` and columns we might not want displayed, such as `BirthDate`. To change the settings for a column, we create a property in our metadata class and apply attributes, as shown in Listing 34-3.

Listing 34-3. Hiding and Renaming Columns

```
using System.ComponentModel;
using System.ComponentModel.DataAnnotations;

namespace DynamicDataApp {

    [DisplayName("Sales Staff")]
    public class EmployeeMetaData {

        [ScaffoldColumn(false)]
        public object BirthDate { get; set; }

        [DisplayName("First Name")]
        public object FirstName { get; set; }

        [DisplayName("Last Name")]
        public object LastName { get; set; }
    }

    [MetadataType(typeof(EmployeeMetaData))]
```

```
        public partial class Employee {
        }
}
```

The ASP.NET Dynamic Data system only looks for the name of the property, so it doesn't matter what type the property has. I have used `object` as the property type in my example. Once you have a property, you can apply attributes. We use the `DisplayName` attribute as we did for the table so that the following changes the names that will be used for the `FirstName` and `LastName` columns:

```
[DisplayName("First Name")]
public object FirstName { get; set; }

[DisplayName("Last Name")]
public object LastName { get; set; }
```

You can hide a column by using the `ScaffoldColumn` attribute and passing `false` as the parameter, like this statement, which hides the `BirthDate` column:

```
[ScaffoldColumn(false)]
public object BirthDate { get; set; }
```

If you update your metadata file to match Listing 34-3 and then build and run the project, the display for the `Sales Staff` table will change to reflect these changes, as illustrated by Figure 34-26.

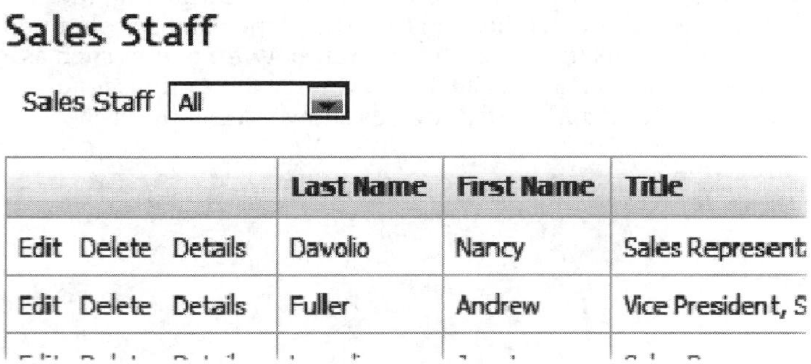

Sales Staff

Sales Staff [All ▼]

			Last Name	First Name	Title
Edit	Delete	Details	Davolio	Nancy	Sales Represent
Edit	Delete	Details	Fuller	Andrew	Vice President, S

Figure 34-26. Changing the name and visibility of columns

Selecting Tables to Be Displayed

When we created the original example, we edited a statement in the `Global.asax.cs` file, as follows:

```
DefaultModel.RegisterContext(typeof(NorthwindEntities), new ContextConfiguration()
{ ScaffoldAllTables = true});
```

The last part of this statement, where we set the value of the `ScaffoldAllTables` property to `true`, tells the Dynamic Data system that we want all the tables that are referenced by our data model to be included in our application.

If we want to be more restrictive, we can rely on our metadata file to specify which tables should be included. To do this, we need to change the property in the Global.asax.cs file like this:

```
DefaultModel.RegisterContext(typeof(NorthwindEntities), new ContextConfiguration()
{ ScaffoldAllTables = false});
```

To specify a table should be included, we use the ScaffoldTable attribute, as shown in Listing 34-4.

Listing 34-4. Including a Table with the ScaffoldTable Attribute

```
using System.ComponentModel;
using System.ComponentModel.DataAnnotations;

namespace DynamicDataApp {

    [DisplayName("Sales Staff")]
    [ScaffoldTable(true)]
    public class EmployeeMetaData {

        [ScaffoldColumn(false)]
        public object BirthDate { get; set; }

        [DisplayName("First Name")]
        public object FirstName { get; set; }

        [DisplayName("Last Name")]
        public object LastName { get; set; }
    }

    [ScaffoldTable(true)]
    public class OrderMetaData {
    }

    [MetadataType(typeof(EmployeeMetaData))]
    public partial class Employee {
    }

    [MetadataType(typeof(OrderMetaData))]
    public partial class Order {
    }
}
```

The ScaffoldTable attribute takes a single bool parameter, which must be true for the table to be included in the application. In Listing 34-4, I have applied this attribute to the existing EmployeeMetaData class and created and registered a new metadata class for the Orders table. If we compile and run the application now, we will see that only these tables have been included, as shown by Figure 34-27.

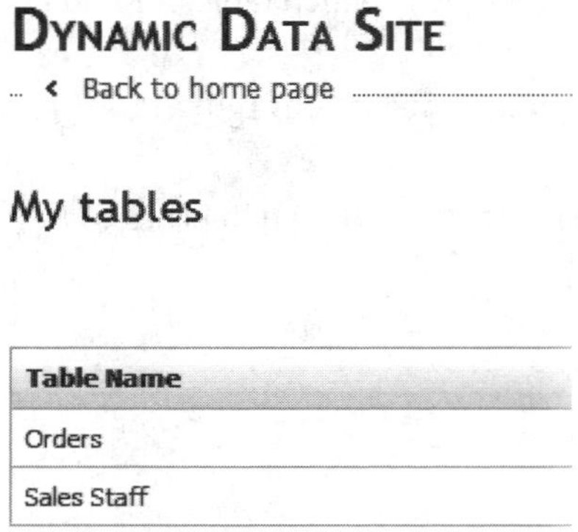

DYNAMIC DATA SITE

... ‹ Back to home page ....

My tables

Table Name
Orders
Sales Staff

Figure 34-27. The restricted set of tables

Customizing the Display Template

The appearance of an ASP.NET Dynamic Data application is controlled by a series of templates. The template for the application home page is `Default.aspx`, and it is at the top level of the Visual Studio project. The templates for the screens for listing the contents of a table, editing a record, and so on, are in the `DynamicData\PageTemplates` folder. The name of the template tells you what the templates are used for: `Details.aspx`, `Edit.aspx`, and so on. In this section, we'll make a couple of template changes just to give you an idea of how it is done.

First, we'll change the name of the application itself. It defaults to `Dynamic Data Site`, as you can see in Figure 34-27. This name is used on all the pages and is taken from a master template file called `Site.master`, changes to which affect all pages in the application. To edit this file, right-click `Site.master` in the Solution Explorer, and select View Designer from the pop-up menu. This will open a standard ASP.NET design surface so that you can make changes. I have edited the title at the top of the page to **Northwind Data**, as shown in Figure 34-28.

|h1.DDMainHeader|

NORTHWIND DATA

‹ Back to home page

ScriptManager - ScriptManager1	

Figure 34-28. Editing the master template

The second change we'll make is in the `Default.aspx` file, changing the default My Tables title into something more apt for our example. Right-click the item in the Solution Explorer, select View Designer from the pop-up menu, and change My Tables to **Staff & Orders Tables**, as shown by Figure 34-29.

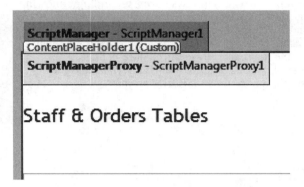

Figure 34-29. Editing the home page template

We can see the effect of these changes when we run the application. Select Start Without Debugging from the Visual Studio Debug menu, and you will see something similar to the application shown in Figure 34-30.

NORTHWIND DATA

⟨ Back to home page ···

Staff & Orders Tables

Table Name
Orders
Sales Staff

Figure 34-30. Customizing the ASP.NET Dynamic Data application

Between the metadata classes and the templates, you can customize most aspects of an ASP.NET Dynamic Data application, meaning that you get the speed of rapid creation combined with the flexibility of being able to tailor almost every aspect of your application's appearance and operation.

Summary

In this chapter, we looked at two of the user interface components from the ASP.NET suite of technologies. The first, Web Forms, follows a similar model to the Windows Forms technology, allowing you build web applications by using controls, configuring them using properties, and responding to their operation using events. Web Forms is a very mature technology with a very wide adoption, especially in corporate intranet environments. We also looked at ASP.NET Dynamic Data, a relatively new addition to ASP.NET that makes it quick and simple to create fully featured data-centric applications. Web Forms can be used to create data applications, but the ASP.NET Dynamic Data feature is, to my mind, a simpler and more elegant approach for most ASP.NET projects.

■ ■ ■

Silverlight

Silverlight is Microsoft's answer to Adobe Flash. A reduced .NET implementation is installed on the user's machine and is used to deliver .NET content contained within web pages. Silverlight supports the mainstream browsers, such as IE, Chrome, Safari, and Firefox and works on Windows and Mac OS X machines.

To a C# programmer, the attraction of Silverlight is that it is based on .NET. The Silverlight runtime doesn't have all the features of the .NET Framework, but it does have many of the core features that programmers rely on every day, including LINQ to Objects, LINQ to XML, the collection classes, generic classes, and more. There is a heavy emphasis on handling media and glossy user interactions. Silverlight user interfaces are based on Windows Presentation Foundation (WPF), and network communications can be performed using Windows Communication Foundation (WCF). There are fewer namespaces available in Silverlight, and some classes have fewer members, but with a few exceptions, you can use most of the knowledge you have gained from this book in Silverlight.

It isn't all good news, though. Silverlight doesn't have the penetration of Flash. At the time of this writing, the latest estimates are that Silverlight is installed on roughly 50 percent of Internet clients, as opposed to the 99 percent of clients that have installed Flash. A 50 percent penetration rate is pretty good, but it means you have to consider your target audience when using Silverlight, and, in particular, you have to take into account how motivated the user is to get your service and how much influence the user has over their environment. Your ideal audience is highly motivated to use your service and able to install Silverlight if they don't have it. You are likely to have low user adoption if you target a different audience. In particular, be wary of targeting large corporate users (who in general are not allowed to install new software) and casual audiences (who generally can't be bothered to install new software).

I like Silverlight. In particular, I like the way you can use the C# and .NET building blocks to create highly interactive web clients in much the same way that you would build a regular Windows/WPF program. As we go through this chapter, you will see just how similar the development process is and how integration with other .NET features, such as WCF, can ease the development burden even further. Flash may be dominant, but if you have invested time, effort, and money on C# and .NET, Silverlight is worthy of serious consideration for your projects.

■ **Note** You must install the Silverlight 4 Tools for Visual Studio 2010 before you can follow the examples in this chapter. See Chapter 2 for details.

Creating the Swimming Calculator

Silverlight user interfaces are based on a cut-down version of WPF, which excludes some controls and restricts some advanced features such as complex event handling. The Silverlight 4 Tools for Visual Studio 2010 package adds some new controls, so in the main, you have access to most of the functionality of WPF, and you will find that you can easily create Silverlight interfaces using a basic knowledge of WPF. In this section, we'll quickly create the same swimming calculator example we used in the previous chapter. This will let us see some of the differences in the XAML code that Silverlight generates and understand how Silverlight is contained inside a web page.

Creating the Project

Create a new project using the Silverlight Application template, which you will find in the Silverlight category, as shown in Figure 35-1.

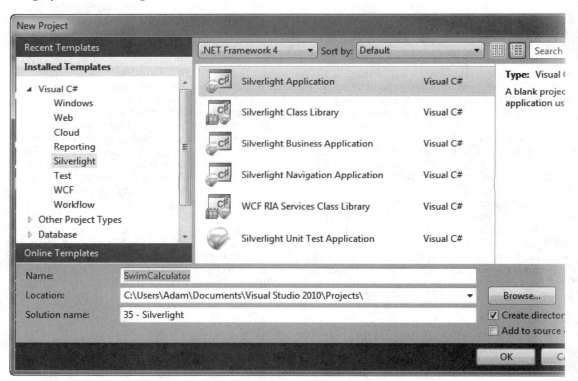

Figure 35-1. *Creating the Silverlight project*

Set the name of the project to **SwimCalculator**, and click the OK button. A second dialog box will appear, as shown in Figure 35-2.

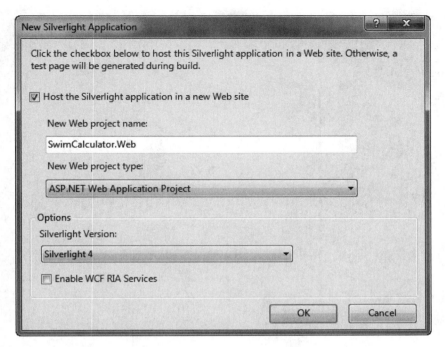

Figure 35-2. The New Silverlight Application dialog box

The New Silverlight Application dialog box allows you to specify how the Silverlight project will be created. Ensure that the "Hosting the Silverlight application in a new Web site" check box is selected. This will create an ASP.NET project that will contain a web page that in turn contains our Silverlight project. You can other web pages, which can contain static HTML, Web Forms, or other Silverlight applications. If you don't select this box, then a web page will be generated dynamically each time you test your application.

The next two controls on the dialog box let you set the name and the type of the project. The default name is the name of the Silverlight project with `.Web` appended. We are only going to build a simple application, so we don't care about the details of the web project type. This would be more interesting if we were building a more complex project, in which case we could select between different default configurations.

The remaining controls allow you to target a specific version of Silverlight (we will be using Silverlight 4, which is the latest release at the time of writing) and to enable WCF services; leave this last option unchecked. We will return to using WCF and Silverlight in the "Using a WCF RIA Service" section later in the chapter.

Click OK to create the projects. You'll see something similar to the pair of projects shown in Figure 35-3. The SwimCalculator project is where we will develop our Silverlight application. The `MainPage.xaml` file will contain our XAML layout, and the `MainPage.xaml.cs` code-behind file will contain our program logic. This is similar to the project layout we saw when using WPF.

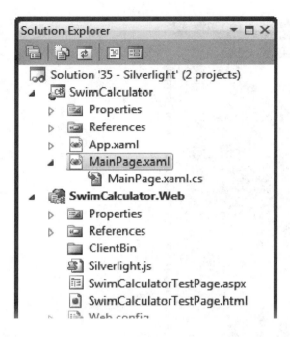

Figure 35-3. *The paired Silverlight projects*

The SwimCalculator.Web project is an ASP.NET web site. When you compile the SwimCalculator project, the output is copied into the ClientBin folder of the SwimCalculator.Web project. If you open the SwimCalculatorTestPage.aspx file, you will see that it contains an object tag that loads your Silverlight application. You can add other items to this file, such as Web Forms controls, and they will be processed by the ASP.NET development server and displayed in the browser when you run your application. Silverlight can run independently of ASP.NET. This is demonstrated by the SwimCalculatorTestPage.html file, which contains only JavaScript and HTML.

Defining the Layout

To make things a little different from the WPF example, we will use some of the rich layout controls that are available. The WPF/Silverlight layout controls are flexible enough that you can achieve the same layout using several different arrangements of layouts and configurations. As you become more experienced with laying out controls, you'll find that you settle on a general approach that you will reuse, relying on some controls heavily and excluding others from your repertoire entirely. In the following sections, we'll use two of my favorites: the Grid and StackPanel controls.

Adding Grid Columns

When we create a Silverlight or WPF program, the design surface contains a Grid control by default. This control lets you divide up the design surface into regions, into which you can place other controls. To create a region, click the design surface to select the Grid control, and then move your mouse over the blue borders that appear on the top and left sides of the control. You'll see either a vertical (if you are moving over the top border) or horizontal line (if you are moving over the left border). If you click, the line that was shown divides the Grid, creating rows and columns. Create three lines to form four columns, as shown in Figure 35-4.

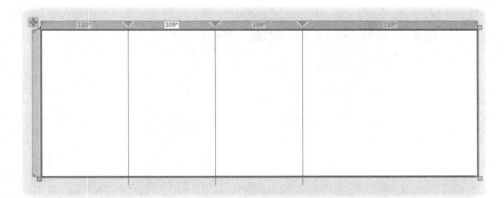

Figure 35-4. Creating columns in the Grid control

You will see a number at the top of each column that you created. The asterisk (*) that follows each number tells you that this is a relative width. If you place your mouse over the number, you will see a small menu appear, as shown in Figure 35-5. This menu allows you to change the mode.

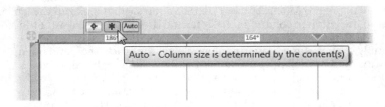

Figure 35-5. Setting the size mode for a column

The first icon, like crosshairs, fixes the column width to a specific number of pixels. The Auto icon sets the width of the column to be large enough to accommodate the contents of the column. The relative mode, which we will use, lets you allocate the width of the column as a ratio. You can change the width by dragging the column divider in the design surface, but it is easier (and more accurate) to simply edit the XAML. If you look at the XML for the Grid control, you will see that it contains some ColumnDefinition elements, like this:

```
<Grid x:Name="LayoutRoot" Background="White">
    <Grid.ColumnDefinitions>
        <ColumnDefinition Width="110*" />
        <ColumnDefinition Width="109*" />
        <ColumnDefinition Width="109*" />
        <ColumnDefinition Width="219*" />
    </Grid.ColumnDefinitions>
</Grid>
```

We are going to allocate the widths so that the first three columns each accounts for 20 percent of the design surface and the middle column accounts for the remaining 40 percent. I like to express my ratios as percentages, so I have edited my XML as follows:

```
<Grid x:Name="LayoutRoot" Background="White">
    <Grid.ColumnDefinitions>
        <ColumnDefinition Width="20*" />
        <ColumnDefinition Width="20*" />
        <ColumnDefinition Width="20*" />
        <ColumnDefinition Width="40*" />
    </Grid.ColumnDefinitions>
</Grid>
```

Be careful to leave the asterisks in place when you edit the width values. If you remove one of these, the column width will be interpreted as a fixed number rather than a ratio.

Adding the StackPanel Controls

A StackPanel is a simple layout control that organizes controls into vertical or horizontal stacks; that is, the controls are placed one after the other in order. We are going to use vertical StackPanel controls in the first two columns of our Grid control to organize the Label and TextBox controls that make up the left side of the display. Drag a StackPanel to the leftmost column in the Grid, and drop it there. We want the StackPanel to fill the column entirely and to resize as the column resizes. We could do this using the design surface, but it is quicker to simply change some property values. Select the StackPanel, and open the Layout section of the Properties window. For each property in the Layout section, right-click the black diamond, and select "Reset value" from the pop-up menu. The Width and Height properties will reset to Auto, and the HorizontalAlignment and VerticalAlignment properties will reset to Stretch, making sure that the StackPanel will fill the Grid column in which it resides and resize when the column resizes. The Margin property defines how much space there is around a control. We don't want any margin at all, so resetting it to zero removes any border around the StackPanel. The Grid.ColumnSpan property defines how many columns in the Grid the StackPanel covers. We want it to fill only one column, so resetting it completes our layout of this first StackPanel. When you have reset the values, you should see something very similar to Figure 35-6 on your design surface.

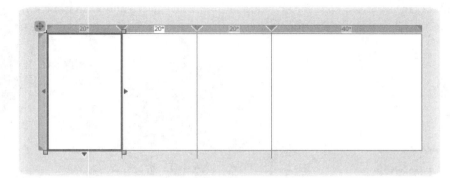

Figure 35-6. *Adding the first* StackPanel *control*

Repeat this process to add a StackPanel to the second Grid column, but be careful not to reset the Grid.Column property, which specifies which column the control is assigned to. If you reset this value, you will end up with two StackPanel controls in the first column and none at all in the second.

Adding the TextBox Controls

We are going to add four TextBox controls to the StackPanel in the second column of the Grid control. Simply drag a TextBox from the Toolbox and drop it onto the second column, and it will be added to the StackPanel. Repeat this process until you have four TextBox controls in a vertical stack, as shown in Figure 35-7.

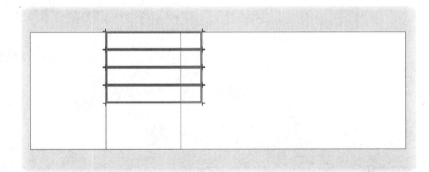

Figure 35-7. *Adding the* TextBox *controls*

You can see that the default width of the TextBox controls is greater than our column, so select all four TextBox control and clear the Width property value (or manually change it to Auto). We want them to be slightly taller than the default, so change the Height property to be 28. We also want them to be spaced out slightly, so change the Margin property so that there is a 10-pixel margin at the top of each control. To do this, select all four TextBox controls, and click the down arrow in the Margin property value box. This will display the Margin editor, which is shown in Figure 35-8. You can see how each value will affect the margin given to the selected control or controls.

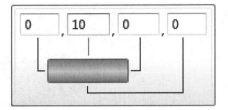

Figure 35-8. *Editing the Margin property*

The remaining configuration is similar to the steps we have taken in the previous chapters. Change the names given to the controls so that they are minutesTextBox, lapsTextBox, lengthTextBox, and caloriesTextBox in order from top to bottom; set the Text properties to 0, 0, 20, and 1070; and right-align the text in the controls. When you have finished, your design surface should look like the one in Figure 35-9.

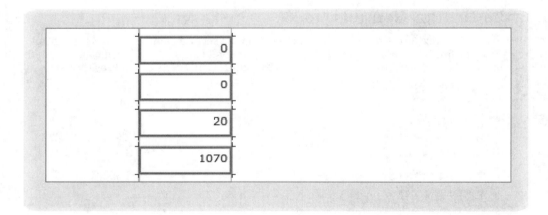

Figure 35-9. *The configured TextBox controls*

Adding the Label Controls

Adding the Label controls is very similar to the process we used for adding the TextBox controls. Drag four Label controls from the Toolbox to the first column in the Grid. Select all four Label controls, and change the properties to the values shown in Table 35-1.

Table 35-1. Property Changes for the Label Controls

Property	Value
Width	Auto
Height	28
Margin	0, 10, 5, 0
HorizontalContentAlignment	Right

Changing the HorizontalContentAlignment property right-aligns the text in the Label controls. Change the Content property for each control in sequence to Minutes:, Laps:, Length (m):, and Cals/hr:. When you have finished configuring the controls, your design surface should look like Figure 35-10.

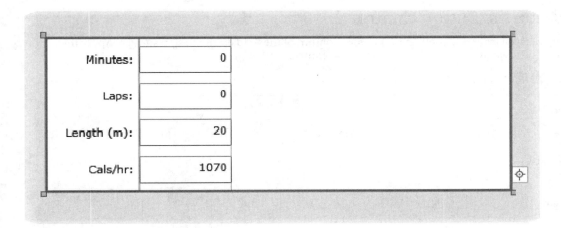

Figure 35-10. The configured Label controls

Adding the TextBlock Control

You can see the pattern emerging now. Having created the super-structure for our layout using the Grid and StackPanel controls, we can now drag them from the Toolbox and format them, where formatting largely means resetting property values so that a control adheres to the geometry of its parent Grid column or StackPanel. The TextBlock is no different. Once you have dragged the control to the rightmost column in the Grid, change the properties shown in Table 35-2.

Table 35-2. Property Changes for the TextBlock Control

Property	Value
Text	<Empty>
Width Height	Auto
HorizontalAlignment VerticalAlignment	Stretch
Margin	10, 10, 10, 10
NameName	resultsTextBlock

Adding the Button Control

Drag a Button from the Toolbox to the third column of the Grid on the design surface. Apply the property changes shown in Table 35-3 to configure the control.

Table 35-3. Property Changes for the Button Control

Property	Value
Name	convertButton
Context	>
Width Height	Auto
HorizontalAlignment VerticalAlignment	Stretch
Margin	10, 10, 10, 10
Grid.ColumnSpan	1
Text	Size 26

When you have made the property changes, your design surface should look like the one in Figure 35-11.

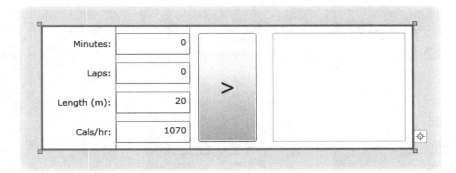

Figure 35-11. The configured Button control

Adjusting the Layout

You can see in the previous section how we can use layout controls as an alternative to absolute positioning. Although positioning controls yourself is the easiest approach for simple projects, you'll find that layout controls become increasingly important to you as you build increasingly complex projects.

There are two advantages to using layouts. The first is that when the size of your Silverlight or WPF program changes (because the user resizes a window, for example), the layouts can be used to ensure that your controls are resized in a sensible way. If a Grid column is set to take 20 percent of the space available to the Grid control and the controls in the column are set to Stretch with the control, then you can rely on the controls to resize nicely together.

The second advantage, which is more apt to our goals in this chapter, is that it makes it easier to correct a layout if you make mistakes or need to make adjustments. The layout shown in Figure 35-11 is perfectly serviceable, but there are some minor imperfections that we might like to correct. First, notice that the space between the Button and the TextBlock is twice the width of the space between the TextBox controls. This has arisen because there is no margin around the TextBox controls, but there is a 10-pixel margin around both the Button and the TextBlock. There are many different ways that we could correct this, but a neat trick is to change the StackPanel that holds the TextBox controls. Select the StackPanel (this is most easily done using the Document Outline window, which we saw in Chapter 33), and change the Margin property so that there is a 10-pixel border on the right side of the control. You'll see that the four TextBoxes snap to their new size.

A second imperfection is that there is a little too much blank space to the left of the Label controls. I thought that they'd require 20 percent of the available space, but it seems that was an over-estimation. We can fix this by changing the ration of the space allocated to the first column in the Grid. Select the Grid control and edit the XAML so that the first column allocation is smaller, say 17* instead of 20*. You'll see all the controls respond, preserving the layout. When you have made your changes, your design surface should look like Figure 35-12.

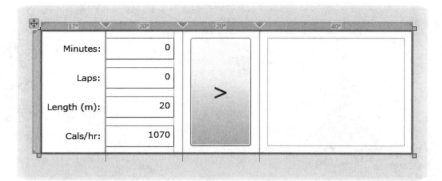

Figure 35-12. The adjusted layout

Using layout controls lets you organize regular controls relative to one another, and this tends to give greater flexibility for change. For a simple project like our example, absolute and relative layouts end up working out pretty much the same, but when you have a complex interface, you'll find that the flexibility inherent in relative layouts can save you a lot of time when you need to make changes or corrections.

Wiring the Button

The only control we need to wire in our Silverlight application is the Button. We don't have Menu or StatusBar controls in Silverlight the way that we do in WPF. To wire the Button, double-click the control in the design surface to generate the handler method for the Click event, and update the code-behind file to match Listing 35-1, which contains the same set of calculations that we have used in each chapter of this part of the book.

Listing 35-1. Handing the Button Click Event

```
using System.Text;
using System.Windows;
using System.Windows.Controls;

namespace SwimCalculator {
    public partial class MainPage : UserControl {
        public MainPage() {
            InitializeComponent();
        }

        private void convertButton_Click(object sender, RoutedEventArgs e) {
            // extract the values from the controls
            int minutesCompleted = int.Parse(minutesTextBox.Text);
            int lapsCompleted = int.Parse(lapsTextBox.Text);
            int lapLength = int.Parse(lengthTextBox.Text);
            int caloriesPerHour = int.Parse(caloriesTextBox.Text);
```

```
            // ensure that we have values that are greater than zero
            if (minutesCompleted <= 0 || lapsCompleted <= 0 ||
                lapLength <= 0 || caloriesPerHour <= 0) {

                // we cannot proceed - we have one or more bad values
                return;
            }

            // perform the calculations we need for the results
            float distance = (lapsCompleted * lapLength) * 0.00062137119223733f;
            float caloriesBurned = (minutesCompleted / 60f) * caloriesPerHour;
            float pace = (minutesCompleted * 60) / lapsCompleted;

            StringBuilder resultBuilder = new StringBuilder();
            resultBuilder.AppendFormat("Distance completed: {0:F2} miles\n", distance);
            resultBuilder.AppendFormat("Calories burned: {0:F0} calories\n",
                caloriesBurned);
            resultBuilder.AppendFormat("Average pace: {0:F0} seconds/lap", pace);

            // compose and set the results
            resultsTextBlock.Text = resultBuilder.ToString();
        }
    }
}
```

Adding a Child Window

If you select Start Without Debugging from the Visual Studio Debug menu, you can see that we have a working Silverlight application, as shown in Figure 35-13.

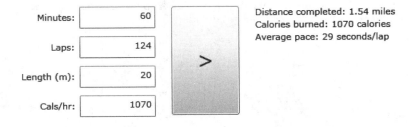

Figure 35-13. *The working Silverlight application*

We don't have any way to tell the user if they provide a value that we can't process. We don't have a StatusBar control as we did for the WPF version of this program, for example. We could use the TextBlock to display errors as well as results, but a more elegant solution is to add a pop-up dialog box to our Silverlight application, which is what we will do in this section.

Start by right-clicking the Silverlight project in the Solution Explorer (the one called SwimCalculator if you followed my example), and select Add ➤ New Item from the pop-up menu. Select the Silverlight Child Window template, and give the item the name ErrorWindow.xaml, as shown in Figure 35-14.

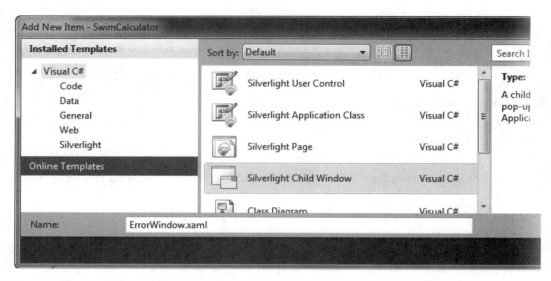

Figure 35-14. *Creating a child window item*

The Child Window template is a preconfigured pop-up window for Silverlight. It has an OK button and a Cancel button by default. We want to display a message, so we are going to remove the Cancel button and add a TextBlock to contain the error description. I am not going to walk through the steps to do this. You have seen enough layout examples to be able to do this yourself, and it doesn't matter if you end up with a slightly different result to mine. However, make sure you set the name of your TextBlock control to be errorMessageTextBlock. My design surface is shown in Figure 35-15.

Figure 35-15. *The edited child window design surface*

We don't need to change the code-behind file for the child window. The OK button is already wired and dismisses the dialog box for us. We can now edit our program logic to display an error message if we can't process the values in the TextBox controls. Listing 35-2 shows the modified `MainPage.xaml.cs` file.

Listing 35-2. Adding Support for the Child Window

```
using System.Text;
using System.Windows;
using System.Windows.Controls;

namespace SwimCalculator {
    public partial class MainPage : UserControl {
        public MainPage() {
            InitializeComponent();
        }

        private void convertButton_Click(object sender, RoutedEventArgs e) {
            // extract the values from the controls
            int minutesCompleted = int.Parse(minutesTextBox.Text);
            int lapsCompleted = int.Parse(lapsTextBox.Text);
            int lapLength = int.Parse(lengthTextBox.Text);
            int caloriesPerHour = int.Parse(caloriesTextBox.Text);

            // ensure that we have values that are greater than zero
            if (minutesCompleted <= 0 || lapsCompleted <= 0 ||
                lapLength <= 0 || caloriesPerHour <= 0) {

                // we cannot proceed - we have one or more bad values
                ErrorWindow myErrorWindow = new ErrorWindow();
                myErrorWindow.errorMessageTextBlock.Text
                    = "Cannot calculate - use values greater than zero";
                myErrorWindow.Show();
                return;
            }

            // perform the calculations we need for the results
            float distance = (lapsCompleted * lapLength) * 0.00062137119223733f;
            float caloriesBurned = (minutesCompleted / 60f) * caloriesPerHour;
            float pace = (minutesCompleted * 60) / lapsCompleted;

            StringBuilder resultBuilder = new StringBuilder();
            resultBuilder.AppendFormat("Distance completed: {0:F2} miles\n", distance);
            resultBuilder.AppendFormat("Calories burned: {0:F0} calories\n",
                caloriesBurned);
            resultBuilder.AppendFormat("Average pace: {0:F0} seconds/lap", pace);

            // compose and set the results
            resultsTextBlock.Text = resultBuilder.ToString();
        }
    }
}
```

The changes are shown in bold. First, I create a new object of the child windows type. This is ErrorWindow, taken from the name we gave the item when we added it to the project:

```
ErrorWindow myErrorWindow = new ErrorWindow();
```

Next, we set the Text property of the TextBlock control in the child window. You could add a method to the ErrorWindow class to handle this or simply access the TextBlock control as a field of the ErrorWindow object, like this:

```
myErrorWindow.errorMessageTextBlock.Text
    = "Cannot calculate - use values greater than zero";
```

Finally, we show the child window by calling the Show method:

```
myErrorWindow.Show();
```

Notice that I have left the return statement in the code so that the convertButton_Click method returns after I have displayed the child window. Silverlight has no notion that I am using the child window to display an error, and if I did not return from the method, I'd get an exception when the zero value was used in the subsequent code statements. If we compile and run our project and then enter a zero value into one of the fields, we see the dialog box shown in Figure 35-16.

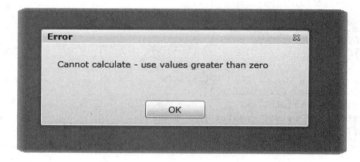

Figure 35-16. *Displaying the child window*

The dialog box disappears when the user clicks the OK button, leaving the user free to try another set of values.

Using a WCF RIA Service

The WCF RIA Rich Internet Applications (RIA) Services feature lets you easily build distributed services that are consumed by Silverlight clients. You could build and manage WCF services directly, as we did in Chapter 21, but taking advantage of the WCF RIA services makes things much easier and is the simplest way of working with databases in Silverlight. In this section, I'll show you how to create a simple Silverlight application that uses a WCF RIA service to read data from the Northwind sample database.

Creating the Project

Create a new project using the Silverlight Application template. Give the project the name **DataApp**, and when the New Silverlight Application dialog box appears, ensure that the Enable ECF RIA Services option is selected, as shown in Figure 35-17.

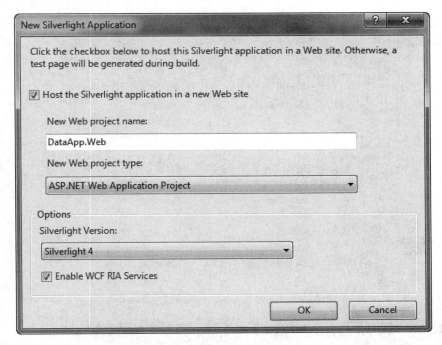

Figure 35-17. Enabling WCF RIA services

Click OK to create the project. As with the previous example, you will have created a Silverlight project and an ASP.NET web site project.

Creating the Data Model

We are going to create an Entity Framework data model on the server side of our project by adding it to the web site project (DataApp.Web if you used the default name). Right-click the DataApp.Web project in the Solution Explorer window, and select Add ➤ New Item from the pop-up menu. Select the ADO.NET Entity Data Model template from the list, and follow the instructions for creating the data model in Chapter 30.

Creating the Domain Service Class

A domain service is an advanced WCF feature that makes application business logic available to a WCF client. We are going to add a domain service class to our project so that our Silverlight client can read the data from the Northwind database. Add a new item to the DataApp.Web project using the Domain Service Class template (you'll find it in the Web template section), using the name EmployeeDomainService.cs, as shown in Figure 35-18.

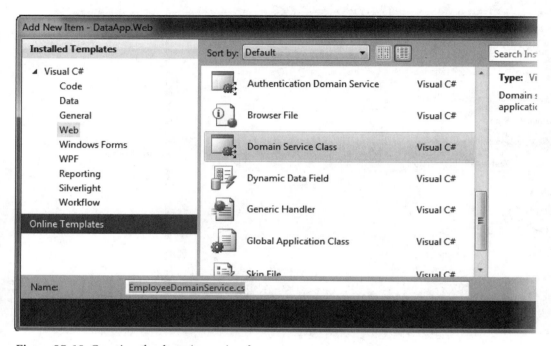

Figure 35-18. *Creating the domain service class*

When you click the OK button, you will be presented with the Add New Domain Service Class dialog box. This is how we pick the entity classes from our data model that will be included in our RIA service. We are going to work with the Employees and Orders tables, so we need to select the corresponding entity types—Employee and Order.

Figure 35-19. *The Add New Domain Service Class dialog box*

■ **Tip** If the dialog box in Figure 35-19 doesn't contain any entity types when you create your class, the most likely cause is that you have not compiled your project since creating the entity domain model. Select Build Solution from the Visual Studio Build menu, and try adding the domain service class again.

If you just select the boxes to the left of the entity types, then the RIA service will be created with methods that let your Silverlight class get the data from the underlying tables. If you select the Enable Editing option, you'll also get methods to insert, update, and delete objects from the data model as well. Select the Enable Editing options for the Employee and Order items, as shown in Figure 35-19, and then click OK to dismiss the dialog box.

You will two new files in your project. The first is EmployeeDomainService.cs, and the other is EmployeeDomainService.metadata.cs. The first contains the methods that your Silverlight application will use to access the RIA service, and the second is where you add attributes to restrict the range of field values when new entity objects are created by the client. We are not going to look at the metadata in this chapter, but it works in a similar manner to the same feature in the ASP.NET Dynamic Data system, which we saw in Chapter 34.

If you open EmployeeDomainService.cs, you will see the methods that have been generated for us. For both of the entity types we selected, there are methods to get the data (GetEmployees and GetOrder), insert new entity objects (InsertEmployee and InsertOrder), update existing objects (UpdateEmployee and UpdateOrder), and, finally, delete objects (DeleteEmployee and DeleteOrder).

There are two things of note. By default the GetXXX methods return all the data in a table. This can be a lot of data, and it can be worth filtering the data using a LINQ query in the GetXXX method. If you don't, you run the risk of transferring large amounts of data from the server to the Silverlight client, which may be more than the network or the client can cope with.

The second thing to note is that the other methods (InsertXXX, UpdateXXX, and DeleteXXX) are filled out for you but that the changes to the data model are not made permanent in the database without a call to the SaveChanges method. See Chapter 30 for details of this method and how to apply it.

We are only going to be working with the Employees data, which is why it's called the domain service class, but I wanted to show you how a single service class can be used to provide access to more than one kind of entity data.

Creating the Silverlight Client

Adding data to our Silverlight client is much the same as for the other user interface technologies we have seen in this part of this book. For variety, we will include a Label and a ComboBox, which we will use to filter the employee data that is displayed by city.

Open your MainPage.xaml file, and drag your components from the Toolbox to the design surface so that it looks like Figure 35-20. I have created two rows in the Grid control, added a StackPanel to the lower row, and added a Label and a ComboBox to the StackPanel.

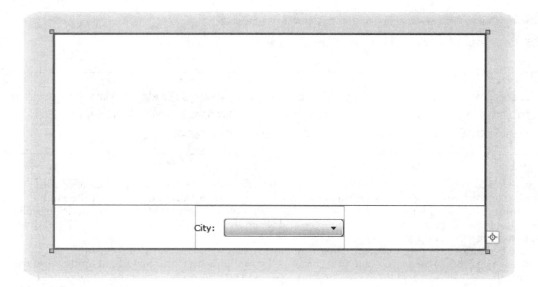

Figure 35-20. The client design surface

You have done enough layouts at this point not to need detailed instructions, but if you just can't make it work, then you can see the XAML from Figure 35-20 in the source code downloads for this chapter, available from Apress.com.

Adding the Data

The simplest way to add the data we want to our application is by using the Data Sources view, which you can open by selecting Show Data Sources from the Visual Studio Data menu. There should be two data sources available—one for the Employee data and one for the Order data, as shown in Figure 35-21.

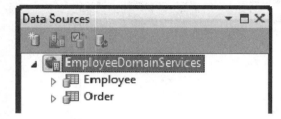

Figure 35-21. *The WCF RIA data source items*

Drag the Employee data source to the top row of the Grid on the design surface. A DataGrid control will appear on the design surface when you drop it. You'll some columns matching properties from the Employee entity object.

Configuring the DataGrid Control

First we need to put the DataGrid into the layout properly. To do that, switch to the Properties window, and reset the following properties:

- Width
- Height
- HorizontalAlignment
- VerticalAlignment
- Margin
- Grid.RowSpan

To reset a property, right-click the black diamond to the right of the property name, and select Reset Value from the pop-up list. When all the values have been reset, your DataGrid control should be nicely homed in the top row of the layout Grid.

Changing the Columns

We also need to change the settings for the columns. By default, they are arranged in alphabetical order. Select the DataGrid on the design surface, and click the ellipsis (...) button in the Columns property value. This will open the Collection Editor dialog box, which we saw in Chapter 33. Rearrange the columns so that the first three are FirstName, LastName, and City, and then click the OK button to close the dialog box. When you have made these changes, your design surface should look like Figure 35-22.

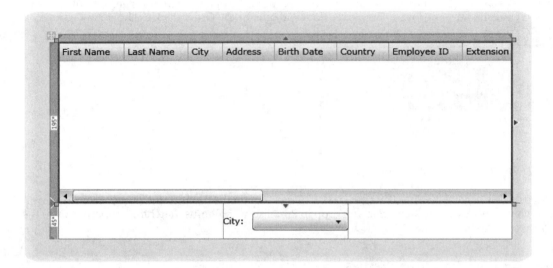

Figure 35-22. *The configured DataGrid control*

You should also see a small database icon at the lower-left corner of the design surface. This is a DomainDataSource object, which we will use to filter data based on the ComboxBox selection in the following sections. If you compile and run the project, you'll see that the data is loaded from the database and displayed in the DataGrid control. Once again, the data support that .NET provides for its user interface technologies has made this a relatively painless and quick process. Bear in mind that we have not had to configure or manage the network connections between the Silverlight client and the ASP.NET service, issue database queries, or convert data to and from C# objects. Everything works in a pleasant and seamless manner.

Configuring the ComboBox Control

We are going to use the ComboBox control to filter the data displayed in the DataGrid by the value of the City field. We start by adding the list of cities that will be available in the drop-down list.

Select the ComboBox control in the design surface, switch to the Properties window, and click the ellipsis (...) button belonging to the Items property. This will open the Collection Editor dialog box again. Click the Add button to create a new item in the list and change the value of the Content property to All. Repeat this process so that you have items for the following city names as well:

- London

- Redmond

- Seattle

- Tacoma

Click OK to dismiss the Collection Editor when you have added all the items. Return to the Properties window for the ComboBox control, and change the value of the SelectedIndex property to 0. This has the effect of selecting the first item (All) by default when the display is created. The design surface will update so that All is shown as the selected value for the ComboBox, as shown in Figure 35-23.

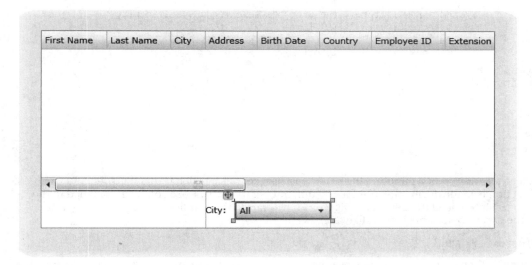

Figure 35-23. *Configuring the ComboBox control*

Wiring the ComboBox Control

All that remains is for us to filter the displayed data based on the selection in the ComboBox. Select the ComboBox, and select the Events view in the Properties window. Double-click in the value area for the SelectionChanged property to create a new handler method. Add the code statements as shown in Listing 35-3.

Listing 35-3. Wiring the ComboBox

```
using System.Windows.Controls;

namespace DataApp {
    public partial class MainPage : UserControl {
        public MainPage() {
```

```
        InitializeComponent();
    }

    private void comboBox1_SelectionChanged(object sender,
        SelectionChangedEventArgs e) {

        if (comboBox1 != null) {
            // get the selected city from the ComboBox
            string selectedCity =
                ((ComboBoxItem)comboBox1.SelectedItem).Content.ToString();

            // remove any filters that are in place
            employeeDomainDataSource.FilterDescriptors.Clear();

            // add a new filter if the user has selected a specific city
            if (selectedCity != "All") {
                employeeDomainDataSource.FilterDescriptors.Add(
                    new FilterDescriptor(
                        "City",
                        FilterOperator.IsEqualTo,
                        selectedCity));
            }
        }
    }
}
```

There is an oddity when handling the SelectionChanged event, which is that it is triggered when the initial selection is made during the interface layout, but before the ComboBox object is assigned to the instance variable we need to refer to. This is why I have started the handler code by checking to see whether the ComboBox variable is null, like this:

```
if (comboBox1 != null) {
```

If it is null, then we assume that the user has not made a selection and ignore the event. If the user *has* made a selection, then I next read the selected value from the ComboBox, like this:

```
string selectedCity = ((ComboBoxItem)comboBox1.SelectedItem).Content.ToString();
```

The ComboBox control can contain a wide range of item types, which makes the process of reading the value slightly indirect. The SelectedItem property returns a ComboBoxItem. I read the Content property to get the value assigned to this item and then call the ToString method to convert it to a string value.

The DomainDataSource object supports a system of filters, the collection of which is accessed using the FilterDescriptors property. I call the Clear method on this collection to remove any previous filters that might have been applied. If the user has switched the filter from London to Seattle, I want to remove the London filter before I apply the Seattle filter. No data will be displayed if I don't. Here is the statement that clears the filter collection:

```
employeeDomainDataSource.FilterDescriptors.Clear();
```

The remaining statements check to see whether a filter is needed and, if so, create one:

```
if (selectedCity != "All") {
```

```
employeeDomainDataSource.FilterDescriptors.Add(
    new FilterDescriptor(
        "City",
        FilterOperator.IsEqualTo,
        selectedCity));
}
```

I don't need to apply a filter if the user has selected the All item in the ComboBox. If the user has selected any other item, then I create a new FilterDescriptor object and add it to the DomainDataSource by calling the Add method on the result of the FilterDescriptors property. The FilterDescriptor constructor takes three parameters—the name of the property that you want to filter on, a value from the FilterOperator enumeration that specifies what kind of comparison to make (IsEqualTo, IsNotEqualTo, Contains, and so on), and the value to compare to. My filter selects data rows that have a City value that is equal to the name the user selected in the ComboBox.

Testing the Application

If you compile and run the project, you will see the completed Silverlight example. The data is loaded from the database, via the ASP.NET server, and delivered to Silverlight seamlessly. When the user selects a value using the ComboBox control, the data is filtered so that only matching data is displayed, as shown in Figure 35-24.

First Name	Last Name	City	Address	Birth Date	Country	Employee I
Steven	Buchanan	London	14 Garrett Hill	3/4/1955	UK	5
Michael	Suyama	London	Coventry House Miner Rd.	7/2/1963	UK	6
Robert	King	London	Edgeham Hollow Winchester Way	5/29/1960	UK	7
Anne	Dodsworth	London	7 Houndstooth Rd.	1/27/1966	UK	9

City: London ▼

Figure 35-24. The completed Silverlight/WCF RIA client

Using Silverlight Out-of-Browser Support

A very nice feature of Silverlight is that your users can install and run your Silverlight clients outside the browser. In this section, I'll show you how to enable this support and demonstrate how it appears to the user. As the foundation, we'll use the Silverlight swimming calculator that we created at the start of the chapter.

Configuring the Out-of-Browser Support

Load the SwimCalculator project into Visual Studio. Right-click the project in the Solution Explorer, and open the project properties by selecting Properties from the pop-up menu. On the Silverlight tab, select the "Enabling running application out of the browser" box, as shown in Figure 35-25.

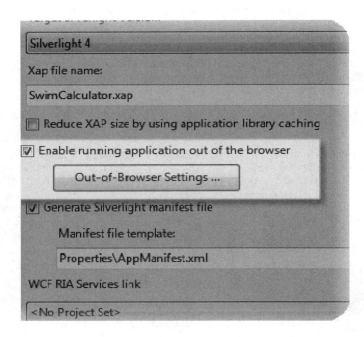

Figure 35-25. *Enabling Silverlight out-of-browser support*

If you click the Out-of-Browser Settings button, you can configure some options for how your program will be run, as shown in Figure 35-25.

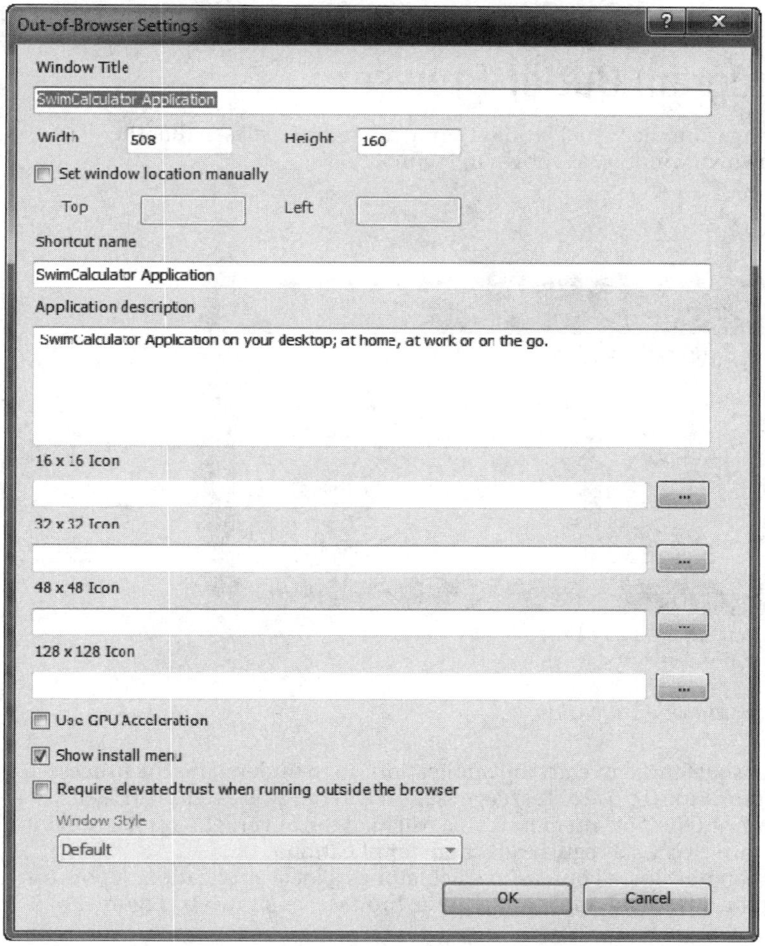

Figure 35-26. *The Out-Of-Browser Settings dialog box*

The meaning of each option is self-evident. You need not make any changes to these options. I tend to set at least the Width and Height options to match the size of my XAML design surface. An 800 by 600 window is the default if you don't specify a size. Click OK to close the dialog box and then recompile your project.

Using a Silverlight Program Out-of-Browser

If you select Start Without Debugging from the Visual Studio Debug menu, you will see that the Silverlight application appears in its own window, as shown in Figure 35-27.

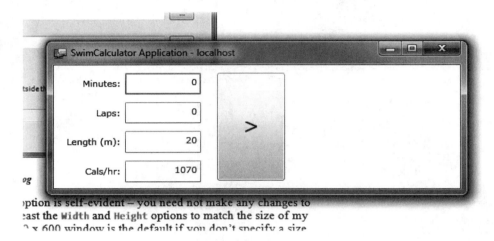

Figure 35-27. The out-of-browser calculator application

The user won't be able to use Visual Studio to start the application, so to understand the process from their perspective, right-click the SwimCalculatorTestPage.aspx file in the SwimCalculator.Web project, and select View in Browser from the pop-up menu. This will load the Silverlight application into the browser, much as we saw when we created a regular Silverlight application.

The difference is that the user can now install our swim calculator as a local application. A pop-up menu will appear if you right-click the Silverlight application in the browser, as shown by Figure 35-28.

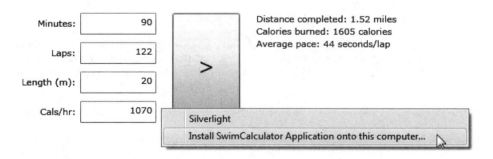

Figure 35-28. The Silverlight install menu

When you user selects the Install menu item, a dialog box appears to confirm the installation, as shown in Figure 35-29. If the user clicks OK, then the application is installed locally and started.

Figure 35-29. The Silverlight local installer

The user doesn't have to install the application to use it. They can continue to use it in the web page, but if they do install it, then there will be a regular icon in the Start menu or on the desktop that they can use to launch your program without needing the browser at all. To uninstall your application, the user right-clicks and selects the "Remove this application" menu, as shown in Figure 35-30.

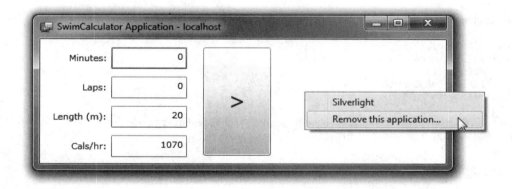

Figure 35-30. Uninstalling the application

Making Installation Part of the Interface

You don't have to rely on the user knowing to right-click to install your application. You can provide support for the user to install your application as part of your program. To demonstrate this, I have added a Button to the swim calculator layout, as shown by Figure 35-31.

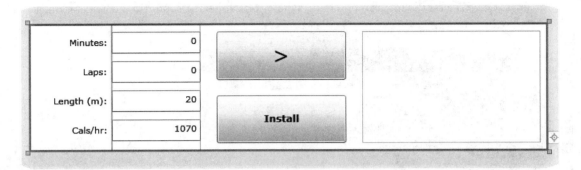

Figure 35-31. *The modified swim calculator layout*

I realize that this is not the most elegant of additions, but it will serve our purposes. The name given to the new Button control in the layout is installButton, and Listing 35-4 demonstrates the additions to the code-behind required to support it. I have omitted the convertButton_Click method for brevity, but it is unchanged from Listing 35-2.

Listing 35-4. Adding Installation Support

```
using System.Text;
using System.Windows;
using System.Windows.Controls;

namespace SwimCalculator {
    public partial class MainPage : UserControl {
        public MainPage() {
            InitializeComponent();
        }

        private void convertButton_Click(object sender, RoutedEventArgs e) {
            // method body removed for brevity
        }

        private void UserControl_Loaded(object sender, RoutedEventArgs e) {
            if (Application.Current.IsRunningOutOfBrowser) {
                installButton.Visibility = System.Windows.Visibility.Collapsed;
                convertButton.SetValue(Grid.RowSpanProperty, 2);
            } else {
                // set the inital state of the install button
                setButtonState();
                // register a handler for the event invoked when the install state changes
                Application.Current.InstallStateChanged += (innerSender, eventArgs) => {
                    setButtonState();
                };
            }
        }
    }
```

```
        private void setButtonState() {
            installButton.IsEnabled
                = Application.Current.InstallState == InstallState.NotInstalled;
        }

        private void installButton_Click(object sender, RoutedEventArgs e) {
            if (Application.Current.InstallState == InstallState.NotInstalled) {
                Application.Current.Install();
            }
        }
    }
}
```

The UserControl_Loaded method is an event handler for the Loaded method of the top-level UserControl in the XAML layout. It is called when the interface is loaded. I don't want the Install button to be shown if the application is already running out-of-browser, so I use the Application class to check the application status, like this:

```
if (Application.Current.IsRunningOutOfBrowser) {
```

The Application class has a static property called Current, which returns an Application object that describes this instance of the Silverlight program. The IsRunningOutOfBrowser property returns true if the program is OOB and false otherwise. If we are running OOB, then I hide installButton and make the convertButton larger to cover the gap in the layout, like this:

```
installButton.Visibility = System.Windows.Visibility.Collapsed;
convertButton.SetValue(Grid.RowSpanProperty, 2);
```

If we are not running out-of-browser, then I want to set the Install button state so that it is active only if the application isn't already installed. Remember that the user may installed the program but chosen to use it in the browser anyway. I call the setButtonState method, which I added to the code-behind file; it enables or disables the Button based on the installation state, which we get from the Application class, like this:

```
installButton.IsEnabled = Application.Current.InstallState ==
InstallState.NotInstalled;
```

I set the IsEnabled property of the installButton object based on the value of the Application.InstallState property, which returns a value from the InstallState enumeration. The InstallState enumeration defines values that you can use to determine whether an application has been installed. The NotInstalled state means that it has not.

The Application class defines an event you can listen to for notification of when the installation state changes. This means I can disable my Install button in the browser when the user installs the application and enable it again if they uninstall. I register interest in the event like this:

```
Application.Current.InstallStateChanged += (innerSender, eventArgs) => {
    setButtonState();
};
```

When the status is changed and the event is invoked, I call the setButtonState method to ensure that my button status accurately reflects the application installation status. The final addition is a handler method for the Click event of the installButton object, which is as follows:

```
private void installButton_Click(object sender, RoutedEventArgs e) {
    if (Application.Current.InstallState == InstallState.NotInstalled) {
        Application.Current.Install();
    }
}
```

I check the installation status when the user click the button, and if the application has not been installed, then I call the Install method of the Application object obtained through the Application.Current property. This opens the same installation dialog box as was shown in Figure 35-29. With these additions, the browser version of the swim calculator looks like Figure 35-32 when the program has not been installed.

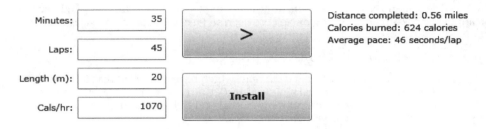

Figure 35-32. The browser layout when the program is not installed

When the program has been installed, the Install button is disabled, as shown in Figure 35-33.

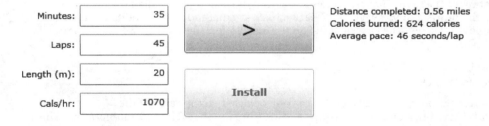

Figure 35-33. *The browser layout when the program is installed*

And, finally, Figure 35-34 shows the layout of the program when it is being run out-of-browser.

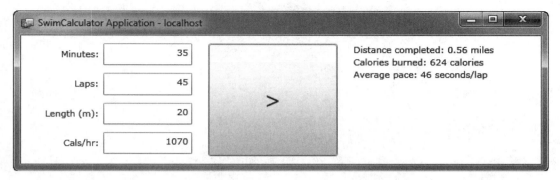

Figure 35-34. Hiding the Install button when running out-of-browser

Using Other Out-of-Browser Features

Silverlight supports some special features for out-of-browser programs, including access to local storage, application updates, detecting networks, Outlook-style toast notification windows, and more. See the .NET Framework documentation for details at http://msdn.microsoft.com/en-us/library/dd550721(VS.95).aspx.

Summary

In this chapter, we took an introductory look at Silverlight, the .NET technology for creating highly interactive web applications. We saw how some of the core C# features and .NET Framework classes are available when writing Silverlight applications and how WPF provides the foundation for the user interface. We also looked at how WCF RIA services can simplify the use of remote services in Silverlight and how to generate service classes and methods that hide the WCF mechanics so that we can work with regular C# objects. Lastly, we look at the way that Silverlight clients can be installed and used outside the web browser, which is a nice way of getting the lightweight features of Silverlight but delivering a full Windows experience. Silverlight may not have the market penetration that Flash enjoys, but the tight integration with ASP.NET and other .NET features, such as WPF and WCF, goes some way to balancing this shortfall.

PART 6

■ ■ ■

Advanced Topics

In this, the final part of the book, we will look at some advanced topics that don't really belong elsewhere. Chapter 36 shows you how to take advantage of key features of the Windows operating system to make your programs better operating system citizens and to improve your users' experience. Chapter 37 explores the .NET Framework Class Library support for cryptography. I'll show you how to encrypt and decrypt data and perform other common cryptographic operations. The last chapter, Chapter 38, is focused on testing and debugging—but not using the regular techniques. C# and .NET have some interesting (and rarely used) features that can dramatically improve the quality of your code and reduce the time it takes to track down bugs. Many readers will be tempted to skip over this chapter, but I recommend you take the time to read it. There is some very useful information there that will help you on your road to becoming a professional C# programmer.

CHAPTER 36

■ ■ ■

Windows Integration

Stand-alone .NET programs can do a lot, but to coexist with other programs, you have to integrate closely with Windows. The .NET Framework Class Library provides a range of convenient classes that you can use to work with some key Windows platform services and features, and in this chapter I'll show you how to use some of them to make your program a first-class Windows citizen. We will start by looking at the Windows event log, move on to gain elevated privileges for our program, and then see how to create, install, and use a Windows service. We finish this chapter by using C# and .NET to access the quintessential Windows feature—the registry. Table 36-1 provides the summary for this chapter.

Table 36-1. *Quick Problem/Solution Reference for Chapter 36*

Problem	Solution	Listings
Read entries from an event log.	Create a new EventLog object, and then use LINQ to query the Entries property.	36-1
Write to an event log.	Create an event source, and use the EventLog.WriteEntry method.	36-2, 36-3
Gain elevated privileges.	Use the ProcessStartInfo and Process classes.	36-4
Create a Windows service.	Derive from the ServiceBase class.	36-5 through 36-8
Search the registry.	Use the static Registry properties to obtain RegistryKey objects.	36-9
Get and set registry values.	Use the static methods of the Registry class.	36-10

Using the Windows Event Log

The event log is the central logging system of the Windows operating system. Applications can write entries to the log to record problems, progress, and changes in state. The administrator of a Windows machine can manually review the logs or set up actions to be performed when a specific kind of event is recorded. This can include running a program, sending an e-mail, or displaying a message. In this section, I'll show you the .NET Framework Class Library provides support for reading from and writing to the event log.

Reading an Event Log

The EventLog class in the System.Diagnostics namespace provides access to the Windows event logs. To read the entries in an event log, you create a new EventLog object, passing the name of the log as a string parameter. You can then read the contents of the log through the Entries property, which returns a collection containing all the items in the log, ordered in the sequence they were created in. Listing 36-1 provides a demonstration.

Listing 36-1. Reading an Event Log

```
using System;
using System.Collections.Generic;
using System.Diagnostics;
using System.Linq;

class Listing_01 {

    static void Main(string[] args) {

        // create an EventLog object for the Application log
        EventLog appLog = new EventLog("Application");

        // use the Cast extension method to create a LING-suitable data source
        IEnumerable<EventLogEntry> logEntries = appLog.Entries.Cast<EventLogEntry>();

        // perform a LINQ query on the log entries
        IEnumerable<EventLogEntry> results = from e in logEntries
                                             where e.EntryType == EventLogEntryType.Warning
                                             select e;

        // enumerate the first few events
        foreach (EventLogEntry entry in results.Take(3)) {
            Console.WriteLine("Event Source: {0}", entry.Source);
            Console.WriteLine("Message: {0}", entry.Message);
            Console.WriteLine("---------------");
        }

        // wait for input before exiting
        Console.WriteLine("Press enter to finish");
        Console.ReadLine();
    }
}
```

Windows has three default logs: Application, System, and Security. I have opened the Application log in Listing 36-1, which is a kind of catchall for application-related items. The Entries property returns an EventLogEntryCollection object, which contains an EventLogEntry object for each entry in the event log.

■ **Note** Your program must have administration privileges to access the Security log, which is given special protection by Windows.

There can be a lot of entries in an event log. As I write this, there are more than 8,000 entries in my Application log on a system that was recently installed and that is used only to write books. Most of the events are of little value. For example, I have many hundreds of events that report that the Microsoft Office system has successfully validated my license codes.

However, we can use our old friend LINQ to filter the contents of an event log for interesting items. The .NET support for the event log predates the introduction of generic types, so we need to convert the value of the Entries property to an IEnumerable<EventLogEntry> using the LINQ Cast extension method (this method is described in Chapter 27). I use the result of the cast operation as the data source for a LINQ query, where I select those EventLogEntries whose EntryType property has the Warning value from the EventLogEntryType enumeration. I then use the LINQ Take extension method to select the first three results and a foreach loop to enumerate them. Compiling and running Listing 36-1 produces the following results:

```
Event Source: Windows Search Service
Message: The Windows Search Service is starting up and attempting to remove the
old search index {Reason: Full Index Reset}.


---------------
Event Source: Microsoft-Windows-User Profiles Service
Message: Windows detected your registry file is still in use by other applications or
services. The file will be unloaded now. The applications or services that
 hold your registry file may not function properly afterwards.

 DETAIL -
 1 user registry handles leaked from \Registry\User\S-1-5-21-4043041569-14014688
4-403651058-1000:
Process 468 (\Device\HarddiskVolume2\Windows\System32\winlogon.exe) has opened k
ey \REGISTRY\USER\S-1-5-21-4043041569-140146884-403651058-1000


---------------
Event Source: Microsoft-Windows-ApplicationExperienceInfrastructure
Message: The application (Microsoft SQL Server 2008, from vendor Microsoft) has
the following problem: After SQL Server Setup completes, you must apply SQL Server 2008
Service Pack 1 (SP1) or a later service pack before you run SQL Server 2
008 on this version of Windows.
---------------
Press enter to finish
```

The EventLogEntry class provides a number of properties that are useful in filtering the contents of a log. The most useful are described in Table 36-2.

Table 36-2. Useful Members of the EventLogEntry Class

Member	Description
Category	Returns the category associated with the event; this is application-specific.
Data	Returns the binary data associated with the event.
EntryType	Returns the type of the event, expressed as a value from the EventLogEntryType enumeration (see Table 36-3 for the set of values).
Message	Returns a string describing the event.
Source	The source name associated with the event; see the "Writing to an Event Log" section for examples of Source values.
TimeGenerated	Returns a DateTime value representing the time that the event was created.

If you are looking or filtering for broad categories of events, then the value of the EntryType property is a good place to start. This property contains a value from the EventLogEntryType enumeration. I filtered for the Warning value in Listing 36-1. Table 36-3 describes the full set of values available.

Table 36-3. EventLogEntryType Values

Value	Description
Error	The event represents a significant problem that the user or administrator should be aware of, usually a loss of data or reduced application functionality.
Warning	The event represents a nonurgent problem that may later lead to more significant issues.
Information	The event represents an informational event, which is usually the successful completion of an action.
SuccessAudit	The event represents a successful audited operation, such a user logging on to the system.
FailureAudit	The event represents a successful audited operation, such as a failed login attempt.

Writing to an Event Log

The EventLog class also supports writing events to a log. In this part of the chapter, I'll show you how to prepare and then write events from your program to the event log.

Creating the Event Source

Each event has an event source associated with it (this is the value returned by the Source property of the EventLogEntry class). Before we can write events, we have to create an event source for our program. Unfortunately, this requires administrative privileges. Listing 36-2 shows you how to check for, and create, an event source for your program.

Listing 36-2. Creating an Event Source

```
using System;
using System.Diagnostics;

class Listing_02 {

    static void Main(string[] args) {

        string eventSource = "C# Intro Source";

        if (!EventLog.SourceExists(eventSource)) {
            // we need to create the source
            Console.WriteLine("Need to create source {0}", eventSource);
            // create the source
            EventLog.CreateEventSource(eventSource, "Application");
            Console.WriteLine("Created source {0}", eventSource);
        } else {
            Console.WriteLine("Source already exists: {0}", eventSource);
        }

        // wait for input before exiting
        Console.WriteLine("Press enter to finish");
        Console.ReadLine();
    }
}
```

The static EventLog.SourceExists method checks the event logs to see whether a source has already been created. It returns true if the source exists, and false otherwise. The static EventLog.CreateEventSource method creates a new event source. This method takes the name of the source you want to create and the name of the log you want to write to as a parameter. Compiling Listing 36-2 and running the program with administration privileges produces the following result:

```
Need to create source C# Intro Source
Created source C# Intro Source
Press enter to finish
```

Event sources are persistent (although you can remove them with the DeleteEventSource method). Once you have created the event source, you can use it indefinitely, as the output from running Listing 36-2 a second time demonstrates:

```
Source already exists: C# Intro Source
Press enter to finish
```

Requiring administration privileges to check and create event sources is an inconvenience. I find the best way of dealing with this is to execute a program like Listing 36-2 as part of the program installer, which is usually granted elevated permissions anyway, but see the "Using Elevated Privileges" section later in this chapter for an alternative approach.

Writing Events

Events are written to the event log using the static EventLog.WriteEntry method, as demonstrated by Listing 36-3.

Listing 36-3. Writing an Entry to an Event Log

```
using System;
using System.Diagnostics;
using System.Text;

class Listing_03 {

    static void Main(string[] args) {

        // define the event source
        string eventSource = "C# Intro Source";

        // write an event to the log
        EventLog.WriteEntry(
            eventSource,
            "This is a test event",
            EventLogEntryType.Information,
            1,
            0,
            Encoding.ASCII.GetBytes("Here is some data"));

        Console.WriteLine("Event written to log");

        // wait for input before exiting
        Console.WriteLine("Press enter to finish");
        Console.ReadLine();
    }
}
```

There are ten overloaded versions of the WriteEntry method. I have used the most complete version in Listing 36-3, which takes parameters for the event source, a message to describe the event, the type of the event, a program-specific event code and category, and a byte array for any supporting data that should be logged.

Notice that I don't have to specify which of the event logs the event should be written to. This is because the association between the event source and the event log was made in Listing 36-2 when I created the event source, and any event written using the C# Intro Source event source will be written to the Application log. Compiling and running Listing 36-3 places a new event in the Application event log. The following is copied from the XML view of the Windows Event Viewer tool:

```
<Event xmlns="http://schemas.microsoft.com/win/2004/08/events/event">
    <System>
        <Provider Name="C# Intro Source" />
        <EventID Qualifiers="0">0</EventID>
        <Level>4</Level>
        <Task>0</Task>
        <Keywords>0x80000000000000</Keywords>
        <TimeCreated SystemTime="2010-08-30T13:30:16.000000000Z" />
        <EventRecordID>8302</EventRecordID>
        <Channel>Application</Channel>
        <Computer>Shuttle</Computer>
        <Security />
    </System>
    <EventData>
        <Data>This is a test event</Data>
        <Binary>4865726520697320736F6D652064617461</Binary>
    </EventData>
</Event>
```

Using Elevated Privileges

There are times when you need to perform actions as an administrator. This can include creating an event source prior to using an event log (as we saw in the previous section), reading and writing files belonging to another user, or making administrative changes to the system (changing passwords, and so on). It is widely considered a security risk (and bad form) to require your program to have administrator rights to perform regular tasks, and Windows doesn't allow a program to gain temporarily elevated privileges. When you need to perform an action as an administrator, the best approach is to start a new process that will perform only the required action and request elevated privileges. Listing 36-4 provides a demonstration that uses the technique in Listing 36-2 to check for (and create, if required) an event log event source.

Listing 36-4. Using Elevated Privileges

```
using System;
using System.Collections.Generic;
using System.Linq;
using System.Text;
using System.Diagnostics;
```

```
class Listing_04 {

    static void Main(string[] args) {

        // define the event source
        string eventSource = "C# Intro Source 2";

        // check the command-line arguments
        if (args.Length > 0 && args[0] == "adminTask") {
            // we have started to perform the admin tasks
            performAdminTasks(eventSource);
            // it is important that we return at this point - we
            // should not perform any task other than those that
            // require administration rights
            return;
        }

        // if we get here, then we are the main program - we have
        // no admin rights
        // - our first task is to create the admin instance of the program
        ProcessStartInfo pstartInfo = new ProcessStartInfo("Listing_04.exe");
        pstartInfo.Arguments = "adminTask";
        pstartInfo.Verb = "runas";
        // start the process and wait for it to complete
        Process.Start(pstartInfo).WaitForExit();


        // we can now be sure that the event source for the event log
        // has been created - write an event to the log
        // write an event to the log
        EventLog.WriteEntry(
            eventSource,
            "This is a test event",
            EventLogEntryType.Information,
            1,
            0,
            Encoding.ASCII.GetBytes("Here is some data"));

        Console.WriteLine("Event written to log");

        // wait for input before exiting
        Console.WriteLine("Press enter to finish");
        Console.ReadLine();
    }

    private static void performAdminTasks(string eventSource) {
        // perform the tasks that require admin rights
        if (!EventLog.SourceExists(eventSource)) {
            // create the source
            EventLog.CreateEventSource(eventSource, "Application");
        }
```

```
    }
}
```

The behavior of the program in Listing 36-4 depends on the command-line arguments it is started with. The code statements in the listing are broken into two groups: a group that needs elevated privileges (shown in bold) and a group that doesn't. When the first command-line argument is adminTask, the elevated statements are executed; otherwise—and this is the tricky part—the ProcessInfo and Process classes are used to start the same program but with the adminTask command-line argument.

So, you run the program as a normal user, and there is no command-line argument. The program runs a second instance of itself as administrator and checks that the event log source exists and then exits. The first instance waits for this to happen and then continues to write an event to the event log. The details of how the ProcessInfo and Process classes work are beyond the scope of this book, but you can use this technique verbatim to get the desired effect. Before the elevated instance of the program is started, the user is automatically prompted by Windows, as shown in Figure 36-1.

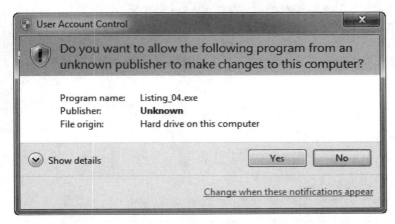

Figure 36-1. The elevated privilege UAC dialog box

If the user clicks the No button on the dialog box, then the second instance of the program won't be started, and your elevated tasks won't be performed. You should take care to catch and handle the exceptions that might arise if this happens in your code.

Creating a Windows Service

A Windows service is a long-lived program that doesn't require any user input. Services are useful if you want some piece of your project functionality to continue without needing the user to keep a window open. Visual Studio provides a convenient template for creating Windows services, and in this section I'll show you how to create, install, and use such a service.

■ **Note** The template for creating a Window Service is not included in the Express edition of Visual Studio 2010. The example in this section was created using the Ultimate edition, and the support is available in all of the commercial Visual Studio editions.

Creating the Service Class

The easiest way to create a service is using the Visual Studio 2010 template. Create a new Visual Studio project using the Windows Service template, as shown in Figure 36-2.

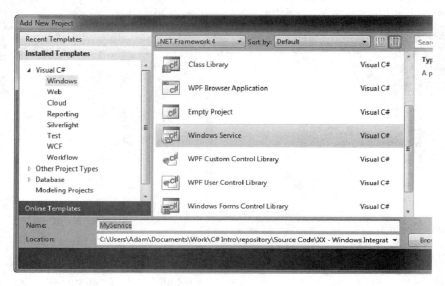

Figure 36-2. Creating a Windows Service project

Name the project **MyService**, and click the OK button. Visual Studio has a design surface view for service projects. Right-click anywhere on the design surface, and select Properties to see the properties for the service. This is similar to the design approach we saw for Windows Forms. Change the values of both the Name and ServiceName properties to MyCalculatorService.

We are done with the design view for the moment, so either click the link to switch to the code view or select Service1.cs in the Solution Explorer window. Then right-click and select View Code from the menu. Listing 36-5 shows the initial code for the service.

Listing 36-5. An Empty Windows Service Class

```
using System;
using System.Collections.Generic;
using System.ComponentModel;
using System.Data;
```

```
using System.Diagnostics;
using System.Linq;
using System.ServiceProcess;
using System.Text;

namespace MyService {
    public partial class MyCalculatorService : ServiceBase {
        public MyCalculatorService() {
            InitializeComponent();
        }

        protected override void OnStart(string[] args) {

        }

        protected override void OnStop() {
        }
    }
}
```

As you can see from the listing, the base class for services is System.ServiceProcess.ServiceBase. The template has created a default constructor and has overridden the OnStart and OnStop methods. The OnStart method is called when the service is started, and, as you might guess, the OnStop method is called when the service is stopped. This is the basic life cycle for a service, but the ServiceBase class defines additional methods you can override. The most useful of the life-cycle methods are described in Table 36-4.

Table 36-4. Useful ServiceBase Life-Cycle Methods

Method	Description
OnStart(string[])	Called when the service has been asked to start. The service should use this method to begin operations. The string array contains the parameters passed to the service.
OnStop()	Called when the service has been asked to stop. The service should use this method to stop operations.
OnPause()	Called when the services has been asked to pause.
OnContinue()	Called when the service has been asked to resume from a prior pause request.
OnShutDown()	Called when the system is shutting down.

Aside from OnStart, the life-cycle methods will be called only if a corresponding property is set for the service class. To enable OnPause and OnContinue, for example, the CanPauseAndContinue property must be set to true. You can set these properties using the design view or manually in the code-behind file.

You must return from the life-cycle methods promptly; otherwise, Windows will categorize your service as nonresponsive. This means you should perform complex operations in the background; see Chapters 24 and 25 for details of how to do this.

Adding the Service Functionality

Since Windows Vista, services have not been allowed to interact with the user, but this doesn't mean they can't be useful. To demonstrate this, I am going to use our example service to create and publish a WCF service just like the one we created in Chapter 21. The Windows service will be the host for the WCF service, which will be able to handle client requests as long as the Windows service is running. This is a better approach than we saw in Chapter 21, which required a console window to keep the WCF service running. I start by defining the WCF service contract in the code file ICalculatorServer.cs, as shown in Listing 36-6. I am not going to explain the meaning of the contract; see Chapter 21 for details.

Listing 36-6. The WCF Service Contract

```
using System;
using System.Collections.Generic;
using System.Linq;
using System.Text;
using System.ServiceModel;

namespace MyService {

    [ServiceContract]
    public interface ICalculatorServer {

        [OperationContract]
        int PerformAddition(int x, int y);

        [OperationContract]
        int PerformMultiplcation(int x, int y);

        [OperationContract]
        int PerformSubtraction(int x, int y);

        [OperationContract]
        float PerformDivision(int x, int y);
    }
}
```

We need an implementation of the service contract, which is shown in Listing 36-7. This is identical to the implementation I used in Chapter 21. I have created a code file called CalculatorImpl.cs to contain this class.

Listing 36-7. The WF Service Contract Implementation

```
using System;
```

```
using System.Collections.Generic;
using System.Linq;
using System.Text;

namespace MyService {

    class CalculatorImpl : ICalculatorServer {

        public int PerformAddition(int x, int y) {
            int result = x + y;
            Console.WriteLine("Addition Request: {0} + {1} = {2}",
                x, y, result);
            return result;
        }

        public int PerformMultiplcation(int x, int y) {
            int result = x * y;
            Console.WriteLine("Multiplcation Request: {0} * {1} = {2}",
                x, y, result);
            return result;
        }

        public int PerformSubtraction(int x, int y) {
            int result = x - y;
            Console.WriteLine("Subtraction Request: {0} - {1} = {2}",
                x, y, result);
            return result;
        }

        public float PerformDivision(int x, int y) {
            float result = ((float)x) / ((float)y);
            Console.WriteLine("Division Request: {0} / {1} = {2}",
                x, y, result);
            return result;
        }
    }
}
```

All that remains is to extend our service class to define the WCF service and start and stop it in response to the service life-cycle calls. Listing 36-8 shows these changes. I have also removed the unused using statements for brevity.

Listing 36-8. Enhancing the Service Class

```
using System;
using System.ServiceModel;
using System.ServiceModel.Description;
using System.ServiceProcess;

namespace MyService {
    public partial class MyCalculatorService : ServiceBase {
```

```
        // define the service host field
        ServiceHost myServiceHost;

        public MyCalculatorService() {
            InitializeComponent();

            // define the WCF service
            // define the URI that will be used to publish the service
            Uri serviceAddress = new Uri("http://localhost:13000/WCF");

            // create the ServiceHost object
            myServiceHost = new ServiceHost(typeof(CalculatorImpl), serviceAddress);

            // add the end point with the HTTP binding
            myServiceHost.AddServiceEndpoint(typeof(ICalculatorServer),
                new WSHttpBinding(), "CalculatorServer");

            // add support for getting the meta-data via HTTP
            ServiceMetadataBehavior smb = new ServiceMetadataBehavior();
            smb.HttpGetEnabled = true;
            myServiceHost.Description.Behaviors.Add(smb);
        }

        protected override void OnStart(string[] args) {
            // start handling requests
            myServiceHost.Open();
        }

        protected override void OnStop() {
            // stop handling requests
            myServiceHost.Close();
        }
    }
}
```

The WCF service is defined in the constructor for the service, and the Open method of the ServiceHost object is called when the service OnStart method is called. When the OnStop service method is called, then I use the Close method on the ServiceHost to stop the WCF service.

Adding the Service Installer

Services have to be installed before they can be run, and the simplest way of handling the installation is to use the Visual Studio features to take care of it for you. Open the design view by double-clicking the Service1.cs item in the Solution Explorer, right-click anywhere on the surface, and then select the Add Installer item from the pop-up menu, as illustrated by Figure 36-3.

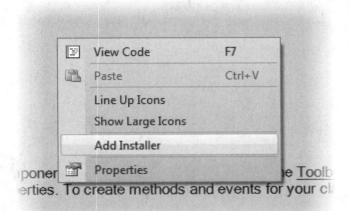

Figure 36-3. Adding an installer from the design surface

Selecting this item adds some new references to your project and creates the `ProjectInstaller.cs` item. Double-click `ProjectInstaller.cs` to open its design surface. There are two items on the surface, `serviceProcessInstaller1` and `serviceInstaller1`, as shown by Figure 36-4.

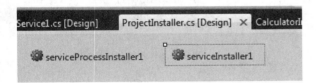

Figure 36-4. Two items on the installer design surface

We will use these two items to configure our surface. Open the Properties view for the `serviceProcessInstaller1` item, and change the `Name` property to `MyCalculatorService`. Change the `Account` property `LocalSystem`. This is the account that will be used to execute our service and that has some elevated privileges we require.

Click the `serviceInstaller1` item, and change the `StartType` property to `Automatic`. This will ensure that our service is started when the machine it is installed on starts.

Add the MSI Installer

We could now install our service using command-line tools, but a more elegant approach is to have Visual Studio create a standard Windows MSI application installer for us. Add a new project to the solution using the Setup Project template, which you can find under Other Project Types ➤ Setup and Deployment ➤ Visual Studio Installer, as shown by Figure 36-5.

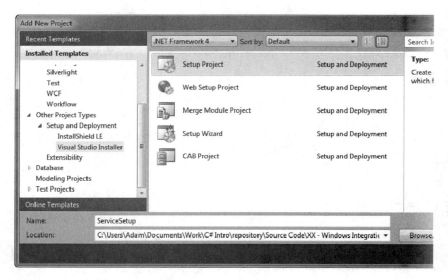

Figure 36-5. Adding a setup project

Set the name of the project to be ServiceSetup, and click the OK button to create the project. Right-click the ServiceSetup item in the Solution Explorer window, and select Add and Project Output from the pop-up menus. Make sure that the MyService project is selected from the drop-down box at the top of the window that appears, and select "Primary output" from the list, as shown in Figure 36-6.

Figure 36-6. Selecting the project output

Right-click the ServiceSetup in the Solution Explorer again, and select View and then Custom Actions from the pop-up menus. This opens the Custom Actions window. Right-click the Custom Actions item, and select Add Custom Action, as shown in Figure 36-7.

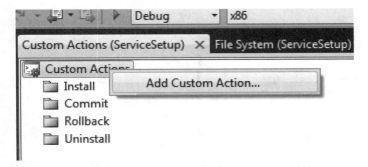

Figure 36-7. Adding a custom action

The Select Item in Project dialog box will appear. Select Application Folder from the Look In drop-down list, as shown in Figure 36-8, and click the OK button.

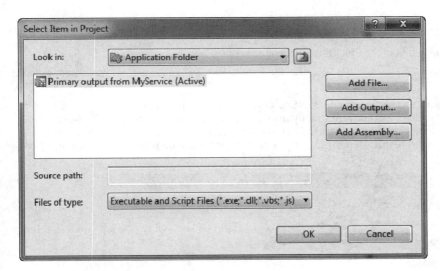

Figure 36-8. The Select Item in Project dialog box

Installing the Service

Right-click the ServiceSetup item in the Solution Explorer, and select Build from the menu. This will compile the Windows service project and then build the installer file. To install the service, right-click ServiceSetup and select Install. You'll see a standard Windows program installer, as shown in Figure 36-9. Follow the steps to install the service.

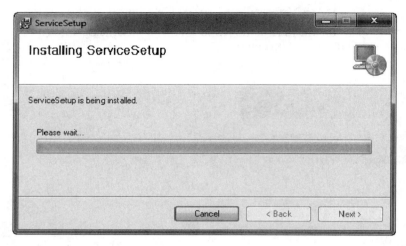

Figure 36-9. *The service installer*

Installing a service requires elevated privileges, so you will have to approve a User Account Control dialog box as part of the service installation.

■ **Tip** You can uninstall the service from the Programs and Features control panel.

When the installer has completed, open the Services control panel, and, all being well, you should see your service. The service won't start automatically until you reboot your machine, so right-click the service, and select Start to start it manually. Figure 36-10 shows you how the service appears on my machine—you may see different results depending on the service you have installed and running.

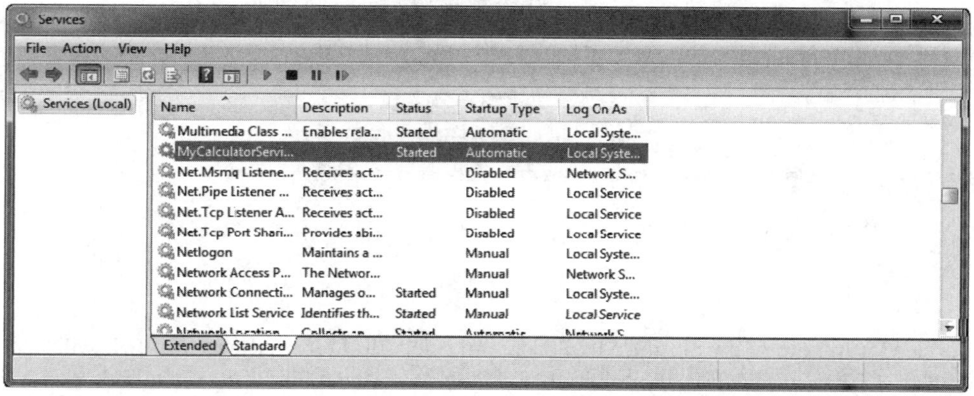

Figure 36-10. *The installed service*

Creating the Client

The process of creating the WCF client is identical to the process described in the "Creating the WCF Client" section of Chapter 21. After all, I have taken the WCF service from that chapter and wrapped it in a Windows service. The WCF service will process client requests while the Windows service is running.

Using the Windows Registry

The Windows registry is a storage facility for information about users, applications, and the settings for Windows itself. You don't need the registry to build and deploy a C# .NET program, but, like the other features in this chapter, being able to work with the registry can make coexisting with other Windows applications easier. In this section, I'll show you how to use the classes in the Microsoft.Win32 namespace to search, read from, and write to the Windows registry. I am going to assume you are already familiar with the registry and the havoc and destruction that can arise if you make changes. I suggest you skip this section if you are new to the registry. The registry is not for the fainthearted, and you can do irreparable damage to your system.

Searching the Registry

The Registry class contains six static properties, each of which relates to one of the root keys of the registry. These properties are described in Table 36-5.

Table 36-5. *The Six Static Registry Properties*

Property	Description
ClassesRoot	Stores information about document types and associated properties
CurrentConfig	Contains hardware configuration information
CurrentUser	Contains information about the preferences of the current user
LocalMachine	Contains the configuration for the local machine
PerformanceData	Contains the data for the Windows performance counters
Users	Contains information about each user of the system

Each of these properties returns a RegistryKey object, which represents the relevant root registry key. The RegistryKey class contains a number of members that you can use to get details of the key and its immediate subkeys; these are described in Table 36-6.

Table 36-6. Useful RegistryKey Members

Member	Description
GetSubKeyNames()	Returns a string array containing the names of the subkeys to this key
GetValueNames()	Returns a string array containing the names of the values for this key
OpenSubKey(string)	Returns a RegistryKey representing the specified subkey
GetValue(string)	Returns the value of the specified value name

Listing 36-9 demonstrates using these methods to recursively read the registry. This example looks for value names that contain the string Environment.

Listing 36-9. Searching the Registry

```
using System;
using Microsoft.Win32;
using System.Security;

class Listing_09 {

    static void Main(string[] args) {

        // get one of the root registry
        RegistryKey rootKey = Registry.CurrentUser;

        // process the key
        processSubKeys(rootKey, rootKey.GetSubKeyNames(), "Environment");

        // wait for input before exiting
        Console.WriteLine("Press enter to finish");
        Console.ReadLine();
    }

    private static void processSubKeys(RegistryKey key, string[] subKeyNames,
        string targetString) {

        // if there are values for this key, then process them
        processValues(key, key.GetValueNames(), targetString);
        // process each of the subkeys
        foreach (string subKeyName in subKeyNames) {
            try {
                // open the subkey
                RegistryKey subKey = key.OpenSubKey(subKeyName);
```

```
                    // recurse and process this key
                    processSubKeys(subKey, subKey.GetSubKeyNames(), targetString);
                } catch (SecurityException) {
                    // this is just part of the registry we are not entitled to read
                    Console.WriteLine("Cannot open subkey {0} for key {1}",
                        subKeyName, key.Name);
                }
            }
        }
    }

    private static void processValues(RegistryKey key, string[] valueNames,
        string targetString) {

        foreach (string valName in valueNames) {
            if (valName.Contains(targetString)) {
                // we have a match - print out the value
                Console.WriteLine("Key: {0}, Value Name: {1}, Value: {2}",
                    key.Name, valName, key.GetValue(valName));
            }
        }
    }
}
```

Not all parts of the registry are accessible to all users, so you must be prepared to handle the exceptions that arise when you try to open a subkey to which you have no access. You can see that I have done this by catching the System.Security.SecurityException in Listing 36-9. Compiling and running Listing 36-9 produces the following results on my machine. The results you get will depend on the contents of your registry.

```
Key: HKEY_CURRENT_USER\Software\Microsoft\Microsoft SQL Server\100\Tools\Shell\General,
Value Name: OnEnvironmentStartup, Value: 5
Cannot open subkey S-1-5-21-4043041569-140146884-403651058-1000 for key
HKEY_CURRENT_USER\Software\Microsoft\Protected Storage System Provider
Key: HKEY_CURRENT_USER\Software\Microsoft\VCSExpress\10.0\General, Value Name:
OnEnvironmentStartup, Value: 5
Key: HKEY_CURRENT_USER\Software\Microsoft\VCSExpress\10.0\Profile\LazyImport\{e8b06f41-6d01-
11d2-aa7d-00c04f990343}\ResetCategories, Value Name:
AutomationProperties\Environment\WebBrowser, Value: 1
Key: HKEY_CURRENT_USER\Software\Microsoft\VisualStudio\10.0\General, Value Name:
 OnEnvironmentStartup, Value: 5
Key: HKEY_CURRENT_USER\Software\Microsoft\VisualStudio\10.0_Config\Setup\VS, Value Name:
VS7EnvironmentLocation, Value: C:\Program Files (x86)\Microsoft VisualStudio
10.0\Common7\IDE\devenv.exe
Key: HKEY_CURRENT_USER\Software\Microsoft\VisualStudio\10.0_Config\Setup\VS, Value Name:
EnvironmentPath, Value: C:\Program Files (x86)\Microsoft Visual Studio
10.0\Common7\IDE\devenv.exe
Key: HKEY_CURRENT_USER\Software\Microsoft\VisualStudio\10.0_Config\Setup\VS, Value Name:
EnvironmentDirectory, Value: C:\Program Files (x86)\Microsoft Visual Studio
10.0\Common7\IDE\
```

```
Key: HKEY_CURRENT_USER\Software\Microsoft\VWDExpress\10.0\General, Value Name:
OnEnvironmentStartup, Value: 5
Press enter to finish
```

Reading and Modifying the Registry

In addition to the six root key properties, the `Registry` class provides static methods for reading and writing registry values, and these provide the most convenient way of getting and setting the value of specific registry entries. Listing 36-10 provides a demonstration.

Listing 36-10. Reading and Modifying the Registry Using the Registry Class

```csharp
using System;
using Microsoft.Win32;

class Listing_10 {

    static void Main(string[] args) {

        // define the key name
        string keyName = @"HKEY_CURRENT_USER\Software\Apress\Introduction to C#";

        // set a value for the key
        Registry.SetValue(keyName,
            "Windows Integration Example",
            "Test Value");

        // read the value back
        string value = (string)Registry.GetValue(keyName,
            "Windows Integration Example",
            "Default Value");

        // print out the value
        Console.WriteLine("Value: {0}", value);

        // wait for input before exiting
        Console.WriteLine("Press enter to finish");
        Console.ReadLine();
    }
}
```

The SetValue method takes the name of the key, the name of the value, and the value itself as parameters. The GetValue method retrieves a value and takes the name of the key, the name of the value, and a default value to use whether a value has not been previously set. In Listing 36-10, I set and then get the same value. Note that when using these static methods, you can specify the key name fully, including the root key, in this case HKEY_CURRENT_USER. Compiling and running Listing 36-10 produces the following output:

```
Value: Test Value
Press enter to finish
```

Using the Windows Registry Editor, we can see the key that Listing 36-10 created, as shown by Figure 36-11.

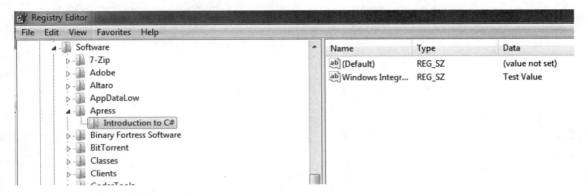

Figure 36-11. *Viewing a key with the Registry Editor*

Summary

In this chapter, we looked at the ways in which the .NET Framework Class Library provides support for accessing key features of the Windows operating system. Using C#, we have been able to use the event log, gain elevated privileges, create and install a Windows service, and make use of the registry. These features are not directly required by C# or .NET, but they can be very useful in making a C# program better fit into the Windows ecosystem.

■ ■ ■

CHAPTER 37

Cryptography and Security

When the .NET Framework was first released, it contained an extensive set of security and cryptographic features. Of particular note was the ability to apply strict controls over the use of your .NET assemblies through a sophisticated policy system. The security features were very comprehensive and so complicated that pretty much no one ever used them. With .NET 4, almost all the security features have been deprecated and are no longer supported, which leaves only the cryptographic features. Fortunately, the same attention to detail that went into the abandoned policy system was also applied to the cryptographic support, which means there is a comprehensive range of algorithms and support classes available for the C# programmer.

In this chapter, we will take a look at how the cryptography features can be used to address common security concerns, including encryption (used to protect data from unwanted eyes), hash codes (used to ensure that data has not been modified), and techniques for generating random data securely and keeping the content of strings hidden.

I have a warning, though, before we start. The security and cryptography features of any programming language have two fatal flaws: the programmer and the user. It is incredibly easy to create a program that appears to have solved a security problem but doesn't—either because it has been badly implemented or because it is badly used.

As a general rule, cryptographic features are used to transform a problem so that it might be easier to solve. For example, imagine you and I need to send data to one another that no one else should be able to read. An obvious approach would be for you to encrypt the data and for me to decrypt it. This is like putting a password on the data, where the password is known as the *encryption key*. For the most commonly used kinds of encryption, I need to use the same password to decrypt the data as you used to encrypt it. And so the problem has changed from how to exchange data in private to how to exchange the key securely. If you e-mail it to me, would the same people who want to read our data be able to read the key and decrypt the data anyway? Can you trust me not to write the key on my whiteboard in a public office? If we meet in person, are bad people likely to be listening to us?

A-ha, you say—what about public key cryptography? Doesn't that solve the problem? And, of course, the answer is that it doesn't; it just changes it in a different way. Public key cryptography means you encrypt the data using a key that can be safely shared with everyone, while I decrypt it using a key that is known only to me. It relies on some very clever math. The problem becomes making sure that you are using *my* public key and verifying that it is me you are exchanging the data with, ensuring that my key hasn't been stolen, and so on.

I could continue, but you get the idea. Cryptographic features must be used with caution. Simply exploring the cryptographic features of .NET is very different from using them to solve a real-world problem. This chapter will help you do the former, but a lot of careful thought and learning is required to do the latter. There are no recent books that I would recommend for .NET security, but for older titles I suggest either my own book, written with Allen Jones, called *Programing .NET Security* and published by O'Reilly, or Jason Bock's book *.NET Security*, published by Apress. Table 37-1 provides the summary for this chapter.

Table 37-1. *Quick Problem/Solution Reference for Chapter 37*

Problem	Solution	Listings
Create or use an encryption key and initialization vector.	Instantiate a `SymmetricAlgorithm` object, and read or set the `Key` and `IV` properties.	37-1, 37-2
Encrypt data.	Use a `SymmetricAlgorithm` with a `CryptoStream` object, and write the data that is to be encrypted to the stream.	37-3
Decrypt data.	Use a `SymmetricAlgorithm` with a `CryptoStream` object, and read the data that is to be decrypted from the stream.	37-4
Encrypt or decrypt data without creating keys.	Use the Data Protection API, which generates keys automatically for Windows users.	37-5
Generate or validate a hash code.	Create a `HashAlgorithm` object, and use the `ComputeHash` method.	37-6, 37-7, 37-8
Securely generate random data.	Use the `RandomNumberGenerator` class.	37-9
Work securely with strings.	Use the `SecureString` class.	37-10

Encrypting and Decrypting Data

Perhaps the most common cryptographic task is to encrypt data that can then be later decrypted. The .NET Framework Class Library provides a good range of encryption algorithms, and in this section I'll demonstrate how to use them to encrypt and decrypt data. There are two broad categories of encryption algorithm: *symmetric* and *asymmetric*. Symmetric encryption algorithms use the same secret *key* (effectively a password) to both encrypt and decrypt the data that the systems or users involved must have agreed on in advance. With asymmetric algorithms, also called *public key* algorithms, each user has different keys to encrypt and decrypt the data. The encryption key can be shared freely, and the decryption key must kept secret, even from the person you are sharing data with. In this chapter, I am going to stick with symmetric encryption, which is the simplest to use and demonstrate. Asymmetric algorithms are much more complicated, have many more security issues to worry about, and require significantly more computation to encrypt and decrypt data.

Creating and Using Encryption Keys

The base class for encryption in .NET is the abstract `SymmetricAlgorithm` class, which is in the `System.Security.Cryptography` namespace. Each algorithm that is supported by the .NET Framework is represented by another abstract class that derived from `SymmetricAlgorithm`, and different implementations of that algorithm are then implemented by concrete classes. This will be clearer if you look at Table 37-2, which shows the algorithms, the abstract classes, and the implementation classes.

Table 37-2. The Symmetric Algorithm Classes

Encryption Algorithm	Abstract Class	Implementation Classes
AES	Aes	AesCryptoServiceProvider AesManaged
DES	DES	DESCryptoServiceProvider
RC2	RC2	RC2CryptoServiceProvider
Rijndael	Rijndael	RijndaelManaged
Triple DES	TripleDES	TripleDESCryptoServiceProvider

The implementation classes whose name ends in Managed are written using one of the .NET languages, whereas the classes whose name ends in CryptoServiceProvider rely on the native Windows implementations.

If you don't know which algorithm you need, then I recommend you use AES. All of the algorithm implementation classes are instantiated using the default constructor, and it is usual to upcast the object to the SymmetricAlgorithm type, like this:

```
SymmetricAlgorithm myAlgorithm = new AesManaged();
```

Once you have created a SymmetricAlgorithm object, you can read the Key property to obtain a randomly generated encryption key. Or, if you have agreed a key in advance, set this property to your key value. Listing 37-1 demonstrates generating a key.

Listing 37-1. Generating an Encryption Key

```
using System;
using System.Security.Cryptography;
using System.Text;

class Listing_01 {

    static void Main(string[] args) {

        SymmetricAlgorithm myAlgorithm = new AesManaged();

        // print out the key
        Console.WriteLine("Key: {0}", Convert.ToBase64String(myAlgorithm.Key));

        // print out the IV
        Console.WriteLine("IV: {0}", Convert.ToBase64String(myAlgorithm.IV));

        // wait for input before exiting
        Console.WriteLine("Press enter to finish");
        Console.ReadLine();
```

```
        }
}
```

Listing 37-1 also reads the IV property to get the *initialization vector* for the algorithm object. The IV is used to make breaking the encryption more difficult and is not a secret. It is usually sent along with the encrypted data or agreed on in advance when the key is decided upon. Listing 37-1 prints out values for the key and the IV without performing any encryption, which is useful when you need to create a key and IV in advance. Both the key and the IV are expressed as byte arrays, so I have used the static `Convert.ToBase64String` method to convert the values into encoded strings that can be easily read and shared. Compiling and running Listing 37-1 produces the following results:

```
Key: Mg4/3QM2Z7fWHWpaFpSl362ERWDLVzt95lxByOG1qPQ=
IV: BvwVkCwsetgeMBls1FWZNg==
Press enter to finish
```

To use these values, we simply create another algorithm object and set the Key and IV properties, as demonstrated by Listing 37-2.

Listing 37-2. Setting an Encryption Key and IV

```
using System;
using System.Security.Cryptography;
using System.Text;

class Listing_02 {

    static void Main(string[] args) {

        SymmetricAlgorithm myAlgorithm = new AesManaged();

        // decode the key and IV
        byte[] key = Convert.FromBase64String(
            "Mg4/3QM2Z7fWHWpaFpSl362ERWDLVzt95lxByOG1qPQ=");
        byte[] iv = Convert.FromBase64String("BvwVkCwsetgeMBls1FWZNg==");

        // set the properties on the algorithm object
        myAlgorithm.Key = key;
        myAlgorithm.IV = iv;

        // wait for input before exiting
        Console.WriteLine("Press enter to finish");
        Console.ReadLine();
    }
}
```

Using base 64 encoding is a little unusual, but I find it ideal for reading and sharing keys and IVs. Every modern programming language and platform can convert to and from the encoding, and it creates compact and easily read strings. Once we have created an algorithm object and created or set the key and IV, we can encrypt and decrypt data.

Encrypting Data

The easiest way to encrypt data is through the `CryptoStream` class in the `System.Security.Cryptography` namespace. This class uses a `SymmeticAlgorithm` object to encrypt or decrypt streaming data and can be used in conjunction with other stream classes to write data in memory, to files, and to the network. When used with a `MemoryStream` class, `CryptoStream` can be used to encrypt data in memory, as demonstrated by Listing 37-3. To encrypt data in a file, replace `MemoryStream` with a `FileStream` object, and to encrypt data to be transmitted over a network, replace the `MemoryStream` with a stream object obtained from a network connection. See Chapters 20 and 21 for examples.

Listing 37-3. Encrypting Data in Memory Using MemoryStream

```csharp
using System;
using System.IO;
using System.Security.Cryptography;

class Listing_03 {

    static void Main(string[] args) {

        // create a new SymmeticAlgoritm object
        SymmetricAlgorithm myAlgorithm = new AesManaged();

        // read and print out the key and IV values
        Console.WriteLine("Key: {0}", Convert.ToBase64String(myAlgorithm.Key));
        Console.WriteLine("IV: {0}", Convert.ToBase64String(myAlgorithm.IV));

        // create a memory stream
        MemoryStream memStream = new MemoryStream();

        // create a CryptoStream that uses the MemoryStream
        CryptoStream myCryptoStream
            = new CryptoStream(memStream,
                            myAlgorithm.CreateEncryptor(),
                            CryptoStreamMode.Write);

        // create a StreamWriter so we can work with strings and not bytes
        StreamWriter myStreamWriter = new StreamWriter(myCryptoStream);

        // write some secret data
        myStreamWriter.Write("The gold is hidden in the kitchen");

        // close the writer and read the encrypted data from the memory stream
        myStreamWriter.Close();
        byte[] encryptedData = memStream.ToArray();

        // encode and print out the data
        Console.WriteLine("Data: {0}", Convert.ToBase64String(encryptedData));

        // wait for input before exiting
        Console.WriteLine("Press enter to finish");
```

```
            Console.ReadLine();
        }
}
```

The CryptoStream class takes three constructor parameters. The first is the Stream that should be written to or read from. For this example, I have used a MemoryStream object, which stores data in memory. The second argument is an implementation of the ICryptoTransform interface. You can get the implementations you need by calling the CreateEncryptor and CreateDecryptor method on your SymmetricAlgorithm object. The final argument is a value from the CryptoStreamMode enumeration, which defines the values Read (used when decrypting data) and Write (used when encrypting data).

The CryptoStream class works on byte values, so for convenience, I have created a StreamWriter that lets me write data to the stream using C# strings. I write a secret message to the StreamWriter using the Write method. This passes the byte data from my message to the CryptoStream class, which uses the SymmetricAlgorithm object to encrypt my data. The encrypted data is then written to the MemoryStream. I retrieve the encrypted data from the MemoryStream by calling the ToArray method and then encode the result using base 64 to make it easier to work with. Compiling and running Listing 37-3 produces the following results:

```
Key: i9zrkg4sws97Xly/c4Cw9nPVf85s70A//ZpnWGGV5UM=
IV: TlcaDtlqR+c3mLsDTtePmg==
Data: FZQuZQNzBC58xNDKjZTXZrS7W8pMPzfmFmR3dzbv3voLI90tOdg/7WoOVUmtFtIY
Press enter to finish
```

The results you see will be different because I am using a randomly generated key and IV. The encrypted data changes each time the key and IV change, meaning that all three values in the results will be different each time Listing 37-3 is run.

Decrypting Data

The process of decrypting data is, as you might expect, the reverse of encryption. We need to know four things to decrypt data: the algorithm used to encrypt the data, the values of the key and IV, and the encrypted data. Listing 37-4 demonstrates how to decrypt the data we created in Listing 37-3.

Listing 37-4. Decrypting Data

```
using System;
using System.IO;
using System.Security.Cryptography;

class Listing_04 {

    static void Main(string[] args) {

        // define the key, IV and data
        byte[] myKey = Convert.FromBase64String(
            "i9zrkg4sws97Xly/c4Cw9nPVf85s70A//ZpnWGGV5UM=");
        byte[] myIV = Convert.FromBase64String(
            "TlcaDtlqR+c3mLsDTtePmg==");
```

```
byte[] myEncryptedData = Convert.FromBase64String(
    "FZQuZQNzBC58xNDKjZTXZrS7W8pMPzfmFmR3dzbv3voLI9OtOdg/7WoOVUmtFtIY");

// create the SymmetricAlgorithm object
SymmetricAlgorithm myAlgorithm = new AesCryptoServiceProvider();
// set the key and IV values
myAlgorithm.Key = myKey;
myAlgorithm.IV = myIV;

// create a MemoryStream using the encrypted data
MemoryStream memStream = new MemoryStream(myEncryptedData);
memStream.Seek(0, SeekOrigin.Begin);

// create a CryptoStream that will decrypt the data
CryptoStream cryptoStream
    = new CryptoStream(
        memStream,
        myAlgorithm.CreateDecryptor(),
        CryptoStreamMode.Read);

// create a StreamReader so we can work with strings and not bytes
StreamReader myReader = new StreamReader(cryptoStream);

// read the secret data
string mySecret = myReader.ReadToEnd();

// print out the secret message
Console.WriteLine("Secret message: {0}", mySecret);

// wait for input before exiting
Console.WriteLine("Press enter to finish");
Console.ReadLine();
    }
}
```

Notice that I encrypted the data using the AesManaged class but decrypt it using AesCryptoServiceProvider. You can mix and match these implementations, and generally the crypto service classes offer better performance. Listing 37-4 uses the values generated by Listing 37-3 and decrypts the data. Compiling and running Listing 37-4 produces the following results:

```
Secret message: The gold is hidden in the kitchen
Press enter to finish
```

Using the Windows Data Protection API

The Windows Data Protection API (DPAPI) allows you to encrypt and decrypt data using keys that are generated automatically by the operating system. This is useful if, for example, you want to encrypt data that only the current user should be able to decrypt. You don't have to worry about generating a key that the user has to remember, because you use a key that is already associated with their Windows credentials.

■ **Note** To use DPAPI, you must add the System.Security assembly to your Visual Studio project.

The ProtectedData class in the System.Security.Cryptography namespace can be used to encrypt and decrypt data. The Protect method encrypts a byte array, and the Unprotect method decrypts it, as demonstrated by Listing 37-5.

Listing 37-5. Encrypting and Decrypting Using the ProtectedData Class

```
using System;
using System.Security.Cryptography;
using System.Text;

class Listing_05 {

    static void Main(string[] args) {

        // define the data to encrypt
        string secretMessage = "The password is 1234";

        // get the bytes from the data
        byte[] secretMessageBytes = Encoding.Default.GetBytes(secretMessage);

        // encrypt the data using DPAPI
        byte[] encryptedData = ProtectedData.Protect(
            secretMessageBytes,
            null,
            DataProtectionScope.CurrentUser);

        // decrypt the data again
        byte[] decryptedData = ProtectedData.Unprotect(
            encryptedData,
            null,
            DataProtectionScope.CurrentUser);

        // print out the decrypted message
        Console.WriteLine("Decrypted message: {0}",
            Encoding.Default.GetString(decryptedData));

        // wait for input before exiting
        Console.WriteLine("Press enter to finish");
        Console.ReadLine();
    }
}
```

The Protect method takes three parameters. The first is the byte array containing the data that you want to encrypt. The second is an optional byte array that is used to make the encrypted data more difficult to crack. If you use this feature, you will need to use the same data to decrypt the data again, which in some ways defeats the convenience offered by the DPAPI. You can ignore this feature by using null. The third parameter is a value from the DataProtectionScope enumeration. The CurrentUser value means that the data can be decrypted only by the user account used to encrypt it, while the LocalMachine value means that the data can be decrypted by any user on the computer used to encrypt the data.

Data is decrypted using the Unprotect method, which also takes three parameters. The first is the encrypted data; the second is the entropy data, if any, used in the encryption; and the final argument is the value from the DataProtectionScope enumeration that was used during encryption. Compiling and running Listing 37-5 produces the following results:

```
Decrypted message: The password is 1234
Press enter to finish
```

There are no versions of the Protect and Unprotect methods that work with streams, so you must read blocks of data from streams and process them manually. Chapter 20 explains how to read byte arrays from Stream objects.

Using Hash Codes

Hash codes are used to ensure the integrity of data. If you have downloaded a software package from a web site, you will have seen a hash code published alongside the download. This is so you can verify that files you download are the ones that were originally published and that no one has tampered with or altered the data in any way.

The base class in the .NET Framework Class Library is HashAlgorithm, which is the System.Security.Cryptography namespace. The class hierarchy for hash algorithms follows the same style as for encryption algorithms—an abstract class derived from HashAlgorithm for each algorithm available, which are in turn derived for each implementation. Table 37-3 lists the available hash algorithm classes.

Table 37-3. *The Hash Algorithm Classes*

Hash Algorithm	Abstract Class	Implementation Classes
MD5	MD5	MD5Cng MD5CryptoServiceProvider
MD160	RIPEMD160	RIPEMD160Managed
SHA-1	SHA1	SHA1Cng SHA1CryptoServiceProvider SHA1Managed
SHA-256	SHA256	SHA256Cng SHA256CryptoServiceProvider

Hash Algorithm	Abstract Class	Implementation Classes
		SHA256Managed
SHA-384	SHA384	SHA384Cng SHA384CryptoServiceProvider SHA384Managed
SHA-512	SHA512	SHA512Cng SHA512CryptoServiceProvider SHA512Managed

The implementation classes whose names end with Cng are implemented using the oddly named *Cryptography Next Generation* (CNG) Windows API, which is a replacement for the Cryptography API. CNG was added to Windows Vista and won't be available if you deploy your program to earlier versions of Windows. Use the managed versions if you are in doubt about the versions of Windows available.

The most widely used hash algorithm is the Secure Hash Algorithm (SHA). The different versions of the SHA algorithm produce hash codes of different sizes where the number represents the bits of data in the hash code. The SHA-512 hash codes are 512 bits long, for example. The exception is SHA-1, which is the original SHA standard. This has a 160-bit hash code. It is possible that two different pieces of data can produce the same hash code. As a general rule, the longer the hash code is, the less likely it is that this will happen, but the more computation will be required to generate and verify the code. If you are in doubt about which hash algorithm to use, then I recommend SHA-256 as a reasonable balance between security and performance for most projects.

Generating a Hash Code

To generate a hash code, you create an object from one of the algorithm implementation classes and call the ComputeHash method. Listing 37-6 provides a demonstration.

Listing 37-6. Generating a Hash Code

```
using System;
using System.Security.Cryptography;
using System.Text;

class Listing_06 {

    static void Main(string[] args) {

        // create the algorithm object
        HashAlgorithm myHashAlgorithm = new SHA256Managed();

        // create the data we want to hash
        string myData = "This is my message";

        // compute the hash code for the data
        byte[] hashCode = myHashAlgorithm.ComputeHash(Encoding.Default.GetBytes(myData));
```

```
        // print out the hash code
        Console.WriteLine("Hash code: {0}", Convert.ToBase64String(hashCode));

        // wait for input before exiting
        Console.WriteLine("Press enter to finish");
        Console.ReadLine();
    }
}
```

Listing 37-6 uses the SHA256Managed implementation class to generate a hash code for a string. There is no version of the ComputeHash method that takes a string parameter, so I have used the Encoding class to convert the string to a byte array. When you validate the hash code, you must be sure to use the same encoding; otherwise, the hash codes won't match. The hash code is generated as a byte array, so I have used base 64 encoding to convert it to something that we can use more easily. If you encode the hash code like this (or using any other encoding), you must use the same encoding during validation, or, once again, the hash codes won't match. Compiling and running Listing 37-6 produces the following results:

```
Hash code: MxG3wL2Rtsc6OCEt6K3jHFGRDxdICtIS7SuXmKNbdOc=
Press enter to finish
```

You can also generate hash codes for streams of data, which allows for easy hashing of the contents of files. Listing 37-7 provides a demonstration of generating a hash code for a file called datafile.txt, which I have added to the Visual Studio project. The content of the file is as follows:

```
This is a data file.
Here is some data.
This is the end of the data.
```

Listing 37-7. Generating a Hash Code for a File

```
using System;
using System.IO;
using System.Security.Cryptography;

class Listing_07 {

    static void Main(string[] args) {

        // open a stream to the file
        Stream myStream = File.OpenRead(@"..\..\datafile.txt");

        // create the hash algorithm object
        HashAlgorithm myHashAlgorithm = new SHA256Managed();

        // generate the hash code for the data
        byte[] hashCode = myHashAlgorithm.ComputeHash(myStream);
```

```
        // print out the hashcode
        Console.WriteLine("Hash code: {0}", Convert.ToBase64String(hashCode));

        // wait for input before exiting
        Console.WriteLine("Press enter to finish");
        Console.ReadLine();
    }
}
```

I create a `Stream` from the file using the `System.IO.File` class. You can find details of this class and other ways to open files in Chapter 20. I create my `HashAlgorithm` object and then pass the `Stream` as a parameter to the `ComputeHash` method. The contents of the file are read in, and the hash code is returned as a byte array. Once again, I encode the bytes using base 64 so we can read them more readily. The result of compiling and running Listing 37-7 is as follows:

```
Hash code: jgtZ8C7iFrBr7YRGBqKtN8e8zNTw9Fq791QyOKz2+/E=
Press enter to finish
```

Verifying a Hash Code

To validate a hash code, we need the data and the hash code that the person who sent us the data has generated. We then use the same hash algorithm to generate our own hash code, and if the two match, we can be confident that the data we received is the data that was sent to us and has not been modified in any way. Listing 37-8 demonstrates validating the checksum we generate in Listing 37-7.

Listing 37-8. Validating a Hash Code

```
using System;
using System.IO;
using System.Linq;
using System.Security.Cryptography;

class Listing_08 {

    static void Main(string[] args) {

        // define the hash code we were sent
        string originalHashCodeString = "jgtZ8C7iFrBr7YRGBqKtN8e8zNTw9Fq791QyOKz2+/E=";
        // decode the hash code to get the bytes
        byte[] originalHashCode = Convert.FromBase64String(originalHashCodeString);

        // open a stream to the file
        Stream myStream = File.OpenRead(@"..\..\datafile.txt");

        // create the hash algorithm object
        HashAlgorithm myHashAlgorithm = new SHA256Managed();

        // generate the new hash code for the data
```

```
    byte[] newHashCode = myHashAlgorithm.ComputeHash(myStream);

    // compare the hash codes byte by byte
    bool hashCodeIsValid = newHashCode.SequenceEqual(originalHashCode);

    // print out the hashcode
    Console.WriteLine("Hash code is valid: {0}", hashCodeIsValid);

    // wait for input before exiting
    Console.WriteLine("Press enter to finish");
    Console.ReadLine();
  }
}
```

Listing 37-8 follows the same steps as Listing 37-7 to generate a hash code for the file. I then use the SequenceEqual LINQ extension method to compare the sequence of bytes in each hash code to see whether they are the same. This is a handy way of comparing the contents of two arrays.

The two hash codes won't match if even one bit of data in the file has been changed since the first hash code was generated. If they are identical, then the codes will match. Since my file is the same, I get the following output when I compile and run Listing 37-8:

```
Hash code is valid: True
Press enter to finish
```

Generating Secure Random Numbers

In Chapter 26, I showed you how to generate pseudorandom numbers. These are quick to generate but are not useful for cryptographic purposes because the sequence of values generated can be predicted. If you need to generate truly random numbers—for keys or passwords, for example—then you should use the RandomNumberGenerator class in the System.Security.Cryptography namespace. Listing 37-9 demonstrates the use of this class.

Listing 37-9. Generating Secure Random Numbers

```
using System;
using System.Security.Cryptography;

class Listing_09 {

    static void Main(string[] args) {

        // create a new number generator
        RandomNumberGenerator rng = RandomNumberGenerator.Create();

        // define a byte array to fill with random data
        byte[] randomData = new byte[10];

        // generate random data
```

```
            rng.GetBytes(randomData);

            // print out the data
            Console.WriteLine(BitConverter.ToString(randomData));

            // wait for input before exiting
            Console.WriteLine("Press enter to finish");
            Console.ReadLine();
        }
    }
```

The static `Create` method returns a new implementation of the `RandomNumberGenerator` class. You generate random data by passing a byte array to the `GetBytes` method, which will fill the array with new data. If you want to ensure that none of the data values is zero, you can use the `GetNonZeroBytes` method. Compiling and running Listing 37-9 produces the following results. Your results will be different, of course, because this is random data:

```
64-88-FB-45-8E-C5-94-9B-D7-EE
Press enter to finish
```

I used the `System.BitConverter` class to create the string representation of the byte array. This is a handy class, although you can't use it easily with encrypted data because the data values produce nonprinting characters.

Working Securely with Strings

When dealing with sensitive information, the standard C# `string` type can be a problem. The contents of the string are stored in memory unencrypted. When you have finished with a string, its contents remain in memory until the garbage collector disposes of the data and the operating system's virtual memory system can temporarily copy the region of memory that contains your sensitive data to the hard disk. Although unlikely, each of these behaviors makes it possible that someone can read your secret data.

The solution is to use the `SecureString` class from the `System.Security` namespace. This class uses the Data Protection API (DPAPI) that we saw earlier in the chapter to encrypt string data. Listing 37-10 provides a demonstration that reads a password from the keyboard.

Listing 37-10. Using the SecureString Class

```
using System;
using System.Security;
using System.Runtime.InteropServices;

class Listing_10 {

    static void Main(string[] args) {

        // create the SecureString
        SecureString secString = new SecureString();
```

```
        // give instruction to the user
        Console.WriteLine("Type password and press enter");

        // define the variable that will hold details of the key press
        ConsoleKeyInfo keyInfo;

        // read from the keyboard
        while ((keyInfo = Console.ReadKey(true)).Key != ConsoleKey.Enter) {
            // append the character to the secure string
            secString.AppendChar(keyInfo.KeyChar);
            // print an asterisk to the user to give feedback
            Console.Write('*');
        }

        // get the unecrypted contents of the secure string
        string unencryptedPassword =
            Marshal.PtrToStringBSTR(Marshal.SecureStringToBSTR(secString));

        // print out the password that the user entered
        Console.WriteLine("\nThe password is: {0}", unencryptedPassword);

        // wait for input before exiting
        Console.WriteLine("Press enter to finish");
        Console.ReadLine();
    }
}
```

SecureString objects are created using the default constructor, and you can add characters using the AppendChar method. One key difference between string and SecureString is that you can change the contents of a SecureString once you have created it. Table 37-4 describes the methods of the SecureString class that you can use to modify the contents.

Table 37-4. Selected SecureString Members

Member	Description
AppendChar(char)	Appends the specified character to the end of the string
Clear()	Deletes the contents of the string
InsertAt(int, char)	Inserts the specified character at the specified index in the string
RemoveAt(int)	Removes the character at the specified location
SetAt(int, char)	Replaces the character at the specified index

Reading the contents of a SecureString object is difficult. The memory that contains the value is outside of the current process, which means you have to use a special (and advanced) technique to access it, using this statement:

```
string unencryptedPassword =
Marshal.PtrToStringBSTR(Marshal.SecureStringToBSTR(secString));
```

I am not going to explain how this statement works, other than to say that when you use it, you will create an unsecure string value that presents a risk that your content can be read after all, so you should read the contents of a SecureString with caution.

There are classes that use SecureString directly, meaning that you don't have to read the contents of the string to make use of it. A good example is the System.Diagnostics.ProcessStartInfo class, which you can use to start a Windows process using a different account. The Password property of this class is of the SecureString type.

Summary

In this chapter, we saw how to use the .NET cryptography features to perform common cryptographic operations, such as encryption, decryption, and hash code validation. The .NET Framework Class Library contains implementations of many encryption and has algorithms, some of which are implemented using underlying Windows features and others of which are written using .NET itself. We have also seen how to use the Data Protection API to encrypt data using keys that are maintained by Windows on behalf of users, which alleviates the user needing to remember additional information beyond their Windows credentials.

CHAPTER 38

■ ■ ■

Testing and Debugging

Every programmer knows about *bugs*—mistakes in code that lead to errors, unexpected behavior, and outright crashes. One approach to finding bugs is to use a debugger. Visual Studio has a very nice debugger that you can use to look at your program as it runs. If you want to see the debugger at work, select Start Debugging from the Visual Studio Debug menu, and start exploring.

The problem with a debugger is that it is *reactive*. You write your program and then use the debugger to try to re-create any problems that your testing process highlighted. If you are working from user feedback, you have to try to simulate the environment they were working in and the steps they took in order to get to the point where the debugger can show you the problem. A debugger is a valuable and useful tool, and if you have to spend hours tracking down some complex issue, the Visual Studio debugger is one of the best. In this chapter, we'll look at a .NET feature that is complementary to the Visual Studio debugger but which you control using code statements.

■ **Note** Unfortunately, some of the features in this chapter are not available in the Express edition of Visual Studio. This is one area where Microsoft differentiates between the free and commercial versions of its product.

A complement to traditional debugging is to test your program as it is being written and to make some of the assumptions that you create in your code explicit so that they can be tested—ideally before your program falls into the hands of users. Some of the topics in this chapter are not intended to be a replacement for traditional debugging, but rather, they aim to reduce the frequency with which you have to break out the debugger and spend the afternoon trying to re-create esoteric running conditions. Table 38-1 provides the summary for this chapter.

Table 38-1. Quick Problem/Solution Reference for Chapter 38

Problem	Solution	Listings
Check the assumptions and logic in your code.	Use the Debug and Trace classes.	38-1 through 38-6
Check your code against a set of best practice guidelines and rules.	Use code analysis.	38-7 through 38-10
Define behavior contracts in your code that are then enforced through static or runtime checking.	Use code contracts.	38-11 through 38-15

Using the Debug and Trace Classes

The System.Diagnostics namespace contains two classes that you can use to debug your programs and test your program's logic. In this section, we will look at these two classes, see how they can be used, and explore the differences between them.

Using the Debug Class

The Debug class allows you to add debugging statements to your code that you can use to check your program logic and assumptions. These statements are included in your program only when you do a debug build of your project and are excluded when you do a release build. (I'll show you how to switch between debug and release builds at the end of this section.) This means that you can add statements that help you understand the way that a program is functioning without affecting the performance of the release versions of your code. Let's start with the example class that we want to work with, shown in Listing 38-1.

Listing 38-1. The Calculator Class

```
class Calculator {

    public int CalculateSum(int x, int y) {
        return x + y;
    }

    public int CalculateProduct(int x, int y) {
        return x * y;
    }

    public int CalculateSubtraction(int x, int y) {
        return x - y;
    }

    public int CalculateDivision(int x, int y) {
        return x / y;
    }
}
```

This seems like a simple enough class. There are four methods, and each of them takes two int parameters, performs a simple math operation, and returns an int result. Here is some code that uses the Calculator class:

```
using System;

class CalculatorTest {

    static void Main(string[] args) {

        // create a new Calculator object
        Calculator calc = new Calculator();
```

```
        // perform some calculations
        int sumResult = calc.CalculateProduct(10, 20);
        int productResult = calc.CalculateSum(10, 20);
        int subtractionResult = calc.CalculateSubtraction(10, 20);
        int divisionResult = calc.CalculateDivision(10, 20);

        // write out the results
        Console.WriteLine("Sum Result: {0}", sumResult);
        Console.WriteLine("Product Result: {0}", productResult);
        Console.WriteLine("Subtraction Result: {0}", subtractionResult);
        Console.WriteLine("Division Result: {0}", divisionResult);

        // wait for input before exiting
        Console.WriteLine("Press enter to finish");
        Console.ReadLine();
    }
}
```

Compiling and running the test class and the Calculator class gives us the following results:

```
Sum Result: 200
Product Result: 30
Subtraction Result: -10
Division Result: 0
Press enter to finish
```

It all looks good, but as we'll see, I have created some implied rules that you need to know in order to use my class without causing an exception or getting odd behavior.

The first implied rule is that the second parameter to the CalculateDivision method can't be zero. See what happens if we add the following statement to the CalculatorTest class:

```
int divisionResult = calc.CalculateDivision(10, 0);
```

We get a System.DivideByZero exception, which is not ideal. We could fix this by testing the value of the parameter in the CalculateDivision method, like this:

```
public int CalculateDivision(int x, int y) {
    if (y == 0) {
        // we can't perform this operation - throw an exception
        throw new ArgumentOutOfRangeException("y");
    }
    return x / y;
}
```

We still get an exception when the second parameter is zero, but at least the exception is slightly more useful. But we may have been addressing the wrong problem. What if the design of your program means that there should never have been a zero value in the first place? In such cases, throwing an exception doesn't really help. We are already in an defective state because a zero value has arisen elsewhere in the system when it shouldn't have, so it seems unlikely that the code that generated the zero value is in a position to handle either the original exception or our new exception properly.

Making Assertions

We can use the Debug class to test for conditions like these. Listing 38-2 shows the static Debug.Assert method applied to the CalculateDivision method.

Listing 38-2. Applying the Debug.Assert Method to a Method

```
using System.Diagnostics;

class Calculator {

    public int CalculateSum(int x, int y) {
        return x + y;
    }

    public int CalculateProduct(int x, int y) {
        return x * y;
    }

    public int CalculateSubtraction(int x, int y) {
        return x - y;
    }

    public int CalculateDivision(int x, int y) {
        Debug.Assert(y != 0, "Second parameter is zero");
        return x / y;
    }
}
```

This version of the Assert method takes a bool parameter and a string parameter. The bool is used to evaluate a condition that you require to be true for your program to work as designed or intended. In the listing, I have *asserted* that the parameter y should not be zero. If the condition evaluates to true, that is, the value of y is not zero, then the program continues as normal. If the condition evaluates to false, that is, y is zero, then execution of the program is stopped and a dialog box appears, displaying the string that was the second parameter to the Assert method, as shown in Figure 38-1.

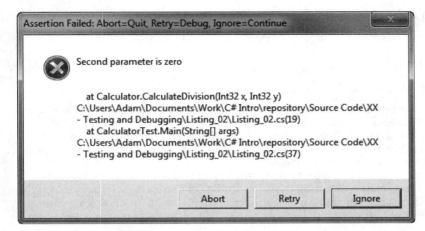

Figure 38-1. The dialog box shown by the Debug.Assert method

The meaning of the three buttons is misleading. Clicking the Abort button will terminate your program. Clicking the Ignore button will continue the execution of your program. In the example, this means that a System.DivideByZero exception will be thrown. Clicking the Retry button will prompt you to choose a debugger to debug your program with, as shown in Figure 38-2.

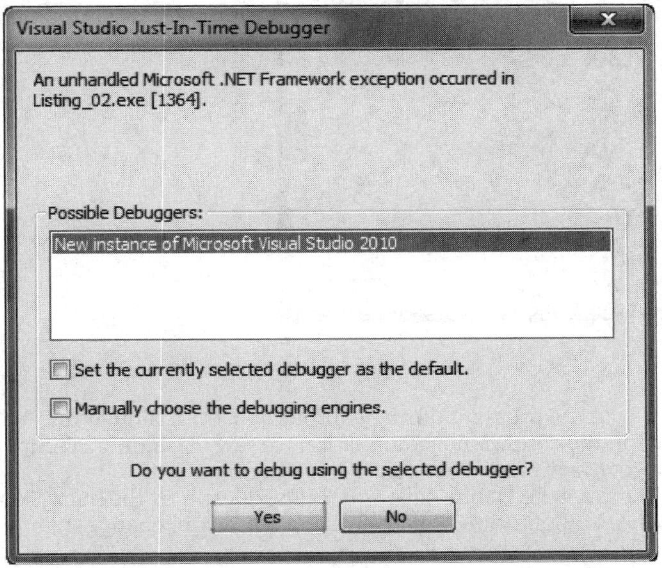

Figure 38-2. Selecting a debugger

If you already have Visual Studio open, you can start debugging, use that instance, or create a new instance debug with that one. Selecting the debugger you want to use and clicking the Yes button starts the debugging process.

Disabling Debug Statements

Once we have added an Assert statement, we can test until we find where the zero value arises and then remove the Assert method call. It would be nice if we could leave the statement there. After all, if the zero value is a big deal, then we always want to know when it arises. But such a statement will provide a miniscule amount of drag on the performance of our program, and we don't want our users to see the dialog box that is displayed when a zero value does arise.

Fortunately, we don't need to remove the Assert statement. It is removed for us when we compile our program for release. When you create a new project, Visual Studio configures it such that the Debug build mode is used. This includes all sorts of additional information that is useful for debugging your program. All that additional information is striped out when you switch to the Release mode, and so are the calls to the Debug class.

To switch to the Release mode, select the Configuration Manager item from the Build menu. This will show the Configuration Manager dialog box, as shown by Figure 38-3. Click the item in the Configuration column for the project you want to change, and select Release from the drop-down list.

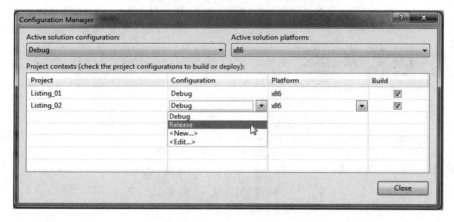

Figure 38-3. Changing the build configuration

The Assert call in the example is omitted from the program during compilation, even though the statement is still in the code file. This is similar to the conditional compilation we saw in Chapter 26 but doesn't require as much forethought. We still get the DivideByZero exception when we run the program—changing the build setting simply removes the Debug calls and, sadly, doesn't fix the bugs. To change back to the Debug build mode, open the Configuration Manager dialog box again, change the setting for your project back to Debug, and rebuild your project.

Changing the build setting also changes where your compiled program resides on the disk. In Debug mode, you can find the output of your project in the bin\Debug directory within your project folder. In Release mode, you will find the output in the bin\Release directory. When relying on the build mode to change the behavior of the program, by suppressing the Assert dialog boxes, for example, it is very important to make sure you ship the contents of the correct directory to your users.

Using Debug Listeners

The Debug class maintains a list of listener objects that are notified when you call the Assert method (or the other Debug methods that we'll see later). The dialog box appears when you call Assert because this is the behavior of the default listener object. It takes the parameter you passed to the Assert method and uses it in the dialog box.

We can access the set of listener objects through the Debug.Listeners property, which returns a TraceListenerCollection, which is a collection of TraceListener objects. This is the base class for objects that want to listen to debug messages.

We can remove the default listener and add our own. The simplest way to do this is to use the TextWriterTraceListener class, which will receive messages from the Debug class and write them to a Stream, to a TextWriter, or directly to a file. Listing 38-3 demonstrates removing the default and adding our own listener.

Listing 38-3. Replacing the Default Debug Listener

```
using System;
using System.Diagnostics;

class CalculatorTest {

    static void Main(string[] args) {

        // remove the default listener
        Debug.Listeners.Clear();
        // create a new listener
        TextWriterTraceListener listener = new TextWriterTraceListener(Console.Out);
        // register our new listener
        Debug.Listeners.Add(listener);

        // create a new Calculator object
        Calculator calc = new Calculator();

        // perform a calculation that we know will cause a problem
        int divisionResult = calc.CalculateDivision(10, 0);

        // write out the result
        Console.WriteLine("Division Result: {0}", divisionResult);

        // wait for input before exiting
        Console.WriteLine("Press enter to finish");
        Console.ReadLine();
    }
}
```

To remove any existing listeners, we call the Clear method on the collection returned from the Debug.Listeners property. The Debug class can have multiple listeners, so care should be taken when calling the Clear method to prevent removing a listener that you wanted to keep. Here is the statement that removes the listeners:

```
Debug.Listeners.Clear();
```

The TextWriterTraceListener class has three constructor overloads, which are described in Table 38-2.

Table 38-2. The Constructors for the TextWriterTraceListener *Class*

Constructor	Description
TextWriterTraceListener(Stream)	Debug messages are written to the specified Stream object.
TextWriterTraceListener(TextWriter)	Debug messages are written to the specific TextWriter object.
TextWriterTraceListener(string)	Debug messages are written to the file whose name is specified.

In the listing, I have created an instance using the static Console.Out property as the constructor parameter, like this:

```
TextWriterTraceListener listener = new TextWriterTraceListener(Console.Out);
```

The Console.Out property returns a Stream object that, if you write to it, sends data to be written to the command window used to start the program. This trick doesn't work with Windows Forms or WPF programs. You should write your debug messages to a file for such programs, either by creating a Stream using the File class or by using the TextWriterTraceListener constructor that takes a file name as a parameter. If I had wanted to write to a file called myFile.txt, I would have used this:

```
TextWriterTraceListener listener = new TextWriterTraceListener("myFile.txt");
```

Having created the TextWriterTraceListener, I register it with the Debug class as follows:

```
Debug.Listeners.Add(listener);
```

Once I have added my TextWriterTraceListener, messages from the Assert method will be passed to my object, which will in turn be written to the console. If we compile and run the listing, we get the following results:

```
Fail: Second parameter is zero

Unhandled Exception: System.DivideByZeroException: Attempted to divide by zero.
   at Calculator.CalculateDivision(Int32 x, Int32 y) in C:\Listing_03\Listing_03.cs:line 20
   at CalculatorTest.Main(String[] args) in C: \Listing_03\Listing_03.cs:line 35
Press any key to continue . . .
```

You can see that the message is written to the console and that this is followed by the exception that is caused by the zero value parameter. Our new listener doesn't stop the execution of the program. There are several overloaded versions of the Assert method, as described in Table 38-3.

Table 38-3. Debug.Assert Overloads

Method Overload	Description
Assert(bool)	Sends an empty message to the listeners if the bool is false.
Assert(bool, string)	Sends the message specified by the string to the listeners if the bool is false.
Assert(bool, string, string)	Sends a message consisting of a short description (the first string parameter) and a detailed description (the second string parameter) to the listeners if the bool is false.
Assert(bool, string, string, params object[])	As with the previous overload, except that the composite formatting feature is used to format the second string argument using the contents of the object array.

The TextWriterTraceListener class writes the short message and the detailed message on the same line of the output. For example, if we change our call to Assert, as follows:

```
Debug.Assert(y != 0, "Bad parameter value", "The {0} parameter is {1}", "second",
y);
```

then we get the following output from the TextWriterTraceListener when running the example:

```
Fail: Bad parameter value The second parameter is 0
```

Other Debug Methods

The Debug class contains other members besides the Assert method. The most useful are described in Table 38-4.

Table 38-4. Useful Debug Members

Member	Description
Fail(string) Fail(string, string)	Send the single- or two-part message to the listeners. There is no condition to evaluate with this method; the message is always sent.
Indent() Unindent()	Increases or decreases the indentation level for subsequent messages; see the example after the table.
WriteLineIf(bool, string) WriteLineIf(bool, object)	Sends the string message or the value of the object's ToString method to the listeners if the bool is true.

Member	Description
WriteLineIf(bool, string, string) WriteLineIf(bool, object, string)	As for the overloads listed earlier, with the addition of the category specified by the third parameter. See the example after the table.
WriteLine(string) WriteLine(object) WriteLine(string, string) WriteLine(string, object)	The WriteLine method works sends a string message or the contents of an object's ToString method to the listeners, with or without a category. There is no condition when using this method; the message is always sent.

The WriteLineIf method works in a similar way to the Assert method, although the message is sent when the bool parameter is true. The WriteLine method always writes its message. There is no condition to evaluate. Both of these methods provide support for specifying a category, which can be used to provide additional context in your debug output.

Indenting Debug Output

You can add structure to your debug output using the Indent and Unindent methods. The Indent method increases the indentation level for messages, and the Unindent method reduces it again. These methods are useful when combined with WriteLine, as shown by Listing 38-4.

Listing 38-4. Indenting and Using the WriteLine and WriteLineIf Methods

```
using System;
using System.Diagnostics;

class Calculator {

    public int CalculateSum(int x, int y) {
        return x + y;
    }

    public int CalculateProduct(int x, int y) {
        return x * y;
    }

    public int CalculateSubtraction(int x, int y) {
        return x - y;
    }

    public int CalculateDivision(int x, int y) {
        Debug.WriteLine("Entered CalculateDivision Method");
        Debug.Indent();
        Debug.WriteLine("Parameters are: {0} {1}", x, y);
        Debug.WriteLineIf(y == 0, "Second parameter is zero");
        Debug.Unindent();
        Debug.WriteLine("Exiting CalculateDivision Method");
        return x / y;
```

```
    }
}
```

I realize that the debug statements in Listing 38-4 outnumber the actual code statements, but it can be like this in real projects as well, especially if there is a suspicion that an elusive bug is related to a small region of code. Compiling and running Listing 38-4 produces the following results:

```
Entered CalculateDivision Method
    Parameters are: 10 0
    Second parameter is zero
Exiting CalculateDivision Method

Unhandled Exception: System.DivideByZeroException: Attempted to divide by zero.
    at Calculator.CalculateDivision(Int32 x, Int32 y) in C:\Listing_04\Listing_04.cs:line 25
    at CalculatorTest.Main(String[] args) in C:\Listing_04\Listing_04.cs:line 44
Press any key to continue . . .
```

Using Categories

The WriteLine and WriteLineIf methods have overloads that support categories. These are useful for differentiating between different kinds of debug output, as demonstrated by Listing 38-5.

Listing 38-5. Using Categories for Debugging Statements

```csharp
using System.Diagnostics;

class Calculator {

    public int CalculateSum(int x, int y) {
        return x + y;
    }

    public int CalculateProduct(int x, int y) {
        return x * y;
    }

    public int CalculateSubtraction(int x, int y) {
        return x - y;
    }

    public int CalculateDivision(int x, int y) {
        Debug.WriteLine("Entered CalculateDivision Method", "Trace");
        Debug.Indent();
        Debug.WriteLine(string.Format("Parameters are: {0} {1}", x, y), "Parameters");
        Debug.WriteLineIf(y == 0, "Second parameter is zero", "Error");
        Debug.Unindent();
        Debug.WriteLine("Exiting CalculateDivision Method", "Trace");
        return x / y;
    }
}
```

```
}
```

In this example, I have added categories to show that some statements are used to trace the flow of the program, some are used to report on method parameter values, and others report errors. Compiling and running Listing 38-5 produces the following results:

```
Trace: Entered CalculateDivision Method
    Parameters: Parameters are: 10 0
    Error: Second parameter is zero
Trace: Exiting CalculateDivision Method

Unhandled Exception: System.DivideByZeroException: Attempted to divide by zero.
    at Calculator.CalculateDivision(Int32 x, Int32 y) in C:\Listing_05\Listing_05.cs:line 25
    at CalculatorTest.Main(String[] args) in C:\Listing_05\Listing_05.cs:line 44
```

I find this feature useful for processing debug log files after a test has been run; it is a simple matter to separate the error statements from the other categories.

Using the Trace Class

The Trace class is very similar to the Debug class, except that calls to the Trace class are not usually removed during compilation. This means you can provide instrumentation to track the health of your program even when it has been shipped to users. Listing 38-6 has a simple demonstration of using the Trace class.

Listing 38-6. Using the Trace Class

```
using System;
using System.Diagnostics;

class Calculator {

    public int CalculateSum(int x, int y) {
        return x + y;
    }

    public int CalculateProduct(int x, int y) {
        return x * y;
    }

    public int CalculateSubtraction(int x, int y) {
        return x - y;
    }

    public int CalculateDivision(int x, int y) {
        Trace.WriteLine("Entered CalculateDivision Method", "Trace");
        Trace.Indent();
        Trace.WriteLine(string.Format("Parameters are: {0} {1}", x, y), "Parameters");
```

```
        Trace.WriteLineIf(y == 0, "Second parameter is zero", "Error");
        Trace.Unindent();
        Trace.WriteLine("Exiting CalculateDivision Method", "Trace");
        return x / y;
    }
}

class CalculatorTest {

    static void Main(string[] args) {

        // remove the default listener
        Trace.Listeners.Clear();
        // create a new listener
        TextWriterTraceListener listener = new TextWriterTraceListener(Console.Out);
        // register our new listener
        Trace.Listeners.Add(listener);

        // create a new Calculator object
        Calculator calc = new Calculator();

        // perform a calculation that we know will cause a problem
        int divisionResult = calc.CalculateDivision(10, 0);

        // write out the result
        Console.WriteLine("Division Result: {0}", divisionResult);

        // wait for input before exiting
        Console.WriteLine("Press enter to finish");
        Console.ReadLine();
    }
}
```

You can see from the listing that you can use the Trace class exactly as you would the Debug class. Adding listeners is the same (and uses the same kind of listener class), the method signatures are the same, and the abilities to indent, provide categories, and evaluate conditions are the same. If we compile and run Listing 38-6, we can see that the output is the same:

```
Trace: Entered CalculateDivision Method
    Parameters: Parameters are: 10 0
    Error: Second parameter is zero
Trace: Exiting CalculateDivision Method

Unhandled Exception: System.DivideByZeroException: Attempted to divide by zero.
    at Calculator.CalculateDivision(Int32 x, Int32 y) in C:\Listing_06\Listing_06.cs:line 25
    at CalculatorTest.Main(String[] args) in C:\ Listing_06\Listing_06.cs:line 44
Press any key to continue . . .
```

The key difference between the Trace and Debug classes is that Trace statements are left in during compilation by default. I say *by default*, because you can actually enable and disable the Trace and Debug classes by changing the properties for your project. If you right-click your project in the Solution Explorer window and select the Build tab on the settings pane, you will see the "Define DEBUG constant" and "Define TRACE constant" check boxes, as shown in Figure 38-4.

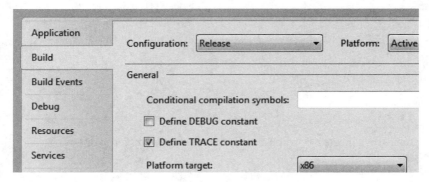

Figure 38-4. *Enabling and disabling the DEBUG and TRACE constants*

You can see from Figure 38-4 that for the Release build, the DEBUG constant is not selected and the TRACE constant is selected. For a Debug build, both are selected, which is why calls to the Debug class don't work in release builds. You can use the project properties to override these defaults by using the check boxes.

Using Static Code Analysis

The paid-for editions of Visual Studio include a static code analyzer, which checks the statements in your code against a set of predefined rules and reports any statement that contravenes any of the rules.

■ **Note** This feature is not available with Visual Studio 2010 Express.

Static code analysis can be a force for good or a force for evil. It is easy to become obsessed with correcting all the errors reported by the analyzer, even when it doesn't pay dividends to do so. I love static code analysis and believe they can really improve the quality of code, but I have lost countless hours of my life settling arguments between developers fighting over the output. Pragmatism is the key with this feature. Only make changes that are sensible, apply only those rules that you care about, and don't become obsessed.

Selecting the Code Analysis Rules

To select the rules used to inspect your code, right-click your project in the Solution Explorer window, and select Properties from the pop-up menu. Click the Code Analysis tab on the left side of the window, and you will see the options for static code analysis, shown in Figure 38-5.

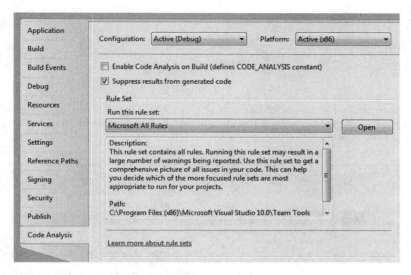

Figure 38-5. Code analysis settings

You can have different code analysis settings for different build settings: Debug, Release, and so on. For each build setting, you can decide whether code analysis should be performed automatically when you build your project and which rules should be used. I have selected Microsoft All Rules from the drop-down list. As the name suggests, this is the set of all rules that Microsoft provides with Visual Studio. Being able to perform code analysis when your project is built can be especially useful if you have a team build environment, which will reject source changes unless they conform to a set of analysis rules. You can inspect the rules by clicking the Open button; we'll return to that in a later section.

Performing Static Analysis

Once you have selected the rule set you want to apply, you can perform code analysis by selecting the Run Code Analysis item from the Build menu. This will recompile your project and analyze your code. Listing 38-7 shows the code that we'll analyze in this section.

Listing 38-7. The Code That Will Be Analyzed

```
class Calculator {

    public int CalculateSum(int x, int y) {
        return x + y;
    }

    public int CalculateProduct(int x, int y) {
        return x * y;
    }

    public int CalculateSubtraction(int x, int y) {
        return x - y;
```

```
    }

    public int CalculateDivision(int x, int y) {
        return x / y;
    }

}
```

When you run code analysis, the results are shown in the Error List window. This will usually pop up when you build your project, but you can also select it from the View menu. Figure 38-6 shows part of the output from applying the Microsoft All Rules set to Listing 38-7.

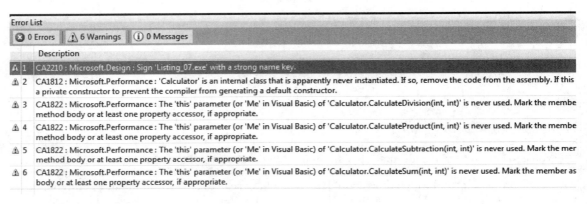

Figure 38-6. The results of code analysis

Not all the detail from the code analysis output will fit into a printed page, but if you run the analysis yourself, you will see that the output includes details of where each rule violation has been found and in which file.

You can see that there is a lot of repetition in the errors shown in Figure 38-6. This is pretty common for some kinds of rule because programmers, me included, tend to write groups of methods together, cookie-cutter style, and so one rule violation tends to be repeated several times.

For example, the first example of rule CA1822 tells me that the CalculateDivision method in the Calculator class doesn't refer to any instance variables and that I should make the method static to improve performance. CA1822 is part of the Microsoft.Performance group of rules that are focused on improving performance. The next three violations are the same rule, reported for the CalculateProduct, CalculateSubtraction, and CalculateSum methods.

Dealing with a Rule Violation

You have some choices when code analysis shows you have broken a rule. The obvious thing to do is to change the code. There really is no good reason why the methods in the Calculator class shouldn't be static, so I can go ahead and make the change shown by Listing 38-8.

Listing 38-8. Changing Code to Fix a Rule Violation

```
class Calculator {
```

```
public static int CalculateSum(int x, int y) {
    return x + y;
}

public static int CalculateProduct(int x, int y) {
    return x * y;
}

public static int CalculateSubtraction(int x, int y) {
    return x - y;
}

public static int CalculateDivision(int x, int y) {
    return x / y;
}
}
```

You can see that I have changed the methods in the Calculator class. If I run the analysis again, I don't see CA1822 errors anymore.

But it isn't always possible, or desirable, to change the code. There might be a good reason why a piece of code is written a certain way. It might work around a bug, and it might be a placeholder for future work that, once completed, will conform to the rule. Or you might like to change the code, but you can't—perhaps it is a legacy code base or it belongs to another team that works on a different schedule than you (this is often the case with shared components such as billing systems and general ledgers).

These situations fall into two broad categories. You don't want to change a particular area of code, but you are interested in seeing other violations of the same type elsewhere in your project. Or, a rule just doesn't apply to you at all, and you don't ever want to see it reported again.

Suppressing a Single Occurrence

If you are getting code violations in part of your project where you don't want to change but you still want to see those errors elsewhere, then you can use the suppression feature. Run code analysis on your project, select the instance of the warning that relates to the code you don't want to change, and right-click. Select Suppress Message(s) from the pop-up menu, and then select In Source, as shown in Figure 38-7.

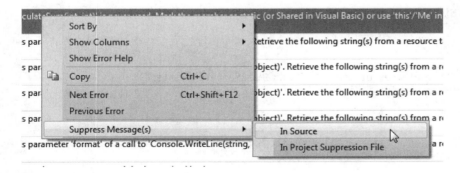

Figure 38-7. *Suppressing a code analysis warning*

I have selected the warning about the `CalculateSum` method not being static. Doing so changes the code, as shown in Listing 38-9.

Listing 38-9. Suppressing an Analysis Error

```
using System.Diagnostics.CodeAnalysis;

class Calculator {

    [SuppressMessage("Microsoft.Performance", "CA1822:MarkMembersAsStatic")]
    public int CalculateSum(int x, int y) {
        return x + y;
    }

    public int CalculateProduct(int x, int y) {
        return x * y;
    }

    public int CalculateSubtraction(int x, int y) {
        return x - y;
    }

    public int CalculateDivision(int x, int y) {
        return x / y;
    }
}
```

The `SupressMessage` attribute (from the `System.Diagnostics.CodeAnalysis` namespace) has been applied to the `CalculateSum` method. This attribute is read by the code analyzer and means that violations of rule CA1822 will no longer be reported for this method. You can repeat this process for each rule violation. If I did this for each of the members in the `Calculator` class, I would end up with the following:

```
using System.Diagnostics.CodeAnalysis;

class Calculator {

    [SuppressMessage("Microsoft.Performance", "CA1822:MarkMembersAsStatic")]
    public int CalculateSum(int x, int y) {
        return x + y;
    }

    [SuppressMessage("Microsoft.Performance", "CA1822:MarkMembersAsStatic")]
    public int CalculateProduct(int x, int y) {
        return x * y;
    }

    [SuppressMessage("Microsoft.Performance", "CA1822:MarkMembersAsStatic")]
    public int CalculateSubtraction(int x, int y) {
        return x - y;
    }
```

```
    [SuppressMessage("Microsoft.Performance", "CA1822:MarkMembersAsStatic")]
    public int CalculateDivision(int x, int y) {
        return x / y;
    }
}
```

The SuppressMessage attributes can quickly start to overwhelm the actual code statements, and this is especially true if you suppress more than one kind of error. You can separate the attributes from the code by choosing the In Project Suppression File menu item, as shown in Figure 38-7. This creates a new code file called GlobalSupressions.cs and writes the SuppressMessage attributes there. Listing 38-10 shows the contents of the file when I suppress the CA1822 message for the four methods in the Calculator class.

Listing 38-10. Using the Global Suppression File

```
// This file is used by Code Analysis to maintain SuppressMessage
// attributes that are applied to this project.
// Project-level suppressions either have no target or are given
// a specific target and scoped to a namespace, type, member, etc.
//
// To add a suppression to this file, right-click the message in the
// Error List, point to "Suppress Message(s)", and click
// "In Project Suppression File".
// You do not need to add suppressions to this file manually.

[assembly: System.Diagnostics.CodeAnalysis.SuppressMessage("Microsoft.Performance",
"CA1822:MarkMembersAsStatic", Scope = "member", Target =
"Calculator.#CalculateSubtraction(System.Int32,System.Int32)")]
[assembly: System.Diagnostics.CodeAnalysis.SuppressMessage("Microsoft.Performance",
"CA1822:MarkMembersAsStatic", Scope = "member", Target =
"Calculator.#CalculateDivision(System.Int32,System.Int32)")]
[assembly: System.Diagnostics.CodeAnalysis.SuppressMessage("Microsoft.Performance",
"CA1822:MarkMembersAsStatic", Scope = "member", Target =
"Calculator.#CalculateProduct(System.Int32,System.Int32)")]
[assembly: System.Diagnostics.CodeAnalysis.SuppressMessage("Microsoft.Performance",
"CA1822:MarkMembersAsStatic", Scope = "member", Target =
"Calculator.#CalculateSum(System.Int32,System.Int32)")]
```

Using a separate suppression file keeps your source code clean, but it can be easy to forget that you have suppressed a message for a particular method. It can pay dividends to review this file to ensure that all the suppressed errors need to be suppressed.

Suppressing Every Occurrence

The simplest way to suppress a rule for an entire project is to create a custom set of rules and disable warnings for the rule or rules that you don't want applied. Right-click your project in the Solution Explorer window, select Properties, and then select the Code Analysis tab on the left side of the window. Select the rule set that you want to use as the basis for your customizations from the drop-down list, and click the Open button. This will open the rule set editor, as shown by Figure 38-8.

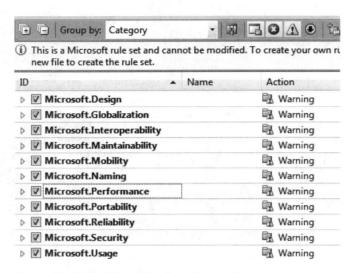

Figure 38-8. The Visual Studio rule set editor

Before making any changes, select Save from the File menu. You can't edit the rule sets provided by Microsoft, so you have to create your own. Save the rule set file somewhere convenient. Open the Properties window, and change the values for Description and Name properties to something meaningful. I have set my Name property to Adam's Rules and the Description property to Excludes CA1822. Open the group for the rule that you want to edit. I am going to edit CA1822, which is in the Microsoft.Performance group, and click the Action column for the rule you want to suppress. Select None from the drop-down menu, as shown by Figure 38-9.

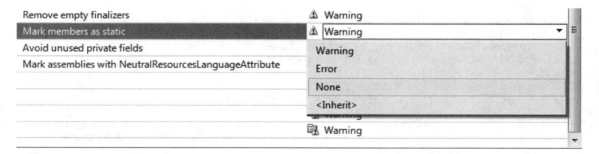

Figure 38-9. Disabling a rule

Save the rule set to reflect the change, and return to the properties page for your project. Select Browse from the drop-down list of rule sets, and select the file you created a moment ago. The name of the rules set and the description will be displayed. Save the changes to the project properties, and select Run Code Analysis from the Build menu. The new rule set will be applied, which in my case excludes CA1822, so I no longer get warnings about my nonstatic methods in the Calculator class.

Using Code Contracts

The final feature we will look at in this chapter is *code contracts*, which are much like more sophisticated versions of the Debug and Trace methods we saw at the start of the chapter. Code contracts let you specify conditions that must be true in your code at given points, but code contracts have finer-grained meanings, such as a condition being true only when a method is entered or exited but not during the execution of the method.

The strength of the code contracts feature comes from the two different ways that contracts can be evaluated—statically and when your program is running. Using both techniques to check the same set of contracts dramatically increases the chances of finding situations that would lead to errors or unexpected behavior in your program.

Installing and Enabling Code Contract Support

The support for code contracts comes in two parts—a set of classes that are part of the .NET Framework Class Library (in the System.Diagnostics.Contracts namespace) and a set of extensions for Visual Studio 2010. For reasons that are not entirely clear, Microsoft has chosen not to include the extensions to Visual Studio in the installation, and you have to download the missing pieces from this URL:

http://msdn.microsoft.com/en-us/devlabs/dd491992.aspx

There are two versions available—one for the Express edition of Visual Studio and one for the paid-for versions. If you go to the previously shown URL, you will see links for each version, as shown in Figure 38-10.

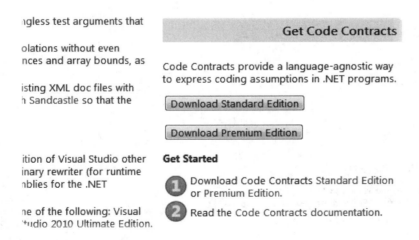

Figure 38-10. Downloading the code contract feature

The version for Visual Studio Express doesn't contain the static contract checker, which is described in the "Using the Static Checker" section. It does contain the runtime checker, which can still be useful and is described in the "Using the Runtime Checker" section.

Download and install the appropriate version for your version of Visual Studio. Start Visual Studio, load the project you want to work on, right-click in the Solution Explorer window, and select Properties. You will see a new Code Contracts tab at the bottom of the Properties window. This tab lets you switch the static and runtime contract checking on and off. To use the code contracts feature, you start by writing contracts into your code and then use either the runtime or static analyzer to enforce them.

Writing Code Contracts

Code contracts are similar to the Debug statements that we used at the start of the chapter, except that where a Debug statement lets you check the logic of your application at a single point in the execution of your program, code contracts let you define and enforce rules about the state of your application over a period of time. There are four types of contract—preconditions, postconditions, assertions, and invariants. Each of these is described in the following sections.

Using Precondition Contracts

A precondition defines something that must be true upon entry to a method. If we return to our simple Calculator class, a precondition might be that the second int parameter is not zero. We define a code contract precondition using the static Contract.Requires method, as shown in Listing 38-11.

Listing 38-11. Defining a Code Contract Precondition

```
using System.Diagnostics.Contracts;

class Calculator {

    public int CalculateSum(int x, int y) {
        return x + y;
    }

    public int CalculateProduct(int x, int y) {
        return x * y;
    }

    public int CalculateSubtraction(int x, int y) {
        return x - y;
    }

    public int CalculateDivision(int x, int y) {
        Contract.Requires(y != 0, "Second parameter is zero");
        return x / y;
    }
}
```

In Listing 38-11, I have added a precondition contract to the CalculateDivision method using this statement:

```
Contract.Requires(y != 0, "Second parameter is zero");
```

Precondition statements must go at the start of your method. The Requires method takes two parameters. The first is a bool, which is the condition you want to check for; in this case, I want to be sure that the second parameter to my method isn't zero. The second parameter to the Requires method is the message that should be displayed if the contract is broken. In this case, my message is Second parameter is zero. Precondition contracts are placed at the start of your method. You can check any condition you are interested in. The Requires method may seem similar to some of the Debug methods we saw earlier, and they do have a lot in common. The differences will become apparent when we come to the other contracts and the way in which contracts are enforced. You can have as many precondition contracts as you need. Here is an example of multiple conditions applied to the CalculateSum method:

```
public int CalculateSum(int x, int y) {
    Contract.Requires(x > 0, "First parameter is zero");
    Contract.Requires(x > y, "First parameter is not > than second parameter");
    return x + y;
}
```

These preconditions check that the first parameter isn't zero and that the value of the first parameter is greater than the value of the second. I could have combined these into a single Requires call, but then I would have lost the benefit of having granular messages that tell me exactly which of my precondition contracts has been broken.

Using Postcondition Contracts

Postcondition contracts specify some fact that must be true when your method exits. Postconditions are defined using the static Contract.Ensures method and must be placed at the start of your method along with your preconditions. Placing postconditions at the start of the method feels a little odd at first, especially when the most common use for postcondition contracts is to check some characteristic of the result, which in many methods won't have been defined until after the contracts are specified. Fortunately, there is a neat trick for dealing with this, as demonstrated in Listing 38-12.

Listing 38-12. Defining a Postcondition Code Contract

```
using System.Diagnostics.Contracts;

class Calculator {

    public int CalculateSum(int x, int y) {
        Contract.Ensures(Contract.Result<int>() > 0, "Result is <= zero");
        return x + y;
    }

    public int CalculateProduct(int x, int y) {
        return x * y;
    }

    public int CalculateSubtraction(int x, int y) {
        return x - y;
    }

    public int CalculateDivision(int x, int y) {
```

```
        Contract.Requires(y != 0, "Second parameter is zero");
        return x / y;
    }
}
```

The Ensures method takes two parameters: a bool (for the condition to evaluate) and a string (for the message to use if the contract is broken). You can reference the result of your method by using the static Contract.Result<T> method, where T is the result that your method returns. In the case of the example, I have called Contract.Result<int>(). The postcondition I have created checks to see that the result of the CalculateSum method is greater than zero. You can have multiple postcondition contracts, and a single method can contain preconditions and postconditions, like this:

```
public int CalculateSum(int x, int y) {
    Contract.Requires(x <= y, "First parameter > second parameter");
    Contract.Ensures(Contract.Result<int>() > 0, "Result is <= zero");
    Contract.Ensures(Contract.Result<int>() < 50, "Result is >= fifty");
    return x + y;
}
```

Postcondition contracts are one of the areas in which code contracts are more sophisticated than the Debug and Trace classes, especially since you can create conditions that depend on the result of your method without changing the way that the result is calculated.

Using Assertion Contracts

Code contract assertions are the same as those offered by the Debug and Trace classes. They allow you to check the state of your program at a particular point in the code. Assertions are created using the static Contract.Assert method, as demonstrated by Listing 38-13.

Listing 38-13. Defining an Assertion Code Contract

```
using System.Diagnostics.Contracts;

class Calculator {

    public int CalculateSum(int x, int y) {
        Contract.Ensures(Contract.Result<int>() > 0, "Result is <= zero");
        // ... other code statements
        int variable1 = 10, variable2 = 10;
        // do something with the local variables
        Contract.Assert(variable1 != variable2, "Parameter values are the same");
        // ... more code statements
        return x + y;
    }

    public int CalculateProduct(int x, int y) {
        return x * y;
    }

    public int CalculateSubtraction(int x, int y) {
```

```
        return x - y;
    }

    public int CalculateDivision(int x, int y) {
        Contract.Requires(y != 0, "Second parameter is zero");
        return x / y;
    }
}
```

Like the other Contract methods, Assert takes a bool parameter for the condition and a string message to use when the contract is broken. I have defined two local variables in the CalculateSum method and created an assertion that states that the values must not be the same.

Using Invariant Contracts

The final kind of contract is the invariant, which is a condition that applies to your entire object and which should never occur. Invariant contracts are put into a single method, which is annotated with the ContractInvariantMethod attribute. Individual contracts are defined using the static Contract.Invariant method. Listing 38-14 provides a demonstration of using invariant contracts.

Listing 38-14. Defining an Invariant Code Contract

```
using System.Diagnostics.Contracts;

class Calculator {
    private int lastResult = 0;

    [ContractInvariantMethod]
    private void InvariantContracts() {
        Contract.Invariant(lastResult > 0, "Variable lastResult <= 0");
    }

    public int CalculateSum(int x, int y) {
        Contract.Ensures(Contract.Result<int>() > 0, "Result is <= zero");
        // ... other code statements
        int variable1 = 10, variable2 = 10;
        // do something with the local variables
        Contract.Assert(variable1 != variable2, "Parameter values are the same");
        // ... more code statements
        return lastResult = x + y;
    }

    public int CalculateProduct(int x, int y) {
        return lastResult = x * y;
    }

    public int CalculateSubtraction(int x, int y) {
        return lastResult = x - y;
    }
```

```
    public int CalculateDivision(int x, int y) {
        Contract.Requires(y != 0, "Second parameter is zero");
        return lastResult = x / y;
    }
}
```

I've changed each method in the Calculator class so that the result returned from each method is also set as the value for the lastResult field. To demonstrate an invariant contract, I have defined a private method called InvariantContracts and used the ContractInvariantMethod attribute to tell the code contracts system that the method contains invariant code contracts.

The contract I have specified is that the value of lastResult should always be greater than zero. Invariant contracts are checked at the end of each public method, so for my example, I can rely on the contract being enforced after any call to one of the CalculateXXX methods. A method marked with the ContractInvariantMethod attribute can contain more than one invariant contract, and there can be more than one method marked with the attribute. Invariant contracts can be extremely useful in ensuring that you understand the behavior of your objects throughout the lifetime of your program, and although this feature is useful during the design and coding feature, I have found it invaluable during debugging to establish where an unwanted state change has originated from.

Using the Static Checker

The static code contract checker analyzes the contents of your code files and tries to figure out whether any of the contracts will be broken. Static analysis can be a powerful technique, but the best results come when you combine the static checker with the runtime equivalent described in the next chapter.

■ **Note** The static checker is not available for use with the Express edition of Visual Studio 2010.

To enable static checking, open the Properties window for your project, click the Code Contracts tab, and check the Perform Static Contract Checking option, as shown by Figure 38-11.

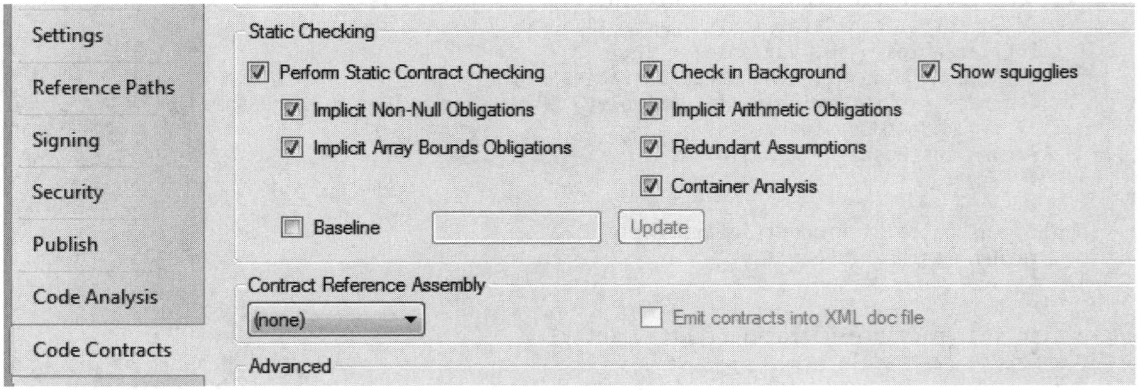

Figure 38-11. Enabling static contract checking

A number of other options are available. Check them all to get the widest enforcement of your contracts, as shown in the figure. Because the static checker examines source code, I have included some statements to Listing 38-15 that use the Calculator class we created in Listing 38-14.

Listing 38-15. The Calculator Class and a Test Class

```
using System;
using System.Diagnostics.Contracts;

class Calculator {
    private int lastResult = 0;

    [ContractInvariantMethod]
    private void InvariantContracts() {
        Contract.Invariant(lastResult > 0, "Variable lastResult <= 0");
    }

    public int CalculateSum(int x, int y) {
        Contract.Ensures(Contract.Result<int>() > 0, "Result is <= zero");
        // ... other code statements
        int variable1 = 10, variable2 = 10;
        // do something with the local variables
        Contract.Assert(variable1 != variable2, "Parameter values are the same");
        // ... more code statements
        return lastResult = x + y;
    }

    public int CalculateProduct(int x, int y) {
        return lastResult = x * y;
    }

    public int CalculateSubtraction(int x, int y) {
        return lastResult = x - y;
    }

    public int CalculateDivision(int x, int y) {
        Contract.Requires(y != 0, "Second parameter is zero");
        return lastResult = x / y;
    }
}

class CalculatorTest {

    static void Main() {

        // create a new Calculator object
        Calculator calc = new Calculator();

        // perform some calculations
        int sumResult = calc.CalculateProduct(10, 20);
        int productResult = calc.CalculateSum(10, -20);
        int subtractionResult = calc.CalculateSubtraction(10, 20);
```

```
        int divisionResult = calc.CalculateDivision(10, 20);

        // write out the results
        Console.WriteLine("Sum Result: {0}", sumResult);
        Console.WriteLine("Product Result: {0}", productResult);
        Console.WriteLine("Subtraction Result: {0}", subtractionResult);
        Console.WriteLine("Division Result: {0}", divisionResult);

        // wait for input before exiting
        Console.WriteLine("Press enter to finish");
        Console.ReadLine();
    }
}
```

All you need to do now is recompile your project. The static checking is done as part of the build process, and problems are reported in the Error List window. This may appear automatically as you build, but you can select it from the View menu if it doesn't. Figure 38-12 shows the contract warnings that are reported for Listing 38-15.

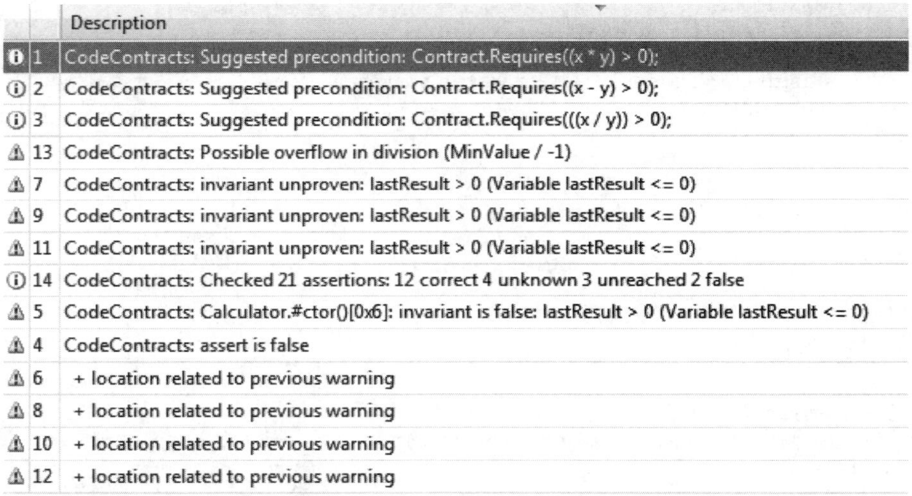

		Description
❶	1	CodeContracts: Suggested precondition: Contract.Requires((x * y) > 0);
ⓘ	2	CodeContracts: Suggested precondition: Contract.Requires((x - y) > 0);
ⓘ	3	CodeContracts: Suggested precondition: Contract.Requires(((x / y)) > 0);
⚠	13	CodeContracts: Possible overflow in division (MinValue / -1)
⚠	7	CodeContracts: invariant unproven: lastResult > 0 (Variable lastResult <= 0)
⚠	9	CodeContracts: invariant unproven: lastResult > 0 (Variable lastResult <= 0)
⚠	11	CodeContracts: invariant unproven: lastResult > 0 (Variable lastResult <= 0)
ⓘ	14	CodeContracts: Checked 21 assertions: 12 correct 4 unknown 3 unreached 2 false
⚠	5	CodeContracts: Calculator.#ctor()[0x6]: invariant is false: lastResult > 0 (Variable lastResult <= 0)
⚠	4	CodeContracts: assert is false
⚠	6	+ location related to previous warning
⚠	8	+ location related to previous warning
⚠	10	+ location related to previous warning
⚠	12	+ location related to previous warning

Figure 38-12. Static contract check results

Visual Studio reports the code file and line where the problem has been detected, but I have omitted these to make Figure 38-12 fit on the page. The code analysis has shown several issues. Once you have the list of issues, then you can start to make changes to your code to fix the problem. I can't show you how to resolve the contract issues because they will always be specific to your project and the contracts you have defined.

The static checker isn't able to check all contracts, and you'll see some that are marked as *unproven*. This means that the checker couldn't figure out whether the contract would be broken or not. Even so, static analysis can pick up a lot of contract violations and is well worth the time to check through the results and consider changes.

Using the Runtime Checker

The runtime checker checks for contract violations as your program is executed. This approach doesn't have a problem with unproven contracts, but it is only able to test the parts of the code that are used, which means you have to create thorough test scenarios to fully exercise all of the possible outcomes in your code. In practice, that is very hard to do, so a combination of static and runtime checking tends to be a pragmatic compromise. To enable runtime checking, go the Code Contracts section of your project Properties page, and check the Perform Runtime Contract Checking option, as shown in Figure 38-13. Ensure that you also check the Asset on Contract Failure option, as shown in the figure.

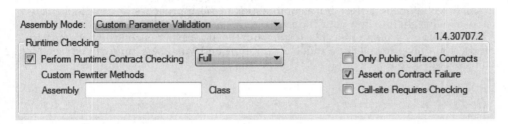

Figure 38-13. Enabling the runtime contract checker

When you run your program, contract violations cause an assert dialog box to appear, similar to the one created by the Debug class. Figure 38-14 shows an example.

Figure 38-14. A contract assert dialog box

The buttons on the dialog box work the same way as the buttons on the Debug dialog box; the Abort button terminated the program, the Retry button starts a debugger, and the Ignore button ignores the contract violation and continues executing your code. The dialog box will reappear if further contract violations are found as the program continues to run.

Summary

In this chapter, we looked at some of the C#, .NET, and Visual Studio features that you can use to improve the quality of your source code and reduce the likelihood of errors or unexpected behavior in your program. No single technique is perfect, but a combination of the approaches we have looked at can provide a great deal of insight into how your code will operate and the implicit assumptions that we all make when writing code. Few programmers like testing, but the more experienced you become with C# and .NET, the more you will appreciate how much of your time and your users' time can be saved by improving the quality of your code.

Index

■ B

■ D

■ G

■ L

■ N

■ P

■ S

■ T

■ V

■ W

You Need the Companion eBook

Your purchase of this book entitles you to buy the companion PDF-version eBook for only $10. Take the weightless companion with you anywhere.

We believe this Apress title will prove so indispensable that you'll want to carry it with you everywhere, which is why we are offering the companion eBook (in PDF format) for $10 to customers who purchase this book now. Convenient and fully searchable, the PDF version of any content-rich, page-heavy Apress book makes a valuable addition to your programming library. You can easily find and copy code—or perform examples by quickly toggling between instructions and the application. Even simultaneously tackling a donut, diet soda, and complex code becomes simplified with hands-free eBooks!

Once you purchase your book, getting the $10 companion eBook is simple:

❶ Visit **www.apress.com/promo/tendollars/**.

❷ Complete a basic registration form to receive a randomly generated question about this title.

❸ Answer the question correctly in 60 seconds, and you will receive a promotional code to redeem for the $10.00 eBook.

233 Spring Street, New York, NY 10013

Offer valid through 11/10.